WHEATER'S
Functional Histology

For my children Alex and Katie.
B.Y.

For my parents Frank and Vi Heath, and my brother Graham,
for their guidance and encouragement in the pursuit of excellence.
J.W.H.

Dedicated to the memory of

Paul Richard Wheater
1951-1989

and

John Young
1923-2005

Commissioning Editor: Inta Ozols
Development Editor: Alison Whitehouse
Project Manager: Glenys Norquay
Design Manager: Andy Chapman
Marketing Manager (UK): Jeremy Bowes
Marketing Manager (USA): John Gore
Editorial Assistant: Katie Sotiris

WHEATER'S
Functional Histology
A Text and Colour Atlas

Fifth edition

Barbara Young

BSc Med Sci Hons, PhD, MB BChir, MRCP(UK), FRCPA
Consultant Pathologist, Western Infirmary, Glasgow, UK

James S. Lowe

BMedSci, BM BS, DM, FRCPath
Professor of Neuropathology, University of Nottingham Medical School, Nottingham, UK

Alan Stevens

MB BS, FRCPath
Consultant Histopathologist, Queen's Medical Centre, Nottingham, UK

John W. Heath

BSc Hons, PhD
Associate Professor in Anatomy, The University of Newcastle, New South Wales, Australia

DRAWINGS BY

Philip J. Deakin

BSc Hons (Sheffield), MB ChB (Sheffield)
General medical practitioner, Sheffield, UK

CHURCHILL LIVINGSTONE
An Imprint of Elsevier

Wheater's Functional Histology, 5/e
Young et al.

CHURCHILL LIVINGSTONE
An imprint of Elsevier

Original ISBN: 978-0-4430-6850-8

Previous editions copyrighted 1979, 1987, 1993, 2000

First Indian Reprint 2006
Reprinted 2007

Indian Reprint ISBN: 978-81-312-0354-5

Published by Elsevier, a division of Reed Elsevier India Private Limited,
Sri Pratap Udyog, 274, Captain Gaur Marg, Sriniwaspuri, New Delhi - 110065 (India)

Printed and bound by Gopsons Papers Ltd., India.

PREFACE *to the fifth edition*

When we set out to write this 5th edition of *Functional Histology*, we were determined to retain all the features that made the previous editions so popular. With this in mind we have kept the general layout much as it has been previously with the bulk of the information incorporated into the figure captions. Short bursts of introductory text are still to be found at the beginning of major sections and give a general overview of the material to be covered. We have updated the text and captions as needed, incorporating new knowledge, in particular in the areas of cell and molecular biology where there have been numerous major advances in the past few years. However, we have been very careful not to include unnecessary detail, as we are all well aware of the limitations on students' time. To this end we have kept this new edition about the same length as the previous one.

Throughout the book we have improved light and electron micrographs and included new micrographs of areas not previously covered. To make interpretation of the micrographs easier, we have included a key of the labelling in each double page spread so that the reader can quickly identify the labelled structures. At the ends of chapters or sections of chapters we have added more summary tables that are intended as quick aids to revision of the main text. Medical education is changing and in particular becoming more integrated. To accommodate this we have included greater emphasis on clinical relevance. Clinical correlations have been greatly expanded and are highlighted in coloured text boxes. The aim is to use clinical examples to reinforce the relevance of the histological structures rather than to provide a miniature textbook of pathology.

To improve the user-friendliness of the book we have included three Appendices at the end of the book. Appendix 1 becomes the Introduction to Microscopy section that was previously part of Chapter 1. The pre-existing Notes on Staining Techniques, with some updating, becomes Appendix 2. A new Appendix 3 is a short glossary of common terms used in the book and in the practice of Histology. It is hoped that grouping this "reference material" at the end of the book will make it more easily accessible to the reader.

We hope our readers will continue to find this book a valuable resource that is pertinent to students in a wide range of courses and that it will fire their enthusiasm for a fascinating field of study.

Barbara Young
James S. Lowe
Alan Stevens
John W. Heath

Glasgow and Nottingham (UK)
Newcastle (Australia)
2006

PREFACE *to the first edition*

Histology has bored generations of students. This is almost certainly because it has been regarded as the study of structure in isolation from function; yet few would dispute that structure and function are intimately related. Thus, the aim of this book is to present histology in relation to the principles of physiology, biochemistry and molecular biology.

Within the limits imposed by any book format, we have attempted to create the environment of the lecture room and microscope laboratory by basing the discussion of histology upon appropriate micrographs and diagrams. Consequently, colour photography has been used since it reproduces the actual images seen in light microscopy and allows a variety of common staining methods to be employed in highlighting different aspects of tissue structure. In addition, some less common techniques such as immunohistochemistry have been introduced where such methods best illustrate a particular point.

Since electron microscopy is a relative new technique, a myth has arisen amongst many students that light and electron microscopy are poles apart. We have tried to show that electron microscopy is merely an extension of light microscopy. In order to demonstrate this continuity, we have included resin-embedded thin sections photographed around the limit of resolution of the light microscope; this technique is being applied increasingly in routine histological and histopathological practice. Where such less conventional techniques have been adopted, their rationale has been outlined at the appropriate place rather than in a formal chapter devoted to techniques.

The content and pictorial design of the book have been chosen to make it easy to use both as a textbook and as a laboratory guide. Wherever possible, the subject matter has been condensed into units of illustration plus relevant text; each unit is designed to have a degree of autonomy whilst at the same time remaining integrated into the subject as a whole. Short sections of non-illustrated text have been used by way of introduction, to outline general principles and to consider the subject matter in broader perspective.

Human tissues were mainly selected in order to maintain consistency, but when suitable human specimens were not available, primate tissues were generally substituted. Since this book stresses the understanding of principles rather than extensive detail, some tissues have been omitted deliberately, for example the regional variations of the central nervous system and the vestibulo-auditory apparatus.

This book should adequately encompass the requirements of undergraduate courses in medicine, dentistry, veterinary science, pharmacy, mammalian biology and allied fields. Further, it offers a pictorial reference for use in histology and histopathology laboratories. Finally, we envisage that the book will also find application as a teaching manual in schools and colleges of further education.

Paul R. Wheater
H. George Burkitt
Victor G. Daniels

Nottingham 1979

INTERNATIONAL ADVISORY PANEL

SOUTH ASIA ADVISORY PANEL

INDIA

Dr. (Mrs) Pritha S. Bhuiyan, MS, PGDME
Professor & Head
Department of Anatomy
Seth G.S. Medical College & KEM Hospital
Mumbai, Maharashtra

Dr. Pari Plavi
Associate Professor
Department of Anatomy
Gandhi Medical College
Secunderabad, Andhra Pradesh

Dr. R.N. Kulkarni
Professor & Head
Department of Anatomy
M.S. Ramaiah Medical College
Bangalore, Karnataka

Dr. R.R. Badagandi, MS
Professor & Head
Department of Anatomy
S.D.M. College of Medical Sciences & Hospital
Dharwad, Karnataka

Dr. Ramaiah, MS
Professor & Head
Department of Anatomy
V.I.M.S. Government Medical College
Bellary, Karnataka

Dr. Roopa Kulkarni
Professor
Department of Anatomy
M.S. Ramaiah Medical College
Bangalore, Karnataka

Dr. Sarada Devi
Professor
Department of Anatomy
Bhaskar Medical College
Hyderabad, Andhra Pradesh

Dr. S. Swayam Jothi
Professor
Department of Anatomy
Katuri Medical College
Guntur, Andhra Pradesh

Dr. Seema Madan
Professor & Head
Department of Anatomy
Gandhi Medical College
Secunderabad, Andhra Pradesh

Dr. (Mrs) Shashi Wadhwa,
MS, PhD, FASc, FNASc
Professor
Department of Anatomy
All India Institute of Medical Sciences
New Delhi

Dr. V. Balasubramanyam
Professor & Head
Department of Anatomy
St. John's Medical College
Bangalore, Karnataka

PAKISTAN

Dr. Atiya Khalid
Professor & Head
Department of Anatomy & Histology
King Edward Medical University
Lahore, Pakistan

Dr. Kishwar Sultana
Chairperson
Department of Anatomy
Baqai Medical University
Karachi, Pakistan

Dr. Masood Ahmed
Vice Principal & Professor
Department of Anatomy
Baqai Medical University
Karachi, Pakistan

Dr. Rehana Azim
Professor & Head
Department of Anatomy
Fatima Jinnah Medical College for Women
Lahore, Pakistan

ACKNOWLEDGEMENTS

In addition to all those people acknowledged in the previous editions, we would like, for this edition, to thank many people who contributed materials or helped in other ways. Without their generous help and expertise this book would not have been possible. We owe a huge debt of gratitude to Anne Kane of the Department of Pathology, Queen's Medical Centre, Nottingham for her expert work with digital images. We also thank Trevor Gray, Phil Hinson, Liz Bakowski and Carol Dunn of the same department, the former two for the provision of several of the new electron micrographs and the latter two for cutting and staining sections for new light micrographs. Irene Smith and Kim Huxley, also of Nottingham, are thanked for their help with word processing. Lindsay Paterson, Senior Cytogeneticist in the Department of Medical Genetics at the Royal Hospital for Sick Children, Yorkhill, Glasgow kindly provided the photograph for Fig 2.6. We also thank Dr Jeannette MacFarlane, Consultant Paediatric Pathologist at the Royal Hospital for Sick Children, Yorkhill, Glasgow for the glass slides for Figs 19.12 and 19.33a and b. Professor Tomas Garcia-Caballero of the Universidade de Santiago de Compostela, Spain kindly donated Fig 13.1. At the Department of Pathology, Western Infirmary, Glasgow, the pathologists generously allowed access to the files to source materials for photography and all of the scientific staff, too numerous to mention individually, tirelessly cut and stained sections for photography. Figures 12.18, 14.17 and 19.22 are all pathological images taken from *Basic Histopathology* 4th edition, Stevens, Lowe and Young, Churchill Livingstone.

We would also like to thank our International Advisory Panel for their help with producing this book. In seeking their advice we aimed to increase the accessibility of the material to the widest possible readership. We have incorporated as many of their valuable suggestions as space and our subject matter allowed.

Finally, we thank our families and friends for their forbearance and support throughout this challenging project, which consumed much time.

CONTENTS

PART ONE

The Cell

1. *Cell structure and function*

Introduction to the cell

This book is about the structure and function of normal mammalian, mainly human, cells and tissues. The major tool in the study of histology is the microscope and students will find a brief description of how microscopes work aimed at the absolute novice in Appendix 1 at the back of this book. Various staining procedures are used to prepare tissues to make them visible through the microscope and these are described in Appendix 2. The student is strongly urged to read these appendices first; it really will make all that follows much more comprehensible. Appendix 3 is a glossary of common histological terms and like the other appendices can be dipped into at any time.

Histology is the study of normal structure. Structure always follows function and histology is therefore a tool for determining the function of different tissues and organs. When tissues malfunction, e.g. in certain disease states such as cancer or inflammation, there are often specific changes in the microscopic structure of the tissues. The study of these changes is known as ***histopathology***. Obviously a sound knowledge of normal structure is essential for an understanding of pathology.

The ***cell*** is the functional unit of all living organisms. The simplest organisms such as bacteria and algae consist of a single cell. More complex organisms consist of many cells as well as ***extracellular matrix*** (e.g. the matrix of bone). The cells of multicellular organisms, such as humans, show a great variety of functional and morphological specializations, which have developed during the process of evolution by amplification of one or other of the basic functions common to all living cells. The process by which cells assume specialised structure and function is known as ***differentiation***. Despite this extraordinary range of morphological forms, all ***eukaryotic*** cells conform to a basic structural model, which is the subject of this chapter. Students will be well aware that the term ***eukaryote*** refers to the group of organisms whose cells have a defined nucleus surrounded by a nuclear membrane. This group includes most living organisms other than bacteria. ***Prokaryotes*** (mainly bacteria) have some major structural differences and are not discussed here.

Human (and all other eukaryotic) cells consist of a ***nucleus*** and ***cytoplasm***. The cytoplasm contains a number of ***organelles*** each with a defined function. The nucleus may be considered the largest organelle.

Fig. 1.1 The cell *(illustration opposite)*
(a) EM ×16 500 (b) Schematic diagram

The basic structural features common to all cells are illustrated in this electron micrograph (a) of a fibroblast and diagram (b). All cells are bounded by an external lipid membrane, called the ***plasma membrane*** or ***plasmalemma PM***, which serves as a dynamic interface with the external environment. In this example, the cell interacts with two types of external environment; adjacent cells **C**, from which it is separated by the intercellular space **IS** and extracellular matrix as represented by collagen fibrils **F**. The functions of the plasma membrane include transfer of nutrients and metabolites, attachment of the cell to adjacent cells and extracellular matrix, and communication with the external environment.

The nucleus **N** is the largest organelle and its substance, often referred to as the ***nucleoplasm***, is bounded by a membrane system called the ***nuclear envelope*** or ***membrane*** **NE**. The nucleus contains the genetic material of the cell. The cytoplasm contains a variety of other organelles, most of which are also bounded by membranes. An extensive system of flattened membrane-bound tubules, saccules and flattened cisterns, collectively known as the ***endoplasmic reticulum*** **ER**, is widely distributed throughout the cytoplasm. A second discrete system of membrane-bound saccules, the ***Golgi apparatus*** **G**, is typically located close to the nucleus (best seen in the adjacent cell). Scattered free in the cytoplasm are a number of relatively large, elongated organelles called ***mitochondria*** **M** which have a smooth outer membrane and a convoluted inner membrane system. In addition to these major organelles, the cell contains a variety of other membrane-bound structures, including intracellular transport vesicles **V** and a lysosome **L**. The cytoplasmic organelles are suspended in a fluid medium called the ***cytosol*** in which many metabolic reactions take place. Within the cytosol, there is a network of minute tubules and filaments, collectively known as the ***cytoskeleton***, which provides structural support for the cell and its organelles, as well as providing a mechanism for transfer of materials within the cell and movement of the cell itself.

Thus the cell is divided into a number of membrane-bound compartments, each of which has its own particular biochemical environment. Membranes therefore serve to separate incompatible biochemical and physiological processes. In addition, enzyme systems are found anchored in membranes so that membranes are themselves the site of many specific biochemical reactions.

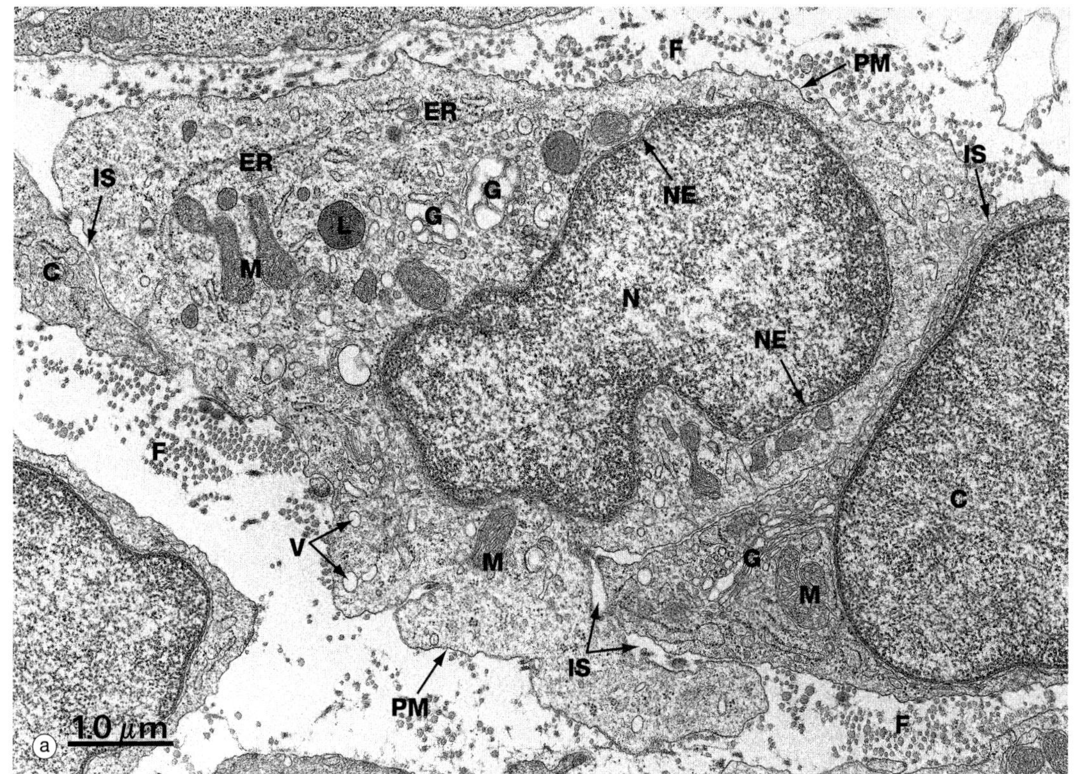

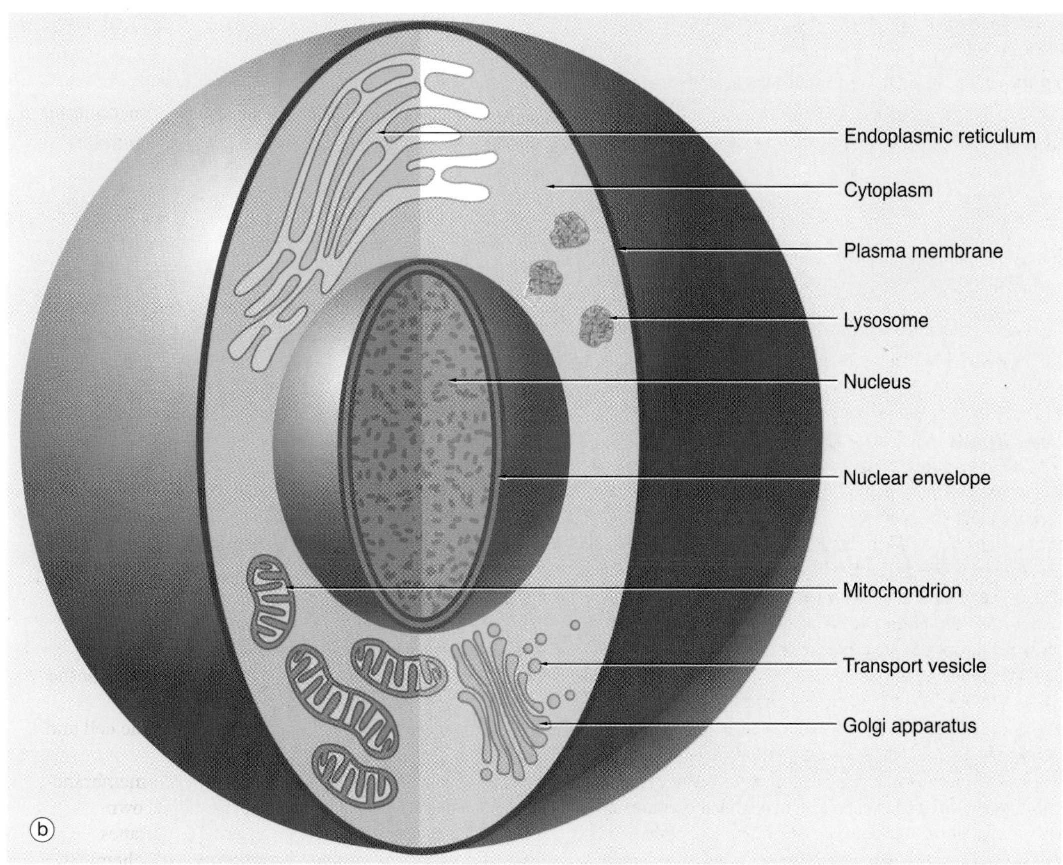

C adjacent cells **ER** endoplasmic reticulum **F** collagen fibrils **G** Golgi apparatus
IS intercellular space **L** lysosome **M** mitochondria **N** nucleus **NE** nuclear envelope
PM plasma membrane **V** secretory vesicles

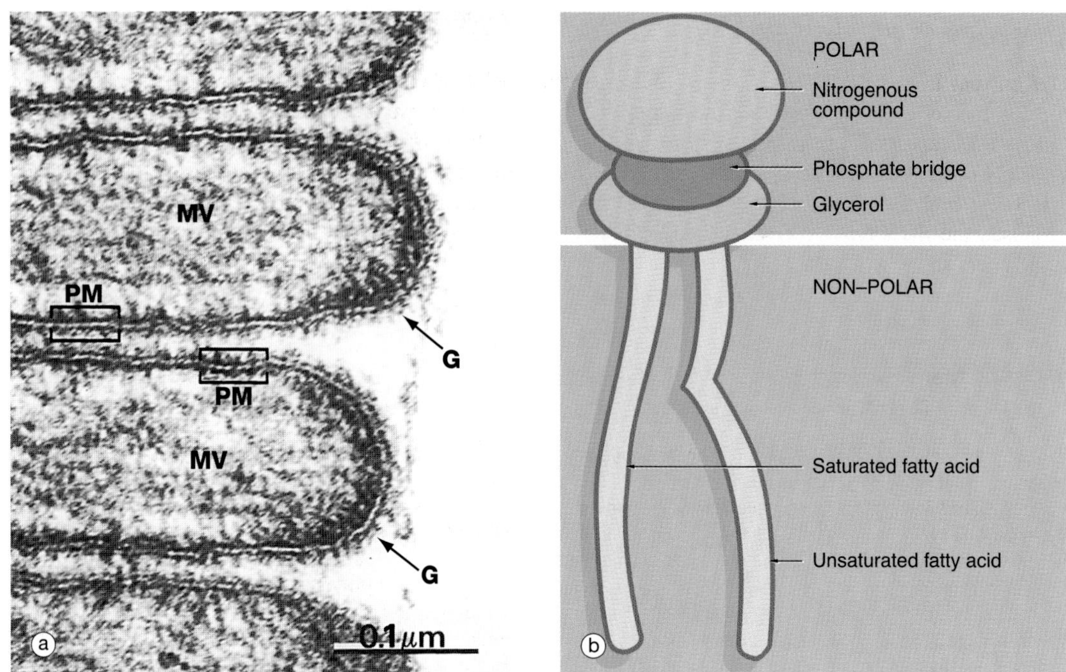

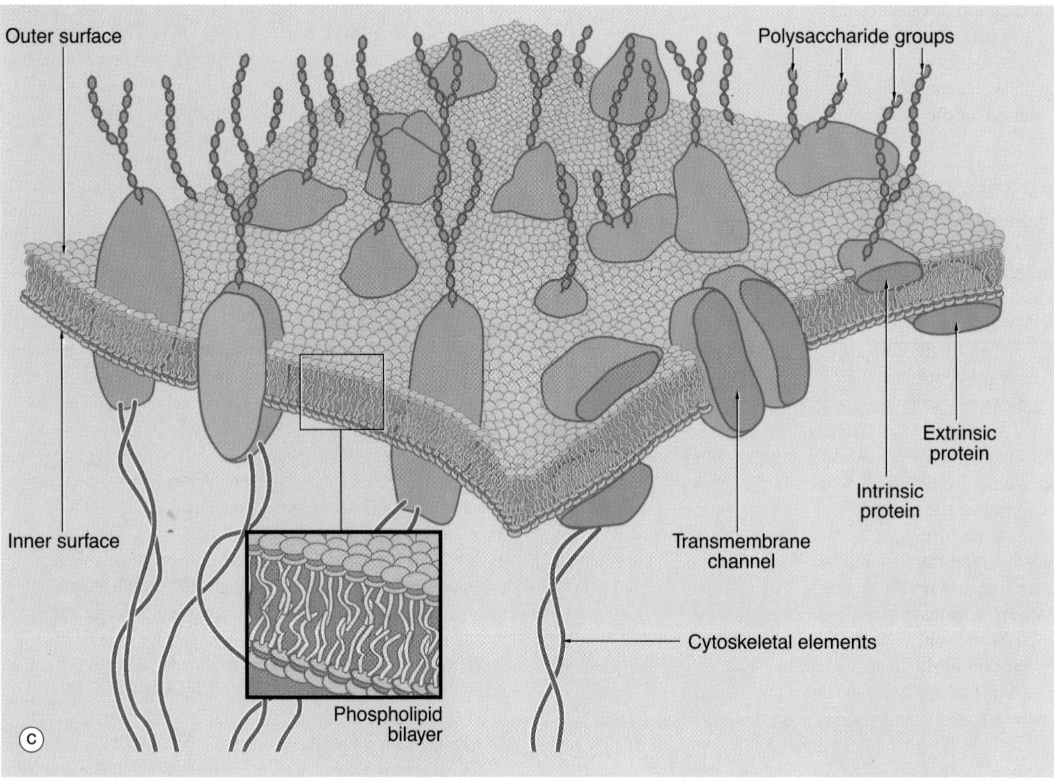

G glycocalyx **MV** microvilli **PM** plasma membrane

Membrane structure

Our current knowledge of membrane structure is the result of many years of study. The permeability of membranes to lipids gave the first indication that cell membranes were composed of lipid as well as protein. Later it was calculated that there was sufficient lipid in the cell membrane to form a bilayer, and an early model was developed of a lipid bilayer sandwiched between two layers of protein. This model, however, failed to explain selective membrane permeability to non-lipid-soluble molecules. Singer and Nicholson, in the early 1970s, proposed the ***fluid mosaic model*** of membrane structure which has been confirmed by many independent researchers and is now generally accepted.

Fig. 1.2 Membrane structure *(illustrations opposite)*
(a) EM ×210 000 (b) Phospholipid structure (c) Fluid mosaic model of membrane structure

Cell membranes consist of a bilayer of phospholipid molecules that are ***amphipathic***, i.e. they consist of a polar, ***hydrophilic*** (water-loving) head and a non-polar, ***hydrophobic*** (water-hating) tail. The polar heads are mainly derived from glycerol conjugated to a nitrogenous compound such as choline, ethanolamine or serine via a phosphate bridge as shown in diagram (b). The phosphate group is negatively charged, whereas the nitrogenous group is positively charged. The non-polar tail of the phospholipid molecule consists of two long-chain fatty acids, each covalently linked to the glycerol component of the polar head. In most mammalian cell membranes, one of the fatty acids is a straight-chain saturated fatty acid, while the other is an unsaturated fatty acid which is 'kinked' at the position of the unsaturated bond. Because of their amphipathic nature, phospholipids in aqueous solution will spontaneously form a bilayer with the hydrophilic (polar) heads directed outwards and the hydrophobic tails forced together inwards. The weak intermolecular forces that hold the bilayer together allow individual phospholipid molecules to move relatively freely within each layer.

The fluidity and flexibility of the membrane is increased by the presence of unsaturated fatty acids, which prevent close packing of the hydrophobic tails. Cholesterol molecules are also present in the bilayer in an almost 1:1 ratio with phospholipids. Cholesterol molecules themselves are amphipathic and have a kinked conformation, thus preventing overly dense packing of the phospholipid fatty acid tails while at the same time filling the gaps between the 'kinks' of the unsaturated fatty acid tails. Cholesterol molecules thus stabilize and regulate the fluidity of the phospholipid bilayer. Cholesterol molecules are not necessarily evenly distributed within the plasma membrane (see below).

Protein molecules make up almost half of the total mass of the membrane. Some protein molecules are incorporated within the membrane (***intrinsic*** or ***integral proteins***) whereas others are held to the inner or outer surface by weak electrostatic forces (***extrinsic*** or ***peripheral proteins***). Some intrinsic proteins span the entire thickness of the membrane (***transmembrane proteins***) to be exposed to each surface. Transmembrane proteins are held within the membrane by a hydrophobic central zone, which allows the protein to float freely in the plane of the membrane. The parts of these proteins protruding beyond the lipid bilayer are hydrophilic. Some membrane proteins are anchored to cytoplasmic structures by the cytoskeleton. Transmembrane proteins have a variety of functions including cell–cell adhesion, cell matrix adhesion, communication and formation of pores or channels for the transport of materials into and out of the cell.

On the external surface of the plasma membranes of animal cells, many of the membrane proteins and some of the membrane lipids are conjugated with short chains of polysaccharide (carbohydrate); these ***glycoproteins*** and ***glycolipids***, respectively, project from the surface of the bilayer forming an outer coating which may be analogous to the cell walls of plants, bacteria and fungi. This polysaccharide layer has been termed the ***glycocalyx*** and appears to vary in thickness in different cell types. The glycocalyx appears to be involved in cell recognition phenomena, in the formation of intercellular adhesions and in the adsorption of molecules to the cell surface; in some situations the glycocalyx also provides mechanical and chemical protection for the plasma membrane.

The electron micrograph in (a) provides a high magnification view of the plasma membrane **PM** of the minute surface projections (***microvilli***) **MV** of a lining cell from the small intestine. The characteristic trilaminar appearance is made up of two outer electron-dense layers separated by an electron-lucent layer. The outer dense layers are thought to correspond to the hydrophilic 'heads' of phospholipid molecules, while the electron-lucent layer is thought to represent the intermediate hydrophobic layer mainly consisting of fatty acids and cholesterol. On the external surface of the plasma membrane the glycocalyx **G**, seen as a fuzzy edge to the cell membrane. This is an unusually prominent feature of small intestinal lining cells where it incorporates a variety of digestive enzymes.

Plasma membranes mediate the flow of both materials and information into and out of the cell, a function of vital importance to the cell. This topic is dealt with in detail in the section 'Import, export and intracellular transport' later in this chapter.

The nucleus

The nucleus may be considered the largest organelle in the cell and is usually the most obvious feature of the cell seen under the light microscope. The nucleus is the control centre of the cell, containing the blueprint from which all the other components of the cell are constructed. This blueprint is stored in the form of ***deoxyribonucleic acid (DNA)*** arranged in the form of ***chromosomes***. When a cell divides, the first step in this process is replication of the DNA so that a copy of the cell blueprint goes to each of the daughter cells. Cell division is the subject of Chapter 2.

Fig. 1.3 Nucleus *(illustrations opposite)*
(a) EM ×15 000 (b) H & E ×480 (c) Azan ×320 (d) Acridine orange ×320

Micrograph (a) illustrates the nucleus of a ***plasma cell***, a type of cell that secretes large amounts of a protein called ***antibody***. Typical of protein-secreting cells, the cytoplasm contains plentiful ribosome-studded or ***rough endoplasmic reticulum*** **ER** and many ***mitochondria*** **M**, which produce the energy required for such a metabolically active cell.

The nucleus contains DNA (making up less than 20% of its mass), protein called ***nucleoprotein*** and some ***ribonucleic acid (RNA)***. Nucleoprotein is of two major types: low molecular weight, positively charged ***histone proteins*** which bind tightly to DNA and control the coiling and expression of the genes encoded by the DNA strand, and ***non-histone proteins***, including enzymes for the synthesis of DNA and RNA and regulatory proteins. All nucleoproteins are synthesised in the cytoplasm and imported into the nucleus. Nuclear RNA includes newly synthesised ***messenger, transfer*** and ***ribosomal RNA (mRNA, tRNA*** and ***rRNA*** respectively) that has not yet passed into the cytoplasm.

Except during cell division, the ***chromosomes***, each a discrete length of DNA with bound histone proteins, exist as coiled and supercoiled strands that cannot be visualised individually. Nuclei are heterogeneous structures with electron-dense (dark, see Appendix 1) and electron-lucent (light) areas. The dense areas, called ***heterochromatin*** **H**, consist of tightly coiled inactive chromatin found in irregular clumps often around the periphery of the nucleus. In females, the inactivated X-chromosome may form a small discrete mass, the ***Barr body***. Barr bodies are occasionally seen at the edge of the nucleus in female cells when cut in a favourable plane of section. The electron-lucent nuclear material, called ***euchromatin*** **E**, represents that part of the DNA that is active in RNA synthesis. Collectively, heterochromatin and euchromatin are known as ***chromatin***, a name derived from the strong colour of nuclei when stained for light microscopy. The chromatin is a highly organised but dynamic structure with individual chromosomes tending to clump in particular areas of the nucleus, known as chromosome territories. Segments of the chromosome are coiled and uncoiled as different genes are brought into contact with the enzymes that make the RNA copy of the DNA, i.e. ***transcription***. Histone proteins also exist as variant forms or can be chemically modified in ways that promote or suppress expression of a particular gene. Permanent switching on or off of a particular set of genes in this way leads to differentiation of a cell. This is also one of the mechanisms by which ***genomic imprinting*** occurs.

The specimen shown in micrograph (b) is of brain tissue which has been stained with ***haematoxylin and eosin*** (H & E), the 'standard' histological staining method. Haematoxylin is blue in colour and eosin is pink. Haematoxylin, a basic dye which binds to negatively charged DNA and RNA, is principally employed to demonstrate nuclear form. Eosin, an acidic dye, has affinity for positively charged structures such as mitochondria and many other cytoplasmic constituents (see also Appendix 2). ***Acidophilic*** (positively charged) structures are therefore ***eosinophilic*** when stained by the H & E method. The nerve cells seen in micrograph (b) contain huge nuclei **Nnc** with relatively pale-stained, dispersed nuclear chromatin and easily seen blue-stained nucleoli **Nu**. In contrast, the surrounding support cells have small nuclei **Nsc** with intensely stained heterochromatin and no visible nucleoli.

Micrograph (c) also shows nerve tissue, but stained by the Azan method which contains a basophilic dye giving the nucleus and nucleolus a red colour, and a blue green acidophilic dye. Note the similarities in the two micrographs despite the different stains.

In micrograph (d), the specimen has been stained with a dye that combines with DNA and RNA. When viewed using a ***fluorescence microscope***, the DNA is seen as yellow-green fluorescence and the RNA as orange-red fluorescence, thereby highlighting the nuclei and cytoplasm, respectively. The micrograph shows plasma cells and lymphocytes in a smear of bone marrow aspirate; the plasma cells, which are very active in protein synthesis, have plentiful cytoplasmic RNA, whereas the quiescent lymphocytes have almost none.

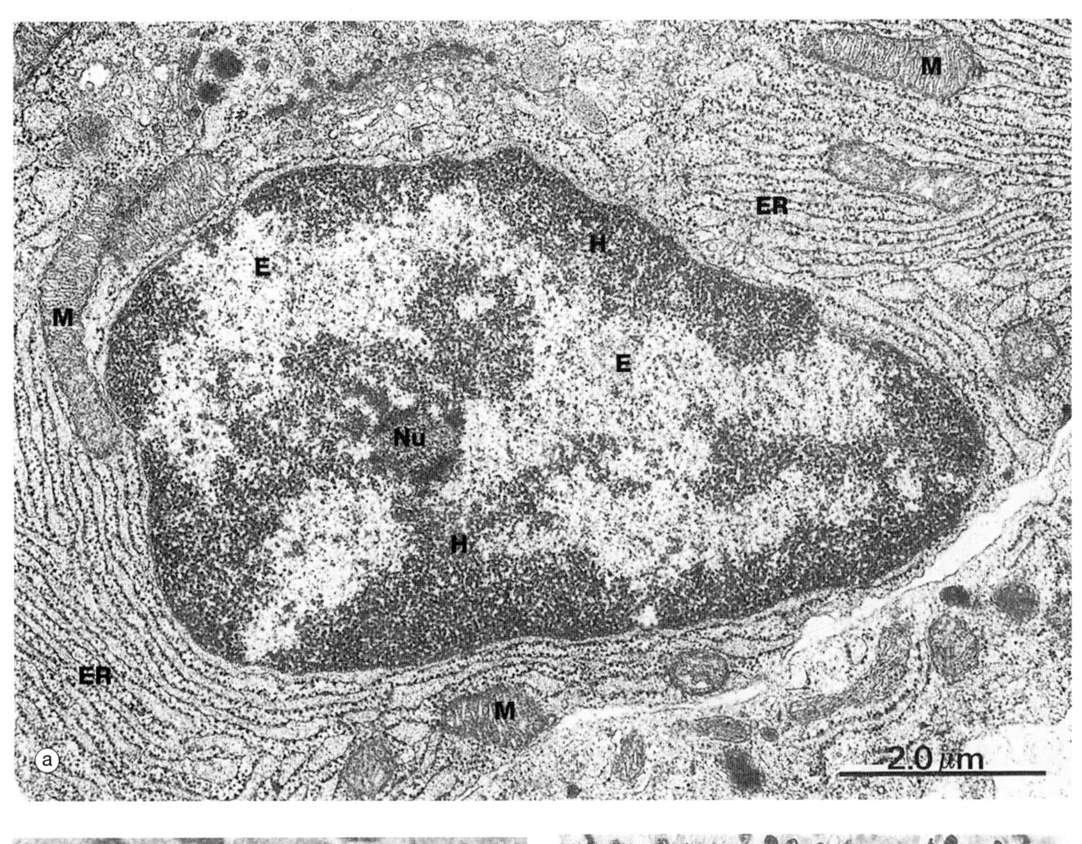

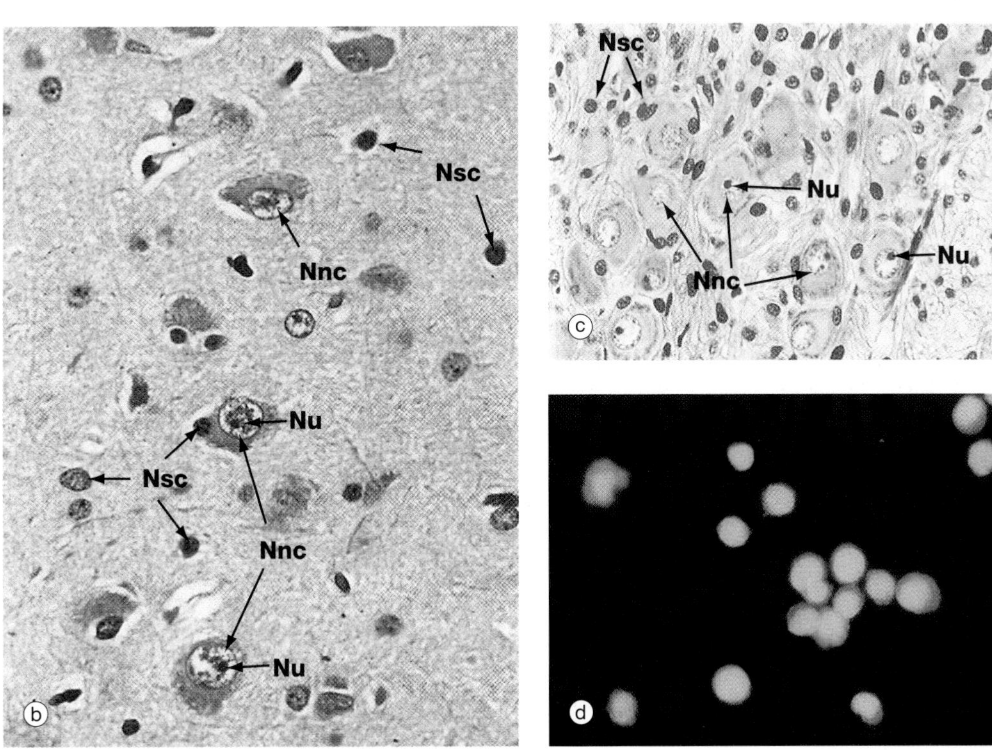

E euchromatin **ER** endoplasmic reticulum **H** heterochromatin **M** mitochondrion
Nnc nerve cell nucleus **Nsc** support cell nucleus **Nu** nucleolus

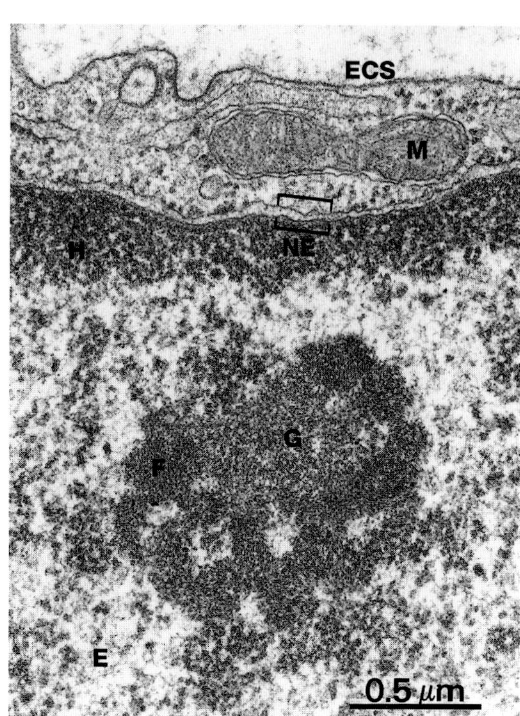

Fig. 1.4 The nucleolus
EM ×37 000

Many nuclei, especially those of cells highly active in protein synthesis, contain one or more dense structures called ***nucleoli*** which are the sites of ribosomal RNA synthesis and ribosome assembly. Ribosomal RNA and proteins, synthesised in the cytoplasm and imported back into the nucleus, are assembled into subunits. The subunits then pass back to the cytoplasm to aggregate into complete ribosomes. This micrograph shows a typical nucleolus. Ultrastructurally, nucleoli are quite variable in appearance. In this example the nucleolus consists of reticular ***nucleolonema*** with dense ***filamentous components*** **F** and paler ***granular components*** **G**. The filamentous components are thought to be the sites of ribosomal RNA synthesis, while ribosome assembly takes place in the granular components. The function of coiled bodies, which are often found associated with the nucleolus, remains to be elucidated. Note also euchromatin **E** and heterochromatin **H** within the nucleus, which is bounded by the nuclear envelope **NE**. A thin rim of cytoplasm containing a mitochondrion **M** separates the nucleus from the extracellular space **ECS**.

Nuclear appearance characteristic of cell type and state

In general the shape and appearance of a cell nucleus is typical of a particular cell type. For instance smooth muscle cell nuclei are long ovals with squared off ends, often called 'cigar-shaped', while epithelial cells usually have round nuclei and nerve cells have large nuclei and prominent nucleoli. The appearance of the nucleus may also be modified by circumstances. For example epithelial cells dividing to heal a wound will have larger nuclei with larger nucleoli than a resting cell, an appearance often called '***regenerative***' or '***reactive***', which reflects the increased protein and DNA synthesis required for cell division.

The nuclei of ***malignant cells*** that form cancers also look different from their normal counterparts. These malignant cells have larger than normal, dark-staining nuclei due to increased amounts of chromatin: many malignant cells have extra or even double the normal number of chromosomes. These features assist in the histopathological diagnosis of cancer.

E euchromatin **ECS** extracellular space **ER** endoplasmic reticulum
F filamentous component of nucleolus **G** granular component of nucleolus **H** heterochromatin
M mitochondrion **N** nucleus **NE** nuclear envelope **NP** nuclear pore **PM** plasma membrane
R ribosome

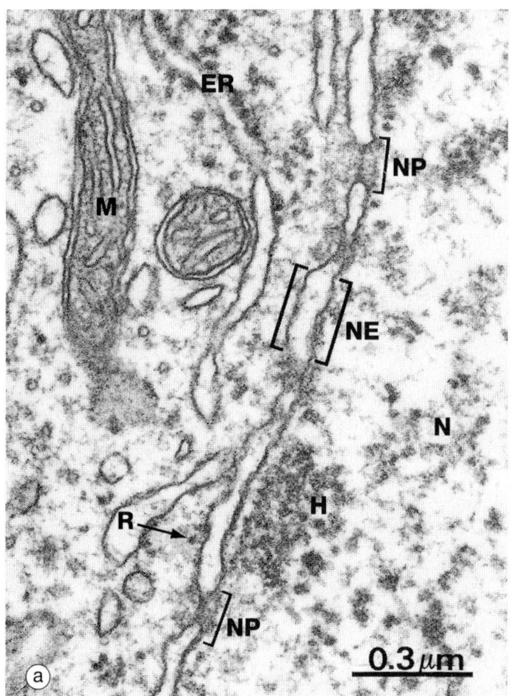

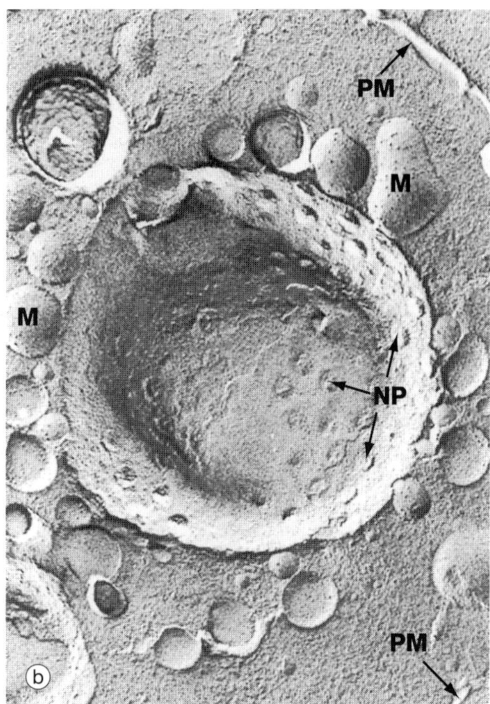

Fig. 1.5 Nuclear envelope
(a) EM ×59 000 (b) Freeze-etched preparation SEM ×34 000

The ***nuclear envelope*** **NE**, which encloses the nucleus **N**, consists of two layers of membrane with the ***intermembranous*** or ***perinuclear space*** between. The inner and outer nuclear membranes have the typical phospholipid bilayer structure but contain different integral proteins. The outer lipid bilayer is continuous with the endoplasmic reticulum **ER** and has ribosomes **R** on its cytoplasmic face. On the inner aspect of the inner nuclear membrane, there is an electron-dense layer of intermediate filaments, the ***nuclear lamina***, consisting of polypeptides called ***lamins*** that link inner membrane proteins and heterochromatin **H**.

The nuclear envelope contains numerous ***nuclear pores*** **NP** at the margins of which the inner and outer membranes become continuous. Each pore contains a ***nuclear pore complex***, an elaborate cylindrical structure consisting of approximately 50 proteins forming a central pore. Nuclear pores permit and regulate the exchange of metabolites, macromolecules and ribosomal subunits between nucleus and cytoplasm. Ions and small molecules diffuse freely through the nuclear pore. Larger molecules, such as mRNA moving from nucleus to cytoplasm and histones from cytoplasm to nucleus, dock to the nuclear pore complex by means of a targeting sequence and are moved through the pore by an energy dependent process. The nuclear pore complex may also hold together the two lipid bilayers of the nuclear envelope. Note that mitochondria **M** are also identifiable in the cytoplasm.

Micrograph (b) shows an example of a technique called ***freeze-etching***. Briefly, this method involves the rapid freezing of cells which are then fractured. Internal surfaces of the cell are exposed in at random, the fracture lines tending to follow natural planes of weakness. Surface detail is obtained by 'etching' or sublimating excess water molecules from the specimen at low temperature. A thin carbon impression is then made of the surface and this mirror image is viewed by conventional electron microscopy. Freeze-etching provides a valuable tool for studying internal cell surfaces at high resolution. In this preparation, the plane of cleavage has included part of the nuclear envelope in which nuclear pores **NP** are clearly demonstrated. Note also the outline of the plasma membrane **PM** and mitochondria **M**.

Protein synthesis

Proteins are not only a major structural component of cells, but as enzymes, transport and regulatory proteins, mediate many metabolic processes. Thus the nature and quantity of proteins within a cell determine its activity. All cellular proteins are replaced continuously. Many cells also synthesise proteins for export including glandular secretions and extracellular structural proteins like collagen. Protein synthesis is, therefore, an essential and continuous activity of all cells and the major function of some cells.

The principal organelles involved in protein synthesis are the nucleus and ***ribosomes***. Every cell contains within its DNA the code for every protein that individual could produce. Production or ***expression*** of selected proteins only is characteristic of differentiated cells. The presence of a particular protein within a cell is one possible method of identifying different cell types, e.g. the presence of actin and myosin in muscle cells.

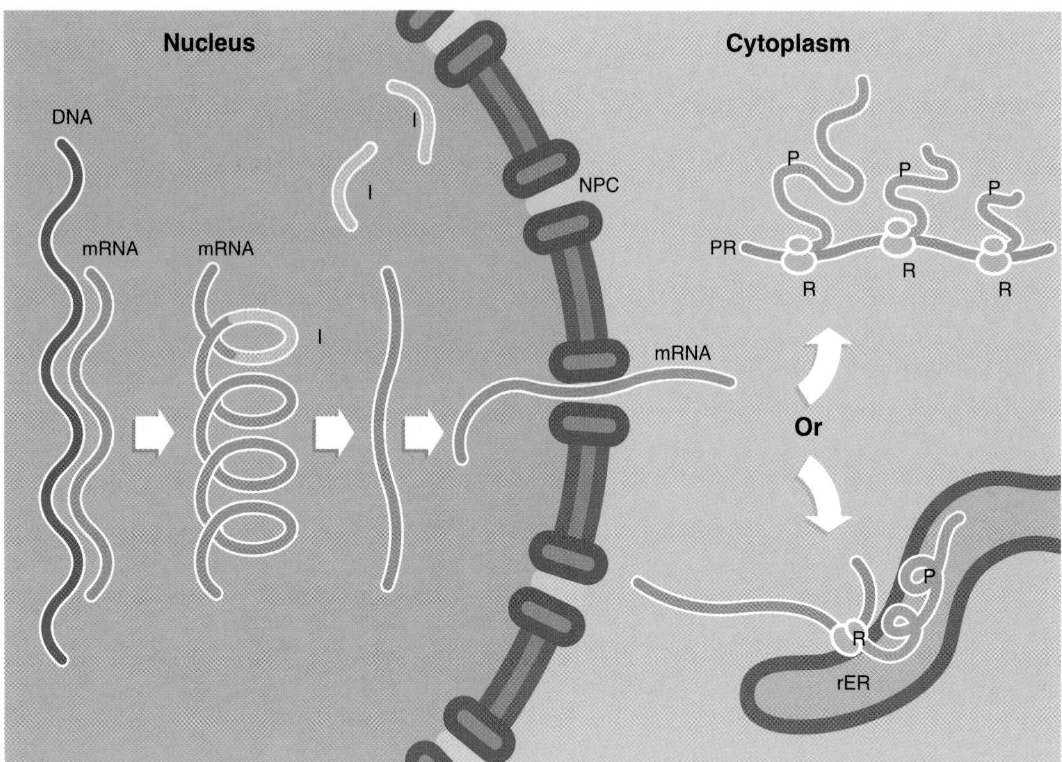

Fig. 1.6 Protein synthesis

Protein synthesis occurs in several steps. First, the DNA template is copied to form a complementary ***messenger RNA*** (**mRNA**) copy, a process known as ***transcription***. A fairly recent discovery is that the DNA template contains non-coding sequences or ***introns*** **I** which are cut or spliced out of the mRNA before it passes through the nuclear pore complex **NPC** into the cytoplasm. Here the mRNA binds to ***ribosomes*** **R**, organelles that read the mRNA sequence and ***translate*** it into the specific sequence of amino acids which characterises a particular protein.

Ribosomes are minute cytoplasmic organelles, each composed of two subunits of unequal size. Each subunit consists of a strand of RNA (***ribosomal RNA***, **rRNA**) with associated ribosomal proteins forming a globular structure. The two subunits together look something like a brioche. Ribosomes align mRNA strands so that ***transfer RNA*** (**tRNA**) molecules may be brought into position and their amino acids added sequentially to the growing polypeptide chain **P**. Other ribosomal proteins are enzymes which promote peptide bond formation between amino acids. Thus the DNA code is converted first into RNA and then into a specific protein. Ribosomes are often found attached to mRNA molecules in small spiral-shaped aggregations called ***polyribosomes*** or ***polysomes*** **PR**, formed by a single strand of mRNA with ribosomes attached along its length. Each ribosome in a polyribosome is making a separate molecule of the protein, an example of the amazing efficiency with which cellular resources are often utilised.

Ribosomes and polyribosomes may also be attached to the surface of endoplasmic reticulum. The endoplasmic reticulum consists of an interconnecting network of membranous tubules, vesicles and flattened sacs (***cisternae***) which ramifies throughout the cytoplasm. Much of its surface is studded with ribosomes, giving a 'rough' appearance leading to the name ***rough endoplasmic reticulum*** (**rER**). Proteins destined for export, as well as lysosomal proteins, are synthesised by ribosomes attached to the surface of the rER and pass through the membrane into its lumen. Integral membrane proteins are also synthesised on rER and inserted into the membrane at this point, the extracellular part of the protein protruding into the lumen of the rER and the intramembranous part held firmly in place by hydrophobic attraction. It is within the rER that proteins are folded to form their tertiary structure, intrachain disulphide bonds are formed and the first steps of glycosylation take place. In contrast, proteins destined for the cytoplasm, nucleus and mitochondria are synthesised on free ribosomes.

DNA deoxyribonucleic acid **I** intron **M** mitochondrion **mRNA** messenger ribonucleic acid
N nucleus **NE** nuclear envelope **NPC** nuclear pore complex **Nu** nucleolus **P** polypeptide chain
PR polyribosome **R** ribosome **rER** rough endoplasmic reticulum

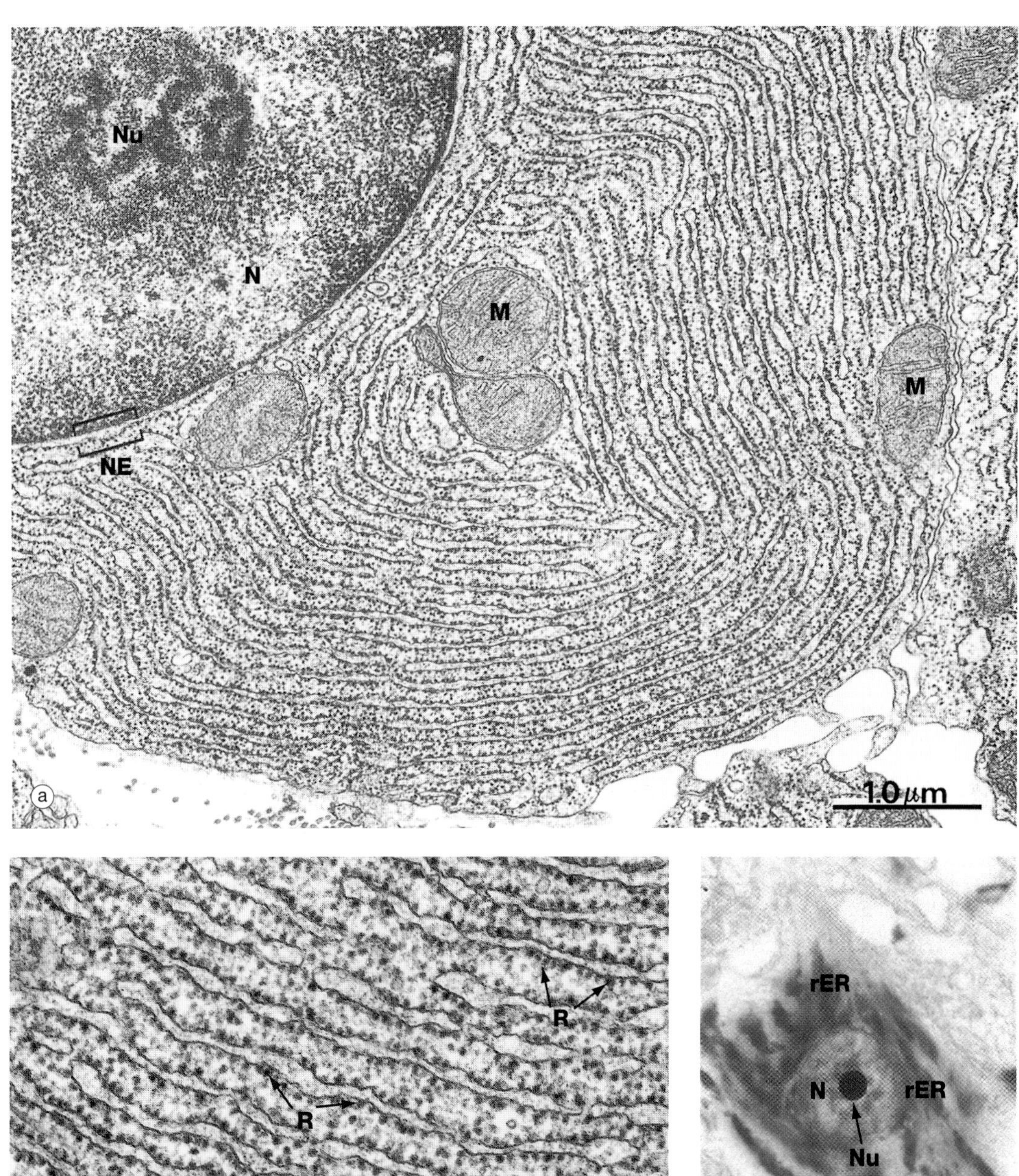

Fig. 1.7 Rough endoplasmic reticulum
(a) EM ×23 000 (b) EM ×50 000 (c) Cresyl violet ×800

These micrographs illustrate rough endoplasmic reticulum **rER** in a cell specialised for the synthesis and secretion of protein; in such cells rER tends to be profuse and to form closely packed parallel laminae of flattened cisternae. In micrograph (a), the dimensions of the rER can be compared with that of mitochondria **M** and the nucleus **N**. The nucleus typically contains a prominent nucleolus **Nu**. Note the close association between the rER and the outer lipid bilayer of the nuclear envelope **NE** with which it is in continuity. The chromatin in the nucleus is mainly dispersed (euchromatin), consistent with prolific protein synthesis.

Micrograph (b) shows part of the rER at high magnification. Numerous ribosomes **R** stud the surface of the membrane system and there are plentiful ribosomes lying free in the intervening cytosol. Micrograph (c) shows a nerve cell at high magnification stained by the basophilic dye, cresyl violet. The basophilic clumps in the cytoplasm represent areas of plentiful rough endoplasmic reticulum **rER**. The nuclear envelope can be distinguished due to the basophilia of the numerous ribosomes that stud its outer surface. The nucleus **N** contains a prominent nucleolus **Nu** and dispersed chromatin.

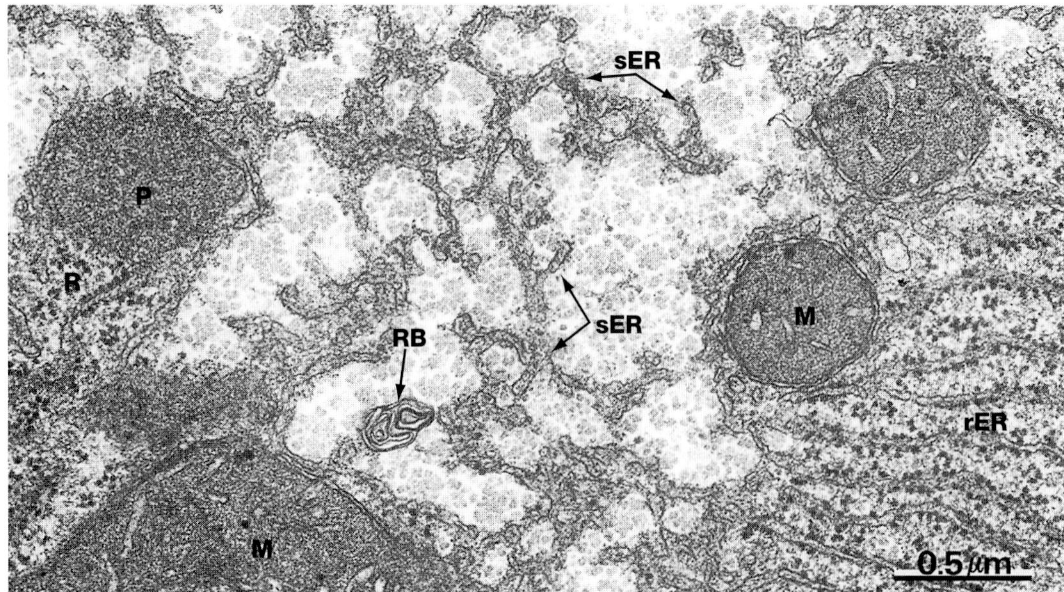

Fig. 1.8 Smooth endoplasmic reticulum
EM ×40 000

Smooth endoplasmic reticulum **sER** is continuous with and similar to rER except that it lacks ribosomes. The principal functions of smooth endoplasmic reticulum are lipid biosynthesis and membrane synthesis and repair. Fatty acids and triglycerides are mostly synthesised within the cytosol, whereas cholesterol and phospholipids are synthesised in sER. In liver cells, smooth endoplasmic reticulum is rich in cytochrome P450 and plays a major role in the metabolism of glycogen and detoxification of various noxious metabolic by-products, drugs and alcohol. In muscle cells, where it is called ***sarcoplasmic reticulum***, sER is involved in the storage and release of calcium ions that activate the contractile mechanism (see Ch. 6).

Most cells contain only scattered elements of sER interspersed with the other organelles. Cell types with prominent sER include liver cells and those cells specialised for lipid biosynthesis, such as the steroid hormone-secreting cells of the adrenal glands and the gonads. In this micrograph from the liver, most of the membranous elements are sER but it is continuous with rough endoplasmic reticulum **rER** in the lower right of the field. This field also includes several mitochondria **M**, a peroxisome **P** (see Fig. 1.14), free ribosomes and polyribosomes **R** and a whorl of membrane in a residual body **RB** (see Fig. 1.11).

Import, export and intracellular transportation

Movement of materials into and out of cells and between separate compartments of a cell involves crossing lipid membranes. The plasma membrane thus controls the interaction of the cell with the external environment, mediating the exchange of nutrients and waste products, secretions and signalling mechanisms. Lipid membranes also separate different compartments of the cell, many of which contain mutually incompatible biochemical reactions. For instance, the process of protein synthesis and export which takes place in the rough endoplasmic reticulum (rER) and Golgi apparatus must be kept separate from the garbage disposal and recycling plant, the ***lysosome***. Likewise, microorganisms phagocytosed by cells must be killed and disposed of without damage to normal structures and mechanisms.

Information must also cross membranes telling the cell when to divide, release secretions, contract or perform many other functions. Many of the mechanisms used for transport of cargo also serve to transmit messages to the interior of the cell. There are also dedicated mechanisms for the transfer of information, such as the transient depolarisation of the plasma membrane along the length of a nerve axon in the conduction of a nerve impulse. Histologically, these transport processes can only be observed indirectly: for example, cells suspended in hypotonic solutions swell due to passive uptake of water, whereas cells placed in hypertonic solutions tend to shrink due to outflow of water. Radioisotope labelling techniques can be used to follow active transport processes. Bulk transport, however, is readily observable by microscopy (see Fig. 1.12). Both active and passive transport processes are enhanced if the area of the plasma membrane is increased by folds or projections of the cell surface as exemplified by the absorptive cells lining the small intestine (see Fig. 1.2).

The main mechanisms by which materials and information are transported across lipid membranes are outlined below. As mentioned above, cargo transport mechanisms are also used to transport signalling molecules into cells to interact with intracellular receptors.

- **Passive diffusion**. This type of transport is entirely dependent on the presence of a concentration gradient across the plasma membrane. Lipids and lipid-soluble molecules such as ethanol pass freely through plasma membranes, which also offer little barrier to the diffusion of gases such as oxygen and carbon dioxide. The plasma membrane is, in general, impermeable to hydrophilic molecules. Nevertheless, some small molecules, including water and urea, and inorganic ions such as bicarbonate, are able to pass down osmotic and electrochemical gradients through the membrane via hydrophilic regions, the nature of which remains obscure. Lipid soluble hormones such as oestrogen and testosterone also enter the cell in this way to deliver their signal to the cell by interacting with nuclear receptors.
- **Facilitated diffusion**. This type of transport is also concentration-dependent and involves the movement of hydrophilic molecules, such as water, ions, glucose and amino acids. This process is strictly passive but requires the presence of protein carrier molecules (known as ***pores*** or ***channels***). ***Aquaporins*** are an important example of facilitated diffusion. These channels allow water to cross plasma membranes at a much faster rate than by diffusion alone. There are many different aquaporin molecules, some of which are highly specific for water molecules, while others allow the passage of other small molecules such as urea or glycerol. Some facilitated diffusion pores are ***gated*** which means that the pore is open or closed depending on different physiological conditions e.g. open only at a particular pH.
- **Active transport**. This mode of transport is not only independent of concentration gradients, but also often operates against extreme concentration gradients. The classic example of this form of transport is the continuous movement of sodium out of the cell by the ***sodium pump***, a transmembrane protein complex (***Na^+-K^+ ATPase***) which exchanges a sodium for a potassium ion across the membrane. ATP is converted to ADP in the process to generate the energy required.
- **Bulk transport**. Transport of large molecules or small particles into, out of or between compartments within the cell is mediated by subcellular, transient structures known as ***coated vesicles***. In brief, these structures can be used to transport proteins embedded in the membrane of the vesicle (e.g. proteins destined for the plasma membrane) or soluble cargo within the lumen of the vesicle. This mechanism is dependent on the fluidity and deformability of lipid membranes and the mobility of intrinsic membrane proteins within the plane of the membrane. To form a coated vesicle, ***coat proteins*** bind to the membrane and induce it to form a bud that is pinched off to form a separate organelle containing its burden of cargo. The vesicle quickly sheds its coat proteins and is moved by elements of the cytoskeleton to its target site. Here the vesicle fuses with the target membrane releasing its contents. Specific examples such as ***endocytosis***, ***exocytosis*** and ***intracellular transport vesicles*** are given in Figs 1.9–1.12.
- **Transmembrane signalling**. Signalling molecules bind and activate ***membrane receptors***, which are usually enzymes. The activated enzyme modifies a range of cytoplasmic molecules, which pass the message to the intracellular site.
- Another method of information transfer occurs between nerve cells, or between a nerve cell and a muscle cell. A chemical ***neurotransmitter*** is released from a nerve cell and binds to a receptor on the adjacent nerve or muscle cell, opening an ion channel and thus depolarising the membrane. In this case, a specific chemical interaction is converted to an electrical signal at the cell membrane.

M mitochondria **P** peroxisome **R** ribosomes **RB** residual body **rER** rough endoplasmic reticulum **sER** smooth endoplasmic reticulum

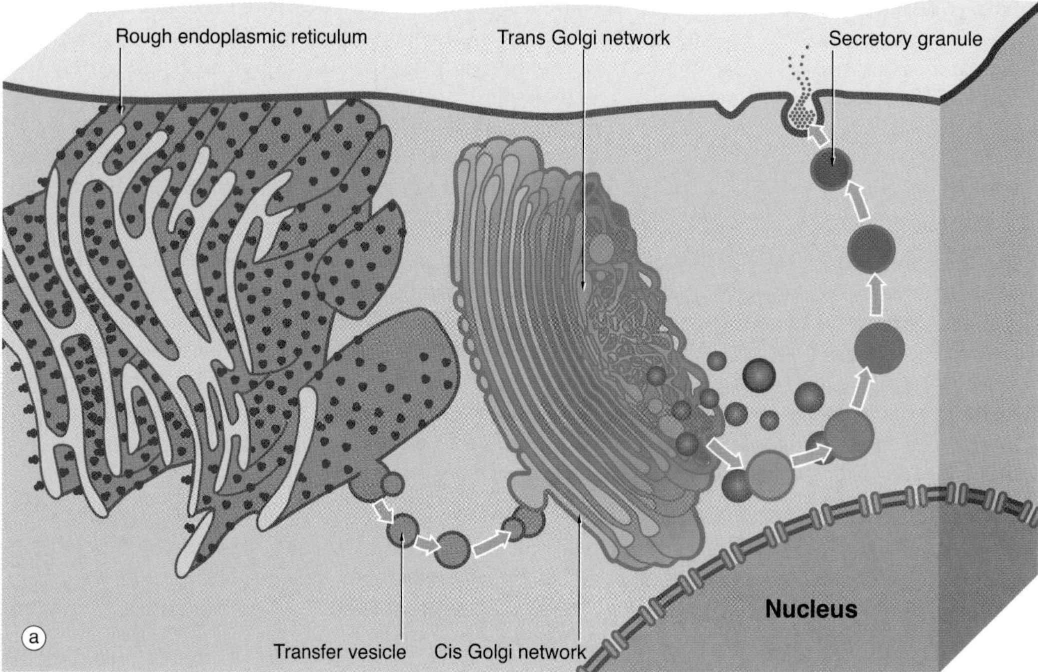

Fig. 1.9 Golgi apparatus
(a) Schematic diagram (b) EM ×30 000 (c) H & E ×300 (d) Immunoperoxidase ×100 (e) Iron haematoxylin ×400

Diagram (a) illustrates the main structural features of the ***Golgi apparatus*** or ***stack*** and summarises the mechanism by which secretory products are packaged within membrane-bound vesicles. A cell may contain one or more Golgi stacks and these may break up and reform during different phases of the cell cycle or in different physiological states. The Golgi apparatus consists of stacked, saucer-shaped membrane-bound cisternae. The outermost cisternae take the form of a network of tubules known as the ***cis*** and ***trans Golgi networks***. Proteins synthesised in the rough ER are transported to the Golgi apparatus in coated vesicles; the coat protein in this case is known as ***coat protein complex II (COP II)***. On arrival at the convex ***forming face*** or ***cis Golgi network*** of the Golgi apparatus, the coat proteins disengage and the vesicles fuse with the membrane of the forming face. In the Golgi apparatus the glycosylation of proteins, begun in the rER, is completed by sequential addition of sugar residues and the proteins are packaged for transport to their final destination. There are two current theories as to how this happens. The most accepted theory postulates that each cisterna is enriched for the specific enzyme to add a specific sugar and that proteins are passed from cisterna to cisterna by formation of a series of ***coat protein complex I (COP I)*** coated vesicles which then fuse with the next cisterna in the stack. Alternatively, there is now some evidence to show that the medial cisternae mature, with specific enzymes being moved backwards to less mature cisternae by means of coated vesicles. It is possible that both mechanisms operate depending on circumstances. On arrival at the concave ***maturing face*** or ***trans Golgi network***, the proteins are accurately sorted into secretory vesicles destined for the extracellular space (e.g. hormones, neurotransmitters, collagen) or the plasma membrane (e.g. cell surface receptors, adhesion molecules) or intracellular organelles such as lysosomes. The sorting of cargo into secretory vesicles is dependent on binding of specific adapter molecules to the cargo, which then bind to specific coat proteins. Secretory vesicles become increasingly condensed as they migrate through the cytoplasm to form mature ***secretory granules***, which are then liberated at the cell surface by exocytosis. A group of membrane proteins called ***SNAREs*** regulate docking and fusion of coated vesicles to their target membrane.

Micrograph (b) illustrates a particularly well-developed Golgi apparatus; transfer vesicles **T** and elements of the rough endoplasmic reticulum **rER** are seen adjacent to the forming face. A variety of larger vesicles **V** can be seen in the concavity of the maturing face, some of which appear to be budding from the Golgi cisternae **C**; such vesicles could be either secretory granules or lysosomes. Note the proximity of the Golgi apparatus to the nucleus **N**; the nuclear membrane **NM** is particularly well demonstrated in this micrograph.

Micrograph (c) illustrates a group of plasma cells from inflamed tissue; these cells are responsible for antibody production as part of the body's immune defences (see Ch. 11). The plentiful rER is strongly basophilic and the protein is acidophilic so that there is staining with both eosin and haematoxylin giving a purplish or amphophilic colour to the cytoplasm. The well-developed Golgi complex **G** consists of lipid (membrane), which is dissolved out during preparation. Thus the Golgi is unstained and appears as a pale area (negative image) adjacent to the nucleus **N**.

Plasma cells **P** are also shown in micrograph (d), a section of tonsil. This example of the ***immunoperoxidase method*** demonstrates plasma cells that have cytoplasm that is packed with IgG. This method of staining is important in diagnostic histopathology and is described in Appendix 2.

The staining method in micrograph (e) is used here to demonstrate secretory granules in the cells of the pancreas, which secretes digestive enzymes. The secretory cells are grouped around a minute central duct **D**, and the secretory granules, which are stained black, are concentrated towards the luminal aspect of the cell. The nuclei **N** of the secretory cells have dispersed chromatin and prominent nucleoli and are arranged around the periphery of the secretory unit.

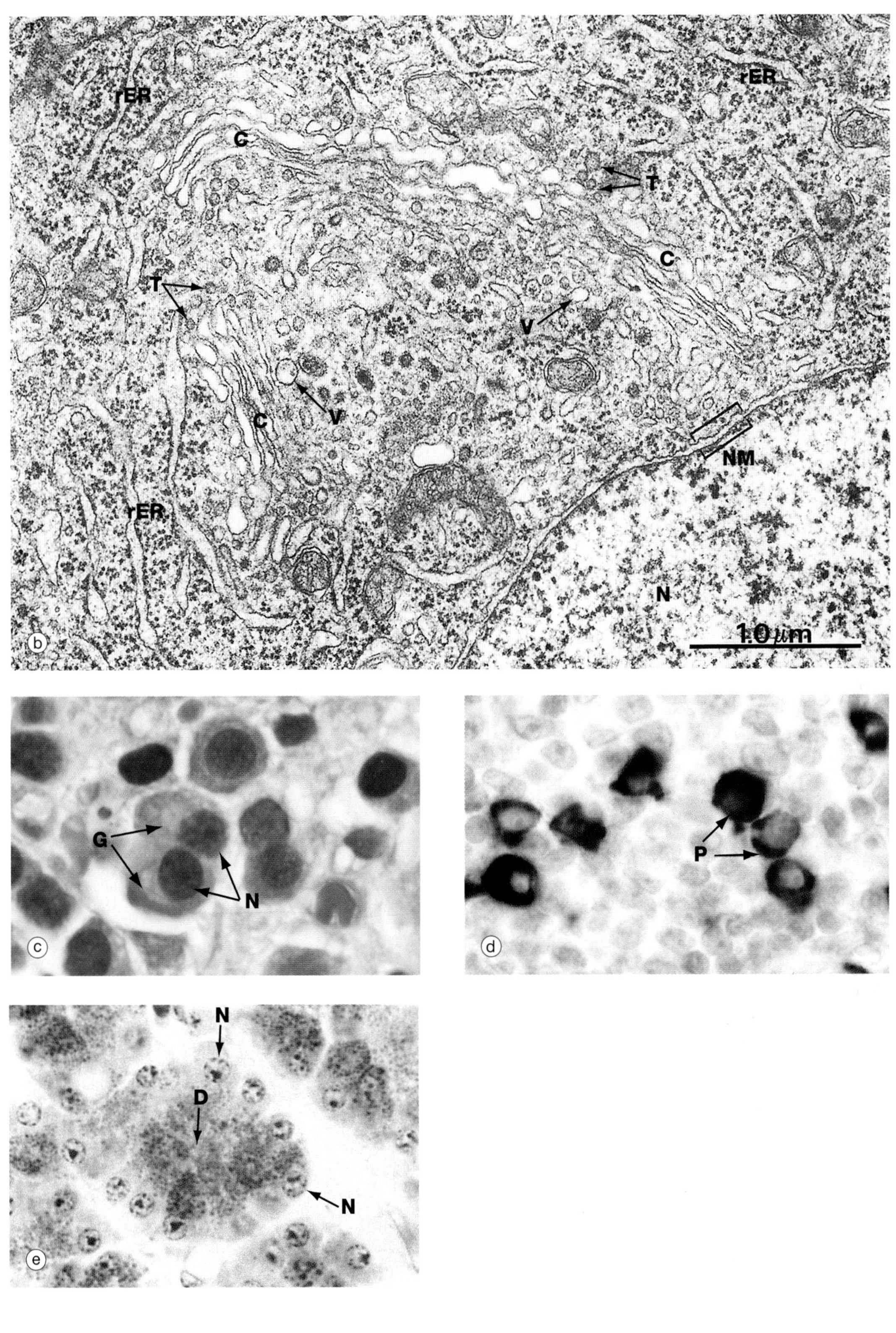

C Golgi cisternae **D** central duct **G** Golgi apparatus **N** nucleus **NM** nuclear membrane
P plasma cell **rER** rough endoplasmic reticulum **T** transfer vesicles **V** vesicles

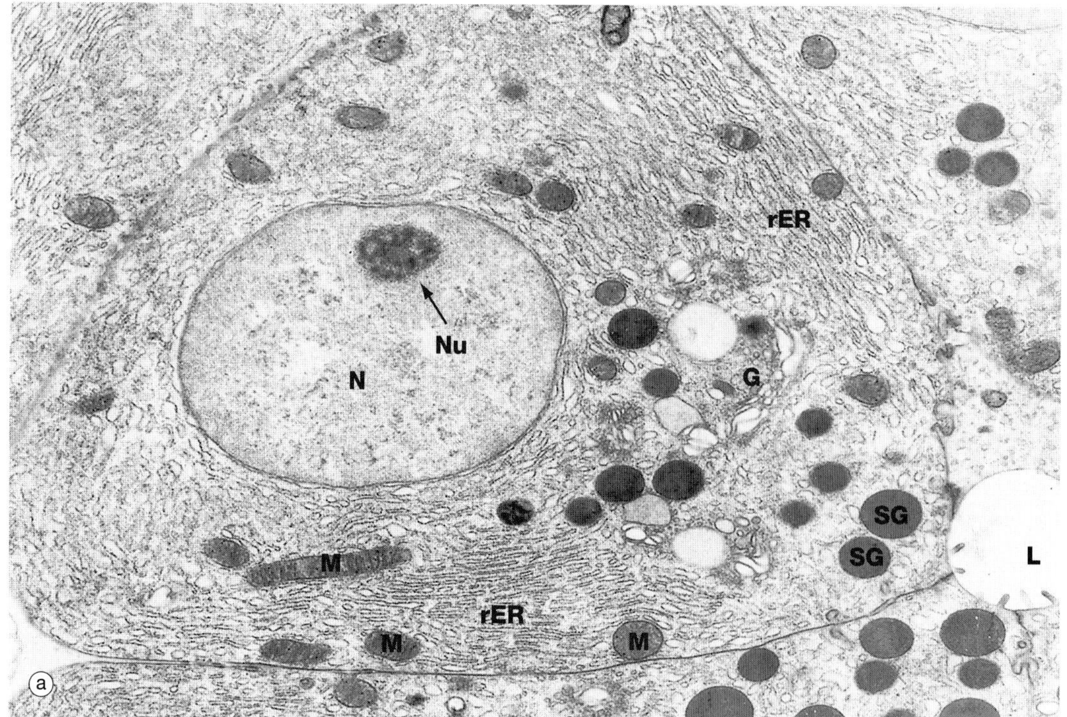

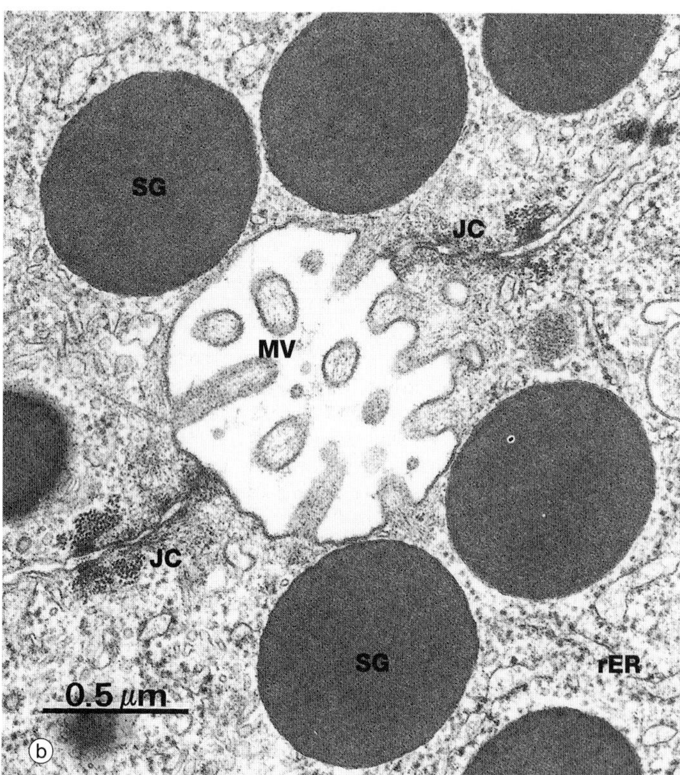

Fig. 1.10 Exocytosis
(a) EM ×14 000 (b) EM ×41 500

Micrographs (a) and (b) illustrate typical protein-secreting cells from the pancreas, which produces digestive enzymes. The nucleus **N** has dispersed chromatin and a prominent nucleolus **Nu.** The rough endoplasmic reticulum **rER** and Golgi apparatus **G** are prominent. Mitochondria **M** supply energy**.** Membrane bound secretory granules **SG** (or vesicles) become increasingly electron dense as they approach the glandular lumen **L**. At the cell apex, secretory granules dock with the plasma membrane forming a transient opening (***porosome***) through which the secretory product exits. The empty secretory vesicle is recycled. Exocytosis may be continuous (***constitutive secretion***) or dependent on a signal (***regulated secretion***), as in this case where digestive enzymes are secreted in response to food in the duodenum.

Micrograph (b) shows secretory granules **SG** approaching the apices of two pancreatic secretory cells and converging on a tiny excretory duct formed by junctional complexes **JC** (see Fig. 5.10) joining adjacent cells. Stubby microvilli **MV** protrude into the excretory duct.

B bacterium **CL** clathrin **CP** coated pit **CV** coated vesicle **G** Golgi apparatus
JC junctional complex **L** gland lumen **Li** ligand **M** mitochondrion **MV** microvilli
MVB multivesicular body **N** nucleus **Nu** nucleolus **P** phagosome **PL** phagolysosome
R receptor **RB** residual body **RE** recycling endosome **rER** rough endoplasmic reticulum
SE sorting endosome **SG** secretory granules

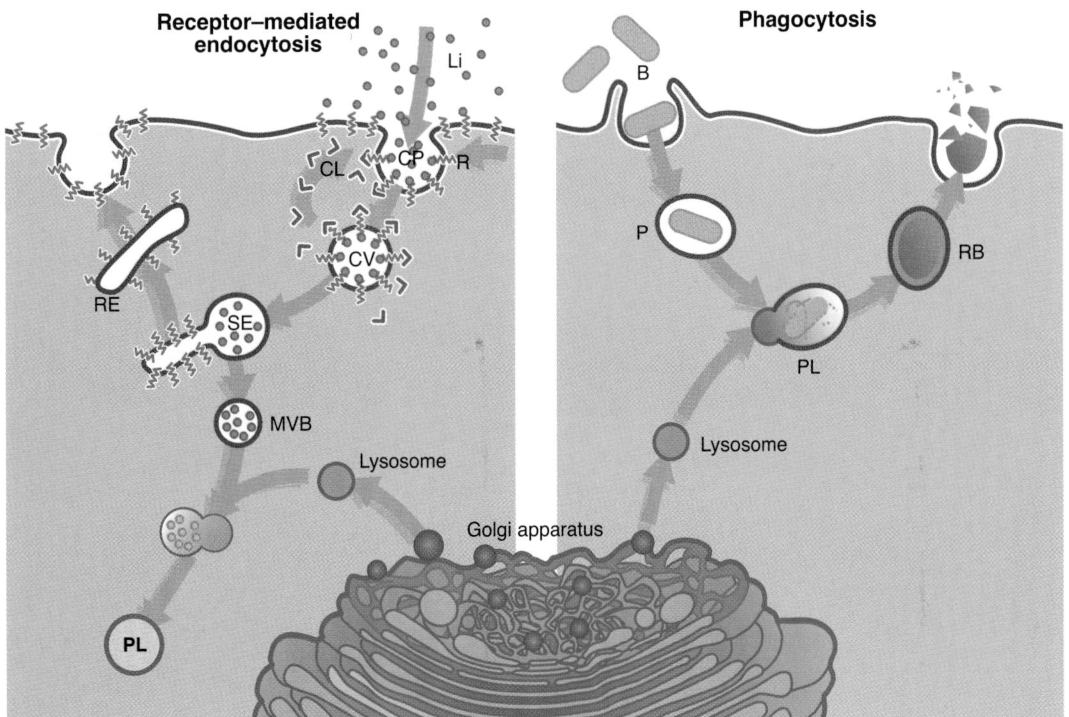

Fig. 1.11 Endocytosis

Cells take up particulate matter and large macromolecules by a variety of processes, collectively known as ***endocytosis.*** The best known of these mechanisms is ***phagocytosis***, which is used by cells of the defence system to ingest and kill pathogenic organisms. ***Receptor-mediated endocytosis***, which uses the coated vesicle mechanism, is probably much more widespread. ***Pinocytosis*** and ***macropinocytosis***, which non-specifically sample the extracellular fluid, and various other types of endocytosis, including the role of ***caveolae***, are less well understood. The diagram summarises the main steps of receptor-mediated endocytosis and phagocytosis. Actin microfilaments and microtubules play an important role in moving vesicles around the cell.

Receptor-mediated endocytosis

Receptor-mediated endocytosis is used extensively for uptake of specific molecules (***ligands* Li**) that bind to cell surface receptors **R**. A well-known example is the ***low-density lipoprotein*** (LDL) receptor. The receptors are intrinsic membrane proteins with extracellular and cytoplasmic domains. The cytoplasmic tail of the receptor binds to the coat protein ***clathrin* CL** in a ***coated pit* CP.** The receptors with bound ligand are concentrated in the coated pit, which then buds off to form a ***coated vesicle* CV**. The vesicles very quickly lose their clathrin coat and fuse with ***sorting endosomes* SE**, which are dynamic tubulovesicular structures usually found close to the plasma membrane. The acid pH in the lumen of sorting endosomes encourages dissociation of receptor and ligand; these are then quickly separated so that most of the membrane and its intrinsic receptors are shuttled to ***recycling endosomes* RE** and from there back to the cell surface. Some membrane receptors may go through this whole cycle up to 300 times and the expression of receptors on the cell surface can be regulated by this mechanism. The remaining part of the sorting endosome, which contains the unbound LDL, converts into a ***late endosome***, often called a ***multivesicular body* MVB**. Multivesicular bodies are moved towards the Golgi apparatus where they fuse with lysosomes. Degradative enzymes within the lysosomes, now called ***phagolysosomes* PL** digest the protein component of the LDL, freeing cholesterol for incorporation into membranes.

Phagocytosis

Bacteria **B** are taken up by specialised phagocytic cells, such as neutrophil polymorphs and monocytes, through the process of phagocytosis. The bacterium binds to cell surface receptors, triggering the formation of pseudopodia that extend around the organism until they fuse leaving the engulfed bacterium in a membrane-bound ***phagosome* P** within the cytoplasm. At this stage, recycling of membrane and receptors back to the plasma membrane takes place. The phagosome then fuses with a lysosome to become a ***phagolysosome* PL** (sometimes called a ***secondary lysosome***) and the bacterium is subjected to the toxic activities of the lysosomal enzymes. These enzymes also break down the components of the dead bacteria, which may be released into the cytoplasm, expelled from the cell by exocytosis or remain in the cytoplasm as a residual body **RB**.

Lysosomes are also involved in the degradation of cellular organelles, many of which have only a finite lifespan and are therefore replaced continuously; this lysosomal function is termed ***autophagy***. Most autophagocytic degradation products accumulate and become indistinguishable from the residual bodies of endocytosis. With advancing age, residual bodies accumulate in the cells of some tissues and appear as brown lipofuscin granules (see Fig. 1.15).

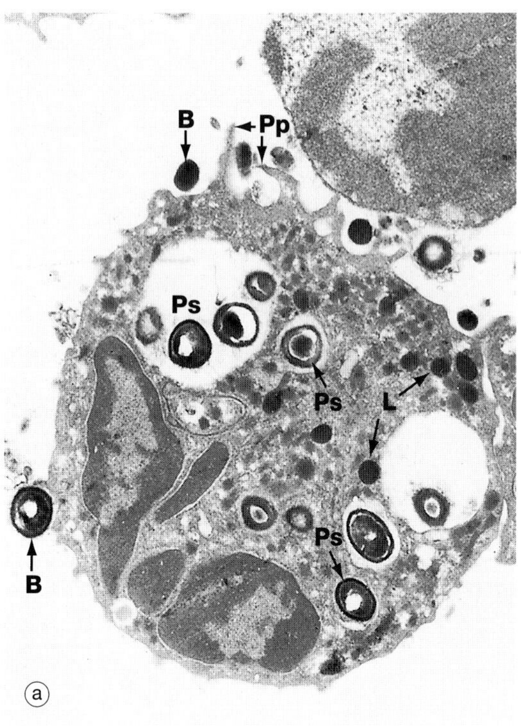

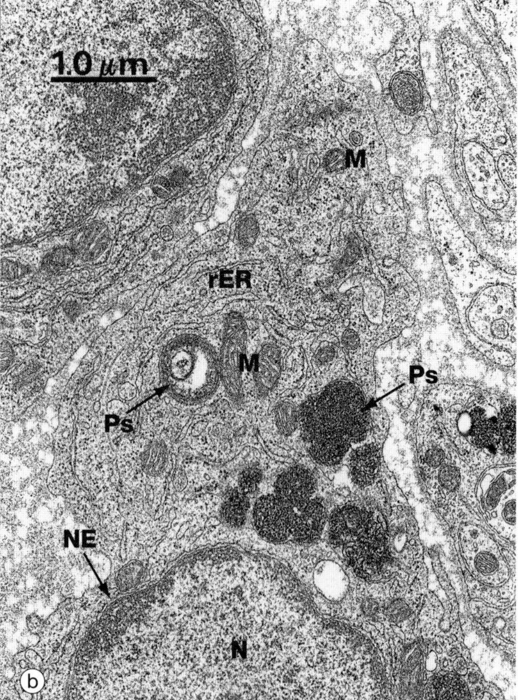

Fig. 1.12 Phagocytosis
(a) EM ×11 750 (b) EM ×14 000

Micrograph (a) illustrates a professional phagocytic white blood cell, a ***neutrophil polmorph*** (see Ch. 3), in the process of engulfing and destroying bacteria **B**. Note the manner in which pseudopodia **Pp** embrace the bacteria before engulfment. Note also phagosomes **Ps** containing bacteria in various stages of degradation. Several lysosomes **L** are also visible.

Micrograph (b) is a high power view of phagosomes **Ps** in the cytoplasm of a macrophage, another professional phagocyte found in almost all tissues. The large, irregularly shaped membrane-bound phagosomes contain coiled fragments of plasma membrane and other cellular constituents derived from damaged cells. This macrophage is performing its function as a scavenger cell by phagocytosing dead and damaged cells and recycling their components. Note also the cell nucleus **N** with its easily identified nuclear envelope **NE**, mitochondria **M** and rough endoplasmic reticulum **rER**.

Microbial tricks in intracellular infections

Phagocytosis is a vital component of the ***innate immune system*** (see Ch. 11). Phagocytosis of bacteria in most cases results in bacterial cell death with lysis of the dead organisms. However, some pathogenic organisms have learned to use the phagocytic mechanism to their own advantage to gain entry to the cell and to grow there in a protected environment safe from other elements of the immune system. For instance, ***Mycobacterium tuberculosis***, the agent responsible for the important worldwide infection tuberculosis, is able to grow and divide within macrophages. Some pathogens have evolved ingenious mechanisms to avoid death and destruction within the phagolysosome. ***Listeria monocytogenes***, a rare cause of food poisoning, is able to disrupt the phagosomal membrane and escape into the cell cytoplasm. ***M. tuberculosis*** can prevent the phagosome from fusing with a lysosome and lives and divides safely within the phagosome. Some viruses, on the other hand, gain entry to the cell by receptor-mediated endocytosis. Both poliovirus and adenovirus use this mechanism, casting their protein coats inside the endosome and allowing their genome to escape into the cytoplasm.

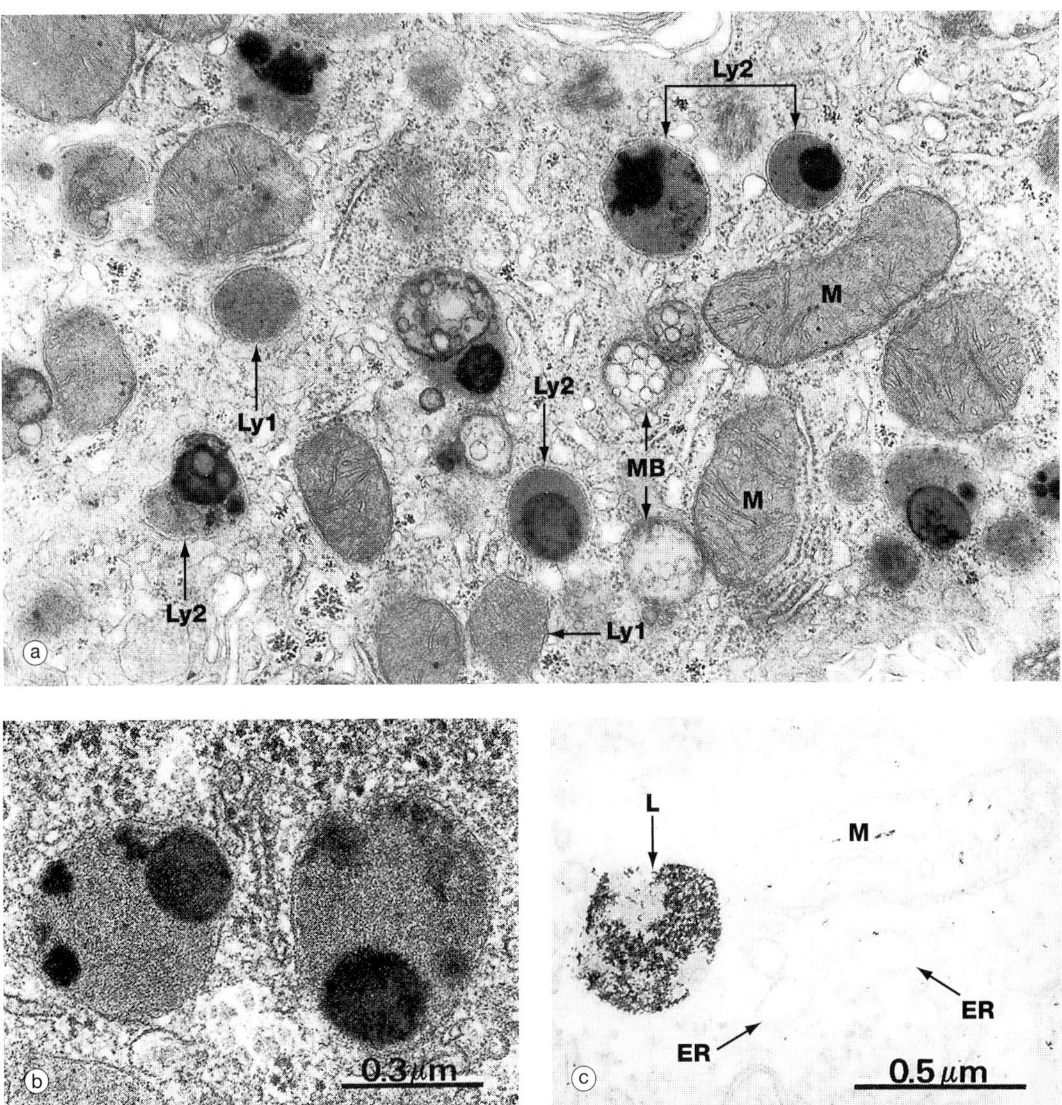

Fig. 1.13 Lysosomes
(a) EM ×27 000 (b) EM ×60 000 (c) Histochemical method for acid phosphatase: EM ×50 000

These micrographs show the typical features of lysosomes and residual bodies. Micrograph (a) shows part of the cytoplasm of a liver cell. Lysosomes **Ly1** vary greatly in size and appearance but are recognised as membrane-bound organelles containing an amorphous granular material. Phagolysosomes or secondary lysosomes **Ly2** are even more variable in appearance but are recognisable by their diverse particulate content, some of which is extremely electron-dense. The distinction between residual bodies and secondary lysosomes is often difficult. Late endosomes or multivesicular bodies **MB** are also seen in this micrograph. Note the size of lysosomes relative to mitochondria **M**.

Micrograph (b) shows two secondary lysosomes at higher magnification, allowing the limiting membrane to be visualised. Both contain electron-dense particulate material and amorphous granular material.

The lysosomal enzymes comprise more than 40 different degradative enzymes including proteases, lipases and nucleases. These are collectively known as acid hydrolases because they are optimally active at a pH of about 5.0. This may be a protective mechanism for the cell should lysosomal enzymes escape into the cytosol where they would be less active at the higher pH. Histochemical methods can be used to demonstrate sites of enzyme activity within cells and thus act as markers for organelles that contain these enzymes. Such a method has been used in micrograph (c) to demonstrate the presence of ***acid phosphatase***, a typical lysosomal enzyme; enzyme activity is represented by the electron-dense area within a lysosome **L**. Other organelles remain unstained, but the outline of a mitochondrion **M** and saccules of endoplasmic reticulum **ER** can nevertheless be identified.

B bacteria **ER** endoplasmic reticulum **L** and **Ly1** lysosomes **Ly2** secondary or phagolysosomes **M** mitochondrion **MB** multivesicular body **N** nucleus **NE** nuclear envelope **Pp** pseudopodia **Ps** phagosome **rER** rough endoplasmic reticulum

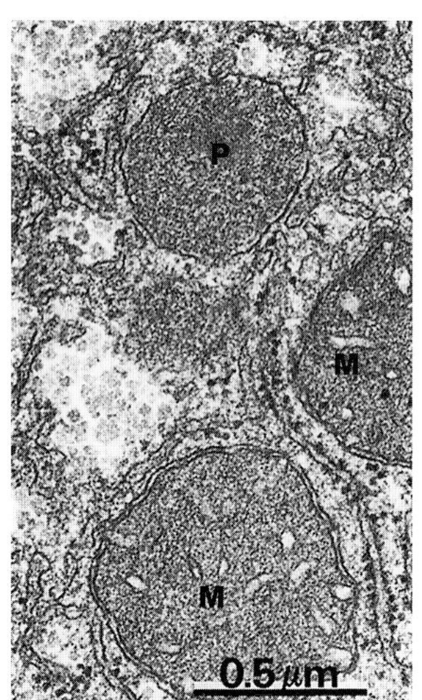

Fig. 1.14 Peroxisomes
EM ×40 000

Peroxisomes or ***microbodies*** are small, spherical, membrane-bound organelles that closely resemble lysosomes in size and ultrastructure. However, they contain an entirely different set of enzymes which can be demonstrated by histochemical techniques. Peroxisomes contain ***oxidases*** involved in certain catabolic pathways (e.g. β oxidation of long-chain fatty acids) which result in the formation of hydrogen peroxide, a potentially cytotoxic by-product. Nonetheless, hydrogen peroxide is used by certain phagocytic cells of the defence system to kill ingested microorganisms. Peroxisomes also contain ***catalase***, which regulates hydrogen peroxide concentration, utilising it in the oxidation of a variety of potentially toxic substances including phenols and alcohol.

The peroxisomes of many species have a central crystalloid structure called a ***nucleoid*** which contains the enzyme ***urate oxidase***. This is not present in humans, who thus lack the ability to metabolise urates. The peroxisomes of the liver and kidney are particularly large and abundant, reflecting the functions of these organs in lipid metabolism and management of metabolic waste products. In this micrograph, note the fine, granular electron-dense contents of a peroxisome **P**, the size of which can be compared to that of adjacent mitochondria **M**.

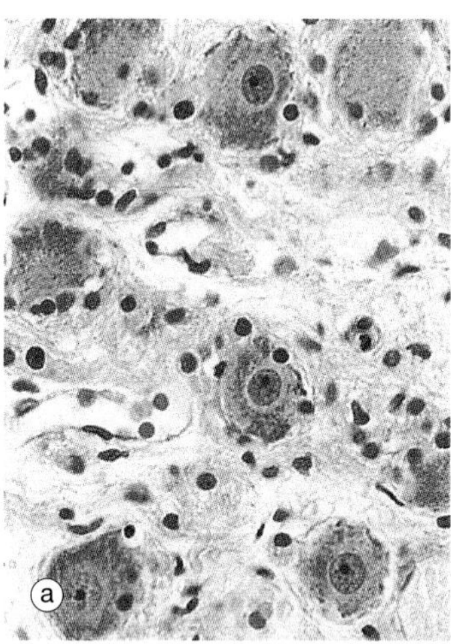

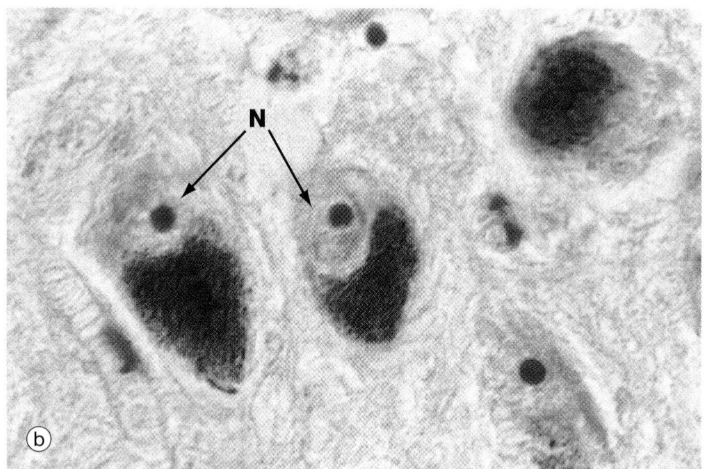

Fig. 1.15 Cellular pigments: lipofuscin and melanin
(a) H & E ×320 (b) Modified Azan ×600

Most mammalian tissues have minimal intrinsic colour: thus the need for staining for microscopy. A few tissues, however, contain intracellular pigments such as ***lipofuscin***, which probably represents an insoluble degradation product of organelle turnover. With increasing age, it accumulates as brown granular material in the cytoplasm, particularly of sympathetic ganglion cells, as seen in micrograph (a), other neurones and cardiac muscle cells; it is thus sometimes referred to as 'age pigment'. Another natural pigment is ***melanin***, which is mainly responsible for skin colour (see Ch. 9). This brown pigment is also present in nerve cells in certain brain regions such as the substantia nigra, shown in micrograph (b) where the cell cytoplasm is largely obscured by its content of brown melanin pigment. This specimen has been stained by the Azan method to pick out the nuclei **N** which are stained pale blue with prominent magenta nucleoli.

Mutation in a single gene may have widespread effects

Lysosomal storage diseases are rare congenital disorders mainly caused by a mutation in the gene coding for one or other lysosomal enzyme. This may lead to either production of a defective enzyme or no enzyme at all. Predictably, the enzyme substrate collects in cells and in some cases can be identified in tissues submitted for a diagnostic biopsy, e.g. ***Tay–Sachs disease, Gaucher's disease***. Some of these conditions are associated with a typical phenotype or appearance of the affected person, e.g. ***Hurler syndrome***.

M mitochondrion **N** nucleus **P** peroxisome

Energy production and storage

All cellular functions are dependent on a continuous supply of energy, which is derived from the sequential breakdown of organic molecules during the process of ***cellular respiration***. The energy released during this process is ultimately stored in the form of ***ATP*** (adenosine triphosphate) molecules. In all cells, ATP forms a pool of readily available energy for all the metabolic functions of the cell. The main substrates for cellular respiration are simple sugars and lipids, particularly glucose and fatty acids. Cellular respiration of glucose (***glycolysis***) begins in the cytosol, where it is partially degraded to form pyruvic acid, yielding a small amount of ATP. Pyruvic acid then diffuses into specialised membranous organelles called ***mitochondria*** where, in the presence of oxygen, it is degraded to carbon dioxide and water; this process yields a large quantity of ATP. In contrast, fatty acids pass directly into mitochondria where they are also degraded to carbon dioxide and water; this also generates a large amount of ATP. Glycolysis may occur in the absence of oxygen and is then termed ***anaerobic respiration***, whereas mitochondrial respiration is dependent on a continuous supply of oxygen and is therefore termed ***aerobic respiration***. Mitochondria are the principal organelles involved in cellular respiration in mammals and are found in large numbers in metabolically active cells, such as those of liver and skeletal muscle.

When there is excess fuel available, most cells convert glucose and fatty acids into glycogen and triglycerides respectively for storage. The amounts of each vary in different cell types. For example, nerve cells contain very little of either, most of the body's limited store of glycogen is found in muscle and liver cells and triglycerides can be stored in almost unlimited amounts in fat (adipose) cells.

Fig. 1.16 Mitochondria

Mitochondria vary considerably in size and shape but are most often elongated, cigar-shaped organelles. Mitochondria are very mobile, moving around the cell by means of microtubules, a component of the cytoskeleton (see below). They tend to localise at intracellular sites of maximum energy requirement. The number of mitochondria in cells is highly variable; liver cells contain as many as 2000 mitochondria, whereas inactive cells contain very few. The numbers of mitochondria in a cell are modified by mitochondrial division and fusion. In some cells fused mitochondria may form an interconnected network throughout the cytoplasm.

Each mitochondrion consists of four compartments:

- The ***outer membrane*** is relatively permeable as it contains a pore-forming protein, known as ***porin***, which allows free passage of small molecules. The outer membrane contains enzymes that convert certain lipid substrates into forms that can be metabolised within the mitochondrion.
- The ***inner membrane***, which is thinner than the outer, is thrown into complex folds and tubules called ***cristae*** that project into the inner cavity. In some cell types mitochondria typically have tubular cristae (see Fig. 17.18).
- The inner cavity filled by the ***mitochondrial matrix***. The matrix contains a number of dense ***matrix granules***, thought to be binding sites for calcium, which is stored in mitochondria.
- The ***intermembranous space*** between the two membranes also contains a variety of enzymes.

Aerobic respiration takes place within the matrix and on the inner membrane, a process enhanced by the large surface area provided by the cristae. The matrix contains most of the enzymes involved in oxidation of fatty acids and the Krebs cycle. The inner membrane contains the cytochromes, the carrier molecules of the electron transport chain, and the enzymes involved in ATP production.

As organelles, mitochondria have several unusual features. The mitochondrial matrix contains one or more circular strands of DNA resembling the chromosomes of bacteria. The matrix also contains ribosomes with a similar structure to bacterial ribosomes. Mitochondria synthesise 37 of their own constituent proteins, others being synthesised by the usual protein synthetic mechanisms of the cell. In addition, mitochondria undergo self-replication in a manner similar to bacterial cell division. It has thus been proposed that mitochondria are derived from bacteria which formed a symbiotic relationship with eukaryotic cells during the process of evolution.

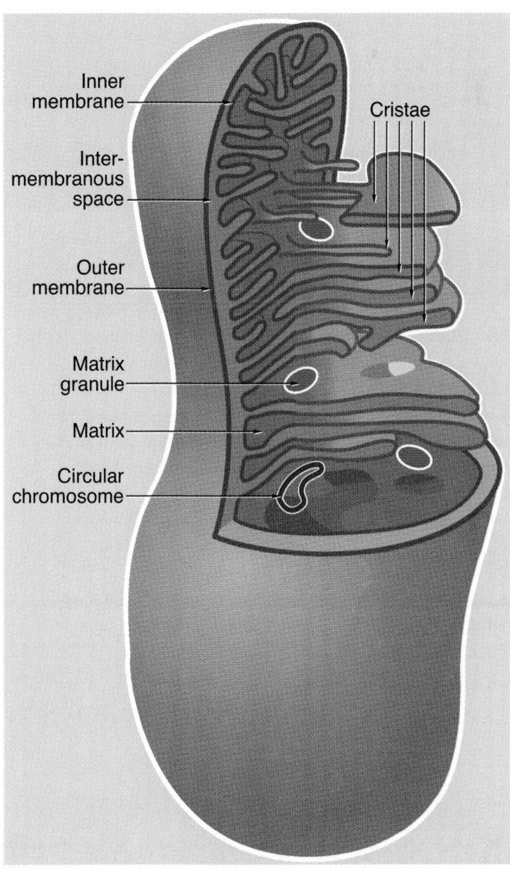

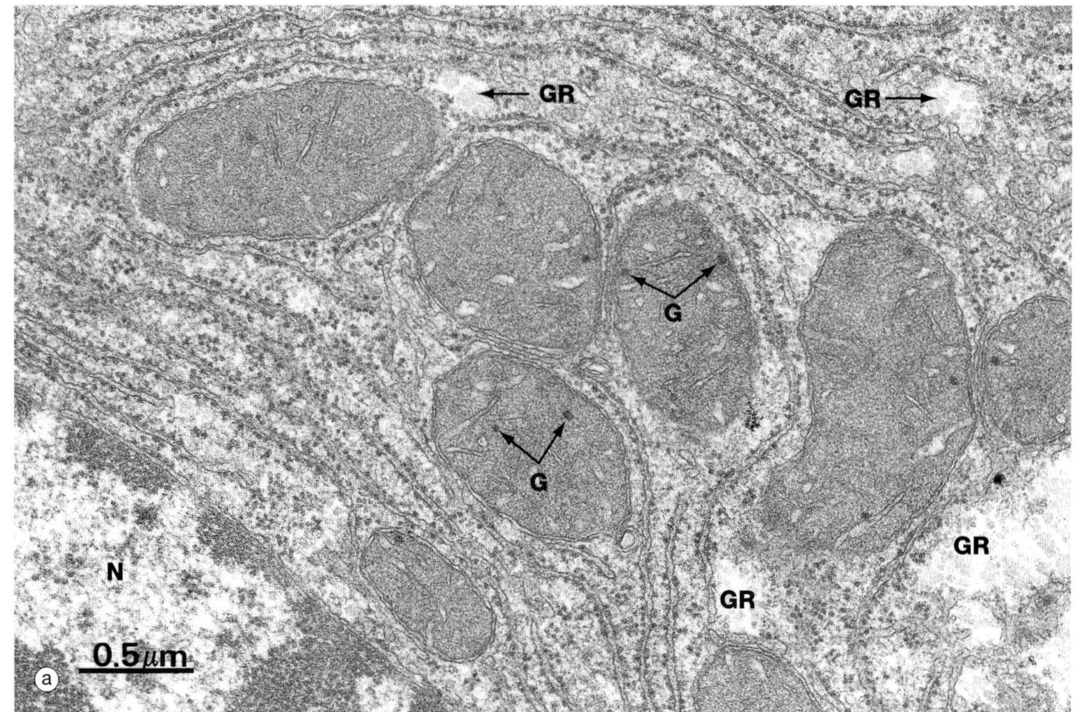

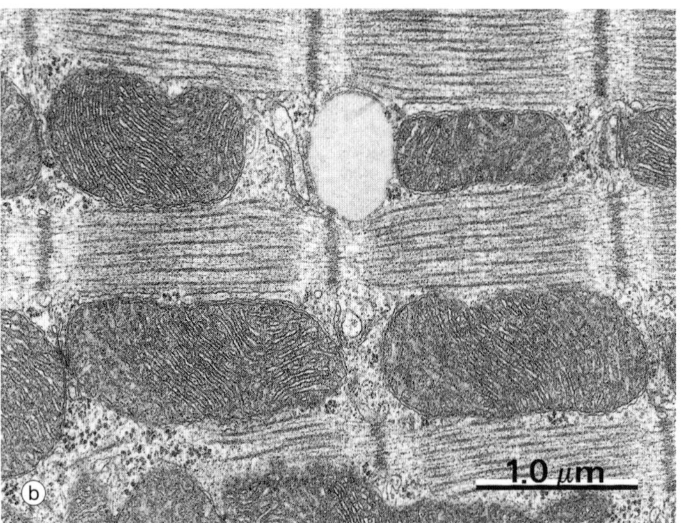

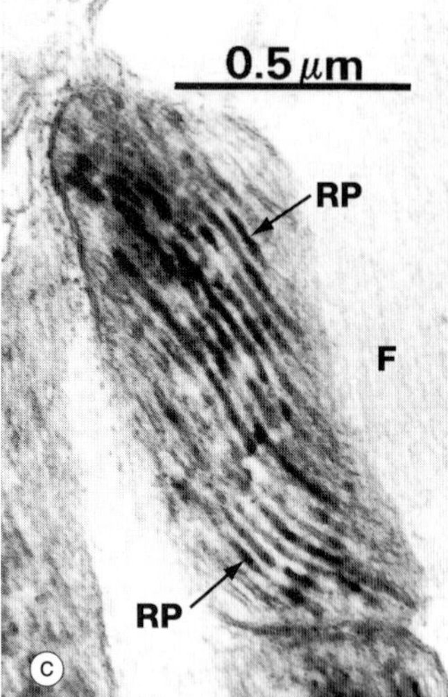

Fig. 1.17 Mitochondria
(a) EM ×34 000 (b) EM ×25 000 (c) Histochemical method for cytochrome oxidase: EM ×50 000

All mitochondria conform to the same general structure but vary greatly in size, shape and arrangement of cristae; these variations are often characteristic of the cell type. Mitochondria move freely within the cytosol and tend to aggregate in intracellular sites with high-energy demands where their shape often conforms to the available space.

Micrograph (a) of liver cell cytoplasm shows the typical appearance of mitochondria when cut in different planes of section; note their relatively dense matrix containing a few matrix granules **G**. ***Glycogen rosettes*** **GR** are also seen in this micrograph (see Fig. 1.19). Part of the nucleus **N** is seen in the bottom left corner.

Mitochondria from heart muscle cells can be seen in micrographs (b) and (c). The cristae are densely packed, reflecting the metabolic activity of the cell. In some cells the cristae have a characteristic shape, those of heart muscle being laminar. Micrograph (c) uses a histochemical technique to localise a mitochondrial enzyme, cytochrome oxidase. The electron dense reaction product **RP** is located in the intermembranous space. The actin and myosin filaments **F** are essentially unstained in this preparation.

F actin and myosin filaments **G** matrix granules **GR** glycogen rosettes **L** lumen **M** mitochondrion **N** nucleus **PM** plasma membrane **RP** reaction product **S** striations

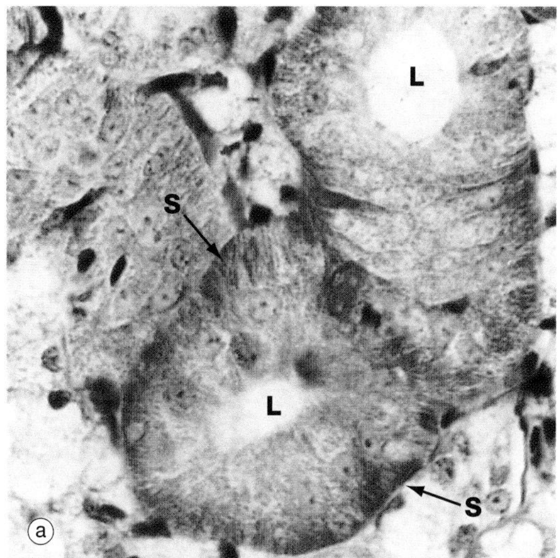

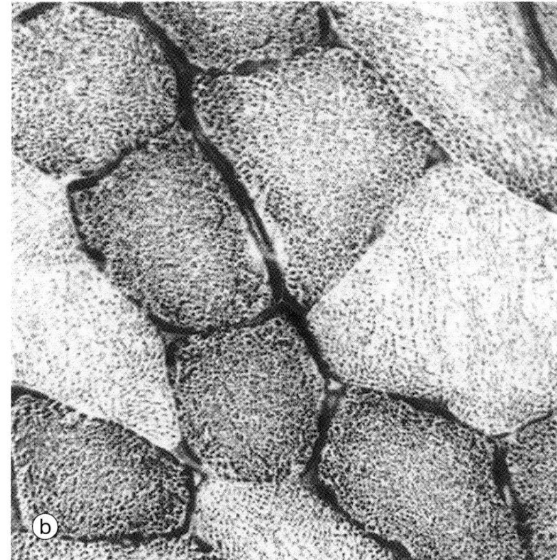

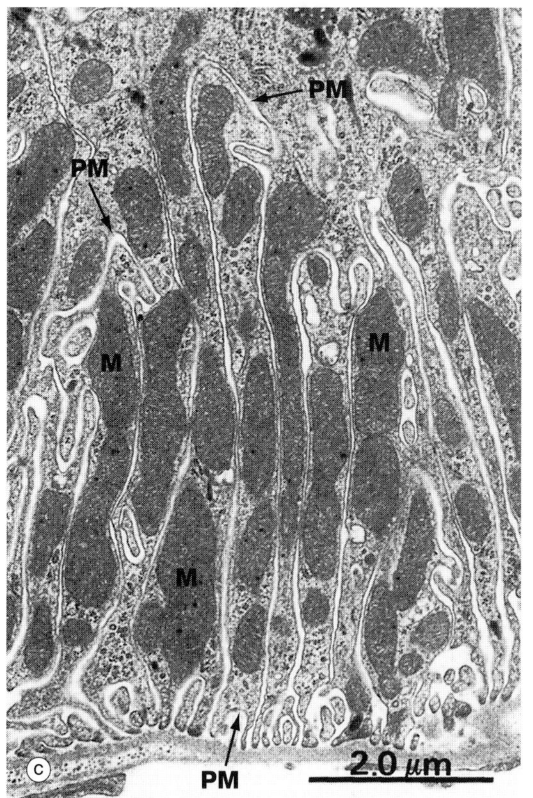

Fig. 1.18 Mitochondria
(a) Iron haematoxylin ×480 (b) Succinate dehydrogenase ×480 (c) EM ×13 000

Mitochondria are, in general, not seen individually by light microscopy. However, they are acidophilic and with the standard H & E stain are responsible for much of the eosinophilia (pink staining) of cytoplasm. In some cells, the mitochondria are profuse and may be concentrated in one region of the cell where they can be demonstrated directly and indirectly by various staining methods.

Micrograph (a) shows a salivary gland duct made up of cells that are extremely active in secretion and reabsorption of a variety of inorganic ions. This takes place at the base of the cells (i.e. the surface away from the lumen **L**) and is powered by ATP produced by elongated mitochondria associated with numerous basal interdigitations between adjacent cells; a strategy which greatly increases the plasma membrane surface area. The cells have been stained by a modified haematoxylin method, which stains not only basophilic structures (i.e. DNA and RNA) but also acidophilic structures such as mitochondria that can be seen as striations **S** in the basal aspect of the cells.

In specimen (b), which shows skeletal muscle cells in transverse section, an enzyme histochemical method for succinate dehydrogenase has been employed. Succinate dehydrogenase is an enzyme of the citric acid cycle that is exclusive to mitochondria and therefore provides a marker for them. In skeletal muscle there are three muscle cell types, which differ from each other in mitochondrial concentration. Such a staining method can be used to demonstrate their relative proportions (see also Fig. 6.14), as shown here by the different intensity of staining for mitochondria in different cells.

Micrograph (c) shows the base of an absorptive cell from a kidney tubule where there is intense active transport of ions. The basal plasma membranes **PM** of adjacent cells form interdigitations that greatly increase their surface area, and elongated mitochondria **M** are packed into the intervening spaces. Micrographs (a) and (c) demonstrate an example of the same structure, interdigitation of a membrane, being used for the same purpose in two different situations to maximise ion transportation.

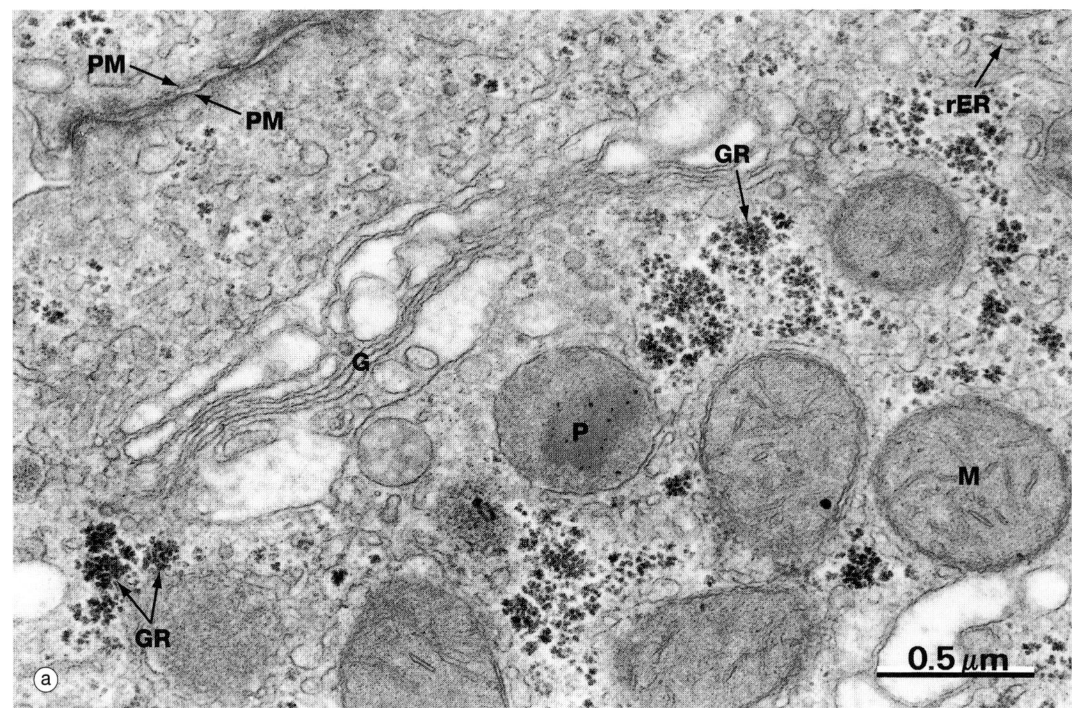

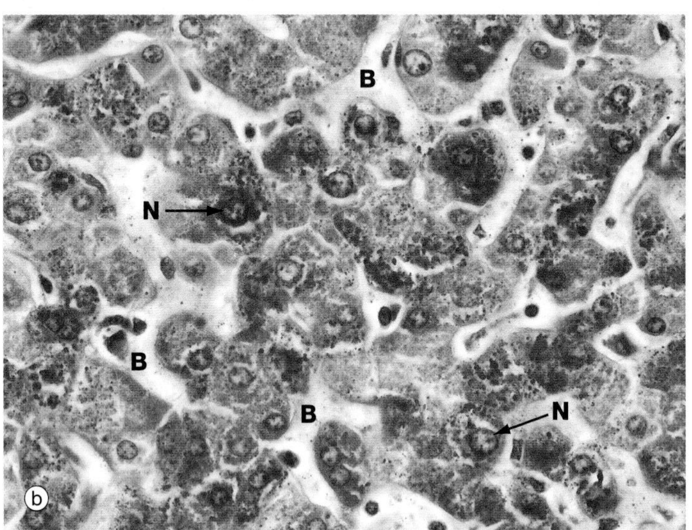

Fig. 1.19 Glycogen
(a) EM ×47 000 (b) PAS/haematoxylin ×600

Glycogen is present in large amounts in liver cells (hepatocytes). In micrograph (a), plentiful glycogen granules are present, appearing either as irregular single granules (called **β *particles)*** or as aggregations termed ***glycogen rosettes*** **GR** (also called **α *particles***). Compare the size of the ribosomes on the rough endoplasmic reticulum **rER** with glycogen granules, which are slightly larger on average. A prominent Golgi apparatus **G** can be seen near the plasma membrane **PM**. Note that although the Golgi apparatus is classically found near the nucleus it is not at all unusual to find it in other areas of the cytoplasm, especially in cells like hepatocytes which contain multiple Golgi stacks. Several mitochondria **M** and a peroxisome **P** can also be seen in this field.

Micrograph (b) has been stained by a histochemical method to demonstrate the presence of glycogen, which is stained magenta (see Appendix 2). The specimen is of liver, the cytoplasm of each liver cell being packed with glycogen. The section has been counterstained (i.e. stained with a second dye) to demonstrate the liver cell nuclei **N** (blue). It also stains the nuclei of the cells lining the blood channels **B** between the rows of liver cells; these nuclei are smaller and more condensed and hence stain more intensely.

Lipid biosynthesis

Lipids are synthesised by all cells in order to maintain the constant turnover of cell membranes. Cells may also synthesise lipid as a means of storing excess energy as cytoplasmic droplets, for lipid transport, e.g. chylomicron production by cells of the small intestine and in the form of steroid hormones, for sending information to other cells. The precursor molecules (fatty acids, triglycerides and cholesterol) are available to the cell from dietary sources, from mobilisation of lipid stored in other cells or can be synthesised by most cells using simple sources of carbon such as acetyl CoA and other intermediates of glucose catabolism. Fatty acids and triglycerides are mostly synthesised within the cytosol, whereas cholesterol and phospholipids are synthesised in areas of smooth endoplasmic reticulum (see Fig. 1.8).

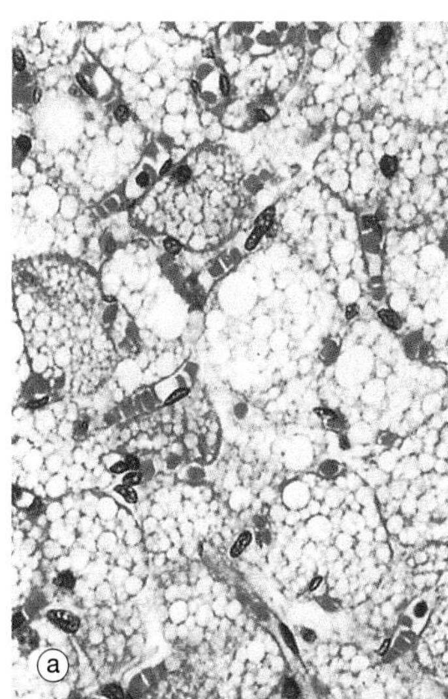

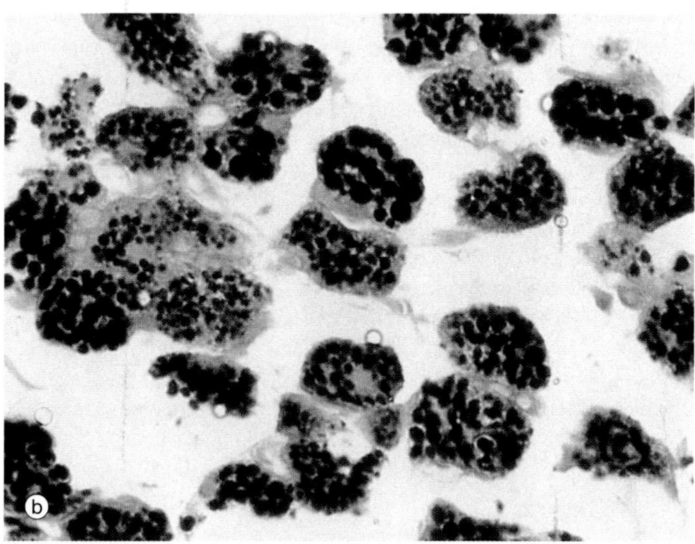

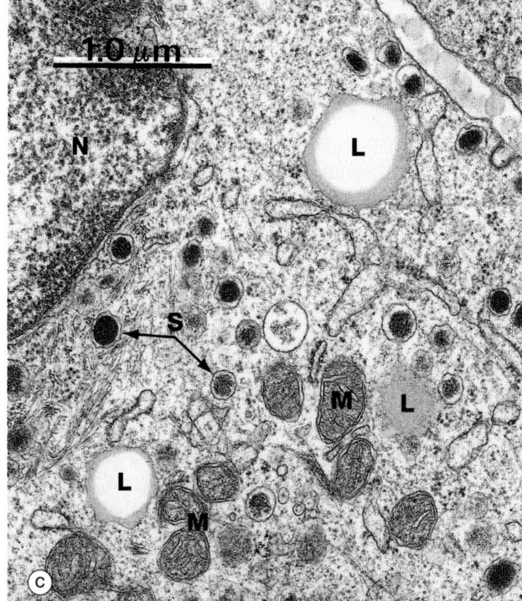

Fig. 1.20 Lipid
(a) H & E ×320 (b) Osmium ×320 (c) EM ×24 000

Routine processing methods for microscopy generally extract lipid from tissues. Therefore lipid droplets within cells appear as unstained vacuoles, as in micrograph (a). Lipids are therefore best demonstrated in frozen sections stained by specific lipid methods such as osmium tetroxide, as in micrograph (b), which stains lipid droplets black. Both micrographs show brown adipose tissue at similar magnifications (see also Fig. 4.13). Lipid droplets **L**, as seen in electron micrograph (c) of the cytoplasm of a neuroendocrine cell, can be identified as homogeneous, rounded (really spherical in three dimensions) globules of lipid. The lipid forms droplets for the same reason that lipid membranes separate themselves from the cytoplasm, i.e. hydrophobic forces tend to exclude water as in the old saying 'oil and water don't mix'. As lipid droplets accumulate and enlarge, the same hydrophobic forces tend to make them fuse together to form larger droplets which may eventually occupy the entire cytoplasm and push the nucleus to the edge of the cell, as in ***adipocytes*** (fat cells) (see Fig. 4.16). Note also that lipid droplets do not have a limiting membrane in contrast to mitochondria **M**, the nucleus **N** and secretory granules **S** of the 'dense core' type that are characteristic of neuroendocrine cells (see Ch. 17).

B blood channels **G** Golgi apparatus **GR** glycogen rosette **L** lipid droplets **M** mitochondrion
N nucleus **P** peroxisome **PM** plasma membrane **rER** rough endoplasmic reticulum
S secretory granules

The cytoskeleton and cell movement

Every cell has a supporting framework of minute filaments and tubules, the ***cytoskeleton***, which maintains the shape and polarity of the cell. Nevertheless, the cell membrane and intracellular organelles are not rigid or static structures but are in a constant state of movement to accommodate processes such as endocytosis, phagocytosis and secretion. Some cells (e.g. white blood cells) propel themselves about by amoeboid movement; other cells have actively motile membrane specialisations such as cilia and flagella (see Ch. 5); while other cells (e.g. muscle cells) are highly specialised for contractility. In addition, cell division is a process that involves extensive reorganisation of cellular constituents. The cytoskeleton incorporates features that accommodate all these dynamic functions.

The cytoskeleton of each cell contains structural elements of three main types, ***microfilaments***, ***microtubules*** and ***intermediate filaments***, as well as many accessory proteins responsible for linking these structures to one another, to the plasma membrane and to the membranes of intracellular organelles.

- **Microfilaments.** Microfilaments are extremely fine strands (approximately 7 nm in diameter) of the protein ***actin.*** Each actin filament consists of two strings of bead-like subunits twisted together like a rope. The globular subunits are stabilised by calcium ions and associated with ATP molecules to provide energy for contraction. Actin filaments are best demonstrated histologically in skeletal muscle cells where they form a stable arrangement of bundles with another type of filamentous protein called ***myosin***. Contraction occurs when the actin and myosin filaments slide relative to one another due to the rearrangement of intermolecular bonds, fuelled by the release of energy from associated ATP molecules (see Ch. 6). Cells not usually considered to be contractile also contain the globular subunits of actin (***G-actin***) which assemble readily into microfilaments (***F-actin***) and then dissociate, thereby providing a dynamic structural framework for the cell. Membrane specialisations such as ***microvilli*** (see Fig. 5.16) also contain a skeleton of actin filaments. Beneath the plasma membrane, actin, in association with various transmembrane and linking proteins (predominantly filamin), forms a robust supporting meshwork called the ***cell cortex***, which protects against deformation yet can be rearranged to accommodate changes in cell morphology. Actin plays a central role in cell movement, pinocytosis and phagocytosis. Actin may also bind to intrinsic plasma membrane proteins to anchor them in position.
- **Intermediate filaments.** Intermediate filaments (10–15 nm in diameter) are, as their name implies, intermediate in size between microfilaments and microtubules. These proteins have a purely structural function and consist of filaments of protein that self-assemble into larger filaments and bind intracellular structures to each other and to plasma membrane proteins. In humans there are more than 50 different types of intermediate filament, but these can be divided into different classes, with some classes characteristic of particular cell types. This feature is used in diagnostic pathology to identify different varieties of tumour. For example, ***cytokeratin*** intermediate filaments are characteristic of epithelial cells where they form a supporting network within the cytoplasm and are anchored to the plasma membrane at intercellular junctions. Likewise, ***vimentin*** is found in cells of mesodermal origin, ***desmin*** in muscle cells, ***neurofilament proteins*** in nerve cells and ***glial fibrillary acidic protein*** in glial cells. ***Lamin*** intermediate filaments form a structural layer on the inner side of the nuclear membrane.
- **Microtubules.** Microtubules (24 nm in diameter) are much larger than microfilaments but, like them, are made up of globular protein subunits which can readily be assembled and disassembled to provide for alterations in cell shape and position of organelles. The microtubule subunits are of two types, ***alpha*** and ***beta tubulin***, which polymerise to form a hollow tubule; when seen in cross-section, 13 tubulin molecules make up a circle. Microtubules originate from a specialised microtubule organising centre, the ***centriole***, found in the ***centrosome*** (see below), and movement may be effected by the addition or subtraction of tubulin subunits from the microtubules, making them longer or shorter. ***Microtubule-associated proteins*** (***MAPs***) stabilise the tubular structure and include ***capping proteins***, which stabilise the growing ends of the tubules. The motor proteins ***dynein*** and ***kinesin*** move along the tubules towards and away from the cell centre, respectively. These motors attach to membranous organelles (e.g. mitochondria, secretory vesicles), and move them about within the cytoplasm rather like an engine pulling cargo along a railway track. The function of the spindle during cell division is a classic example of this process on a large scale (see Fig. 2.3). The centrosome, consisting of a pair of centrioles, each of nine triplets of microtubules, organises the microtubules of the cell spindle during cell division (see Figs 1.24 and 1.25). In cilia nine pairs of microtubules form a cylindrical structure, and movement occurs by rearrangement of chemical bonds between adjacent microtubule pairs (see Fig. 5.15).

M mitochondrion **MF** microfilaments **N** nucleus **R** ribosomes

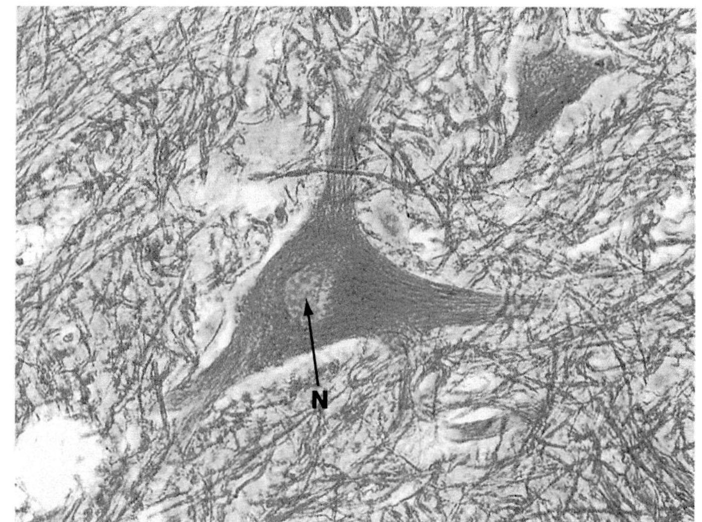

Fig. 1.21 Cytoskeleton
Silver impregnation method ×600

Individual elements of the cytoskeleton are not easily visualised by light microscopy. However, in cells with prominent aggregations of cytoskeletal elements, e.g. nerve cells or cells undergoing division, these can be demonstrated by impregnation with silver or gold. In this micrograph of a nerve cell body, the silver-impregnated cytoskeleton, which appears brown in colour, can be seen radiating from the vicinity of the nucleus **N** into various cytoplasmic extensions.

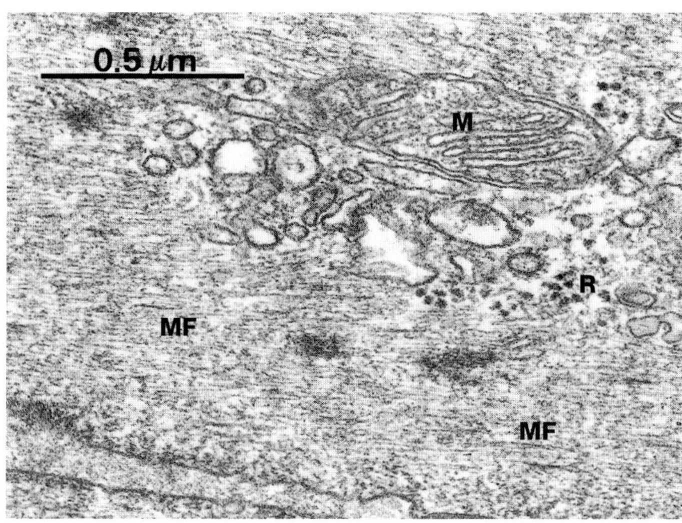

Fig. 1.22 Microfilaments
EM ×76 500

In general, individual microfilaments are difficult to demonstrate due to their small diameter (approximately 7 nm) and diffuse arrangement among other cytoplasmic components. In this example from a smooth muscle cell, a cell type in which cytoplasmic microfilaments are a predominant feature, parallel arrays of microfilaments **MF** are readily seen. The diameter of microfilaments may be compared with the diameter of a mitochondrion **M** and ribosomes **R**.

Abnormalities of the cytoskeleton can produce life-threatening diseases

A number of blistering diseases of the skin are caused by abnormalities of the cytoskeleton. In the rare congenital disorder ***epidermolysis bullosa simplex***, mutations have been found in the genes coding for cytokeratins 5 and 15. These intermediate filaments normally provide basal epidermal cells of the skin with resistance to trauma and in this condition clumps of abnormal intermediate filaments can be seen within the cells. The result is a loss of cohesion between the basal epithelial cells and the underlying basement membrane, causing blister formation and fluid loss. In ***bullous pemphigoid***, there are antibodies to a particular protein, known forgettably as BPAG1, that links intermediate filaments to hemidesmosomes (see Ch. 5) resulting again in lack of cohesion of the epidermal cells and thus the formation of blisters. This is a relatively common example of an ***autoimmune disease***, where, usually for unknown reasons, the components of the body's defence system, the immune system (Ch. 11), attack normal body components to cause disease. Other autoimmune diseases include rheumatoid arthritis, primary biliary cirrhosis and systemic lupus erythematosus (SLE).

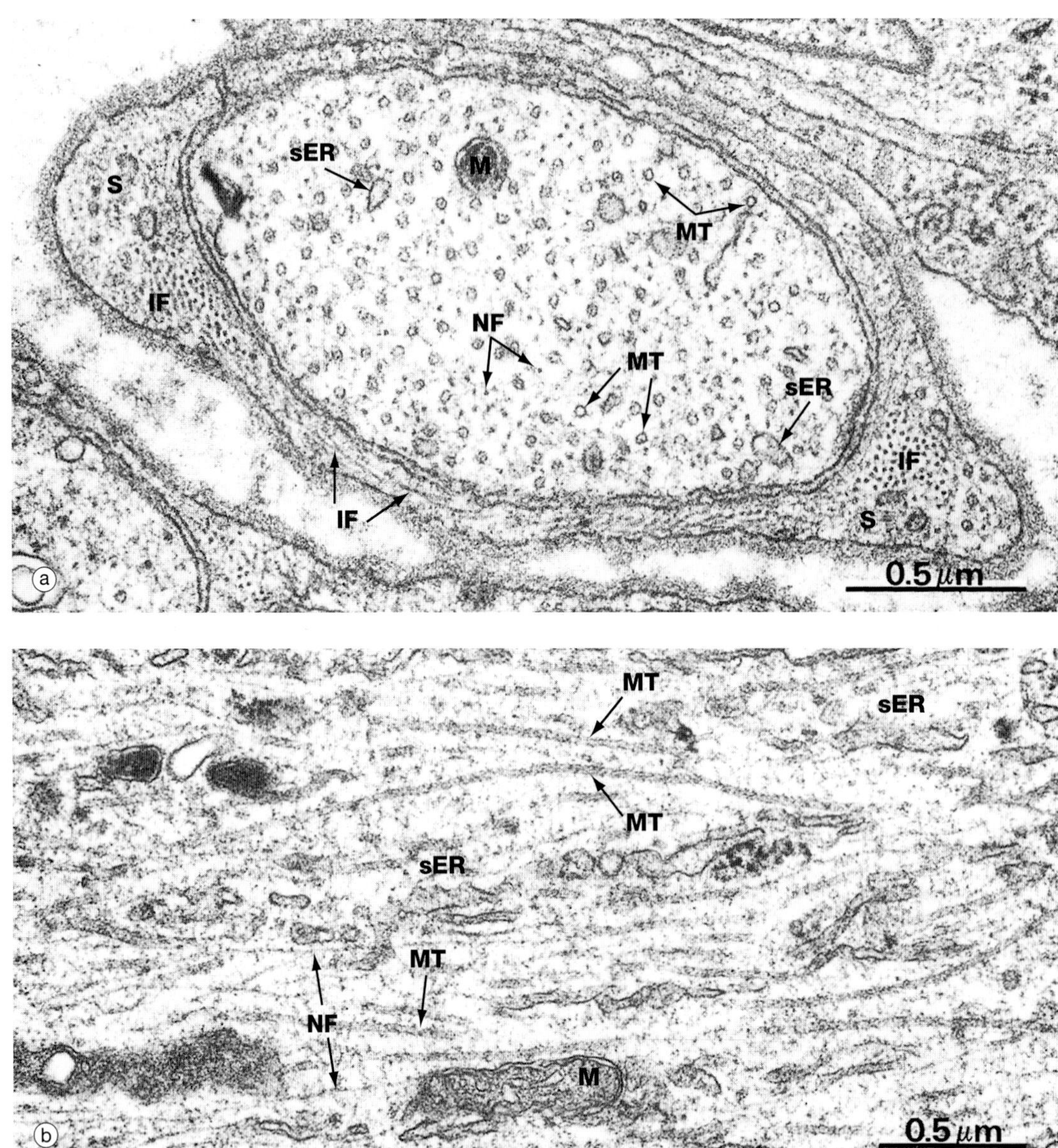

Fig. 1.23 Intermediate filaments and microtubules
(a) EM: TS ×53 000 (b) EM: LS ×40 000

These micrographs are taken from nervous tissue; nerve cells contain both intermediate filaments and microtubules, allowing comparison of size and morphology. Each nerve cell has an elongated cytoplasmic extension called an axon (see Ch. 7), which in the peripheral nervous system is ensheathed by a supporting Schwann cell. Micrograph (a) shows an axon in transverse section wrapped in the cytoplasm of a Schwann cell **S**. Micrograph (b) shows part of an axon in longitudinal section. The axonal microtubules provide structural support and transport along the axon.

In longitudinal section, microtubules **MT** appear as straight, unbranched structures, and in transverse section they appear hollow. Their diameter can be compared with small mitochondria **M** and smooth endoplasmic reticulum **sER**.

Intermediate filaments (known as ***neurofilaments*** in this case) are a prominent feature of nerve cells, providing internal support for the cell by cross-linkage with microtubules and other organelles. The neurofilaments **NF** are dispersed among and in parallel with the microtubules, but are much smaller in diameter and are not hollow in cross-section. Intermediate filaments **IF** are also seen in the Schwann cell cytoplasm in micrograph (a) both in transverse and longitudinal view.

C centriole **F** filament **G** Golgi apparatus **IF** intermediate filament **MT** microtubule **N** nucleus **NF** neurofilament **S** Schwann cell **sER** smooth endoplasmic reticulum **T** triplet

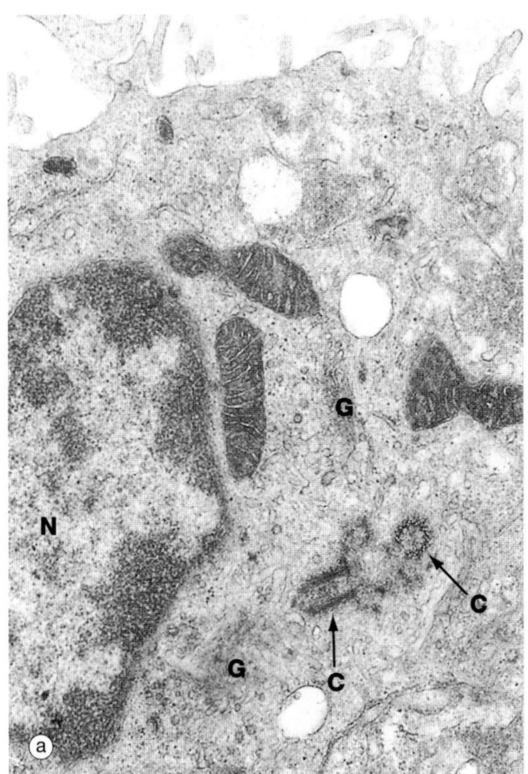

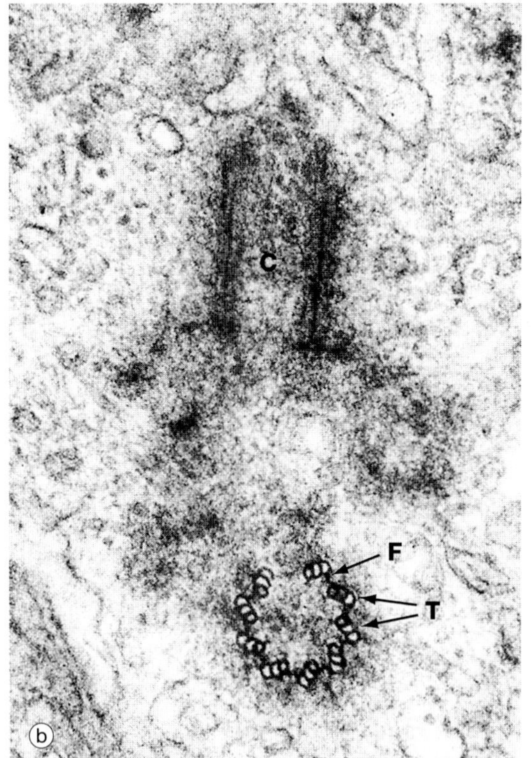

Fig. 1.24 Centrosome
(a) EM ×9200 (b) EM ×48 000 (c) Schematic diagram

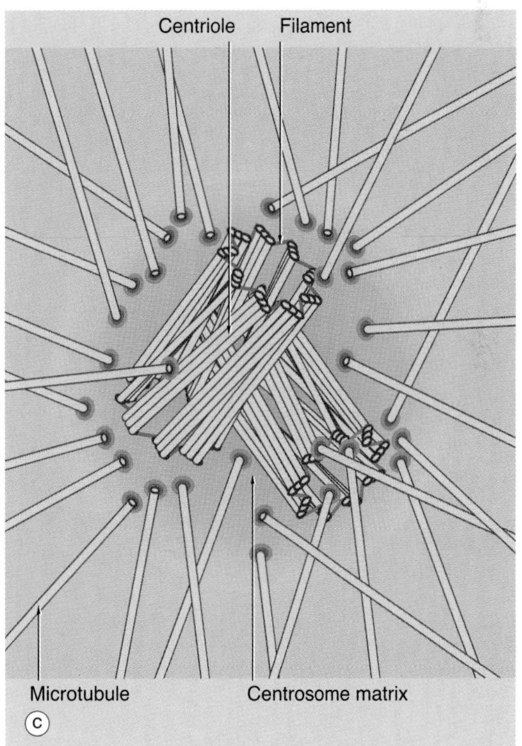

The ***centrosome*** includes a pair of ***centrioles*** **C** and the ***centrosome matrix*** or ***pericentriolar material***. The centrosome matrix is a zone of cytoplasm distinguishable by its different texture. It is usually centrally located in the cell adjacent to the nucleus **N** and often surrounded by the Golgi apparatus **G**. The pair of centrioles are also known as a ***diplosome***. There are also fifty or more ***δ-tubulin ring complexes***, which form a nucleus for the polymerisation of microtubules. Thus the centrioles, themselves composed of microtubules, act as a ***microtubule organising centre***. Microtubules radiate outwards from the centrioles in a star-like arrangement, often called an ***aster***.

Each centriole is cylindrical in form, consisting of nine triplets of parallel microtubules. In transverse section, as in the lower half of micrograph (b) and in diagram (c), each triplet **T** is seen to consist of an inner microtubule, which is circular in cross-section, and two further microtubules, which are C-shaped in cross-section. Each of the inner microtubules is connected to the outermost microtubule of the adjacent triplet by fine filaments **F**, thus forming a cylinder. The two centrioles of each diplosome are arranged with their long axes at right angles to each other, as can be seen in these micrographs.

Structures apparently identical to centrioles form the ***basal bodies*** of cilia and flagella (see Figs 5.14, 18.6 and 18.7), both of which are moved by microtubules. Cilia are a cell surface specialisation, each cilium comprising a minute hair-like cytoplasmic extension containing microtubules. Cilia move in a wave-like fashion for the purpose of moving secretions across a tissue surface. Flagella are the long tails responsible for the motility of sperm.

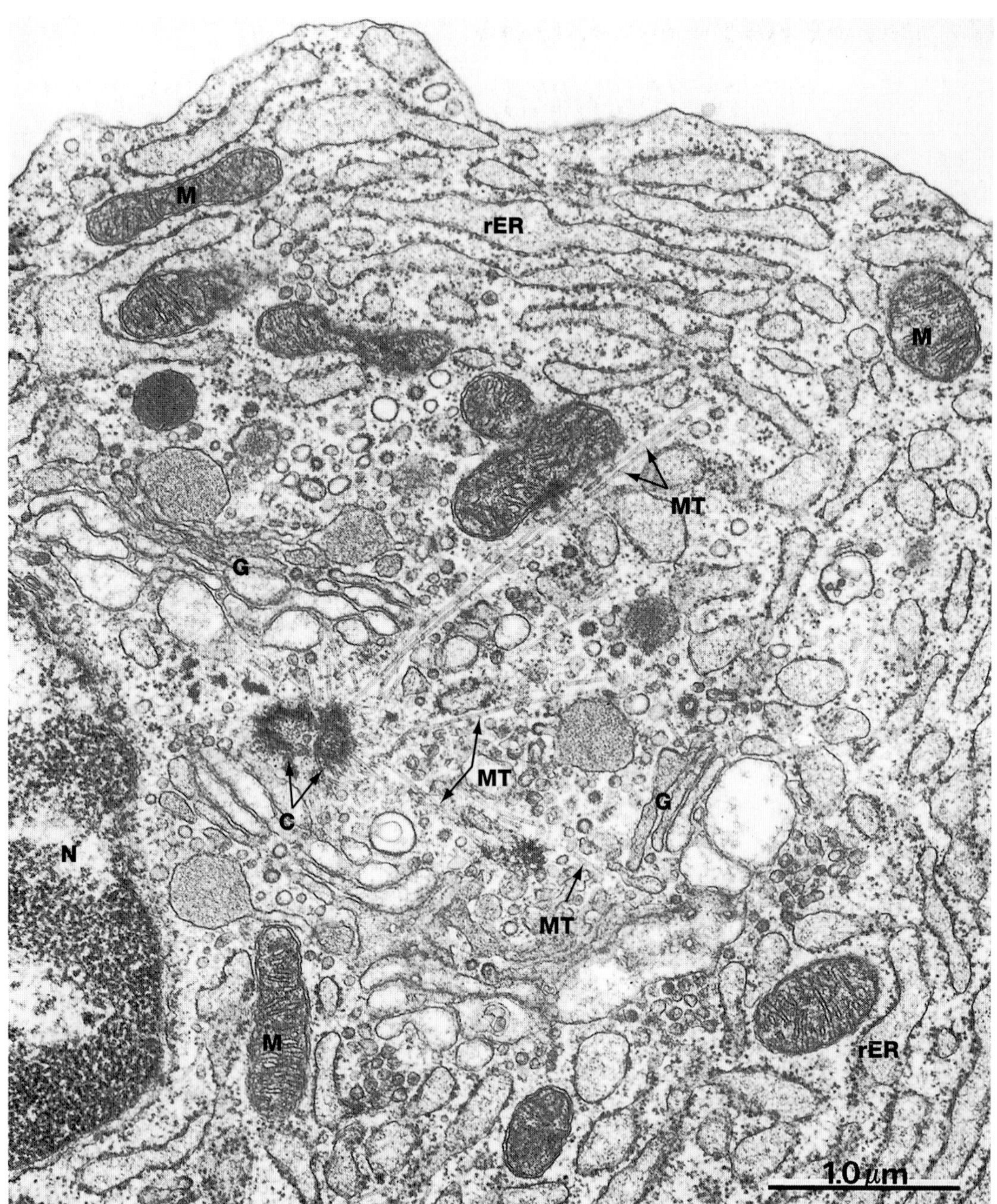

Fig. 1.25 Centrosome and microtubules
EM ×30 000

This micrograph shows the centrosome acting as an organising centre for the microtubules of the cytoskeleton. The centrosome consists of two centrioles **C** (both cut somewhat obliquely in this specimen), typically located at the centre of the cell close to the nucleus **N**. Several microtubules **MT** are seen radiating from the centrosome towards the cell periphery. Centrioles appear to be necessary for microtubule function. For example, prior to cell division the pair of centrioles is duplicated, the pairs migrating towards opposite ends of the cell. Here they act as organising centres for the microtubules of the spindle that controls distribution of chromosomes to the daughter cells. Likewise, a centriole, known as a basal body, is found attached to the microtubules at the base of cilia.

Other features of this micrograph, which is from an antibody-secreting plasma cell, include profuse rough endoplasmic reticulum **rER** distended with secretory product, several saccular profiles of an extensive Golgi complex **G** and scattered mitochondria **M**.

C centriole **G** Golgi complex **M** mitochondrion **MT** microtubules **N** nucleus
rER rough endoplasmic reticulum

Fig. 1.26 Summary of functions of cellular organelles

Organelle	Brief description	Functions
Nucleus	Double membrane-bound large structure containing chromatin	Chromosomes (DNA) contain the genetic blueprint for every protein in the body
Nuclear envelope/membrane	Double lipid bilayer with nuclear pore complexes	Separates and mediates transport between nucleus and cytoplasm
Nucleolus	Dense non-membrane-bound structure in nucleus	Ribosomal RNA synthesis and ribosome assembly
Ribosomes	Small structures free in cytoplasm or bound to endoplasmic reticulum. Consist of two subunits of ribosomal RNA	Protein synthesis – formation of peptide bonds between amino acids to make polypeptide chains using messenger RNA as template
Endoplasmic reticulum	Extensive membrane system within the cell: may be rough (rER) with associated ribosomes, or smooth (sER)	Modification and folding of proteins synthesised on ribosomes (rER), synthesis of some lipids (sER)
Golgi apparatus/stack	Stacks of flattened membrane-bound cisternae	Final assembly and glycosylation of proteins and dispatch to their ultimate destination
Mitochondria	Double membrane-bound organelles with folded inner membrane	Energy production mainly in the form of ATP
Plasma membrane	Lipid bilayer containing intrinsic proteins and with an external coat of carbohydrate	Divides cell from external environment and mediates interactions with external environment
Cytoskeleton	Microfilaments, intermediate filaments and microtubules	Maintain cell shape and orientation, cell movement, movement of organelles around the cell, movement of chromosomes during cell division
Transport/secretory vesicles	Membrane-bound vesicles often with a protein coat e.g. COP I, clathrin	Transport materials between different cell compartments and to plasma membrane for export
Phagosomes/endosomes – including sorting and recycling endosomes	Membrane-bound vesicles containing material imported into cell	Phagocytosis/endocytosis and transport of cargo to intracellular destination e.g. lysosome
Lysosomes	Membrane-bound vesicles containing hydrolytic enzymes	Killing of pathogenic organisms (in phagocytic cells) and degradation of waste products
Peroxisomes	Membrane-bound vesicle containing oxidases and catalase	Production of hydrogen peroxide for killing pathogens, detoxification of certain toxic materials
Lipid droplets	Non-membrane-bound spherical aggregates of lipid of variable size	Energy storage
Glycogen granules	Non-membrane-bound granules and aggregates of granules (rosettes)	Energy storage
Lipofuscin	Brown pigment in cytoplasm	Waste product
Melanin	Brown pigment in cytoplasm	Skin pigmentation

The integrated function of cells in tissues, organs and organ systems

As mentioned at the outset, cells are the functional units of all living organisms; indeed the most primitive organisms merely consist of single cells. In multicellular organisms, however, individual cells become specialised (***differentiated***) and grouped together to perform specific functions. Multicellular organisms would obviously disintegrate if the cells were not organised into specific structures and held together by ***intercellular junctions*** (see Ch. 5) and ***extracellular matrix*** (see Ch. 4). Cells of similar morphology and function along with extracellular matrix form ***tissues***, which are relatively homogeneous in overall structure; examples include cartilage, bone and muscle. Extracellular matrix such as the calcified matrix of bone and the fibrous matrix of the deep layer of the skin (the dermis) can impart great strength to tissues. Other cell types such as blood cells and tissue macrophages migrate throughout the body either in the blood or other body fluids or through the extracellular matrix. ***Organs*** are anatomically discrete collections of tissues that together perform certain specific functions (e.g. liver, kidney, eye, and ovary). Tissues and organs may constitute integrated functional systems forming major anatomical entities (e.g. central nervous system, female reproductive tract, gastrointestinal tract, urinary system) or be more diffusely arranged (e.g. immune defence system, diffuse neuroendocrine system). Despite the foregoing, the terms tissue, organ and system are not necessarily mutually exclusive and may in some cases be used interchangeably depending on the functional implications. Part 2 of this book describes five basic tissues: blood, supporting/connective tissue, epithelia, muscle and nervous tissues. These are constituents of all organs and organ systems. In tissues and organs the functionally specialised cells are often called the ***parenchyma*** and the less specialised supporting tissue, the ***stroma***.

Within tissues and organs, cells interact with one another in numerous ways during embryological development and growth, maintenance of structural integrity, response to injury (inflammation and repair), integration and control of tissue and organ functions and the maintenance of overall biochemical and metabolic integrity (***homeostasis***). Various types of intercellular junctions also serve as conduits for information exchange in the form of electrical excitation or chemical messengers. Within tissues, cellular functions are integrated by a great variety of local chemical mediators (***paracrine signalling***) or by direct contact between cells and interaction between messaging molecules bound to the cell surface. At the level of systems and of the whole body, functions are coordinated via circulating chemical messengers (***hormones***) and/or via the nervous system (***synaptic signalling***). The great pleasure to be derived from the study of histology is that all structures, from the subcellular to organ systems, reflect these functional requirements and interrelationships. It really is all very cleverly arranged.

2. *Cell cycle and replication*

Introduction

The development of a single, fertilised egg cell to form a complex, multicellular organism involves cellular replication, growth and progressive specialisation (***differentiation***) for a variety of functions. The fertilised egg (***zygote***) divides by a process known as ***mitosis*** to produce two genetically identical daughter cells, each of which divides to produce two more daughter cells and so on. Some of these daughter cells progressively specialise and eventually produce the ***terminally differentiated*** cells of mature tissues, such as muscle or skin cells. Most tissues however retain a population of relatively undifferentiated cells (***stem cells***) that are able to divide and replace the differentiated cell population as required. The interval between mitotic divisions is known as the ***cell cycle***. All body cells divide by mitosis except for male and female germ cells, which divide by ***meiosis*** to produce ***gametes*** (see Fig. 2.5).

In the fully developed organism, the terminally differentiated cells of some tissues, such as the neurones of the nervous system, lose the ability to undergo mitosis. In contrast, the cells of certain other tissues, e.g. the stem cells of gut and skin, undergo continuous cycles of mitotic division throughout the lifespan of the organism replacing cells lost during normal wear and tear. Between these extremes are cells such as liver cells that do not normally divide but retain the capacity to undergo mitosis should the need arise (***facultative dividers***).

Cell division and differentiation are balanced by cell death both during the development and growth of the immature organism and in the mature adult. In these circumstances, cell death occurs by a mechanism known as ***apoptosis*** (Fig. 2.7).

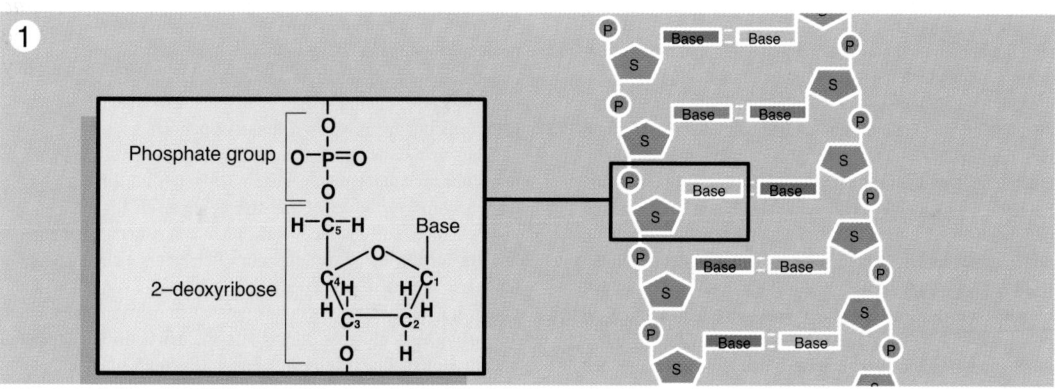

Fig. 2.1 The cell cycle

Historically, only two phases of the cell cycle were recognised: a relatively short mitotic phase (***M phase***) and a non-dividing phase (***interphase***), which usually occupies most of the life cycle of the cell. With the development of radioisotopes, it was found that there is a discrete period during interphase when nuclear DNA is replicated; this phase, described as the synthesis or ***S phase***, is completed some time before the onset of mitosis. Thus interphase may be divided into three separate phases. Between the end of the M phase and the beginning of the S phase is the first gap or ***G_1 phase***; this is usually much longer than the other phases of the cell cycle. During the G_1 phase, cells differentiate and perform their specialised functions as part of the whole tissue. The interval between the end of the S phase and the beginning of the M phase, the second gap or ***G_2 phase***, is relatively short and is the period in which cells prepare for mitotic division.

Stem cells in some tissues progress continually through the cell cycle to accommodate tissue growth or cell turnover, whereas terminally differentiated cells leave the cell cycle after the M phase and enter a state of continuous differentiated function designated as ***G_0 phase***. Facultative dividers enter the G_0 phase but retain the capacity to re-enter the cell cycle when suitably stimulated. Liver cells are a prominent example of facultative dividers with differentiated hepatocytes acting as stem cells in cases of massive liver injury. Some liver cells appear to enter a protracted G_2 phase in which they perform their normal differentiated functions despite the presence of a duplicated complement of DNA. These cells may be seen histologically as binucleate cells.

In general, the S, G and M phases of the cell cycle are relatively constant in duration, each taking up to several hours to complete, whereas the G_1 phase is highly variable, in some cases lasting for several days or weeks. The G_0 phase may last for the entire lifespan of the organism.

G_0 terminally differentiated cell **G_1** gap phase 1 **G_2** gap phase 2 **M** mitotic phase
S synthesis phase

Mitosis

Division of ***somatic cells*** (all body cells except for the germ cells) occurs in two phases. Firstly, the chromosomes duplicated in S phase are distributed equally between the two potential daughter cells; this process is known as ***mitosis***. Secondly, the dividing cell is cleaved into genetically identical daughter cells by cytoplasmic division or ***cytokinesis***. Although mitosis is always equal and symmetrical, cytokinesis may, in some situations, result in the formation of two daughter cells with grossly unequal amounts of cytoplasm or cytoplasmic organelles. In other circumstances, mitosis may occur in the absence of cytokinesis, as in the formation of binucleate and multinucleate cells.

Fig. 2.2 Chromosomes during mitosis *(illustrations opposite)*

The nuclei of all somatic cells of an individual contain the same fixed complement of ***deoxyribonucleic acid (DNA)***, a quantity called the ***genome***. The DNA is arranged into chromosomes, with each species having a set number. DNA is a very large molecular weight polymer consisting of many ***deoxyribonucleotides*** with a double-stranded structure. Each strand consists of a backbone of alternating ***deoxyribose* S** and phosphate **P** moieties. Each deoxyribose unit is covalently bound to a ***purine*** or ***pyrimidine*** base, which is in turn non-covalently linked to a complementary base on the other strand, thus linking the strands together. The bases are of four types, ***adenine* A**, ***cytosine* C**, ***thymine* T** and ***guanine* G**, with adenine only linking to thymine and cytosine only linking to guanine, thus making each strand complementary to the other (diagram 1). Linked in this way, the strands assume a double helical conformation around a common axis, the internucleotide phosphodiester bonds running in opposite directions (i.e. antiparallel) and the planes of the linked bases lying at right angles to the axis (diagram 2). The sequence of bases in either strand of the DNA molecule forms the genetic code for the individual. The bases are read in groups of three called ***codons***, each coding for one amino acid. In human cells, there are 46 chromosomes (the ***diploid*** number) comprising 22 homologous pairs, the ***autosomes***, and 2 ***sex chromosomes***, either XX in the female or XY in the male. The members of each pair of autosomes have the same length of DNA and code for the same proteins.

Histologically, individual chromosomes are not visible within the cell nucleus during interphase. During S phase, each chromosome is duplicated (as shown in diagram 3). The resulting identical chromosomes, now known as ***chromatids***, remain attached to one another at a point called the ***centromere***, and become even more tightly coiled and condensed when they may be visualised with the light microscope (see Figs 2.3 and 2.4).

The extremely long DNA molecule making up each chromosome binds to a range of ***histone proteins*** that hold the chromosome in a supercoiled and folded conformation, compact enough to be accommodated within the nucleus. Thus the 2 nm diameter double helix is coiled and packed through several orders of three-dimensional complexity to form an elongated structure some 300 nm in diameter and very much shorter in length than the otherwise uncoiled molecule would be. This is the form in which the chromosome is structured during the G_1 and G_0 phases of the cell cycle, during which ***gene transcription*** (the prerequisite for protein synthesis) occurs.

Diagram 4 shows further detail of the structure of mitotic chromosomes and their supercoiled three-dimensional structure. Note the position of the kinetochore (see Fig. 2.3) that provides attachment for the microtubules of the cell spindle during cell division and seems also to control the progression of mitosis. Examination of the chromosomes of dividing cells, ***karyotyping***, can give diagnostic information about the chromosomal complement of an individual or of a malignant tumour (see Fig. 2.6).

Stem cells

In tissues with a regular turnover of cells, the dividing cells are relatively undifferentiated cells and are known as ***stem cells***. Some of the progeny of these cells undergo further cell division and finally differentiate to become the various types of mature cells, while others remain undifferentiated to maintain the pool of stem cells.

Stem cell research is currently a very controversial area. Embryonic stem cells are theoretically ***totipotent***, i.e. able to differentiate into any other cell type while many stem cells found in adults are either ***multipotent,*** able to produce cells of several lineages, or ***unipotent***, producing only a single cell type. Thus multipotent haemopoeitic stem cells can produce all the formed elements of the blood while unipotent epidermal stem cells of the skin can produce only epithelial cells. Recent research has hinted that under certain circumstances haemopoietic stem cells can produce other cell types. The advantages of such cells in the treatment of degenerative diseases are obvious – imagine being able to grow a new kidney or even a new limb to order. However, the ethical minefield created by the possible applications of such technology, especially the use of embryonic cells, is equally apparent.

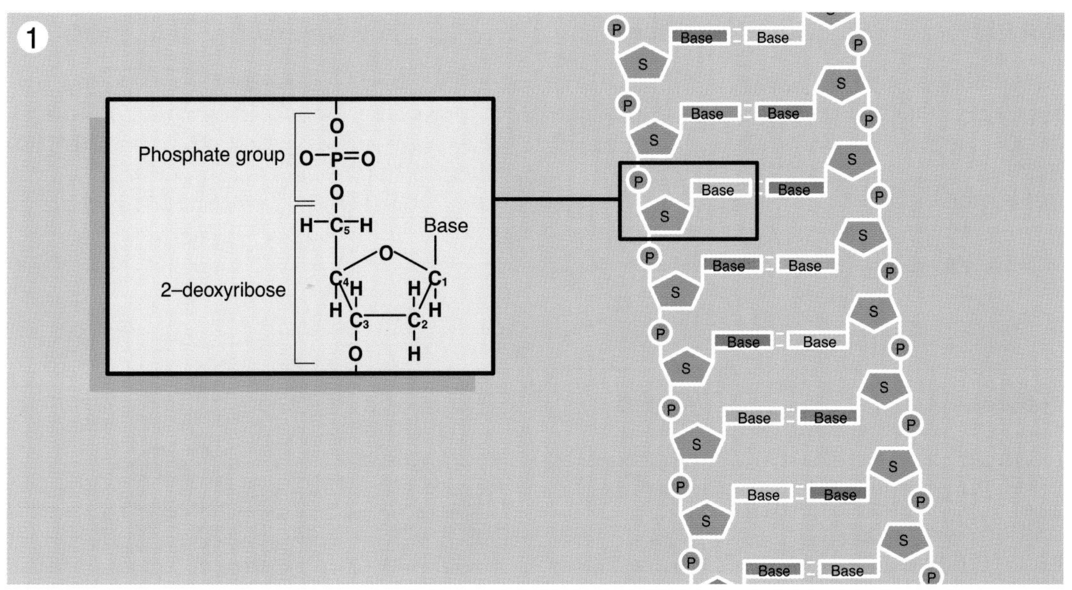

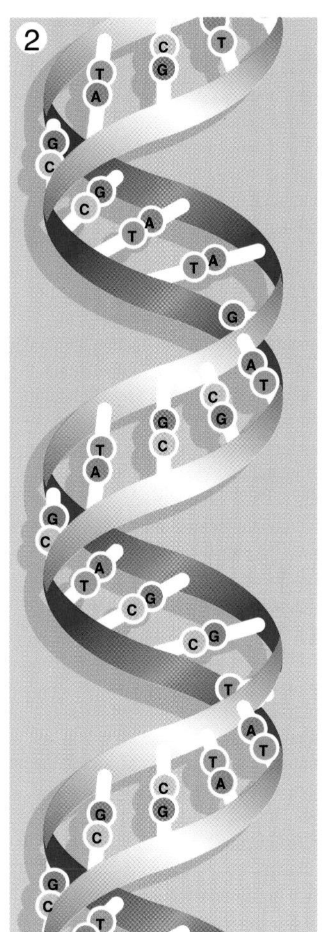

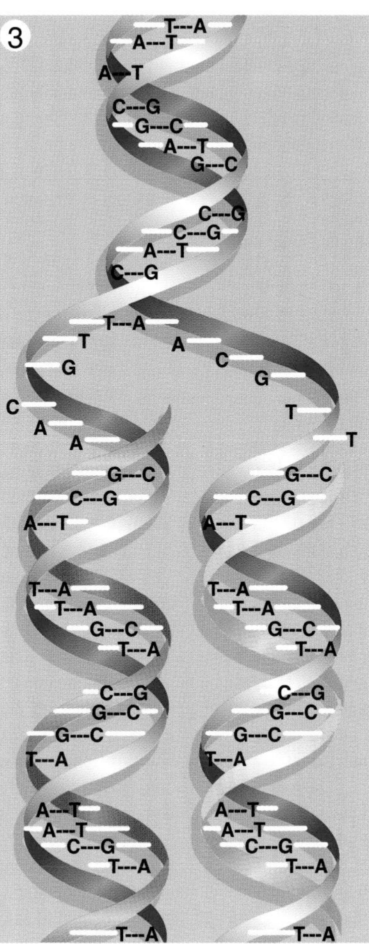

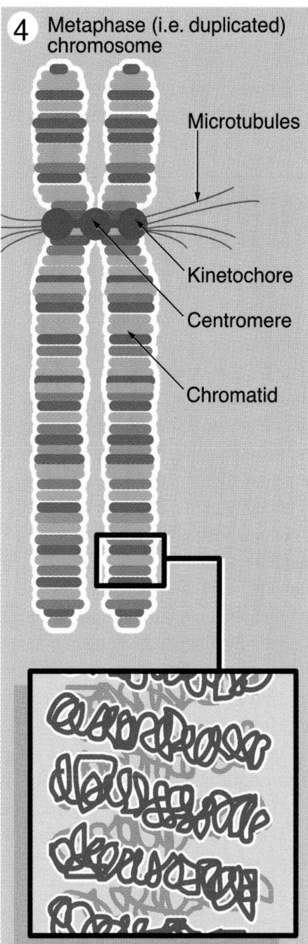

A adenine **C** cytosine **G** guanine **P** phosphate **S** deoxyribose **T** thymine

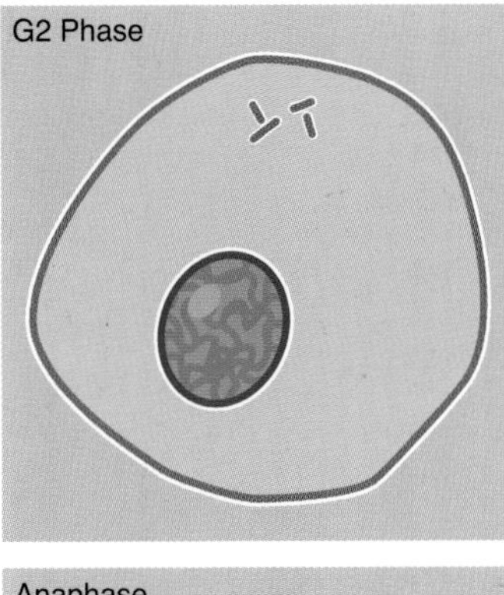

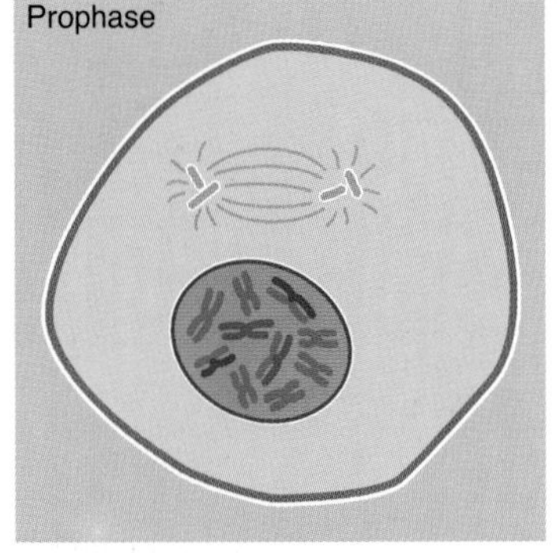

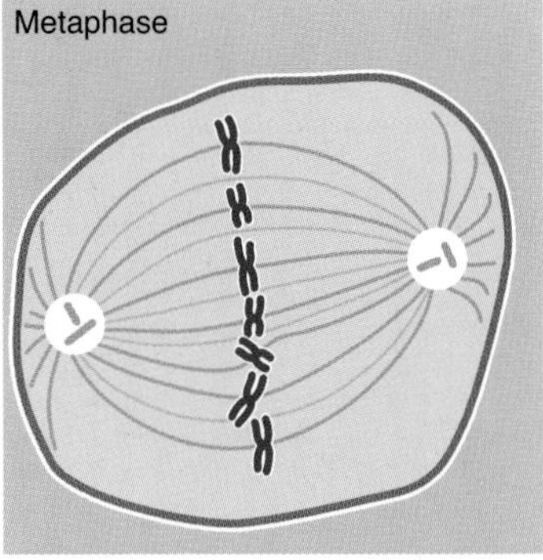

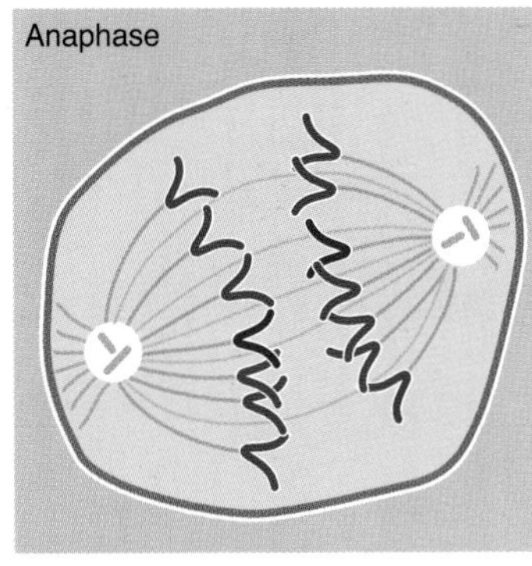

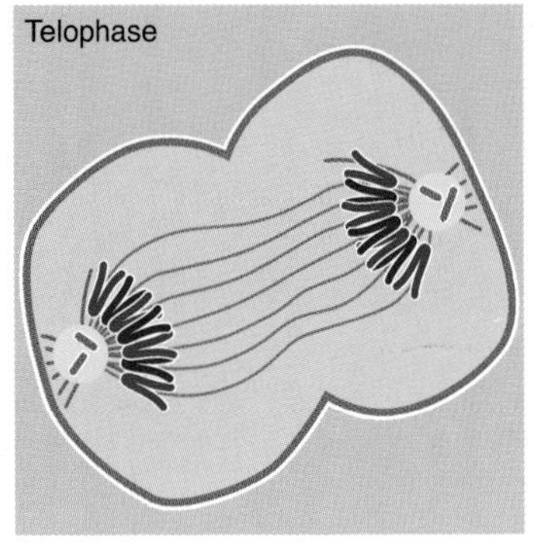

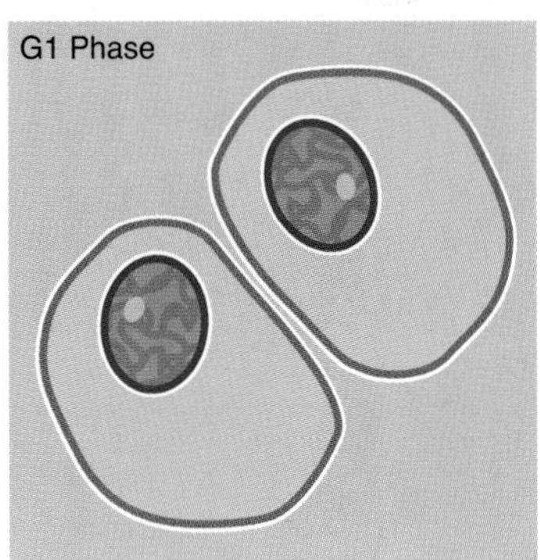

(a)

Fig. 2.3 Mitosis
(a) Schematic diagram (b) Mitotic series Giemsa ×800 *(opposite)*

The series of micrographs, shown opposite, illustrates the mitotic process in actively dividing immature blood cells from a smear preparation of human bone marrow. Mitosis is a continuous process that is traditionally divided into four phases, ***prophase***, ***metaphase***, ***anaphase*** and ***telophase***, each stage being readily recognisable with the light microscope. Cell division requires the presence of a structure called the ***mitotic apparatus***, which comprises a spindle of longitudinally arranged microtubules extending between a pair of centrioles (see Figs 1.24 and 1.25) at each pole of the dividing cell. The mitotic apparatus is visible within the cytoplasm only during the M phase of the cell cycle since it disaggregates shortly after completion of mitosis.

Prophase. The beginning of this stage of mitosis is defined as the moment when the chromosomes (already duplicated during the preceding S phase) first become visible within the nucleus. As prophase continues, the chromosomes become increasingly condensed and shortened and the nucleoli disappear. Dissolution of the nuclear envelope marks the end of prophase. During prophase, the microfilaments and microtubules of the cytoskeleton disaggregate into their protein subunits. The centrosome has already divided during the preceding interphase, and in prophase the two pairs of centrioles migrate towards opposite poles of the cell while simultaneously a spindle of microtubules is formed between them (***interpolar microtubules***).

Metaphase. The nuclear envelope having disintegrated, the mitotic spindle moves into the nuclear area and each duplicated chromosome becomes attached, at a site called the ***kinetochore***, to another group of microtubules of the mitotic spindle (***kinetochore*** or ***chromosome microtubules***). The kinetochore is a DNA and protein structure on each duplicated chromosome, located at the centromere, the structure which binds the duplicated chromosomes (chromatids) together (see also diagram 4, Fig. 2.2). Other microtubules attach the chromosome arms to the spindle. The chromosomes then become arranged in the plane of the spindle equator, known as the ***equatorial*** or ***metaphase plate***. The kinetochore also controls entry of the cell into anaphase so that the process of mitosis does not progress until all chromatid pairs are aligned at the cell equator. This is sometimes called the ***metaphase checkpoint*** and prevents the formation of daughter cells with unequal numbers of chromosomes.

Anaphase. The splitting of the centromere, which binds the chromatids of each duplicated chromosome, marks this stage of mitosis. The mitotic spindle becomes lengthened by addition of tubulin subunits to its interpolar microtubules while ***astral microtubules*** joining the centrosome to the cell cortex (the area underlying the plasma membrane) shorten. The centrioles are thus pulled apart and the chromatids of each duplicated chromosome are drawn to opposite ends of the spindle, thus achieving an exact division of the duplicated genetic material. By the end of anaphase, two groups of identical chromosomes are clustered at opposite poles of the cell.

Telophase. During the final phase of mitosis, the chromosomes begin to uncoil and to regain their interphase conformation. The nuclear envelope reassembles and nucleoli again become apparent. The process of cytokinesis also takes place during telophase. The plane of cytoplasmic division is usually defined by the position of the spindle equator, thus producing two cells of equal size. The plasma membrane around the spindle equator becomes indented to form a circumferential furrow around the cell, the ***cleavage furrow***, which progressively constricts the cell until it is cleaved into two daughter cells. A ring of microfilaments is present just beneath the surface of the cleavage furrow and cytokinesis occurs as a result of contraction of this filamentous ring. In early G_1 phase, the mitotic spindle disaggregates and in many cell types the single pair of centrioles begins to duplicate in preparation for the next mitotic division.

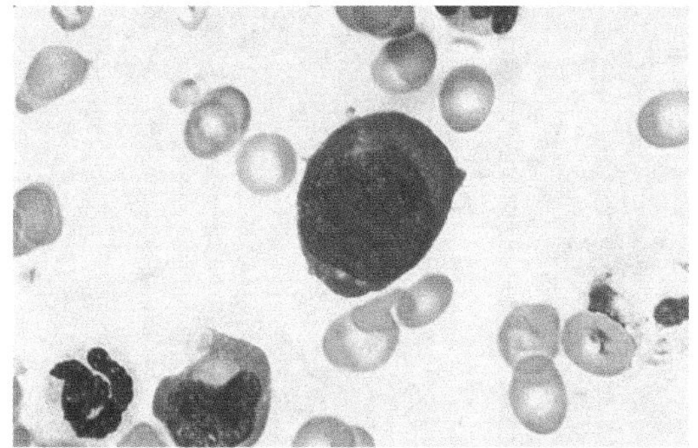

1. Interphase

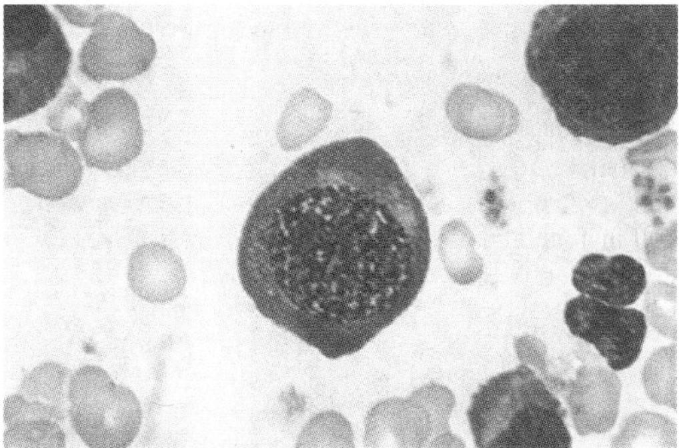

2. Early prophase

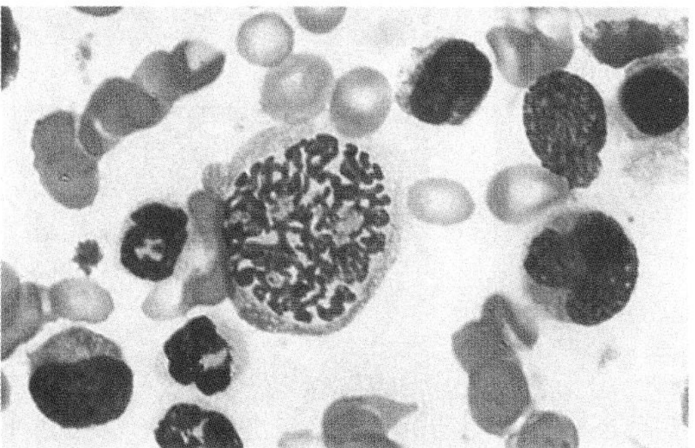

3. Late prophase

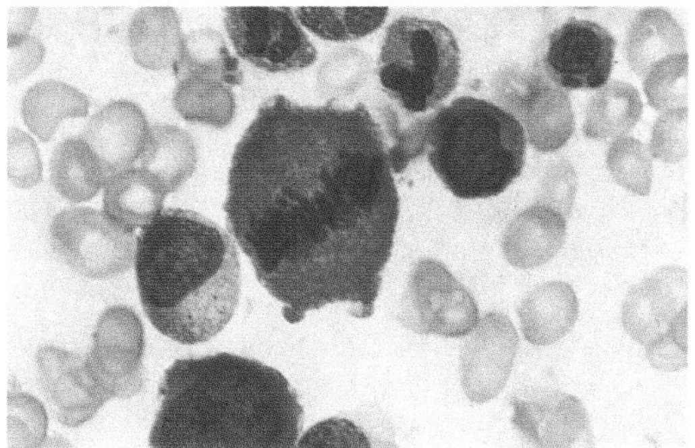

4. Metaphase

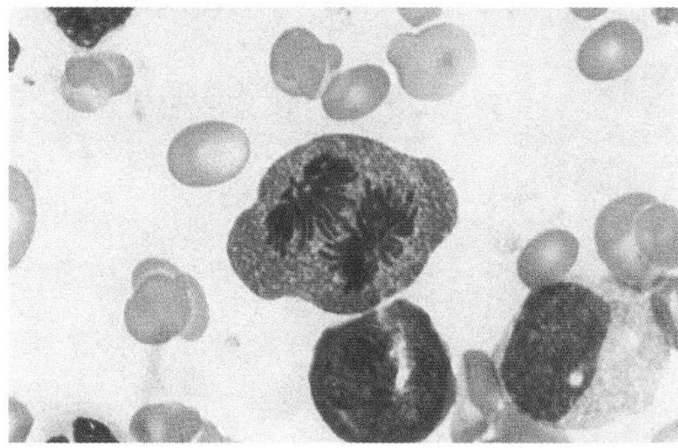

5. Early anaphase

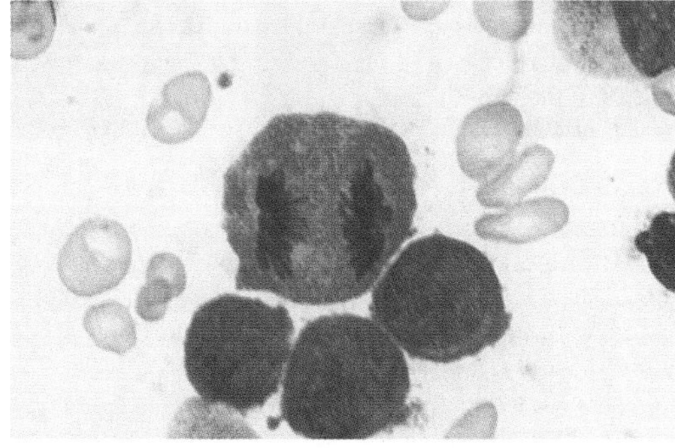

6. Late anaphase

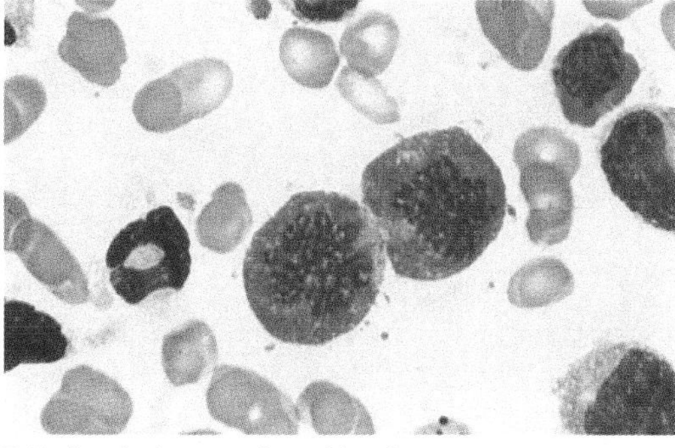

7. Early telophase and cytokinesis

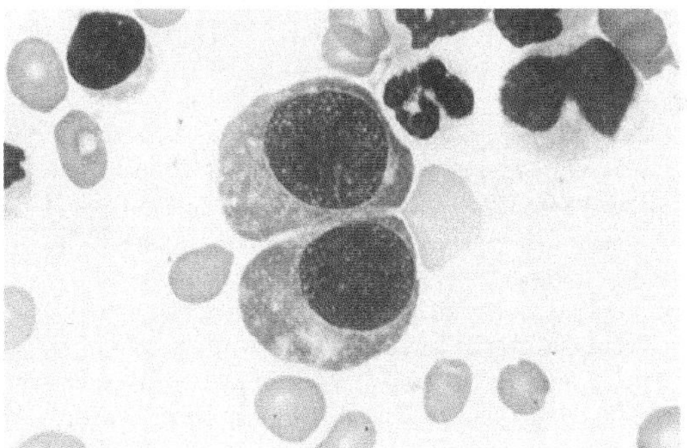

8. Late telophase and cytokinesis

(b)

Fig. 2.4 Mitotic figures in tissue sections

(a), (b) H & E ×400 (c) H & E ×600 (d) EM ×30 000 *(opposite)*

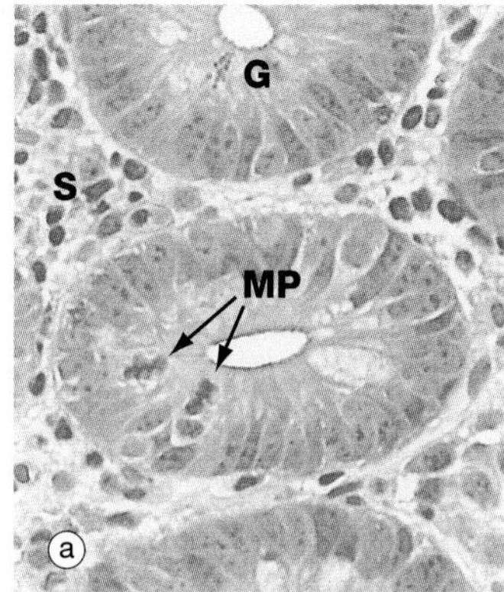

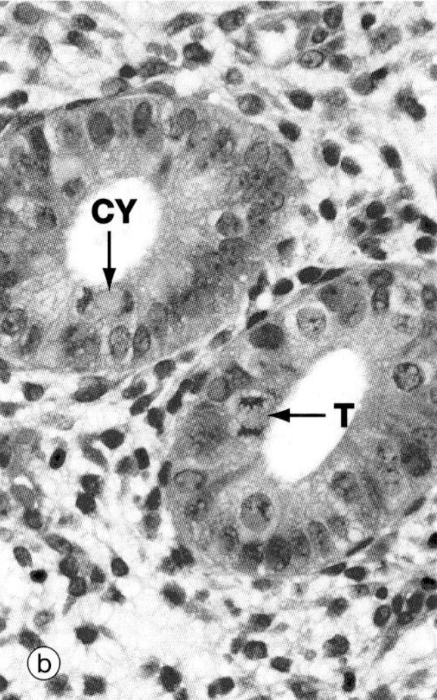

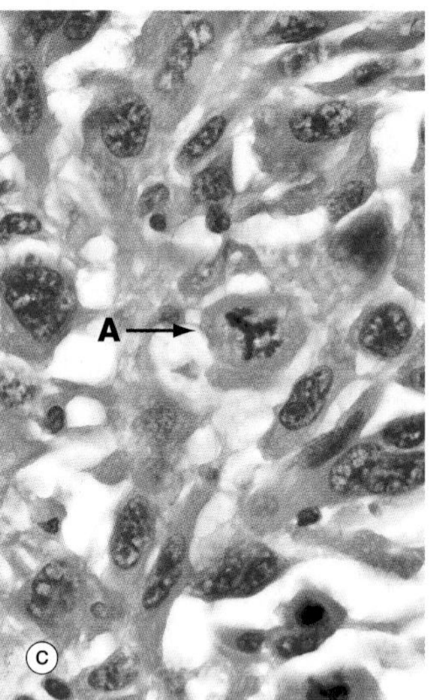

Micrographs (a) and (b) show the typical appearance of mitotic figures in normal tissue sections. In contrast to smear preparations where the entire cell is visualised, the process of preparing a tissue section cuts through the cell in a random plane. Thus it is more difficult to recognise mitotic figures with certainty in tissue sections. In many adult tissues such as skeletal muscle or adipose tissue, mitosis is not seen, as these cells do not normally divide. Other tissues such as uterine endometrium regularly undergo cell division as part of their normal functions.

Micrographs (a) and (b) illustrate normal proliferative phase endometrium (see Ch. 19). During this phase of the monthly cycle, the endometrial glands **G** and stroma **S** proliferate by mitosis to form a thicker lining for the uterus in preparation for implantation of a fertilised egg. In (a) two glandular epithelial cells are at the metaphase plate **MP** stage of mitosis while in micrograph (b) a single cell is in telophase **T** and a second cell is entering cytokinesis **CY**. Micrograph (c) shows an abnormal mitotic figure **A** in a malignant tumour of the kidney (see **Cancer** below). Compare this tripolar mitosis with the normal metaphase plates in micrograph (a).

Micrograph (d) shows an electron microscopic view of part of a dividing cell, in this case a supporting Schwann cell in the developing nervous system. The plasma membrane **PM** can be identified, but the nuclear membrane has dissolved and condensed chromatin **C** has spread out into the cytoplasm. Mitochondria **M**, smooth endoplasmic reticulum **sER** and ribosomes **R** are seen in the peripheral cytoplasm. In the centre of the nuclear material, numerous microtubules **MT** can be seen in transverse section representing part of the spindle apparatus. Taken together, these features probably indicate that the cell is in anaphase, the plane of section being through one end of the dividing nuclear material and oriented at right angles to the spindle axis.

Cancer

Cancers or ***malignant tumours*** are common causes of illness and death in most societies and the diagnosis of cancer is an important part of the workload of diagnostic histopathology. Cancers cause disease by growing in an uncontrolled fashion within the body and replacing or destroying normal tissues. Importantly, as well as growing at their site of origin, cancers are able to ***metastasize*** or spread to other areas of the body such as the lungs or liver. Thus a primary cancer of the breast can spread to the lungs causing death from respiratory failure or a cancer of the prostate may replace the bone marrow with consequent failure of production of white blood cells, causing death from overwhelming infection.

The many features of malignant tumours are well described in standard pathological texts but one common feature is the abnormal mitotic figure (Fig. 2.4c), which is not seen in normal tissue but is frequently a feature of malignant tumours (and some ***premalignant*** conditions). Abnormal mitotic figures are a visually obvious example of the many genetic abnormalities that are found in cancer cells, where there is loss of control of cell division and of cell death (see Figs 2.7 and 2.8). These genetic abnormalities or mutations may be caused by infections (e.g. Epstein–Barr virus), toxins (e.g. cigarette smoke), radiation (e.g. sunlight) or may be inherited. Intensive research in this area continues and more causes and mechanisms of cancer are uncovered almost daily.

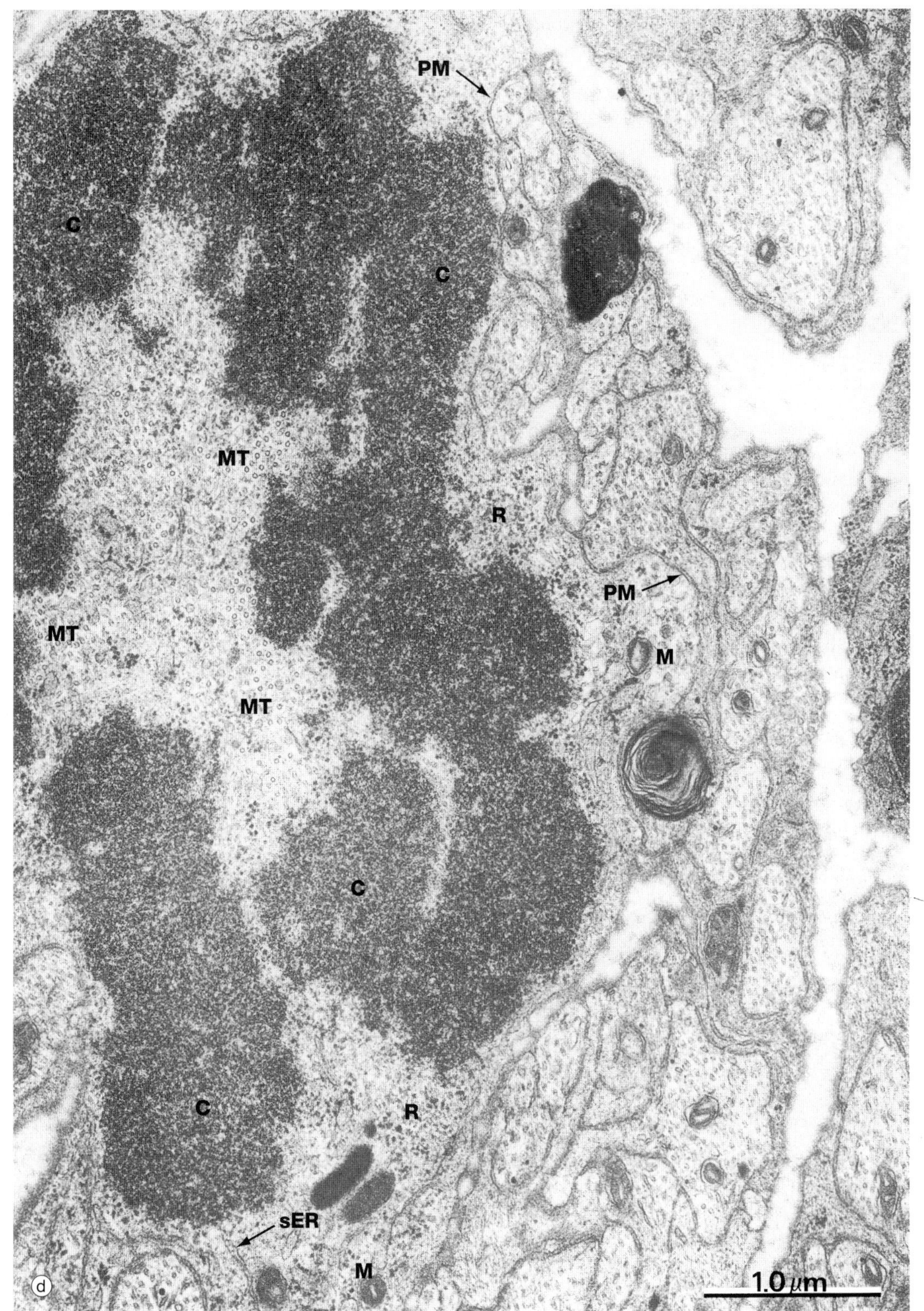

A abnormal mitotic figure **C** chromatin **CY** cytokinesis **G** gland **M** mitochondria **MP** metaphase plate **MT** microtubules **PM** plasma membrane **R** ribosomes **S** stroma **sER** smooth endoplasmic reticulum **T** telophase

Meiosis

In all somatic cells, cell division (mitosis) results in the formation of two daughter cells, each one genetically identical to the mother cell. Somatic cells contain a full complement of chromosomes (the ***diploid number***) which function as homologous pairs as described earlier. The process of sexual reproduction involves the production by ***meiosis*** of specialised male and female cells called ***gametes***. Meiotic cell division is thus also called ***gametogenesis***. Each gamete contains the ***haploid number*** of chromosomes (23 in humans) i.e. one from each homologous pair. When the male and female gametes fuse at fertilisation to form a ***zygote*** the diploid number of chromosomes (46 in humans) is restored. The member of each chromosome pair assigned to a particular gamete is entirely random, so that a particular gamete contains a mix of chromosomes from the mother and father of the individual forming the gamete. This mixing of chromosomes contributes to the genetic diversity of the next generation. Further genetic diversity and therefore evolutionary advantage is added by the mechanism of ***crossing over*** (see below). The process of meiosis is outlined below and compared to mitosis in Fig. 2.5 opposite.

- The first step in meiosis is the duplication of the chromosomes as for mitosis.
- This is immediately followed by crossing over of the chromatids, so that genetic information is exchanged between the two chromosomes of the homologous pair. In any individual, one of each pair of chromosomes is derived from the father and one from the mother. Crossing over mixes up these paternally and maternally derived ***alleles*** (alternative forms of the same gene) so that the haploid gamete ends up with only one of each chromosome pair but each individual chromosome include alleles from each parent (see Fig. 2.5). The mechanism of crossing over is called ***chiasma formation***. As well as generating great genetic diversity, this mixing up of genes explains the conviction of many teenagers that they must be adopted.
- The first meiotic division then proceeds, involving separation of the pairs of chromatids still joined together at the centromere. Thus at the end of the first meiotic division, each daughter cell contains a half complement of duplicated chromosomes, one from each homologous pair of chromosomes.
- The second meiotic division involves splitting of the chromatids by pulling apart the centromeres. The chromatids then migrate to opposite poles of the spindle.

Thus, meiotic cell division of a single diploid germ cell gives rise to four haploid gametes. In the male, each of the four gametes undergoes morphological development into a mature ***spermatozoon***. In the female, unequal distribution of the cytoplasm results in one gamete gaining almost all the cytoplasm from the mother cell, while the other three acquire almost none; the large gamete matures to form an ***ovum*** and the other three, called ***polar bodies***, degenerate.

During both the first and second meiotic divisions, the cell passes through stages that have many similar features to prophase, metaphase, anaphase and telophase of mitosis. Unlike mitosis, however, the process of meiotic cell division can be suspended for a considerable length of time. For example, in the development of the human female gamete, the germ cells enter prophase of the first meiotic division during the fifth month of fetal life and then remain suspended until some time after sexual maturity; the first meiotic division is thus suspended for between 12 and 50 years!

The primitive germ cells of the male, the ***spermatogonia***, are present only in small numbers in the male gonads before sexual maturity. After this, spermatogonia multiply continuously by mitosis to provide a supply of cells, which then undergo meiosis to form male gametes. In contrast, the germ cells of the female, called ***oogonia***, multiply by mitosis only during early fetal development, thereby producing a fixed complement of cells with the potential to undergo gametogenesis.

Chromosomes are not the only source of genes in the germ cells. Mitochondria also contain DNA that codes for some intrinsic mitochondrial proteins required for energy production. Because the spermatozoa shed their mitochondria at the time of fertilisation, only maternal mitochondrial genes are passed on to the offspring. A number of inherited diseases are known to be transmitted through mitochondrial DNA.

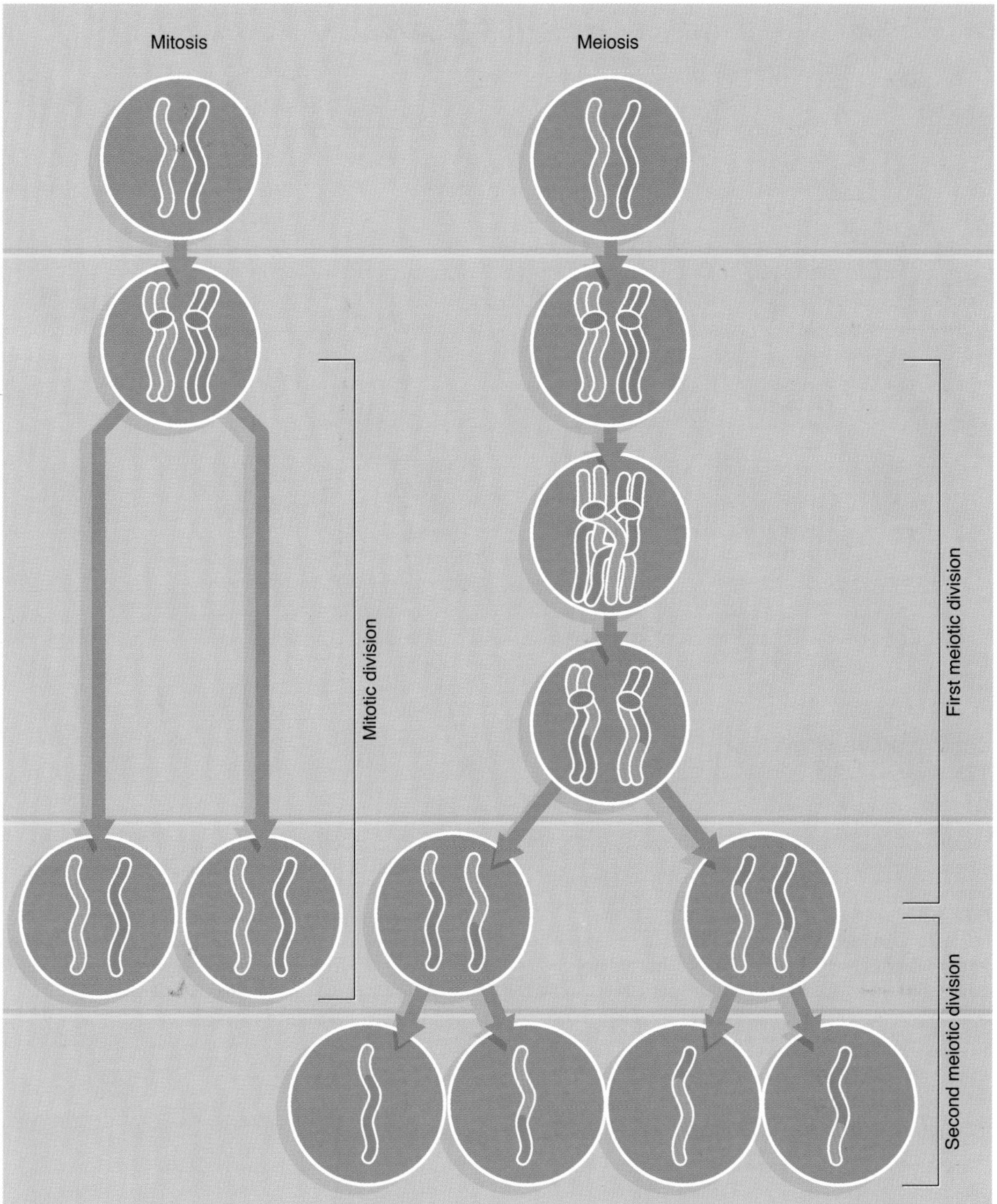

Fig. 2.5 Comparison of mitosis and meiosis

This diagram compares the behaviour of each homologous pair of chromosomes during mitosis and meiosis. The progress of only one homologous pair is represented here. The key differences between the two forms of cell division are as follows:

- Meiosis involves one reduplication of the chromosomes followed by two sequential cell divisions. Thus a diploid cell produces four haploid germ cells (gametes).
- Crossing over occurs only in meiosis, to rearrange alleles such that every gamete is genetically different. In contrast, the products of mitosis are genetically identical.

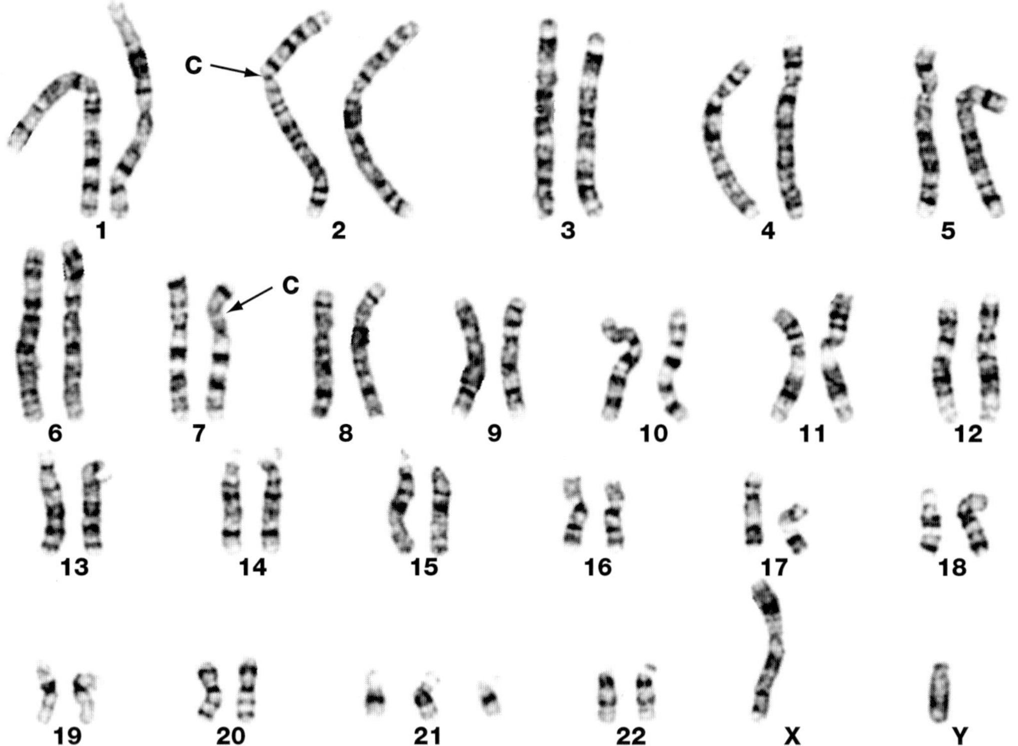

Fig. 2.6 Human karyotype
Leishman's ×1000

This micrograph illustrates the chromosomes of a human cell grown in vitro and harvested at the onset of mitosis. The cell has been disrupted and the chromosomes stained to reveal their characteristic cross-banding pattern. This approach allows the investigator to identify chromosomes 1, 2 etc. At this stage the chromosomes are duplicated and the two chromatids (not visible at this magnification) are joined at the centromere **C**. Each member of a homologous pair of mitotic chromosomes is identical in length, centromere location and banding pattern. Study of the chromosomes in this fashion, ***karyotyping***, can reveal structural and numerical chromosomal abnormalities, known as ***cytogenetic abnormalities***. In this particular case there are three copies of chromosome 21, i.e. this is a trisomy 21 karyotype. All the other chromosomes are normal. There is one X and one Y chromosome demonstrating that the fetus is male.

Common cytogenetic abnormalities

The complex processes of meiotic cell division sometimes malfunction. It is unknown how many fetuses are conceived each year with genetic abnormalities so serious that the condition is lethal in utero and results in an early, perhaps even unrecognised miscarriage. Most cytogenetic defects are thought to be lethal in this way and only a very few such as Trisomy 21 (i.e. three copies of chromosome 21, also known as Down syndrome), trisomy 18 (Edward syndrome) and Trisomy 13 (Patau syndrome) give rise to live births. In the two latter conditions the infant usually dies within the first year, but individuals with Down's syndrome may live to middle age or longer.

Trisomies arise usually due to failure of the homologous chromosome pairs to separate during the first meiotic division (***nondisjunction***) or failure of the two sister chromatids to separate during the second meiotic division (***anaphase lag***). Thus the resulting gamete has two copies of the relevant chromosome and when fertilisation occurs a third copy is added. In most cases the extra chromosome is from the mother and there is a greatly increased incidence of Down's syndrome with increasing maternal age, although the exact mechanism is as yet unclear. Karyotyping of fetal cells is widely available to detect cytogenetic abnormalities by the techniques of ***amniocentesis*** or ***chorionic villous sampling***.

Apoptosis

Apoptosis is an essential part of normal fetal development, growth of juveniles and control of cell numbers in adults, where it exactly balances cell division. Apoptosis also occurs in a number of pathological conditions. This process has characteristic microscopic features and is a highly controlled and ordered mechanism that removes cells in a way that causes minimal disruption to the surrounding tissue. Apoptosis is brought about by different mechanisms than those causing ***necrosis***, a mode of cell and tissue death that occurs only in pathological conditions. A well-known example of necrosis is myocardial infarction, where heart muscle dies from lack of

oxygen due to blockage of a coronary artery. Apoptosis is an active process requiring the expenditure of energy, while necrosis is characterised by the inability of cells to produce the energy (ATP) required to maintain homeostasis. When apoptosis occurs during development of the embryo or fetus it is often referred to as ***programmed cell death***.

Control of apoptosis is very finely balanced and a wide variety of triggers may initiate the process. The signal for apoptosis may be the binding of an external signal molecule to a membrane receptor (the 'death receptor' known as ***Fas***), or may arise from intracellular signals such as DNA damage, leading to the release of the enzyme ***cytochrome c*** from the mitochondria into the cytoplasm. Within the cell many regulatory proteins control apoptosis including members of the ***bcl-2*** and ***inhibitors of apoptosis (IAP)*** families. The end result of all these various signals is a common mechanism known as the ***caspase cascade***. The activated enzymes of the caspase cascade cleave cellular proteins such as the lamins of the nucleus as well as activating additional enzymes such as ***DNAase*** to cleave ***DNA***.

Examples of apoptosis include:

- Some cell types have a preset limited lifetime and inevitably undergo apoptosis as part of their life cycle, e.g. epithelial cells in the skin or the lining of the gastrointestinal tract.
- Other cells are triggered to destroy themselves if they behave in ways which are 'inappropriate'; for example, developing T lymphocytes that are capable of reacting to normal body components are triggered to self-destruct in the thymus, a process known as clonal deletion (see Ch. 11). Failure of clonal deletion may lead to autoimmune disorders such as autoimmune thyroiditis or pernicious anaemia.
- During development certain cells are programmed to die by apoptosis, e.g. in humans the webs between the fingers and toes disappear and the tadpole loses its tail as it matures into a frog.
- Certain tissues in adults grow and regress in a cyclical fashion, such as the growth of ovarian follicles before ovulation in females followed by regression of the corpus luteum by apoptosis to form a corpus albicans (see Ch. 19).
- Apoptosis is a common mode of cell death of abnormal cells such as those infected by viruses or with genetic mutations. Failure of apoptosis may be as important in cancer as unrestricted cell division.

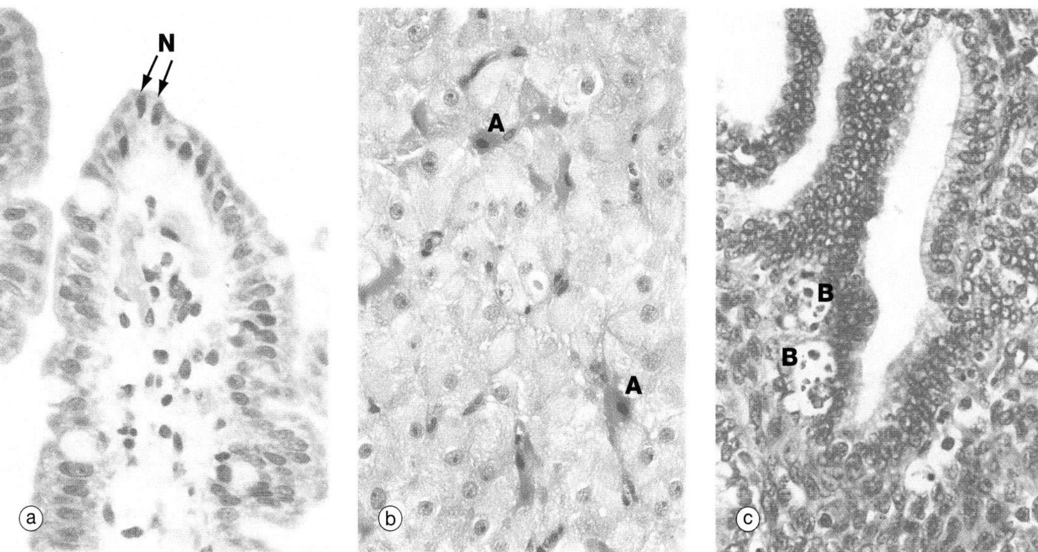

Fig. 2.7 Apoptosis in normal tissues
H & E (a) ×300 (b) ×200 (c) ×300

These three micrographs illustrate the typical features of apoptotic cells in normal tissues. Specimen (a) shows the tip of a villus in the small intestine. Several nuclei **N** in the epithelial cells at the tip are more darkly stained than the neighbouring cells, indicating that these cells are beginning the process of apoptosis prior to being shed from the surface. Micrograph (b) is a corpus luteum, formed from an ovarian follicle after discharge of an ovum (see Ch. 19). If the ovum is not fertilised the corpus luteum will involute, a process that involves progressive death of its constituent cells leaving a fibrotic scar known as a corpus luteum. In this micrograph several apoptotic cells **A** can be identified by their condensed nuclei and eosinophilic cytoplasm.

Micrograph (c) shows a later stage of apoptosis in epithelial cells of endometrial glands at the beginning of menstruation (see Ch. 19). Two cells have undergone apoptosis and reached the stage of forming easily identified apoptotic bodies **B**. The apoptotic bodies have been phagocytosed by adjacent cells, which are themselves about to undergo the same process as the superficial part of the endometrium is shed.

A apoptotic cell **B** apoptotic body **C** centromere **N** nucleus

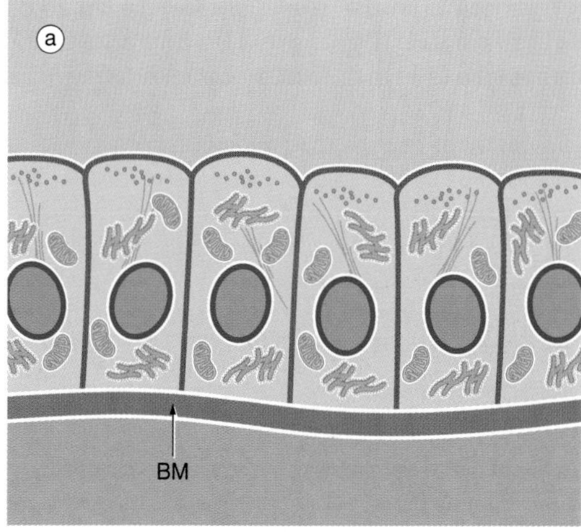

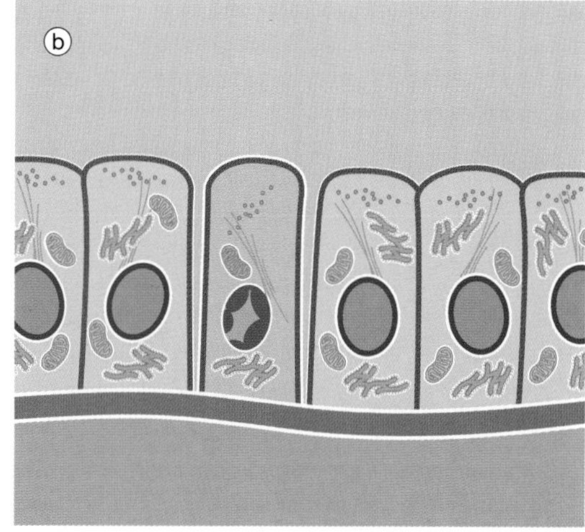

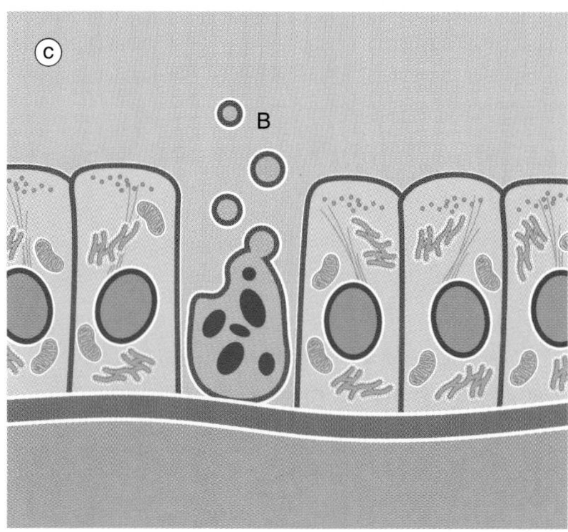

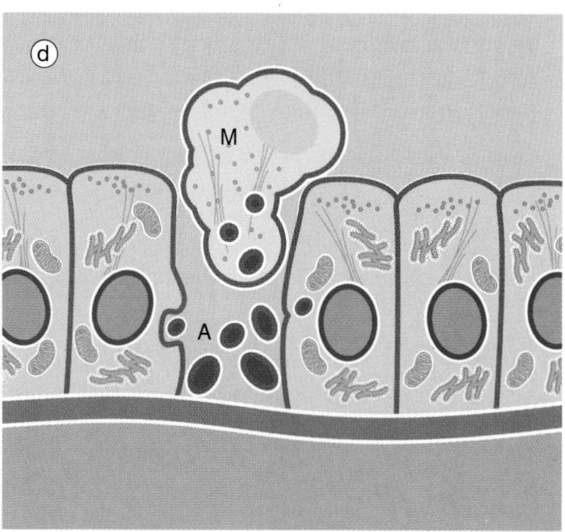

Fig. 2.8 The mechanism of apoptosis

Although a variety of extrinsic and intrinsic triggers may initiate apoptosis, at the molecular level the final common pathway is the activation of the caspase cascade. Caspases are a set of enzymes found in inactive form in all cells. When the first in the series is activated, by cleaving off a short protein sequence, it is then able to activate the next enzyme in the series and so on. Because each enzyme is able to activate many copies of the next enzyme, the reaction is greatly amplified. This enzyme cascade mechanism is also seen in other situations requiring a rapid but controlled response, such as the blood clotting mechanism (the coagulation cascade) and the complement cascade.

The process of apoptosis is shown in this diagram of simple columnar epithelial cells resting on basement membrane **BM**. When a normal cell (a) receives a signal to initiate apoptosis, the characteristic change by light microscopy (b) is condensation of the nuclear chromatin (***pyknosis***) to form one or more dark-staining masses found against the nuclear membrane. At the same time the cell shrinks away from its neighbours with loss of cell–cell contacts and increasing eosinophilia (pink staining) of the cytoplasm. The cytoplasmic organelles are still preserved at this stage. As the process continues (c), the nuclear material breaks into fragments (***karyorrhexis***). This is accompanied by dissolution of the nuclear membrane. Cytoplasmic blebs **B** break away from the cell surface and eventually the entire cell breaks up (***karyolysis***) (d) to form membrane-bound fragments. Some of the cell fragments contain nuclear material and are known as ***apoptotic bodies*** **A**. These apoptotic bodies may be phagocytosed by tissue ***macrophages*** **M**, scavenger cells derived from the bone marrow and found in virtually every tissue in the body, or by their neighbouring cells.

In some circumstances, part of the cell remains as a normal tissue component after apoptosis. For instance, in the skin, epithelial cells undergo apoptosis as part of their normal life cycle, but for some considerable time after the nucleus has disappeared, the cell cytoplasm filled with keratin intermediate filaments remains as an anucleate 'squame' to form a waterproof coating on the surface of the skin.

A apoptotic bodies **B** cytoplasmic blebs **BM** basement membrane **M** macrophage

PART TWO

Basic tissue types

3. *Blood*

Introduction

Blood consists of a variety of cells suspended in a fluid medium called ***plasma***. It functions as a vehicle for the transport of gases, nutrients, metabolic waste products, cells and hormones throughout the body. Because the blood is composed not only of cells and molecules involved in transport processes but also cells and molecules in the process of being transported, laboratory analysis of blood plays a large role in diagnosis of disease. A typical sample of plasma is composed of 90% water, 8% protein, 1% inorganic salts, 0.5% lipids and 0.1% sugar, the rest being made of lesser components. Salts are constantly exchanged with the extracellular fluid of body tissues. The three main groups of protein in plasma are the blood coagulation proteins, albumin, and the globulins. The globulins can be divided into alpha globulins (proteases, antiproteases and transport proteins) beta globulins (transferrin, other transport proteins) and gamma globulins (mainly immunoglobulins). The plasma proteins are nearly all derived from synthesis in the liver, with the exception of the immunoglobulins which are synthesised by plasma cells (Ch. 11). Collectively, the plasma proteins exert a colloidal osmotic pressure within the circulatory system which helps to regulate the exchange of fluid between plasma and the extracellular space. In general, the molecular components of plasma cannot be demonstrated by light or electron microscopy.

Blood cell types

The cells of blood are of three major functional classes: ***red blood cells*** (***erythrocytes***), ***white blood cells*** (***leucocytes***) and ***platelets*** (***thrombocytes***). All are formed in the ***bone marrow***, the process being known as ***haemopoiesis***.

Erythrocytes contain large amounts of oxygen-carrying haemoglobin, are primarily involved in the transport of oxygen and carbon dioxide, and function exclusively within the vascular system. The whole mass of red blood cells and their precursors in the bone marrow is called the ***erythron***.

The leucocytes constitute an important part of the defence and immune systems of the body and, as such, act mainly outside blood vessels in the tissues; thus the leucocytes found in circulating blood are merely in transit between their various sites of activity.

Platelets play a vital role in the control of bleeding (***haemostasis***) by plugging defects in blood vessel walls and contributing to the activation of the blood-clotting cascade.

Histological methods used to study blood and bone marrow

The standard method of examination of the blood is to make a ***spread*** (also called a ***smear***) on a glass slide. After fixation, a polychromatic ***Romanowsky-type staining technique*** such as the ***Giemsa***, ***Wright*** or ***Leishman method*** is used for examination with the light microscope. Four distinctive staining characteristics can be identified according to the affinity of the various cellular organelles for the different stains employed in these methods:

- **Basophilia** (deep blue) – affinity for the basic dye ***methylene blue***; this is a characteristic of DNA in nuclei and RNA in the cytoplasm, i.e. ribosomes
- **Azurophilia** (purple) – affinity for azure dyes; this is typical of lysosomes, one of the granule types found in leucocytes
- **Eosinophilia** (pink) – affinity for the acidic dye ***eosin*** (thus also described as ***acidophilia***); this is a particular feature of haemoglobin which fills the cytoplasm of erythrocytes
- **Neutrophilia** (salmon pink/lilac) – affinity for a dye once erroneously believed to be of neutral pH; characteristic of the specific cytoplasmic granules of neutrophil leucocytes.

Anaemia

Failure to maintain an adequate haemoglobin concentration is termed ***anaemia***. There are several common causes of anaemia, including lack of factors required to make haemoglobin, (e.g. iron, or vitamins B_{12} and folic acid), excessive loss or inappropriate destruction of erythrocytes, or failure of bone marrow to manufacture enough cells. Erythrocyte morphology may be altered in certain types of anaemia. Lack of iron leads to cells that are smaller than normal (***microcytes***) while lack of B_{12} and folate leads to cells that are larger than normal (***macrocytes***). Abnormally rounded and fragile erythrocytes (***spherocytes***) may be caused by mutations in genes coding for proteins in the red cell cytoskeleton.

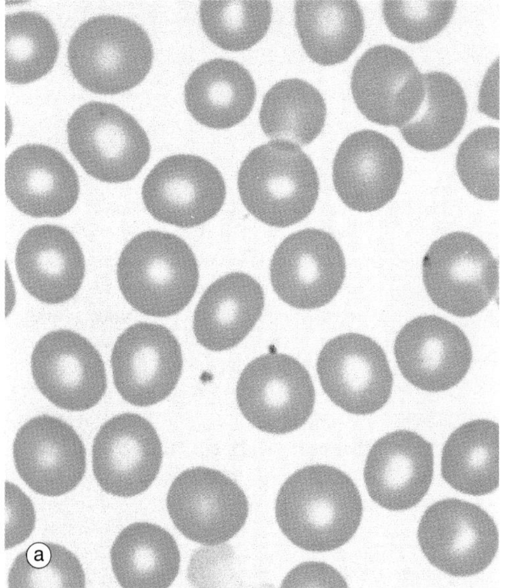

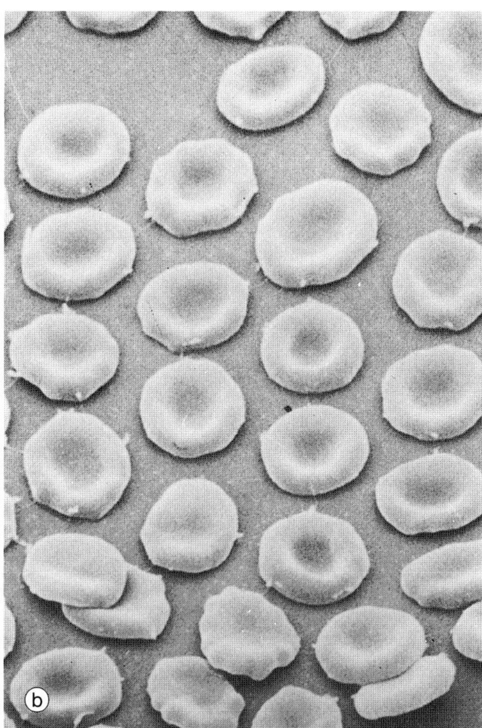

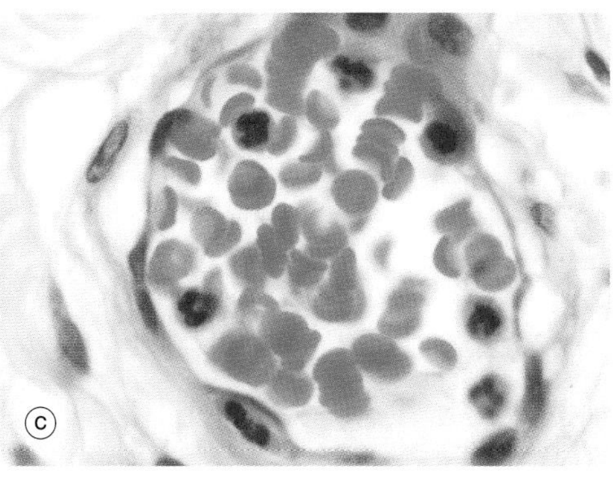

Fig. 3.1 Erythrocytes
Giemsa ×1200 (b) Scanning EM ×2400 (c) H & E ×400

The erythrocyte is highly adapted for its principal function of oxygen and carbon dioxide transport. During differentiation in the bone marrow, large quantities of the iron-containing respiratory pigment ***haemoglobin*** are synthesised. Before release into the blood circulation, the erythrocyte nucleus is extruded and, by maturity, all cytoplasmic organelles degenerate. The fully differentiated erythrocyte therefore simply consists of an outer plasma membrane enclosing haemoglobin and the limited number of enzymes necessary for maintenance of the cell.

Micrograph (a) demonstrates the characteristic appearance of erythrocytes in a stained spread of peripheral blood. The cells are stained pink (eosinophilia/acidophilia) due to their high content of haemoglobin, a basic protein. The pale staining of the central region of the erythrocyte is a result of its biconcave disc shape.

Scanning electron microscopy shown in micrograph (b) reveals the biconcave disc shape of erythrocytes which provides a 20–30% greater surface area than a sphere relative to cell volume, thus significantly enhancing gaseous exchange. This shape, along with the fluidity of the plasma membrane, allows the erythrocyte to deform readily, and thus erythrocytes (average diameter 7.2 μm) are able to pass through the smallest capillaries (3–4 μm in diameter). In tissue sections erythrocytes are seen within blood vessels as shown in micrograph (c). They have a high affinity for eosin and appear as intensely pink-stained in H & E preparations. Sectioning in different planes results in different shapes.

The erythrocyte plasma membrane is composed of a lipid bilayer incorporating various globular proteins conforming to the standard fluid mosaic model of membrane structure (see Fig. 1.2). Blood group substances are carried on the surface. Immediately beneath the plasma membrane is a meshwork of proteins forming a cytoskeleton anchored to the membrane by one or more membrane-incorporated proteins; the main skeletal protein is the long fibre-like protein, ***spectrin***. The biconcave shape of erythrocytes is determined in part by the cytoskeleton and in part by its water content, the latter being related to the concentration of inorganic ions within the cell.

The binding, transport and delivery of oxygen by haemoglobin are not dependent on erythrocyte metabolism. However, erythrocytes use energy to maintain normal electrolyte gradients across the plasma membrane, maintain the iron atoms of haemoglobin in a divalent form and for maintenance of the sulphydryl groups of red cell enzymes and haemoglobin in a reduced, active form. The energy required for this process is derived from anaerobic metabolism of glucose. The absence of mitochondria precludes aerobic energy production and erythrocytes are therefore totally dependent on glucose as an energy source.

The lifespan of an erythrocyte averages 120 days and is partly governed by its ability to maintain the biconcave shape. Without the appropriate organelles, erythrocytes are unable to replace deteriorating enzymes and membrane proteins, leading to diminished ability to pump sodium ions from the cell, uptake of water and the development of an abnormal spheroidal shape. Such cells are removed from the circulation by the spleen and liver (see Ch. 11).

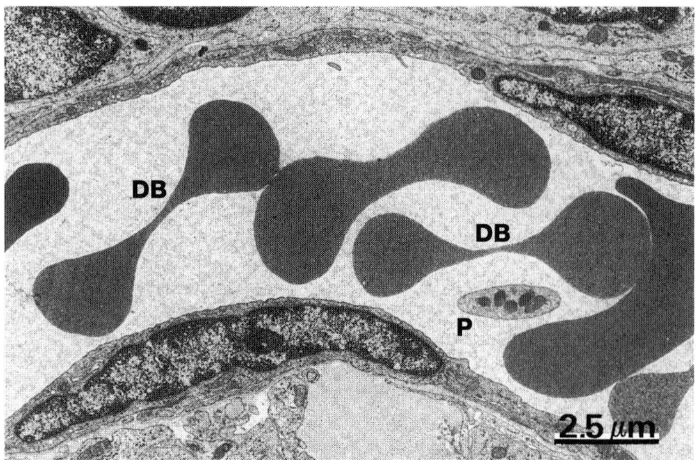

Fig. 3.2 Erythrocytes
EM ×6000

This electron micrograph illustrates erythrocytes within a capillary. The observed shape of the erythrocyte depends on the plane of section through the cell. The classic 'dumb-bell' shape **DB** is only seen when the erythrocyte is cut through its thin central zone; more frequently, irregularly shaped erythrocytes are seen reflecting the deformation which occurs in small blood vessels. The high electron density of erythrocytes is due to the iron atoms of haemoglobin. Note the total absence of organelles. A platelet **P** is also seen in this field.

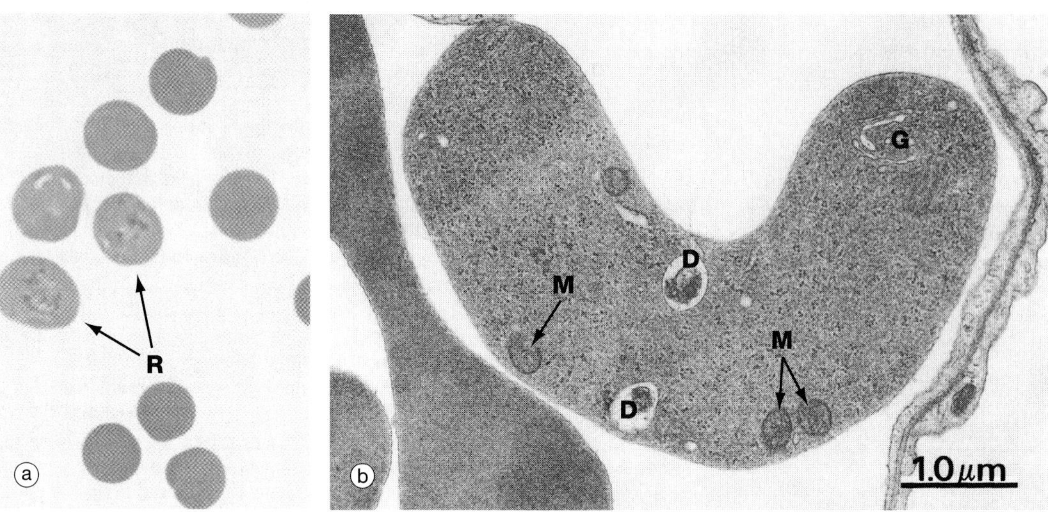

Fig. 3.3 Reticulocytes
(a) Cresyl blue/eosin ×1200 (b) EM ×16 000

Reticulocytes are immature red blood cells which have shed their nucleus, but still retain residual nuclear material. Reticulocytes are the immature form in which erythrocytes are released into the circulation from the bone marrow. They still contain sufficient mitochondria, ribosomes and Golgi elements to complete the cytoskeleton and the remaining 20% of haemoglobin synthesis. Final maturation into erythrocytes occurs within 24–48 hours of release. The rate of release of reticulocytes into the circulation generally equals the rate of removal of spent erythrocytes by the spleen and liver. Since the lifespan of circulating erythrocytes is about 120 days, reticulocytes constitute slightly less than 1% of circulating red blood cells.

Reticulocytes cannot normally be seen in routinely stained blood spreads. A special procedure is performed to demonstrate reticulocytes in which a fresh blood sample is incubated with the basic dye, brilliant cresyl blue. A blue-stained ***reticular*** precipitate **R** is formed in the reticulocytes due to the interaction of the dye with RNA remnants. This technique, called ***supravital staining***, is illustrated in micrograph (a). Diagnostic detection of reticulocytes is now usually done using automated systems such as flow cytometry.

Reticulocytes are slightly larger than mature erythrocytes. Micrograph (b) shows the ultrastructure of a reticulocyte with an adjacent mature erythrocyte for comparison. Overall the cytoplasmic density is lower, due to a lower concentration of haemoglobin. Scattered ribosomes can still be seen as well as a few mitochondria **M**, a couple of degenerating mitochondria **D** and a small Golgi remnant **G**.

When severe erythrocyte loss occurs, such as after haemorrhage or haemolysis, the rate of erythrocyte production in the bone marrow increases and the proportion of reticulocytes in circulating blood rises (***reticulocytosis***). Clinically, the reticulocyte percentage is a useful indicator of erythropoiesis. In cases of anaemia, an elevated reticulocyte count indicates normal marrow function, while a decreased count may mean impaired erythropoiesis.

D degenerating mitochondrion **DB** dumb-bell-shaped erythrocyte **G** Golgi remnants
M mitochondrion **P** platelet **R** reticular precipitate in reticulocyte

White cell series

Five types of leucocyte are normally present in the circulation. These are traditionally divided into two main groups based on their nuclear shape and cytoplasmic granules:

- **Granulocytes**
  Neutrophils
  Eosinophils
  Basophils

- **Mononuclear leucocytes**
  Lymphocytes
  Monocytes

Granulocytes are so named for their prominent cytoplasmic secretory granules. Each of the three different types of granulocyte has type-specific granules, the names ***neutrophil***, ***eosinophil*** and ***basophil*** being derived from the staining characteristics of these ***specific granules***. The granulocytes have a single multilobed nucleus, which conveyed to early microscopists the erroneous impression that these cells were multinucleate and led to the confusing description of the other main group of leucocytes as mononuclear cells (see below). The multilobed nucleus may assume many morphological shapes leading to the use of the term ***polymorphonuclear leucocyte*** or ***polymorph*** as a synonym for the term granulocyte. To confuse matters further, the term polymorph is often used to refer to neutrophils since they exhibit the greatest degree of nuclear polymorphism and are by far the most prolific of the polymorphs. Granulocytes are also referred to as ***myeloid cells*** due to their exclusive origin from bone marrow; this should not, however, be taken to imply that they are the only white blood cells to be formed in the bone marrow.

Lymphocytes and ***monocytes*** have non-lobulated nuclei and were described as mononuclear leucocytes by early microscopists to distinguish them from the polymorphs whose multilobed nuclei were originally believed to represent multiple nuclei. Again, to distinguish this group from the granulocytes, the term ***agranulocytes*** was also employed since cytoplasmic granules were not readily seen with early microscopic methods; unfortunately this may give the erroneous impression that these cells are devoid of cytoplasmic granules.

The leucocytes have important roles as components of the body defense systems however this activity takes place in the tissues, not in the blood. All leucocytes carry surface proteins which are capable of binding to complementary receptors on endothelial cells in blood vessels (Ch. 8). This binding then allows cells to actively migrate using amoeboid movement into the tissues. Neutrophils do not normally enter tissues in large numbers and a moderate number constantly circulate, generally only entering tissues in response to a disease stimulus in the process of ***acute inflammation***. Eosinophils, basophils and monocytes constantly enter certain tissues in normal states and circulate in the blood in relatively low numbers. Lymphocytes constantly enter tissues from the blood in normal states and leave tissues via the lymphatic system, to reach the lymphoid system (Ch. 11).

Functionally, neutrophils and monocytes are highly phagocytic and engulf microorganisms, cell debris and particulate matter in a non-specific manner; this activity may be enhanced and directed by immune responses to specific foreign agents (see Ch. 11). Lymphocytes play the key role in all immune responses and, in contrast to the other leucocytes, their activity is always directed against specific foreign agents.

White cell count in disease

In general, all the leucocytes perform their functions in the tissues and merely use the blood as a vehicle for transit between sites of formation, storage and activity. It follows, therefore, that increased demand for particular leucocytes in various sites is reflected in increased numbers in the circulation. The absolute and differential white cell count is therefore a useful pointer to diagnosis and is an important laboratory investigation. Automated assays are generally used to perform white cell counts using advanced cytometric techniques that do not use microscopy.

- Raised neutrophil count (blood ***neutrophilia***) indicates an acute inflammatory response and is especially seen in association with bacterial infections.
- Raised eosinophil count (blood ***eosinophilia***) is seen in response to allergy and in infections with certain parasites.
- Raised lymphocyte count (blood ***lymphocytosis***) is seen in response to viral infections.
- Malignant tumours can form from the bone marrow cells that make white blood cells, termed ***leukaemias***. In these conditions it is common to find a very raised white cell count corresponding to circulating malignant cells.
- Reduction in white cells in the blood may indicate defective function of the bone marrow.

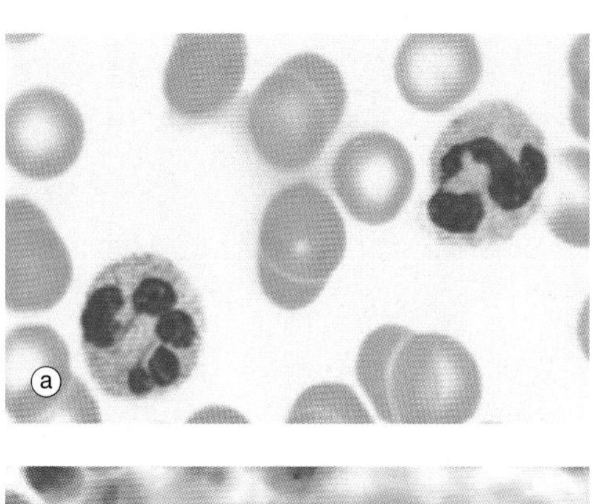

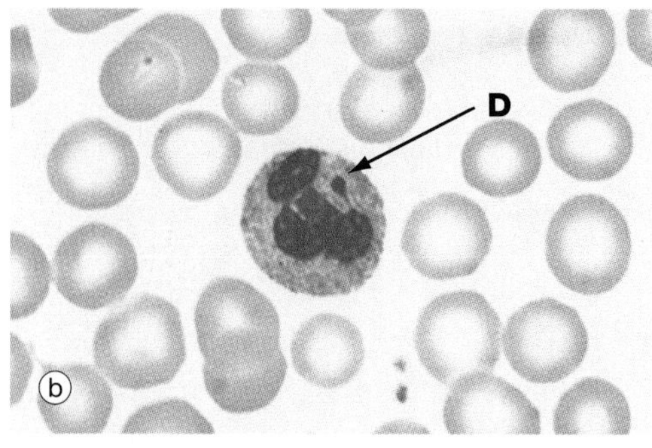

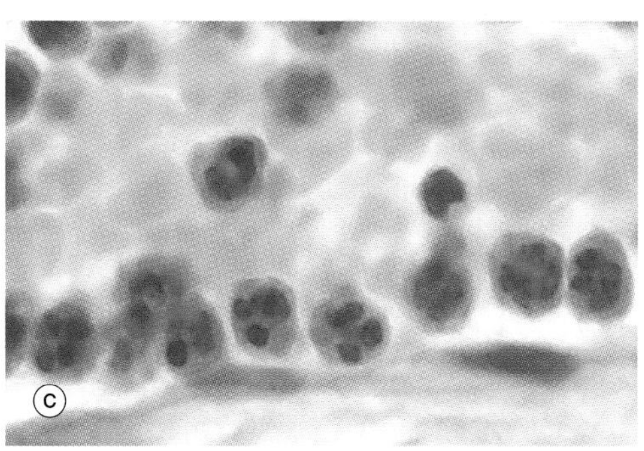

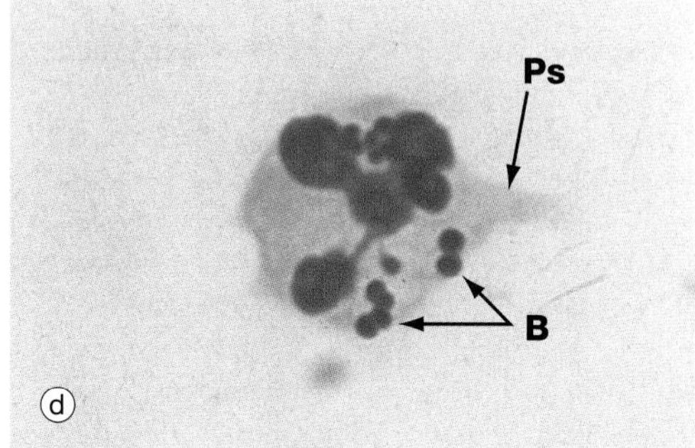

Fig. 3.4 Neutrophils
(a) Giemsa ×1200 (b) Giemsa ×1200 (c) Histochemical method for chloroacetate esterase ×700 (d) Giemsa ×2400

Neutrophils are the most common type of leucocyte in blood and constitute 40–75% of circulating leucocytes. They generally only leave the circulation in large numbers in response to disease. Being highly motile and phagocytic, their principal function is in the acute inflammatory response to tissue injury where they secrete enzymes that degrade tissue components, ingest and destroy damaged tissue and kill invading microorganisms, particularly bacteria.

The most prominent feature of the neutrophil is the highly lobulated nucleus. When mature, there are usually five lobes connected by fine strands of nuclear material. In less mature neutrophils the nucleus is generally not as lobulated. In micrograph (a), two neutrophils in different stages of maturity are illustrated.

In neutrophils of females, the condensed, quiescent X-chromosome or Barr body (see Fig. 1.3) exists in the form of a small drumstick-shaped appendage of one of the nuclear lobes. This is known as the ***drumstick chromosome*** **D** and is shown in micrograph (b); it is visible in about 3% of neutrophils in peripheral blood films of females.

Neutrophils contain different types of membrane-bound granules that can release their contents by exocytosis or fuse to phagosomes containing ingested particles. Granules contain antimicrobial proteins, proteases, components of the respiratory burst oxidase system, and a series of receptors for cell adhesion, extracellular matrix proteins, and bacteria. Only the main granule proteins are mentioned below.

The cytoplasm of neutrophils is lightly stippled with purplish granules called ***azurophilic granules***; these are often referred to as ***primary granules*** as they are the first granules to appear during neutrophil differentiation. They are not simply modified lysosomes as was once believed. These granules contain a number of microbicidal agents including ***myeloperoxidase*** and ***neutrophil defensins***. They are believed to mainly contribute to the killing and degradation of engulfed microorganisms rather than secreting contents.

The most numerous granules in the cytoplasm are the ***secondary granules***, also termed ***specific granules***. They are smaller than primary granules (0.2–0.8 μm), are rich in antimicrobial substances, and contain lysozyme, gelatinase, collagenase, lactoferrin, cathelicidins, transcobalamin-1 and membrane proteins.

Small ***tertiary granules***, also termed ***gelatinase granules***, mainly secrete enzymes to degrade tissue. They contain gelatinase which breaks down extracellular matrix and also insert adhesion molecules into the cell membrane.

Neutrophils also possess ***secretory granules*** which mainly act as a reservoir of membrane-associated receptors needed for neutrophil function in acute inflammation. They also contain alkaline phosphatase and albumin and are believed to form in neutrophils by endocytosis.

Several histochemical methods can be used to highlight neutrophils in tissue sections, for example chloroacetate esterase staining, micrograph (c). However for specific markers immunohistochemical staining is required, for example to detect human neutrophil lipocalin or specific neutrophil defensins.

Micrograph (d) illustrates a neutrophil which has engulfed some coccoid bacteria **B**; note the pseudopodium **Ps**, a typical feature of highly motile cells. This specimen was obtained experimentally by incubating fresh blood with bacteria. In vivo, neutrophils die after engulfing bacteria and do not re-enter the circulation.

B bacteria **D** drumstick chromosome **P** primary granule **Ps** pseudopodium **S** secondary granules

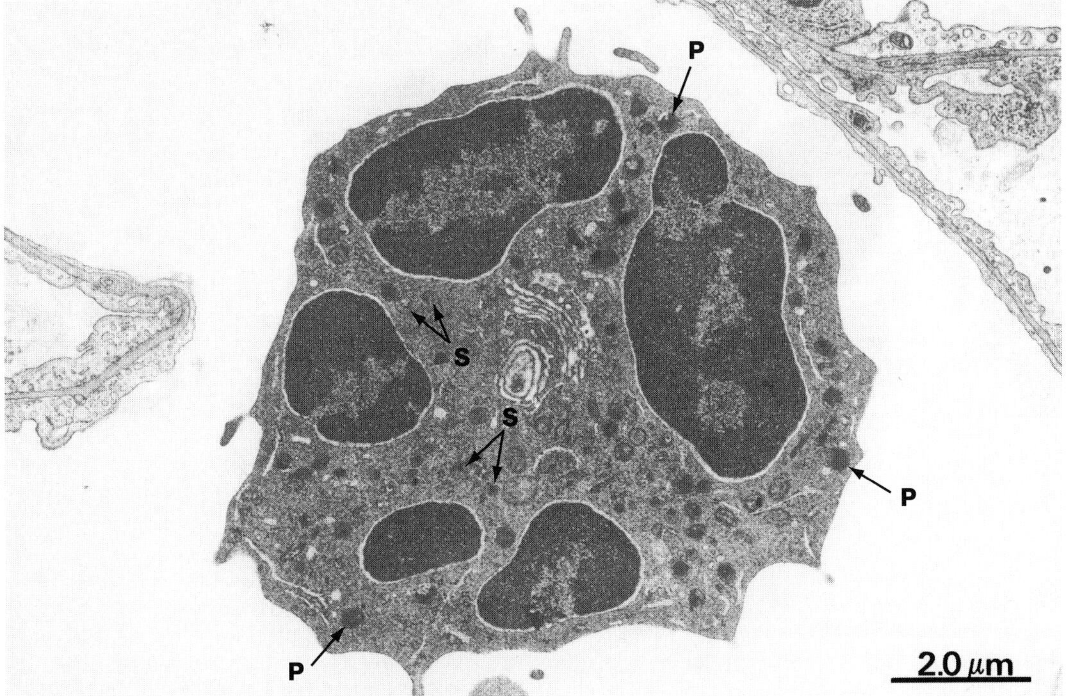

Fig. 3.5 Neutrophil
EM ×10 000

With electron microscopy, neutrophils have three distinguishing features. Firstly, the nucleus has up to five lobes which in section may appear as separate nuclei. The chromatin is highly condensed reflecting a low degree of protein synthesis. Secondly, the cytoplasm contains many membrane-bound granules. The primary granules **P** are large, spheroidal and electron-dense, and although morphologically similar to the lysosomes do not show their biochemical features. The secondary granules **S** are more numerous, small and often rod-like, and of variable density and shape. Tertiary granules and secretory granules cannot be readily distinguished from other membrane vesicles by distinctive ultrastructural features. Thirdly, all other cytoplasmic organelles are scarce although the cytoplasm is particularly rich in dispersed glycogen.

Since the neutrophil has few organelles for protein synthesis, it has a limited capacity to regenerate secreted proteins and specific enzymes which are depleted by phagocytic activity. The neutrophil is thus incapable of continuous function and degenerates after a single burst of activity. Defunct neutrophils are the main cellular constituent of ***pus*** and are therefore sometimes referred to as ***pus cells***.

The paucity of mitochondria and the abundance of glycogen in neutrophils reflect the importance of the anaerobic mode of metabolism. Energy production via glycolysis permits neutrophils to function in the poorly oxygenated environment of damaged tissues whilst the hexose monophosphate pathway generates microbicidal oxidants.

Neutrophils are highly motile cells moving through the extracellular spaces in a crawling fashion with an undulating pseudopodium typically thrust out in the line of advance (see Fig. 3.4d). Motility and endocytotic activity are reflected in a large content of the contractile proteins, actin and myosin, tubulin and microtubule-associated proteins.

Neutrophil function

Neutrophils in the circulation are attracted by chemotactic factors (***chemotaxins***) released from damaged tissue or generated by the interaction of antibodies with antigens on the surface of the microorganisms (see Ch. 11). Chemotaxins stimulate neutrophils and signal to fuse secretory granules with the cell surface, thereby expressing stored cell adhesion proteins that allow the neutrophil to stick to vascular endothelial cells and start to move into the tissues.

The coating of organisms with antibodies and complement enhances neutrophilic phagocytic activity, the phenomenon being known as ***opsonisation***. Neutrophils have surface receptors that bind to opsonins and stimulate internalisation by phagocytosis.

As the first step in phagocytosis, an organism is surrounded by pseudopodia which then fuse to completely enclose it in an endocytotic vesicle called a ***phagosome***. This then fuses with cytoplasmic granules, in particular the primary granules, which discharge their contents exposing the organism to a potent mixture of antimicrobial proteins. Killing is greatly enhanced by the generation of hydrogen peroxide and superoxide by enzymatic reduction of oxygen (respiratory burst oxidase).

Neutrophils also secrete granule contents into the extracellular environment by ***degranulation***. The binding of a significant proportion of receptors on the neutrophil with substances such as products from damaged tissues, inflammation or bacteria activates intracellular secondary messengers to stimulate membrane fusion and exocytosis (degranulation). This happens first to the secretory granules, then to gelatinase granules and finally to specific granules. Primary granules are mainly involved in intracellular bacterial killing but can also be secreted into the extracellular space.

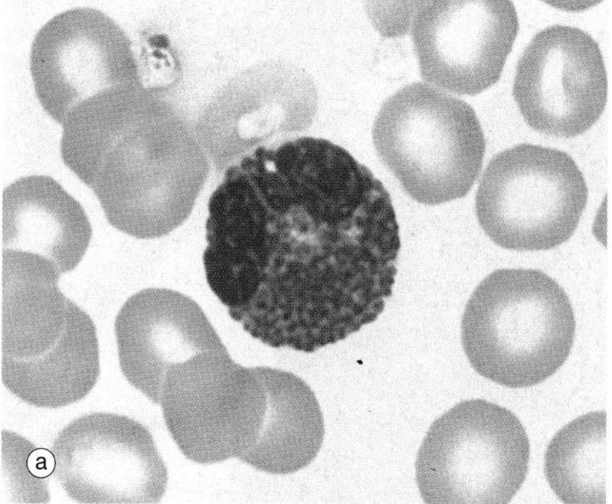

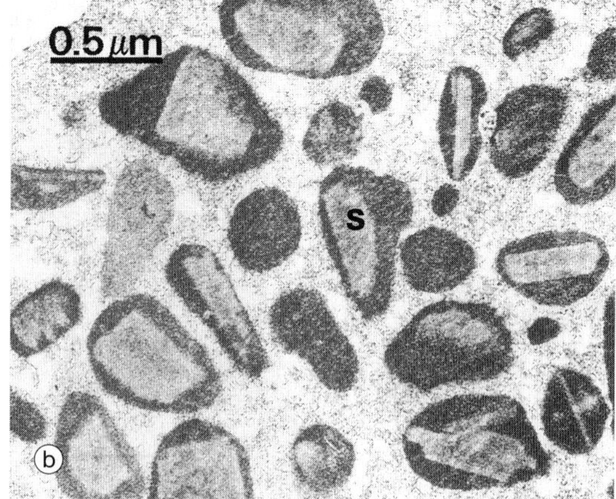

Fig. 3.6 Eosinophils

(a) Giemsa ×1600 (b) Human: EM ×25 000 (c) Mouse: EM ×20 000 (opposite) (d) Rat: EM ×25 000 (opposite)

Eosinophils account for 1–6% of leucocytes in circulating blood; their numbers exhibit a diurnal variation, being greatest in the morning and least in the afternoon. The production of eosinophils by the bone marrow is stimulated by the cytokine interleukin 5 (IL-5), produced by activated lymphocytes, and to a lesser extent, interleukin 3 (IL-3) and granulocyte monocyte-colony stimulating factor (GM-CSF). Eosinophils circulate in the blood for about 8–12 hours and emigrate from capillaries to enter the tissues, where the majority of eosinophils reside. This migration of eosinophils is stimulated by chemotaxis. The cytokines eotaxin, IL-5 and eosinophil chemotactic factor of anaphylaxis (ECF-A) are able to stimulate recruitment of eosinophils into tissues from the circulation.

Under normal conditions such tissue-based eosinophils are found in the spleen, lymph nodes and the gastrointestinal tract. Eosinophils enter other tissues when stimulated by disease, especially in association with mucosal inflammatory or allergic responses. Eosinophils survive in tissues for several days, and longer if stimulated by IL-5. Eosinophils undergo apoptotic cell death in tissues and are removed by local macrophages.

The eosinophil (12–17 µm in diameter) is larger than the neutrophil and is easily recognised by its large specific granules, which stain bright red with eosin and a more brick-red with Romanowsky methods. Most cells have a bilobed nucleus but, as seen in micrograph (a), this is often partly obscured by the densely packed cytoplasmic granules.

The most characteristic ultrastructural feature of eosinophils is the large, ovoid, specific granules **S**, each containing an elongated crystalloid. In humans, as illustrated in micrograph (b), the crystalloids are relatively electron-lucent and irregular in form but in many other mammals they have a more regular, discoid shape. Micrograph (c) shows an eosinophil within the tissues of a mouse; in this species the crystalloids are also relatively electron-lucent. Micrograph (d) shows the specific granules of a rat eosinophil, the crystalloids of which are very electron-dense.

The specific granules are membrane-bound and of uniform size and the matrix contains a variety of hydrolytic enzymes including histaminase. The crystalloid has a cubic lattice structure and consists of an extremely alkaline (i.e. basic) protein called the ***major basic protein***, other basic proteins, hydrolytic lysosomal enzymes and a peroxidase (different from the myeloperoxidase of neutrophils) termed ***eosinophil peroxidase (EPO)***.

Smaller granules are also present in mature eosinophils and contain aryl sulphatase and acid phosphatase; the concentration of the former is eight times greater in eosinophils than in other white cells and appears to be secreted independently of phagocytosis and degranulation.

As seen in micrograph (c), the characteristic bilobed nucleus **N** is readily seen with the electron microscope. The cytoplasm contains a fairly extensive smooth endoplasmic reticulum **sER**, clusters of ribosomes **R** and a little rough endoplasmic reticulum **rER**. Glycogen is abundant and there is a scattering of mitochondria **M**.

Eosinophil function

The eosinophil plasma membrane has different immunoglobulin and complement receptors from other leucocytes. All eosinophils have receptors for IgE; this is not present on neutrophils. IgG and complement receptors are also present.

Eosinophils are able to modulate inflammatory responses at several levels and have a central role in the induction and maintenance of inflammatory responses due to ***allergy***, for example in allergic rhinitis (hay fever) and asthma.

Eosinophils can act as pro-inflammatory leucocytes. They have important roles in defence against ***helminthic parasites*** which is mediated by release of basic granule proteins as well as the production of leukotrienes. Degranulation occurs when eosinophils are exposed to mediators such as PAF (platelet activating factor) or antigen–antibody complexes. Increased numbers of circulating eosinophils (eosinophilia) has long been recognised as a diagnostic clue to the presence of helminthic infections.

Eosinophils are able to modulate local immune responses by production and release of cytokines including tumour necrosis factor (TNF), transforming growth factor (TGF), granulocyte monocyte-colony stimulating factor (GM-CSF) and interleukins 4, 5 and 8 (IL-4, IL-5, IL-8). Importantly, the production of factors such as TNF and leukotrienes may have adverse local effects in causing tissue damage. Eosinophils also have a minor role as antigen presenting cells.

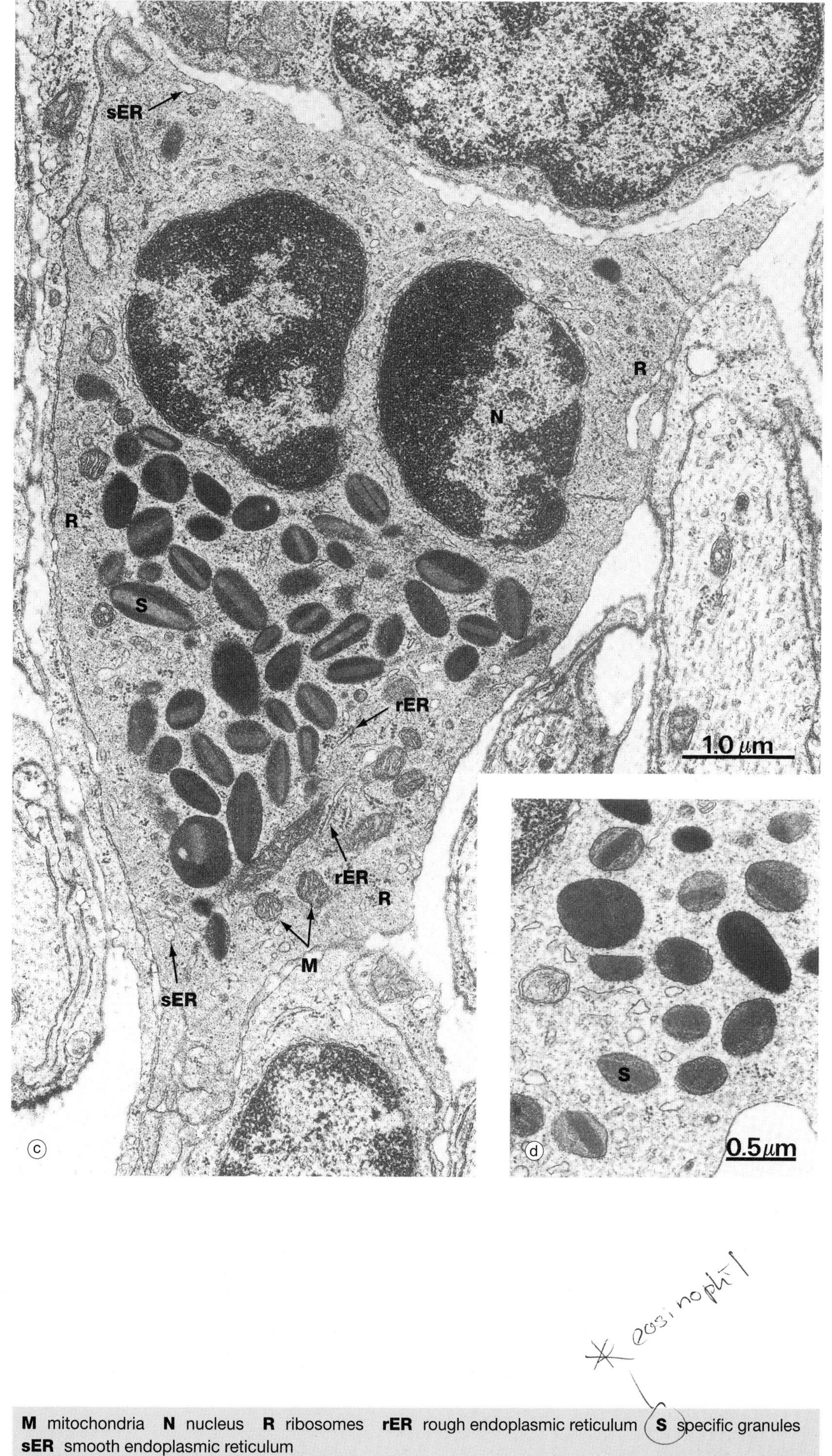

✱ eosinophil

M mitochondria **N** nucleus **R** ribosomes **rER** rough endoplasmic reticulum **S** specific granules **sER** smooth endoplasmic reticulum

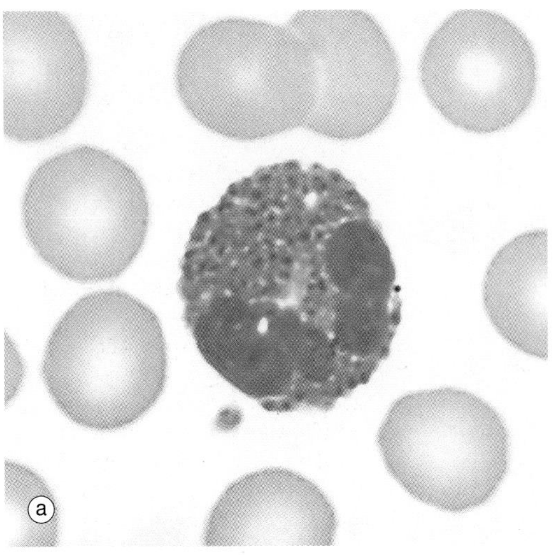

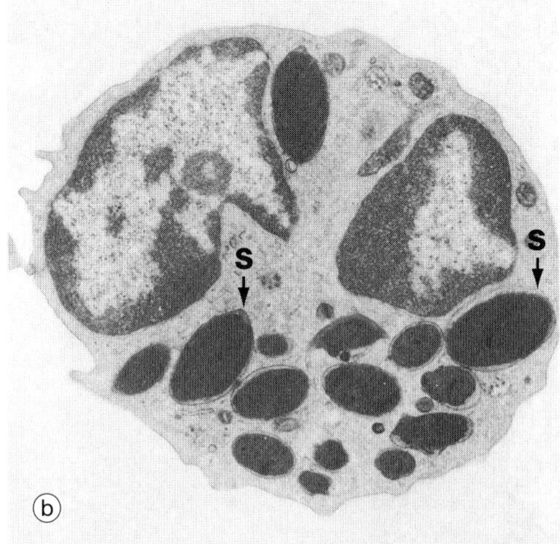

Fig. 3.7 Basophils
(a) Giemsa ×1500 (b) EM ×10 500

Basophils are the least common leucocyte and constitute less than 1% of leucocytes in circulating blood. They are characterised by large intensely basophilic cytoplasmic granules and share many structural and functional similarities with tissue mast cells (see Fig. 4.18). The exact relationship between mast cells and basophils has been and remains controversial, but they do seem to share a common bone marrow precursor.

Basophils are formed in the bone marrow, sharing a common precursor with the other granulocytes up to the myeloblast stage; from here, development proceeds through analogous stages as for neutrophils and eosinophils. Interleukin 3 (IL-3) promotes basophil formation from bone marrow cells while IL-3 and stem cell factor (SCF) promote mast cell proliferation and maturation, and prevent death in tissues. Effete mast cells are removed from tissues by apoptotic cell death and are not believed to re-enter the blood again as basophils.

The basophil (14–16 μm in diameter) is intermediate in size between the neutrophil and eosinophil. Like the latter, it has a bilobed nucleus but this is usually obscured by numerous large, densely basophilic (deep blue) specific granules which are larger, but fewer in number, than those of eosinophils. The granules are highly soluble in water and tend to be dissolved away during common blood spread preparation, thus adding to the difficulty of identifying basophils in blood spreads. Special techniques of fixation, embedding and staining may thus need to be used. When stained with the basic dye, ***toluidine blue***, the granules bind the dye which changes colour to red, a phenomenon described as ***metachromasia*** (see Fig. 4.18).

With electron microscopy, the characteristic bilobed nucleus of the basophil is easily seen. The large specific granules **S** are membrane-bound, round or oval in shape and filled with closely packed, electron-dense material; the granules of basophils are larger and fewer in number than those of mast cells.

A small population of smaller granules is also found near the nucleus. The cytoplasm also contains free ribosomes, mitochondria and glycogen whilst the plasma membrane exhibits blunt, irregularly spaced surface projections.

Basophil function

The cytoplasmic granules of basophils and mast cells contain proteoglycans consisting of sulphated glycosaminoglycans linked to a protein core; this accounts for their metachromatic staining property. The proteoglycans are a variable mixture of ***heparin*** and ***chondroitin sulphate***. The granules also contain ***histamine*** and many other mediators of inflammatory processes such as ***slow reacting substance of anaphylaxis (SRS-A)***, ***eosinophil chemotactic factor of anaphylaxis (ECF-A)***. Granules also contain a tryptase.

Basophil infiltration, mast cell proliferation and degranulation are features of a variety of immunological and other disorders. Mast cells and basophils act as effector cells in allergic disorders mediated by IgE and T helper lymphocytes (Ch. 11) as well as in the immune responses to parasites.

Basophils and mast cells have high affinity membrane receptors specific for the Fc segment of IgE, a class of immunoglobulin which is produced by plasma cells in response to a variety of environmental antigens (allergens). Exposure to allergen results in the antigen forming bridges between adjacent IgE molecules which triggers rapid exocytosis of granule contents (degranulation). The release of histamine and other vasoactive mediators is thus responsible for the so-called ***immediate hypersensitivity (anaphylactoid) reaction*** characteristic of allergic rhinitis (hay fever), some forms of asthma, urticaria and anaphylactic shock. Nevertheless, there are other IgE-independent stimuli for mast cell degranulation.

Elevated serum levels of mast cell tryptase are detected in anaphylaxis.

Basophils may account for up to 15% of infiltrating cells in allergic dermatitis and skin allograft rejection, a phenomenon known as ***cutaneous basophil hypersensitivity***; this is induced by sensitised lymphocytes and is thus a type of cell-mediated hypersensitivity (see Ch. 11). In this case degranulation is slow rather than rapid as in immediate hypersensitivity reactions.

S specific granules

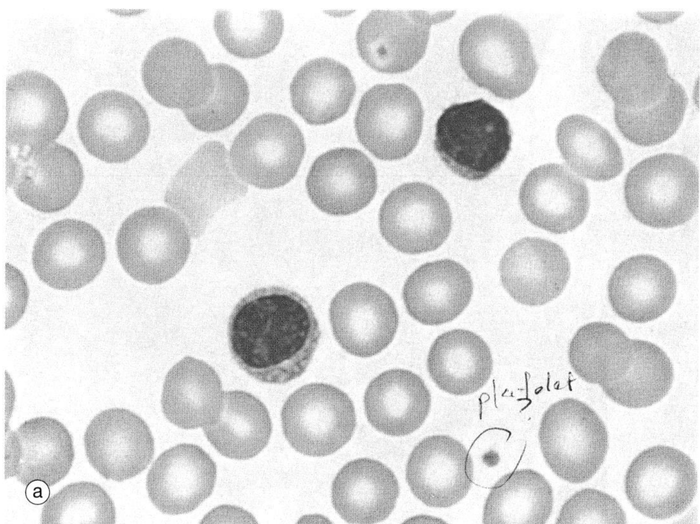

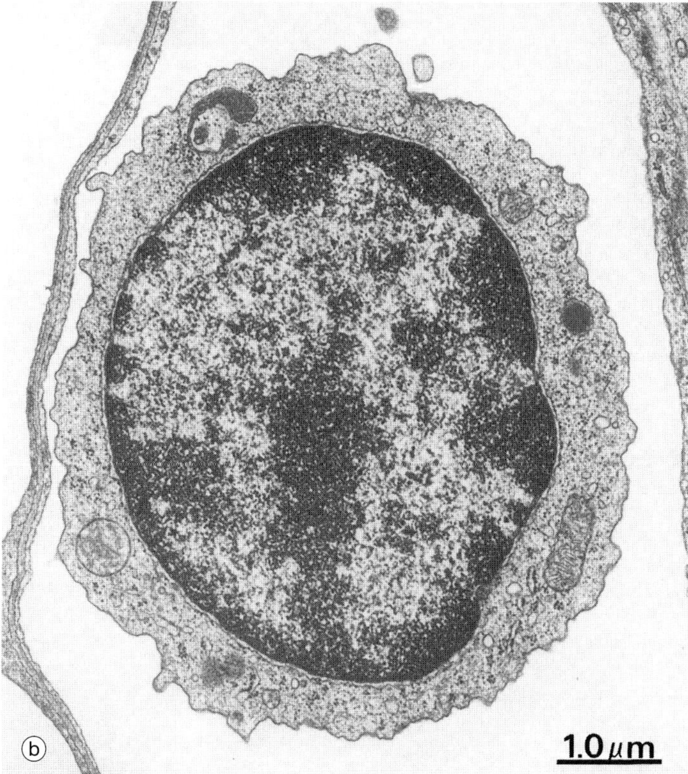

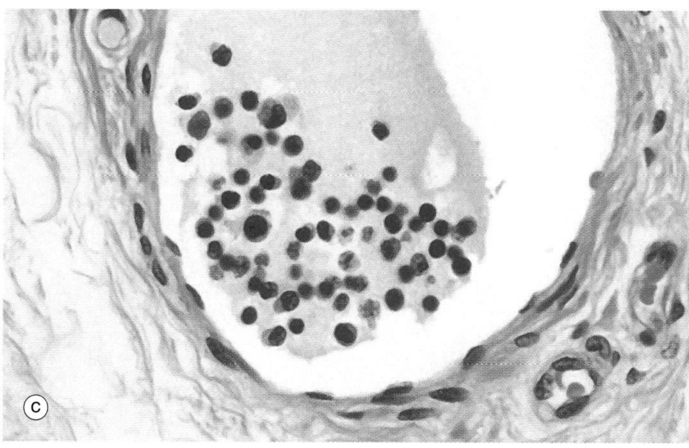

Fig. 3.8 Lymphocytes
(a) Giemsa ×800 (b) EM ×15 000 (c) H & E ×650

Lymphocytes are the smallest cells in the white cell series, being only slightly larger than erythrocytes. They are the second most common leucocyte in circulating blood and make up 20–50% of the differential white cell count.

Lymphocytes play the central role in all immunological defense mechanisms and are described in detail in Ch. 11. Lymphocytes circulate between various lymphoid tissues and all other tissues of the body via the blood and lymphatic vessels. There is a constant recirculation of lymphoid cells through tissues and back to the circulation as part of immune surveillance. Most of the lymphocytes in the blood are in a relatively inactive functional and metabolic state.

Lymphocytes are characterised by a round, densely stained nucleus and a relatively small amount of pale basophilic, non-granular cytoplasm. The amount of cytoplasm depends upon the state of activity of the lymphocyte, and in circulating blood there is a predominance of 'small' inactive lymphocytes (6–9 μm in diameter). 'Large' lymphocytes (9–15 μm in diameter) make up about 3% of lymphocytes in peripheral blood. Large lymphocytes represent activated B or T lymphocytes en route to the tissues where they will become antibody-secreting plasma cells; they also include ***natural killer cells.***

Micrograph (a) illustrates small and large lymphocytes. In the large lymphocyte, the cytoplasm is readily visible but in the small lymphocyte the cytoplasm is almost too sparse to be seen.

Micrograph (b) shows a small circulating lymphocyte in a pulmonary capillary. The nucleus is typically rounded but slightly indented and the chromatin is moderately condensed; nucleoli are not usually present. The sparse cytoplasm contains a few mitochondria, a rudimentary Golgi apparatus, minimal endoplasmic reticulum and a comparatively large number of free ribosomes which account for the basophilia of light microscopy. The plasma membrane exhibits small cytoplasmic projections which, with the scanning electron microscope, appear as short microvilli.

Micrograph (c) shows lymphocytes in a small lymphatic vessel (see Ch. 8). Only cell nuclei are readily seen.

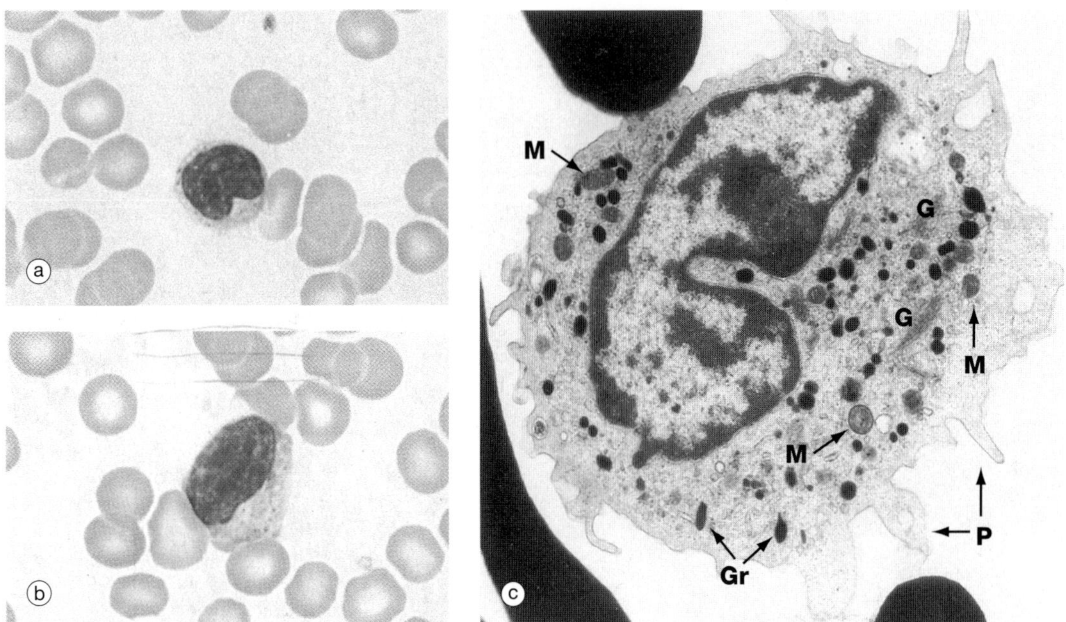

Fig. 3.9 Monocytes
(a) Giemsa ×1000 (b) Giemsa ×1000 (c) EM ×20 000

Monocytes are the largest of the white cells (up to 20 μm in diameter) and constitute from 2 to 10% of leucocytes in peripheral blood where they circulate for 3–4 days before emigrating into tissues. They are motile phagocytic cells and are the precursors of ***macrophages*** found in peripheral tissues and organs (Ch. 4).

Monocytes are characterised by a large, eccentrically placed nucleus which is stained less intensely than that of other leucocytes. As seen in these light micrographs, nuclear shape is variable but there is often a deep indentation of that aspect of the nucleus adjacent to the centre of the cell; nuclear indentation tends to become more pronounced as the cell matures, so as to give a horseshoe appearance. Two or more nucleoli may be visible. The extensive cytoplasm stains pale greyish blue with Romanowsky methods and contains numerous small purple stained lysosomal granules and cytoplasmic vacuoles which may confer a 'frosted-glass' appearance. With the electron microscope, the cytoplasm is seen to contain a variable number of ribosomes and polyribosomes and relatively little rough endoplasmic reticulum. The Golgi apparatus **G** is well-developed and located with the centrosome in the vicinity of the nuclear indentation. Small elongated mitochondria **M** are prolific. Numerous small pseudopodia **P** extend from the cell, reflecting phagocytic ability and amoeboid movement.

The cytoplasmic granules **Gr** of monocytes are electron-dense and homogeneous. Half resemble primary (azurophilic) granules of neutrophils and contains myeloperoxidase, acid phosphatase, elastase, and cathepsin-G. The other half are secretory granules containing plasma proteins, membrane adhesion proteins, and tumour necrosis factor alpha (TNF-α). Granules contain the CD68 antigen, useful in identifying macrophages in tissue sections by immunohistochemistry.

Monocytes are capable of continuous lysosomal activity and regeneration which utilises aerobic and anaerobic metabolic pathways depending on the availability of oxygen in the tissues.

Monocyte–macrophage system

Monocytes migrate to peripheral tissues where they assume the role of macrophages. This has led to the concept of a single functional unit, the ***monocyte–macrophage system*** (***mononuclear phagocyte system***), consisting of circulating monocytes, their bone marrow precursors, and tissue macrophages both free and fixed (***histiocytes***). Included in the system are the Kupffer cells of the liver, microglia of the CNS, Langerhans cells of the skin, alveolar macrophages in lung, antigen-presenting cells of the lymphoid organs and the osteoclasts of bone.

Monocyte function

Monocytes appear to have little function in circulating blood. They respond by chemotaxis to the presence of factors from damaged tissue, microorganisms and inflammation by migration into the tissues and differentiation into macrophages; with their capacity for phagocytosis and content of hydrolytic enzymes, they engulf and destroy tissue debris and foreign material as part of the process of healing.

Most monocytes that migrate into a tissue die by apoptosis. They can survive and proliferate as macrophages if they are stimulated by growth factors, such as macrophage colony-stimulating factor (M-CSF), granulocyte-macrophage colony-stimulating factor (GM-CSF) or IL-3.

Macrophages become active when exposed to interferon-gamma (IFN-γ) a cytokine produced by T lymphocytes (Ch. 11). They can then process antigen, presenting it to the immune system, and can secrete cytokines that are involved in tissue healing and repair.

Lipopolysaccharide (LPS) which is a component of Gram-negative bacteria also stimulates monocytes/macrophages to secrete the powerful cytokine, TNF-α. This is one mediator of so-called 'septic shock'.

G Golgi apparatus **Gr** cytoplasmic granules **M** mitochondrion **P** pseudopodia

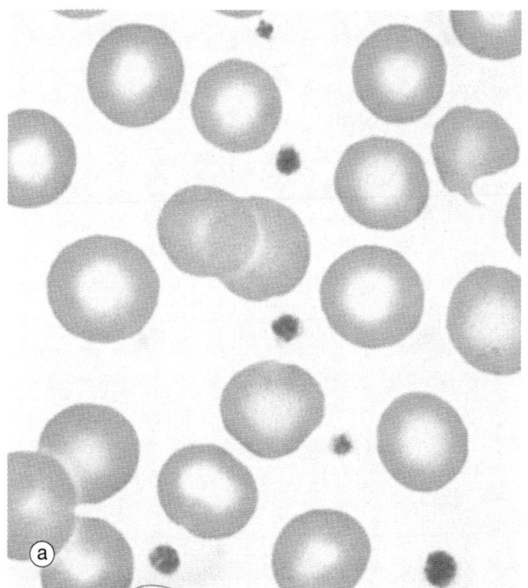

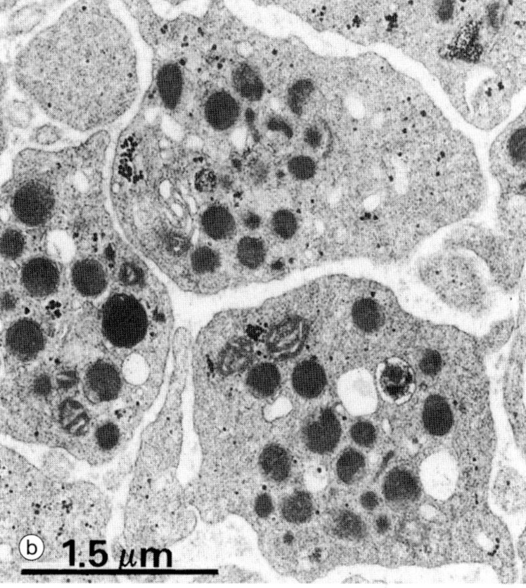

Fig. 3.10 Platelets
(a) Giemsa ×1600 (b) EM ×18 000

Platelets (thrombocytes) are small, non-nucleated cells formed in the bone marrow from the cytoplasm of cells called ***megakaryocytes***. Their numbers in circulating blood range from 150 000 to 400 000/mL. Platelets have a variety of functions essential to the normal process of hemostasis. Firstly, they form plugs to occlude sites of vascular damage by adhering to collagenous tissue at the margin of a wound; later the platelet plug is reinforced by fibrin. Secondly, they promote clot formation by providing a surface for the assembly of coagulation protein complexes. Thirdly, platelets secrete factors that modulate coagulation and vascular repair.

Platelets are round or oval, biconvex discs varying in size from about 1.5 to 3.5 μm in diameter. In blood spreads, as in micrograph (a), their shape is not clearly seen and they are often partially clumped together. The cytoplasm has a purple-stained, granular appearance due to their numerous organelles which are concentrated towards the centre of the cell; the peripheral cytoplasm is very poorly stained and therefore barely visible. Platelets contain most of the cytoplasmic organelles of other cells including mitochondria, microtubules, glycogen granules, occasional Golgi elements and ribosomes as well as enzyme systems for both aerobic and anaerobic respiration. The most conspicuous organelles, as seen in micrograph (b), are the electron-dense granules which constitute about 20% of platelet volume and are of four types:

- **Alpha granules** are variable in size and shape and contain many proteins, both megakaryocyte-derived and derived by endocytosis from plasma. Granule membrane contains several membrane adhesion molecules. Important proteins include ***glycoprotein (GP)Ib-IX-V complex, platelet integrin αIIbβ3 (GPIIb-IIIa)***, ***platelet factor 4, platelet-derived growth factor and beta thromboglobulin***; these granules also contain coagulation factors including fibrinogen, taken up from the plasma by endocytosis.
- **Dense granules** are very electron-dense and contain ***serotonin*** which is absorbed from the plasma having been produced by enterochromaffin cells of the gut (see Ch. 17). They also contain ADP.
- **Lysosomes** are membrane-bound vesicles containing usual lysosomal enzymes (Ch. 1).
- **Microperoxisomes** are small in number and have peroxidase activity, probably catalase.

The platelet plasma membrane expresses cell adhesion molecules involved in platelet:platelet interactions, adhesion to extracellular matrix or binding of coagulation factors. Many of these proteins are held within granules until expressed on the surface following granule fusion with exocytosis.

Platelets contain a well-developed cytoskeleton. At the periphery of the cell is a ***marginal band of microtubules*** which depolymerise at the onset of platelet aggregation. The cytoplasm is rich in the contractile proteins actin and myosin which are involved in the functions of clot retraction and extrusion of granule contents as part of degranulation.

Located deep to the marginal band of microtubules and also scattered throughout the cytoplasm is the ***dense tubular system (DTS)*** consisting of narrow membranous tubules which contain a homogeneous electron-dense substance. This system is believed to be an intracellular store of calcium which is released into the platelet cytosol following signaling from platelet surface receptors and secondary messengers.

Platelets contain a system of interconnected membrane channels the ***surface-connected canalicular system (SCCS)*** which is in continuity with the external environment via external pits. Alpha granules fuse with the SCCS as part of secretion of their contents.

Platelet disorders

Lack of circulating platelets (***thrombocytopaenia***) leads to a bleeding tendency while excess of platelets (***thrombocytosis***) leads to risk of inappropriate blood clotting (***thrombosis***). Some people have inherited problems with platelet function, for example defects in expression of cell adhesion proteins, or defects in the secretion of factors from platelet granules.

Haemopoiesis

Haemopoiesis is the process by which mature blood cells develop from precursor cells. In the human adult, haemopoiesis takes place in the bone marrow mainly of the skull, ribs, sternum, vertebral column, pelvis and the proximal ends of the femurs. Before maturity, however, haemopoiesis occurs in other sites at different stages in development. In the early embryo, primitive blood cells arise in the yolk sac and, later, the liver. From the third to seventh months, the spleen is the major site of haemopoietic activity. As the bones develop during the fourth and fifth months of intrauterine life, granulocyte and platelet formation begins in the marrow cavities with erythropoiesis becoming established by the seventh month. By birth, haemopoiesis is almost exclusive to the bone marrow although the liver and spleen may resume activity in times of need. From birth to maturity, the number of active sites of haemopoiesis in bone marrow diminishes although all bone marrow retains haemopoietic potential.

It has been shown that all blood cell types are derived from a single primitive stem cell type called a ***multipotential (pluripotential) stem cell***. The multipotential cells replicate at a slow rate differentiating into five discrete types of ***unipotential stem cells***, each committed to a different developmental lineage: erythrocytes, granulocytes, lymphocytes, monocytes and platelets. Unipotential stem cells (which are not readily distinguishable from each other histologically) divide at a rapid rate to provide histologically recognisable precursors of the mature cell types.

In vitro culture systems are used to study haemopoiesis, progenitor cells being described as ***colony forming units (CFU)***. The rate of division of these cells is modulated by hormones called ***poietins*** (e.g. erythropoietin) and locally produced ***colony stimulating factors*** and ***interleukins***.

Bone marrow

Bone marrow consists of a meshwork of vascular sinuses and highly branched fibroblasts (see Ch. 4) with the interstices packed with haemopoietic cells. The production of blood cells by the bone marrow is astronomical with an estimated daily output of about 2.5 billion erythrocytes, a comparable number of platelets, some 50–100 billion granulocytes (1.0 billion/kg body weight per day) as well as large numbers of monocytes and immunologically naive lymphocytes. In addition to its haemopoietic function, the bone marrow, along with the spleen and liver, is one of the major sites of removal of aged and defective erythrocytes from the circulation. The bone marrow also plays a central role in the immune system, being the site of B lymphocyte differentiation (the mammalian equivalent of the bursa of Fabricius of birds) as well as containing large numbers of antibody-secreting plasma cells (see Ch. 11).

Examination of the bone marrow

Bone marrow is usually studied by taking an aspirate from an active area of haemopoiesis (e.g. sternum, iliac crest or, in children, tibia). This is made into a spread, fixed and stained as for peripheral blood films. These processes induce artefactual alterations, particularly in respect of cell size and morphology, and this must be taken into account when comparing blood or marrow spreads with tissue sections and ultrastructural preparations.

Bone marrow is also studied by taking a needle biopsy of bone (trephine biopsy). This is normally performed from the iliac crest of the pelvis and is useful when aspiration has given a 'dry tap'.

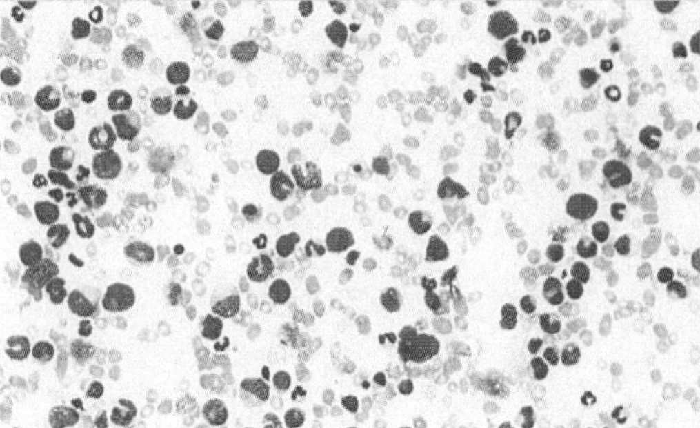

Fig. 3.11 Bone marrow smear Giemsa ×200

This micrograph shows the general appearance of a smear made from an aspirate of bone marrow. Nucleate cells of developing erythrocyte and leucocyte cell lines make up a considerable proportion of the cells, in contrast to smears of peripheral blood where nucleate cells (i.e. mature leucocytes) are few and far between. Cells of the same lineage are relatively easy to identify as they tend to be drawn out into trails from the various colony forming units in the marrow; this is better seen at lower magnification than shown here.

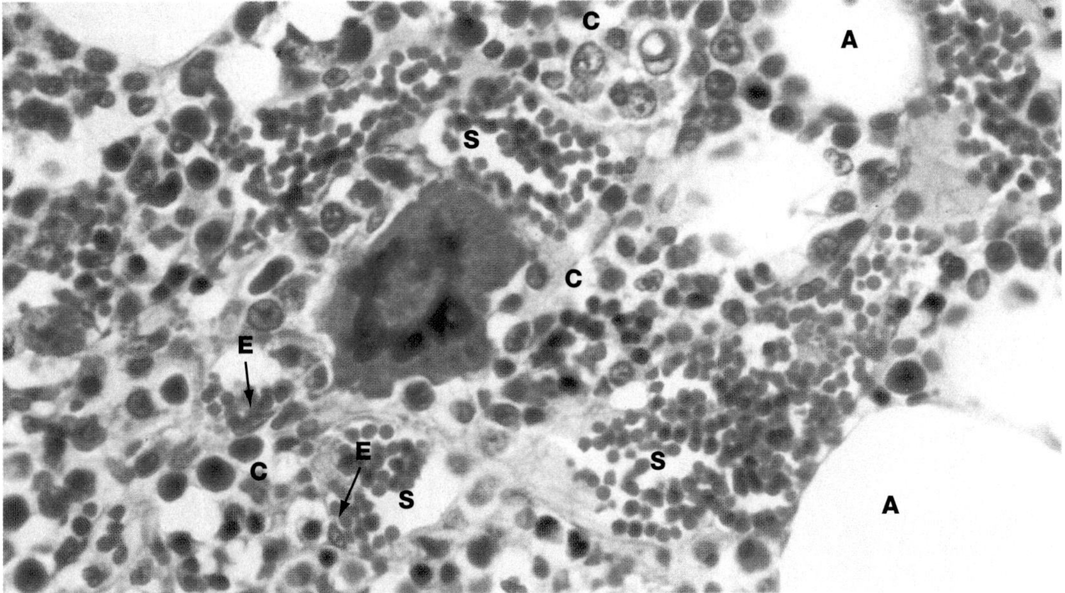

Fig. 3.12 Bone marrow
H & E ×640

Active bone marrow is crammed with dividing stem cells and the precursors of mature blood cells, the predominance of maturing erythrocytes conferring a deep red colour: hence the name ***red marrow***. With increasing age, the marrow of peripheral long bones becomes less active and is progressively dominated by fat cells, so that in mature mammals much of the marrow is inactive and yellow in colour; ***yellow marrow*** may, however, be reactivated if the need arises for increased haemopoiesis.

Active bone marrow consists of two main components: a framework of reticulin (see Fig. 4.8) and specialised mesenchymal cells termed ***marrow stromal cells*** which provide an appropriate microenvironment for the developing blood cells; and a system of interconnected blood sinusoids which drain towards the central vein.

The bone marrow sinuses are of the continuous endothelium type (see Ch. 8) but an unusual feature is that the underlying basement membrane is discontinuous. The sinus endothelial cells are active in endocytosis and probably control passage of all materials into and out of the haemopoietic compartment. In places, the endothelial cytoplasm is so thin that the endothelial barrier is little more than the inner and outer layers of plasma membrane, and such sites may provide the route of exit of mature blood cells into the circulation.

Beyond the endothelium and its basement membrane is a discontinuous layer of marrow stromal cells with extensive branched cytoplasmic processes which embrace the outer surface of the sinus wall as well as ramifying throughout the haemopoietic spaces. The stromal cells synthesise reticulin fibres, which along with the cytoplasmic processes, form a meshwork which supports the haemopoietic cells. By the accumulation of lipid, stromal cells also give rise to the fat cells (adipocytes) characteristically found in the bone marrow. Macrophages are also present within the haemopoietic cords and are involved in phagocytosis of cellular debris and cells that are eliminated in division through programmed cells death and apoptosis. The haemopoietic compartment also contains typical noncellular supporting elements (see Ch. 4) including collagen fibres and the large molecular weight proteins laminin and fibronectin which bind the haemopoietic cells to the fibrous elements of the marrow stroma. Ground substance proteoglycans may have the function of binding growth factors and other modulators of haemopoiesis.

This micrograph illustrates haemopoietic cords **C** separated by broad sinusoids **S** which are filled with erythrocytes and occasional leucocytes. Note the nuclei of occasional flattened endothelial cells **E** which line the sinusoids. Of the haemopoietic cells, only one can be reliably identified, namely a huge megakaryocyte (responsible for platelet formation) near the centre of the field. Note also a few scattered adipocytes **A**.

Bone marrow stem cells are used in the treatment of individuals with haematological malignancies after ablation of the patient's marrow with radiation and chemotherapy. The marrow stem cells are purified from aspirated donor bone marrow or peripheral blood using a fluorescence activated cell sorter. Fluorescent labelled antibodies to a set of surface markers specific for stem cells are used to identify the stem cells and to purify them from all the other marrow components. When the stem cells are injected into the recipient, the bone marrow microenvironment is very important for their growth. Specific surface receptors on the stem cells must interact with chemokines expressed on the surface of the marrow endothelial cells for stem cell growth and for engraftment to occur.

A adipocytes **C** haemopoietic cords **E** endothelial cell **S** sinusoids

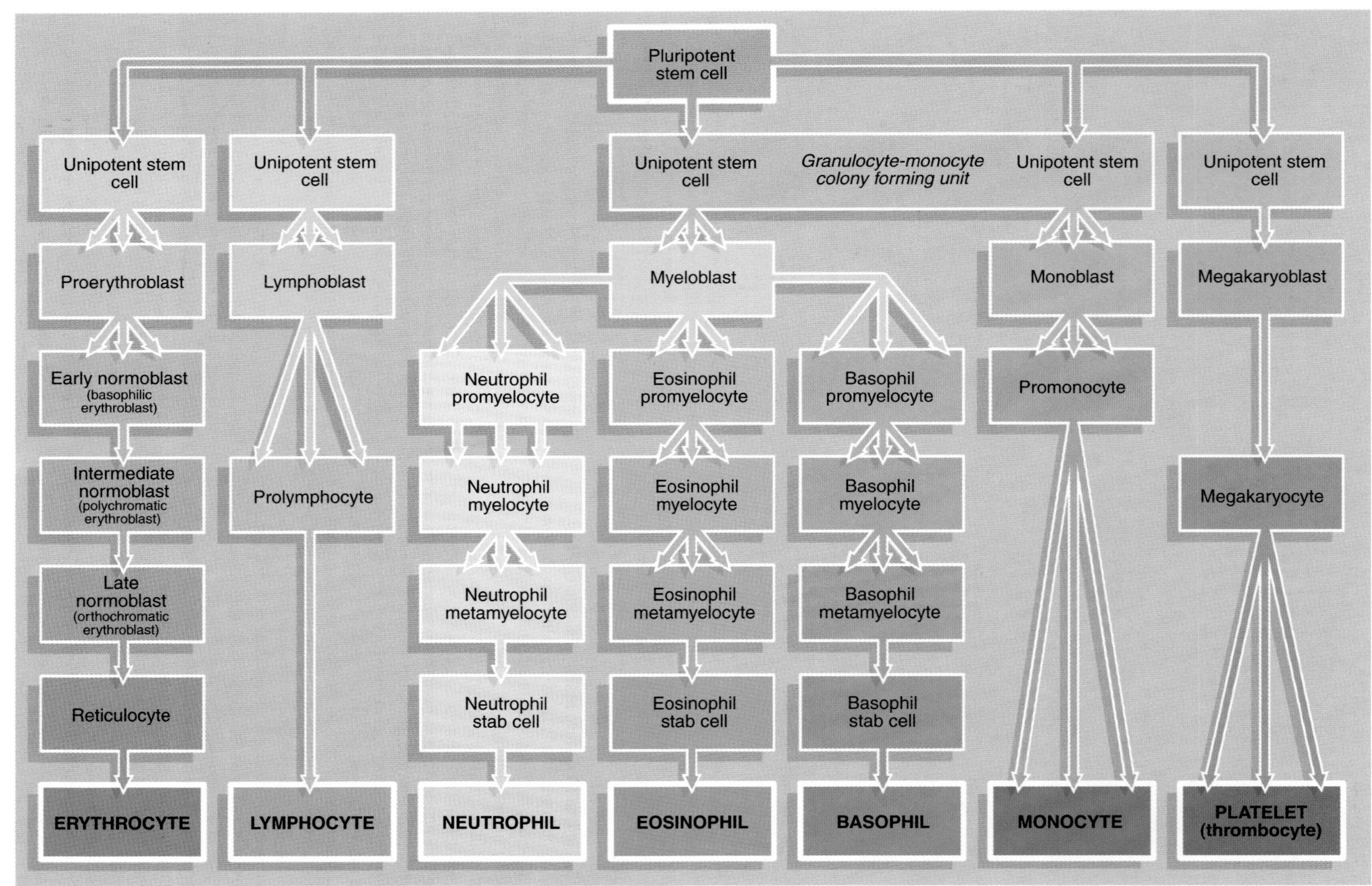
Pluripotent stem cell
Unipotent stem cell
Unipotent stem cell
Unipotent stem cell
Granulocyte-monocyte colony forming unit
Unipotent stem cell
Unipotent stem cell
Proerythroblast
Lymphoblast
Myeloblast
Monoblast
Megakaryoblast
Early normoblast (basophilic erythroblast)
Neutrophil promyelocyte
Eosinophil promyelocyte
Basophil promyelocyte
Promonocyte
Intermediate normoblast (polychromatic erythroblast)
Prolymphocyte
Neutrophil myelocyte
Eosinophil myelocyte
Basophil myelocyte
Megakaryocyte
Late normoblast (orthochromatic erythroblast)
Neutrophil metamyelocyte
Eosinophil metamyelocyte
Basophil metamyelocyte
Reticulocyte
Neutrophil stab cell
Eosinophil stab cell
Basophil stab cell
ERYTHROCYTE
LYMPHOCYTE
NEUTROPHIL
EOSINOPHIL
BASOPHIL
MONOCYTE
PLATELET (thrombocyte)

Fig. 3.13 Haemopoiesis *(illustration opposite)*

This diagram summarises the main developmental stages in blood cell formation. Such a classification is somewhat arbitrary since the process of haemopoiesis is a continuum of proliferation and progressive differentiation from stem cell to the mature form found in circulating blood.

Red cell formation (erythropoiesis). The process of erythropoiesis is directed towards producing a cell devoid of organelles but packed with haemoglobin. The first recognisable erythrocyte precursor is known as the proerythroblast, a large cell with numerous cytoplasmic organelles and no haemoglobin. Further stages of differentiation are characterised by three main features:

- decreasing cell size and nuclear extrusion
- progressive loss of organelles; the presence of numerous ribosomes at early stages accounts for the marked cytoplasmic basophilia (blue staining) which steadily decreases as the number of ribosomes falls
- progressive increase in the cytoplasmic haemoglobin content; this accounts for the increasing eosinophilia (pink staining) of the cytoplasm towards maturity.

Haemoglobin synthesis begins during the ***early normoblast*** (***basophilic erythroblast***) stage and is complete by the end of the reticulocyte stage. Cell division ceases with the early normoblast stage, after which the nucleus progressively condenses and is finally extruded at the late normoblast (orthochromatic erythroblast) stage. The early normoblast stage also marks the beginning of the progressive loss of cytoplasmic organelles, only remnants of which remain by the reticulocyte stage. This process, accompanied by progressive haemoglobin synthesis, is represented morphologically by the transition from basophilia through polychromasia (intermediate normoblast) to the eosinophilia (orthochromasia) of the mature erythrocyte.

The process of erythropoiesis from stem cell to erythrocyte takes about 1 week. The rate of erythropoiesis is controlled by the hormone erythropoietin secreted by the kidney and by the availability of red cell components, particularly iron, folic acid, vitamin B_{12} and protein precursors.

The ***erythroblastic island*** is the unit of erythropoiesis within the bone marrow and consists of one or two macrophages surrounded by erythrocyte progenitor cells. In bone marrow aspirates, the erythroblastic islands are broken up and ultrastructural studies of bone marrow sections are required to demonstrate their structure. The plasma membranes of the macrophages exhibit long cytoplasmic processes and deep invaginations which accommodate the dividing erythroid cells. As the erythroid cell differentiates, it migrates outwards along the cytoplasmic process of the macrophage leaving less mature cells in its wake.

Approaching maturity, the erythroblast makes contact with the nearby sinusoidal endothelium and passes through spaces in its cytoplasm to enter the circulation. The nucleus is extruded prior to entry into the bloodstream and is phagocytosed by perisinusoidal macrophages. Cell culture studies indicate that endothelial cells, macrophages and fibroblasts are all essential for erythropoiesis, the fibroblasts being responsible for the production of various growth factors.

Granulocyte formation (granulopoiesis). The ***myeloblast*** is the earliest recognisable stage in granulopoiesis, the inappropriate name of myeloblast being derived from an outdated view that granulocytes were the only white cells formed in ***myeloid tissue*** (bone marrow). Myeloblasts give rise to ***promyelocytes*** which are characterised by the development of azurophilic granules; since the azurophilic granules develop before the specific granules, they are referred to as primary granules.

The next stage in differentiation is the myelocyte which is marked by the development of specific granules, the process continuing through a further three cell divisions. The relative number and proportion of primary granules progressively decreases and the proportion of specific (secondary) granules progressively increases. From the myelocyte stage through the ***metamyelocyte*** stage to the mature granulocyte forms, the nucleus becomes increasingly segmented. The immediate precursors of mature granulocytes tend to have an irregular horseshoe or sometimes ring-shaped nucleus and are termed ***stab cells*** or ***band forms***.

On reaching maturity, neutrophils enter the bloodstream where some appear to circulate whilst others become adherent to the endothelial walls of small vessels (***marginated pool***) entering the circulating pool in response to exercise and stress; exit from the circulation appears to occur in a random manner. The bone marrow contains a huge pool of stored neutrophils which can be rapidly mobilised should the need arise. Corticosteroids increase the rate of release from the bone marrow and reduce the rate of exit from the circulation.

Lymphocyte formation (lymphopoiesis). Only two precursor stages, the lymphoblast and the prolymphocyte, are recognisable in the development of lymphocytes. The main feature of lymphopoiesis is a progressive diminution in cell size.

Unlike other blood cell types, lymphocytes also proliferate outside the bone marrow. This occurs in the tissues of the immune system in response to specific immunological stimulation (see Ch. 11).

Monocyte formation (monopoiesis). There is considerable evidence that monocytes and granulocytes have a common progenitor, the granulocyte-monocyte colony forming unit (CFU-GM) and that growth of colonies requires the presence of colony stimulating factors (CSFs) with functions analogous to that of erythropoietin in erythropoiesis.

Two morphological precursors of monocytes are recognised, ***monoblasts*** and ***promonocytes***, with at least three cell divisions occurring before the mature monocyte stage is reached. Monopoiesis is characterised by a reduction in cell size and progressive indentation of the nucleus. Mature monocytes leave the bone marrow soon after their formation and there is no reserve pool as for neutrophils. Monocytes spend an average of 3–4 days in the circulation before migrating into the tissues in an apparently random fashion after which they are unable to re-enter the circulation.

Platelet formation (thrombopoiesis) (see Fig. 3.16). In bone marrow spreads, the earlier phases of thrombopoiesis may be recognisable only with great difficulty, the characteristic, detailed features of each stage having been described using techniques of fixation and staining which are rarely applied in routine haematological practice. The recognition of such stages is of little practical value except in certain pathological conditions.

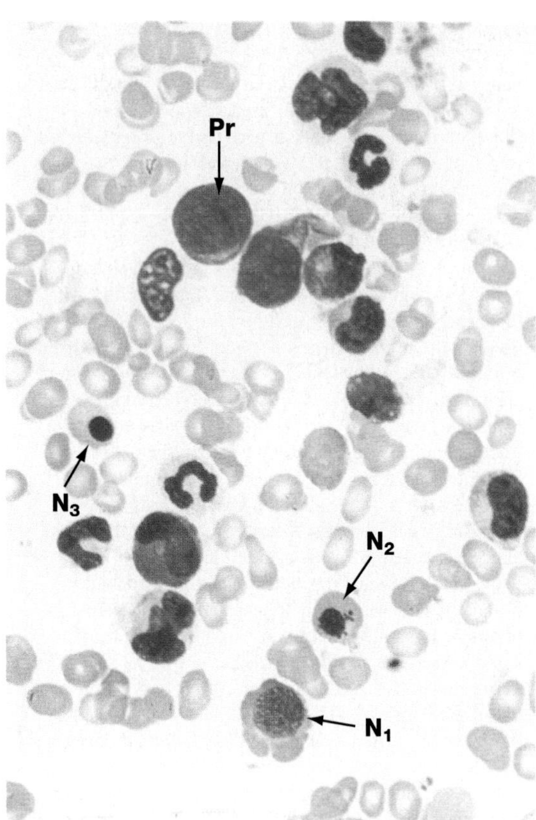

Fig. 3.14 Erythropoiesis
Giemsa ×1200

This bone marrow smear illustrates several stages in erythropoiesis. The proerythroblast **Pr** is the first recognisable erythrocyte precursor; the cell has a large, intensely stained, granular nucleus containing one or more paler nucleoli. The sparse cytoplasm is strongly basophilic due to its high content of RNA and lack of haemoglobin. A narrow, pale zone of cytoplasm close to the nucleus represents the Golgi apparatus.

Three increasingly differentiated normoblast forms can also be recognised. An early normoblast (basophilic erythroblast) $\mathbf{N_1}$ can be distinguished from the proerythroblast stage by its smaller size and smaller nucleus which has more condensed chromatin. More advanced in the maturation sequence is an intermediate normoblast (polychromatophilic erythroblast) $\mathbf{N_2}$, the cytoplasm of which exhibits both basophilia and eosinophilia (i.e. polychromasia), the latter due to increasing haemoglobin content. The nucleus is also condensed and is accompanied by several small fragments called ***Howell–Jolly bodies***, an unusual finding in normal erythropoiesis. With further haemoglobin synthesis and degeneration of cytoplasmic ribosomes, the late normoblast (orthochromatic erythroblast) stage $\mathbf{N_3}$ is reached and by this time the nucleus is extremely condensed prior to being extruded from the cell.

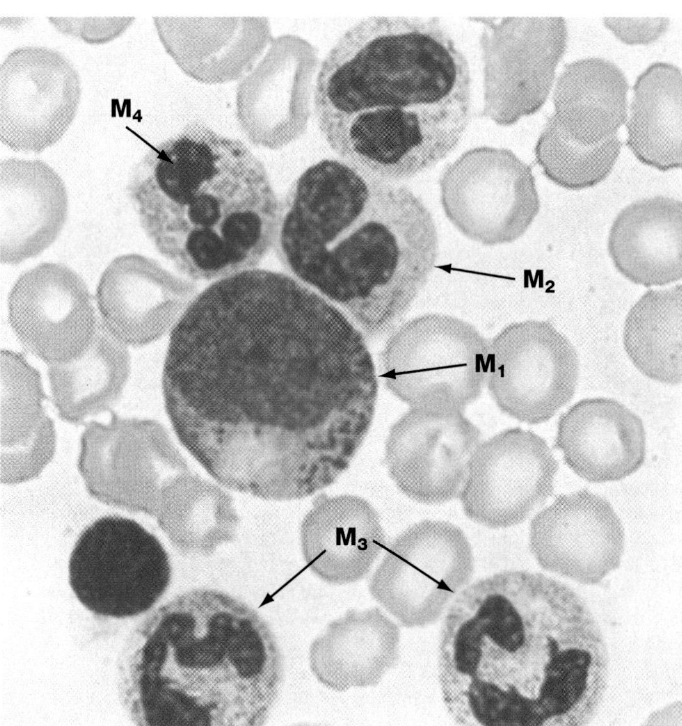

Fig. 3.15 Granulocyte precursors
Giemsa ×1600

This micrograph illustrates three phases of neutrophil granulocyte development. A neutrophil myelocyte $\mathbf{M_1}$ is recognised by its large, eccentrically located nucleus, a prominent Golgi apparatus (pale cytoplasmic zone beneath nucleus) and cytoplasm containing many azurophilic (primary) granules. The next stage towards maturity, the metamyelocyte $\mathbf{M_2}$, is a smaller cell characterised by indentation of the nucleus and loss of prominence of the azurophilic granules. The final stage before maturity, the stab cell $\mathbf{M_3}$, has a more highly segmented nucleus approaching that of the mature neutrophil $\mathbf{M_4}$.

I intermediate zone **M_1** neutrophil myelocyte **M_2** metamyelocyte **M_3** stab cell
M_4 mature neutrophil **N** perinuclear zone **N_1** basophilic erythroblast
N_2 polychromatophilic erythroblast **N_3** orthochromatic erythroblast **P** pseudopodia
Pr proerythroblast

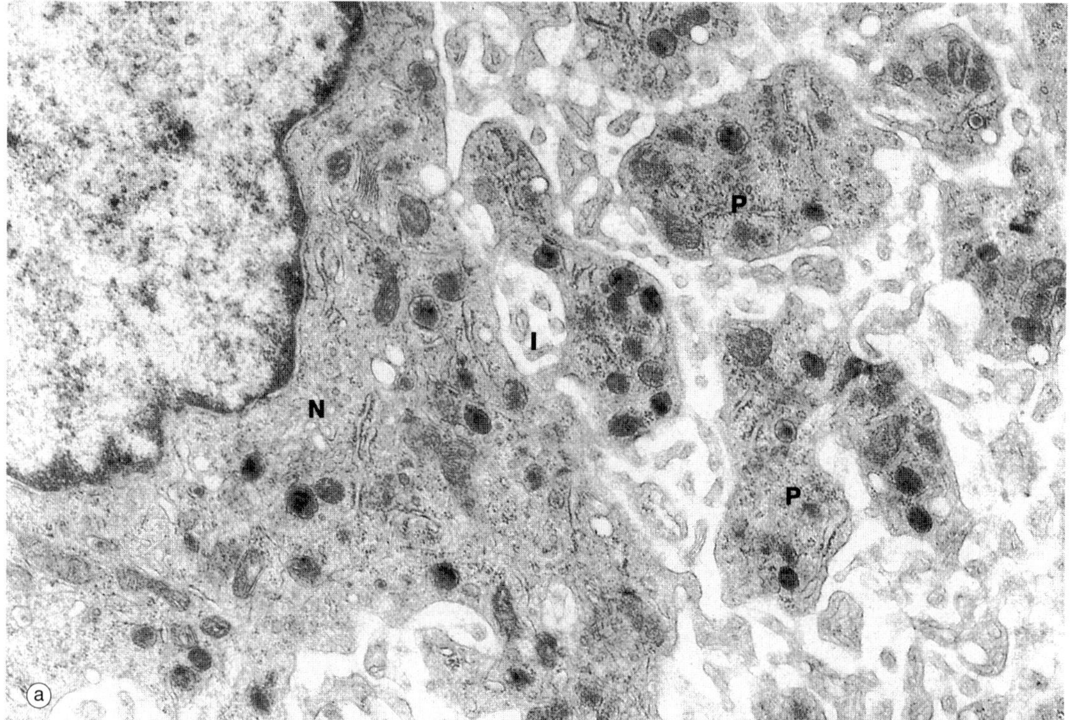

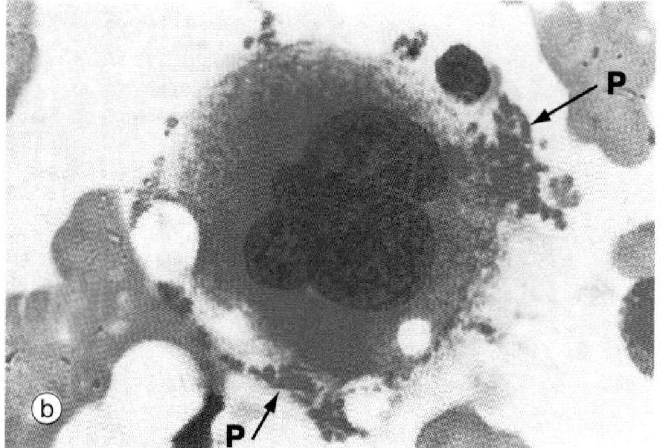

Fig. 3.16 Megakaryocytes and platelet formation
(a) EM ×22 500 (b) Giemsa ×800

Megakaryocytes are responsible for platelet production and are the largest cells seen in bone marrow aspirates (30–100 μm in diameter).

These huge cells are polyploid, cells undergoing a process in which there is nuclear replication without cytokinesis (***endomitosis***), resulting in a large irregular, multilobular nucleus containing clumped dispersed chromatin devoid of nucleoli. The extensive cytoplasm is filled with fine basophilic granules reflecting a profusion of cytoplasmic organelles. With light microscopy, the margin of the cell is often difficult to define clearly due to ruffles, blebs and the elongated pseudopodia **P** from which platelets will form.

The precursor of the megakaryocyte in the bone marrow is the ***megakaryoblast*** which undergoes as many as seven reduplications of nuclear and cytoplasmic constituents without cell division, each associated with increasing ploidy, nuclear lobulation and cell size.

Cytoplasmic maturation involves the elaboration of granules, vesicles and ***demarcation membranes***, and progressive loss of free ribosomes and rough endoplasmic reticulum.

The megakaryocyte cytoplasm is divided into three zones:

- **A perinuclear zone N** contains the Golgi apparatus and associated vesicles, rough and smooth endoplasmic reticulum, developing granules, centrioles and spindle tubules; the zone remains attached to the nucleus after platelet shedding.
- **The intermediate zone I** contains an extensive system of interconnected tubules known as the demarcation membrane system (DMS). These are invaginations of the plasma membrane which act as a reservoir of membrane to allow the extension of long pseudopodia from which platelets form.
- **The outer marginal zone** is filled with cytoskeletal filaments and is traversed by membranes connecting with the demarcation membrane system.

Platelets are formed not by budding, as often described, but rather by fragmentation of the megakaryocyte pseudopodia. Platelets appear to be released in at least two different ways.

- From the bone marrow, megakaryocytes exude pseudopodia called ***proplatelets*** into the sinusoidal lumens which then fragment to enter the circulation.
- Mature megakaryocytes also appear to enter the bone marrow sinusoids intact and pass to the pulmonary vascular bed where they fragment into platelets.

The process of platelet release appears dependent on activation of proteases called caspases. After platelet release, the megakaryocytes, which now are composed of a nucleus surrounded by some cytoplasm, undergo cell death by apoptosis.

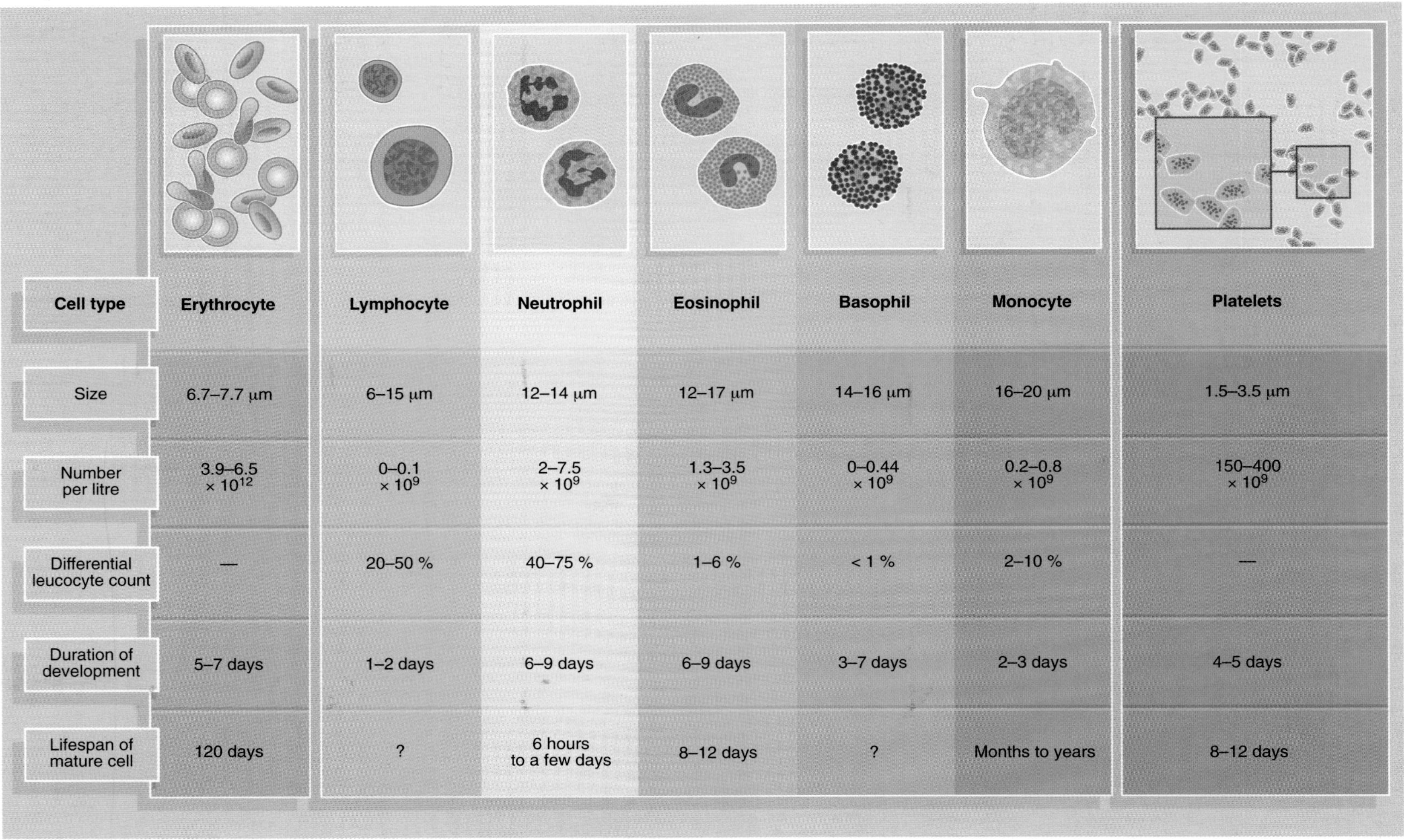

Cell type	Erythrocyte	Lymphocyte	Neutrophil	Eosinophil	Basophil	Monocyte	Platelets
Size	6.7–7.7 μm	6–15 μm	12–14 μm	12–17 μm	14–16 μm	16–20 μm	1.5–3.5 μm
Number per litre	3.9–6.5 $\times 10^{12}$	0–0.1 $\times 10^{9}$	2–7.5 $\times 10^{9}$	1.3–3.5 $\times 10^{9}$	0–0.44 $\times 10^{9}$	0.2–0.8 $\times 10^{9}$	150–400 $\times 10^{9}$
Differential leucocyte count	—	20–50 %	40–75 %	1–6 %	< 1 %	2–10 %	—
Duration of development	5–7 days	1–2 days	6–9 days	6–9 days	3–7 days	2–3 days	4–5 days
Lifespan of mature cell	120 days	?	6 hours to a few days	8–12 days	?	Months to years	8–12 days

Fig. 3.17 Mature cell types in circulating blood

4. Supporting/connective tissues

Introduction

Connective tissue is the term traditionally applied to a basic type of tissue of mesodermal origin which provides structural and metabolic support for other tissues and organs throughout the body. In addition to a mechanical structural role, connective tissues mediate the exchange of nutrients, metabolites and waste products between tissues and the circulatory system. The connective tissues generally contain blood and lymphatic vessels. The traditional term 'connective tissue' thus hardly does justice to the wide range of functions of this type of tissue and it is now probably more appropriate to use the term supporting tissue.

All supporting/connective tissues are composed of a population of specialised ***support cells***, some of which produce an abundant ***extracellular matrix***. The extracellular matrix is the dominant component of certain supporting tissues that determines the physical properties of each type. Extracellular matrix consists of a gel-like arrangement of organic material called ***ground substance*** within which are embedded a variety of ***fibres***.

Supporting tissues occur in many different forms with diverse physical properties. In most organs, loose supporting tissues act as a biological packing material between cells and other tissues with more specific functions. Dense forms of supporting tissue provide tough physical support in the dermis of the skin, comprise the robust capsules of organs such as the liver and spleen, and are the source of great tensile strength in ligaments and tendons. Cartilage and bone, both major skeletal components, are highly specialised forms of supporting tissue that are considered separately in Chapter 10. Supporting tissues have important metabolic roles such as the storage of fat (white adipose tissue) and the regulation of body temperature in the newborn (brown adipose tissue). Cells of the immune system enter support tissues where they assist in defence against pathogenic microorganisms. In response to tissue damage, the processes of tissue repair are largely a function of supporting tissues.

The cells of supporting/connective tissue

The cells of supporting tissue are derived from precursor cells in primitive supporting tissue (***mesenchyme***) and may be divided into several types, each with different functions. A dominant common function is synthesis and maintenance of extracellular matrix material.

- The most common support cell is termed the ***fibroblast*** which is responsible for secreting the extracellular matrix in most tissues.
- ***Chondrocytes*** and ***osteocytes*** are responsible for secreting the extracellular matrix in cartilage and bone respectively (Ch. 10).
- ***Myofibroblasts*** have a contractile function as well as a role in secretion of extracellular matrix.
- A group of highly modified support cells are responsible for the storage and metabolism of fat. These are known as ***adipocytes*** and may collectively form ***adipose tissue***.

Cells with defence and immune functions are commonly encountered in the support tissues. This includes the mast cells, tissue macrophages, all types of white blood cells and antibody-secreting plasma cells. Some of these cells migrate into support tissues and remain static, performing their local function. Other immune cells migrate through support tissue and are *en route* to perform their function elsewhere.

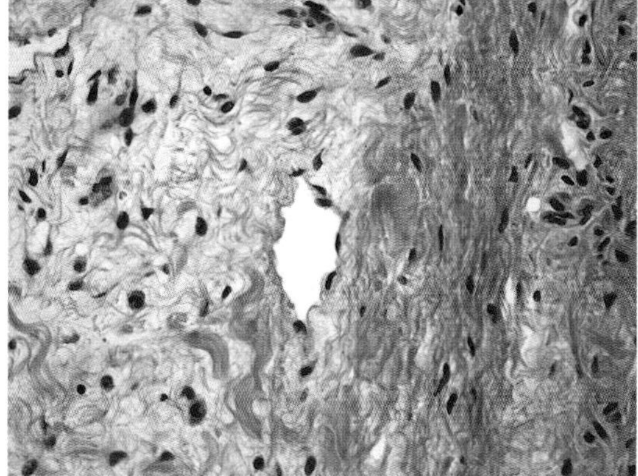

Fig. 4.1 Components of support tissue
H & E ×400

The components of support tissue are seen in this micrograph of support tissues from the submucosa of the bowel wall.

The main component is extracellular matrix material which is largely composed of organized bundles of fibrous proteins, seen as wavy bundles of pink-stained material. Ground substance is unstained and seen as the pale spaces between the pink-staining fibrous protein.

The cell density of support tissues is generally low, reflected in the scattered cell nuclei seen in this type of tissue. The cells seen here are mainly fibroblasts with a few cells of the immune defense system. In the centre of this micrograph is a small blood vessel.

The fibres of supporting/connective tissue

The fibrous components of supporting tissue are of two main types: ***collagen*** (including ***reticulin*** which was formerly considered a separate fibre type) and ***elastin***.

Collagen

Collagen is the main fibre type found in most supporting tissues and is the most abundant protein in the human body. Its most notable function is the provision of tensile strength. Collagen is secreted into the extracellular matrix in the form of ***tropocollagen*** which consists of three polypeptide chains (alpha chains) bound together to form a helical structure 300 nm long and 1.5 nm in diameter. In the extracellular matrix, the tropocollagen molecules polymerise to form collagen. At least 27 different types of collagen (designated by Roman numerals I–XXVII) have now been delineated on the basis of morphology, amino acid composition and physical properties.

- **Type I collagen** is found in fibrous supporting tissue, the dermis of the skin, tendons, ligaments and bone, in a variable arrangement from loose to dense according to the mechanical support required. The tropocollagen molecules are aggregated to form fibrils strengthened by numerous intermolecular bonds. Parallel collagen fibrils are further arranged into strong bundles 2–10 μm in diameter which confer great tensile strength to the tissue; these bundles are visible with the light microscope.
- **Type II collagen** is found in hyaline cartilage and consists of fine fibrils which are dispersed in the ground substance.
- **Type III collagen** makes up the fibre type known as reticulin which was previously thought to represent a separate species of fibre because of its affinity for silver salts. Reticulin fibres form the delicate branched 'reticular' supporting meshwork in highly cellular tissues such as the liver, bone marrow and lymphoid organs.
- **Type IV collagen** does not form fibrils but rather a mesh-like structure and is an important constituent of basement membranes.
- **Type VII collagen** forms anchoring fibrils that link to basement membrane.

The remaining collagen types are present in various specialised situations.

Elastin

Elastin is an important structural protein which is arranged as fibres and/or discontinuous sheets in the extracellular matrix particularly of skin, lung and blood vessels where it confers the properties of stretching and elastic recoil. Elastin is synthesised by fibroblasts in a precursor form known as ***tropoelastin*** which undergoes polymerisation in the extracellular tissues. Deposition of elastin in the form of fibres requires the presence of microfibrils of the structural glycoprotein ***fibrillin*** (see below) which become incorporated around and within the elastic fibres.

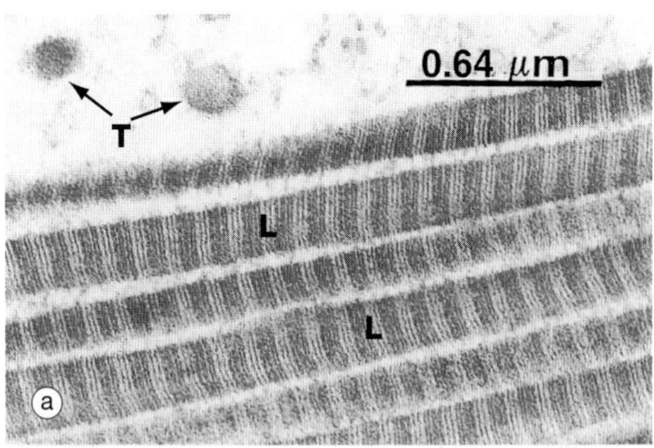

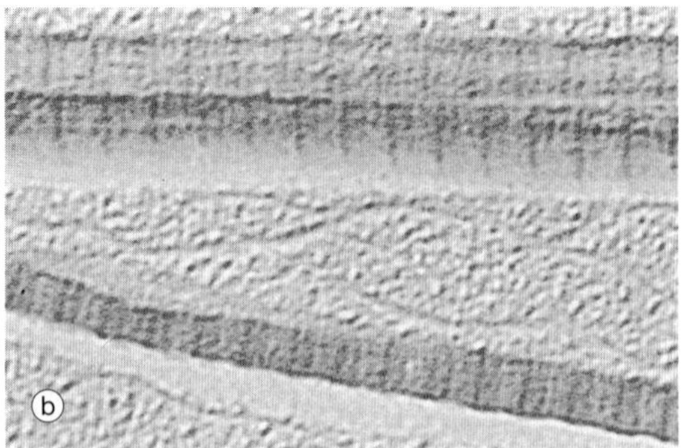

Fig. 4.2 Collagen
(a) EM ×32 000 (b) SEM ×32 000 (teased preparation)

The typical appearance of type I collagen, the most common variety, is shown in these specimens. The characteristic feature is a pattern of cross-banding with a periodicity of approximately 64 nm which results from the polymerisation of tropocollagen molecules (300 nm in length) such that each molecule overlaps the next by approximately one-quarter of its length. In micrograph (a) collagen fibres are shown in transverse **T** and longitudinal **L** section.

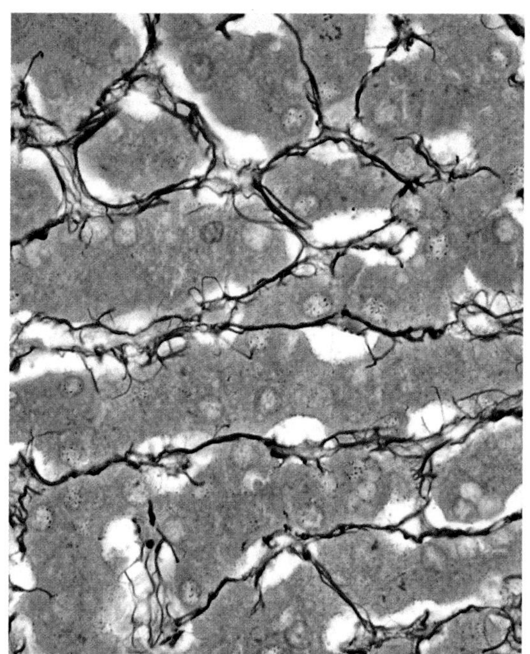

Fig. 4.3 Reticulin fibres
Silver impregnation method/neutral red ×800

Reticulin fibres form a delicate supporting framework for many highly cellular organs such as endocrine glands, lymph nodes and the liver. In such organs, a fine network of branching fibres ramifies throughout the parenchyma usually anchored to a dense, collagenous capsule and septa which traverse the tissue. Reticulin is a non-banded form of collagen designated collagen type III.

Reticulin fibres are usually poorly stained in standard preparations but are able to adsorb metallic silver by which they are stained black. This phenomenon led early histologists to believe that reticulin had a completely different chemical composition from that of collagen. Reticulin is the earliest type of collagen fibre to be produced during the development of all supporting tissues and is also present in varying quantities in most mature supporting tissues.

This micrograph shows the fine reticulin scaffolding of the liver; the framework provides support for hepatocytes (the purple-stained plates of cells), and the sinusoids through which blood flows.

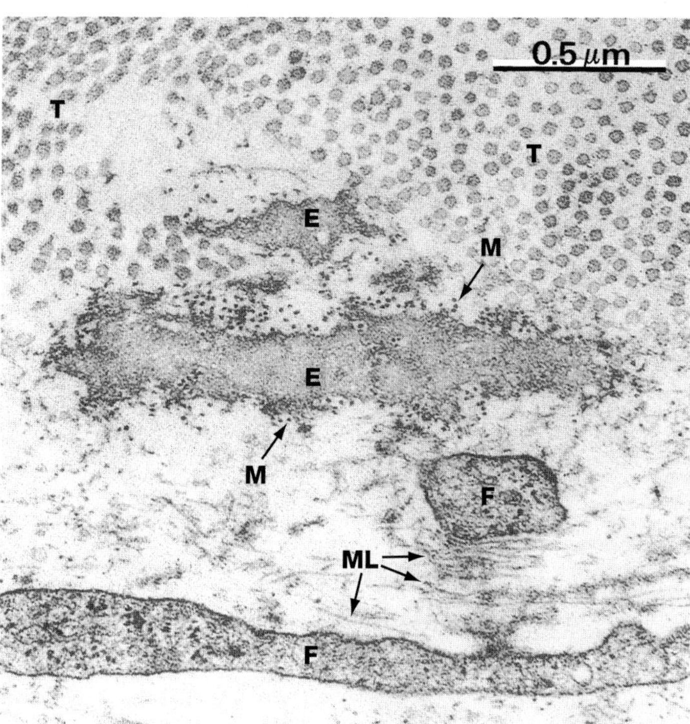

Fig. 4.4 Elastin
EM ×50 000

This micrograph shows elastin **E** in the delicate supporting tissue underlying the epithelium of mouse trachea. The field also contains collagen fibrils **T** (cut in transverse section) and the fine cytoplasmic extensions of fibroblasts **F** responsible for elaboration of the extracellular constituents.

The elastin is not made up of fibrils but rather is an amorphous mass of polymerised tropoelastin. Microfibrils **M** of the structural glycoprotein fibrillin, which is involved in the process of elastin deposition, can just be discerned at this magnification (in transverse section) lying within and around the elastin. Microfibrils can also be seen in the lower part of the field cut in longitudinal section **ML** in association with small amounts of elastin.

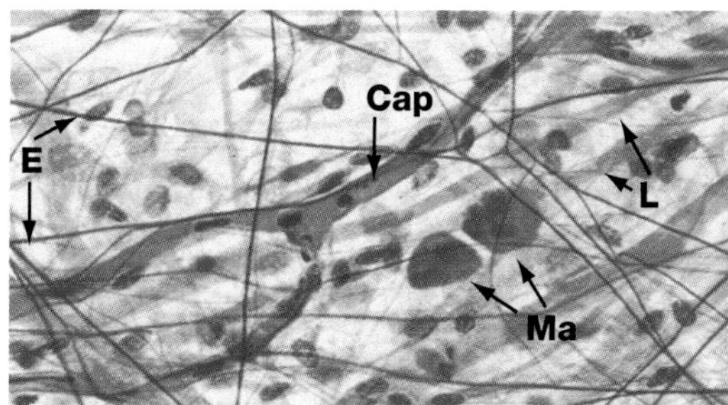

Fig. 4.5 Elastin fibres
Spread preparation, elastin/H & E ×320

In most tissues, elastin occurs as short branching fibres which form an irregular network throughout the tissue. This is not easily seen in tissue sections but is better demonstrated in ***spread preparations*** such as in this micrograph in which elastin fibres **E** are stained black, collagen fibres **L** are stained pink and nuclei are stained blue. A branched capillary **Cap** crosses the field and two densely stained mast cells **Ma** are also seen (see Ch. 11).

Cap capillary **E** elastin fibre **F** fibroblast **L** collagen fibres in longitudinal section
M microfibrils in transverse section **Ma** mast cells **ML** microfibrils in longitudinal section
T collagen fibres in transverse section

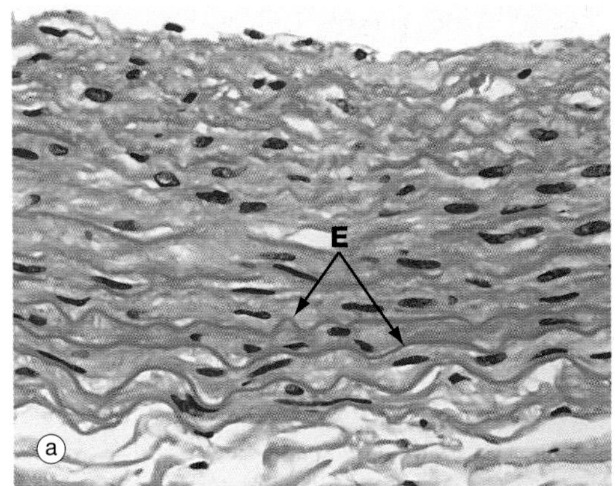

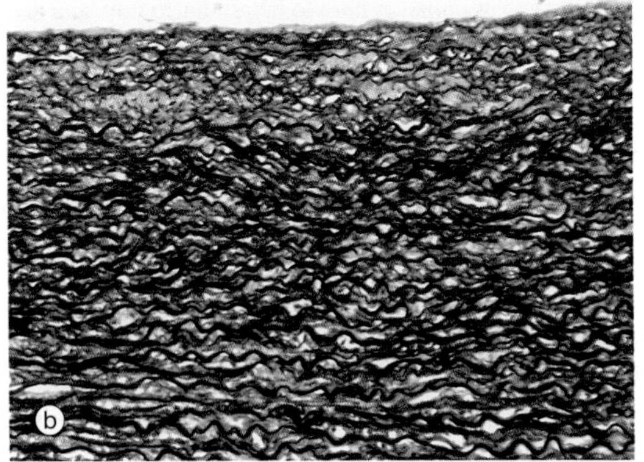

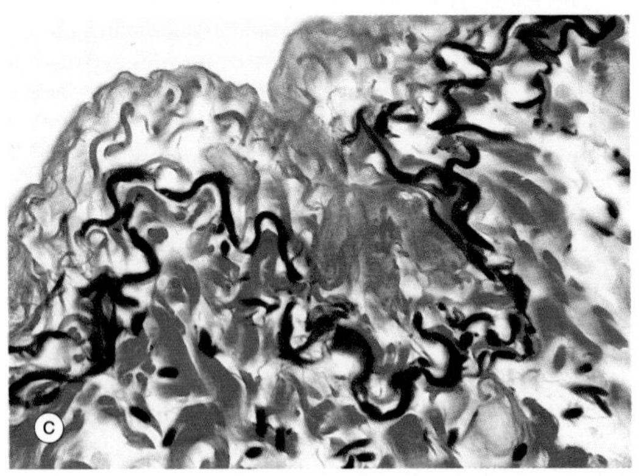

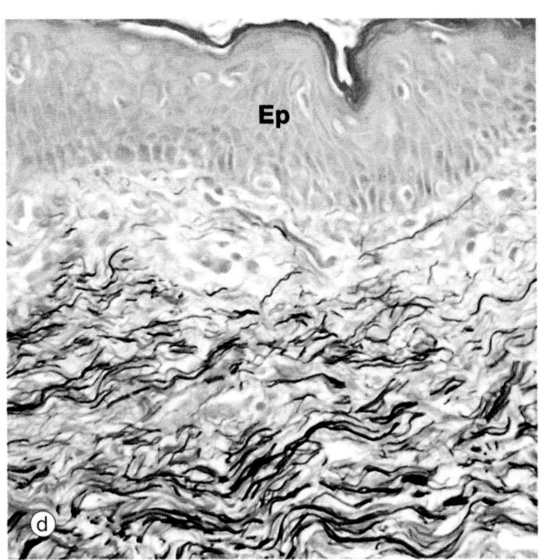

Fig. 4.6 Elastin fibres
(a) H & E ×300 (b) elastin/eosin ×200 (c) Elastic van Gieson ×400 (d) Elastic van Gieson ×200

Elastin is found in varying proportions in most supporting tissues conferring elasticity to enable recovery of tissue shape following normal physiological deformation. Elastin is thus present in large amounts in tissues such as lung, skin and urinary bladder. It is also important as a constituent of the wall of blood vessels.

Micrograph (a) shows the wall of one type of large artery, this being made up mainly of smooth muscle cells, collagen and thick sheets of elastin (see Ch. 8). Like the collagen and smooth muscle cytoplasm, the elastin **E** is eosinophilic; it is only recognisable in this situation because the elastin sheets are comparatively more eosinophilic than other components of the extracellular matrix and because the elastin has a wave-like conformation due to relaxation of the vessel wall.

Micrograph (b) shows a histological section stained specifically for elastin; with this method, elastin is stained black and collagen is stained red. This is the wall of another type of large artery (see Ch. 8). The functional properties of this type of large artery are largely determined by the amount of elastin in its wall which allows stretching and recoil to smooth the pulse pressure generated by the heart.

Micrograph (c) shows part of the periphery of the lung in which a layer of black-stained elastic fibres is woven into the collagen support tissues. The lung contains abundant elastic which helps to expel air from the lungs (see Ch. 12). Energy is stored in stretched elastic on inhalation and released on exhalation when the elastic fibres recoil.

Micrograph (d) shows a section of skin, stained to show elastin. The surface epithelium (**Ep**) is anchored to the support tissues of the dermis below. The pink-stained coarse, closely packed, bundles of collagen in the dermis are interwoven by elastic fibres, stained black. Most of the elastic fibres are cut in longitudinal section making them readily identifiable. The elastic fibres in the dermis allow the skin to stretch and recoil, keeping it wrinkle-free.

Diseases due to disorders of collagen

There are several inherited diseases caused by mutations in genes coding for collagen. The main effect is reduced tensile strength in support tissues leading to abnormal tissue laxity or susceptibility to injury.

Ehlers–Danlos syndromes are characterised by abnormal skin laxity and hypermobility of joints which can predispose to recurrent joint dislocations. There are several genetic subtypes of disease and six main forms have been described characterised by distinct clinical associations. In some individuals, disease is caused by mutation in a collagen gene or in an enzyme related to collagen metabolism.

Ground substance

Ground substance derived its name from being an amorphous transparent material which has the properties of a semi-fluid gel. Tissue fluid is loosely associated with ground substance, thereby forming the medium for passage of molecules throughout supporting tissues and for the exchange of metabolites with the circulatory system.

Ground substance consists of a mixture of long, unbranched polysaccharide chains of seven different types, each composed of repeating disaccharide units. One of the disaccharide units is usually a uronic acid and the other an amino sugar (either N-acetyl glucosamine or N-acetyl galactosamine) thus giving rise to the modern term ***glycosaminoglycans*** (***GAGs***); these were formerly called ***mucopolysaccharides***. The glycosaminoglycans are acidic (negatively charged) due to the presence of hydroxyl, carboxyl and sulphate side groups on the disaccharide units.

Hyaluronic acid is the predominant GAG in the loose supporting tissues and is the only one without sulphate side groups; the other GAGs (***chondroitin-4-sulphate***, ***chondroitin-6-sulphate***, ***dermatan sulphate***, ***heparan sulphate***, ***heparin sulphate*** and ***keratan sulphate***) differ from hyaluronic acid in that they are covalently linked to a variety of protein molecules to form proteoglycans (formerly known as ***mucoproteins***); these proteoglycans are huge molecules consisting of 90–95% carbohydrate. Further, the proteoglycans may form non-covalent links with hyaluronic acid chains to form even larger molecular complexes.

Unlike many proteins, GAG molecules are not flexible enough to form globular aggregates but remain in an expanded form, thus occupying a huge volume for relatively small mass. In addition, their highly charged side groups render them extremely hydrophilic, thus attracting a large volume of water and positive ions, particularly sodium, which constitute ***extracellular fluid***. The extracellular fluid imparts the characteristic turgor of supporting tissue.

In summary, ground substance is basically composed of glycosaminoglycans in the form of hyaluronic acid and proteoglycans. These huge molecules are entangled and electrostatically linked to one another and their water of hydration, to form a flexible gel through which metabolites may diffuse. The size of the spaces between the GAG molecules and the nature of electrostatic changes determine the permeability characteristics of any particular supporting tissue, a fact of particular significance in the structure of basement membranes. The mechanical properties of ground substance are reinforced by the fibrous proteins of the extracellular tissue to which the components of ground substance are also bound.

The structural glycoproteins

The structural glycoproteins are a group of molecules composed principally of protein chains bound to branched polysaccharides; much has yet to be learned about their role in the function of extracellular material. The structural glycoproteins include two fibril-forming molecules, ***fibrillin*** and ***fibronectin***, and a number of non-filamentous proteins including ***laminin***, ***entactin*** and ***tenascin*** which function as links between cells and extracellular matrix.

Fibrillin forms microfibrils 8–12 nm in diameter which, in certain specialised situations, e.g. the mesangium of the kidney (see Ch. 16), appear to enhance adhesion between other extracellular constituents. Fibrillin is a constituent of elastic fibres where it appears to play a role in the orderly deposition of the fibres.

Fibronectin plays a part in controlling the deposition and orientation of collagen in extracellular matrix and the binding of the cell to the extracellular material. Cell membranes incorporate a group of transmembrane protein complexes called ***integrins*** which act as ***cell adhesion molecules***. One of these, the ***fibronectin receptor***, establishes bonds within the cell to the actin filaments of the cytoskeleton and binds with fibronectin externally. The fibronectin in turn binds with collagen and the glycosaminoglycan, heparin sulphate, thus establishing structural continuity between the cytoskeleton and the extracellular matrix.

Laminin is a major component of basement membranes, binding with specific cell adhesion molecules so as to form links between cell membranes and other constituents of the basement membrane. Entactin, another non-fibrillary protein, has the function of binding laminin to type IV collagen in basement membranes. Tenascin also binds to integrins and is important in the embryo where it appears to be involved in control of nerve cell growth.

E elastin **Ep** epithelium

Basement membranes

Basement membranes are sheet-like arrangements of extracellular matrix proteins which act as an interface between the support tissues and parenchymal cells. Such basement membranes are associated with epithelial and muscle cells, as well as forming a limiting membrane around the central nervous system. The term derives from the fact that the first basement membranes to be recognised were those lying beneath the basal cells of surface epithelia. In the context of muscle and nervous tissue, the term ***external lamina*** may also be applied.

Epithelia in particular are composed of closely packed cells with minimal intercellular material between them. The basement membrane provides metabolic support as well as binding the epithelium to the underlying supporting tissue. Basement membrane is also involved in the control of epithelial growth and differentiation, forming a barrier to downward epithelial growth; this is only breached if epithelia undergo malignant transformation. Epithelium is devoid of blood vessels and the basement membrane must therefore permit the flow of nutrients, metabolites and other molecules to and from the epithelium. Where an epithelium acts as a selective barrier to the passage of molecules from one compartment to another (e.g. between the lumen of blood vessels and surrounding tissues), the basement membrane assumes a critical role in regulating permeability. This reaches an extreme of sophistication in the kidney where the glomerular basement membrane is part of the highly selective filter for molecules passing from the bloodstream into the urine.

The main constituents of basement membranes and external laminae are the glycosaminoglycan ***heparan sulphate***, the fibrous protein ***collagen type IV***, and the structural glycoproteins ***fibronectin***, ***laminin*** and ***entactin***. Fibronectin appears to be produced by fibroblasts of the supporting tissue but the remainder are at least partly, if not exclusively, elaborated by the tissues being supported.

With the electron microscope, the basement membrane is seen to consist of three layers. A relatively electron-lucent layer, the ***lamina lucida*** (ranging from 10 to 50 nm in width), abuts the basal cell membrane of the parenchymal tissue. The intermediate layer is electron-dense and is thus known as the ***lamina densa***; depending on the tissue, this varies from 20 to 300 μm in thickness. Beyond the lamina densa is a broad, relatively electron-lucent layer known as the ***lamina fibroreticularis*** which merges with the underlying supporting tissue.

The structural framework of both lamina lucida and lamina densa is a fine meshwork of collagen type IV which is exclusive to basement membranes. Another major constituent of these layers is laminin which binds the type IV collagen to the other basement membrane constituents and to laminin receptors in the parenchymal basal plasma membranes. Entactin mediates the binding of laminin to type IV collagen. The fibroreticular layer probably represents a condensation of the underlying supporting tissue. Its collagen content is mainly of type III (reticulin) which, via the fibrillar glycoprotein fibronectin, is also bound to integrins in the parenchymal basal plasma membrane.

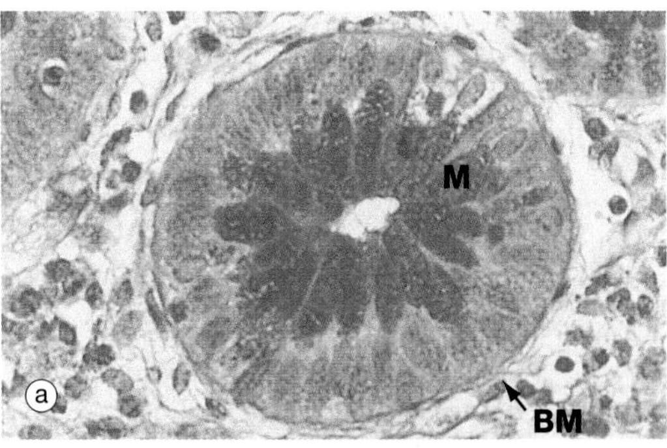

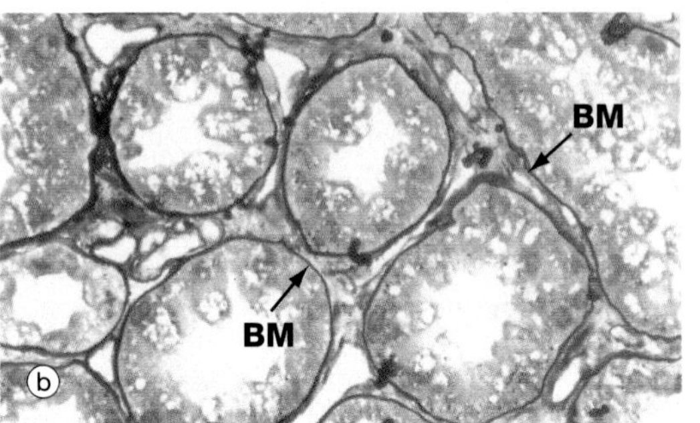

Fig. 4.7 Basement membrane
(a) PAS/haematoxylin ×400 (b) Jones' methenamine silver ×100

With the light microscope, basement membranes can be seen beneath certain epithelial tissues where they happen to be relatively thick or where histochemical or other methods have been employed which are specific for particular basement membrane constituents.

Micrograph (a) shows a duodenal crypt lined by mucus-secreting cells and is stained by the PAS method. This has affinity for the complex carbohydrates of the proteoglycans in the basement membrane **BM** as well as the mucus **M** at the luminal aspect of the crypt lining cells. In micrograph (b), a silver impregnation method which has affinity for reticulin demonstrates the basement membrane **BM** of the renal tubules.

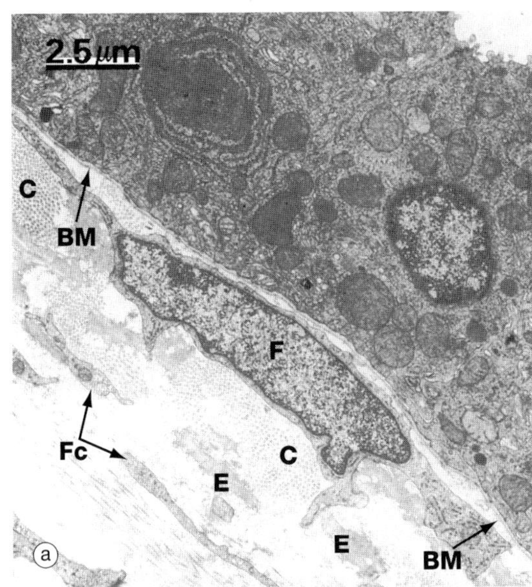

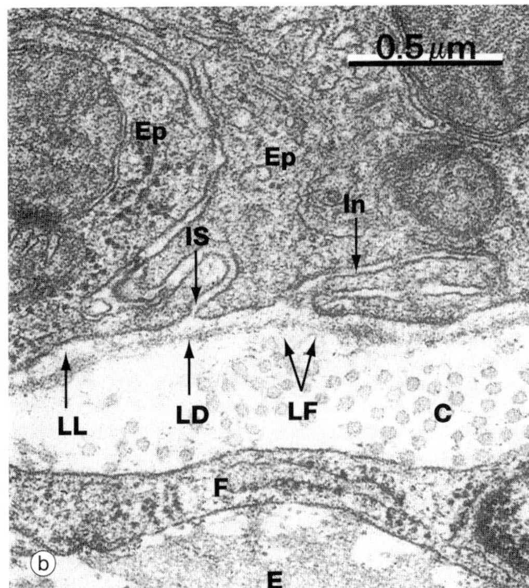

Fig. 4.8 **Basement membrane**
(a) EM ×5000 (b) EM ×45 000

Micrograph (a) shows the epithelial lining of mouse trachea. A basement membrane **BM** can be clearly seen separating it from the underlying supporting tissue which contains the cell body and nucleus of a fibroblast **F**, numerous fine fibroblastic cytoplasmic processes **Fc**, bundles of collagen fibrils **C** (cut in transverse section) and elastin fibres **E**.

At higher magnification in micrograph (b), the three layers of the basement membrane can be seen. The relatively electron-lucent ***lamina lucida*** **LL** abuts the basal epithelial cell membrane. The intermediate layer is electron-dense and represents the ***lamina densa*** **LD**. Beyond the lamina densa is the broad, relatively electron-lucent ***lamina fibroreticularis*** **LF** which merges with the fibrous and fibrillary (reticular) components of the underlying supporting tissue. In this field, note collagen fibrils **C**, part of a fibroblast **F** and elastin **E**. The basement membrane typically passes uninterrupted beneath the intercellular space **IS** between two epithelial cells **Ep** and beneath a basal invagination **In** of one of these cells.

The lamina densa was formerly known as the ***basal lamina***. The terms ***basal lamina*** and ***basement membrane*** were often used interchangeably until it was realised that all three layers seen with the electron microscope represent the single layer seen with the light microscope. This has led to considerable terminological confusion and, if used, the term basal lamina should be confined to its meaning as lamina densa.

Disorders of basement membranes

Basement membranes are involved in several disease processes.

Renal function
In the kidney (Ch. 16) the fused basement membranes of endothelial cells and podocytes forms the filtration barrier for the ultrafiltrate in the glomerulus. If the glomerular basement membrane becomes abnormal then renal function is impaired. In patients with diabetes mellitus there is thickening of the glomerular basement membrane which becomes abnormally permeable to small proteins.

Cancer
Epithelial tissues grow and regenerate and are anchored to, but separated from, support tissues by a basement membrane. Genetic changes in epithelial cells lead to abnormal growth (neoplasia) forming cancers. A malignant tumour can grow from the site of origin and spread into local tissues (invasion). This is achieved by cancer cells secreting factors that facilitate destruction of basement membrane, allowing cells to grow into the extracellular matrix.

Genetic diseases
Mutations in genes coding for components of basement membrane have been shown for renal disease (Alport's disease), muscle disease (congenital muscular dystrophy), and skin disease (junctional epidermolysis bullosa).

Autoimmune disease
In the condition termed Goodpasture's syndrome, autoantibodies are produced to a component of the basement membrane common to glomeruli and lung, leading to renal and lung disease.

BM basement membrane **C** collagen **E** elastin **Ep** epithelial cell **F** fibroblast
Fc fibroblast cytoplasmic process **In** basal invagination **IS** intercellular space **LD** lamina densa
LF lamina fibroreticularis **LL** lamina lucida **M** mucus

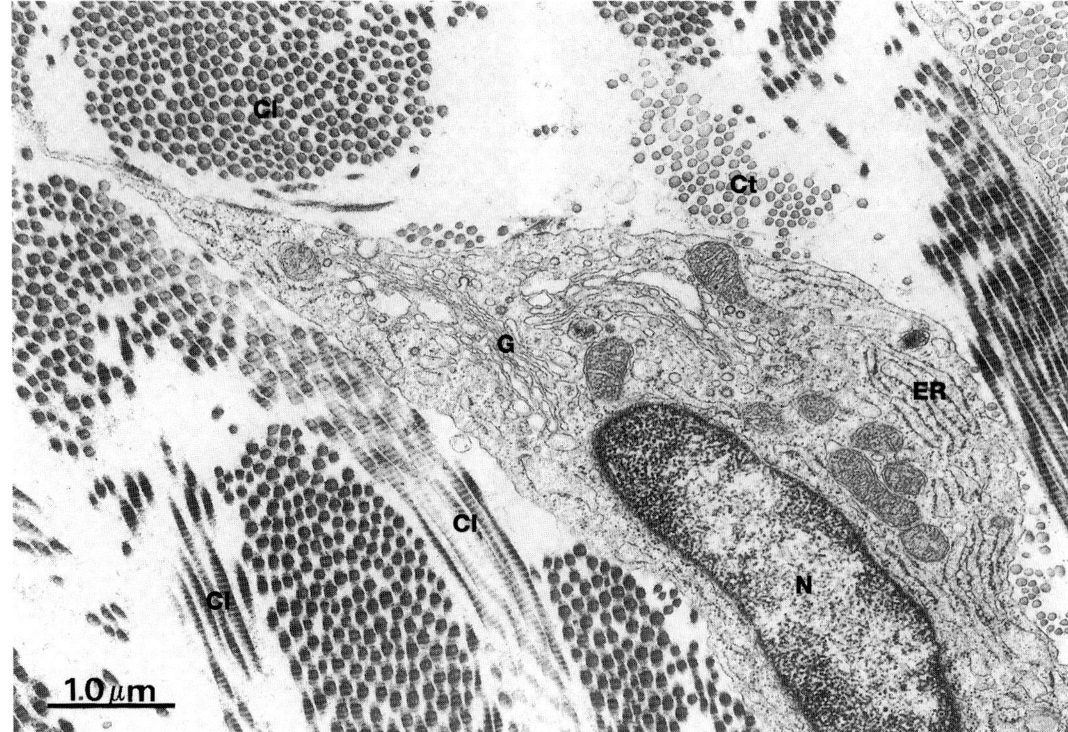

Fig. 4.9 Fibroblasts
EM ×18 500

This micrograph illustrates the body of a mature fibroblast within loose collagenous supporting tissue. The nucleus **N** is moderately condensed, and nucleoli are not a prominent feature. The small quantity of cytoplasm is mostly occupied by rough endoplasmic reticulum **ER**, reflecting the dominant protein-secreting function of this type of cell. The Golgi apparatus **G** is visible and a few mitochondria are present.

Bundles of collagen fibrils are seen in transverse **Ct** and longitudinal section **Cl** in the extracellular matrix.

During active synthesis of extracellular fibres, the fibroblast cytoplasm becomes markedly expanded and the rough endoplasmic reticulum and Golgi apparatus become much more prominent features. Fibroblasts synthesise and secrete the precursors of the glycosaminoglycans, collagen, elastin and all other extracellular constituents; however, in the mature, relatively inactive fibroblast, few secretory vesicles are found.

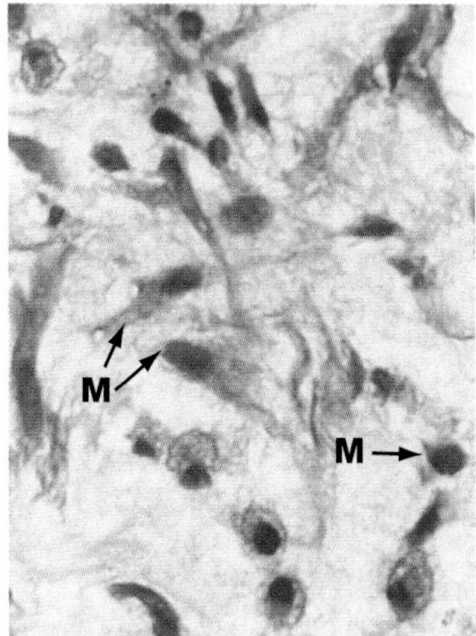

Fig. 4.10 Primitive mesenchyme
H & E ×400

Primitive mesenchyme is the embryological tissue from which all types of supporting connective tissue, including that of the skeleton, are derived. Mesenchymal cells are relatively unspecialised and are capable of differentiation into all the cell types found in mature supporting tissue. Some mesenchymal cells remain in fully mature supporting tissue and act as stem cells (see Ch. 2).

Mesenchymal cells **M** have an irregular, star (stellate) or spindle (fusiform) shape with delicate branching cytoplasmic extensions which form an interlacing network throughout the tissue. The oval nuclei have dispersed chromatin and visible nucleoli. The extracellular material consists almost exclusively of ground substance and does not contain mature fibres. Thus, mesenchyme represents a very loose variant of supporting tissue. The circulatory system of the embryo is poorly developed until a late stage and mesenchyme permits free diffusion of metabolites to and from developing tissues.

Cl collagen fibrils in longitudinal section **Ct** collagen fibrils in transverse section
ER rough endoplasmic reticulum **G** Golgi apparatus **M** mesenchymal cells **N** nucleus

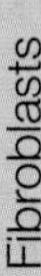

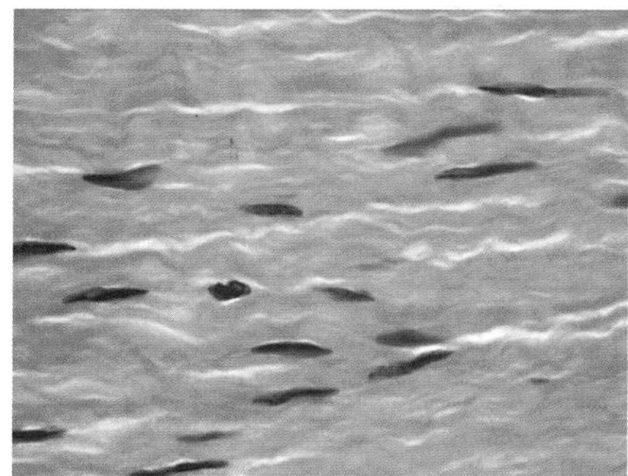

Fig. 4.11 Mature fibroblasts
H & E ×320

This micrograph demonstrates the typical histological appearance of mature fibroblasts in collagenous supporting tissue; collagen fibres are stained pink in this preparation. The fibroblast nuclei are condensed and elongated in the direction of the collagen fibres. The cytoplasm is small in volume and barely visible, the cell being long and thin with fine cytoplasmic processes extending into the matrix to meet up with those of other fibroblasts; these are not generally visible in this type of section by light microscopy. The main function of fibroblasts is to maintain the integrity of supporting tissues by continuous slow turnover of the extracellular matrix constituents.

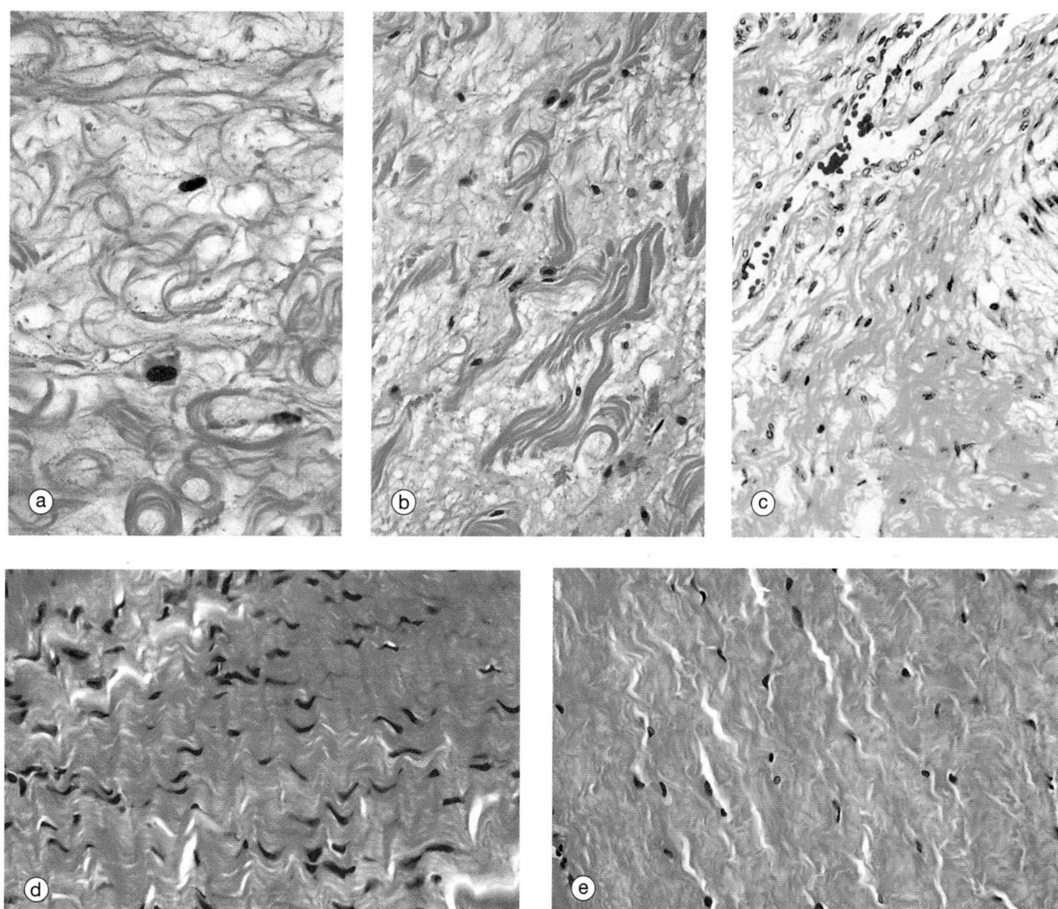

Fig. 4.12 Variation in collagenous tissue
(a) H & E ×350 (b) H & E ×320 (c) Masson's trichrome ×320 (d) H & E ×330 (e) H & E ×330

These micrographs illustrate variations in collagenous tissue. In the past descriptive classifications have been employed, e.g. 'dense regular connective tissue', 'dense irregular connective tissue', 'loose (areolar) connective tissue' etc., but in reality supporting tissues exhibit a great diversity of density and regularity and such rigid descriptions have outlived their usefulness.

The first two micrographs show relatively loosely arranged collagen fibres from submucosa of the bowel. There are thicker collagen bundles in (b). Fibroblasts are sparse compared to matrix. Collagen is acidophilic due to its positively charged side groups; thus in standard H & E preparations, collagen is eosinophilic (i.e. pink-stained). Such loose support tissue has been termed ***areolar connective tissue***. With the trichrome stain (c), collagen stains green or blue (depending on the variant of the stain used).

Micrograph (d) is from fascia surrounding muscle demonstrating a typical dense arrangement of collagen fibres where mechanical support is the primary function. The collagen fibres are arranged in a regular manner to provide a well organised anchorage to transmit forces of contraction. Fibroblast nuclei are elongated in the direction of the collagen fibres. Micrograph (e) is dense collagenous tissue from the dural coat of the brain where it serves a barrier as well as a support function.

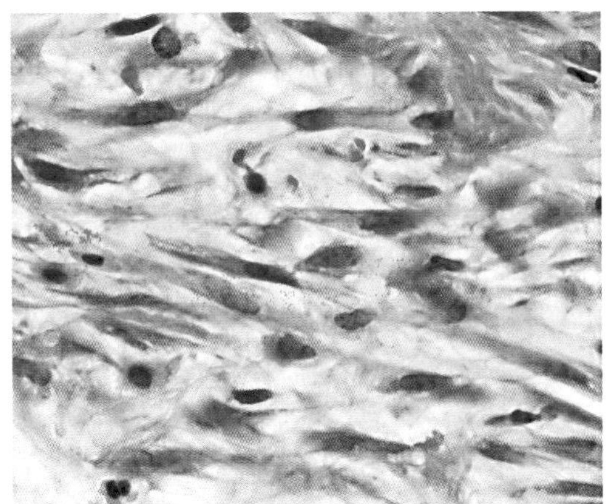

Fig. 4.13 Active fibroblasts: healing wound
H & E ×400

These cells are fibroblasts and myofibroblasts in a healing wound. The nuclei are large and with prominent nucleoli reflecting active protein synthesis. The cytoplasm is extensive and the purple-stained, granular appearance is evidence of an extensive system of rough endoplasmic reticulum involved in protein synthesis. The relative absence of formed collagen fibres in the extracellular matrix permits the meshwork of cytoplasmic extensions between fibroblasts to be seen more easily than is usual in less active supporting tissues.

Fibroblasts with a contractile function (myofibroblasts) play an important role in contraction and shrinkage of the resultant scar tissue.

Healing and repair

Following damage to cells and tissues there is an inflammatory response which is responsible for eliminating the damaging agent and clearing away dead tissues.

Repair to damaged tissues is mainly delivered by support cells from connective tissues. Briefly, there is a local proliferation of mesenchymal cells from the margins of residual normal tissue to form fibroblasts and myofibroblasts. These grow out to replace the area of tissue damage. This proliferation is also associated with growth of new capillary blood vessels to supply nutrients. The fibroblasts and myofibroblasts secrete extracellular matrix material, ground substance and collagen, to replace the damaged area by fibrocollagenous material. This is the basis of the formation of a collagenous scar. Over time there is remodelling of collagen to maximise strength of collagen and link it to adjacent tissues.

This process is termed ***healing by repair***. Specialised tissues damaged by disease, such as muscle or lung, are replaced by strong but non-functional ***collagenous scar***.

Adipose tissue

Most supporting tissues contain cells which are adapted for the storage of fat; these cells, called ***adipocytes***, are derived from primitive mesenchyme where they develop as ***lipoblasts***. Adipocytes are found in isolation or in clumps throughout loose supporting tissues or may constitute the main cell type as in adipose tissue.

Stored fat within adipocytes is derived from three main sources: dietary fat circulating in the bloodstream as chylomicrons; triglycerides synthesised in the liver and transported in blood; and triglycerides synthesised from glucose within adipocytes. Adipose tissue is often regarded as an inactive energy store, however it is an extremely important participant in general metabolic processes in that it acts as a temporary store of substrate for the energy-deriving processes of almost all tissues. Adipose tissue, therefore, generally has a rich blood supply. The rate of fat deposition and utilisation within adipose tissue is largely determined by dietary intake and energy expenditure, but a number of hormones and the sympathetic nervous system profoundly influence the fat metabolism of adipocytes.

In addition to their energy-storage role adipocytes have an important endocrine role. Through secretion of several proteins adipocytes modulate energy metabolism and influence general metabolism in coordination with hormones such as insulin to regulate body mass. Adipose tissue is responsible for the secretion of several proteins, collectively known as adipocytokines. These include leptin, adipsin, resistin, adiponectin, tumor necrosis factor alpha, and plasminogen-activator inhibitor type 1.

There are two main types of adipose tissue:

- **White adipose tissue.** This type of adipose tissue comprises up to 20% of total body weight in normal, well-nourished male adults and up to 25% in females. It is distributed throughout the body particularly in the deep layers of the skin (see Ch. 9). In addition to being an important energy store, white adipose tissue acts as a thermal insulator under the skin and functions as a cushion against mechanical shock in such sites as around the kidneys.
- **Brown adipose tissue.** This highly specialised type of adipose tissue is found in newborn mammals and some hibernating animals, where it plays an important part in body temperature regulation. Only small amounts of brown adipose tissue are found in human adults.

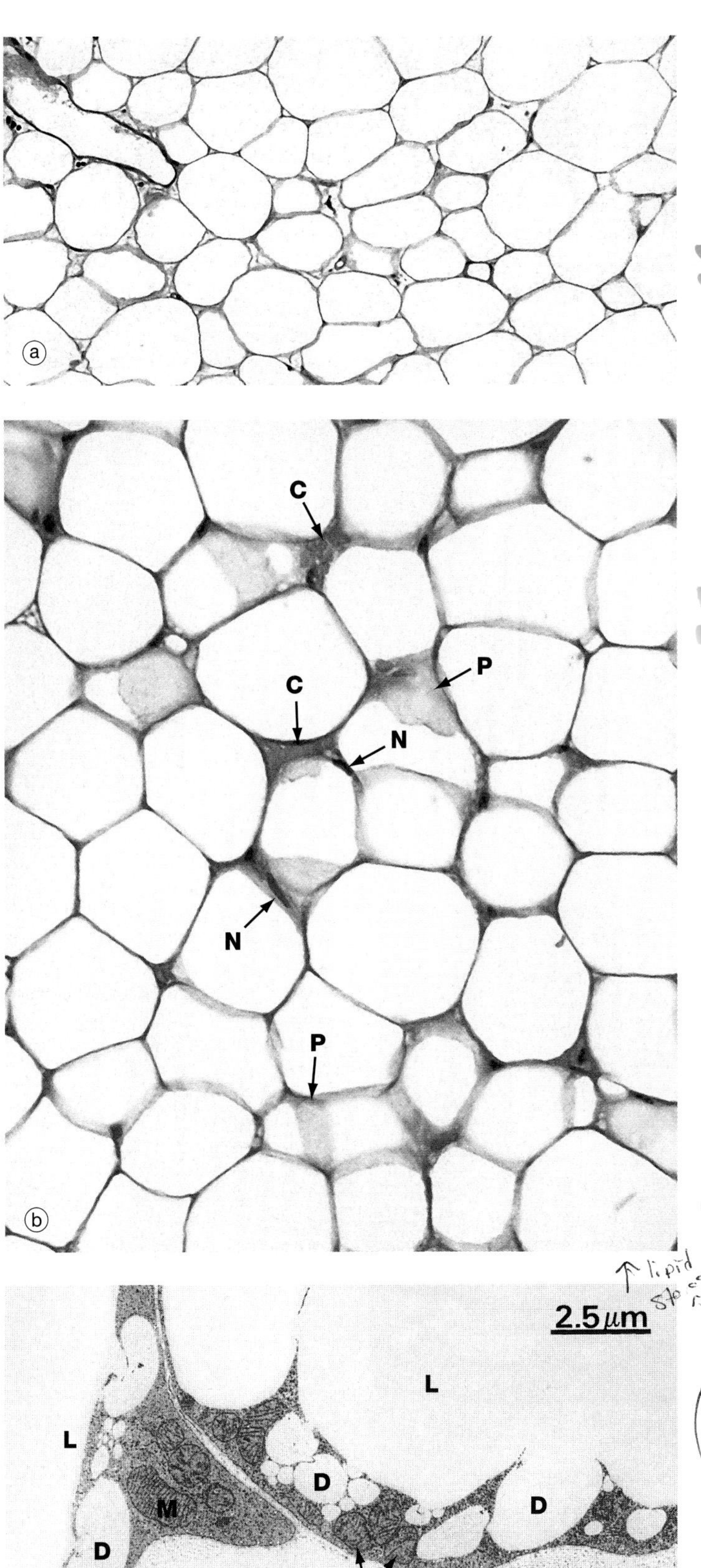

Fig. 4.14 White adipose tissue
(a) H & E ×240 (b) H & E ×480
(c) EM ×6000

The typical appearance of white adipose tissue is illustrated in micrographs (a) and (b). At low magnification adipose tissue is pale staining because virtually all the cell is occupied by lipid, which is dissolved out in standard wax-embedded tissue preparations. The cell membrane and a thin rim of peripheral cytoplasm gives a chicken-wire appearance.

Fat stored in adipocytes accumulates as lipid droplets which fuse to form a single large droplet which distends and occupies most of the cytoplasm. The adipocyte nucleus **N** is compressed and displaced to one side of the stored lipid droplet and the cytoplasm is reduced to a small rim around the periphery. In some cells, tangential slicing of the top or bottom of a cell is seen as a sheet of pink-stained cytoplasm **P**. Note the minute dimensions of blood capillaries **C** compared with the size of the surrounding adipocytes.

The electron micrograph (c) shows the periphery of two adjacent adipocytes. Contrary to the impression given by light microscopy, the main lipid droplet **L** in each cell has an irregular outline with numerous tiny droplets **D** at the periphery in the process of fusion with the main droplet. The lipid is not bounded by a membrane. The thin rim of cytoplasm contains the usual organelles, most notably mitochondria **M**. Each adipocyte is surrounded by an external lamina. In the adjacent extracellular tissue a fibroblast cytoplasmic process **F** and collagen fibrils **Co** can be seen.

Adipocytes have receptors for insulin, glucocorticoids, growth hormone and noradrenalin (norepinephrine) that modulate uptake and release of fat. Adipocytes secrete the hormone ***leptin*** that is involved in regulation of appetite.

C capillary **Co** collagen fibrils **D** small lipid droplet **F** fibroblast cytoplasmic process
L large lipid droplet **M** mitochondrion **N** nucleus **P** cytoplasm of adipocyte

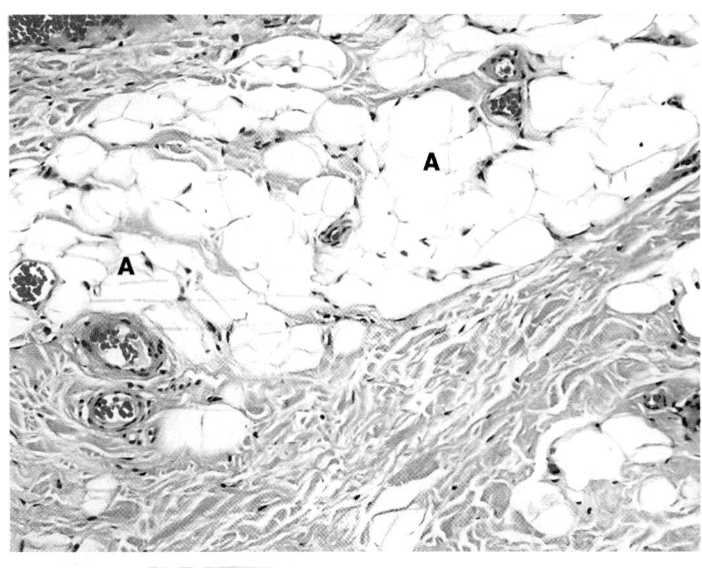

Fig. 4.15 Fibroadipose tissue
H & E ×200

This micrograph demonstrates the typical appearance of adipocytes **A** scattered within collagenous supporting tissue. Adipocytes occur either singly or in groups, particularly in the tissues supporting the lining of the gastrointestinal tract as shown here. Like the adipocytes of white adipose tissue, the size of adipocytes in loose supporting tissue depends on the equilibrium between dietary fat intake and energy expenditure.

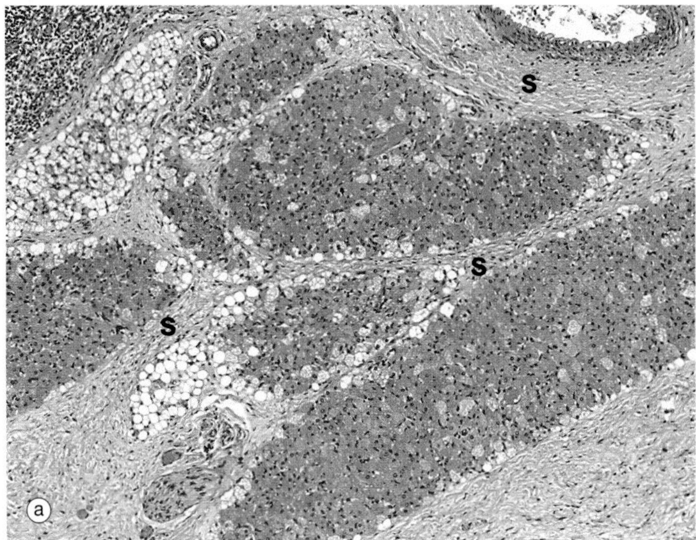

Fig. 4.16 Brown adipose tissue
(a) H & E ×100 (b) H & E ×200

These micrographs demonstrate the typical histological appearance of brown adipose tissue. As seen in micrographs (a) and (b), brown adipose tissue is arranged in lobules separated by fibrous septa **S** which convey blood vessels and sympathetic nerve fibres.

At low magnification two types of cell can be seen. Many cells, and especially cells at the centre of lobules, are pink-stained due to cytoplasm packed with mitochondria. Other cells, and especially those at the periphery of lobules have a pale-stained cytoplasm which is due to the presence of multiple vesicles containing lipid.

Brown adipose tissue is involved in non-shivering thermogenesis, an increase in metabolic activity induced by cold stress. Brown adipose tissue is characterised by expression of a unique uncoupling protein termed UCP1 (thermogenin). This protein, in association with several other modulating factors, serves to uncouple mitochondrial metabolism from production of ATP to produce heat.

A adipocyte **C** capillary **L** lipid droplet **M** mitochondrion **S** septum

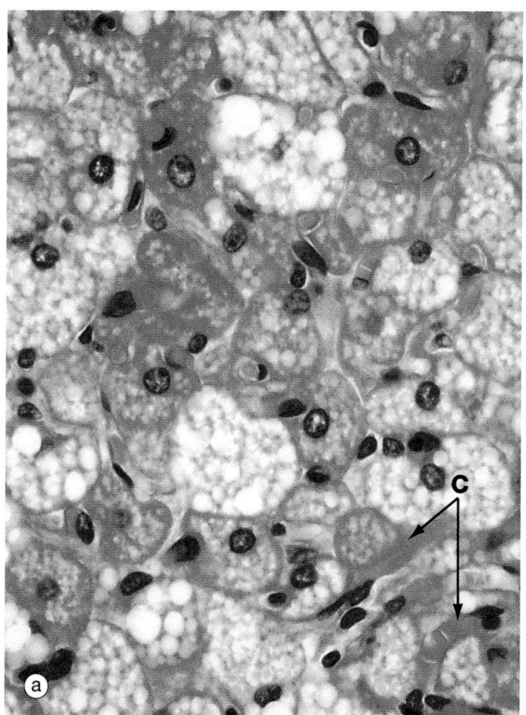

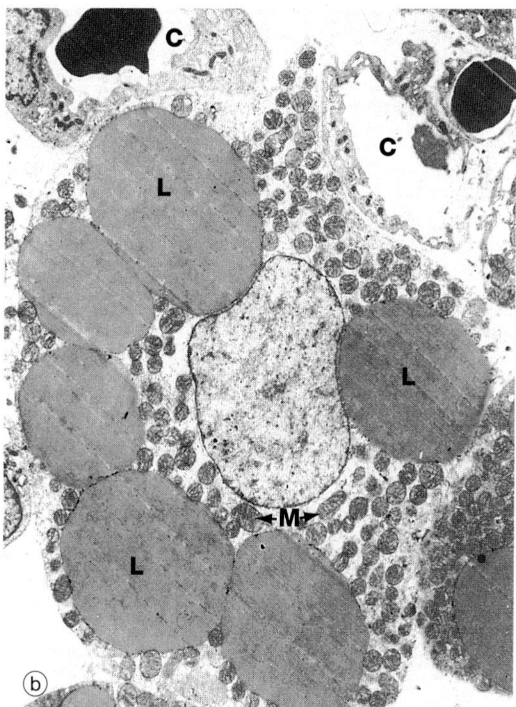

Fig. 4.17 Brown adipose tissue
(a) H & E ×400 (b) Rabbit, EM ×4070

At high magnification in micrograph (a), the nuclei of brown adipocytes are seen to be eccentrically located within the cell but, unlike those of white adipocytes, the nuclei are large and surrounded by a significant quantity of strongly eosinophilic cytoplasm. The stored lipid is contained within multiple droplets, all of which have been dissolved away during tissue processing. Note the rich network of capillaries **C** between the brown adipocytes.

The electron micrograph (b) shows brown adipose tissue taken from a newborn rabbit and readily demonstrates the multilocular nature of stored lipid **L**. The cytoplasm of brown adipocytes is crammed with mitochondria **M** which have numerous, closely packed cristae. These mitochondria are extremely rich in cytochromes, part of the electron transport chain involved in oxidative energy production; this accounts for the brown colour of brown adipose tissue when examined macroscopically.

Unlike the metabolism of other tissues, in brown adipose cells the process of electron transport is readily uncoupled from the phosphorylation of ADP to form ATP. The energy derived from oxidation of lipids, and energy released by electron transport in the uncoupled state, is dissipated as heat which is rapidly conducted to the rest of the body by the rich vascular network of brown adipose tissue. Note the intimate association of capillaries **C** with the brown adipocyte in this micrograph.

Using these metabolic processes, neonatal humans and other mammals utilise brown adipose tissue to generate body heat during the vulnerable period after birth. Brown adipose tissue undergoes involution in early infancy and in adult humans is found only in restricted sites such as around the adrenal gland and great vessels in retroperitoneal fat. The production of heat by brown adipose tissue is controlled directly by the sympathetic nervous system.

Obesity

Among affluent societies there is concern about the rapid increase in prevalence of obesity – the so-called 'obesity epidemic'. A syndrome has been characterised termed '***the metabolic syndrome***' which comprises abdominal obesity, lipid changes in blood, high blood pressure, insulin resistance, and a proinflammatory/prothrombotic state.

The obesity epidemic has been attributed to the rising prevalence of metabolic syndrome which in turn is a major contribution to the development of cardiovascular diseases such as atheroma. Adipocytes are not merely fat storage cells and have complex metabolic roles including the ability to secrete a variety of wide-acting cytokines. Factors which increase the mass of adipocytes are believed to contribute to development of the metabolic syndrome.

Obesity has been mainly linked to environmental factors such as overeating and physical inactivity. Obesity has also been linked to genetic factors. In rare familial cases obesity has been caused by mutations in leptin, leptin receptor, prohormone convertase, pro-opiomelanocortin or melanocortin-4 receptor. Sporadic human obesity has been linked to several genetic loci.

Tumours derived from support cells

Tumours are caused by changes in the genome of cells that leads them to undergo poorly regulated growth. Local overgrowth produces a mass of cells termed a neoplasm or tumour. Tumours may be confined to the part in which they arise (benign) or may develop further loss of growth control that allows cells to invade local tissues or spread widely in the body (malignant).

Tumours of support cells are commonly seen. They are often referred to as the group of ***soft tissue tumours***.

An abnormal growth of adipocytes is responsible for the commonly encountered benign tumour termed a ***lipoma***. Although they can arise in almost any site in the body, the commonest presentation is as a subcutaneous soft mass. Histologically these lesions are composed of mature unilocular 'white' adipose tissue, indistinguishable from normal adipose tissue.

Malignant tumours of adipocytes are rare and called ***liposarcomas***. These are highly malignant lesions that often arise deep within the retroperitoneal tissues.

Benign tumours of fibroblasts are sometimes seen, termed ***fibromas***. Malignant tumours of fibroblasts are termed ***fibrosarcomas*** and may arise at any site.

The defence cells of supporting tissue

The supporting tissues not only contain cells responsible for their synthesis, maintenance and metabolic activity, but also a variety of cells with defence and immune functions. Traditionally, these cells have been divided into two categories: fixed (intrinsic) cells and wandering (extrinsic) cells.

The intrinsic defence cells of supporting tissue are the ***tissue-fixed macrophages*** (***histiocytes***) and ***mast cells***. Tissue-fixed macrophages are now generally believed to be derived from circulating monocytes (see Fig. 3.9), which have become at least temporarily resident in supporting tissues. Mast cells are functionally analogous to basophils (see Fig. 3.7), but there are structural differences which suggest that mast cells are not merely basophils resident in the tissues.

The wandering category of defence and immune cells includes all the remaining members of the white blood cell series (see Ch. 3). Although leucocytes (white blood cells) are usually considered as a constituent of blood, their principal site of activity is outside the blood circulation, particularly within loose supporting tissues. Leucocytes are normally found only in relatively small numbers, but in response to tissue injury and other disease processes their numbers increase greatly. The supporting tissues of those regions of the body which are subject to the constant threat of pathogenic invasion, such as the gastrointestinal and respiratory tracts, contain a large population of leucocytes, maintaining constant surveillance.

The reticuloendothelial concept

The term ***reticuloendothelial system*** has long been used to describe a diverse group of cells found in many tissues but in particular the bone marrow, liver, spleen, lymph nodes and thymus. The main functional characteristic of these cells is their ability to phagocytose particulate matter, microorganisms, and effete (worn out or dead) cells, e.g. aged blood cells. Another important function is storage of iron and certain metabolic products. Such phagocytic cells are found lining certain blood- and lymph-filled spaces, such as the sinusoids of the liver (see Fig. 15.9), bone marrow (see Fig. 3.12) and spleen (see Fig. 11.19), and in this context they have some features in common with the ***endothelial cells*** which line all blood and lymphatic vessels (see Ch. 8).

Certain highly cellular tissues, such as lymph nodes and the haemopoietic cords of bone marrow, have a supporting framework of reticulin fibres (see Fig. 4.3) upon which are draped cells with long cytoplasmic processes morphologically similar to primitive mesenchymal cells (see Fig. 4.10); these cells are traditionally described as ***reticulum*** or ***reticular cells***. Some if not all of these cells are probably responsible for synthesis of the reticulin framework, being thus analogous to fibroblasts; many of these cells, if not all, may also exhibit considerable phagocytic activity.

Because of the close structural and functional association of these cell types with the haemopoietic, macrophage-monocyte (see Fig. 3.9) and immune systems, they were thought to represent a single functional system. Consequently, 'reticuloendothelial' and related terms became widely and often indiscriminately applied to tissues and cells within these systems. Scientific advances have rendered the concept imprecise. However it is important to understand the meaning of this term. A search of PubMed for papers written in 2005 will reveal continued usage of the term reticuloendothelial system to describe a distributed phagocytic cell network mainly located in the bone marrow, spleen, liver, and lymph nodes. In certain inherited storage diseases abnormal metabolic products can also accumulate in cells of the reticuloendothelial system leading to enlargement of liver and spleen.

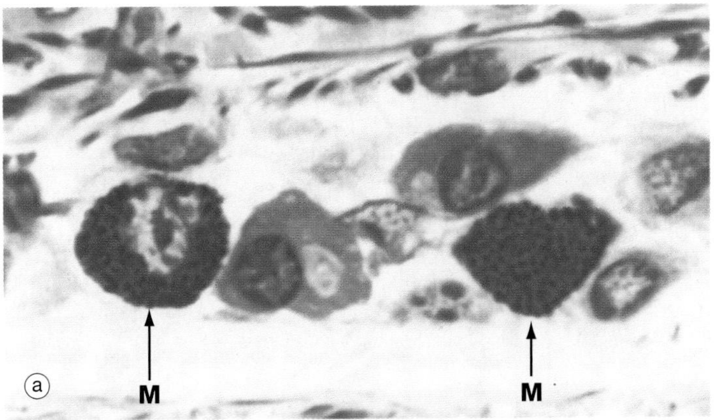

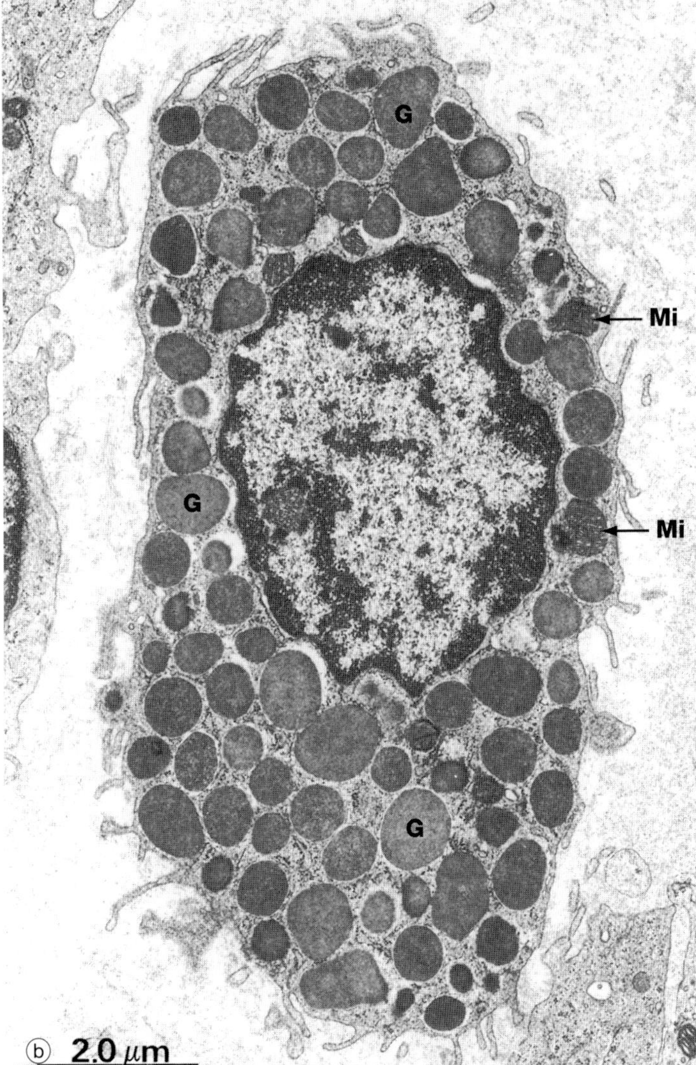

Fig. 4.18 Mast cells
(a) Thin section, toluidine blue ×1200 (b) EM ×12 000

Mast cells are found in all supporting tissues but are particularly prevalent in the skin, gastrointestinal lining, the serosal lining of the peritoneal cavity and around blood vessels. Their major constituents and functions are very similar to those of basophils to which they are probably related and which are described in detail with Fig. 3.7. Mast cells are long-lived with the ability to proliferate in the tissues. Mast cell degranulation results in the release of histamine and other vasoactive mediators which induce the immediate hypersensitivity (anaphylactoid) response (characteristic of urticaria, allergic rhinitis and asthma) and anaphylactic shock.

Mast cells are not readily identified in routine histological sections due to the water solubility of their densely basophilic granules which tend to be lost during preparation. Thus special techniques of fixation, embedding and staining must be employed. With suitable staining, however, the characteristic feature of mast cells is an extensive cytoplasm packed with large granules which are nevertheless smaller in size, though more numerous, than those of basophils. When stained with certain blue basic dyes such as ***toluidine blue***, the granules bind to the dye changing its colour to red. This property is known as ***metachromasia***.

The light micrograph (a) demonstrates two mast cells **M** in the supporting tissue underlying the tracheal surface. A pale nucleus can be seen in one cell but the plane of section is outside the nucleus of the other. Note the large, densely p acked granules which exhibit metachromasia.

In the electron micrograph (b), mast cell granules **G** are seen to be membrane-bound and to contain a dense amorphous material. The granules are liberated from the cell by exocytosis when stimulated during an inflammatory or allergic response. The cytoplasm contains a few rounded mitochondria **Mi** and a little rough endoplasmic reticulum. The non-segmented nucleus has less condensed chromatin than that of basophils. Other differences from basophils include a more uniform distribution of their thin surface processes, a greater number of cytoplasmic filaments and a lack of glycogen granules.

G mast cell granule **M** mast cell **Mi** mitochondrion

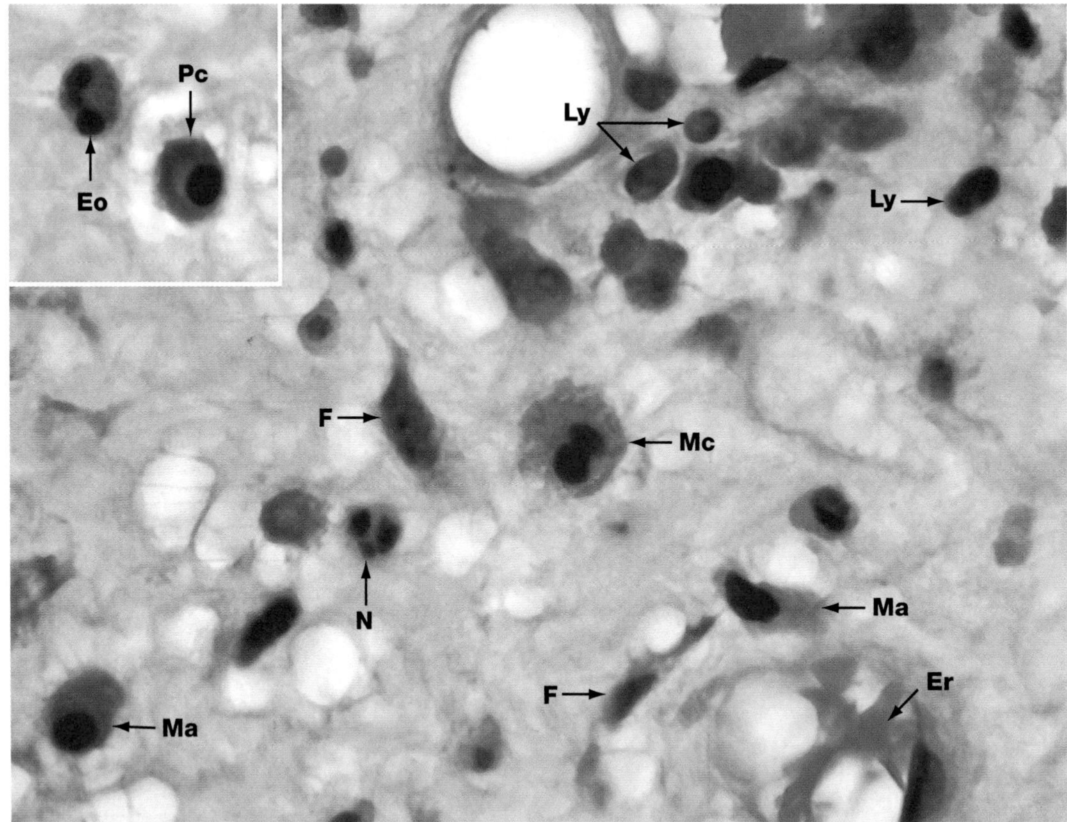

Fig. 4.19 Leucocytes in loose supporting tissue
H & E ×640

The appearance of leucocytes within tissue sections differs greatly from the appearance seen in blood smears (see Ch. 3). In this micrograph, a variety of leucocytes are seen in the loose supporting tissue supporting the lining epithelium of the nasal mucosa, a site which is normally rich in such cells even in the absence of inflammation.

Fibroblasts **F** are identified by their relatively large, elongated nuclei. Erythrocytes **Er** within small blood vessels are intensely eosinophilic (red stained) but difficult to discriminate as they are clumped together.

Of the granulocytes, neutrophils are only rarely seen in the tissues except in acute or chronic inflammation. Neutrophils **N** are recognised by their multilobed nuclei and poorly stained cytoplasm. Eosinophils **Eo** may be present in large numbers in normal supporting tissues, such as in the nose or gut, and are recognised by their bilobed nuclei and strongly eosinophilic cytoplasmic granules. Mast cells **Ma** can be identified by a uniform purple-stained cytoplasm and often eccentric rounded nucleus.

Lymphocytes **L** are easily recognised by their small, densely stained nuclei and a thin halo of poorly stained cytoplasm. Lymphocyte nuclei are approximately 7–8 μm in diameter and provides a useful reference for the size of other cells in tissue sections. Plasma cells **Pc**, responsible for antibody synthesis (see Ch. 11), are recognised by their large nuclei and extensive amphophilic (purple stained) cytoplasm containing a pale stained perinuclear area which represents a well developed and active Golgi apparatus. The amphophilia of plasma cells is attributable to large amounts of rough endoplasmic reticulum (basophilic) and of protein (antibody, acidophilic) resulting in a purple colour.

Large mononuclear phagocytes, analogous to the monocytes of blood, are distributed throughout all supporting tissues where they may exhibit intense phagocytic activity; these cells are also known as macrophages, tissue-fixed macrophages, and histiocytes when present in supporting tissue. Inactive macrophages are small and drape themselves on the fibres of the extracellular matrix and may be difficult to distinguish from fibroblasts. In contrast, actively phagocytic macrophages are plump and may move in an amoeboid manner through the ground substance. When they have been actively phagocytic, macrophages may be recognised by their large size and content of engulfed material; note, however, that active macrophages have an extremely variable appearance, depending on the nature of their phagocytic activity. The macrophage shown in this tissue **Mc** has a granular pale purple cytoplasm possibly representing mucous material that has been phagocytosed from the local environment.

Eo eosinophil **Er** erythrocytes **F** fibroblast **L** lysosome **Ly** lymphocyte **M** mitochondrion **Ma** mast cell **Mc** macrophage **N** neutrophil **P** latex particle **Pc** plasma cell **Pp** pseudopodia **R** residual body **rER** rough endoplasmic reticulum

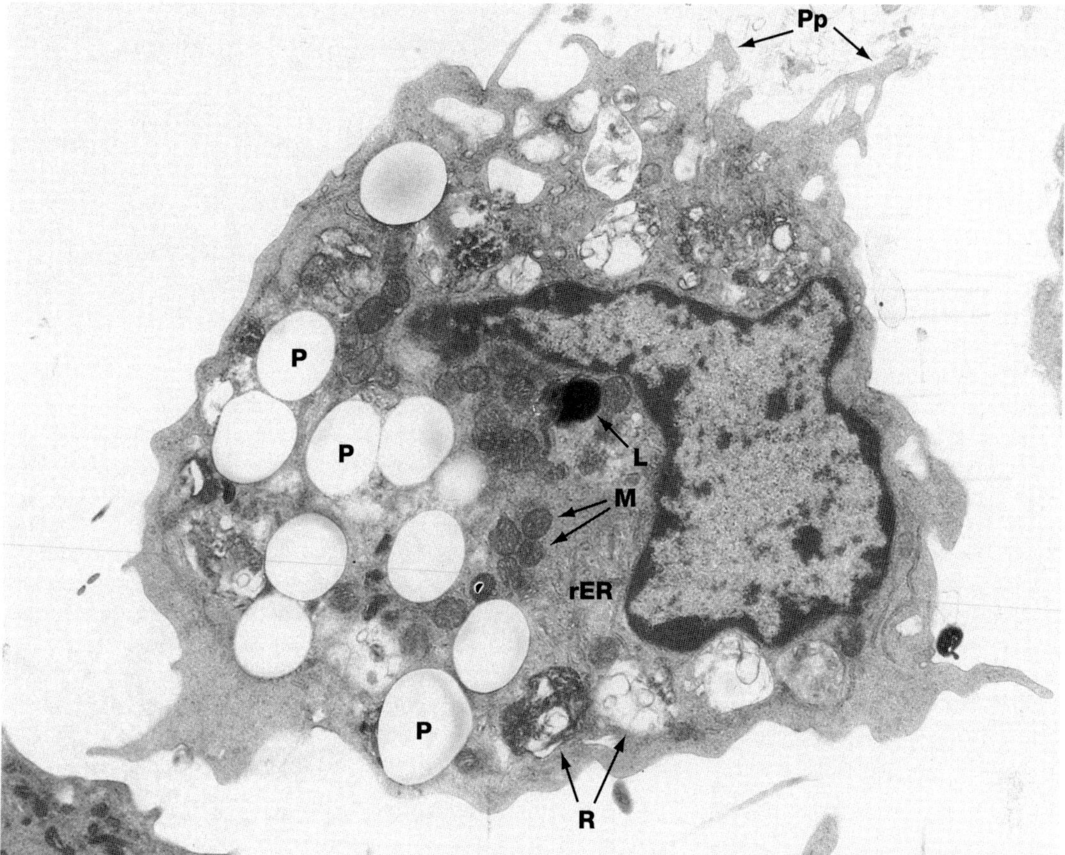

Fig. 4.20 Macrophage
EM ×11 600

The ultrastructural features of macrophages vary widely according to their state of activity and tissue location. This micrograph shows an active macrophage obtained from the peritoneum of a rat which had previously been injected intraperitoneally with latex particles; a number of particles **P** have been engulfed by the macrophage.

The macrophage nucleus is irregular with heterochromatin typically clumped around the nuclear envelope. The cytoplasm contains a few mitochondria **M** and a variable amount of free ribosomes and rough endoplasmic reticulum **rER**. In quiescent macrophages, lysosomes **L** are abundant but their number is much reduced in actively phagocytic cells; lysosomes are later regenerated by the Golgi apparatus. The macrophage cytoplasm contains an assortment of phagosomes and residual bodies **R**. Residual material may be released from the macrophage by exocytosis. Such material may remain sequestered in the tissues, as occurs with the dyes used in tattooing of the skin, or the material may be returned to the circulation for excretion or re-use in biosynthetic processes. Actively phagocytic cells exhibit irregular cytoplasmic projections or pseudopodia **Pp** which are involved in amoeboid movement and phagocytosis.

In addition to their role as tissue scavengers, macrophages play an important role in immune mechanisms (see Ch. 11) since they are often the first cells to make contact with antigens. Macrophages process antigenic material before presenting it to lymphocytes; lymphocytes are then stimulated to undergo specific immune responses. Macrophages involved in this way are described as ***antigen presenting cells***. As a result of various immune mechanisms, antigenic material may become combined or coated with substances such as antibodies and complement which are then collectively known as ***opsonins***. Opsonins are recognised by surface receptors on the macrophage surface and this greatly enhances the phagocytic ability of macrophages and other phagocytes such as neutrophils (see Ch. 3), a process which is known as ***opsonisation***. Other substances such as ***lymphokines***, which are released during the immune response, act directly upon macrophages to increase greatly their metabolic and phagocytic activity.

Macrophages also secrete a variety of cytokines that act to enhance local and systemic immune responses. This is especially in response to cytokine stimulation by activated T cells.

In some disease states macrophages may develop a large voluminous cytoplasm when they are termed ***epithelioid macrophages***. In other pathological situations macrophages can fuse to form ***multinucleate giant cells***.

5. *Epithelial tissues*

Introduction

The epithelia are a diverse group of tissues that include both ***surface epithelia*** and ***solid organs***. Surface epithelia cover or line all body surfaces, cavities and tubes and thus form the interfaces between different biological compartments. As such, epithelia mediate a wide range of activities such as selective diffusion, absorption, secretion, physical protection and containment; many of these major functions may be exhibited at a single epithelial surface. For example, the epithelial lining of the small intestine is primarily involved in absorption of the products of digestion, but the epithelium also protects itself from noxious intestinal contents by the secretion of a surface coating of mucus. The majority of epithelial cells contain ***cytokeratin*** intermediate filaments, and this can be used to recognise an epithelial phenotype using immunohistochemistry, a technique often used in diagnostic histopathology to classify difficult malignant tumours.

Surface epithelia form continuous sheets comprising one or more layers of cells. Epithelial cells are bound to adjacent cells by a variety of membrane specialisations called ***cell junctions*** that provide physical strength and mediate exchange of information and metabolites. All epithelia are supported by a ***basement membrane*** of variable thickness. Basement membranes (see Ch. 4) separate epithelia from underlying supporting tissues and are never penetrated by blood vessels; epithelia are thus critically dependent on the diffusion of oxygen and metabolites from adjacent supporting tissues. Thus epithelial cells are ***polarised*** with one side facing the basement membrane and underlying supporting tissues (the ***basal surface***) and the other facing outwards (the ***apical surface***). For instance the epidermis of the skin is exposed to the external environment and the epithelial lining of the gastrointestinal tract is exposed to the partially digested food in the lumen of the gut.

Classification of epithelia

Surface epithelia are traditionally classified according to three morphological characteristics:

- The number of cell layers: a single layer of epithelial cells is called ***simple epithelium***, whereas epithelium composed of several layers is a ***stratified epithelium***.
- The shape of the component cells: this is based on the appearance in sections taken at right angles to the epithelial surface; cells are thus either ***squamous*** (flattened), ***cuboidal*** or ***columnar***. In stratified epithelia the shape of the outermost layer of cells determines the descriptive classification.
- The presence of surface specialisations such as cilia and keratin. For example the epithelial surface of the skin is classified as ***stratified squamous keratinising epithelium*** since it consists of many layers of cells, the surface cells of which are flattened (squamous) in shape, and it is covered by an outer layer of the proteinaceous material, ***keratin*** that is synthesised by the epithelial cells (see Fig. 5.6).

Epithelium may be derived from ectoderm, mesoderm or endoderm although in the past it was thought that true epithelia were only of ectodermal or endodermal origin. Two types of epithelium derived from mesoderm were not considered to be true epithelium, i.e. the lining of blood and lymphatic vessels (***endothelium***) and the linings of the serous body cavities (***mesothelium***). By both morphological and functional criteria, such distinction has little practical value; nevertheless, the terms endothelium and mesothelium are still used to describe these types of epithelium.

Glandular epithelia

Epithelium that is primarily involved in secretion is often arranged into structures called ***glands***. Glands are merely invaginations of epithelial surfaces, which are formed during embryonic development by proliferation of epithelium into the underlying tissues. For example glandular epithelium is characteristic of the lining of the gastrointestinal tract.

As mentioned above, some solid organs are composed largely of epithelial cells with a supporting tissue framework. Some of these organs are connected to the surface epithelium of the gastrointestinal tract by a branching system of ducts and belong to the category of ***exocrine glands***, e.g. the salivary glands. ***Endocrine glands*** on the other hand have lost their connection to the epithelial surface from which they developed and release their secretions directly into the blood e.g. the thyroid gland.

Simple epithelia

Simple epithelia are defined as surface epithelia consisting of a single layer of cells. Simple epithelia are almost always found at interfaces involved in selective diffusion, absorption and/or secretion. They provide little protection against mechanical abrasion and thus are not found on surfaces subject to such stresses. The cells comprising simple epithelia range in shape from extremely flattened to tall columnar, depending on their function. For example, flattened simple epithelia are ideally suited to diffusion and are therefore found in the air sacs of the lung (alveoli), the lining of blood vessels (endothelium) and lining body cavities (mesothelium). In contrast, highly active epithelial cells, such as the cells lining the small intestine, are generally tall since they must accommodate the appropriate organelles. Simple epithelia may exhibit a variety of surface specialisations, such as microvilli and cilia, which facilitate their specific surface functions.

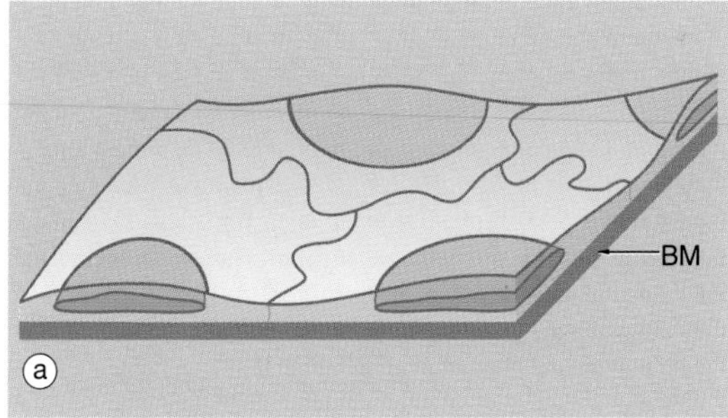

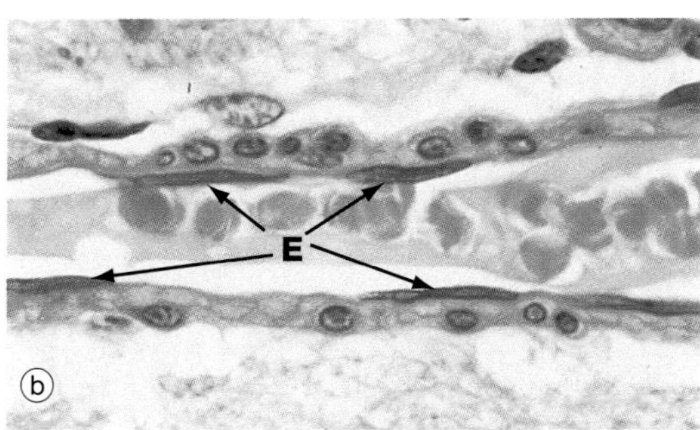

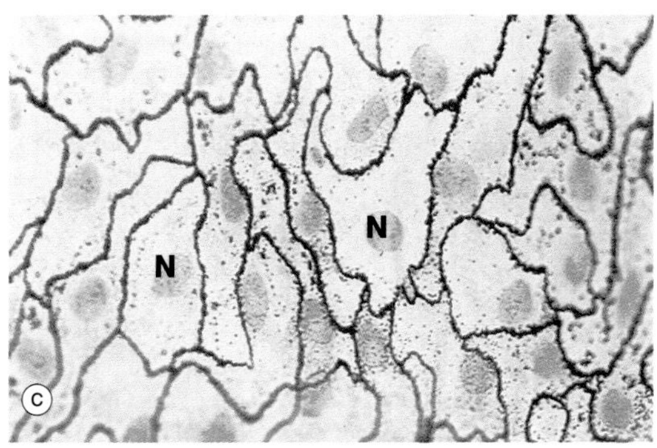

Fig. 5.1 Simple squamous epithelium
(a) Diagram (b) H & E ×800 (c) Spread preparation, silver method/neutral red ×320

Simple squamous epithelium is composed of flattened, irregularly shaped cells forming a continuous surface that is sometimes called ***pavemented epithelium***; the term 'squamous' derives from the comparison of the cells to the scales of a fish. Like all epithelia, this delicate lining is supported by an underlying basement membrane **BM** as shown diagrammatically.

Simple squamous epithelium is found lining surfaces involved in passive transport (diffusion) of either gases (as in the lungs) or fluids (as in the walls of blood capillaries). Simple squamous epithelium also forms the delicate lining of the pleural, pericardial and peritoneal cavities where it allows passage of tissue fluid into and out of these cavities. Although these cells appear simple in form they have a wide variety of important roles.

Micrograph (b) shows a small blood vessel and illustrates the typical appearance of simple squamous epithelium in section. The epithelial lining cells **E** (known as endothelium in the circulatory system) are so flattened that they can only be recognised by their nuclei, which bulge into the vessel lumen. The supporting basement membrane is thin and, in H & E stained preparations, has similar staining properties to the endothelial cell cytoplasm; hence it cannot be seen in this micrograph.

In the preparation used in micrograph (c), the mesothelial lining of the peritoneal cavity has been stripped from the underlying tissues and spread onto a slide thus permitting a surface view of simple squamous epithelium. The intercellular substance has been stained with silver thereby outlining the closely interdigitating and highly irregular cell boundaries. The nuclei **N** are stained a slightly darker pink.

BM basement membrane **E** epithelial lining cells **N** nucleus

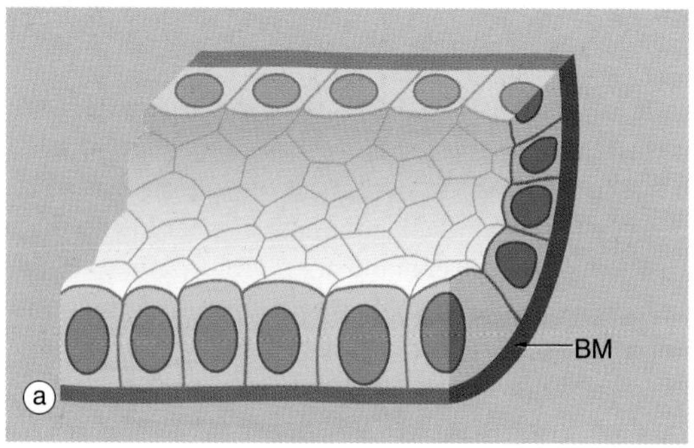

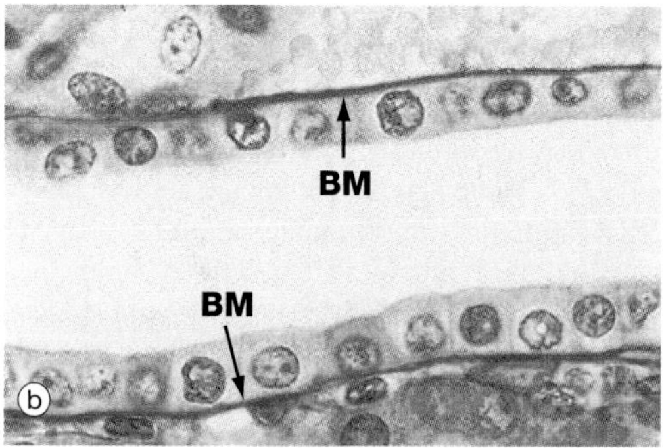

Fig. 5.2 Simple cuboidal epithelium
(a) Diagram (b) Azan ×400

Simple cuboidal epithelium represents an intermediate form between simple squamous and simple columnar epithelium; the distinction between tall cuboidal and low columnar is often arbitrary and is of descriptive value only. In the section perpendicular to the basement membrane **BM**, the epithelial cells appear square, leading to its traditional description as cuboidal epithelium; on surface view, however, the cells are actually polygonal in shape. The nucleus is usually round and located in the centre of the cell.

Simple cuboidal epithelium usually lines small ducts and tubules that may have excretory, secretory or absorptive functions; examples are the collecting tubules of the kidney and the small excretory ducts of the salivary glands and pancreas.

Micrograph (b) shows the cells lining a collecting tubule in the kidney. Although the boundaries between individual cells are indistinct, the nuclear shape provides an approximate indication of the cell size and shape. The underlying basement membrane **BM** appears as a prominent blue line with the Azan staining method in contrast to basement membranes stained with the standard H & E stain that are generally indistinguishable.

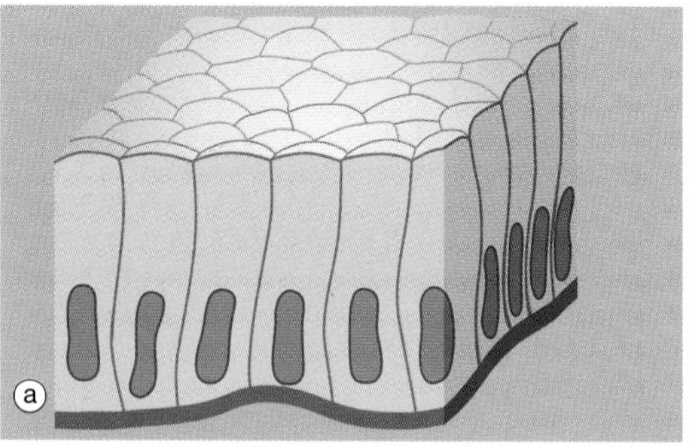

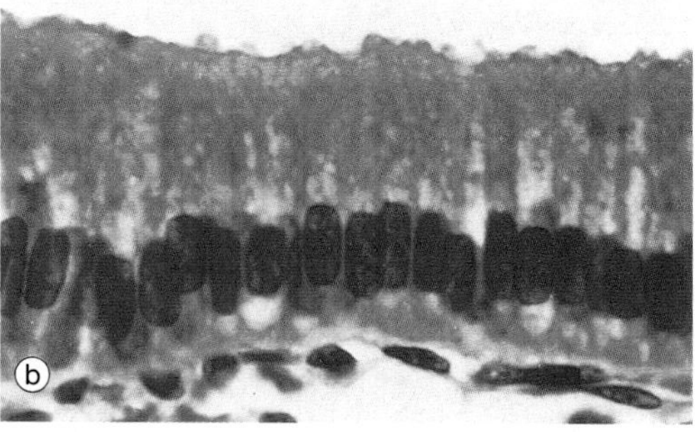

Fig. 5.3 Simple columnar epithelium
(a) Diagram (b) H & E ×800

Simple columnar epithelium is similar to simple cuboidal epithelium except that the cells are taller and appear columnar in sections at right angles to the basement membrane. The height of the cells may vary from low to tall columnar depending on the site and/or degree of functional activity. The nuclei are elongated and may be located towards the base, the centre or occasionally the apex of the cytoplasm: this is known as ***polarity*** of the nucleus. Simple columnar epithelium is most often found on absorptive surfaces such as in the small intestine, although it may constitute the lining of secretory surfaces such as that of the stomach.

Micrograph (b) illustrates an unusually tall example of simple columnar epithelium and is taken from the lining of the gall bladder where it has the function of absorbing water, thus concentrating bile. Note the typically elongated nuclei that in this location exhibit basal polarity.

BM basement membrane **C** cilia **G** goblet cell

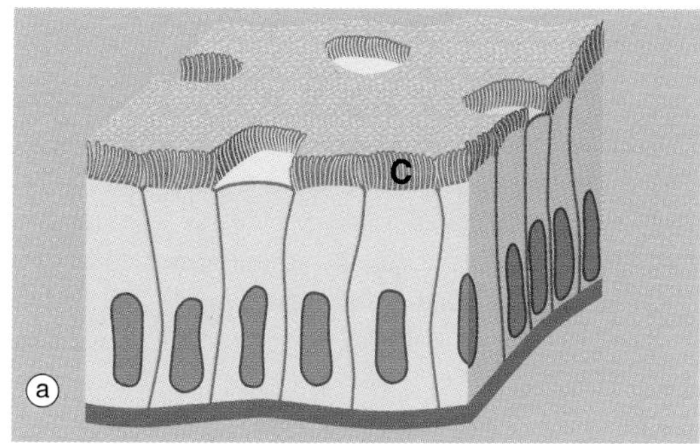

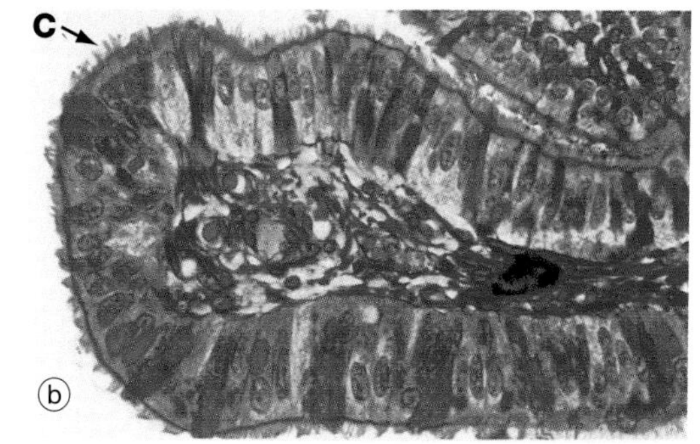

Fig. 5.4 Simple columnar ciliated epithelium
(a) Diagram (b) Azan ×320

Some simple columnar epithelia have surface ***cilia* C** on the majority of the cells (see also Fig. 5.14). Among the ciliated cells are scattered non-ciliated cells that usually have a secretory function.

Cilia are much larger than microvilli (see Fig. 5.15) and are readily visible with the light microscope. Each cilium consists of a finger-like projection of the plasma membrane, its cytoplasm containing modified microtubules. Each cell may have up to 300 cilia that beat in a wave-like manner synchronised with the adjacent cells. The waving motion of the cilia propels fluid or minute particles over the epithelial surface.

Simple columnar ciliated epithelium is found mainly in the female reproductive tract. Micrograph (b) taken from the Fallopian tube (oviduct) shows one of its numerous folds covered by simple columnar ciliated epithelium. The predominant cell type in this epithelium is tall columnar and ciliated, the nuclei being located towards the apical aspect of the cells. The less numerous, blue stained cells with basally located nuclei are not ciliated and have a secretory function. Ciliary action facilitates transport of the ovum from the ovary towards the uterus.

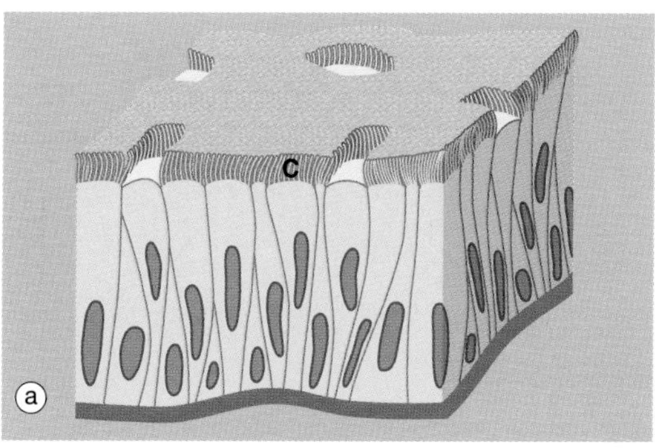

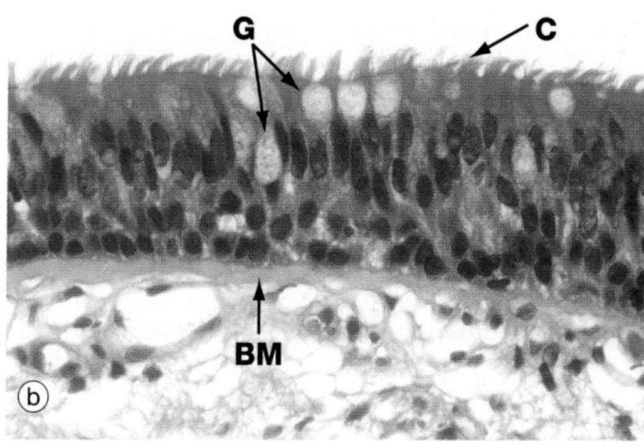

Fig. 5.5 Pseudostratified columnar ciliated epithelium
(a) Diagram (b) H & E ×200

Another variant of simple columnar epithelium is described in which the majority of cells are also usually ciliated **C**. The term ***pseudostratified*** is derived from the appearance of this epithelium in section, which conveys the erroneous impression that there is more than one layer of cells. In fact, this is a true simple epithelium since all the cells rest on the basement membrane. The nuclei of these cells, however, are disposed at different levels, thus creating the illusion of cellular stratification. Scattered stem cells (see Ch. 2) are found throughout the epithelium: these generally are devoid of cilia (i.e. less differentiated) and do not extend to the luminal surface.

Pseudostratified columnar ciliated epithelium may be distinguished from true stratified epithelia by two characteristics. Firstly, the individual cells of the pseudostratified epithelium exhibit polarity, with nuclei being mainly confined to the basal two-thirds of the epithelium. Secondly, cilia are never present on true stratified epithelia.

Pseudostratified epithelium is almost exclusively confined to the airways of the respiratory system in mammals and is therefore often referred to as ***respiratory epithelium***. Micrograph (b) illustrates the lining of a bronchus. In the respiratory tract, the cilia propel a surface layer of mucus containing entrapped particles towards the pharynx in what is often described as the ***mucociliary escalator***. The mucus is secreted by nonciliated ***goblet cells* G** found amongst the ciliated cells (see also Figs 5.18 and 5.19).

Stratified epithelia

Stratified epithelia are defined as epithelia consisting of two or more layers of cells. Stratified epithelia have mainly a protective function and the degree and nature of the stratification are related to the kinds of physical stresses to which the surface is exposed. In general, stratified epithelia are poorly suited for absorption and secretion by virtue of their thickness, although some stratified surfaces are moderately permeable to water and other small molecules. The classification of stratified epithelia is based on the shape and structure of the surface cells since cells of the basal layer are usually cuboidal in shape. ***Transitional epithelium*** is a stratified epithelium found only in the urinary outflow tract with special features to make it waterproof as well as expansile.

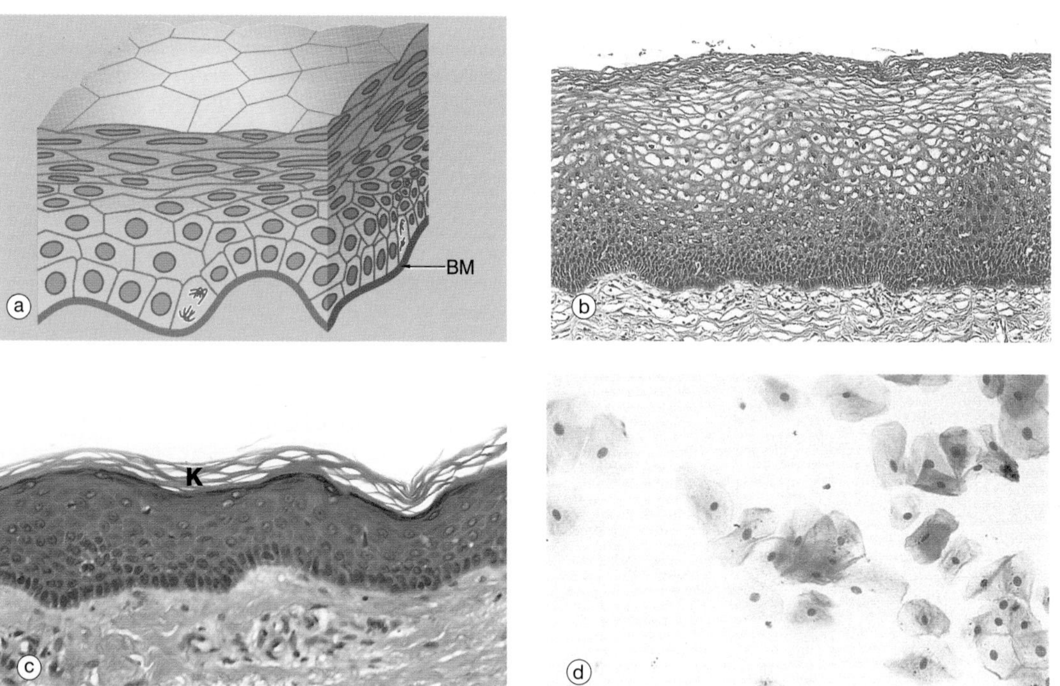

Fig. 5.6 Stratified squamous epithelium
(a) Diagram (b) H & E ×100 (c) H & E ×200 (d) Papanicolaou ×400

Stratified squamous epithelium consists of a variable number of cell layers that exhibit maturation from a cuboidal basal layer adherent to the underlying basement membrane to a flattened surface layer. The basal cells include continuously dividing stem cells, their offspring migrating towards the surface where they are ultimately shed. Stratified squamous epithelium is well adapted to withstand abrasion since loss of surface cells does not compromise the underlying tissue; it is poorly adapted to withstand desiccation. This type of epithelium lines the oral cavity, pharynx, oesophagus, anal canal, uterine cervix and vagina, sites which are subject to mechanical abrasion but which are kept moist by glandular secretions.

The epithelium in micrograph (b) is from the uterine cervix. Note the cuboidal basal layer and the maturation through the large polygonal cells of the intermediate layers to the flattened superficial squamous cells.

Keratinising stratified squamous epithelium (micrograph c) constitutes the epithelial surface of the skin (the ***epidermis***) and is adapted to withstand the constant abrasion and desiccation to which the body surface is exposed. During maturation, the epithelial cells accumulate cross-linked cytokeratin intermediate filaments in a process called ***keratinisation*** resulting in the formation of a tough, non-living surface layer of ***squames*** consisting of the protein ***keratin*** **K** wrapped in residual plasma membrane (see Ch. 9). The nuclei of the maturing epithelial cells become progressively condensed (pyknotic) and eventually disappear. Keratinisation may be induced in normally non-keratinising stratified squamous epithelium such as that of the oral cavity when exposed to excessive abrasion (e.g. poorly-fitting false teeth).

Micrograph (d) shows a smear made from normal cells scraped from the uterine cervix as it projects into the vagina. The degenerate, scaly superficial cells stain pink with this staining method, while the living cells from deeper layers stain blue.

BM basement membrane **K** keratin layer **Ke** abnormal keratinisation **U** umbrella cell

Carcinoma

Cancer is the colloquial term for almost any malignant tumour. The term ***carcinoma*** refers specifically to malignant tumours arising from epithelium, while ***lymphoma*** specifies malignant tumours of lymphoid tissue, ***sarcoma*** describes tumours arising from muscle, blood vessels and supporting tissues such as bone. Classification of malignant tumours is important because different tumours behave differently and respond to different treatments. Further classification of carcinomas gives us ***adenocarcinomas***, arising from glandular epithelium, ***transitional cell carcinomas*** from transitional epithelium and ***squamous cell carcinomas*** (see Fig. 5.7) that derive from stratified squamous epithelium as well as other less common types.

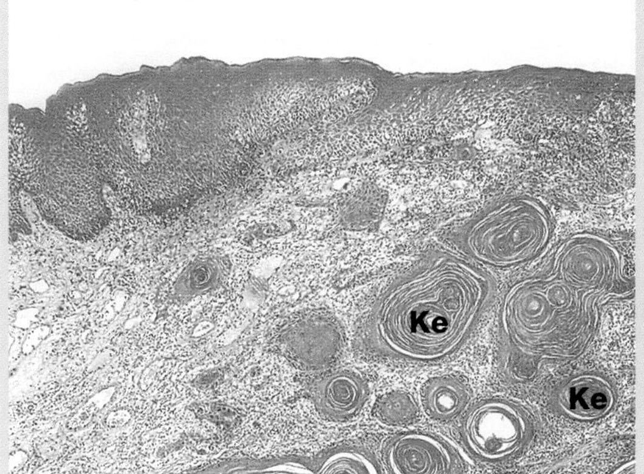

Fig. 5.7 Squamous cell carcinoma

This micrograph is a typical squamous cell carcinoma arising in the skin and taken at lower magnification than Fig. 5.6c of normal skin. Note the disorganised abnormal squamous epithelium that has penetrated through the basement membrane and is invading the underlying dermis. The nests of malignant squamous cells contain central swirls of keratin (keratin pearls) **Ke**, recapitulating the normal keratin production of the epidermis of the skin. Keratinisation is a feature by which squamous carcinoma may be recognised.

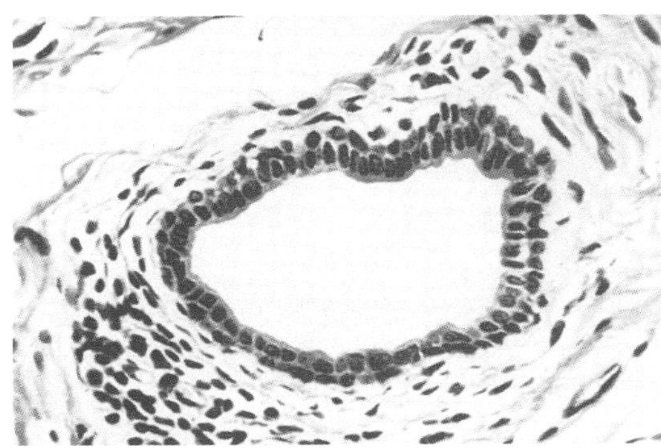

Fig. 5.8 Stratified cuboidal epithelium
H & E ×320

Stratified cuboidal epithelium is a thin, stratified epithelium that usually consists of only two or three layers of cuboidal cells. This type of epithelium is usually confined to the lining of the larger excretory ducts of exocrine glands such as the salivary glands. Stratified cuboidal epithelium is probably not involved in significant absorptive or secretory activity but merely provides a more robust lining than would be afforded by a simple epithelium.

Fig. 5.9 Transitional epithelium
(a) Diagram (b) H & E ×320

Transitional epithelium (or ***urothelium***) is a form of stratified epithelium found only in the urinary tract in mammals where it is highly specialised to accommodate a great degree of stretch and to withstand the toxicity of urine. This epithelial type is so named because it has some features intermediate (transitional) between stratified cuboidal and stratified squamous epithelia. In the non-distended state, transitional epithelium appears to be about four to five cell layers thick. The basal cells are roughly cuboidal, the intermediate cells are polygonal and the surface cells (***umbrella*** or ***dome cells*** **U**) are large and rounded and may contain two nuclei. In the stretched state, transitional epithelium often appears only two or three cells thick (although the actual number of layers remains constant) and the intermediate and surface layers are extremely flattened.

Micrograph (b) shows the appearance of transitional epithelium from the lining of a contracted bladder. The shape and apparent size of the basal and intermediate cells vary considerably depending on the degree of distension, but the cells of the surface layer usually retain characteristic features. Firstly, the surface cells are large and pale stained with a scalloped surface outline often overlapping two or more of the underlying cells and thus known as umbrella cells. Secondly, the luminal surface of the cells appears thickened and more densely stained.

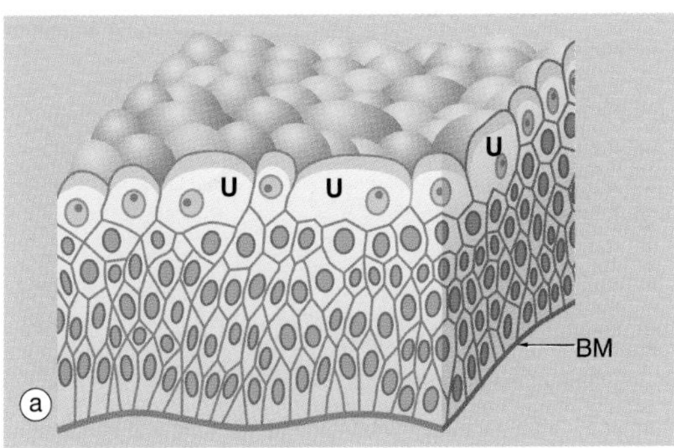

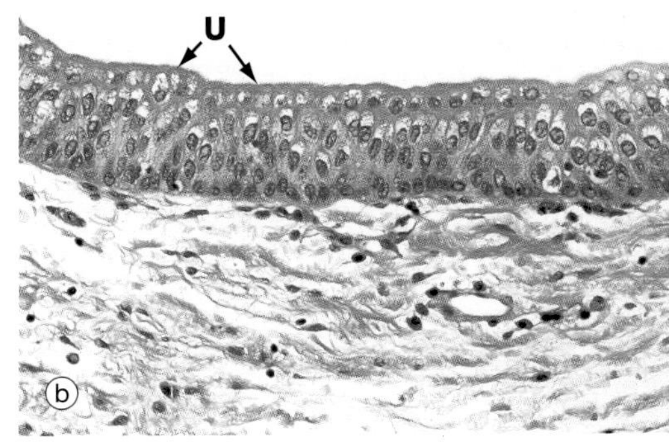

Membrane specializations of epithelia

The plasma membranes of epithelial cells exhibit a variety of specialised structures that allow them to perform their function as a barrier with selective permeability. In some cases the epithelial barrier is very impermeable, e.g. the transitional epithelium of the bladder, while other epithelia such as the lining of the small intestine or the convoluted tubules of the kidney promote movement of selected ions and molecules across the epithelium.

Intercellular surfaces

The adjacent or lateral surfaces of epithelial cells are linked by ***cell junctions*** so that the epithelium forms a continuous cohesive layer. Cell junctions also operate as communication channels governing such functions as growth and cell division. The various types of cell junction are composed of transmembrane proteins that interact with similar proteins on adjacent cells and are linked to intracellular structures on the cytoplasmic side.

Cell junctions are of three functional types:

- **Tight junctions (occluding junctions)** block the passage of molecules between adjacent cells. These are located immediately beneath the luminal surface of simple columnar epithelium (e.g. intestinal lining) where they seal the intercellular spaces so that luminal contents cannot penetrate between the lining cells. Each tight junction forms a continuous circumferential band or zonule around the cell and is thus also known as a ***zonula occludens***.
- **Zonula adherens (adhering belt)** and ***desmosomes*** give the epithelium strength by linking the cytoskeletons of adjacent cells. Adhering junctions bind to the actin cytoskeleton of the cell. In simple columnar epithelia, the ***zonula adherens*** forms a continuous band around the cell just deep to the zonula occludens to form a contractile circumferential band near the apical surface of the cell. Desmosomes (***macula adherens*** or ***spot adhering junctions***) also provide strong attachment between adjacent cells, but in this case they link the intermediate filaments (***keratins*** in epithelium) to form a robust structural framework for the entire epithelium. Desmosomes are found circumferentially arranged around columnar epithelial cells deep to the adhering junction. The combination of zonula occludens, zonula adherens and desmosomes is known as a ***junctional complex.*** The junctional complex essentially divides the plasma membrane of the cell into the apical and basolateral surfaces. Desmosomes are also widely scattered elsewhere in epithelial intercellular interfaces.
- **Communicating junctions**, also known as ***gap*** or ***nexus junctions***, provide a conduit for the passage of small molecules directly between adjacent cells. These junctions allow signalling by the passage of small molecules between adjacent cells to coordinate and synchronise functions of the epithelium.

Adhering junctions and communicating junctions are not exclusive to epithelia and are also present in cardiac and visceral muscle where they appear to serve similar functions.

Luminal surfaces

The luminal or ***apical surfaces*** of epithelial cells may incorporate three main types of specialisation: ***cilia***, ***microvilli*** and ***stereocilia***. Cilia are actively motile structures that are easily resolved by light microscopy. In contrast, microvilli are shorter projections of the plasma membrane that cannot be individually resolved with the light microscope. A single cell may have thousands of microvilli or only a few. Stereocilia are merely extremely long microvilli usually found only singly or in small numbers; stereocilia are not motile and are thus quite inappropriately named.

Basal surfaces

The interface between all epithelia and underlying supporting tissues is marked by a non-cellular structure known as the ***basement membrane*** (see Ch. 4) that provides structural support for the epithelium and constitutes a selective barrier to the passage of materials between epithelium and supporting tissue. ***Hemidesmosomes***, a variant of desmosomes, bind the base of the cell to the underlying basement membrane by linking to the cell's intermediate filament network.

BM basement membrane **CJ** communicating junctions **D** desmosome **HD** hemidesmosome
IF intermediate filaments **Mf** microfilaments **Mv** microvillus **TJ** tight junction **TW** terminal web
ZA zonula adherens

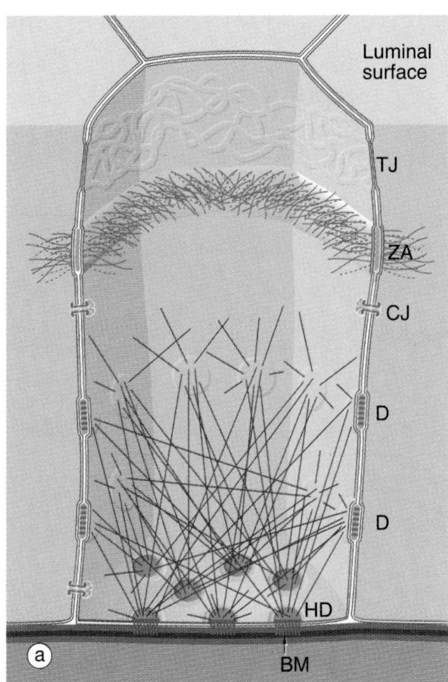

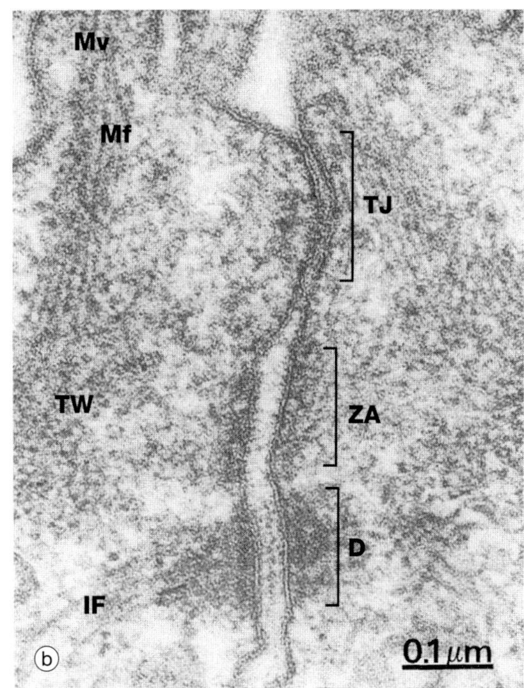

Fig. 5.10 Intercellular junctions
(a) Schematic diagram (b) Junctional complex, EM ×125 000

The illustration (a) demonstrates, in a highly schematic manner, the three-dimensional organisation of the various intercellular junctions and their interaction with the cytoskeleton. In simple cuboidal and simple columnar epithelia, a junctional complex encircles each cell sealing the intercellular spaces and holding the cells tightly together.

As seen in micrograph (b) of intestinal columnar epithelium, the junctional complex at the luminal end of the lateral plasma membrane is made up of three components: a tight junction **TJ** (zonula occludens), an adhering belt (zonula adherens) **ZA** and a row of desmosomes **D**. The bases of microvilli **Mv** covering the surface of the small intestinal lining cells can be identified. Each microvillus contains a core of actin microfilaments **Mf** which insert into the terminal web **TW** (see Fig. 5.15). As mentioned opposite, actin microfilaments are anchored to the zonula adherens and keratin intermediate filaments **IF** bind to desmosomes.

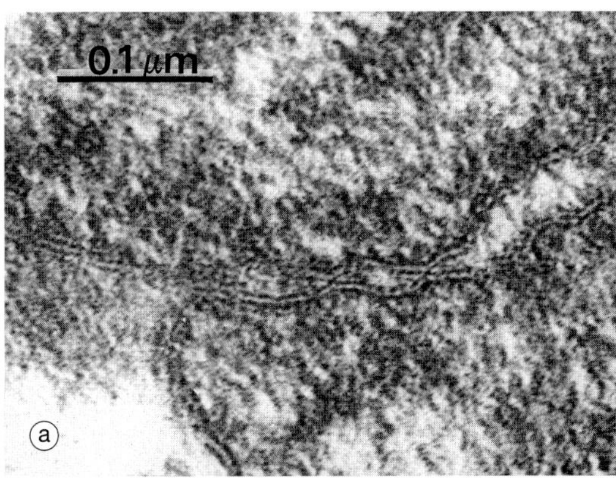

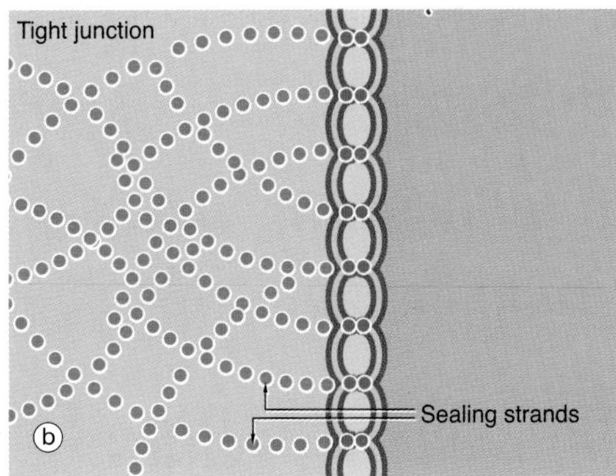

Fig. 5.11 Tight junctions
(a) EM × 190 000 (b) schematic diagram

The tight junction (occluding junction or zonula occludens) forms a collar around each cell immediately beneath the apical surface, blocking passage of luminal contents between cells. As seen in this electron micrograph, the outer electron-dense layers of opposing cell membranes come extremely close together and in places, appear to fuse completely. At the molecular level, transmembrane proteins form the so-called ***sealing strands*** that 'stitch' the membranes together in the manner of two pieces of cloth haphazardly stitched together on a sewing machine (see diagram b). Continuing this analogy, each 'stitch' comprises two molecules of the transmembrane protein ***claudin,*** one an integral part of each opposing plasma membrane, linked tightly together. On the cytoplasmic side of the plasma membrane, the tight junctions are linked to the actin cytoskeleton.

As well as sealing the intercellular space from the luminal environment, tight junctions maintain the polarisation of the cell by separating the proteins of the apical and basolateral plasma membrane compartments. Structurally similar but discontinuous strips of tight junction called ***fascia occludens*** are found between the endothelial cells lining blood vessels, except in the vessels of the brain where they are of the continuous (zonula occludens) type.

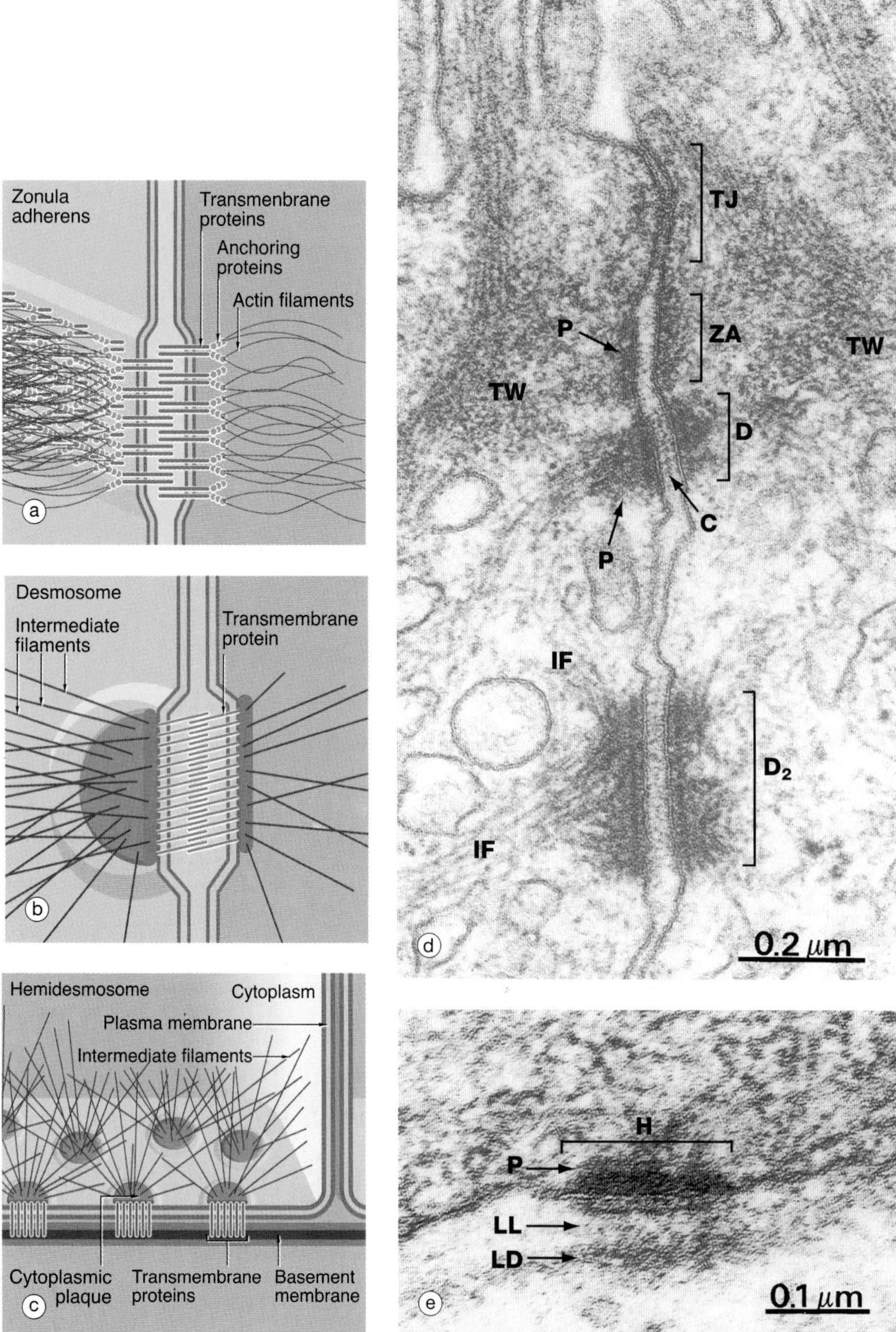

Fig. 5.12 Adhering junctions
(a), (b) and (c) Diagrams (d) EM × 95 000 (e) EM ×150 000

Adhering junctions provide anchorage points for cytoskeletal elements, linking the cytoskeletons of individual cells into a strong transcellular network. These junctions are of three types; the adhesion belt (zonula adherens) and the desmosome (macula adherens) link adjacent cells and the ***hemidesmosome*** links the cell to the underlying basement membrane. The zonula adherens forms a single continuous band lying deep to the tight junction at the luminal end of the lateral plasma membranes of columnar epithelium. Deep to the zonula adherens there is ring of desmosomes, the third component of the junctional complex. Larger desmosomes are also scattered over the intercellular surfaces of all epithelial cells. Adhering junctions consist of three components: ***transmembrane proteins*** bind to similar proteins on adjacent cells (zonula adherens and desmosomes) or to extracellular matrix (hemidesmosomes), and ***anchoring proteins*** on the cytoplasmic side of the junction that link the transmembrane proteins to the third component, the ***cytoskeleton***.

- **Zonula adherens** (a) have transmembrane proteins that are ***cadherins***. The cadherins span the plasma membranes of the cells and bind to identical cadherins on adjacent cells. The cytoplasmic tails of the cadherins bind to anchor proteins (***catenins***, ***vinculin*** and ***α-actinin***) which in turn bind to actin molecules. The intracellular component of the zonula adherens can be seen as a small electron-dense ***plaque*** **P** on the cytoplasmic side of the plasma membrane.
- **Desmosomes** (b) also use cadherins as their transmembrane proteins. The overlapping segments of the cadherin molecules in the intercellular space

form an electron-dense line **C**. On the cytoplasmic side, anchoring proteins (***desmoplakin*** and ***plakoglobin***) bind to intermediate filaments **IF** forming a prominent electron-dense plaque **P** on the inner aspect of the desmosome. Desmosome numbers are greatest in stratified squamous epithelia, that have to withstand the greatest friction.

- **Hemidesmosomes** (c) are modified desmosomes that are found at the basal surface of the cell. In this case the transmembrane proteins are ***integrins***, the extracellular components of which bind to extracellular ***laminins*** in the basement membrane (see Ch. 4). The intracellular component of the integrins binds to the anchor protein, ***plectin*** and thus to the intermediate filament keratin. Again the intracellular component can be seen as an electron-dense plaque **P**.

Micrograph (d) from the intestinal lining illustrates a junctional complex comprising tight junction **TJ**, zonula adherens **ZA** and desmosome **D**. At a deeper level, a larger desmosome $\mathbf{D_2}$ is seen. Note the small electron-dense plaque **P** of the zonula adherens and the larger plaques **P** of the desmosomes. The electron-dense line created by overlapping cadherin molecules **C** is also visible in the desmosomes.

Micrograph (e) illustrates a hemidesmosome **H** along the basal plasma membrane of an epithelial cell. On the cytoplasmic aspect of the plasma membrane is the protein plaque **P**. The underlying lamina densa **LD** is thickened and more electron-dense than usual as is the lamina lucida **LL** which contains an electron-dense line. This appearance is the result of binding of the extracellular component of the integrins to the laminins of the basement membrane.

Fig. 5.13 Gap junctions

(a) EM × 80 000 (b) Diagram

Communicating or gap junctions are broad patches where adjacent plasma membranes are closely opposed leaving a narrow intervening gap 2–4 nm in diameter. A gap junction **G** is demonstrated in micrograph (a) taken from intestinal epithelium.

As seen in diagram (b), each gap junction contains numerous transmembrane channels (***connexons***) that permit the passage of inorganic ions and other small molecules (approximately 1.5 nm in diameter) from the cytoplasm of one cell to another. Large molecules and negatively charged ions are denied access. Gap junctions are thought to be important in the control of growth, development, cell recognition and differentiation. Gap junctions also provide the means of electrical coupling of visceral and cardiac muscle cells permitting synchronous contraction.

Each connexon is made up of six transmembrane proteins known as ***connexins***. Each connexon aligns with a connexon of a neighbouring cell to form a direct channel between the two cells. There are more than 20 different connexin proteins in humans and these form specific connexons in different tissues with specificity for different molecules and ions. Connexons may be opened or closed depending on the intracellular concentration of calcium ions, the pH or on extracellular signals. For instance the neurotransmitter dopamine closes gap junctions between certain nerve cells in the retina. A rise in intracellular calcium concentration, a feature of cell death, also closes connexons and this mechanism appears to provide a means of sealing off apoptotic cells and their potentially noxious contents from adjacent viable cells.

Communicating junctions are more numerous in embryonic epithelia where they appear to be involved in exchange of chemical messengers, in cell recognition, differentiation and control of cell position. They are also probably involved in the passage of nutrients from cells deep in the epithelium (adjacent to supporting tissues and blood vessels) to cells more remote from the nutritional supply.

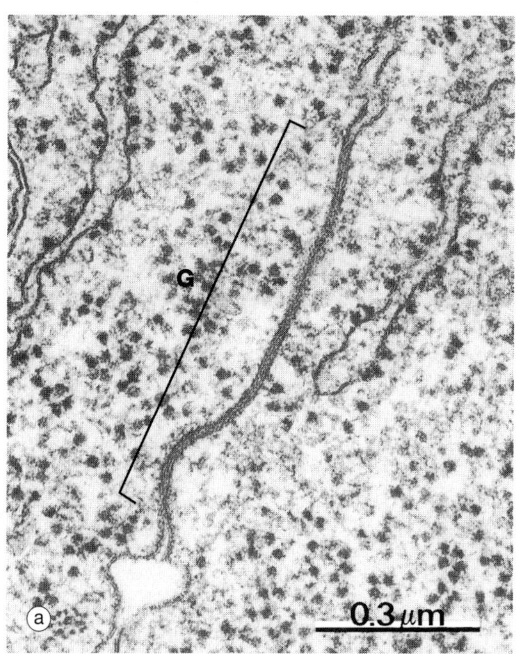

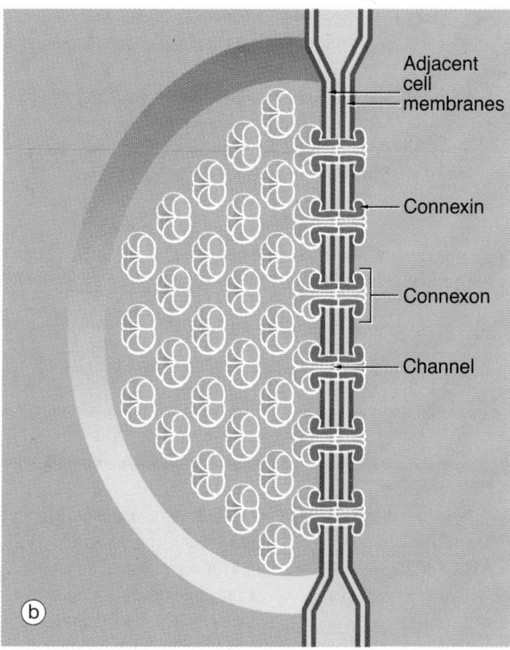

C overlapping cadherins **D** spot desmosome $\mathbf{D_2}$ individual desmosome **G** gap junction
H hemidesmosome **IF** intermediate filaments **LD** lamina densa **LL** lamina lucida
P cytoplasmic plaque **TJ** tight junction **TW** terminal web **ZA** zonula adherens

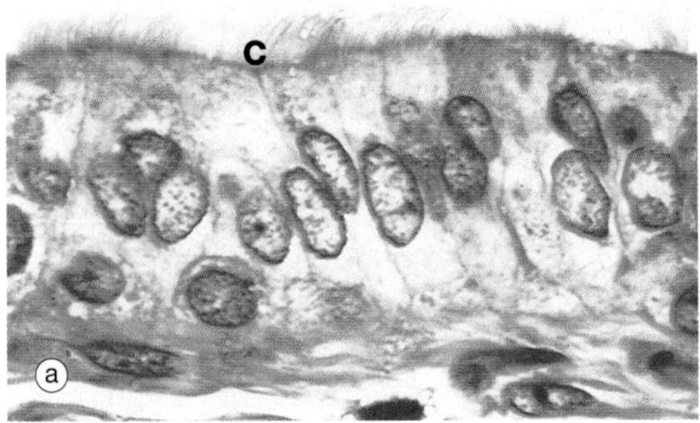

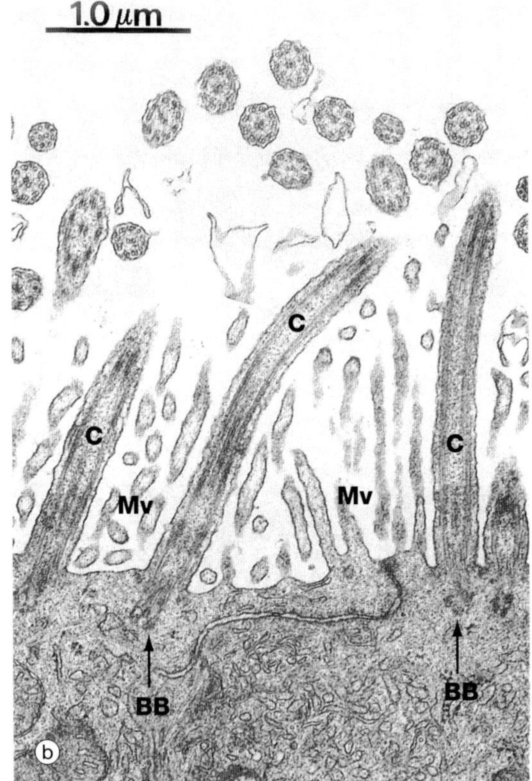

Fig. 5.14 Cilia
(a) Thin section, toluidine blue ×800 (b) EM ×20 000
(c) Schematic diagram

Cilia are motile structures that project from the apical surfaces of certain epithelial cells, notably in the respiratory and female reproductive tracts. Cilia beat with a wave-like synchronous rhythm propelling surface films of mucus or fluid in a consistent direction over the epithelial surface. In the airways, mucus traps debris from inspired air and the cilia move the mucus towards the throat where it is swallowed thus keeping the airways clean. In the Fallopian tubes, ciliary action propels the ovum from the ovary to the uterus. Cilia are up to 10 μm long (up to half the height of the cell). A single epithelial cell may have up to 300 cilia usually of similar length.

Micrographs (a) and (b) show ciliated cells from the respiratory tract. Cilia **C** are readily visible with light microscopy. In micrograph (b), the proximal parts of three cilia **C** are seen in longitudinal section and, more superficially, the tips of a number of others otherwise lying outside the plane of section. Small surface microvilli **Mv** are seen between the cilia. Each cilium is bounded by plasma membrane and, as shown in (c), contains a central core called the ***axoneme*** consisting of 20 microtubules arranged as a central pair surrounded by nine peripheral doublets. At the base of the cilium, the microtubule doublets are continuous with the ***basal body*** consisting of nine microtubule triplets. Each peripheral doublet of the cilium axoneme is continuous with the two inner microtubules of the corresponding triplet of the basal body. The basal bodies **BB** are easily seen in (b).

Each axoneme doublet consists of one complete microtubule closely applied to a second incomplete C-shaped tubule. From each complete tubule, pairs of 'arms' consisting of the protein ***dynein***, an ATPase, extend towards the incomplete tubule of the adjacent doublet. Ciliary action results from bending of the doublets first in one direction and then in the other and is fuelled by dynein-catalysed conversion of ATP to ADP.

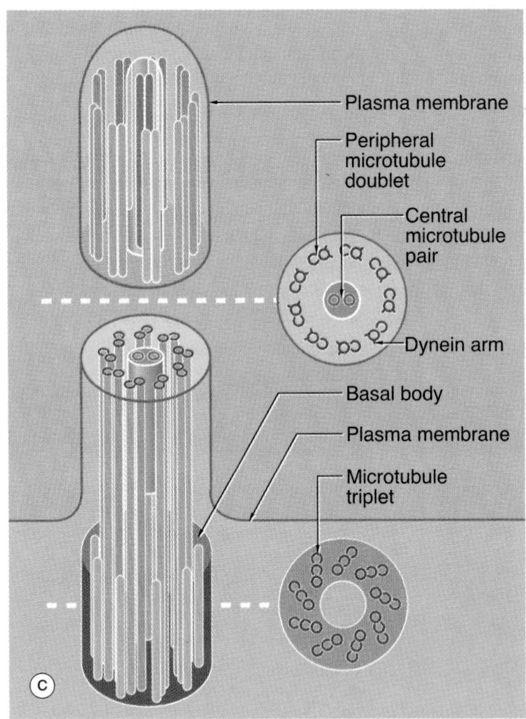

Kartagener's syndrome

Patients with Kartagener's syndrome (or primary ciliary dyskinesia) have bronchiectasis, sinusitis and dextrocardia along with infertility in affected males. These abnormalities arise due to inherited abnormalities in cilia including lack of the dynein arms, missing central microtubule pairs or absence of one of the many other proteins critical for ciliary function. The lung and sinus problems arise due to infections caused by ineffective clearance of mucus. The infertility in males is due to malfunction of the tails of spermatozoa, which have a similar structure to cilia (see Ch. 18). The dextrocardia is due to an inability to determine the right-left axis, a function also mediated by ciliary motion during embryonic development.

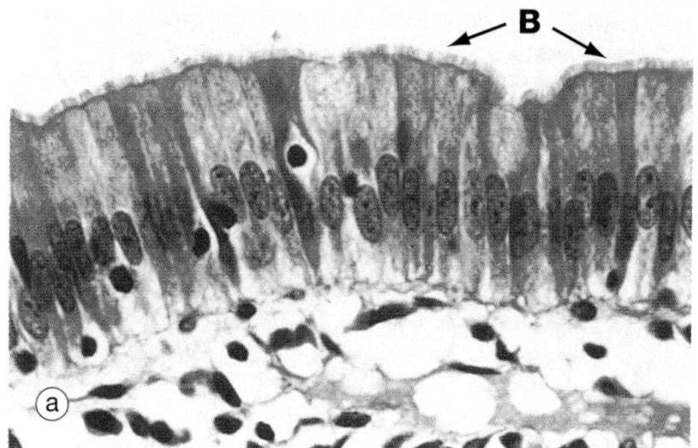

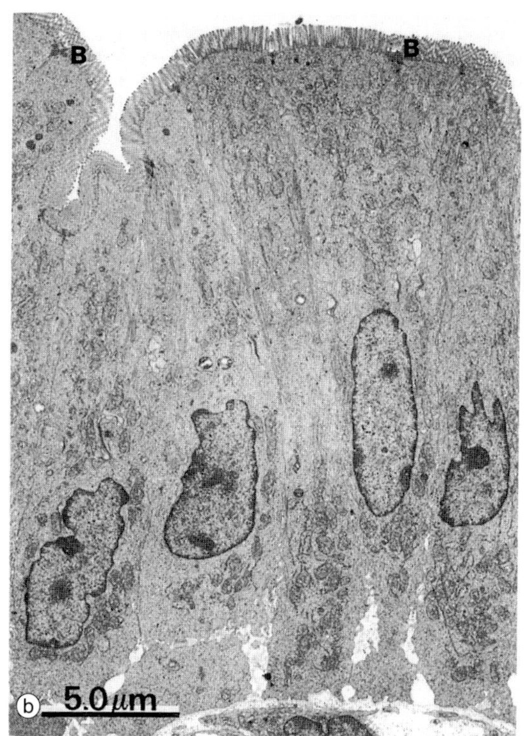

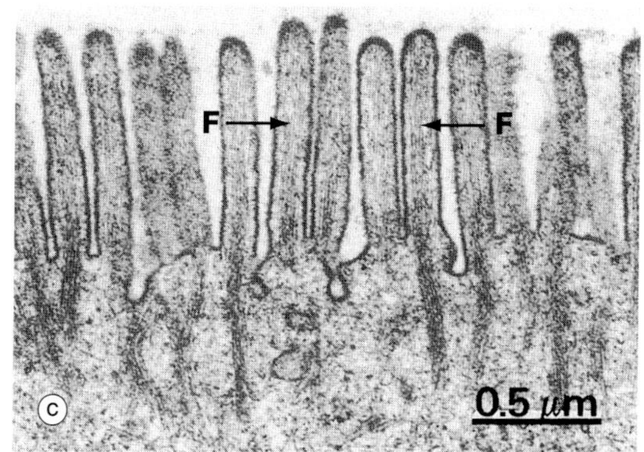

Fig. 5.15 Microvilli
(a) H & E × 320 (b) EM × 4000 (c) EM × 30 000

Microvilli are minute finger-like projections of the luminal plasma membrane found in many epithelia, particularly those specialised for absorption where their presence may increase the surface area as much as 30-fold. Microvilli are only 0.5–1.0 μm in length and are thus very short in relation to the size of the cell, a feature contrasting markedly with cilia. Furthermore, individual microvilli are too small to be resolved by light microscopy. Microvilli should not be confused with villi; the difference between the two is made clear in Fig. 14.18.

Most epithelia have only a small number of irregular microvilli. However, in the small intestine and proximal renal tubules the epithelial cells have up to 3000 regular microvilli per cell and these can be seen with the light microscope as so-called ***striated*** or ***brush borders***. Micrographs (a) and (b) illustrate the typical features of microvilli constituting the brush border **B** of cells lining the small intestine.

As seen at higher magnification in micrograph (c), the cytoplasmic core of each microvillus contains actin microfilaments **F** which insert into the ***terminal web***, a specialisation of the actin cytoskeleton lying immediately beneath the cell surface. At the periphery of the cell the terminal web is anchored to the zonula adherens (see Fig. 5.12). At the tip of the microvillus, the filaments attach to an electron-dense part of the plasma membrane. The microfilaments maintain stability of microvilli and may also mediate some contraction and elongation of the microvilli.

Fig. 5.16 Stereocilia
H & E ×320

Extremely long microvilli, readily visible with light microscopy, are found in small numbers in parts of the male reproductive tract such as the epididymis (shown in this micrograph). Originally, these structures were thought to be an unusual form of cilia and were termed stereocilia; however, electron microscopy has shown that they do not have the internal structure of cilia but merely an actin microfilament skeleton like that of microvilli. Stereocilia **S** are thought to facilitate absorptive processes in the epididymis but the reason for their unusual form is not known.

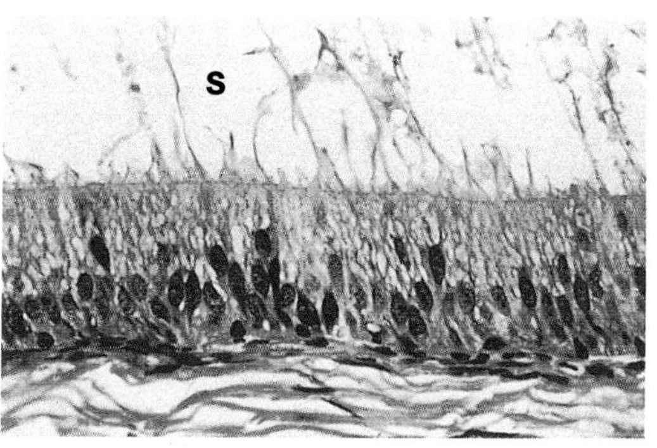

B brush border **BB** basal body **C** cilia **F** microfilaments **Mv** microvilli **S** stereocilia

Fig. 5.17 Goblet cell
PAS/haematoxylin ×800

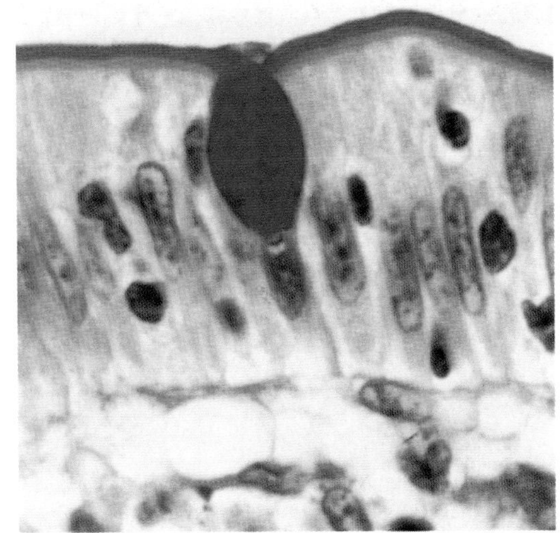

Goblet cells are modified columnar epithelial cells that synthesise and secrete mucus. Goblet cells are scattered amongst the cells of many simple epithelial linings, particularly those of the respiratory and gastrointestinal tracts, and are named for their resemblance to drinking goblets.

The distended apical cytoplasm contains a dense aggregation of mucigen granules which, when released by exocytosis, combine with water to form the viscid secretion called mucus. Mucigen is composed of a mixture of neutral and acidic proteoglycans (mucopolysaccharides) and therefore can be readily demonstrated by the PAS method which stains carbohydrates magenta. The 'stem' of the goblet cell is occupied by a condensed, basal nucleus and is crammed with other organelles involved in mucigen synthesis.

In this example from the lining of the small intestine, note the tall columnar nature of the surrounding absorptive cells. The PAS-positive surface coating is not only due to secreted mucus but also to the presence of a thick glycocalyx (see Ch. 1) on the numerous microvilli which characterise small intestine absorptive cells.

Fig. 5.18 Goblet cell
EM ×5000

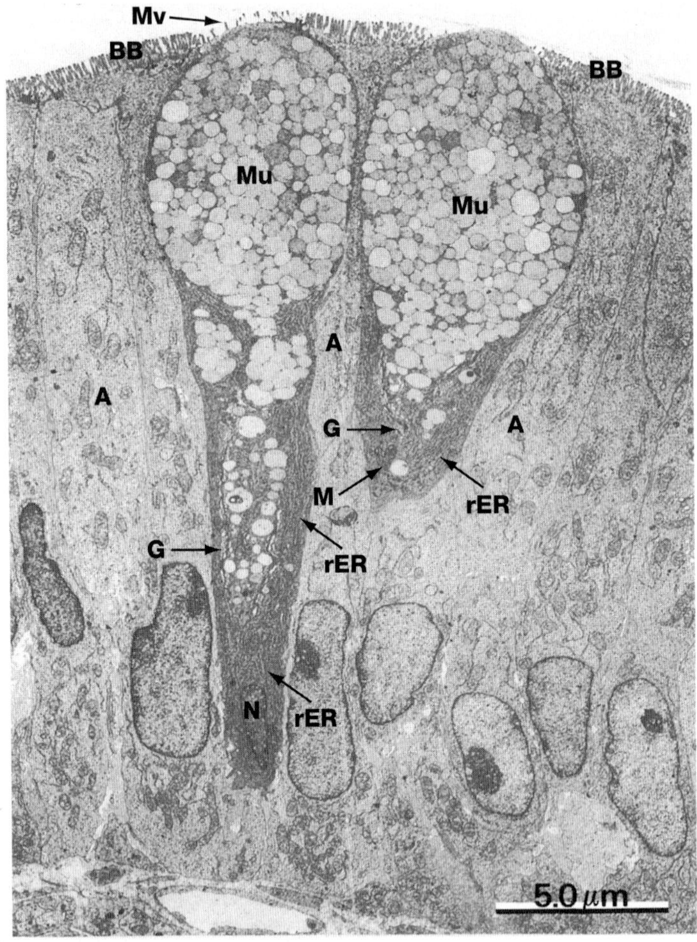

This micrograph shows two goblet cells among columnar absorptive cells **A** (or enterocytes) of the small intestine. The nucleus of the goblet cell on the right is outside the plane of section, the nucleus **N** of the other being typically highly condensed (see also Fig. 14.23 showing a goblet cell in horizontal section). The cytoplasm is packed with rough endoplasmic reticulum **rER**; a few mitochondria **M** are present. A prominent Golgi apparatus **G** is found in the supranuclear region although it is barely visible at this magnification.

The protein component of mucigen is synthesised by the rough endoplasmic reticulum and passed to the Golgi apparatus where it is combined with carbohydrate and packaged into membrane-bound, secretory granules containing mucigen **Mu**. Goblet cells secrete at a steady basal rate and may be stimulated by local irritation to release their entire mucigen contents. Sparse microvilli **Mv** are seen at the surface of the goblet cell and may be associated with the secretory process. Note the microvilli forming the brush border **BB** of the absorptive cells.

Mucus has a variety of functions. In the upper gastrointestinal tract it protects the intestinal lining cells from autodigestion whilst in the lower tract it lubricates the passage of faeces. In the respiratory tract it protects the lining from drying, contributes to the humidification of inspired air and acts as a sticky surface trap for fine dust particles and microorganisms.

A absorptive cells **BB** brush border **G** Golgi apparatus **M** mitochondria **Mu** mucigen granules **Mv** microvilli **N** nucleus **rER** rough endoplasmic reticulum

Exocrine glands

As discussed earlier in this chapter, epithelial cells are the major component of all the glands of the body. The simplest glands can be easily recognised as an invagination of a surface epithelium. However increasingly complex glandular structures have evolved over time and some of the most elaborate have lost contact with the epithelial surface completely. This gives us the two major subdivisions in the classification of glands: ***exocrine glands***, which release their contents onto an epithelial surface either directly or via a duct, and ***endocrine glands***, which have no duct system but by releasing their secretions into the bloodstream can act on distant tissues. Endocrine glands are dealt with briefly at the end of this chapter and in much more detail in Chapter 17.

This section deals with exocrine glands, which vary from microscopic such as sweat glands of the skin to large solid organs such as the liver weighing approximately 1.5 kg. The duct system of the liver ramifies throughout the solid gland and empties its secretions (bile) into the duodenum. In contrast the simple tubular glands (crypts) of the large bowel (see also Ch. 14) consist entirely of the secretory component and empty directly onto the surface of the bowel. Indeed the simplest exocrine glands of all are single mucus-secreting cells such as goblet cells.

Exocrine glands may be subclassified according to two major characteristics as described below.

1. The morphology of the gland

Exocrine glands can be divided into the ***secretory component*** and the ***duct***.

- The duct system may be branched (***compound gland***) or unbranched (***simple gland***).
- The secretory component may be ***tubular*** or ***acinar*** (roughly spherical).
- Both types of secretory component may also be ***coiled*** or ***branched***.
- Almost any combination of duct and secretory component may occur (see Figs 5.19 to 5.26).

2. The means of secretion

Secretion from exocrine glands may occur in one of three ways:

- **Merocrine (eccrine) secretion** involves the process of exocytosis and is the most common form of secretion; proteins are usually the major secretory product.
- **Apocrine secretion** involves the discharge of free, unbroken, membrane-bound vesicles containing secretory product; this is an unusual mode of secretion and applies to lipid secretory products in the breasts and some sweat glands.
- **Holocrine secretion** involves the discharge of whole secretory cells with subsequent disintegration of the cells to release the secretory product. Holocrine secretion occurs principally in sebaceous glands.

In general, all glands have a continuous basal rate of secretion, which is modulated by nervous and hormonal influences. The secretory portions of some exocrine glands are surrounded by contractile cells that lie between the secretory cells and the basement membrane. The contractile mechanism of these cells is similar to that of muscle cells and has given rise to the term ***myoepithelial cells*** as these cells share characteristics of both epithelial and muscle cells.

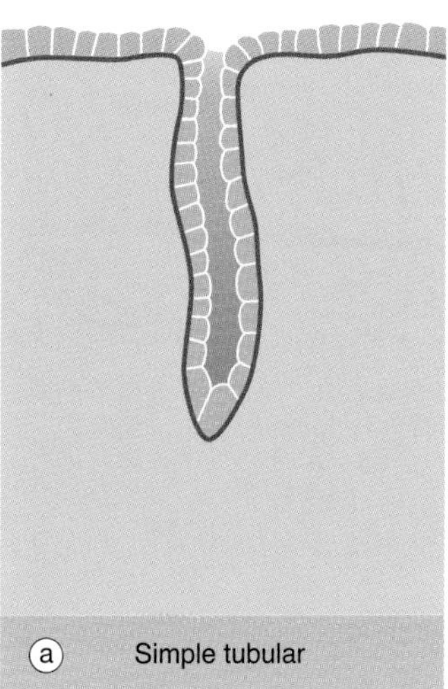

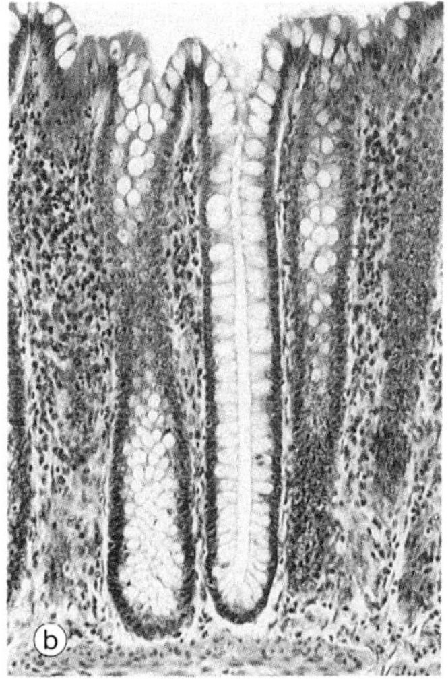

Fig. 5.19 Simple tubular glands
(a) Diagram (b) H & E ×50

This example of simple tubular glands is taken from the large intestine. This type of gland has a single, straight tubular lumen into which the secretory products are discharged. In this example, secretory cells line the entire duct; the secretory cells are goblet cells. At other sites mucus is secreted by columnar cells that do not have the classic goblet shape but nonetheless function in a similar manner.

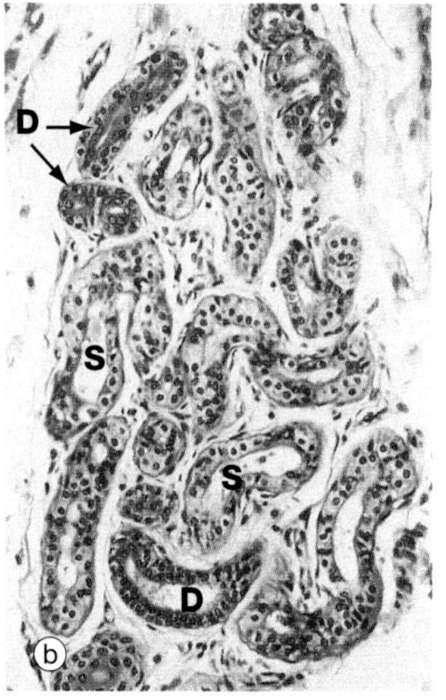

Fig. 5.20 Simple coiled tubular glands
(a) Diagram (b) H & E ×80

Sweat glands are almost the only example of simple coiled tubular glands. Each consists of a single tube that is tightly coiled in three dimensions; portions of the gland are thus seen in various planes of section. Sweat glands have a terminal secretory portion **S** lined by simple cuboidal epithelium, which gives way to a non-secretory (excretory) duct **D** lined by stratified cuboidal epithelium.

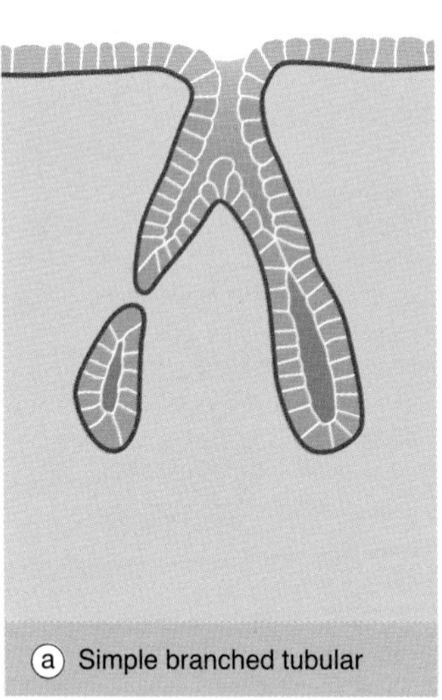

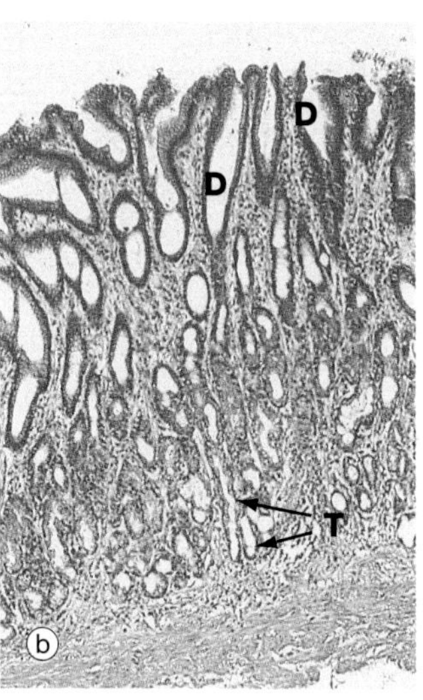

Fig. 5.21 Simple branched tubular glands
(a) Diagram (b) H & E ×60

Simple branched tubular glands are found mainly in the stomach. The mucus-secreting glands of the pyloric part of the stomach are shown in this example. Each gland consists of several tubular secretory portions **T**, which converge onto a single, unbranched duct **D** of wider diameter. Mucus-secreting cells also line the duct but unlike those of the large intestine (see Fig. 5.19), these mucus cells do not have a goblet shape.

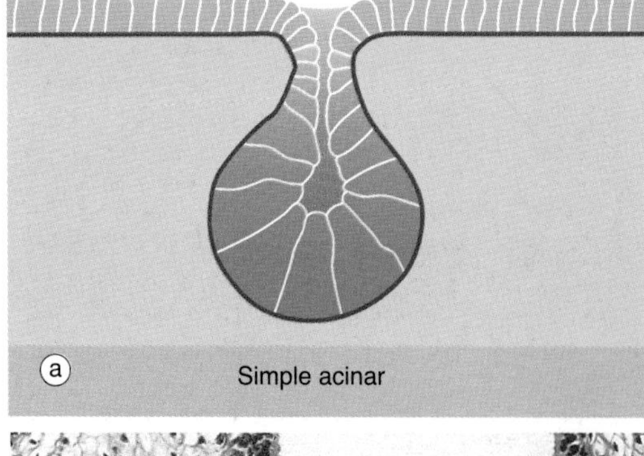

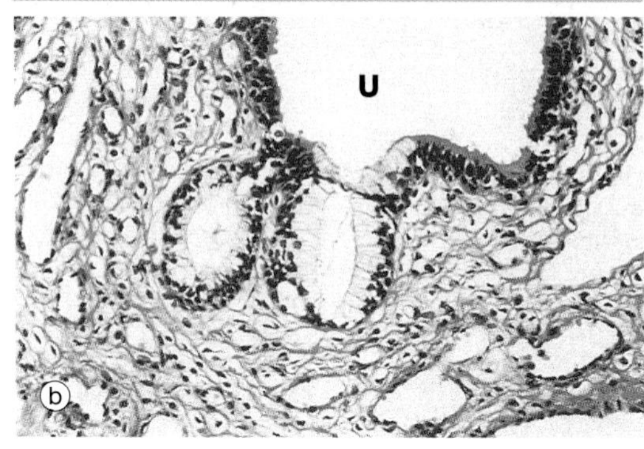

Fig. 5.22 Simple acinar glands
(a) Diagram (b) H & E ×128

Simple acinar glands occur in the form of pockets in epithelial surfaces and are lined by secretory cells. In this example of the mucus-secreting glands of the penile urethra, the secretory cells are pale stained compared to the non-secretory cells lining the urethra **U**. Note that the term ***acinus*** can be used to describe any rounded exocrine secretory unit.

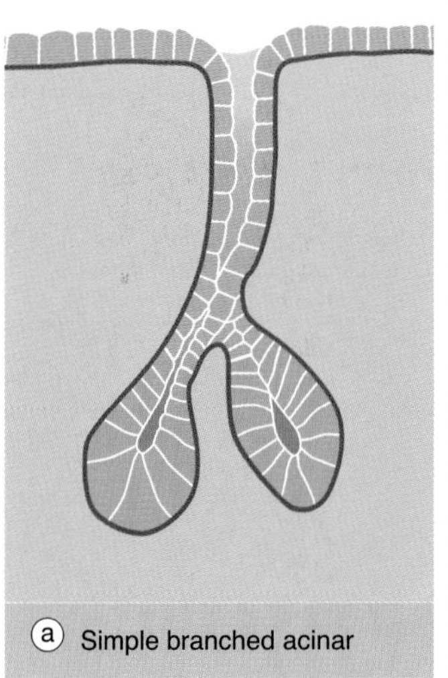

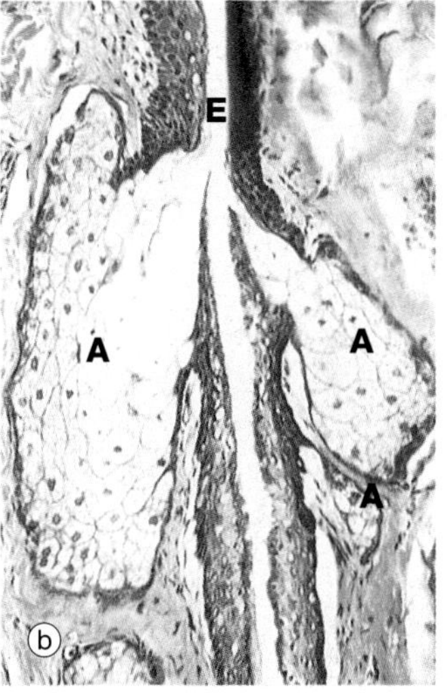

Fig. 5.23 Simple branched acinar gland
(a) Diagram (b) Masson's trichrome ×80

Sebaceous glands provide a good example of simple branched acinar glands. Each gland consists of several secretory acini **A** that empty into a single excretory duct; the excretory duct **E** is formed by the stratified epithelium surrounding the hair shaft. The mode of secretion of sebaceous glands is holocrine, i.e. the secretory product, sebum, accumulates within the secretory cells and is discharged by degeneration of the cells.

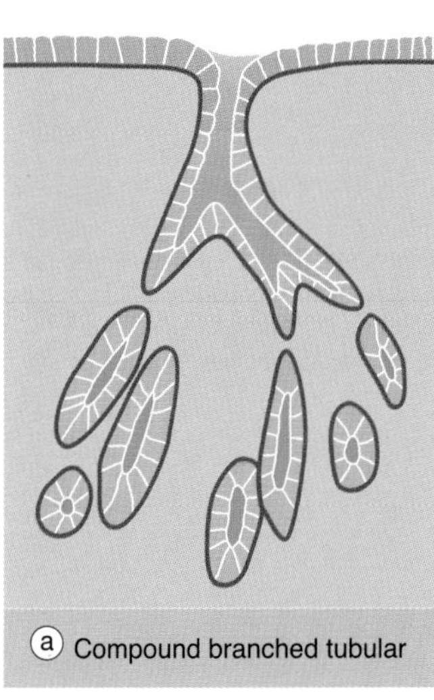

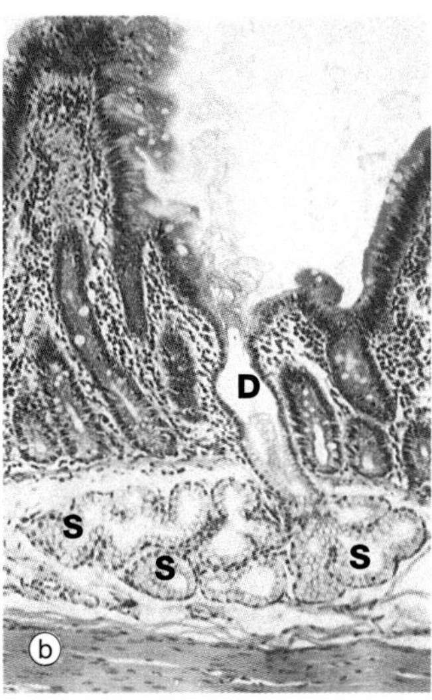

Fig. 5.24 Compound branched tubular gland
(a) Diagram (b) H & E ×20

Brunner's glands of the duodenum, as shown in this example, are described as compound branched tubular glands. Although difficult to visualise here, the duct system **D** is branched, thus defining the glands as compound glands and the secretory portions **S** have a tubular form, which is branched and coiled.

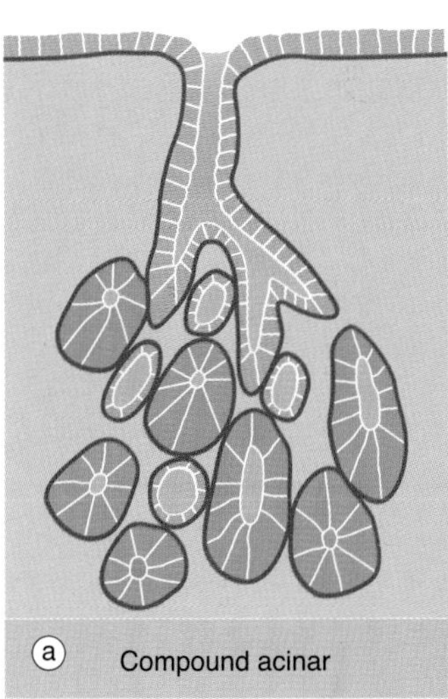

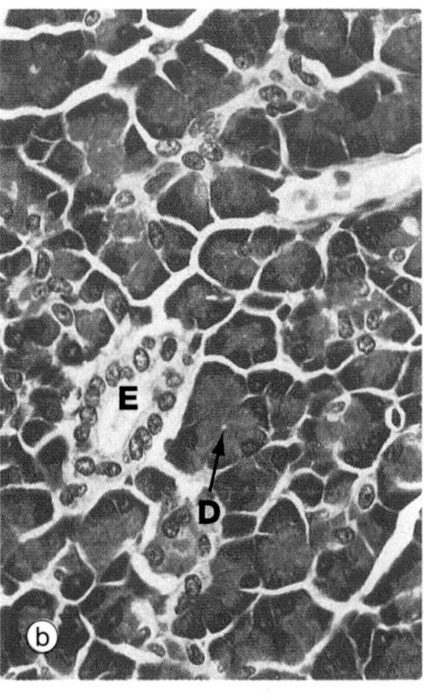

Fig. 5.25 Compound acinar gland
(a) Diagram (b) Chrome alum haematoxylin/phloxine ×320

Compound acinar glands are those in which the secretory units are acinar in form and drain into a branched duct system. The pancreas shown in this micrograph consists of numerous acini, each of which drains into a minute duct. These minute ducts **D**, which are just discernible in the centre of some acini, drain into a system of branched excretory ducts **E** of increasing diameter and lined by simple cuboidal epithelium.

A acinus **D** duct **E** excretory ducts **S** secretory portion **T** tubular secretory portion **U** urethra

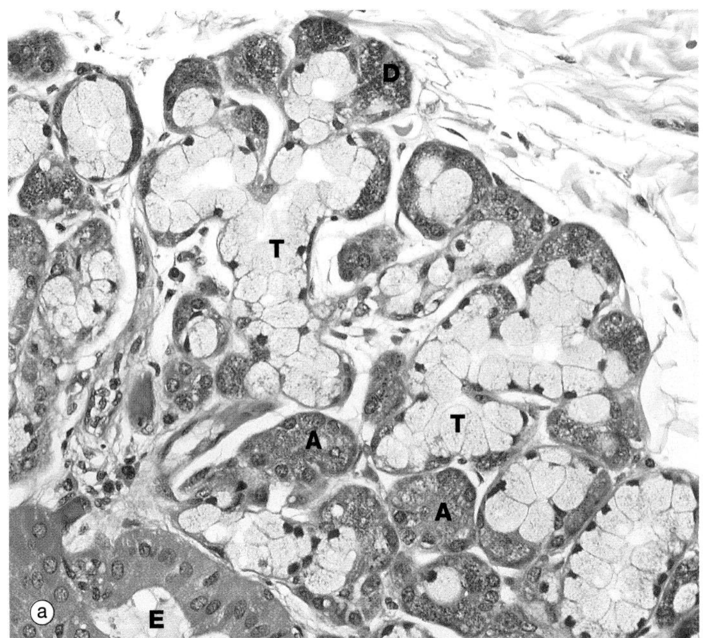

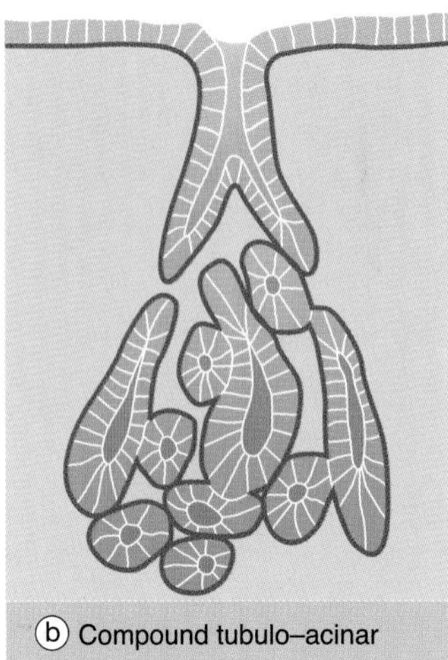

Fig. 5.26 Compound tubulo–acinar gland
H & E ×200

Compound tubulo–acinar glands have three types of secretory units; namely branched tubular, branched acinar and branched tubular with acinar end-pieces called ***demilunes***. The submandibular salivary gland shown here is the classic example. It contains two types of secretory cells, mucus-secreting cells and serous cells; the former are pale but the latter, which have a protein-rich secretion (digestive enzymes), stain strongly due to their large content of rough endoplasmic reticulum. Generally, the mucous cells form tubular components **T** whereas the serous cells form acinar components **A** and demilunes **D**. Part of an excretory duct **E** is also seen in the lower left corner of the micrograph.

Adenocarcinoma

Just as stratified squamous epithelium gives rise to squamous cell carcinoma, tumours arising in glandular epithelium (***adenocarcinomas***) have features that recapitulate to some extent the normal glandular structure of the affected organ. Thus adenocarcinomas are common in the stomach, colon, uterine endometrium and endocervix as well as in solid glands such as the thyroid, breast, liver, prostate and pancreas. All adenocarcinomas have features in common such as the tendency to form glands and to secret mucus, but as in other malignant tumours the copy is a poor likeness of the original consisting of abnormal glands made up of highly atypical cells. Nevertheless it is often possible for the experienced pathologist to identify a particular adenocarcinoma as arising in for instance the breast, prostate or colon as they often have a characteristic appearance.

Endocrine glands

As described earlier, endocrine (or ductless) glands release their secretions directly into the bloodstream rather than via a duct. Endocrine glands are the source of many of the body's chemical messengers, ***hormones*** that act at a distance from their source. For example insulin, secreted by the pancreas (see Ch. 17), acts on muscle and adipose tissue throughout the body to control the metabolism of glucose. Other hormones may act only on a single tissue; thus thyroid-stimulating hormone (TSH) secreted by the pituitary gland is widely disseminated in the blood but only the thyroid gland has the necessary receptors to respond.

Endocrine glands are very varied in their size, location and appearance and are described in more detail in Chapter 17.

- Many are solid organs but some consist of widely distributed single cells.
- Most endocrine glands release more than one hormone product.
- Several endocrine glands consist of more than one type of secretory cell.
- The pancreas is both an endocrine and an exocrine gland because it contains nests of endocrine cells (islets of Langerhans) embedded in a large exocrine gland, the exocrine pancreas (see Ch. 15).
- In general secretion of hormones by endocrine glands is controlled by metabolic factors (e.g. blood glucose levels), the secretion of other hormones (e.g. TSH controls secretion of thyroxine) and the nervous system (e.g. the secretion of adrenaline by the adrenal medulla) or a mixture of all of these factors.

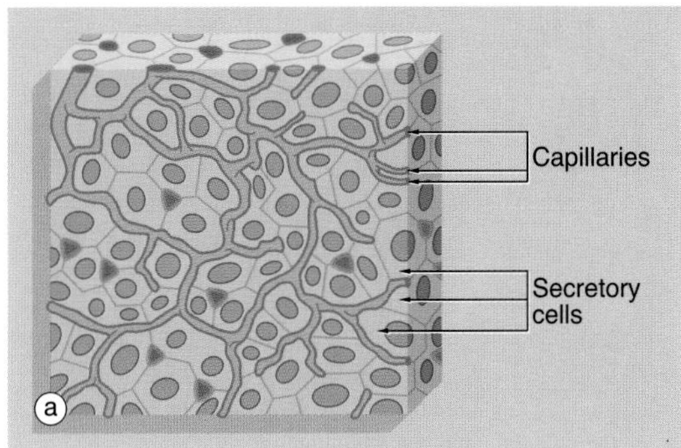

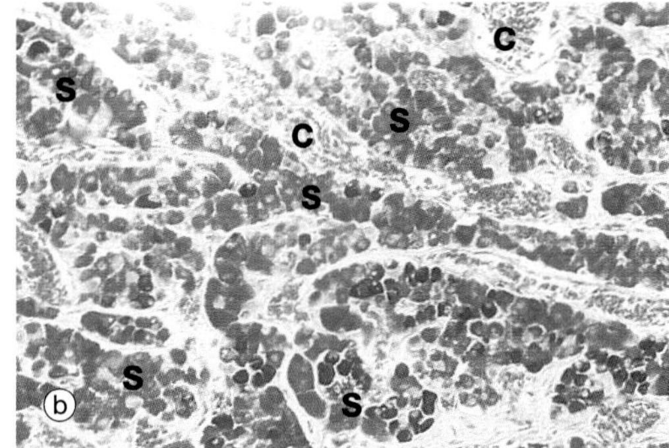

Fig. 5.27 Endocrine gland
(a) Diagram (b) Isamine blue eosin ×128

Most endocrine glands consist of clusters or cords of secretory cells surrounded by a rich network of small blood vessels. Each cluster of endocrine cells is surrounded by a basement membrane, reflecting its epithelial origin. Endocrine cells release hormones into the intercellular spaces from which they diffuse rapidly into surrounding blood vessels and from there throughout the body.

Micrograph (b) of the anterior pituitary gland shows the typical features of endocrine glands. The secretory cells **S** are arranged in cords and clusters and are surrounded by delicate supporting tissue containing a rich network of broad capillaries **C**. The basement membrane surrounding each group of endocrine cells is not visible at this magnification. Like many other endocrine glands, the secretory cells of the pituitary are of several different types; in this case, the majority are acidophilic (red stained), while some stain blue (basophilic) and some stain very little (chromophobes).

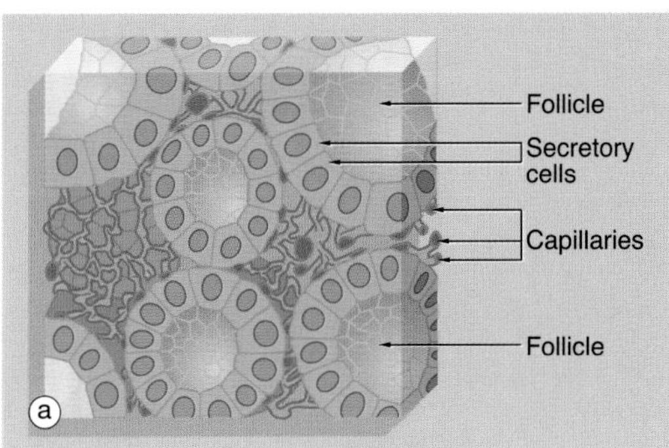

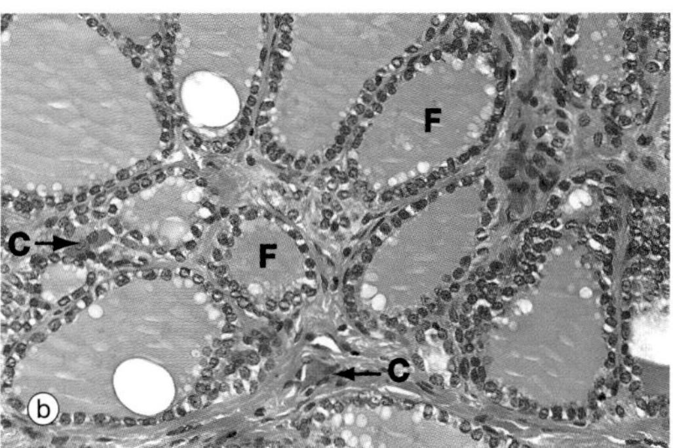

Fig. 5.28 Follicular endocrine gland
(a) Diagram (b) H & E ×150

The thyroid gland is an unusual endocrine gland in that it stores hormone (***thyroxine***) within roughly spherical cavities enclosed by the secretory cells; these units are called ***follicles***. Secretion of stored hormone involves reabsorption of hormone from the follicular lumen, release into the surrounding interstitial spaces, and then diffusion into the rich capillary network that embraces each follicle.

Micrograph (b) shows typical thyroid follicles **F** of variable size. The secretory cells lining the follicles are of flattened cuboidal shape. Stored thyroxine is bound to a glycoprotein (***thyroglobulin***), which is strongly eosinophilic. The relatively sparse interfollicular supporting tissue is mainly occupied by capillaries **C** which can be identified by the strongly eosinophilic (pink stained) erythrocytes within them.

A acinus **C** capillaries **D** demilune **E** excretory duct **F** follicle **S** secretory cells
T tubular secretory component

Fig. 5.29 Epithelium: major types and locations

Type of epithelium	Subclassification	Site
Squamous	Simple	Lining blood vessels (endothelium), lining body cavities (mesothelium), alveoli of lungs, Bowman's capsule and loop of Henlé of kidney
Squamous	Stratified	Lining oral cavity, epiglottis, oesophagus, anus, cervix, vagina, vulva, glans penis, cornea
Squamous	Stratified, keratinising	Skin (epidermis)
Cuboidal	Simple	Collecting tubules of kidney, rete testis, small ducts of exocrine glands, surface of ovary
Cuboidal	Stratified	Larger ducts of exocrine glands
Columnar	Simple	Gall bladder, collecting ducts of kidney, endocervix
Columnar	Pseudostratified, ciliated	Respiratory tract including nose and sinuses
Columnar	Simple ciliated	Fallopian tubes
Transitional	None	Lower urinary tract (renal pelvis, ureters, bladder and urethra)
Glandular	Simple	Colon, stomach, eccrine sweat glands
Glandular	Compound	Sebaceous glands, Brunner's glands of duodenum, small salivary glands, breast, prostate
Glandular – solid organs	Exocrine	Major salivary glands, liver, pancreas (acinar tissue)
Glandular – solid organs	Endocrine	Thyroid, anterior pituitary, adrenal, pancreas (islets of Langerhans)

6. *Muscle*

Introduction

Although all cells are capable of some sort of movement, the dominant function of several cell types is to generate motile forces through contraction. In these specialised contractile cells, motile forces are generated by the interaction of the proteins ***actin*** and ***myosin*** (contractile proteins). Certain forms of contractile cell function as single-cell contractile units:

- **Myoepithelial cells** are an important component of certain secretory glands (Ch. 5) where they function to expel secretions from glandular acini.
- **Pericytes** are smooth muscle-like cells that surround blood vessels (Ch. 8).
- **Myofibroblasts** are cells that have a contractile role in addition to being able to secrete collagen. This type of cell is generally inconspicuous in normal tissues but comes to be a dominant cell type when tissues undergo repair after damage in the formation of a scar.

Other forms of contractile cell function by forming multicellular contractile units termed muscles. Such muscle cells can be divided into three types:

- **Skeletal muscle** is responsible for the movement of the skeleton and organs such as the globe of the eye and the tongue. Skeletal muscle is often referred to as ***voluntary muscle*** since it is capable of voluntary (conscious) control. The arrangement of the contractile proteins gives rise to the appearance of prominent cross-striations in some histological preparations and so the name ***striated muscle*** is often applied to skeletal muscle. The highly developed functions of the cytoplasmic organelles of muscle cells has led to the use of a special terminology for some muscle cell components: plasma membrane or plasmalemma = ***sarcolemma***; cytoplasm = ***sarcoplasm***; endoplasmic reticulum = ***sarcoplasmic reticulum***.
- **Smooth muscle** is so named because, unlike other forms of muscle, the arrangement of contractile proteins does not give the histological appearance of cross-striations. This type of muscle forms the muscular component of visceral structures such as blood vessels, the gastrointestinal tract, the uterus and the urinary bladder, giving rise to the alternative name of ***visceral muscle***. Since smooth muscle is under inherent autonomic and hormonal control, it is also described as ***involuntary muscle***.
- **Cardiac muscle** has many structural and functional characteristics intermediate between those of skeletal and smooth muscle and provides for the continuous, rhythmic contractility of the heart. Although striated in appearance, cardiac muscle is readily distinguishable from skeletal muscle and should not be referred to by the term 'striated muscle'.

Muscle cells of all three types are surrounded by an external lamina (see Ch. 4). In all muscle cell types, contractile forces developed from the internal contractile proteins are transmitted to the external lamina via link proteins which span the muscle cell membrane. The external lamina binds individual muscle cells into a single functional mass.

Skeletal muscle

Skeletal muscles have a wide variety of morphological forms and modes of action; nevertheless all have the same basic structure. Skeletal muscle is composed of extremely elongated, multinucleate contractile cells, often described as ***muscle fibres***, bound together by collagenous supporting tissue. Individual muscle fibres vary considerably in diameter from 10 to 100 μm and may extend throughout the whole length of a muscle reaching up to 35 cm in length.

Skeletal muscle contraction is controlled by large motor nerves, individual nerve fibres branching within the muscle to supply a group of muscle fibres, collectively described as a ***motor unit.*** Excitation of any one motor nerve results in simultaneous contraction of all the muscle fibres of the corresponding motor unit. The structure of ***neuromuscular junctions*** is described in Fig. 7.12. The vitality of skeletal muscle fibres is dependent on the maintenance of their nerve supply which, if damaged, results in atrophy of the fibres. Skeletal muscle contains highly specialised stretch receptors known as neuromuscular spindles which are shown in Fig. 7.30.

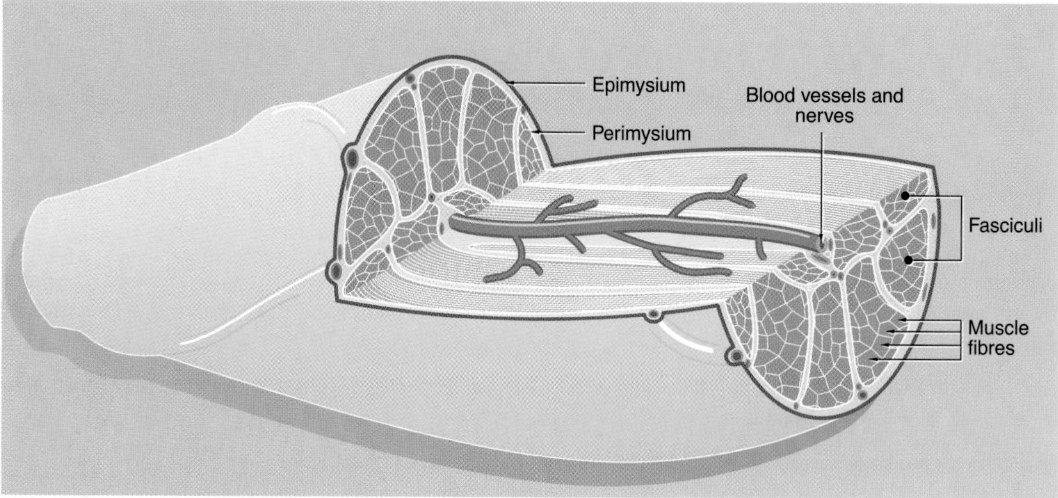

Fig. 6.1 Skeletal muscle

This diagram illustrates the arrangement of the basic components which make up a typical skeletal muscle.

The individual muscle cells (muscle fibres) are grouped together into elongated bundles called ***fasciculi*** with delicate supporting tissue called ***endomysium*** occupying the spaces between individual muscle fibres.

Each fascicle is surrounded by loose collagenous tissue called ***perimysium***. Most muscles are made up of many fasciculi and the whole muscle mass is invested in a dense collagenous sheath called the ***epimysium***. Large blood vessels and nerves enter the epimysium and divide to ramify throughout the muscle in the perimysium and endomysium.

The size of the fasciculi reflects the function of the particular muscle concerned. Muscles responsible for fine, highly controlled movements, e.g. the external muscles of the eye, have small fasciculi and a relatively greater proportion of perimysial supporting tissue. In contrast, muscles responsible for gross movements only, e.g. the muscle of the buttocks, have large fasciculi and relatively little perimysial tissue. Muscle fibres are anchored to the support tissue so that contractile forces can be transmitted. The connective tissue framework contains both collagen and elastic fibres. This connective tissue becomes continuous with that of the tendons and muscle attachments (see Ch. 10), which distribute and direct the motive forces of the muscle to bone, skin etc. as appropriate.

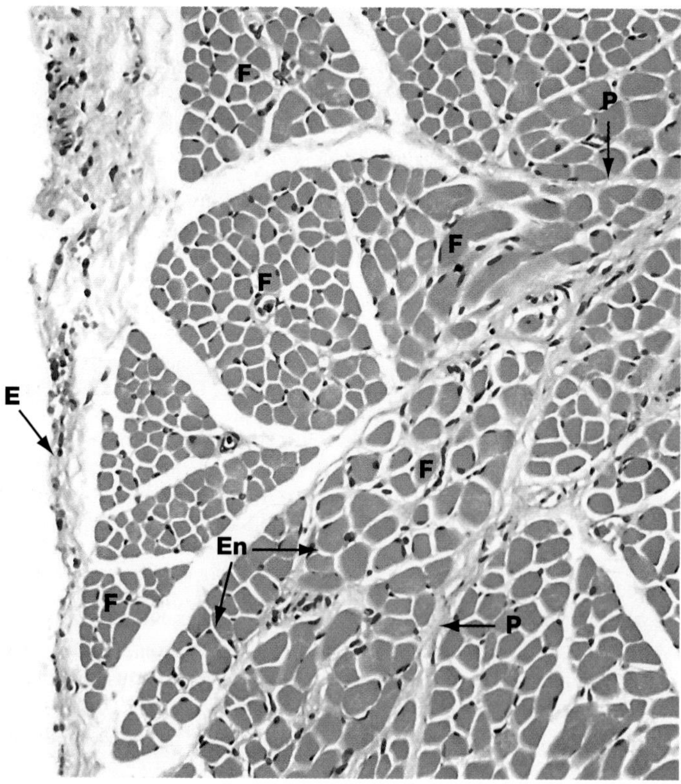

Fig. 6.2 Skeletal muscle
H & E ×150

This micrograph shows the arrangement of muscle fibres in skeletal muscle composed of several fasciculi.

The individual pink-stained muscle cells (fibres) are cut in transverse section, the spaces between them being occupied by small amounts of barely visible endomysial supporting tissue. The endomysium, which consists mainly of reticulin fibres and a small amount of collagen conveys numerous small blood vessels, lymphatics and nerves throughout the muscle.

Surrounding individual fasciculi **F** is the perimysium **P** composed of collagen and through which larger vessels and nerves run.

The epimysium **E** is a collagenous sheath that binds the fascicles into a single muscle. The endomysium **En** is barely visible as the delicate support tissue surrounding each muscle fibre.

B blood vessel **C** capillary **E** epimysium **En** endomysium **F** fascicle **P** perimysium

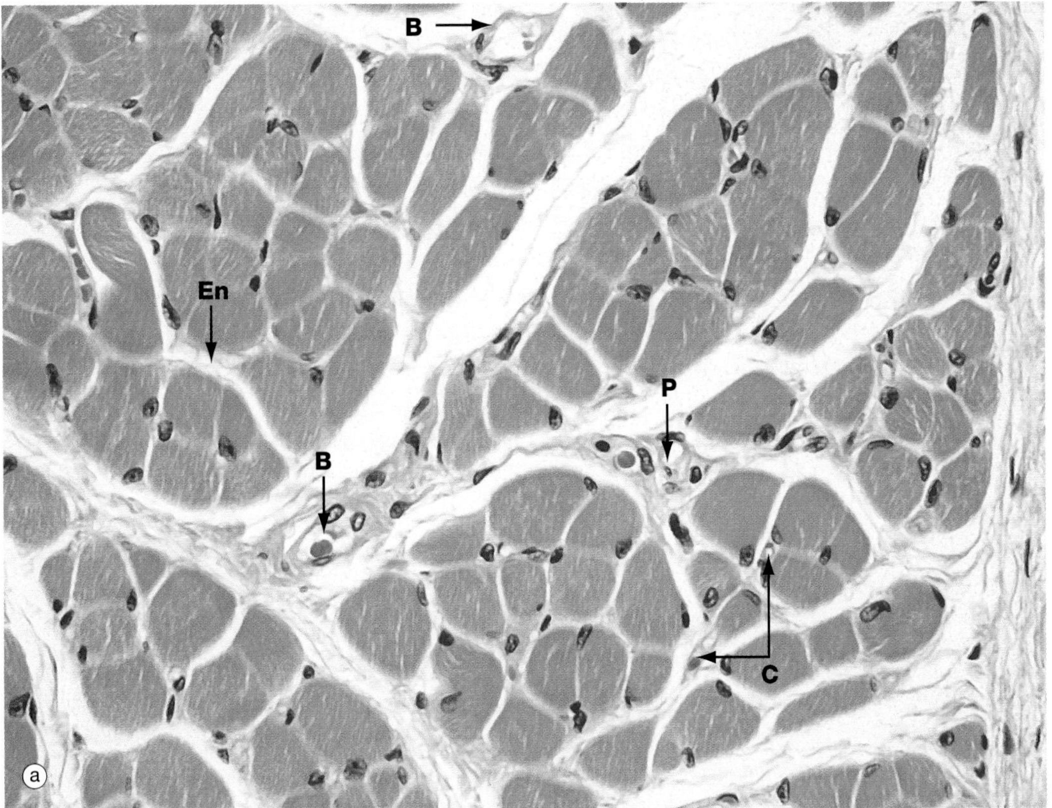

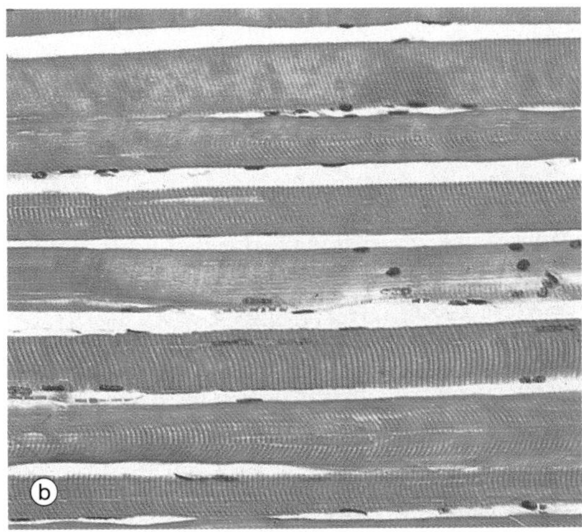

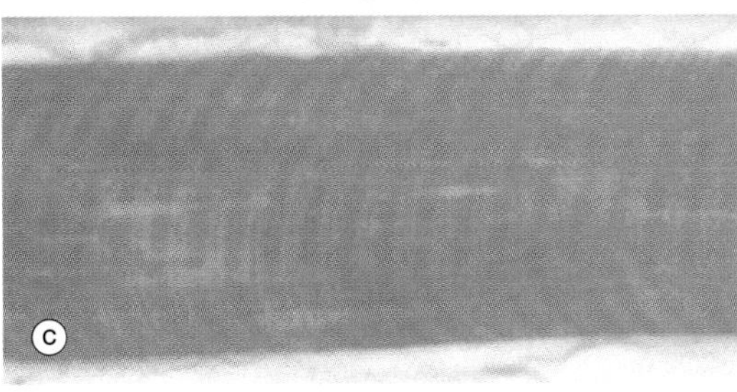

Fig. 6.3 Skeletal muscle
(a) H & E TS ×300 (b) H & E LS ×310
(c) H & E LS ×500

These micrographs show skeletal muscle from human limb muscles. Micrograph (a) in transverse section shows the muscle to be made up of numerous small fasciculi.

The spaces between the fasciculi are filled with loose collagenous tissue, the perimysium **P**, which is continuous with the delicate endomysium **En**, separating individual muscle fibres in each fasciculus. The supporting tissue of skeletal muscle also contains elastin fibres (not distinguishable in this preparation) which are most numerous in muscles attached to soft tissues as in the tongue and face. Note the rich network of capillaries **C** in the endomysium. Small blood vessels **B** together with nerves run in the perimysium.

Micrograph (b) demonstrates the characteristic histological features of skeletal muscle fibres in longitudinal section. Skeletal muscle fibres are extremely elongated, unbranched cylindrical cells with numerous flattened nuclei located at fairly regular intervals just beneath the sarcolemma (plasma membrane).

Each muscle fibre has multiple nuclei arranged at the cell periphery. However in transverse section, as in micrograph (a) most fibre profiles appear to contain a single nucleus while some do not because the plane of section has cut between the zones containing a nucleus.

In routine histological preparations stained with H & E it is often possible to see the striations in skeletal muscle when cut in longitudinal section. Micrograph (c) shows a detail of a skeletal muscle fibre with visible striations. Special stains are required for better resolution of these structures, illustrated later.

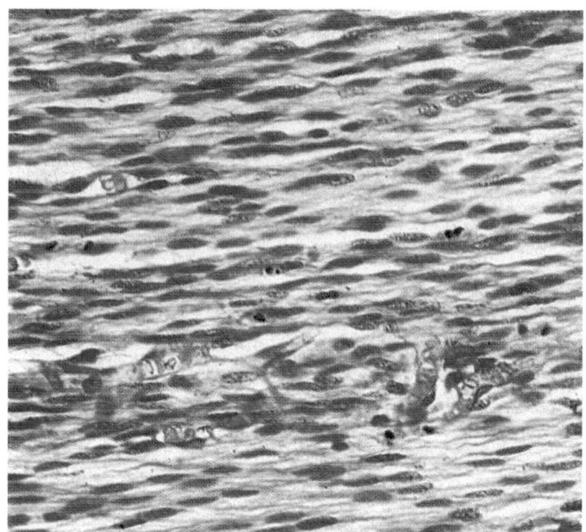

Fig. 6.4 Skeletal muscle embryogenesis
H & E ×150

During embryological development, mesenchymal cells in each myotome differentiate into long, mononuclear skeletal muscle precursors called myoblasts which then proliferate by mitosis. Subsequently, the myoblasts fuse end to end forming elongated multinucleate cells called myotubes, as seen in this micrograph which may eventually contain up to 100 nuclei.

Mature muscle cells can regenerate if damaged, by proliferation of stem cells which remain in adult muscles. These muscle stem cells resemble myoblasts and are called satellite cells. They enter mitosis after muscle damage and several fuse to form differentiated muscle fibres. Muscle fibres which are the result of regeneration after damage have nuclei in the centre of the fibre rather than at the periphery.

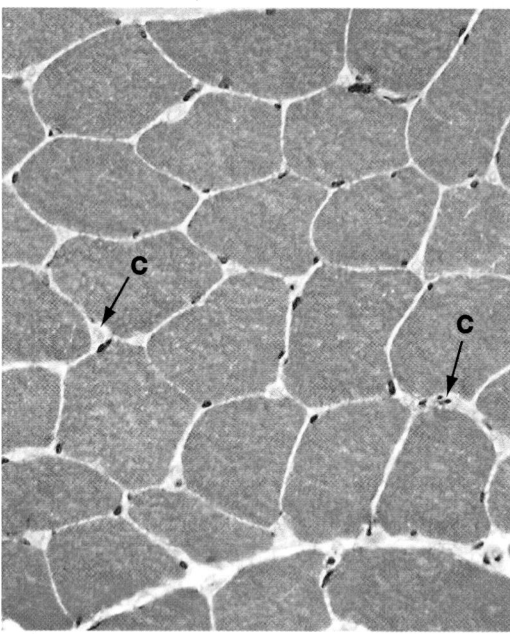

Fig. 6.5 Skeletal muscle
Frozen section, H & E ×500

In research and clinical diagnosis of muscle disease fixed, paraffin-embedded tissues are not usually used as they cause artefact to develop and limit investigation of muscle structure. Fresh frozen section is the preferred method for preparation of muscle for investigation by light microscopy.

This micrograph shows a frozen section of skeletal muscle from human vastus lateralis. Tissue shrinkage is minimised. In this transverse section the extreme peripheral location of the nuclei of skeletal muscle fibres is well seen. In cross-section muscle fibres appear polyhedral with flattening of adjacent cells. In normal muscle the cross-sectional areas of individual fibres are approximately the same. In the endomysial spaces, the numerous minute capillaries **C** are just recognisable. Compare the huge diameter of the muscle fibres which may be as great as 0.1 mm in diameter with that of the capillaries, the latter being approximately 7 μm across.

Muscular dystrophy

In muscular dystrophy there is weakness and wasting of muscles due to disease caused by a defective protein involved in muscle function. One of the important groups of protein involved in muscle function is that associated with the cell membrane of skeletal muscle. A complex of large proteins act to link the contractile proteins within the cell through the cell membrane with structural proteins in the external lamina. Thus contraction forces within each muscle fibre are transmitted to the collagenous support tissues to bring about movement.

One of the most important of these link proteins is called ***dystrophin***. Immunostaining for this protein, seen here as a brown stain, shows it closely associated with the muscle cell membrane. Some people have a mutation in the gene for dystrophin that results in inefficient linking of contractile forces to the support tissues in muscle. Muscle does not function correctly and fibres undergo progressive damage with repeated contraction, ultimately leading to death of muscle cells. The disease is called ***Duchenne muscular dystrophy***.

Mutation in genes coding for proteins in the link complex is an important cause of the group of muscular dystrophies. Other genes coding for contractile and other structural proteins also cause muscular dystrophy.

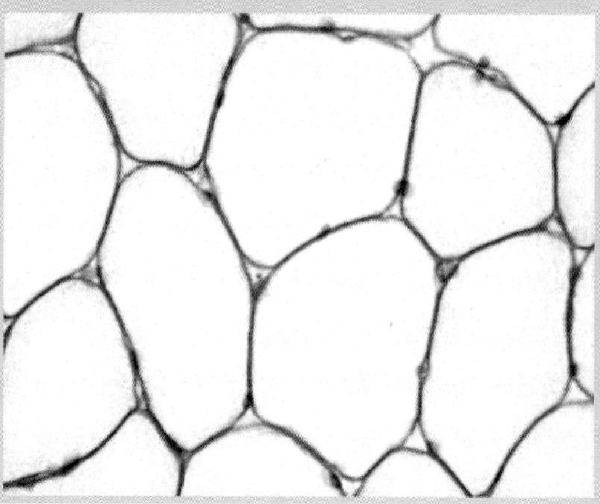

Fig. 6.6 Skeletal muscle
Dystrophin immunostain ×525

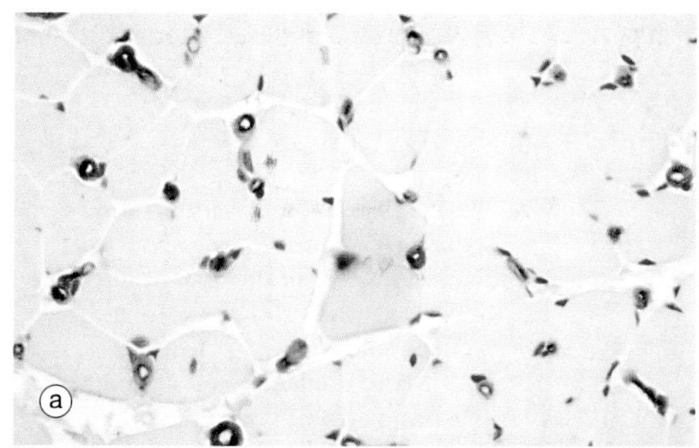

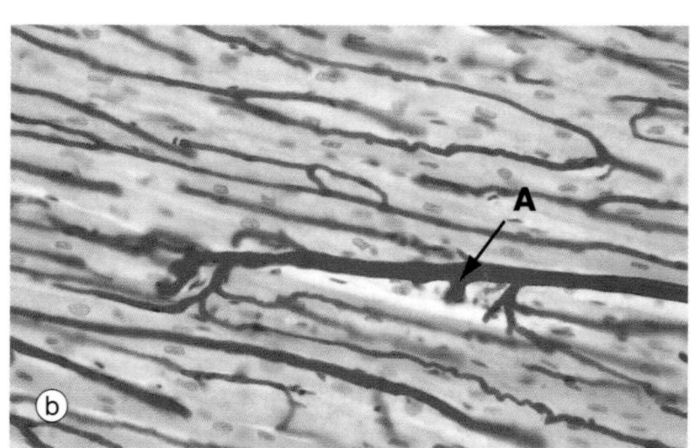

Fig. 6.7 Skeletal muscle blood supply
(a) Immunostain CD34 ×350
(b) Perfusion preparation/haematoxylin ×300

Micrograph (a) shows skeletal muscle cut in transverse section and stained to show the endothelial cells using an immunohistochemical technique. This highlights the distribution of capillaries. Each muscle fibre is in close contact with 1–3 capillaries, seen as the small circular brown-stained profiles.

The capillaries run along the muscle fibres, a feature best illustrated in micrograph (b) which is a perfusion preparation of muscle in which the vessels have been injected with red gel. Muscle nuclei can be seen stained blue with haematoxylin. A small artery **A** running in perimysium can be seen giving off capillaries which branch out and run along the length of the muscle fibres.

The high energy requirements of skeletal muscle demand an extensive capillary network.

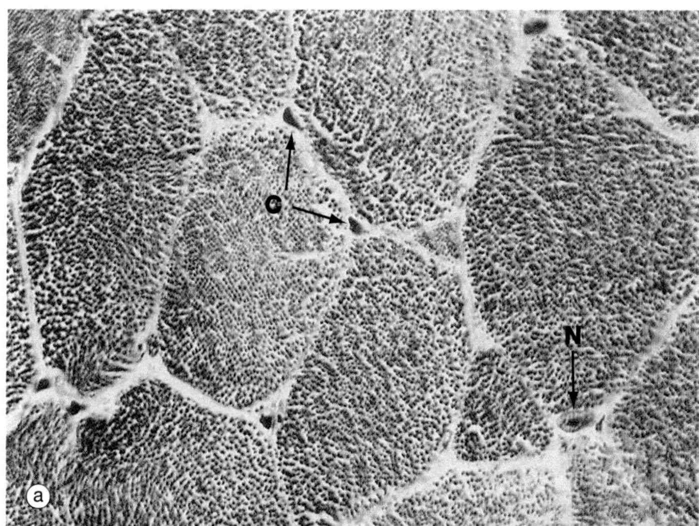

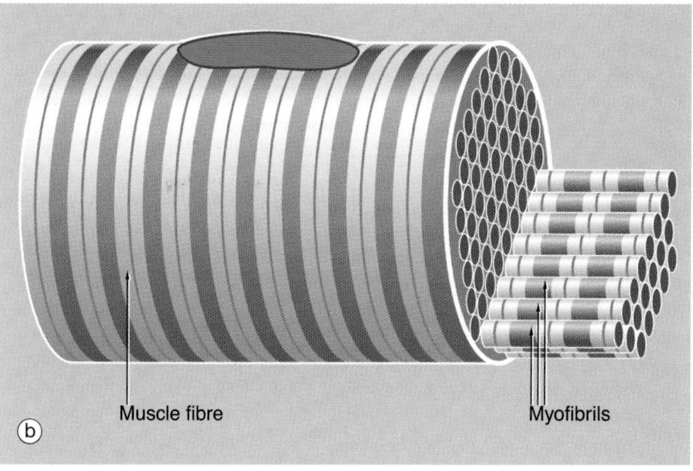

Fig. 6.8 Skeletal muscle
(a) TS, iron haematoxylin ×1200
(b) Schematic diagram

Micrograph (a) shows a transverse section through several skeletal muscle fibres at very high magnification. The plane of section includes only one skeletal muscle nucleus **N**. Note the presence of erythrocytes in endomysial capillaries **C**.

In preparations such as this, the transversely sectioned muscle fibres are seen to be packed with numerous dark dots. These represent the cut ends of myofibrils, elongated cylindrical structures which lie parallel to one another in the sarcoplasm.

As shown diagrammatically in part (b), each myofibril exhibits a repeating pattern of cross-striations which is a product of the highly ordered arrangement of the contractile proteins within it; this can only be seen with electron microscopy (see Fig. 6.9). Furthermore, the parallel myofibrils are arranged with their cross-striations in register, giving rise to the regular striations seen with light microscopy in longitudinal sections of skeletal muscle as in Fig. 6.3.

A small artery **C** capillary **N** nucleus

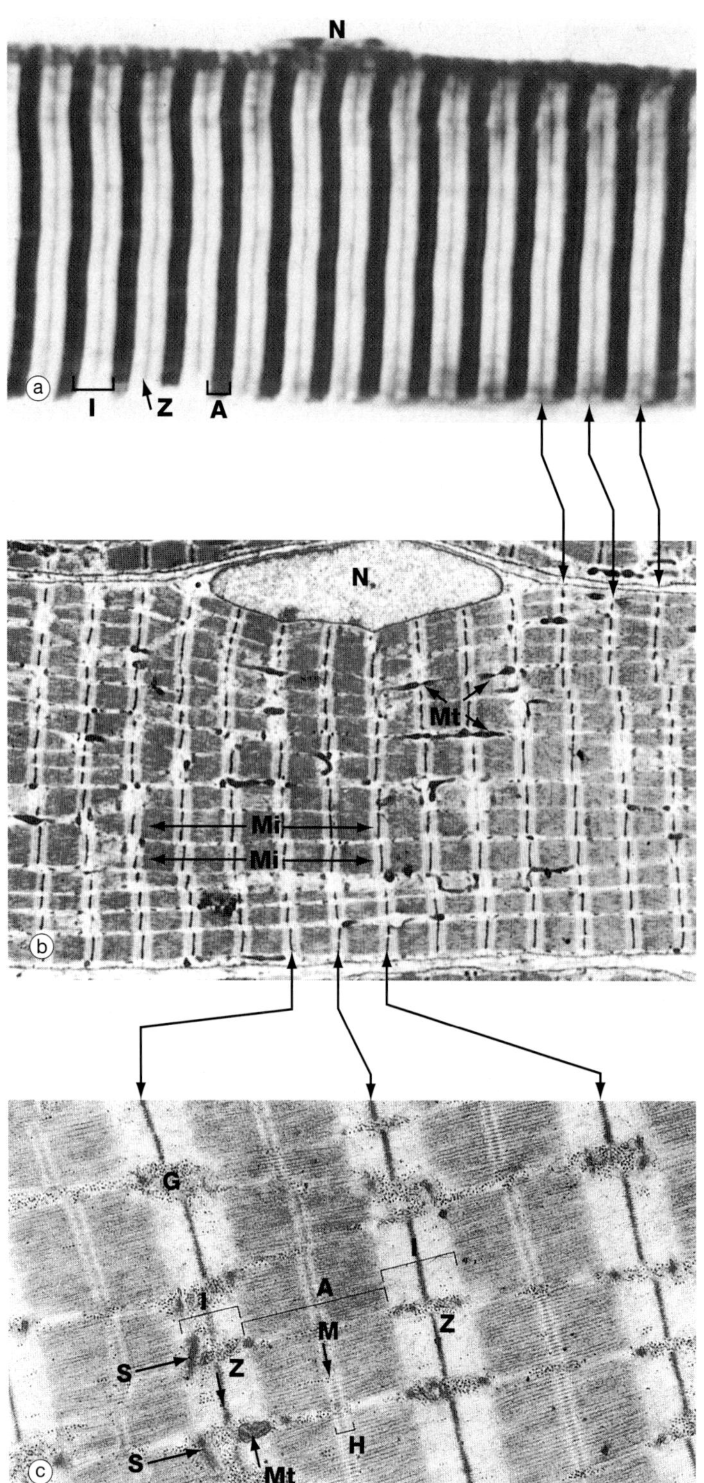

Fig. 6.9 Skeletal muscle
(a) Heidenhain's haematoxylin ×1200 (b) EM ×2860 (c) EM ×18 700

This series of micrographs shows the arrangement of the contractile proteins within skeletal muscle and explains the striations seen with light microscopy.

Micrograph (a) shows the striations of a skeletal muscle fibre at a magnification close to the limit of resolution. They are composed of alternating broad light **I** bands (isotropic in polarised light) and dark (anisotropic) **A** bands. Fine dark lines called **Z** bands (Zwischenscheiben) can be seen bisecting the light **I** bands. Note the nucleus **N** at the extreme periphery of the cell.

Micrograph (b) shows the electron microscopic appearance of muscle with a nucleus **N** situated in a similar position. The sarcoplasm is filled with myofibrils **Mi** oriented parallel to the long axis of the cell. These are separated by a small amount of sarcoplasm containing rows of mitochondria **Mt** in a similar orientation.

Each myofibril has prominent regular cross-striations arranged in register with those of the other myofibrils and corresponding to the I, A and Z bands seen in light microscopy. The Z bands are the most electron-dense and divide each myofibril into numerous contractile units, called ***sarcomeres***, arranged end to end.

With further magnification in micrograph (c), the arrangement of the contractile proteins (***myofilaments***) may be seen in each sarcomere. The dark **A** band is bisected by the lighter **H** (Heller) band, which is further bisected by a more dense **M** (Mittelscheibe) band. Irrespective of the degree of contraction of the muscle fibre, the A band remains constant in width. In contrast, the **I** and **H** bands narrow during contraction and the **Z** bands are drawn closer together. These findings are explained by the ***sliding filament*** theory (Fig. 6.10). Mitochondria **Mt** and numerous glycogen granules **G** provide a rich energy source in the scanty cytoplasm between the myofibrils. The mature muscle cell contains little rough endoplasmic reticulum; it contains, however, a smooth membranous system **S** which is involved in activation of the contractile mechanism (see Figs 6.11–6.13).

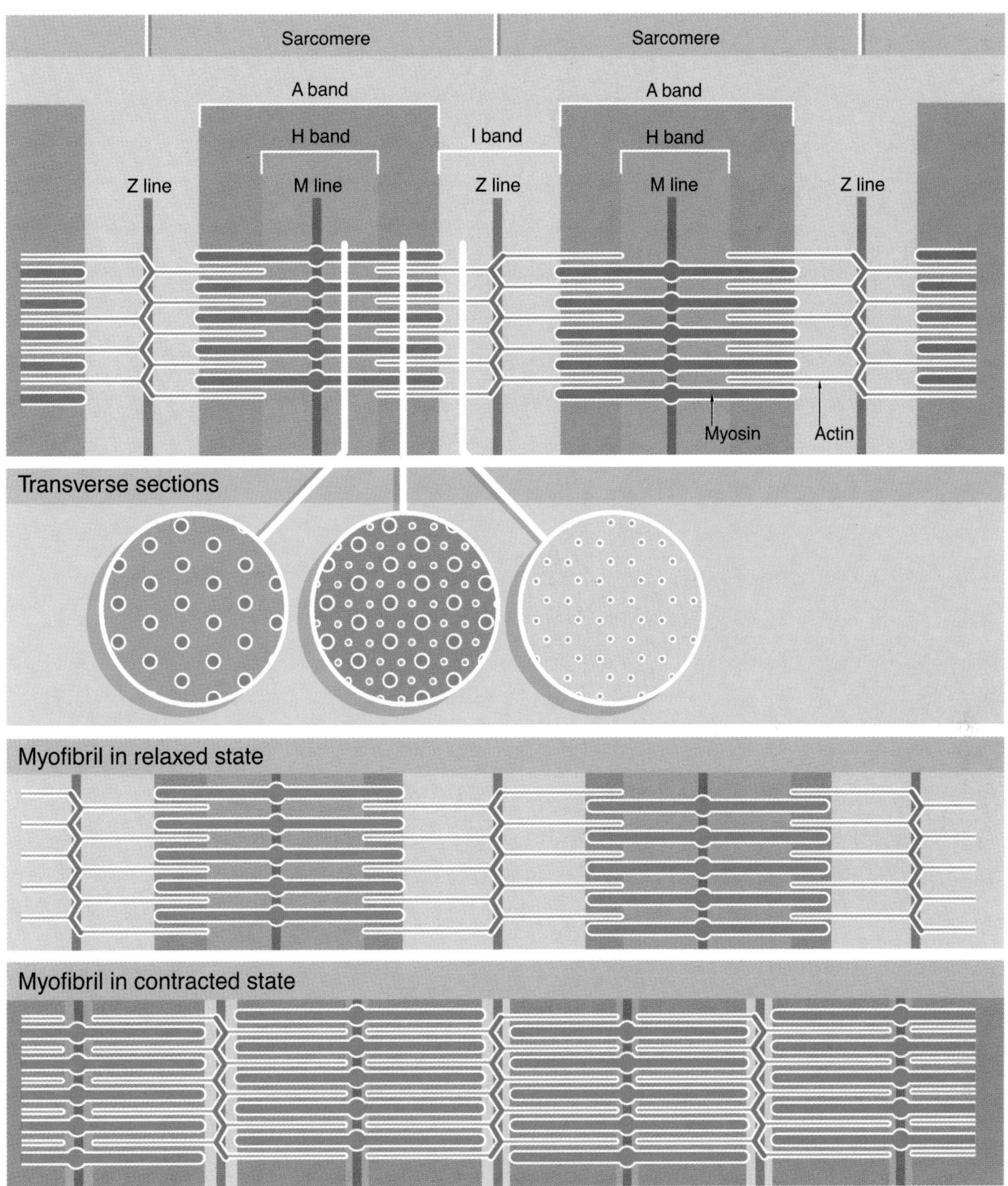

Fig. 6.10 The arrangement of myofilaments in the sarcomere

The sarcomere consists of two types of myofilaments, thick filaments and thin filaments. Each type remains constant in length irrespective of the state of contraction of the muscle. The thick filaments, which are composed mainly of the protein ***myosin***, are maintained in register by their attachment to a disc-like zone represented by the M line. Similarly the thin filaments, which are composed mainly of the protein ***actin***, are attached to a disc-like zone represented by the Z line. The I and H bands, both areas of low electron density, represent areas where the thick and thin filaments do not overlap one another.

The widely accepted sliding filament theory proposes that using energy released from ATP, the thick and thin filaments slide over one another, thus causing shortening of the sarcomere.

A large number of accessory proteins are also present in the sarcomere where they play roles in filament alignment and regulation of contraction.

A A band **G** glycogen granules **H** H band **I** I band **M** M band **Mi** myofibril
Mt mitochondrion **N** nucleus **S** sarcoplasmic reticulum **Z** Z band

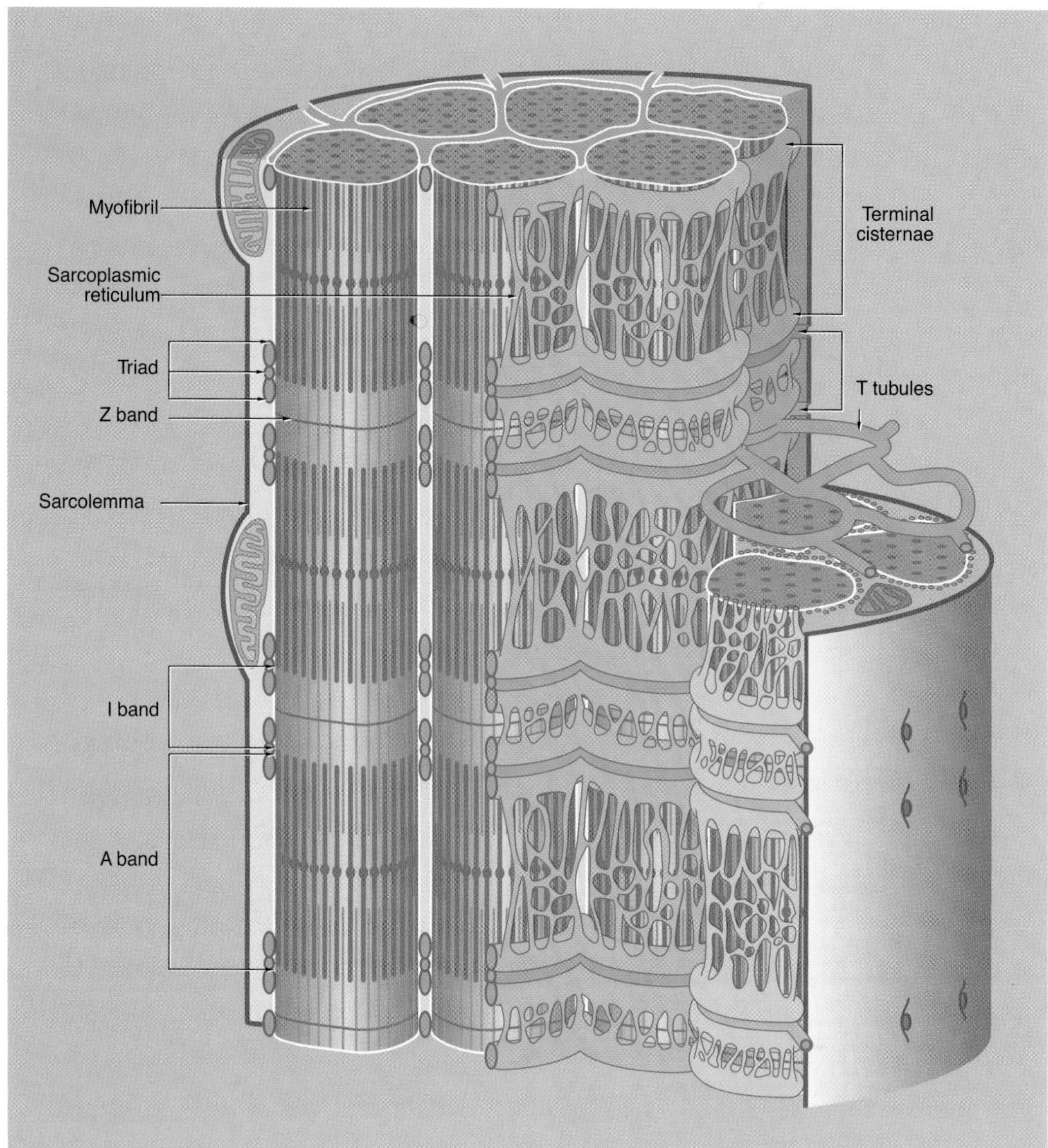

Fig. 6.11 **The conducting system for contractile stimuli**

To permit the synchronous contraction of all sarcomeres in the muscle fibre, a system of tubular extensions of the muscle cell plasma membrane (sarcolemma) extends transversely into the muscle cell to surround each myofibril at the region of the junction of the A and I bands. Known as the ***T system***, its lumen is continuous with the extracellular space. (In amphibian skeletal muscle, which was the first to be studied, the T tubules are disposed at the Z bands; the same applies in cardiac muscle.)

Between the T tubules, a second membrane system derived from smooth endoplasmic reticulum, the ***sarcoplasmic reticulum***, forms a membranous network which embraces each myofibril. On either side of each T tubule, the sarcoplasmic reticulum exhibits a flattened cisternal arrangement, each pair of ***terminal cisternae*** and a T tubule forming a triad near the junction of the I and A bands of each sarcomere.

Calcium ions are concentrated within the lumen of the sarcoplasmic reticulum. Depolarisation of the sarcolemma of the muscle fibre is rapidly disseminated throughout the sarcoplasm by the T tubule system. This promotes the release of calcium ions from the sarcoplasmic reticulum into the sarcoplasm surrounding the myofilaments. Calcium ions activate the sliding filament mechanism resulting in muscle contraction.

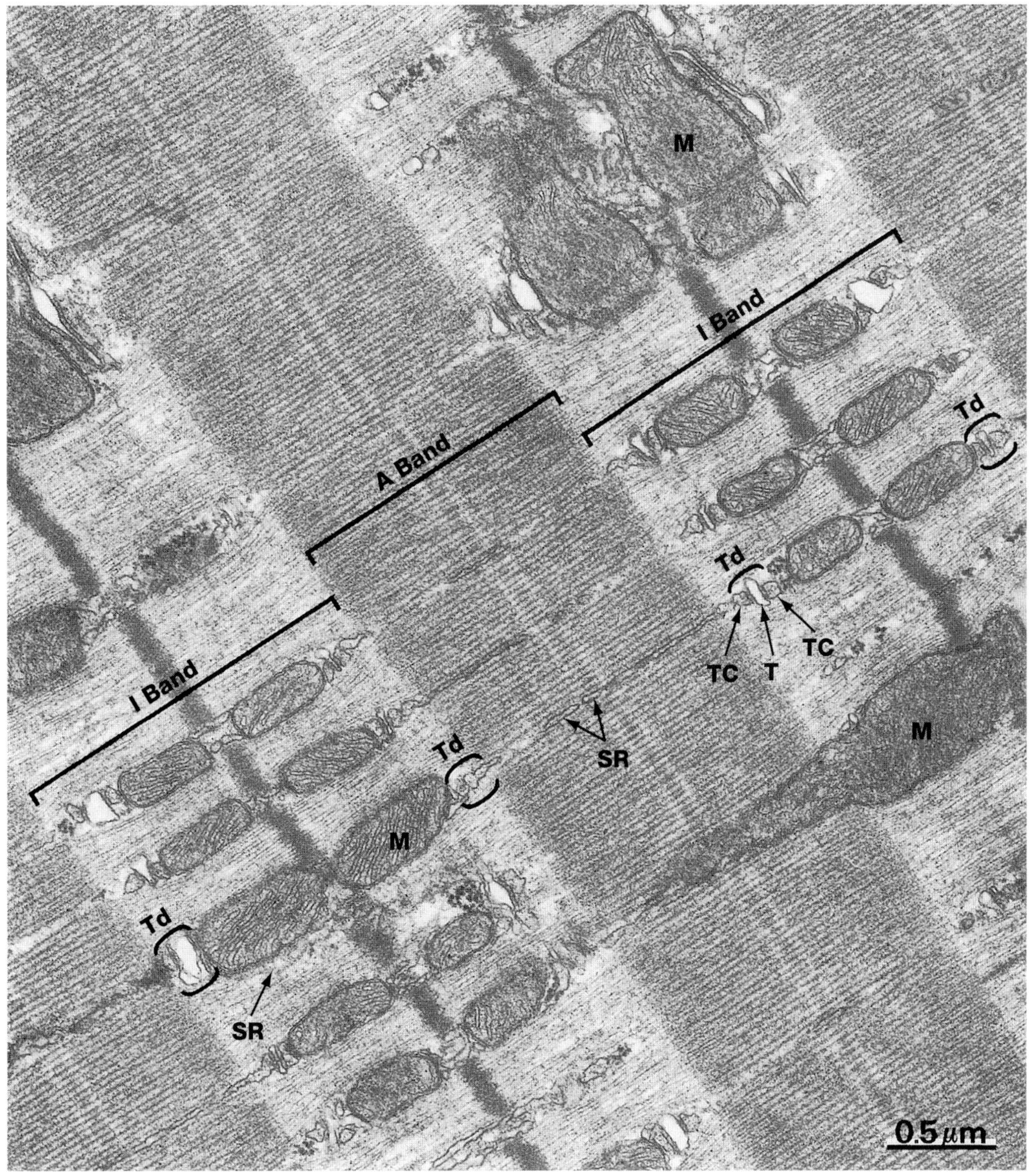

Fig. 6.12 Skeletal muscle
EM ×33 000

This electron micrograph of mammalian skeletal muscle cut in longitudinal section demonstrates the main elements of the conducting system. In the vicinity of the junction of the **A** and **I** bands (and depending on the state of contraction) are tubular triads **Td** each comprising a central flattened tubule of the T system **T** and a pair of terminal cisternae **TC** of the sarcoplasmic reticulum. Within the A bands can be seen tubular elements of the sarcoplasmic reticulum **SR** connecting the terminal cisternae. Likewise within the I bands, similar though less regular longitudinal tubular profiles of sarcoplasmic reticulum are seen. The conducting system of 'slow-twitch' (red) fibres as shown here (see Fig. 6.13) is more regular than that of 'fast-twitch' (white) fibres where this pattern is more difficult to discern. Note the distribution of mitochondria **M**, regularly arranged between the sarcomeres within the I bands in immediate association with those parts of the actin and myosin filaments which interact during the process of contraction. The reason for this appearance is evident in the following micrograph.

M mitochondrion **T** T tubule **TC** terminal cisterna **Td** triad **SR** sarcoplasmic reticulum

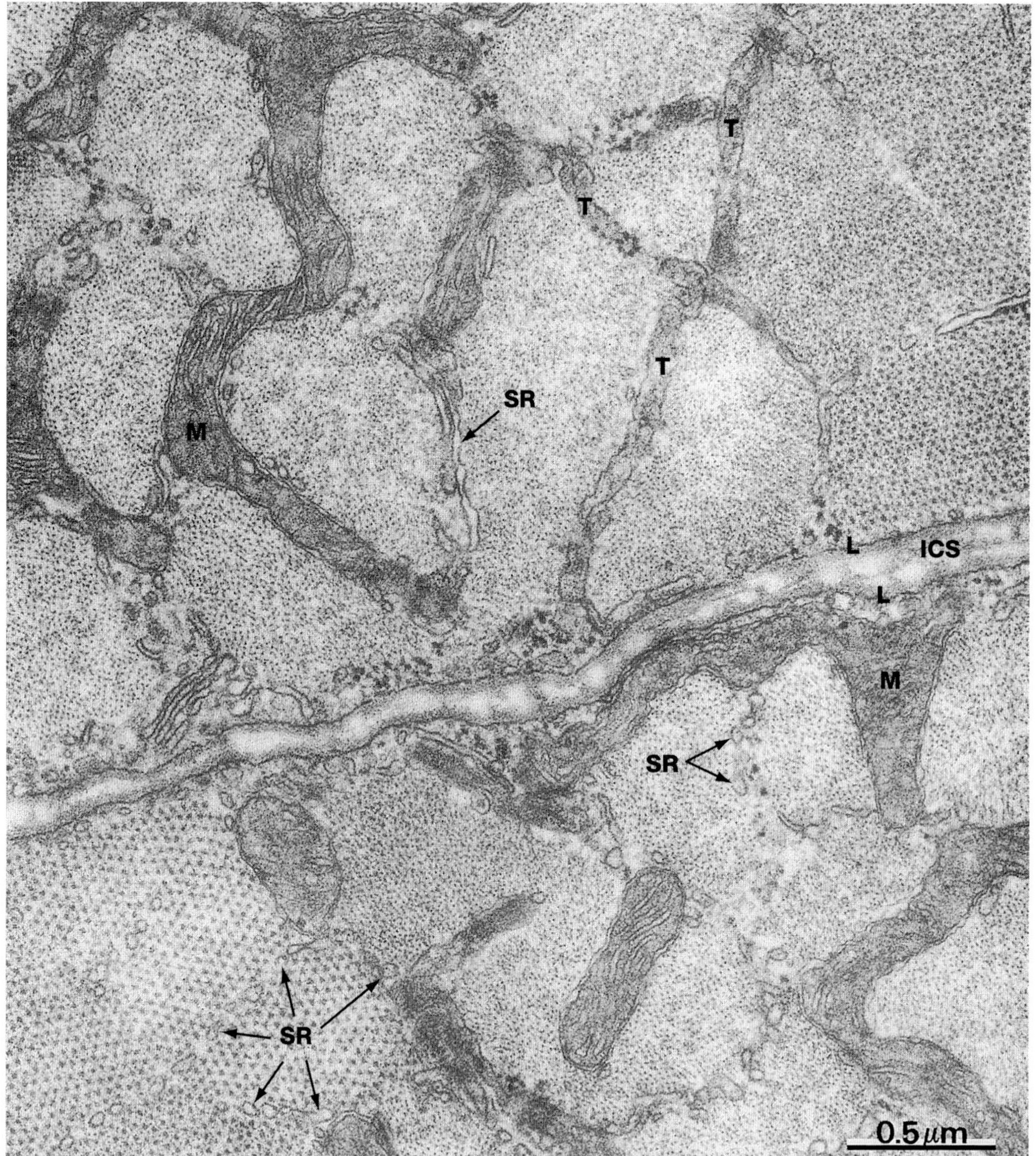

Fig. 6.13 Skeletal muscle
×44 000

This micrograph shows parts of two skeletal muscle cells cut in transverse section in the vicinity of the junction of A and I bands; the intercellular space **ICS** bisects the field. Note the external lamina **L** adjacent to the sarcolemma. Sarcomeres at the upper right and lower left of this field have been sectioned through the end part of the A band and thus show both actin and myosin filaments. The remaining sarcomeres are cut through the I band and contain only actin filaments. This results from the fact that the bands of all sarcomeres within any one muscle cell are not exactly in register with one another.

Each sarcomere is ensheathed by a network of tubules of the sarcoplasmic reticulum **SR**. The plane of section has also included a part of a broader diameter T tubule system **T** which branches to encompass several different sarcomeres. Direct communication of T tubules with the intercellular space is difficult to see here as the tubules appear to ramify into a complex tubular system just beneath the plasmalemma; the continuity of T tubule lumen and the intercellular space has been convincingly demonstrated, however, by experimental techniques. Note the extraordinary serpentine branched mitochondria **M** which lie between the sarcomeres within the I bands, giving rise to the mitochondrial appearance seen in longitudinal section in the previous micrograph.

A aerobic muscle fibre (type I) **An** anaerobic muscle fibre (type II) **I** intermediate type muscle fibre **ICS** intercellular space **L** external lamina **M** mitochondrion **SR** sarcoplasmic reticulum **T** tubule system

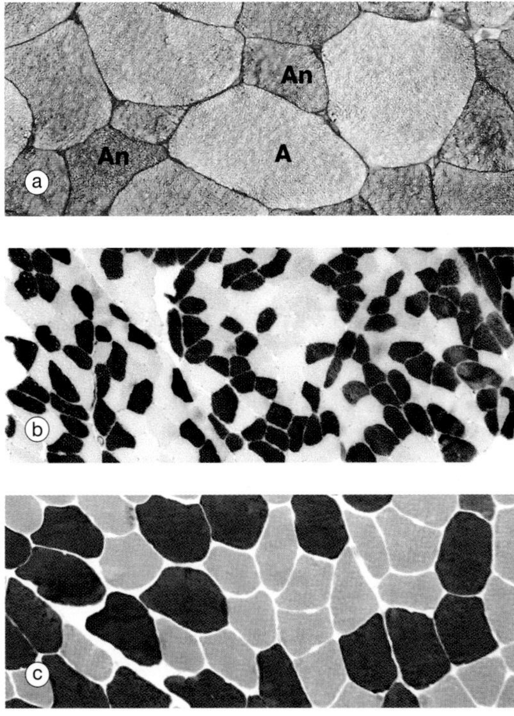

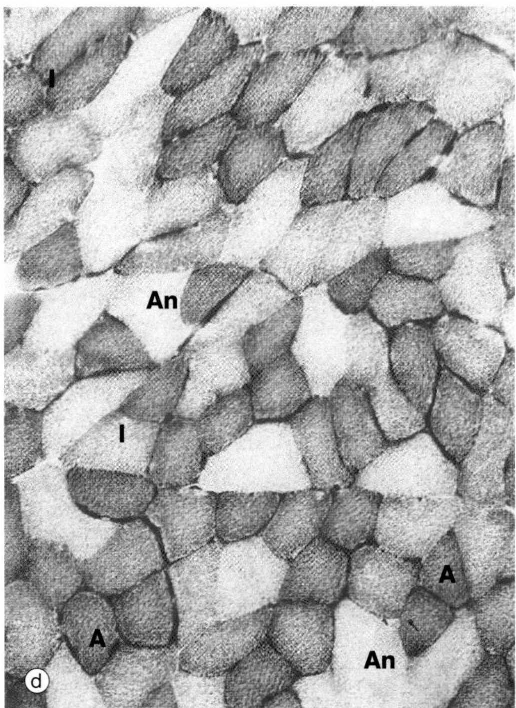

Fig. 6.14 Skeletal muscle

TS: histochemical techniques (a) PAS ×500 (b) ATPase pH 4.2 ×90 (c) ATPase pH 9.4 ×180 (d) succinate dehydrogenase ×200

The mode of activity of skeletal muscle varies from one part of the body to another. Some muscles, such as those involved in the maintenance of posture, are required to contract almost continuously while others, such as the extra-ocular muscles, make rapid short-lived movements. In humans, distinction between these types cannot be made on gross examination of the muscle. In domestic poultry, however, the extremes are easily identified by a difference in colours; for example, leg muscles are red and flight (breast) muscles are white.

Correspondingly, 'slow-twitch' and 'fast-twitch' muscle fibre types can be demonstrated by nerve stimulation studies. The metabolic requirements of each fibre type differ markedly, the slow red fibres mainly relying on aerobic metabolism and the fast white fibres using predominantly anaerobic pathways. Most muscles contain a mixture of these extreme fibre types as well as an intermediate type. There are significant interspecies differences.

Aerobic (***type I***) muscle fibres **A** contain abundant mitochondria. They also contain a large content of myoglobin, an oxygen-storage molecule analogous to haemoglobin, which accounts for the red colour of such fibres.

In contrast, anaerobic (***type II***) muscle fibres **An** contain few mitochondria and relatively little myoglobin. These muscle fibres are, however, rich in glycogen and glycolytic enzymes. These characteristics account for the 'white' colour of such fibres. Anaerobic fibres predominate in muscles responsible for intense but sporadic contraction such as the biceps and triceps of the arms.

Type I and II fibres can also be identified by the nature of their myosin ATPase, which differs in its protein structure between different fibre types. In the preparation in micrograph (b), type I fibres are dark and type II fibres are light. This low magnification shows the checkerboard pattern of the fibre types within a muscle fascicle. Micrograph (c) has been stained at a pH that reveals type I fibres as pale and type II fibres as dark (the opposite to micrograph b). Such histochemical staining is used routinely in diagnosis of muscle disease.

The activity of the specific mitochondrial enzyme succinate dehydrogenase, which catalyses one of the stages of Krebs cycle, demonstrates the relative proportions of mitochondria within the muscle fibres. In micrograph (d), note the presence of intensely stained small-diameter aerobic fibres **A**, poorly stained large-diameter anaerobic fibres **An** and intermediate fibres **I**.

The type of metabolism of each fibre is determined by the frequency of impulses in its motor nerve supply. Any one motor nerve supplies fibres of one type only and all the fibres of a particular motor unit are of the same metabolic type. Indeed, if the motor nerve supply to one type of fibre is experimentally transplanted to supply another fibre type, this fibre type will become converted to the metabolic pattern of the former.

Smooth muscle

In contrast to skeletal muscle, which is specialised for relatively forceful contractions of short duration and under fine voluntary control, smooth muscle is specialised for continuous contractions of relatively low force, producing diffuse movements resulting in contraction of the whole muscle mass rather than contraction of individual motor units. Contractility is an inherent property of smooth muscle, occurring independently of neurological innervation often in a rhythmic or wave-like fashion. Superimposed on this inherent contractility are the influences of the autonomic nervous system, hormones and local metabolites which modulate contractility to accommodate changing functional demands. For example, the smooth muscle of the intestinal wall undergoes continuous rhythmic contractions which result in waves of constriction passing along the bowel, propelling the luminal contents distally. This activity is enhanced by parasympathetic stimulation and influenced by a variety of hormones released in response to changes in the nature and volume of the gut contents. The structure of autonomic neuromuscular junctions is described in Chapter 7.

The cells of smooth muscle are relatively small with only a single nucleus. The fibres are bound together in irregular branching fasciculi, the arrangement varying considerably from one organ to another according to functional requirements.

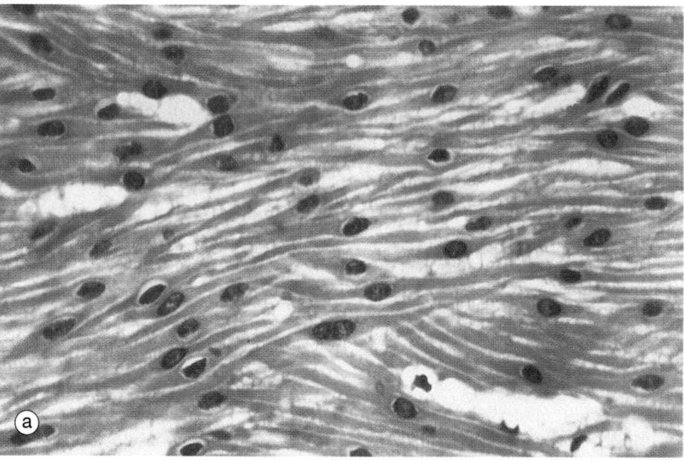

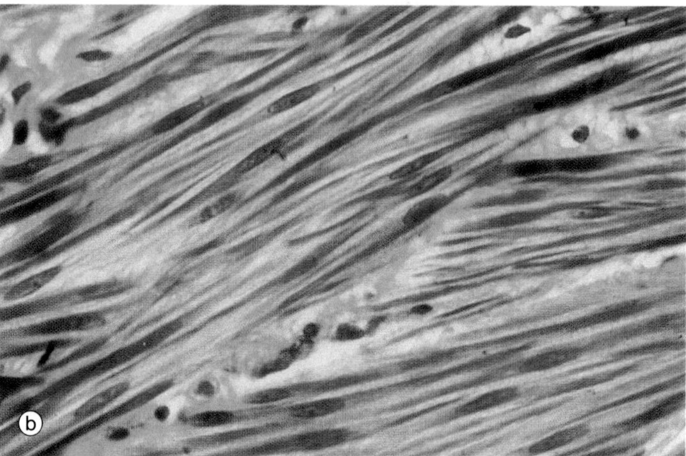

Fig. 6.15 Smooth muscle
(a) LS, H & E ×480 (b) LS, Masson's trichrome ×480

As seen in these micrographs, smooth muscle fibres are elongated, spindle-shaped cells with tapered ends which may occasionally be bifurcated. Smooth muscle fibres are generally much shorter than skeletal muscle fibres and contain only one nucleus which is elongated and centrally located in the cytoplasm at the widest part of the cell; however, depending on the contractile state of the fibres at fixation, the nuclei may sometimes appear to be spiral-shaped.

Smooth muscle fibres are bound together in irregular, branching fasciculi and these fasciculi, rather than individual fibres, are the functional contractile units. Within the fasciculi, individual muscle fibres are arranged roughly parallel to one another with the thickest part of one cell lying against the thin parts of adjacent cells.

The contractile proteins of smooth muscle are not arranged in myofibrils as in skeletal and cardiac muscle, and thus visceral muscle cells are not striated.

Between individual muscle fibres and between fasciculi is a network of supporting collagenous tissue; this is well demonstrated in micrograph (b) in which the collagen is stained blue.

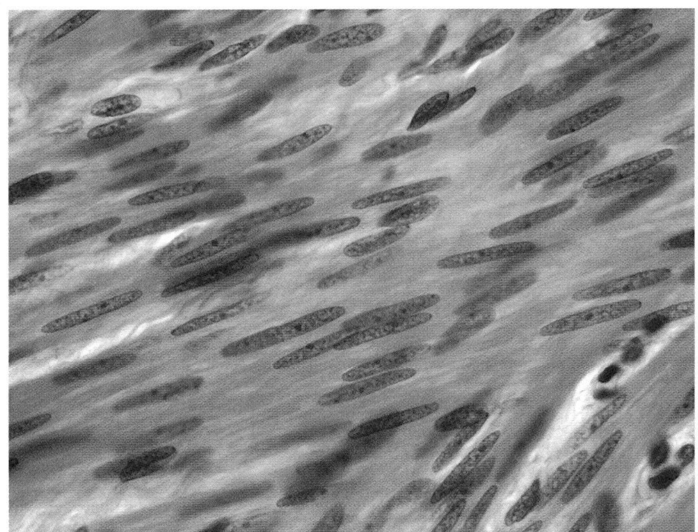

Fig. 6.16 Smooth muscle
LS, H & E ×500

This micrograph illustrates smooth muscle from the bowel wall cut in longitudinal section. In this case, the fibres are arranged in a highly regular manner and packed so closely that it is difficult to identify individual cell outlines although cell shape can be deduced from that of the nuclei.

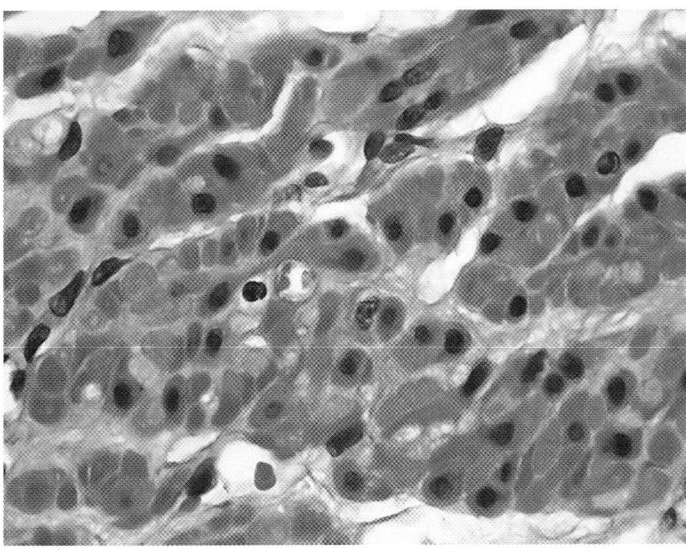

Fig. 6.17 Smooth muscle
TS, H & E ×500

This micrograph shows smooth muscle in transverse section at very high magnification. The spindle-shaped cells are sectioned at various different points along their length which gives the erroneous impression that they are of differing diameters. Nuclei are only included in the plane of section where fibres have been cut through their widest diameter. Note the plump nuclear shape and central location of nuclei within the cytoplasm.

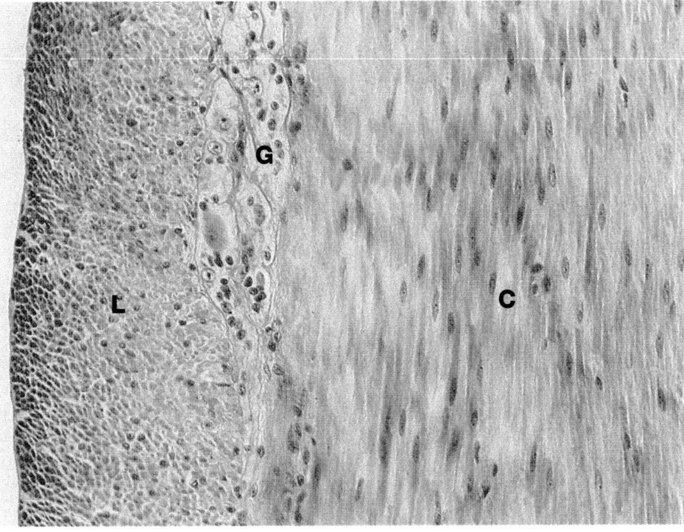

Fig. 6.18 Smooth muscle
Masson's trichrome ×150

In many tubular visceral structures, such as the ileum seen in this micrograph, smooth muscle is disposed in layers with the cells of one layer arranged at right angles to those of the adjacent layer. This arrangement permits a wave of contraction to pass down the tube, propelling the contents forward; this action is called ***peristalsis***.

Typically, the longitudinal outer smooth muscle layer **L** is closely applied to the inner circular layer **C** with only a minimal amount of supporting tissue between; in this specimen the collagen is stained blue. The supporting tissue contains clumps of large cells with pale nuclei which represent ***parasympathetic ganglia*** **G** (see Fig. 7.19).

C inner circular muscle layer **G** ganglion cells **L** outer longitudinal muscle layer

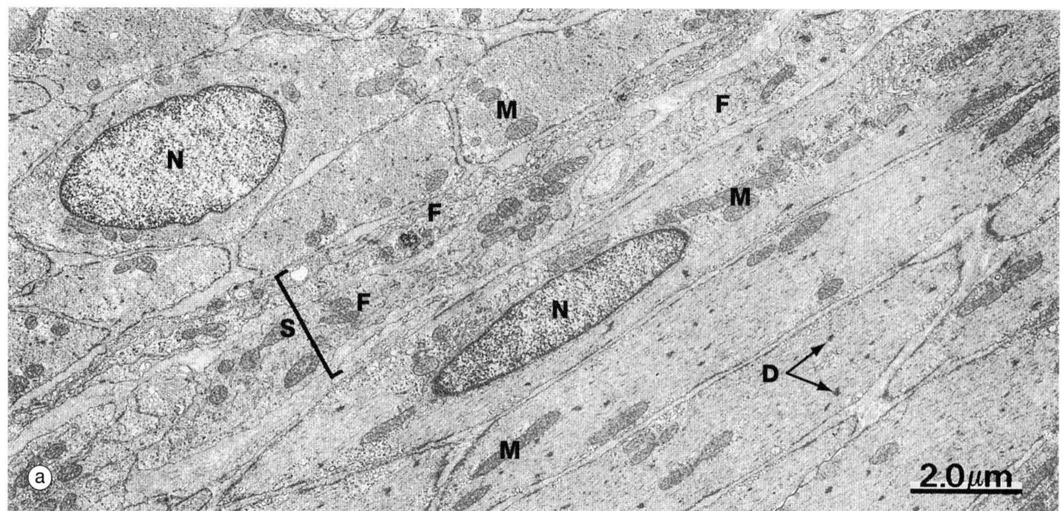

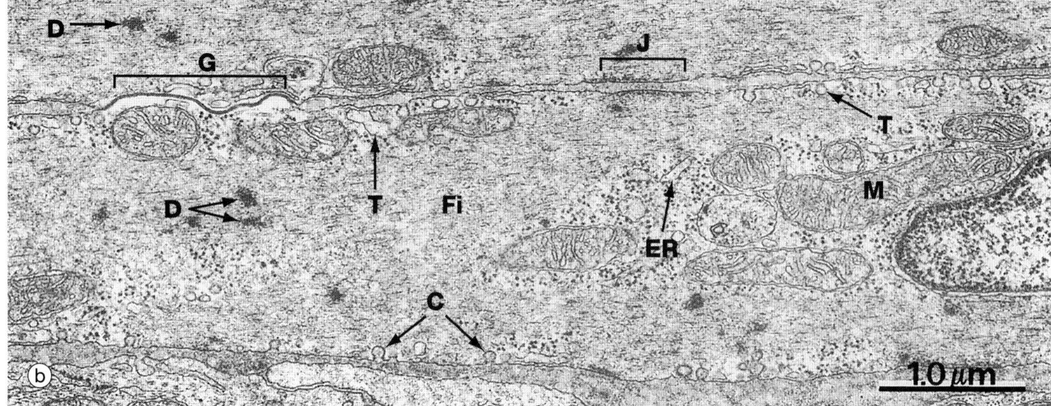

Fig. 6.19 Smooth muscle
(a) EM ×8000 (b) EM ×21 000

At low magnification, micrograph (a) demonstrates the spindle-shaped and elongated central nuclei **N** of smooth muscle cells. The cells at the lower right are cut longitudinally and those at the upper left transversely. Between them is a band of supporting tissue **S** containing the cytoplasmic processes of fibroblasts **F**. Note the relative sparsity of mitochondria **M** and other intracellular organelles.

At high magnification in micrograph (b), details of the plasma membrane and endomembrane system can be seen. The plasma membrane contains numerous flask-shaped invaginations. In some areas these are irregular in shape and size and may be involved in pinocytosis. In other areas, the invaginations are regular in shape and distribution and are called ***caveolae*** **C**.

The endomembrane system contains some elements which represent a poorly developed Golgi and endoplasmic reticulum **ER**. Other vesicular and tubular structures **T** are seen near the plasma membrane, often in association with caveolae; these probably constitute a system analogous to the sarcoplasmic reticulum of skeletal muscle, with the caveolae being analogous to the T tubule system.

Thick and thin filaments **Fi** of myosin and actin criss-cross the cytoplasm of each cell and are anchored to the cell membrane at attachment junctions (***focal adhesion densities***) **J**. Filaments are also attached within the cytoplasm to ***focal densities*** **D** which are believed to hold filaments in register.

The narrow intercellular spaces are of almost uniform width but at numerous sites the plasma membranes of adjacent cells form specialised cell junctions. Nexus (gap) junctions **G** mediate spread of excitation throughout visceral muscle (see Fig. 5.13).

C caveolae **D** focal density **ER** endoplasmic reticulum **F** fibroblast **Fi** filaments
G gap junction **J** attachment junction **M** mitochondrion **N** nucleus **S** supporting tissue
T intracellular tubule

Smooth muscle contraction

Smooth muscle does not show the longitudinally organised system of contractile proteins that is seen in striated muscle, but has an arrangement where bundles of contractile proteins criss-cross the cell, being inserted into anchoring points (focal densities) within the cytoplasm as well as anchoring to the cell membrane as focal adhesion densities.

Tension generated by contraction is transmitted through anchoring densities in the cell membrane to the surrounding external lamina, thus allowing a mass of smooth muscle cells to function as one unit. The intermediate filaments of smooth muscle, ***desmin***, are also inserted into the focal densities (Fig. 6.20).

The contraction mechanism of smooth muscle differs from that for striated muscle. Because the contractile proteins are arranged in a criss-cross lattice inserted around the cell membrane, contraction results in shortening of the cell, which assumes a globular shape in contrast to its elongated shape in the relaxed state (Fig. 6.20).

The mechanism of smooth muscle contraction is as follows:

- Thin filaments of actin are associated with ***tropomyosin***.
- Thick filaments composed of myosin only bind to actin if one chain is phosphorylated.
- Ca^{2+} ions in the cytosol of smooth muscle cells cause contraction as in striated muscle, but the control of Ca^{2+} ion movements is different. In relaxed smooth muscle, free Ca^{2+} ions are normally sequestered in sarcoplasmic reticulum throughout the cell. On membrane excitation, free Ca^{2+} ions are released into the cytoplasm and bind to a protein called ***calmodulin*** (a calcium-binding protein). The calcium-calmodulin complex then activates an enzyme called myosin light-chain kinase, which phosphorylates myosin and permits it to bind to actin. Actin and myosin subsequently interact by filament sliding to produce contraction in a similar way to that for skeletal muscle.
- Contraction of smooth muscle can be modulated by surface receptors activating internal second messenger systems. Expression of different receptors allows smooth muscle in different sites to respond to several different hormones.
- Compared with skeletal muscle, smooth muscle is able to maintain a high force of contraction for very little ATP usage.

Most smooth muscle is present in the walls of hollow viscera (e.g. gut, ureter, Fallopian tube) where it is arranged in sheets with cells aligned circumferentially or longitudinally, with contraction resulting in reduction of the lumen diameter.

In these so-called ***unitary smooth muscles***, cells tend to generate their own low level of rhythmic contraction, which may also be stimulated by stretch and is transmitted from cell to cell via the gap junctions. Such smooth muscle is richly innervated by the autonomic nervous system (see Ch. 7), which increases or decreases levels of spontaneous contraction rather than actually initiating it. Physiologically, this is termed ***tonic smooth muscle*** and is characterised by slow contraction, no action potentials and a low content of fast myosin.

A second arrangement of smooth muscle is typified by that in the iris of the eye. Here, rather than simply modulating spontaneous activity, autonomic innervation precisely controls contraction, resulting in opening and closing of the pupil. Similar neurally controlled or multi-unit smooth muscle is found in the vas deferens and some large arteries. Physiologically, this is termed ***phasic smooth muscle*** and is characterised by rapid contraction associated with an action potential.

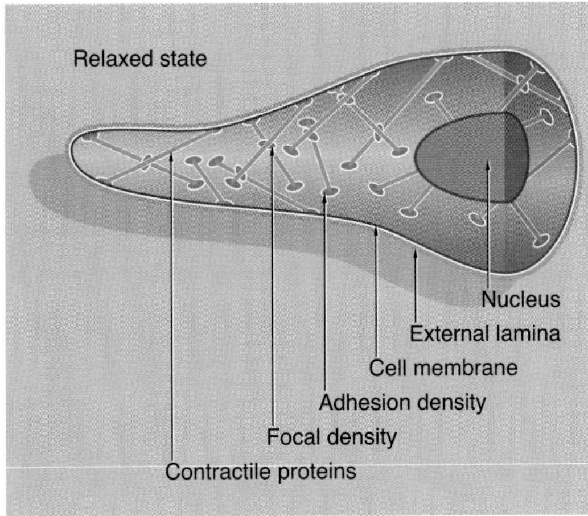

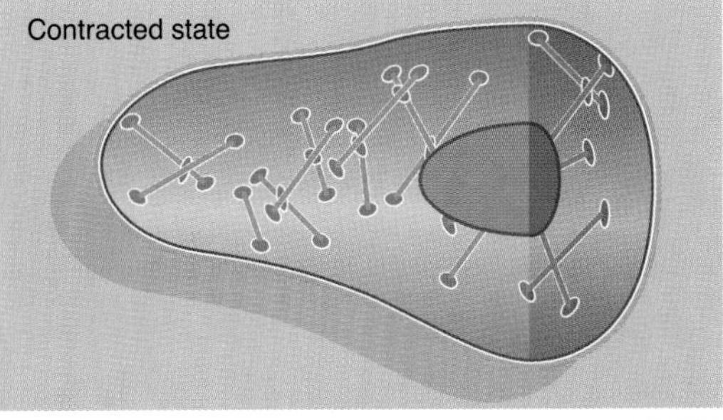

Fig. 6.20 Smooth muscle contraction

Contractile proteins are inserted into focal densities and focal adhesion densities around the cell membrane. In the relaxed state the cell is elongated. With contraction the smooth muscle adopts a globular shape.

Cardiac muscle

Cardiac muscle or ***myocardium*** exhibits many structural and functional characteristics intermediate between those of skeletal and visceral muscle. Like the former, its contractions are strong and utilise a great deal of energy, and like the latter the contractions are continuous and initiated by inherent mechanisms, although they are modulated by external autonomic and hormonal stimuli.

Cardiac muscle fibres are essentially long cylindrical cells with one or at most two nuclei, centrally located within the cell. The ends of the fibres are split longitudinally into a small number of branches, the ends of which abut onto similar branches of adjacent cells giving the impression of a continuous three-dimensional cytoplasmic network; this was formerly described as a syncytium before the discrete intercellular boundaries were recognised.

Between the muscle fibres, delicate collagenous tissue analogous to the endomysium of skeletal muscle supports the extremely rich capillary network necessary to meet the high metabolic demands of strong continuous activity.

Cardiac muscle fibres have an arrangement of contractile proteins similar to that of skeletal muscle and are consequently striated in a similar manner. However, this is often difficult to see with light microscopy due to the irregular branching shape of the cells and their myofibrils. Cardiac muscle fibres also have a system of T tubules and sarcoplasmic reticulum analogous to that of skeletal muscles. In the case of cardiac muscle, however, there is a slow leak of calcium ions into the cytoplasm from the sarcoplasmic reticulum after recovery from the preceding contraction; this causes a succession of automatic contractions independent of external stimuli. The rate of this inherent rhythm is then modulated by external autonomic and hormonal stimuli.

Between the ends of adjacent cardiac muscle cells are specialised intercellular junctions, called ***intercalated discs***, which not only provide points of anchorage for the myofibrils but also permit extremely rapid spread of contractile stimuli from one cell to another. Thus, adjacent fibres are triggered to contract almost simultaneously, thereby acting as a functional syncytium. In addition, a system of highly modified cardiac muscle cells constitutes the pacemaker regions of the heart and ramifies throughout the organ as the ***Purkinje system***, thus coordinating contraction of the myocardium as a whole in each cardiac cycle; this is illustrated and described in more detail in Chapter 8.

Cardiac muscle cells in certain locations in the heart are responsible for secreting hormones into the bloodstream.

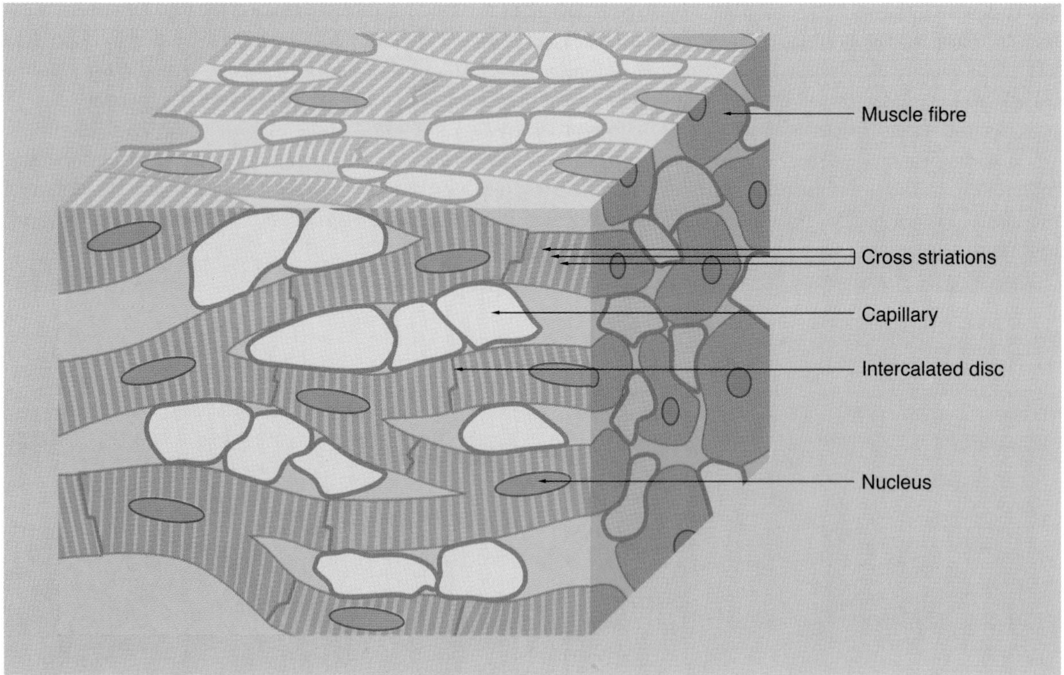

Fig. 6.21 Cardiac muscle

IC intercalated disc **N** nucleus

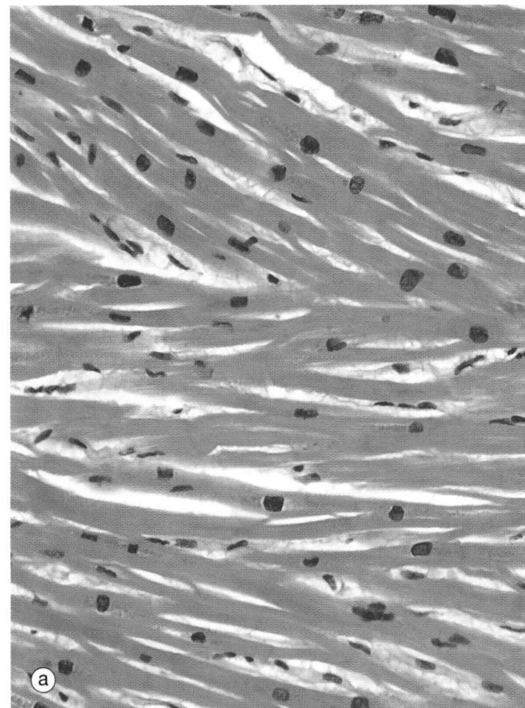

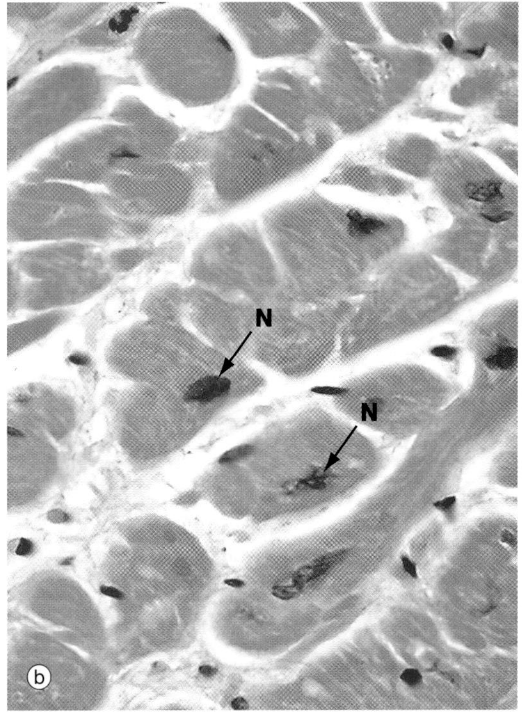

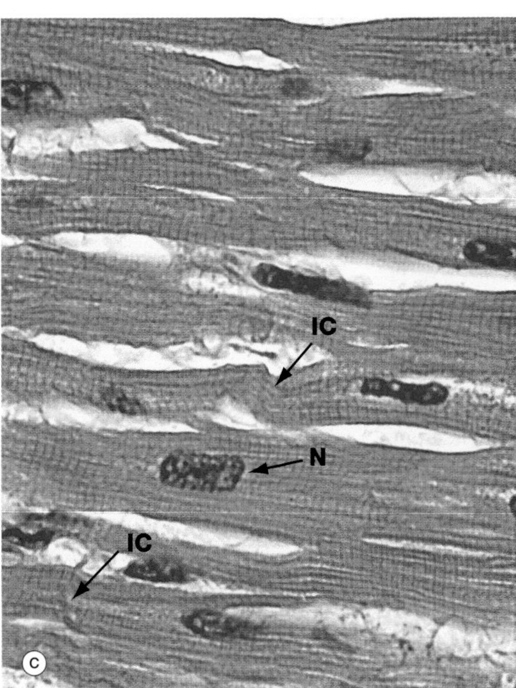

Fig. 6.22 Cardiac muscle
(a) LS, H & E ×198 (b) TS, H & E ×480 (c) LS, H & E polarised light ×480

In longitudinal section in micrograph (a), cardiac muscle cells are seen to contain one or two nuclei **N** and an extensive cytoplasm which branches to give the appearance of a continuous three-dimensional network. The elongated nuclei are mainly centrally located, a characteristic well demonstrated in transverse section as in micrograph (b).

Fine wisps of collagenous tissue run between fibres together with an extensive capillary supply, not seen at this resolution.

Micrograph (c) has been taken from an H & E stained section but viewed using polarised light to create optical contrast to reveal the striations. In routine light microscopy striations in cardiac muscle are generally not as easy to demonstrate as in skeletal muscle. The branching cytoplasmic network is readily seen with intercalated discs (**IC**) marking the intercellular boundaries just being visible. Note the delicate supporting tissue filling the intercellular spaces.

Cardiac muscle and disease

The heart muscle has high metabolic demands as it is constantly contracting to supply the body with blood. The blood supply to the heart itself is through three main coronary arteries which are prone to ***atheroma***, leading to narrowing and a reduction in blood flow. If there is a critical failure of blood flow to the myocardium, the cardiac muscle cells may be deprived of oxygen and other nutrients and die. Sudden occlusion of a coronary artery may lead to sudden reduction in blood supply to the heart causing death of cardiac muscle in a large area of the heart, termed a ***myocardial infarct***. In the normal heart, conduction of depolarisation for contraction runs along the muscle cells themselves. This is interrupted in the case of an area of infarction. A common complication of a myocardial infarct is the development of disturbances of the heart rhythm, for example ***ventricular fibrillation***. Loss of a significant portion of muscle mass from the heart can cause heart failure.

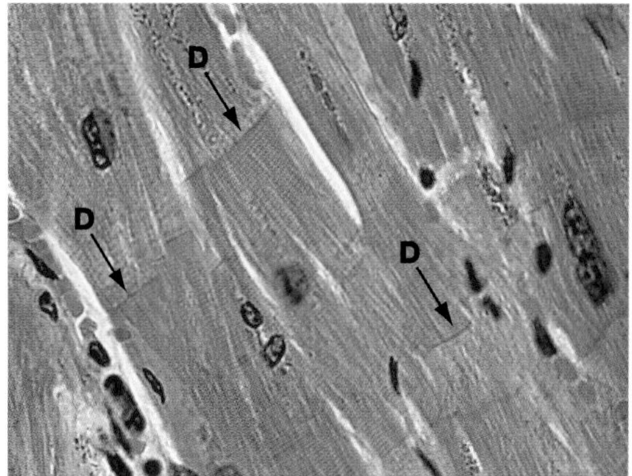

Fig. 6.23 Cardiac muscle
LS, H & E ×500

The branching pattern of cardiac muscle cells is demonstrated. Individual cells are attached to each other end-to-end by specialised cell junctions termed ***intercalated discs*** (see also Figs 6.26 and 6.27). These can just be seen as transverse bands **D** within the muscle cells. A red-brown pigment seen in these cardiac cells is termed ***lipofuscin*** and is derived from turnover of cell material within lysosomes, so-called 'wear-and-tear pigment'. This pigment gradually accumulates in the human heart with age and can be responsible for the heart muscle appearing brown in colour (see also Ch. 1).

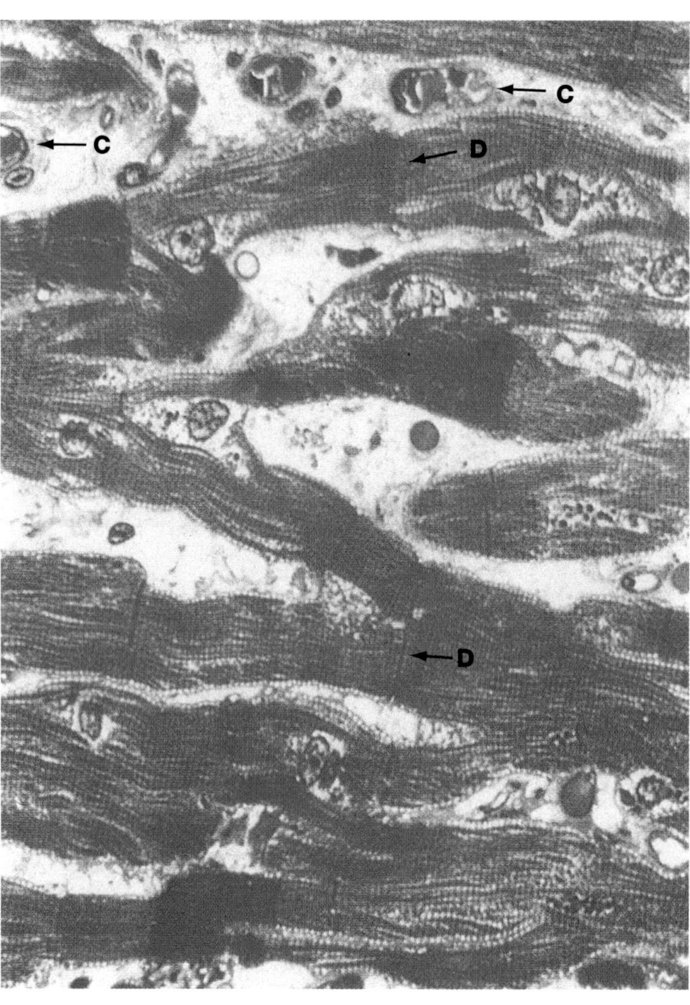

Fig. 6.24 Cardiac muscle
Thin section, toluidine blue ×640

This micrograph illustrates an extremely thin resin-embedded section at very high magnification. The branching cytoplasmic network of cardiac muscle cells is readily seen with prominent intercalated discs **D** marking the intercellular boundaries.

With this method of preparation it is easy to see the typical cross-striations.

Also note the delicate supporting tissue filling the intercellular spaces containing an extensive network of blood capillaries **C**.

C capillary **C_1–C_6** cardiac muscle cells **D** intercalated disc **F** fibroblast **G** glycogen **L** lipid **M** mitochondria **SR** sarcoplasmic reticulum **T** T tubule

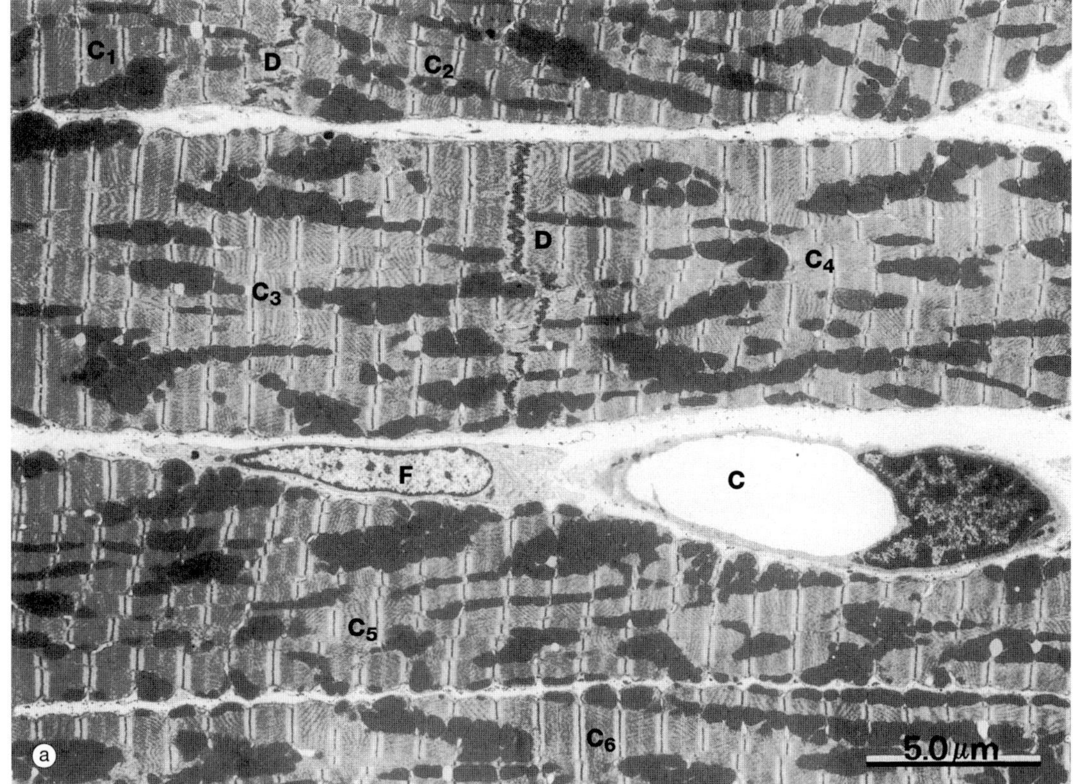

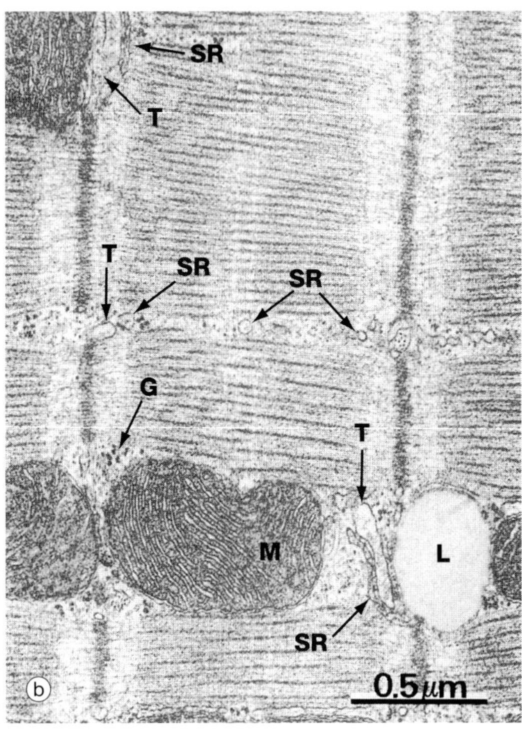

Fig. 6.25 Cardiac muscle
(a) EM ×5000 (b) EM ×38 000

Micrograph (a) illustrates portions of six cardiac muscle cells labelled $\mathbf{C}_1$ to $\mathbf{C}_6$. None of their nuclei are included in the plane of section. Cells $\mathbf{C}_1$ and $\mathbf{C}_2$ abut one another end to end and are demarcated by an intercalated disc **D**. Cells $\mathbf{C}_3$ and $\mathbf{C}_4$ are demarcated in a similar fashion. The intercellular space contains a capillary **C** and a fibroblast **F**.

The sarcomeres of cardiac muscle have an identical banding pattern to that of skeletal muscle. The sarcomeres are not, however, arranged into single columns making up cylindrical myofibrils as in skeletal muscle, but form a branching myofibrillar network continuous in three dimensions throughout the cytoplasm. The branching columns of sarcomeres are separated by sarcoplasm containing rows of mitochondria and sarcoplasmic reticulum. The great abundance of mitochondria in cardiac muscle reflects the enormous metabolic demands of continuous cardiac muscle activity.

Conduction of excitatory stimuli to the sarcomeres of cardiac muscle is mediated by a system of T tubules and sarcoplasmic reticulum essentially similar in arrangement to that of skeletal muscle. The T tubules, however, ramify throughout the cardiac muscle cytoplasm at the Z lines and their origins are seen as indentations in the sarcolemma which thus has a somewhat scalloped outline.

The conducting system can be seen at high magnification in micrograph (b). T tubules **T** and sarcoplasmic reticulum **SR** form poorly defined triads compared with those of skeletal muscle. Note the typical closely packed cristae of the mitochondria **M**, a lipid droplet **L** and glycogen granules **G**.

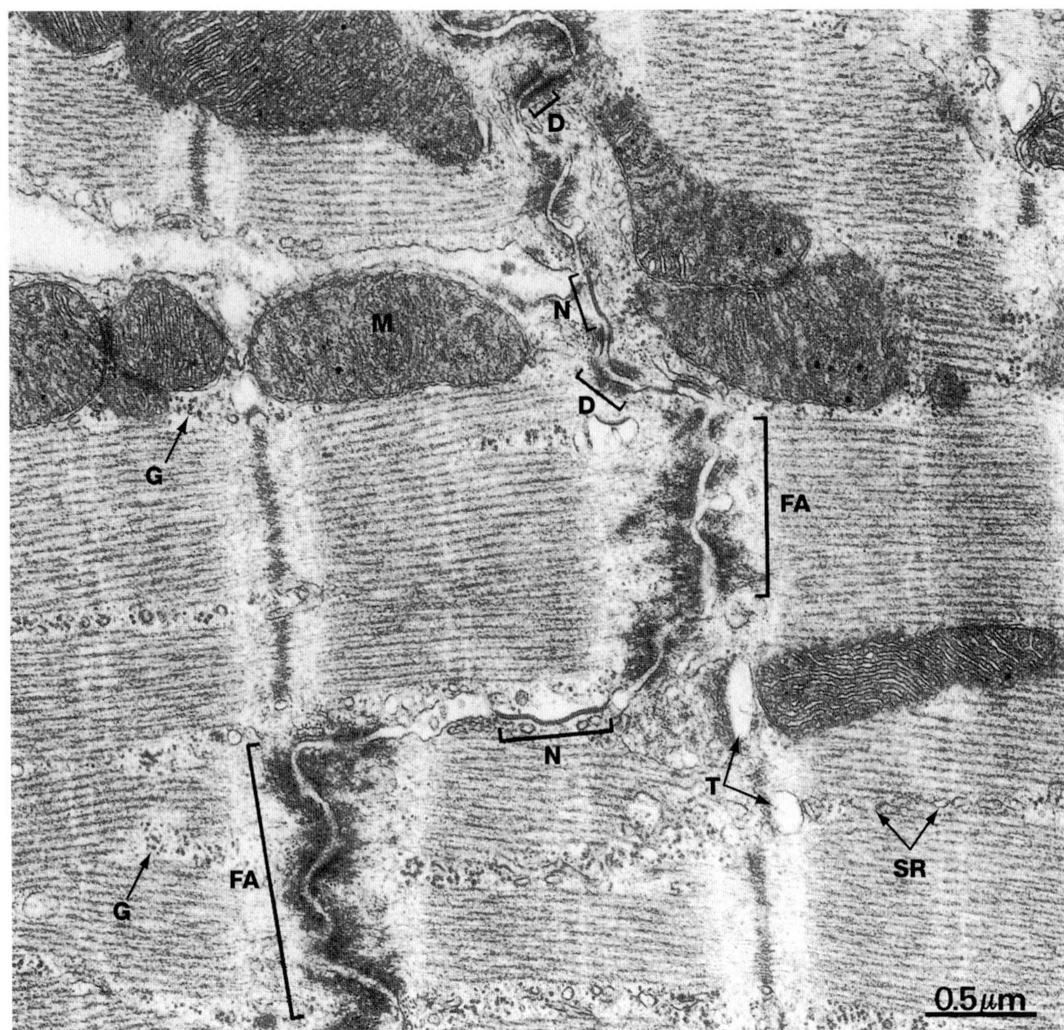

Fig. 6.26 Cardiac muscle: intercalated disc in LS view
EM ×31 000

Intercalated discs are specialised transverse junctions between cardiac muscle cells at sites where they meet end to end; they always coincide with the Z lines. Intercalated discs bind the cells, transmit forces of contraction and provide areas of low electrical resistance for the rapid spread of excitation throughout the myocardium.

The intercalated disc is an interdigitating junction and consists of three types of membrane-to-membrane contact. The predominant type of contact, the ***fascia adherens*** **FA**, resembles the zonula adherens of epithelial junctional complexes (see Fig. 5.12) but is more extensive and less regular. The actin filaments at the ends of terminal sarcomeres insert into the fasciae adherentes and thereby transmit contractile forces from cell to cell. Desmosomes **D** occur less frequently and provide anchorage for intermediate filaments of the cytoskeleton. Gap (nexus) junctions **N** (see Fig. 5.13) are present mainly in the longitudinal portions of the interdigitations and are sites of low electrical resistance through which excitation passes from cell to cell.

Note the similarity of the sarcomeres of cardiac and skeletal muscle (see Fig. 6.9). The mitochondria **M** are elongated or spheroidal and have abundant closely packed cristae rich in oxidative enzyme systems. The sarcoplasm within and between the sarcomeres is rich in glycogen granules **G**. Lace-like profiles of sarcoplasmic reticulum **SR** and parts of T tubules **T** can be identified.

D desmosome **E** endothelial cell **EL** external lamina **F** fibroblast **FA** fascia adherens
G glycogen **ID** interdigitation **L** leucocyte **M** mitochondria **N** nexus or gap junction
S sarcomere **SR** sarcoplasmic reticulum **T** T tubule

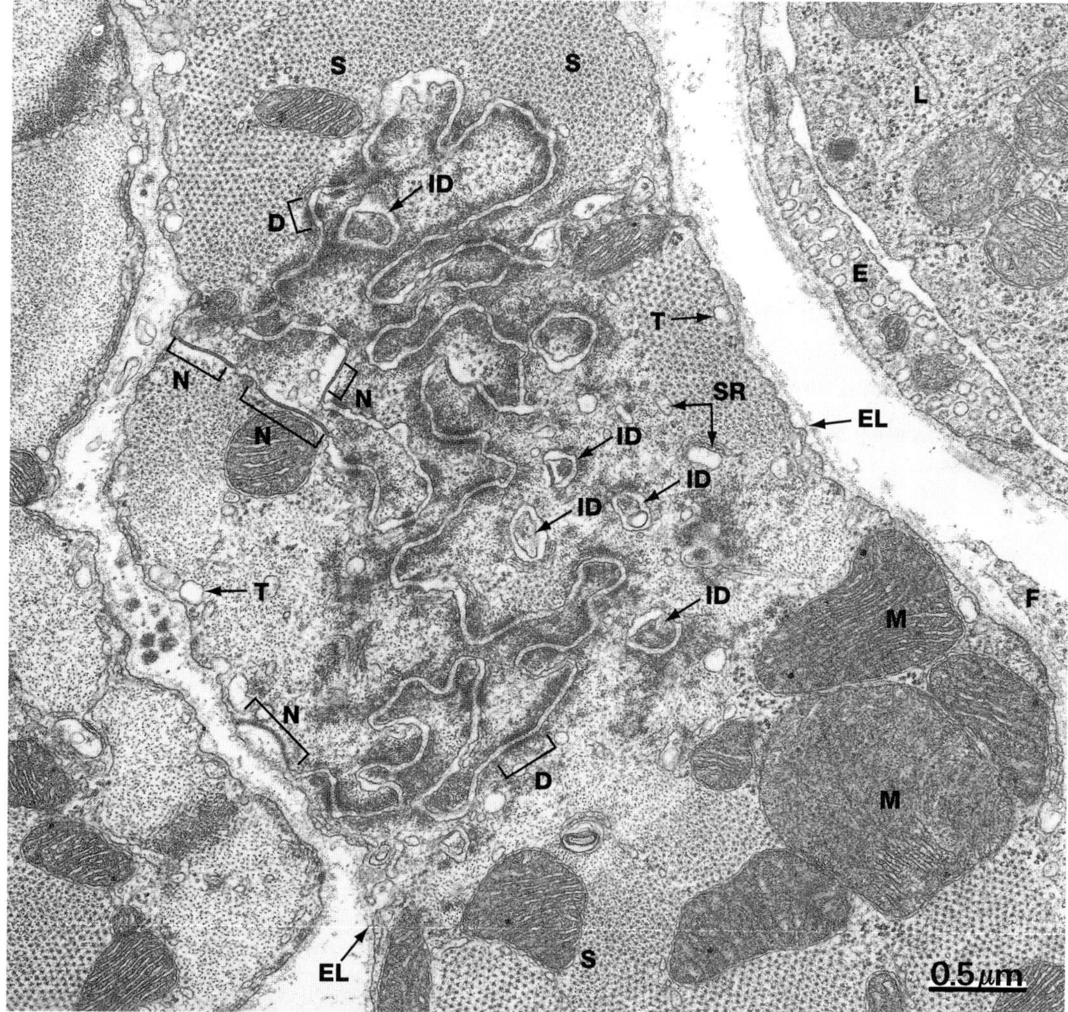

Fig. 6.27 Cardiac muscle: intercalated disc in TS view
EM ×27 000

The end-to-end junction between cardiac muscle cells is not simply a flat surface. In contrast, each junction is a highly convoluted set of finger-like interdigitations, maximising the surface area in contact between each cell.

This rich structure can be appreciated in this micrograph which shows a transverse section through cardiac muscle in the vicinity of a Z line incorporating an intercalated disc. The tortuous course of the intercellular junction as well as islands of apparently isolated paired cell membranes **ID** reflect the manner in which the ends of the cardiac muscle cells interdigitate with one another. Most of the intercellular junction comprises fasciae adherentes with interspersed desmosomes **D** and some nexus junctions **N**.

The dot-like regular lattice are the contractile proteins of the sarcomeres **S** with the thick filaments surrounded by thin filaments cut in transverse section. Mitochondria **M** are prominent.

Beneath the cell membrane are dilated tubules **T** representing part of the T tubule system. Elements of the sarcoplasmic reticulum **SR** can be seen surrounding the sarcomeres. Beyond the plasma membrane lies the external lamina **EL**. A fibroblast cytoplasmic extension **F** is present in the extracellular space at the right of the field. At the upper right is an endomysial capillary, its endothelium **E** containing numerous pinocytotic vesicles; the lumen contains a leucocyte **L**.

7. *Nervous tissues*

Introduction

The nervous system is designed to deliver rapid and precise communication between different parts of the body by the action of specialised nerve cells called ***neurones***. These highly specialised cells are interconnected and function to gather and process information and then generate appropriate response signals. The nervous system is divided into two main parts:

- The **central nervous system** (**CNS**) comprising the brain and spinal cord.
- The **peripheral nervous system** (**PNS**) comprising the nerves which run between the CNS and other tissues, together with nerve 'relay stations' termed ***ganglia***.

Functionally, the nervous system is divided into the somatic nervous system which is involved in voluntary functions, and the autonomic nervous system which exerts control over many involuntary functions. Histologically, however, the entire nervous system merely consists of variations in the arrangement of neurones and their supporting tissues.

The functions of the nervous system depend on a fundamental property of neurones called ***excitability***. As in all cells, the resting neurone maintains an ionic gradient across its plasma membrane thereby creating an electrical potential. Excitability involves a change in membrane permeability in response to appropriate stimuli such that the ionic gradient is reversed and the plasma membrane becomes ***depolarised***; a wave of depolarisation, known as an ***action potential***, then spreads along the plasma membrane. This is followed by the process of repolarisation in which the membrane rapidly re-establishes its resting potential.

The sites of intercommunication between neurones are termed ***synapses***. Depolarisation of one neurone causes it to release chemical transmitter substances, ***neurotransmitters***, which initiate an action potential in the adjacent neurone. Within the nervous system, neurones are arranged to form pathways for the conduction of action potentials from receptors to effector organs via integrating neurones. Neurotransmitters not only mediate neurone-to-neurone transmission but also act as chemical intermediates between the nervous system and effector organs which also exhibit the property of excitability.

The effector organs of voluntary nervous pathways are generally skeletal muscle while those of involuntary pathways are usually smooth muscle, cardiac muscle and muscle-like epithelial cells (myoepithelial cells) within some exocrine glands.

This chapter encompasses the cell and tissue types found in the nervous system and includes the structure of the peripheral nervous system and relatively simple types of sensory receptor. Details of the arrangement of nervous tissue in the central nervous system are the subject of Chapter 20, while the structure of the highly specialised organs of sensory reception associated with the cranial nerves, e.g. eye and ear, is presented in Chapter 21.

Diseases of the nervous system

Selective vulnerability
Neurones have a very high metabolic demand and are especially vulnerable to deprivation of oxygen or nutrients by obstructing the blood supply. Relatively short periods of deprivation of nutrients lead to nerve cell death.

Epilepsy
The regulation of neuronal excitability within the brain may become abnormal, leading to an uncontrolled spread of depolarisation termed an epileptic seizure.

Neurodegenerative diseases
A series of diseases mainly seen in old age characterised by progressive degeneration and death of nerve cells, often limited to specific neuronal systems. Alzheimer's disease, motor neurone disease and Parkinson's disease fall in this group.

Demyelinating diseases
The transmission of signals in the nervous system is largely by way of long nerve cell processes which are insulated by cells making a substance called myelin. These specialised myelin-forming cells can be the target of specific diseases, leading to loss of function of effective signaling between nerve cells. Multiple sclerosis is the main disease in this group.

Stroke
The vascular supply to the brain is vital in maintaining its function. If blood vessels become blocked or bleed there is corresponding damage to the functioning nerve cells. Stroke is one of the major causes of morbidity and death in affluent societies.

Drugs and the blood–brain barrier
There is a highly specialised barrier to the diffusion of substances from the blood into the brain which functionally relates to the arrangement of support cells and basement membrane around capillaries in the CNS. Certain drugs do not get into the brain because of this barrier.

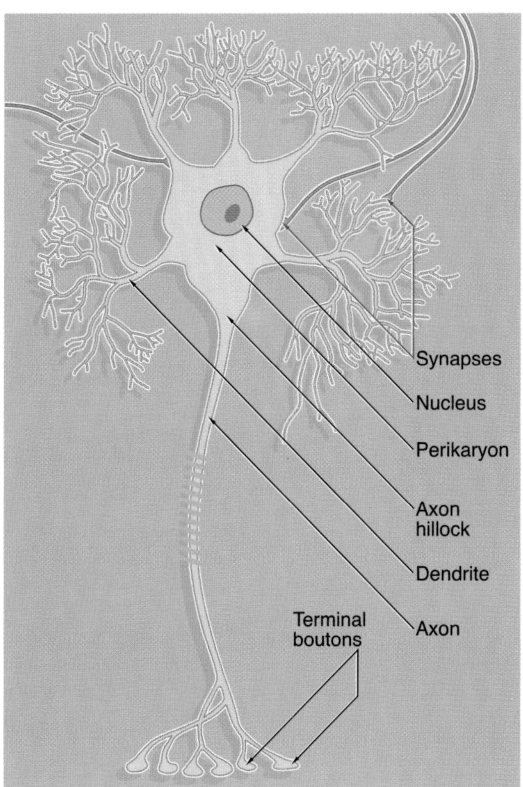

Fig. 7.1 The neurone

Despite great variation in size and shape in different parts of the nervous system, all neurones have the same basic structure as shown in this idealised diagram. The neurone consists of a large ***cell body*** containing the nucleus surrounded by cytoplasm known as the ***perikaryon***. Processes of two types extend from the cell body, namely a single ***axon*** and one or more ***dendrites***.

Dendrites are highly branched, tapering processes which either end in specialised sensory receptors (as in primary sensory neurones) or form synapses with neighbouring neurones from which they receive stimuli. In general, dendrites function as the major sites of information input into the neurone.

Each neurone has a single axon arising from a cone-shaped portion of the cell body called the ***axon hillock*** The axon is a cylindrical process up to 1 metre in length terminating on other neurones or effector organs by way of a variable number of small branches which end in small swellings called ***terminal boutons***.

Action potentials arise in the cell body as a result of integration of afferent (incoming) stimuli; action potentials are then conducted along the axon to influence other neurones or effector organs. Axons are commonly referred to as ***nerve fibres***.

In general, the cell bodies of all neurones are located in the central nervous system; exceptions are the cell bodies of most primary sensory neurones and the terminal effector neurones of the autonomic nervous system where, in both cases, the cell bodies lie in aggregations called ***ganglia*** in peripheral sites.

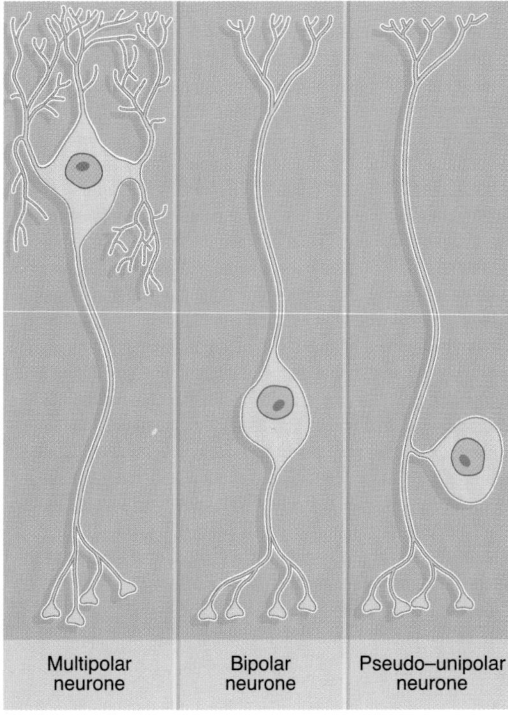

Multipolar neurone | Bipolar neurone | Pseudo–unipolar neurone

Fig. 7.2 Basic neurone types

Throughout the nervous system, neurones have a wide variety of shapes which fall into three main patterns according to the arrangement of the axon and dendrites with respect to the cell body.

The most common form is the ***multipolar neurone*** in which numerous dendrites project from the cell body; the dendrites may all arise from one pole of the cell body or may extend from all parts of the cell body. In general, intermediate, integratory and motor neurones conform to this pattern.

Bipolar neurones have only a single dendrite which arises from the pole of the cell body opposite to the origin of the axon. These unusual neurones act as receptor neurones for the senses of smell, sight and balance.

Most other primary sensory neurones are described as ***pseudo-unipolar neurones*** since a single dendrite and the axon arise from a common stem of the cell body; this stem is formed by the fusion of the first part of the dendrite and axon of a bipolar type of neurone during embryological development.

As a general rule, neurone impulses are conveyed along dendrites towards the nerve cell body (afferent) while axons usually convey impulses away from the nerve cell body (efferent).

Origin and regeneration of nerve cells

Neurones are derived in embryogenesis from primitive neuroblasts. Neurones are terminally differentiated cells that, for all practical purposes, do not regenerate in the event of cell death. Studies have shown cell division in neurones in the adult brain, although the biological significance of this remains uncertain. However, regeneration of axons and dendrites can occur in the event of damage, provided the neurone cell body remains viable. This is the basis of nerve grafting used to treat peripheral nerve injuries.

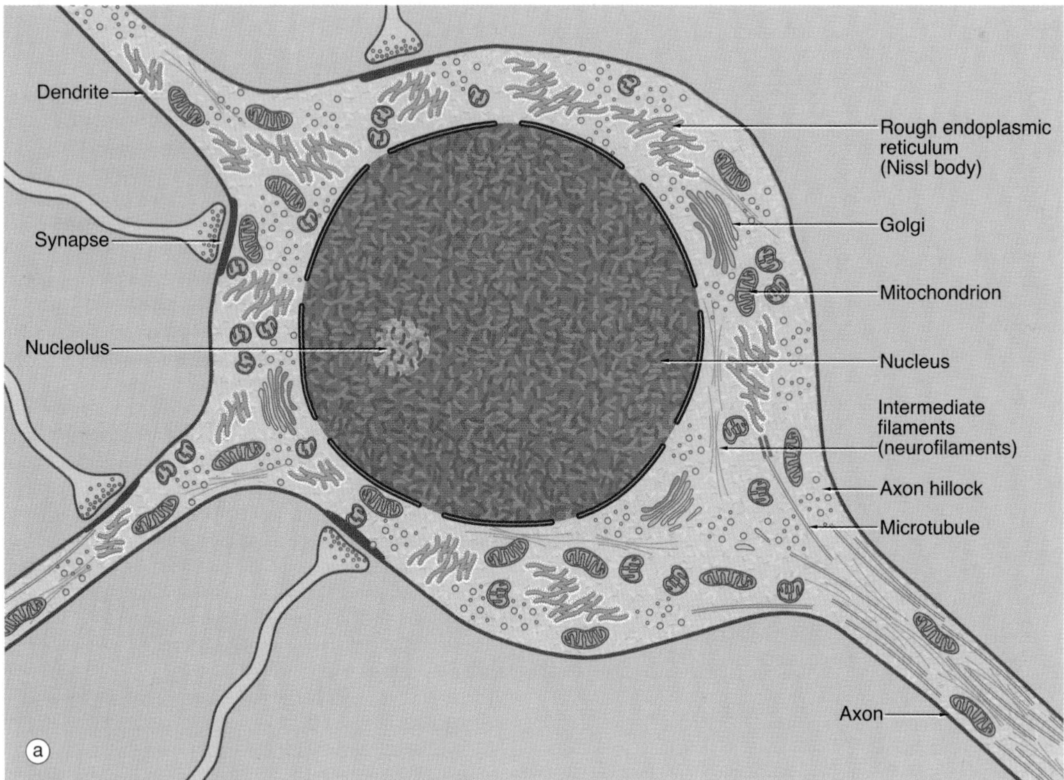

Fig. 7.3 Ultrastructure of the neurone
(a) Schematic diagram (b) EM ×19 000 *(opposite)*

The diagram (a) illustrates the main ultrastructural features of the neurone, in this case a multipolar neurone with an axon and two dendrites. The nucleus is large, round or ovoid and usually centrally located within the perikaryon. Reflecting the intense metabolic activity of the neurone (and consequent need to replace proteins which are rapidly turned over), the chromatin is completely dispersed and the nucleolus is a conspicuous feature.

The cytoplasm of the cell body contains large aggregations of rough endoplasmic reticulum which correspond to the ***Nissl substance*** of light microscopy (see Fig. 7.4); the rough endoplasmic reticulum extends into the dendrites but not into the axon hillock or axon. Rough endoplasmic reticulum is a much more prominent feature in large neurones, such as somatic motor neurones, than in smaller neurones such as those of the autonomic nervous system. A diffuse Golgi apparatus is found adjacent to the nucleus. Smooth endoplasmic reticulum is not a prominent feature of the perikaryon, but tubules, cisternae and vesicles are prominent in the axon and dendrites. The mitochondria of the perikaryon are numerous and have the usual rod-like appearances; those of the axon are extremely slender and elongated.

Neurones are very metabolically active and expend much energy in maintaining ionic gradients across the plasma membrane. Neurones synthesise neurotransmitter substances or their precursors in the perikaryon from where they are transported along the axon to the synapse to be released when appropriately stimulated.

Numerous intermediate filaments (neurofilaments) and microtubules are arranged in parallel bundles throughout the perikaryon and along the length of the axon and dendrites. The electron micrograph (b) shows part of the cell body of a neurone and includes a portion of the nucleus **N**. At the lower right, part of the neuronal plasma membrane **PM** is seen including a synapse **S** with the terminal bouton **TB** of an adjacent neurone. Features of the cytoplasm of the perikaryon are areas of rough endoplasmic reticulum **rER**, free ribosomes **R** and scattered mitochondria **M**. An extensive Golgi complex **G** is represented by several stacks of flattened membranous cisternae. Associated with the Golgi are several multivesicular bodies **MB** involved in transport to other organelles including lysosomes **L**. Microtubules **T** can be identified in oblique section but neurofilaments are not readily identifiable.

The cytoskeleton of the neurone is vital for axonal transport

The cytoskeleton of neurones is highly organised. Neurofilament proteins, the intermediate filaments of nerve cells, act as a scaffold to maintain the shape of the axon and cell body. There is a highly organised network of microtubules, which transport material up and down the axon. ***Slow axonal transport*** carries cytoskeletal elements.

Fast axonal transport carries membrane-bound organelles, such as neurosecretory vesicles, at speeds of 400 mm/day and is mediated by microtubular transport mechanisms. Anterograde movement (from the cell body) uses the molecule kinesin as a molecular motor while retrograde movement (to the cell body) uses the molecule dynein.

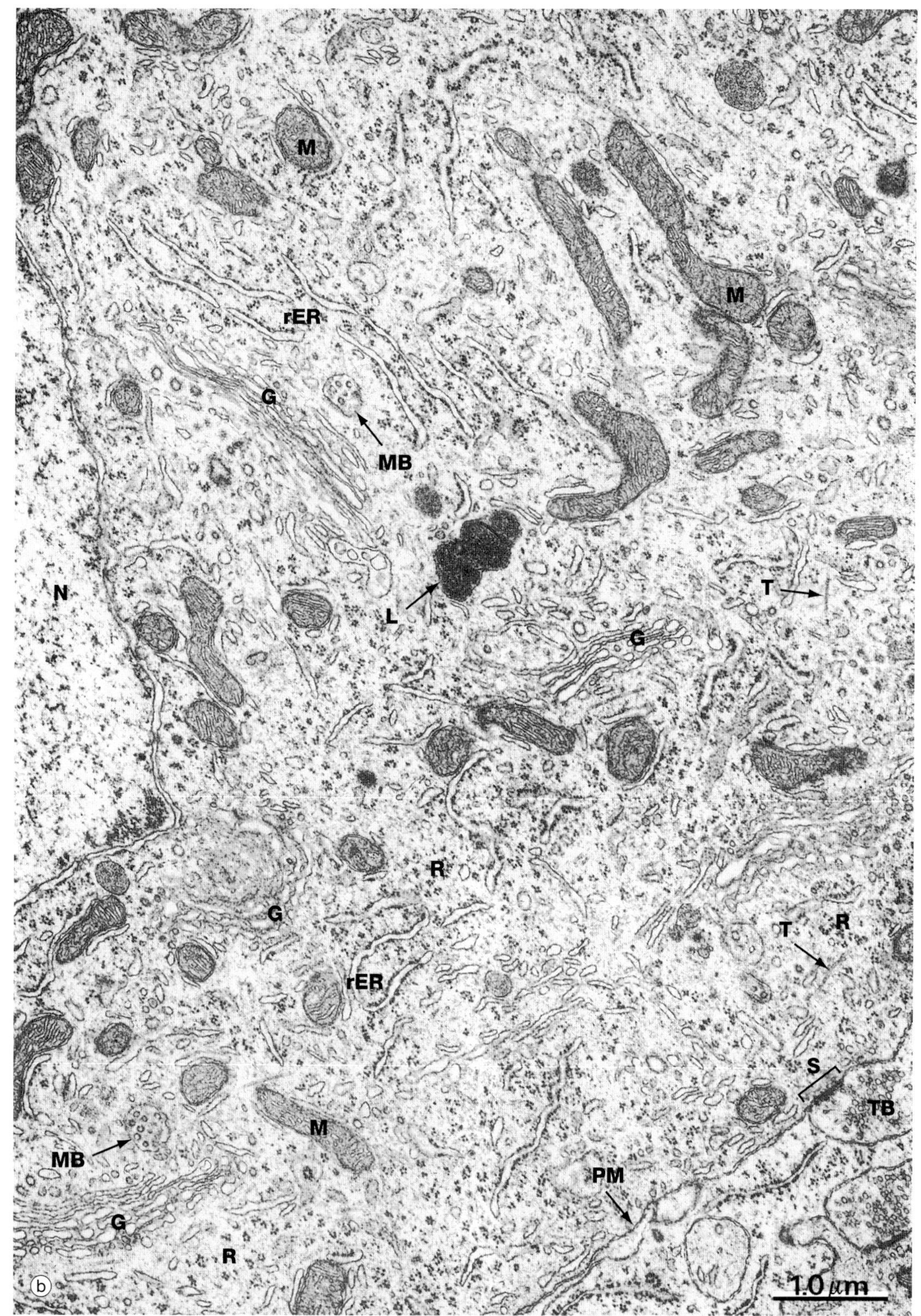

G Golgi complex **L** lysosomes **M** mitochondria **MB** multivesicular bodies **N** nucleus
PM plasma membrane **R** free ribosomes **rER** rough endoplasmic reticulum **S** synapse
T microtubules **TB** terminal bouton

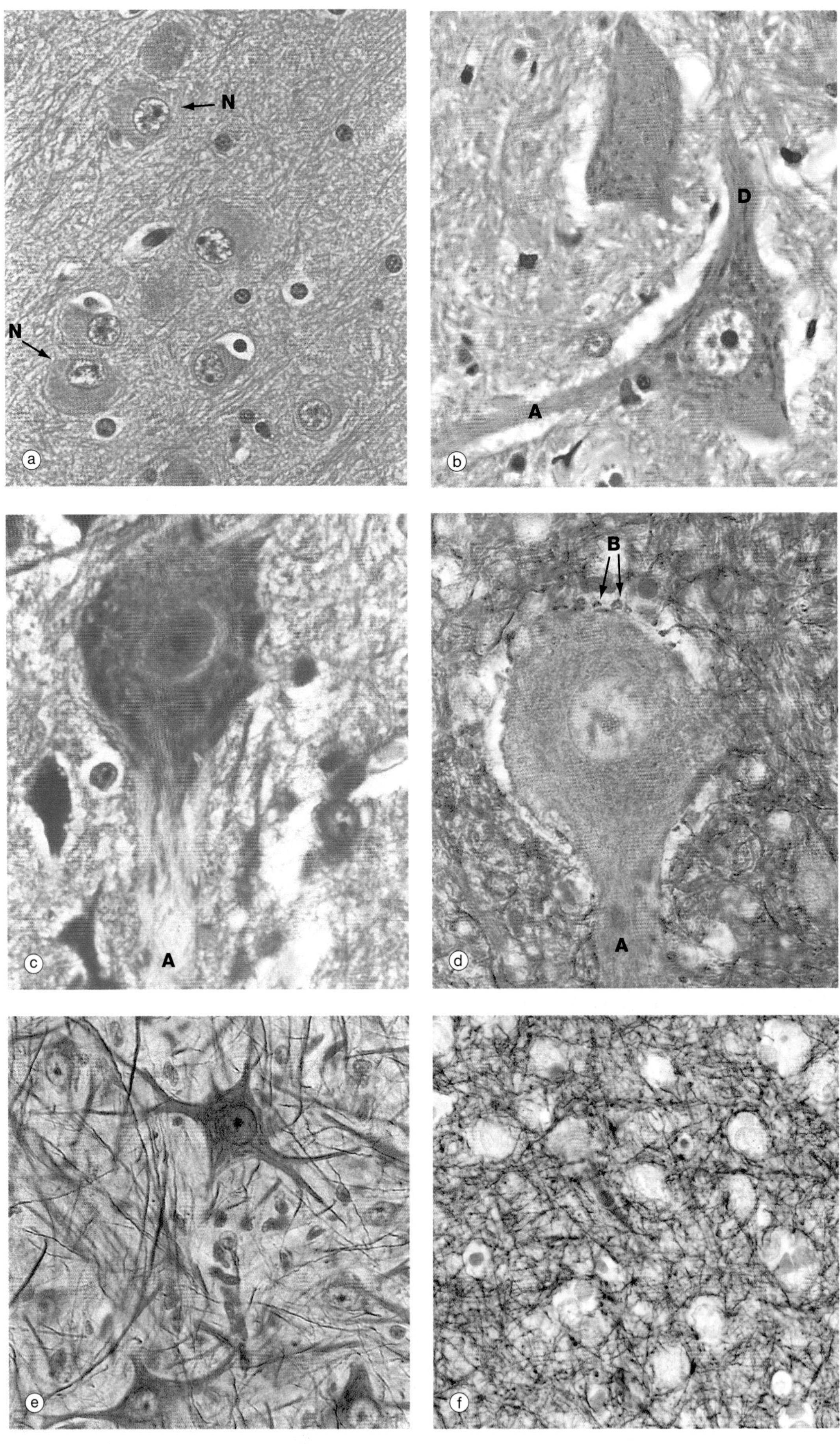
N
N
a
D
A
b
A
c
B
A
d
e
f

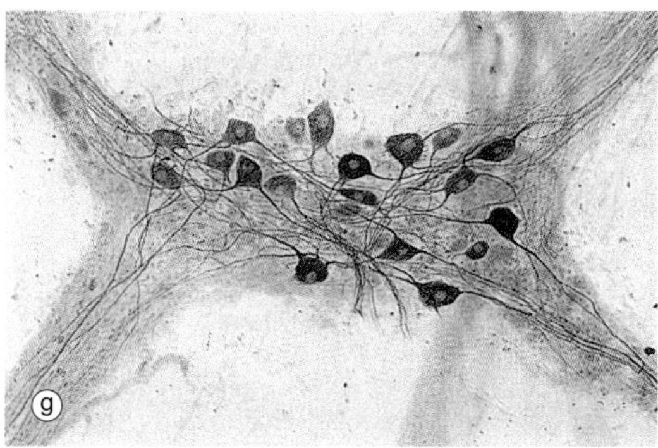

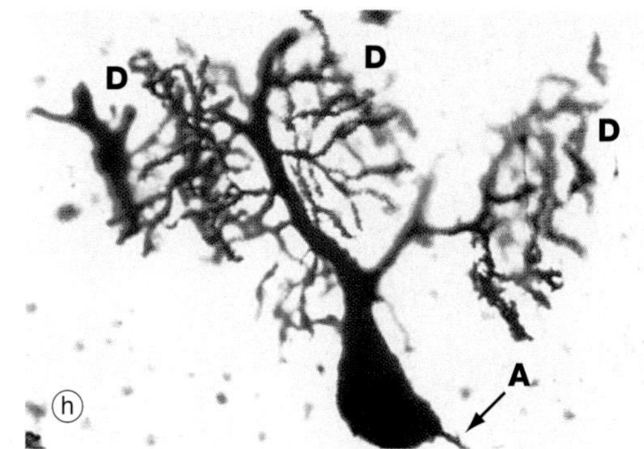

Fig. 7.4 Neurones and methods of study with light microscopy *(Micrographs (a) to (f) opposite)*
(a) H & E ×480 (b) H & E ×1200 (c) Nissl method ×1200 (d) Gold method ×1200 (e) Gold/toluidine blue ×600 (f) Immunochemistry neurofilament protein ×480 (g) Spread preparation, gold method ×320 (h) Golgi–Cox ×320

Special staining techniques are required to show the rich structural detail of the nervous system.

Heavy metal impregnation techniques with gold and silver are valuable in the study of neurone morphology, and were widely employed by the pioneers of neuro-anatomy such as Cajal and Golgi from whom they take their names. Likewise, ***spread preparations*** often permit the examination of complete neurones and their cytoplasmic processes.

Immunohistochemistry can also be used to identify neurone-specific proteins, e.g. neurofilament protein, and γγ enolase (neurone-specific enolase).

Micrographs (a) and (b), stained with H & E, show neurones **N** in the central nervous system; the nuclei are huge in comparison with those of surrounding support cells; dispersed chromatin and prominent nucleoli reflect a high level of protein synthesis. Neurones have extensive cytoplasm which is basophilic (blue stained) due to extensive ribosomal RNA. In (b) the RNA can be seen gathered into small patches termed Nissl substance which extends into dendrites **D** but not the axon **A**. In H & E preparations virtually no detail can be seen of cytoplasmic processes which merge into a fibrillary background termed the ***neuropil*** composed of nerve cell processes as well as those of support cells.

In micrograph (c), the Nissl method stains RNA, identifying the rough endoplasmic reticulum (Nissl substance) as dark blue material giving the neuronal cytoplasm a mottled appearance; DNA in the nucleus and nucleoli has similar staining properties. Note the axon **A** which lacks Nissl substance.

A very similar neurone is shown in micrograph (d) using a heavy metal impregnation technique that highlights small axons. Numerous axons from other neurones with tiny terminal boutons **B** can be seen forming synapses with the cell body.

Micrograph (e) employs another gold method which provides excellent detail of neuronal shape and shows the presence of the cytoskeleton in the dendrites and axons; the blue counter-stain demonstrates the nuclei of surrounding support cells. Note that detail of neuronal processes is lost when these pass out of the plane of section.

Micrograph (f) shows an area of the brain stained with an antibody to neurofilament protein. This highlights the complex network of axons within the neuropil between neurones. Neurones are seen as clear spaces containing a nucleus in this preparation.

Spread preparations, as shown in micrograph (g), also outline the complexity of nerve cell processes, both axons and dendrites. This example shows neurones in a small peripheral ganglion, their main cytoplasmic processes being very clearly delineated.

Finally, micrograph (h) illustrates a very thick section stained by a silver impregnation method and shows a Purkinje cell in the cerebellar cortex. These cells have a single small axon **A** at one pole and an extraordinary, finely branching dendritic tree **D** at the other pole. Note that the base of the dendritic system is in this case much larger than that of the axon.

Myelinated and non-myelinated nerve fibres

In the peripheral nervous system, all axons are enveloped by highly specialised cells called ***Schwann cells*** which provide both structural and metabolic support. In general, small diameter axons (e.g. those of the autonomic nervous system and small pain fibres) are simply enveloped by the cytoplasm of Schwann cells; these nerve fibres are said to be ***non-myelinated***. Large diameter fibres are wrapped by a variable number of concentric layers of the Schwann cell plasma membrane forming a ***myelin sheath***; such nerve fibres are said to be ***myelinated***. Within the central nervous system, myelination is similar to that in the peripheral nervous system except that the myelin sheaths are formed by cells called ***oligodendrocytes*** (see Fig. 7.25). There are however distinct chemical differences between central and peripheral myelin. In all nerve fibres, the rate of conduction of action potentials is proportional to the diameter of the axon; myelination greatly increases axon conduction velocity compared with that of a non-myelinated fibre of the same diameter.

A axon **B** terminal bouton (synapse) at the end of axons **D** dendrite **N** neurone

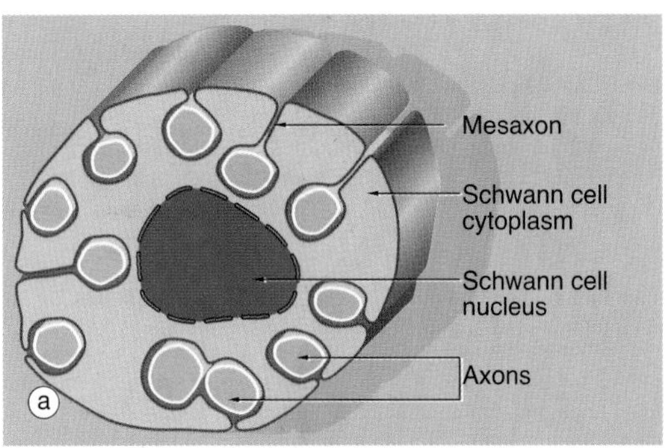

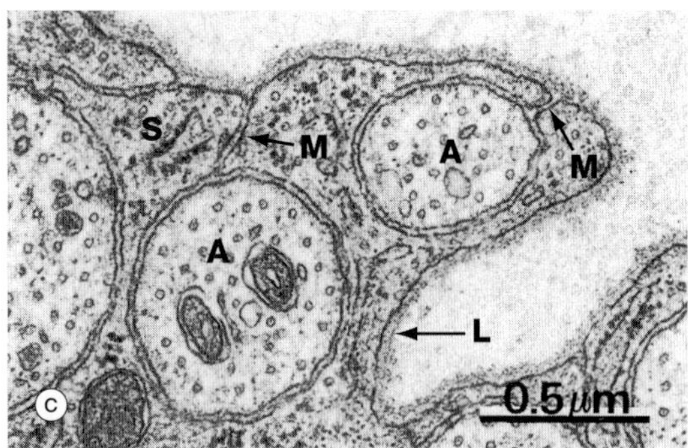

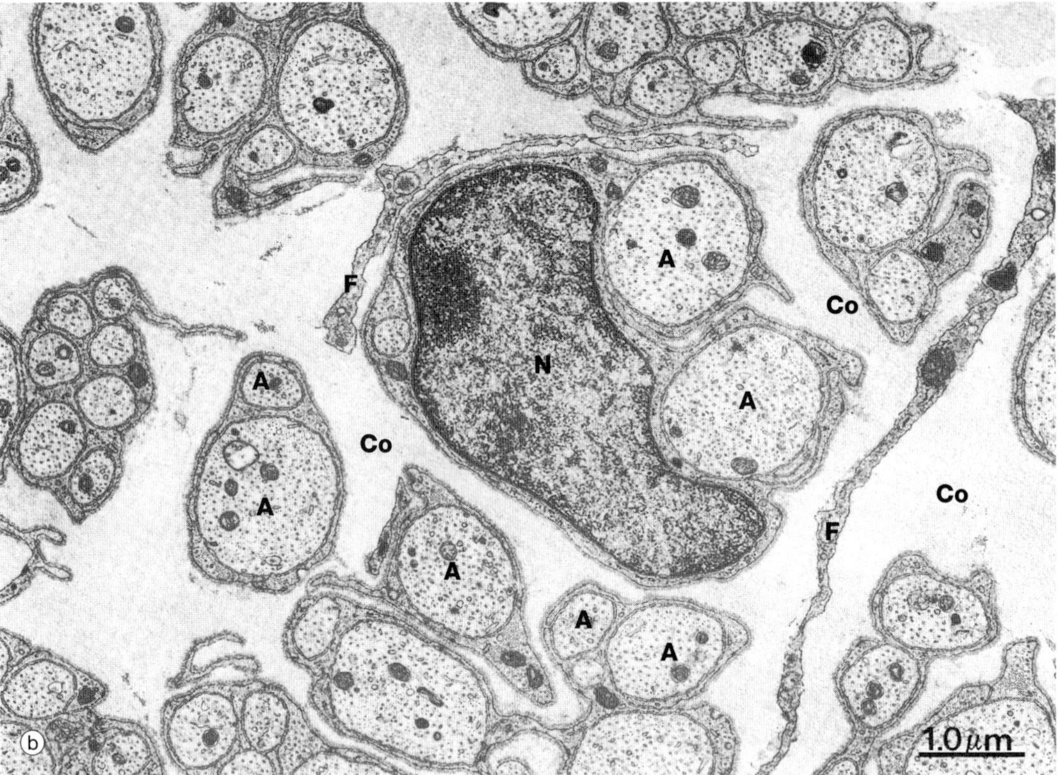

Fig. 7.5 Non-myelinated nerve fibres
(a) Diagram (b) EM ×15 000 (c) EM ×36 000

The relationship of non-myelinated axons with their supporting Schwann cell is illustrated in diagram (a). One or more axons become longitudinally invaginated into the Schwann cell so that each axon is embedded in a channel, invested by the Schwann cell plasma membrane and cytoplasm. The Schwann cell plasma membrane becomes apposed to itself along the opening of the channel, thus effectively sealing the axon within an extracellular compartment bounded by the Schwann cell. The zone of apposition of the Schwann cell membrane is called the ***mesaxon***. Note that more than one axon may occupy a single channel within the Schwann cell. Each Schwann cell extends for only a short distance along the nerve tract and at its termination the ensheathment is continued by another Schwann cell with which it interdigitates closely end to end.

At low magnification in micrograph (b), non-myelinated axons **A** of various sizes are seen ensheathed by Schwann cells; one of the Schwann cells has been sectioned transversely through its nucleus **N**. Note the variable number of axons enclosed by each Schwann cell. Delicate cytoplasmic extensions of fibroblasts **F** and collagen fibrils **Co** cut in cross-section can be seen in the endoneurium.

At high magnification in micrograph (c), part of the cytoplasm of a Schwann cell **S** is shown ensheathing several axons **A**; axons are readily identified by their content of smooth endoplasmic reticulum and microtubules, seen in cross-section. Several mesaxons **M** can be seen. The external surface of the Schwann cell is bounded by an external lamina **L** equivalent to lamina densa in epithelia.

A axon **C** Schwann cell cytoplasm **Ci** inner Schwann cell cytoplasm **Co** collagen **F** fibroblast
L external lamina **M** mesaxon **My** myelin sheath **N** Schwann cell nucleus **S** Schwann cell

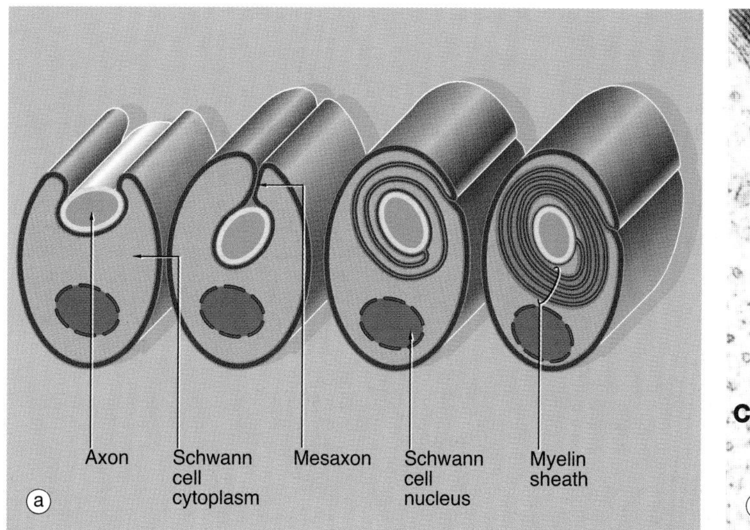

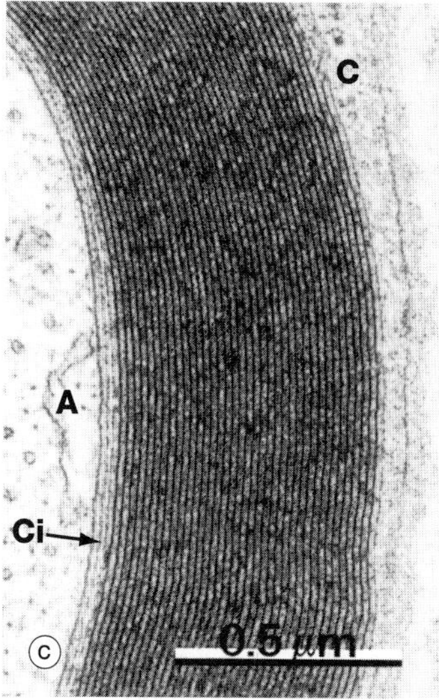

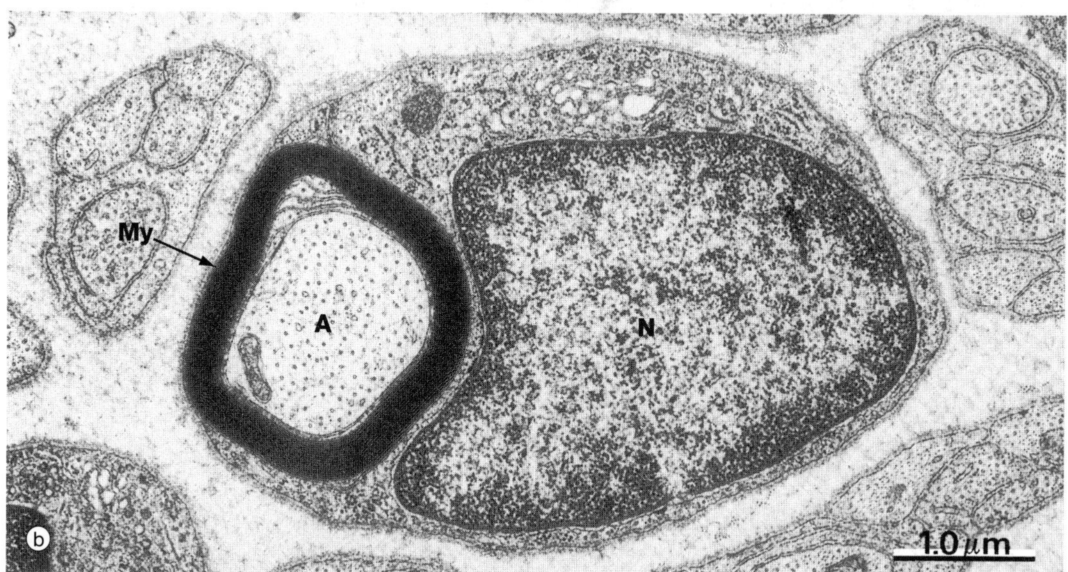

Fig. 7.6 Myelinated nerve fibre
(a) Diagram (b) EM ×20 000 (c) EM ×46 000

In peripheral nerves, myelination begins with the invagination of a single nerve axon into a Schwann cell; a mesaxon is then formed. As myelination proceeds, the mesaxon rotates around the axon thereby enveloping the axon in concentric layers of Schwann cell cytoplasm and plasma membrane. The cytoplasm is then excluded so that the inner leaflets of plasma membrane fuse with each other and the axon becomes surrounded by multiple layers of membrane which together constitute the myelin sheath. The single segment of myelin produced by each Schwann cell is termed an ***internode***; this ensheaths the axon between one node of Ranvier and the next (see Fig. 7.7).

In micrograph (b), a myelinated nerve fibre from the PNS is sectioned transversely at the level of the nucleus of an ensheathing Schwann cell **N**. The single axon **A** is enveloped by many layers of fused Schwann cell plasma membrane forming the myelin sheath **My**.

Micrograph (c) shows that the compact myelin sheath consists of many regular layers of membrane. The darker lines, termed the ***major dense lines***, arise by fusion of cytoplasmic leaflets. The intervening ***intraperiod*** lines represent closely apposed external membrane leaflets. The substantial lipid content of these modified membrane layers insulate the underlying axon **A**, preventing ion fluxes across the axonal plasma membrane except at the nodes of Ranvier. The main bulk of the Schwann cell cytoplasm **C** encircles the myelin sheath. However, a thin layer of Schwann cell cytoplasm also persists immediately surrounding the axon **CI**.

In the CNS, oligodendrocytes are responsible for myelination; a single oligodendrocyte, however, forms multiple myelin internodes, which contribute to the ensheathment of as many as 50 individual axons (see Fig. 7.25).

Specific proteins bind cell membranes to form myelin sheaths

The layers of cell membrane that form myelin are bound together by special proteins that differ between CNS and PNS. In the CNS ***proteolipid protein*** links the exoplasmic surfaces, while cytoplasmic surfaces are linked by ***myelin basic protein***. In the PNS ***P0 protein*** associates with ***myelin basic protein*** to form the major dense line. PNS myelin also contains ***peripheral myelin protein-22***.

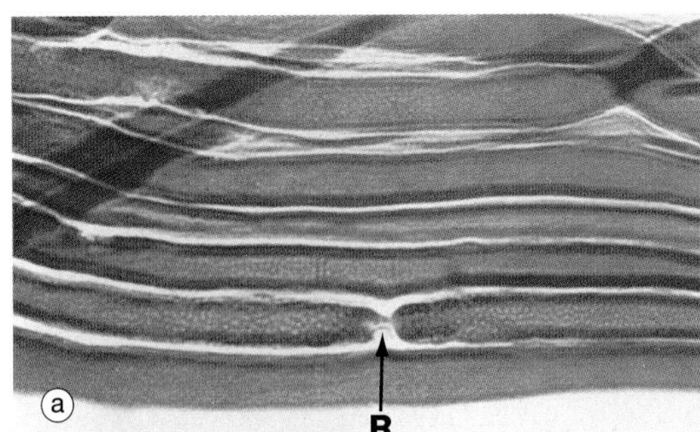

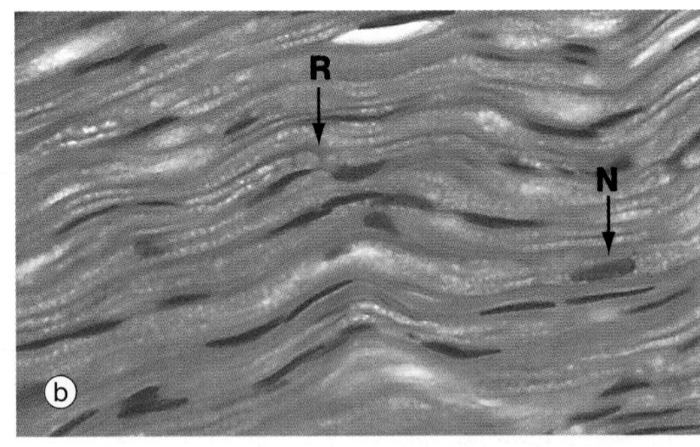

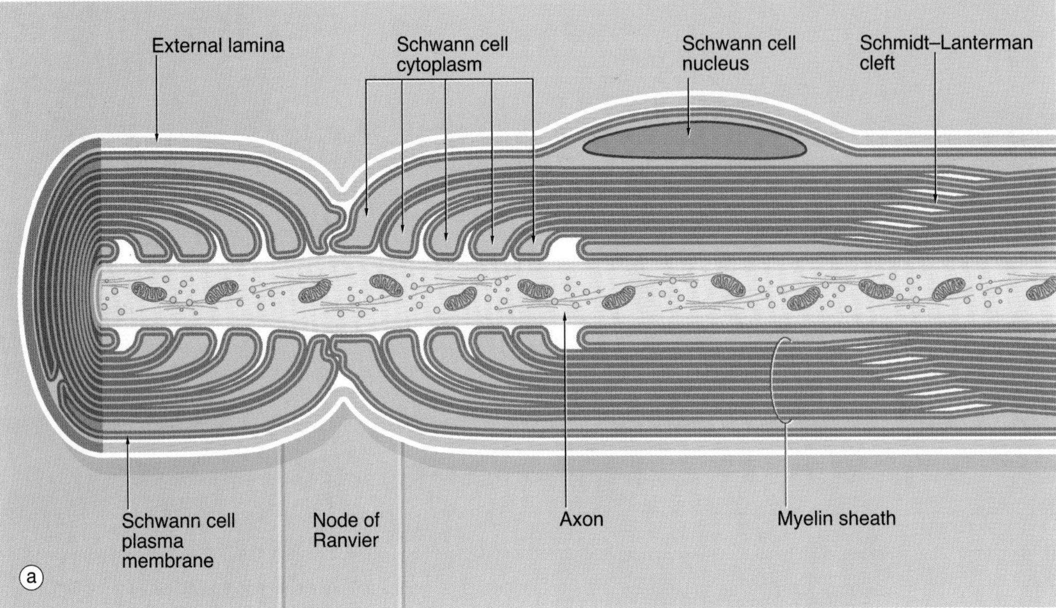

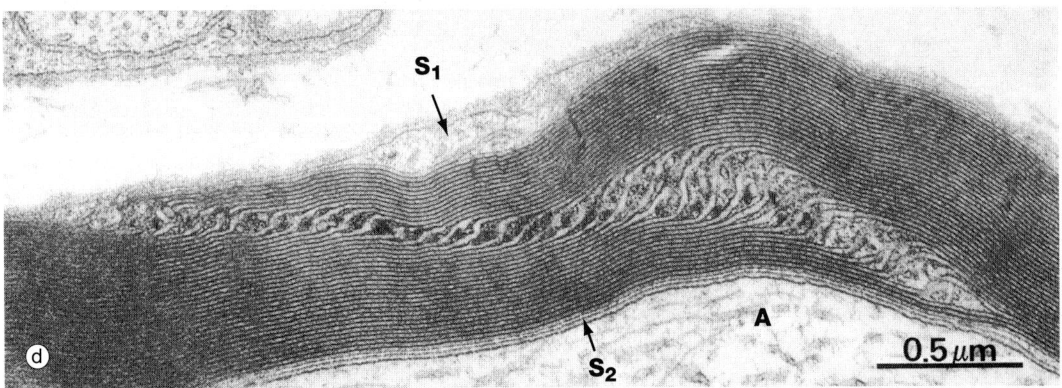

Disorders of myelin

Several diseases specifically affect formation of myelin, either in the CNS, the PNS or both.

- In ***multiple sclerosis*** there is immune-mediated destruction of myelin confined to the CNS. This leads to slowing of axonal conduction and neurological dysfunction. Signs and symptoms relate to the location of affected white matter. Histological examination of an affected area shows loss of myelin staining in areas called ***plaques of demyelination***.
- In ***Guillain–Barré syndrome*** there is immune-mediated destruction of myelin in the peripheral nervous system. Illness is often triggered by an infective condition. Patients develop rapidly progressive weakness of limbs and weakness of respiratory muscles. Histological examination of affected nerve shows loss of myelin with preservation of axons. Conduction velocity in affected nerves is greatly slowed.
- Mutation in genes coding for myelin proteins is the basis of several inherited disorders of the nervous system.

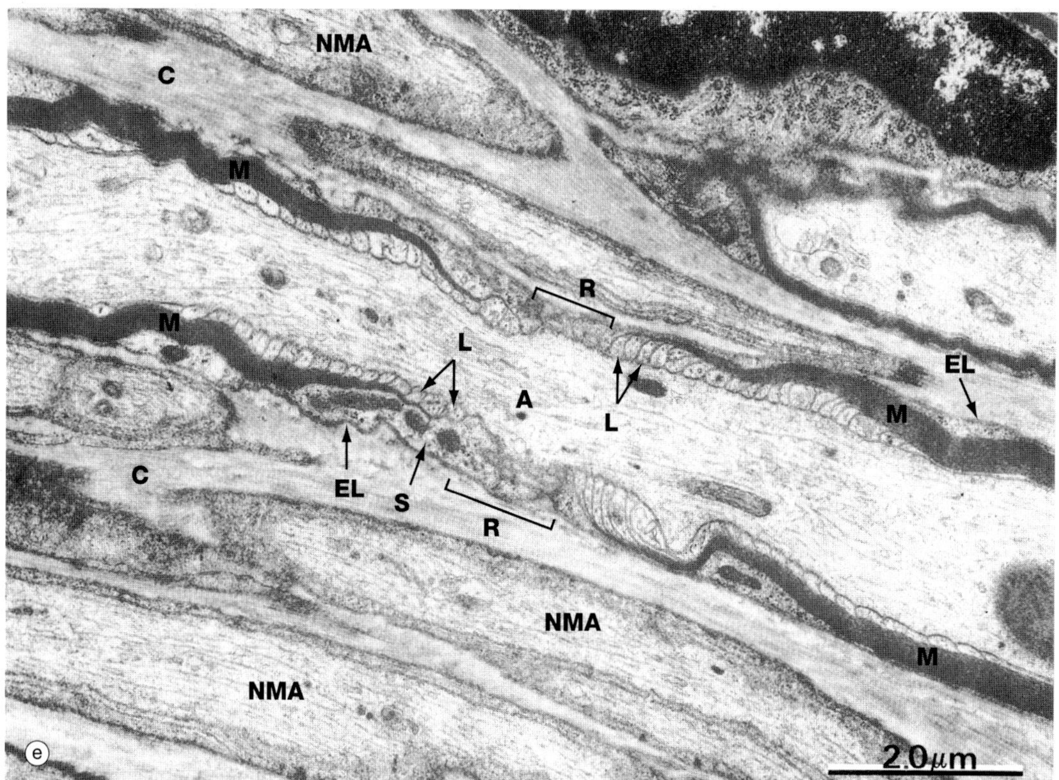

Fig. 7.7 Nodes of Ranvier and Schmidt–Lanterman incisures *(illustrations (a) to (d) opposite)*
(a) Teased preparation, Sudan black ×320 (b) H & E ×320 (c) Schematic diagram (d) EM ×42 000 (e) EM ×14 000

The myelin sheath of an individual axon is provided by many Schwann cells (oligodendrocytes in the CNS), each Schwann cell covering only a segment of the axon. Between the Schwann cells there are short intervals at which the axon is not covered by a myelin sheath; these points are known as ***nodes of Ranvier***.

Micrograph (a) shows a node of Ranvier **R** in a teased preparation of myelinated axons. With this method, only the lipid of the myelin has been stained, and thus Schwann cell nuclei are not seen.

Micrograph (b) shows axons in longitudinal section stained with H & E. Due to a fixation artefact, myelin sheaths appear 'bubbly'; the lipid is mostly dissolved out during preparation and is therefore unstained. A node of Ranvier **R** is identifiable in the large axon in midfield. These are very difficult to see in such routine preparations. Most of the elongated nuclei **N** are those of Schwann cells.

Diagram (c) illustrates the manner in which Schwann cells terminate at the node of Ranvier, so exposing the axon to the surrounding environment. Note the manner in which cytoplasmic processes of adjacent Schwann cells interdigitate at the node; also note the continuation of the Schwann cell basement membrane (external lamina) across the node. The myelin sheath prevents the nerve action potential from being propagated continuously along the axon and the action potential travels by jumping from node to node. This mode of conduction, known as saltatory conduction, greatly enhances the conduction velocity of axons. The internodal length is related to the diameter of the axon and may be up to 1.5 mm in the largest fibres.

Micrograph (e) illustrates the ultrastructure of a node of Ranvier **R**. The axon **A** is characterised by numerous neurofilaments, microtubules and elongated mitochondria. A myelin sheath **M** can be identified at each end of the field, the myelin becoming progressively thinner as it approaches the node. This is because, as it approaches the node, each compact major dense line expands to form a small membrane loop **L** containing Schwann cell cytoplasm, the loops directly abutting the axonal plasma membrane. Externally, a broader layer of Schwann cell cytoplasm **S** containing mitochondria envelops the nodal area. Note the external lamina **EL** of the Schwann cell and collagen fibrils **C** in surrounding endoneurium. Several non-myelinated axons **NMA** are seen nearby.

At certain points within the internodal myelin sheath, narrow channels of cytoplasm are retained and connect the main bulk of the Schwann cell cytoplasm peripherally to the narrow zone of Schwann cell cytoplasm adjacent to the axon. These uncompacted regions are known as ***Schmidt–Lanterman incisures*** or ***clefts***; in longitudinal section, as in electron micrograph (d), the incisure passes obliquely across the width of the compact sheath. The axon is marked **A**, the peripheral Schwann cell cytoplasm $\mathbf{S_1}$ and the periaxonal Schwann cell cytoplasm $\mathbf{S_2}$.

A axon **C** collagen fibrils **EL** external lamina **L** membrane loop **M** myelin sheath
N Schwann cell nucleus **NMA** non-myelinated axon **R** node of Ranvier **S** Schwann cell cytoplasm
$\mathbf{S_1}$ peripheral Schwann cell cytoplasm $\mathbf{S_2}$ periaxonal Schwann cell cytoplasm

Synapses and neuromuscular junctions

Synapses are highly specialised intercellular junctions which allow communication by linking neurones of each nervous pathway. Similar intercellular junctions link neurones and their effector cells such as muscle fibres; where neurones synapse with skeletal muscle they are referred to as ***neuromuscular junctions*** or ***motor end plates***. Individual neurones intercommunicate via a widely variable number of synapses depending on their location and function within the nervous system. Classically, the axon of one neurone synapses with the dendrite of another neurone (***axodendritic synapse***), but axons may synapse with the cell bodies of other neurones (***axosomatic synapses***) or other axons (***axoaxonic synapses***); dendrite-to-dendrite and cell body-to-cell body synapses have also been described. For a given synapse, the conduction of an impulse is unidirectional but the response may be either excitatory or inhibitory depending on the specific functional nature of the synapse and its location.

The mechanism of conduction of the nerve impulse involves the release from one neurone of a chemical neurotransmitter which then diffuses across a narrow intercellular space to induce excitation or inhibition in the other neurone or effector cell of that synapse. Neurotransmitters mediate their effects by interacting with specific receptors incorporated in the opposing plasma membrane.

The chemical nature of neurotransmitters and the morphology of synapses are highly variable in different parts of the nervous system, but the principles of synaptic transmission and the basic structure of synapses are similar throughout the nervous system.

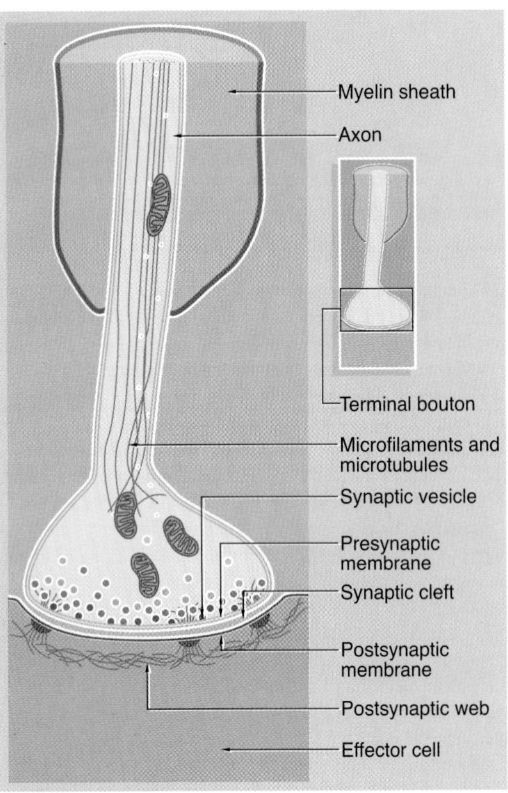

Fig. 7.8 Synapse

This diagram illustrates the general structure of the synapse. The axon responsible for propagating the stimulus terminates at a bulbous swelling or ***terminal bouton***; this is separated from the plasma membrane of the opposed neurone or effector cell by a narrow intercellular gap of uniform width (20–30 nm) called the ***synaptic cleft.*** The terminal boutons are not myelinated. The boutons contain mitochondria and membrane-bound vesicles of neurotransmitter substance known as ***synaptic vesicles*** which are approximately 50 nm in diameter.

There are many different types of neurotransmitter substance which are different in CNS and PNS, for example acetylcholine, noradrenaline (norepinephrine), glutamate, or dopamine. Synaptic vesicles are transported into the synaptic bouton down the axon from the cell body. Vesicles can also be formed in the synaptic bouton by recycling of vesicle membrane. Protein synthesis can also occur in the synaptic bouton.

Synaptic vesicles aggregate towards the ***presynaptic membrane*** and, on arrival of an action potential, dock with the membrane and release their contents into the synaptic cleft by exocytosis (see Ch. 1). The neurotransmitter diffuses across the synaptic cleft to stimulate receptors in the ***postsynaptic membrane.*** Associated with synapses are a variety of biochemical mechanisms such as hydrolytic and oxidative enzymes which inactivate the released neurotransmitter between successive nerve impulses. Transmitter may also be taken up back into the terminal bouton and be recycled into new synaptic vesicles. The cytoplasm beneath the postsynaptic membrane often contains a feltwork of fine fibrils, the ***postsynaptic web***, which may be associated with desmosome-like structures in maintaining the integrity of the synapse.

Synaptic loss and Alzheimer's disease

In Alzheimer's disease, the commonest cause of dementia, an early pathological feature is loss of synapses from the hippocampus and the cerebral cortex. The synapses mediating neurotransmission by acetylcholine (cholinergic system) are particularly affected. The identification of this transmitter deficit has led to development of drugs to maximise the concentration of acetycholine in the remaining synapses. Acetylcholine is rapidly destroyed once secreted into the synaptic cleft by the action of cholinesterases. Cholinesterase inhibitor drugs are now given to patients with Alzheimer's disease to compensate for the synaptic loss by maximising the impact of remaining cholinergic synaptic activity.

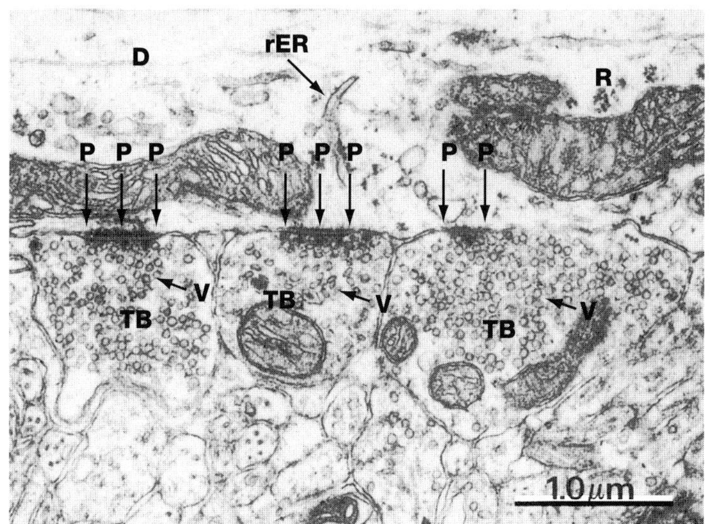

Fig. 7.9 Axodendritic synapse
EM ×22 000

This micrograph from the CNS illustrates three terminal boutons **TB** (probably from different axons) forming synapses with a dendrite **D**. The dendrite can be identified as such by its content of ribosomes **R** and rough endoplasmic reticulum **rER** (which are not present in axons). Note the presence of numerous uniform-sized synaptic vesicles **V** and a few mitochondria within the terminal boutons. The ***postsynaptic density*** **P** contributes to the structural stability of the closely apposed pre- and postsynaptic membranes.

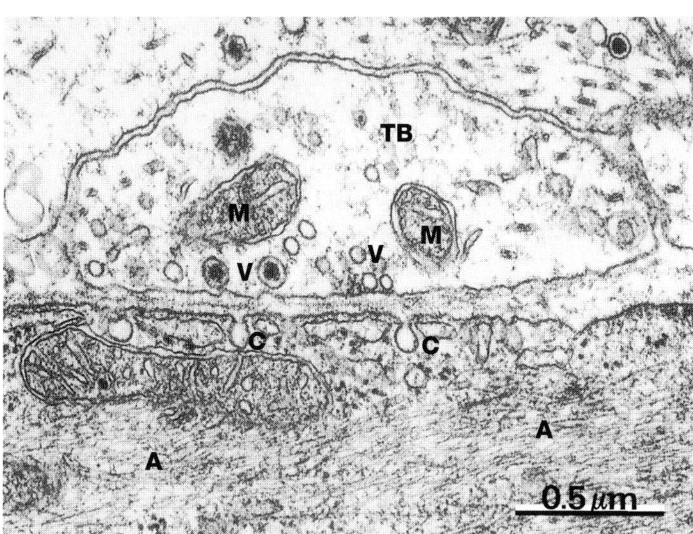

Fig. 7.10 Autonomic synapse
EM ×42 000

This micrograph illustrates a synapse between an autonomic axon and a smooth muscle cell in the intestine. The terminal bouton **TB** contains mitochondria **M** and a number of synaptic vesicles **V** some of which contain a dense central core probably representing an electron-dense carrier protein; such ***dense-cored vesicles*** are a feature of autonomic synapses. Frequently more than one neurotransmitter substance is present in individual autonomic neurones.

The postsynaptic membrane exhibits flask-like invaginations **C** which may represent caveolae. Note the uniform width of the synaptic cleft between the pre- and postsynaptic membranes. The smooth muscle cell contains numerous fine actin microfilaments **A**.

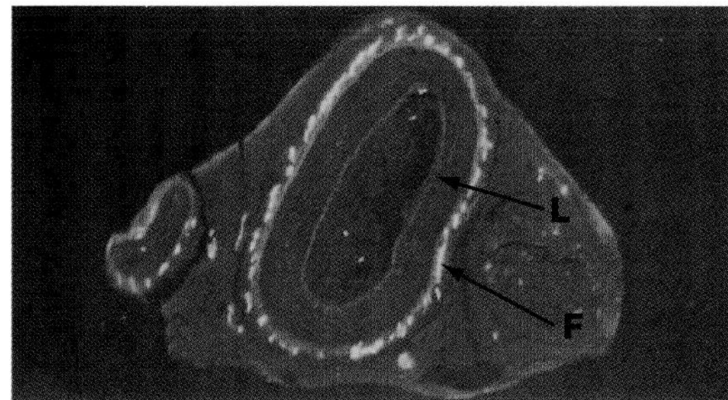

Fig. 7.11 Sympathetic nerve endings
Formalin-induced fluorescence ×80

Noradrenaline is the main postganglionic neurotransmitter in the sympathetic nervous system. When noradrenaline combines with formalin (and some other compounds) it becomes fluorescent and can be visualised by fluorescence microscopy.

This micrograph illustrates formalin-induced fluorescence **F** in the outer layer of large and small arteries, corresponding to the presence of sympathetic noradrenergic nerve endings. Background autofluorescence outlines the general structure; note that the internal elastic lamina **L** (see Fig. 8.10) of the large artery in midfield is particularly autofluorescent.

A actin filaments **C** caveola **D** dendrite **F** fluorescent sympathetic nerves
L internal elastic lamina **M** mitochondrion **P** postsynaptic density **R** ribosomes
rER rough endoplasmic reticulum **TB** terminal bouton **V** synaptic vesicles

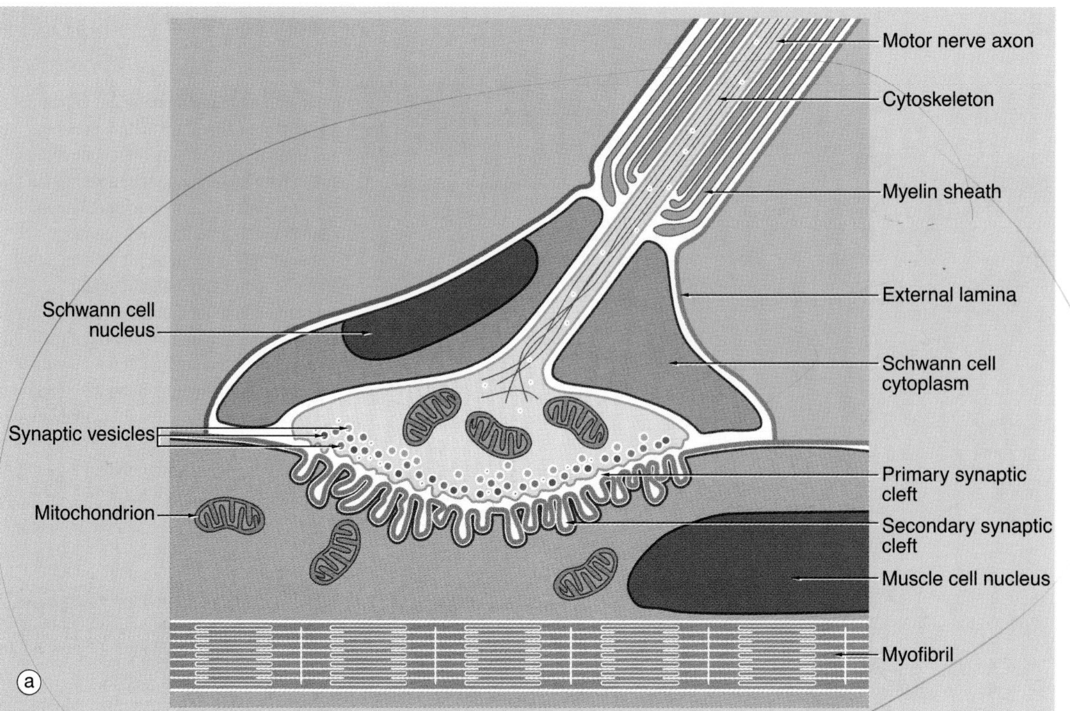

Fig. 7.12 Motor end plates *(illustrations (b) to (e) opposite)*
(a) Schematic diagram (b) Teased preparation, gold method ×320 (c) Teased preparation, gold method ×800 (d) Histochemical method for acetylcholinesterase ×320 (e) EM ×26 000

The motor end plates of skeletal muscle have the same basic structure as other synapses with the addition of several important features. Firstly, one motor neurone may innervate from a few to more than a thousand muscle fibres depending on the precision of movement of the muscle; the motor neurone and the muscle fibres which it supplies together constitute a ***motor unit***.

At low magnification in micrograph (b), the terminal part of the axon of a motor neurone is seen dividing into several branches, each terminating as a motor end plate on a different skeletal muscle fibre near to its midpoint. Micrograph (c) shows the lowermost of these motor end plates at higher magnification. The axonal branch is seen to lose its myelin sheath and divides to form a cluster of small bulbous swellings (terminal boutons) on the muscle fibre surface.

As seen in the diagram, the motor end plate occupies a recess in the muscle cell surface, described as the ***sole plate***, and is covered by an extension of the cytoplasm of the last Schwann cell surrounding the axon. The external lamina (basement membrane) of the Schwann cell merges with that of the muscle fibre, and the delicate collagenous tissue investing the nerve (endoneurium) becomes continuous with the endomysium of the muscle fibre (not illustrated).

Each of the terminal swellings of the cluster making up the motor end plate has the same basic structure as the synapse shown in Fig. 7.8, but the postsynaptic membrane of the neuromuscular junction is deeply folded to form parallel ***secondary synaptic clefts***. The overlying presynaptic membrane is also irregular and the cytoplasm immediately adjacent contains numerous synaptic vesicles. The remaining cytoplasm of the terminal bulb contains many mitochondria and a membrane compartment for recycling secretory vesicles. The sole plate of the muscle fibre also contains a concentration of mitochondria and an aggregation of muscle cell nuclei.

The neurotransmitter of somatic neuromuscular junctions is ***acetylcholine***, the receptors for which are concentrated at the margins of the secondary synaptic clefts. The hydrolytic enzyme acetylcholinesterase is present deeper in the clefts associated with the external lamina and is involved in deactivation of the neurotransmitter between successive nerve impulses. The histochemical technique shown in micrograph (d) defines the location of motor end plates by demonstrating acetylcholinesterase activity which appears as a brown deposit.

Micrograph (e) demonstrates the ultrastructure of a motor end plate, the terminal bouton **TB** typically lying in a depression in the skeletal muscle surface and invested externally by Schwann cell cytoplasm **S** and its external lamina **L**. Note the uniform width of the primary synaptic cleft $\mathbf{C_1}$ and the branching nature of the numerous secondary synaptic clefts $\mathbf{C_2}$. The underlying cytoplasm is packed with mitochondria **M**. Myofibrils **Mf** are seen in transverse section at the lower right of the field. The terminal bouton contains numerous synaptic vesicles **V** of uniform size, other membranous elements representing part of the endoplasmic reticulum and a few mitochondria.

$\mathbf{C_1}$ primary synaptic cleft $\mathbf{C_2}$ secondary synaptic cleft **L** external lamina **M** mitochondrion
Mf myofibrils **S** Schwann cell cytoplasm **TB** terminal bouton **V** synaptic vesicles

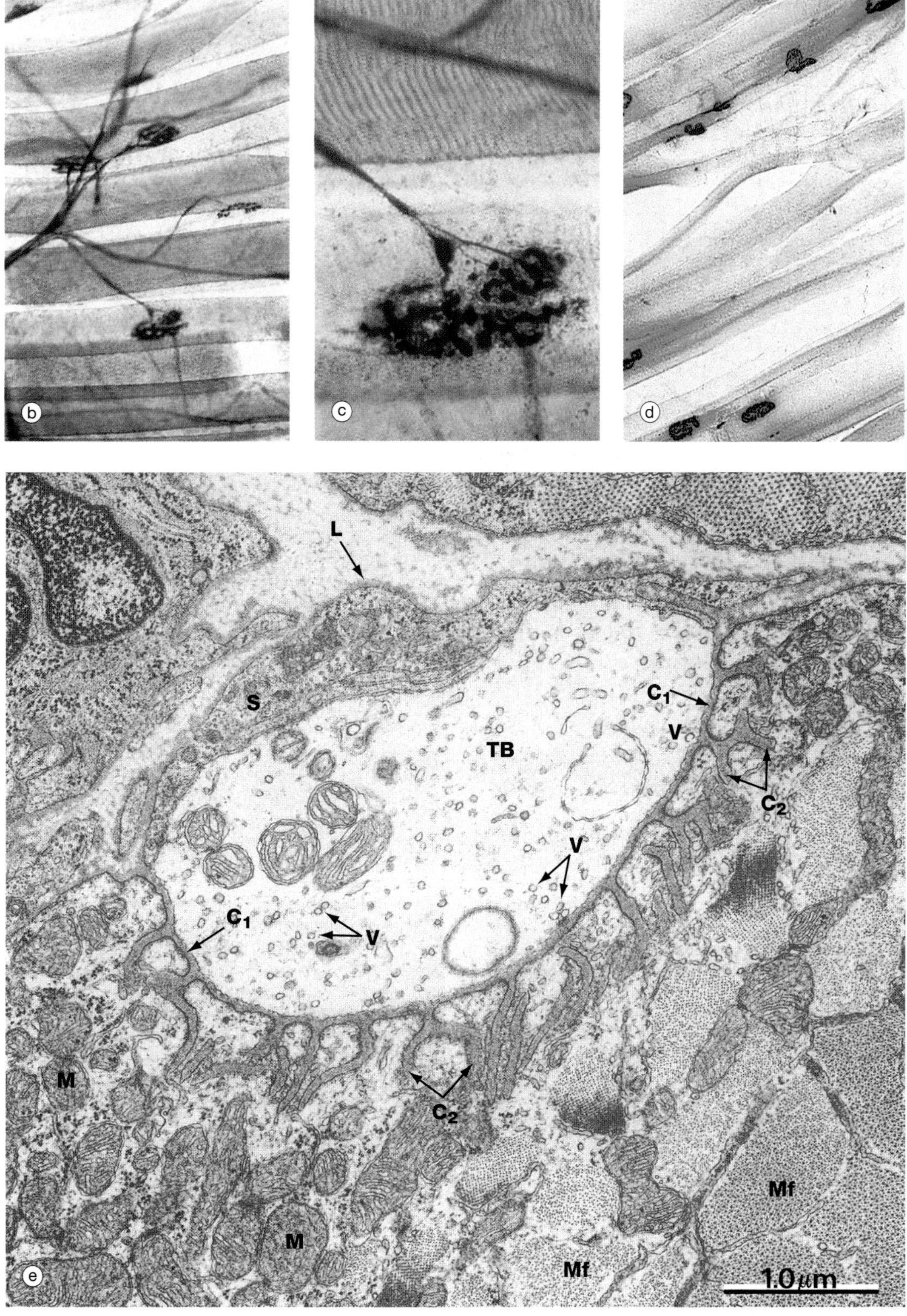

Myasthenia gravis: an autoimmune disease affecting the motor end plate

Myasthenia gravis is the most common primary disorder of neuromuscular transmission. Patients develop fatigue and muscle weakness. Under normal circumstances the motor end plate releases acetylcholine (ACh) which then binds to receptors on the muscle surface to cause depolarisation and muscle contraction. In myasthenia gravis ACh is released normally, but its effect on the post-synaptic membrane is reduced. This is because acetylcholine receptors (AChR) have been depleted by binding to autoantibodies specific for the receptor. Detection of serum antibodies that bind human AChR is used to help diagnose the condition. In some patients with this condition treatment with cholinesterase inhibitors, which prevents ACh breakdown, prolongs the effects of the secreted transmitter substance and leads to improved muscle strength.

Peripheral nervous tissues

Peripheral nerves are anatomical structures which may contain any combination of afferent or efferent nerve fibres of either the somatic or autonomic nervous systems. Each peripheral nerve is composed of one or more bundles (***fascicles***) of nerve fibres. Within the fascicles, each individual nerve fibre, with its investing Schwann cell, is surrounded by a delicate packing of loose vascular supporting tissue called ***endoneurium.*** Each fascicle is surrounded by a condensed layer of robust collagenous tissue invested by a layer of flat epithelial cells called the ***perineurium.*** In peripheral nerves consisting of more than one fascicle, a further layer of loose collagenous tissue called the ***epineurium*** binds the fascicles together and is condensed peripherally to form a strong cylindrical sheath. Peripheral nerves receive a rich blood supply via numerous penetrating vessels from surrounding tissues and accompanying arteries. Larger vessels course longitudinally within the compartments bounded by the perineurium and epineurium with a rich capillary network in the endoneurium.

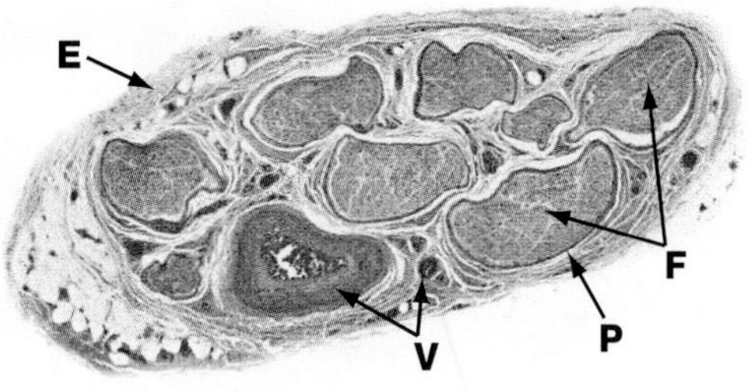

Fig. 7.13 Peripheral nerve
H & E ×20

This micrograph illustrates the typical appearance of a medium-sized peripheral nerve in transverse section. This specimen consists of eight fascicles **F**, each of which contains many nerve fibres. Each fascicle is invested by the perineurium **P**, and the nerve as a whole is encased in a loose collagenous tissue sheath, the epineurium **E**, which is condensed at its outermost aspect. Blood vessels **V** of various sizes can be seen in the epineurial connective tissue.

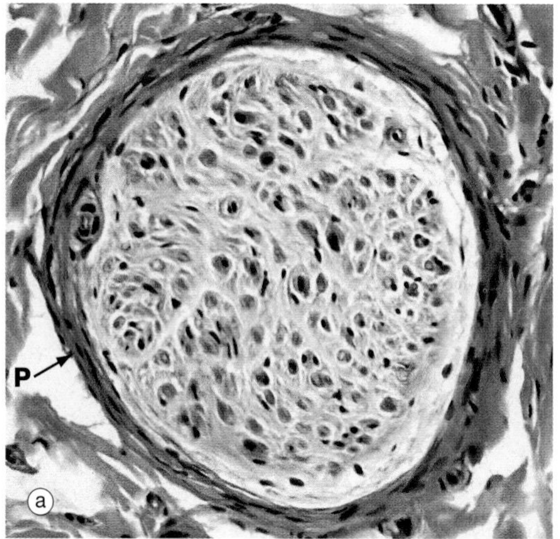

Fig. 7.14 Peripheral nerve
(a) H & E ×150 (b) resin toluidine blue ×120

The peripheral nerves shown in transverse section in micrograph (a) and (b) each consists of a single fascicle invested by the perineurium **P** composed of several layers of flattened cells with elongated nuclei.

In micrograph (a) individual myelin sheaths are just visible as bright pink circular structures, some associated with their Schwann cell nucleus. Most of the nuclei seen within the fascicle are those of Schwann cells which mark the course of individual axons. Fibroblasts of the endoneurium are scattered amongst the much more numerous Schwann cells. It is not possible to distinguish small non-myelinated axons in this type of wax-embedded material stained with H & E. Around the outside of the perineurium are bundles of pink-staining epineurial collagen.

Micrograph (b) is a preparation of nerve embedded in epoxy resin and stained with toluidine blue. This is photographed at a slightly lower magnification than micrograph (a). The myelin sheaths are stained dark blue and can be seen as small ring-shaped structures. Axons run down the centre of each myelin sheath but are not resolved at this magnification. In the centre of the fascicle are small endoneurial blood vessels **V**. The perineurium **P** runs around the fascicle.

Peripheral nerve disease

There are two main patterns of nerve disease, termed peripheral neuropathy. Symptoms include weakness and sensory loss. In one type, there is damage to the Schwann cells and myelin causing reduced conduction velocity in nerves (***demyelinating neuropathy***). In the other main type there is damage to the axons (***axonal neuropathy***). Schwann cells can regenerate after damage and remyelinate axons. Axons can also regenerate providing the neuronal cell body is not damaged.

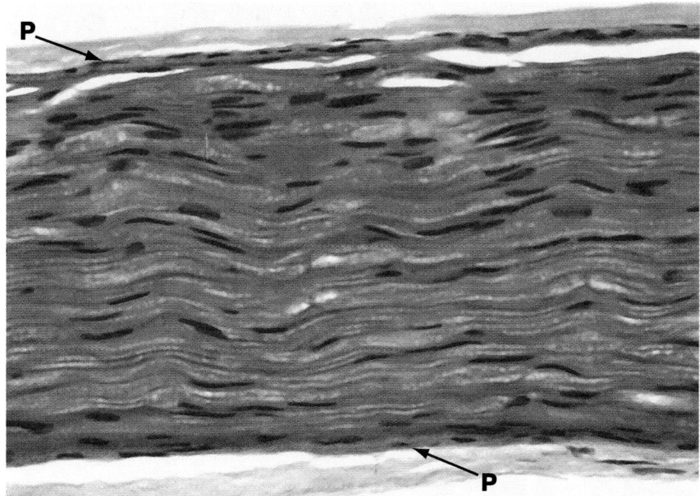

Fig. 7.15 Peripheral nerve
H & E ×320

This micrograph illustrates the typical appearance of a single nerve fascicles in longitudinal section. It contains many nerve fibres. The perineurium **P** is seen on each side. The elongated nuclei are mainly those of Schwann cells but some will also be those of endoneurial fibroblasts. It is not easy to discriminate between these cells in this type of preparation. Nerve fibres often follow an undulating or zig-zag pattern in longitudinal section, as shown here.

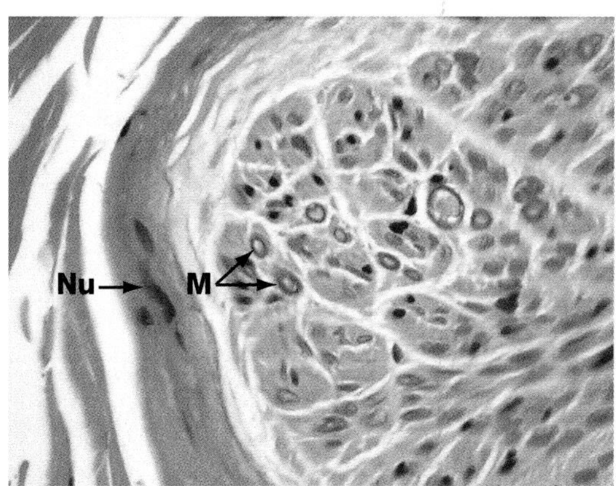

Fig. 7.16 Peripheral nerve
H & E ×480

In routinely fixed and stained preparations, myelin is poorly preserved since it is largely composed of lipid material. Schwann cell cytoplasm is, however, well-preserved and has eosinophilic staining properties.

This is the edge of a peripheral nerve cut transversely; the nerve contains axons of different types and calibre, some of which are myelinated. Heavily myelinated fibres **M** can be identified by a pink ring representing the myelin sheath, with a pale centrally located axon. Small non-myelinated fibres cannot easily be identified. Several flattened nuclei **Nu** of perineurial cells are also seen in the perineurium.

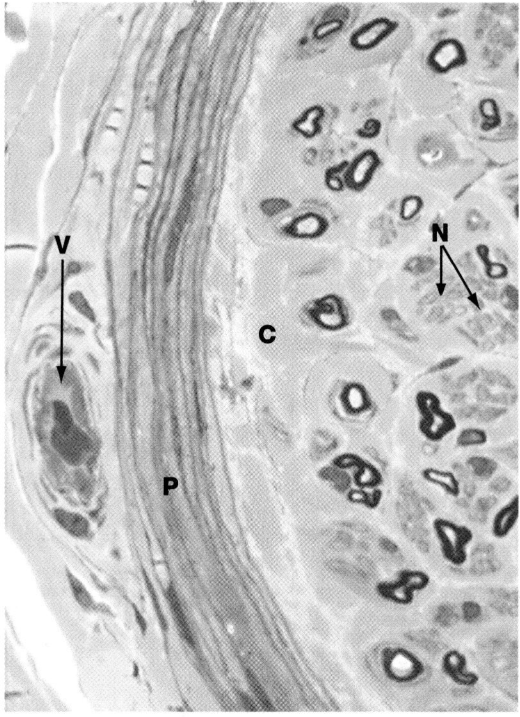

Fig. 7.17 Peripheral nerves in section
Toluidine blue ×500

In material which has been fixed in glutaraldehyde and embedded in epoxy resin, myelin is well preserved and stains darkly with toluidine blue. A mixture of large and small myelinated fibres can be seen as dark-staining ring-like structures. These are often collapsed or elliptical in profile in sections, as here. The axon contained within each myelin sheath is seen as a pale structure but no detail can be resolved at this magnification.

Schwann cell cytoplasm stains a paler shade of blue than the myelin and can be seen surrounding small clusters of small, non-myelinated axons **N**.

In between bundles of nerve fibres is the paler-staining endoneurial collagen **C**.

The perineurium **P** is well shown in this type of preparation and resolves into several layers of epithelial cells separated by thin layers of collagen. The elongated nuclei of perineurial cells are well seen.

Outside the perineurium are bundles of epineurial collagen and a small blood vessel **V**.

C collagen **E** epineurium **F** fascicle **M** myelin **N** non-myelinated fibres
Nu nucleus of perineurial cell **P** perineurium **V** vessel

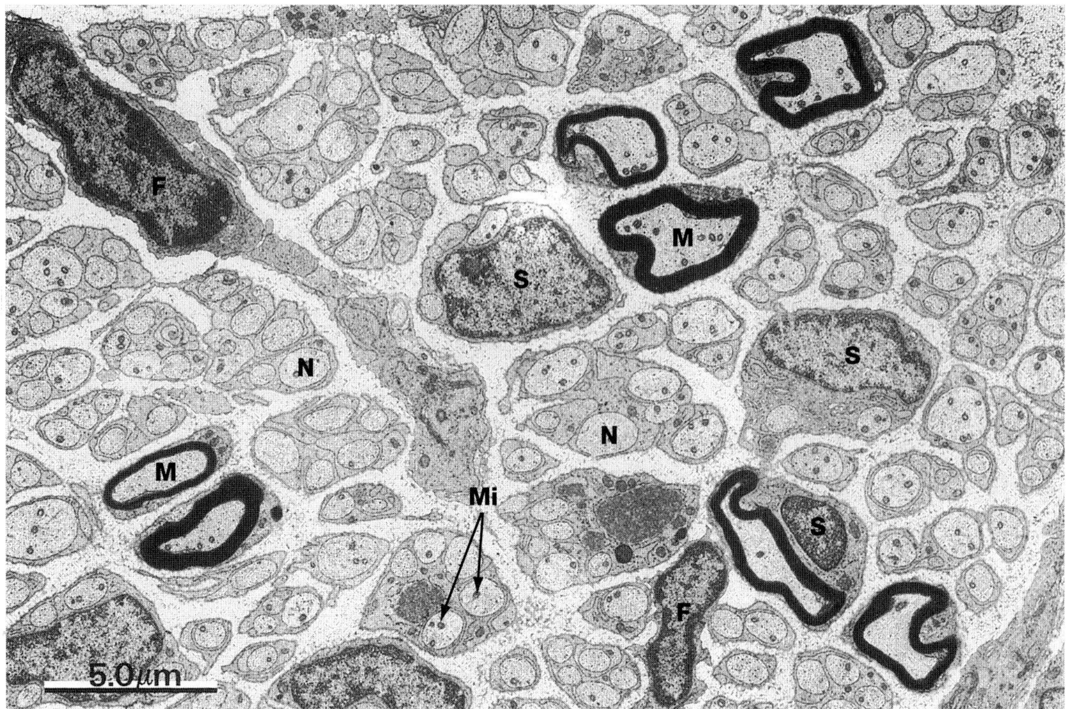

Fig. 7.18 Peripheral nerve
EM ×5000

The ultrastructural features of a typical peripheral nerve are shown in this micrograph. Both myelinated axons **M** and more numerous non-myelinated axons **N** are present both ensheathed by Schwann cells **S.** The axons contain dot-like structures which are mitochondria **Mi**.

The endoneurium mainly consists of loosely arranged collagen fibrils (difficult to identify at this magnification) lying parallel to the nerve fibres. The nuclei of two fibroblasts **F** can be identified and fibroblast processes extend through the endoneurium.

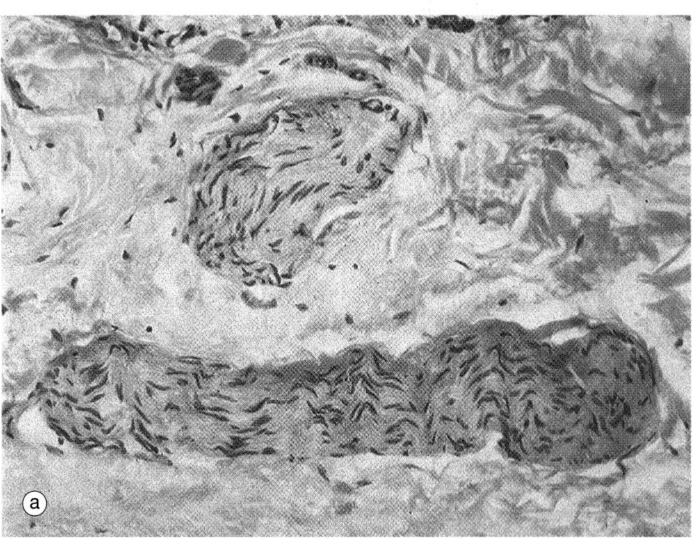

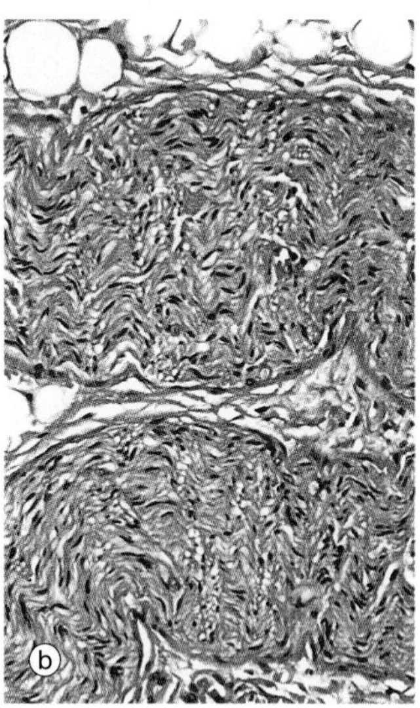

Fig. 7.19 Small peripheral nerves
(a) H & E ×480 (b) H & E ×320

These micrographs illustrate the appearance of small peripheral nerves in the tissues.

Micrograph (a) shows two small nerves in the dermis of the skin, each nerve consisting of a single fascicle of fibres. The nerve at the bottom of the field is cut in longitudinal section; the wavy shape of the Schwann cell nuclei reflects the course of the axons which are thereby protected from damage when the skin is stretched. The nerve in the upper part of the field is cut in oblique section. Note the dense irregular collagenous dermal tissue surrounding the nerves in this specimen.

Micrograph (b) shows a small peripheral nerve in the submucosa of the large bowel. This nerve runs a zigzag course in the tissue and the plane of section has cut it in the long axis as it folds. This allows the nerve to stretch as the bowel moves with peristalsis.

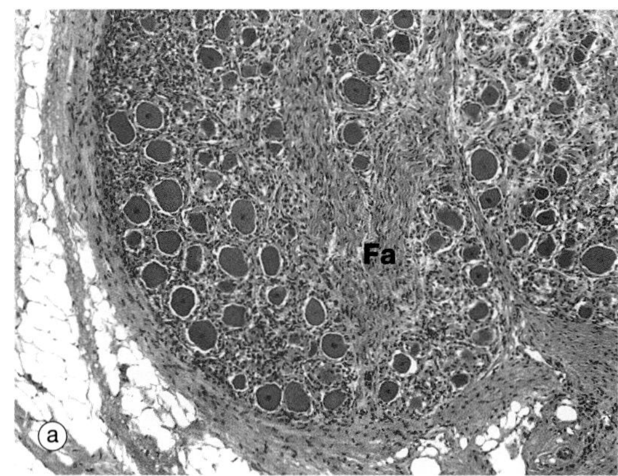

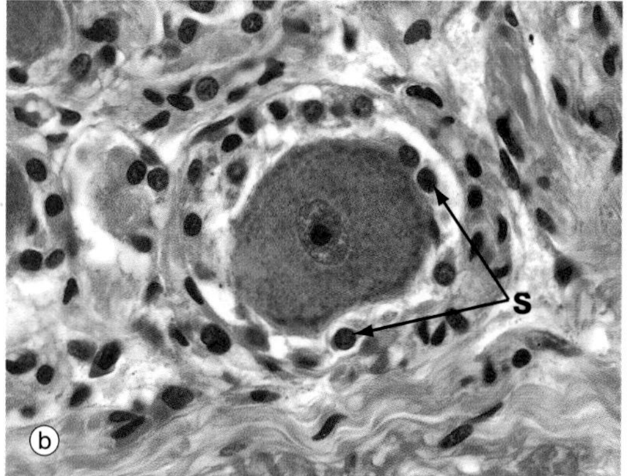

Fig. 7.20 Spinal ganglion
(a) H & E ×128 (b) H & E ×800

Ganglia are discrete aggregations of neurone cell bodies located outside the CNS. The spinal ganglia lie on the posterior nerve roots of the spinal cord as they pass through the intervertebral foramina; they contain the cell bodies of primary sensory neurones which are of the pseudo-unipolar form (see Fig. 7.2).

At low magnification in micrograph (a), note the fascicle **Fa** of nerve fibres passing to the centre of the ganglion, the ganglion cells being located peripherally.

At high magnification in micrograph (b), a nerve cell body is seen to be surrounded by a layer of rounded ***satellite cells*** **Sa** which provide structural and metabolic support and have similar embryological origin to the Schwann cells (neural crest).

The whole ganglion is encapsulated by condensed supporting tissue which is continuous with the perineurial and epineurial sheaths of the associated peripheral nerve.

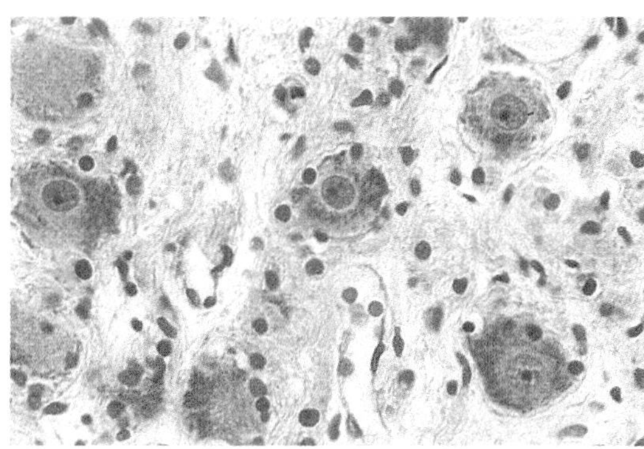

Fig. 7.21 Sympathetic ganglion
H & E ×400

Sympathetic ganglia have a similar structure to that of somatic sensory ganglia with a few minor differences. The ganglion cells are multipolar and thus more widely spaced, being separated by numerous axons and dendrites, many of which pass through the ganglion without being involved in synapses. As seen in this micrograph, the nuclei of the ganglion cells tend to be eccentrically located and the peripheral cytoplasm contains a variable quantity of brown stained lipofuscin granules representing cellular debris sequestered in residual bodies. The satellite cells are smaller in number and irregularly placed due to the numerous dendritic processes of the ganglion cells.

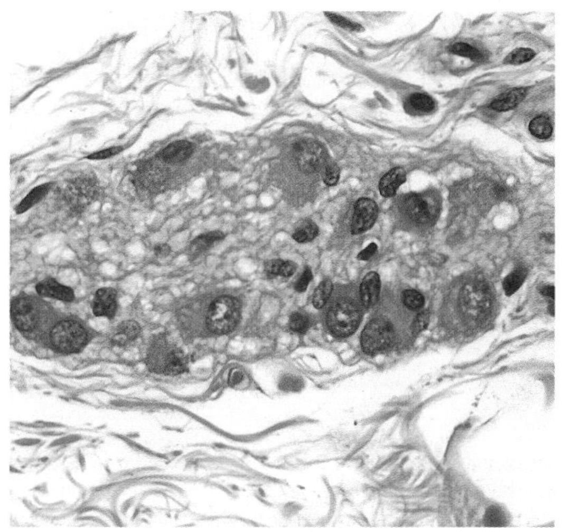

Fig. 7.22 Parasympathetic ganglion
H & E ×400

The cell bodies of the terminal effector neurones of the parasympathetic nervous system are usually located within or near the effector organs. The cell bodies may form well-organised ganglia of moderate size (as in the otic ganglion) but more commonly a few cell bodies are clumped together to form tiny ganglia scattered in the supporting tissue.

This micrograph shows a minute ganglion from the wall of the gastrointestinal tract. Like all neurones, the ganglion cells are recognised by their large nuclei, with dispersed chromatin and prominent nucleoli, and extensive basophilic cytoplasm. As in other ganglia, the neurones are surrounded by small Schwann cells and afferent and efferent nerve fibres.

F fibroblast **Fa** fascicle **M** myelinated axon **Mi** mitochondrion **N** non-myelinated axon
S Schwann **Sa** satellite cell

Central nervous tissues

The central nervous system consists of the brain and spinal cord, each of which can be divided macroscopically into areas of ***grey matter*** and ***white matter***. Grey matter contains almost all the neurone cell bodies and their associated fibres (axons). White matter consists of tracts of nerve fibres in which a substantial number of the axons are myelinated, myelin appearing white in fresh tissue.

Central nervous tissue consists of a vast number of neurones and their processes embedded in a mass of support cells, collectively known as ***neuroglia***, which comprise all the non-neural cells of the CNS. Central nervous tissue proper is devoid of collagenous supporting tissue that is confined to the immediate vicinity of penetrating blood vessels and to the ***meninges*** that invest the outer surface of the brain. The neuroglia, which form almost half the total mass of the CNS, are highly branched cells that occupy the spaces between neurones; the CNS contains little extracellular material. The neuroglia have intimate functional relationships with neurones providing both mechanical and metabolic support.

Four principal types of neuroglia are recognised: ***oligodendrocytes, astrocytes***, ***microglia*** and ***ependymal cells***. Oligodendrocytes are the CNS equivalent of the Schwann cells of the peripheral nervous system and are responsible for the formation of myelin sheaths in the CNS. Astrocytes are highly branched cells that pack the interstices between the neurones, their processes and oligodendrocytes. They provide mechanical support as well as mediating the exchange of metabolites between neurones and the vascular system. They also form part of the blood–brain barrier. Astrocytes also play an important role in repair of CNS tissue after injury or damage by disease. Microglia are the CNS representatives of the monocyte–macrophage system and have defence and immunological functions. Ependymal cells make up a specialised epithelium which lines the ventricles and spinal canal.

Although each functional zone of the CNS has its own particular histological appearance, the basic organisation of grey and white matter remains consistent throughout; only the principles of organisation are discussed in this chapter. The various regions of the central nervous system are the subject of Chapter 20.

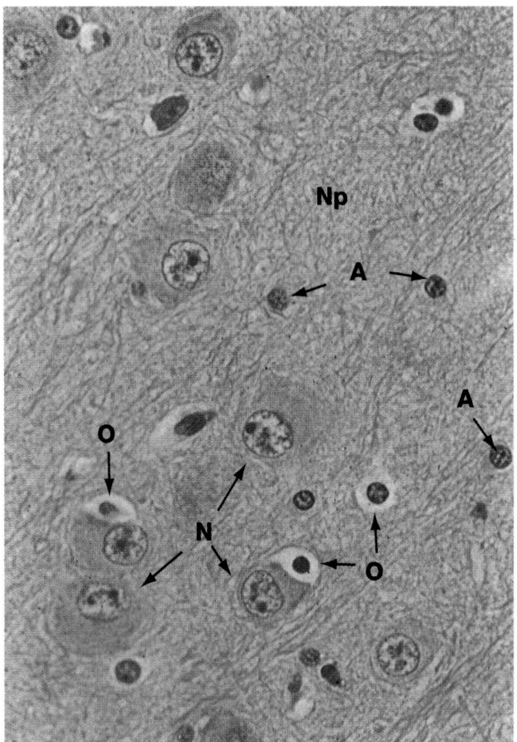

Fig. 7.23 Grey matter
H & E ×480

Common staining methods usually permit neurones **N** to be readily distinguished from glial cells. Although the size and morphology of neurones vary greatly in different regions of the brain, they are usually recognisable by their large nuclei, with prominent nucleoli and dispersed chromatin. There is extensive basophilic granular cytoplasm, one or more processes of which may be visible.

Neuroglia are difficult to differentiate with certainty by common staining methods. In the mature CNS, as in this specimen, oligodendroglia have small round condensed nuclei; their cytoplasm is unstained by routine methods including H & E. As described later, in grey matter oligodendrocytes are not only scattered between the nerve cell bodies along with the astrocytes but also tend to be aggregated around the neurone cell bodies. Thus the cells marked **O** can be presumed to be oligodendrocytes. Others marked **A** are probably astrocytes.

The nuclei of both neurones and neuroglia are surrounded by a feltwork of axons and dendrites arising from and converging upon the neurones. This is described as the ***neuropil* Np.** Most neuropil fibres are devoid of myelin (being so close to the neurone cell bodies) accounting for the eosinophilia of neuropil.

A astrocyte **C** astrocyte cytoplasmic extension **IF** intermediate filament bundle **M** myelinated axon **N** neurone **Np** neuropil **O** oligodendrocyte

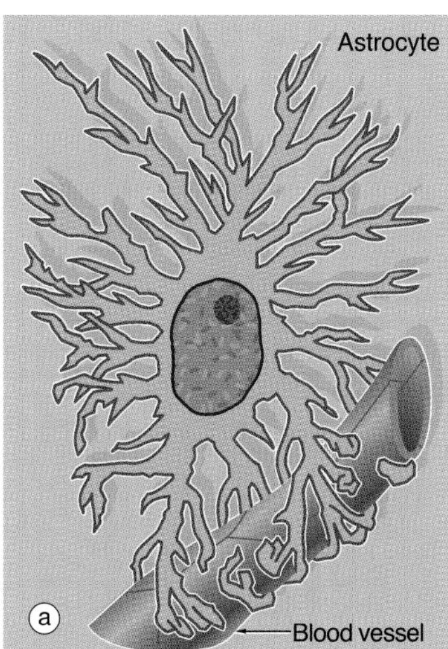

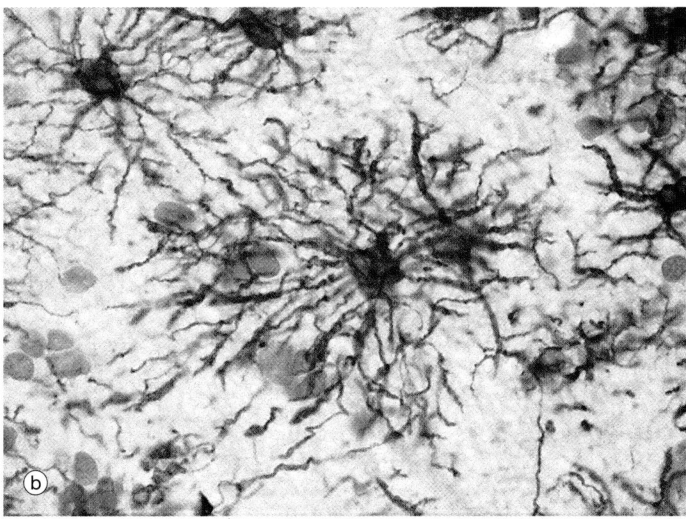

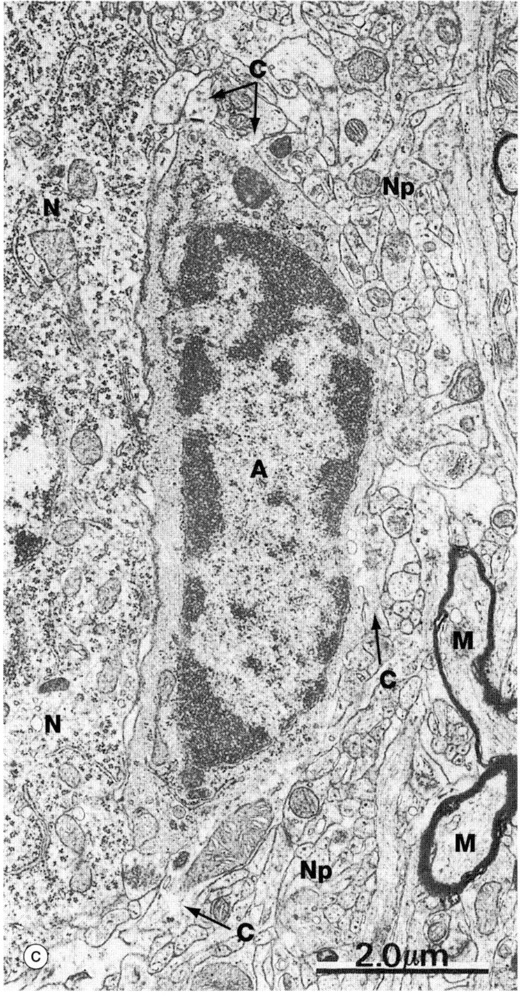

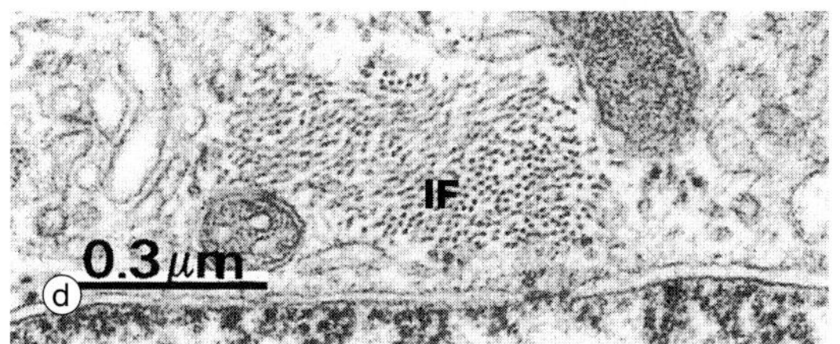

Fig. 7.24 Astrocytes

(a) Diagram (b) Immunoperoxidase method for glial fibrillary acidic protein ×400 (c) EM ×12 000 (d) EM ×57 500

Immunochemical staining for GFAP seen in micrograph (b) identifies the presence of ramified neuroglia, the astrocytes. These cells, which are the most numerous glial cells in grey matter, have long branched processes which occupy much of the interneuronal spaces in the neuropil. In grey matter, many of the astrocyte processes end in terminal expansions adjacent to the non-synaptic regions of neurones. Other processes of the same astrocytes terminate upon the basement membranes of capillaries; these ***perivascular feet*** cover most of the surface of the capillary basement membranes and form part of the blood–brain barrier (a). Similar foot processes invest the basement membrane that lies between the CNS and the innermost layer of the meninges, the ***pia mater*** (see Fig. 7.29) forming a relatively impermeable barrier called the ***glia limitans***.

In grey matter, astrocytes mediate metabolic exchange between neurones and blood and regulate the composition of the intercellular environment of the CNS.

All astrocytes contain bundles of intermediate filaments and microtubules. These are particularly prominent in the astrocytes of white matter which have relatively few, straight cytoplasmic processes and are known as ***fibrous astrocytes***. By contrast, those of grey matter have numerous short highly branched cytoplasmic processes and are described as ***protoplasmic astrocytes***. The intermediate filaments consist of a protein characteristic of astrocytes called ***glial fibrillary acidic protein*** (***GFAP***) which is demonstrated in micrograph (b).

Micrograph (c) shows an astrocyte **A** lying adjacent to a nerve cell body **N** in the cerebral cortex. The astrocyte cytoplasm contains many ribosomes, a little rough endoplasmic reticulum, and a few small mitochondria and lysosomes. The origins of several cytoplasmic extensions **C** can be identified. The cytoplasm appears moderately electron-dense due to its content of intermediate filaments **IF**, which can be seen at higher magnification in micrograph (d). Typically of CNS grey matter, the adjacent neuropil **Np** contains numerous neuronal and glial processes in various planes of section; some myelinated axons **M** are included in the field.

Fig. 7.25 CNS myelin and oligodendrocytes

(a) TS, solochrome cyanin ×480 (b) LS, solochrome cyanin ×480 (c) immunoperoxidase alpha B crystallin ×480 (d) EM ×13 000 (e) Schematic diagram

Oligodendrocytes were named by the early neurohistologists using classical heavy metal impregnation methods which showed that they had a small number of short, branched processes (Greek: *oligos* = few, *dendron* = tree). It is now known that oligodendrocytes are the cells responsible for myelination of axons in the CNS and the dendrites previously described are the short pedicles that connect the cell body to the myelin sheaths.

A single oligodendrocyte can contribute to the myelination of up to 50 axons which may belong to the same or different fibre tracts, illustrated in the diagram (e). Conversely, any one axon will require the services of numerous different oligodendrocytes since the myelin internodes along its length are synthesised by different cells. The mechanism of myelin sheath formation is very similar to that of Schwann cells in peripheral nerve (see Fig. 7.6). Oligodendrocytes are thus the predominant type of neuroglia in white matter as well as being abundant in grey matter.

Micrograph (a) shows CNS myelin in cross section, stained blue with solochrome cyanin. The ring-shaped profiles each surround an axon, not visible in this preparation. The nucleus of oligodendrocytes can be seen as rounded red-stained profiles, best seen in micrograph (b). Oligodendrocytes develop an artefactual vacuolation in wax-embedded material leaving a clear 'halo' around the nuclei.

Micrograph (c) shows the cytoplasm of oligodendrocytes as detected by immunostaining for alpha B crystallin. Short cell processes can be seen on several cells. The general background staining reflects detection of myelin.

Oligodendrocytes also aggregate closely around nerve cell bodies in the grey matter where they are thought to have a support function analogous to that of the satellite cells which surround nerve cell bodies in peripheral ganglia (see Fig. 7.20).

Oligodendrocytes are relatively large cells with dispersed nuclear chromatin. The cytoplasm contains numerous ribosomes, microtubules and a large Golgi apparatus.

The electron micrograph (d) shows an oligodendrocyte **O** lying adjacent to a nerve cell body **N** with a neuronal dendrite **D** at the upper right. The oligodendrocyte contains prominent rough endoplasmic reticulum, ribosomes and Golgi apparatus **G**. The commencement of one cytoplasmic process **C** is seen. The remainder of the field shows the complexity of the neuropil **Np** comprising glial and neuronal processes, including some myelinated axons **M**.

Myelin sheath formation begins in the CNS of the human embryo at about 4 months gestational age with the formation of most sheaths at least commenced by about the age of 1 year. From this time, successive layers continue to be laid down, with final myelin sheath thickness being achieved by the time of physical maturity.

Oligodendrocyte precursor cells are present in the adult CNS and can proliferate to bring about remyelination of areas of myelin loss due to disease.

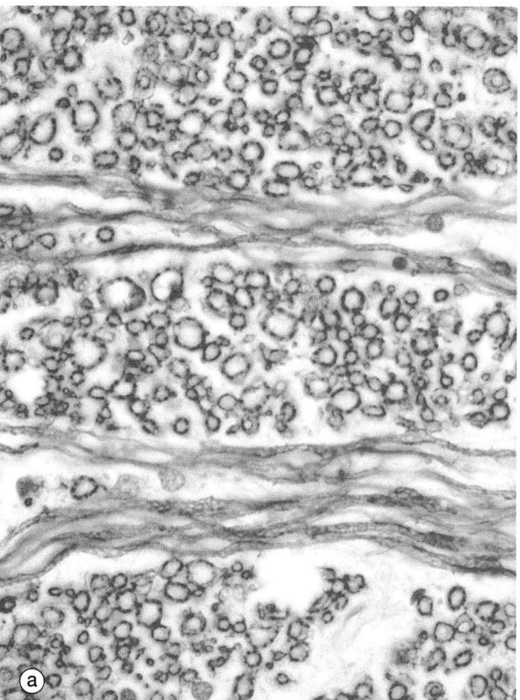

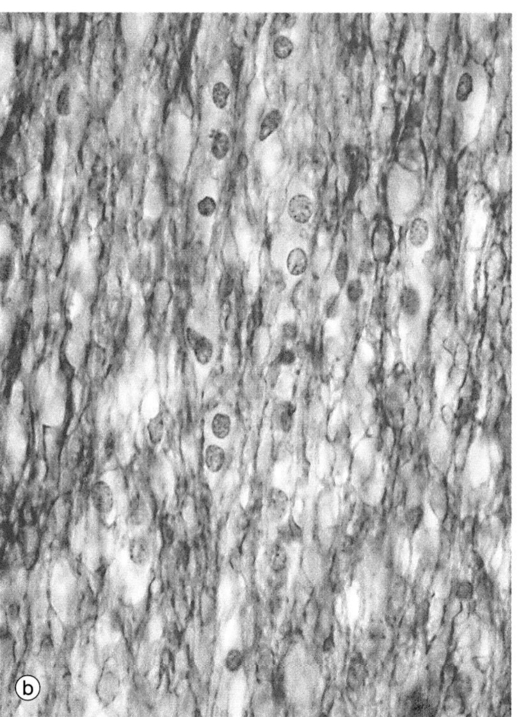

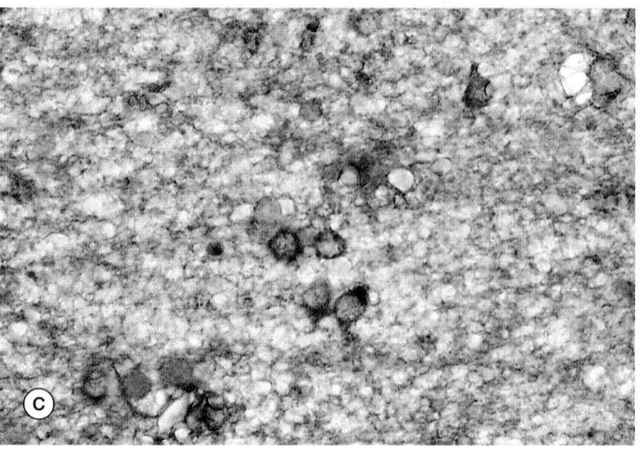

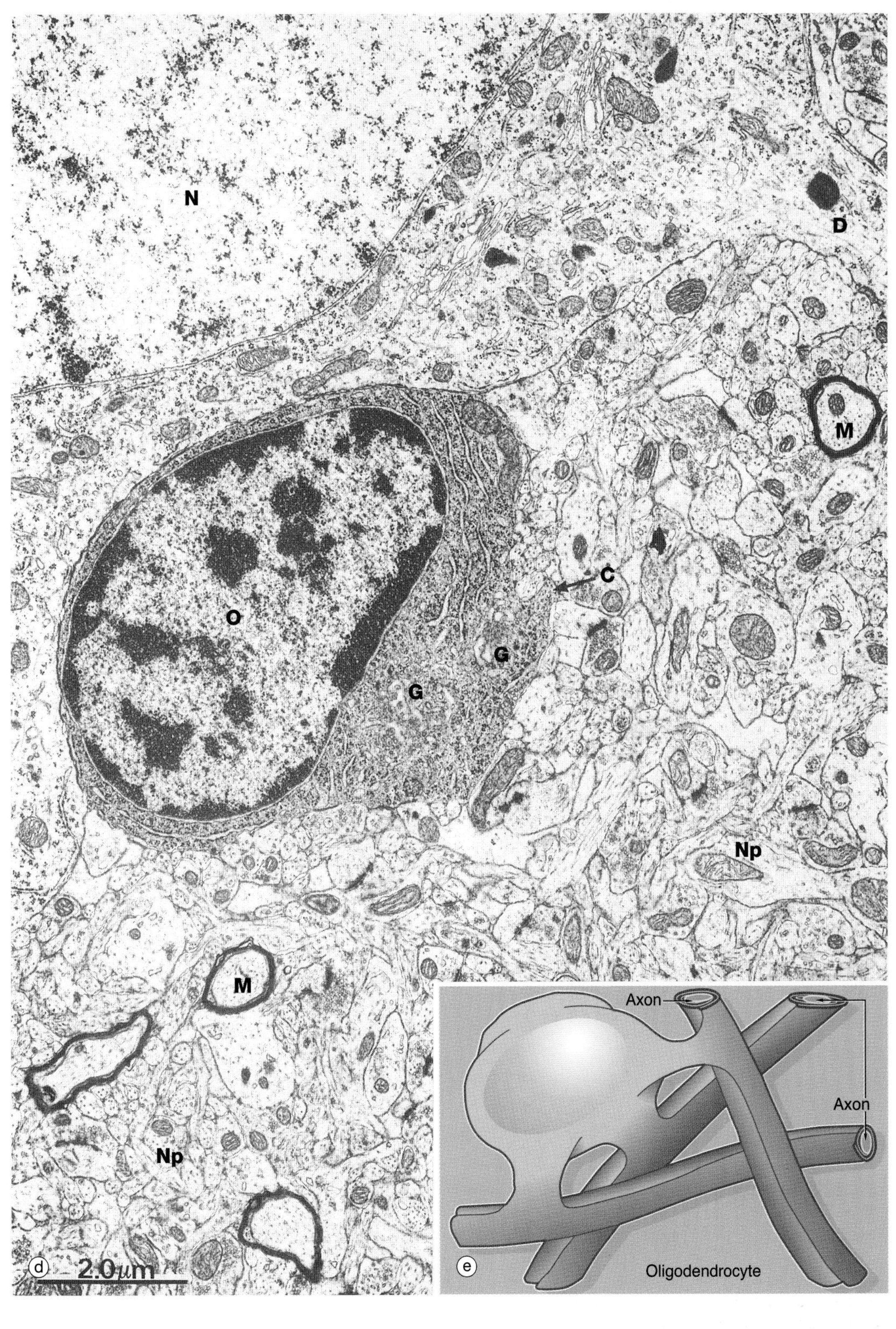

C cytoplasmic process of oligodendrocyte **D** neuronal dendrite **G** Golgi apparatus
M myelinated axon **N** nerve cell body **Np** neuropil **O** oligodendrocyte

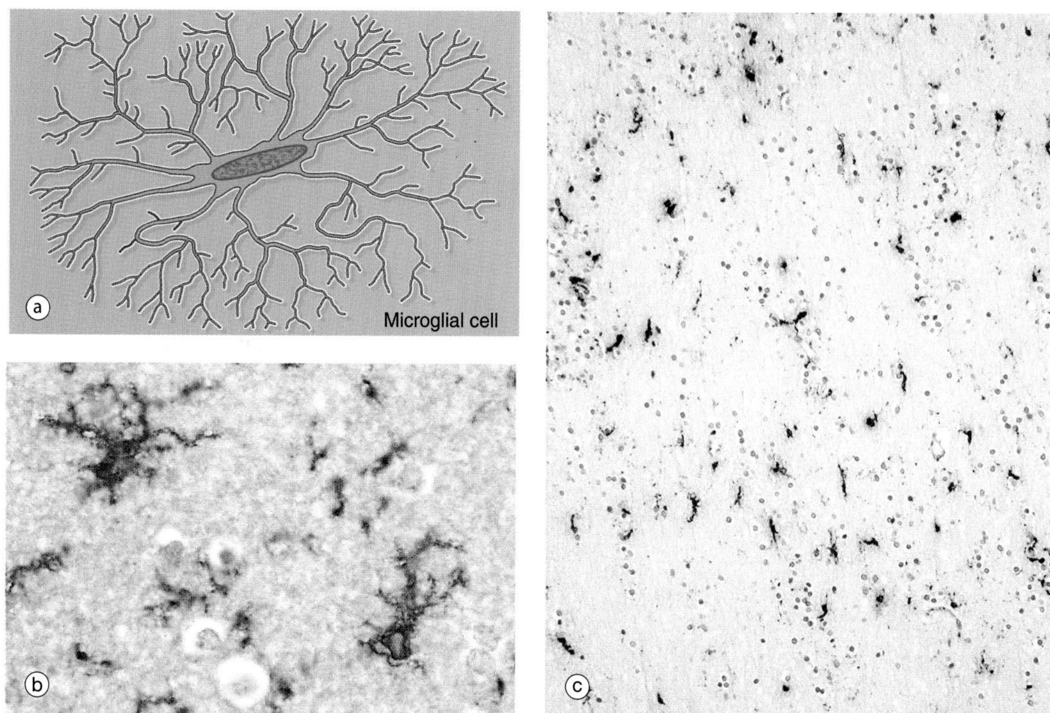

Fig. 7.26 Microglia
(a) Diagram (b) Ricinus communis agglutinin ×450 (c) Immunohistochemical staining CD68 ×120

Microglia are small cells, derived from cells of mesenchymal origin which invade the CNS at a late stage of fetal development. As shown in the diagram, microglia have elongated nuclei and relatively little cytoplasm which forms fine, highly branched processes. In consequence, they are difficult to identify in conventional preparations for light microscopy. Immunostaining provides the best way to see microglia. Micrograph (b) shows the ramified profile of microglia cells identified by staining using ricinus communis agglutinin which binds to sugars on the membrane of this cell type. Micrograph (c) highlights the distribution of this cell type in white matter from the cerebral hemisphere. The rounded nuclei in the background are mainly oligodendrocytes.

In response to tissue damage, microglia transform into large amoeboid phagocytic cells and are thus considered to be the CNS representatives of the macrophage-monocyte defence system (see Fig. 3.9). CD68 stains cells of macrophage lineage, including microglial cells. Other macrophages, distinct from microglia, are present in the space surrounding the CNS capillaries but separated from the CNS compartment proper by the perivascular feet of astrocytes. A small population of macrophages is also present adherent to the ependymal surfaces.

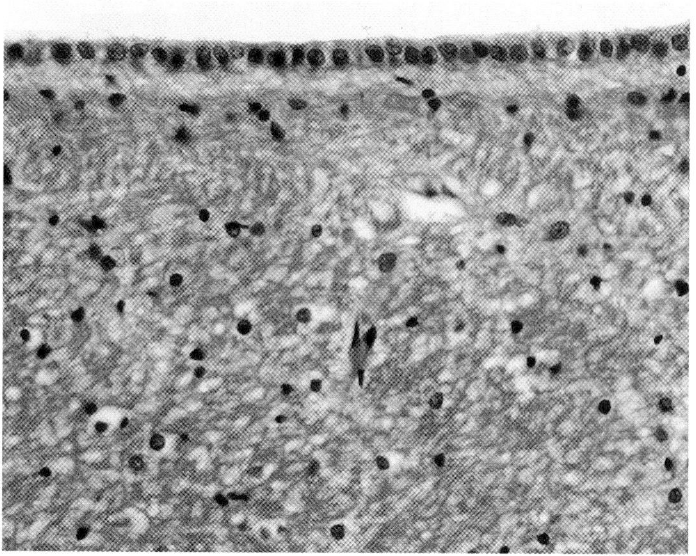

Fig. 7.27 Ependyma
H & E ×400

Ependymal cells form the epithelial lining of the ventricles and spinal canal. Cuboidal or low columnar in shape, the cells are tightly bound together at their luminal surfaces by the usual epithelial junctional complexes. Unlike other epithelia, however, ependymal cells do not rest on a basement membrane but, rather, the bases of the cells taper and then break up into fine branches which ramify into an underlying layer of processes derived from astrocytes. At the luminal surface, there is a variable number of cilia. Microvilli are also present and probably have absorptive and secretory functions.

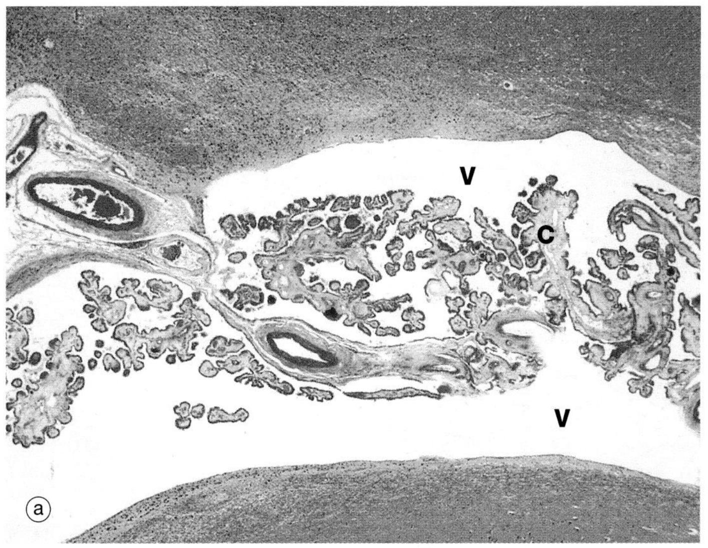

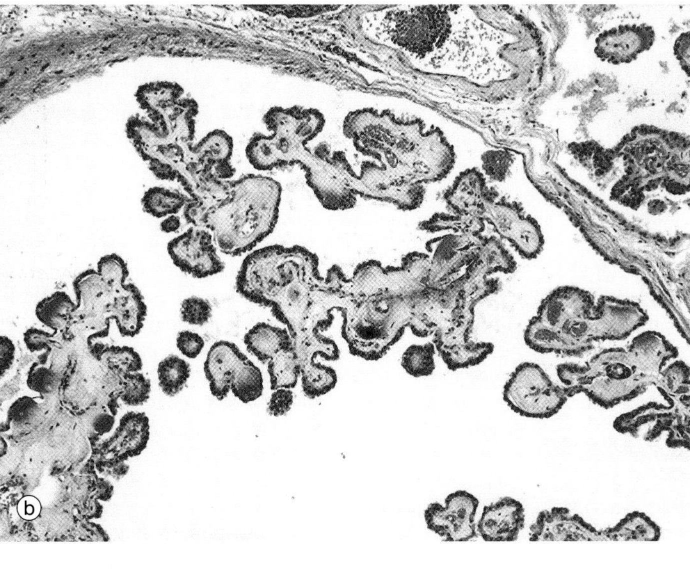

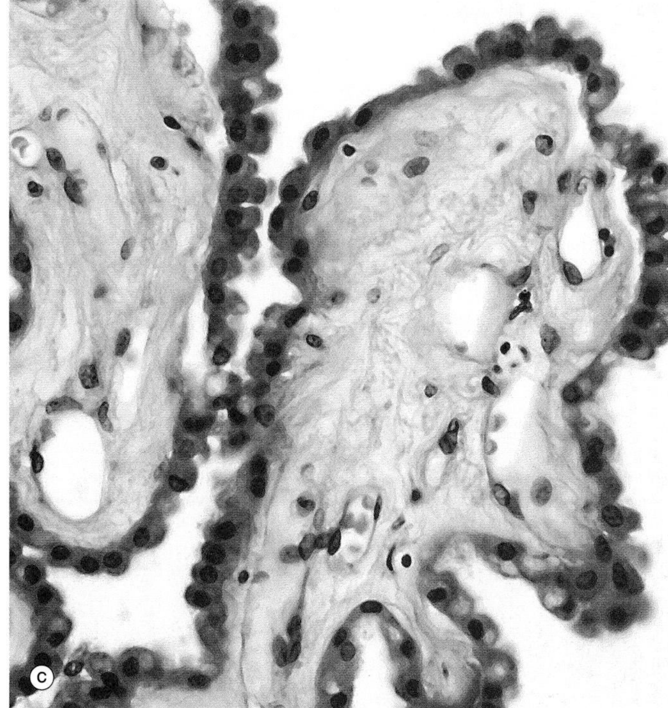

C choroid plexus **V** ventricle

Fig. 7.28 Choroid plexus
(a) H & E ×128 (b) H & E ×250
(c) H & E ×450

The choroid plexus is a vascular structure arising from the wall of each of the four ventricles of the brain and responsible for the production of ***cerebrospinal fluid (CSF)***. CSF drains from the interconnected ventricular cavities via three channels connecting the fourth ventricle with the subarachnoid space which surrounds the CNS. CSF is produced at a constant rate and is reabsorbed from the subarachnoid space into the superior sagittal venous sinus via finger-like projections called ***arachnoid villi***. Thus the CNS is suspended in a constantly circulating fluid medium which acts as a shock absorber.

Each choroid plexus consists of a branching system of blood vessels which run in fronds composed of collagenous tissue and covered by a cuboidal or columnar epithelium. The choroid plexus is therefore a villous structure. Micrograph (a) shows the choroid plexus **C** within a ventricle of the brain **V**.

Micrograph (b) shows the complex folded structure composed of vessels running in a collagenous stroma with overlying epithelium. Micrograph (c) shows detail of one of the choroid plexus processes. The capillaries and vessels of the choroid plexus are large, thin-walled and sometimes fenestrated. The epithelial cells rest on a basal lamina. At the ultrastructural level, long, bulbous microvilli project from the luminal surfaces of the choroid plexus epithelial cells and the cytoplasm contains numerous mitochondria, features which suggest that the elaboration of CSF is an active process.

The mode of CSF secretion involves active secretion of sodium ions by choroid epithelial cells into the CSF, followed by passive movement of water from the local vessels. Continuous tight junctions (zonula occludens) contribute to a ***blood–CSF barrier*** preventing ingress of almost all other molecules.

Fig. 7.29 Meninges *(illustrations opposite)*
(a) Diagram (b) H & E ×40 (c) H & E ×198 (d) H & E ×480 (e) Immunohistochemistry GFAP ×480

The brain and spinal cord are invested by three layers of supporting tissue collectively called the meninges. The surface of the nervous tissue is covered by a delicate layer called the ***pia mater*** containing collagen fibres, fine elastin fibres and occasional fibroblasts separated from the processes of underlying astrocytes by a basement membrane. The basement membrane is completely invested by astrocytic processes, the two layers forming the impermeable glia limitans (see also Fig. 7.24). Overlying the pia mater is a thicker fibrous layer, the ***arachnoid mater***, which derives its name from the presence of cobweb-like strands which connect it to the underlying pia mater; since the pia and arachnoid are structurally continuous, they are often considered as a single unit, the ***pia-arachnoid*** or ***leptomeninges***. The space between the pia and arachnoid layers is called the ***subarachnoid space*** and in places forms large cisterns. The subarachnoid space is connected with the ventricular system by three foramina and CSF circulates continuously from the ventricles into the subarachnoid space. The subarachnoid space (i.e. apposed surfaces of the pia and arachnoid layers, and their interconnecting fibres) is lined by flattened arachnoidal cells. The outer surface of the arachnoid mater is also lined by flat cells.

As shown in the diagram, arteries and veins passing to and from the CNS pass in the subarachnoid space loosely attached to the pia mater and invested by subarachnoid mesothelium. As the larger vessels extend into the nervous tissue, they are surrounded by a delicate sleeve of pia mater. Between the penetrating vessels and the pia there is a ***perivascular space*** which is continuous with the subarachnoid space in some animals but not in humans. In humans, the epithelium of the pia blends with the adventitia of the vessel as it penetrates the brain, separating the perivascular space from the subarachnoid space.

External to the arachnoid mater is a dense fibroelastic layer called the ***dura mater*** which is lined on its internal surface by flat cells. The dura is closely applied to, but not connected with, the arachnoid layer and a potential space, the ***subdural space***, can develop between the two layers. In the cranium, the dura mater merges with the periosteum of the skull, whereas around the spinal cord the dura is suspended from the periosteum of the spinal canal by the ***denticulate ligaments***, the intervening ***epidural space*** being filled with loose, fibrofatty tissue and a venous plexus.

The pia and arachnoid layers of the brain meninges are illustrated in micrographs (b) and (c), the dura mater typically remaining adherent to the skull when the brain is removed from the cranial cavity. The pia mater **P** is attached to the surface of the brain and continues into the sulci **S** and around the penetrating vessels. The arachnoid mater **A** appears to be a completely separate layer and bridges the sulci. Meningeal vessels lie in the subarachnoid space. At high magnification in micrograph (c), delicate fibrous strands **F** can be discerned traversing the subarachnoid space **SS** to connect the pia and arachnoid layers. Two small vessels **V** can be seen in the subarachnoid space. A penetrating vessel is also seen surrounded by a perivascular space **PVS**. The perivascular space is extremely narrow although it often appears artefactually wider as in this micrograph. The CNS contains no lymphatics and interstitial fluid is thought to drain outwards from the brain substance to join the subarachnoid CSF via the perivascular spaces and to contribute as much as 20% of its volume.

As seen in micrograph (d), the capillaries of the CNS are similar to those elsewhere in the body with flattened endothelial cells resting on a basement membrane. The endothelial cells are not fenestrated and are bound together by continuous tight intercellular junctions (zonula occludens) except in the choroid plexus where this is discontinuous. Externally, the basement membranes are covered by the perivascular foot processes of astrocytes shown in micrograph (e) where brown-stained processes form a continuous layer. A thin layer of the pia mater extends down into the CNS around smaller arteries, veins, arterioles and venules but is not present around the capillaries of the CNS.

Perfusion studies show that the CNS capillaries are impermeable to certain plasma constituents, especially larger molecules, forming a ***blood–brain barrier***. The capillary endothelium plays the central role since junctions between endothelial cells are sealed; the endothelial cells exhibit little or no pinocytosis. Luminal surface membranes contain various enzymes which destroy neurotoxic metabolites and neuroactive humoral substances. Maintenance of barrier-type endothelium appears to be under the control of astrocyte foot processes. The blood–brain barrier provides neurones with a relatively constant biochemical and metabolic environment, protection against endogenous and exogenous toxins and infective agents and insulates the neurones from circulating neurotransmitters and other humoral agents. The capillaries of the choroid plexus, the pituitary and pineal glands and the vomiting centre of the hypothalamus are, however, devoid of this barrier to allow specialised functions.

Meningeal spaces and disease

The meningeal spaces are the site of several disease processes.

- The subarachnoid space contains the cerebrospinal fluid. In ***bacterial meningitis*** infective organisms gain entrance to the CSF and there is an inflammatory response. A count of lymphocytes, monocytes and neutrophils in the CSF, usually performed on a sample drawn from the lumbar thecal space (lumbar puncture), is helpful in diagnosis of meningitis.
- The subarachnoid space contains the main blood vessels supplying the brain. If there is damage to these vessels, for example rupture due to a weakness of the vessel wall, then blood enters the CSF, termed ***subarachnoid haemorrhage***.
- The subdural space lies between the dura and the arachnoid. Veins traverse this tissue plane. In the elderly and in patients with impaired blood clotting minor trauma can tear veins and cause bleeding into this space, termed a ***subdural haemorrhage***.
- The dura is firmly attached to the inner surface of the skull. If there is bleeding associated with skull fracture then blood can accumulate in the tissue plane outside the dura, termed an ***extradural haemorrhage***.

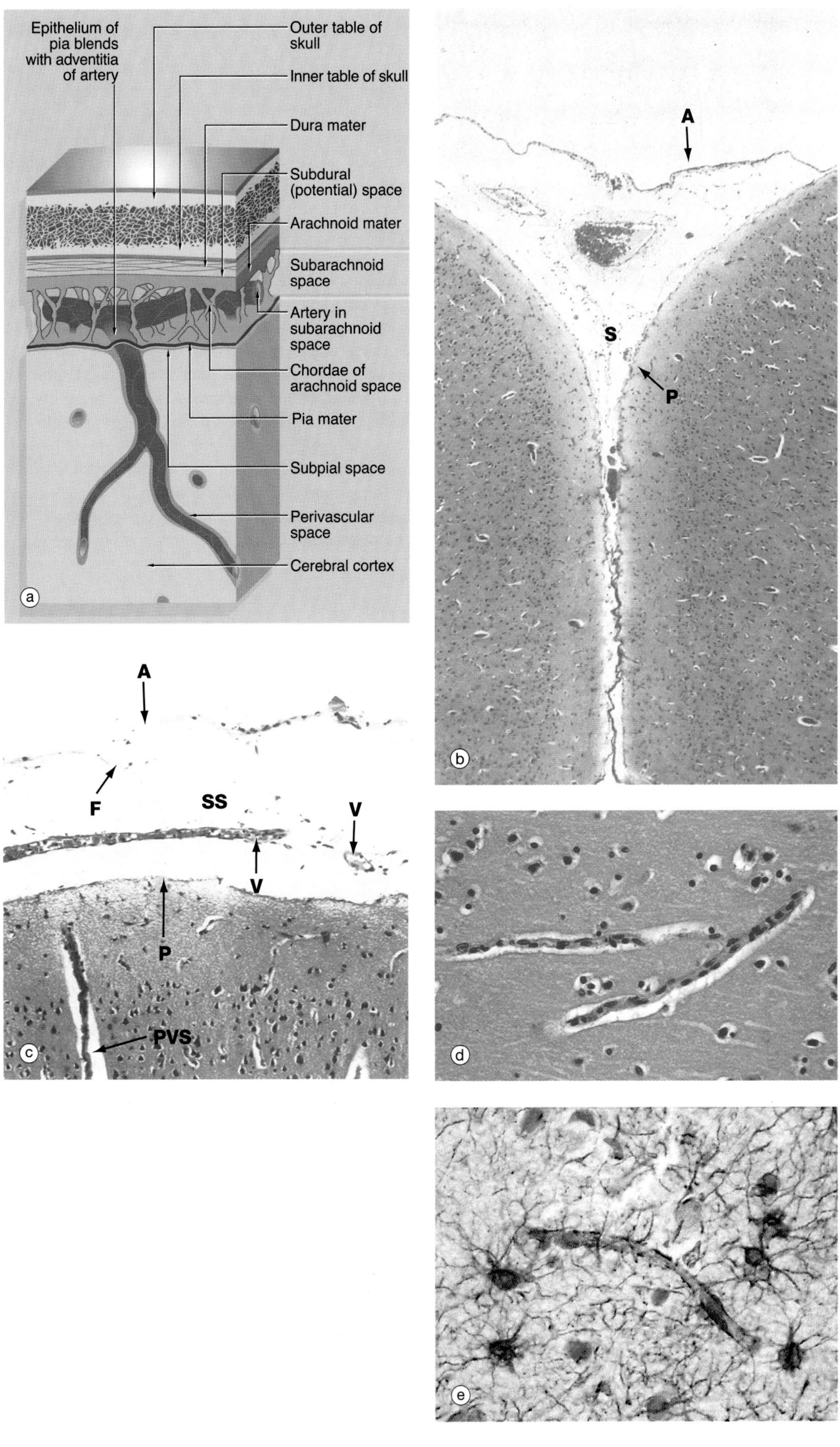

A arachnoid mater **F** fibrous strand **P** pia mater **PVS** perivascular space **S** sulcus
SS subarachnoid space **V** vessels

Sensory receptors

Sensory receptors are nerve endings or specialised cells which convert (transduce) stimuli from the external or internal environments into afferent nerve impulses; the impulses pass into the CNS where they initiate appropriate voluntary or involuntary responses.

No classification system for sensory receptors has yet been devised which adequately incorporates either functional or morphological features. A widely used functional classification divides sensory receptors into three groups: ***exteroceptors***, ***proprioceptors*** and ***interoceptors***. Exteroceptors are those which respond to stimuli from outside the body and include receptors for touch, light pressure, deep pressure, cutaneous pain, temperature, smell, taste, sight and hearing. Proprioceptors are located within the skeletal system and provide conscious and unconscious information about orientation, skeletal position, tension and movement; such receptors include the vestibular apparatus of the ear, tendon stretch receptors and neuromuscular spindles. Interoceptors respond to stimuli from the viscera and include the chemoreceptors of blood, vascular (pressure) baroreceptors, the receptors for the state of distension of hollow viscera such as the gastrointestinal tract and urinary bladder, and receptors for such nebulous senses as visceral pain, hunger, thirst, well-being and malaise.

The structure of the receptors involved in some of these sensory modalities is poorly understood. Sensory receptors may be classified morphologically into two groups, ***simple*** and ***compound***. Simple receptors are merely free, branched or unbranched nerve endings such as those responsible for cutaneous pain and temperature; they are rarely visible with the light microscope unless special staining methods are employed. Compound receptors involve organisation of associated non-neural tissues to complement the function of the neural receptors. The degree of organisation may range from mere encapsulation to highly sophisticated arrangements such as in the eye and ear. By tradition, the eye, ear and receptors for the senses of smell and taste are described as the ***organs of special sense***; they are the subject of Chapter 21.

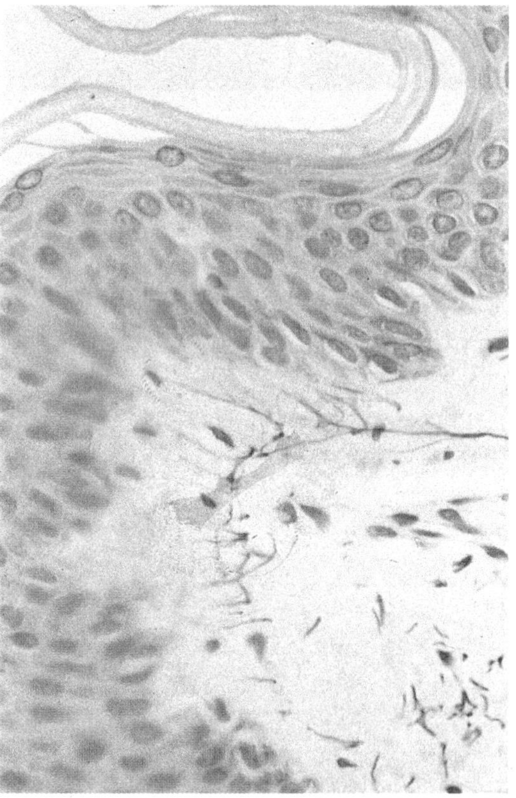

Fig. 7.30 Free nerve endings
Silver/haematoxylin ×480

Free nerve endings are the simplest form of sensory receptor, merely consisting of numerous small terminal branches of afferent nerve fibres. Such free nerve endings are found in supporting tissues throughout the body subserving a variety of relatively unsophisticated sensory modalities such as temperature, touch and pain. The afferent fibres are of relatively small diameter with slow rates of conduction; although some of these fibres are myelinated, the nerve endings are devoid of myelin.

In the skin, free nerve endings are found along the dermo-epidermal junction. Some exhibit a terminal expansion which is intimately associated with non-neuronal cells called ***Merkel cells*** scattered in the basal layers of the epidermis (see Fig. 9.7). The adjacent Merkel cell cytoplasm contains vesicles with ultrastructural features similar to those found in synapses in which transmitter substances such as dynorphin have been demonstrated. Merkel nerve endings are served by large-diameter myelinated fibres and are thought to be responsible for the sensation of touch. A variety of different arrangements of free nerve endings is also incorporated in the follicles of fine and coarse hairs acting as touch receptors, the most sophisticated type being those associated with the whiskers of animals such as cats and rodents.

This thick section of skin stained by a heavy metal impregnation method shows a nerve fibre with many fine terminal branches extending as free nerve endings into the dermo-epidermal junction; Merkel cells cannot be readily identified in this micrograph.

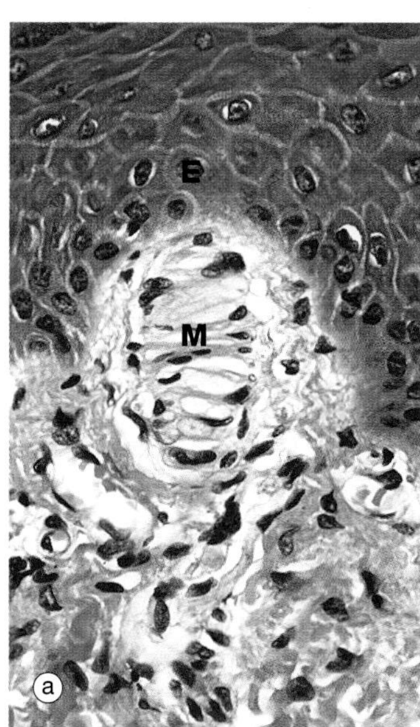

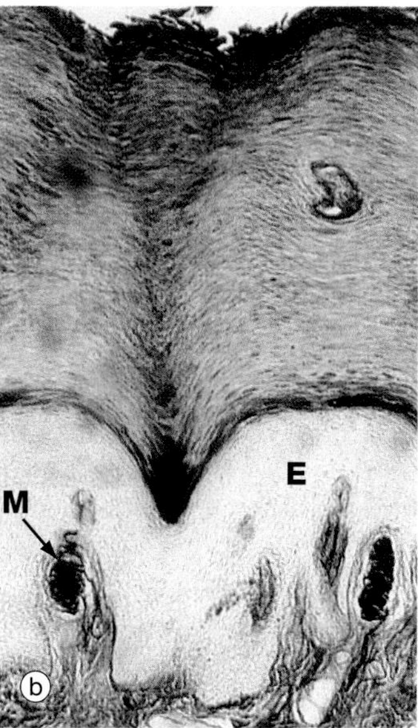

Fig. 7.31 Meissner's corpuscles
(a) H & E ×320
(b) Silver method ×150

Meissner's corpuscles are small, encapsulated, sensory receptors found in the dermis of the skin, particularly of the fingertips, soles of the feet, nipples, eyelids, lips and genitalia. They are involved in the reception of light discriminatory touch, the degree of discrimination depending on the proximity of receptors to one another.

As seen in micrograph (a), Meissner's corpuscles **M** are oval in shape and are usually located in the dermal papillae immediately beneath the epidermis **E**. The receptors consist of a delicate collagenous tissue capsule surrounding a mass of plump, oval cells arranged transversely and probably representing specialised Schwann cells. Non-myelinated branches of large myelinated sensory fibres ramify throughout the cell mass in a helical manner as shown by the heavy metal impregnation technique in micrograph (b).

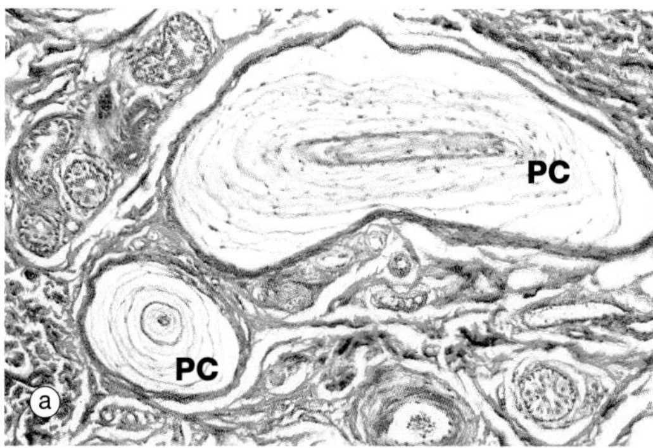

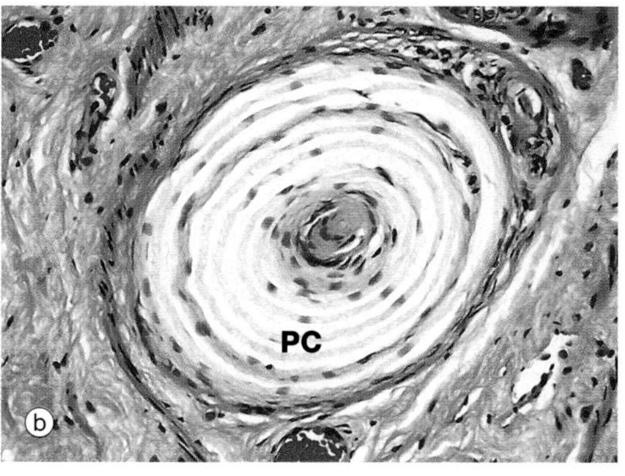

Fig. 7.32 Pacinian corpuscles
(a) Masson's trichrome ×80 (b) H & E ×100

Pacinian corpuscles **PC** are large encapsulated sensory receptors responsive to pressure or coarse touch, vibration and tension, and are found in the deeper layers of the skin, ligaments and joint capsules, in some serous membranes, mesenteries, some viscera and in some erogenous areas.

Pacinian corpuscles range from 1 to 4 mm in length and in section have the appearance of an onion. These organs consist of a delicate capsule enclosing many concentric lamellae of flattened cells (probably modified Schwann cells) separated by interstitial fluid spaces and delicate collagen fibres. Towards the centre of the corpuscle the lamellae become closely packed and the core contains a single large unbranched non-myelinated nerve fibre with several club-like terminals which becomes myelinated as it leaves the corpuscle. Distortion of the Pacinian corpuscle produces an amplified mechanical stimulus in the core which is transduced into an action potential in the sensory neurone.

Two other simple encapsulated mechanoreceptors are described. ***Ruffini corpuscles*** are robust spindle-shaped structures found particularly in the soles of the feet. ***Krause end bulbs*** are delicate receptors found in the lining of the oropharynx and the conjunctiva of the eye.

E epidermis **M** Meissner's corpuscle **PC** Pacinian corpuscle

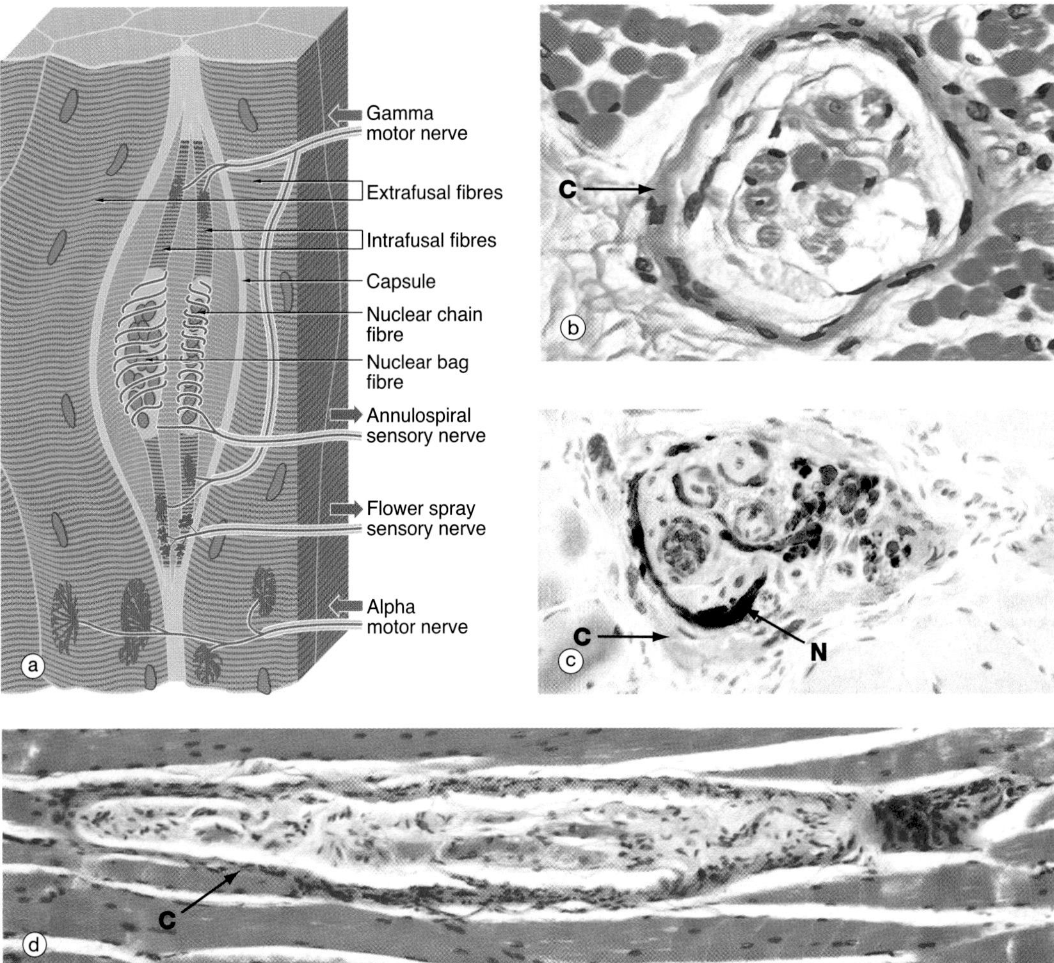

Fig. 7.33 Neuromuscular spindle
(a) Schematic diagram (b) TS, H & E ×350 (c) TS, S100 immunostaining ×350 (d) LS, H & E ×150

Neuromuscular spindles are stretch receptor organs within skeletal muscles which are responsible for the regulation of muscle tone via the spinal stretch reflex.

Neuromuscular spindles are encapsulated, lymph filled, fusiform structures up to 6mm long but less than 1 mm in diameter. They lie parallel to the muscle fibres, embedded in endomysium or perimysium. Each spindle contains from two to 10 modified skeletal muscle fibres called ***intrafusal fibres*** which are much smaller than skeletal muscle fibres proper (***extrafusal fibres***). The intrafusal fibres have a central non-striated area in which their nuclei tend to be concentrated. Two types of intrafusal fibres are recognised. In one type, the central nuclear area is dilated, these fibres being known as ***nuclear bag fibres***. In the other type, there is no dilatation and the nuclei are arranged in a single row giving rise to the name ***nuclear chain fibres***.

Associated with both types of intrafusal fibres are sensory receptors of two types. Firstly, branched, non-myelinated endings of large, myelinated sensory fibres are wrapped around the central non-striated area of the intrafusal fibres forming ***annulospiral endings***. Secondly, ***flower-spray endings*** of smaller, myelinated sensory fibres are located on the striated portions of the intrafusal fibres.

Together, these sensory receptors are stimulated by stretching of the intrafusal fibres which occurs when the extrafusal muscle mass is stretched. This stimulus evokes reflex contraction of the extrafusal muscle fibres via large (alpha) motor neurones of a simple two-neurone spinal reflex arc. Contraction of the extrafusal muscle mass thus removes the stretch stimulus from the intrafusal stretch receptors and equilibrium is restored.

The sensitivity of the neuromuscular spindle is modulated by higher centres via small (gamma) motor neurones arising from the extrapyramidal system. These gamma motor neurones innervate the striated portions of the intrafusal fibres thus controlling their state of contraction. Contraction of the intrafusal fibres increases the sensitivity of the intrafusal receptors to stretching of the extrafusal mass.

In any one histological section, it is impossible to demonstrate all the structural features of a neuromuscular spindle, but many of the features of the organ are shown in these micrographs. The most easily recognisable features are the discrete capsule **C** which is continuous with the endomysium of the surrounding muscle and the small size of the intrafusal muscle fibres, best seen in longitudinal section in micrograph (d). Note the nerve fibres **N** passing to and from the spindle immunostained in micrograph (c).

C capsule of spindle **N** nerve fibre

PART THREE

Organ systems

8. *Circulatory system*

Introduction

The circulatory system mediates the continuous movement of all body fluids, its principal functions being the transport of oxygen and nutrients to the tissues, and transport of carbon dioxide and other metabolic waste products from the tissues. The circulatory system is also involved in temperature regulation and the distribution of molecules, such as hormones, and cells, such as those of the immune system. The circulatory system has two functional components: the blood vascular system and the lymph vascular system.

The ***blood circulatory system*** comprises a circuit of vessels through which blood flow is initiated by continuous action of a central muscular pump, the ***heart***. The ***arterial system*** provides a distribution network to the tiny peripheral microcirculation, the capillaries and postcapillary venules, which are the main sites of interchange of gas and metabolite molecules between the tissues and the blood. The ***venous system*** carries blood from the capillary system back to the heart.

The ***lymph vascular system*** is a network of drainage vessels for returning excess extravascular fluid, the ***lymph***, to the blood circulatory system, and for transporting lymph to the lymph nodes for immunological screening (see Ch. 11). The lymphatic system has no central pump but in all but the tiniest lymphatics there is an intrinsic pumping system effected by contractile smooth muscle fibres in the lymph vessel wall, combined with a valve system preventing back flow.

The whole circulatory system has a common basic structure:

- An inner lining comprising a single layer of extremely flattened epithelial cells called ***endothelium*** supported by a basement membrane and delicate collagenous tissue; this constitutes the ***tunica intima***.
- An intermediate predominantly muscular layer, the ***tunica media***.
- An outer principally supporting tissue layer called the ***tunica adventitia***.

The tissues of the thick walls of large vessels (e.g. aorta) cannot be sustained by diffusion of oxygen and nutrients from their lumina, and are supplied by small arteries (***vasa vasorum***) which run in the tunica adventitia and sends arterioles and capillaries into the tunica media.

The muscular content exhibits the greatest variation from one part of the system to another. For example, it is totally absent in capillaries but comprises almost the whole mass of the heart. Blood flow is predominantly influenced by variation in activity of the muscular tissue.

The heart

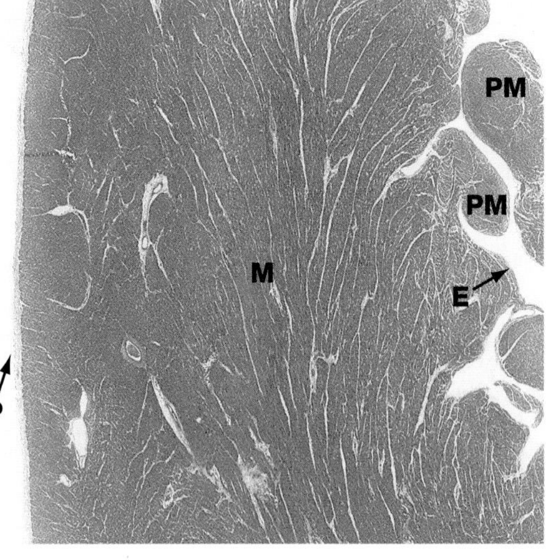

Fig. 8.1 Heart – left ventricle wall
H & E ×3

This low power micrograph shows the three basic layers of the heart wall, in this case the left ventricle. The tunica intima equivalent of the heart is the ***endocardium*** **E**, normally a thin layer in a ventricle. The tunica media equivalent is the ***myocardium*** **M**, made up of cardiac-type muscle (see Ch. 6); in the left ventricle this layer is very prominent, but is less thick in the right ventricle and atria which operate at much lower pressures. Note the origins of the ***papillary muscles*** **PM**, extensions of the myocardium which protrude into the left ventricular cavity and provide attachment points of the ***chordae tendinae*** which tether the cusps of the atrio-ventricular valves. The equivalent of the tunica adventitia is the ***epicardium*** or ***visceral pericardium*** **P**, usually a thin layer (as here), but in some areas containing adipose tissue (see Fig. 8.2a).

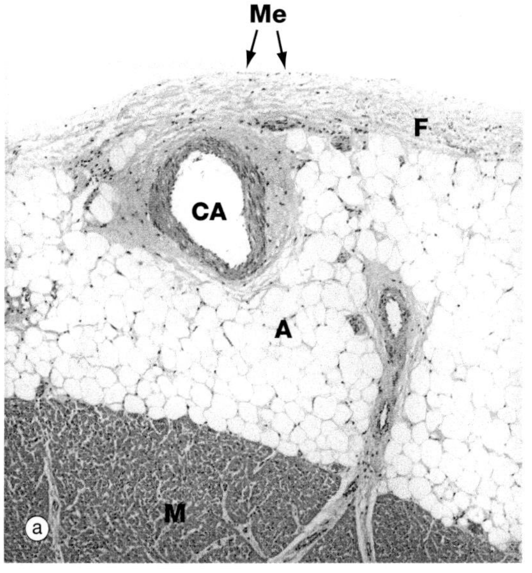

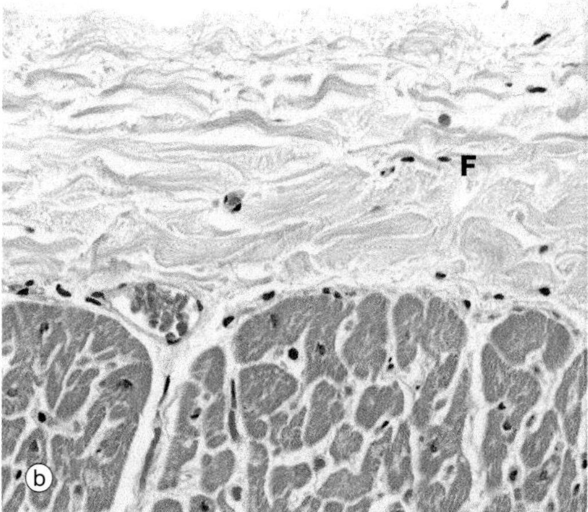

Fig. 8.2 Heart: epicardium (visceral pericardium)
(a) H & E ×200 (b) H & E ×480

The constant layer of the epicardium is a dense sheet of fibrocollagenous tissue **F** which also contains elastic fibres. On its outer surface is a flat monolayer of mesothelial cells **Me** (not clearly seen here) responsible for secretion of lubricating fluid. Micrograph (a) shows an area where the epicardium contains a large branch of the coronary artery **CA**, with a smaller branch penetrating the myocardium **M**. Note that while in areas containing artery branches, there is a variable layer of adipose tissue **A**. Micrograph (b) shows the appearance of the epicardium over most of the heart surface where the fibrocollagenous layer lies directly on the myocardium without adipose tissue.

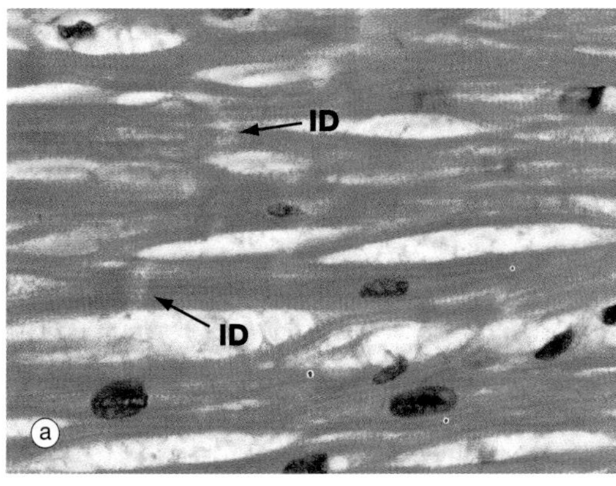

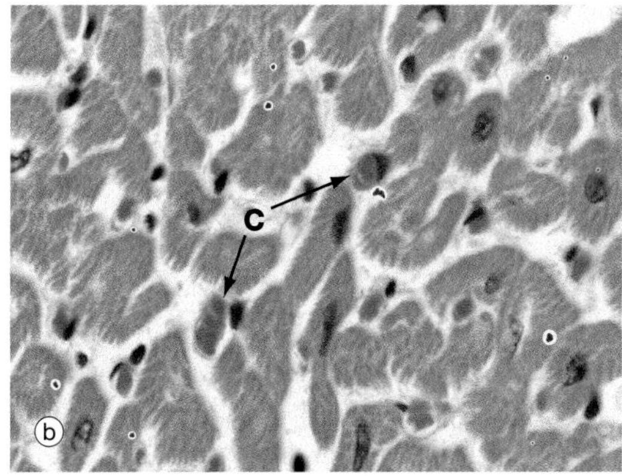

Fig. 8.3 Myocardium
(a) LS ×300 (b) TS ×300

In longitudinal section (a), cardiac muscle fibres form an interconnecting network, joined to each other by ***intercalated discs*** **D**, and having central nuclei and regular cytoplasmic striations. The discs and striations can be clearly seen using special methods such as the immunocytochemical technique for α-B crystallin and in thin resin sections stained with toluidine blue (see Fig. 6.24).

In transverse section (b), the extensive and intimate capillary network **C** between the myocardial fibres is easily seen, in this section distended with red blood cells (see also Fig. 6.21). This is a reflection of the high and constant oxygen demand of the myocardium, particularly in the left ventricle shown in these two pictures.

The structural details of the cardiac muscle of the myocardium are given in Ch. 6.

A adipose tissue **C** capillaries **CA** coronary artery **D** intercalated disc **E** endocardium
F fibrous tissue **M** myocardium **Me** mesothelial cells **P** pericardium **PM** papillary muscles

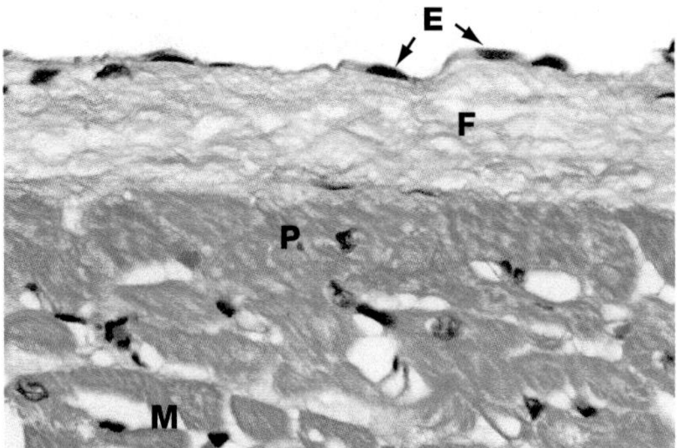

Fig. 8.4 Endocardium
H & E ×300

The endocardium has a surface layer of flattened endothelial cells **E** supported by a fibrous layer **F**, containing variable amounts of elastic tissue, which merges with the collagen fibres surrounding adjacent cardiac muscle **M** and the larger ***Purkinje fibres*** **P** (see Fig. 8.6). The endocardium shown here is from the wall of the left ventricle. The endocardium of the atria is much thicker, and has more elastic fibres.

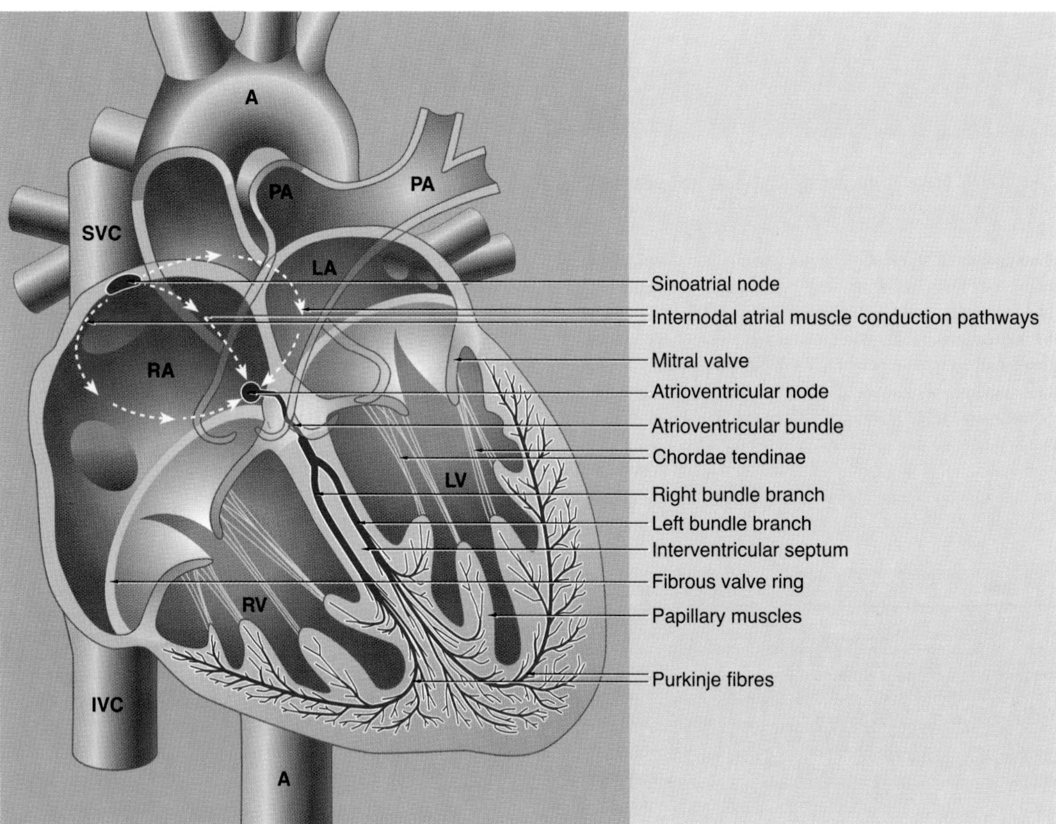

Fig. 8.5 Heart – conduction system

The coordinated contraction of the heart is largely effected by a specialised conducting system of modified cardiac muscle fibres. The initial impulse originates spontaneously in the ***sino-atrial node*** situated in the right atrial wall near the entry of the superior vena cava, but the impulse rate is controlled by the autonomic nervous system. The impulse passes through the muscle of the atria, causing them to contract, and reaches the ***atrioventricular node*** in the medial wall of the right atrium just above the tricuspid valve ring, at the base of the interatrial septum. Both the sinoatrial and atrioventricular nodes are irregular meshworks of very small specialised myocardial fibres, with electrochemical stimuli being transmitted via gap junctions. The nodal fibres are embedded in collagenous fibrous tissue which contains blood vessels and many autonomic nerve fibres.

From the atrioventricular node, the impulse is passed along a specialised bundle of conducting fibres, the ***atrioventricular bundle*** (***of His***), which initially divides into right and left bundle branches, that then (halfway down the interventricular septum) become Purkinje fibres which run immediately beneath the endocardium before penetrating the myocardium (see Figs 8.4 and 8.6).

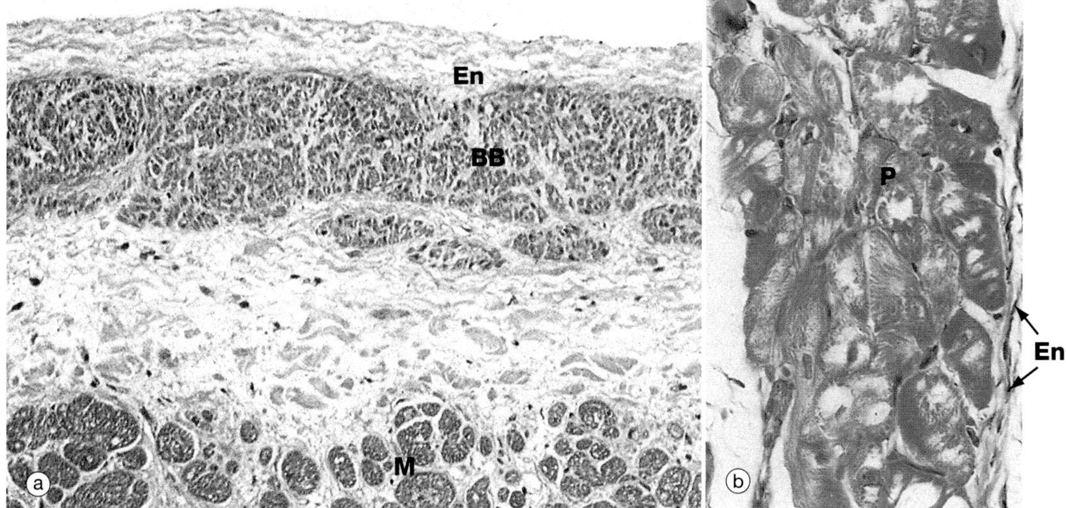

Fig. 8.6 Heart
(a) Bundle branch H & E ×150 (b) Purkinje fibres H & E/elastin ×400

Micrograph (a) shows the left branch bundle of conducting fibres **BB** running in the interventricular septum just beneath the endocardium **En** lining the left ventricular cavity. At this level the conducting fibres are separated from the myocardial fibres **M** of the septum by a layer of fibrous tissue. The conducting fibres are specialised cardiac muscle fibres, and contain comparatively few myofibrils, which are mainly located beneath the cell membrane, but abundant glycogen granules and mitochondria. This makes these fibres paler staining than normal myocardial fibres by most stains.

Micrograph (b) shows the distal extension of the branch bundle, the Purkinje fibres **P** beneath the thin endocardium **En**. These fibres are larger than cardiac muscle fibres and have a pale staining central area with most of the red-staining myofibrils around the periphery of the cell. Unlike myocardial fibres, Purkinje and other conducting fibres have no T tubule system, and connect with each other by desmosomes and gap junctions rather than intercalated discs.

Common disorders of myocardium

The myocardial cells have a high-energy demand and therefore a high and constant oxygen requirement. When deprived of oxygen, individual cardiac muscle cells die and cannot be replaced. When the reduction in oxygenation (due to progressively inadequate arterial supply) is slow and progressive, a few muscle cells die at a time and the patient develops the symptom complex called ***angina of effort*** (a characteristic crushing central chest pain on exertion, disappearing on rest). With progressively more severe ischaemia of the myocardium, the angina symptoms appear with minimal or no exertion. Histologically, the dead muscle fibres are replaced by collagenous fibrous tissue, and remaining muscle fibres enlarge and increase their work rate ('hypertrophy') to compensate. The reduction in flow of arterial blood to the heart is due to the arterial disease, ***atherosclerosis***, reducing the lumen of the coronary arteries.

When a coronary artery suddenly becomes completely occluded (e.g. by thrombosis), a substantial mass of the heart muscle cells dies, for example the muscle comprising the entire anterior wall of the left ventricle and the anterior part of the interventricular septum if the anterior descending branch of the left coronary artery is blocked. This is called ***myocardial infarction***. This sudden loss of contractile mass greatly reduces the force of contraction of the left ventricle, leading to low output left heart failure. Death of some component of the conducting bundles of Purkinje fibres can also lead to potentially fatal abnormalities of cardiac rhythm (***dysrhythmia***). Histologically, all the muscle fibres in the affected area die and are eventually replaced by collagenous fibrous tissue, which is strong but not contractile, so the patient may have persistent left heart failure.

A aorta **BB** bundle branch **E** endothelial cell **En** endocardium **F** fibrous layer
IVC inferior vena cava **LA** left atrium **LV** left ventricle **M** myocardium **P** Purkinje fibres
PA pulmonary artery **RA** right atrium **RV** right ventricle **SVC** superior vena cava

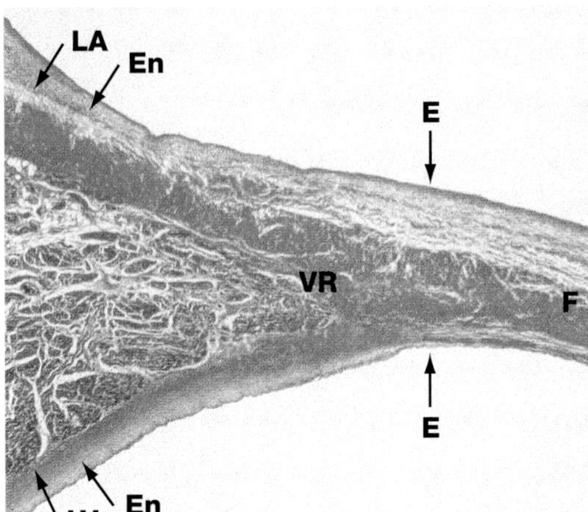

Fig. 8.7 Heart valve
H & E ×15

The heart valves consist of leaflets of fibroelastic tissue, the surfaces covered by a thin layer of endothelium **E** continuous with that lining the heart chambers and great vessels. This micrograph shows the left atrioventricular valve (the mitral valve) arising at the junction of the walls of the left atrium **LA** and left ventricle **LV**. The fibroelastic layer of the endocardium **En** condenses to form the valve ring **VR** and from this arises the central fibroelastic sheet of the valve, the ***lamina fibrosa*** **F**.

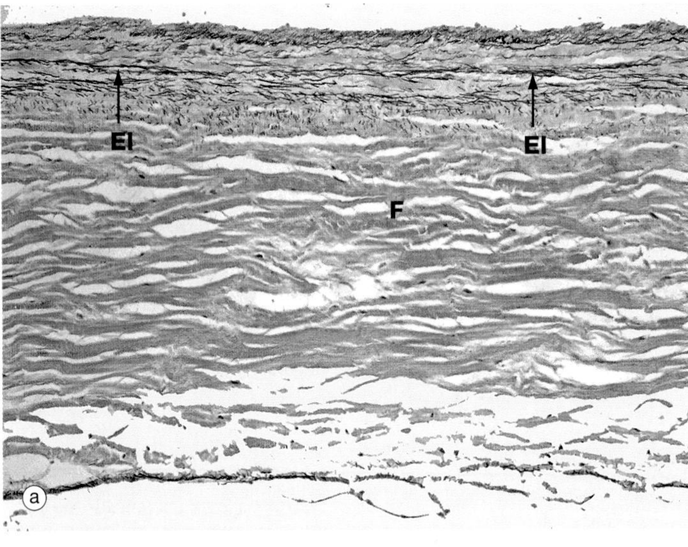

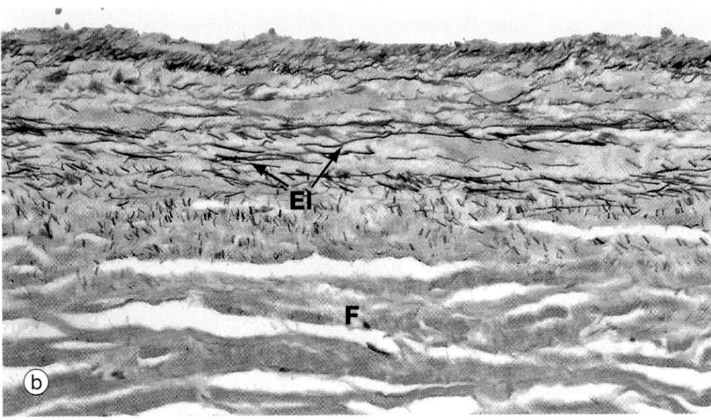

Fig. 8.8 Heart valve
(a) EVG ×30 (b) EVG ×75

The valves are sheets of fibroelastic tissue covered on both sides by endocardium; there is a dense central plate of collagen (the lamina fibrosa **F**) containing scattered elastic fibres (black in this stain) as shown in micrograph (a) at low magnification. In the left atrioventricular valves (as here), there is a distinct elastic lamina towards the atrial surface (**El**) in micrograph (b), and the collagen (red staining here) is particularly prominent on the ventricular surface where the chordae tendinae **CT** are attached.

Common disorders of heart valves

The aortic valve normally has three cusps, but occasionally there are only two (bicuspid) due to a developmental anomaly. Bicuspid aortic valves are particularly prone to develop fibrous thickening within which calcium salts, are deposited to make fibrocalcific nodules. These severely distort the cusps, which also tend to fuse. This disease, called ***calcific aortic valve disease***, interferes with valve function, reducing flow of blood through the valve during systole (***aortic stenosis***) and allowing blood to leak back from the aorta into the left ventricle during diastole (***aortic regurgitation***). Thrombosis may occur on the free margins of heart valves and, if there is subsequent bacteraemia, they may become infected (***valvitis*** or ***endocarditis***). Depending on the bacterium involved, the infected thrombus may erode the valve, leading to severe valve failure, or fragments of the thrombus may break off and pass in the circulation to distant sites where they may block arteries (***embolism***).

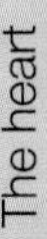

The arterial system

The function of the arterial system is to distribute blood from the heart to capillary beds throughout the body. The cyclical pumping action of the heart produces a pulsatile blood flow in the arterial system. With each contraction of the ventricles (***systole***), blood is forced into the arterial system causing expansion of the arterial walls; subsequent recoil of the arterial walls assists in maintenance of arterial blood pressure between ventricular beats (***diastole***). This expansion and recoil is a function of elastic tissue within the walls of the arteries. The flow of blood to various organs and tissues may be regulated by varying the diameter of the distributing vessels. This function is performed by the circumferentially disposed smooth muscle of vessel walls and is principally under the control of the sympathetic nervous system and adrenal medullary hormones.

The walls of the arterial vessels conform to the general three-layered structure of the circulatory system but are characterised by the presence of considerable elastin and the smooth muscle wall is thick relative to the diameter of the lumen. There are three main types of vessel in the arterial system:

- **Elastic arteries.** These comprise the major distribution vessels and include the aorta, the innominate (brachiocephalic trunk), common carotid and subclavian arteries and most of the large pulmonary arterial vessels.
- **Muscular arteries.** These are the main distributing branches of the arterial tree, e.g. the radial, femoral, coronary and cerebral arteries.
- **Arterioles.** These are the terminal branches of the arterial tree which supply the capillary beds.

There is a gradual transition in structure and function between the three types of arterial vessel rather than an abrupt demarcation. In general, the amount of elastic tissue decreases as the vessels become smaller and the smooth muscle component assumes relatively greater prominence.

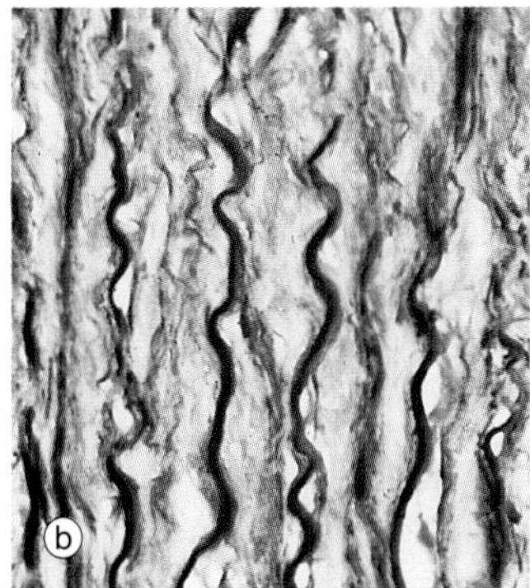

Fig. 8.9 Elastic artery: aorta
(a) Elastic van Gieson ×33 (b) Elastic van Gieson ×320

The highly elastic nature of the aortic wall is demonstrated in these preparations in which the elastic fibres are stained brownish-black. In micrograph (a), the three basic layers of the wall can be seen: the tunica intima **I**, the broad tunica media **M** and the tunica adventitia **A**.

The tunica intima consists of a single layer of flattened endothelial cells (not seen at this magnification) supported by a layer of collagenous tissue rich in elastin disposed in the form of both fibres and discontinuous sheets. The subendothelial supporting tissue contains scattered fibroblasts and other cells with ultrastructural features akin to smooth muscle cells and known as ***myointimal cells***. Both cell types are probably involved in elaboration of the extracellular constituents. The myointimal cells are not invested by basement membrane and are thus not epithelial (myoepithelial) in nature. With increasing age, the myointimal cells accumulate lipid and the intima progressively thickens; if this process continues, ***atherosclerosis*** will develop (see page 158).

The tunica media is particularly broad and extremely elastic. At high magnification in (b), it is seen to consist of concentric fenestrated sheets of elastin (stained black) separated by collagenous tissue (stained reddish-brown) and smooth muscle fibres (stained yellow). As seen in micrograph (a), the collagenous tunica adventitia (stained reddish-brown) contains small vasa vasorum **V** which also penetrate the outer half of the tunica media.

Blood flow within elastic arteries is highly pulsatile; with advancing age the arterial system becomes less elastic thereby increasing peripheral resistance and thus arterial blood pressure.

A tunica adventitia **E** endothelium **El** elastic lamina **En** endocardium **F** lamina fibrosa
I tunica intima **LA** left atrial wall **LV** left ventricular wall **M** tunica media **V** vasa vasorum
VR valve ring

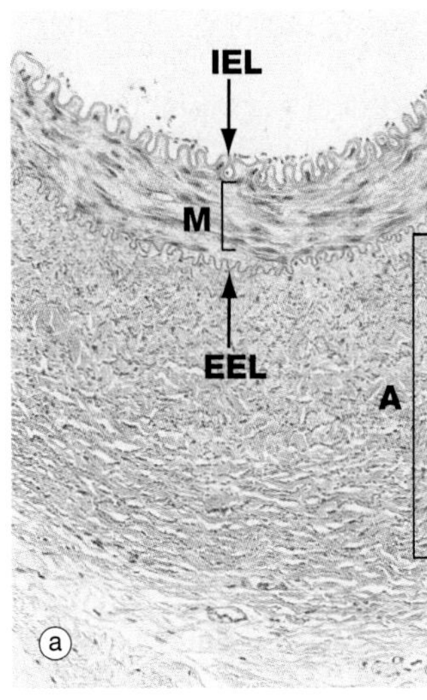

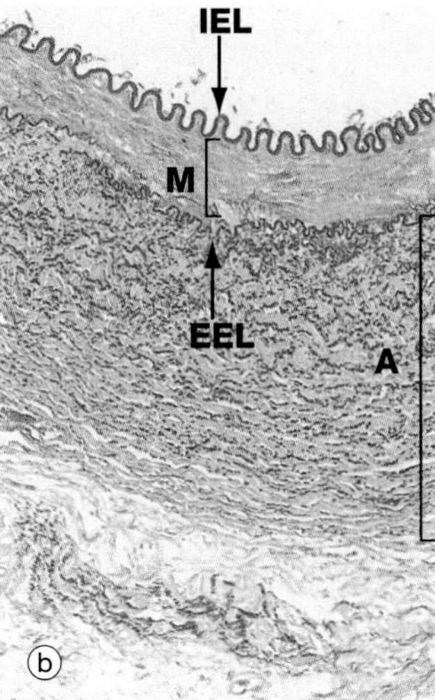

Fig. 8.10 Muscular artery
(a) H & E ×100 (b) EVG ×100

In muscular arteries the elastic tissue is largely concentrated as two well-defined elastic sheets. One sheet is the ***internal elastic lamina*** **IEL** between the tunica intima and the tunica media. The less prominent and more variable ***external elastic lamina*** **EEL** lies between the tunica media **M** and the adventitia. The tunica intima is usually a very thin layer, not visible at low magnification, and the tunica media **M** is composed of concentrically arranged smooth muscle fibres with scanty elastic fibres **F** between them. The tunica adventitia **A** is of variable thickness, and is composed of collagen and a variable amount of elastic tissue; in larger muscular arteries, this layer may contain prominent vasa vasorum.

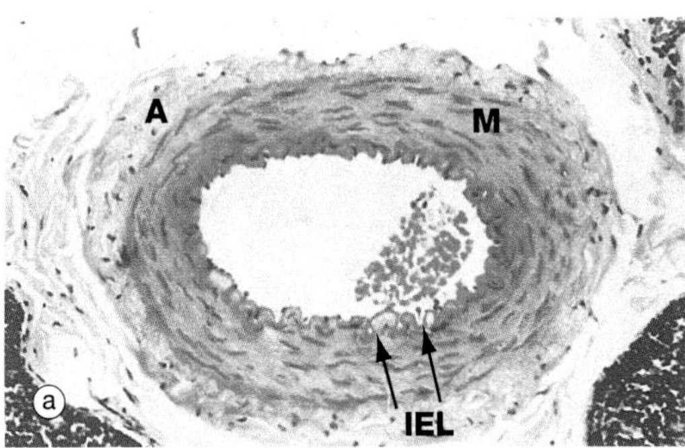

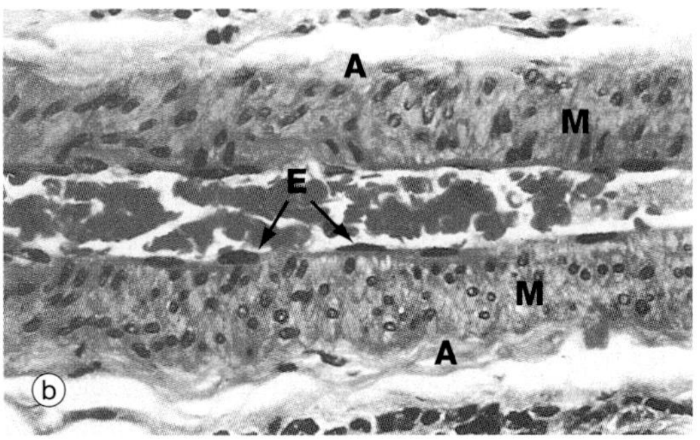

Fig. 8.11 Small muscular artery
(a) H & E, TS ×128 (b) H & E, LS ×320

In a small muscular artery, the diameter is approximately 0.5 to 2 mm and a thin but distinct internal elastic lamina is present but there is usually little or no external elastic lamina. The tunica media has 3–10 concentric layers of smooth muscle and contains almost no elastic fibres.

Micrograph (a) shows an artery in transverse section. The distinction between tunica media **M** and the adventitia **A** is obvious. The internal elastic lamina **IEL** can just be distinguished as a densely staining wavy line.

Micrograph (b) is a smaller artery at higher magnification. The nuclei of the intimal endothelial cells are visible **E** but the elastic lamina has largely disappeared.

Common disease of arteries

Elastic and muscular arteries develop the common disease called ***atherosclerosis*** in which lipid material infiltrates the tunica intima and accumulates in macrophages. This stimulates the proliferation of intimal fibroblasts and myointimal cells, with collagen deposition, to produce a ***plaque*** which thickens the intima. If severe, and in a small diameter artery, this intimal thickening can severely reduce the artery lumen and limit the blood flow. These plaques commonly rupture further occluding the vessel lumen. The intimal surface is also roughened, predisposing to the aggregation of platelets and fibrin to form a ***thrombus*** which may increase the size of the plaque and further compromise the vessel lumen.

A further consequence of severe atheroma in elastic arteries is that the muscle cells in the tunica media are replaced by non-contractile and non-elastic collagen, leading to a weakness in the artery wall, which may bulge and rupture (***aneurysm***).

A adventitia **At** arteriole **BM** basement membrane **C** capillaries **E** endothelial cells **EEL** external elastic lamina **F** elastic fibre **I** tunica intima **IEL** internal elastic lamina **M** tunica media **Ma** metarteriole **S** arteriovenous shunt **SM** smooth muscle cell **V** venule

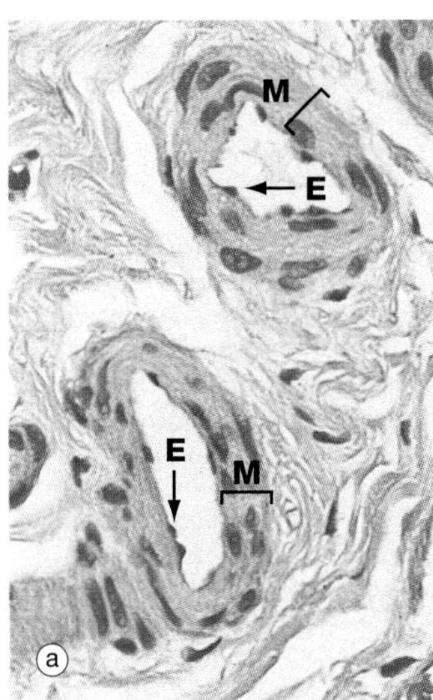

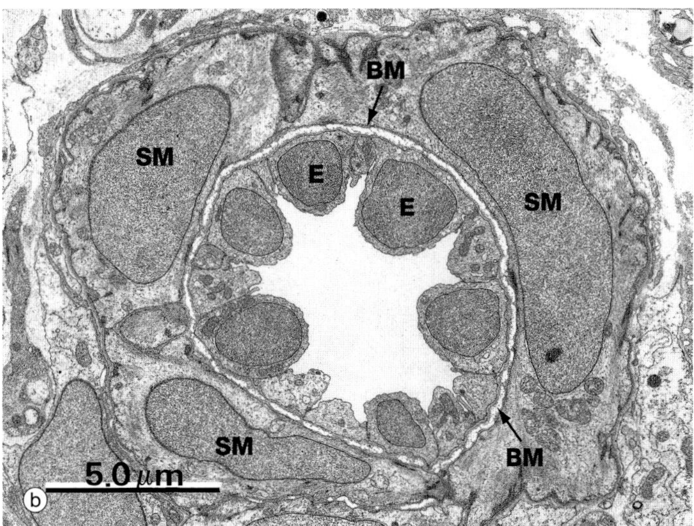

Fig. 8.12 Arterioles
(a) Large arteriole H & E ×100 (b) small arteriole EM ×5250

Small muscular arteries give way to large arterioles, which eventually become small arterioles. These transitions are gradual, with no sharp demarcations, and involve loss of the internal elastic lamina, and progressive reduction of the number of muscle layers in the media. Micrograph (a) shows two large arterioles with a thin intima lined by endothelial cells **E** and a tunica media **M** comprising only 2–3 layers of muscle. The adventitia is thin and merges imperceptibly with surrounding supporting collagenous fibrous tissue.

Micrograph (b) is an electron micrograph of a small arteriole, with a single layer of smooth muscle cells **SM** separated from endothelium **E** by basement membrane **BM**. The endothelium is prominent because the arteriole is constricted.

The microcirculation

The microcirculation is that part of the circulatory system concerned with the exchange of gases, fluids, nutrients and metabolic waste products. Exchange occurs mainly within the ***capillaries***, extremely thin-walled vessels forming an interconnected network. Blood flow within the capillary bed is controlled by the arterioles and muscular sphincters at the arteriolar-capillary junctions called ***precapillary sphincters***. The capillaries drain into a series of vessels of increasing diameter, namely ***postcapillary venules***, ***collecting venules*** and small ***muscular venules*** which make up the venous component of the microcirculation.

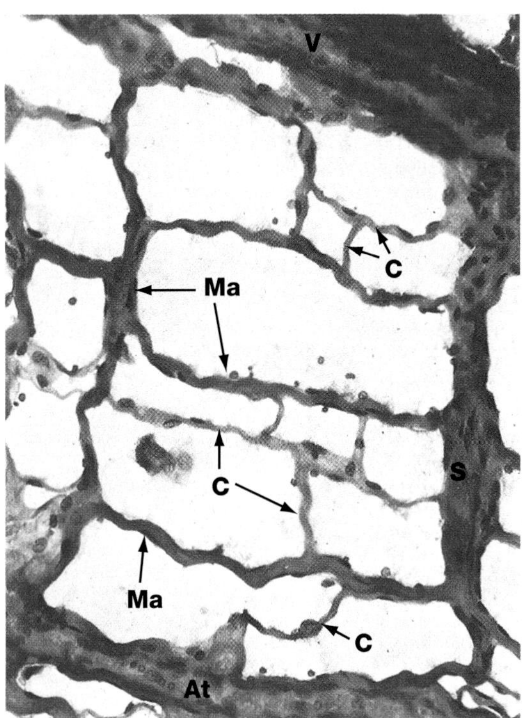

Fig. 8.13 The microcirculation – mesenteric spread
H & E ×120

This micrograph demonstrates an anastomosing network of capillaries between an arteriole **At** and a venule **V**. The capillary network comprises small diameter capillaries **C**, consisting of only a single layer of endothelial cells and basement membrane, and larger diameter capillaries known as ***metarterioles*** **Ma** characterised by a discontinuous outer layer of smooth muscle cells.

Note that small capillaries arise from both arterioles and metarterioles. At the origin of each capillary there is a sphincter mechanism, the precapillary sphincter, which is involved in regulation of capillary blood flow. Note also a direct wide-diameter communication between the arteriole and venule, an ***arteriovenous shunt*** **S**. Metarterioles also form direct communications between arterioles and venules. Contraction of the smooth muscle of the shunts and metarterioles directs blood through the network of small capillaries. Thus regulation of blood flow in the microcirculation is mediated by arterioles, metarterioles, precapillary sphincters and arteriovenous shunts. The smooth muscle activity of these vessels is modulated by the autonomic nervous system and circulating hormones, e.g. adrenal catecholamines.

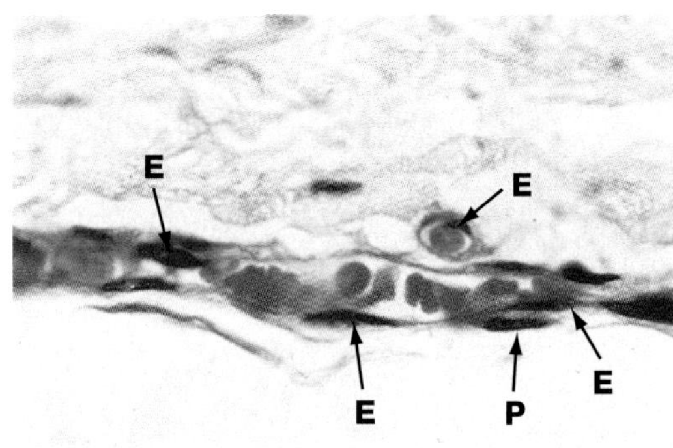

Fig. 8.14 Capillaries
H & E ×800

The vessels seen here in longitudinal section and transverse section illustrate the characteristic features of capillaries.

A single layer of flattened endothelial cells lines the capillary lumen. The thin layer of cytoplasm is difficult to resolve by light microscopy. The flattened endothelial cell nuclei **E** bulge into the capillary lumen; in longitudinal section the nuclei appear elongated whereas in transverse section they appear more rounded in shape. Muscular and adventitial layers are absent. Occasional flattened cells called ***pericytes*** **P** embrace the capillary endothelial cells and may have a contractile function. Note that the diameter of capillaries is similar to that of the red blood cells contained within them.

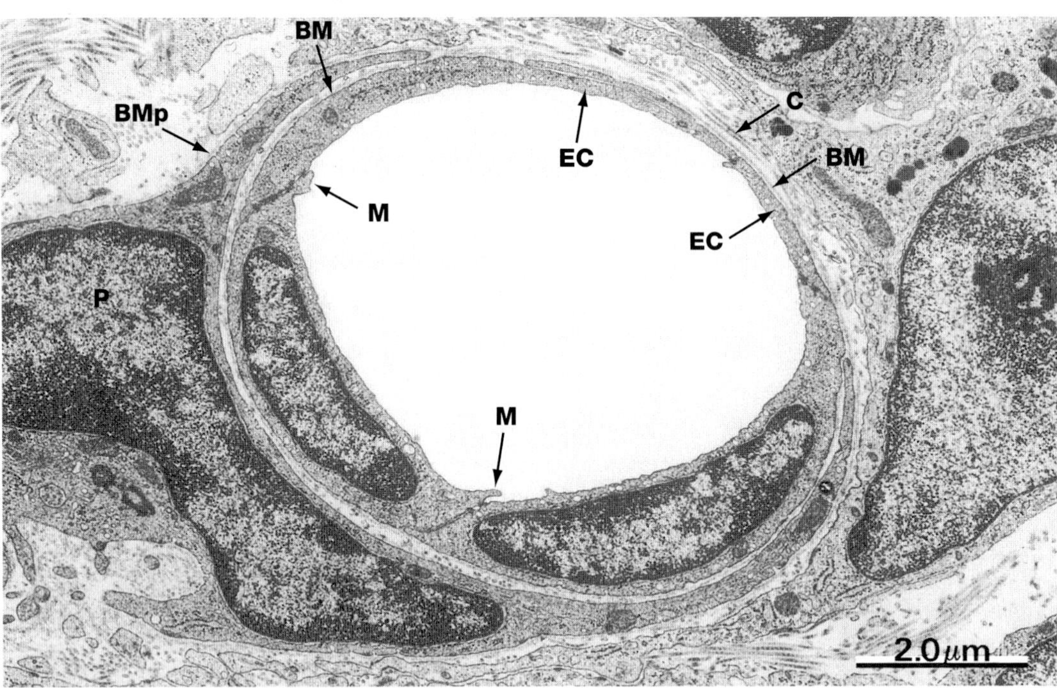

Fig. 8.15 Capillary: continuous endothelium type
EM ×12 000

This electron micrograph illustrates the ultrastructure of capillaries of the continuous endothelium type, the type found in most tissues.

Endothelial cells **E** are seen to encircle the capillary lumen, their plasma membranes approximating one another very closely and bound together by scattered tight junctions of the fascia occludens type (see Fig. 5.11). Small cytoplasmic flaps called ***marginal folds*** **M** extend across the intercellular junctions at the luminal surface. The capillary endothelium is supported by a thin basement membrane **BM** and adjacent collagen fibrils **C**. A pericyte **P** embraces the capillary. The pericyte is supported by its own basement membrane **BMp**.

Exchange between the lumen of the continuous-type capillary and the surrounding tissues is believed to occur in three ways. Passive diffusion through the endothelial cell cytoplasm mediates exchange of gases, ions and low molecular weight metabolites. Proteins and some lipids are transported by pinocytotic vesicles. White blood cells pass through the intercellular space between the endothelial cells in some way negotiating the endothelial intercellular junctions. Some researchers maintain that the intercellular spaces also permit molecular transport. In capillaries of the continuous endothelial type, the basement membrane is thought to present little barrier to exchange between capillaries and surrounding tissues.

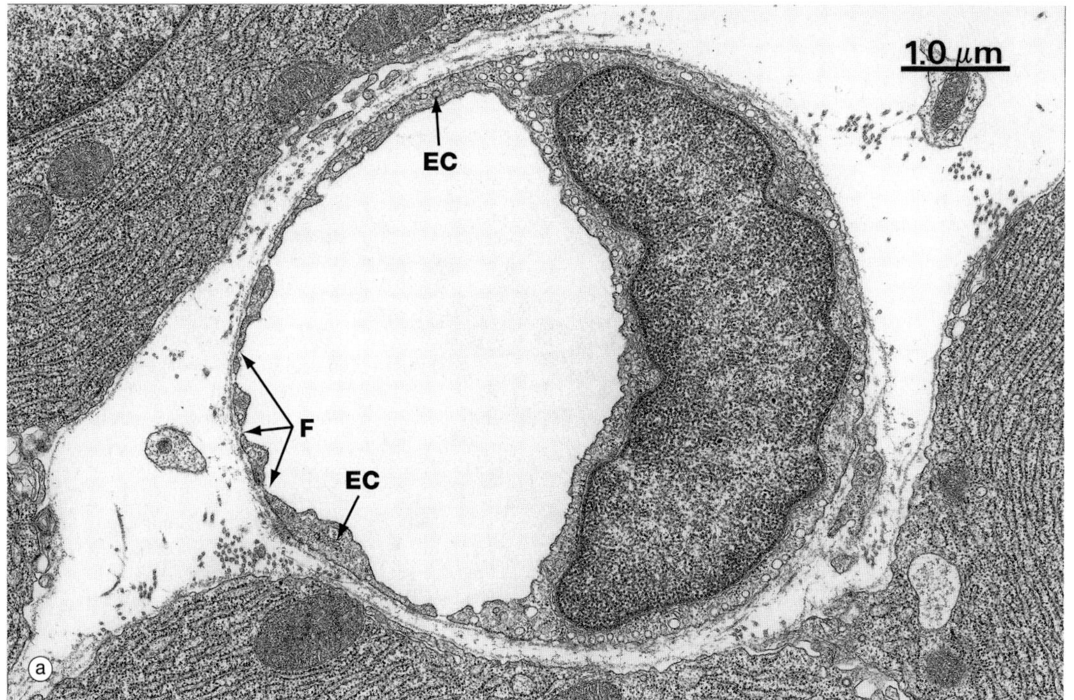

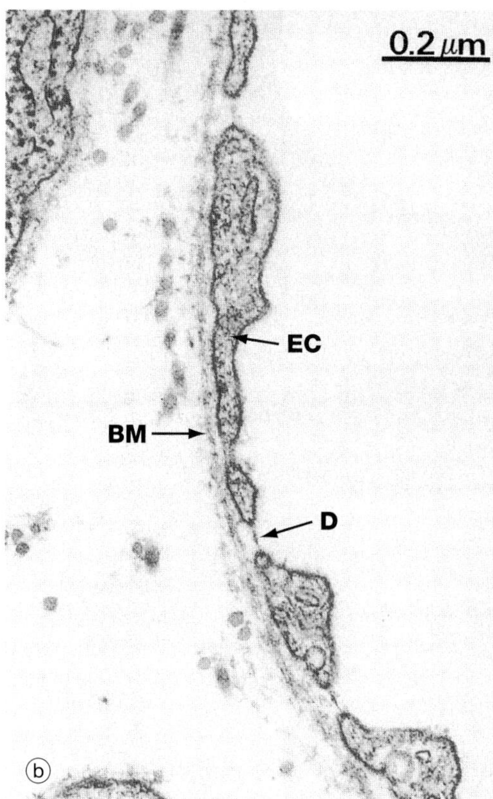

Fig. 8.16 Fenestrated capillary
(a) EM ×15 000 (b) EM ×60 000

Fenestrated capillaries are found in some tissues where there is extensive molecular exchange with the blood; such tissues include the small intestine, endocrine glands and the kidney.

At low magnification (a), fenestrations **F** appear as pores through attenuated areas of the endothelial cytoplasm **EC**; however, only a small proportion of these areas are fenestrated. At high magnification (b), the fenestrations appear to be traversed by a thin electron-dense line **D** which may constitute a diaphragm; the biochemical and functional nature of this is not understood. Fenestrated capillaries without a diaphragm are found in the glomerli of the kidney (see Fig. 16.15).

The permeability of fenestrated capillaries is much greater than that of continuous endothelium-type capillaries and molecular labelling techniques have demonstrated that fenestrations permit the rapid passage of macromolecules smaller than plasma proteins from the lumina of fenestrated capillaries into surrounding tissues.

Like continuous endothelium-type capillaries, all fenestrated capillaries are supported by a basement membrane **BM** which is continuous across the fenestrations. However, the endothelium of the sinusoids of the bone marrow, spleen and liver has large fenestrations without diaphragms and an underlying discontinuous basement membrane. Pericytes are rarely found in association with fenestrated capillaries.

BM basement membrane **BMp** pericyte basement membrane **C** collagen **D** diaphragm **E** endothelial cell nucleus **EC** endothelial cell cytoplasm **F** fenestrations **M** marginal fold **P** pericyte

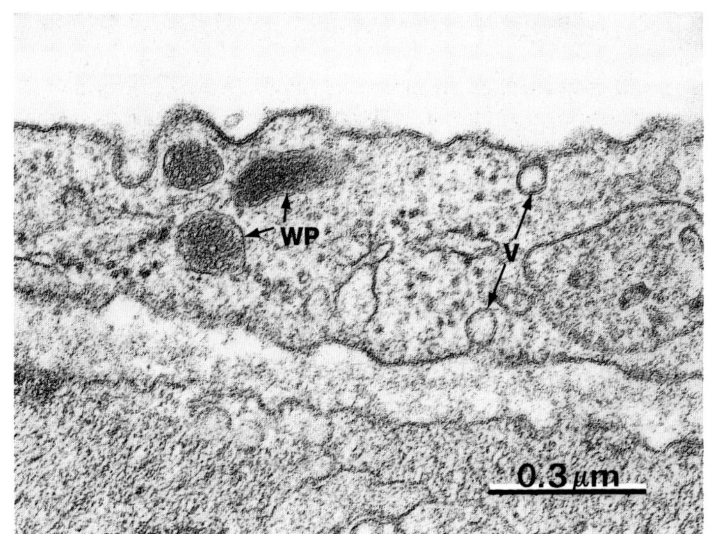

Fig. 8.17 Endothelial cell
EM ×68 000

Endothelial cells are flat polygonal cells connected to each other by junctional complexes. They have numerous ***pinocytotic vesicles*** **V** and specialised membrane-bound organelles called ***Weibel–Palade bodies*** **WP** which store Von Willebrand factor. Endothelial cells have many metabolic functions (see box), many concerned with the fine control of blood coagulation and thrombosis and with local control of blood vessel constriction/dilatation and vessel wall permeability. Endothelial cell damage may lead to pathological thrombosis or haemorrhage, or exudation of some components of blood into the extravascular tissues.

Summary of functions of endothelial cells

- Act as a permeability barrier.
- Synthesise collagen and proteoglycans for basement membrane maintenance.
- Synthesise and secrete molecules which promote protective thrombus formation, e.g. von Willebrand factor (Factor VIII).
- Synthesise and secrete molecules which minimise pathological thrombus formation, e.g. prostacyclin, thrombomodulin, nitrous oxide (which inhibits platelet adhesion and aggregation).
- Secrete vasoactive factors controlling blood flow, e.g. nitrous oxide, prostacyclin, vasoactive peptides such as endothelin.
- Produce molecules which mediate the acute inflammatory reaction, e.g. interleukins 1, 6 and 8, cell adhesion molecules.
- Produce some growth factors, e.g. fibroblast growth factor, platelet-derived growth factor, blood cell colony stimulating factor.

Fig. 8.18 Cell migration from the microcirculation
(a) EM ×6000 (b) H & E ×600

Fluids and cells pass from the circulation into the tissues in the microcirculation, mainly capillaries and postcapillary venules. Electron micrograph (a) shows a lymphocyte in the process of migration through the wall of a postcapillary venule (see Fig. 8.19). Its pseudopodium **Ps** has lifted the marginal fold **MF** at the contact point of two endothelial cells **E**. In contrast to capillaries, intercellular junctional complexes are relatively uncommon between endothelial cells in postcapillary venules, and this facilitates leucocyte emigration.

Micrograph (b) shows a markedly dilated postcapillary venule in an area of tissue damage. Neutrophils in the circulation have migrated to the periphery of the erythrocyte stream and have become attached to the endothelial cell surface ('***margination***') prior to emigration into the tissues.

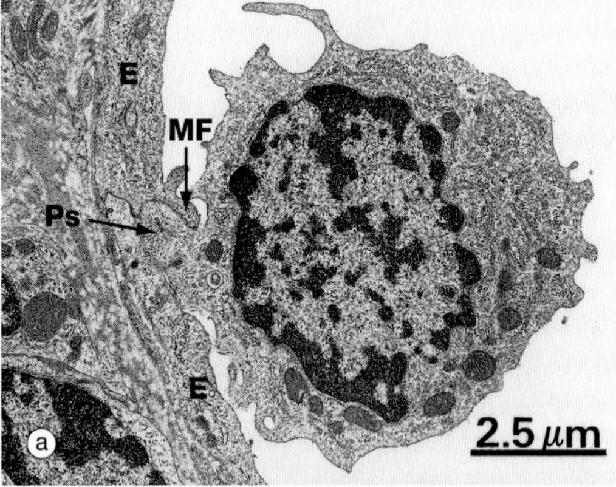

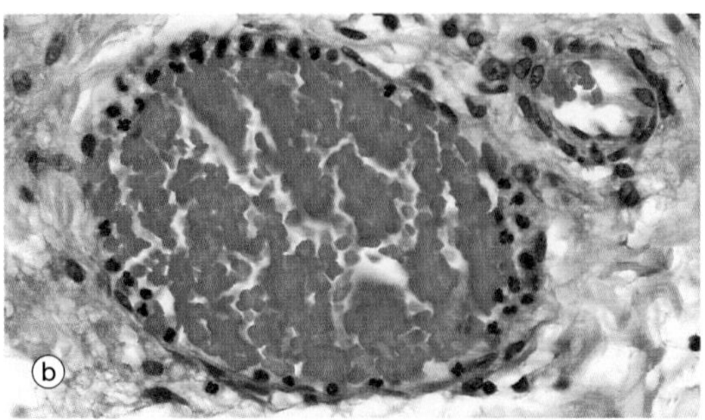

The venous system

The systemic venous system is a low-pressure component of the blood circulatory system responsible for carrying blood from the capillary networks to the right atrium of the heart. The force impelling the blood towards the heart, often against a gravity gradient, is a combination of contraction of the smooth muscle of the vein wall and external compression of veins by contraction of skeletal muscles, particularly in the lower limbs. Backflow of blood is prevented by valves, particularly in small and medium-sized veins, derived from the intima of the vessel. Valve failure in the veins of the legs is the basis for the development of varicose veins.

The structure of the venous system conforms to the general three-layered arrangement elsewhere in the circulatory system, but the elastic and muscular components are much less prominent features. A major part of the total blood volume is contained within the venous system. Variations in relative blood volume, due for example to dilation of capillary beds or haemorrhage, may be compensated by changes in the capacity of the venous system. These changes are mediated by smooth muscle in the tunica media which controls the luminal diameter of muscular venules and veins.

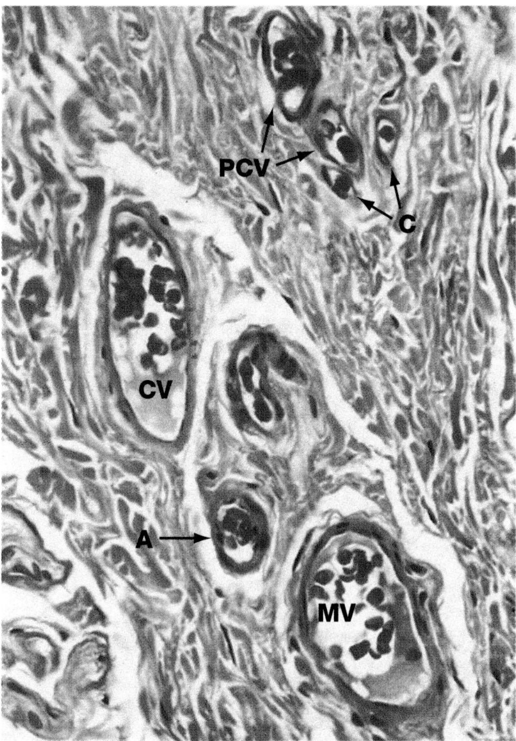

Fig. 8.19 Postcapillary, collecting and muscular venules
H & E ×480

The capillaries drain into a series of thin-walled vessels which form the first part of the venous system. ***Postcapillary venules*** **PCV** are the smallest of these vessels and are formed by the confluence of several capillaries **C**. Postcapillary venules have a similar structure to large capillaries with an endothelium and pericytes but no smooth muscle layer. Blood flow in postcapillary venules is sluggish and it appears that these vessels are the main site of migration of white cells into and out of the circulation. Postcapillary venules drain into ***collecting venules*** **CV** which are structurally similar but larger, with more surrounding pericytes. Collecting venules drain into vessels of increasing diameter which eventually acquire a wall of smooth muscle cells two or three layers thick; at this stage the vessels are called ***muscular venules*** **MV**. This micrograph also shows a small arteriole **A** with only a single layer of smooth muscle cells in the wall; its wall structure is similar to that of muscular venules, but the lumen is considerably smaller.

A arteriole **C** capillaries **CV** collecting venule **E** endothelial cell **MF** marginal fold
MV muscular venules **PCV** postcapillary venules **Ps** pseudopodium of lymphocyte
V pinocytotic vesicle **WP** Weibel–Palade body

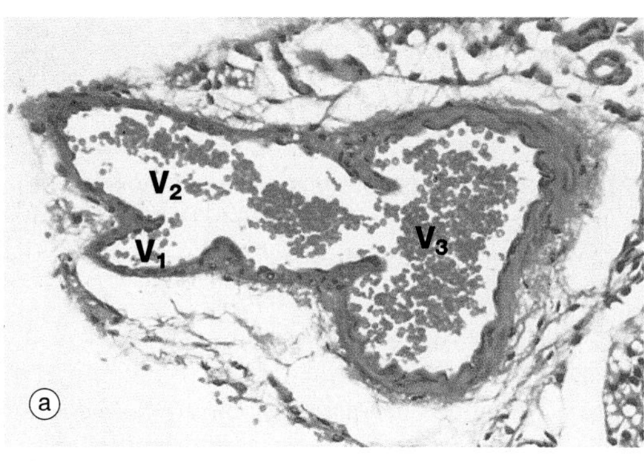

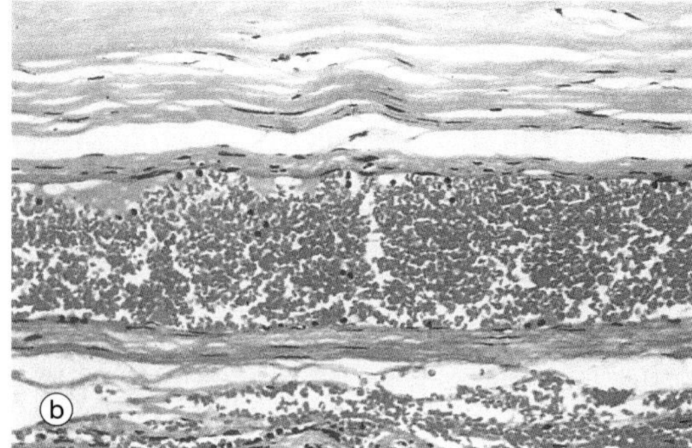

Fig. 8.20 Muscular venules and small veins
(a) H & E ×128 (b) H & E ×128

Micrograph (a) illustrates the confluence of a small muscular venule $\mathbf{V_1}$ with a larger muscular venule $\mathbf{V_2}$ which then joins a small vein $\mathbf{V_3}$ cut in transverse section. Note the valve at the junction of the large venule and vein. Muscular venules are characterised by a clearly defined intimal layer devoid of elastic fibres and a tunica media consisting of one or two layers of smooth muscle fibres. Veins are characterised by a thicker muscular wall and a poorly developed internal elastic lamina. Note that the tunica adventitia of these vessels is continuous with the surrounding collagenous supporting tissue.

Micrograph (b) shows a small vein cut in longitudinal section and fixed whilst still distended with blood. The wall of the vein consists of two to three layers of smooth muscle fibres. Note the wide diameter of the lumen relative to the thickness of the wall.

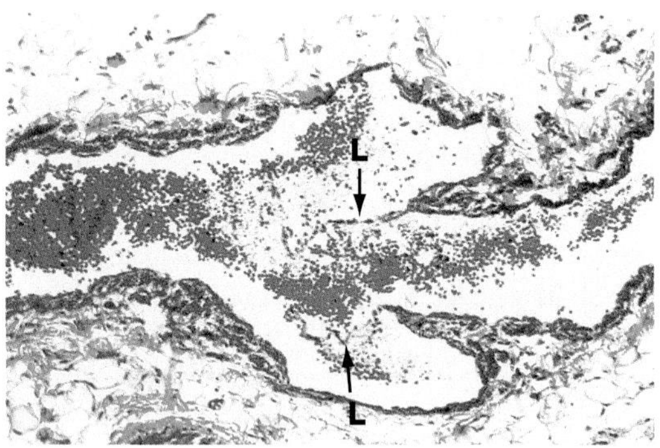

Fig. 8.21 Vein with valve
Masson's trichrome ×128

This micrograph demonstrates a valve in a small vein. The valve consists of delicate semilunar projections of the tunica intima of the vein wall; the projections are composed of fibroelastic tissue lined on both sides by endothelium. Each valve usually consists of two leaflets **L**, the free edges of which project in the direction of blood flow. Valves only occur in veins of more than 2 mm in diameter, particularly those draining the extremities.

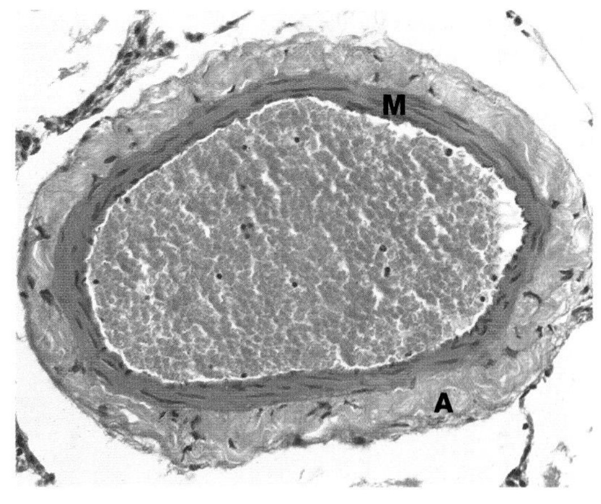

Fig. 8.22 Medium-sized vein
H & E ×180

This micrograph shows a medium-sized vein distended with red blood cells. The tunica intima consists of little more than the endothelial cell layer supported by a very narrow band of supporting intimal fibrous tissue. The tunica media **M** is thin compared with that of an equivalent sized artery (compare with Fig. 8.11a) and consists of only 2–4 layers of smooth muscle fibres arranged circumferentially. In veins, the tunica adventitia **A** is usually the thickest layer of the vessel wall, and is composed of collagenous fibrous tissue, the collagen fibres usually running predominantly in a longitudinal direction.

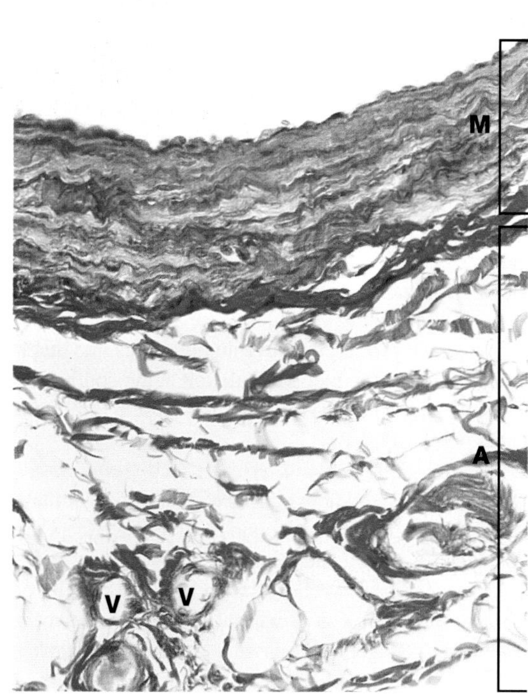

Fig. 8.23 Large muscular vein
Elastic van Gieson ×250

Large veins such as the femoral and renal veins again have a very narrow tunica intima, but the media **M** is more substantial, consisting of several layers of smooth muscle (stained yellow in this stain) separated by layers of collagenous connective tissue (red) and scanty elastic fibres (black).

The tunica adventitia **A** is broad and is composed of collagen (red) and contains numerous vasa vasorum **V**. Elastic fibres are particularly prominent at the junction between media and adventitia, but there are no distinct elastic laminae as there are in arteries.

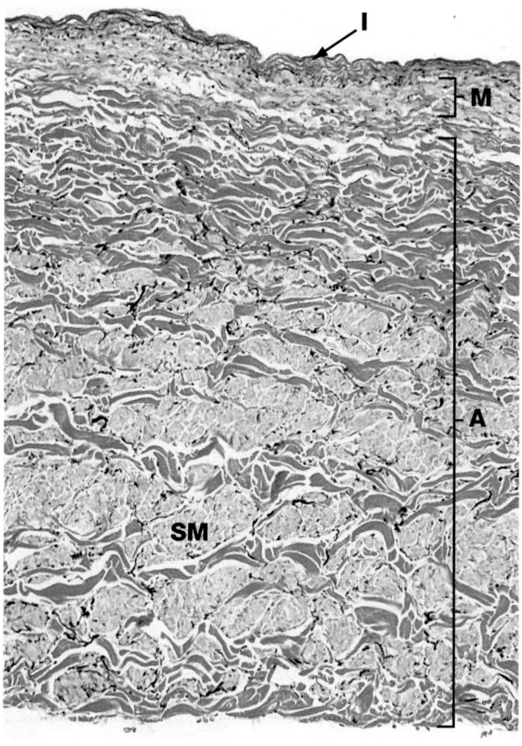

Fig. 8.24 Inferior vena cava
Elastic van Gieson ×100

The ***superior*** and ***inferior venae cavae*** are the largest veins in the body, and return deoxygenated blood from all areas of the body (except the lungs) to the right atrium of the heart. They have the thickest walls of all veins, comprising a distinct intima of fibroelastic tissue **I**, a narrow tunica media **M** composed of smooth muscle cells (predominantly circular), beneath which is a thick adventitia **A** composed of collagen (red) and numerous thick bundles of longitudinally arranged smooth muscle fibres (yellow) **SM**. There are elastic fibres (black) scattered throughout all layers of the vena caval wall, and in some areas there is a variable internal elastic lamina between intima and media.

A adventitia **I** tunica intima **L** valve leaflet **M** tunica media **SM** smooth muscle
V vasa vasorum $\mathbf{V_1}$ and $\mathbf{V_2}$ muscular venules $\mathbf{V_3}$ small vein

The lymph vascular system

The lymph vascular system drains excess fluid, the ***lymph***, from extracellular spaces and returns it to the blood vascular system. Lymph is formed in the following manner. At the arterial end of blood capillaries, the hydrostatic pressure of blood exceeds the colloidal osmotic pressure exerted by plasma proteins. Water and electrolytes therefore pass out of capillaries into the extracellular space; some plasma proteins also leak out through the endothelial wall. At the venous end of blood capillaries, the pressure relationships are reversed and fluid tends to be drawn back into the blood vascular system. In this way, about 2% of plasma passing through the capillary bed is exchanged with the extracellular tissue fluid. The rate of tissue fluid formation at the arterial end of capillaries generally exceeds the re-uptake of fluid at the venous end. The excess fluid, lymph, is drained by a system of lymph capillaries which converge to form progressively larger diameter lymphatic vessels.

As lymphatics get larger they acquire smooth muscle cells in their walls, and these contribute to the movement of lymph by pumping it onwards, the valves preventing back flow. Lymph eventually passes into much larger ducts (thoracic and right lymphatic ducts) which empty lymph into the blood circulation at the confluence of the internal jugular and subclavian veins of both sides. These large ducts have a substantial muscle layer with longitudinal and circular layers, but the layers are ill demarcated.

Along the course of the larger lymphatic vessels are aggregations of lymphoid tissues called ***lymph nodes*** where lymph is sampled for the presence of foreign material (antigen) and where activated cells of the immune system and antibodies join the general circulation (see Ch. 11). Lymphatic vessels are found in all tissues except the central nervous system, cartilage, bone, bone marrow, thymus, placenta, cornea and teeth.

Lymphatic capillaries differ from blood capillaries in several respects which reflect the greater permeability of lymphatic capillaries. In particular, the endothelial cell cytoplasm of lymphatics is extremely thin, the basement membrane is rudimentary or absent and there are no pericytes. Fine collagenous filaments known as ***anchoring filaments*** link the endothelium to the surrounding supporting tissue preventing collapse of the lymphatic lumen.

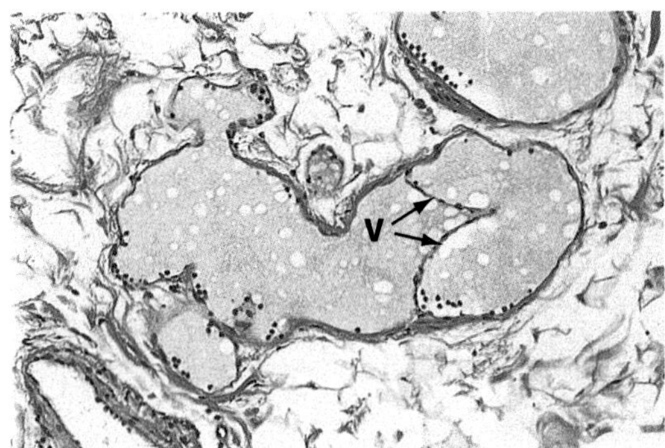

Fig. 8.25 Valve of a lymphatic vessel
H & E ×40

A characteristic feature of the lymphatic system is the numerous delicate valves in small and medium-sized vessels. The structure of these valves **V** is similar to that of valves in the venous system, but the supporting tissue core consists merely of reticulin fibres and a little ground substance. Note the presence of lymphocytes at the periphery of the lumina.

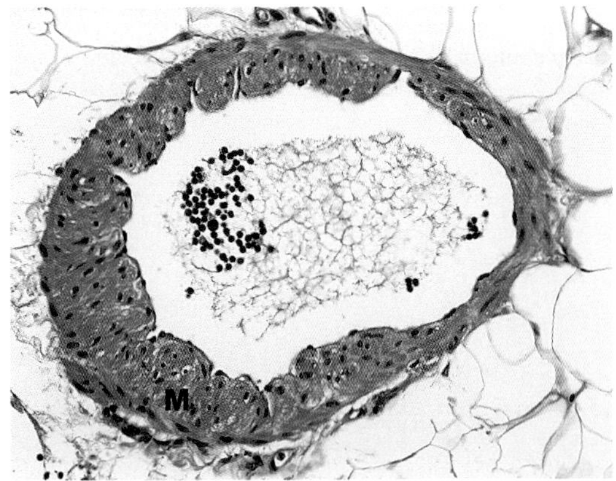

Fig. 8.26 Medium-sized lymphatic vessel
H & E ×40

Fig. 8.25 shows small lymphatic vessels containing a very small amount of smooth muscle in their walls. As lymphatics become larger, the muscle layer **M** becomes thicker and its contraction makes a greater contribution to the movement of lymph along the vessel, with backflow prevented by valves. The muscle layers are most prominent in the largest lymphatic vessels which empty into the venous system (the ***thoracic duct*** and ***right lymphatic duct***).

M smooth muscle layer **V** lymphatic valve

9. *Skin*

Introduction

The skin is the largest organ in the body, both in weight and surface area, and shows marked variation in structure at different sites in the body surface. Some regional variations are illustrated at the end of the chapter, but others will emerge during the description of the normal histology. The skin varies greatly in thickness; the thickest skin is on the upper back (approximately 5 mm) whilst the thinnest is the delicate skin on the upper and lower eyelids (less than 1 mm).

Skin has the following functions:

- **Protection.** The skin provides protection against a wide variety of external damaging stimuli, including ultraviolet light, chemical, thermal and mechanical insults. The most frequent mechanical insult is the frictional/shearing forces normally experienced by the soles and ventral aspect of the toes in walking, and to a lesser extent the palms and ventral aspects of the fingers during use of the hands. In these areas, skin structure is modified to resist these potentially damaging shearing forces (see Fig. 9.17). The skin also provides a barrier against excessive wetting, and also against bacterial and fungal invasion. Bacteria and fungi live on the skin surface, but cannot penetrate into underlying tissues unless the skin is breached.
- **Sensation.** The skin is the largest sensory organ in the body, and contains a range of different receptors for touch, pressure, pain and temperature (see Ch. 7). As a regional variation in structure, sensory receptors are most numerous in skin which has most physical contact with solid objects in the environment, again the soles and palms, and the ventral surfaces of fingers and toes (see Fig. 7.31).
- **Thermoregulation.** In most mammals the skin has an important role in heat conservation through the thick pelt of hairs on the surface. In man, body hair is scanty and this heat conservation property is minimal, although subcutaneous adipose tissue offers some insulation against heat loss. If there is a requirement for heat to be lost, this is achieved by increasing the blood flow through the rich vascular network in the skin, and by the secretion of sweat, a watery secretion of the eccrine glands (see p. 179), onto the skin surface, and subsequent evaporation producing a cooling effect.
- **Metabolic functions.** The most important metabolic function of the skin is the synthesis of vitamin D3 (cholecalciferol) by the action of ultraviolet light on the precursor, 7-dehydrocholesterol. Cholecalciferol is further processed in the liver and kidney to produce the active agent 1,25-dihydroxycholecalciferol which is important in calcium metabolism and bone formation. The adipose tissue in the subcutis is a major store of energy in the form of triglycerides.
- **Sexual attractant.** This greatly underestimated function has spawned an enormous industry in products claiming to improve the texture and appearance of skin, hair and nails, and other products which hide or minimise defects.

Skin structure

The skin has three main layers:

- **Epidermis** – a self-regenerating stratified squamous epithelium which produces a surface layer of the protein, ***keratin***, which is the component of skin in direct contact with external environment.
- **Dermis** – a layer of fibrocollagenous and elastic tissue which contains blood vessels, nerves and sensory receptors.
- **Subcutis or hypodermis** – the deepest layer of skin which is mainly adipose tissue, but also contains the larger vessels which supply and drain the dermal blood vasculature.

In addition there are the ***skin appendages***, specialised structures such as hair follicles, sweat glands and sebaceous glands which arise as downgrowths into the dermis from the epidermis during embryological development. These skin appendages mainly occupy the dermis and, occasionally, the upper subcutis.

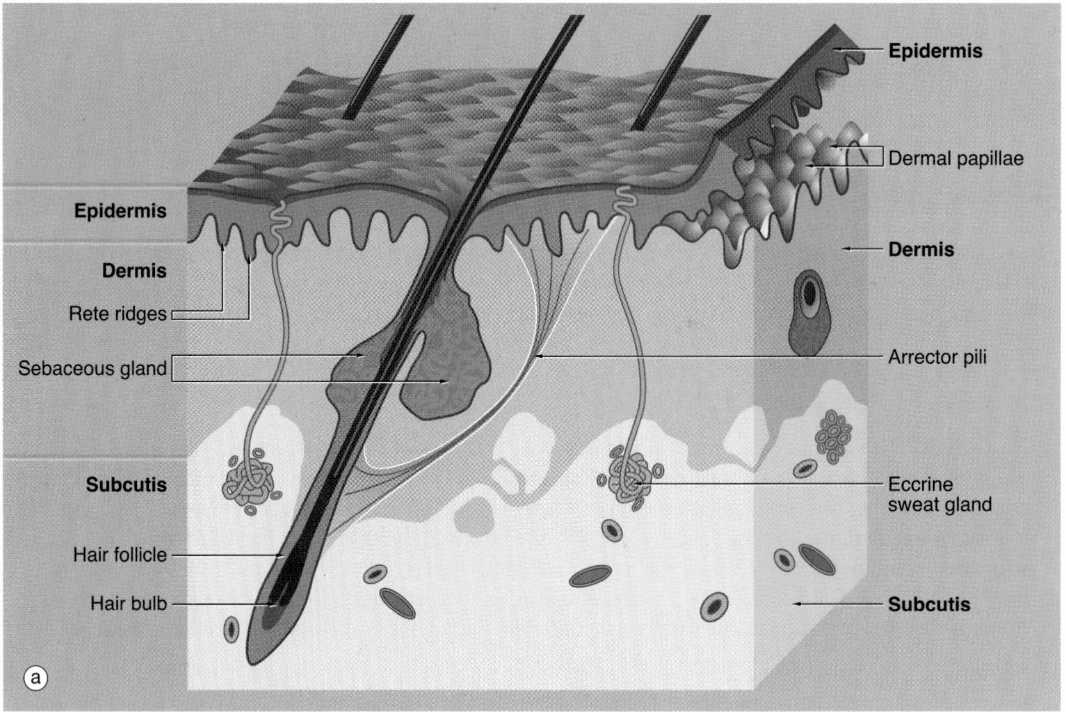

Fig. 9.1 Skin architecture
(a) Diagram (b) H & E ×15

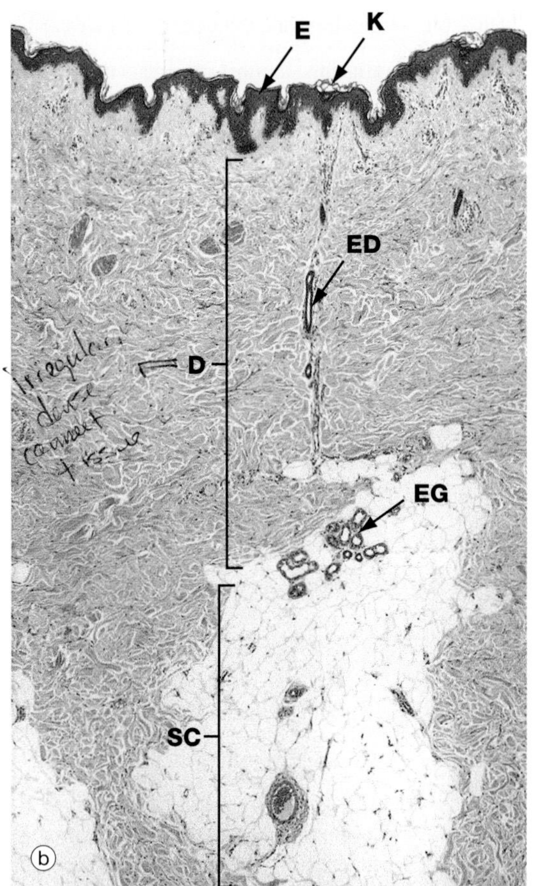

These two illustrations show the basic structure of the skin, with the three component layers, ***epidermis***, ***dermis*** and ***subcutis***.

The surface layer in contact with the exterior is the epidermis **E**, a highly specialised self-regenerating stratified squamous epithelium which produces a protein ***keratin*** **K** that is tough and protective and is also partially water-resistant. The epidermis also contains non-epithelial cells which protect against sunlight (***melanocytes***), recognise external antigens (***Langerhans cells***), and provide touch receptors (***Merkel cells***). The epidermis is tightly bound to the underlying layer (dermis) by a specialised basement membrane, and additional resistance to frictional shearing force is provided by a series of epidermal downgrowths (***rete ridges***) which penetrate the upper dermis to provide stronger tethering. These are most developed where exposure to shearing forces is almost constant e.g. sole, palm.

The dermis **D** is a tough layer of horizontally arranged collagen and elastic fibres, with fibroblasts; the dermis adjacent to the epidermis is less dense and contains numerous small blood vessels and in some areas, sensory nerve endings and sense organs.

The third layer is the subcutis **SC**, a layer of adipose tissue often compartmentalised by downwards extensions of dermal collagen. The subcutis acts as a shock absorber and thermal insulator, as well as holding fat stores.

The dermis and subcutis contain an assortment of skin appendages, i.e. hair follicles, sebaceous glands, eccrine glands **EG** and ducts **ED** and, in some areas, apocrine glands.

Fig. 9.2 Epidermis
(a) Masson's trichrome ×600 (b) H & E ×1000
(c) Epoxy resin section toluidine blue ×1200

Micrograph (a) shows the cells of the full-thickness of the epidermis from a friction-prone area with marked keratin production, (b) shows the regimented cells of the basal layer (stratum basale), and (c) shows the keratinocytes of the prickle cell layer (stratum spinosum).

The ***basal layer*** (***stratum basale***) **B** is the layer responsible, by repeated mitotic division, for the constant regeneration of the other layers of the epidermis. The cells are arranged as a regimented single layer of cuboidal or low columnar cells which connect to the cells of the prickle cell layer **S** above and the basement membrane between epidermis and dermis **D** below. The basal aspect of each basal cell is highly irregular and bound to the basement membrane by hemidesmosomes.

The ***prickle cell layer*** (***stratum spinosum***) **S** is composed of polyhedral keratinocytes with large pale staining nuclei and prominent nucleoli, an indicator of their active protein synthetic function. They are synthesising a fibrillar protein, the intermediate filament ***cytokeratin***, which accumulates in the cells in the form of aggregates called ***tonofibrils***. These bundles of tonofibrils converge into the numerous ***desmosomes*** that form the strong contacts between adjacent keratinocytes. There are very few tonofibrils in the basal cells, and the numbers increase in the keratinocytes as the granular layer **G** is approached.

The tonofibril-packed desmosomal bridges connecting keratinocytes can be easily seen in (c), explaining the name 'prickle cell layer.'

The cells of the ***granular layer*** (***stratum granulosum***) **G** begin to lose their polyhedral shape and become progressively more flattened nearer the surface. They contain dense basophilic and electron-dense granules called ***keratohyaline granules***. These are distinct from the cytokeratin tonofibrils and contain proteins rich in sulphur-containing amino acids such as cysteine and other proteins such as involucrin which interact with the cytokeratin tonofibrils. The combination of tonofibrils with keratohyaline produces ***keratin***. At the surface, the granular layer cells lose their nuclei and cytoplasm, leaving the masses of formed keratin which comprise the surface coating of the skin.

The ***keratin layer*** (***stratum corneum***) **C** is normally composed of flat flakes and sheets of keratin, coated with an anti-wetting agent synthesised by the cells of the granular layer. At the interface between the acellular keratin layer and underlying granular layer, some residue of cell structure may remain, particularly desmosomes.

In micrograph (a) the epidermis is thick, with prominent prickle cell **S** and granular cell **G** layers and abundant thick surface keratin **C**, all indications that the skin was taken from an area regularly exposed to friction e.g. sole.

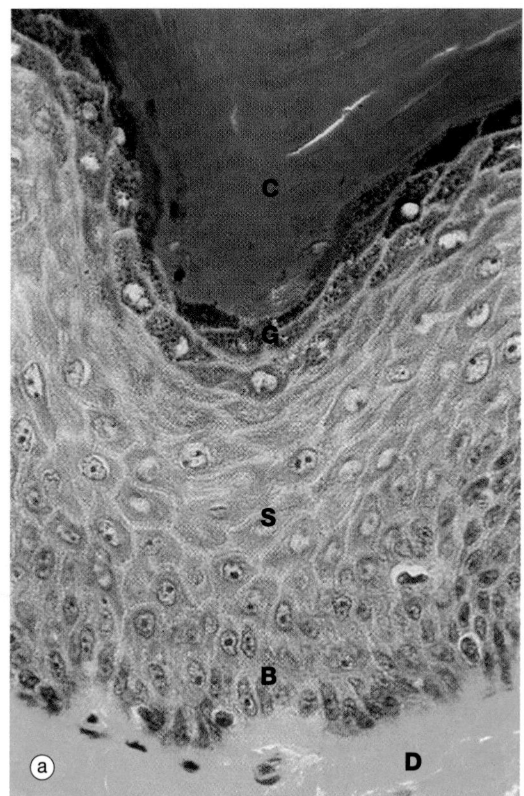

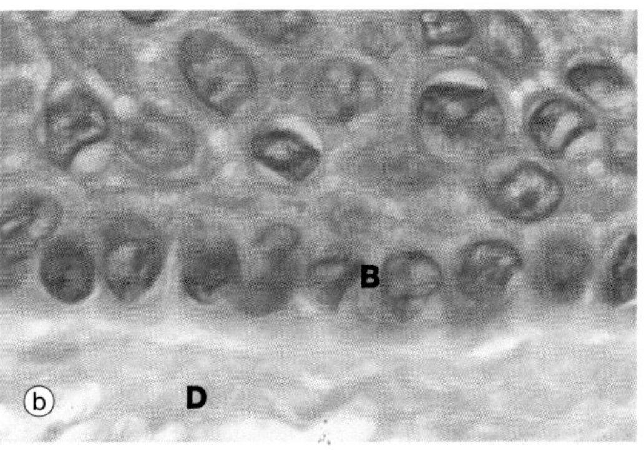

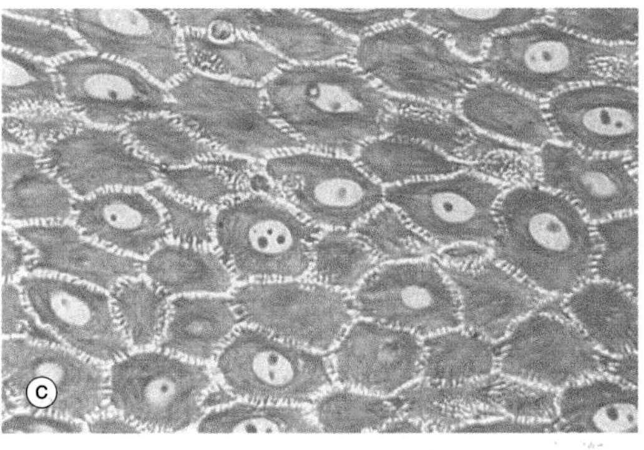

B basal layer (stratum basale) **C** keratin layer (stratum corneum) **D** dermis **E** epidermis **ED** eccrine duct **EG** eccrine gland **G** granular layer (stratum granulosum) **K** keratin **S** prickle cell layer (stratum spinosum) **SC** subcutis

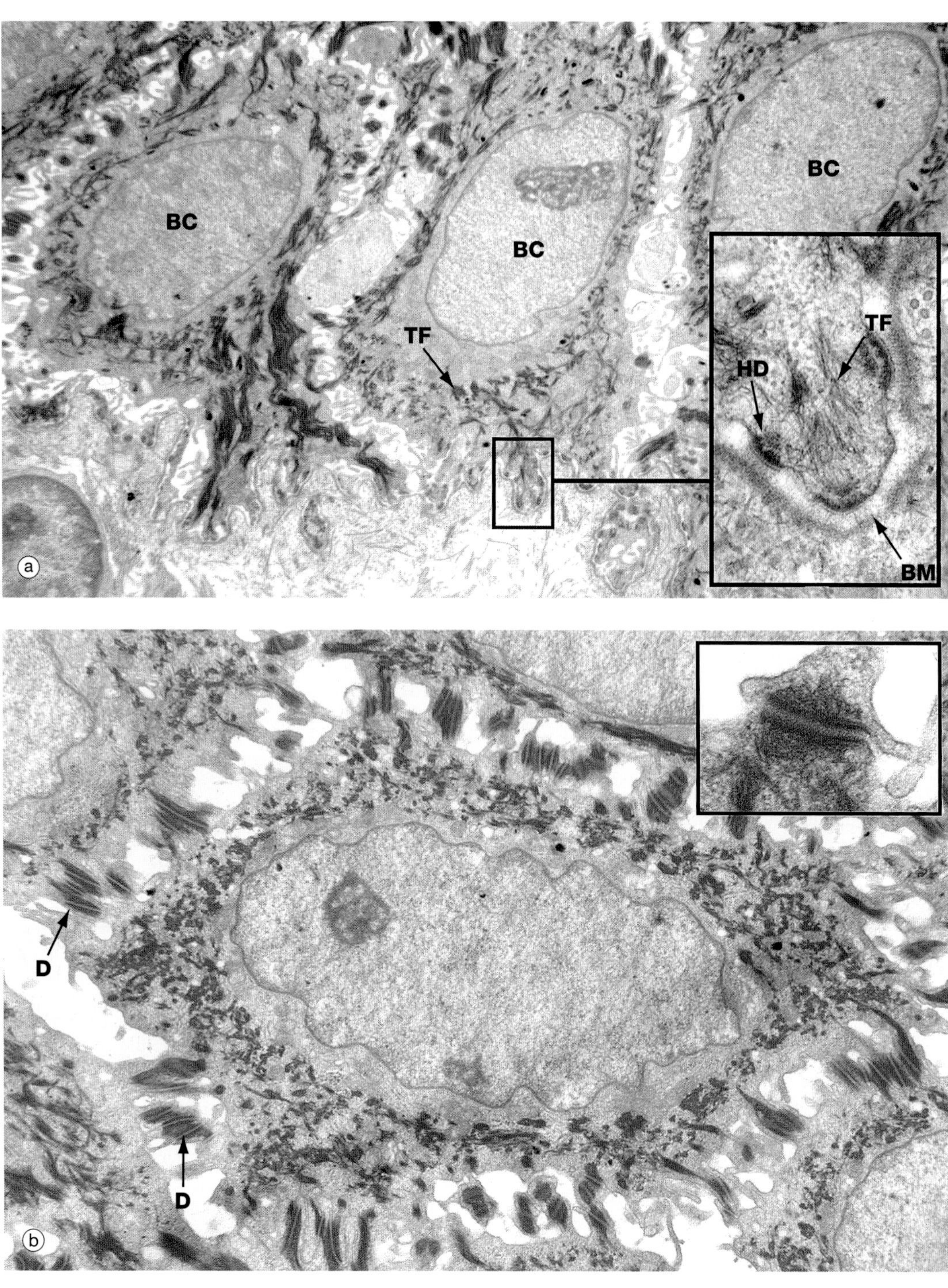

BC basal cell **BM** basement membrane **D** desmosome **HD** hemidesmosome
K keratohyaline granules **N** nucleus **TF** tonofibrils

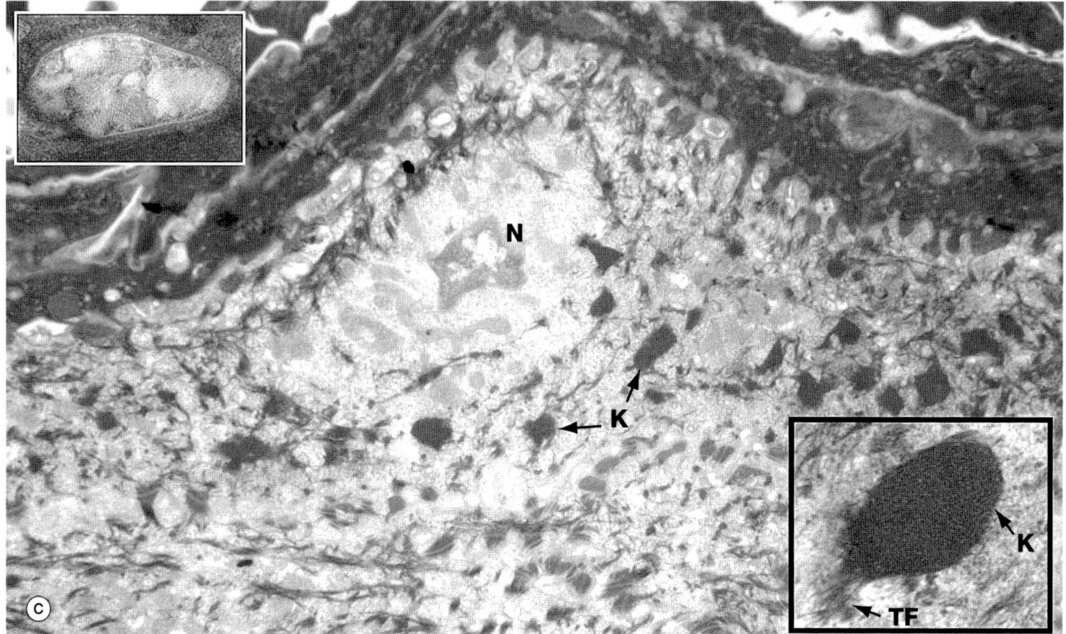

Fig. 9.3 Keratinocytes – ultrastructure *(illustrations (a) and (b) opposite)*
(a) basal keratinocytes EM ×10 000, inset ×30 000 (b) keratinocytes from prickle cell layer EM ×15 000, inset ×40 000 (c) Keratinocyte from granular layer EM ×12 000 insets ×50 000

Micrograph (a) shows a row of three basal cells **BC** sitting on the epidermal basement membrane which can only just be discerned as a highly convoluted line in the low magnification main picture. The basal cells (of which the central cell is the most typical example) are low columnar with prominent nuclei and nucleoli, and a perinuclear zone containing ribosomes and mitochondria; tonofibrils **TF** are present towards the periphery of the cell. The inset shows the linkage of the basal surface of the cell to the basement membrane **BM** by hemidesmosomes **HD** into which scanty tonofibrils **TF** are inserted. Basal cells link to each other and to overlying keratinocytes of the prickle cell layer by desmosomes. The pale staining cytoplasmic processes in the spaces between basal cells are extensions of the cytoplasm of melanocytes (see Fig. 9.5).

Micrograph (b) shows a single keratinocyte from the prickle cell layer. It has abundant electron dense tonofibrils which extend into the many desmosomes **D** that link it firmly to adjacent keratinocytes. The inset shows a desmosome linking the cytoplasmic processes of two keratinocytes. Electron dense tonofibrils from each cell are attached to the desmosome.

Micrograph (c) shows a flattening keratinocyte in the granular layer immediately beneath the keratin layer. The cell is degenerate with only an ill-defined remnant of the nucleus **N**. The cytoplasm contains both linear cytokeratin tonofibrils and electron dense round or ovoid keratohyaline granules **K**, one of which is shown merging with tonofibrils **TF** at higher magnification in the inset bottom right. Also present, but difficult to see in the low magnification main picture, are lamellated pale-staining ovoid bodies (about 500 nm long) called ***keratinosomes*** or ***Odland bodies***, one of which is shown at higher magnification in the inset top left. These contain a hydrophobic glycolipid which is released in the lower layers of keratin to coat and bind together the keratin flakes, rendering them relatively water repellent.

Psoriasis

The transition of keratinocytes from replicating basal cells, through the keratinocytes of the prickle cell layer, to the flattening and degenerating granular layer cells packed with tonofibrils and keratohyaline granules, can be regarded as a well-ordered maturation sequence culminating in the production of a tough water-resistant keratin layer on the surface of the skin. The normal transit time from basal cell to formed keratin is 50–60 days, but in one important disease this is significantly shortened to about 7 days. This disease is ***psoriasis***, a common skin condition of unknown cause but with an element of multifactorial inheritance. In psoriasis, the maturation process is so rushed that there is insufficient time for full development of tonofibrils and keratohyaline in the prickle cell layers, and a proper granular layer does not form. Instead of normal keratin there is a surface opaque white scale composed of a mixture of keratin and the nuclear and cytoplasmic debris of the keratinocytes (immature granular layer cells shed prematurely). The rapidly proliferating epidermis is thickened to produce raised red patches under the white scale.

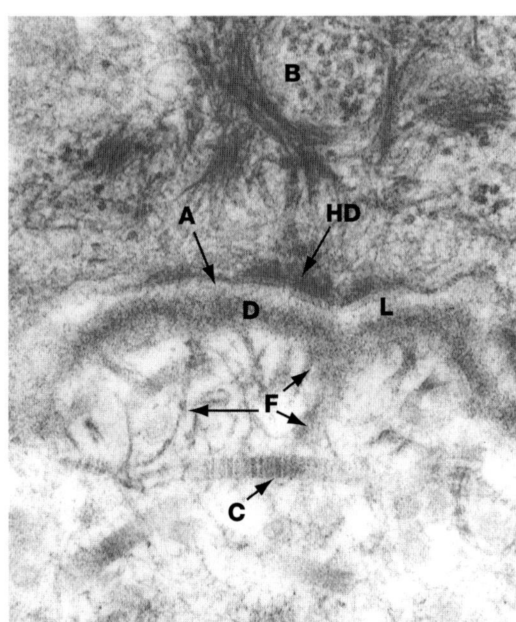

Fig. 9.4 Dermo-epidermal basement membrane
EM ×64 000

At the junction between the basal surface of basal keratinocytes and the underlying dermis is a basement membrane comprising a ***lamina lucida*** **L**, a ***lamina densa*** **D** and a ***fibro-reticular lamina***. The latter is ill-defined and contains anchoring fibrils **F** of mainly type VII collagen which connect the lamina densa to type IV collagen fibres **C** in the dermis, and finer ***fibrillin*** microfilaments which link to dermal elastic fibres. The basal cell **B** is tethered to the lamina densa by hemidesmosomes **HD** with fine anchoring protein filaments **A** which cross the lamina lucida.

Disorders of epidermal basement membrane

Any disease which damages the epidermal basement membrane can lead to separation of epidermis from dermis. For a while the space between is occupied by fluid, leading to blister formation. In two groups of disorders, the abnormality in the basement membrane is at molecular level.

In ***bullous pemphigoid*** and related disorders, the affected patient has an antibody which reacts against a specific antigen (BPAG) located in the hemidesmosomes and lamina lucida; an antigen-antibody reaction occurs triggering a sequence of changes damaging the basement membrane and leading to separation of the epidermis and blistering.

Epidermolysis bullosa has a number of forms, all leading to blistering; many are hereditary, and have different molecular/genetic abnormalities as their basis. In one form the anchoring fibrils are abnormal and deficient possibly due to mutations in the type VII collagen gene.

In another form, separation occurs within the cytoplasm near the basal surface of the basal cell and is thought to be due to a keratin gene mutation affecting connection of tonofibrils to hemidesmosomes.

Melanocytes

Melanocytes are the cells responsible for producing the pigment ***melanin*** which is responsible for skin coloration (and the colour of the hair – see Fig. 9.8d). The pigment exists in various forms from yellowish brown to black, and is thought to have a protective function against damage from excessive ultraviolet light. Melanin is synthesised from the amino acid tyrosine by the melanocyte within specific cytoplasmic organelles called ***melanosomes***, which are transferred to the keratinocytes through a complex network of melanocytes' cytoplasmic processes. These processes can frequently be seen in electron micrographs of the epidermis running in the narrow spaces between adjacent keratinocytes. The mechanism of transfer of melanosomes between melanocyte and keratinocyte is unknown. The melanosomes within the keratinocyte usually form a cap sitting over the nucleus, and probably deposit melanin when exposed to UV light.

Melanocytes are present as scattered cells in the basal layer and are more numerous in areas which are most exposed to light, for example they are more numerous on the face than on the buttocks. There is no great difference in numbers of melanocytes between white and dark-skinned races, but they are considerably more synthetically active in darker-skinned people. In pale-skinned people, the melanocytes can be stimulated into producing more melanin by gradually increasing exposure to UV light. This may produce a socially desirable suntan but constant forced stimulation of melanocytes has its drawbacks (see opposite).

A anchoring filaments **B** basal keratinocyte **BM** basement membrane **C** collagen fibres type IV **D** lamina densa **F** anchoring fibrils (type VII collagen) **HD** hemidesmosome **L** lamina lucida **M** melanocyte **P** premelanosomes and melanosomes

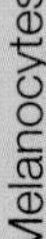

Fig. 9.5 Melanocytes
(a) H & E ×1000 (b) EM ×15 000 (c) EM ×300 000

Micrograph (a) shows normal epidermis with scattered melanocytes **M** in the basal layer. They are round cells with clear cytoplasm.

The low power electron micrograph (b) shows a pale staining melanocyte **M** between two tonofibril-containing basal keratinocytes **B**; all are sitting on an indistinct basement membrane **BM**. The cytoplasm of the melanocyte has no tonofibrils but contains scanty tiny round or oval dark-staining bodies **P**. These are the premelanosomes and melanosomes responsible for the synthesis of melanin. Tyrosine is converted into dihydroxyphenylalanine (DOPA) and then polymerised into melanin, which later links to protein to form melanoprotein.

The high magnification electron micrograph (c) shows the ultrastructural features of a premelanosome. They are round or cylindrical electron-dense structures with distinct transverse striations and sometimes faint longitudinal striations. Sometimes an indistinct surrounding membrane can be seen.

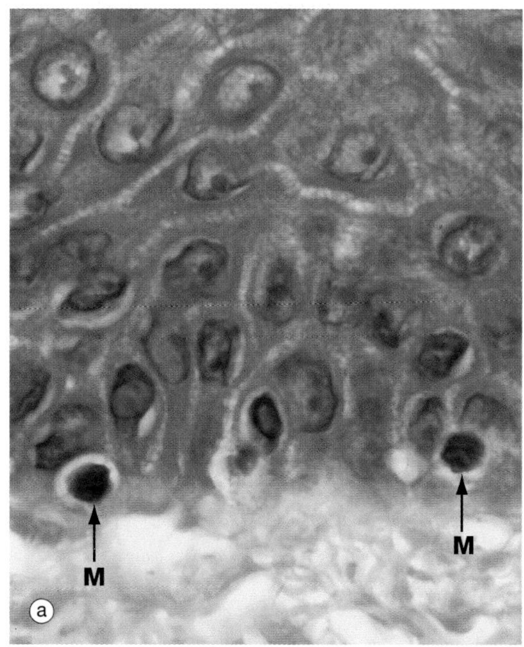

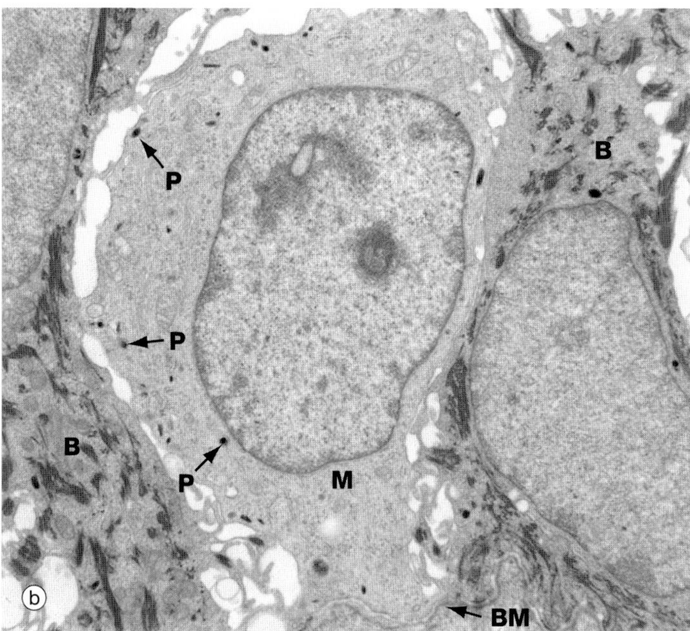

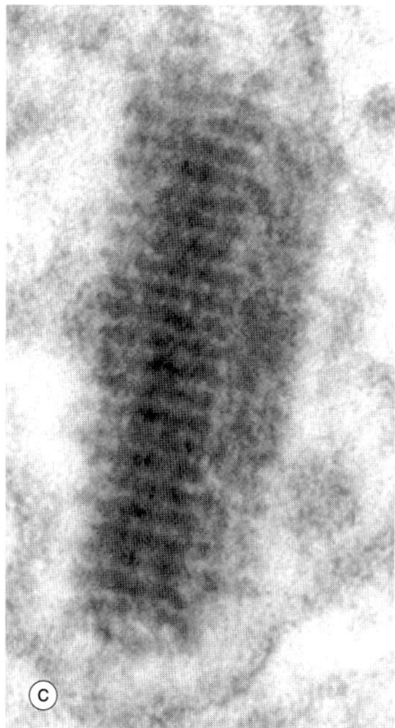

Disorders of melanocytes

Vitiligo is a common disease in which symmetrical areas of depigmentation of the skin occur, often on the hands, fingers and face. The disease destroys all the melanocytes in the affected skin and the skin becomes glaringly white; the keratinocytes are not affected. Vitiligo is due to an autoimmune destruction of melanocytes, and is associated with other autoimmune diseases.

'***Moles***' or ***naevi*** are benign accumulations of melanocytes in the dermis (***intradermal naevus***), epidermis (***junctional naevus***) or both (***compound naevus***). ***Malignant melanoma*** is a dangerous malignant tumour of melanocytes, particularly affecting pale-skinned people who are exposed to excessive UV light.

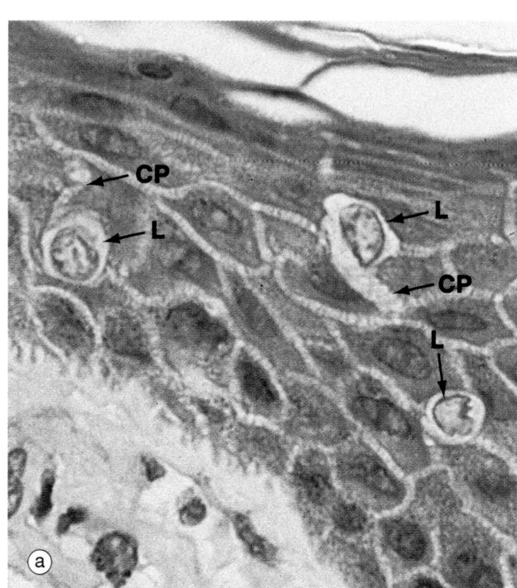

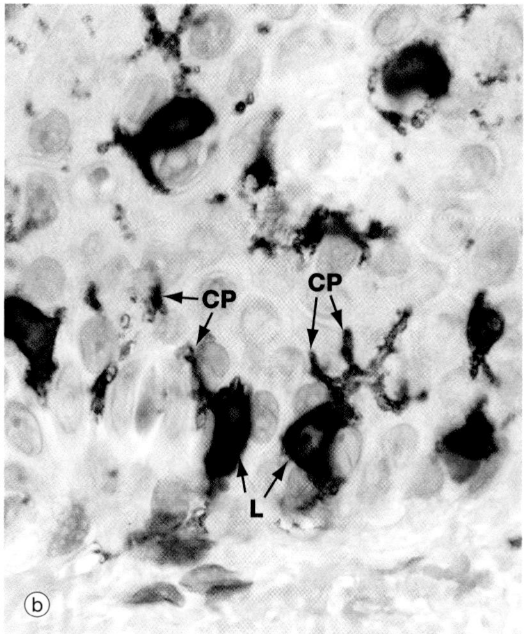

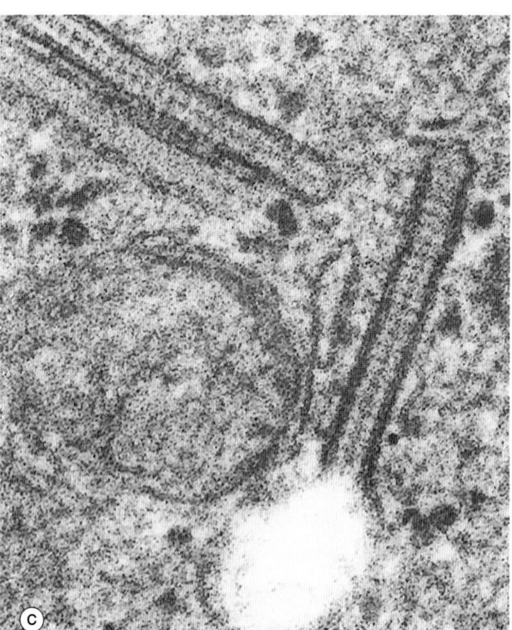

Fig. 9.6 Langerhans cells
(a) H & E ×700 (b) Immunocytochemistry CD1a ×700
(c) Birbeck granule EM ×100 000

Langerhans cells are intraepidermal antigen-recognition and processing cells, and are present in all layers of the epidermis but are most easily recognised in the prickle cell layer. They are also present in the upper dermis, particularly around small blood vessels. Micrograph (a) shows pale-staining Langerhans cells **L** in the epidermis; they have irregularly lobulated nuclei and almost clear cytoplasm. Cytoplasmic processes **CP** extend from the cell and insinuate between keratinocytes of all layers. The extensive network of cytoplasmic processes is highlighted in the immunocytochemical preparation shown in (b). Electron micrograph (c) shows the typical cytoplasmic organelle of Langerhans cells, the ***Birbeck granule***, a rod-like structure with regular cross-striations, one end of which frequently distends in a vesicle so that they resemble a tennis racket. Their function is not known.

Langerhans cells and skin disease

Langerhans cells are the skin's antigen-recognition and processing cells, and express a large number of lymphocyte and macrophage surface markers (see Ch. 11). They constantly monitor the environment on the epidermal surface and in spaces between epidermal cells with their dendritic cytoplasmic processes, and are potent stimulators of cell-mediated immunological responses in the skin. They are therefore active and present in increased numbers in epidermis and upper dermis in many inflammatory skin diseases, particularly ***contact allergic dermatitis***. Langerhans cells also play an important role in the rejection mechanisms in skin allografts, and it has been suggested that their activity may have a protective effect against the development of epidermal tumours. Some chemical carcinogens, immunosuppressive agents and excessive ultraviolet light have all been shown to reduce the number and effectiveness of Langerhans cells, and these are all factors which predispose to the development of epidermal tumours.

CP cytoplasmic processes **L** Langerhans cells **M** Merkel cells **N** nerve twig

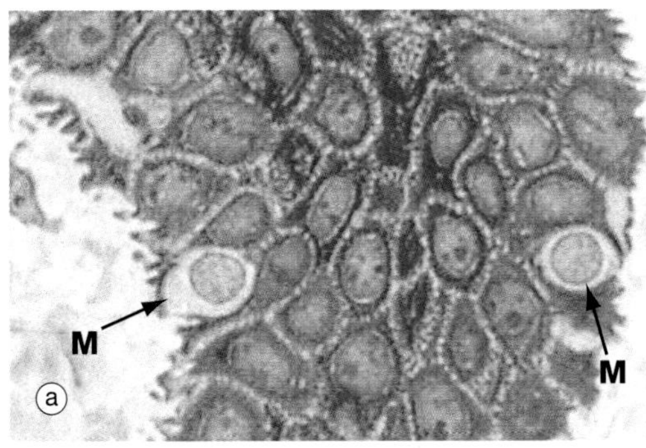

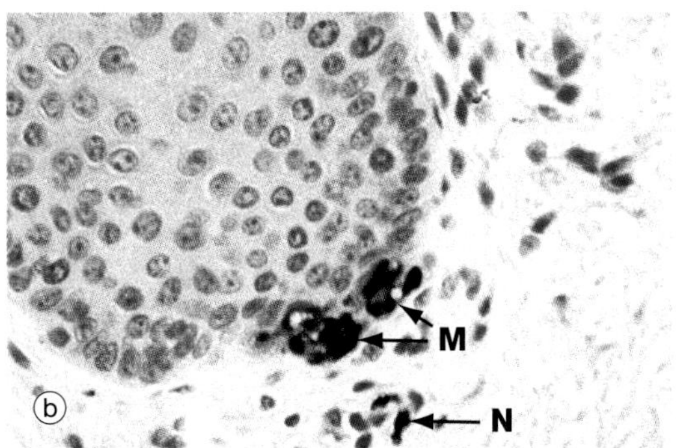

Fig. 9.7 Merkel cell
(a) Epoxy resin thin section – toluidine blue ×1000 (b) Immunocytochemistry ×700

Merkel cells are intra-epidermal touch receptors and contain neuroendocrine-type membrane-bound vesicles (dense core granules) in their cytoplasm, particularly near their base where they make synaptic junctions with myelinated sensory nerve twigs in the upper dermis. They are very scanty in adult skin and are difficult to find.

Micrograph (a) shows two Merkel cells **M** in the basal layer of epidermis in a thin epoxy resin section. They are rounded cells with pale-staining cytoplasm and round pale-staining nuclei. The immunocytochemical preparation shown in (b) illustrates two Merkel cells **M** and a tiny dermal nerve twig **N** related to one of them.

Epidermal skin appendages

Skin appendages first develop in the second trimester of intrauterine development as simple downgrowths of the surface epithelium (epidermis) into the developing subepithelial layers of mesoderm which will eventually become dermis and subcutis. The skin appendages include:

- **Hair follicles** which produce long thin cylindrical structures (hair shafts) composed largely of keratin arranged in an organised manner. In normal coarse hair, each hair shaft is composed of a central ***medulla*** surrounded by a ***cortex***, with a surface ***cuticle*** composed of a single layer of flattened scales. In the animal kingdom the function of hair is thermoregulation (particularly heat conservation) and display; only the latter function can be ascribed to hair in humans. The structure of the hair follicle is complex (Fig. 9.8), and hair growth is cyclical, with three phases – a phase of active growth (***anagen***), a phase of involution (***catagen***) and a resting phase (***telogen***). In the scalp, most hairs are in the anagen phase with their bases located in subcutis; telogen hairs have their bases in mid-dermis.
- **Sebaceous glands** occur in two forms. The majority are associated with hair follicles, and develop as lateral protrusions from the hair follicle at about the junction between its upper third and lower two thirds. Sebaceous glands secrete a mixture of lipids called ***sebum***, which may provide some waterproofing of the skin surface and hair shafts; the sebum is secreted into the hair follicle (see Fig. 9.9c). At some sites in the skin (areolae and nipples, labia minora of vulva, eyelids) and in the buccal and labial mucosa, the sebaceous glands are independent of hair follicles and open directly onto the skin or mucosal surface.
- **Eccrine sweat glands** are widespread throughout the skin. They are located around the junction between dermis and subcutis and synthesise a thin watery liquid (sweat) which is passed along eccrine ducts and deposited onto the skin surface. Evaporation of this sweat reduces body temperature.
- **Apocrine glands** are confined to a few localised areas, mainly in the axillary and groin regions. Like eccrine sweat glands, the secretory component is located in lower reticular dermis or subcutis, and a duct system carries the secretion to be discharged into the upper part of the hair follicle above the sebaceous duct. Apocrine gland secretions in humans have no definite function, but in animals they are responsible for scent production, used in territory marking and as a sexual attractant.

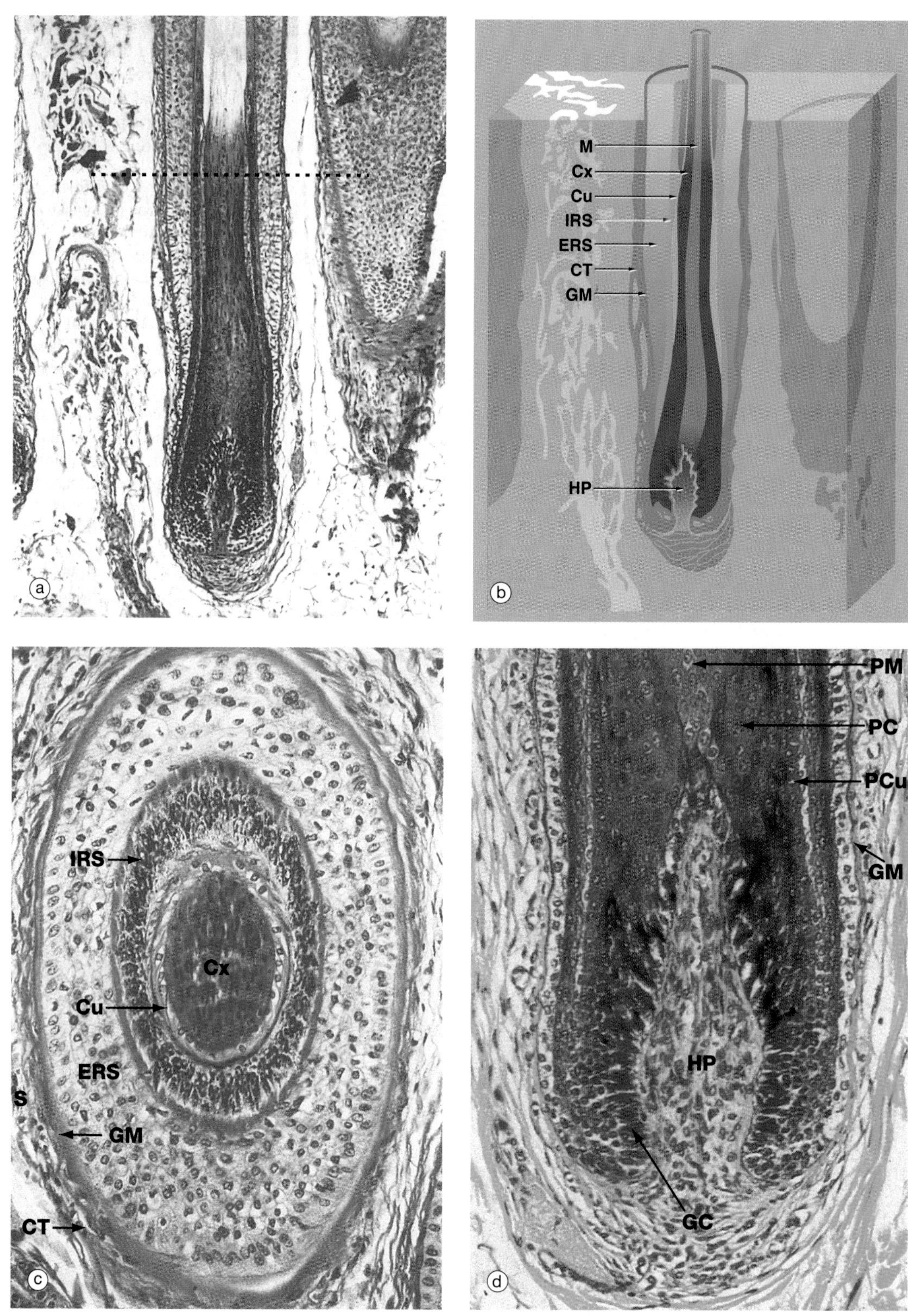

CT connective tissue sheath **Cu** cuticle **Cx** cortex **ERS** external root sheath
GC germinative cells **GM** glassy membrane **HP** hair papilla **IRS** internal root sheath **M** medulla
PC precortical cells **PCu** precuticular cells **PM** premedullary cells

Fig. 9.8 Hair follicle *(illustrations opposite)*
(a) H & E ×120 (b) Explanatory diagram for (a) (c) Transverse section of follicle H & E ×300 (d) Hair bulb Masson's trichrome ×198

The hair follicle is a tubular structure consisting of five concentric layers of epithelial cells. At the base, there is a bulbous expansion, the ***hair bulb***, enclosing the ***hair papilla* HP**. As they are pushed towards the skin surface from the hair bulb, the inner three epithelial layers undergo keratinisation to form the hair shaft whilst the outer two layers form an epithelial sheath. At the hair bulb, all the layers merge to become indistinguishable from one another; the mass of cells destined to form the hair is known as the ***hair matrix***.

During active hair growth, the epithelial cells surrounding the dermal papilla proliferate to form the four inner layers of the follicle whilst the outermost layer merely represents a downward continuation of the stratum basale of the surface epithelium. The whole epithelial mass surrounding the dermal papilla constitutes the ***hair root***.

The cells of the innermost layer of the follicle undergo moderate keratinisation to form the ***medulla* M** or core of the hair shaft; the medullary layer is often not distinguishable in fine hairs. The medulla is surrounded by a broad, highly keratinised layer, the ***cortex* Cx**, which forms the bulk of the hair. The third cell layer of the follicle undergoes keratinisation to form a hard, thin ***cuticle* Cu** on the surface of the hair. The cuticle consists of overlapping keratin plates, an arrangement which is said to prevent matting of the hair.

The fourth layer of the follicle constitutes the ***internal root sheath* IRS**; the cells of this layer become only lightly keratinised and disintegrate at the level of the sebaceous gland ducts leaving a space into which sebum is secreted around the maturing hair. The outermost layer, the ***external root sheath* ERS**, does not take part in hair formation; this layer is separated from the sheath of connective tissue **CT** surrounding the follicle by a thick, specialised basement membrane known as the ***glassy membrane* GM**.

In the growing follicle, large active melanocytes (see Fig. 9.5) are scattered amongst the proliferating cells with melanin being incorporated in the cortex of the hair shaft. Black, brown and yellow forms of melanin are produced in various combinations to determine final hair colour. In infancy, childhood and females, body hair is fine and soft and known as ***vellus*** in contrast to the coarser hair of the scalp which is known as ***terminal hair***. Male sex hormone production at puberty is responsible for the development of further terminal pubic and axillary hair in both sexes and for the replacement of vellus hair with terminal hair on the mature male body.

The cross-sectional shape of hairs also varies between races. The straight hair of the Mongol races is round in cross-section, the wavy hair characteristic of Europeans is oval as in (c) and the curly hair of black skinned peoples is more kidney-shaped.

In addition, the structure of hair follicles depends on the type of hair being produced. For example, the follicles of the scalp and other terminal hairs tend to be long and straight, whereas those of the body, which produce fine, downy hair (vellus), are relatively short and plump; curly hair may be produced by curved follicles or follicles in which the hair bulb lies at an angle to the hair shaft.

Micrograph (c) is a transverse section through the hair follicle at the level shown by a broken line in (a).

The broad external root sheath **ERS** is separated from the fibrous root sheath **CT** by the glassy membrane **GM**. Passing inwards, the internal root sheath **IRS** is recognised by its content of eosinophilic (keratohyaline) granules; the outermost cells of the internal root sheath have a more homogeneous appearance. Deep to the internal root sheath is the thin, pale stained cuticle layer **Cu** which surrounds the strongly stained cortex **Cx**. A medulla is not present in this specimen.

Micrograph (d) shows the hair bulb, the distended base of the hair follicle, which is invaginated by a stromal core of connective tissue, the ***dermal papilla* DP**, containing abundant small blood vessels and myelinated and non-myelinated nerve twigs. This nourishes a basal layer of palisaded active ***germinative cells* GC** which, in people with dark coloured hair (as here), contains melanocytes that supply the hair-forming epithelial cells with melanin. Between the dermal papillae and the germinative epithelium is a distinct thin membrane continuous with the thicker ***glassy membrane* GM** higher up the follicle. The germinative epithelium gives rise to three groups of epithelial cells: the ***premedullary epithelium* PM**, the ***precortical epithelium* PC** and the ***precuticular epithelium* PCu**, which in turn give rise to the medulla, cortex and cuticle, respectively. In the active (anagen) growth phase, the hair bulbs are prominent, with a well-formed dermal papilla, and are located in subcutis. In resting phase (telogen) hair follicles, the hair bulbs are small and have no dermal papilla. The growth cycle of hairs varies from site to site: scalp hair follicles have an anagen growth phase of more than two years and a very short telogen resting phase of a few months. Pubic hair, coarse trunk hair, eyelashes and eyebrows have a short growth phase and a relatively long resting phase, preventing excessive growth of hair at these sites. Only scalp hair can grow to a great length.

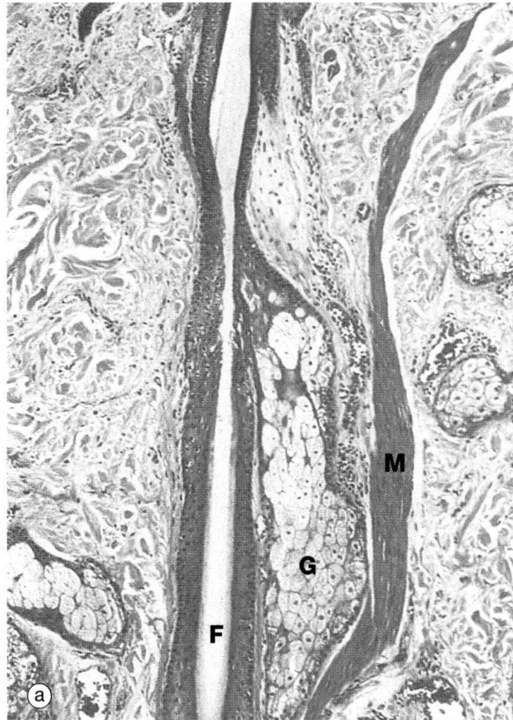

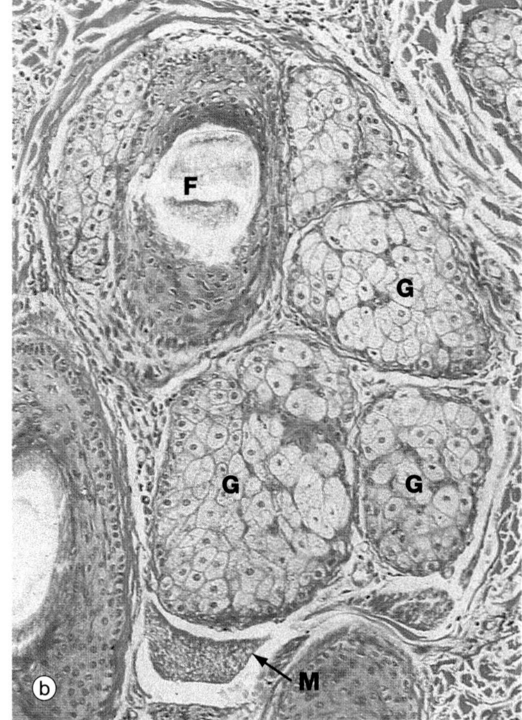

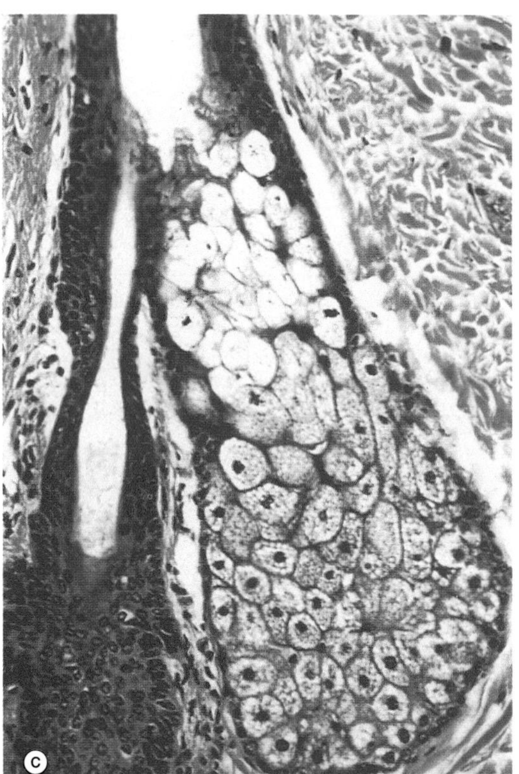

Fig. 9.9 Sebaceous glands
(a) H & E ×33 (b) H & E ×150 (c) H & E ×198

Micrograph (a) illustrates the relationship of a sebaceous gland **G** and an ***arrector pili muscle*** **M** to a hair follicle **F**. At a point about one-third of its length from the surface, each hair follicle is surrounded by one or more sebaceous glands which discharge their secretions onto the hair shaft and thence onto the skin surface. As seen in micrograph (b), sebaceous glands lie within the fibrous sheath surrounding the hair follicle, and the glandular epithelium represents an outgrowth of the external root sheath.

The arrector pili muscle of each follicle consists of a bundle of smooth muscle fibres. The muscle inserts at one end into the sheath of the follicle at a point below the sebaceous glands, and at the other end into the dermal papillary area beneath the epidermis. Each hair follicle and its associated arrector pili muscle and sebaceous glands is known as a ***pilosebaceous unit***.

More detail of sebaceous gland structure can be seen in micrograph (c). Each sebaceous gland has a branched acinar form, the acini converging upon a short duct which empties into the hair follicle beside the maturing hair. Each acinus consists of a mass of rounded cells which are packed with lipid-filled vacuoles; during tissue preparation the lipid is largely removed leaving the cytoplasm of these cells poorly stained. Towards the duct, the lipid content of the acinar cells increases greatly and the distended cells degenerate, so releasing their contents, ***sebum***, into the duct by the process known as holocrine secretion (see Ch. 5). Cells lost by holocrine secretion are replaced by mitosis in the basal layer of the acinus.

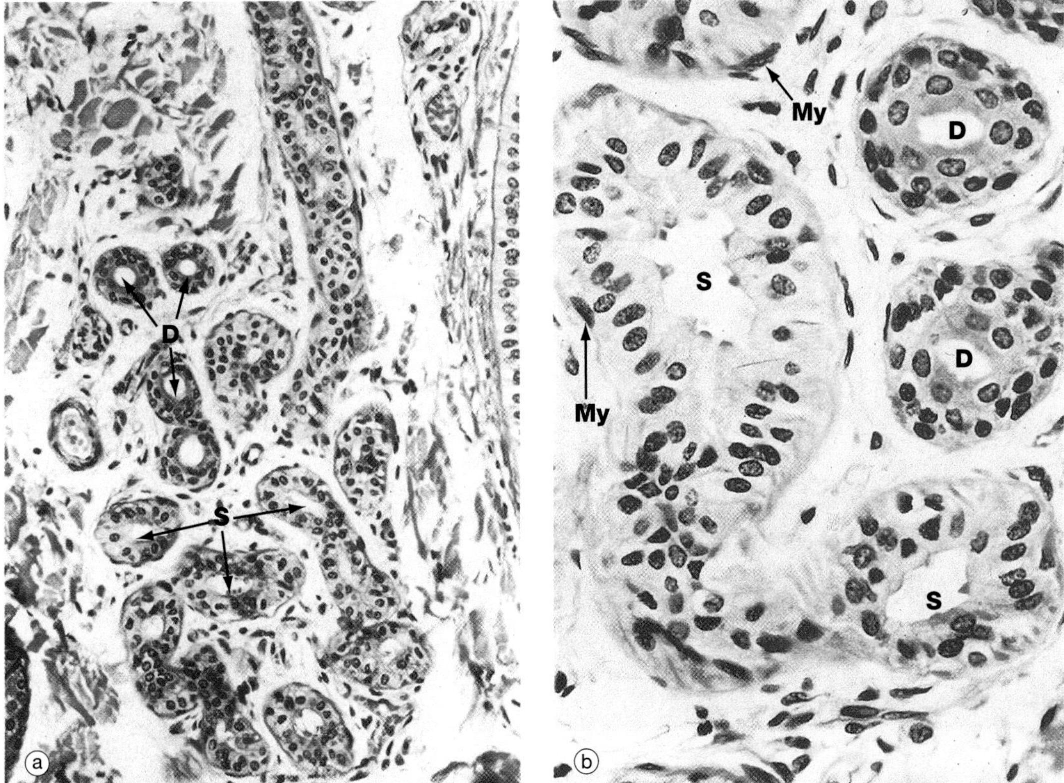

Fig. 9.10 Eccrine sweat glands and ducts
(a) H & E ×198 (b) H & E ×480

Eccrine glands occur everywhere in the skin and are particularly frequent on the palms, soles, forehead and axillae. They arise as downgrowths from the epidermis during the second trimester of intrauterine life, and their function is to secrete a watery fluid called ***sweat***. The evaporation of sweat from the skin surface provides a means of lowering body temperature, and is an important component of the thermoregulatory system. Sweat contains significant quantities of sodium and chloride ions, some other ions, urea and some small molecular weight metabolites; thus sweating may be considered as a minor route of excretion.

Histologically, the entire eccrine unit has two main components. The main secretory component is a coiled ***secretory gland*** situated in the deep reticular dermis or upper subcutis. The secretions formed there are passed into a coiled eccrine duct close to the secretory gland; the duct then becomes straight as it ascends vertically through the dermis towards the skin surface. As it passes through the epidermis, the duct (here called the acrosyringium) becomes slightly coiled again, a feature which is particularly apparent as it passes through the thick epidermis of the sole. The ***secretory gland component*** **S** has an inner layer of large columnar or pyramidal cells with central oval nuclei and pale-staining cytoplasm, interspersed with smaller, rarer darker-staining cells best identified by a specific stain for mucopolysaccharides such as the PAS reaction. The clear cells secrete the bulk of the watery sweat, and the smaller cells secrete a glycoprotein.

The lateral walls of the secretory cells show prominent interdigitations which separate in places to form canaliculi that open into the gland lumen.

The glands have an attenuated outer layer of contractile ***myoepithelial cells*** **My**, which form a discontinuous layer between the secretory cells and the basement membrane. They are spindle shaped and are arranged with their long axes parallel with the long axis of the coiled tubular gland.

The ***eccrine ducts*** **D** appears darker staining and have an obvious double layer of epithelial cells, the inner layer being larger and more cuboidal, and with prominent microvilli lining the lumen. The luminal aspect often has a characteristic eosinophilic appearance (sometimes called the cuticle). This is partly due to the presence of a compact layer of circumferentially arranged tonofilaments in the cuboidal duct epithelial cells at the base of the abundant microvilli. The duct epithelium is biochemically active and modifies the composition of sweat, probably reabsorbing some sodium and ions and water molecules.

D eccrine ducts **F** hair follicle **G** sebaceous gland **M** arrector pili muscle **My** myoepithelial cells
S eccrine secretory gland

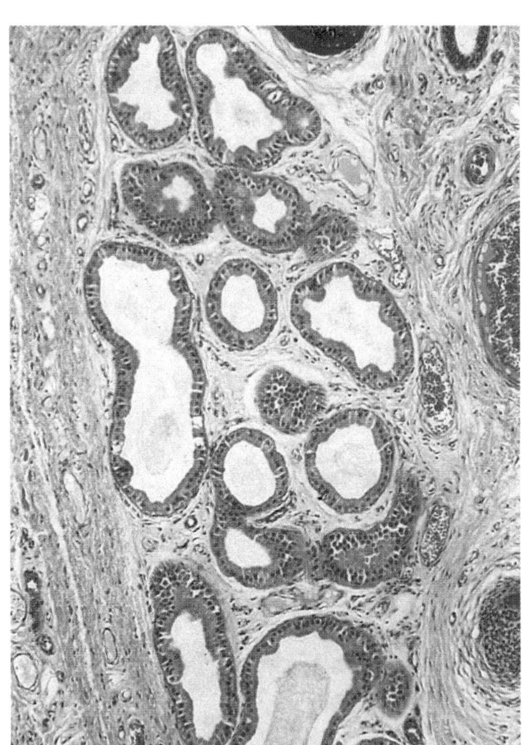

Fig. 9.11 Apocrine glands
H & E ×128

Apocrine glands are mainly confined to the areolae of the breasts and the axillae and genital regions where they produce a viscid, milky secretion which becomes malodorous after the action of skin commensal bacteria.

Apocrine glands are large glands, which always secrete into an adjacent hair follicle via a duct which is histologically similar to that of eccrine sweat glands. The secretory portion of the gland is of the coiled, tubular type with a widely dilated lumen. The secretory cells are usually low cuboidal and have an eosinophilic cytoplasm. The budding appearance of the apical cytoplasm of some cells gave rise to the belief that the mode of secretion was of the apocrine type, but recent evidence suggests that this appearance may be due to a fixation artefact and that the original interpretations were erroneous. Like eccrine sweat glands, apocrine glands have a discontinuous layer of myoepithelial cells between the base of the secretory cells and the prominent basement membrane.

Apocrine glands do not become functional until puberty and in women undergo cyclical changes under the influence of the hormones of the menstrual cycle.

Apocrine glands are analogous to the odiferous glands of many mammals but their biological significance in humans is unknown.

Dermis and subcutis

The ***dermis*** and ***subcutis*** (also known as the ***hypodermis***) are the layers beneath the epidermis. The overall thickness of skin is dependent on the thickness of the dermal and subcutaneous layers; in the eyelids both layers are very thin and the skin is consequently thin and highly flexible, whereas in the back and buttocks the dermis is thick and the subcutis variable but usually thick.

The dermis is composed of collagen and elastic fibres, and is responsible for the tone and texture of the skin. In the young, the skin is tight and firm because of the quality of the collagen and elastin, but with increasing age, and particularly exposure to sunlight, the collagen and elastin in upper dermis progressively degenerate, and the skin loses much of its texture and may wrinkle. The dermis also contains the skin appendages, most of the vascular supply to the skin, and nerves and sensory nerve endings.

The subcutis is predominately composed of adipose tissue, in many areas compartmentalised by vertical fibrous septa running from the deep reticular dermis to the fibrous tissue layer which frequently underlies the subcutis. In some areas of the body, the subcutis contains the lower parts of anagen hair follicles (e.g. scalp), apocrine glands (e.g. axilla and groin) and eccrine glands (e.g. palms and soles). In parts of the face, the subcutis also contains sheets of skeletal muscle, the muscles of facial expression.

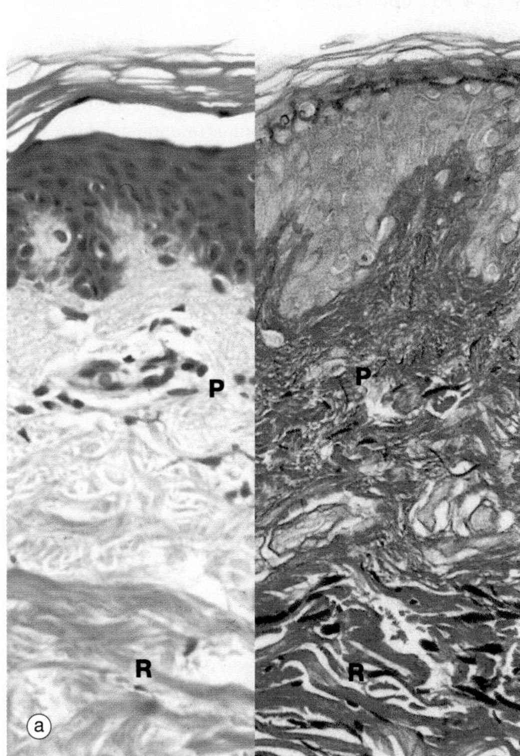

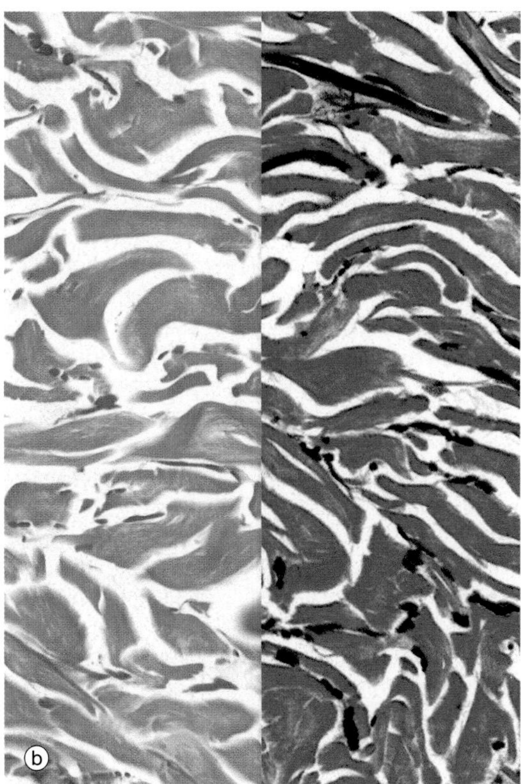

Fig. 9.12 Dermis

(a) Papillary dermis: H & E and EVG ×140 (b) Reticular dermis: H & E and EVG ×280

The dermis is composed of bundles of collagen fibres and strands of elastic fibres embedded in scanty amounts of acellular ground substance, together with occasional inactive fibroblasts which synthesised the collagen, elastic fibres and matrix. The dermis contains the vascular supply (see Fig. 9.14) and innervation of the skin, and has two layers, a superficial ***papillary dermis*** beneath the epidermis and a deeper ***reticular dermis*** which borders the subcutis. Micrograph (a) shows the papillary dermis **P** which is loose and contains very fine interlacing collagen and elastic fibres that stain red and black respectively in the EVG stain. It contains arterioles, capillary loops and venules, as well as lymphatics and fine nerve twigs from the sensory nerve endings such as Meissner's corpuscles (see Fig. 7.31).

Beneath the narrow papillary dermis is the thicker layer, the reticular dermis **R**.

Micrograph (b) shows the reticular dermis in which the collagen bundles and elastic fibres are much larger than in papillary dermis. The reticular dermis also contains blood vessels and nerves, and the skin appendages. Lymphocytes, mast cells and macrophages are present but scarce in normal dermis, but increase in number in many skin diseases.

The reticular dermis varies greatly in thickness at different sites; it is thickest on the back, and thinnest in the eyelids.

P papillary dermis **R** reticular dermis

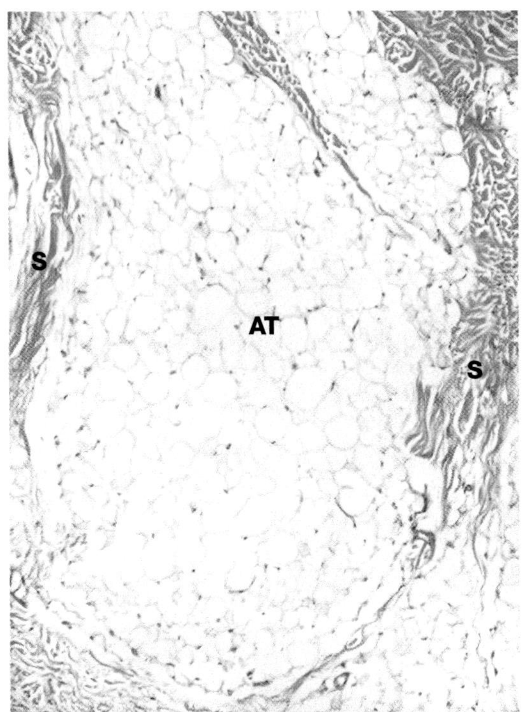

Fig. 9.13 Subcutis
H & E ×110

This photomicrograph shows the subcutis from the skin of the upper thigh of a woman. It is composed of mature adipose tissue **AT**, partially compartmentalised by collagenous fibrous septa **S** which pass vertically from the lower reticular dermis.

The thickness of the subcutis, and the degree of compartmentalisation by fibrous septa, varies from site to site. At this site, the subcutis normally contains no hair follicles or apocrine glands.

Innervation and nerve endings of the skin

The skin is an important sensory organ, and consequently is richly innervated and supplied with a range of nerve endings of different types.

Afferent nervous system

The afferent nervous system in the skin comprises both myelinated and non-myelinated fibres, and is responsible for transmitting impulses from the various nerve endings, and therefore the perception of cutaneous sensation. The sensory nerve endings in the skin are in the form of both free nerve endings and specialised encapsulated nerve endings, the 'capsules' being modifications of Schwann cells; these specialised nerve endings in the skin are ***Meissner's, Pacinian*** and ***Ruffini's corpuscles***, and are illustrated and discussed in more detail in Chapter 7.

Free nerve endings (see Fig. 7.30) may be myelinated or non-myelinated, and are mainly responsible for pain and itch sensations, and detecting temperature. They occupy the papillary dermis and send twigs into the epidermis where some of them associate with Merkel cells (see Fig. 9.7) and act as slowly adapting mechanoreceptors. Free nerve endings also ramify around hair follicles, in the perifollicular fibrous sheath, and some penetrate into the external root sheath.

Meissner's corpuscles (see Fig. 7.31) are rapidly adapting mechanoreceptors responsible for touch sensation. They are particularly prominent in the papillary dermis of the pulps of the fingers and toes, and soles and palms.

Pacinian corpuscles (see Fig. 7.32) are responsible for detection of deep pressure and vibration. In the skin they are usually found deep in the subcutis, singly or in small clusters, being particularly numerous in the palms and soles.

Ruffini corpuscles are small simple dermal mechanoreceptors, particularly common in the soles.

Efferent nervous system

The efferent nervous system is of non-myelinated fibres from the sympathetic component of the autonomic nervous system. It supplies the blood vessels in the skin, and is responsible for vessel diameter and hence blood flow. They also provide a supply to the skin appendages, particularly to arrector pili muscles and the eccrine sweat glands.

A arterial component of glomus **AT** adipose tissue **S** fibrous septum **V** venous component of glomus

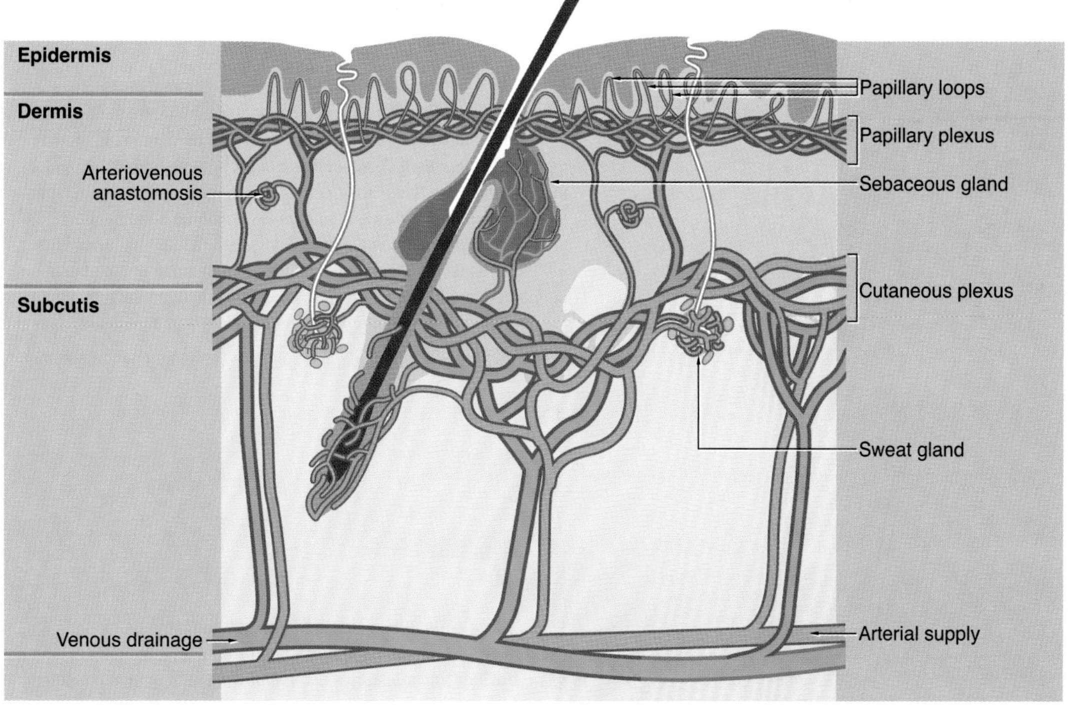

Fig. 9.14 The skin circulation

The circulation of the skin has an unusual arrangement which accommodates several different, sometimes conflicting, functional requirements: nutrition of the skin and appendages, increased blood flow to facilitate heat loss in hot conditions, and decreased blood flow to minimise heat loss in cold conditions whilst nevertheless maintaining adequate nutritional flow.

The arteries supplying the skin are located deep in the subcutis from which they give rise to branches passing upwards to form two plexuses of anastomosing vessels. The deeper plexus lies at the junction of the subcutis and dermis and is known as the ***cutaneous plexus***; the more superficial plexus lies at the junction between papillary and reticular dermis (see Fig. 9.12) and is known as the ***subpapillary plexus***. Branches of the cutaneous plexus supply the fatty tissue of the subcutis, the deeper aspect of the dermis and capillary networks which envelop the hair follicles and deep sebaceous glands and sweat glands. The subpapillary plexus supplies the upper aspect of the dermis and the capillary networks around the superficial appendages. The subpapillary plexus also gives rise to a capillary loop in each dermal papilla. The venous drainage of the skin is arranged into plexuses broadly corresponding to the arterial supply.

Numerous shunts provide direct arteriovenous communications which play an important role in thermoregulation by controlling blood flow to the appropriate part of the dermis.

The skin has a rich lymphatic drainage which forms plexuses corresponding to those of the blood vascular system.

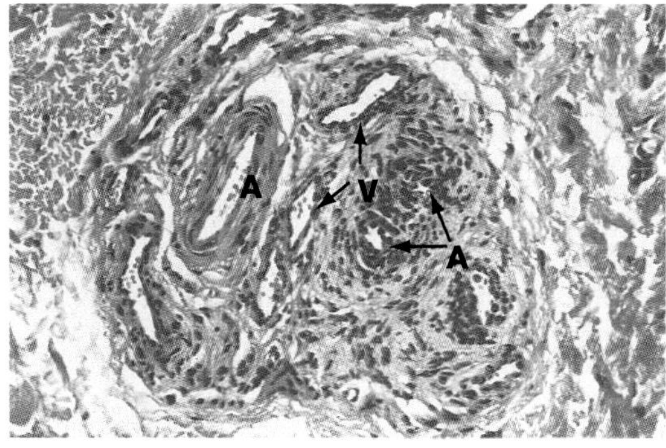

Fig. 9.15 Glomus body
H & E ×128

In the dermis of the fingertips, and other odd peripheral sites prone to excessive cold such as the external ear, the flow in arteriovenous shunts is controlled by structures called ***glomus bodies***. The glomus consists of a highly convoluted segment of an arteriovenous shunt enveloped by condensed collagenous tissue. In histological section, one or more convolutions of the arterial **A** and venous **V** elements of the shunt are usually seen. Just before the arteriovenous junction, the wall of the artery becomes greatly thickened and its smooth muscle cells assume an epithelioid appearance.

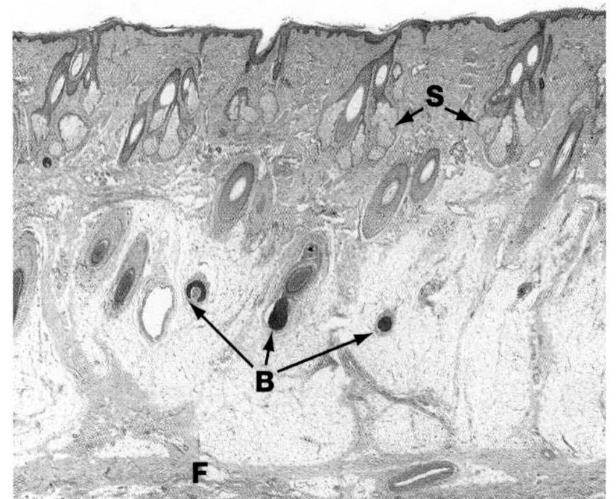

Fig. 9.16 Scalp
H & E ×12

This low power photomicrograph shows the full thickness of the skin of the scalp. The dermis is a broad layer containing the upper parts of the abundant hair follicles with their associated sebaceous glands **S**. The subcutis is similarly broad and contains the deeper parts of the hair follicles, particularly the hair bulbs **B**. The section does not contain complete pilo-sebaceous units because they are arranged obliquely; the owner has curly hair. The fibrous tissue layer **F** deep to the subcutis merges with the periosteum of the skull.

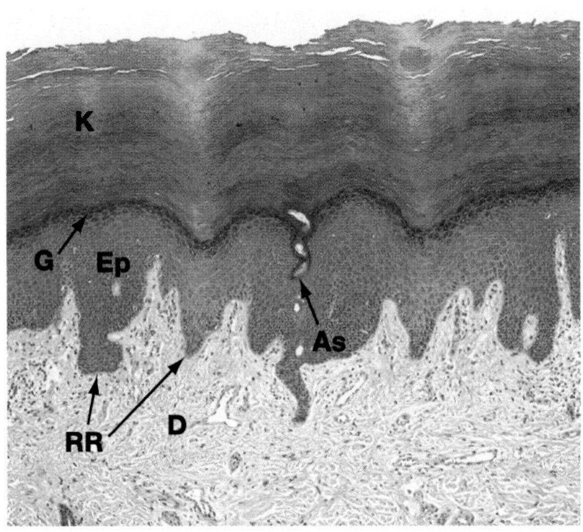

Fig. 9.17 Sole
H & E ×24

The skin of the soles and palms is glabrous, i.e. completely devoid of hair and hair follicles. Because both are areas subject to regular shearing and frictional forces, the skin is structurally modified to resist these forces. The epidermis **Ep** is thick, with a prominent granular layer **G** producing a thick layer of compact keratin **K**, the stratum corneum; elongated epidermal rete ridges **RR** extend into dermis **D**, providing a large area of attachment of epidermis to dermis to minimise separation due to the shearing forces during walking. Note the intraepidermal part of a sweat duct, the acrosyringium **As**, spiralling through epidermis. Sweat glands and nerve endings are numerous at both sites.

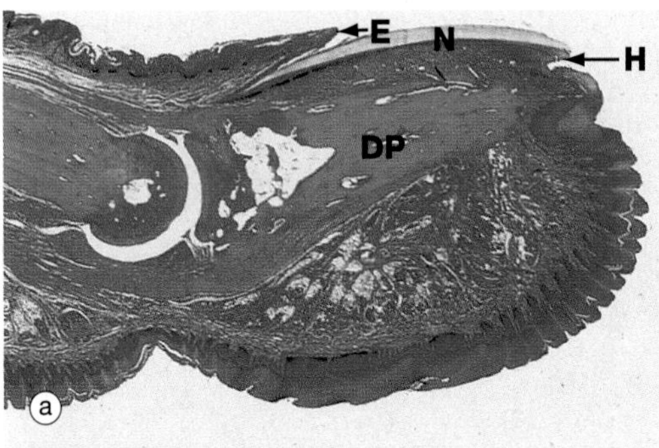

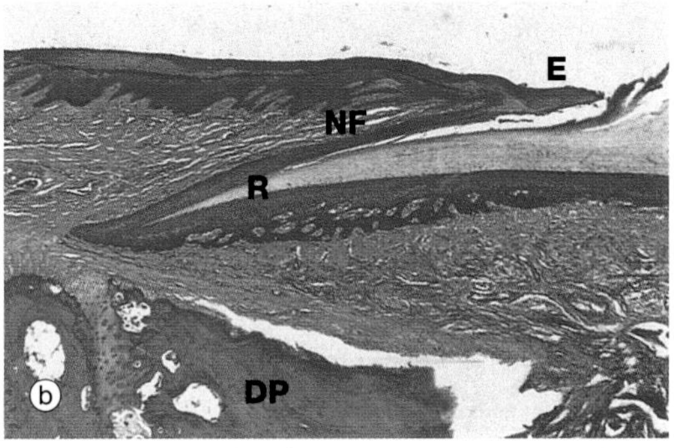

Fig. 9.18 Fingernail (monkey)
(a) H & E ×5 (b) H & E ×20

The dorsal skin surface of the tip of each finger and toe forms a highly specialised appendage, the nail **N**, consisting of a dense keratinised plate, the ***nail plate***, which rests on a stratified squamous epithelium called the ***nail bed***. The proximal end of the nail, the ***nail root*** **R**, and the underlying nail bed extend deeply into the dermis to lie in close apposition to the distal interphalangeal joint, and the dermis beneath the nail plate is firmly attached to the periosteum of the distal phalanx **DP**.

Nail growth occurs by proliferation and differentiation of the epithelium underlying the nail root (known as the ***nail matrix***), and the nail plate slides distally over the rest of the nail bed which does not actively contribute to nail growth. Reflecting its proliferative activity, the nail matrix is thicker than that of the rest of the nail bed and exhibits pronounced epidermal ridges as seen in micrograph (b); on the surface, the distal part of the nail matrix is marked by the white crescent-shaped ***lunular*** at the base of the nail.

The skin overlying the root of the nail is known as the ***nail fold*** **NF** and its highly keratinised free edge is known as the ***eponychium*** **E**. The skin beneath the free end of the nail is known as the ***hyponychium*** **H**.

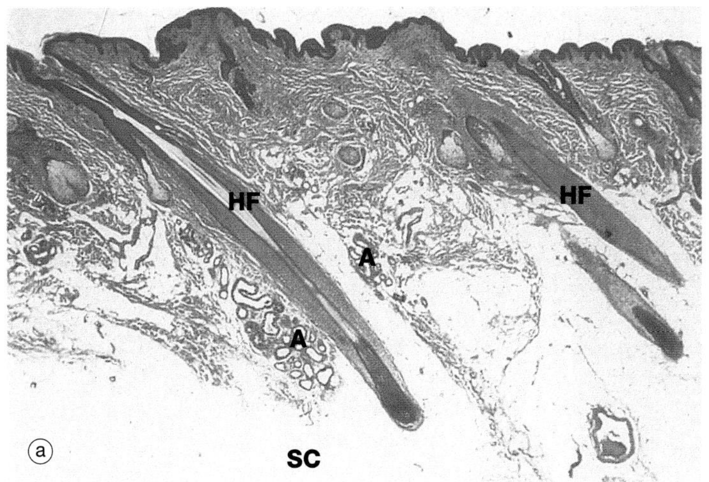

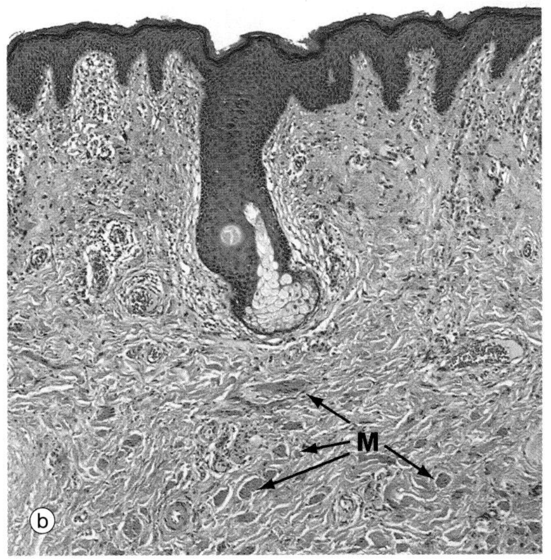

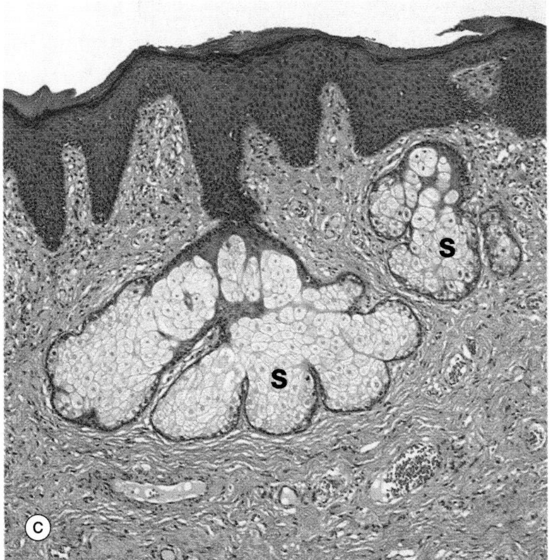

Fig. 9.19 Vulva
(a) Mons pubis H & E ×12 (b) Labium majus H & E ×60 (c) Labium minus H & E ×80

The vulva comprises the ***mons pubis***, ***labia majora*** and ***labia minora***, and the ***vestibule*** with its vestibular glands which mark the junction between vulva and vaginal canal. The vulva is also the site of the opening of the female urethra, and the location of the erectile ***clitoris***, the female homologue of the penis. The squamous epithelium of the labia minora is continuous with the squamous epithelium of the lower vagina (see Fig. 19.26).

Micrograph (a) shows the mons pubis skin with abundant oblique hair follicles **HF** (producing curly hair) and some apocrine glands **A**. This area has a thick pad of subcutaneous adipose tissue **SC**.

The labia majora are longitudinal folds of skin which extend posteriorly from the mons pubis; the outer surface of the fold has the same type of skin as the mons pubis i.e. with abundant pilosebaceous units, oblique hair follicles and apocrine glands in the subcutis, as shown in (a). On the inner surface, the hair follicles progressively disappear but sebaceous glands persist.

Micrograph (b) shows the inner surface of a labium majus, with the residue of a pilosebaceous unit in the upper dermis, and numerous clumps of small smooth muscle fibres **M** in mid and deep dermis. The labia majora are the female homologue of the male scrotum, and the labial muscle fibres are the homologue of the dartos muscle of the scrotum.

The labia minora are internal to the labia majora and are thin flaps of skin which is devoid of hair and hair follicles.

Micrograph (c) shows the outer aspect of a labium minus. It has a keratinising stratified squamous epidermis and scattered sebaceous glands **S** which open directly onto the skin surface rather than into the necks of hair follicles as they do in hair-bearing skin (see Fig. 9.9). On the inner aspect, the labia minora have a thinner epidermis and keratin layer. The vaginal orifice is one of the sites of a muco-cutaneous junction, where the skin of the labia minora of the vulva meets the mucosa of the vaginal canal; similar muco-cutaneous junctions exist at the oral, nasal and anal orifices.

A apocrine gland **As** acrosyringium **B** hair bulb **D** dermis **DP** distal phalanx **E** eponychium **Ep** epidermis **F** fibrous layer **G** granular layer **H** hyponychium **HF** hair follicles **K** keratin **M** smooth muscle fibres **N** nail **NF** nail fold **R** nail root **RR** rete ridges **S** sebaceous glands **SC** subcutaneous adipose tissue

10. *Skeletal tissues*

Introduction

The skeletal system is composed of highly specialised forms of supporting/connective tissue, based on collagen and acellular matrix, and the synthetic cells which produce them. ***Bone*** provides a rigid protective and supporting framework, the rigidity resulting from the deposition of calcium salts within the collagen and matrix. ***Cartilage*** has different forms and provides a smooth articular surface at bone ends, as well as structural support in special areas (e.g. trachea, pinna) and is also important in one form of new bone formation.

Joints are composite structures which join the bones of the skeleton and, depending on the function and structure of individual joints, permit varying degrees of movement. ***Ligaments*** are robust but flexible bands of collagenous tissue which contribute to the stability of joints. ***Tendons*** provide strong, pliable connections between muscles and their points of insertion into bones.

The functional differences between the various tissues of the skeletal system relate principally to the different nature and proportion of the ground substance and fibrous elements of the extracellular matrix. The cells of all the skeletal tissues, like the cells of the less specialised supporting/connective tissues, have close structural and functional relationships and a common origin from primitive mesenchymal cells (see Ch. 4).

Cartilage

The semi-rigid nature of cartilage stems from the predominance of proteoglycan ground substance in the extra-cellular matrix.

Proteoglycans (see Ch. 4), disposed in ***proteoglycan aggregates*** of 100 or more molecules, make up the ground substance and account for the solid, yet flexible, consistency of cartilage. Sulphated glycosaminoglycans (GAGs, chondroitin sulphate and keratan sulphate) predominate in the proteoglycan aggregates with molecules of the non-sulphated GAG, hyaluronic acid, forming the central backbone of the complex. The different types of cartilage vary in the amount and nature of fibres in the ground substance: ***hyaline cartilage*** contains few fibres, ***fibro-cartilage*** contains abundant collagen fibres, and ***elastic cartilage*** contains elastic fibres.

Cartilage formation commences with the differentiation of stellate-shaped, primitive mesenchymal cells (see Fig. 4.10) to form rounded cartilage precursor cells called ***chondroblasts***. Subsequent mitotic divisions give rise to aggregations of closely packed chondroblasts which grow and begin synthesis of ground substance and fibrous extracellular material. Secretion of extracellular material traps each chondroblast within the cartilaginous matrix thereby separating the chondroblasts from one another. Each chondroblast then undergoes one or two further mitotic divisions to form a small cluster of mature cells separated by a small amount of extracellular material. Mature cartilage cells, known as ***chondrocytes***, maintain the integrity of the cartilage matrix.

Most mature cartilage masses acquire a surrounding layer called the ***perichondrium***, composed of collagen fibres and spindle-shaped cells which resemble fibroblasts. These have the capacity to transform into chondroblasts and form new cartilage by ***appositional growth***. There is also very limited capacity in mature cartilages masses for ***interstitial growth*** by further division of chondrocytes trapped within the previously formed matrix, and subsequent deposition of more matrix material. The hyaline cartilage of the articular surfaces of joints does not have perichondrium on the surface, and has no capacity to regenerate new cartilage after damage. In general, mature cartilage has a very limited capacity to repair and regenerate, partly because of its poor blood supply.

Most cartilage is devoid of blood vessels and consequently the exchange of metabolites between chondrocytes and surrounding tissues depends on diffusion through the water of solvation of the ground substance. This limits the thickness to which cartilage may develop while maintaining viability of the innermost cells; in sites where cartilage is particularly thick (e.g. costal cartilage), ***cartilage canals*** convey small vessels into the centre of the cartilage mass.

The role of cartilage in bone formation is discussed in Figs 10.17 and 10.18.

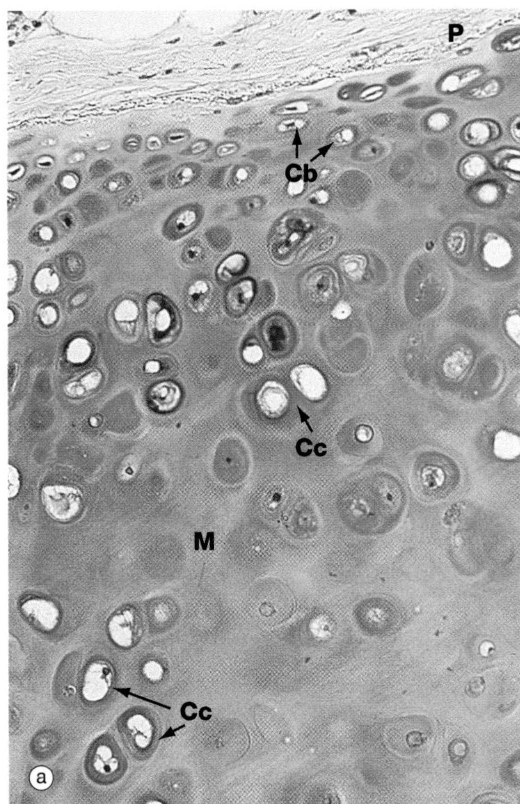

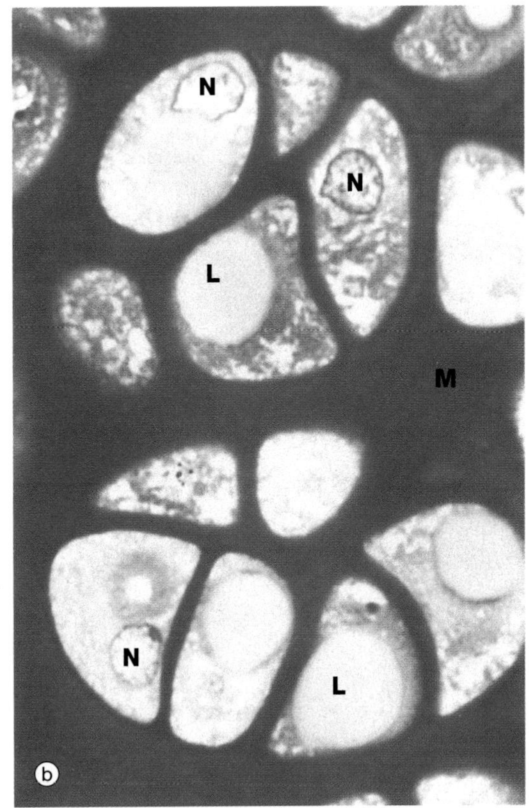

Fig. 10.1 Hyaline cartilage
(a) H & E ×150 (b) Thin epoxy resin section, toluidine blue ×1200

Hyaline cartilage is the most common type of cartilage and is found in the nasal septum, larynx, tracheal rings, most articular surfaces and the sternal ends of the ribs. It also forms the precursor of bone in the developing skeleton. Mature hyaline cartilage is characterised by small aggregations of chondrocytes embedded in an amorphous matrix of ground substance reinforced by collagen fibres.

Micrograph (a) shows a hyaline cartilage mass with its outer perichondrium **P**. The ***chondrocytes*** of the formed cartilage **Cc** are arranged in clusters, usually of 2–4 cells, each cluster being separated from its neighbours by amorphous cartilage matrix **M**. The perichondrium is composed of parallel collagen fibres containing a few spindle-shaped nuclei of inactive fibrocytes, but on its inner surface these cells are transforming into small ***chondroblasts*** **Cb** which are in the process of enlarging, dividing and synthesising new cartilage matrix.

The matrix of hyaline cartilage appears fairly amorphous since the ground substance and collagen have similar refractive properties. With the exception of articular cartilage, the collagen of hyaline cartilage, designated as collagen type II (see Ch. 4), is not cross-banded and is arranged in an interlacing network of fine fibrils; this collagen cannot be demonstrated by light microscopy.

The thin epoxy resin section of hyaline cartilage in micrograph (b) shows the cellular details of mature chondrocytes.

Note that the chondrocytes fully occupy the spaces in the matrix **M**, each space containing a single chondrocyte. Mature chondrocytes are characterised by small nuclei **N** with dispersed chromatin and basophilic, granular cytoplasm, reflecting a well developed rough endoplasmic reticulum. Lipid droplets **L**, often larger than the nuclei, are a prominent feature of larger chondrocytes; the cytoplasm is also rich in glycogen. These characteristics reflect the active role of chondrocytes in synthesis of both the ground substance and fibrous elements of the cartilage matrix. In fully formed cartilage, the constituents of the extracellular matrix are continuously turned over, the integrity of the matrix being thus absolutely dependent on the viability of the chondrocytes.

Cb chondroblasts **Cc** chondrocytes **L** lipid droplet **M** cartilage matrix **N** nucleus
P perichondrium

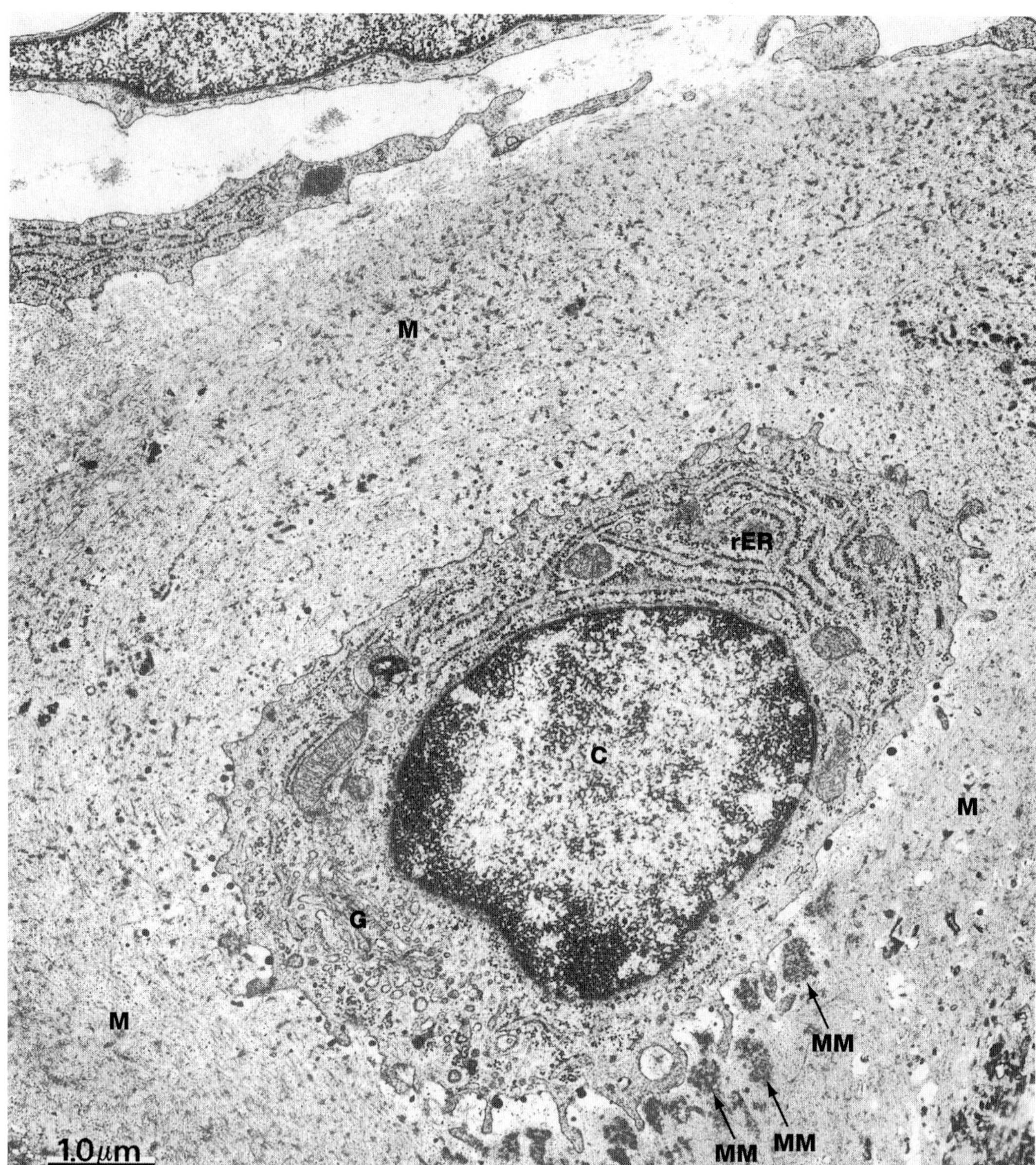

Fig. 10.2 Chondrocytes
EM ×16 000

This micrograph illustrates a chondrocyte **C** lying within its lacuna and surrounded by cartilage matrix **M**. Typical of cells active in protein synthesis (in this case matrix turnover), chondrocytes have prominent rough endoplasmic reticulum **rER** which is distended with secretory material. A well-developed Golgi apparatus **G** is present. Glycogen granules are scattered in the cytoplasm. Note that the chondrocyte completely fills its lacuna within the matrix. Small cytoplasmic extensions mediate the constant interaction between chondrocytes and matrix. At this magnification, the fibrous elements of the matrix can just be discerned. The electron-dense material adjacent to the deep aspect of the cell **MM** represents recently secreted matrix material.

C chondrocyte **G** Golgi apparatus **M** cartilage matrix **MM** new matrix **P** perichondrium **rER** rough endoplasmic reticulum

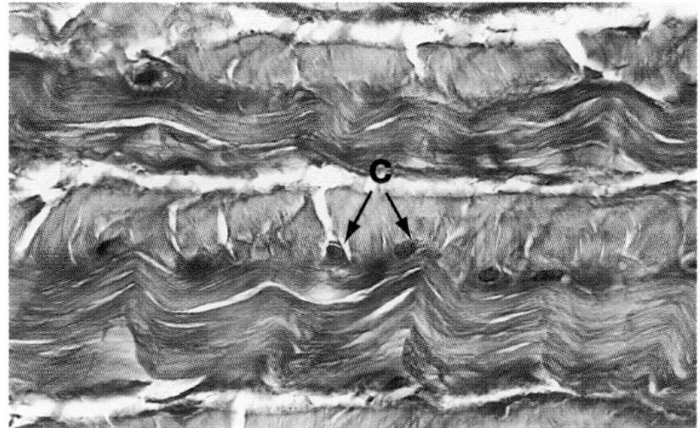

Fig. 10.3 Fibrocartilage
H & E/Alcian blue ×320

Fibrocartilage, which has features intermediate between cartilage and dense fibrous supporting tissue, is found in the intervertebral discs, some articular cartilages, the pubic symphysis, and in association with dense collagenous tissue in joint capsules, ligaments and the connections of some tendons to bone. Fibrocartilage consists of alternating layers of hyaline cartilage matrix and thick layers of dense collagen fibres oriented in the direction of the functional stresses.

This micrograph is taken from the same specimen of intervertebral disc illustrated in Fig. 10.30. Pink stained collagen characteristically permeates the blue stained cartilage ground substance. Chondrocytes **C** are typically arranged in rows between the dense collagen layers within lacunae in the glycoprotein matrix.

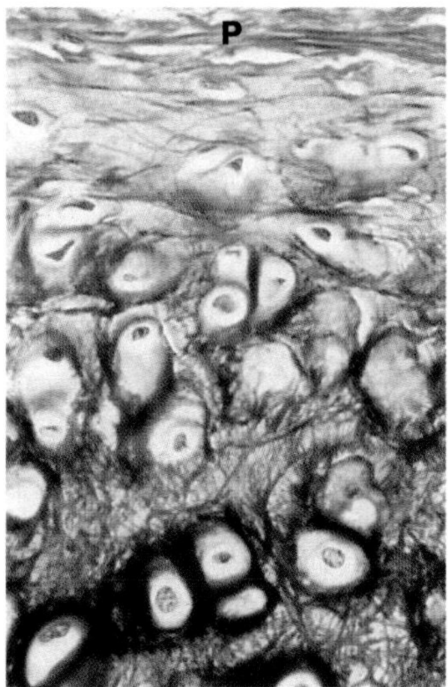

Fig. 10.4 Elastic cartilage
Elastic van Gieson ×128

Elastic cartilage occurs in the external ear and external auditory canal, the epiglottis, parts of the laryngeal cartilages and the walls of the Eustachian tubes.

The histological structure of elastic cartilage is similar to that of hyaline cartilage, its elasticity, however, being derived from the presence of numerous bundles of branching elastic fibres in the cartilage matrix; this network of elastic fibres (stained black in this preparation) is particularly dense in the immediate vicinity of the chondrocytes. Collagen (stained red) is also a major constituent of the cartilage matrix and makes up the bulk of the perichondrium **P** intermingled with a few elastic fibres.

Development and growth of elastic cartilage occurs by both interstitial and appositional growth in the same manner as for hyaline cartilage.

Bone

Bone is composed of cells and a predominantly collagenous extracellular matrix (type I collagen) called ***osteoid*** which becomes mineralised by the deposition of ***calcium hydroxyapatite***, thus giving the bone considerable rigidity and strength. The cells of bone are:

- **Osteoblasts** – which synthesise osteoid and mediate its mineralisation; they are found lined up along bone surfaces.
- **Osteocytes** – which represent largely inactive osteoblasts trapped within formed bone; they may assist in nutrition of bone.
- **Osteoclasts** – phagocytic cells which are capable of eroding bone and which are important, along with osteoblasts, in the constant turnover and refashioning of bone.

Osteoblasts and osteocytes are derived from a primitive mesenchymal (stem) cell called the ***osteoprogenitor cell***. Osteoclasts are multinucleate phagocytic cells derived from the macrophage-monocyte cell line.

Bone forms the strong and rigid endoskeleton to which skeletal muscles are attached to permit movement. It is also acts as a calcium reservoir and is important in calcium homeostasis. Bone is heavy and its architecture is optimally arranged to provide maximum strength for the least weight. Most bones have a dense rigid outer shell of ***compact bone***, the ***cortex***, and a central ***medullary*** or ***cancellous*** zone of thin interconnecting narrow bone trabeculae. The number, thickness and orientation of these bone trabeculae are dependent upon the stresses to which the particular bone is exposed; for example, there are many thick intersecting trabeculae in the constantly weight-bearing vertebrae, but very few in the centre of the ribs which are not subjected to constant stress. The spaces in the medullary bone between trabeculae is occupied by haemopoietic bone marrow (see Fig. 3.12).

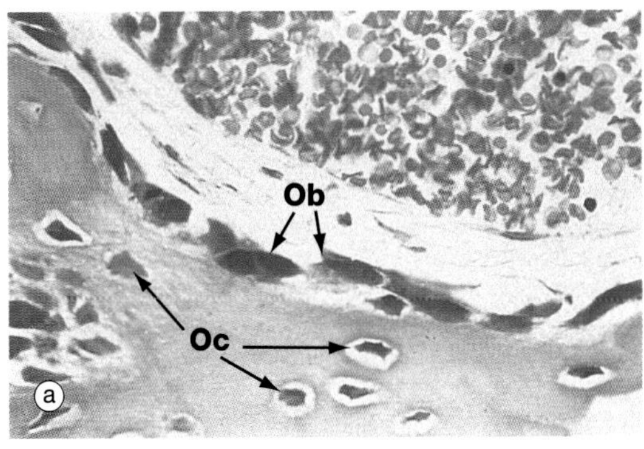

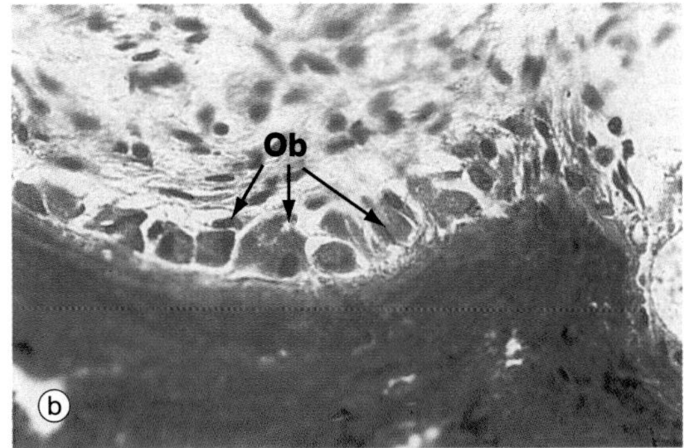

Fig. 10.5 Active osteoblasts and osteoid
(a) H & E ×320 (b) Undecalcified resin section, Goldner's trichrome stain ×320

These micrographs illustrate osteoblasts actively depositing new osteoid on a bone surface. When active, the osteoblasts **Ob** are large broad spindle-shaped or cuboidal cells with abundant basophilic cytoplasm containing much rough endoplasmic reticulum and a large Golgi apparatus. These features reflect a high rate of protein (type I collagen) and proteoglycan synthesis. In (a), the tissue has been decalcified before sectioning and staining, so the distinction between mineralised bone and the newly formed unmineralised osteoid cannot be seen. In (b), which has not been decalcified, the mineralised bone (blue) can easily be distinguished from the new osteoid (red) which is being produced by the row of cuboidal osteoblasts; there is always a short delay between osteoid production and its mineralisation.

When inactive, osteoblasts are narrow attenuated spindle-shaped cells lying on the bone surface. In (a) the burst of new bone formation is nearly over, and the osteoblasts are becoming spindle-shaped again and will soon become virtually undetectable, only the long narrow nucleus being visible histologically. A few cells are being incorporated in the newly formed bone as osteocytes **Oc**.

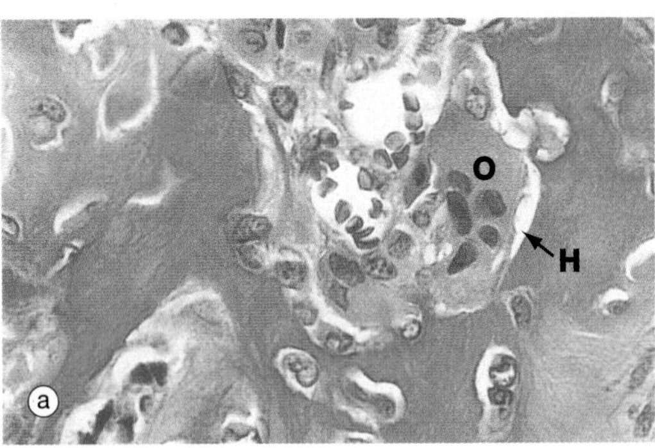

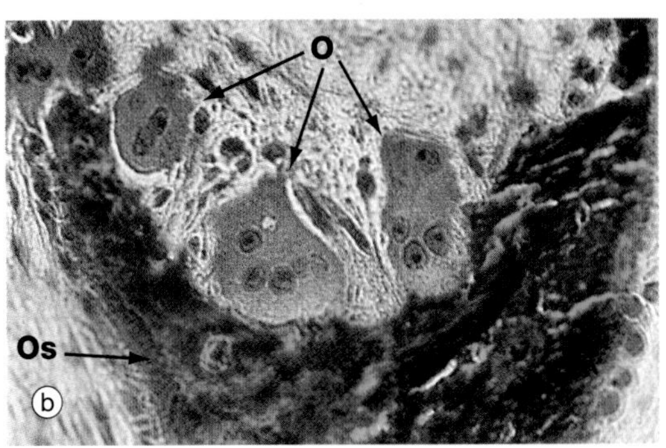

Fig. 10.6 Osteoclasts
(a) H & E ×400 (b) Undecalcified resin section, Goldner's trichrome ×320

Resorption of bone is performed by large multinucleate cells called osteoclasts **O** which are often seen lying in depressions resorbed from the bone surface called ***Howship's lacunae*** **H**. The aspect of the osteoclast in apposition to bone is characterised by fine microvilli which form a ***ruffled border*** that is readily visible with the electron microscope. The ruffled border secretes several organic acids which dissolve the mineral component while lysosomal proteolytic enzymes are employed to destroy the organic osteoid matrix.

Osteoclastic resorption contributes to bone remodelling in response to growth or changing mechanical stresses upon the skeleton. Osteoclasts also participate in the long-term maintenance of blood calcium homeostasis by their response to parathyroid hormone and calcitonin (see Ch. 17). Parathyroid hormone stimulates osteoclastic resorption and the release of calcium ions from bone, whereas calcitonin inhibits osteoclastic activity.

Both (a) and (b) are taken from bone showing excessive osteoclastic activity due to disease (Paget's disease – see opposite). Micrograph (b) also shows uncoordinated new osteoid **Os** formation by a row of osteoblasts.

H Howship's lacuna **L** lamellar bone **O** osteoclasts **Ob** osteoblasts **Oc** osteocytes **Os** osteoid **W** woven bone

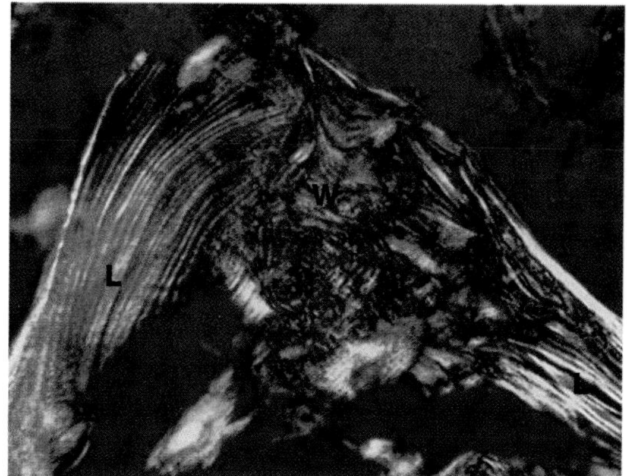

Fig. 10.7 Woven and lamellar bone – polarising microscopy
Eosin ×120

Bone exists in two main forms, woven bone **W** and lamellar bone **L**. Woven bone is an immature form with randomly arranged collagen fibres in the osteoid. Lamellar bone is composed of regular parallel bands of collagen arranged in sheets. Woven bone is produced when osteoblasts produce osteoid rapidly, as in fetal bone development and in adults when there is pathological rapid new bone formation, e.g. healing fracture and Paget's disease. The rapidly formed woven bone is eventually remodelled to form lamellar bone, which is physically stronger and more resilient. Virtually all bone in a healthy adult is lamellar.

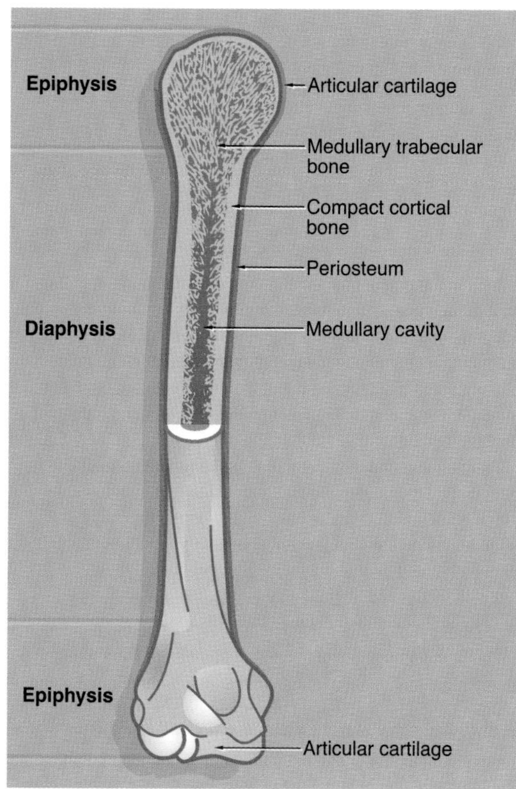

Fig. 10.8 Long bone

This diagram illustrates the general structure of long bones in the mature skeleton and the gross morphological appearance of the two types of lamellar bone found in the mature skeleton, i.e. compact (cortical) bone and cancellous (medullary) bone. Compact bone forms the dense walls of the shaft or ***diaphysis*** while cancellous bone occupies part of the large central ***medullary cavity***. Cancellous bone consists of a network of fine, irregular plates called ***trabeculae*** separated by intercommunicating spaces.

The articular (joint) surfaces of the expanded ends, or ***epiphyses***, of long bones are protected by a layer of specialised hyaline cartilage called ***articular cartilage***. The external surface of the bone is invested in a dense fibrous layer called the ***periosteum*** into which are inserted muscles, tendons and ligaments. The inner surfaces of the bone, including the trabeculae of cancellous bone, are invested by a delicate layer called the ***endosteum***. The endosteum and periosteum contain cells of the osteogenic series which are responsible for growth, continuous remodelling and repair of bone fractures.

Prior to the attainment of skeletal maturity, the long bones grow in length by the process of endochondral ossification which occurs at a ***growth*** or ***epiphysial plate*** situated at each end of the bone at the junction of the diaphysis (shaft) and epiphysis.

Diseases of osteoblasts and osteoclasts

The maintenance and refashioning of bone is the result of co-ordinated activity of osteoblasts depositing new bone and osteoclasts eroding redundant bone. Some diseases are the result of excessive unbalanced activity of one or other of the cell types, commonly osteoclasts.

In ***hyperparathyroidism***, excessive uncontrolled secretion of parathormone by the parathyroid gland (see Fig. 17.13) stimulates increase in numbers and erosive activity of osteoclasts. This leads to diffuse destruction of bone, producing radiological areas of lucency ('brown tumours') and predisposition to fracture. A serious side effect of excessive bone erosion is the release of large amounts of ionic calcium into the bloodstream, producing severe symptoms of ***hypercalcaemia***.

Paget's disease is a disease of unknown cause in which there is random and haphazard excessive osteoclastic erosion of bone occurring in waves, followed by increased osteoblastic activity attempting to replace eroded bone (see Fig. 10.6). However, the new osteoid and bone formation does not always occur where bone has previously been eroded, so the architecture of the bone is grossly distorted (usually with woven bone – see Fig. 10.7) and the bone is structurally weak.

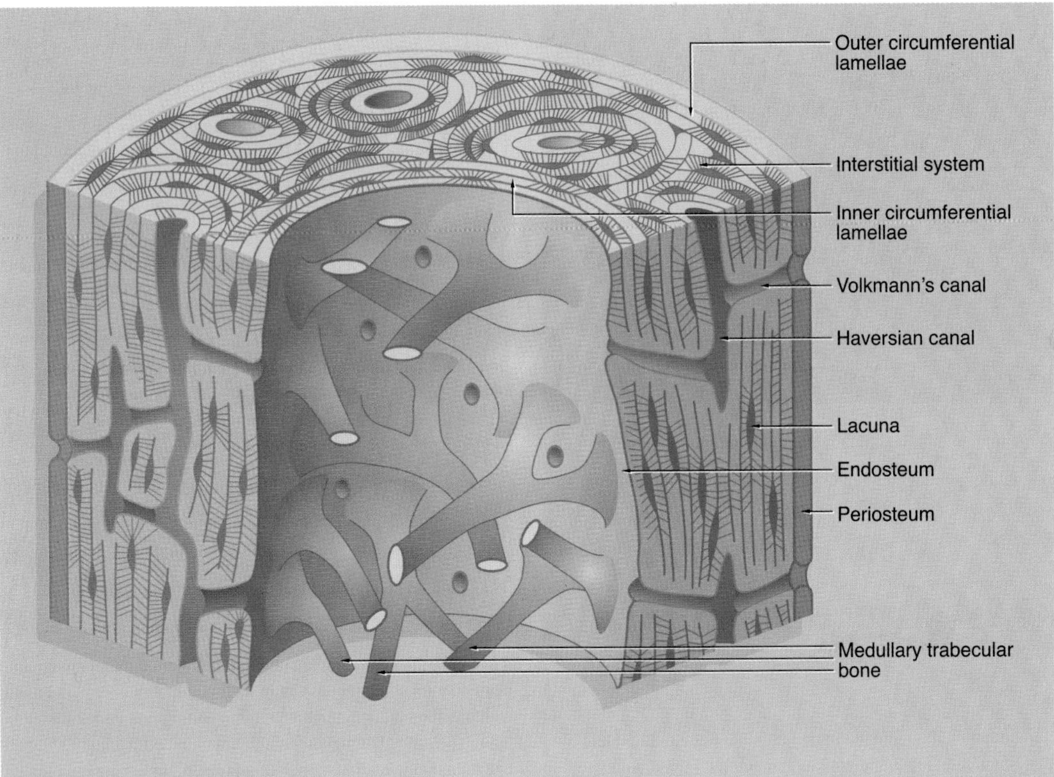

Fig. 10.9 Cortical (compact) bone

Compact bone is made up of parallel bony columns which, in long bones, are disposed parallel to the long axis, i.e. in the line of stress exerted on the bone. Each column is made up of concentric bony layers or ***lamellae*** disposed around a central channel containing blood vessels, lymphatics and nerves. These neurovascular channels are known as ***canals of Havers*** or ***Haversian canals***, and with their concentric lamellae form ***Haversian systems***. The neurovascular bundles interconnect with one another, and with the endosteum and periosteum, via ***Volkmann's canals*** which pierce the columns at right angles (or obliquely) to the Haversian canals.

Each Haversian system (***osteon***) develops by osteoclastic tunnelling of a mass of compact bone to form a broad channel into which blood vessels and nerves grow, after which it becomes lined internally by active osteoblasts which lay down concentric lamellae of bone.

With the deposition of successive lamellae, the diameter of the Haversian canal decreases and osteoblasts are trapped as osteocytes in spaces called ***lacunae*** in the matrix. The osteocytes are thus arranged in concentric rings within the lamellae. Between adjacent lacunae and the central canal are numerous minute interconnecting canals called ***canaliculi*** which contain fine cytoplasmic extensions of the osteocytes.

As a result of the continuous resorption and redeposition of bone, complete newly formed Haversian systems are disposed between partly resorbed systems formed earlier. The remnants of lamellae no longer surrounding Haversian canals form irregular ***interstitial systems*** between intact Haversian systems.

At the outermost aspect of compact bone, Haversian systems give way to concentric lamellae of dense cortical bone laid down partly by the osteoblasts of the periosteum (***outer circumferential lamellae***). Similar circumferential lamellae line the inside of the cortical bone (***inner circumferential lamellae***) where it abuts the marrow cavity.

The inner surface of cortical bone (***endosteum***) is composed of the innermost layer of the inner circumferential lamellae with a layer of inactive flat osteoblasts on its surface. When activated, these cells enlarge to become active cuboidal osteoblasts and synthesise new lamellar osteoid which, on mineralisation, forms another layer of inner circumferential lamella. This occurs regularly as part of the constant dynamic refashioning of bone, and is particularly prominent during bone growth, and in response to increased or altered stress on the cortical bone, for example in the leg bones during periods of increased physical training for running and other sports.

The ends of the interconnecting network of trabecular or cancellous bone, which occupy part of the central marrow cavity of bone, are attached to the inner circumferential lamellae of the cortical bone (see Fig. 10.13). The inactive osteoblasts of the endosteum also extend onto the surface of the trabecular bone, and similarly deposit new osteoid when required for strengthening or remodelling.

Small blood vessels and nerves enter the cortical bone from the marrow space through defects in the endosteum and inner circumferential lamellae, which connect with Volkmann's canals, which in turn connect with the Haversian canals.

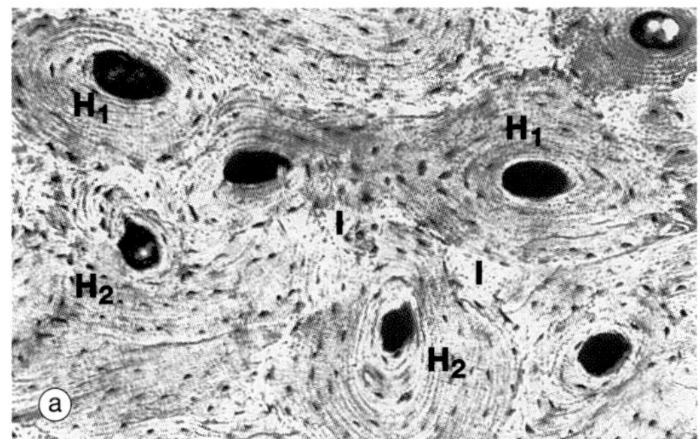

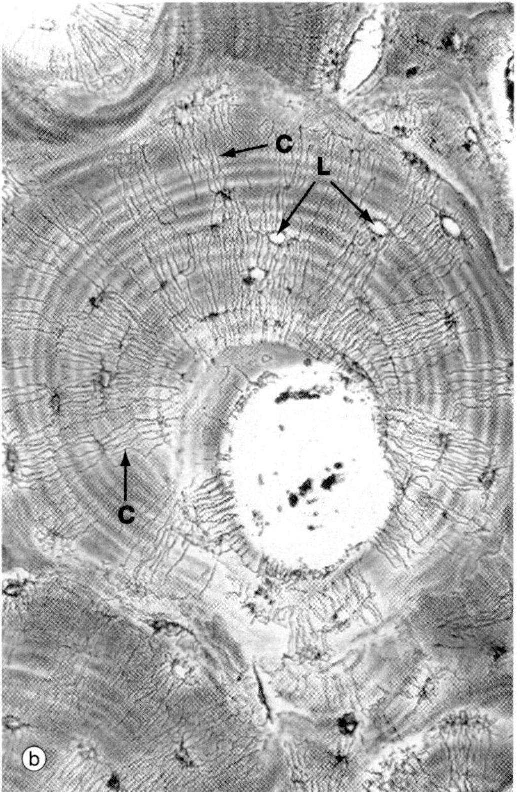

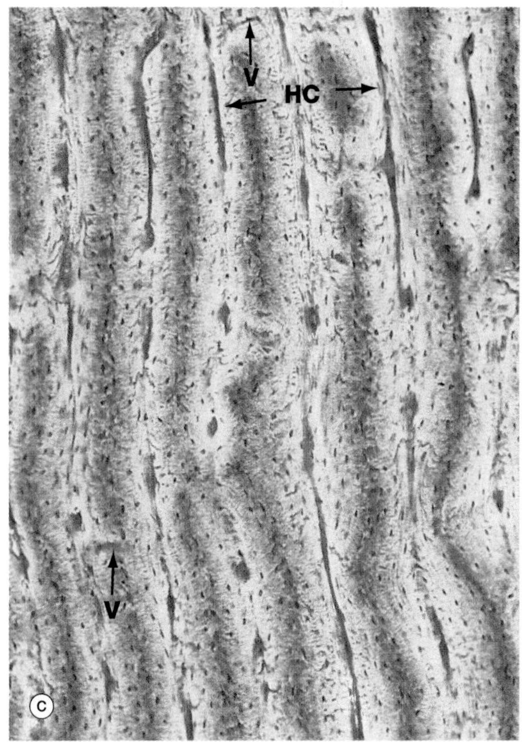

Fig. 10.10 Cortical (compact) bone
Ground sections, unstained (a) TS ×80 (b) TS ×600 (c) LS ×150

These ground sections illustrate many of the features described in the preceding figure. In micrograph (a), the bone has been cut transversely thereby demonstrating newly formed Haversian systems $\mathbf{H_1}$ and older, partly resorbed Haversian systems $\mathbf{H_2}$; irregular interstitial systems **I**, representing the remnants of former Haversian system, fill the spaces between the Haversian systems. Concentric rings of flattened lacunae can be seen to surround the central Haversian canals which appear as very dark areas in this preparation.

Micrograph (b) focuses on a single Haversian system, the central canal being surrounded by concentric lamellae of bone matrix containing empty lacunae **L**. Fine canaliculi **C** radiate from each lacuna to anastomose with those of adjacent lacunae. In life, the osteocytes do not completely fill the lacunae, the remaining narrow space being filled with extracellular bone fluid. Fine cytoplasmic processes of the osteocytes pass in the canaliculi to communicate via gap junctions with the processes of osteocytes in adjacent lamellae. The canaliculi provide passages for circulation of extracellular fluid and diffusion of metabolites between the lacunae and vessels of the Haversian canals.

Osteocytes maintain the structural integrity of the mineralised matrix and mediate short-term release or deposition of calcium for the purpose of calcium homeostasis in the body as a whole. The activity of osteocytes in calcium regulation is controlled directly by plasma calcium concentration and indirectly by the hormones parathormone and calcitonin secreted by the parathyroid and thyroid glands, respectively (see Ch. 17). Osteoblasts and osteocytes also appear to respond to minute piezo-electric currents induced by bone deformation, increasing or decreasing local bone formation as appropriate and inducing complementary activity in local osteoclasts via the secretion of local humoral factors. In this fashion bone is remodelled to adapt to mechanical stresses imposed on it.

Micrograph (c) shows compact bone cut in longitudinal section, the plane of section including some Haversian canals **HC** and traces of the interconnecting Volkmann's canal system **V**. These appear dark in colour as in micrograph (a) due to an optical artefact related to air trapped in the section. For the same reason, the tiny osteocyte lacunae appear as brown specks elongated in shape and arranged in concentric layers around the Haversian canals.

C bone canaliculi $\mathbf{H_1}$ and $\mathbf{H_2}$ Haversian systems **HC** Haversian canals **I** interstitial system **L** lacunae **V** Volkmann's canal

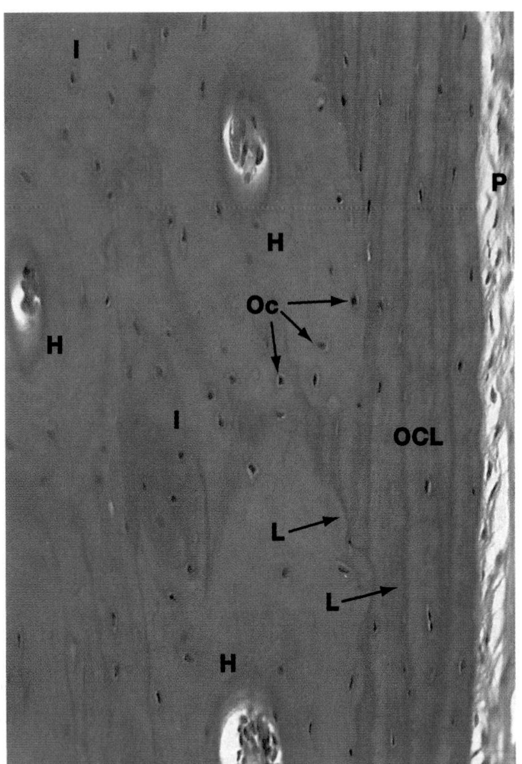

Fig. 10.11 Cortical (compact) bone
H & E ×198

This micrograph shows compact cortical bone, with periosteum **P** on its outer surface. The outer circumferential lamellae **OCL** lie between the periosteum and three Haversian systems **H**, seen here in transverse section. At the centre of each Haversian system is a canal containing blood vessels, and between adjacent systems are irregular interstitial lamellae **I**. The lamellae of the Haversian systems are not clearly seen in this section, but fine basophilic cement lines **L**, rich in proteoglycan ground substance, can be seen in the outer circumferential lamellae and defining the outer limits of each Haversian system.

Osteocytes **Oc** have dark staining nuclei and lie in lacunae from which canaliculi radiate (not seen in this preparation but see Fig. 10.10b). Fine cytoplasmic processes of osteocytes occupy the canaliculi and communicate with those of adjacent osteocytes. Unlike the chondrocytes of cartilage, osteocytes and their processes do not usually completely occupy the lacunae and canaliculi but are surrounded by a narrow space filled with fluid.

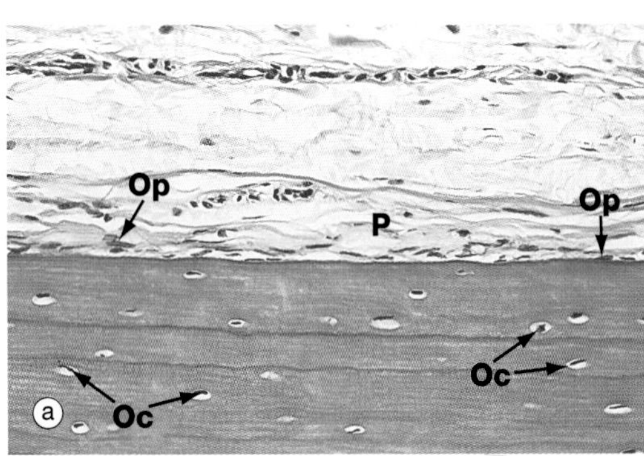

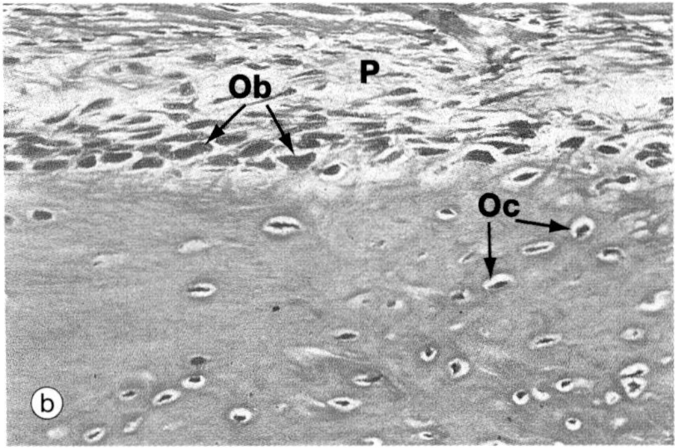

Fig. 10.12 Periosteum
(a) Inactive: H & E ×128 (b) Active: H & E ×200

The outer surface of most bone is covered by a layer of condensed fibrous tissue, the periosteum **P** which contains cells capable of converting into osteoprogenitor cells and osteoblasts. When no new bone is being formed on the bone surface, these cells are insignificant flattened cells with spindle-shaped nuclei, but when there is active new bone formation at the periosteal surface, these cells proliferate and increase in size to become osteoblasts. Micrograph (a) shows an inactive periosteum, with barely detectable inactive osteoprogenitor cells **Op** and mature formed bone containing established osteocytes **Oc**. Micrograph (b) shows active periosteum with new bone being formed by active periosteal osteoblasts **Ob** some of which are being incorporated into newly formed bone to become osteocytes **Oc**.

AC articular cartilage **C** cortical bone **FM** fatty marrow **H** Haversian systems **HM** haemopoietic marrow **I** interstitial lamellae **L** cement lines **Ob** osteoblasts **Oc** osteocytes **OCL** outer circumferential lamellae **Op** osteoprogenitor cells **P** periosteum **T** trabecular bone **V** blood sinusoids

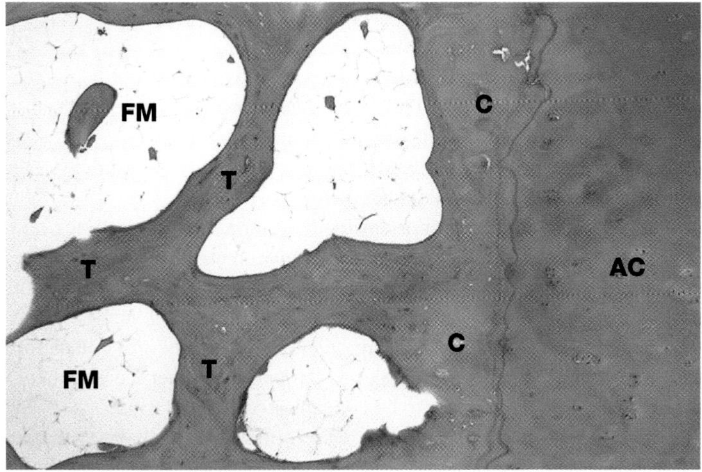

Fig. 10.13 Bone – cortex and trabecular
H & E ×50

This micrograph from the head of the femur shows the origin of the trabecular (cancellous) bone **T** from the compact cortical bone **C**. As this end of the bone forms part of a synovial joint (see Fig. 10.25), the outer cortical plate is articular hyaline cartilage **AC**. On the shaft of this long bone, the outer layer would be fibrous periosteum. Note the marrow spaces **FM** filled with adipose tissue ('fatty' or 'yellow' marrow).

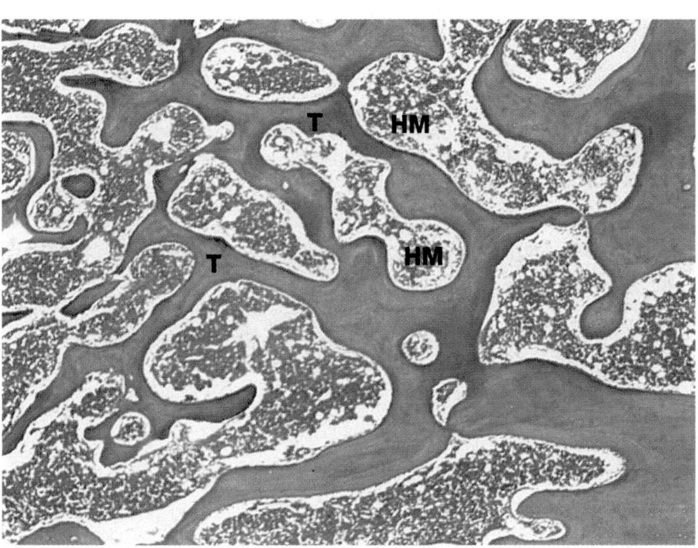

Fig. 10.14 Bone – trabecular
H & E ×50

The trabecular (cancellous) bone is a network of interconnecting struts orientated in a position to provide the maximum strength for the minimum mass. They are composed of lamellar bone with scanty lacunae containing osteocytes. These exchange metabolites via canaliculi which communicate with each other and with blood sinusoids in the haemopoietic (red) marrow spaces **HM**. The trabeculae **T** have a thin external coating of endosteum containing flat inactive osteoblasts.

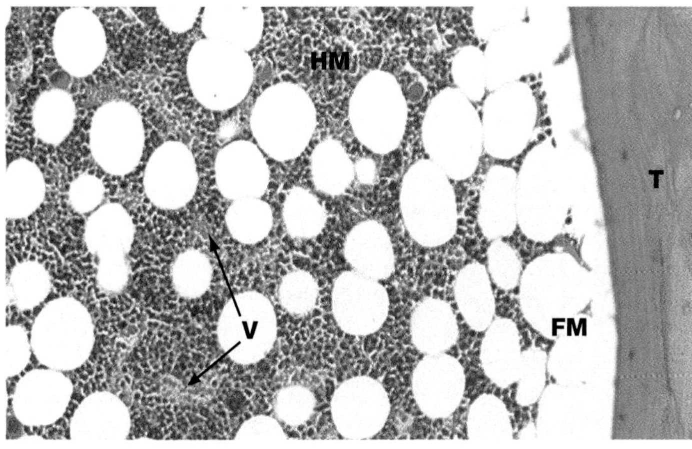

Fig. 10.15 Bone – marrow
H & E ×200

This micrograph shows part of a bone trabeculum **T** of lamellar bone and the marrow space. In this micrograph, as in Fig. 10.14, the marrow space contains a mixture of fatty marrow **FM** composed of adipose tissue, and haemopoietic ('red') marrow **HM** composed of red and white blood cell precursors in intimate contact with numerous thin-walled blood vessels (sinusoids) **V**.

Bone matrix and mineralisation

Mature compact bone is made up of about 70% inorganic salts and 30% organic matrix by weight. Collagen makes up over 90% of the organic component, the remainder being ground substance proteoglycans and a group of non-collagen molecules which appear to be involved in regulation of bone mineralisation.

The collagen of bone is almost exclusively in the form of type I fibres. Spaces within this three-dimensional structure, often referred to as ***hole zones***, are the initial site of mineral deposition.

Ground substance proteoglycans contribute a much smaller proportion of the matrix than in cartilage and mainly consist of chondroitin sulphate and hyaluronic acid in the form of proteoglycan aggregates. As well as controlling the water content of bones, ground substance is probably involved in regulating formation of collagen fibres in a form appropriate for subsequent matrix mineralisation. The remaining non-collagen organic material includes ***osteocalcin*** (***Gla protein***), involved in binding calcium during the mineralisation process, ***osteonectin*** which may serve some bridging function between collagen and the mineral component, ***sialoproteins*** (rich in sialic acid) and certain proteins which appear to be concentrated from plasma.

The mineral component of bone mainly consists of calcium and phosphate in the form of hydroxyapatite crystals. These are conjugated to a small proportion of magnesium carbonate, sodium and potassium ions but also have affinity for heavy metal and radioactive environmental pollutants.

Collagen and the other organic matrix constituents are synthesised by the rough endoplasmic reticulum of osteoblasts, packaged by the Golgi apparatus and secreted from the cell surface resulting in the production of osteoid. After a maturation phase lasting several days, amorphous (non-crystalline) calcium phosphate salts begin to precipitate in the hole zones of the collagen. These mineralisation foci expand and coalesce into hydroxyapatite crystals by further remodelling. Nevertheless, 20% or more of the mineral component remains in the amorphous form providing a readily available buffer in whole body calcium homeostasis.

The concentration of calcium and phosphate ions in bony extracellular fluid is greater than required for spontaneous deposition of calcium salts, and a variety of inhibitors including ***pyrophosphate*** play a crucial role in controlling bone mineralisation. The deposition of calcium appears to be associated with membrane-bound vesicles derived from osteoblast plasma membrane called ***matrix vesicles***; these contain ***alkaline phosphatase*** and other phosphatases which may play a role in neutralising the inhibitory effect of pyrophosphate.

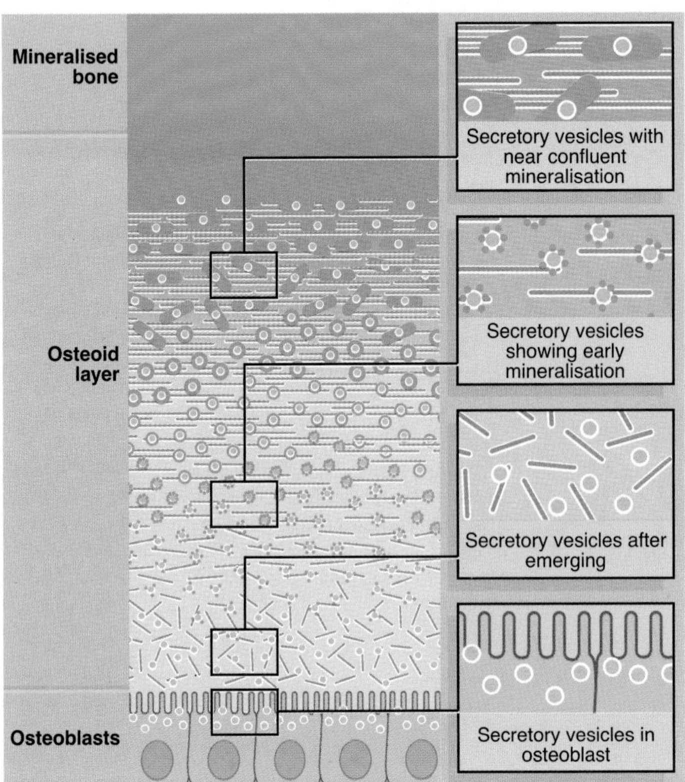

Fig. 10.16 Mineralisation of bone

This diagram shows the events believed to occur in the mineralisation of osteoid to form mineralised bone. The active cuboidal osteoblasts secrete osteoid collagen (red) but also matrix vesicles (yellow). The matrix vesicles are the focus for deposition of hydroxyapatite crystals (green), the first step in mineralisation. Continued accretion of mineral on these early foci leads eventually to confluent mineralisation of the osteoid collagen and supporting glycosaminoglycan matrix.

The matrix vesicles are rich in the enzymes alkaline phosphatase and pyrophosphatase which can both produce phosphate ions from a range of molecules. The phosphate ions accumulate in the matrix vesicles with calcium ions and form the raw material for the production of hydroxyapatite.

Osteomalacia

Osteomalacia is a disease which results from failure of normal mineralisation of newly formed osteoid. Successful and speedy mineralisation requires the presence of adequate concentrations of calcium and phosphate ions. If there is a deficiency of calcium ions, mineralisation of osteoid cannot take place and osteomalacia develops; such a calcium deficiency may be the result of inadequate dietary intake (for example, in some vegans) or malabsorption due to disease of the small intestine. Osteomalacia due to phosphate deficiency is less common, and is usually the result of kidney disease leading to uncontrolled loss of phosphate ions in the urine. Severe osteomalacia produces bone trabeculae which are only mineralised at their centre, the bulk being soft non-rigid osteoid. The bone is soft and prone to fracture.

Bone development and growth

The fetal development of bone occurs in two ways, both of which involve replacement of primitive collagenous supporting tissue by bone. The resulting woven bone is then extensively remodelled by resorption and appositional growth to form the mature adult skeleton, which is made up of lamellar bone. Thereafter, resorption and deposition of bone occur at a much reduced rate to accommodate changing functional stresses and to effect calcium homeostasis. The long bones, vertebrae, pelvis and bones of the base of the skull are preceded by the formation of a continuously growing cartilage model which is progressively replaced by bone; this process is called ***endochondral ossification*** and the bones so formed are called ***cartilage bones***. In contrast, the bones of the vault of the skull, the maxilla and most of the mandible are formed by the deposition of bone within primitive mesenchymal tissue; this process of direct replacement of mesenchyme by bone is known as ***intramembranous ossification*** and the bones so formed are called ***membrane bones***. Bone development is controlled by growth hormone, thyroid hormone and the sex hormones.

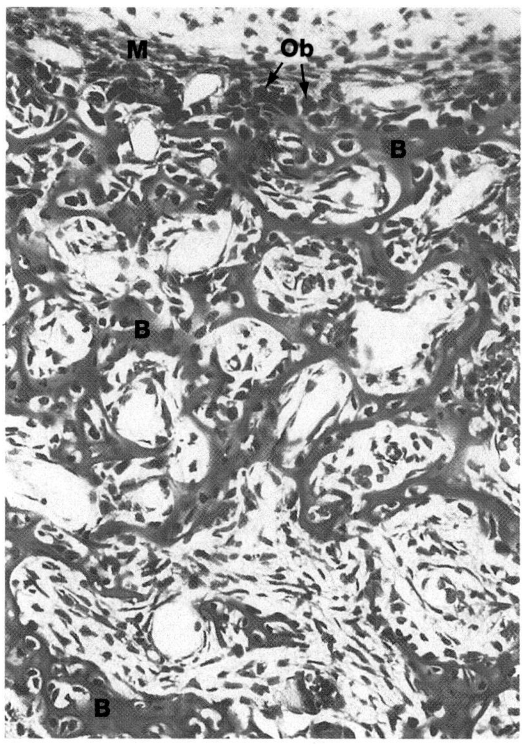

Fig. 10.17 Intramembranous ossification
H & E ×75

Intramembranous bone formation occurs within 'membranes' of condensed, primitive mesenchymal tissue. Mesenchymal cells differentiate into osteoblasts **Ob** which begin synthesis and secretion of osteoid at multiple ***centres of ossification***; mineralisation of osteoid follows closely. As osteoid is laid down, osteoblasts are trapped in lacunae to become osteocytes and their fine cytoplasmic extensions shrink to form the fine processes contained within the canaliculi. Osteoprogenitor cells at the surface of the centres of ossification undergo mitotic division to produce further osteoblasts which lay down more bone. Progressive bone formation results in the fusion of adjacent ossification centres to form bone which is spongy in gross appearance.

The collagen fibres of developing bone are randomly arranged in interlacing bundles, giving rise to the term woven bone. The woven bone then undergoes progressive remodelling into lamellar bone by osteoclastic resorption and osteoblastic deposition to form mature compact or trabecular bone. The primitive mesenchyme remaining in the network of developing bone differentiates into bone marrow.

This preparation from the developing skull vault of a cat fetus illustrates spicules of woven bone **B**, separated by primitive mesenchymal tissue. Note the condensed primitive mesenchyme **M** which delineates the outer margin of the developing bone eventually to become the periosteum.

B woven bone **M** primitive mesenchyme **Ob** osteoblast

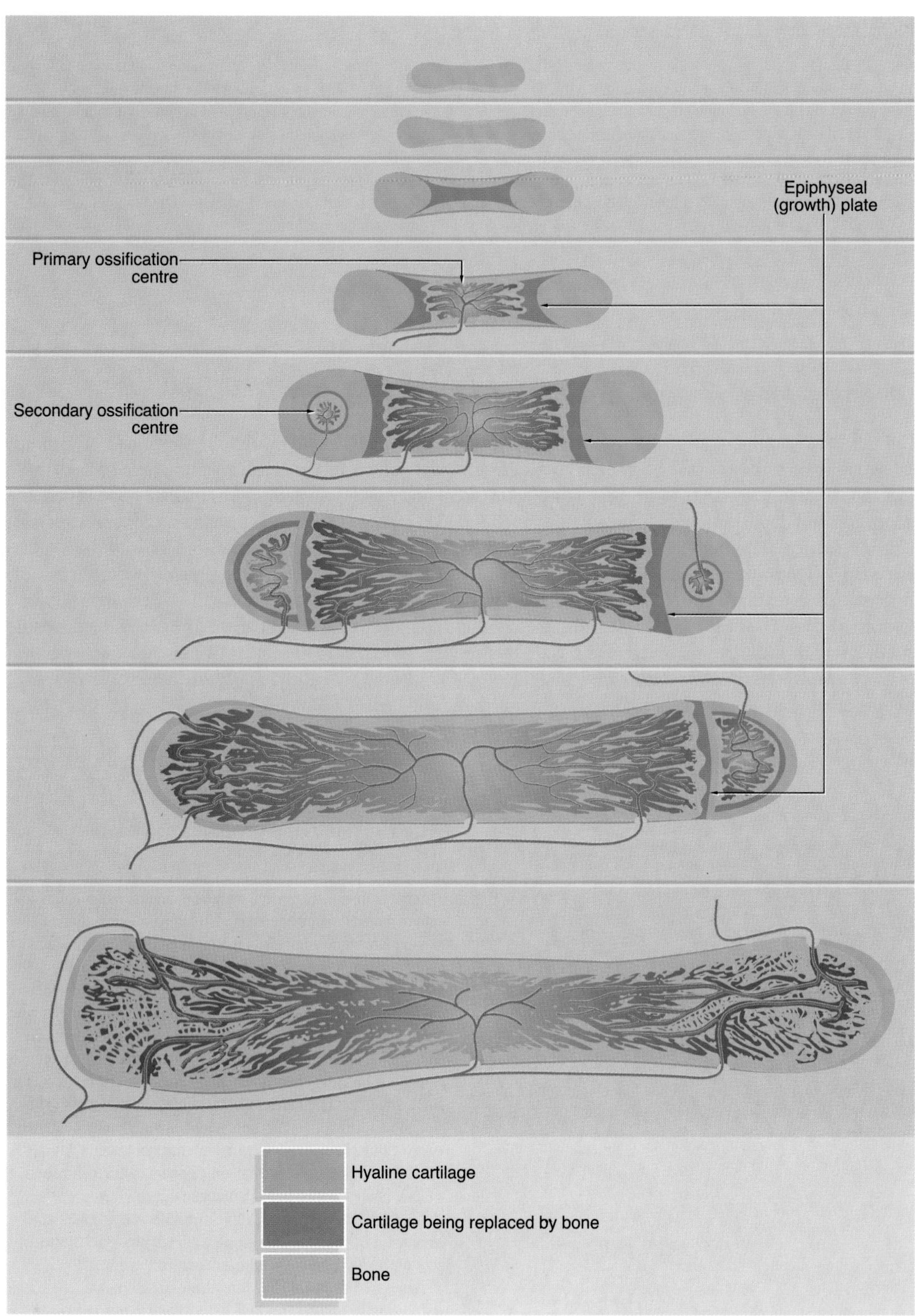
Epiphyseal
(growth) plate
Primary ossification
centre
Secondary ossification
centre
Hyaline cartilage
Cartilage being replaced by bone
Bone

Fig. 10.18 Endochondral ossification *(illustration opposite)*

Endochondral ossification is a method of bone formation that permits functional stresses to be sustained during skeletal growth. It is well demonstrated in the development of the long bones.

A small model of the long bone is first formed in solid hyaline cartilage. This undergoes mainly appositional growth to form an elongated, dumb-bell shaped mass of cartilage consisting of a shaft (diaphysis) and future articular portions (epiphyses) surrounded by perichondrium.

Within the shaft of the cartilage model the chondrocytes enlarge greatly, resorbing the surrounding cartilage so as to leave only slender perforated trabeculae of cartilage matrix. This cartilage matrix then becomes calcified and the chondrocytes degenerate leaving large, interconnecting spaces. During this period, the perichondrium of the shaft develops osteogenic potential and assumes the role of periosteum. The periosteum then lays down a thin layer of bone around the surface of the shaft. At the same time, primitive mesenchymal cells and blood vessels invade the spaces left within the shaft after degeneration of the chondrocytes. The primitive mesenchymal cells differentiate into osteoblasts and blood-forming cells of the bone marrow. The osteoblasts form a layer of cells on the surface of the calcified remnants of the cartilage matrix and commence the formation of irregular, woven bone.

The ends of the original cartilage model have by now become separated by a large site of ***primary ossification*** in the shaft. The cartilaginous ends of the model, however, continue to grow in diameter. Meanwhile, the cartilage at the ends of the shaft continues to undergo regressive changes followed by ossification so that the developing bone now consists of an elongated, bony diaphysial shaft with a semilunar cartilage epiphysis at each end. The interface between the shaft and each epiphysis constitutes a ***growth*** or ***epiphysial plate***. Within the growth plate, the cartilage proliferates continuously, resulting in progressive elongation of the bone. At the diaphysial aspect of each growth plate, the chondrocytes mature and then die, the degenerating zone of cartilage being replaced by bone. Thus the bony diaphysis lengthens and the growth plates are pushed further and further apart. On reaching maturity, hormonal changes inhibit further cartilage proliferation and the growth plates are replaced by bone, causing fusion of the diaphysis and epiphyses.

In the meantime, in the centre of the mass of cartilage of each developing epiphysis, regressive changes and bone formation similar to that in the diaphysial cartilage occur along with appositional growth of cartilage over the whole external surface of the epiphysis. This conversion of central epiphysial cartilage to bone is known as ***secondary ossification***. A thin zone of hyaline cartilage always remains at the surface as the articular cartilage.

Under the influence of functional stresses, the calcified cartilage remnants and the surrounding irregular woven bone are completely remodelled so that the bone ultimately consists of a compact outer layer with a medulla of cancellous bone.

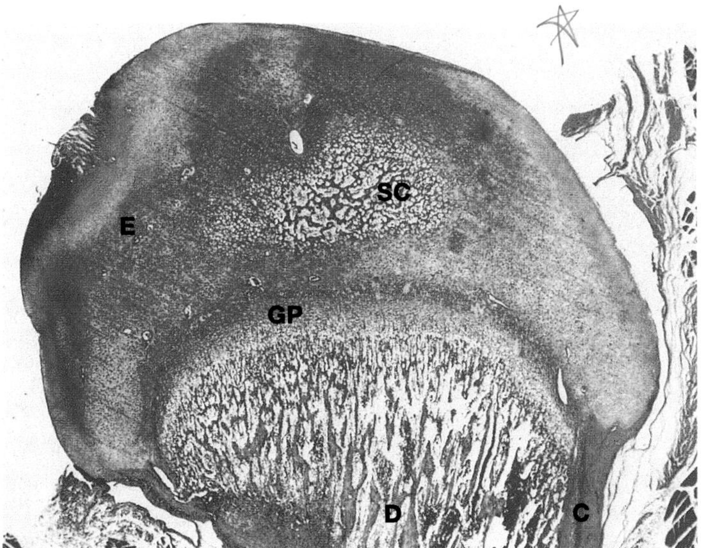

Fig. 10.19 Epiphysis
H & E/Alcian blue ×12

This micrograph illustrates the head of a kitten femur at an advanced stage of development.

The cartilaginous epiphysis **E** is separated from the diaphysis **D** by the epiphysial growth plate **GP**. Note the thickening cortical bone **C** at the outer aspect of the diaphysis and the trabeculae of bone in the medulla. Note also the centre of secondary ossification **SC** in the epiphysial cartilage.

Epiphysial growth plates provide for growth in length of long bones while accommodating functional stresses in the growing skeleton. The next three micrographs focus, at higher magnification, on particular areas of the epiphysial plate.

C compact cortical bone **D** diaphysis **E** epiphysis **GP** epiphysial growth plate
SC secondary ossification centre

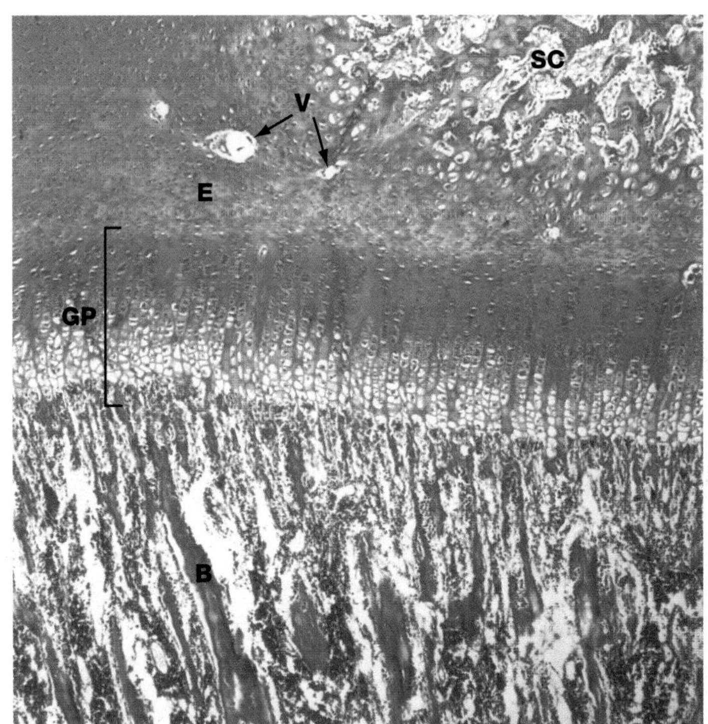

Fig. 10.20 Epiphysial growth plate
H & E/Alcian blue ×40

At higher magnification, the epiphysial growth plate **GP** shows a progression of morphological changes between the epiphysial cartilage **E** and the newly forming bone **B** of the diaphysis. Similar, but less stratified, morphological changes are seen between the epiphysial cartilage and the centre of secondary ossification **SC** within the epiphysis although this does not represent a growth plate. The Alcian blue counter-stain has been employed as it has particular affinity for the ground substance of cartilage. Note blood vessels **V**, cut in transverse section, passing into the secondary ossification centre via cartilage canals.

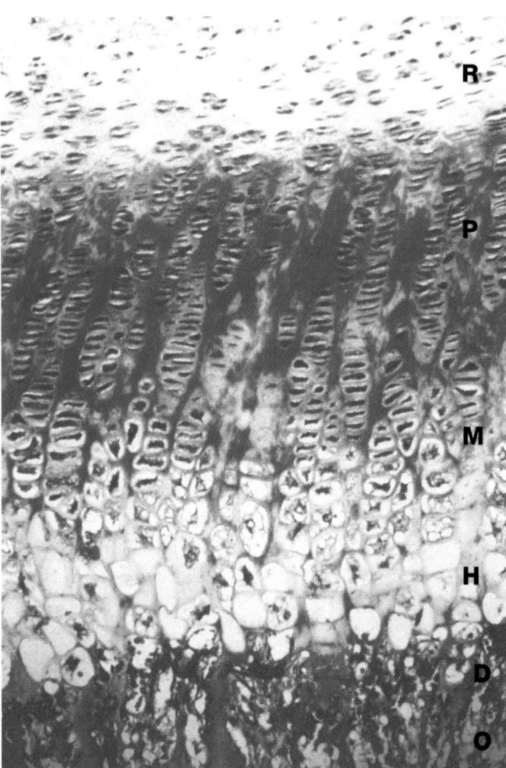

Fig. 10.21 Epiphysial growth plate
H & E/Alcian blue ×120

The dynamic process of endochondral ossification is summarised in this micrograph of the epiphysial growth plate at high magnification. The transition between epiphysial cartilage and new bone occurs in six functional and morphological stages:

- **Zone of reserve cartilage R:** this consists of typical hyaline cartilage (see Fig. 10.1) with the chondrocytes arranged in small clusters surrounded by a large amount of moderately stained matrix.
- **Zone of proliferation P:** the clusters of cartilage cells undergo successive mitotic divisions to form columns of chondrocytes separated by strongly stained matrix rich in proteoglycans.
- **Zone of maturation M:** cell division has ceased and the chondrocytes increase in size.
- **Zone of hypertrophy and calcification H:** the chondrocytes become greatly enlarged and vacuolated and the matrix becomes calcified.
- **Zone of cartilage degeneration D:** the chondrocytes degenerate and the lacunae of the calcified matrix are invaded by osteogenic cells and capillaries from the marrow cavity of the diaphysis.
- **Osteogenic zone O:** the osteogenic cells differentiate into osteoblasts which congregate on the surface of the spicules of calcified cartilage matrix where they commence bone formation. This transitional zone is known as the ***metaphysis***.

Fig. 10.22 Endochondral ossification – metaphysis
H & E/Alcian blue ×198

The metaphysis is the name given to the area where the shaft of a long bone joins the epiphyseal growth plate. Here the blue-stained spicules of calcified cartilage matrix are surrounded by active osteoblasts **Ob** and newly formed woven bone, stained pink. Further growth of metaphyseal woven bone is followed by extensive remodelling to produce mature trabecular bone.

At physical maturity, endochondral ossification ceases, and the diaphysis fuses with the epiphysis, obliterating the growth plates. From this point, no further endochondral ossification or bone lengthening are possible. Although bones grow in length by endochondral ossification, growth in diameter of the shaft occurs by appositional growth at the periosteal surface and complementary osteoclastic resorption at the endosteal (medullary) aspect. Note that the marrow spaces between the developing trabeculae are already populated by numerous small haemopoietic cells (red marrow).

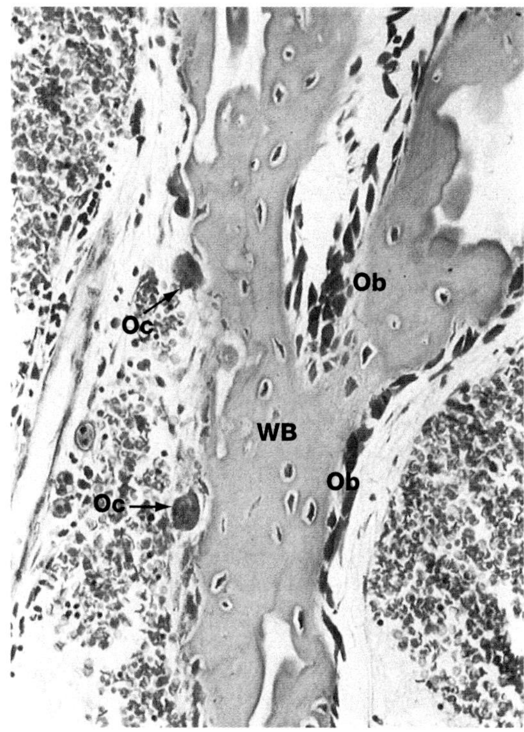

Fig. 10.23 Bone remodelling and repair
H & E ×480

This micrograph illustrates an irregular spicule of woven bone **WB** from a fetus. Some of the surfaces of the spicule exhibit osteoblastic proliferation and activity **Ob** whereas other surfaces are in the process of being resorbed by osteoclasts **Oc**.

Woven bone is not only the first type of bone to be formed during skeletal development but is also the first bone to be laid down during the repair of a fracture. At the fracture site, a blood clot initially forms, later being replaced by highly vascular collagenous tissue (***granulation tissue***) which becomes progressively more fibrous. Mesenchymal cells then differentiate into chondroblasts and progressively replace this ***fibrous granulation tissue*** with hyaline cartilage. This firm but still flexible bridge is known as the ***provisional callus***. The provisional callus is then strengthened by deposition of calcium salts within the cartilage matrix. Meanwhile, osteoprogenitor cells in the endosteum and periosteum are activated and lay down a meshwork of woven bone within and around the provisional callus; the provisional callus thus becomes transformed into the ***bony callus***. ***Bony union*** is achieved when the fracture site is completely bridged by woven bone. Under the influence of functional stresses, the bony callus is then slowly remodelled to form mature lamellar bone.

B bone **D** cartilage degeneration **E** epiphyseal cartilage **GP** epiphysial growth plate
H hypertrophy zone **M** maturation zone **O** osteogenic zone **Ob** osteoblast **Oc** osteoclast
P proliferative zone **R** reserve cartilage zone **SC** secondary ossification centre **V** blood vessels
WB woven bone

Joints

Joints may be classified into two main functional groups, ***synovial*** and ***non-synovial***, both of which may show wide morphological variations.

Synovial joints

In this type of joint there is extensive movement of the bones upon one another at the articular surfaces. The articular surfaces are maintained in apposition by a fibrous capsule and ligaments, and the surfaces are lubricated by ***synovial fluid***. Synovial joints are known as ***diarthroses***. In some diarthroses such as the temporomandibular and knee joints, plates of fibrocartilage may be completely or partially interposed between the articular surfaces but remain unattached to the articular surfaces.

Non-synovial joints

These joints have limited movement, the articulating bones having no free articular surfaces, instead being joined by dense collagenous tissue. This may be of three types:

- **Dense fibrous tissue.** This forms the sutures between the bones of the skull and permits moulding of the fetal skull during its passage through the birth canal. The sutures are progressively replaced by bone with advancing age. Such fibrous tissue joints are called ***syndesmoses***, and when replaced by bone are called ***synostoses***.
- **Hyaline cartilage.** This type of joint, called a ***synchondrosis*** or ***primary cartilaginous joint***, unites the first rib with the sternum and is the only synchondrosis found in the human adult.
- **Fibrocartilage.** The opposing surfaces of some bones are covered by hyaline cartilage but, instead of a synovial space, are directly connected to each other by a plate of fibrocartilage. Such fibrocartilaginous joints are called ***symphyses*** or ***secondary cartilaginous joints*** and occur in the pubic symphysis and at the intervertebral discs. The fibrocartilage disc of the pubic symphysis develops a central cavity and the intervertebral discs have a fluid-filled central cavity.

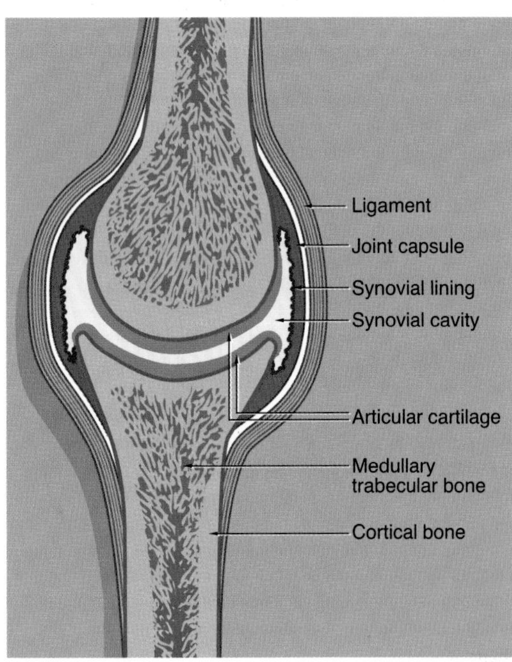

Fig. 10.24 Typical synovial joint

In synovial joints the articulating bone surfaces are covered by a thick layer of hyaline cartilage (***articular cartilage***) which has smooth low-friction surfaces and also offers a degree of resistance to compressive forces, hence can act as shock-absorbers in weight-bearing joints. The joint is enclosed within a fibrocollagenous joint capsule, which is lined internally by a specialised secretory cell layer, the ***synovium***, which secretes a small amount of lubricant fluid into the synovial cavity, aiding the smooth articulation of the cartilage-covered bone surfaces. Excessive movement at the joint is limited by the fibrous joint capsule, and by external fibro-elastic ligaments, which prevent over-flexion and over-extension.

In some joints such as the knee there are internal ligaments (the ***cruciate ligaments***), which prevent excessive joint movement, particularly excessive twisting rotation.

Muscles attach to bones via tendinous attachments (see Fig. 10.33) and these may also play a role in stabilising synovial joints.

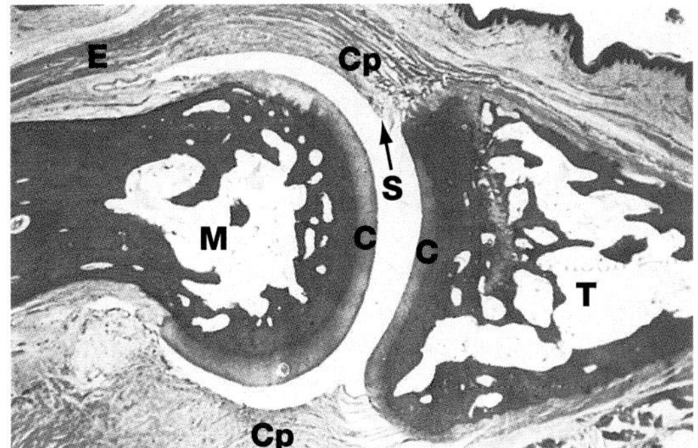

Fig. 10.25 Synovial joint (monkey)
H & E ×12

This micrograph illustrates a typical synovial joint, in this case the distal interphalangeal joint of the finger. The articular surfaces of the terminal phalanx **T** and the middle phalanx **M** are covered by hyaline cartilage **C**. The joint space is artefactually widened. In vivo, the articular surfaces are maintained in close contact by a fibrous capsule **Cp** which is inserted into the articulating bones at some distance beyond the articular cartilages. The ***synovium*** **S** is a specialised layer of collagenous tissue which lines the inner aspect of the capsule. Note the extensor tendon **E** which inserts into the base of terminal phalanx.

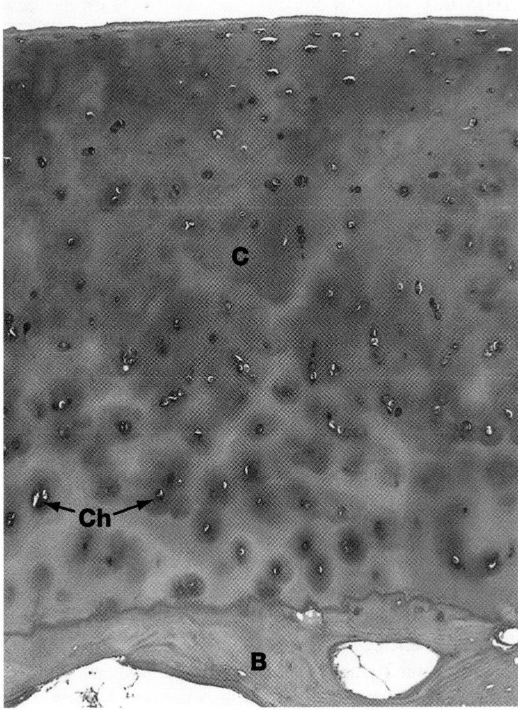

Fig. 10.26 Articular cartilage
H & E ×35

This photomicrograph shows the articular cartilage on the surface of the head of the femur from a young adult. It is composed of hyaline cartilage **C** and is attached to the cortical bone **B** of the head of the femur. The bluish colour of the cartilage on H & E staining is due to the presence of glycosaminoglycans in the matrix; it is these, together with the collagen of the matrix, which provides the resistance to compression, which is such an important property of hyaline cartilage. Both the glycosaminoglycans and collagen are synthesised and maintained by the chondrocytes **Ch** (see Fig. 10.1).

In this young person the articular cartilage layer is thick and healthy; in older people the cartilage near the surface undergoes degenerative changes as a result of wear and tear, eventually leading to arthritis (see below).

Diseases of synovial joints (arthritis)

Osteoarthritis is a degenerative disease of synovial joints due to excessive wear and tear leading initially to degenerative change in the articular cartilages of both opposing bone ends which participate in the joint. Eventually the cartilage is eroded completely, and the cortical bone of one bone end is in frictional contact with the cortical bone of the opposing bone. Both areas of cortical bone undergo refashioning to become thick layers with hard surfaces (eburnation), and continued use of the joint may produce tiny eroded bone fragments which float in the fluid of the joint cavity and eventually become deposited in the synovium of the joint capsule.

Rheumatoid arthritis is a destructive disease of synovial joints in which the synovium lining the joint capsule becomes thickened and heavily infiltrated with lymphocytes and plasma cells, and the articular cartilage is destroyed and replaced by fibrovascular tissue (pannus).

There are many other causes of arthritis, including ***bacterial infection*** and deposition of urate crystals (***gout***).

B cortical bone **C** hyaline cartilage **Ch** chondrocytes **Cp** fibrous joint capsule **E** extensor tendon **M** middle phalanx **S** synovium **T** terminal phalanx

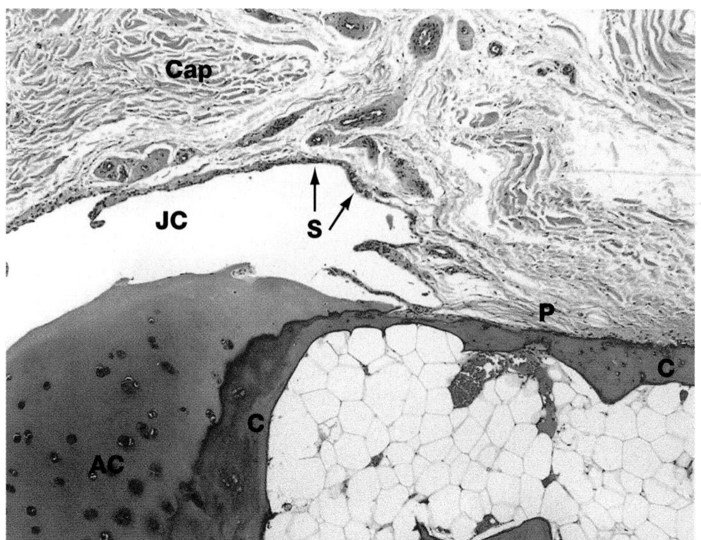

Fig. 10.27 Joint capsule and synovium
H & E ×24

This photomicrograph shows the relationship between the articular surfaces of bone and the joint capsule. The bone end is cortical bone **C** covered by articular cartilage **AC** protruding into the joint cavity **JC**. The cavity is contained by a dense collagenous fibrous capsule **Cap** lined internally by a layer of synovium **S** which secretes the serous fluid which lubricates the articulation of the joint.

The collagen fibres of the joint capsule merge with those of the periosteum **P** over the shaft of the bone.

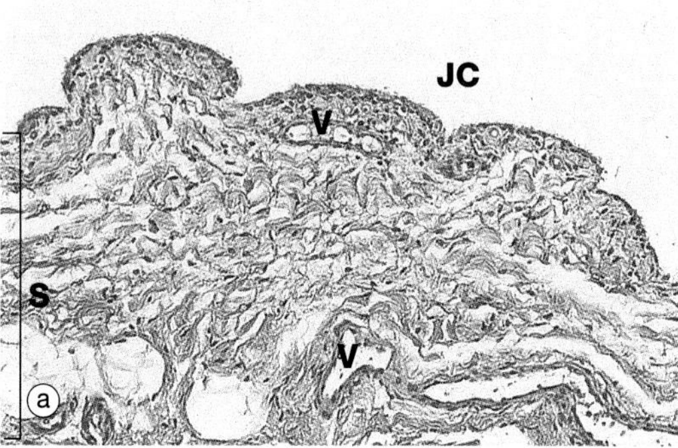

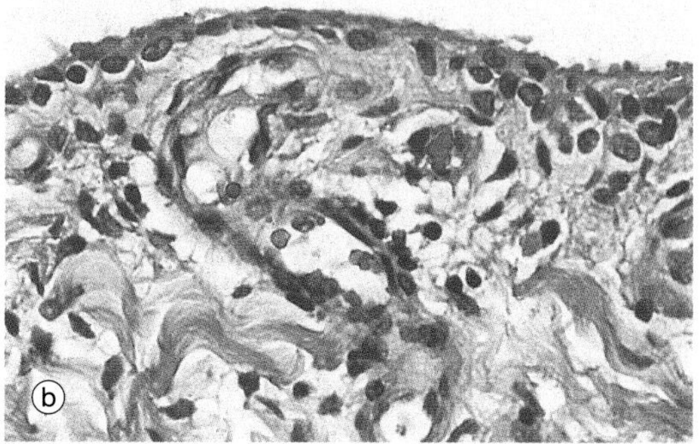

Fig. 10.28 Synovium
(a) H & E ×100 (b) H & E ×400

The inner surface of the capsule of synovial joints and tendon sheaths is lined by a specialised collagenous tissue, the synovium, which is responsible for the elaboration of the synovial fluid that lubricates the movement of articular surfaces. Depending on the location, the bulk of the synovial tissue may be of loose collagenous type (***areolar synovium***), of more dense collagenous type (***fibrous synovium***) or predominantly composed of fat (***adipose synovium***) as in the case of intra-articular fat pads.

As seen in micrograph (a), the surface of the synovium **S** is thrown up into folds and small villi which may extend for some distance into the joint cavity **JC**. The synovial tissue contains numerous blood vessels **V**, lymphatics and nerves.

As seen in micrograph (b), the free surface of the synovium is characterised by a discontinuous layer of cells up to four cells deep. These ***synovial cells*** are not connected by junctional complexes and do not rest on a basement membrane, and the synovial surface therefore does not constitute an epithelium. The synovial cells are of mesenchymal origin. The majority are plump with an extensive Golgi complex and numerous lysosomes, features suggestive of macrophages (***type A synoviocytes***). The remainder have profuse rough endoplasmic reticulum and represent fibroblasts (***type B synoviocytes***). Also in this micrograph, note the rich network of capillaries and the thick strands of collagen which would define this as fibrous synovium.

In the normal joint, the synovial fluid is little more than a thin film covering the articular surfaces. In that the articular space is not demarcated from the synovium by an epithelium, the synovial fluid represents a highly specialised fluid form of synovial extracellular matrix rather than a secretion in the usual sense. Its major constituents are hyaluronic acid and associated glycoproteins secreted by the type B synoviocytes and its fluid component is a transudate from synovial capillaries. This arrangement facilitates the continuous exchange of oxygen, carbon dioxide and metabolites between blood and synovial fluid which is the major source of metabolic support for articular cartilage. Normal synovial fluid also contains a small number of leucocytes (less than 100/mL), predominantly monocytes.

AC articular cartilage **AF** annulus fibrosus **B** vertebral body **C** compact cortical bone **Cap** joint capsule **JC** joint cavity **NP** nucleus pulposus **P** periosteum **S** synovium **V** blood vessels

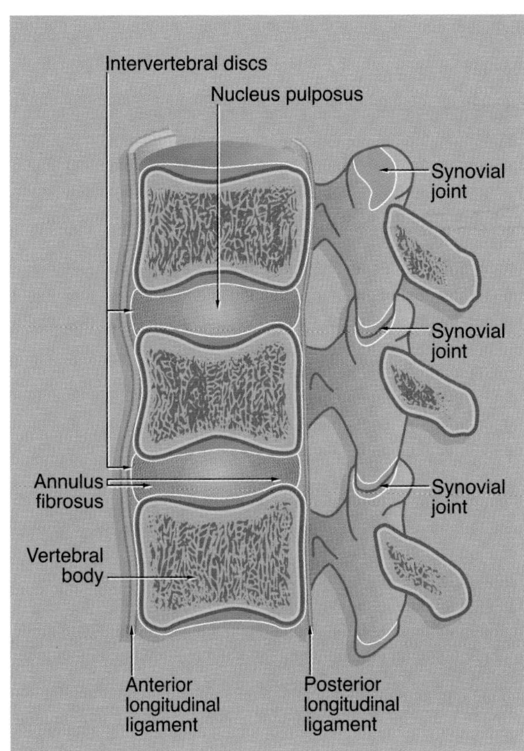

Fig. 10.29 The intervertebral joints

The vertebrae articulate by means of two different types of joints:

- The vertebral bodies are united by symphysial joints, the ***intervertebral discs***, which permit movement between the vertebral bodies while maintaining a union of great strength. The fibrocartilage of each intervertebral disc is arranged in concentric rings forming the ***annulus fibrosus***. Within the disc, there is a central cavity containing a viscous fluid, the ***nucleus pulposus***, which acts as a shock absorber. The annulus fibrosus is reinforced peripherally by circumferential ligaments. A thick ligament extending down the anterior aspect of the spinal column merges with and further reinforces the annulus fibrosus and a similar, but thinner, ligament reinforces the posterior aspect.
- The vertebral arches articulate with each other by pairs of synovial joints known as ***facet*** or ***zygapophyseal joints***. Strong elastic ligaments connecting the bony processes of the vertebral arches contribute to the stability of the spinal column.

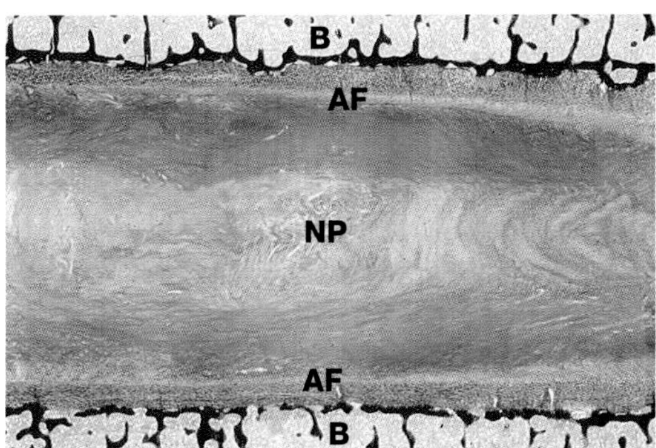

Fig. 10.30 Intervertebral disc
Haematoxylin von Kossa ×4

The intervertebral disc lies between the surfaces of adjacent vertebral bodies **B**, and acts as a shock absorber. It is composed of an outer compact region of dense fibrocollagenous tissue containing occasional chondrocytes, the ***annulus fibrosus*** **AF**, with a variable thin layer of hyaline cartilage between it and the bone. The annulus fibrosus surrounds a central area of semi-fluid gelatinous matrix, the ***nucleus pulposus*** **NP**.

Disc degeneration and prolapse

The intervertebral discs act as shock absorbers, supporting and springing the vertebral column. In bipeds (like humans) they are particularly vulnerable to damage because of the weight they have to support and the rotational and flexional/extensional forces they are subjected to in daily human activities. These can lead to weakening of the annulus fibrosus which may give way, allowing the soft central nucleus pulposus to extrude (***disc prolapse***) through into the spaces beneath the ligaments (see Fig. 10.29) and elsewhere. This leads to soft tissue swelling around the protrusion, and this may involve the spinal nerves emerging from the spinal column. Nerve damage may produce severe pain symptoms in the leg (e.g. ***sciatica***).

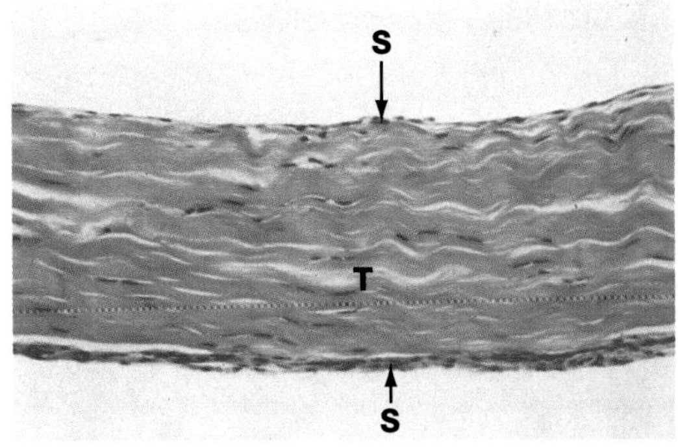

Fig. 10.31 Tendon
H & E ×128

Tendons are tough flexible straps or cords which connect muscles to bone. They are composed of compact linear collagen fibres with the compressed nuclei of inactive fibroblasts (tenocytes) between the collagen bundles. Tendon **T** is poorly vascularised and heals slowly when damaged, and also contains tiny nerve fibres and tendon stretch receptors. Some tendons have a thin outer layer of synovium **S**; these tendons run for part of their course through a cylindrical fibrous sheath which is lined internally by synovium. The synovia secrete lubricatory fluid.

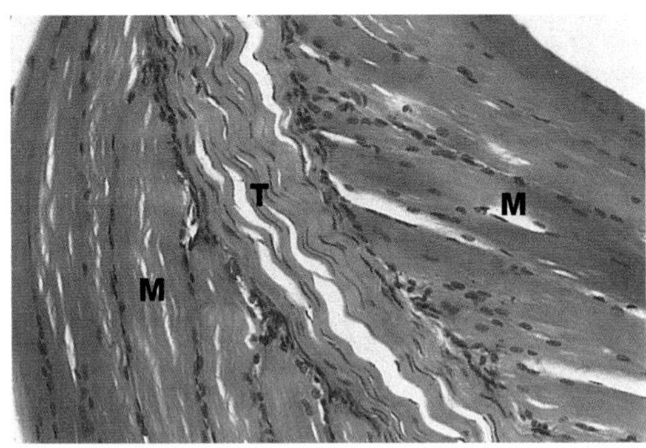

Fig. 10.32 Tendon/muscle interface
H & E ×128

This micrograph shows two masses of skeletal muscle **M** inserted into a common tendon **T**. Within the muscle close to the tendon, some of the muscle fibres show splitting of their ends, with some of the collagen fibres from the tendon that penetrate the muscle forming a complex interdigitation with the split muscle fibres (***myotendinous junction***), thus increasing the surface area for anchorage and thus the strength of the attachment.

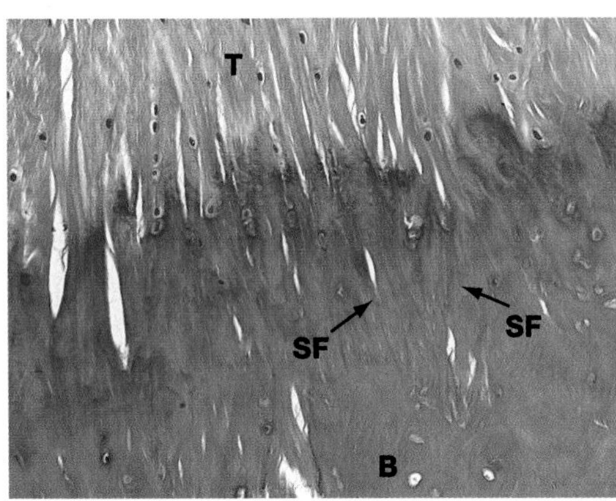

Fig. 10.33 Tendon insertion into bone
H & E ×280

Tendons sometimes attach to bone by the tendon collagen fibres intermingling with the collagen of the periosteum, a few of the fibres penetrating into the bone. At other sites the collagen fibres of the tendon **T** penetrate directly into the bone **B** in the form of Sharpey's fibres **SF**, as shown here.

Diseases of tendon

Tendons have to withstand enormous forces, particularly in athletes and people with strenuous occupations. The following are common:

- **Ruptured Achilles tendon** – the Achilles tendon connects the powerful muscles of the calf to the heel, and can be partially or completely torn across in strenuous movements of the foot, particularly acute dorsiflexion. Because tendon has a poor vascular supply, natural healing (replacing tendon with weaker fibrous scar) is slow and uncertain.
- **Tendonitis** – for example extensor tendonitis at the elbow ('tennis elbow'), particularly occurs where tendon fibres insert directly into bone (see Fig. 10.33). It produces pain, tenderness and sometimes swelling at the site of insertion, and is probably due to avulsion of the tendon fibres as they insert into bone.
- **Tenosynovitis** – occurs in long cylindrical tendons which run through tendon sheaths, for example the flexor and extensor tendons of the hands. The synovium of both tendon surface and sheath lining becomes thickened and rough (probably due to repeated frictional damage).

B bone **M** skeletal muscle **S** synovium **SF** Sharpey's fibres **T** tendon

11. *Immune system*

Introduction

All living tissues are subject to the constant threat of invasion by disease-producing foreign agents and micro-organisms (pathogens), i.e. bacteria, viruses, fungi, protozoa and multicellular parasites such as worms. These organisms may invade the body, multiply and destroy functional tissue causing illness and potentially death. Three main lines of defence have consequently evolved:

- Protective surface mechanisms.
- The innate immune system.
- The adaptive immune system.

Protective surface mechanisms

These provide the first line of defence and, while intact, provide excellent protection from many disease-causing organisms. However pathogens may enter the body via breaches in the skin or mucosal linings of the gut, respiratory and genitourinary tracts. The skin constitutes an impenetrable barrier to most microorganisms unless breached by injury such as abrasion or burning. The mucous surfaces of the body, such as the conjunctivae and oral cavity, are protected by a variety of antibacterial substances including the enzyme ***lysozyme***, which is secreted in tears and saliva. A layer of surface mucus that is continuously removed by ciliary action and replaced by goblet cells protects the respiratory tract. Maintenance of an acidic environment in the stomach, vagina and, to a lesser extent, the skin, inhibits the growth of pathogens in these sites. When such defences fail and an infection takes hold, the two other main types of defence mechanism are activated.

The innate immune system

The innate immune response provides a rapid reaction to infections and, characteristically, the same magnitude of response each time the same pathogen is encountered i.e. there is no learning in the innate system. The cells, proteins and peptides involved circulate in the blood of healthy individuals in sufficient amounts to overcome many trivial infections and to contain more serious infections until an adaptive immune response can develop. The cellular components include neutrophils, eosinophils, basophils, and macrophages, as well as tissue-resident cells such as histiocytes and mast cells. The proteins and peptides of the innate response include ***complement***, ***acute phase proteins*** and ***cytokines*** such as interferon. The end results of these various modes of defence include the release of molecules toxic to microorganisms, phagocytosis and intracellular killing of organisms or the action of ***natural killer cells*** to kill virus-infected or malignant cells. The innate immune response causes a pathological condition known as ***inflammation***, familiar to anyone who has ever had a cut finger. ***Acute inflammation*** is characterised by vascular changes, including dilatation and enhanced permeability of capillaries and increased blood flow, resulting in the production of a fibrin-rich ***inflammatory exudate***, thus bringing the proteins and cells required for early defences to the site of infection.

The adaptive immune system

The adaptive immune system is characterised by the ability to learn, so that second and subsequent encounters with a pathogen elicit a greater, more specific and faster response. This is the basis of life-long immunity to certain infections after an initial episode or vaccination. The adaptive system builds on and is intimately associated with the innate immune system. Adaptive immunity depends on cell division to produce large numbers of lymphocytes with specificity for a particular pathogen (or ***antigen***) and thus takes 3–5 days to develop a significant response. Lymphocytes are able to kill or disable pathogens either by a ***cellular response*** (***T lymphocytes*** or ***T cells***) or a ***humoral response (B lymphocytes*** or ***B cells***). Adaptive immunity increases the power and amplifies some of the mechanisms of the innate response. For instance, ***antibody*** produced by B lymphocytes coats bacteria (***opsonisation***) to facilitate phagocytosis by neutrophils and directly activates the complement cascade. The adaptive immune response is also controlled by the innate response, as T lymphocytes require the services of ***antigen presenting cells*** (***APCs***) such as macrophages and dendritic cells for activation.

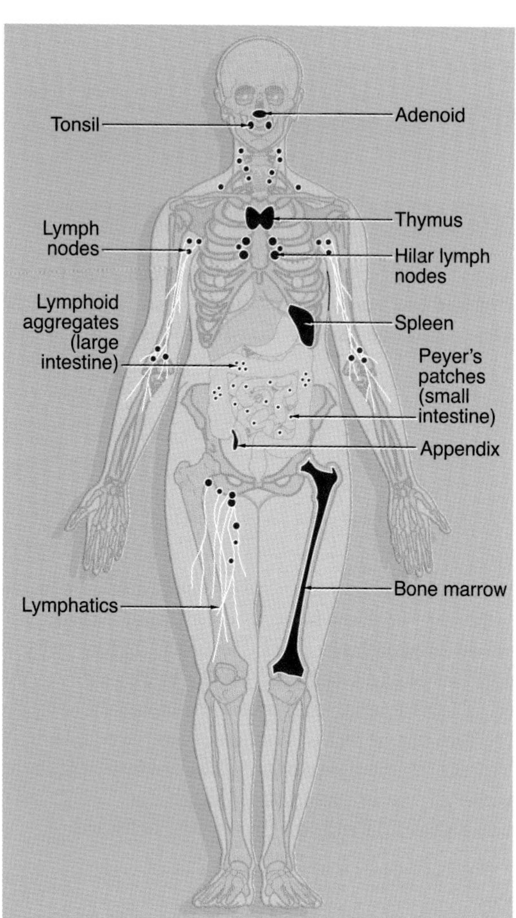

Fig. 11.1 The organs of the immune system

The components of both the innate and adaptive systems are found throughout the body. Both types of cells are produced in the bone marrow from haemopoietic stem cells (see Ch. 3). The cells of the innate immune system circulate in the blood and migrate quickly into damaged or infected tissues. As well as circulating in the blood, the cells of the adaptive immune system form specialised lymphoid tissues and also constitute a significant component of other tissues. The major lymphoid organs include:

- **The thymus**, situated in the anterior mediastinum, is the site of maturation of immature T lymphocytes.
- **The bone marrow** is not only the home of lymphocyte stem cells but is also the site of B lymphocyte maturation.
- **The lymph nodes**, found at the junctions of major lymphatic vessels, are the sites where both T and B lymphocytes may interact with antigen and antigen presenting cells (APC) from the circulating lymph and undergo activation and cell division.
- **The spleen**, found in the left upper quadrant of the abdomen, is the location where T and B lymphocytes may interact with blood-borne antigen and undergo stimulation and cell division.

Mucosal associated lymphoid tissue (***MALT***) includes the ***tonsils*** and ***adenoids*** in the oropharynx, ***Peyer's patches*** and ***lymphoid aggregates*** of the small and large intestines respectively and a diffuse population of lymphocytes and plasma cells in the mucosae of the gastrointestinal, respiratory and genitourinary tracts. These specialised lymphoid tissues respond to antigens entering the body through these mucosae.

The thymus and bone marrow, where immature lymphocytes acquire the receptors to recognise antigen, are known as ***primary lymphoid tissues***. The spleen, lymph nodes and organised lymphoid tissues of MALT where lymphocytes are activated in response to antigen are the ***secondary lymphoid tissues***.

Lymphocytes

Lymphocytes comprise some 20–50% of white cells in the circulation. Most circulating lymphocytes measure 6–9 μm (i.e. about the same size as erythrocytes) and are called ***small lymphocytes***. About 3% are ***large lymphocytes***, measuring 9–15 μm. The light and electron microscopic features of lymphocytes are described in Figure 3.8. Briefly, small lymphocytes have a round to ovoid nucleus occupying about 90% of the cell volume with a thin rim of basophilic (bluish) cytoplasm.

Lymphocytes constantly patrol the body, circulating in the blood, lymph and other extracellular fluids and pausing in the organised lymphoid tissues. Secondary lymphoid tissues are organised to optimise the chances of an antigen meeting a potentially reactive lymphocyte and facilitating activation. If an antigen binds to a lymphocyte surface receptor the lymphocyte will be activated and a specific response to that antigen is triggered. Obviously the immune response must be tightly controlled so as to be active when there is a potentially serious infection but not react against harmless components of everyday life such as food proteins or even against normal components of the body (***autoimmunity***).

The effectiveness of the adaptive immune system in recognising the huge range of pathogenic organisms found in nature depends upon the unique ability of lymphocytes to produce an equally huge range of antigen receptors i.e. ***surface immunoglobulin*** (***sIg***) for B cells and the ***T cell receptor*** (***TCR***) for T cells. The ability of antibody to bind to antigen is determined by the physico-chemical properties of the antibody. Put simply, the shape and electrical charge of the binding site of the antibody must be complementary to the antigen and the closer the fit of binding site to antigen, the stronger the bond formed and the more likelihood of the lymphocyte being stimulated. The TCR binds to antigen by similar reciprocity of shape and charge but it must also bind to the ***major histocompatibility complex*** (see Figs 11.2 and 11.3). During maturation of lymphocytes, alternate components of the antigen binding part of the antigen receptor genes are spliced together (rearranged) in a random fashion. Thus a huge range of possible antigen specificities are generated before the lymphocytes have a chance to meet external antigen.

The role of T lymphocytes

T cells have a number of effector and regulatory functions. Both T and B cells are derived from stem cells in the bone marrow. Immature T lymphocytes migrate from the bone marrow to the thymus where they develop into mature T lymphocytes. The process of maturation includes proliferation, rearrangement of TCR genes, and acquisition of the surface receptors and accessory molecules of the mature T cell (see Fig. 11.5). At this stage, T cells with the ability to react with 'self-antigens' (normal body components) are removed by apoptosis, creating a state of ***self-tolerance***. Mature T cells then populate the secondary lymphoid tissues and from there continuously recirculate via the bloodstream in the quest for antigen.

T lymphocytes are divided into several functional subsets known as ***T helper cells***, ***cytotoxic T cells*** and ***suppressor T cells***. These subsets can be identified in the laboratory by means of their surface receptors and accessory molecules (see Fig 11.5).

- **T helper cells (TH cells).** These T lymphocytes 'help' other cells to perform their effector functions by secreting a variety of mediators known as ***interleukins***. TH cells thus provide 'help' to B cells, cytotoxic T cells (see below) and macrophages.
- **Cytotoxic T cells (TC cells).** These lymphocytes are able to kill virus-infected and some cancer cells. They require interaction with TH cells to become activated and proliferate to form clones of effector cells.
- **Suppressor T cells (TS cells).** The existence of this functional subset is still controversial. These cells may suppress immune responsiveness to self-antigens and possibly switch off the response when antigen is removed.
- **Memory T cells** develop from activated T cells to provide a 'rapid reaction force' for a subsequent encounter with the same antigen.

The role of B lymphocytes

B lymphocytes are derived from precursors in the bone marrow and also mature there. Stimulated B cells mature into ***plasma cells*** that synthesise large amounts of antibody (***immunoglobulin***). Immunoglobulins, which fall into five different structural classes, namely IgG, IgA, IgD, IgM and IgE, are secreted and circulate in the blood. Surface immunoglobulin is the antigen receptor for B lymphocytes and when it binds antigen the B cell is activated, generally with the 'help' of a TH cell responding to the same antigen.

Once activated, the B cell undergoes mitotic division to produce a ***clone*** of cells able to synthesise immunoglobulin of the same antigen specificity. Most of the B cells of such a clone mature into plasma cells. When an antigen is encountered for the first time, this is described as the ***primary immune response***. A few cells from the same clone mature to become ***memory B cells***, small long-lived circulating lymphocytes that are able to respond quickly to any subsequent challenge with the same antigen. Antibody production during this ***secondary immune response*** occurs much more rapidly, is of much greater magnitude and produces IgG rather than IgM. This phenomenon explains the lifetime immunity that follows many common infections; it is also the general principle on which vaccination is based. Antibodies neutralise or destroy invading organisms by a number of methods (see Fig. 11.2).

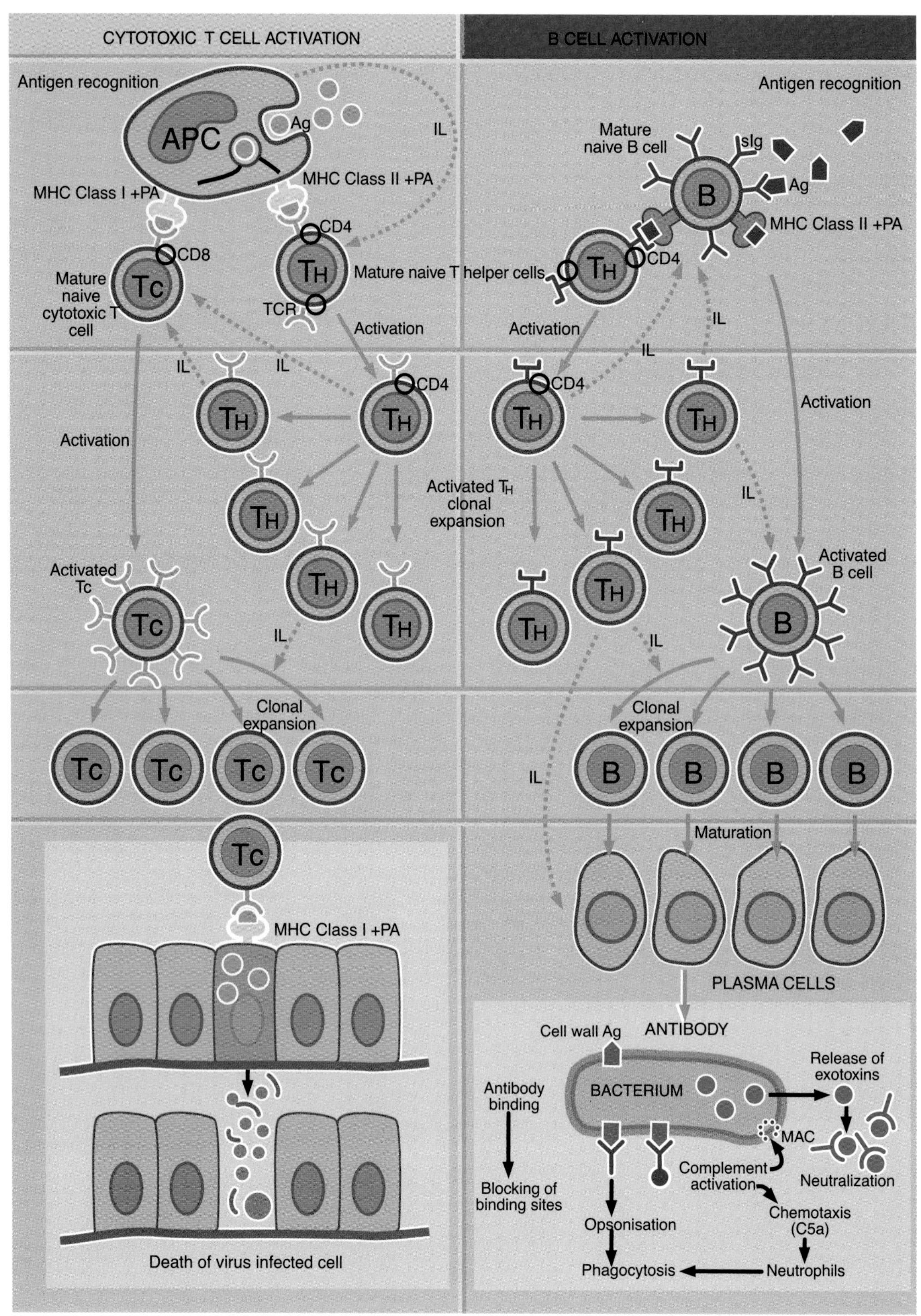

Ag antigen **APC** antigen presenting cell **B** B lymphocyte **IL** interleukin
MAC membrane attack complex **MHC** major histocompatibility complex **PA** processed antigen
sIg surface immunoglobulin **Tc** cytotoxic T cell **TCR** T cell receptor **TH** T helper cell

Fig. 11.2 The basics of the immune response *(illustration opposite)*

This diagram outlines the key steps in the adaptive immune response i.e. recognition of antigen, activation of the response, generation of effector mechanisms, and destruction or inactivation of the antigen.

Activation of the immune system

Initiation of an immune response first requires contact between antigen **Ag** and surface receptors on mature lymphocytes. There are several mechanisms of activation:

1. B lymphocytes interact directly with antigens. They recognise antigen by means of surface immunoglobulin molecules **sIg**. Activation will occur if sIg binds to a protein or polysaccharide antigen with a repeating chemical structure e.g. the polysaccharide coat of the bacterium *Pneumococcus*. Such antigens are often known **as *T cell independent antigens***. Few naturally occurring antigens are of this type (not illustrated).
2. Activation of T cells is dependent on ***antigen presenting cells* APC**. The antigen is taken up by an APC (e.g. macrophage, B lymphocyte, dendritic cell, Langerhans cell of skin) and broken down to short peptides (see Fig. 11.3). Processed antigen **PA** is then bound to a major histocompatibility complex molecule **MHC** and the MHC-peptide complex is incorporated into the cell membrane so that the bound antigenic peptide is exposed to the extracellular fluid. Contact with a mature T cell bearing a T cell receptor **TCR** with appropriate specificity activates the T cell. The type of response depends on whether the peptide is presented bound to MHC class I or II. Antigenic peptides bound to class II MHC molecules induce a ***T helper cell* TH** response needed to activate B cells **B**. B cell receptors (sIg) must also bind to the antigen. TH cells secrete a variety of interleukins **IL** that mediate activation, clonal expansion and maturation of the B cell response.
3. Antigen synthesised within a body cell (e.g. tumour cell, virus-infected cell) is presented on the APC plasma membrane bound to a class I MHC protein where it is recognised by ***cytotoxic T cells* TC**. Cytotoxic T cells are able to kill the abnormal cells directly. TH activation is also required for a TC response to be mounted.

Generation of effector mechanisms

1. Production of antibodies by plasma cells. Mechanisms of antibody-mediated antigen elimination are as follows:
   - Antibody blocks the entry of organisms (such as viruses) into cells by binding to viral surface antigens.
   - Antigen-antibody complexes (***immune complexes***) activate complement to produce (among other factors) the ***membrane attack complex* MAC**, which punctures the outer membrane of the attacking organism.
   - Bound antibody with or without complement ***opsonises*** organisms and facilitates phagocytosis by neutrophils and macrophages.
   - Antibody is essential for ***antibody-dependent cell cytotoxicity*** (**ADCC**) (see below).
   - Antibody bound to toxins inactivates them and facilitates their removal by phagocytic cells.
2. ***Cell-mediated cytotoxicity*** is the destruction by apoptosis of abnormal cells by cytotoxic T cells, natural killer (NK) cells or antibody dependent cytotoxic cells.
3. Certain types of organism such as *Mycobacterium tuberculosis*, the cause of tuberculosis, activate T helper cells to secrete cytokines that in turn activate macrophages. Activated macrophages are more effective at killing phagocytosed organisms. This is the mechanism of ***type IV hypersensitivity*** (***chronic granulomatous inflammation)*** (not illustrated).

Termination of the immune response

There are a number of mechanisms for switching off the immune response when the need for it has been removed. These include removal of antigen, the short life span of plasma cells, the activities of suppressor T cells and a variety of other mechanisms that downregulate the activity of T and B cells.

Immunological memory

When activated lymphocytes undergo clonal expansion during an immune response, some of the cells so generated mature to become memory T and B cells. These lymphocytes have a similar appearance to naive lymphocytes but are able to produce a faster and more effective response to a smaller quantity of antigen. This is known as a secondary immune response and is the basis of lifelong immunity after certain infections and of vaccination.

Fig. 11.3 Lymphocytes and antigen presenting cell

(a) Schematic diagram (b) EM ×18 000 (opposite)

Antigen presenting cells **APC** are vital for the activation of lymphocytes to produce an adaptive immune response. They include macrophages, ***dendritic cells*** and B lymphocytes. Dendritic cells patrol the body surfaces and phagocytose invading pathogens e.g. a bacterium **B**. Dendritic cells carrying antigen migrate via the lymph to the regional lymph nodes. The traffic of both lymphocytes and dendritic cells to the lymph nodes maximises the chances of lymphocytes meeting an antigen they can react to. APC function is shown on the right side of diagram (a). Antigen is taken up by APCs into an early endosome **EE** that fuses with a lysosome containing ***major histocompatibility complex class II*** **MHC II** molecules. The antigen is broken down into short antigenic peptides **AP** that bind to MHC II and the peptide-MHC II complex is transported to the plasma membrane. After fusion of the phagolysosome **PL** with the plasma membrane **PM**, the MHC II-peptide complex is exposed on the cell surface where it may come into contact with helper T cells **TH**. If the T cell receptor **TCR** on the TH cell can bind to that particular MHC II-peptide complex, activation will occur and the adaptive immune response will proceed. Obviously a bacterium, after processing, will generate many different antigenic peptides, but only one peptide and one TH cell is shown here for simplicity.

In general TH cells recognise peptide bound to MHC II and cytotoxic T cells **TC** recognise antigen bound to MHC class I **MHC I**. On the left of diagram (a) processing of intrinsic viral antigen in a virus-infected cell is shown. The viral protein **VPr** is chopped into short peptides **VP** by a ***proteasome*** **Pr** (an organelle that breaks down abnormal proteins). The peptides bind to MHC I and are presented on the cell surface for interaction with a cytotoxic T cell. Almost all body cells express MHC I but usually only APCs express MHC II.

Micrograph (b) illustrates several lymphocytes and an APC in a lymph node. Lymphocytes and APCs exhibit similar features in other lymphoid tissues. The lymphocytes **L** are relatively small with round nuclei and condensed chromatin that tends to be clumped around the periphery. Cell outlines are fairly regular with occasional surface projections. The scanty cytoplasm contains plentiful free ribosomes and a few mitochondria but little endoplasmic reticulum, lysosomes or secretory granules.

The centre of the field is occupied by the large cell body of an antigen presenting cell, in this case an ***interdigitating dendritic cell***. These have numerous long branched cytoplasmic extensions **CE** reaching out between the surrounding lymphocytes so that a single dendritic cell can be in contact with many different lymphocytes. Its nucleus is deeply indented with dispersed chromatin; in this example the plane of section has resulted in a small nuclear extension appearing to be separate from the main part of the nucleus. Typically, the APC cytoplasm contains numerous small lysosomes **Ly** and larger phagosomes **P**.

Dendritic cells include interdigitating dendritic cells in the paracortical area of lymph nodes, ***interdigitating cells*** of the thymus and ***Langerhans cells*** of the skin. ***Follicular dendritic cells*** are accessible to B cells in the germinal centres of lymph nodes. They are similar cells which are able to bind antibody-antigen complexes to their surface without prior processing.

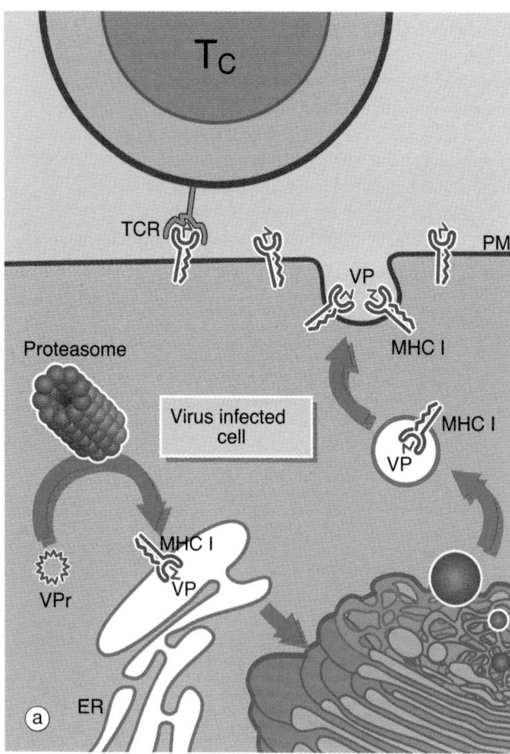

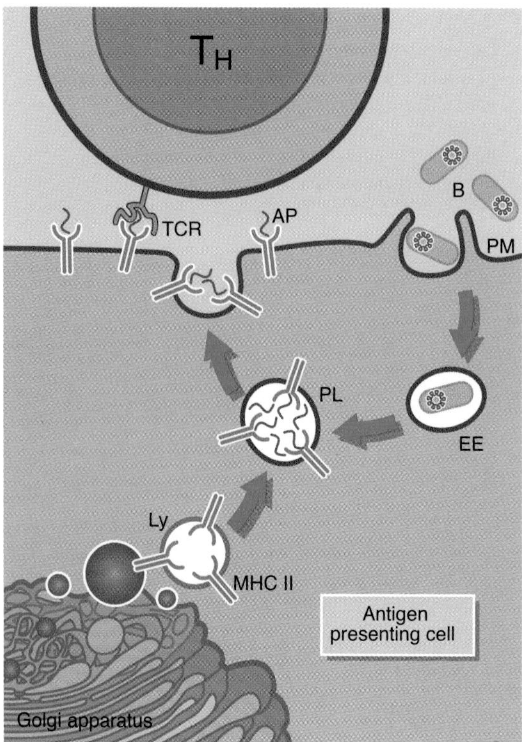

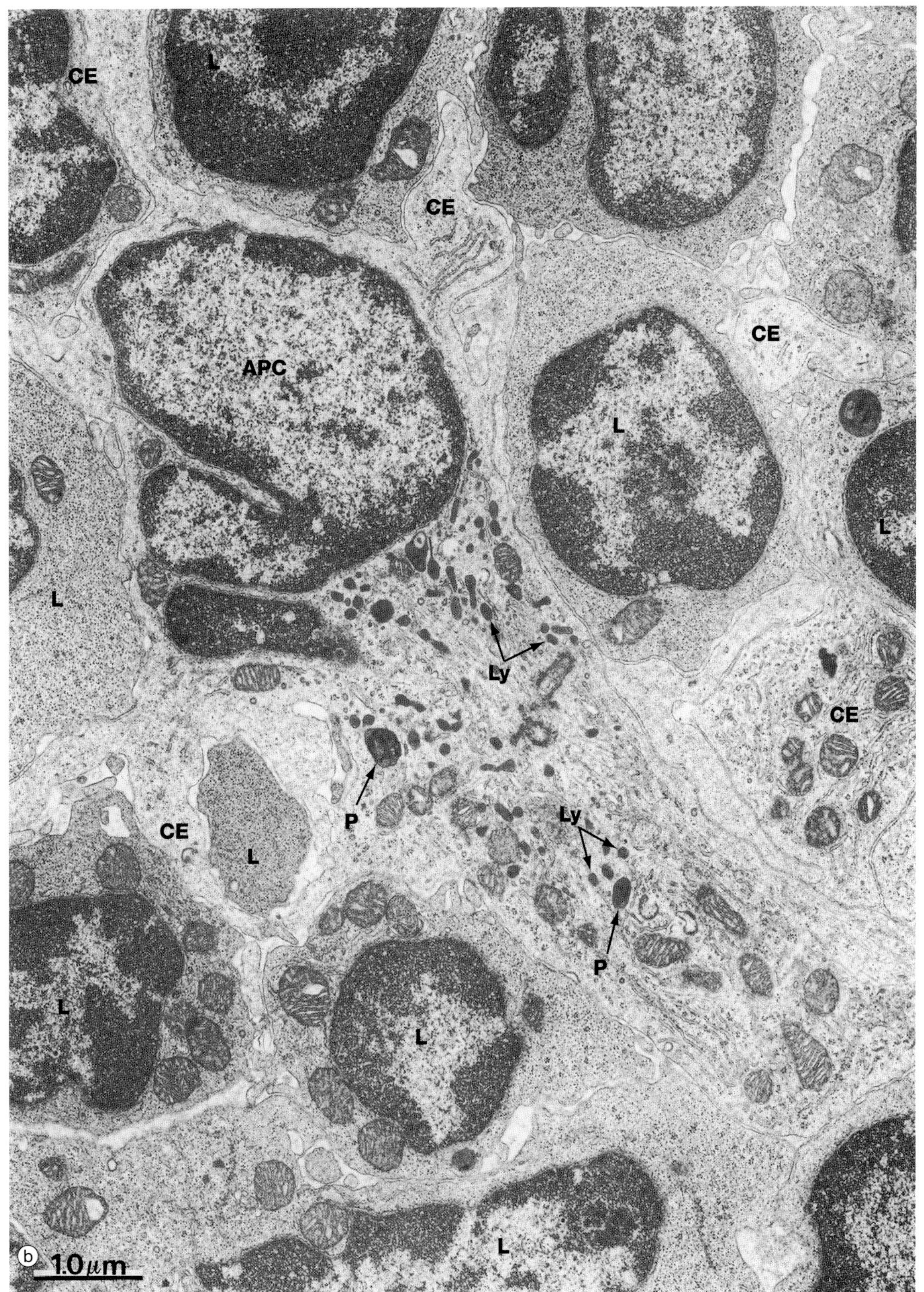

AP antigenic peptide **APC** antigen presenting cell **B** bacterium **CE** cytoplasmic extensions
EE early endosome **ER** endoplasmic reticulum **L** lymphocyte **Ly** lysosome
MHC I major histocompatibility complex class I **MHC II** major histocompatibility complex class II
P phagosome **PL** phagolysosome **PM** plasma membrane **Pr** proteasome **Tc** cytotoxic T cell
TCR T cell receptor **TH** T helper cell **VP** viral peptide **VPr** viral protein

Fig. 11.4 Lymphocyte surface markers

Function	T cell	B cell
Antigen receptor	T cell receptor (TCR)	Surface immunoglobulin (sIg)
Accessory binding molecules	CD4 (T_H) CD8 (T_C) CD2 CD28	CD19 CD21 (CR2) CD81 CD40
Signal transduction	CD3 CD2	Igα Igβ
Other	CD25 (IL-2 receptors)	Fc receptor

Fig. 11.4 Lymphocyte surface markers

Lymphocytes carry on their plasma membranes a wide range of transmembrane proteins that have various functions in controlling the activation of the immune response and are the means by which lymphocytes interact with their environment. They can also be used to identify different types of lymphocyte within the laboratory for diagnostic and research purposes and are thus often called ***surface markers***. Known functions of these molecules include acting as receptors for antigen, acting as cobinding/costimulatory molecules required for the activation of lymphocytes, and signal transmission from the surface to the inside of the cell. Many of these surface markers are named according to the ***CD (cluster of differentiation) system***, an internationally agreed system which may seem confusing but which is infinitely better than the haphazard free-for-all that preceded it. There are well over 100 known CD molecules now. Fortunately, for the purposes of this text, only a few need to be touched on here.

Antigen receptors

Lymphocytes are constantly being produced in the bone marrow, each cell subsequently acquiring the ability to recognise a single particular chemical configuration, i.e. a particular antigen, to which it might be exposed at some time in the future. This huge range of possible antigen specificities is brought about by the random rearrangement of segments of the genes coding for the antigen-binding part of the receptor, a process called ***gene splicing***, which is unique to lymphocytes.

B cells produce small amounts of immunoglobulin that are inserted into the plasma membrane (business end out) and act as the antigen receptor. When this surface immunoglobulin binds to antigen, activation of the B cell is initiated, resulting in the production of clones of plasma cells that secrete large amounts of immunoglobulin specific for that antigen. T cells have a structurally similar antigen receptor, the T cell receptor, which serves the same triggering function when bound to antigen. During T cell development the TCR genes are rearranged in a manner similar to immunoglobulin genes, in order to produce T cells with a wide range of possible antigen specificities.

Accessory binding/costimulatory molecules

Accessory binding molecules are required for the stimulation of both T and B cells. Activation of T cells requires binding between ***accessory molecules*** on the surface of the T cell and their counterparts on the APC. T_H cells are recognisable by the CD4 surface marker which binds to MHC class II molecules on the surface of APCs, thereby providing increased binding affinity and an additional signal to the T cell. CD8 on the surface of the cytotoxic T cells binds in a similar fashion to MHC class I on APCs. Thus, T_H cells are said to be ***MHC class II restricted*** and T_C cells ***MHC class I restricted***.

Other surface molecules that have cobinding and costimulatory activity include CD28 and CD2 on T cells and CD19, CD 21, CD 81 and CD40 on B cells.

Signal transduction molecules

CD3 on T cells is a protein complex closely associated with the TCR. When the TCR binds antigen and CD4/8-MHC binding occurs, CD3 passes the message to the inside of the cell to trigger the intracellular events leading to cell activation. On B cells, molecules known as Igα and Igβ that are associated with the surface immunoglobulin perform the same function.

Other surface markers

These include a diverse range of transmembrane proteins such as receptors for the constant region of the immunoglobulin molecule (Fc receptors), complement receptors, interleukin receptors, CD25 and various others.

Transplantation

Transplantation of organs such as heart, liver and kidneys has transformed the lives of many patients with chronic organ failure. However it is fraught with difficulties due to rejection of the transplanted organ. The immune system of the recipient reacts mainly against the MHC complexes (known as the ***H***uman ***L***eukocyte ***A***ntigens (**HLA**) in humans). Indeed these antigens were first discovered in the context of organ transplantation and it was many years before the function of these molecules became known. Each class of HLA antigens includes a number of different proteins each of which may be coded by a number of different alleles. Thus an individual will have two different variants of each HLA type. The overall HLA makeup is called the ***HLA phenotype*** and no two individuals (except identical twins) have the exact same HLA phenotype. Tissue matching is used to find the closest match possible but most transplants occur between individuals with some degree of ***MHC mismatch***. Immunosuppressive drugs of various types are used to suppress the immune response against the foreign antigens in the donor organ. Unfortunately these drugs also suppress desirable immune responses to pathogens, putting the patient at risk of life-threatening infections and a careful balance is sought between loss of the grafted organ through rejection and danger of infection. The search continues for more specific drugs to control rejection.

Thymus

The thymus is a flattened lymphoid organ located in the upper anterior mediastinum and lower part of the neck. The thymus is most active during childhood, reaching a weight of about 30–40 g at puberty, after which it undergoes slow involution so that in the middle-aged or older adult it may be difficult to differentiate from adipose tissue macroscopically.

In the embryo, the thymus originates from epithelial outgrowths of the ventral wing of the third pharyngeal pouch on each side. These merge in the midline, forming a single organ subdivided into numerous fine lobules. The epithelium develops into a sponge-like structure containing a labyrinth of interconnecting spaces that become colonised by immature T lymphocytes derived from haemopoietic tissue elsewhere in the developing embryo. Towards the centre of the organ, the epithelial framework has a coarser structure with smaller interstices and a much smaller lymphocyte population, so that, on microscopic examination, the gland has a highly cellular outer ***cortex*** and a less cellular central ***medulla***.

The epithelial cells of the thymus provide a mechanical supporting framework for the lymphocyte population. Cortical epithelial cells, known as ***nurse cells***, envelop multiple lymphocytes promoting T cell differentiation and proliferation. Furthermore, the epithelial cells secrete a number of different hormones that regulate T cell maturation and proliferation within the thymus and in other lymphoid organs and tissues. The inner surfaces of the thymic capsule and septa are invested by a continuous layer of thymic epithelial cells resting on a basement membrane. The epithelium also forms sheaths around the blood vessels, creating a barrier to the entry of antigenic material into the thymic parenchyma. This is known as the ***blood–thymus barrier***.

The functions of the thymus include:

- Development of immunocompetent T lymphocytes from bone marrow derived T cell precursors to produce mature T_H and T_C cells.
- Proliferation of clones of mature naïve T cells to supply the circulating lymphocyte pool and peripheral tissues.
- Development of immunological self-tolerance – more than 98% of maturing cells die by apoptosis within the thymus, and many of these are self-reactive.
- Secretion of hormones and cytokines that regulate T cell maturation, proliferation and function within the thymus and peripheral lymphoid tissues. There are various polypeptides with hormonal characteristics, including ***thymulin***, ***thymopoietin*** and various ***thymosins***.

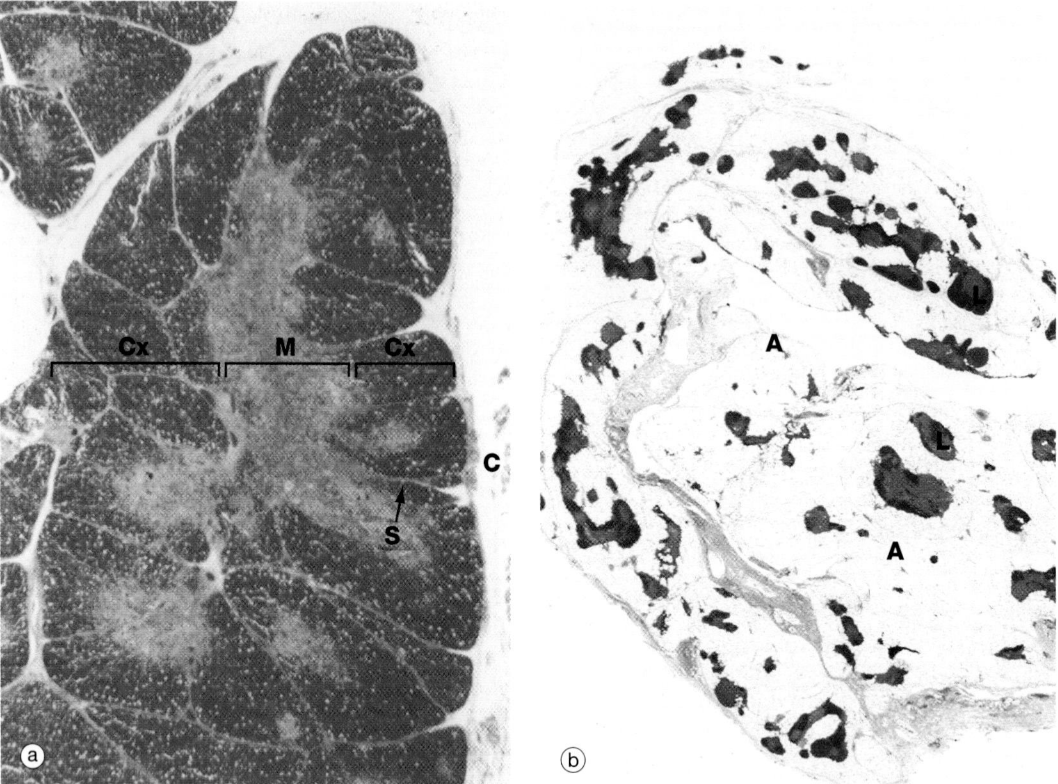

Fig. 11.5 Thymus
(a) H & E ×15 (b) H & E ×15

The infant thymus (a) is a lobulated organ invested by a loose collagenous capsule **C** from which short interlobular septa **S** containing blood vessels radiate into the substance of the organ. The thymic tissue is divided into two distinct zones, a deeply basophilic outer cortex **Cx** and an inner eosinophilic medulla **M**; distinction between the two is most marked in early childhood, as in this specimen.

In the middle-aged adult, the thymus (b) is already well into the process of involution, which involves two distinct processes, fatty infiltration and lymphocyte depletion. Fat cells (adipocytes) first begin to appear at birth, their numbers slowly rising until puberty when the rate of fatty infiltration increases markedly. Fatty infiltration of the interlobular septa occurs first, spreading out into the cortex and later the medulla. Thus in the mature thymus islands of lymphoid tissue **L** are separated by areas of adipose tissue **A**. Lymphocyte numbers begin to fall from about 1 year of age, the process continuing thereafter at a constant rate. Despite this, the thymus continues to provide a supply of mature T lymphocytes to the circulating pool and peripheral tissues. Lymphocyte depletion results in collapse of the epithelial framework. However, cords of epithelial cells persist and continue to secrete thymic hormones throughout life.

The normal process of slow thymic involution associated with aging should be distinguished from ***acute thymic involution***, which may occur in response to severe disease and metabolic stress associated with pregnancy, lactation, infection, surgery, malnutrition, malignancy and other systemic insults. Stress involution is characterised by greatly increased lymphocyte death and is probably mediated by high levels of corticosteroids; thus the size and activity of the adult thymus are often underestimated if examined after prolonged illness.

Numerous small branches of the internal thoracic and inferior thyroid arteries enter the thymus via the interlobular septa, branching at the corticomedullary junction to supply the cortex and medulla. Postcapillary venules in the corticomedullary region have a specialised cuboidal endothelium similar to that of the high endothelial venules of the lymph node (see Fig. 11.14), which allows passage of lymphocytes into and out of the thymus. The venous and lymphatic drainage follow the course of the arterial supply; there are no afferent lymphatics. Sympathetic and parasympathetic fibres derived from the sympathetic chain and phrenic nerves respectively accompany the blood vessels into the thymus.

A adipose tissue **BM** basement membrane **C** capsule **Cx** cortex **E** endothelial cells **Ep** epithelial cell **H** Hassall's corpuscle **L** lymphoid tissue **M** medulla **Ma** macrophage **Mt** mitotic figure **S** septum

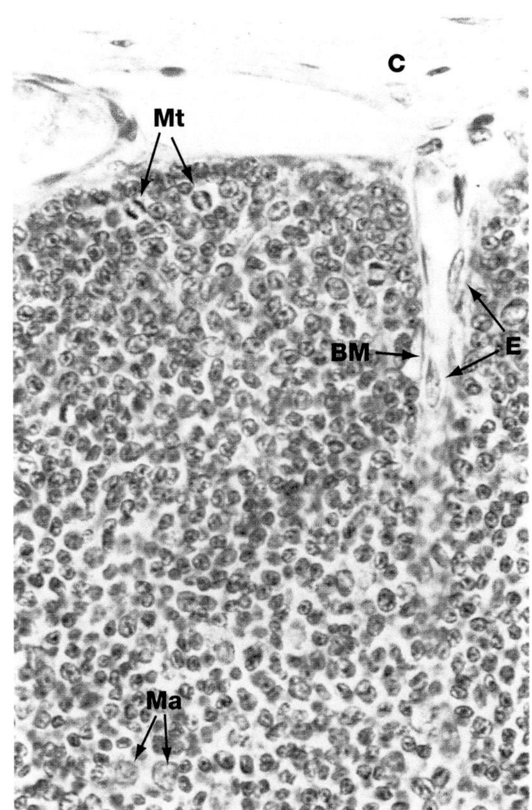

Fig. 11.6 Thymic cortex
H & E ×480

The thymic cortex is packed with immature and maturing T cells, often called ***thymocytes***. In the outer cortex large lymphocytes (***lymphoblasts***) divide by mitosis to produce clones of smaller mature T cells. These undergo further maturation as they move deeper into the cortex towards the medulla. It is during this process that the TCR genes are rearranged and the cells acquire the surface markers or phenotype of mature helper and cytotoxic T cells. Several mitotic figures **Mt** can be seen in the outer cortex in this micrograph. Cells failing to make these adjustments successfully die by apoptosis and are taken up by pale-stained macrophages **Ma** at the corticomedullary junction.

Note also in this micrograph, a small capillary lined by flattened endothelial cells **E** entering the cortex from the capsule **C**. Around the capillary the basement membrane **BM** of epithelial cells can be discerned at the interface between the thymic framework and supporting tissue elements. The epithelial framework of the cortex is more delicate and finely branched than that of the medulla and the cells cannot be distinguished in this micrograph, being obscured by the mass of lymphocytes.

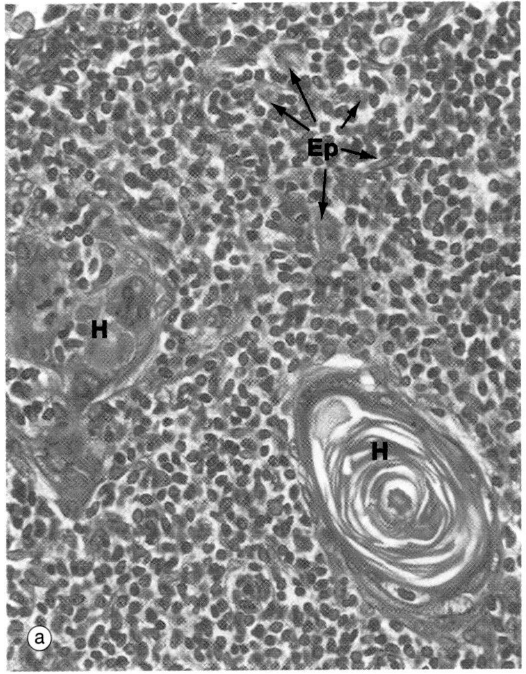

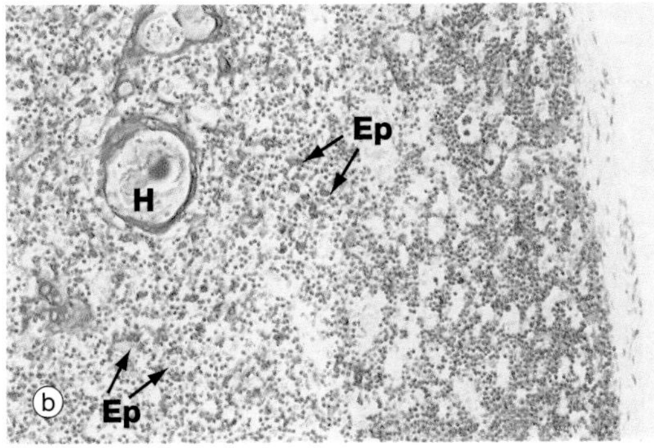

Fig. 11.7 Thymic medulla
(a) H & E ×480 (b) Immunoperoxidase cytokeratin ×100

The dominant feature of the thymic medulla is the robust epithelial component **Ep**. The epithelial cells have large pale-stained nuclei, eosinophilic cytoplasm and prominent basement membranes. A particular feature in the medulla are the lamellated ***Hassall's corpuscles*** **H** that first appear in fetal life and increase in number and size thereafter. These are formed from groups of keratinised epithelial cells and may represent a degenerative phenomenon. The epithelial cells of the thymus are highlighted in micrograph (b) that uses an antibody to keratin to stain the tissue by the immunoperoxidase technique (see Appendix 2). Individual epithelial cells **Ep**, as well as Hassall's corpuscles **H**, are stained brown.

Also found in the medulla is a type of antigen presenting cell, known as a ***thymic interdigitating cell***, which expresses high levels of both class I and II MHC proteins. It appears that these cells present normal self-components, ***self-antigens***, to maturing T cells. Any self-reactive T cells that identify themselves by becoming activated are obliterated by apoptosis. This is known as ***clonal deletion*** or ***negative selection***. Thus the thymus is the organ where self-reactive T cells are removed, preventing the development of autoimmunity.

At the end of their journey through the thymus, the mature T cells enter the blood vessels and lymphatics to join the pool of circulating T lymphocytes and populate the T lymphocyte domains of other lymphoid organs.

Lymph nodes

Mature lymphocytes are distributed throughout the body, where they are arranged in aggregations that exhibit various degrees of structural organisation. Individual lymphocytes are found in most loose supporting tissues and amongst epithelial cells, particularly the epithelium of the gastrointestinal and respiratory tracts. In addition, large non-encapsulated aggregations of lymphocytes are found in the walls of these tracts including the palatine tonsils and the Peyer's patches of the small intestine. Many lymphocytes are, however, located in encapsulated, highly organised structures called ***lymph nodes***, which are interposed along the larger regional vessels of the lymph vascular system. Lymph nodes tend to occur in groups, particularly in areas where the lymphatics converge to form larger trunks as in the neck, axillae, groins, lung hila and para-aortic areas.

Lymph nodes are like singles bars for lymphocytes and antigen, providing the perfect location for lymphocytes to be exposed to a wide variety of antigens and to undergo stimulation. As described earlier, antigen-loaded dendritic cells from skin and mucosal sites migrate in the lymph to the regional lymph nodes where they are able to present antigen to T cells. Free antigen is also carried in the lymph to the nodes. The acute inflammatory process increases the flow of lymph by flooding the infected or damaged tissue with extracellular fluid. Mature naïve lymphocytes constantly traffic between the periphery and organised lymphoid tissues via the blood and lymph circulation to maximise their chances of meeting the right antigen.

The architecture of the lymph node is arranged in such a way as to bring together the necessary elements for stimulation of the adaptive immune response. In this environment stimulated T and B cells undergo clonal expansion and maturation. B cells mature into antibody-secreting ***plasma cells***. Effector lymphocytes and plasma cells leave the nodes in the efferent lymph and recirculate to the damaged or infected tissue.

Lymph node enlargement

Lymph nodes can become enlarged for a wide variety of reasons but by far the most common is infection. The lymph nodes in most cases are not actively infected themselves but are responding to infection in the tissues which they drain. Most readers will have experienced a sore throat at some point in their lives. This may be due either to a viral or a bacterial infection of the mucosa of the pharynx (***pharyngitis***) which may in turn lead to inflammation and enlargement of the tonsils (***tonsillitis***), large aggregates of lymphoid tissue in the throat (see Fig 11.16). In addition the regional lymph nodes in the neck are recruited with increased flow of antigen-bearing lymph and the triggering of an adaptive immune response. These lymph nodes become enlarged and tender and can easily be palpated in the neck, a situation known colloquially as 'enlarged glands'. The end result of all this activity is the recruitment of all the effector mechanisms of the adaptive and innate immune responses and the clearance of the infection with a return to normal good health.

In some situations, however, the infective organism can directly invade and grow in the lymph node. Such infections include *Mycobacterium tuberculosis* (TB), *Mycobacterium avium-intracellulare* (MAIS) and *Toxoplasma gondii*, which typically give rise to a ***granulomatous*** pattern of chronic inflammation.

Another common cause of lymph node enlargement is malignant tumours. Tumours of the immune system itself (***lymphomas*** and ***leukaemias***) are discussed briefly on page 231. However it is common for lymph nodes draining a malignant epithelial tumour to become enlarged. This may simply be a reactive process caused by increased flow of lymph to the nodes, perhaps due to necrosis of the tumour. Much more sinister is the spread of tumour to the lymph nodes, a process known as ***metastasis***. This is so important for ***staging*** a tumour that for many common carcinomas, the local lymph nodes are either sampled or removed in their entirety to assess the presence of tumour deposits in the lymph node. This is routine in the assessment of breast carcinomas and colonic carcinomas. The presence or absence of tumour in the lymph nodes allows a prediction to be made about whether that particular tumour is likely to spread elsewhere (***prognosis***) and allow informed planning of future treatment.

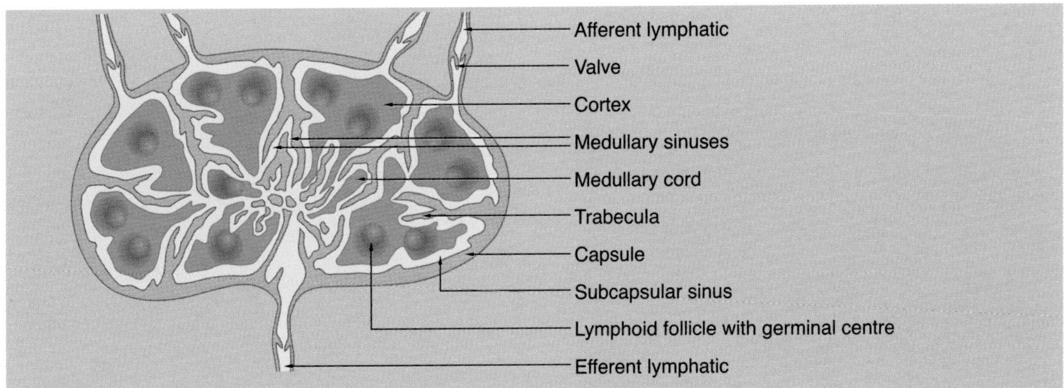

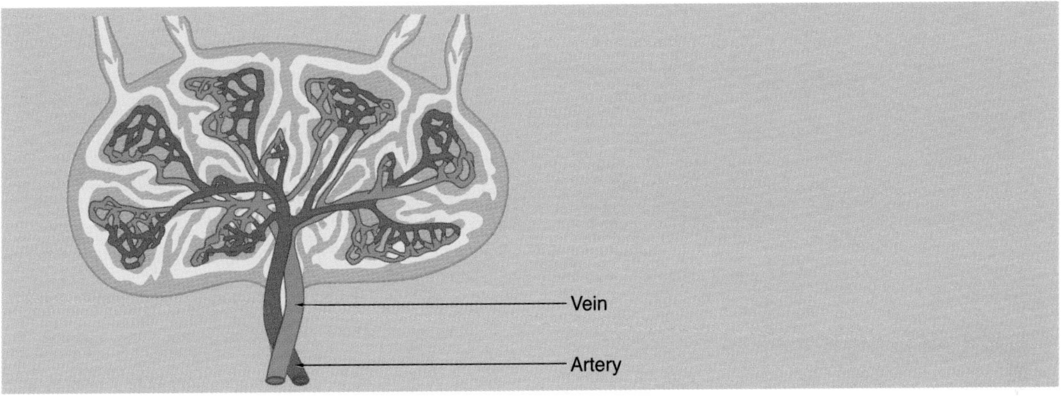

Fig. 11.8 Lymph node structure and vascular organisation

Lymph nodes are small, bean-shaped organs situated in the course of lymphatic vessels such that lymph draining back to the bloodstream passes through one or more lymph nodes. Inactive nodes are only a few millimetres long but may increase greatly in size when mounting an active immunological response. Most lymph nodes in the body show some degree of reactive change in response to the constant barrage of antigen they are exposed to. The outer part of the lymph node is highly cellular and is known as the ***cortex***, whilst the central area, the ***medulla***, is less cellular.

The lymph node is surrounded by a collagenous ***capsule*** from which ***trabeculae*** extend for a variable distance into the substance of the node. ***Afferent lymphatic vessels*** divide into several branches outside the node, then pierce the capsule to drain into a narrow space called the ***subcapsular sinus*** that encircles the node beneath the capsule. From here, a labyrinth of channels called ***cortical sinuses*** passes towards the medulla through the cortical cell mass; sinuses adjacent to the trabeculae pursue a more direct course towards the medulla, but nevertheless form part of the cortical sinus system. The dominant feature of the medulla is the network of broad interconnected lymphatic channels called ***medullary sinuses*** that converge upon the hilum in the concavity of the node. Lymph drains from the hilum into one or more ***efferent lymphatic vessels***, which in turn drain into more proximal nodes before eventually joining the blood stream via the ***thoracic duct*** or ***right lymphatic duct***.

The parenchyma of the lymph node consists of an open meshwork of reticulin fibres, which provides support for an ever-changing population of lymphocytes. The cortex consists of densely-packed lymphocytes. Cellular ***medullary cords*** project into the medulla between the medullary sinuses. In the outer cortex, lymphocytes form a variable number of densely packed ***lymphoid follicles***, many of which show less dense ***germinal centres***. The deep cortex (***paracortical zone***) is devoid of lymphoid follicles.

The blood supply of the lymph node is derived from one or more small arteries which enter at the hilum and branch in the medulla, giving rise to extensive capillary networks corresponding to the cortical follicles, paracortical zone and medullary cords. Lymphocytes enter lymph nodes mainly via the arterial system, gaining access by migrating across the walls of specialised postcapillary venules (***high endothelial venules, HEV***) as described later. The HEV drain into small veins that leave the node via the ***hilum***.

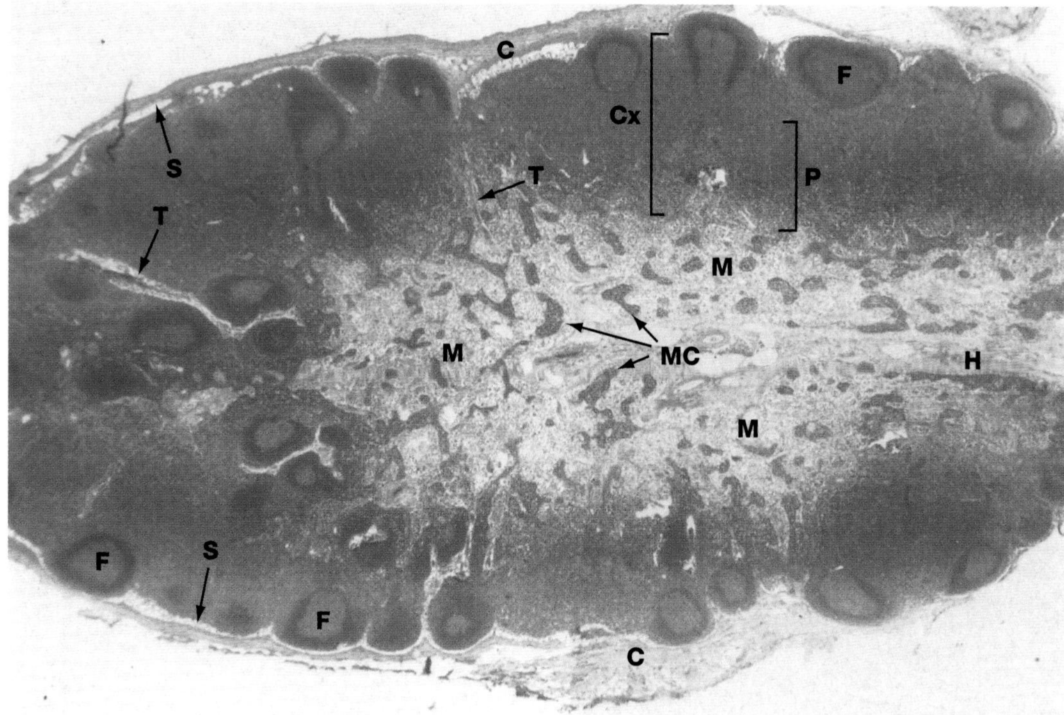

Fig. 11.9 Lymph node structure
H & E ×8

The micrograph illustrates the main histological features of a lymph node. The node is made up of an outer, densely staining cell-rich cortex **Cx** and a pale-stained inner medulla **M** which is continuous with the hilum **H**. The superficial cortex contains a number of dense cellular aggregations, the follicles **F**, many of which have a pale-stained ***germinal centre***. The deeper cortex or paracortex **P** is also densely cellular but has a more homogeneous staining appearance. At the left of the field, some lymphoid follicles appear to be located deep in the paracortex; this is not the case but is a product of the plane of section, which passes at that point through the superficial cortex. Extensions of the cortical cell mass extend into the medulla as ***medullary cords*** **MC**. The superficial cortex, the paracortex, the medulla and the sinuses represent the four different zones of immunological activity in the lymph node, containing mainly B lymphocytes, T lymphocytes, plasma cells and macrophages, respectively.

Several trabeculae **T** extend from the capsule **C** into the substance of the node. The subcapsular sinus **S** is found immediately beneath the capsule and is continuous with the trabecular sinuses. The cortical sinuses are generally difficult to visualise because of their highly convoluted shape and numerous fine extensions that penetrate the cellular mass of the cortex. B cells respond to antigen in the cortex and undergo stimulation, clonal expansion and maturation in the follicles, the presence of germinal centres indicating that an active immune response is underway. Self-reactive B cells are also deleted here and memory cells are generated. T lymphocytes interact with antigen presenting cells in the paracortex and undergo a similar process of activation and clonal expansion. T helper cells migrate towards the cortex to help B cells while activated cytotoxic T cells leave the node to perform their functions in the periphery.

The vascular system provides the main route of entry of lymphocytes into the node as well as supplying its metabolic requirements. Within the paracortex, the postcapillary high endothelial venules have a cuboidal endothelium specialised for the exit of lymphocytes. Recognition by lymphocytes of these exit sites appears to involve the presence of specific complementary ***adhesion molecules*** on the surface of the endothelial cells and lymphocytes. Different groups of lymphocytes home to different tissues. Thus lymphocytes from the mucosa of the gut home to mesenteric lymph nodes, then to the spleen, and back to mucosal tissues. Lymphocytes from the skin home to their regional lymph nodes and then return to the skin. This is made possible by the different adhesion molecules or ***vascular addressins*** in the HEV of the different lymph node groups and the corresponding binding molecules on the lymphocytes.

C capsule **CS** cortical sinus **Cx** cortex **F** follicle **H** hilum **M** medulla **MC** medullary cords **MS** medullary sinus **P** paracortex **S** subcapsular sinus **T** trabecula **TS** trabecular sinus

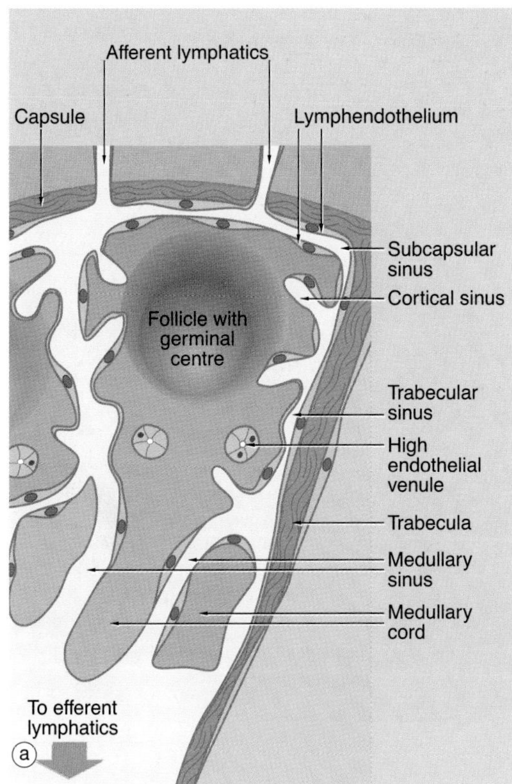

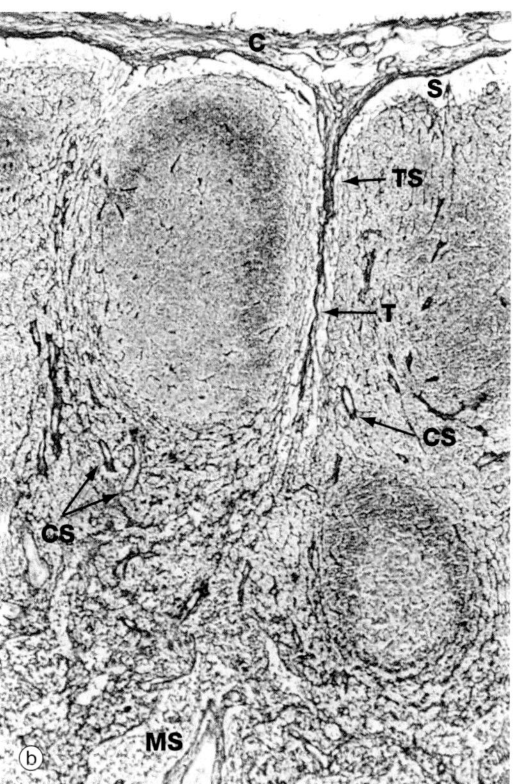

Fig. 11.10 Structure of the lymph node
(a) Schematic diagram (b) Reticulin method ×30

Diagram (a) illustrates the three functional compartments within the lymph node: the ***lymphatic sinuses***, the ***blood vessels*** and the ***interstitial compartment***. A network of lymphatic sinuses permeates the node and is continuous with the lumen of the afferent and efferent lymphatic vessels. The sinuses are lined by a mixture of lymphatic endothelial cells and macrophages and carry lymph, antigen, dendritic cells and macrophages into the node. Blood vessels form a microvascular network in the node. Of particular note are the ***high endothelial venules*** that are the major site of entry of circulating lymphocytes into the node. The interstitial compartment is packed with lymphocytes. Lymphocytes that do not recognise antigen while in the node leave within a few hours in the efferent lymph to rejoin the general circulation. The lymphatic and blood vessel endothelia thus define the boundaries of the three compartments and control passage of cells and molecules between the different compartments.

Micrograph (b) shows the fine reticular architecture of the lymph node; reticulin fibres are stained blackish-brown and lymphocyte nuclei appear lighter brown. The main structural support for the lymph node is derived from the collagenous capsule **C** and trabeculae **T**, which extend into the node. From these, a fine meshwork of reticulin fibres extends throughout the node, providing a supporting framework for the mass of lymphocytes and accessory cells within the cortex and medullary cords. The reticular network is particularly dense in the cortex, except for the follicular areas where it is relatively sparse. The subcapsular sinus **S**, trabecular sinuses **TS**, other cortical sinuses **CS** and medullary sinuses **MS** are kept patent by a fine skeleton of reticulin fibres which traverse the sinuses.

The reticulin framework and collagen of the capsule and trabeculae are laid down by fibroblasts as in other supporting tissues and a few fibroblast-like cells are found on the reticulin network.

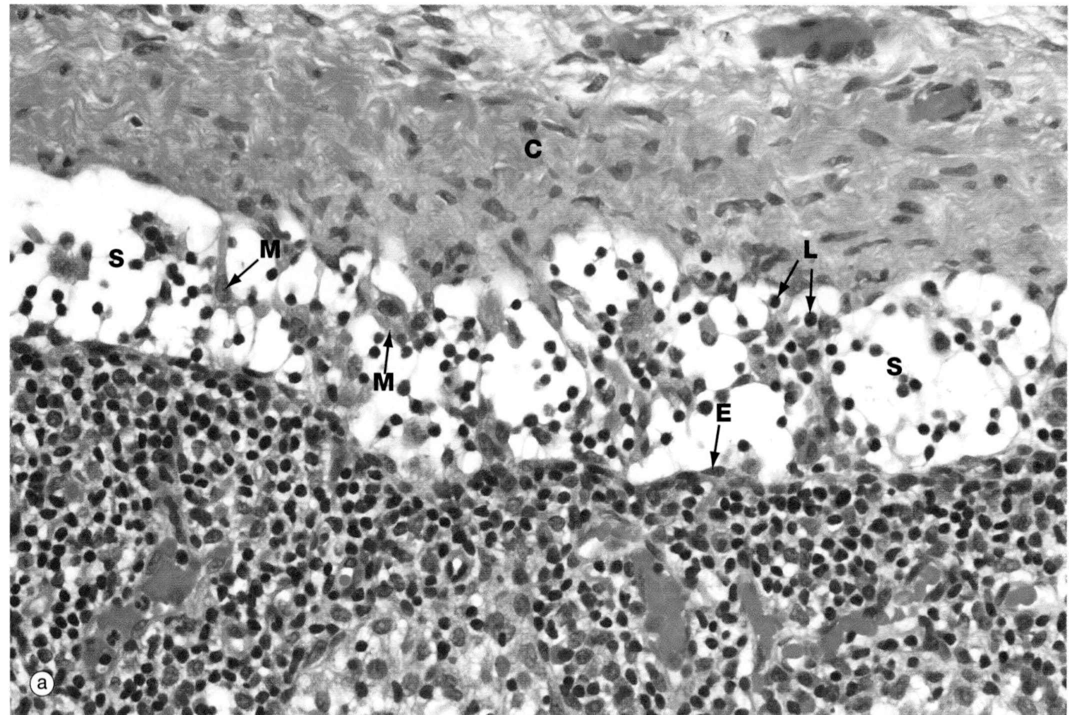

Fig. 11.11 Capsule and subcapsular sinus
(a) H & E ×200 (b) EM ×11 000 with inset ×20 000 *(illustration opposite)*

The fibrous capsule **C** of the lymph node is pierced by branches of afferent lymphatic vessels with valves to ensure one-way flow. The afferent lymphatics bring lymphocytes, antigen-carrying dendritic cells, macrophages and particulate antigen into the node. Micrograph (a) focuses on the subcapsular sinus **S** at high magnification. Endothelial cells **E** lining the sinus can just be identified at this magnification but are much better seen in micrograph (b). The lymph node sinuses are traversed by fine reticulin strands that provide support for large eosinophilic ***sinus macrophages*** **M**. These macrophages filter antigen and other debris from afferent lymph. The macrophages are then able to process antigen and present it to lymphocytes within the node. Lymphocytes **L** and dendritic cells also are found within the subcapsular sinus.

In micrograph (b) the structures of the subcapsular sinus are seen in much more detail. Endothelial cells **E** line the sinus. Reticular fibres **RF** are surrounded by the cytoplasmic projections or dendrites of dendritic cells **DC** that wrap all the way around the reticular fibres and form junctions **J** with themselves (see inset, which is an enlargement of area outlined). A sinus macrophage **M** is draped between the two reticular fibres and within its cytoplasm the machinery for antigen processing is readily apparent i.e. plentiful lysosomes **Ly** and endocytic vacuoles **V**. The macrophage also has plentiful cell processes **P** to increase the surface area. Thus the subcapsular sinus of the lymph node acts as a 'strainer' for antigen entering the node.

C capsule **DC** dendritic reticular cell **E** endothelial cell **J** cell junction **L** lymphocyte
Ly lysosome **M** sinus macrophage **P** macrophage cell process **RF** reticular fibre
S subcapsular sinus **V** endocytic vacuole

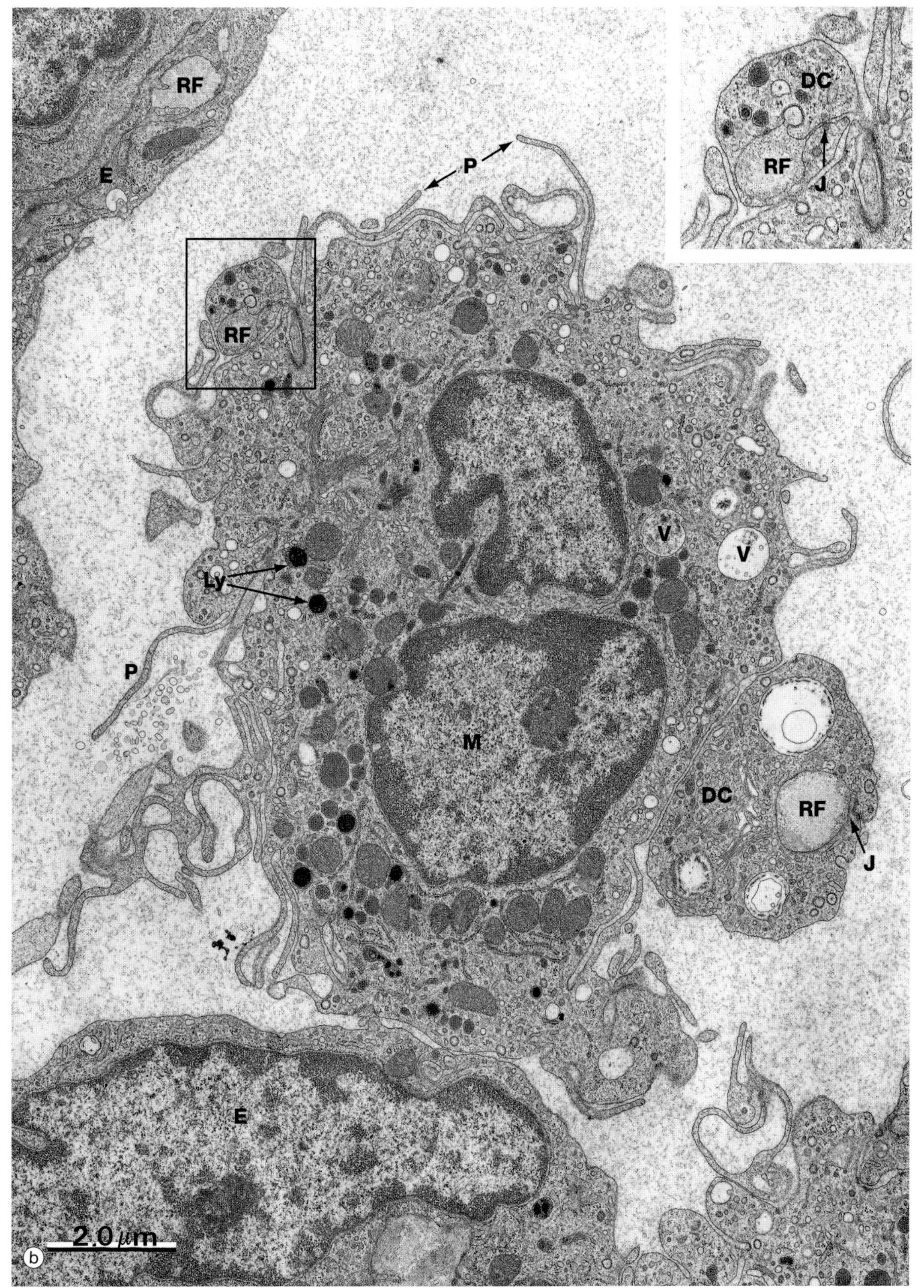
RF
E
P
RF
DC
RF
J
V
V
Ly
P
M
DC
RF
J
E
2.0 μm
b

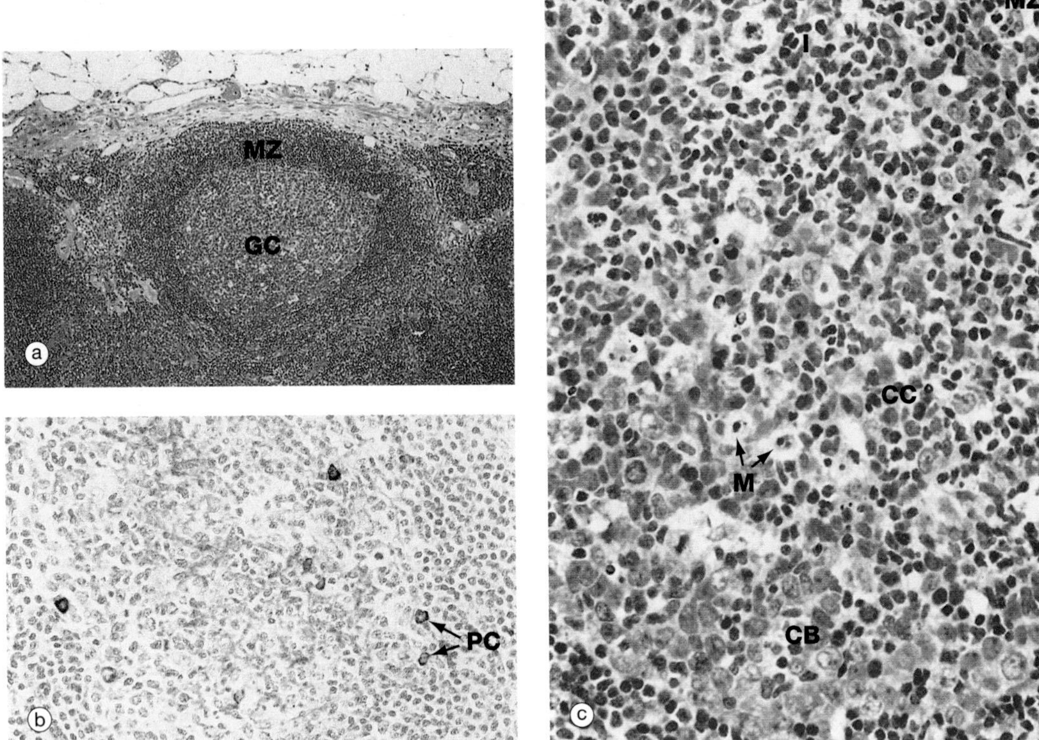

Fig. 11.12 Lymphoid follicle and germinal centre
(a) H & E ×50 (b) Immunoperoxidase IgM ×200 (c) H & E ×300

Micrograph (a) shows a secondary lymphoid follicle with a pale ***germinal centre* GC** and a darker stained ***mantle zone* MZ** surrounding it. The mantle zone is made up of small resting B cells, the condensed nuclear chromatin giving the dark blue colour. The mantle zone is usually asymmetric, with the wider side towards the capsule. Intermixed with the B cells is a scattering of TH cells, follicular dendritic cells and macrophages. Primary follicles which are unstimulated consist entirely of the same cell types as the mantle zone.

The cells of the germinal centre (c) are mainly actively dividing B cells. The germinal centre is not uniform in colour but is darker towards the medulla, reflecting the organisation of the different cell types within it. Resting B cells enter the lymph node via the high endothelial venules and, if they encounter an antigen with which they can react, enter the cycle of blast transformation to produce clones of plasma cells and B memory cells. The first step is activation to give rise to ***centroblasts* CB**, large, mitotically active cells with round nuclei that are found in the darker zone of the germinal centre. These differentiate into ***centrocytes* CC**, found in the pale midzone of the germinal centre. These cells are of variable size and have folded, irregular ('cleaved') nuclei. Mitotic figures are absent in this area. Centrocytes migrate towards the paler capsular zone of the germinal centre where they go through further cycles of division to produce either ***immunoblasts* I** or memory B cells. Immunoblasts move to the medullary cords where they complete their differentiation into plasma cells capable of secreting large amounts of antibody. In the germinal centre a further ingenious device ensures even greater diversity of antibody specificity. Centroblasts undergo increased mutation of the immunoglobulin genes (***somatic hypermutation***), thus creating further variations in immunoglobulin structure. Those centroblasts with the antibody structure that binds most tightly to the antigen (high affinity antibody) are then stimulated to differentiate into plasma cells and memory cells. Memory cells, which resemble small lymphocytes, take up residence in the mantle zone **MZ** of the follicle or may join the recirculating pool of small lymphocytes.

Other cells found in the germinal centres include:

- ***Follicular dendritic cells***, the major antigen presenting cells of the follicles. These are difficult to see in routine H & E stains but their dendritic processes can be demonstrated (stained orange/brown) as in micrograph (b) using an antibody to IgM which is trapped on the plasma membrane. These cells are found in all areas of the germinal centre and also form a meshwork in the mantle zone and in primary follicles. They can retain antigen on their surface for many months and may have a role in maintaining the activity of memory cells as well as stimulating a primary immune response. Occasional plasma cells **PC** are also stained by virtue of their cytoplasmic IgM.
- The interestingly named ***tingible body macrophages* M** are easily seen in routine sections in active germinal centres (c). They contain within their cytoplasm numerous apoptotic bodies derived from B lymphocytes that have not been successful in generating a high affinity antibody.

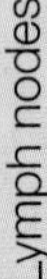

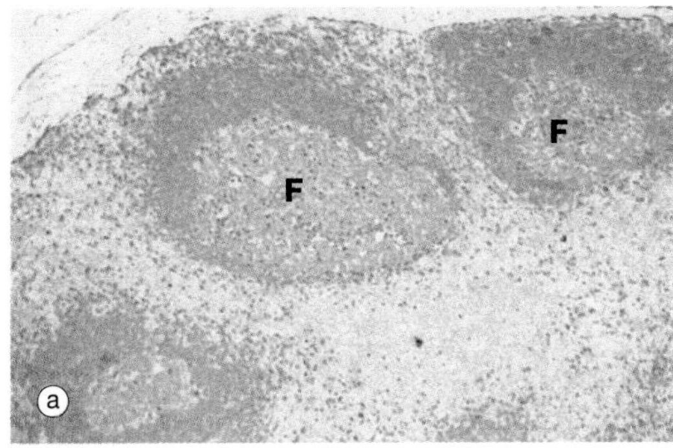

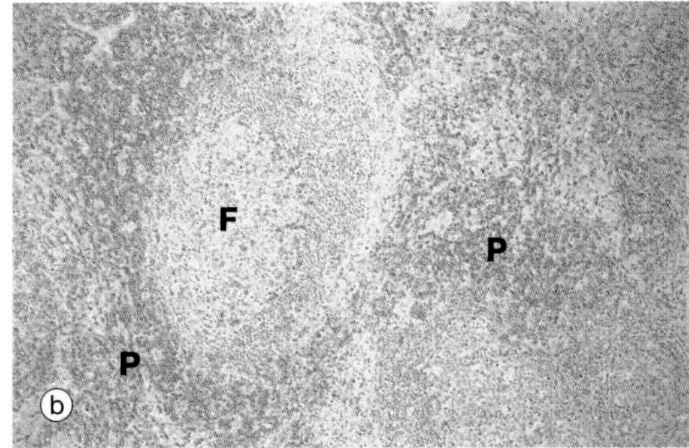

Fig. 11.13 Cortical distribution of T and B lymphocytes
Immunoperoxidase method: (a) CD20 B cells ×50 (b) CD3 T cells ×50

Micrograph (a) employs an immunoperoxidase method for a B lymphocyte surface marker, which stains the cell surface orange. Nuclei are counterstained blue with haematoxylin. The follicles **F** are composed mainly of B cells.

Micrograph (b) uses the same method, in this case with a T cell marker. T lymphocytes make up the majority of the cells in the paracortex **P**, but scattered T cells are also present in the follicles **F**. These are mainly TH cells which must also recognise antigen to provide help for B cell stimulation.

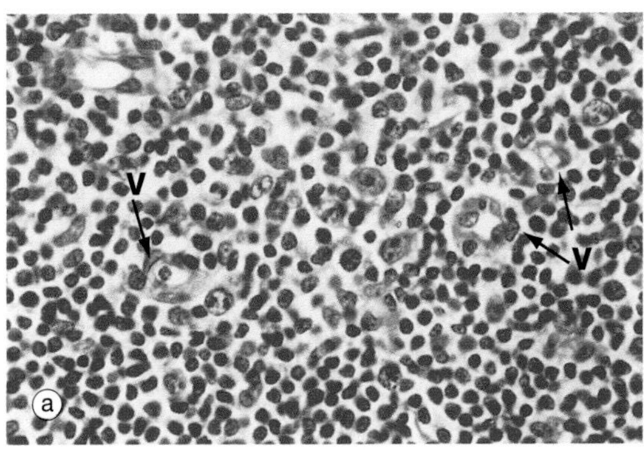

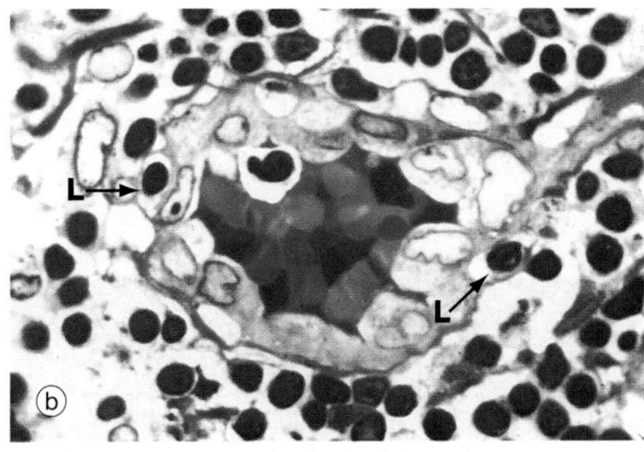

Fig. 11.14 Paracortical zone
(a) H & E ×320 (b) Thin epoxy resin section: toluidine blue ×800

T lymphocytes are the main cell type in the paracortical zone. Circulating T lymphocytes of both helper and cytotoxic subsets enter the lymph node through the walls of high endothelial venules **V** into the paracortical zone; they rejoin the circulation some 6–16 hours later in the efferent lymph.

When activated, T lymphocytes enlarge to form immunoblasts, histologically similar to their B cell counterparts, before mitotic proliferation to produce expanded clones of activated T lymphocytes. Indeed, in a T cell-dominated immunological response, the paracortical zone may be greatly expanded, a pattern known as the ***paracortical reaction***. Activated T cells are then disseminated via the circulation to peripheral sites where much of their activity occurs.

The main antigen-presenting cell in the paracortex is the ***interdigitating dendritic cell***, whose numerous cytoplasmic processes form a meshwork in the paracortex and are in close contact with the naïve T cells circulating through this zone. The interdigitating dendritic cells are derived from macrophage precursors including the Langerhans cells of the skin.

Postcapillary venules of the paracortex have an unusual structure to facilitate the passage of lymphocytes from the blood circulation into the lymph node. Micrograph (b) illustrates a high endothelial venule which is lined by tall cuboidal rather than the usual squamous endothelial cells. These endothelial cells express on their surface specific lymphocyte binding molecules known as ***addressins*** that allow lymphocytes to bind to the endothelium as the first step of migration into the tissue. Several lymphocytes **L** can be seen migrating through the vessel wall between the endothelial cells.

CB centroblasts **CC** centrocytes **F** follicle **GC** germinal centre **I** immunoblasts **L** lymphocytes **M** tingible body macrophages **MZ** mantle zone **P** paracortex **PC** plasma cells **V** high endothelial venule

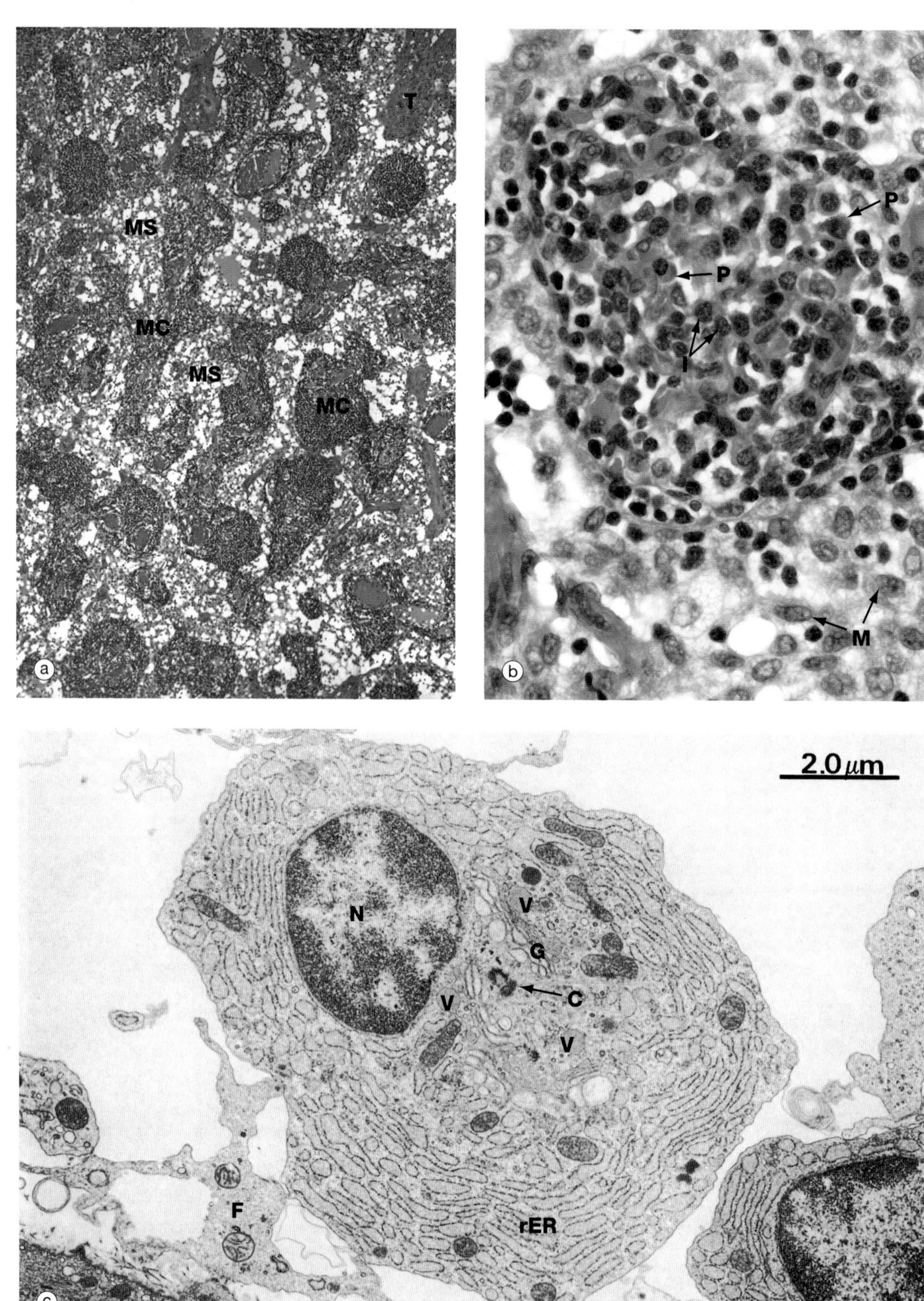

C centrosome **F** fibroblast **G** Golgi apparatus **M** macrophage **MC** medullary cord
MS medullary sinus **N** nucleus **P** plasma cell **PB** plasmablast **rER** rough endoplasmic reticulum
T trabecula **V** secretory vesicle

Fig. 11.15 Medullary cords and sinuses *(illustrations opposite)*
(a) H & E ×40 (b) H & E ×400 (c) EM of plasma cell ×10 000

Micrograph (a) illustrates the structure of the lymph node medulla with branching medullary cords **MC** separated by irregular medullary sinuses **MS**. Throughout the medulla are trabeculae **T** extending from the collagenous supporting tissue of the capsule. Plasma cells and their precursors, plasmablasts, which have migrated from the germinal centres, are the major cell types in the medullary cords. Here, the final stages of maturation to form plasma cells take place. Plasma cells synthesise antibody that is carried to the general circulation in efferent lymph; some plasmablasts also migrate from the node in efferent lymph to take up residence in peripheral tissues.

Micrograph (b) shows a higher power view of the medullary cords and sinuses. In the right and central part of the micrograph there is a medullary cord packed with plasmablasts **PB** and plasma cells **P**. In contrast the sinus, which contains mainly sinus macrophages **M** is paler stained. As in the subcapsular and trabecular sinuses, fine reticular strands traverse the medullary sinuses providing support for sinus macrophages.

Plasma cells are differentiated B lymphocytes specialised for the production of large quantities of antibody. Plasma cells are not usually detectable in the circulating blood but are found in the tissues, in particular the medullary cords of lymph nodes, the white pulp of the spleen, the supporting tissues of mucosal surfaces (e.g. lamina propria of intestine) and the bone marrow.

Micrograph (c) is an electron micrograph of a plasma cell. Plasma cells are large with an eccentric round or oval nucleus **N** the chromatin of which is coarsely clumped in a characteristic 'clock face' pattern. By light microscopy, the cytoplasm is amphophilic (purple) due to its large content of ribosomal RNA and protein which stains with both acidophilic and basophilic dyes (see Fig. 1.9c). With electron microscopy, the ribosomes are seen to be associated with an extensive rough endoplasmic reticulum **rER**. A well-developed Golgi apparatus **G** displaces the nucleus to one side of the cell and with light microscopy is represented by a perinuclear halo. The immunoglobulin protein chains are synthesised in the rER and the carbohydrate element added in the Golgi apparatus. Secretory vesicles **V** then convey the antibody to the surface where it is secreted into the extracellular fluid. Plasma cells do not express surface immunoglobulin (sIg) as they have no need to recognise antigen. In the centre of the cell and surrounded by the Golgi complex is the centrosome **C** from which radiate the microtubules of the cytoskeleton. Note the fine cytoplasmic extensions of fibroblasts **F** in the surrounding tissues.

Mucosa-associated lymphoid tissue (MALT)

Lymphoid tissue is distributed throughout the gastrointestinal tract either as a diffuse population or as non-encapsulated organised aggregations, such as the ***tonsils*** or the ***Peyer's patches*** of the small bowel. Follicles with germinal centres, similar to those of lymph nodes, are found in the organised lymphoid tissues. Smaller lymphoid aggregations and diffuse populations of lymphocytes are also seen in the tracheobronchial tree (see Fig. 12.9) and genitourinary tract. The breast also contains a population of lymphocytes and plasma cells.

The total mass of lymphoid tissue in the gastrointestinal, respiratory and genitourinary tracts is enormous and is collectively known as ***mucosa-associated lymphoid tissue*** (***MALT***). The larger aggregations function in a manner analogous to lymph nodes, sampling antigenic material entering the tracts and initiating both antibody-mediated and cytotoxic immune responses where appropriate; they contain discrete B and T cell zones as well as antigen-processing accessory cells.

The diffusely scattered lymphocytes seen in the lamina propria of the gut and respiratory tree are mainly T lymphocytes. Smaller numbers of B cells are also present, as well as plasma cells. All classes of antibody are produced, with IgA predominating. IgA is secreted into the lumen bound to a carbohydrate moiety, ***secretory piece***, which is synthesised in the epithelium and renders IgA resistant to proteolytic enzymes. This ***secretory IgA*** protects against pathogens in the gut lumen before they breach the tissues. IgA also reaches the gut in bile, being taken up from blood and secreted into bile in a similar fashion. IgG and IgM are also secreted into the lamina propria to deal with organisms that elude the surface protective mechanisms. IgE is also produced and triggers release of histamine from mast cells that are present in large numbers in the lamina propria.

Considerable numbers of lymphocytes are found within the epithelium of the small and large intestines and are present in particularly large numbers in the epithelium overlying Peyer's patches. These lymphocytes are almost exclusively CD8-positive T cells, with most of the rest being NK cells.

The epithelium overlying all MALT aggregations is specialised for the sampling of luminal contents for antigen and acts as the equivalent of the afferent lymphatics of the lymph node. The lymphatics associated with MALT are all efferent from the MALT and pass to regional lymph nodes (e.g. tonsillar, mesenteric, hilar).

MALT acts as an integrated unit with a separate route of lymphocyte circulation in parallel with the peripheral lymphoid circulation. When antigen is encountered, it is carried to local MALT tissue. Stimulated lymphocytes migrate to regional lymph nodes where clonal expansion takes place. Effector cells then pass via the thoracic duct and general circulation to the gastrointestinal and respiratory mucosae. MALT lymphocytes carry surface binding molecules that attach to the addressins on high endothelial venules in MALT tissue but not in peripheral tissue.

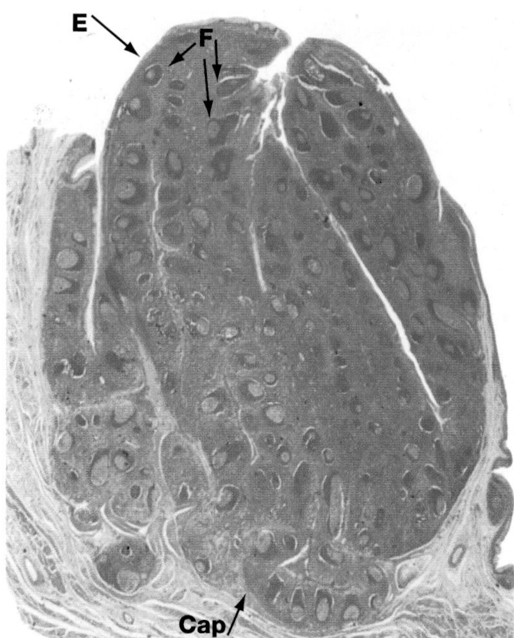

Fig. 11.16 Palatine tonsil
H & E ×6

The palatine tonsils are organised masses of lymphoid tissue that, along with the lingual, pharyngeal and tubal tonsils (adenoids) form ***Waldeyer's ring***.

The luminal surface is covered by stratified squamous epithelium **E** that deeply invaginates the tonsil, forming blind-ended tonsillar crypts. The base of the tonsil is separated from underlying muscle by a dense collagenous hemicapsule **Cap**. The tonsillar parenchyma contains numerous lymphoid follicles **F** with germinal centres similar to those found in lymph nodes. Particulate matter or bacteria entering the crypts from the oropharynx are passed to the follicles, by transcytosis by the epithelial cells of the crypt lining and an immune response is initiated. Efferent lymphatics pass to the deep cervical chain of nodes and activated lymphocytes migrate to the lamina propria of the oral mucosa and nasopharynx and other mucosae.

Antigen uptake occurs in a similar manner in the lingual, pharyngeal and tubal tonsils, the latter being covered with respiratory-type epithelium rather than stratified squamous epithelium.

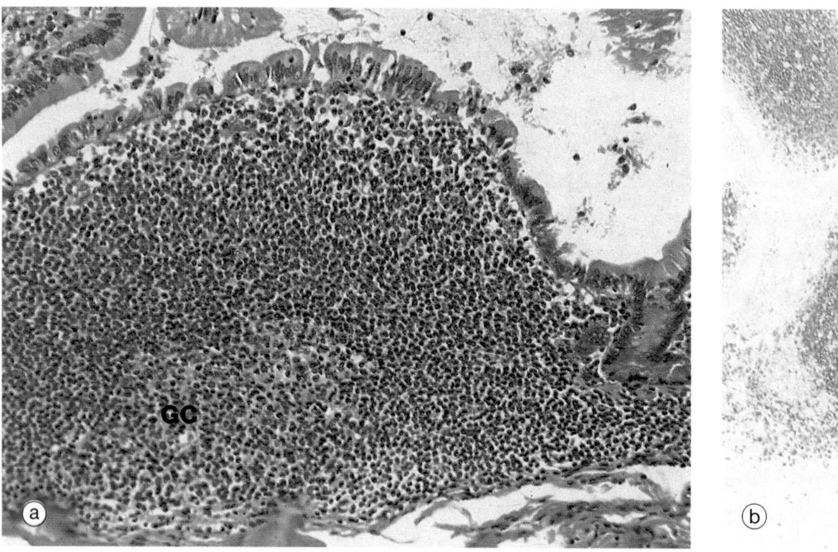

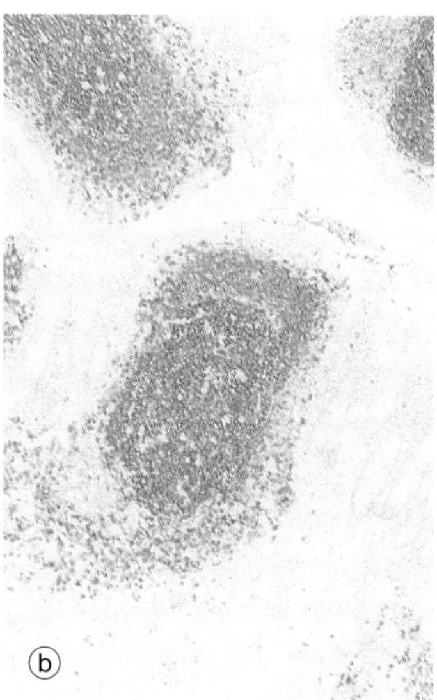

Fig. 11.17 Gut associated lymphoid tissue
(a) Peyer's patch H & E ×150 (b) The appendix: immunoperoxidase CD20 ×40

Organised lymphoid tissue is found in all parts of the normal gastrointestinal system except the stomach. This is often called ***gut associated lymphoid tissue*** or ***GALT***. The largest lymphoid aggregates are the Peyer's patches of the small intestine, which are groups of lymphoid follicles located in the mucosa where they bulge dome-like into the gut lumen. Usually there are few villi overlying Peyer's patches. They are least numerous in the duodenum and most prominent in the terminal ileum. Micrograph (a) illustrates part of a Peyer's patch in the ileum, showing only a single lymphoid follicle. The follicle is similar to those in lymph nodes, consisting of a germinal centre **GC** composed of proliferating and maturing B cells (centroblasts and centrocytes) surrounded by a mantle of small resting lymphocytes. Immediately beneath the epithelium is a zone of mixed lymphocytes and macrophages. The area between follicles is occupied by T lymphocytes and, like its lymph node equivalent, the paracortex, contains high endothelial venules.

The epithelium overlying these ***dome areas*** is specialised for antigen uptake. Scattered among the epithelial cells are low cuboidal ***M cells***, epithelial cells with numerous surface microfolds instead of the usual microvilli. These cells are specialised for transcytosis and take up antigen from the lumen of the gut and transport it into the underlying Peyer's patch. Goblet cells are scanty in these areas.

Antigen entering the Peyer's patch is taken up by antigen presenting cells and presented to T lymphocytes. IgA-committed B cells responding to the antigen migrate via afferent lymphatics to mesenteric lymph nodes where the immunological response is greatly amplified. Activated lymphocytes enter the circulation via the thoracic duct and home to the lamina propria of the gut where they undergo final maturation into plasma cells. During lactation, GALT B cells migrate to the breast, mature into plasma cells and secrete IgA into the milk to protect the newborn.

Micrograph (b) shows lymphoid tissue in the wall of the appendix. The immunoperoxidase method used here stains the B cells brown and confirms that, as in lymph nodes, lymphoid follicles consist mainly of B cells with intervening T cell areas.

Spleen

The spleen is a large lymphoid organ situated in the left upper part of the abdomen. It receives a rich blood supply via a single artery, the ***splenic artery***, and is drained by the ***splenic vein*** into the hepatic portal system.

In humans, the spleen has three main functions:

- Production of immunological responses against blood-borne antigens.
- Removal of particulate matter and aged or defective blood cells, particularly erythrocytes, from the circulation.
- Haemopoiesis in the normal fetus and in adults with certain diseases.

Removal of the spleen in childhood or adolescence renders the individual susceptible to infection by certain pyogenic bacteria but in adults splenectomy has less effect. Presumably adults have been naturally immunised against these organisms.

The spleen performs the same function for blood that lymph nodes perform for lymph. The structure of the spleen allows intimate contacts to be made between blood and lymphocytes, just as the structure of the lymph node facilitates the interaction of afferent lymph and lymphocytes. The histology of the spleen varies according to the animal models used. This description is specific to the human spleen.

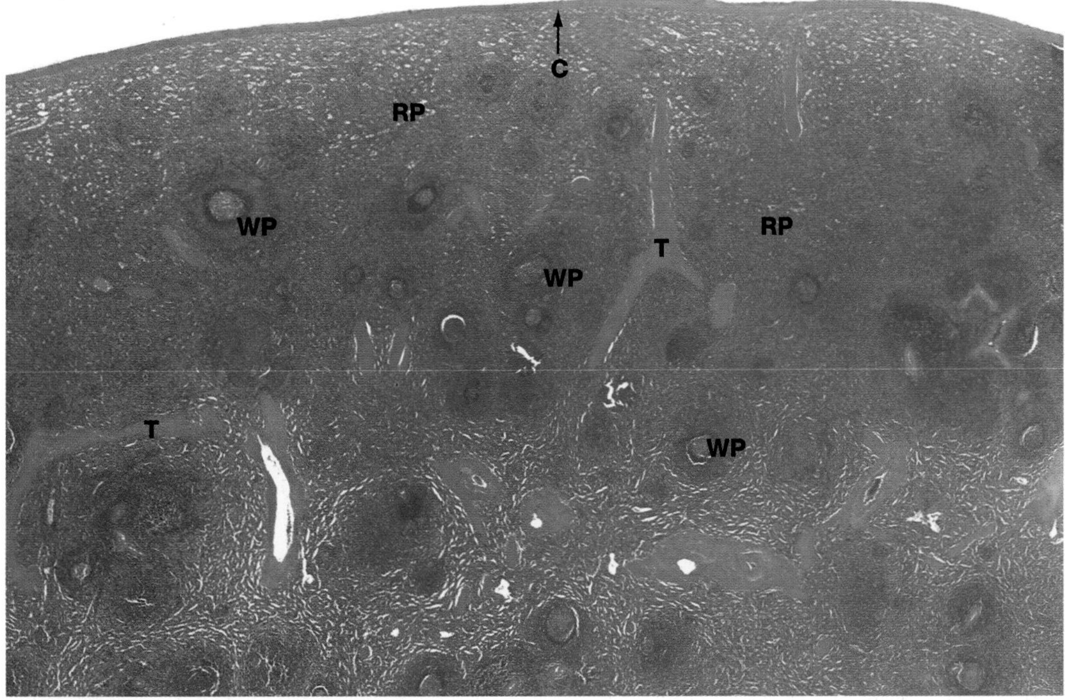

Fig. 11.18 Spleen
H & E ×12

Macroscopically the spleen appears to consist of discrete 0.5–1 mm white nodules, called the ***white pulp***, embedded in a red matrix called the ***red pulp***. Microscopically, as shown here, the white pulp **WP** consists of lymphoid aggregations and the red pulp **RP**, making up the bulk of the organ, is a highly vascular tissue.

The spleen has a thin fibroelastic outer capsule **C** from which short trabeculae **T** extend into the parenchyma. The capsule is thickened at the hilum and is continuous with supporting tissues that sheath the larger blood vessels entering and leaving the organ. In dogs and horses the spleen is also a reservoir of blood and these supporting tissues contain smooth muscle to pump blood out, but in humans only a few smooth muscle cells persist. The splenic artery divides into several major branches, which enter the hilum and branch to form numerous arterioles.

In the white pulp, the T cell areas surround the central arteries, forming the ***periarteriolar lymphoid sheath*** (***PALS***). In humans, this lymphoid tissue is less well organised than in other animals, but the term PALS persists.

C capsule **Cap** hemicapsule **E** epithelium **F** follicle **GC** germinal centre **RP** red pulp **T** trabecula **WP** white pulp

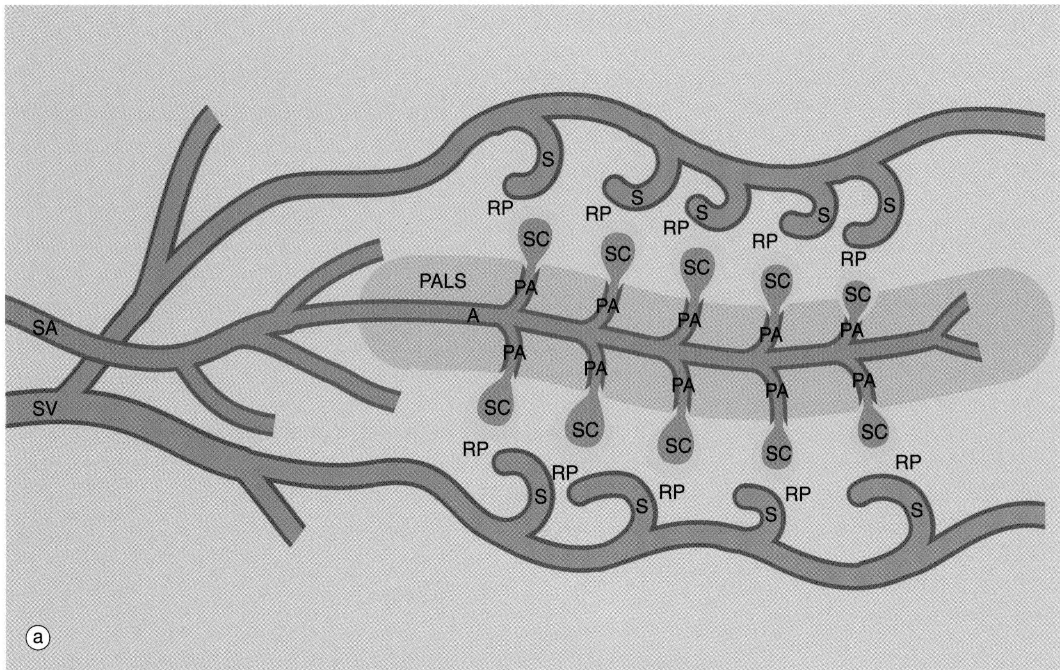

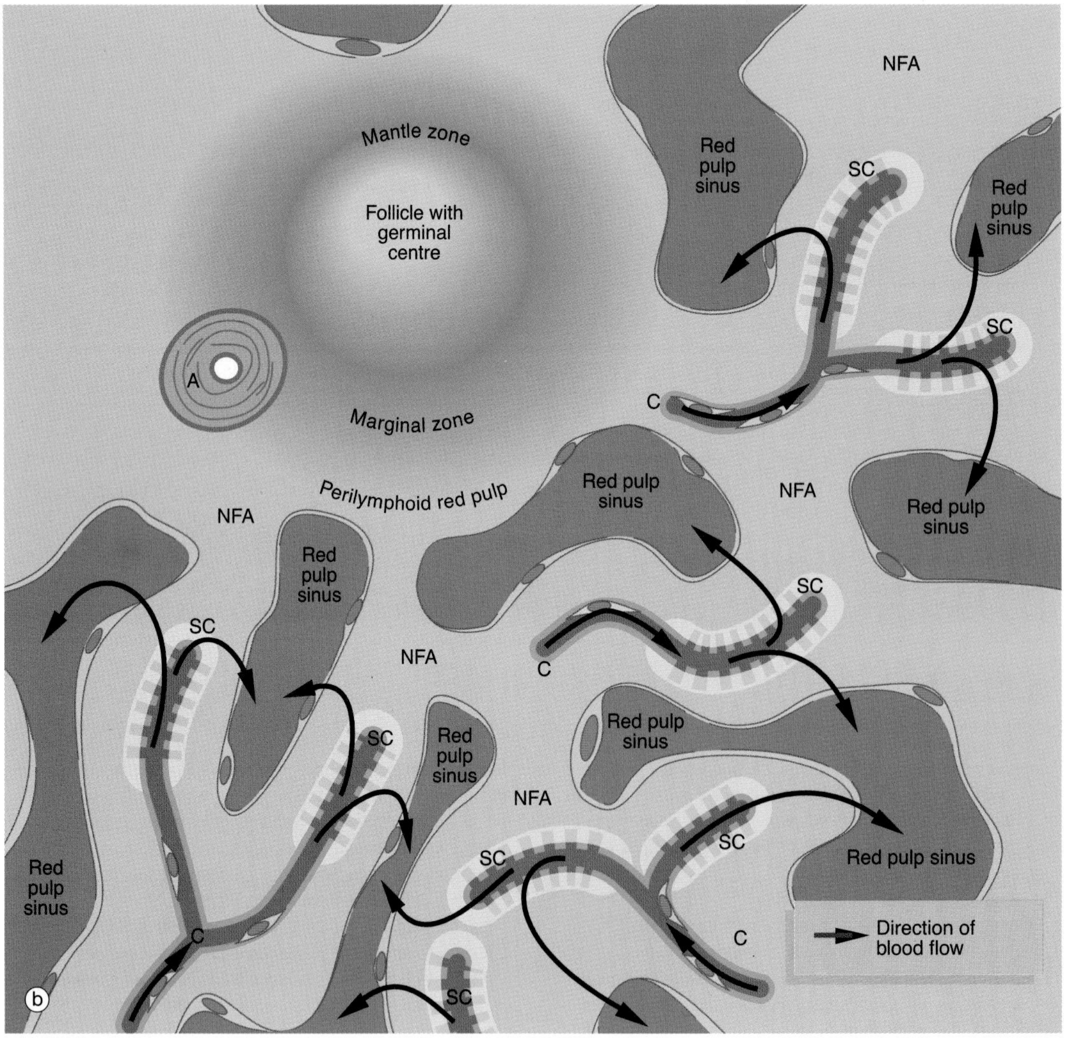

A central artery **C** capillaries **NFA** non-filtering areas **PA** penicilliary arteries **PALS** periarteriolar lymphoid sheath **RP** red pulp **S** sinus **SA** splenic artery **SC** sheathed capillaries **SV** splenic vein

Fig. 11.19 Splenic vasculature and red pulp *(illustrations opposite)*

An overview of the splenic circulation is shown in diagram (a) and a more detailed view of the red pulp in diagram (b). Blood enters the spleen in the splenic artery **SA,** which branches repeatedly within the parenchyma (only a few branches are shown for simplicity). The larger arteries are surrounded by a fibrocollagenous sheath that disappears in the smaller branches. These ***central arteries*** **A**, are so named because they have a cylindrical cuff of lymphoid tissue around them, the ***periarteriolar lymphoid sheath*** **PALS**, consisting mainly of TH cells. The central artery gives off a number of short branches at right angles, which are called ***penicilliary arteries*** **PA**, and these terminate in two to three ***sheathed capillaries*** **SC** (only one is shown for each penicilliary artery). These unique vessels are small blind-ending capillaries with no endothelial lining but surrounded instead by an aggregate of macrophages. Thus the blood arriving in a sheathed capillary must traverse this wall of macrophages before entering the red pulp **RP**. The sheathed capillaries therefore form the first part of the filtering mechanism of the spleen.

Splenic red pulp

The splenic parenchyma is permeated by an interconnected network of sinuses **S** that drain in turn into larger sinuses, tributaries of the splenic vein **SV** and finally the hepatic portal vein. The sinuses are lined by endothelial cells resting upon a basement membrane with numerous narrow slits. The reticulin fibres of the sinusoidal basement membrane are arranged in a circular fashion and are continuous with the reticulin meshwork of the parenchyma (see Fig. 11.20b).

Blood cells entering the parenchyma from the sheathed capillaries squeeze through the walls of the sinuses to drain out of the organ via the splenic vein, an arrangement known as the ***open circulation***. The rate of flow in this system approximates the rate through capillaries elsewhere in the body.

Most of the red pulp parenchyma (diagram (b)) consists of loose tissue supported by reticulin fibres permeated by capillaries **C** terminating as sheathed capillaries **SC**. The parenchyma removes particulate matter and aged or abnormal erythrocytes from the blood, the defective cells being less deformable and thus unable to negotiate the narrow slits in the sinusoidal basement membrane. Trapped cells are removed by the macrophages of the sheathed capillaries and the parenchyma. The mechanism of recognition of effete red cells is probably based on diminished deformability, but immunological mechanisms may also be involved.

Numerous small patches of the red pulp parenchyma (comprising in total a volume comparable to that of the white pulp) are devoid of capillaries and contain mainly T and B lymphocytes and macrophages. Adjacent sinuses are blind-ended and bulb-shaped and their endothelial lining cells have been shown to have characteristics similar to high endothelial venules of lymph nodes. Lymphocytes probably exit these sinuses to enter these non-filtering areas of the red pulp parenchyma **NFA** and these areas should be considered as a functional part of the splenic lymphoid tissue.

Perilymphoid (perifollicular) zones

The zone of red pulp immediately surrounding the white pulp differs from the rest of the red pulp, being devoid of sinuses, having only a sparse reticulin meshwork and containing a large number of red and white blood cells in the same proportion as that of blood. About 10% of blood entering the spleen is believed to pass into this perilymphoid parenchyma, from which it passes much more slowly into the surrounding, more widely spaced sinuses than in the rest of the red pulp. The function of these ***perilymphoid (perifollicular) zones*** is unclear, but the sluggish blood flow may be a means of enhancing the interaction of blood cells, antigens and antibodies.

Tumours of the immune system

Malignant tumours occur in the immune system just as in all other systems of the body. As a group they are called ***lymphomas*** (involving solid organs) and ***leukaemias*** (involving the blood) and exist in many forms with many characteristic clinical presentations and in virtually all age groups. Lymphomas may be systemic or may be localised to a particular lymphoid organ or to non-lymphoid organs such as the skin or brain. They may occur in otherwise healthy individuals, in immunosuppressed people such as AIDS patients or organ transplant recipients or in certain infections. For instance, patients with lymphoma of the stomach (MALT lymphoma or MALToma) almost always have infection of the stomach with ***Helicobacter pylori***, a bacterium also associated with gastritis, peptic ulcer and gastric adenocarcinoma. Interestingly, eradication of the infection may bring about resolution of the lymphoma.

Common clinical presentations include enlargement of some or all lymph nodes (lymphadenopathy), enlargement of the spleen (splenomegaly) and liver (hepatomegaly) as well as fever, weight loss and malaise. Lymphomas of lymphoid tissues are generally divided into Hodgkin's and non-Hodgkin's lymphomas. Non-Hodgkin's lymphomas composed of malignant B lymphocytes may have a follicular (nodular) architecture recapitulating normal lymphoid follicle formation. Lymphomas are also generally classified as high and low grade but interestingly there are no truly benign tumours of lymphoid tissues.

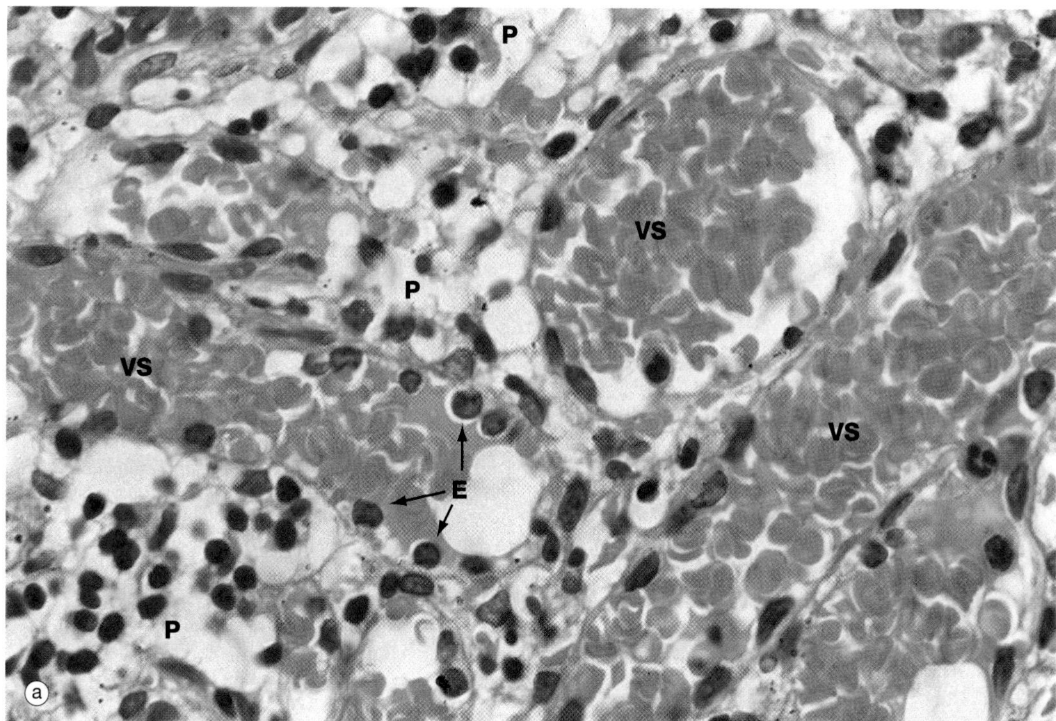

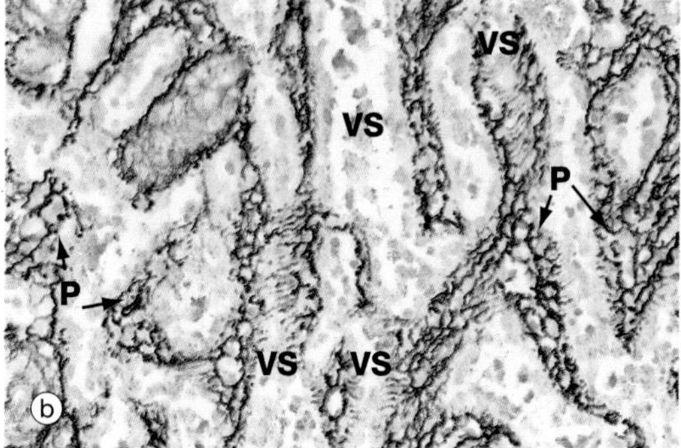

Fig. 11.20 Red pulp
(a) H & E ×800 (b) Reticulin method ×200

Micrograph (a) illustrates the red pulp, consisting of the parenchyma **P** permeated by broad interconnected venous sinuses **VS**. Seen in section, the parenchymal tissue between the sinusoids is considerably narrower than the diameter of the sinusoids, and the area occupied by sinuses is greater than that of the parenchyma; in three-dimensional terms, however, the parenchyma makes up 70% of the volume and the sinuses only 30%. The two-dimensional view gave rise to the misleading term ***cords*** (***of Billroth***) to describe the parenchymal tissue. The three dimensional structure of the red pulp is analogous to a Swiss cheese, with the holes representing the sinuses and the cheese representing the parenchyma.

The parenchyma is composed of the macrophages of sheathed capillaries, other macrophages and blood cells in transit. Non-filtering areas are devoid of sheathed capillaries and contain a greater proportion of lymphocytes. The macrophages are responsible for destruction of aged or damaged blood cells. The different nucleated cell types of the parenchyma cannot be reliably distinguished in this type of preparation.

The venous sinuses are lined by elongated, spindle-shaped endothelial cells **E** lying parallel to the long axes of the sinuses. The venous sinuses have thus been likened to tall wooden barrels with both ends open, with the endothelial cells represented by the wooden staves and hence described as ***stave cells***. Slits occur between the endothelial cells, the endothelial basement membrane being discontinuous over the slits. Blood cells, particularly viable erythrocytes, squeeze between the stave cells to reach the venous sinuses; these drain into progressively larger vessels that converge to form the splenic vein.

Micrograph (b) shows red pulp stained by the reticulin method to demonstrate the supporting framework of the parenchyma **P**. The basement membranes of the venous sinuses **VS** show the greatest concentration of reticulin fibres encircling the endothelium in a manner reminiscent of the steel bands holding together a wooden barrel. Fine reticular strands traverse the parenchyma, linking the whole structure together and providing support for parenchymal macrophages and a small number of fibroblasts responsible for elaboration of the reticulin. In some sinuses, the plane of section is such that the parallel bands of reticulin can be seen encircling the sinuses. Other sinuses are cut in such a way that only the erythrocytes in the lumina are visible.

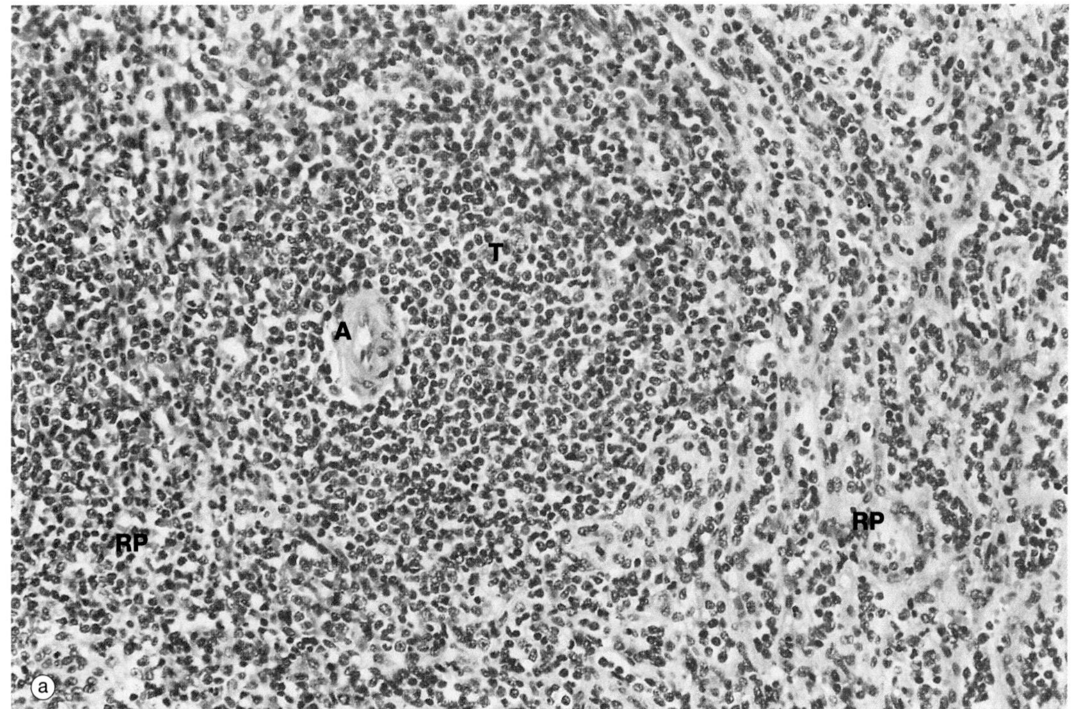

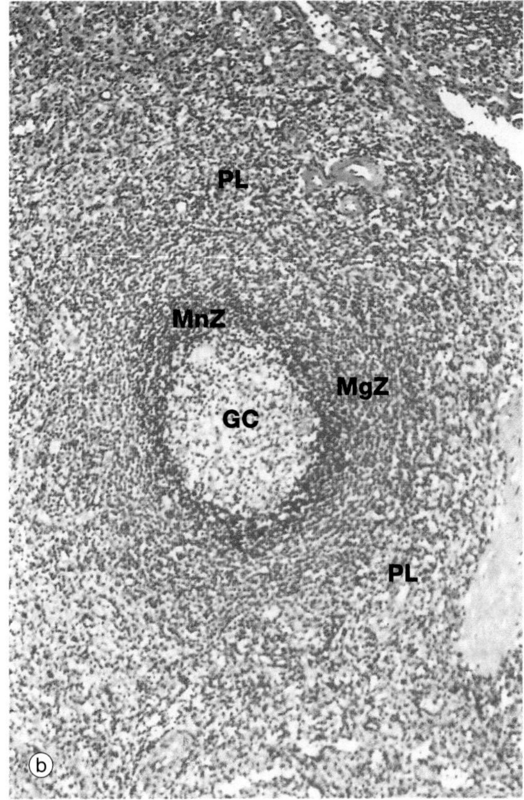

Fig. 11.21 Splenic lymphoid tissue
(a) H & E ×225 (b) H & E ×150

The splenic white pulp is of two types, T cell and B cell, together making up 5–20% of the total mass of the spleen. The functions of these areas appear to be similar to those of the paracortex and superficial cortex of lymph nodes respectively. The non-filtering areas of red pulp parenchyma (see Fig. 11.19) should probably be considered part of the splenic lymphoid tissue mass also, but its immunological function remains to be elucidated.

Micrograph (a) shows a T cell area typically forming an eccentric cylindrical sheath **T** around a central artery **A** and containing small lymphocytes mainly of the T helper subset. This is equivalent to the periarteriolar lymphoid sheath in animals. Note the way the T cell mass merges with the surrounding red pulp parenchyma **RP**. Small lymphatics arise in the T lymphocyte areas, forming a network around the arterioles and then continuing with the larger arteries to the hilum to drain into a group of adjacent lymph nodes.

B cells form follicles usually located in the vicinity of an arteriole, as illustrated in micrograph (b). In young people, many of the follicles exhibit germinal centres **GC** similar to those of the lymph node, although the proportion of follicles with germinal centres diminishes with age. At the follicle periphery is a narrow zone of small lymphocytes called the ***mantle zone*** **MnZ** beyond which is a broader ***marginal zone*** **MgZ** of less densely packed medium-sized lymphocytes supported by a framework of reticulin fibres. The red pulp around the marginal zone, the perilymphoid red pulp **PL**, also contains lymphocytes which may simply be migrating from the sinuses to the white pulp.

A central artery **E** endothelial cells **GC** germinal centre **MgZ** marginal zone **MnZ** mantle zone
P parenchyma **PL** perilymphoid red pulp **RP** red pulp **T** T cell area **VS** venous sinus

12. *Respiratory system*

Introduction

Respiration is a term used to describe two different but interrelated processes: ***cellular respiration*** and ***mechanical respiration***. Cellular respiration is the series of intracellular biochemical processes by which the cell produces energy by metabolism of organic molecules (see Ch. 1). This chapter is concerned with mechanical respiration which involves the following steps:

- Air is drawn into the body (to the ***lungs***) from the atmosphere by inhalation.
- Before it reaches the furthest parts of the lungs the air is cleaned by removal of particulate matter, warmed so that its temperature equals that of the body, and moistened.
- In the lung parenchyma, oxygen is extracted from the air and transferred into the blood vascular system where it bonds tightly with haemoglobin in the red cells for transport in the systemic arterial circulation.
- At the same time that oxygen is passing from air into the blood, carbon dioxide (a side product of cellular metabolic activity) is transferred from the blood to the air.
- After gaseous exchange, the air is returned to the atmosphere by exhalation.

Inhalation and exhalation are achieved by expanding and contracting the thoracic cavity using the ***intercostal muscles*** and the ***diaphragm***, drawing air in when the thoracic cavity expands and driving air out when it contracts.

The respiratory system has two main functional elements, a conducting/cleaning system and a gaseous interchange mechanism.

The ***conducting/cleaning system*** begins as a system of cavities (***nasal cavity***, ***paranasal sinuses*** and ***nasopharynx***) which begin the cleansing, warming and moistening of air drawn in through the anterior ***nares*** (***nostrils***). These cavities are lined by respiratory epithelium with two cell types, one of which secretes mucus which traps particulate matter, and the other bears surface cilia which moves the thin layer of mucus. Abundant blood vessels beneath the epithelium warm the air, and seromucous glands in the submucosa secrete both mucus and a watery fluid which moistens the air. In the nasopharynx is lymphoid tissue which provides immunological surveillance against inhaled antigens. Some air is also taken in through the mouth and therefore bypasses these early cavities.

The air then enters a single tube (the ***trachea***) that divides repeatedly to form airways of ever-decreasing diameter (***primary*** or ***main bronchi***, ***secondary*** or ***lobar bronchi*** and ***tertiary*** or ***segmental bronchi***). In the larger airways the epithelium has a similar structure and function to the upper respiratory tract. The wall of the trachea is held open by hyaline cartilage rings, which become irregular cartilage plates in smaller branches. Smooth muscle is also an important component of the wall and contracts and relaxes to modify the diameter of the airway and therefore the flow of air, particularly in those air passages with less cartilage. The tertiary bronchi ramify into numerous orders of progressively smaller airways called ***bronchioles***, which have muscle but no cartilage in their walls. The smallest bronchioles are called ***terminal bronchioles*** which are the last of the purely conducting tubes.

The ***gaseous interchange system*** is a vast number of blind ending sacs called ***alveoli***, the walls of the sacs containing an extensive network of thin-walled blood vessels, the ***pulmonary capillaries***, gaseous exchange occurring between the air in the alveoli and the blood in the capillaries. This arrangement provides a huge surface area where blood and air are separated by a very thin barrier, allowing exchange of gases between the two compartments. The continuous process of gaseous diffusion requires appropriate gaseous pressure gradients to be maintained across the alveolar/capillary walls. This is achieved by rapid and continuous perfusion of the pulmonary capillaries by deoxygenated venous blood from the right side of the heart and regular replacement of alveolar gases by the process of breathing. Between the end of the purely conducting part of the system (terminal bronchioles) and the alveoli is a series of transitional airways, the ***respiratory bronchioles*** and ***alveolar ducts***, which become increasingly involved in gas exchange. These passages terminate in dilated air spaces called ***alveolar sacs***, which open into the alveoli.

The respiratory tract also contains two elements with separate functions:

- The roof of the nasal cavity contains areas of highly specialised mucosa, the ***olfactory mucosa***, responsible for the detection of smell and the more complex aspects of taste (see Fig. 21.2).
- The ***larynx*** is a specialised structure located at the upper end of the trachea. This utilises forcibly expired air from the respiratory tract below it to generate sound by vibrating the ***true vocal cords***.

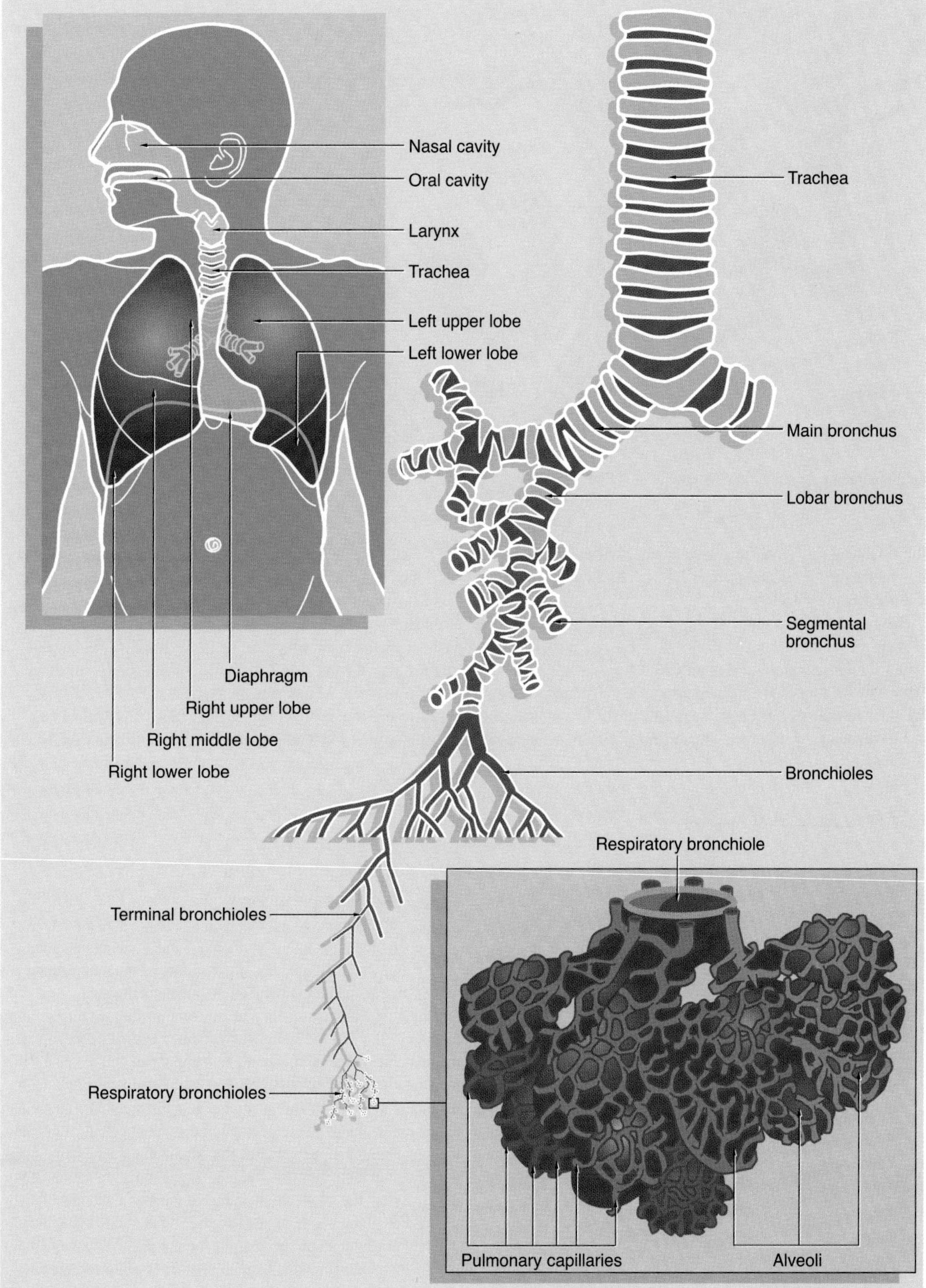

Fig. 12.1 **Structure of the respiratory system**

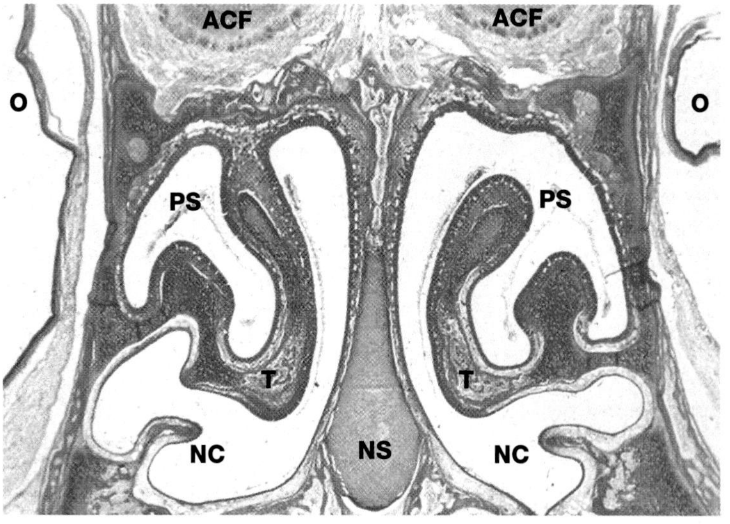

Fig. 12.2 Nasal cavity – kitten
Coronal section H & E/Alcian blue ×12

The nose is subdivided into two nasal cavities **NC** by the cartilaginous ***nasal septum*** **NS**; cartilage is stained blue in this preparation.

The nasal cavities and paranasal sinuses **PS** are lined by respiratory mucosa, the major function of which is to adjust the temperature and humidity of inspired air. Particulate matter entering the nares is usually trapped by the hairs at that site but some smaller particles are caught on the respiratory mucosa. These functions are enhanced by a large surface area provided by the turbinate system of bones **T** which project into the nasal cavities.

Part of the nasal mucosa, the ***olfactory mucosa***. contains receptors for the sense of smell (see Fig. 21.2). Although the olfactory mucosa is extensive in lower mammals, in man it is confined to a relatively small area in the roof of the nasal cavities.

Note the close proximity of the nasal cavities to the orbital cavities **O** and the anterior cranial fossa **ACF**.

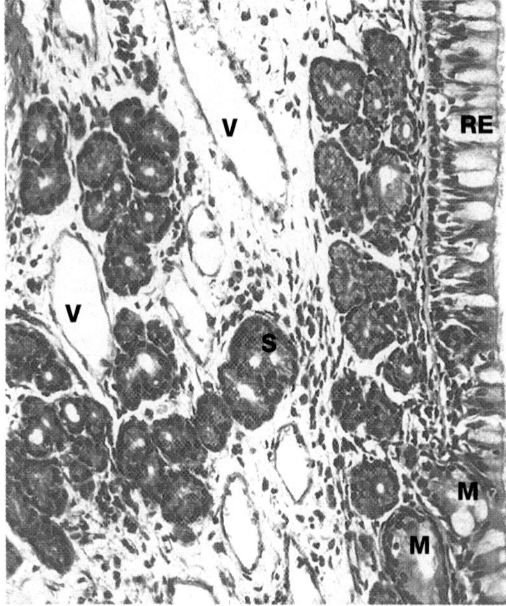

Fig. 12.3 Nasal mucosa
H & E ×200

The mucosa of the nasal cavities (and paranasal sinuses) consists of a pseudostratified columnar ciliated epithelium **RE** containing numerous mucin secreting goblet cells. This is called ***respiratory epithelium*** and is found elsewhere in the conducting part of the respiratory tract. It is supported by a lamina propria rich in blood vessels **V** and serous **S** and mucous **M** glands. The secretions of these glands, and of the epithelial goblet cells, trap small particles in the inspired air in a thin layer of surface mucous, which is propelled towards the pharynx by the co-ordinated movement of the cilia. From the pharynx, most of the mucus is swallowed, and gastric acids destroy any trapped bacteria.

The temperature of the inspired air is adjusted close to that of the body as a result of warming by the rich plexus of blood vessels (mainly thin-walled vessels). The air is also humidified by contact with the gland secretions, particularly those of the serous glands.

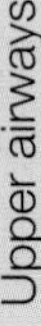

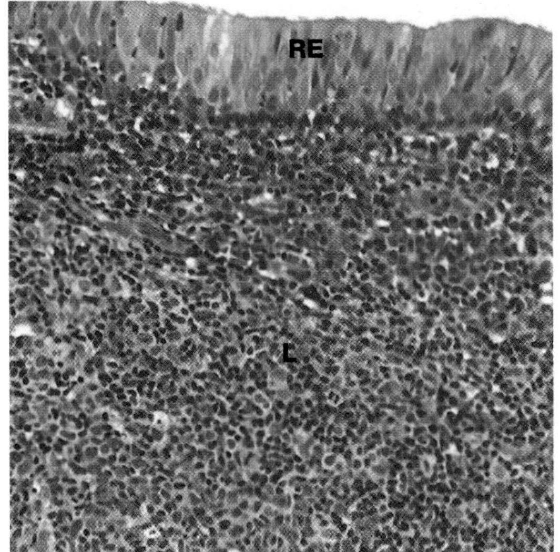

Fig. 12.4 Nasopharynx
H & E ×260

The nasopharynx is lined by pseudostratified ciliated columnar (respiratory) epithelium **RE** similar to that seen in Fig. 12.3, but patches of squamous epithelium occur with increasing age, particularly near the lower end and most markedly in smokers. The lamina propria contains some serous and mucous glands but the dominant feature is large masses of lymphoid tissue **L** which forms a component of ***Waldeyer's ring*** of lymphoid tissue protecting the entry portals of the respiratory and gastro-intestinal systems.

This lymphoid tissue is particularly prominent in children and young adults, and bulges outwards into the lumen producing an appearance similar to that seen in the lingual tonsil (Fig. 13.13) with epithelial crypts. This is called the nasopharyngeal tonsil, or ***adenoid***.

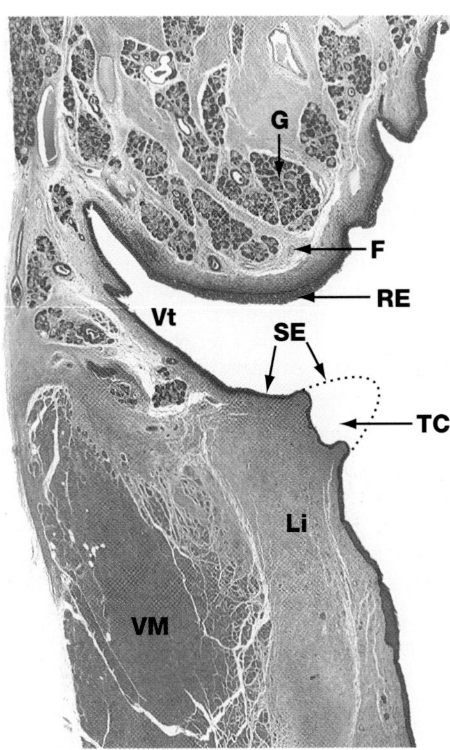

Fig. 12.5 Larynx
H & E ×4

This low power photomicrograph shows the constituents of one half of the larynx. It comprises two folds which protrude into the airway. The upper fold is the ***false vocal cord*** **F** which is covered by columnar ciliated respiratory-type epithelium **RE** and contains seromucous glands **G**. The lower fold is the ***true vocal cord*** **TC**. In this surgically removed human larynx, the sharp tip of the true cord has been removed by diathermy in the distant past, and a dotted line shows its normal outline. The true cord contains the ***vocalis muscle*** **VM** and ***vocalis ligament*** **Li** which are responsible for moving the true cord so that it becomes distant from or closer to the true cord on the other side, thus controlling the pitch of the sound made. The true cords are covered by stratified squamous epithelium **SE** which is more resistant to the effects of physical trauma caused by the free margins of the true cords contacting each other during speech.

Between the true and false cords is a narrow cleft, the ***ventricle*** **Vt** which terminates in a blind-ending ***saccule*** (not shown). The ventricle and saccule are lined by respiratory-type columnar epithelium, and contain seromucous glands.

ACF anterior cranial fossa **F** false cord **G** seromucous gland **L** lymphoid tissue
Li vocalis ligament **M** mucous glands **NC** nasal cavity **NS** nasal septum **O** orbital cavity
PS paranasal sinuses **RE** respiratory type epithelium **S** serous glands **SE** squamous epithelium
T turbinate bones **TC** true cord **V** blood vessels **Vt** ventricle **VM** vocalis muscle

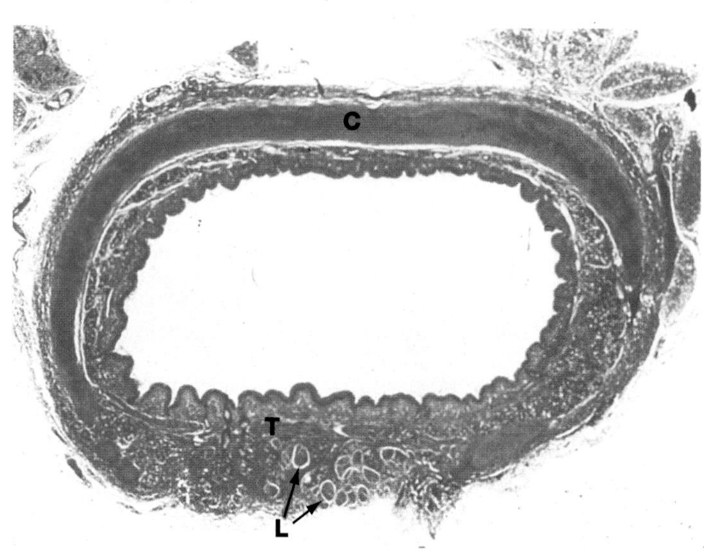

Fig. 12.6 Trachea
H & E/Alcian blue ×9

This specimen from a newborn child shows the general structure of the trachea. This is a flexible tube of fibroelastic tissue and cartilage which permits expansion in diameter and extension in length during inspiration, and passive recoil during expiration.

A series of C-shaped rings of hyaline cartilage **C** (stained blue) support the tracheal mucosa and prevent its collapse during inspiration.

Bands of smooth muscle, called the ***trachealis muscle*** **T**, join the free ends of the rings posteriorly; contraction of the trachealis reduces tracheal diameter and thereby assists in raising intrathoracic pressure during coughing. A few strands of longitudinal muscle **L** can be seen disposed behind the trachealis muscle.

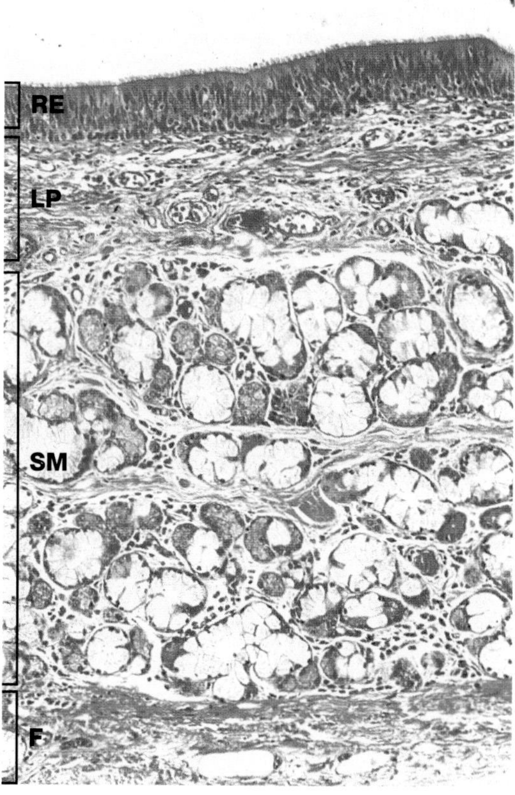

Fig. 12.7 Trachea
H & E ×198

The inner layers of the tracheal wall are shown in this specimen from a young adult. The respiratory epithelium **RE** of the trachea is similar to the rest of the bronchial tree and nasal epithelium. The epithelium of the respiratory system is supported by an unusually thick basement membrane (not visible at this magnification). A variety of cell types is found in the epithelium, including:

- Tall pseudostratified columnar cells with cilia.
- Goblet cells.
- Serous cells identical to the cells of the submucosal serous glands.
- Basal cells which are part of the diffuse neuroendocrine system.
- Basal stem cells which are able to divide and differentiate to replace other cell types.

The various cell types are present in different proportions in different parts of the trachea, with ciliated columnar cells relatively more plentiful in the lower trachea, and goblet and basal cells more common in the upper trachea. Beneath the basement membrane, the lamina propria **LP** consists of loose, highly vascular supporting tissue which becomes more condensed at its deeper aspect to form a band of fibroelastic tissue.

Underlying the lamina propria is the loose submucosa **SM** containing numerous mixed seromucinous glands which decrease in number in the lower parts of the trachea; the serous cells stain strongly with H & E whilst the mucous cells remain poorly stained. The submucosa merges with the perichondrium of the underlying hyaline cartilage rings (not seen in this field) or, as here, with the dense fibroelastic tissue **F** between the cartilage rings.

C cartilage **CC** ciliated cell **El** elastic fibres **F** fibroelastic tissue **G** seromucinous glands **GC** goblet cells **L** longitudinal muscle **LP** lamina propria **M** smooth muscle **Ma** mast cell **RE** respiratory epithelium **SM** submucosa **T** trachealis muscle

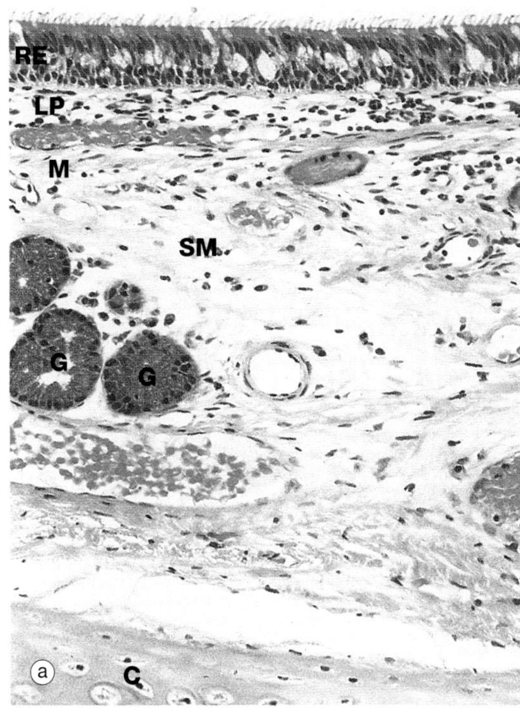

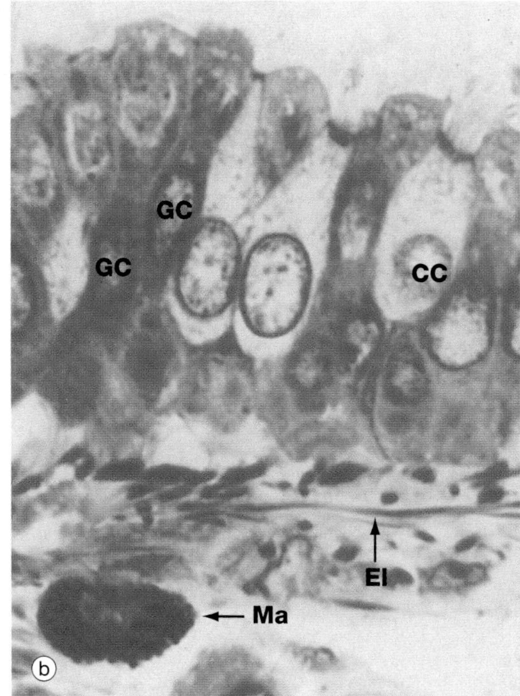

Fig. 12.8 Primary bronchus
(a) H & E ×150 (b) Thin epoxy resin section ×800

The basic structure of the wall of a main bronchus (a) is similar to that of the trachea but differs in several details:

- The respiratory epithelium **RE** is less tall and contains fewer goblet cells.
- The lamina propria **LP** contains more elastin in its upper layers.
- The lamina propria is separated from the submucosa **SM** by a layer of smooth muscle **M** which becomes more prominent in more distal bronchi.
- The submucosa contains fewer seromucinous glands **G**.
- The cartilage support **C** is in flattened interconnected plates rather than distinct rings.

Micrograph (b) shows the epithelial layer at very high magnification. The cells are pseudostratified, the bases of all the cells contacting the basement membrane, but not all the cells reaching the luminal surface. The ciliated **CC** and goblet **GC** cells can be easily distinguished. The underlying lamina propria contains elastic fibres **El**, and occasional mast cells **Ma**.

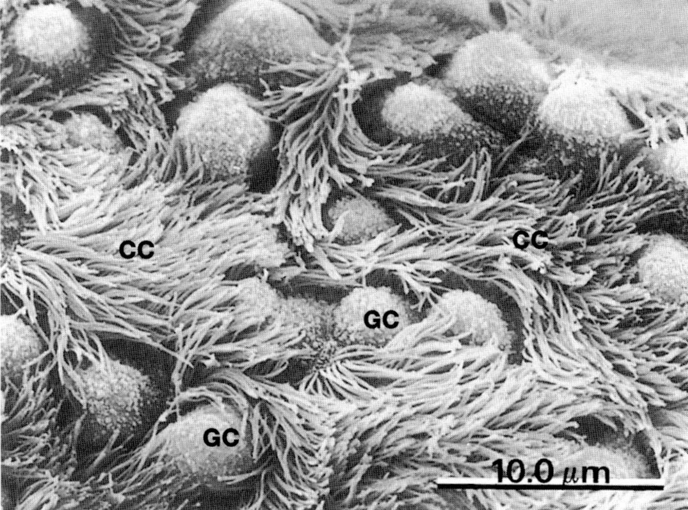

Fig. 12.9 Primary bronchus epithelium
SEM ×2000

This scanning electron micrograph illustrates the surface of a primary bronchus; the film of surface mucus has been removed. The ciliated epithelial cells **CC** have numerous surface cilia, each several microns long, that move in a coordinated fashion sweeping mucous up the bronchus. Scattered goblet cells **GC** are recognisable by their bulbous surface outline, lack of cilia and the presence of small surface projections associated with mucus secretion. The fragile cilia are particularly vulnerable to damage and destruction by inhaled toxic chemicals (cigarette smoke, car exhaust fumes) and by bacterial and viral infections.

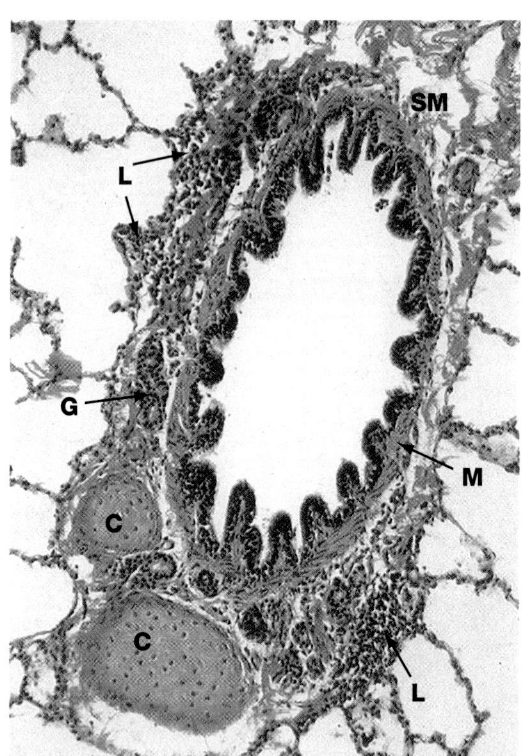

Fig. 12.10 Tertiary (segmental) bronchus
Elastic van Gieson ×75

As the bronchi diminish in diameter, the structure progressively changes to resemble more closely that of large bronchioles. The respiratory epithelium, which is just visible at this magnification, is now tall and columnar with little pseudostratification, and goblet cell numbers are greatly diminished.

The lamina propria is thin, elastic and completely encircled by smooth muscle **M** which is disposed in a spiral manner. This arrangement of smooth muscle permits contraction of the bronchi in both length and diameter during expiration. Seromucinous glands **G** are sparse in the submucosa: they are rarely found in smaller airways.

The cartilage framework **C** is reduced to a few irregular plates: cartilage does not usually extend beyond the tertiary bronchi. Note that the submucosa **SM** merges with the surrounding adventitia and thence with the lung parenchyma. Small aggregations of lymphocytes **L**, part of the mucosa-associated lymphoid tissue (MALT), are seen in the adventitia.

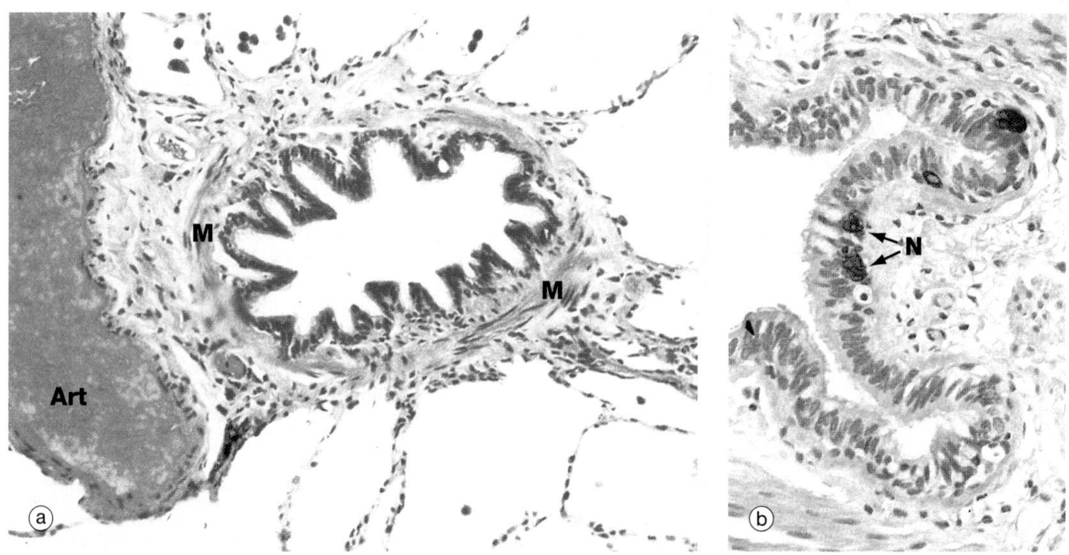

Fig. 12.11 Bronchiole
(a) H & E ×150 (b) Immunoperoxidase chromogranin A ×300

A bronchiole (a) is an airway of less than 1 mm diameter which has neither cartilage or submucosal glands in its wall. The epithelium is composed of ciliated columnar cells and few goblet cells. In the terminal and respiratory bronchioles, goblet cells are replaced by Clara cells (see Fig. 12.12), tall columnar cells with apical secretory granules. The wall is also composed of smooth muscle **M**, the tone of which controls the bore of the tube and therefore resistance to airflow within the lungs. A distended thin-walled pulmonary artery branch **Art** lies next to the bronchiole.

Micrograph (b) shows the presence of neuroendocrine cells **N**, part of the diffuse neuroendocrine system (see Ch. 17), secreting a number of peptide hormones, including serotonin and bombesin, which regulate muscle tone in bronchial and vessel walls.

A alveoli **AD** alveolar duct **AR** alveolar ring **Art** pulmonary artery branch **AS** alveolar sacs
C cartilage **G** seromucinous glands **L** lymphocytes **M** smooth muscle **N** neuroendocrine cells
R respiratory bronchioles **SM** submucosa **T** terminal bronchiole **V** vein

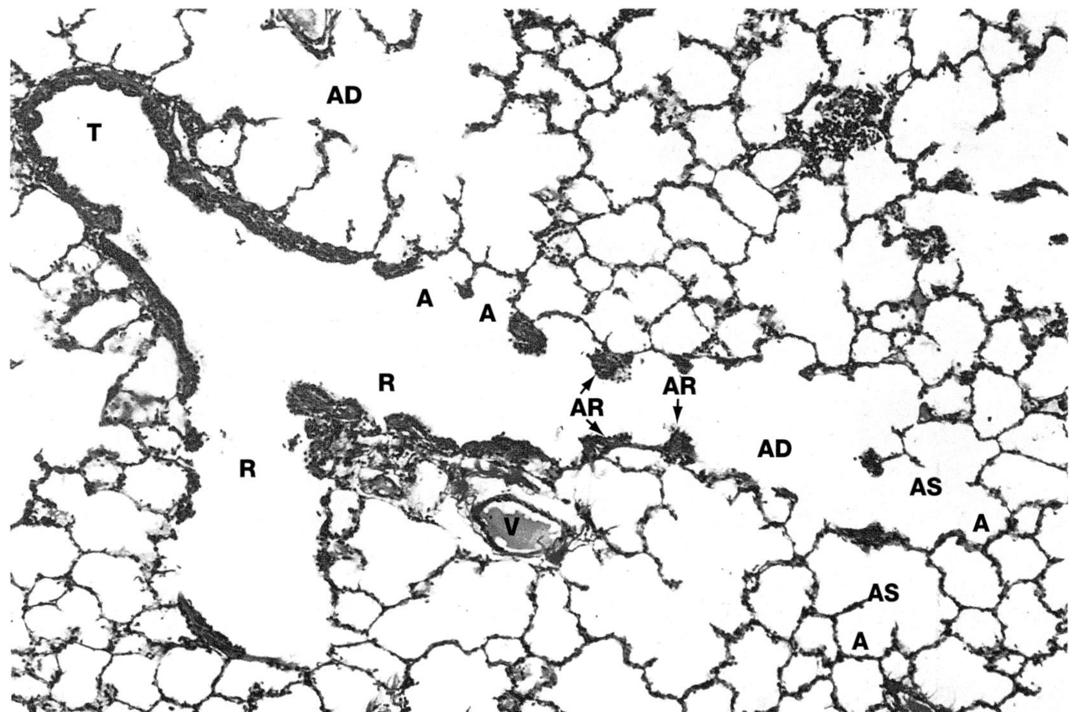

Fig. 12.12 Terminal portion of the respiratory tree
H & E ×40

Terminal bronchioles **T** are the smallest diameter passages of the purely conducting portion of the respiratory tree; beyond this, further branches become increasingly involved in gaseous exchange.

Each terminal bronchiole divides to form short, thinner-walled branches called ***respiratory bronchioles*** **R** which contain a small number of single alveoli **A** in their walls. The epithelium of the respiratory bronchioles is devoid of goblet cells and largely consists of ciliated cuboidal cells and smaller numbers of non-ciliated cells called ***Clara cells***. In the most distal part of the respiratory bronchioles. Clara cells become the predominant cell type. Clara cells have three functions:

- They produce one of the components of ***surfactant***.
- They act as stem cells, i.e. they are able to divide, differentiate and replace other damaged cell types.
- They contain enzyme systems which can detoxify noxious substances.

Each respiratory bronchiole divides further into several ***alveolar ducts*** **AD** which have numerous alveoli **A** opening along their length. The alveolar ducts end in an ***alveolar sac*** **AS**, which in turn opens into several alveoli.

In histological sections, all that can be seen of the walls of the alveolar ducts are small aggregations of smooth muscle cells, collagen and elastic fibres which form rings **AR** surrounding the alveolar ducts and the openings of the alveolar sacs and alveoli. The smooth muscle of the respiratory bronchioles and alveolar ducts regulates alveolar air movements.

Each alveolus consists of a pocket, open at one side, lined by flattened epithelial cells (***pneumocytes***). The wall or ***alveolar septum*** is composed of a central area of alveolar capillaries surrounded by a fine sparse network of elastin and collagen fibres, with the flat epithelial layer of the two adjacent alveoli on each side of the capillary network (see Figs 12.13–12.17). The alveolar septa contain occasional small openings, about 8 μm diameter, the ***alveolar pores (of Kohn)***, which allow some movement of air between adjacent alveoli. The collagen and elastic fibres of the septum condense around the openings of the alveoli and form a supporting meshwork for the lung parenchyma.

Disorders of the tracheobronchial tree

The tracheobronchial mucosa is subjected to many forms of damaging agent, including inhaled chemical toxins, viruses and bacteria. Prolonged or repeated damage to the respiratory epithelial cells leads to their death and replacement by squamous epithelium (***squamous metaplasia***).

Viral infections kill epithelial cells, and lead to vulnerability to secondary bacterial infection (***purulent tracheobronchitis***). Repeated damage to the mucosa leads to a state called ***chronic bronchitis*** in which the bronchial wall is thickened by increase in numbers and activity of seromucous glands, and thickening of the muscle layers. It is commonly associated with ***asthma*** (a combination of severe bronchoconstriction due to bronchial smooth muscle contraction and the production of particularly viscid mucus) and ***emphysema*** (in which alveolar walls are destroyed). The combination of all three is called ***chronic obstructive pulmonary disease*** (***COPD***).

The bronchial tree is an important site for the development of malignant tumours (***bronchial carcinoma***), often originating in areas of squamous metaplasia in the bronchial mucosa in heavy smokers. One particularly aggressive type of bronchial carcinoma derives from the neuroendocrine cells of the bronchial mucosa.

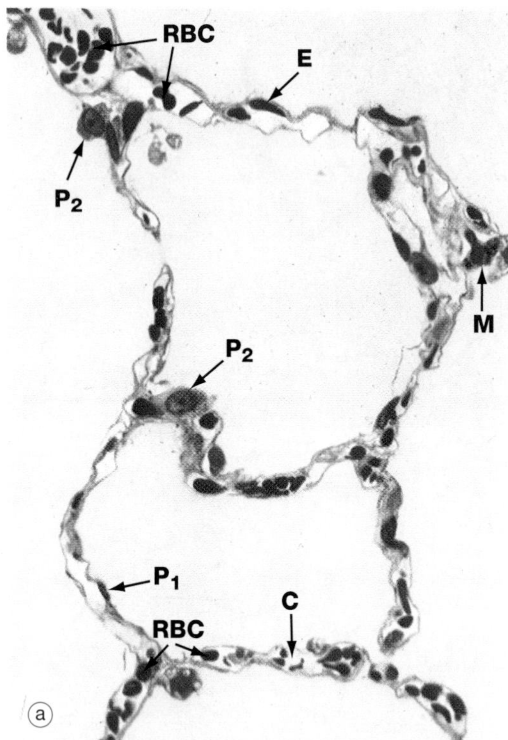

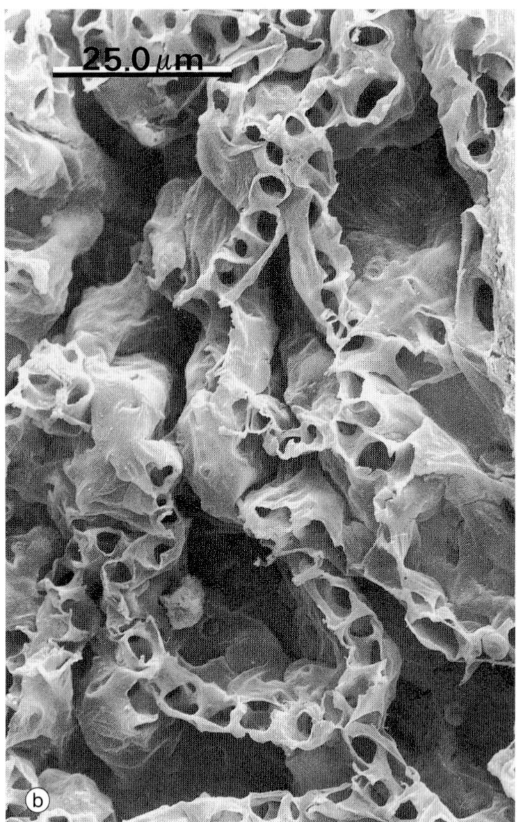

Fig. 12.13 Alveoli
(a) Thin resin section toluidine blue stain ×480
(b) SEM ×500

In general terms, the alveolar wall consists of three tissue components: ***surface epithelium, supporting tissue*** and ***blood vessels***.

The epithelium provides a continuous lining to each alveolus and consists of cells of two types. Most of the alveolar surface area is covered by large, squamous cells called ***type I pneumocytes*** (***alveolar lining cells***); since the cytoplasm of these cells covers such an extensive area, the characteristic densely stained nuclei of type I pneumocytes $\mathbf{P_1}$ are relatively infrequently seen in histological section. A second epithelial cell type, known as the ***type II pneumocyte*** $\mathbf{P_2}$, represents some 60% of cells in the lining epithelium; these cells are rounded in shape and thus occupy a much smaller proportion (about 5%) of the alveolar surface area.

Type I pneumocytes constitute part of the extremely thin gaseous diffusion barrier, whereas type II pneumocytes secrete a surface-active material called ***surfactant*** which reduces surface tension within the alveoli, preventing alveolar collapse during expiration. Clara cells of the respiratory bronchioles probably synthesise other components of surfactant. Type II pneumocytes retain the capacity for cell division and can differentiate into type I pneumocytes in response to damage to the alveolar lining.

Supporting tissue forms an attenuated layer beneath the epithelium and surrounding the blood vessels of the alveolar wall. This layer consists of fine reticular, collagenous and elastic fibres and occasional fibroblasts.

Blood vessels, mainly capillaries **C** (7–10 μm in diameter), form an extensive plexus around each alveolus. In most of the alveolar wall, the basement membrane which supports the capillary endothelium is directly applied to the basement membrane supporting the surface epithelium: in such sites the two basement membranes are fused and the supporting tissue layer is absent. This arrangement provides an interface of minimal thickness between alveolar air and blood.

In micrograph (a) the red blood cells within the capillary lamina are seen as densely stained round or elliptical structures **RBC**. Nuclei of the endothelial cells **E** lining the capillaries are elongated and flat, and usually sparse.

Micrograph (b) is a low magnification scanning electron micrograph of a group of alveoli to show their three-dimensional architecture; the capillaries in the alveolar walls have been distended by injection. At this magnification no cellular detail of the epithelial lining cells can be seen.

A alveolus **C, $\mathbf{C_1}$,** and $\mathbf{C_2}$ capillaries **E** capillary endothelial cells $\mathbf{E_2}$ nuclei of endothelial cells **L** lamellar bodies **M** alveolar macrophage $\mathbf{P_1}$ type I pneumocytes $\mathbf{P_2}$ type II pneumocyte **RBC** red blood cells

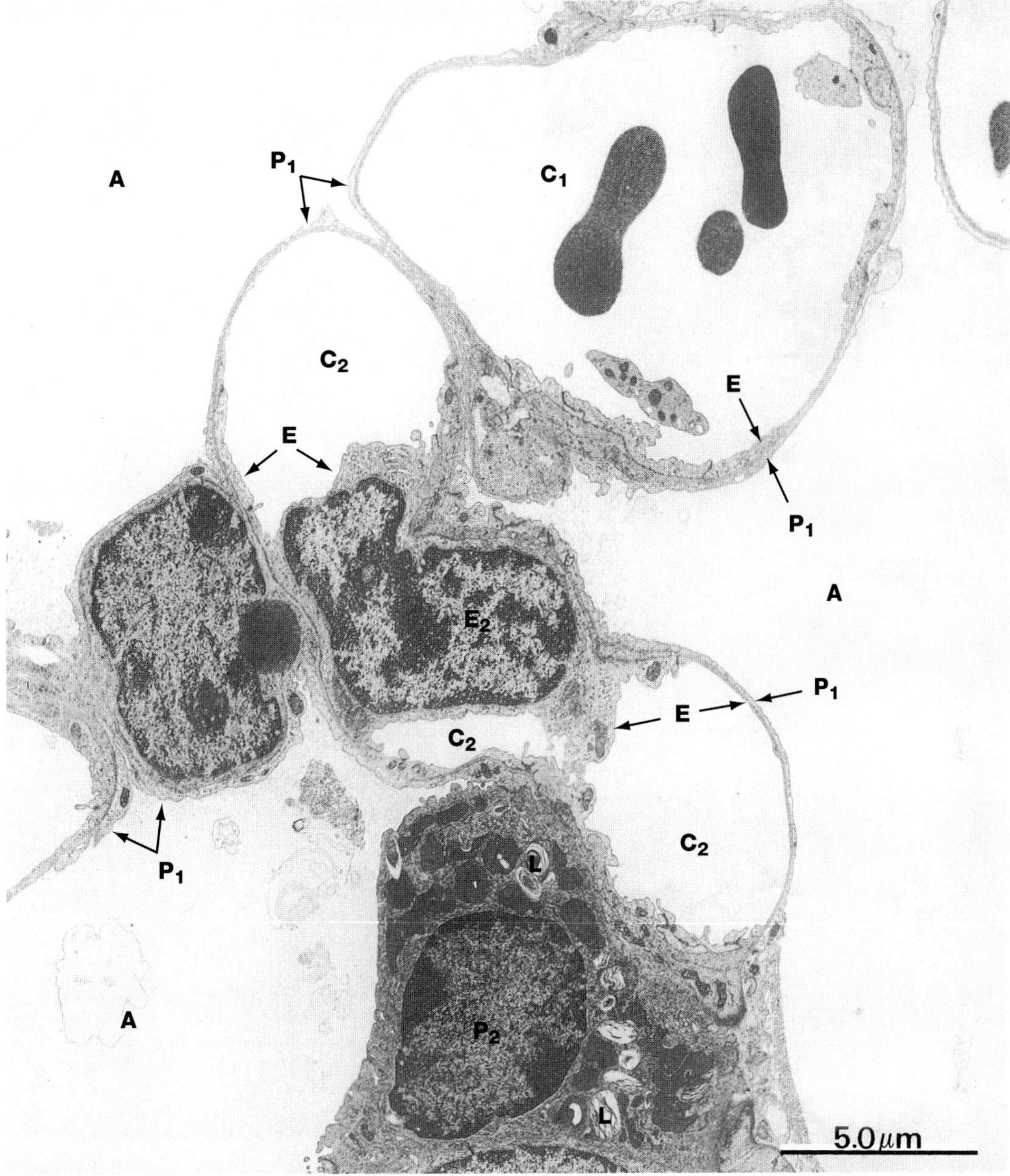

Fig. 12.14 Alveolar wall
EM ×6000

This electron micrograph shows the alveolar wall between three alveoli **A** at low magnification. Capillaries make up the bulk of the alveolar wall, branching and anastomosing to create a basket-like arrangement around each alveolus. This field shows parts of several capillaries, the uppermost $\mathbf{C_1}$ containing erythrocytes and a platelet. The plane of section has cut the lumen of a second capillary $\mathbf{C_2}$ in three places and includes the nucleus of one of its lining endothelial cells $\mathbf{E_2}$. The cytoplasm of type I pneumocytes $\mathbf{P_1}$, which cover most of the alveolar surface, and capillary endothelial cells **E** are both extremely attenuated and distinction between them is best made by tracing their basement membranes. Alveolar lining cells lie on the convex side of the basement membrane, whilst endothelial cells are on the concave side and adjacent to any erythrocytes within the capillary.

A type II pneumocyte $\mathbf{P_2}$ is also seen, typically located at a branching point of the alveolar septum; the cytoplasm is filled with vesicles containing phospholipid in the form of ***lamellar bodies*** **L**. These bodies are discharged into the alveolar air space where they contribute to a surfactant layer at the epithelium/air interface.

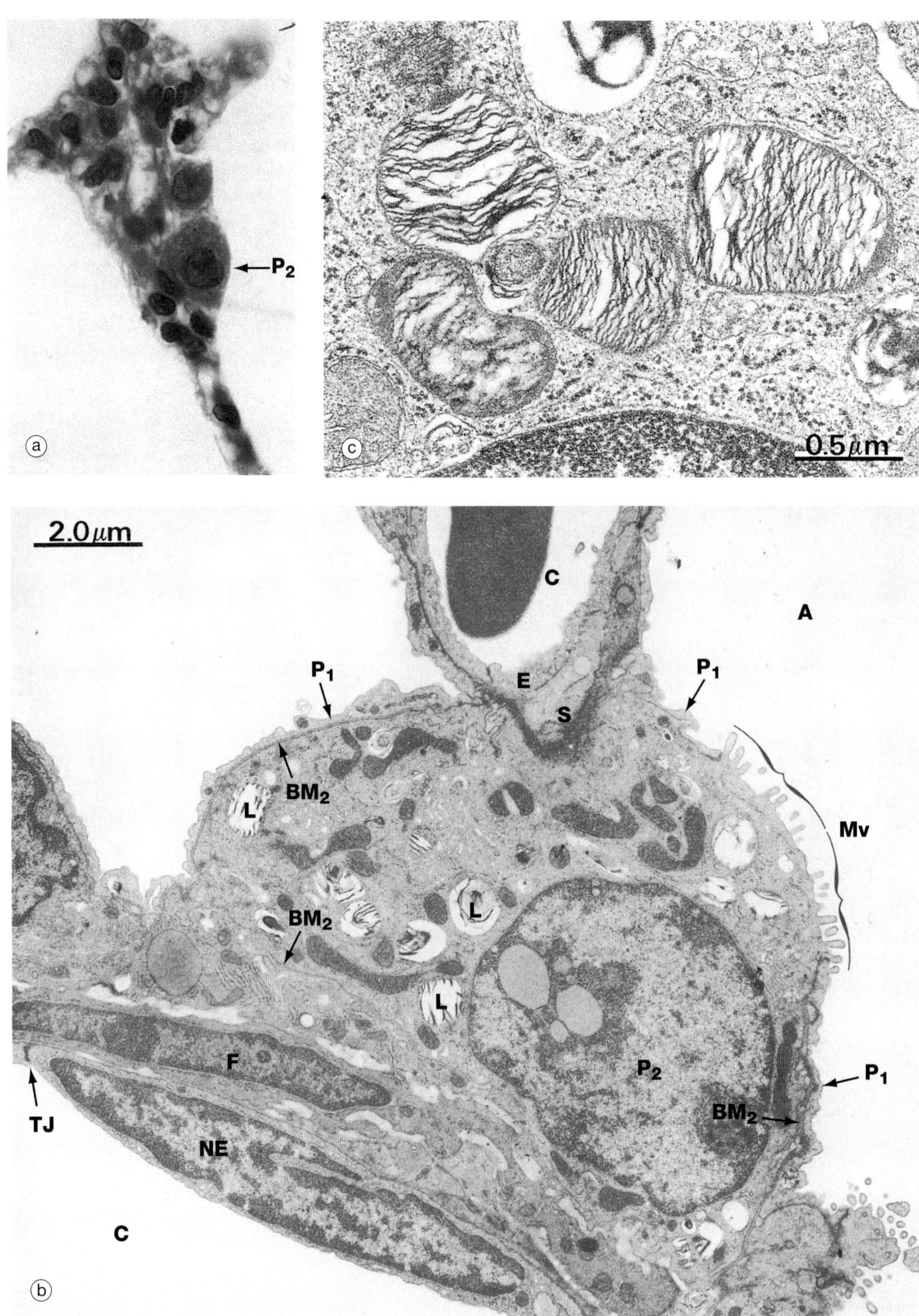

A alveolus **BM** basement membrane **BM_2** basement membrane of type II pneumocyte **C** capillary **E** endothelium **Er** erythrocyte **F** fibroblast **L** lamellar bodies **Mv** microvilli **NE** nucleus of endothelial cell **P_1** type I pneumocyte **P_2** type II pneumocyte **S** supporting tissue **TJ** tight junction

Fig. 12.15 Type II pneumocytes *(illustrations opposite)*
(a) H & E ×400 (b) EM ×9000 (c) EM ×35 000

Micrograph (a) shows the light microscope appearance of type II pneumocytes P_2 or ***surfactant cells***, which are responsible for surfactant production; their nuclei are large and plump with dispersed chromatin and prominent nucleoli. The plentiful eosinophilic cytoplasm is filled with fine unstained vacuoles representing ***lamellar bodies***, the phospholipid of which is dissolved out during tissue preparation. In comparison, the nuclei of type I pneumocytes (alveolar lining cells) and capillary endothelial cells are small, dense and flattened.

Micrograph (b) shows a branching point in an alveolar wall typically containing a type II pneumocyte P_2. recognisable by its lamellar bodies **L**. Most of the type II pneumocyte is surrounded by basement membrane BM_2 and only a small proportion of its surface is exposed directly to the alveolar space **A**, where it exhibits numerous small microvilli **Mv** associated with surfactant secretion. Elsewhere, the alveolar aspect of the type II pneumocyte is invested by a thin layer of cytoplasm of type I pneumocytes P_1 but separated by a common basement membrane. At the top of the field, the type II pneumocyte abuts a capillary **C**, its cytoplasm being separated from that of the capillary endothelium **E** by the basement membranes of each cell and a little intervening supporting tissue **S**. At the lower left of the field, the type II cell rests upon a thin layer of septal supporting tissue containing a fibroblast **F**. Beyond this lies the flattened nucleus of a capillary endothelial cell **NE**, its attenuated cytoplasm spreading out to line the capillary lumen **C**. A tight junction **TJ** is seen where this endothelial cell abuts an adjacent cell. Basement membranes can be traced on both aspects of this alveolar supporting tissue. The surfactant cell contains rough ER, free ribosomes and moderate numbers of elongated mitochondria.

Micrograph (c) shows lamellar bodies at high magnification. These are membrane-bound and the lamellae within them are composed mainly of phospholipids, particularly palmityl phosphatidylcholine. Phospholipid is released by exocytosis, spreading out over the alveolar surface where it combines with other carbohydrate- and protein-containing secretory products (some of which are derived from bronchiolar Clara cells) to form a tubular lattice of lipoprotein described as ***tubular myelin***. In the event of two alveolar surfaces coming together, this overcomes the effects of surface tension which would otherwise cause them to adhere. This allows for normal inflation of the alveoli at birth and for the reinflation of alveoli which collapse after airway obstruction.

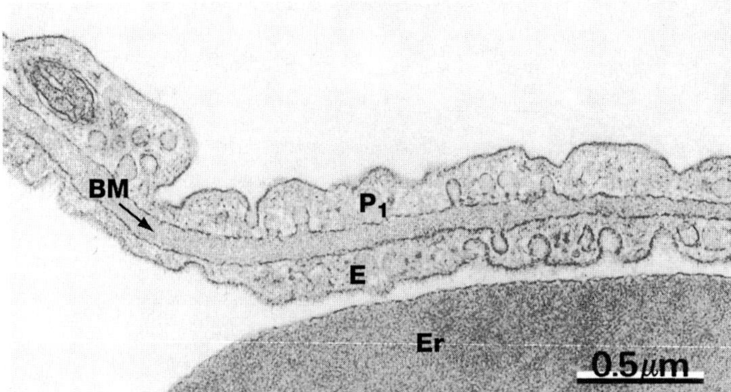

Fig. 12.16 Air–blood barrier
EM ×34 000

This micrograph shows, at high magnification, the components of the diffusion barrier between blood and alveolar air. This consists of the attenuated cytoplasm of a type I pneumocyte P_1, the fused basement membrane **BM** and the thin cytoplasm of a capillary endothelial cell **E**. Note part of an erythrocyte **Er** in the capillary lumen.

Disorders of alveoli

The alveolar walls provide an enormous surface area for exchange of gases between air in the alveoli and the capillaries in the septum wall. Any diseases that reduce the amount of air in the alveoli, or reduce the surface area of the alveoli, or render the alveolar walls thick and impermeable to gases, will lead to inadequate oxygenation of blood (***hypoxia***), carbon dioxide retention, and breathlessness.

All three patterns of disease occur:

In ***lobar pneumonia***, bacteria (usually Streptococci) gain access to the alveoli and proliferate rapidly, spreading to all the alveoli in the lobe very rapidly through the alveolar pores. The body responds by mounting an acute inflammatory reaction which fills the alveolar cavities with a mixed fluid/cellular exudate, thus preventing the entry of air into the alveoli of an entire lung lobe, greatly reducing the capacity for adequate oxygenation.

In ***emphysema***, there is progressive destruction of the alveolar ducts, sacs and alveoli, leading to permanent dilatation of the air spaces but reduction in the surface area for gas exchange. There is also loss of the elastic tissue support for the bronchioles, leading to their collapse and air trapping.

In ***interstitial fibrosis*** the fibroblasts in the alveolar septa, normally scanty, increase in number and in collagen and elastin production. This thickens the alveolar septum, interposing layers of collagen between the cytoplasm of the type I pneumocyte and alveolar capillaries, thus impeding gaseous exchange. This is a diffuse change throughout the lung and leads to slowly progressive hypoxia and breathlessness.

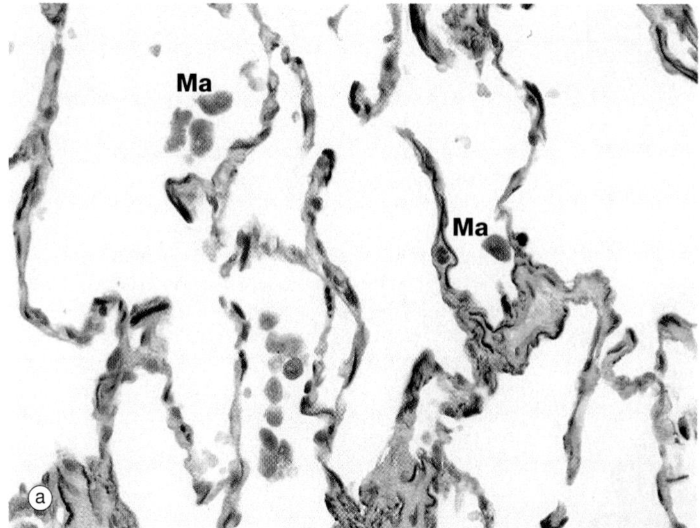

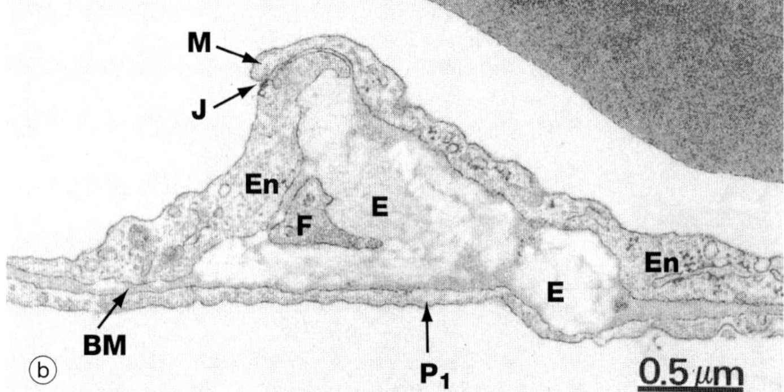

Fig. 12.17 Pulmonary elastic tissue
(a) Elastic van Gieson ×130 (b) EM ×26 000

The staining method used in micrograph (a) demonstrates the large amount of elastin (stained black) in the alveolar walls. At the margins of the openings into the alveoli, the elastin is condensed to form a supporting ring. The elastin and septal collagen of the alveolar wall are continuous with those of adjacent alveoli, forming a fibroelastic supporting framework for the lung parenchyma as a whole. Occasional alveolar macrophages **Ma** can be seen within the lumen of the alveoli.

Micrograph (b) shows part of an alveolar septum containing elements of the elastin meshwork. The septum consists of the thin cytoplasmic layers of a type I pneumocyte $\mathbf{P_1}$ and two capillary endothelial cells **En** separated by a common basement membrane **BM**: note the marginal fold **M** of one endothelial cell overlapping the other, creating a seal and reinforced by a tight junction **J**.

The elastin **E** is an amorphous, moderately electron-dense mass insinuated between the two epithelial layers. This space also contains a fine cytoplasmic extension of a fibroblast **F**.

Lung cancer – cytology

Most lung cancers actually arise within the epithelium of the bronchi and spread from there into the surrounding lung tissue. Thus they are often accessible by bronchoscopy where samples may be taken either by washings or brushings of a lesion. More peripheral lesions may be accessed by the technique of ***fine needle aspiration*** (***FNA***) by passing a long needle into the tumour through the chest wall. Least invasive of all is the examination of sputum coughed up by the patient. All of these specimens may be examined by cytological techniques as seen in this case.

This micrograph demonstrates the difference between normal epithelial cells **Ep** and adenocarcinoma cells **A**. The malignant cells are much larger with prominent nuclei, large nucleoli and scanty cytoplasm. In contrast the much smaller normal epithelial cells exhibit the expected columnar shape. The pseudostratified nature of the normal epithelium is demonstrated by the tapered end of the cell that would normally rest on the basement membrane. The cilia of the luminal surface of the cell can just be discerned at this magnification.

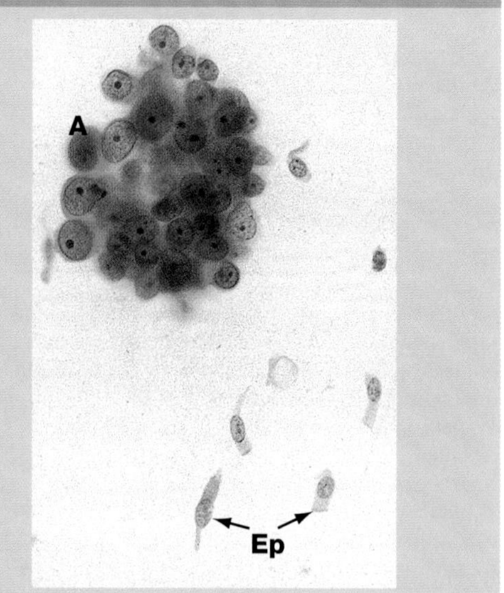

Fig. 12.18 Lung
Fine needle aspiration Giemsa ×400

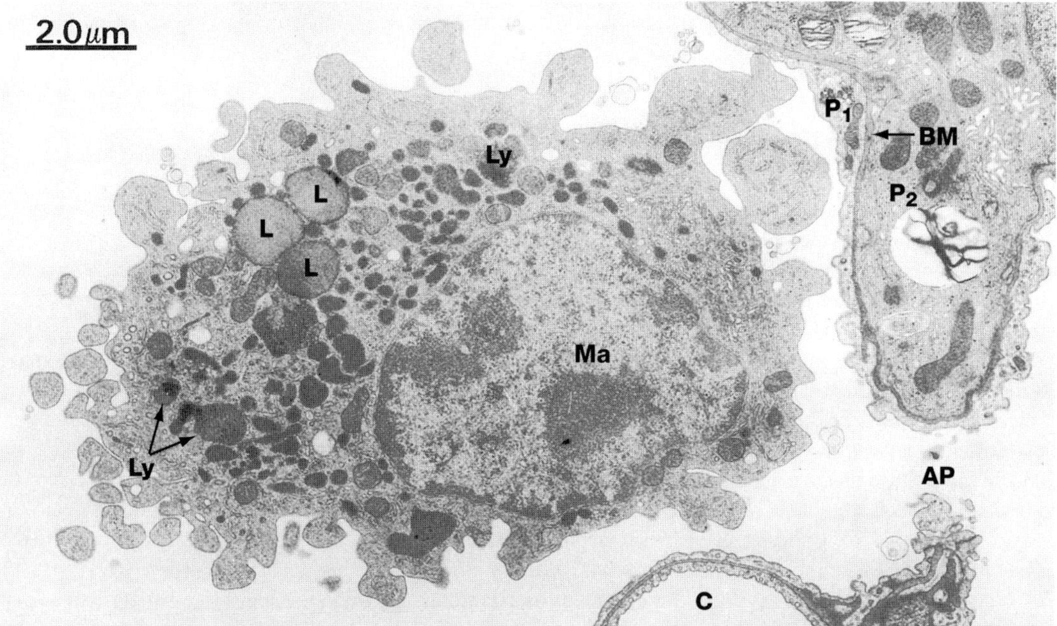

Fig. 12.19 Alveolar macrophage
EM ×8000

The lung contains macrophages, both free within the alveolar spaces and in the alveolar septa. They are derived from circulating blood monocytes, although some may arise by mitotic division of macrophages already present in the lung. Their function is the phagocytosis and removal of unwanted material which gains access to the air spaces, such as inhaled particulate matter and bacteria. The most common particles are carbon, in city dwellers from car exhaust fumes and industrial smoke, and in cigarette smokers. After phagocytosing the particles, most macrophages pass into the airways to become trapped in mucus and coughed up as sputum. Others stay in the septa, and some gain access to the lymphatic system and pass, with their phagocytosed material, to the hilar lymph nodes.

The macrophage **Ma** in this micrograph lies within an alveolus adjacent to a septal capillary **C** and a type II pneumocyte (surfactant cell) $\mathbf{P_2}$ between which is an alveolar pore **AP**. The aspect of the surfactant cell seen here is typically invested by the thin cytoplasm of a type I pneumocyte (alveolar lining cell) $\mathbf{P_1}$, the two being separated by a common basement membrane **BM** (see Fig. 12.15). The alveolar macrophage exhibits the typical features of macrophages elsewhere in the body (see Fig. 4.20), but in particular contains numerous secondary lysosomes **Ly** and lipid droplets **L**.

Industrial lung disease

Although lung macrophages perform a useful function in clearing the air spaces, they also play a role in some industrial lung diseases.

Silicosis of the lungs has many forms depending on the source and nature of the particulate silica which is inhaled. In coal miners, the silica is a component of the fine coal dust that is inhaled during mining, and a similar situation occurs in haematite miners, the silica being a component of iron ore dust. The silica is inhaled into the air sacs as tiny particles that are phagocytosed by macrophages. As described above, many of these macrophages pass into the bronchial mucus and are expectorated or swallowed. However, those that remain in the alveolar septa stay there for many years and the silica is slowly converted into silicic acid which stimulates the proliferation of fibroblasts and the production of excess collagen. The alveolar walls thicken and become fibrotic, interfering with gas exchange, and eventually lung fibrosis becomes extensive. Macrophages that reach the lymph nodes carry the particulate matter there, and fibrosis of lymph nodes may also occur. A special form of silica which can be inhaled is asbestos, a silicate which exists in the form of long crystalline needles. When inhaled, these asbestos particles also stimulate lung fibrosis to produce the disease ***asbestosis***. For the development of silica-based lung fibrosis (***pneumosilicosis***), the inhalation of silica particles must be extensive or prolonged. However, asbestos silica need only be inhaled in small quantities on a few occasions to stimulate the development (usually decades later) of a malignant form of cancer of the pleura (***mesothelioma***).

A adenocarcinoma cells **AP** alveolar pore **BM** basement membrane **C** capillary **E** elastin **En** endothelial cell **Ep** normal epithelial cells **F** fibroblast **J** tight junction **L** lipid droplet **Ly** lysosome **M** marginal fold **Ma** alveolar macrophage $\mathbf{P_1}$ type I pneumocyte $\mathbf{P_2}$ type II pneumocyte

Pulmonary vasculature

The lungs have a double blood supply:

- **Pulmonary vascular system.**
- **Bronchial vascular system.**

The major supply is the pulmonary vascular system. Deoxygenated blood is carried by the systemic veins to the right atrium and into the right ventricle. The right ventricle pumps the blood through the pulmonary valve into the main ***pulmonary arterial trunk*** and then into the ***right*** and ***left pulmonary arteries***. The main right and left pulmonary arteries enter the lungs at the lung hila alongside the main bronchi, and follow the course of the bronchi into the lungs, dividing into progressively smaller branches as the bronchi divide. With each division the arteries become smaller and the structure of their wall changes. The proximal pulmonary arteries, the main pulmonary trunk and large pulmonary arteries, are elastic arteries, similar to the aorta (see Fig. 8.9) but thinner walled, with elastic fibres an important component of the tunica media. Beyond the point where the bronchi lose their cartilage plates to become bronchioles, the pulmonary arteries become muscular arteries, with distinct elastic laminae and a tunica media that is almost completely composed of smooth muscle. The transition from elastic to muscular arteries is gradual. The distal pulmonary arteries continue to follow the distribution of bronchioles, and become progressively smaller as the tunica media becomes thinner, eventually becoming discontinuous in the pulmonary arterioles. The small pulmonary arterioles transfer blood into the pulmonary capillaries (see Figs 12.13 and 12.14) where it becomes oxygenated, and is then passed through pulmonary venules (indistinguishable from arterioles) into a series of gradually enlarging venules and veins. Some of these run in the fibrocollagenous septa of the lung before becoming medium-sized veins with a distinct tunica media and ill-formed elastic laminae. The largest pulmonary veins that leave the lungs at the hilar regions and pass to the left atrium show elastic fibres scattered in the media rather than in distinct elastic laminae.

The bronchial vascular system is minor and provides lung structures such as bronchi with oxygenated blood at systemic pressure. The bronchial arteries are lateral branches of the thoracic aorta and run with the bronchial tree as far as respiratory bronchiole level where they anastomose with the pulmonary vascular system. The small bronchial veins and venules also anastomose freely with pulmonary veins and venules; the main bronchial veins drain into the ***azygos*** and ***hemiazygos veins***.

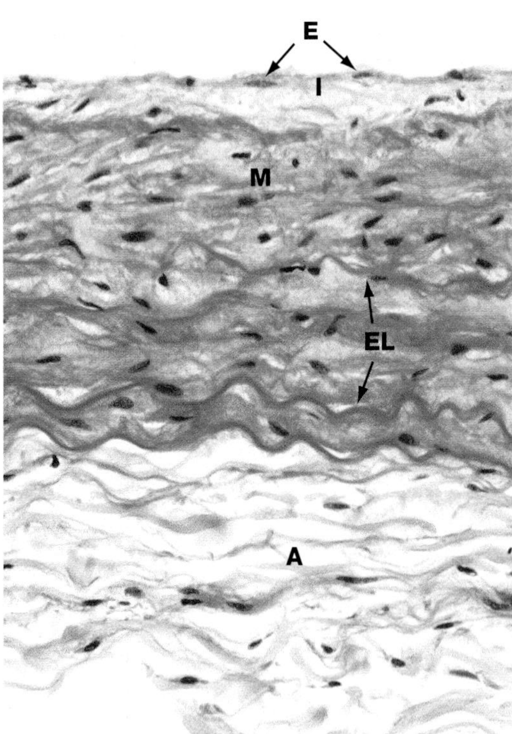

Fig. 12.20 Large (elastic) pulmonary artery
H & E ×300

The pulmonary trunk, main right and left pulmonary arteries and their major lobar branches have a structure similar to that of the aorta (see Fig. 8.9), i.e. an elastic-type artery with prominent elastic lamellae as an important component of the tunica media.

However, because the intravascular pressures are so much less in the pulmonary vascular system, the layers are thinner and less substantial than their equivalents in the aorta. The intima **I** has surface endothelial cells **E**, and the media **M** is composed of smooth muscle cells, collagen, and prominent elastic lamellae **EL**. The adventitia **A** comprises loose fibrocollagenous tissue.

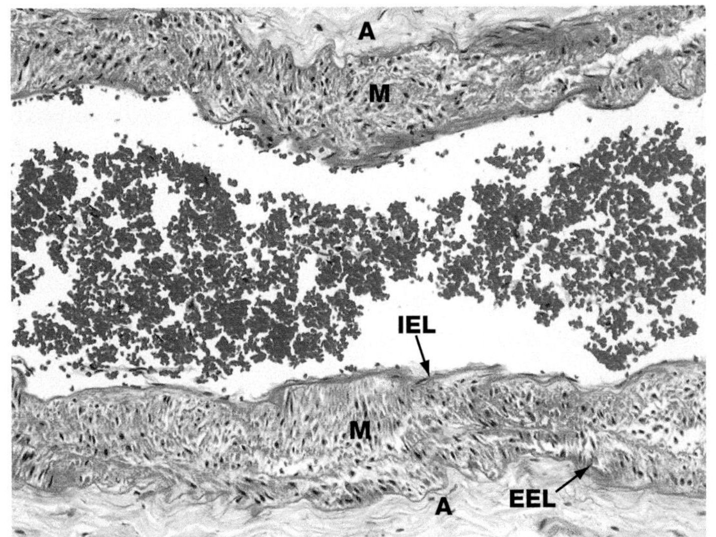

Fig. 12.21 Muscular pulmonary artery
H & E ×100

More distally, the elastic pulmonary artery progressively loses most of the intermixed elastic fibres in the media. Most of the remaining elastic is in the form of internal **IEL** and external **EEL** elastic laminae so that the media **M** is largely composed of smooth muscle and collagen. The intima is thin and indistinct and the fibrocollagenous adventitia **A** merges with the fibrocollagenous support tissue of the lung septa and peribronchial areas.

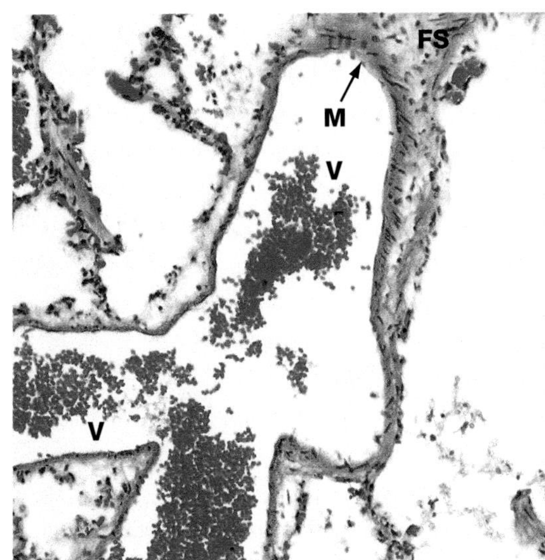

Fig. 12.22 Small pulmonary vein
H & E ×70

Pulmonary capillaries and venules empty recently oxygenated blood into thin-walled pulmonary veins **V**. The amount of smooth muscle media **SM** in the vein wall increases progressively along the venous network and the largest pulmonary veins have a distinct muscular tunica media containing elastic fibres. Small pulmonary veins of the size shown here run in the fibrous septa **FS** of the lungs.

A tunica adventitia **E** endothelial cells **EEL** external elastic lamina **EL** elastic lamellae
FS fibrous septum of lung **I** tunica intima **IEL** internal elastic lamina **M** tunica media
SM smooth muscle **V** pulmonary vein

The pleura

The two cavities in the thorax which house the right and left lungs, the ***pleural cavities***, are lined internally by a thin smooth layer, the ***pleura***, which is also reflected over the external surfaces of the lungs. The part of the pleura which forms the internal lining of the chest cavities is called the ***parietal pleura***, and that which externally coats the lungs, the ***visceral pleura***. The parietal and visceral pleurae are normally in contact, but separated by a potential space containing a small amount of serous fluid that lubricates the movement of visceral upon parietal pleura during breathing.

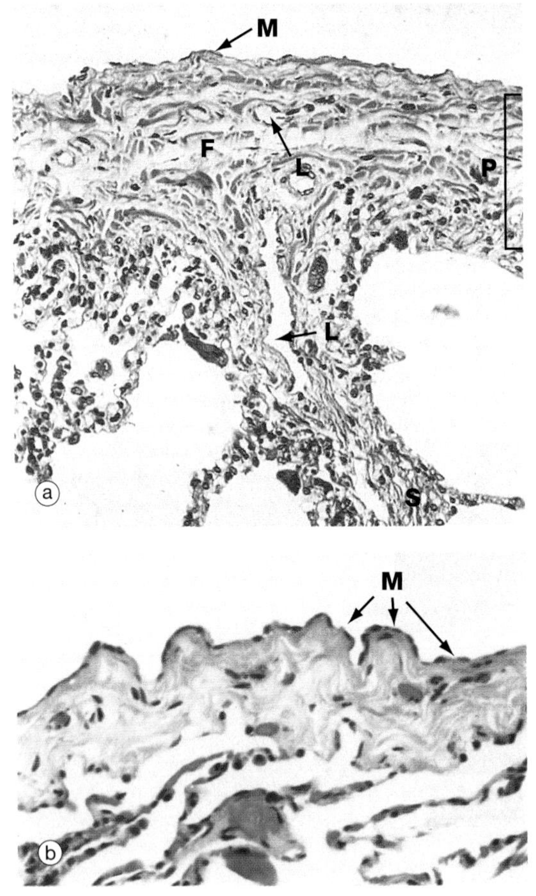

Fig. 12.23 Visceral pleura
(a) H & E ×200 (b) H & E ×380

Micrograph (a) illustrates visceral pleura **P**. The outer surface is lined by a layer of flattened mesothelium **M**, supported by a thin basement membrane. The underlying fibrous supporting tissue **F** consists primarily of collagen and elastin fibres. The fibrous layer of visceral pleura extends into the lung as fibrous septa **S** which are continuous with the fibroelastic framework of the lung parenchyma.

The visceral pleura contains a superficial plexus of lymph vessels which drain via the septa into a deep plexus surrounding the pulmonary blood vessels and airways. Lymph from the deep plexuses drains into the thoracic duct via lymph nodes in the hilar region. Lymph capillaries are not found in alveolar walls, but they are present in the walls of respiratory bronchioles and all larger airways. Several lymph vessels **L** can be seen in the pleura in this micrograph. The visceral pleura also contains numerous small blood vessels and capillaries.

Micrograph (b) is a higher power view of the pleura showing the flattened cuboidal mesothelial cells **M**. These cells stretch to accommodate the movement of the lungs so that the height of the cells varies from flattened to columnar. Ultrastructurally, mesothelial cells have plentiful long surface microvilli which serve to trap hyaluronic acid, thus enhancing the lubrication of the two pleural surfaces. Like other epithelia, mesothelial cells contain prekeratin intermediate filaments.

Disorders of the pleura

The smooth movement of parietal and visceral pleura during inspiration and expiration is impaired when the smooth pleural surfaces become damaged and roughened, particularly during bacterial infections. This produces the symptom called ***pleurisy***, a severe stabbing pain in the chest wall at the site of pleural damage during inspiration and expiration, often accompanied by a scratching noise on auscultation (***pleural friction rub***), in time with respiratory movements. Damage to the pleura can be followed by fibrous scar formation leading the fibrous thickening and often adhesions between the two facing surfaces of the pleura.

Some of the lung's lymphatics run in fibrous septa and empty their contents into the pleural cavity. If the lungs become severely waterlogged (for instance, due to heart failure), these lymphatics can disgorge large quantities of fluid into the pleural cavity (***pleural effusion***). Unfortunately these lymphatics can also carry bacteria and tumour cells into the pleural cavity from the lung, producing infected pleural effusions and malignant pleural effusions respectively. Only one form of primary cancer occurs in the pleura, ***malignant mesothelioma***, which is known to be associated with the inhalation of some forms of asbestos fibre.

F fibrous tissue **L** lymphatic vessel **M** mesothelial cells **P** visceral pleura **S** fibrous septum

13. *Oral tissues*

Introduction

The digestive process commences in the oral cavity with the ingestion, fragmentation and moistening of food, but in addition to its digestive role, the oral cavity is involved in speech, facial expression, sensory reception and breathing. The major structures of the oral cavity, the ***lips***, ***teeth***, ***tongue***, ***oral mucosa*** and the associated ***salivary glands***, participate in all these functions.

Mastication or chewing is the process by which ingested food is made suitable for swallowing. Chewing involves not only coordinated movements of the mandible and the cutting and grinding action of the teeth, but also activity of the lips and tongue, which continually redirect food between the ***occlusal surfaces*** of the teeth. The watery component of saliva moistens and lubricates the masticatory process, while salivary mucus helps to bind the food bolus ready for swallowing.

The entire oral cavity is lined by a protective mucous membrane, the ***oral mucosa***, which contains many sensory receptors, including the taste receptors of the tongue. The epithelium of the oral mucosa is of the stratified squamous type which tends to be keratinised in areas subject to considerable friction such as the palate. The oral epithelium is supported by dense collagenous tissue, the ***lamina propria***. In highly mobile areas such as the soft palate and floor of the mouth, the lamina propria is connected to the underlying muscle by loose submucosal supporting tissue. In contrast, in areas where the oral mucosa overlies bone, such as the hard palate and tooth-bearing ridges, the lamina propria is tightly bound to the periosteum by a relatively dense fibrous submucosa. Throughout the oral mucosa, numerous small accessory salivary glands of both serous and mucous types are distributed in the submucosa.

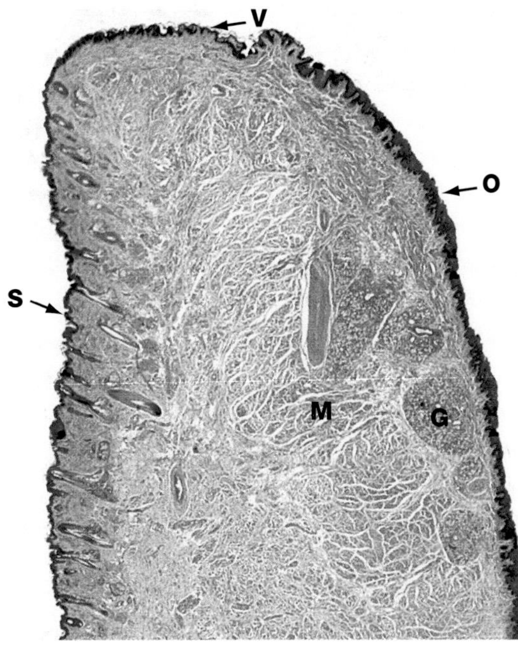

Fig. 13.1 Lip
H & E ×6

This micrograph illustrates a midline section through a human lower lip, the bulk of which is made up of bundles of circumoral skeletal muscle **M** seen in transverse section.

The external surface of the lip is covered by hairy skin **S** which passes through a transition zone to merge with the oral mucosa **O** of the inner surface. The transition zone constitutes the free ***vermilion border*** of the lip **V**, and derives its colour from the richly vascular dermis, which here has only a thin, lightly keratinised epidermal covering. The free border is highly sensitive due to its rich sensory innervation. Since the vermilion border is devoid of sweat and sebaceous glands, it requires continuous moistening by saliva to prevent cracking.

The oral mucosa covering the inner surface of the lip has a thick stratified squamous epithelium and the underlying submucosa contains numerous accessory salivary glands **G** of serous, mucous and mixed seromucous types.

G accessory salivary glands **M** skeletal muscle **O** oral mucosa **S** skin **V** vermilion border

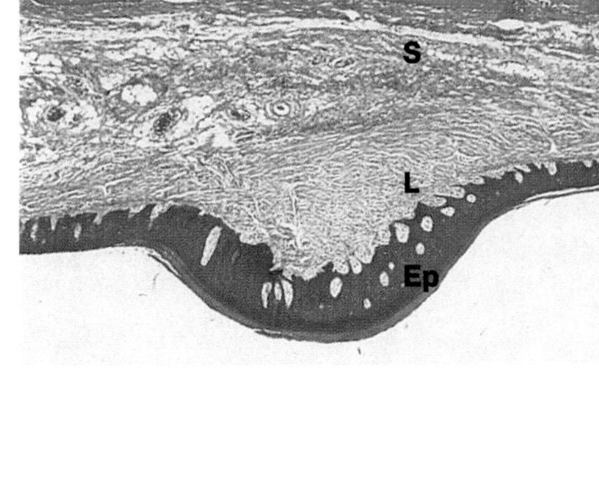

Fig. 13.2 Palatal mucosa
H & E ×28

Like the rest of the mouth, the palate is covered by a thick stratified squamous epithelium **Ep** supported by a tough, densely collagenous lamina propria **L**. To assist mastication, the palatal mucosa is thrown up into transverse folds or ***rugae***, one of which is shown in this micrograph.

The mucosa of the hard palate is bound down to the underlying bone **B** by relatively dense submucosal tissue **S** containing a few accessory salivary glands.

In rodents and many other mammals with a coarse diet, the surface epithelium of particularly exposed areas is keratinised for extra protection, as in this specimen taken from a monkey.

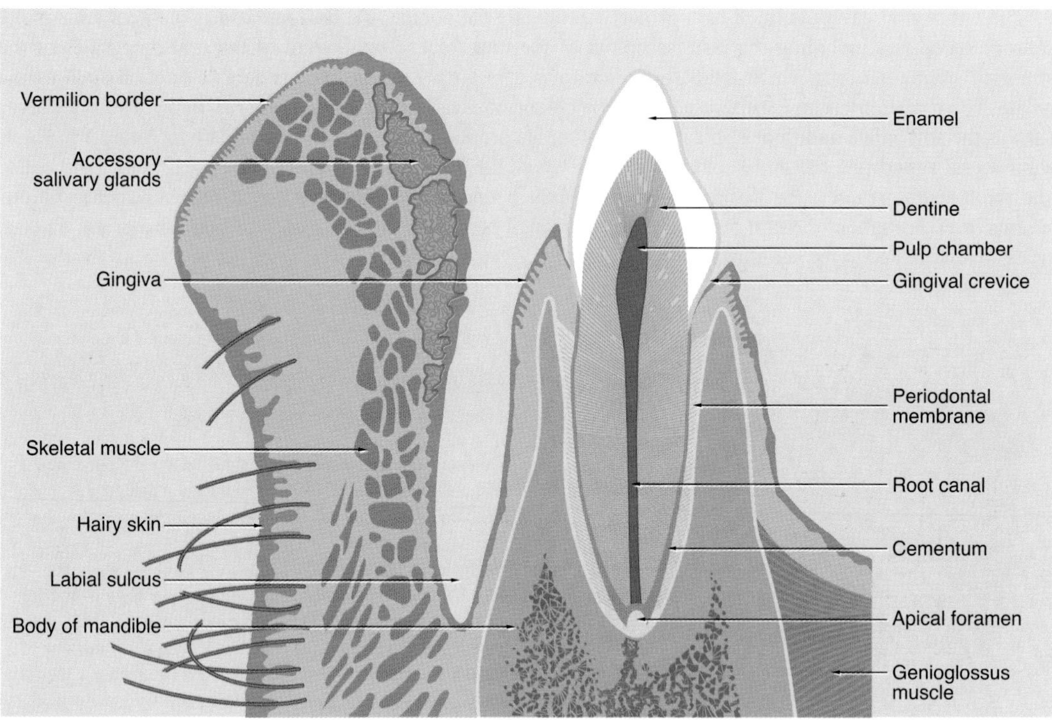

Fig. 13.3 Lip and tooth

This drawing of a section through the lower jaw near the midline illustrates the general arrangement of the lip and a tooth with its supporting structures.

Each tooth may be grossly divided into two segments, the ***crown*** and the ***root***; the crown is that portion which projects into the oral cavity and is protected by a layer of highly mineralised ***enamel*** which covers it entirely. The bulk of the tooth is made up of ***dentine***, a mineralised tissue which has a similar chemical composition to bone. The dentine has a central pulp cavity containing the ***dental pulp*** which consists of specialised supporting tissue containing many sensory nerve fibres. The tooth root is embedded in a bony ridge in the jaw called the ***alveolar ridge***; the tooth socket is known as the ***alveolus***. At the lip or cheek (***buccal***) aspect of the alveolus, the bony plate is generally thinner than at the tongue (***palatal***) aspect. The root of the tooth is invested by a thin layer of ***cementum*** which is connected to the bone of the socket by a thin fibrous layer called the ***periodontal ligament*** or ***periodontal membrane***.

The oral mucosa covering the upper part of the alveolar ridge is called the ***gingiva***, and at the junction of the crown and root of the tooth (the ***neck of the tooth***) the gingiva forms a tight protective cuff around the tooth. The potential space between the gingival cuff and the enamel of the crown is called the ***gingival crevice***. All of the tissues which surround and support the tooth are collectively known as the ***periodontium***.

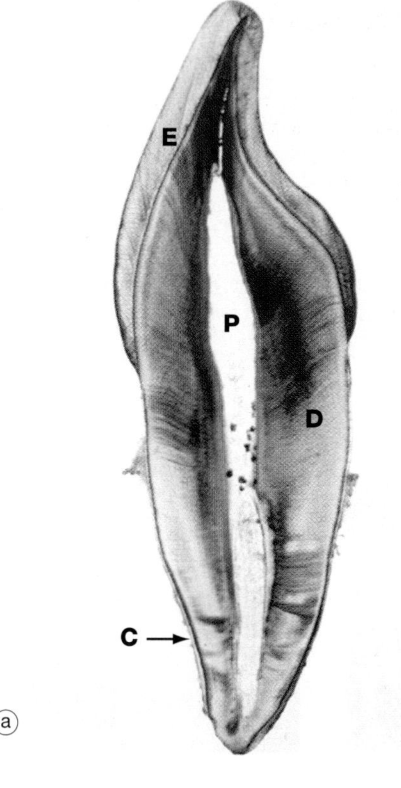

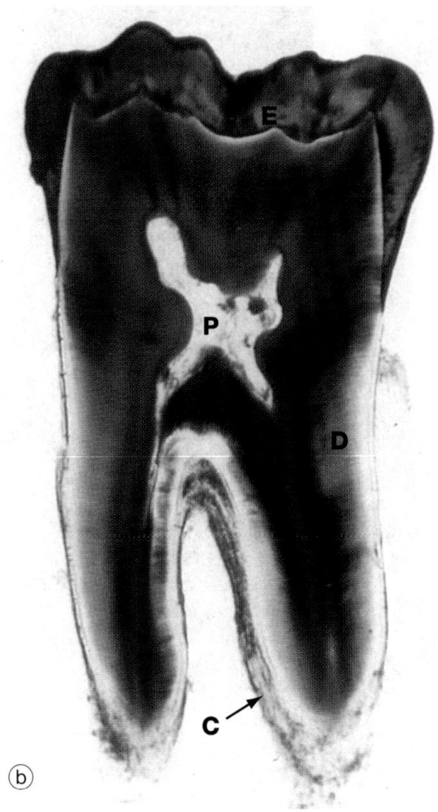

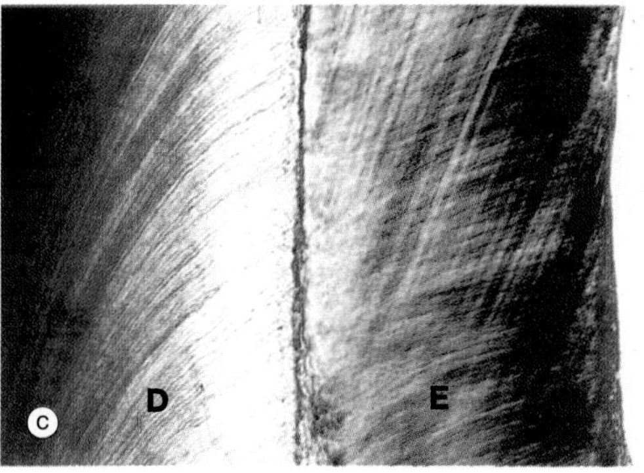

Fig. 13.4 Tooth structure
Undecalcified sections, unstained: (a) ×5 (b) ×5 (c) ×50

These undecalcified sections cut with a diamond wheel demonstrate the arrangement of the calcified tissues of an upper central incisor tooth (micrograph (a)) and a lower molar tooth (micrograph (b)). Micrograph (c) demonstrates the tissues of the crown at high magnification.

The dentine **D**, which forms the bulk of the crown and root, is composed of a calcified organic matrix similar to that of bone. The inorganic component constitutes a somewhat larger proportion of the matrix of dentine than that of bone and exists mainly in the form of hydroxyapatite crystals. Teeth are thus harder than bone. From the pulp cavity **P**, minute parallel tubules, called ***dentine tubules***, radiate to the periphery of the dentine.

The crown of the tooth is covered by enamel **E**, an extremely hard, translucent substance composed of parallel ***enamel rods*** or ***prisms*** of highly calcified material cemented together by an almost equally calcified ***interprismatic material***.

The root is invested by a thin layer of ***cementum*** **C** which is generally thicker towards the apex of the root. The cementum is an amorphous calcified tissue into which the fibres of the periodontal membrane are anchored.

The morphological form of the tooth crown and roots varies considerably in different parts of the mouth; nevertheless, the basic arrangement of the dental tissues is the same in all teeth.

In humans, the ***primary*** (***deciduous***) ***dentition*** consists of 20 teeth, comprising two ***incisors***, one ***canine*** and two ***molars*** in each quadrant. These begin to be formed at the age of 6 weeks during fetal development and erupt between the ages of 6 and 30 months after birth. Between the ages of 6 and 12 years, the deciduous teeth are succeeded by permanent teeth, namely two incisors, one canine and two ***premolars*** in each quadrant. Distal to these will develop three ***permanent molars*** which have no primary precursors; the first permanent molar erupts at age 6, the second at age 12 and the third (wisdom tooth) at age 17–21 years. The sharp points found on the posterior teeth are known as ***cusps***.

B bone **C** cementum **D** dentine **E** enamel **Ep** epithelium **L** lamina propria **P** pulp cavity **S** submucosa

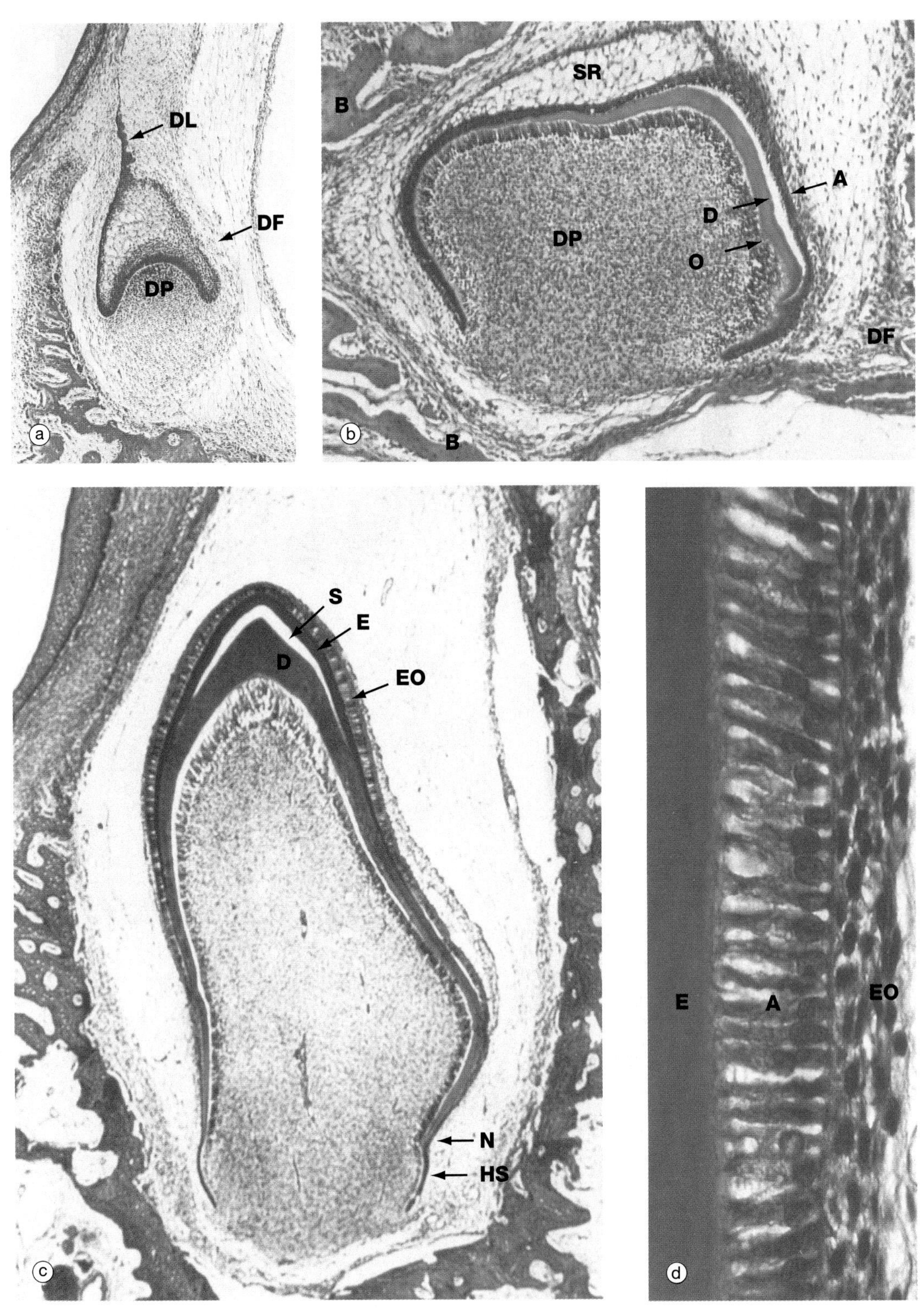

A ameloblasts **B** bone **D** dentine **DF** dental follicle **DL** dental lamina **DP** dental papilla
E enamel **EO** enamel organ **HS** epithelial sheath of Hertwig **N** neck of tooth **O** odontoblasts
S space (enamel) **SR** stellate reticulum

Fig. 13.5 Tooth development *(illustrations opposite)*
(a) H & E: cap stage ×28 (b) H & E: bell stage ×96 (c) H & E: onset of root development ×45 (d) H & E: ameloblasts ×640

This series of micrographs illustrates the important stages of tooth development.

The tissues of the teeth are derived from two embryological sources. The enamel is of epithelial (ectodermal) origin, while the dentine, cementum, pulp and periodontal ligament are of mesenchymal (mesodermal) origin. The first evidence of tooth development in humans occurs at 6 weeks of fetal life with the proliferation of a horseshoe-shaped epithelial ridge from the basal layer of the primitive oral epithelium into the underlying mesoderm in the position of the future jaws; this is known as the ***dental lamina***. In each quadrant of the mouth, the lamina then develops four globular swellings which will become the ***enamel organs*** of the future deciduous central and lateral incisors, canines and first molar teeth. Subsequently, the dental lamina proliferates backwards in each arch, successively giving rise to the enamel organs of the future second deciduous molar and the three permanent molars. The permanent successors of the deciduous teeth will later develop from enamel organs which bud off from the inner aspect of the enamel organs of their deciduous predecessors.

The primitive mesenchyme immediately subjacent to the developing enamel organ proliferates to form a cellular mass, the ***dental papilla*** **DP**. At the same time, the enamel organ becomes progressively cap-shaped, as seen in micrograph (a), enveloping the dental papilla. During the cap stage, the cells lining the concave face of the enamel organ in contact with the dental papilla begin to differentiate into tall columnar cells, ***ameloblasts***, which will be responsible for the production of enamel. This, in turn, induces the differentiation of a layer of columnar ***odontoblasts***, the future dentine-producing cells, in the apical region of the dental papilla. The interface between the differentiating ameloblast and odontoblast layers marks the position and shape of the future junction between enamel and dentine.

As the enamel organ develops further, it assumes a characteristic bell shape as seen in micrograph (b), the free edge of the 'bell' proliferating so as to determine the eventual shape of the tooth crown.

Meanwhile, the cells of the main bulk of the enamel organ become large and star-shaped, forming the ***stellate reticulum*** **SR**, the extracellular matrix of which is rich in glycosaminoglycans. Between the stellate reticulum and ameloblast layer, two or three layers of flattened cells form the ***stratum intermedium***, while the outer surface of the enamel organ consists of a simple cuboidal epithelium called the ***external enamel epithelium***. By the cap stage of development, the dental lamina **DL** connecting the enamel organ with the oral mucosa has become fragmented and, around the whole developing bud, a condensation of mesenchyme forms the ***dental follicle*** **DF** which will eventually become the periodontal ligament.

As ameloblasts and odontoblasts differentiate at the tip of the crown, a layer of dentine matrix is progressively laid down between the ameloblast and odontoblast layers. As the odontoblasts retreat, each leaves a long cytoplasmic extension, the ***odontoblastic process***, embedded within the dentine matrix, thereby forming the dentine tubules. Dentine matrix has a similar biochemical composition to that of bone and undergoes calcification in a similar fashion. Deposition of dentine induces the production of enamel by the adjacent ameloblasts. Each retreating ameloblast lays down a column of enamel matrix, which then undergoes mineralisation resulting in the formation of a dense prismatic structure as described below. With the deposition of dentine and enamel, the overlying stellate reticulum atrophies and the enamel organ is much reduced in thickness. These changes are well demonstrated in micrograph (b). A thin layer of dentine **D** has been laid down by the underlying odontoblastic layer **O** of the highly cellular dental papilla **DP**. The ameloblastic layer **A** is about to lay down enamel in the space next to the dentine; note that in this area, the stellate reticulum has disappeared. Note also the surrounding dental follicle **DF** and early formation of cancellous bone **B**.

By the time that dentine and enamel formation is well underway at the incisal edge or tips of the cusps (as the case may be), the enamel organ will have fully outlined the shape of the whole tooth crown. This is the case in micrograph (c), the neck of the tooth **N** marking the junction of crown and root. A thin, densely stained layer of poorly mineralised enamel **E** can be seen covered at its external surface by the now much thinner enamel organ **EO**. The unstained space **S** between this and the underlying dentine **D** represents fully mineralised enamel laid down earlier but dissolved away during tissue preparation. Although enamel production is confined to the crown, the rim of the 'bell' of the enamel organ nevertheless continues to proliferate, inducing dentine formation and thereby determining the shape of the tooth root. This part of the enamel organ, known as the ***epithelial sheath of Hertwig*** **HS** disintegrates once the outline of the root is completed. The cementum which later forms on the root surface is derived from the dental follicle. As the dentine of the crown and root are progressively laid down, the dental papilla shrinks and eventually becomes the dental pulp contained within the pulp chamber and root canals.

Growth of the tooth root is one of the principal mechanisms of tooth eruption, and root formation is not completed until some time after the crown has fully erupted into the oral cavity.

Micrograph (d) illustrates the characteristic appearance of ameloblasts. Active ameloblasts **A** are tall columnar epithelial cells which form a single layer apposed to the forming surface of the enamel **E**. Each ameloblast elaborates a column of organic enamel matrix which undergoes progressive mineralisation by the deposition of calcium phosphate mainly in the form of hydroxyapatite crystals. Fully formed enamel contains less than 1% organic material and is the hardest and most dense tissue in the body.

Mature enamel consists of highly calcified ***enamel prisms*** separated by ***interprismatic enamel*** consisting of similar crystals orientated in a different direction. Each prism extends from the dentino-enamel junction to the enamel surface. The prisms are made up of groups of long, thin, parallel crystallites of hydroxyapatite covered by a surface layer of organic material.

Underlying the ameloblast layer are several layers of cells, also of epithelial origin, which constitute the remainder of the enamel organ **EO**. As enamel formation progresses, the enamel organ becomes much reduced in thickness compared with earlier stages of its development. At tooth eruption, the enamel organ, including the ameloblasts, degenerates leaving the enamel exposed to the hostile oral environment, completely incapable of regeneration.

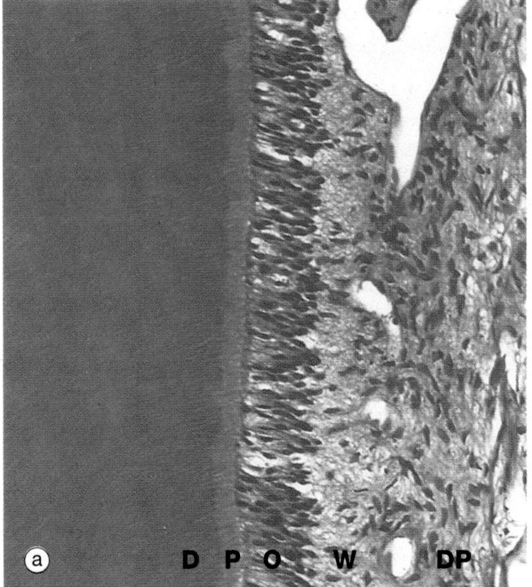

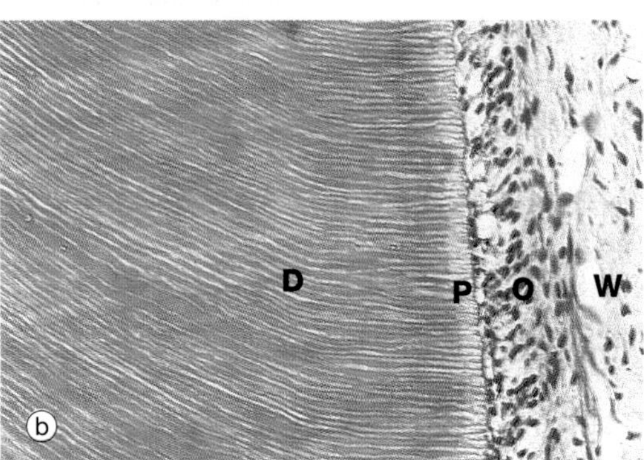

Fig. 13.6 Odontoblasts and dentine
Decalcified sections: (a) H & E ×200 (b) H & E ×128

Dentine, the dense calcified tissue which forms the bulk of the tooth, is broadly similar to bone in composition but is more highly mineralised and thus much harder than bone. The cells responsible for dentine formation, the ***odontoblasts***, differentiate as a single layer of tall columnar cells on the surface of the dental papilla apposed to the ***ameloblast*** layer of the enamel organ. The odontoblasts initiate tooth formation by deposition of organic dentine matrix between the odontoblastic and ameloblastic layers; calcification of this dentine matrix then induces enamel formation by ameloblasts (see Fig. 13.5). Odontoblasts continue to produce dentine which subsequently calcifies. Unlike ameloblasts, each odontoblast leaves behind a slender cytoplasmic extension, the odontoblastic process, within a fine dentine tubule. When dentine formation is complete, the dentine is thus pervaded by parallel ***odontoblastic processes*** radiating from the odontoblast layer on the dentinal surface of the reduced dental papilla which now constitutes the dental pulp. After tooth formation is complete, a small amount of less organised ***secondary dentine*** continues to be laid down, resulting in the progressive obliteration of the pulp cavity with advancing age.

These micrographs illustrate active odontoblasts **O** forming a pseudostratified layer of columnar cells at the dentine surface. Parallel dentine tubules containing odontoblastic processes extend through a narrow pale-stained zone of uncalcified dentine matrix called ***predentine*** **P** into the mature dentine **D**; the dentine tubules are best seen in micrograph (b). Underlying the odontoblastic layer, a relatively acellular layer, called the ***cell free zone of Weil*** **W**, gives way to the highly cellular dental pulp **DP**.

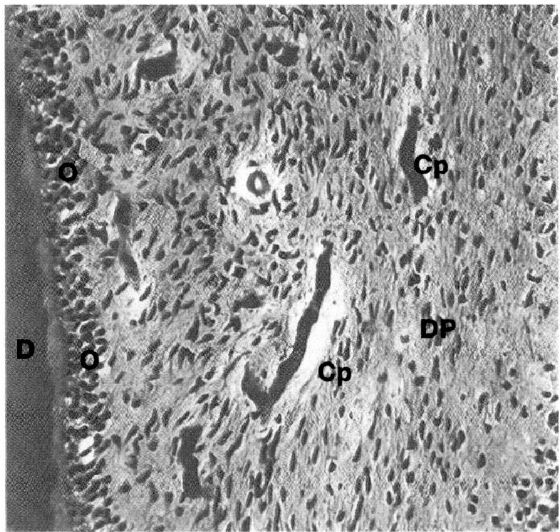

Fig. 13.7 Dental pulp
Decalcified section: H & E ×198

The dental pulp **DP** consists of a delicate supporting/connective tissue resembling primitive mesenchyme (see Fig. 4.10); it contains numerous stellate fibroblasts, reticulin fibres, fine collagen fibres and plentiful ground substance. The pulp contains a rich network of thin-walled capillaries **Cp** supplied by arterioles which enter the pulp canal from the periodontal membrane, usually via one foramen at each root apex. The pulp is also richly innervated by a plexus of myelinated nerve fibres from which fine, non-myelinated branches extend into the odontoblastic layer. Despite the acute sensitivity of dentine, nerve fibres are rarely demonstrable and the mechanism of sensory reception is unknown; it has been suggested that the odontoblastic processes may act as sensory receptors. Odontoblasts **O** and the edge of the dentine **D** can also be identified.

B bone **C** cementum **CE** crevicular epithelium **CEJ** cemento-enamel junction **Cp** capillary
D dentine **Db** organic debris **DP** dental pulp **FG** free gingiva **M** Malassez rests
O odontoblasts **P** predentine **PM** peridontal membrane **W** Weil's zone

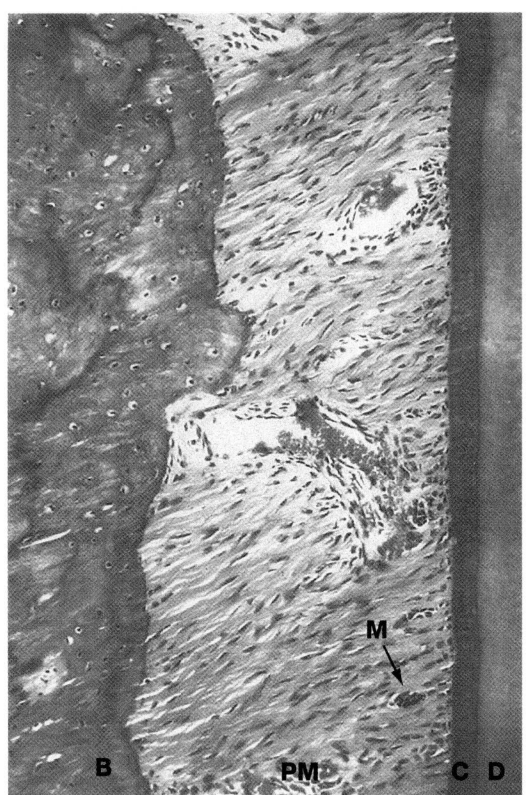

Fig. 13.8 Periodontal membrane and cementum
Decalcified section: H & E ×200

The periodontal membrane **PM** forms a thin fibrous attachment between the tooth root and the alveolar bone. The dentine **D**, comprising the root, is covered by a thin layer of cementum **C** which is elaborated by cells called ***cementocytes*** lying on the surface of the cementum. Cementum consists of a dense, calcified organic material similar to the matrix of bone, and is generally acellular. Towards the root apex, the cementum layer becomes progressively thicker and irregular and cementocytes are often entrapped in lacunae within the cementum.

The periodontal membrane consists of dense collagenous tissue. The collagen fibres, known as ***Sharpey's fibres***, run obliquely downwards from their attachment in the alveolar bone **B** to their anchorage in the cementum at a more apical position on the root surface. The periodontal membrane thus acts as a sling for the tooth within its socket, permitting slight movements which cushion the impact of chewing. The points of attachment of the collagen fibres in both cementum and bone are in a constant state of reorganisation to accommodate changing functional stresses upon the teeth. Osteoclastic resorption is often seen at one aspect of a tooth socket and complementary osteoblastic deposition at the opposite side, thus indicating bodily movement of the tooth through the bone; this is the mechanism which permits tooth movement during orthodontic treatment.

The periodontal membrane is richly supplied by blood vessels and nerves from the surrounding alveolar bone, the apical region and the gingiva. Small clumps of epithelial cells are often found scattered throughout the periodontal membrane; these cells are remnants of Hertwig's sheath (see Fig. 13.5) and are known as ***epithelial rests of Malassez*** **M**.

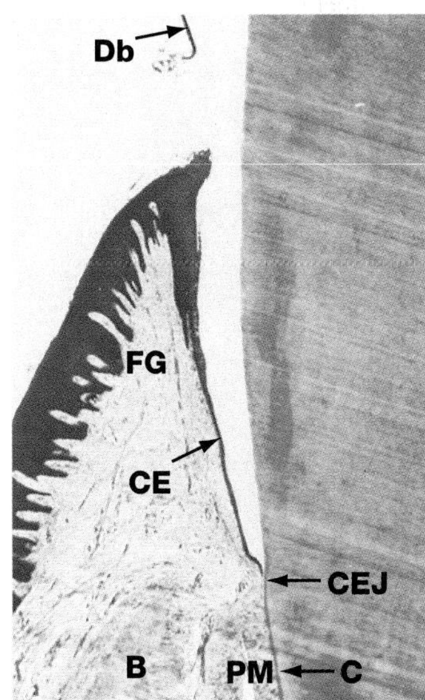

Fig. 13.9 Gingival attachment
Decalcified section: H & E ×320

This micrograph shows the relationship of the gingiva (gum) to the neck of the tooth. During tissue preparation the enamel has been completely dissolved from the surface of the crown, but the extent of the outer surface of the enamel can be visualised by shreds of remaining organic debris **Db** which had been adherent to the tooth surface.

The gingiva may be divided into the ***attached gingiva***, which provides a protective covering to the upper alveolar bone **B**, and the ***free gingiva*** **FG**, which forms a cuff around the enamel at the neck of the tooth. Between the enamel and the free gingiva is a potential space, the ***gingival crevice***, which extends from the tip of the free gingiva to the cemento-enamel junction **CEJ**.

The thick stratified squamous epithelium, which constitutes the oral aspect of the gingiva, undergoes abrupt transition at the tip of the free gingiva to form a thin layer of epithelial cells, tapering to only two or three cells thick at the base of the gingival crevice. This ***crevicular epithelium*** **CE** is easily breached by pathogenic organisms, and the underlying supporting tissue is thus frequently infiltrated by lymphocytes and plasma cells.

Collagen fibres of the periodontal membrane **PM** radiate from the cementum **C** near the cemento-enamel junction into the dense supporting tissue of the free gingiva; these fibres, together with circular fibres surrounding the neck of the tooth, maintain the role of the gingiva as a protective cuff.

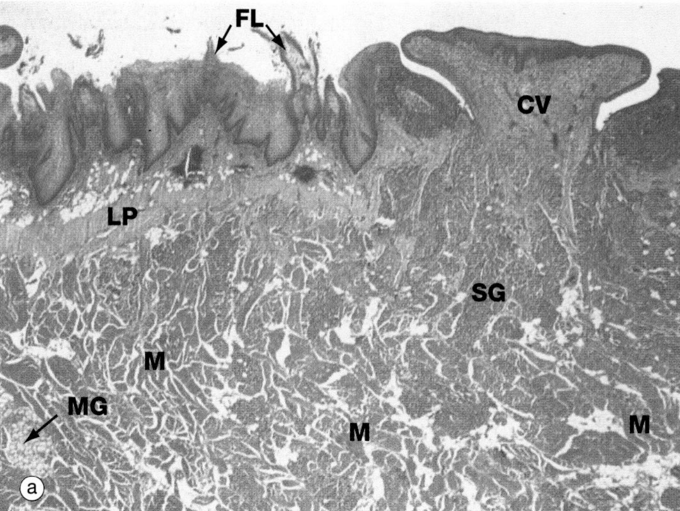

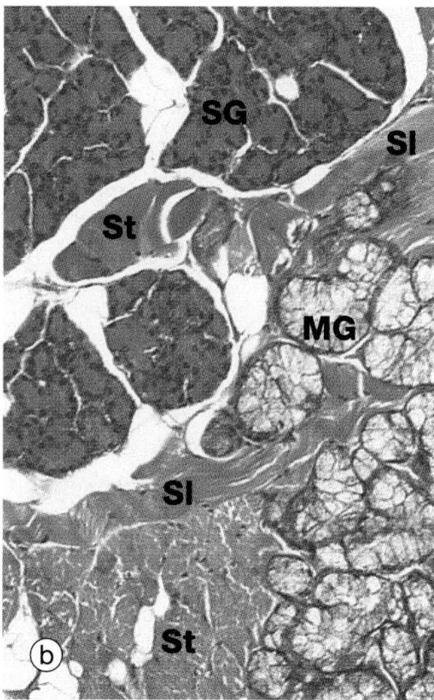

Fig. 13.10 Tongue – anterior two-thirds
(a) H & E ×6 (b) H & E ×100

The tongue is a muscular organ covered by oral mucosa which is specialised for manipulating food, general sensory reception and the special sensory function of taste. The tongue is also vital for speech.

A V-shaped groove, the ***sulcus terminalis***, demarcates the anterior two-thirds of the tongue from the posterior one-third. The mucosa of the anterior two-thirds is formed into papillae of three types. The most numerous, the ***filiform papillae***, appear as short 'bristles' macroscopically. Among them are scattered the small red globular ***fungiform papillae***. Six to 14 large ***circumvallate papillae*** form a row immediately anterior to the sulcus terminalis and these papillae contain most of the taste buds (see Figs 13.12 and 21.1); a circumvallate papilla **CV** and numerous filiform papillae **FL** are seen in micrograph (a). ***Foliate papillae***, which are rudimentary in humans, are found in some animal species.

The body of the tongue consists of a mass of interlacing bundles of skeletal muscle fibres **M** which permit an extensive range of tongue movements. The mucous membrane covering the tongue is firmly bound to the underlying muscle by a dense, collagenous lamina propria **LP**, which is continuous with the epimysium of the tongue muscle.

Numerous small serous and mucous accessory salivary glands are scattered throughout the muscle and lamina propria of the tongue and are seen at higher magnification in micrograph (b); in these preparations the serous glands **SG** are stained strongly, whereas the mucous glands **MG** are poorly stained. Note bundles of skeletal muscle cut in both transverse **St** and longitudinal **Sl** sections.

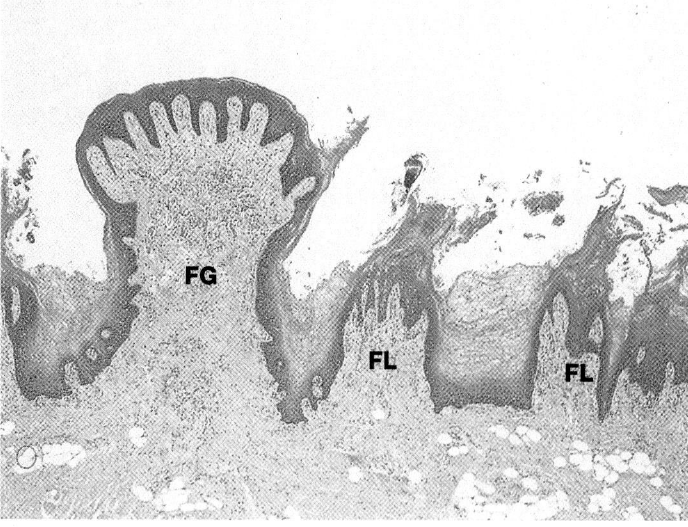

Fig. 13.11 Filiform and fungiform papillae
H & E ×30

This micrograph illustrates several filiform papillae **FL** and a fungiform papilla **FG**. Filiform papillae are the most numerous type and consist of a dense supporting tissue core and a heavily keratinised surface projection. Fungiform papillae have a thin non-keratinised epithelium and a richly vascularised supporting tissue core, giving them a red appearance macroscopically amongst the much more numerous, whitish filiform papillae.

B taste buds **C** cleft **Cr** crypt **CV** circumvallate papillae **E** epithelium **F** lymphoid follicle **FG** fungiform papillae **FL** filiform papillae **L** lymphoid tissue **LP** lamina propria **M** skeletal muscle **MG** mucous glands **SG** serous glands **Sl** skeletal muscle in longitudinal section **St** skeletal muscle in transverse section **VE** von Ebner's gland

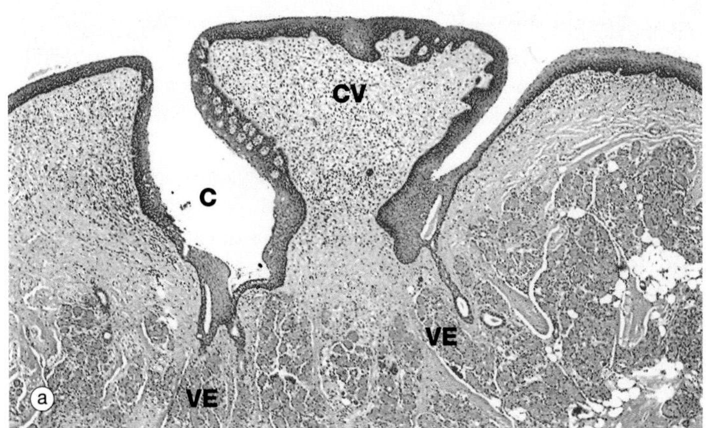

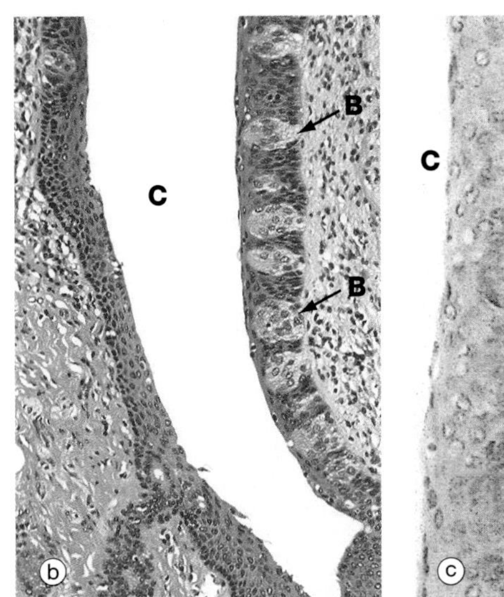

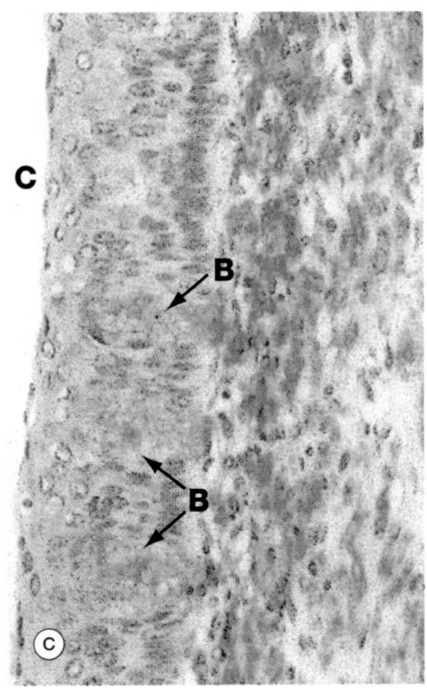

Fig. 13.12 Circumvallate papillae

(a) H & E ×15 (b) H & E ×100
(c) Immunoperoxidase NSE ×100

Circumvallate papillae **CV** are the largest and least common type of papillae on the tongue. They are set into the tongue surface and encircled by a deep cleft **C**. Aggregations of serous glands, called ***von Ebner's glands*** **VE**, open into the base of the circumvallate clefts (micrograph (a)), secreting a watery fluid which dissolves food constituents, thus facilitating taste reception. The stratified epithelium lining the papillary wall of the cleft contains numerous taste buds **B** as shown in micrograph (b) (see also Fig. 21.1).

Micrograph (c) is stained by the immunoperoxidase method for the enzyme neurone-specific enolase (NSE). This demonstrates the neural nature of the taste buds **B** and the meshwork of fine axons (stained brown) in the lamina propria underlying the taste buds which subserve taste sensation.

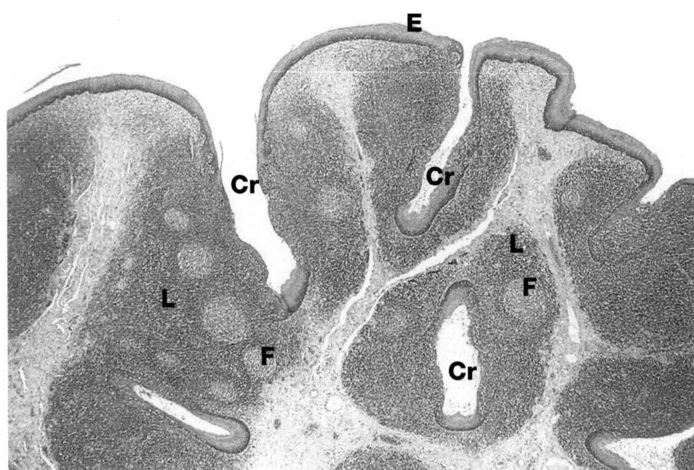

Fig. 13.13 Tongue – posterior third

H & E ×15

The posterior surface of the tongue has a relatively smooth stratified squamous epithelium **E** overlying lymphoid tissue **L** containing lymphoid follicles **F**. This lymphoid tissue is the ***lingual tonsil*** and, with the palatine tonsils and adenoids, completes ***Waldeyer's ring*** of lymphoid tissue guarding the entrance to the gastrointestinal and respiratory tracts. Like the palatine tonsils (see Fig. 11.16), epithelial crypts **Cr** penetrate the lingual tonsil.

Salivary glands

Saliva is produced by three pairs of major salivary glands, the ***parotid***, ***submandibular*** and ***sublingual glands***, and numerous minor ***accessory glands*** scattered throughout the oral mucosa. The minor salivary glands secrete continuously and are in general under local control, whereas the major glands mainly secrete in response to parasympathetic activity which is induced by physical, chemical and psychological stimuli. Daily saliva production in humans is 600–1500 mL.

Saliva is a hypotonic watery secretion containing variable amounts of mucus, enzymes (principally ***amylase*** and the antibacterial enzyme ***lysozyme***), antibodies and inorganic ions. Two types of secretory cells are found in the salivary glands: ***serous cells*** and ***mucous cells***. The parotid glands consist almost exclusively of serous cells and produce a thin watery secretion rich in enzymes and antibodies. The sublingual glands have predominantly mucous secretory cells and produce a viscid secretion. The submandibular glands contain both serous and mucous secretory cells and produce a secretion of intermediate consistency. The overall composition of saliva varies according to the degree of activity of each of the major gland types.

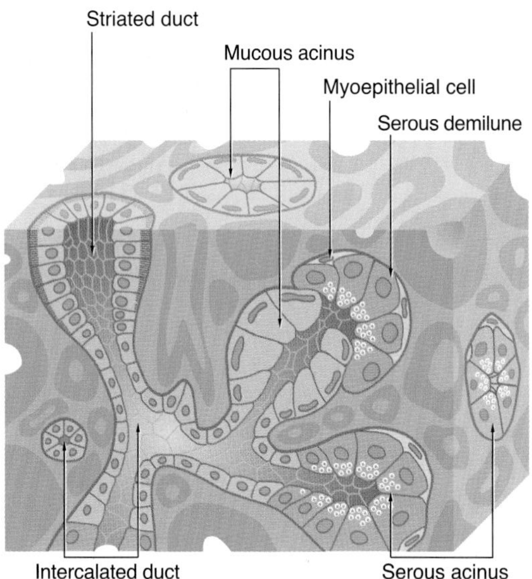

Fig. 13.14 Salivary secretory unit

The salivary secretory unit consists of a terminal branched tubulo-acinar structure composed exclusively of either serous or mucous secretory cells or a mixture of both types. In mixed secretory units where mucous cells predominate, serous cells often form semilunar caps called ***serous demilunes*** surrounding the terminal part of the mucous acini. Myoepithelial cells embrace the secretory units, their contraction helping to expel the secretory product.

The terminal secretory units merge to form small ***intercalated ducts*** which are also lined by secretory cells. They drain into larger ducts called ***striated ducts***, so named because of their striated appearance by light microscopy. The striations result from the presence of numerous interdigitations of the basal cytoplasmic processes of adjacent columnar lining cells.

The serous cells secrete a fluid isotonic with plasma. In the striated ducts ions are reabsorbed and secreted to produce hypotonic saliva containing less Na^+ and Cl^- and more K^+ and HCO_3^- than plasma. The mitochondria, which pack the basal processes, provide the energy for ion transport.

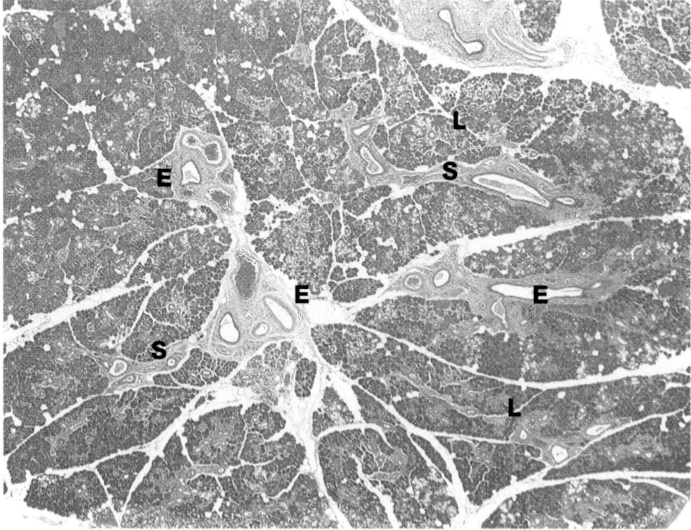

Fig. 13.15 Parotid gland
H & E ×15

The general architecture of the major salivary glands follows the pattern shown in this micrograph of the parotid gland. The gland is divided into numerous lobules **L**, each containing many secretory units. Supporting tissue septa **S** radiate between the lobules from an outer capsule and convey blood vessels, nerves and large excretory ducts **E**. The parotid gland consists mainly of serous secretory units which are darkly stained in this H & E preparation.

A adipocytes **D** striated duct **E** excretory ducts **ID** intercalated duct **L** lobule
M mucous acini **S** septum **SC** serous cells **SD** serous demilunes

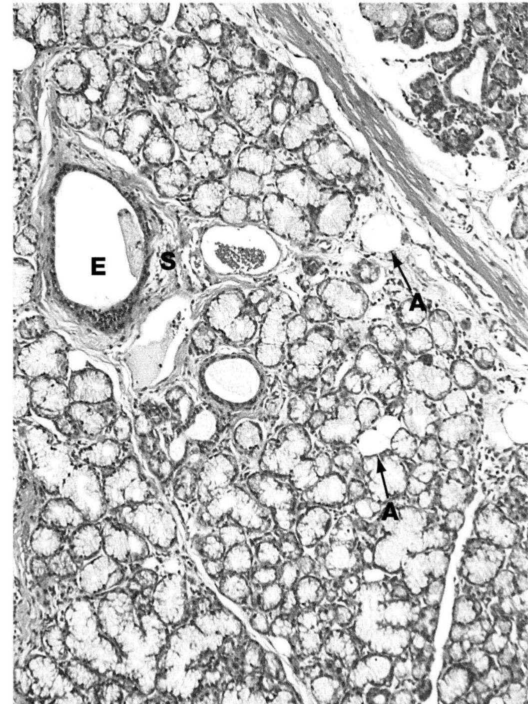

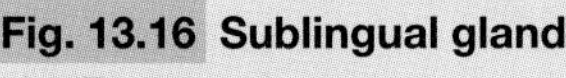

Fig. 13.16 Sublingual gland
H & E ×75

Mucous acini predominate in the sublingual glands making them stain very poorly with H & E, in contrast to the serous units shown in the parotid in Figure 13.15. A large excretory duct **E**, lined by a stratified cuboidal epithelium, is also present in the fibrous tissue septum **S**. The duct is accompanied by blood vessels and nerves. As these ducts merge to form the major excretory duct, the epithelium gradually transforms into stratified squamous epithelium.

Note also that the gland contains occasional adipocytes **A**, a feature found in older individuals. The proportion of fat in the gland generally increases with increasing age.

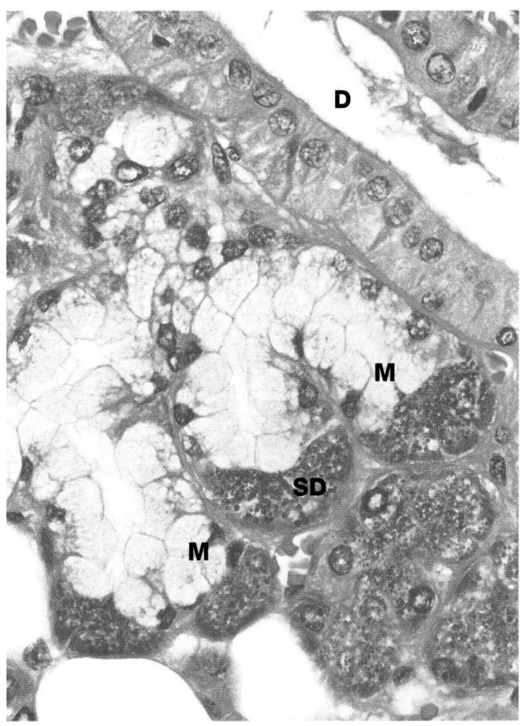

Fig. 13.17 Submandibular gland
H & E ×450

The submandibular gland consists of a mixture of serous and mucous secretory units which are often found in the form of mixed seromucous secretory units as shown here. However, both pure serous and pure mucous secretory units are also found in the submandibular gland. The mixed secretory units consist of mucous acini **M** with serous demilunes **SD**. In H & E stained preparations, ***mucigen*** granules within the mucous acini are poorly stained, whereas the enzyme-containing (***zymogen***) granules of serous acini are strongly stained. The nuclei of mucous cells are characteristically condensed and flattened against the basement membrane, whereas the nuclei of serous cells are rounded with dispersed chromatin and usually occupy a more central position within the cell.

Also running across the corner of the micrograph is a striated duct **D** cut in longitudinal section.

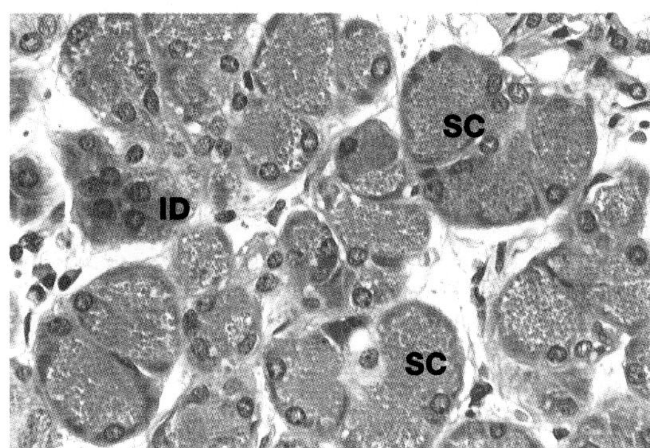

Fig. 13.18 Intercalated duct
H & E ×300

This micrograph of serous secretory units is taken from the parotid gland. A small intercalated duct **ID** with several acini draining into it can be identified. Intercalated ducts have a lining of cuboidal secretory cells.

At this magnification, the serous secretory cells **SC** have plentiful strongly stained apical cytoplasmic granules. The nucleus is pushed to the base of the cell. Adjacent to the nucleus, in EM sections (not illustrated), a large Golgi apparatus, prominent rough endoplasmic reticulum and mitochondria are found in common with other protein-secreting cells (see Fig. 15.15 of a pancreatic secretory cell, which is very similar ultrastructurally).

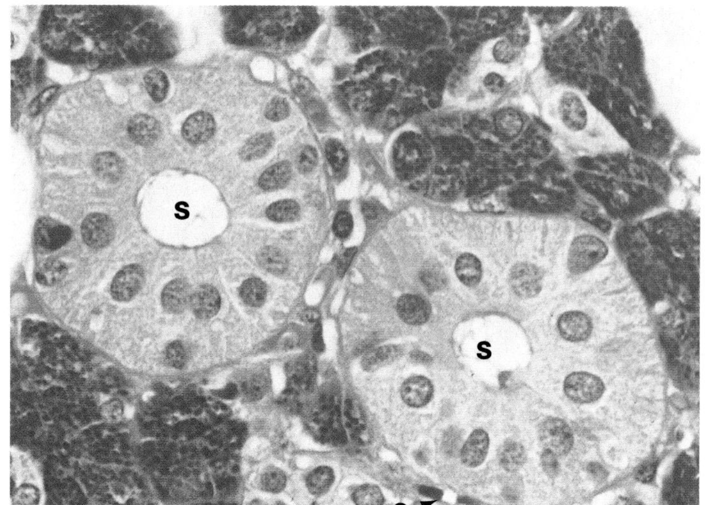

Fig. 13.19 Striated ducts
H & E ×600

The striated ducts are lined by tall columnar cells with large nuclei located towards the apex of the cell. The basal cytoplasm appears striated, reflecting the presence of basal interdigitations of cytoplasmic processes of adjacent cells and associated columns of mitochondria. This feature greatly extends the area of membrane available for exchange of water and ions in a similar fashion to the proximal convoluted tubule of the kidney (see Fig 16.18). The duct epithelium also secretes lysozyme and IgA. In predominantly serous salivary glands, the striated ducts are larger than in predominantly mucous glands, a feature associated with the role of the striated duct in modifying isotonic basic saliva to produce hypotonic saliva. The sparse supporting tissue between the secretory acini contains a rich network of capillaries **C**.

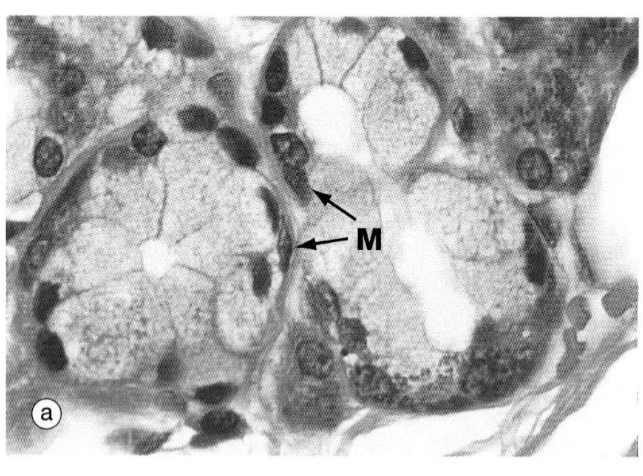

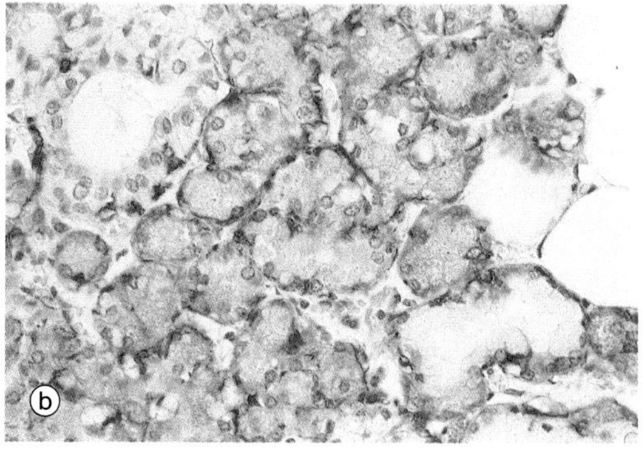

Fig. 13.20 Mucous acinus
(a) H & E ×300 (b) Immunoperoxidase ×200

Both serous and mucous acini are embraced by the processes of contractile cells called ***myoepithelial cells*** which, on contraction, force secretion from the acinar lumen into the duct system. Myoepithelial cells are located between the basal plasma membranes of secretory cells and the basement membrane. These cells are flattened and have long processes which extend around the secretory acinus, but in section they can only be recognised by their large flattened nuclei lying within the basement membrane surrounding the acinus. Micrograph (a) shows the typical appearance of myoepithelial cells **M** embracing mucous acini.

In micrograph (b), a similar section has been stained using the immunoperoxidase technique with an antibody specific for actin, a microfilament characteristic of muscle cells but not usually found in epithelial cells. The myoepithelial cells are stained brown, confirming the presence of cytoplasmic actin which is not seen in the luminal epithelial cells. However, myoepithelial cells also show characteristics of epithelial differentiation, including cytoplasmic cytokeratin intermediate filaments. This technique demonstrates the large numbers of myoepithelial cells surrounding each of the secretory acini.

C capillary **M** myoepithelial cells **S** striated ducts

14. *Gastrointestinal tract*

Introduction

The function of the gastrointestinal system is to break down food for absorption into the body. This process occurs in five main phases: ***ingestion***, ***fragmentation***, ***digestion***, ***absorption*** and ***elimination*** of waste products. Digestion is the process by which food is enzymatically broken down into molecules that are small enough to be absorbed into the circulation; e.g. ingested proteins are first reduced to polypeptides and then further degraded to small peptides and amino acids that can be absorbed.

The gastrointestinal system is essentially a muscular tube lined by a mucous membrane that exhibits regional variations reflecting the changing functions of the system from mouth to anus. The mucous membrane is protective, secretory, absorptive or a combination of these in different parts of the tract (see Fig. 14.3). The muscle gives strength to the wall of the tract as well as moving the food along it. The muscle is arranged somewhat differently in different areas of the tract.

Because of its continuity with the external environment, the gastrointestinal system is a potential portal of entry for pathogenic organisms. Thus the system incorporates a number of defence mechanisms, which include prominent aggregations of lymphoid tissue, known as the ***gut-associated lymphoid system*** (***GALT***), distributed throughout the tract (see Ch. 11).

Fig. 14.1 The parts of the gastrointestinal tract

Ingestion and initial fragmentation of food occur in the ***oral cavity***, resulting in the formation of a bolus of food; this is then conveyed to the ***oesophagus*** by the action of the tongue and pharyngeal muscles during swallowing. Secretion of saliva from major and minor ***salivary glands*** (see Ch. 13) helps in fragmentation and lubricates the food for swallowing.

The oesophagus conducts food from the oral cavity to the ***stomach*** where fragmentation is completed and digestion started. Initial digestion, accompanied by intense muscular action of the stomach wall, converts the stomach contents to a semi-digested liquid called ***chyme***. Chyme is squirted through a muscular sphincter, the ***pylorus***, into the ***duodenum***, the short first part of the ***small intestine***. Digestive enzymes from a large exocrine gland, the ***pancreas***, enter the duodenum together with bile from the liver via the ***common bile duct*** (see Ch. 15). Bile contains excretory products of liver metabolism, some of which act as emulsifying agents necessary for fat digestion. The duodenal contents pass onwards along the rest of the small intestine where the process of digestion is completed and the main absorptive phase occurs. The middle segment of the small intestine is called the ***jejunum*** and the distal segment the ***ileum***. There is no distinct anatomical boundary between these two parts of the small bowel.

The liquid residue from the small intestine passes through the ***ileocaecal valve***, into the ***large intestine***. Here, water is absorbed from the liquid residue, which becomes progressively more solid as it passes towards the anus. The capacious first part of the large intestine is called the ***caecum***, from which projects a blind-ended sac, the ***appendix***. The next part of the large intestine, the ***colon***, is divided anatomically into ***ascending***, ***transverse***, ***descending*** and ***sigmoid*** segments, although histologically the segments are indistinguishable from one another. The terminal portion of the large intestine, the ***rectum***, is a holding chamber for faeces prior to defaecation via the ***anal canal***.

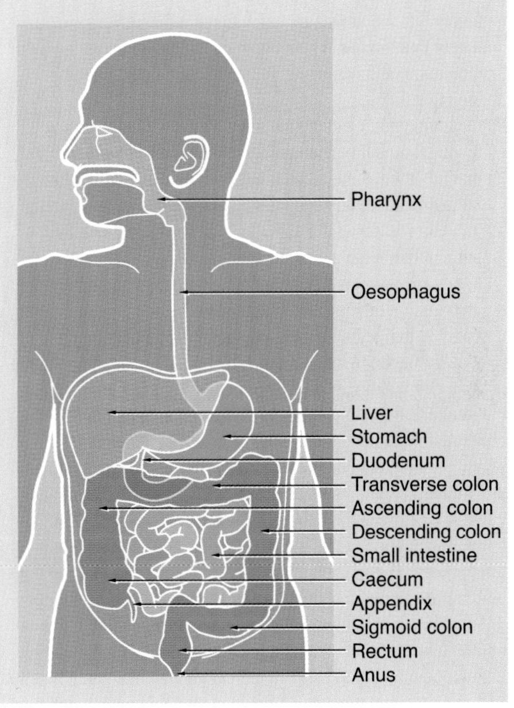

Fig. 14.2 Structure of the gastrointestinal tract

The structure of the gastrointestinal tract conforms to a general plan that is clearly evident from the oesophagus to the anus. The tract is essentially a muscular tube lined by a mucous membrane. There are minor variations in the arrangement of the muscular component in different parts of the gut, but much more striking are the marked changes in the structure and underlying function of the mucosa in the different regions of the tract.

The gastrointestinal tract has four distinct functional layers: ***mucosa***, ***submucosa***, ***muscularis propria*** and ***adventitia***.

- **Mucosa.** The mucosa is made up of three components: the ***epithelium***, a supporting ***lamina propria*** and a thin smooth muscle layer, the ***muscularis mucosae***, which produces local movement and folding of the mucosa. At four points along the tract, the mucosa undergoes abrupt transition from one form to another: the gastro-oesophageal junction, the gastroduodenal junction, the ileocaecal junction and the recto-anal junction.
- **Submucosa.** This layer of loose collagenous supporting tissue supports the mucosa and contains the larger blood vessels, lymphatics and nerves.
- **Muscularis propria.** The muscular wall proper consists of smooth muscle that is usually arranged as an inner circular layer and an outer longitudinal layer. In the stomach only, there is an inner oblique layer of muscle. The action of the two layers, at right angles to one another, is the basis of peristaltic contraction.
- **Adventitia.** This outer layer of loose supporting tissue conducts the major vessels, nerves and variable adipose tissue. Where the gut lies within the abdominal cavity (peritoneal cavity), the adventitia is referred to as the ***serosa*** (***visceral peritoneum***) and is lined by a simple squamous epithelium (***mesothelium***). Elsewhere, the adventitial layer merges with retroperitoneal tissues.

Food is propelled along the gastrointestinal tract by two main mechanisms: voluntary muscular action in the oral cavity, pharynx and upper third of the oesophagus is succeeded by involuntary waves of smooth muscle contraction called ***peristalsis***. Peristalsis and the secretory activity of the entire gastrointestinal system are modulated by the autonomic nervous system and a variety of hormones, some of which are secreted by neuroendocrine cells, located within the gastrointestinal tract itself. These cells constitute a diffuse neuroendocrine system, with cells producing a variety of locally acting hormones found scattered along the whole length of the tract (see also Ch. 17).

Autonomic regulation of certain glandular secretions and the smooth muscle of the gut and its blood vessels is mediated by the enteric nervous system, comprising postganglionic sympathetic fibres and ganglia and postganglionic fibres of the parasympathetic nervous system supplied by the vagus nerve. Contraction of the smooth muscle of the bowel is initiated by pacemaker cells, known as ***interstitial cells of Cajal***, modulated by the autonomic nervous system, particularly the parasympathetic nervous system. As in other organs of the body, parasympathetic efferent fibres synapse with effector neurones in small ganglia located in or close to the organ involved. In the gastrointestinal tract, parasympathetic ganglia are concentrated in plexuses in the wall of the tract. In the submucosa, isolated or small clusters of parasympathetic ganglion cells give rise to postganglionic fibres which supply the mucosal glands and the smooth muscle of the muscularis mucosae; this submucosal plexus, ***Meissner's plexus***, also contains postganglionic sympathetic fibres arising from the superior mesenteric plexus. Larger clusters of parasympathetic ganglion cells are found between the two layers of the muscularis propria, the postganglionic fibres mainly supplying the surrounding smooth muscle. This plexus is known as the ***myenteric plexus*** or ***Auerbach's plexus***.

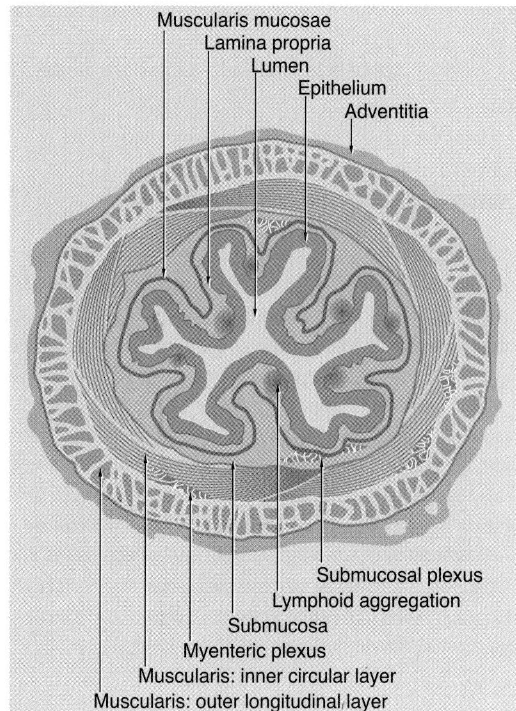

Glands are found throughout the tract at various levels in its wall. In some parts of the tract (i.e. stomach, small and large intestine), the mucosa is arranged into glands that secrete mucus for lubrication among other things. In the lower oesophagus and duodenum, glands penetrate the muscularis mucosae to lie in the submucosa. The pancreas and liver are large glands draining into the gastrointestinal lumen but lying entirely outside its wall (see Ch. 15).

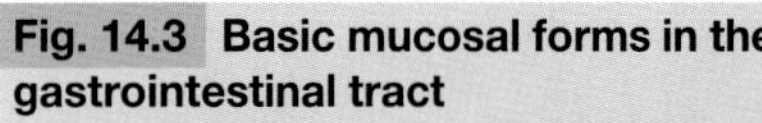

Fig. 14.3 Basic mucosal forms in the gastrointestinal tract
H & E: (a) ×100 (b) ×100 (c) ×128 (d) ×128

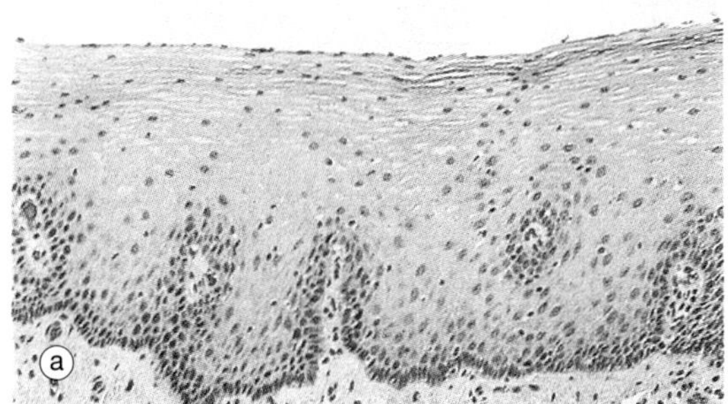

There are four basic mucosal types found in the gastrointestinal tract, which can be classified according to their main function:

Protective. This type is found in the oral cavity, pharynx, oesophagus and anal canal. The surface epithelium is of stratified squamous type and although not keratinised in humans, it may be keratinised in animals that have a coarse diet, e.g. rodents, herbivores.

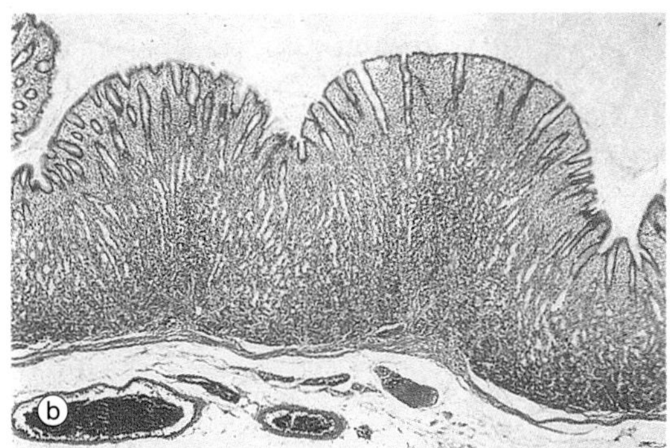

Secretory. This type occurs only in the stomach. The mucosa consists of long, closely packed tubular glands that are simple or branched depending on the region of the stomach.

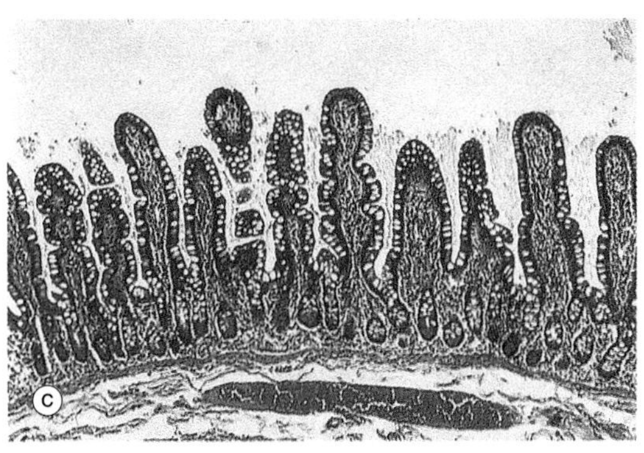

Absorptive. This mucosal form is typical of the entire small intestine. The mucosa is arranged into finger-like projections, called ***villi***, which increase surface area with intervening short glands called ***crypts***. In the duodenum, some crypts extend through the muscularis mucosae to form submucosal glands called ***Brunner's glands***. This is the major histological feature that differentiates the duodenum from the jejunum and ileum.

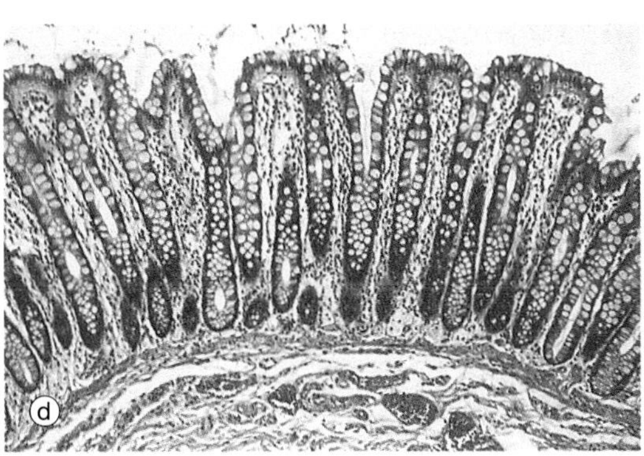

Absorptive/protective. This form lines the entire large intestine. The mucosa is arranged into closely packed, straight tubular glands consisting of cells specialised for water absorption and mucus-secreting goblet cells to lubricate the passage of faeces.

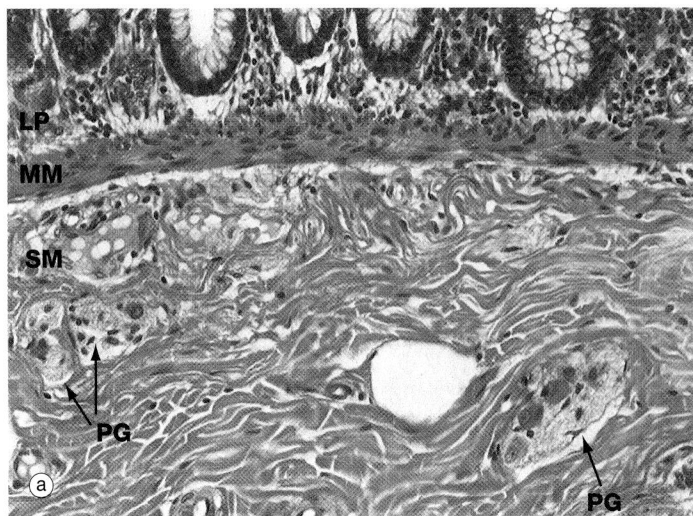

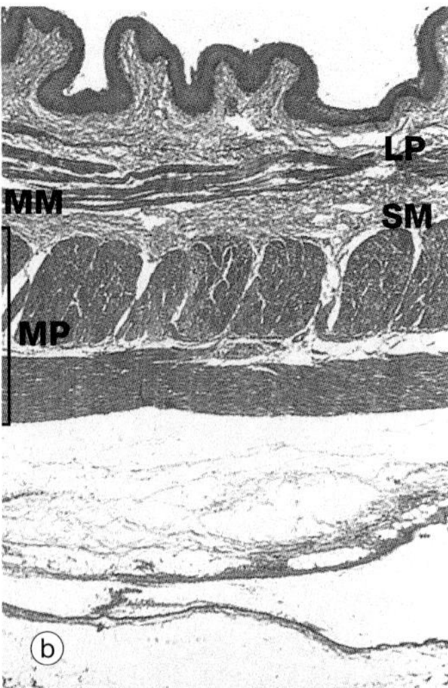

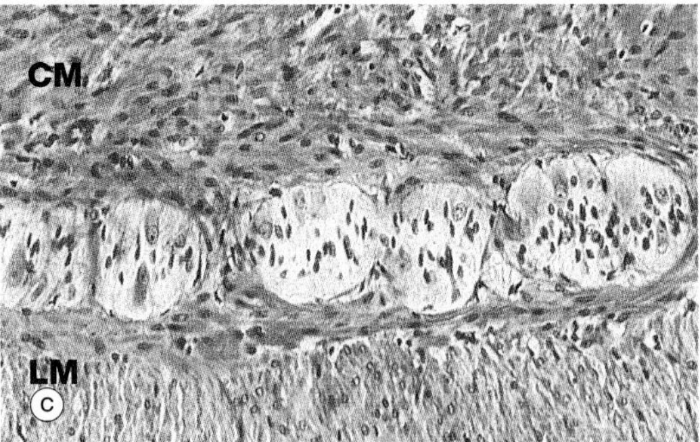

Fig. 14.4 Components of the wall of the gastrointestinal tract
(a) H & E ×480 (b) H & E ×28 (c) H & E ×320

This series of micrographs illustrates the deeper layers of the wall of the gastrointestinal tract.

Micrograph (a) illustrates the muscularis mucosae **MM** clearly demarcating the delicate lamina propria **LP** from the more robust underlying submucosa **SM**; this arrangement is typical of the whole of the gastrointestinal tract.

In most of the gut the ***lamina propria*** consists of loose supporting tissue with a diffuse population of lymphocytes and plasma cells. The exception is the stomach, which normally has few, if any, resident lymphoid cells. At intervals in the oesophagus, small and large bowels and appendix, prominent aggregates of lymphocytes with lymphoid follicles are found. There are also smaller numbers of eosinophils and histiocytes (see Fig. 4.19) to deal with any microorganisms breaching the intestinal epithelium until a specific immune response can be mounted. In the oesophagus, where the function of the mucosa is to protect against friction, the lamina propria is more collagenous than elsewhere and the muscularis mucosae is more prominent. The lamina propria is also typically rich in blood and lymphatic capillaries necessary to support the secretory and absorptive functions of the mucosa.

The ***muscularis mucosae*** consists of several layers of smooth muscle fibres, those in the deeper layers oriented parallel to the luminal surface. The more superficial fibres are oriented at right angles to the surface and in the small intestine the fibres extend up into the villi (Fig. 14.22). The activity of the muscularis mucosae keeps the mucosal surface and glands in a constant state of gentle agitation, which expels secretions from the deep glandular crypts, prevents clogging and enhances contact between epithelium and luminal contents for absorption.

The ***submucosa*** consists of collagenous and adipose supporting tissue that binds the mucosa to the main bulk of the muscular wall. The submucosa contains the larger blood vessels and lymphatics as well as the nerves supplying the mucosa. Tiny parasympathetic ganglia **PG** are scattered throughout the submucosa, forming the ***submucosal (Meissner's) plexus*** from which postganglionic fibres supply the muscularis mucosae.

The typical arrangement of the two layers of the muscular wall proper is seen in micrograph (b), which shows a longitudinal section of the oesophagus. The muscularis propria **MP** is made up of an outer longitudinal layer and a somewhat broader inner circular layer; there has been some artefactual separation of the layers in this micrograph making them easier to visualise. The submucosa **SM** is separated from the lamina propria **LP** by the muscularis mucosae **MM**.

Micrograph (c) illustrates, at high magnification, the junction of outer longitudinal **LM** and inner circular **CM** layers of the muscularis propria in the large intestine; between the layers are clumps of pale-stained parasympathetic ganglion cells of the ***myenteric (Auerbach's) plexus***. The two layers of the muscularis propria undergo synchronised rhythmic contractions that pass in peristaltic waves down the tract, propelling the contents distally. Peristalsis is initiated by the pacemaker cells, the interstitial cells of Cajal, but the level of activity is modulated by the autonomic nervous system, locally produced gastrointestinal tract hormones and other environmental factors. Parasympathetic activity enhances peristalsis while sympathetic activity slows gut motility.

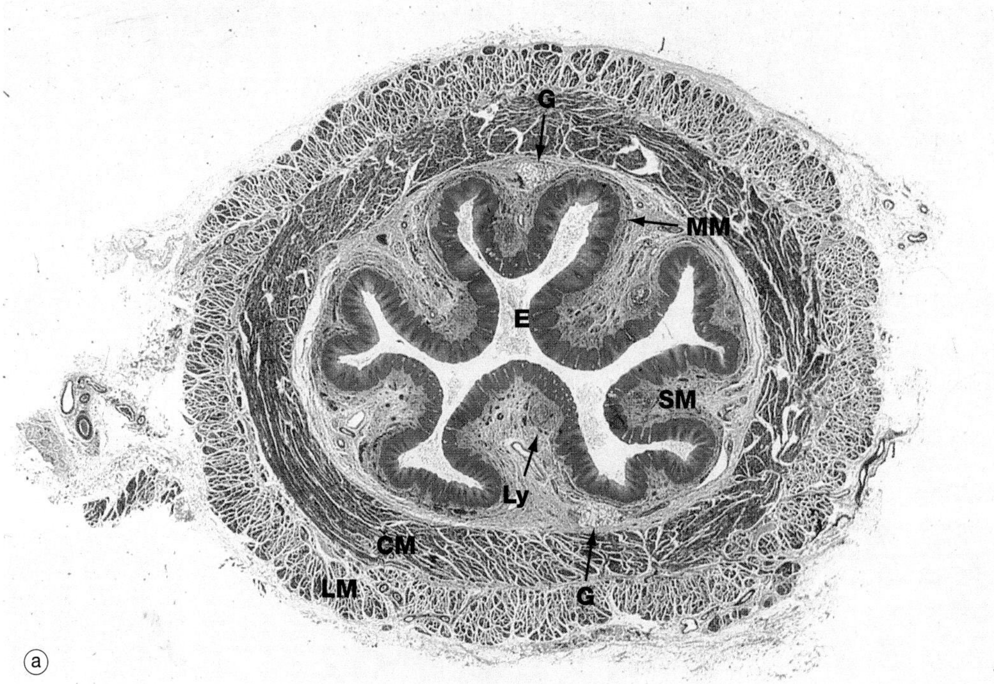

Fig. 14.5 Oesophagus
Masson's trichrome ×9 (b) Masson's trichrome ×320

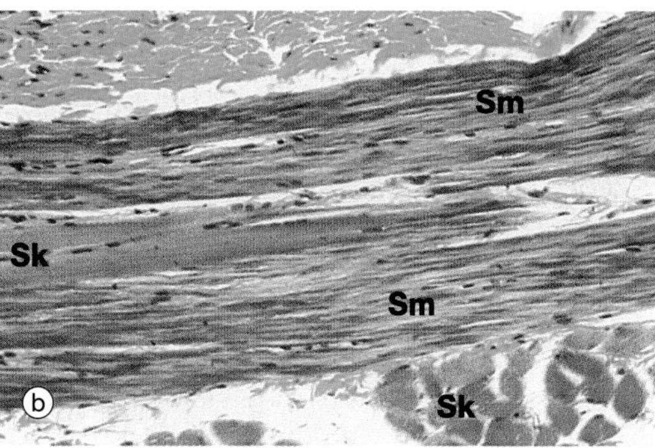

The oesophagus is a strong muscular tube that conveys food from the oropharynx to the stomach. The initiation of swallowing is a voluntary act involving the skeletal musculature of the oropharynx that is then succeeded by a strong peristaltic reflex that conveys the bolus of food or fluid to the stomach. Food and fluid do not normally remain in the oesophagus for more than a few seconds and reflux is usually prevented by a physiological sphincter at the gastro-oesophageal junction. Below the diaphragm, the oesophagus passes a centimetre or so into the abdominal cavity before joining the stomach at an acute angle. Sphincter control appears to involve four complementary factors: diaphragmatic contraction, greater intra-abdominal pressure than intragastric pressure being exerted upon the abdominal part of the oesophagus, unidirectional peristalsis and maintenance of correct anatomical arrangements of the structures.

Micrograph (a) shows the lower third of the oesophagus. In the relaxed state, the oesophageal mucosa is deeply folded; an arrangement that allows marked distension during the passage of a food bolus. The lumen of the oesophagus is lined by a thick protective stratified squamous epithelium **E** (see Fig. 14.3). The underlying lamina propria is quite narrow and contains scattered lymphoid aggregates **Ly**; the muscularis mucosae **MM** is barely visible at this magnification.

The submucosa **SM** is quite loose with many elastic fibres, allowing for considerable distension during passage of a food bolus. The submucosa also contains small seromucous glands **G**, similar to salivary glands, which aid lubrication and are most prominent in the upper and lower thirds of the oesophagus.

The muscularis propria is thick and inner circular **CM** and outer longitudinal **LM** layers of smooth muscle are clearly distinguishable. Since the first part of swallowing is under voluntary control, bundles of skeletal muscle predominate in the muscularis of the upper third of the oesophagus.

Micrograph (b) shows part of the muscularis propria of the upper oesophagus at high magnification in the area of transition from skeletal to smooth muscle fibres. A bundle of smooth muscle fibres **Sm** is seen, with two skeletal muscle fibres **Sk** in their midst. Other skeletal muscle fibres are seen in transverse section in the lower right of the micrograph. The cross-striation of the skeletal muscle are just visible at this magnification. The collagen of the endomysial supporting tissue stains green with this method.

CM inner circular layer of muscularis propria **E** epithelium **G** seromucous gland
LM outer longitudinal layer of muscularis propria **LP** lamina propria **Ly** lymphoid aggregates
MM muscularis mucosae **MP** muscularis propria **PG** parasympathetic ganglion
Sk skeletal muscle fibres **Sm** smooth muscle fibres **SM** submucosa

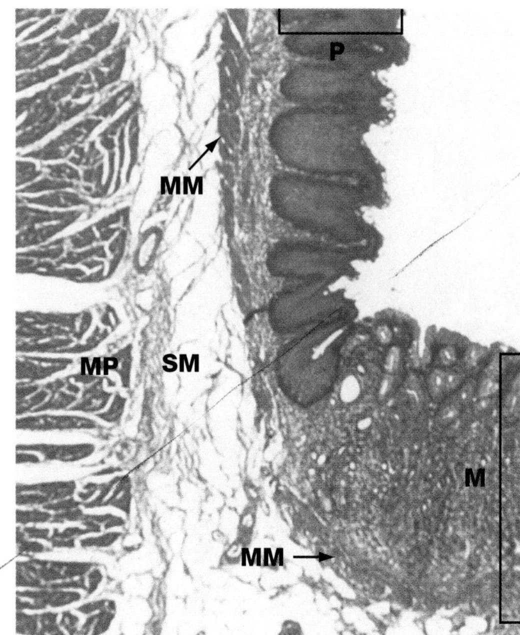

Fig. 14.6 Gastro-oesophageal junction
H & E ×40

At the junction of the oesophagus with the stomach, the mucosa of the tract undergoes an abrupt transition from a protective stratified squamous epithelium **P** to a tightly packed glandular secretory mucosa **M**. The muscularis mucosae **MM** is continuous across the junction, although it is less easily seen in the stomach where it lies immediately beneath the base of the gastric glands. The underlying submucosa **SM** and muscularis propria **MP** continue uninterrupted beneath the mucosal junction. The muscularis propria does not form a defined anatomical sphincter, but rather a physiological sphincter mechanism as described in Fig. 14.5.

Barrett's oesophagus

The importance of the physiologic sphincter at the gastro-oesophageal junction is apparent when the consequences of malfunction are considered. Reflux through the sphincter allows gastric acid into the lower oesophagus causing the well-known symptom of 'heartburn'. With time the epithelium of the lower oesophagus undergoes ***metaplasia***, i.e. it converts to a columnar mucous secreting form, a reaction that may well be protective. Barrett's oesophagus is the term given to this metaplastic columnar epithelium of the lower oesophagus, which is at high risk of developing dysplasia and ***invasive adenocarcinoma***. Oesophageal carcinomas in general have a poor prognosis.

Fig. 14.7 Stomach

Food passes from the oesophagus into the stomach, a distensible organ, where it may be retained for 2 hours or more. In the stomach the food undergoes mechanical and chemical breakdown to form chyme. Solid foods are broken up by a strong muscular churning action, while chemical breakdown is produced by gastric juices secreted by the glands of the stomach mucosa. There is little absorption from the stomach, except for water, alcohol and some drugs. Once chyme formation is completed, the pyloric sphincter relaxes and allows the liquid chyme to be squirted into the duodenum.

In the non-distended state, the stomach mucosa is thrown into prominent longitudinal folds called ***rugae*** that allow distension after eating. Anatomically the stomach is divided into four regions: the ***cardia***, ***fundus***, ***body*** (***corpus***) and ***pylorus*** (***pyloric antrum***). The pylorus terminates in a strong muscular sphincter at the gastroduodenal junction.

The mucosa of the entire stomach has a tubular glandular form but there are three distinctly different histological zones:

- The cardia is a small area of mucus-secreting glands surrounding the entrance of the oesophagus. In some individuals the cardia measures only a few millimetres or may be incomplete or absent altogether.
- The mucosa of the fundus and body forms the major histological region and consists of glands that secrete acid-pepsin gastric juices as well as some protective mucus.
- The glands of the pylorus secrete mucus of two different types and associated endocrine cells secrete the hormone ***gastrin***.

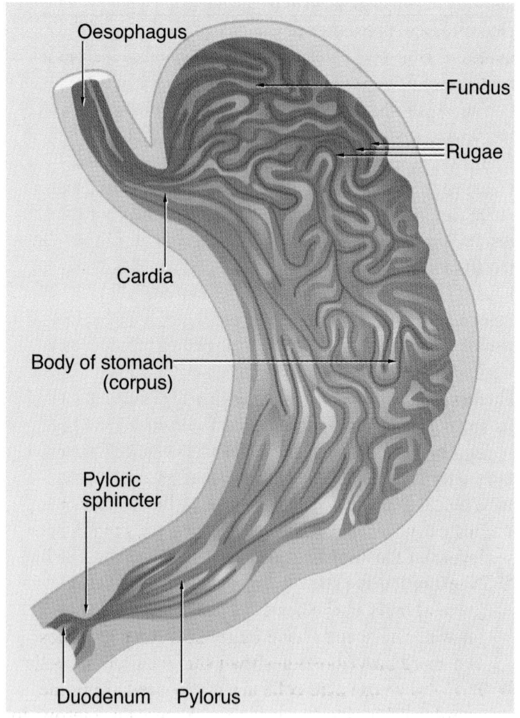

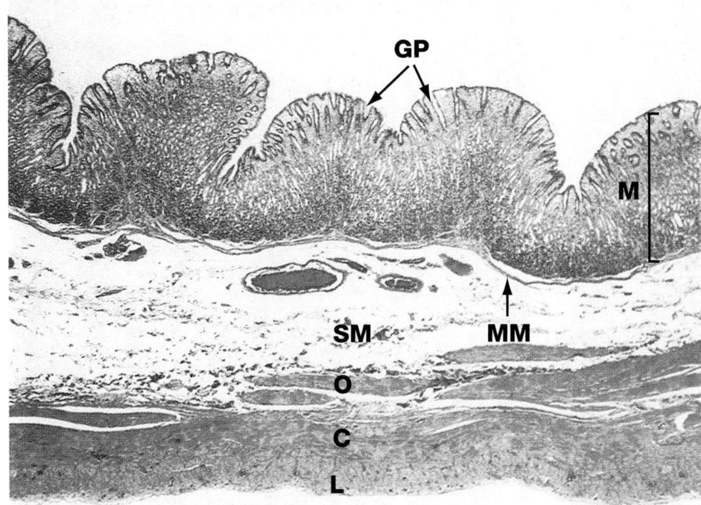

Fig. 14.8 Body of the stomach
H & E ×12

This micrograph illustrates the body of the stomach in the non-distended state. The mucosa **M** is thrown into prominent folds or rugae and consists of ***gastric glands*** that extend from the level of the muscularis mucosae **MM** to open into the stomach lumen via ***gastric pits*** or ***foveoli*** **GP**.

The muscularis propria comprises the usual inner circular **C** and outer longitudinal **L** layers, but the inner circular layer is reinforced by a further inner oblique layer **O**. The submucosa **SM** is relatively loose and distensible and contains the larger blood vessels. The serosal layer, which covers the peritoneal surface, is thin and barely visible at this magnification.

Fig. 14.9 Body of stomach: structure of glands

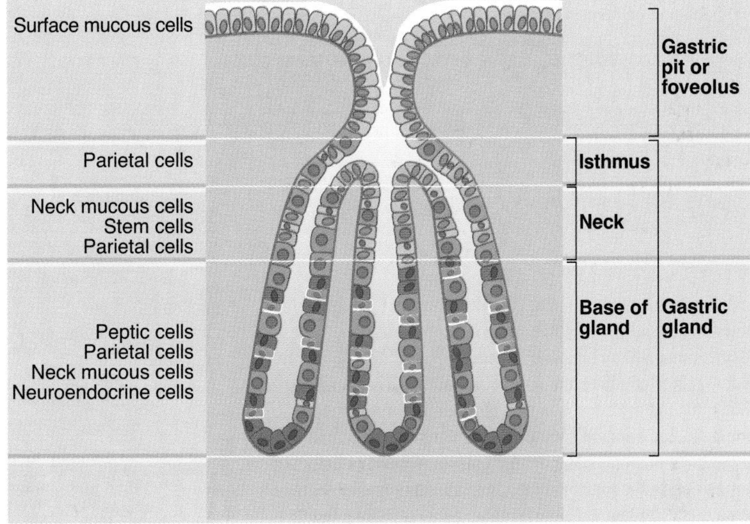

The mucosa of the fundus and body of the stomach consists of straight tubular glands that synthesise and secrete gastric juice. The gastric pits occupy about one-quarter of the thickness of the gastric mucosa and each has between one and seven gastric glands opening into it. Gastric juice is a watery secretion containing ***hydrochloric acid*** (pH 0.9–1.5) and the digestive enzyme ***pepsin***, which hydrolyses proteins into polypeptide fragments. The stomach mucosa is protected from self-digestion by a thick surface covering of mucus, which is maintained at a higher pH than the gastric juice by the secretion of bicarbonate ions by the gastric surface mucous cells.

The gastric glands contain a mixed population of cells:

- **Surface mucous cells** cover the luminal surface of the stomach and partly line the gastric pits. The cytoplasmic mucigen granules that pack these cells are stained poorly by the standard H & E stain. These cells have short surface microvilli and secrete protective bicarbonate ions directly into the deeper layers of the surface mucous coat.
- **Neck mucous cells** are squeezed between the parietal cells in the neck and base of the gastric glands. These cells have larger secretory granules and more polyribosomes than surface mucous cells.
- **Parietal** or **oxyntic cells** are distributed along the length of the glands but tend to be most numerous in the ***isthmus*** of the glands. These large rounded cells have an extensive eosinophilic (oxyntic) cytoplasm and a centrally located nucleus. Parietal cells secrete gastric acid as well as ***intrinsic factor***, a glycoprotein necessary for the absorption of vitamin B_{12} in the terminal ileum.
- **Chief**, **peptic** or **zymogenic cells** are located towards the bases of the gastric glands. Peptic cells are recognised by their condensed, basally located nuclei and strongly basophilic granular cytoplasm, which reflects their large content of ribosomes. These are the pepsin-secreting cells.
- **Neuroendocrine cells**, part of the diffuse neuroendocrine system, are also found in the base of the gastric glands. They secrete serotonin and other hormones (see also Fig. 14.12).
- **Stem cells** are found mainly in the neck of the gastric glands. These undifferentiated cells divide continuously to replace all other types of cell in the glands. The maturing cells then migrate up or down as appropriate. These cells are not easily identified in sections of normal gastric mucosa but become very prominent with plentiful mitotic figures after damage to the mucosa has occurred, e.g. after an episode of gastritis.

C inner circular layer of muscularis propria **GP** gastric pits **L** outer longitudinal layer of muscularis propria **M** mucosa **MM** muscularis mucosae **MP** muscularis propria **O** inner oblique layer of muscularis propria **P** stratified squamous epithelium **SM** submucosa

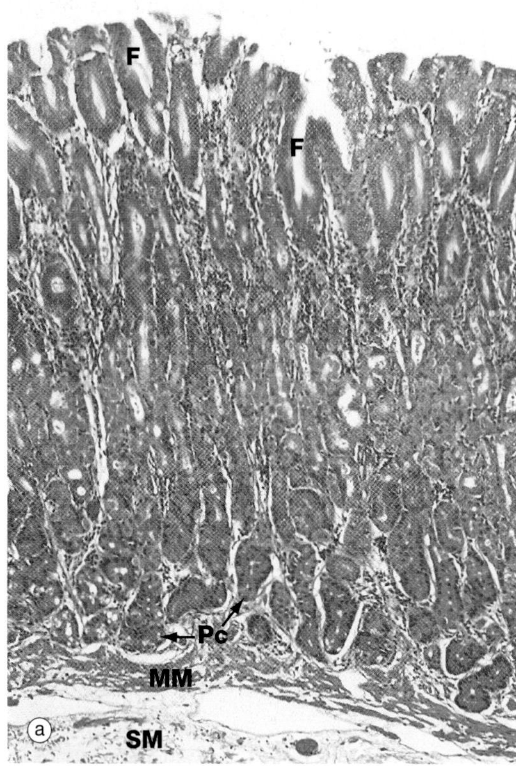

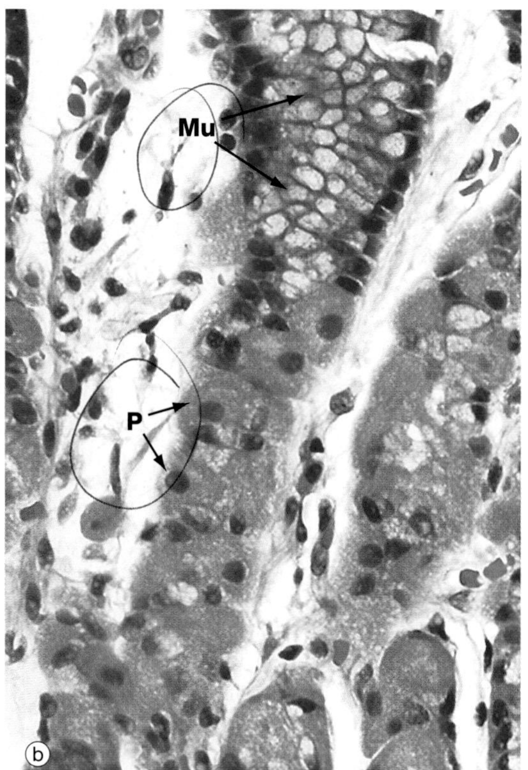

Fig. 14.10 Gastric body mucosa
(a) H& E ×40 (b) H & E ×400 (c) PAS/haematoxylin/orange G TS ×200

Micrograph (a) shows the full thickness of the gastric body mucosa and includes a small amount of submucosa **SM**. The gastric pits or foveolae **F** lined by pale-stained surface mucous cells are easily identifiable. The isthmus and neck of the glands also appear pale due to the predominance of neck mucous cells and parietal cells. The base of the glands, where peptic (chief) cells **Pc** predominate, are stained darker in this H & E preparation. The glands extend down to the muscularis mucosae **MM**. Normal gastric mucosa is virtually devoid of lymphoid cells.

Micrograph (b) is a high-power view of the neck and isthmus of a gastric body gland. The neck mucous cells **Mu** and parietal cells **P** are easily visualised at this magnification. The tall columnar mucus-secreting cells of the stomach are not of the goblet cell type found in small and large intestines. The mucus produced by these mucous cells protects the epithelium from autodigestion by acid gastric juice. The parietal cells are recognised by their copious eosinophilic cytoplasm and central nucleus, which is often described as a 'fried egg appearance'.

In transverse section, as in micrograph (c), the tubular nature of the gastric pits is clearly evident. Between one and seven gastric glands may open into each gastric pit. Note the loose vascular but scanty ***lamina propria*** **L** that supports the gastric pits and glands. The lightly PAS-positive basement membrane **BM** can be distinguished between the epithelium and lamina propria. The mucus of the neck mucous cells stains a strong magenta colour with this staining method.

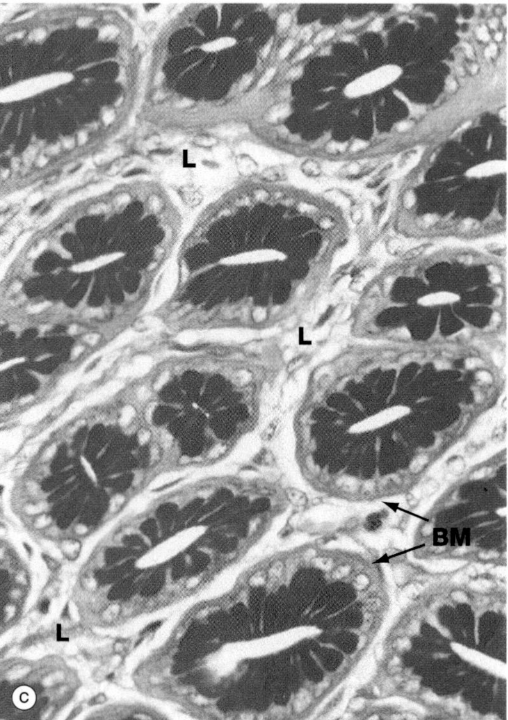

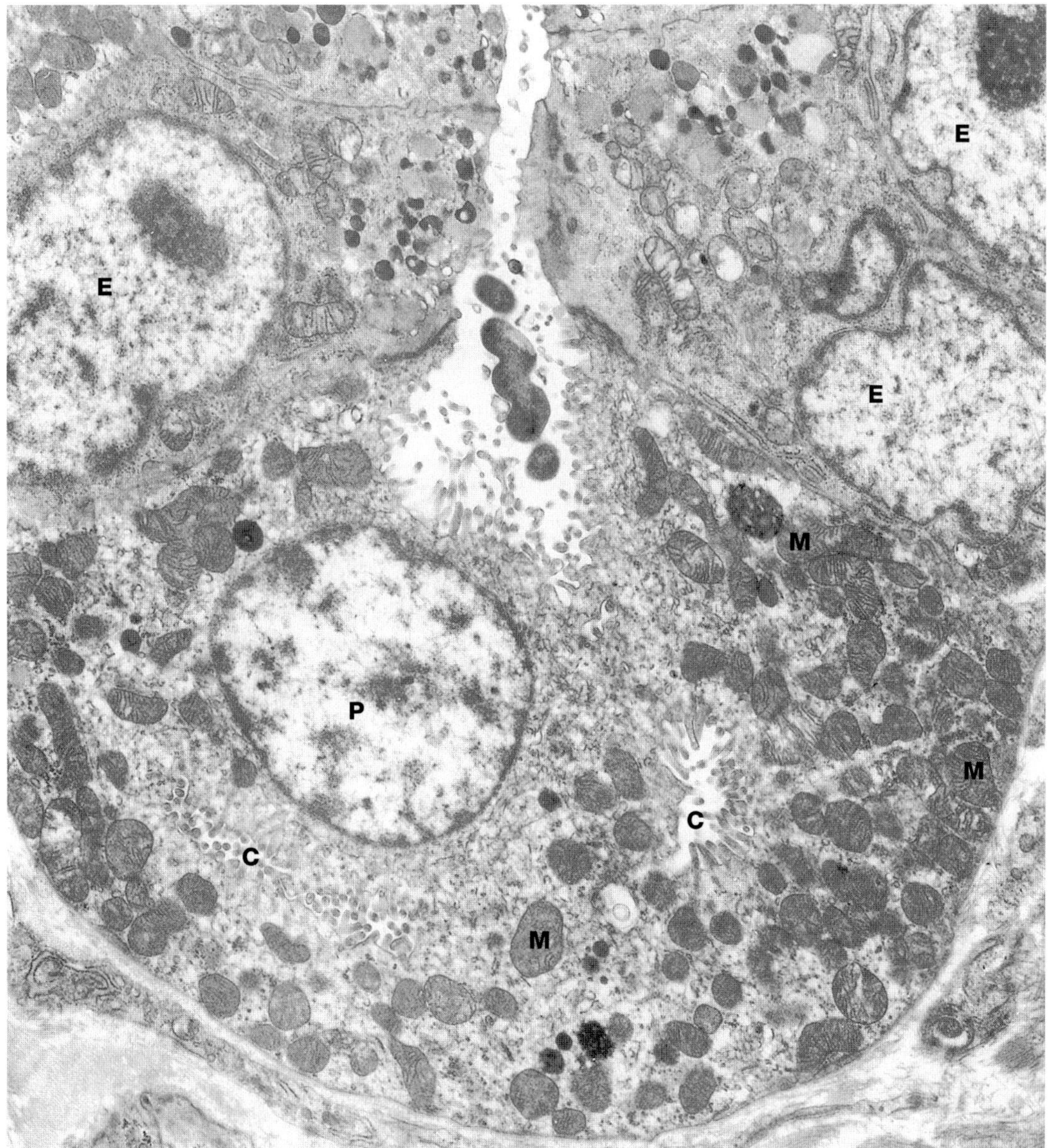

Fig. 14.11 Parietal cell – rat
EM ×9600

This micrograph shows a parietal cell **P** within a gastric gland. The luminal plasma membrane of the parietal cell forms deep, branching ***canaliculi*** **C** that extend throughout the cytoplasm and between adjacent cells. Numerous short microvilli project into the lumina of the intracellular canaliculi, greatly increasing the surface area. The canaliculi are related to a tubulovesicular membrane complex (not well seen in this micrograph) and these two membrane systems secrete hydrochloric acid. In actively secreting cells, as in this case, the canalicular system is more prominent, whereas in resting parietal cells the canalicular system is inconspicuous and the tubulovesicular complex is prominent.

Secretion of hydrochloric acid begins with the production of carbonic acid, which dissociates into hydrogen and bicarbonate ions. The hydrogen ions are actively transported into the lumen of the tubulovesicular complex by the trans-membrane 'proton pump', a H^+/K^+-ATPase. Chloride ions follow passively. The details of the next step are as yet unclear, but there may be fusion of the tubulovesicular complex vesicles with the canalicular system, so that the acid is now within the lumina of the canaliculi. This would explain the increase in the size of the canalicular system and decrease in the tubulovesicular complex that occurs in actively secreting cells. The end result is a hydrogen ion concentration in gastric juice about 1 million times that in plasma. This process is fueled by the many mitochondria **M** of the parietal cells.

Parietal cells also secrete a glycoprotein called ***intrinsic factor***, which is essential for the absorption of vitamin B_{12} in the terminal ileum. Also seen in this micrograph are several neuroendocrine cells **E**, recognised by their small electron-dense secretory granules.

BM basement membrane **C** canaliculus **E** neuroendocrine cell **F** foveola **L** lamina propria **M** mitochondrion **MM** muscularis mucosae **Mu** neck mucous cell **P** parietal cells **Pc** peptic cell **SM** submucosa

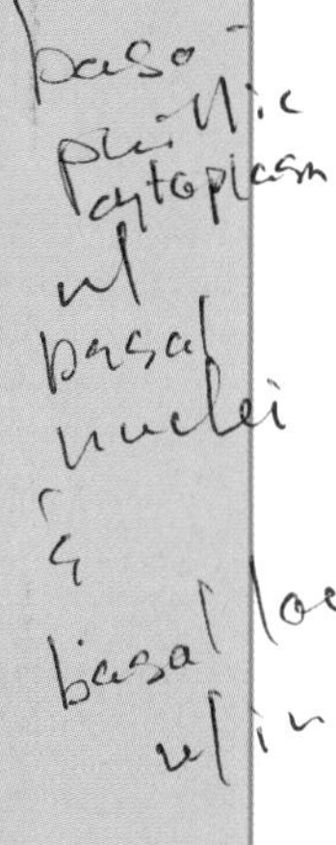

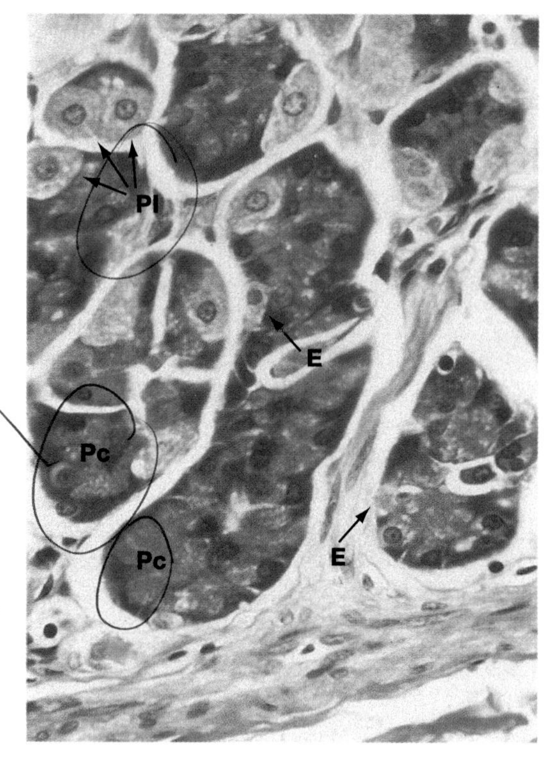

Fig. 14.12 Base of gastric gland
H & E ×320

Peptic (chief) cells **Pc**, which synthesise and secrete the proteolytic enzyme ***pepsin***, are the principal cell type in the basal third of the gastric glands, although some parietal cells **Pl** are also found at this level. Peptic cells have basally located nuclei and extensive granular cytoplasm packed with rough endoplasmic reticulum, the ribosomes accounting for the relative cytoplasmic basophilia. The inactive pepsin precursor, ***pepsinogen***, is synthesised by the ribosomes and stored in numerous secretory granules located towards the luminal surface. Pepsinogen remains inactive until it reaches the lumen of the stomach where it is activated by the low pH of the gastric juices. Secretion of an inactive precursor molecule prevents autodigestion of the gastric glands.

The much larger parietal cells are round with large, centrally located nuclei and eosinophilic (pink-stained) cytoplasm due to the numerous mitochondria that are a feature of highly metabolically active cells.

The secretory activity of both parietal and peptic cells is controlled by the autonomic nervous system and the hormone ***gastrin*** that is secreted by neuroendocrine cells of the pyloric region. A variety of other neuroendocrine cells of the gastrointestinal endocrine system are also scattered in the gastric body mucosa and elsewhere in the gastrointestinal tract. Occasionally, the neuroendocrine cells **E** can be identified in sections fixed with chromium-containing fixatives, as in this example.

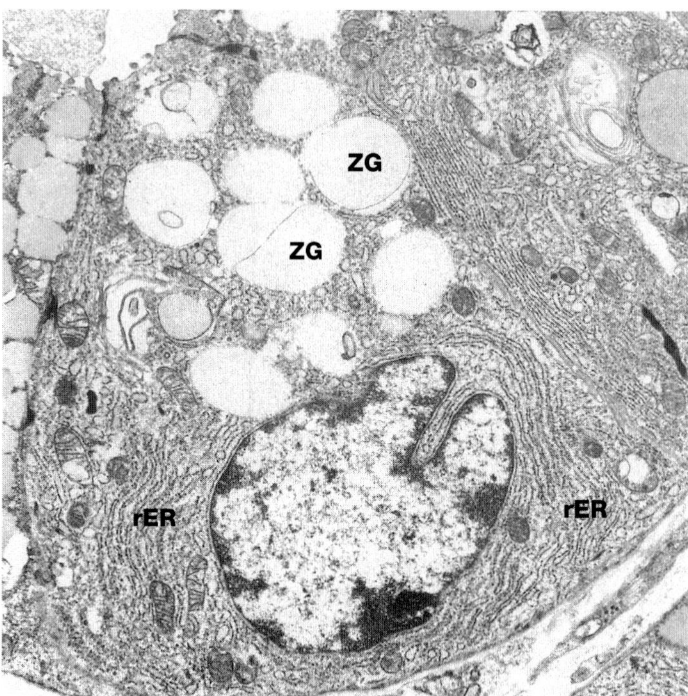

Fig. 14.13 Peptic cell – rat
EM ×7200

This electron micrograph illustrates a peptic (chief) cell at the base of a gastric gland. The ultrastructural features of peptic cells are those of protein-secreting cells in general; these features include an extensive rough endoplasmic reticulum **rER** and membrane-bound secretory vesicles (zymogen granules) **ZG** containing pepsinogen crowded in the apical cytoplasm, thus restricting the nucleus to the base of the cell. The extensive rough endoplasmic reticulum accounts for the basophilia of peptic cells in H & E sections.

B Brunner's glands **CM** inner circular layer of muscularis propria **D** duodenum **E** neuroendocrine cell **G** G cells **LM** outer longitudinal layer of muscularis propria **MM** muscularis mucosae **P** gastric pits **Pc** peptic cell **Pl** parietal cell **PS** pyloric sphincter **rER** rough endoplasmic reticulum **S** stomach **ZG** zymogen granules

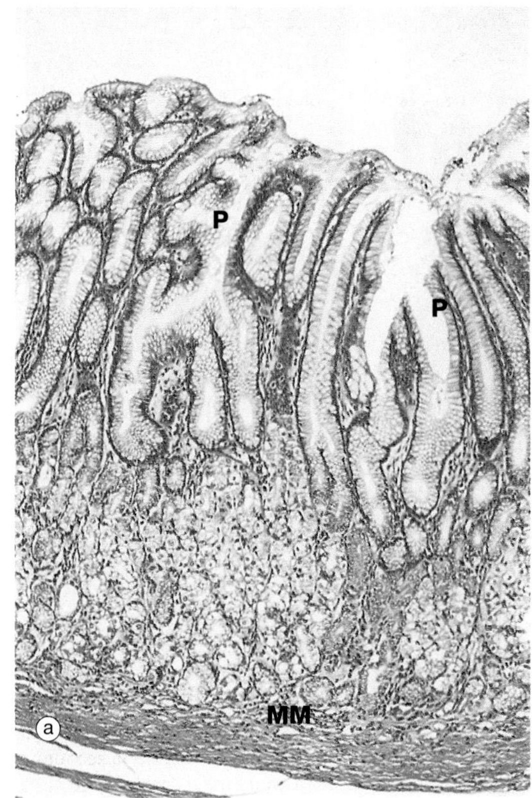

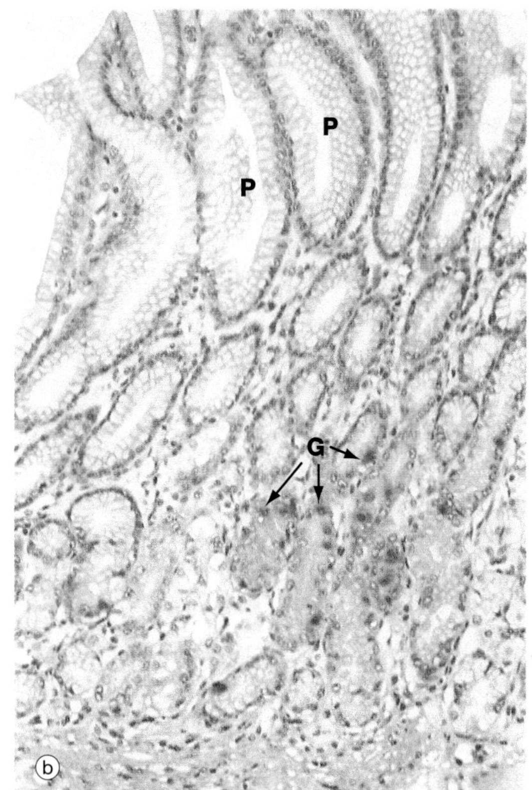

Fig. 14.14 Pyloric stomach
(a) H & E ×75 (b) Immunoperoxidase for gastrin ×150

In contrast to the simple tubular glands of the fundus and body, the pyloric glands are branched and coiled and the gastric pits **P** occupy about half the thickness of the pyloric mucosa (a). The glands are lined almost exclusively by mucus-secreting cells, which are similar to the neck mucous cells of the gastric body and fundus. A small number of acid-secreting parietal cells are also scattered among the pyloric glands. Note the prominent muscularis mucosae **MM** separating the glands from underlying submucosa. As in the body of the stomach, stem cells are found in the neck of the glands but cannot be easily identified by light microscopy.

Scattered among the pyloric mucous cells are neuroendocrine cells that secrete the peptide hormone ***gastrin*** and are thus called ***G cells***. In micrograph (b) an antibody to gastrin has been used to highlight the G cells which contain gastrin in secretory granules in their cytoplasm. The G cells are stained brown **G** and are found mainly in the neck of the glands. The presence of food in the stomach stimulates the secretion of gastrin into the bloodstream; gastrin then promotes secretion of pepsin and acid by the gastric glands of the fundus and body as well as enhancing gastric motility. Other neuroendocrine cells in the pylorus secrete various other hormonal products, including somatostatin, which is involved in the regulation of insulin, glucagon, gastrin and growth hormone secretion.

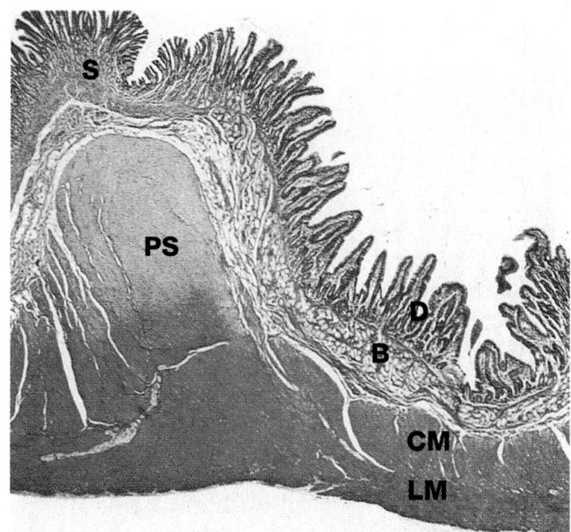

Fig. 14.15 Gastroduodenal junction – monkey
H & E ×12

The pyloric sphincter **PS** marks a sharp transition from the glandular mucosa of the stomach **S** to the villous mucosa of the duodenum **D** and the rest of the small intestine. In addition, the duodenum is distinguished from the jejunum and ileum by the presence of numerous mucus-secreting glands **B**. These glands, known as ***Brunner's glands***, are predominantly found in the submucosa but may extend into the mucosa.

The pyloric sphincter consists of a marked thickening of the circular layer of the muscularis at the gastroduodenal junction. Note the continuity of both the circular **CM** and longitudinal **LM** layers of the muscularis between the pylorus and duodenum.
The inner oblique layer is found only in the body of the stomach.

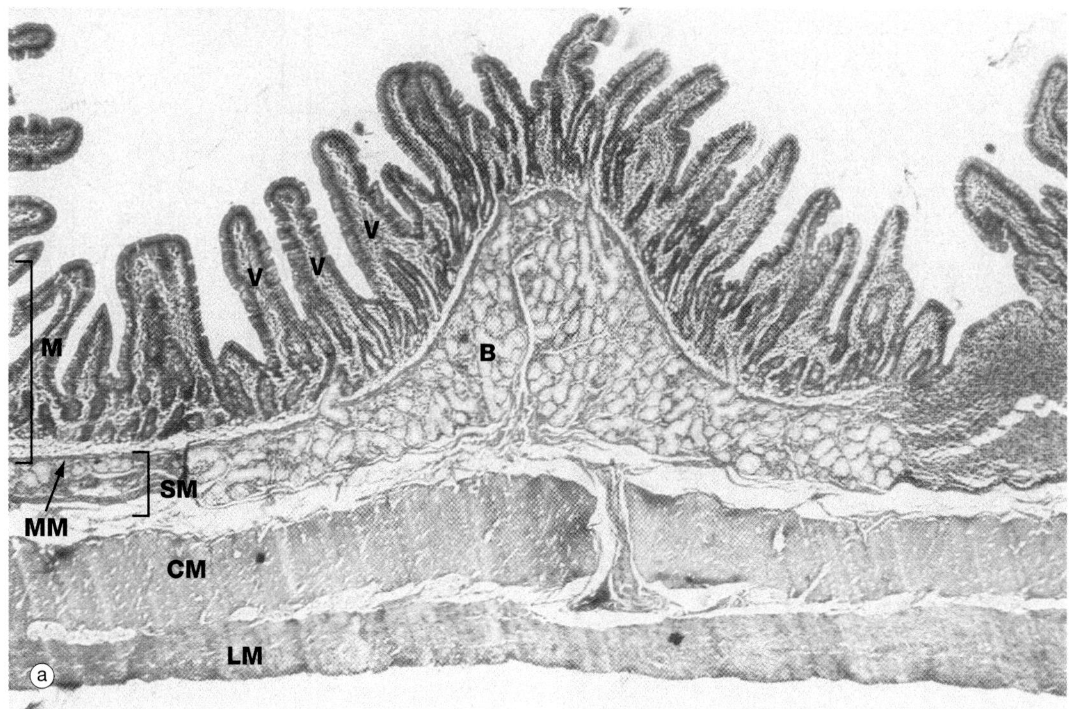

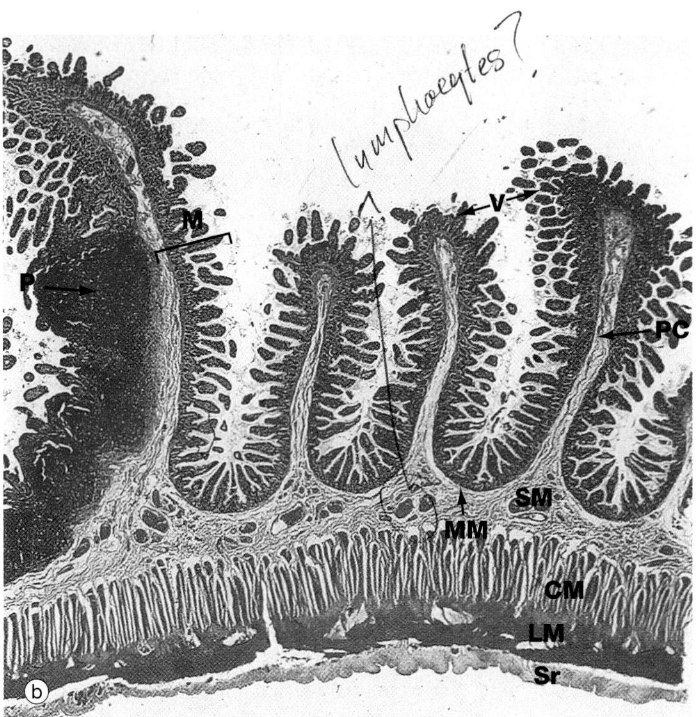

Fig. 14.16 Small intestine – monkey
(a) Duodenum H & E ×20 (b) ileum H & E ×16

The duodenum, seen in micrograph (a), represents the first part of the small intestine and receives partly digested food in the form of acidic chyme from the stomach via the pyloric canal. The main function of the duodenum is to neutralise gastric acid and pepsin and to initiate further digestive processes.

Micrograph (a) illustrates monkey duodenum, the wall of the human duodenum being too thick to be photographed in its entirety. The mucosa **M** has the characteristic villous form of the whole of the small intestine, interspersed with short glands known as ***crypts of Lieberkühn*** extending down to the muscularis mucosae **MM**. The feature unique to the duodenum is the extensive mass of coiled branched tubular ***Brunner's glands*** **B** found mainly in the submucosa **SM**. The ducts of the Brunner's glands pass through the

B Brunner's glands **CM** inner circular layer of muscularis propria **LP** lamina propria
LM outer longitudinal layer of muscularis propria **M** mucosa **MM** muscularis mucosae
P Peyer's patches **PC** plicae circulares **SM** submucosa **Sr** serosa **V** villi

Fig. 14.16 Small intestine – monkey (*cont'd*)
(a) Duodenum H & E ×20 (b) Ileum H & E ×16

muscularis mucosae to open into the crypts between the mucosal villi **V**. The muscularis propria of the duodenum consists of an inner circular layer **CM** and an outer longitudinal layer **LM**, as in the rest of the small intestine.

The tall columnar cells of Brunner's glands have extensive, poorly stained mucigen-filled cytoplasm and basally located nuclei. The presence of chyme in the duodenum stimulates Brunner's glands to secrete a thin alkaline mucus that helps to neutralise the acidic chyme and to protect the duodenal mucosa from autodigestion. Other products of Brunner's glands include lysozyme and epidermal growth factor.

Chyme also stimulates the release of two peptide hormones, ***secretin*** and ***cholecystokinin-pancreozymin*** (***CCK***) from neuroendocrine cells scattered throughout the duodenal mucosa. Secretin and CCK promote pancreatic exocrine secretion into the duodenal lumen via the pancreatic duct; CCK also stimulates contraction of the gall bladder, thus propelling bile into the common bile duct. The pancreatic and common bile ducts merge to empty their contents into the duodenum via a single short duct that opens into the second part of the duodenum via the ***ampulla of Vater***.

Pancreatic juice is alkaline due to a high content of bicarbonate ions and thus helps to neutralise the acidic gastric contents entering the duodenum. The pancreas also secretes a variety of digestive enzymes, including the proteolytic enzymes ***trypsin*** and ***chymotrypsin***; like pepsin in the stomach, these are secreted in an inactive pro-enzyme form. On entering the duodenal lumen, trypsin is activated by the enzyme ***enterokinase*** secreted by the duodenal mucosa; activated trypsin in turn activates chymotrypsin. The pancreatic enzymes, which also include ***amylase*** and ***lipases***, initiate the processes of luminal digestion described in Fig. 14.18. The biliary secretions contain ***bile acids***, which act as emulsifying agents and are particularly important in the absorption of lipids.

Micrograph (b) shows a section of ileum at very low magnification. The mucosa **M** is thrown into transverse folds, the ***plicae circulares*** **PC** (also called ***valvulae conniventes*** or ***folds of Kerckring***), covered with villi **V**. The muscularis mucosae **MM** lies immediately beneath the crypts and is difficult to see at this magnification. The vascular submucosa **SM** extends into the plicae circulares. Beneath it lie the inner circular **CM** and outer longitudinal **LM** layers of the muscularis propria and the serosa **Sr.** Peyer's patches **P** (see Ch. 11) dominate the mucosa at the left of the field.

It is clear from these two micrographs that the small intestine has the same basic structure throughout. The major difference between the duodenum on the one hand, and the jejunum and ileum on the other, is the presence of Brunner's glands in the duodenum. Other qualitative differences include the following:

- The villi tend to be longest in the duodenum and become shorter towards the ileum.
- Lymphoid tissue becomes more prominent in the ileum and is fairly inconspicuous in the duodenum.
- The proportion of goblet cells in the epithelium increases distally.
- Plicae circulares are most prominent and numerous in the jejunum and proximal ileum and are generally absent in the proximal duodenum and distal ileum.

Coeliac disease

Coeliac disease (or coeliac sprue or gluten sensitive enteropathy) is caused by an immunologic response to gluten (gliadin) a component of wheat, oats, barley and rye. Individuals with the condition present with symptoms of malabsorption (weight loss, diarrhoea, steatorrhoea, anaemia and vitamin deficiencies). Blood tests reveal the characteristic anti-endomysial antibodies. Biopsies of the small bowel for diagnosis are usually carried out endoscopically and reveal the typical loss of the normal intestinal villi (compare Fig. 14.17 with Fig. 14.16) and a marked increase in the numbers of lymphocytes and plasma cells in the lamina propria **LP**. Also typical is the marked increase in the numbers of intraepithelial T lymphocytes suggesting that the condition is at least partly due to a cell mediated immune response. Although these histological appearances are very suggestive of coeliac disease they are not specific and the diagnosis must be confirmed by resolution of symptoms and histological changes after a period of time on a gluten-free diet.

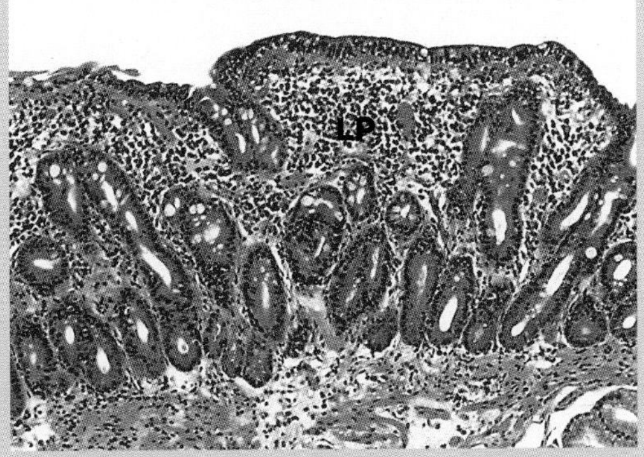

Fig. 14.17 Coeliac disease: atrophic jejunal mucosa
H & E ×100

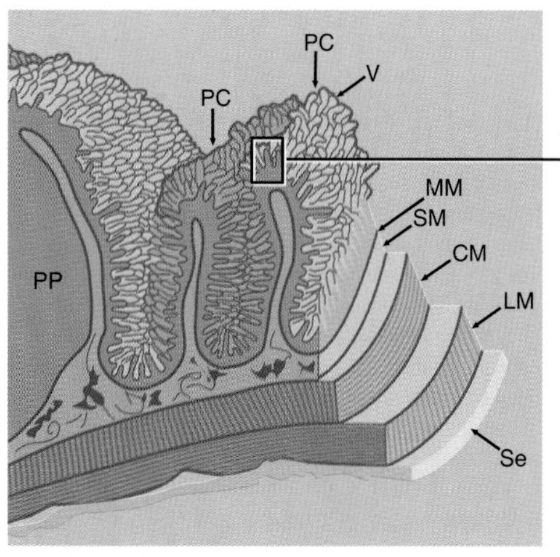

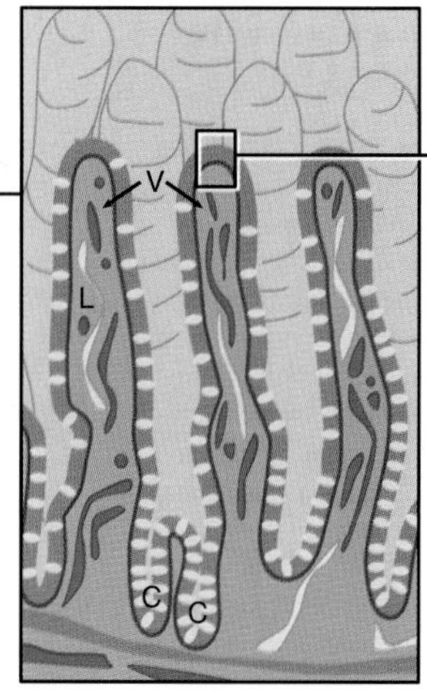

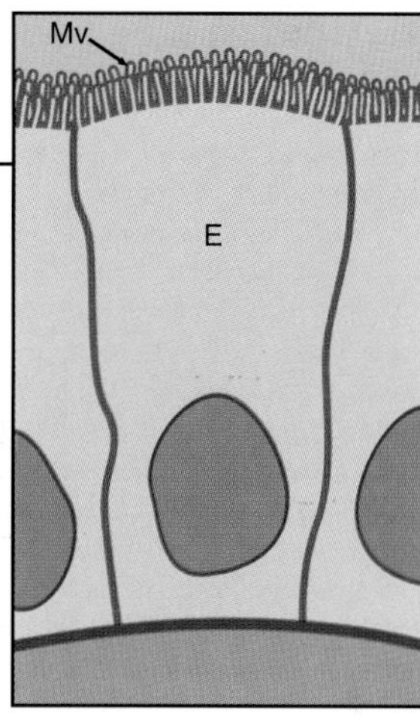

Fig. 14.18 Small intestine

The small intestine, comprising the duodenum, jejunum and ileum, is the principal site for absorption of digestion products from the gastrointestinal tract. Digestion begins in the stomach and is completed in the small intestine in association with the absorptive process. Four factors combine to provide an enormous surface area:

- The small intestine is extremely long (4–6 metres in humans).
- The mucosa and submucosa are thrown up into circularly arranged folds called ***plicae circulares*** **PC** or ***valves of Kerckring*** which are particularly numerous in the jejunum.
- The mucosal surface is made up of numerous finger-like projections called ***villi*** **V**.
- Thousands of ***microvilli*** **Mv** are present at the luminal surface of the ***enterocytes*** **E**, the columnar cells covering the villi; these cells are responsible for the process of absorption and some digestion.

The muscularis mucosae **MM** lies immediately beneath the mucosal crypts and separates the mucosa from the submucosa **SM**. The vascular submucosa extends into, and forms the core of, the plicae circulares. Inner circular **CM** and outer longitudinal **LM** layers of the muscularis are responsible for continuous peristaltic activity of the small intestine. The peritoneal aspect of the muscularis is invested by the loose collagenous serosa **Se**, which is lined on its peritoneal surface by mesothelium identical in appearance to the mesothelial lining of the pleura (see Fig. 12.23).

A prominent feature of the small intestine are 200 or so lymphoid aggregations known as ***Peyer's patches*** **PP** within the lamina propria (see Fig. 11.17).

The mechanisms of digestion and absorption

Digestion occurs within the lumen or at the mucosal surface where it is linked with the process of absorption.

Luminal digestion involves the mixing of chyme with pancreatic enzymes to break up foods into their component parts; the process is facilitated by adsorption of pancreatic enzymes onto the mucosal surface. ***Membrane digestion*** involves enzymes located in the luminal plasma membranes of the enterocytes. The principal means of digestion and absorption of the main food constituents are as follows:

- **Proteins** are first denatured by the gastric acid and then hydrolysed to polypeptide fragments by the enzyme pepsin. In the duodenum, pancreatic enzymes, including ***trypsin***, ***chymotrypsin***, ***elastase*** and ***carboxypeptidases***, continue this process producing small peptide fragments. Membrane-bound ***peptide hydrolases*** complete the digestion to amino acids that are then absorbed. Absorption is by active transport with a different carrier system for each amino acid. In young infants, some proteins are absorbed without prior digestion by the process of endocytosis.
- **Carbohydrates** occur in the diet mainly in the form of starches and the disaccharides, sucrose and lactose. ***Pancreatic amylase*** hydrolyses starch to glucose and the disaccharide maltose in the small intestinal lumen. This process is begun by ***salivary amylase*** in the mouth, although its contribution to digestion is probably minor. Membrane-bound disaccharidases and oligosaccharidases convert the sugars to monosaccharides, mainly glucose, galactose and fructose, which are absorbed by facilitated diffusion.
- **Lipids**, predominantly triglycerides, are converted by the mechanical action of the stomach into a coarse emulsion, which is converted to a fine emulsion in the duodenum by bile acids synthesised in the liver. Each triglyceride molecule is broken down into a monoglyceride and two free fatty acids by pancreatic ***lipases***, although some glycerol and diglycerides are also produced. These smaller lipid molecules are then absorbed and resynthesised back into triglycerides within the enterocytes.

The products of protein and carbohydrate digestion, namely amino acids and monosaccharides, respectively, enter the intestinal capillaries and pass via the portal vein to the liver. In contrast, the reconstituted triglycerides pass into intestinal lymphatics known as ***lacteals*** **L**, and thence via the thoracic duct to the general circulation, bypassing the liver. For lymphatic transport, the triglycerides become coated with phospholipids and proteins to form fine globules known as ***chylomicrons***. A minority of lipid digestion products, such as short-chain fatty acids and glycerol, pass in the portal system to the liver along with almost all the bile acids which are reabsorbed and recirculated.

Fig. 14.19 Duodenum

H & E ×15

This micrograph of the human duodenum is stained by the standard H & E method. The duodenal mucosa has the typical form found elsewhere in the small intestine; namely numerous elongated villi **V**, between the bases of which are shorter crypts **C**. In the distal duodenum the height of the villi is about four times the length of the crypts while in the more distal small bowel the villus:crypt ratio is 2–3:1. The pale stained Brunner's glands occupy the entire submucosa **SM** deep to the muscularis mucosae **MM**. A small component of the Brunner's gland is sometimes found in the lamina propria **LP** where the duct of the gland empties into the base of a mucosal crypt. The Brunner's glands secrete alkaline mucins into the lumen of the small intestine.

As mentioned already, the presence of Brunner's glands is one of the main features that differentiates the duodenum from the rest of the small intestine.

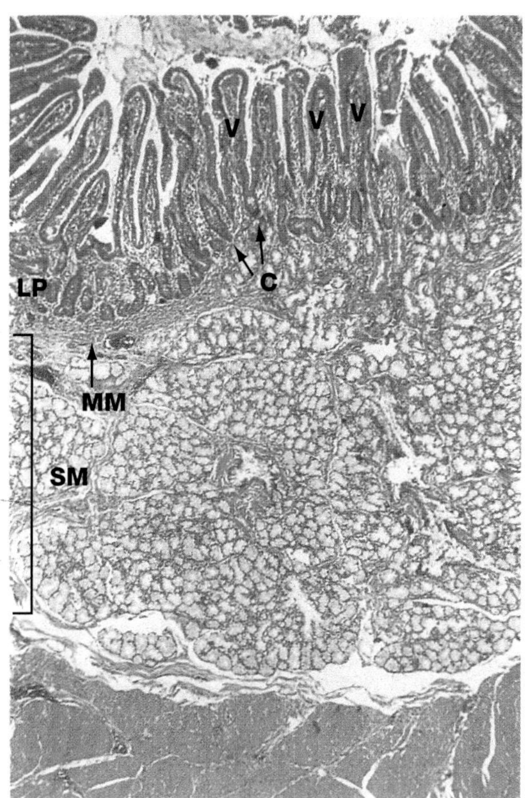

Fig. 14.20 Intestinal villi and crypts

H & E ×150

The intestinal villi **V** are lined by a simple columnar epithelium which is continuous with that of the crypts **C** As in other parts of the gastrointestinal tract, the epithelium includes a variety of cell types, each with its own specific function. Cell types in the small intestine epithelium include:

- **Enterocytes**, the most numerous cell type, are tall columnar cells with surface microvilli that are seen as a brush border in light micrographs. These cells are the main absorptive cells.
- **Goblet cells** are scattered among the enterocytes and produce mucin for lubrication of the intestinal contents and protection of the epithelium.
- **Paneth cells** are found at the base of the crypts and are distinguished by their prominent, eosinophilic apical granules. These cells have a defensive function.
- **Neuroendocrine cells** produce locally acting hormones that regulate gastrointestinal motility and secretion.
- **Stem cells**, found at the base of the crypts, divide continuously to replenish all of the above four cell types.
- **Intraepithelial lymphocytes**, which are mostly T cells, provide defence against invasive organisms.

The lamina propria **LP** extends between the crypts and into the core of each villus and contains a rich vascular and lymphatic network into which digestive products are absorbed. The muscularis mucosae **MM** lies immediately beneath the base of the crypts.

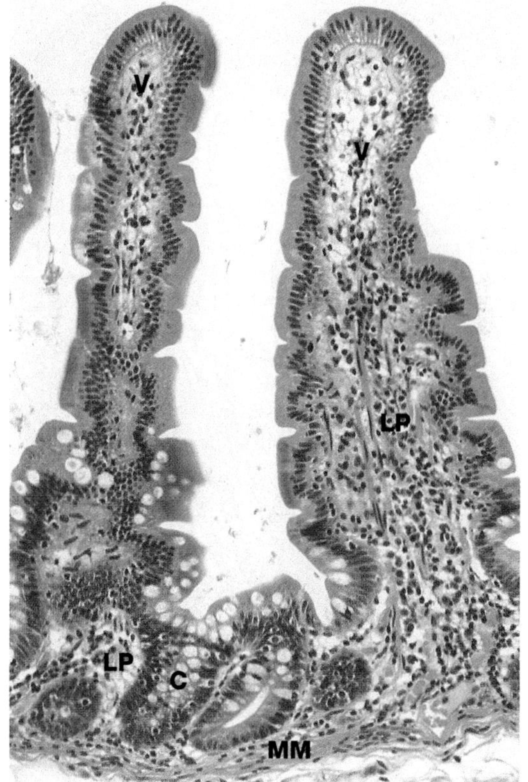

C crypts **CM** inner circular layer of muscularis propria **E** enterocytes **L** lacteal
LP lamina propria **LM** outer longitudinal layer of muscularis propria
MM muscularis mucosae **Mv** microvilli **PC** plicae circulares **PP** Peyer's patch **Se** serosa
SM submucosa **V** intestinal villi

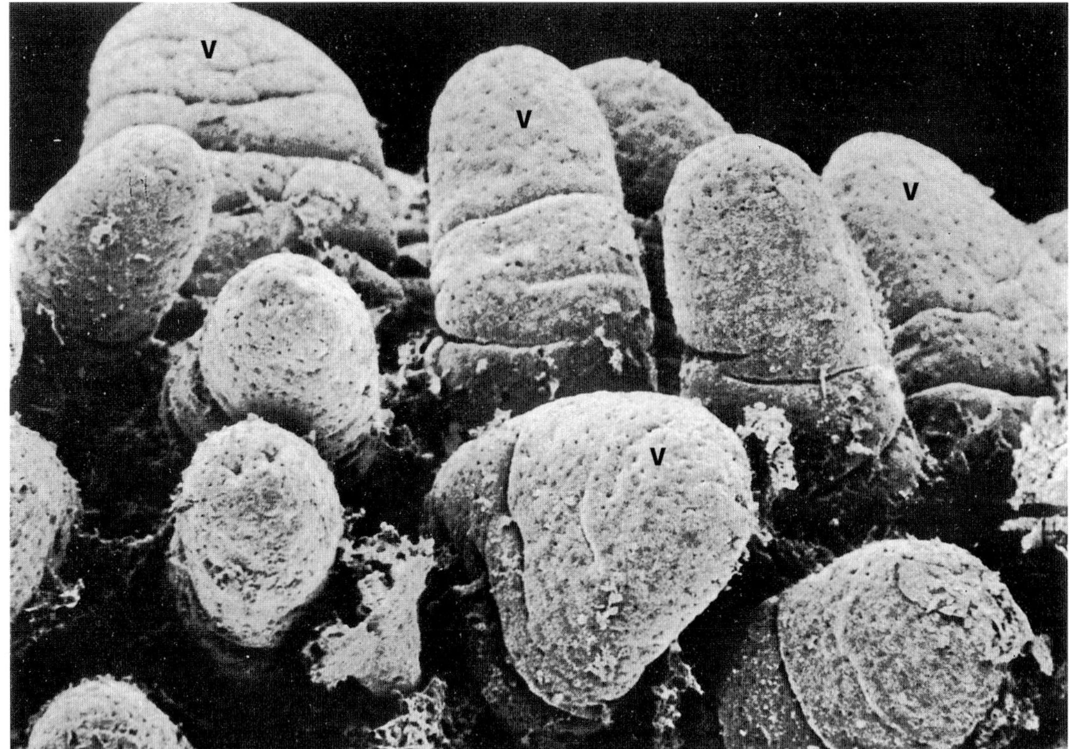

Fig. 14.21 Intestinal villi
SEM ×100

This low power scanning electron micrograph shows villi **V** along the crest of a plica circularis in the small intestine. Note the variability of the shape of the villi: some are finger-shaped, while others have a broader, leaf-like profile. Surface openings of scattered goblet cells stud the villous surface. Fragments of mucus can be seen trapped between the villi.

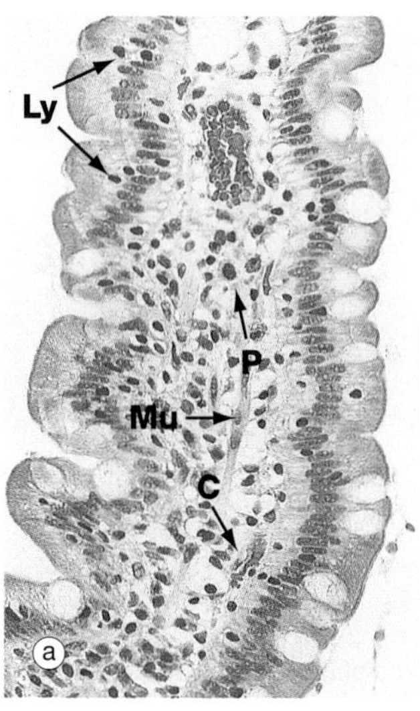

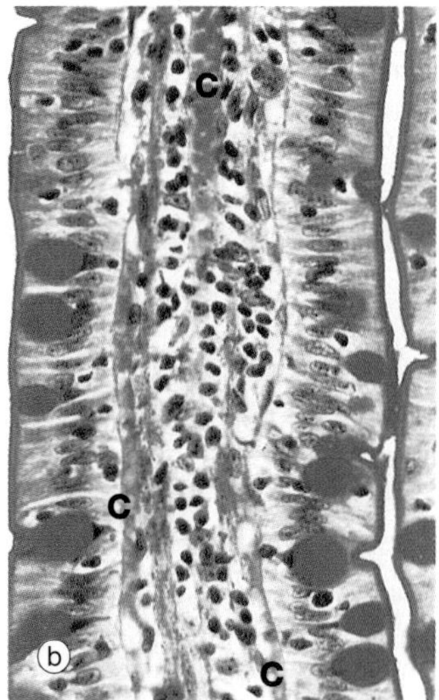

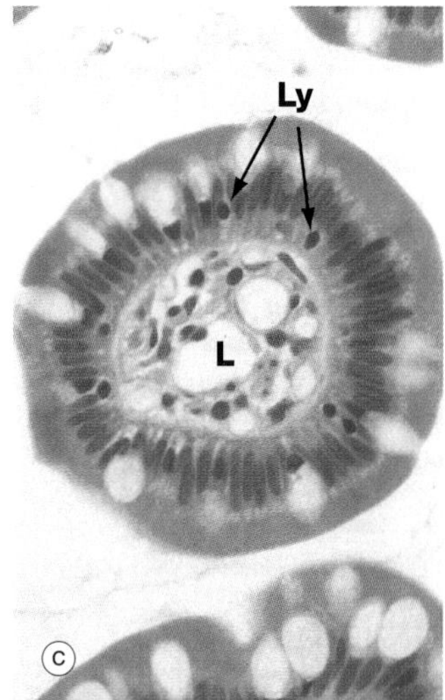

Fig. 14.22 Intestinal villi
(a) H & E LS ×100 (b) PAS/iron haematoxylin/orange G ×320 (c) H & E, TS ×300

These micrographs illustrate the tall columnar enterocytes and goblet cells that cover the intestinal villi, as well as the goblet cells scattered among them. The luminal surface of the enterocytes seen in micrograph (b) is strongly PAS-positive due to a particularly thick glycocalyx and a surface layer of goblet cell-derived mucus; both protect against autodigestion. The glycocalyx is also the site for adsorption of pancreatic digestive enzymes.

T lymphocytes **Ly** are scattered among the enterocytes. Plasma cells **P** in the villous core secrete IgA into the intestinal lumen by transcytosis across epithelial cells.

The cores of the villi are extensions of the lamina propria and consist of loose supporting tissue. Capillaries **C** lie immediately beneath the basement membrane and transport most digestive products to the hepatic portal vein. Tiny lymphatic vessels drain into a single larger vessel called a ***lacteal*** **L**, at the centre of the villus. The lacteals transport absorbed lipid into the circulatory system via the thoracic duct. Smooth muscle fibres **Mu** are seen in the long axis of the villous core in micrograph (a) and represent extensions of the muscularis mucosae.

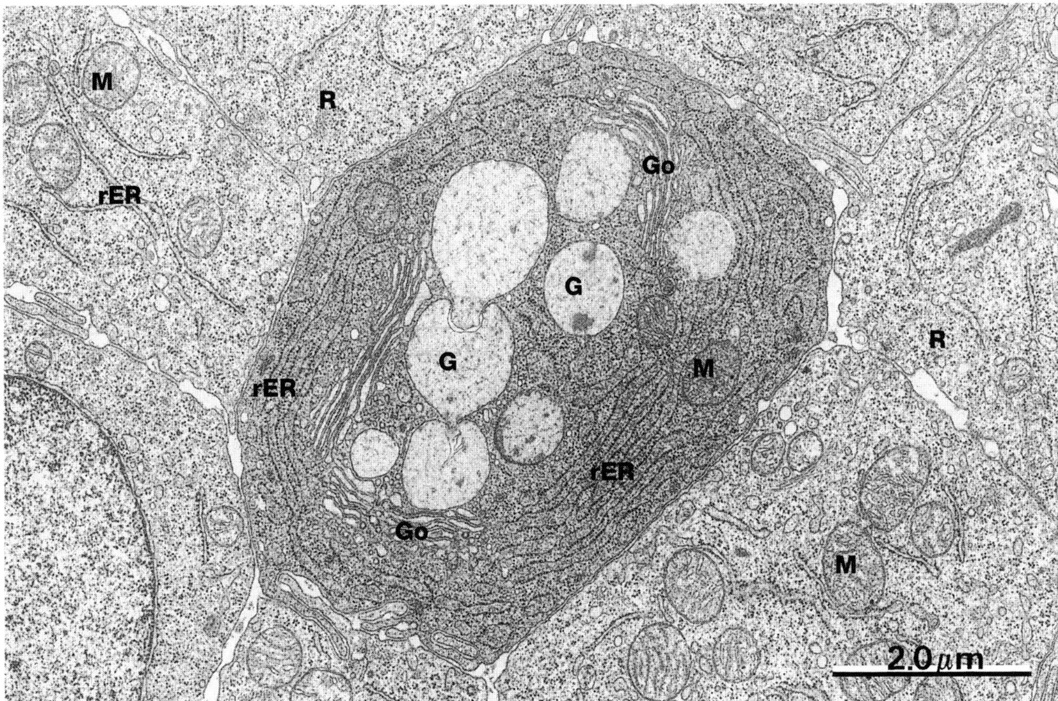

Fig. 14.23 Duodenal epithelium
EM ×14 500

This low power electron micrograph of a horizontal section through the duodenal epithelium demonstrates several important features. In the central area there is a goblet cell containing several mucin-containing granules **G**. The goblet cell appearance by conventional light microscopy is actually an artifact of preparation whereby water is taken up by the granules that consequently expand and compress the surrounding cytoplasm. Adjacent to the mucin granules are three Golgi apparatuses **Go** with plentiful rough endoplasmic reticulum **rER**, features typical of secretory cells. Occasional mitochondria **M** are also seen.

Surrounding the goblet cell are a number of enterocytes. These have much less prominent rER but contain large numbers of free ribosomes **R** and mitochondria **M** (see Fig. 14.25). This micrograph is of duodenal epithelium but jejunal and ileal epithelium is identical.

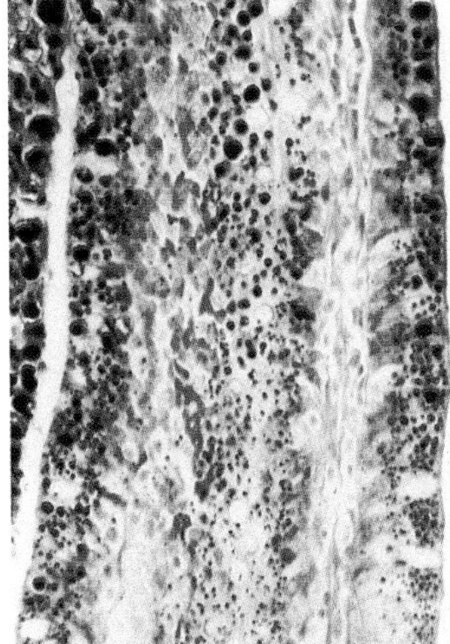

Fig. 14.24 Intestinal villus
Sudan black ×320

This frozen section from the intestine of a rat fed with milk has been stained to demonstrate the presence of absorbed lipids. Ingested triglycerides are emulsified by bile and hydrolysed by the pancreatic enzyme, ***lipase***; the degradation products, mainly free fatty acids and monoglycerides, are absorbed by enterocytes where they are resynthesised into triglycerides in the smooth endoplasmic reticulum. Here, the triglycerides are reconstituted into small globules and form a lipoprotein complex incorporating protein, cholesterol and phospholipids. Membrane-bound vesicles containing multiple droplets bud from the smooth endoplasmic reticulum and pass towards the base of the cell where they are released by exocytosis into the intercellular clefts; from here the small lipoprotein droplets, described as ***chylomicrons***, pass into the lacteals and then into larger lymphatics, eventually entering the general circulation. Note the high concentration of black-stained lipid in the enterocyte cytoplasm and in the chylomicrons within the central lacteal.

C capillary **G** mucin granules **Go** Golgi apparatus **L** lacteal **Ly** lymphocytes **M** mitochondrion **Mu** smooth muscle **P** plasma cell **R** ribosomes **rER** rough endoplasmic reticulum **V** villus

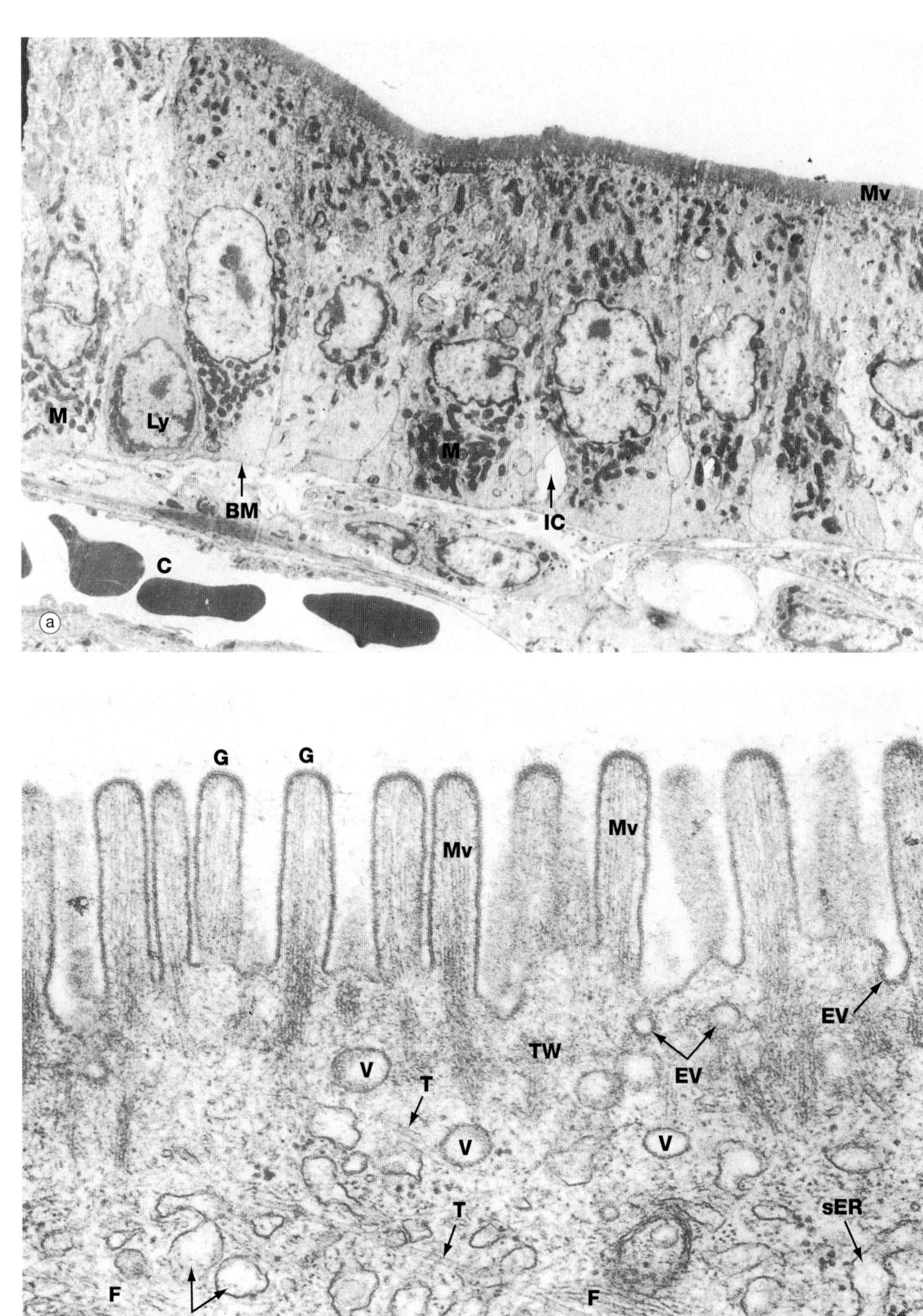

BM basement membrane **BM**$_E$ endothelial basement membrane **C** capillary **Ch** chylomicrons **Co** collagen fibrils **En** endothelium **EV** endocytic vesicle **F** microfilaments **Fi** fibroblast **G** glycocalyx **IC** intercellular cleft **J** junctional complex **LD** lamina densa **Ly** lymphocyte **M** mitochondrion **Mv** microvilli **R** ribosomes **sER** smooth endoplasmic reticulum **T** microtubules **TW** terminal web **V** transport vesicle

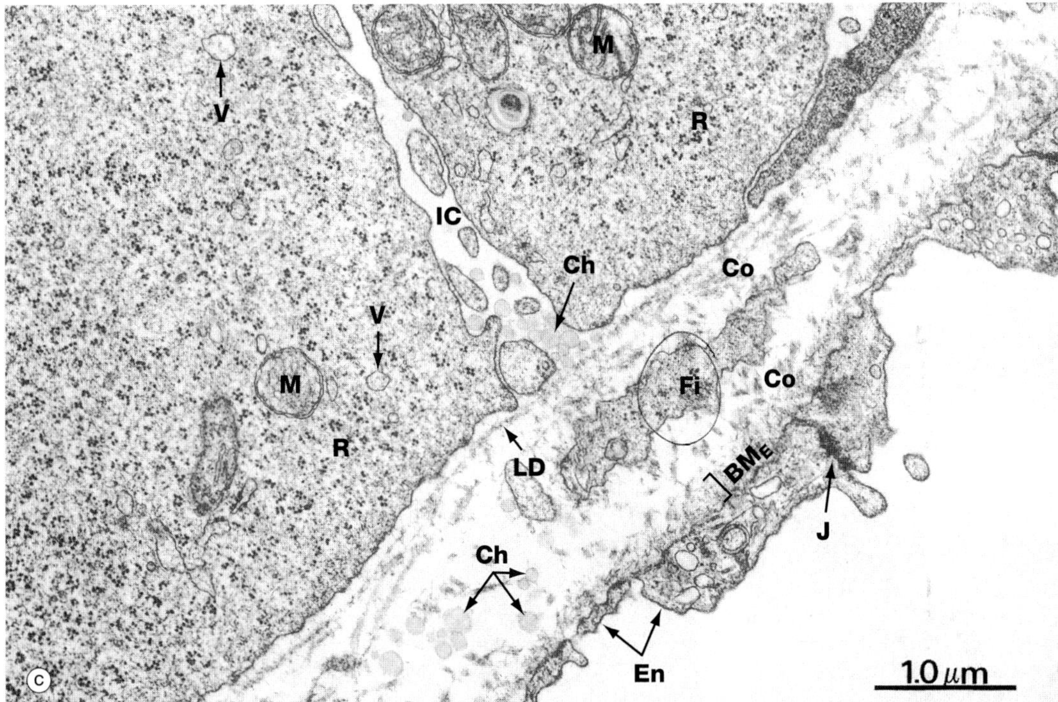

Fig. 14.25 Enterocytes
(a) EM ×4540 (b) EM ×56 000 (c) EM ×22 000 *(illustrations (a) and (b) opposite)*

These micrographs illustrate the main ultrastructural features of enterocytes, the absorptive cells of the small intestine. Micrograph (a) shows the enormous number of ***microvilli*** **Mv** (up to 3000 per cell), which increase the surface area of the plasma membrane exposed to the lumen by some 30 times. The microvilli are of uniform length (approximately 1 μm) and constitute the ***brush border*** of light microscopy (see Figs 14.22 and 5.15). Most absorption in the small intestine occurs by direct passage of low molecular weight digestion products across the luminal plasma membrane. Mitochondria **M** are particularly abundant within enterocytes, reflecting the high energy demands of such processes. Chylomicrons assembled in the enterocytes pass first into the ***intercellular clefts*** **IC**, then across the basement membrane **BM** into the core of the villus and finally into the lacteal. Lymphocytes **Ly** are commonly found in the intercellular clefts between enterocytes where they play an important part in the immunological defence of the tract. Note the close proximity of a blood capillary **C** to the enterocyte basement membrane.

As seen in micrograph (b), the glycocalyx **G** of the enterocyte microvilli is unusually prominent. It provides protection against autodigestion and acts as the site for adsorption of pancreatic digestive enzymes. This micrograph also shows the microfilament cytoskeleton of the microvilli **Mv** extending into the superficial cytoplasm. Here, in the terminal web **TW**, it becomes integrated into the cytoskeleton of the body of the cell. Deeper in the cell, microfilaments **F** and microtubules **T** are readily identified. Enterocytes are tightly bound near their luminal surface by junctional complexes (see Fig. 5.10) which prevent direct access of luminal contents into the intercellular spaces as well as holding the epithelium together.

Endocytic vesicles **EV** are often seen between the bases of microvilli, and transport vesicles **V** are common in the superficial cytoplasm. Endocytosis with transfer to the extracellular fluid at the base of the cell (***transcytosis***) is an important mechanism of uptake of macromolecules from the gut lumen into the blood. An example of transcytosis is the uptake of maternal antibodies from the milk in breast fed infants. Smooth endoplasmic reticulum **sER** is seen deeper in the cytoplasm.

Micrograph (c) illustrates the basal aspect of two enterocytes separated by an intercellular cleft **IC**. Their basement membrane is thin and the lamina densa **LD** appears to be discontinuous. Close beneath the base of the enterocytes is a tiny lymphatic tributary of the central lacteal, its endothelial lining **En** being thin and fenestrated; note the junctional complex **J** binding adjacent endothelial cells and the thin discontinuous endothelial basement membrane $\mathbf{BM_E}$. The delicate supporting tissue between the basement membrane and lymphatic contains fibroblasts **Fi** and fine collagen fibrils **Co**.

The main feature of the basal enterocyte cytoplasm is numerous free ribosomes **R**, scattered mitochondria **M** and membranous vesicles **V** containing lipoprotein droplets en route for exocytosis into the intercellular cleft. The cleft contains numerous small chylomicrons **Ch** that cluster near the lamina densa as if temporarily held up in their passage towards the lymphatic. In the lamina propria, the chylomicrons are larger, probably due to fusion of smaller ones coursing through from the intercellular cleft. Note that the chylomicrons in the extracellular environment are not membrane-bound but have a fine electron-dense limiting layer of protein.

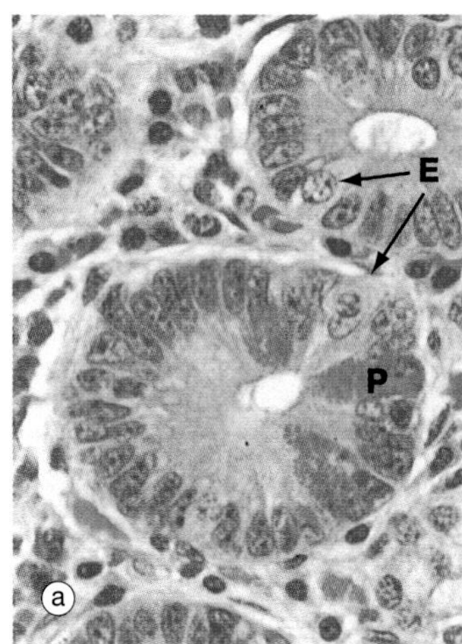

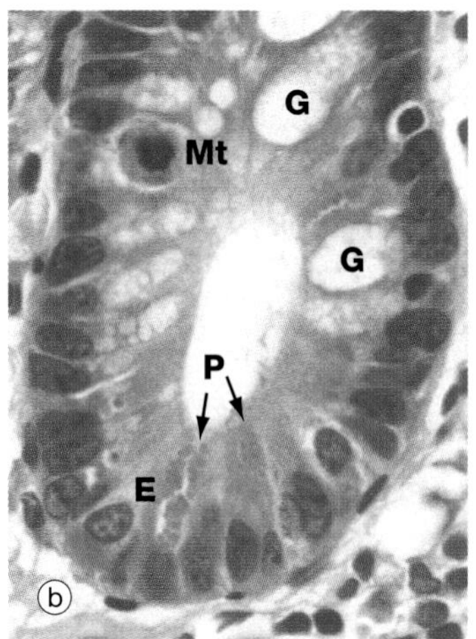

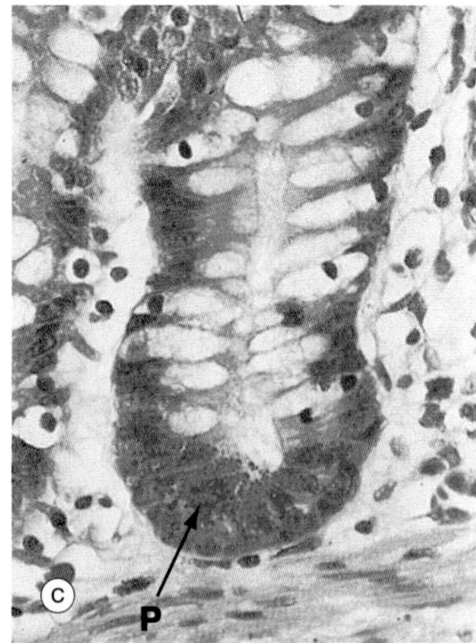

Fig. 14.26 Crypts of Lieberkuhn
(a) H & E, TS ×400 (b) H & E, LS ×300 (c) Phloxine-tartrazine ×320

The majority of cells in the crypt bases are stem cells that divide regularly to replenish the epithelial cells of the villi; immature goblet cells **G** are readily seen in micrograph (b). A single mitotic figure **Mt** is identifiable. With H & E staining (micrograph (a)), Paneth cells **P**, which form part of the innate immune system, exhibit intensely eosinophilic apical cytoplasmic granules; these are stained bright scarlet by the phloxine-tartrazine method (micrograph (c)). The granules of Paneth cells contain antimicrobial peptides (***defensins***), and protective enzymes such as lysozyme and phospholipase A. These products, secreted into the small bowel, provide the first line of defence against any pathogens that survive passage through the stomach. The lumen of the small bowel is virtually sterile. Paneth cells are long-lived (weeks) in comparison to the short lifespan (3–5 days) of enterocytes and goblet cells.

Endocrine cells **E** also contain eosinophilic cytoplasmic granules, which are found in a subnuclear position, in contrast to the granules of Paneth cells. Secretory products of gut endocrine cells include hormones such as secretin, somatostatin and serotonin among others. In general, each endocrine cell produces only one hormone.

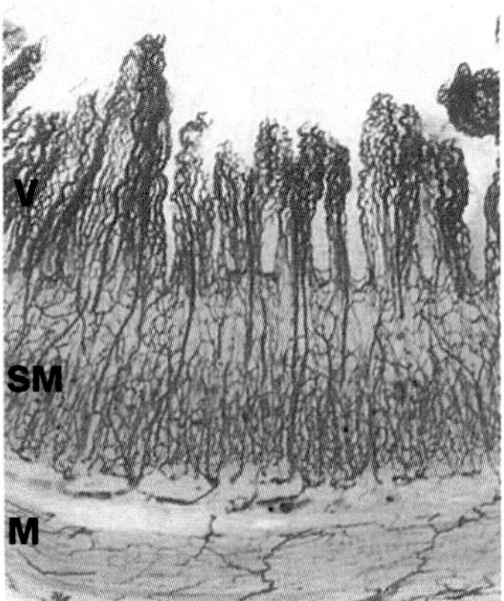

Fig. 14.27 Intestinal villi
Carmine perfused ×10

This specimen of small intestine has been perfused before fixation with a red dye and demonstrates the blood supply of the mucosa. Long loops of branching capillaries originating from a dense capillary network in the submucosa **SM** extend up to the tips of the villi **V**. Note also the capillary network supplying the muscularis propria **M**. Most of the absorbed food products, with the exception of triglycerides, enter the capillaries and pass via the portal vein to the liver.

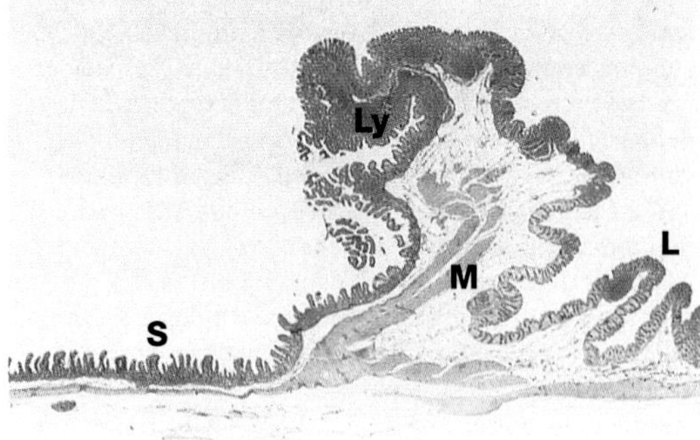

Fig. 14.28 Ileocaecal junction
H & E ×5

Indigestible food residues from the ileum are propelled by peristalsis into the distended first part of the large intestine, the caecum, through the cone-shaped ileocaecal valve. There is an abrupt transition in the lining of the valve from the small intestinal villiform pattern **S** to the glandular form in the large intestine **L**. The ileocaecal valve consists of a thickened extension of the muscularis propria **M** that provides robust support for the mucosa. Lymphoid tissue **Ly** in the form of large Peyer's patches is found in the mucosa.

CM inner circular layer of muscularis propria **E** endocrine cell **G** goblet cell **L** large intestine
LA lymphoid aggregate **LM** outer longitudinal layer of muscularis propria **Ly** lymphoid tissue
M muscularis propria **MM** muscularis mucosae **Mt** mitotic figure **P** Paneth cell **S** small intestine
SM submucosa **T** T lymphocytes **V** villi

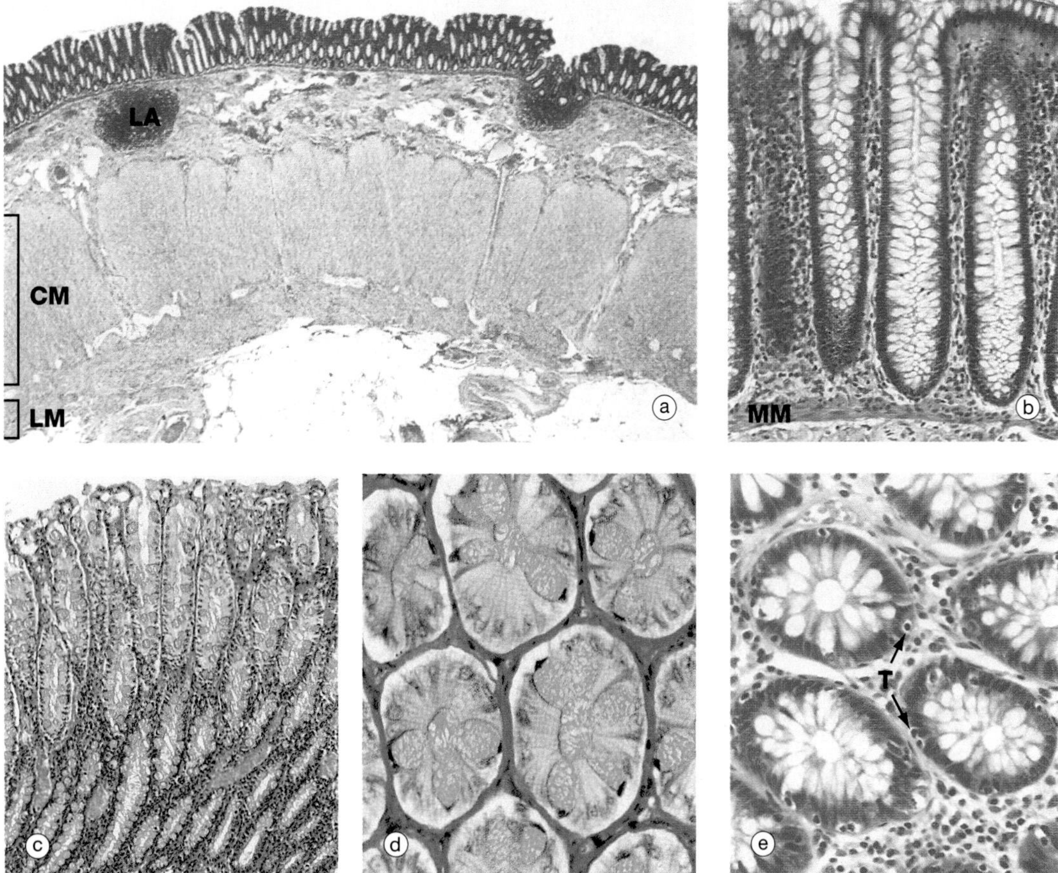

Fig. 14.29 Colon
(a) H & E ×4 (b) H & E ×100 (c) LS, Alcian blue/van Gieson ×80 (d) TS, Alcian blue/van Gieson ×320 (e) TS, H & E ×200

The principal functions of the large intestine are the recovery of water and salt from the faeces and the propulsion of increasingly solid faeces to the rectum prior to defaecation.

As shown in micrograph (a), the muscular wall is consequently thick and capable of powerful peristaltic activity. As in the rest of the gastrointestinal tract, the muscularis propria of the large intestine consists of inner circular **CM** and outer longitudinal layers **LM** but, except in the rectum, the longitudinal layer forms three separate longitudinal bands called ***teniae coli***.

The mucosa is the same from caecum to rectum. It is folded in the non-distended state but it does not exhib it distinct plicae circulares like those of the small intestine. Immediately above the anal valves, the mucosa forms longitudinal folds called the ***columns of Morgagni***. The muscularis mucosae is a prominent feature of the large intestinal mucosa; rhythmic contractions prevent clogging of the glands and enhance expulsion of mucus.

Consistent with its functions of water absorption and faecal lubrication, the mucosa consists of cells of two types: absorptive cells and mucus-secreting goblet cells. As seen in micrograph (b), these are arranged in closely packed straight tubular glands or ***crypts***, which extend to the muscularis mucosae **MM**. As faeces pass along the large intestine and become progressively dehydrated, the mucus becomes increasingly important in protecting the mucosa from trauma. The Alcian blue method (micrograph (c)) stains goblet cell mucus a greenish-blue colour while the absorptive cells remain poorly stained. Goblet cells predominate in the base of the glands, whereas the luminal surface is almost entirely lined by columnar absorptive cells.

Micrographs (d) and (e) show transverse sections through the upper part of large intestinal glands, highlighting the closely packed arrangement of the glands in the mucosa. The tall columnar absorptive cells have oval basal nuclei; in contrast, goblet cell nuclei are small and condensed. Stem cells at the base of the glands continually replace the epithelium. Intraepithelial T lymphocytes **T** are easily seen in (e). Lamina propria fills the space between the glands and contains numerous blood and lymphatic vessels into which water is absorbed. The lamina propria also contains collagen (stained red in (c) and (d)) as well as lymphocytes and plasma cells. These form part of the defence mechanisms against invading pathogens along with intraepithelial lymphocytes and the lymphoid aggregates **LA**, which are smaller than Peyer's patches, found in the lamina propria and submucosa (a).

The large intestine is inhabited by a variety of commensal bacteria that further degrade food residues. Bacterial degradation is an important mechanism for the digestion of cellulose in ruminants, but in humans most cellulose is excreted. Small quantities of fat-soluble vitamins derived from bacterial activity are absorbed in the large intestine.

Carcinoma of the colon and rectum

Malignant tumours arising in glandular epithelium are called ***adenocarcinomas***. Adenocarcinomas of the colon and rectum are common in older patients particularly in developed countries. This is in contrast to adenocarcinomas of the small intestine, which are comparatively rare. Intensive research in recent time has identified a number of predisposing factors including the prior existence of benign tumours (adenomas) in the bowel, the prior existence of ***ulcerative colitis***, inherited syndromes such as ***familial adenomatous polyposis*** and ***Gardner's syndrome***, dietary factors such as a low fibre diet and so on. The sequence of events in the development of some adenocarcinomas is becoming clearer and involves the number of genetic abnormalities (mutations) arising generally in a specific order. The acquisition of these mutations can be detected as the epithelium changes from normal to an adenoma with increasing degrees of dysplasia to invasive carcinoma. This is known as the ***adenoma-carcinoma*** sequence. A typical colorectal adenocarcinoma is shown in Fig. 14.30.

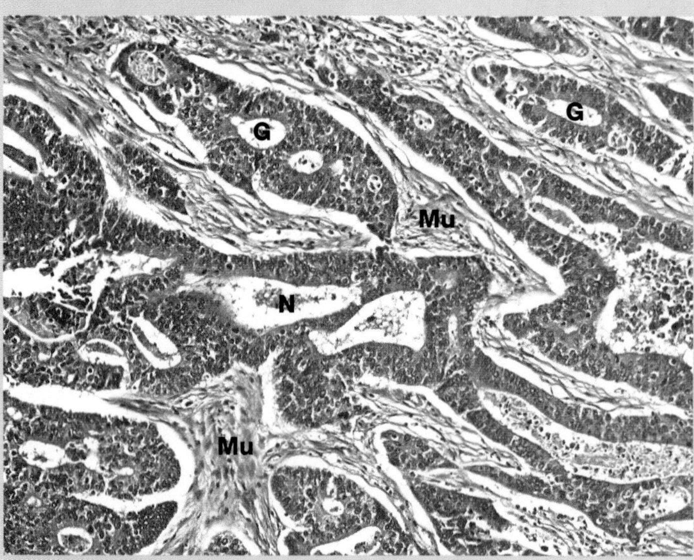

Fig. 14.30 Adenocarcinoma of the colon
H & E ×20

This micrograph shows a typical adenocarcinoma of the colon. Compare this with the normal colonic mucosa seen in Fig. 14.29. In adenocarcinoma the malignant epithelial cells form disorganised abnormal glands that invade into the adjacent tissues. The depth of invasion and indeed the spread to the draining mesenteric lymph nodes is the basis for ***staging*** the tumour i.e. giving a prediction of the likely behaviour of the tumour based on the extent of the tumour. Obviously the further the tumour has spread the worse the outcome is likely to be; a small, superficial adenocarcinoma confined to the colon has a good chance of cure by surgery whereas a tumour that has spread far and wide (***metastasized***) will have a much worse outlook. In this micrograph the malignant glands **G** of the tumour have invaded into the muscularis propria. Small bundles of smooth muscle **Mu** can be identified and there are also areas of necrosis **N** (dead tissue), another feature commonly seen in cancers.

F lymphoid follicle **G** gland **J** recto-anal junction **LP** lamina propria **M** mesentery **Mu** smooth muscle **N** necrosis **RM** rectal mucosa **S** serosa **SM** submucosa **SS** stratified squamous epithelium

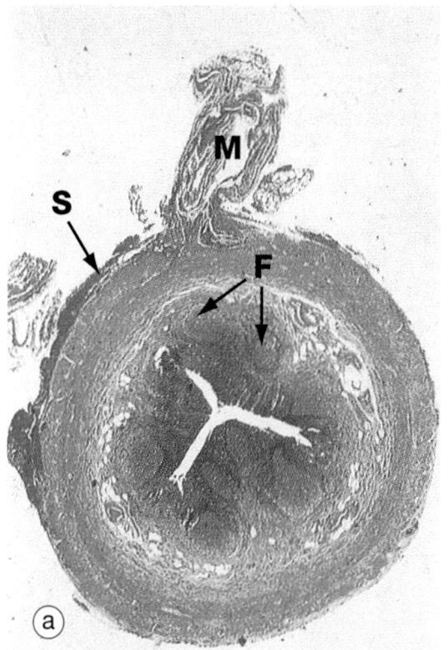

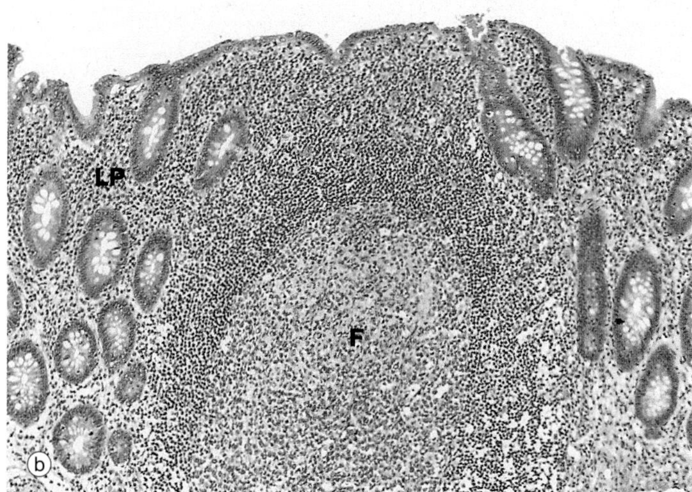

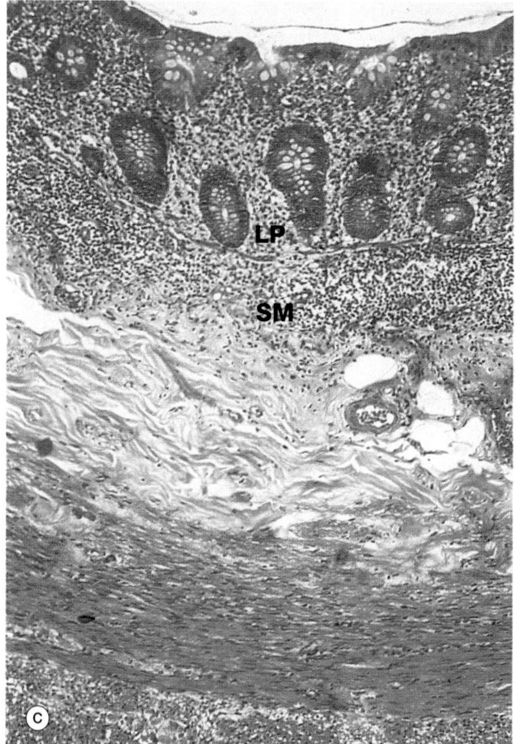

Fig. 14.31 Appendix
(a) H & E ×5 (b) H & E ×75 (c) H & E ×42

The appendix is a small blind-ended tubular sac extending from the caecum just distal to the ileocaecal junction. The general structure of the appendix conforms to that of the rest of the large intestine. In some mammals, the appendix is capacious and involved in prolonged digestion of cellulose, but in humans its function is unknown.

Micrograph (a) illustrates the suspensory mesentery **M** in continuity with the outer serosal layer **S**. The serosa contains extravasated blood resulting from haemorrhage during surgical removal. The mesenteries conduct blood vessels, lymphatics and nerves to and from the gastrointestinal tract.

The most characteristic feature of the appendix, particularly in the young, is the presence of masses of lymphoid tissue in the mucosa and submucosa. As seen in micrographs (b) and (c), the lamina propria **LP** and upper submucosa **SM** are diffusely infiltrated with lymphocytes. Note that the mucosal glands are much less closely packed than in the large intestine. As seen in micrographs (a) and (b), the lymphoid tissue also forms follicles **F** often containing germinal centres (see Ch. 11). These follicles bulge into the lumen and, like the follicles of Peyer's patches in the small intestine, are invested by a simple epithelium of M cells (see Fig. 11.17), which presumably facilitates sampling of antigen in the lumen.

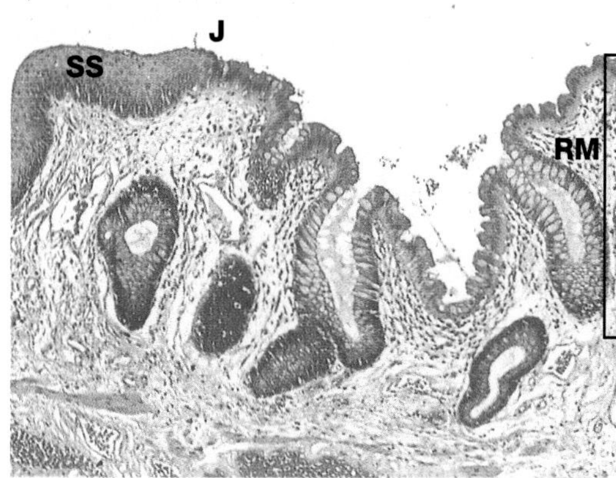

Fig. 14.32 Recto-anal junction
H & E ×60

The rectum is the short dilated terminal portion of the large intestine. The rectal mucosa **RM** is the same as the rest of the large bowel except that it has even more numerous goblet cells. At the recto-anal junction **J**, it undergoes an abrupt transition to become stratified squamous epithelium **SS** in the anal canal. Branched tubular ***circumanal glands*** open at the recto-anal junction into small pits at the distal ends of the columns of Morgagni. The anal canal forms the last 2 or 3 cm of the gastrointestinal tract and is surrounded by voluntary muscle that forms the anal sphincter. Here, the stratified squamous epithelium undergoes a gradual transition to skin containing sebaceous glands and large apocrine sweat glands (see Ch. 9).

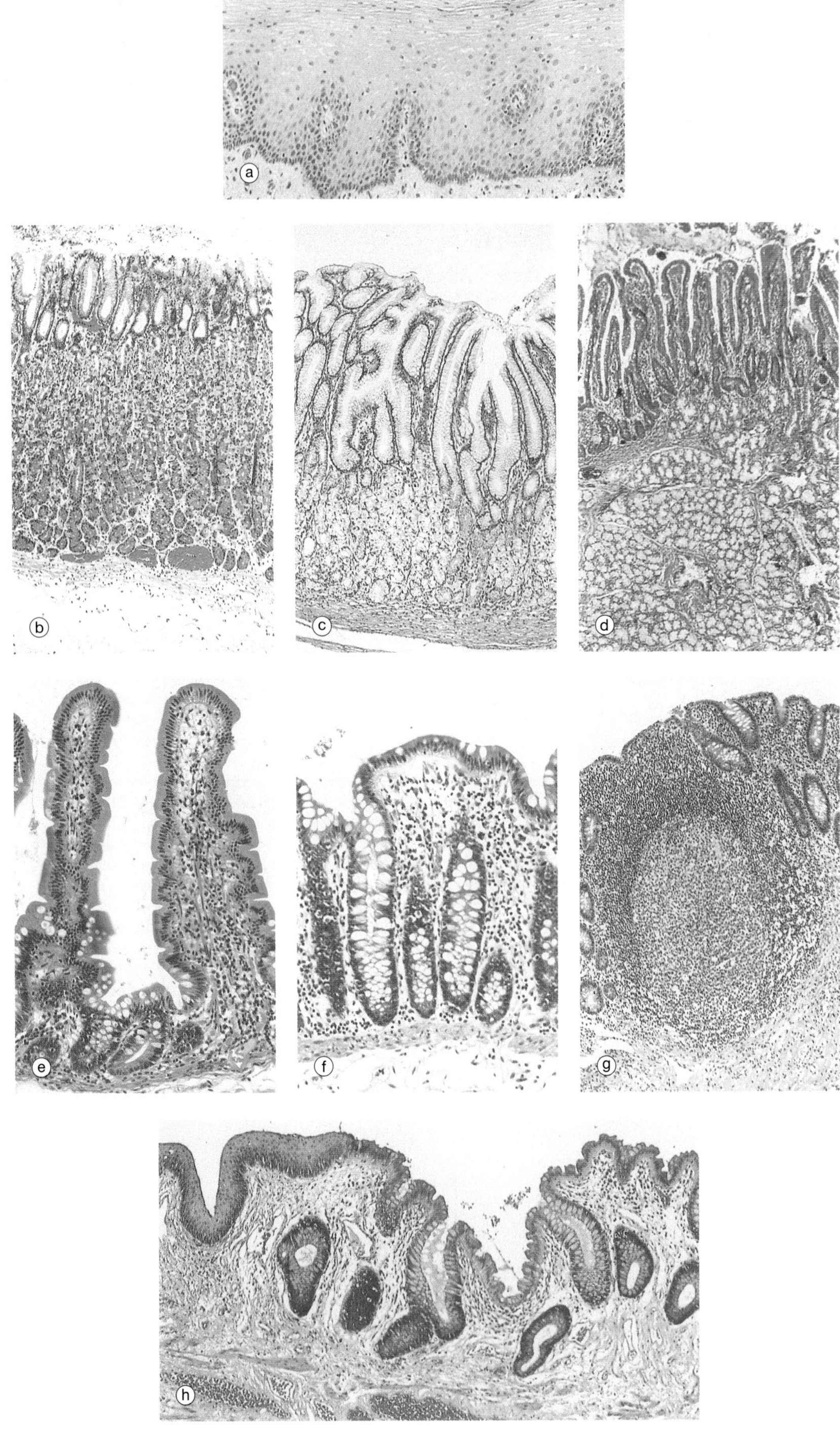
a
b
c
d
e
f
g
h

Fig. 14.33 Comparison of structure of parts of the gastrointestinal tract
(a) H & E ×100 (b) H & E ×50 (c) H & E ×50 (d) H & E ×15 (e) H & E ×100 (f) H & E ×100 (g) H & E ×75 (h) H & E ×60 *(illustrations opposite)*

The table below outlines the main structural features of the different components of the gastrointestinal tract for easy reference and revision. Please note that the epithelium of all segments includes stem cells and neuroendocrine cells, which have not been included in the table for simplicity. Each line of the table refers to the correspondingly labelled micrograph opposite.

Fig. 14.33 (i) Comparison of structure of parts of the gastrointestinal tract

Part of the gastrointestinal tract	Illustration (opposite)	Type of epithelium	Main cell types of epithelium	Other distinctive features
Oesophagus	(a)	Stratified squamous	■ Squamous cells	Submucosal glands
Body/fundus of stomach	(b)	Glandular – straight tubular	■ Surface mucous cells ■ Neck mucous cells ■ Parietal cells ■ Chief (peptic) cells	Lymphoid cells very sparse No lymphoid aggregates
Pylorus and cardia of stomach	(c)	Glandular – coiled, branched tubular	■ Mucous cells ■ May be occasional parietal cells	Lymphoid cells very sparse No lymphoid aggregates
Duodenum	(d)	Glandular with villi and crypts of Lieberkühn	■ Enterocytes with microvilli ■ Goblet cells ■ Paneth cells	Brunner's glands Plicae circulares (distal duodenum)
Jejunum and ileum	(e)	Glandular with villi and crypts of Lieberkühn	■ Enterocytes with microvilli ■ Goblet cells ■ Paneth cells	Peyer's patches become more prominent distally Plicae circulares
Colon and rectum	(f)	Glandular – straight crypts	■ Goblet cells ■ Absorptive cells	Teniae coli
Appendix	(g)	Glandular – straight crypts	■ Goblet cells ■ Tall columnar cells	Prominent lymphoid tissue
Anus	(h)	Stratified squamous	■ Squamous cells	Columns of Morgagni

15. *Liver and pancreas*

Liver and biliary system

The liver, like the pancreas, develops embryologically as a glandular outgrowth of the primitive gut. The major functions of the liver may be summarised as follows:

Fat metabolism

- Oxidising triglycerides to produce energy.
- Synthesis of plasma lipoproteins.
- Synthesis of cholesterol and phospholipid.

Carbohydrate metabolism

- Converting carbohydrates and proteins into fatty acids and triglyceride.
- Regulation of blood glucose concentration by glycogenesis, glycogenolysis and gluconeogenesis.

Protein metabolism

- Synthesis of the plasma proteins, including albumin and clotting factors.
- Synthesis of the non-essential amino acids.
- Detoxification of metabolic waste products, e.g. deamination of amino acids and production of urea.

Storage

- Storage of glycogen, vitamins, iron.

Intermediary metabolism

- Detoxification of various drugs and toxins, such as alcohol.

Secretion

- Synthesis and secretion of bile; bile contains many of the products of the above processes.

The main functional cell in the liver is a form of epithelial cell called the ***hepatocyte***. These cells are arranged as thin plates separated by fine vascular sinusoids through which blood flows. The close association of liver cells and the circulation allows absorption of nutrients from digestion as well as secretion of products into the blood. Blood flow into the liver sinusoids comes from terminal branches of both the ***hepatic portal vein*** and ***hepatic artery***. The liver is therefore unusual in having both arterial and venous blood supplies as well as separate venous drainage. With the exception of most lipids, absorbed food products pass directly from the gut to the liver via the hepatic portal vein. This brings blood that is rich in amino acids, simple sugars and other products of digestion but is relatively poor in oxygen. Oxygen required to support liver metabolism is supplied via the hepatic artery. After passing through the sinusoids, venous drainage of blood from the liver occurs via the ***hepatic vein*** into the vena cava.

The main blood vessels and ducts run through the liver within a branched collagenous framework termed the ***portal tracts***. These tracts also contain the ***bile ducts*** that transport bile away from the liver to be secreted into the small bowel.

Fig. 15.1 Liver *(illustrations opposite)*
(a) Capsule and parenchyma H & E ×70 (b) Architecture H & E ×30

Micrograph (a) shows the structure of the liver which is a solid organ composed of tightly packed, pink-staining plates of epithelial cells termed hepatocytes. The outer surface of the liver is covered by a capsule composed of collagenous tissue **C** called ***Glisson's capsule*** over which is a layer of mesothelial cells **M** from the peritoneum.

The sinusoids can just be seen as pale-stained spaces between the plates of liver cells. The hepatic sinusoids form a very low-resistance system of vascular channels that allows blood to come into contact with the hepatocytes over a huge surface area.

Micrograph (b) shows the overall architecture of the liver at a slightly lower magnification. The liver does not contain much in the way of connective tissue. Most of the collagenous connective tissue in the liver is in the form of the ***portal tracts*** **P** which contain the main blood vessels running into the liver. Larger vessels can be seen containing bright red blood even at this low magnification. The other structures that run in the portal tracts, although not readily seen at this magnification, are branches of the bile ducts.

Less conspicuous than the portal tracts are the centrilobular venules (hepatic venules) **V** that drain the liver. These are tributaries of the hepatic vein and take blood away from the liver.

The very close association of the sinusoidal vasculature of the liver with the hepatocytes is essential for normal function. Certain diseases of the liver cause obliteration of the normal sinusoidal arrangement and this then causes impairment of liver function.

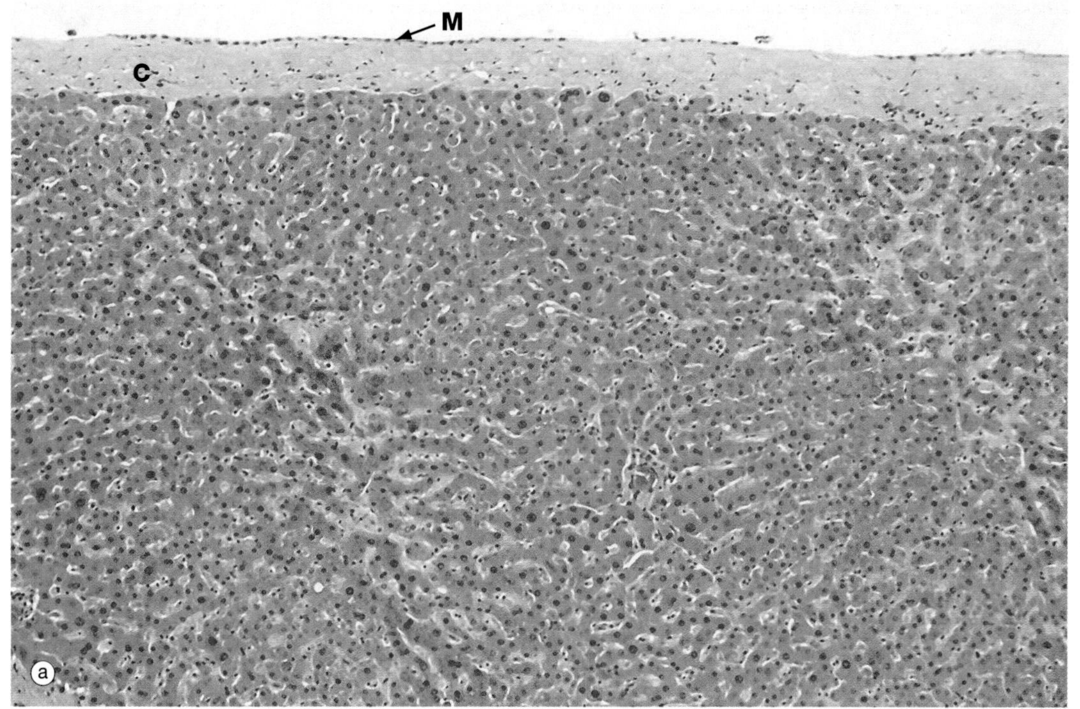

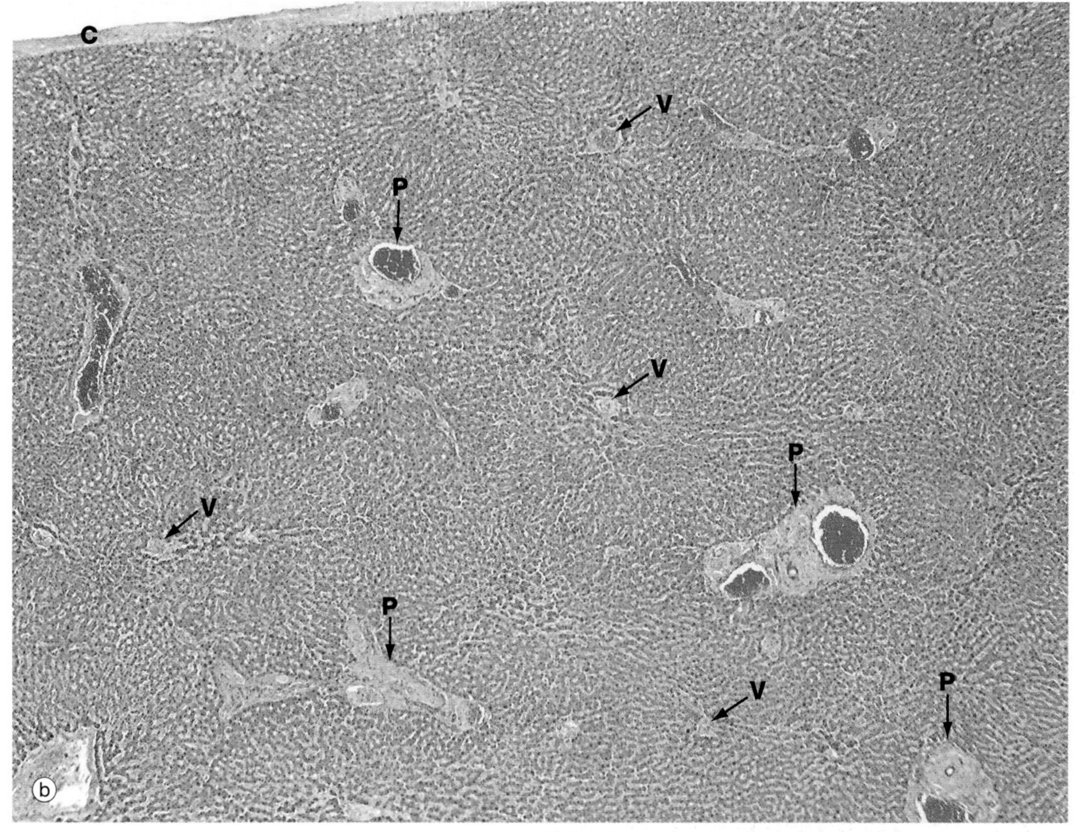

C capsule **M** mesothelial cells **P** portal tract **V** hepatic (centrilobular) venule

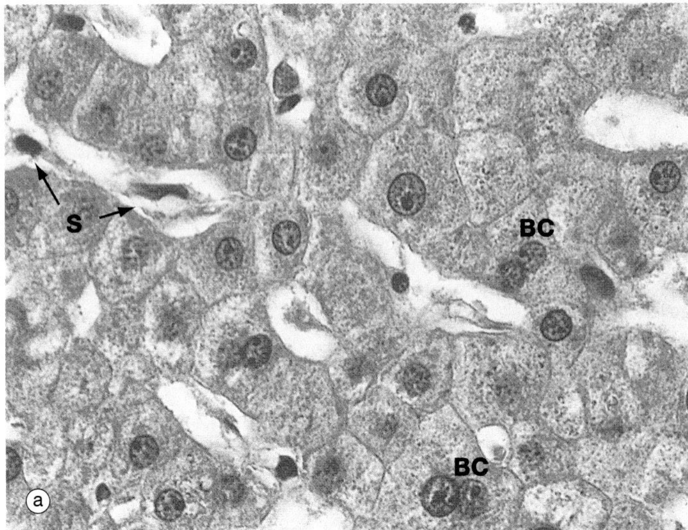

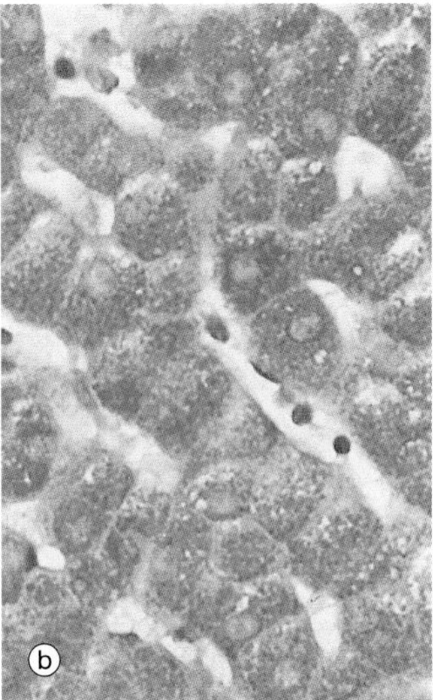

Fig. 15.2 Hepatocytes
(a) H & E ×600 (b) PAS/haematoxylin ×400

Hepatocytes are large polyhedral cells with round nuclei with peripherally dispersed chromatin and prominent nucleoli. The nuclei vary greatly in size, reflecting an unusual cellular feature; more than half the hepatocytes contain twice the normal (diploid) complement of chromosomes within a single nucleus (i.e. they are tetraploid) and some contain four or even eight times this amount (polyploid). Binucleate cells **BC** are also common in normal liver.

The extensive cytoplasm has a variable appearance depending on the nutritional status of the individual. When well-nourished, hepatocytes store significant quantities of glycogen and process large quantities of lipid. Both of these metabolites are partially removed during routine histological preparation, leaving irregular unstained areas within the cytoplasm. The cytoplasm is otherwise strongly eosinophilic due to numerous mitochondria with a fine basophilic granularity due to extensive free ribosomes and rough endoplasmic reticulum. Fine brown granules of the 'wear and tear' pigment lipofuscin (see Fig. 1.15) are present in variable amounts, increasing with age. All these features are seen in micrograph (a).

The sinusoids are lined by flat endothelial lining cells **S** which are readily distinguishable from hepatocytes by their flattened condensed nuclei and attenuated poorly stained cytoplasm.

Micrograph (b) shows glycogen in hepatocytes which, being polysaccharide, is PAS-positive, i.e. stains magenta; the nuclei are counterstained blue.

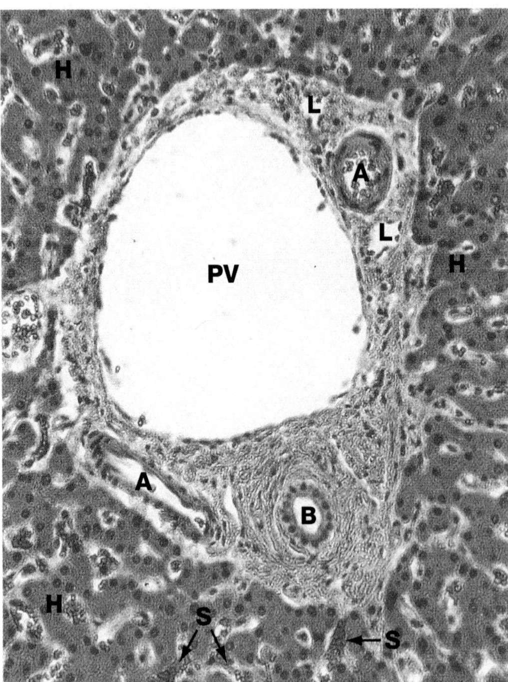

Fig. 15.3 Portal tract
H & E ×150

This micrograph shows a typical portal tract containing three main structures. The largest is a terminal branch of the hepatic portal vein **PV** (***terminal portal venule***) which has a thin wall lined by endothelial cells. Smaller diameter thick-walled vessels are terminal branches of the ***hepatic artery*** **A** with the structure of arterioles.

A network of bile canaliculi is located within each plate of hepatocytes but these are far too small to be seen at this magnification. These drain into bile collecting ducts lined by simple cuboidal or columnar epithelium, known as the ***canals of Hering***, which in turn drain into the ***bile ductules*** **B**. The bile ductules are usually located at the periphery of the tract. The bile ductules merge to form larger, more centrally located ***trabecular ducts*** which drain via intrahepatic ducts into the ***right*** and ***left hepatic ducts***, the ***common hepatic duct*** and then to the duodenum via the ***common bile duct***. Because these three structures are always found in the portal tracts, the tracts are often referred to as ***portal triads***. Lymphatics **L** are also present in the portal tracts, but since their walls are delicate and often collapsed they are less easily identified.

Surrounding the portal tract are anastomosing plates of hepatocytes **H**, between which are the hepatic sinusoids **S** receiving blood from both the hepatic portal and hepatic arterial systems. The layer of hepatocytes immediately bordering the portal tract is known as the limiting plate.

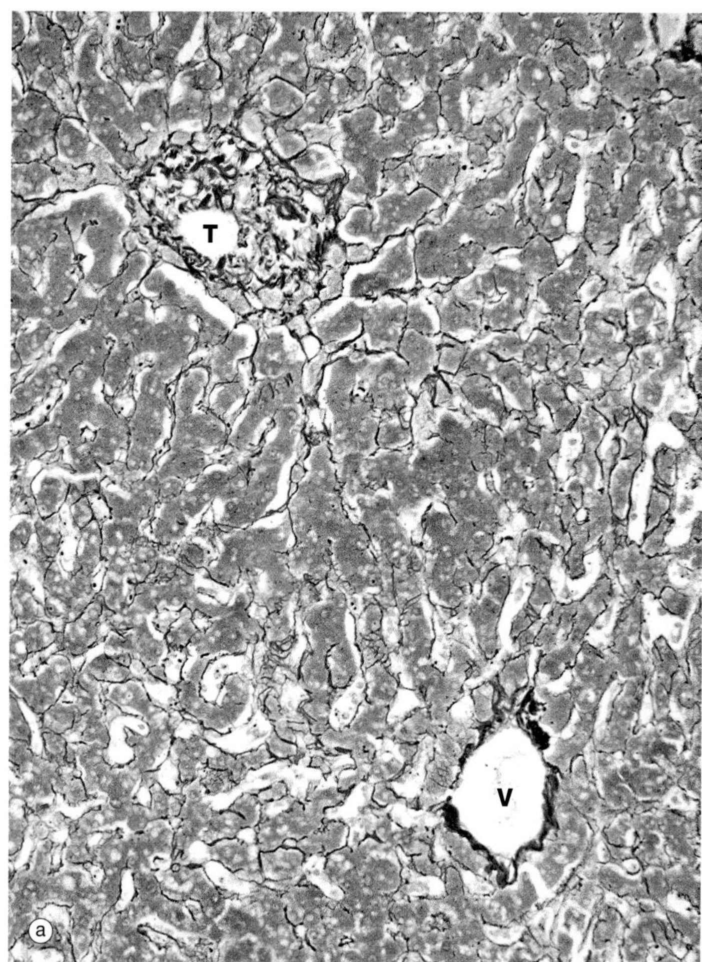

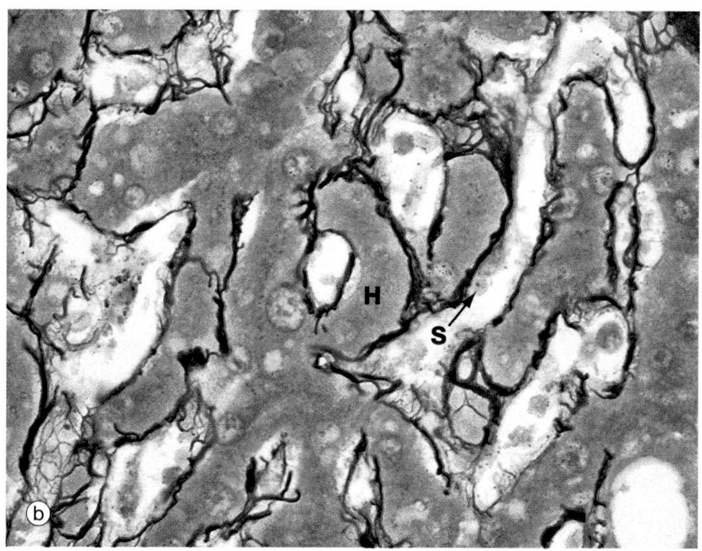

Fig. 15.4 Liver
(a) Reticulin method ×150
(b) Reticulin method ×600

The structural integrity of the liver is maintained by a delicate meshwork of extracellular matrix in the form of a fine meshwork of reticulin fibres (collagen type III).

The reticulin meshwork supports both the hepatocytes and the sinusoidal lining cells (endothelial cells). These micrographs have both been stained by a silver method that shows reticulin as a black stained material.

Micrograph (a) shows how reticulin is present on both sides of liver cell plates. The sinusoids are also bounded by the same reticulin framework. The reticulin merges with the sparse collagenous supporting tissue of the portal tract **T** and terminal hepatic venule **V**.

At the periphery of the liver, the reticulin becomes continuous with Glisson's capsule, which invests the external surface of the liver.

Micrograph (b) shows more detail of the reticulin scaffolding. Single layers of hepatocytes in the liver cell plates **H** lie immediately upon the reticulin framework. On the other side of the reticulin layer are the hepatic sinusoidal spaces. Some sinusoidal lining cells can just be seen **S**.

The sinusoids are lined by a discontinuous, fenestrated endothelium, which has no basement membrane and which is separated from the hepatocytes by a narrow space (***space of Disse***), which drains into the lymphatics of the portal tracts.

A hepatic artery branch **B** bile duct branch **BC** binucleate hepatocyte **H** hepatocyte plate
L lymphatic **PV** portal venule **S** sinusoidal lining cell **T** portal tract
V terminal branch of hepatic vein

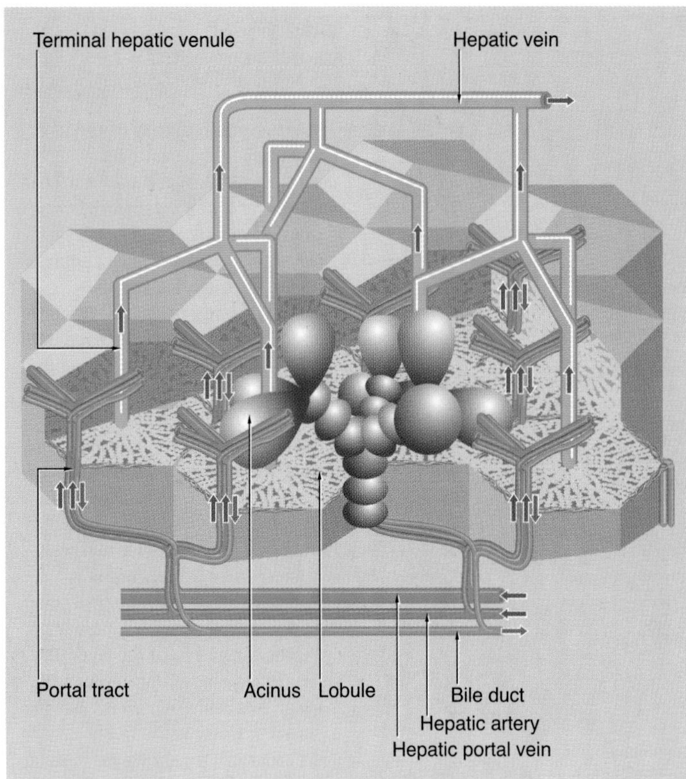

Fig. 15.5 Hepatic vasculature and biliary system

This diagram shows the hepatic vascular and bile collecting systems.

The hepatic portal vein and hepatic artery branch repeatedly within the liver. Their terminal branches run within the portal tracts and empty into the sinusoids. Blood from both systems percolates between plates of hepatocytes in the sinusoids, which converge to drain into a ***terminal hepatic (centrilobular) venule***. These drain to intercalated veins and then to the hepatic vein which drains into the inferior vena cava.

Bile is secreted into a network of minute ***bile canaliculi*** situated between the plasma membranes of adjacent hepatocytes; the canaliculi are too small to be represented in this diagram. The canalicular network drains into a system of bile ducts located in the portal tracts. Bile then flows through the extrahepatic biliary tree and ultimately to the duodenum. The hepatic lobule and acinus are explained in Fig. 15.7 below.

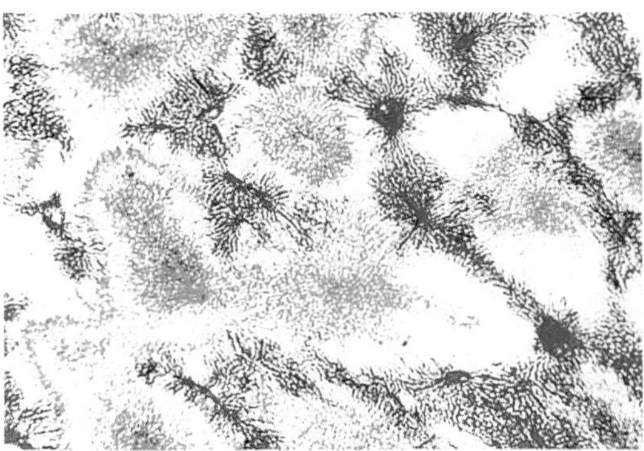

Fig. 15.6 Perfusion method
×20

This preparation shows one of the techniques used by early histologists in mapping hepatic blood flow. The hepatic portal vein (supplying the liver) has been perfused with a red dye and the hepatic vein (draining the liver) has been back-perfused with a blue dye. Thus it can be seen how liver units can be defined by a number of portal tracts peripherally (stained red) with blood draining to a single terminal hepatic venule (stained blue) at the centre.

Fig. 15.7 Liver *(illustrations opposite)*
(a) Diagram of liver lobule (b) Pig, H & E ×20 (c) Human, H & E ×20 (d) Diagram of simple acinus (e) Diagram of acinar agglomerate

The structural unit of the liver can be considered as a conceptually simple ***hepatic lobule***. However the physiology of the liver is more accurately represented by a unit structure known as the ***hepatic acinus***.

The hepatic lobule (a) is roughly hexagonal in shape and is centred on a ***terminal hepatic venule (centrilobular venule)*** **V**. The portal tracts **T** are positioned at the angles of the hexagon. The blood from the portal vein and hepatic artery branches flows away from the portal tract to the adjacent central veins. In some species, such as the pig (b), the lobule is outlined by bands of fibrous tissue **C** giving a well-defined structural unit. In humans (c) and most other species, no such clear structural definition exists, although lobules can be roughly outlined as an hexagonal array of portal tracts **T** arranged around a terminal hepatic venule **V**.

The hepatic acinus (d) is a more physiologically useful model of liver anatomy although more difficult to define histologically. The acinus is a roughly berry-shaped unit of liver parenchyma centered on a portal tract. The acinus lies between two or more terminal hepatic venules and blood flows from the portal tracts through the sinusoids to the venules. The acinus is divided into zones 1, 2 and 3 and the hepatocytes in these zones have different metabolic functions. Zone 1 is closest to the portal tract and receives the most oxygenated blood, while zone 3 is furthest away and receives least oxygen. Liver cells in zone 3 contain high levels of esterases and low levels of oxidative enzymes. Large branches of the portal vein and hepatic artery supply an ***agglomerate of acini*** each of which is in turn composed of several ***complex acini*** which, at the lowest level, are made of ***simple acini*** each supplied by terminal vascular branches. Although the structure looks on paper like a bunch of grapes, it must be remembered that this is a functional grouping and in reality the hepatic parenchyma is uniform and continuous.

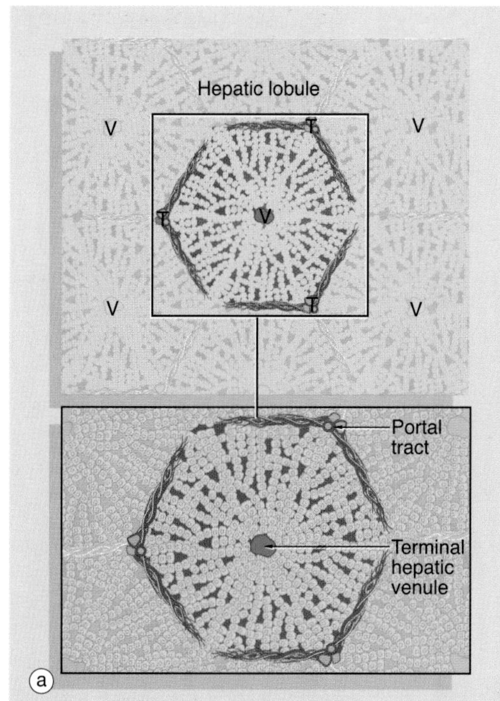

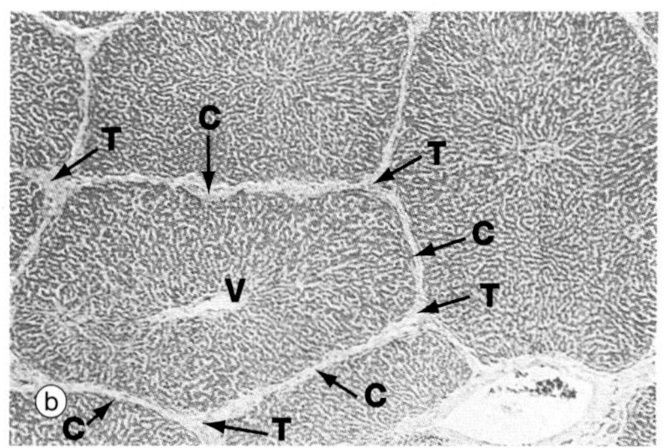

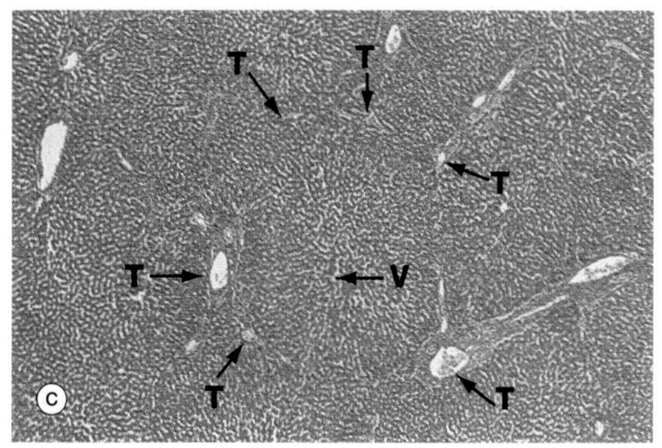

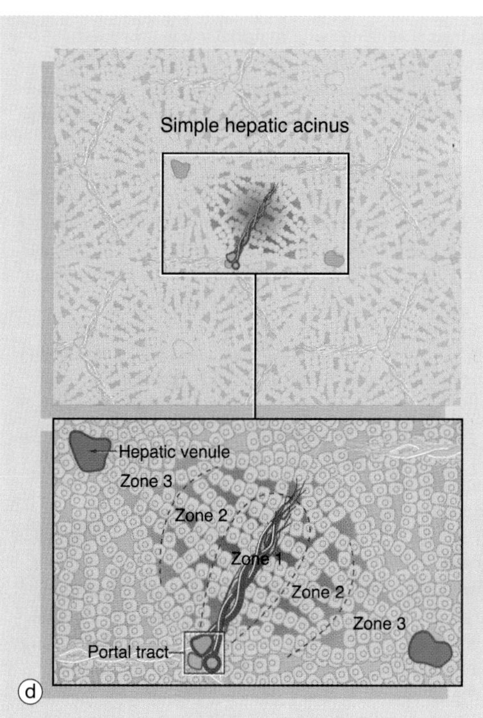

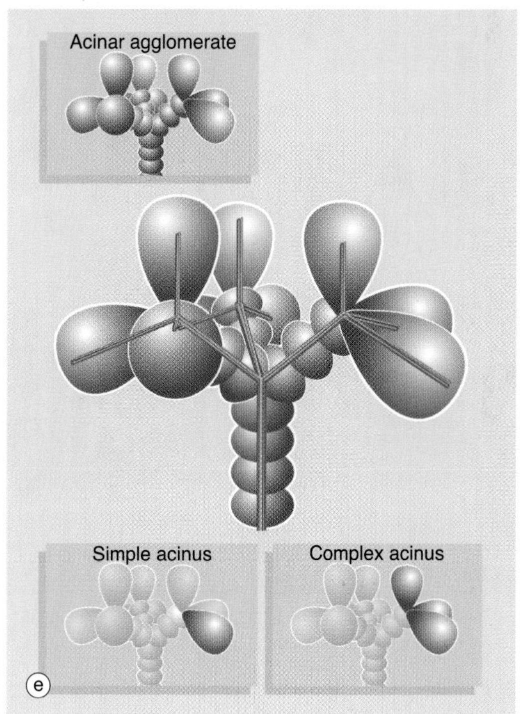

C bands of fibrous tissue **T** portal tract **V** terminal hepatic (centrilobular) venule

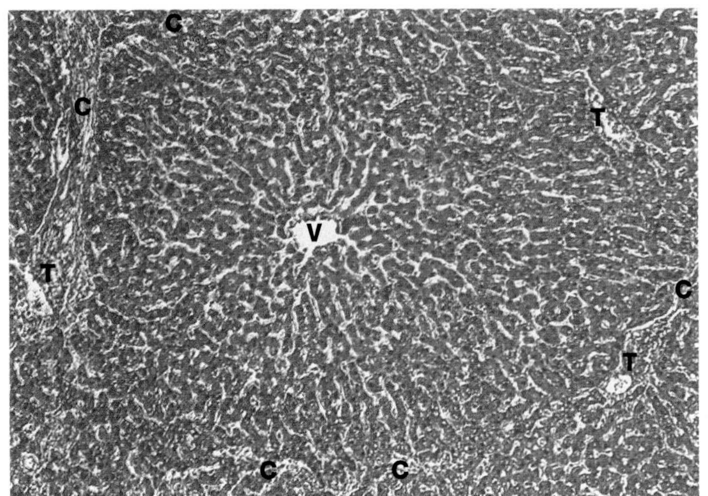

Fig. 15.8 Liver lobule
H & E ×75

This micrograph illustrates a single human liver lobule and includes parts of a number of hepatic acini, each centred on a portal tract. The irregular hexagonal boundary of the lobule is defined by portal tracts **T** and sparse collagenous tissue **C**. Sinusoids originate at the lobule margin and course between plates of hepatocytes to converge upon the terminal hepatic (centrilobular) venule **V**. The plates of hepatocytes are usually only one cell thick and each hepatocyte is thus exposed to blood on at least two sides. The plates of hepatocytes branch and anastomose to form a three-dimensional structure like a sponge.

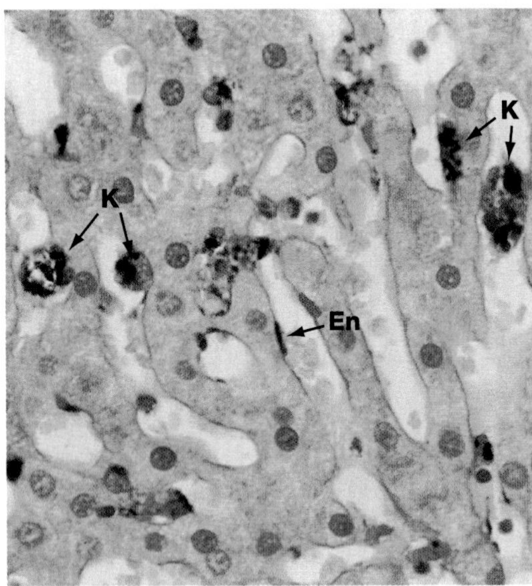

Fig. 15.9 Sinusoid lining cells
Perl's Prussian blue ×48

The sinusoid lining cells include at least three cell types.

The majority of cells lining the hepatic sinusoids are ***endothelial cells*** **En** with flat darkly stained nuclei and thin fenestrated cytoplasm.

Scattered among the endothelial cells are large plump phagocytic cells with ovoid nuclei. Known as ***Kupffer cells*** **K**, these form part of the monocyte-macrophage defence system (see Chs 3 and 4) and, with the spleen, participate in the removal of spent erythrocytes and other particulate debris from the circulation. The phagocytic capability of the Kupffer cells can be demonstrated when they are 'fed', either artificially or under pathological conditions, with appropriate particulate matter. The animal used for this preparation was injected intravenously with a particulate iron-sugar compound, which with this staining method is demonstrated as a dark deposit within the sinusoid lining cells.

The third cell type, known variously as ***stellate cells***, ***Ito cells*** or ***hepatic lipocytes***, cannot be easily distinguished by light microscopy. This cell type has lipid droplets containing vitamin A in their cytoplasm. These cells have the dual functions of vitamin A storage and production of extracellular matrix and collagen. During liver injury, these cells are thought to produce greatly increased amounts of collagen causing the fibrosis which is a characteristic of hepatic cirrhosis.

Hepatic cirrhosis

In diseases where there is repeated liver cell destruction the liver responds by cell division to replace dead liver cells (***regeneration***) and depositing collagenous tissue (***scarring***). The combination of nodules of regenerated liver cells separated by bands of scar tissue is termed ***cirrhosis***.

In cirrhosis the liver cells that are separated from a normal sinusoidal blood flow have reduced function, for example reduced synthesis of albumin and reduced secretion of bile. The scarring and interruption of the low-resistance sinusoidal system has important consequences. Blood from the portal vein cannot drain from the liver and ***portal hypertension*** develops.

The common causes of cirrhosis are diseases in which there is continued liver cell damage and death. ***Chronic ethanol abuse*** is an important cause. Infection with hepatitis viruses B and C lead to ***chronic hepatitis*** and a risk of cirrhosis. Certain autoimmune diseases are also recognised to cause chronic hepatitis and cirrhosis in susceptible patients. Rare causes include excessive storage of iron and copper due to genetic metabolic diseases.

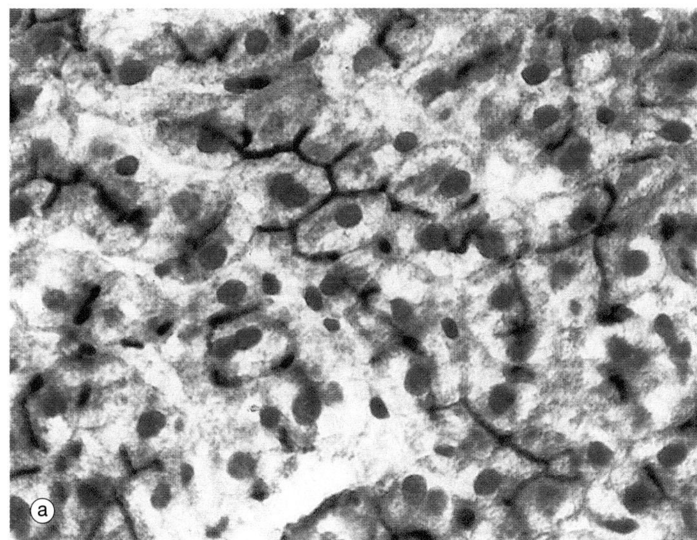

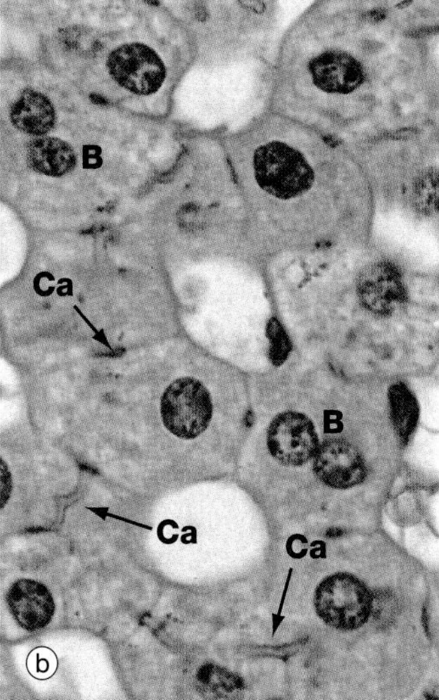

Fig. 15.10 Bile canaliculi
(a) Enzyme histochemical method for ATPase ×480 (b) Iron haematoxylin ×480

Bile is synthesised by all hepatocytes and secreted into a system of minute canaliculi which form an anastomosing network within the plates of hepatocytes. The canaliculi have no discrete structure of their own but consist merely of fine channels formed by the plasma membranes of adjacent hepatocytes; the ultrastructural features are shown in Fig. 15.12. Bile canaliculi of adjacent hepatocyte plates merge to form ***canals of Hering*** before draining into the bile ductules of the portal tracts.

The hepatocyte plasma membranes forming the walls of the canaliculi contain the enzyme ATPase, which suggests that bile secretion is an energy-dependent process. A histochemical method for ATPase has been used in micrograph (a) to demonstrate bile canaliculi (stained brown), which are difficult to demonstrate with routine light microscopy methods. Within each hepatocyte plate, the canaliculi form a regular hexagonal network reminiscent of chicken wire, each hexagon enclosing a single hepatocyte. In micrograph (b), black stain has been deposited in the walls of the canaliculi **Ca**. Note two binucleate hepatocytes **B**.

The biliary canalicular membrane also contains alkaline phosphatase. In diseases that cause obstruction of bile flow, this enzyme is released from the hepatocyte canalicular membrane into the blood where it can be detected. Elevated blood levels of hepatic alkaline phosphatase are therefore a feature of obstructive jaundice.

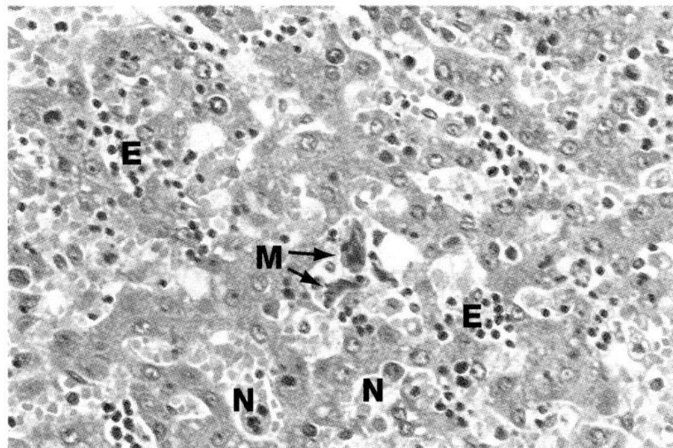

Fig. 15.11 Fetal liver
H & E ×100

In fetal life, the liver and spleen are important sites of haemopoeisis (see Ch. 3). When haemopoeisis in bone marrow begins, some time after the fourth month of gestation, the importance of the liver and spleen for this function gradually declines.

In this micrograph of fetal liver, the hepatocyte plates are two cells thick, a normal finding up to the age of about 7 years. The sinusoids are packed with blood precursors, including megakaryocytes **M** and erythroid **E** and myeloid precursors **N**.

Extramedullary haematopoiesis

In adult life the liver does not normally have haemopoietic tissue. However if the capacity of normal marrow is inadequate for demand then the fetal function of hepatic haemopoiesis can be re-established. Important causes include fibrosis of the bone marrow, replacement of the bone marrow by malignancy or certain genetic disorders of haemoglobin formation (***haemoglobinopathy***). Patients develop haemopoiesis in liver and spleen both of which may become abnormally enlarged.

B binucleate hepatocyte **C** collagenous tissue **Ca** canaliculi **E** erythroid precursors
En endothelial cell **K** Kupffer cell **M** megakaryocyte **N** myeloid precursors **T** portal tract
V terminal hepatic venule

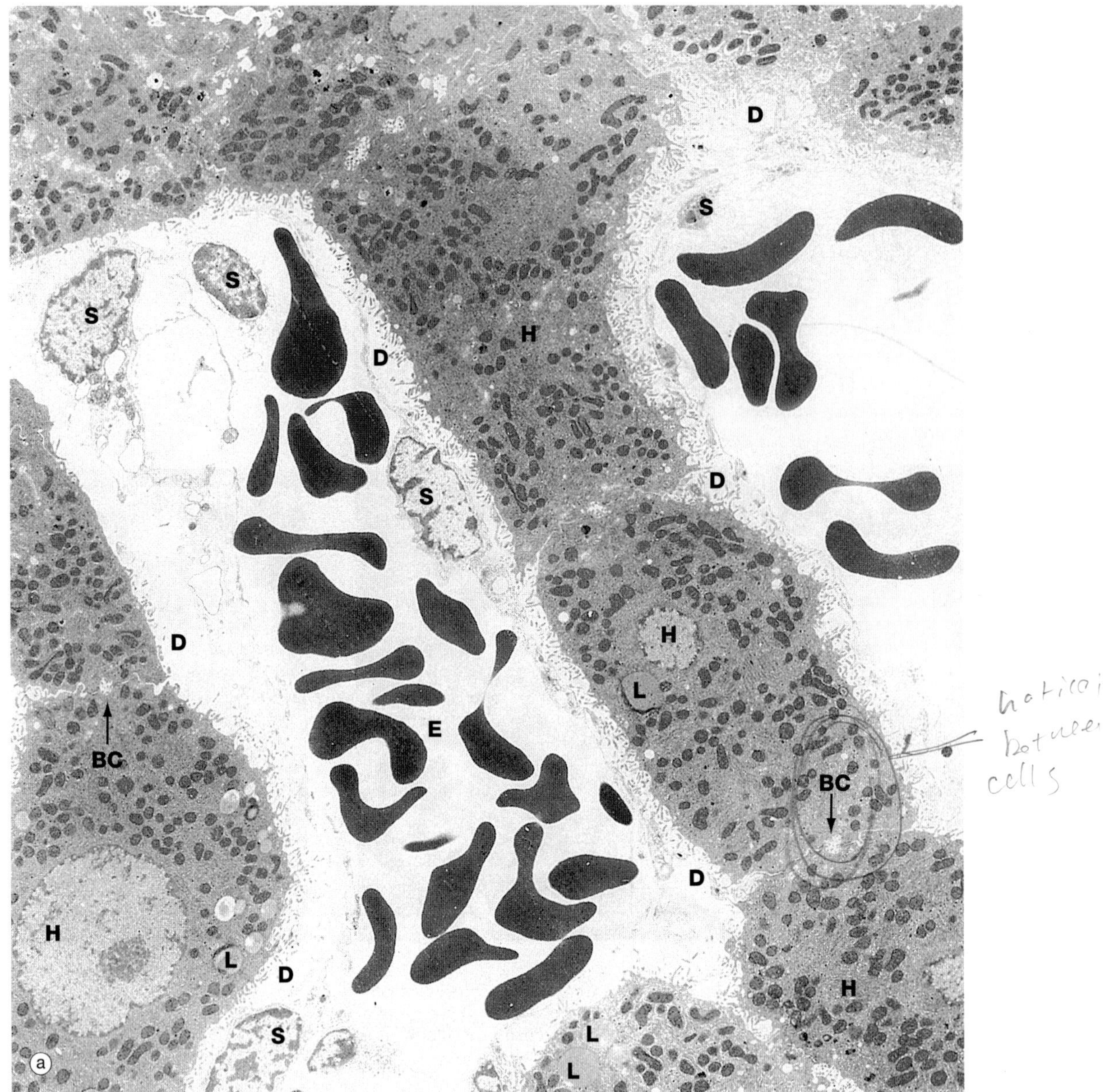

Fig. 15.12 Liver
(a) EM ×4400 (b) EM ×15 200 *(opposite)*

These micrographs demonstrate the main ultrastructural features of the liver. Hepatocytes **H** are exposed on each side to the sinusoids lined by a discontinuous layer of sinusoid lining cells **S**. These are supported by the fine reticulin framework of the liver (see Fig. 15.4) with the space of Disse **D** between the lining cells and the hepatocyte surface. Via the gaps in the sinusoid lining, the space of Disse is continuous with the sinusoid lumen, thus bathing the hepatocyte surface with plasma. Numerous irregular microvilli **Mv** extend from the hepatocyte surface into the space of Disse, greatly increasing the surface area for metabolic exchange. Between the bases of the microvilli are coated pits involved in endocytosis. Erythrocytes **E** can be seen within the sinusoids.

Reflecting their extraordinary range of biosynthetic and degradative activities, the hepatocyte cytoplasm (b) is crowded with organelles, particularly rough endoplasmic reticulum **rER**, smooth endoplasmic reticulum **sER**, Golgi stacks, free ribosomes, mitochondria **M**, lysosomes **Ly** and peroxisomes. Lipid droplets **L** and glycogen rosettes are present in variable numbers depending on nutritional status.

Bile canaliculi **BC** are seen to be formed from the plasma membranes of adjacent hepatocytes, the plasma membranes being tightly bound by junctional complexes **J**; small microvilli project into the canaliculi. The subjacent cytoplasm contains a network of actin filaments, contraction of which reduces canalicular diameter, thus reducing flow rate.

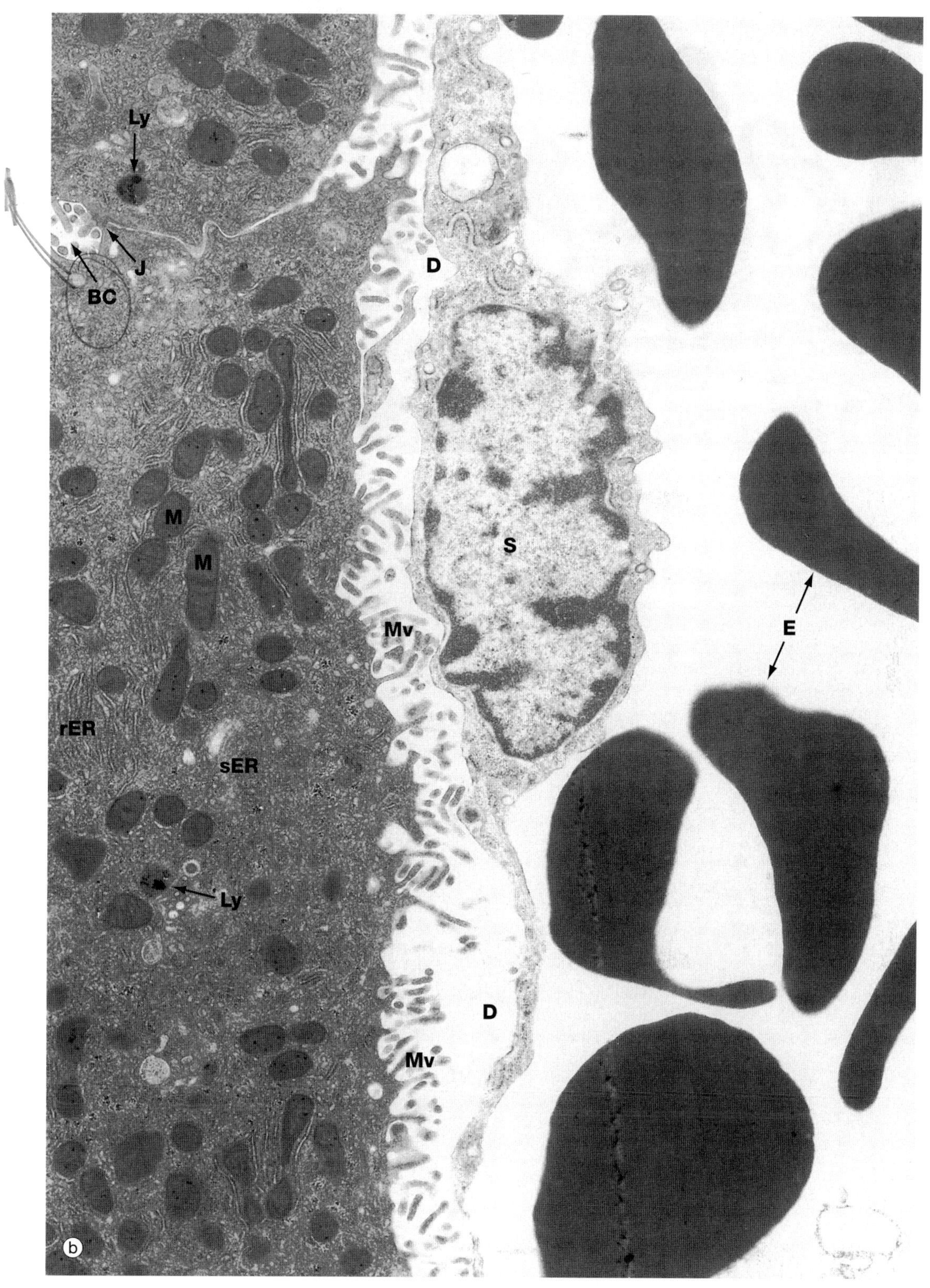

BC bile canaliculus **D** space of Disse **E** erythrocyte **H** hepatocyte **J** junctional complex
L lipid droplet **Ly** lysosome **M** mitochondria **Mv** microvilli **rER** rough endoplasmic reticulum
S sinusoid lining cell **sER** smooth endoplasmic reticulum

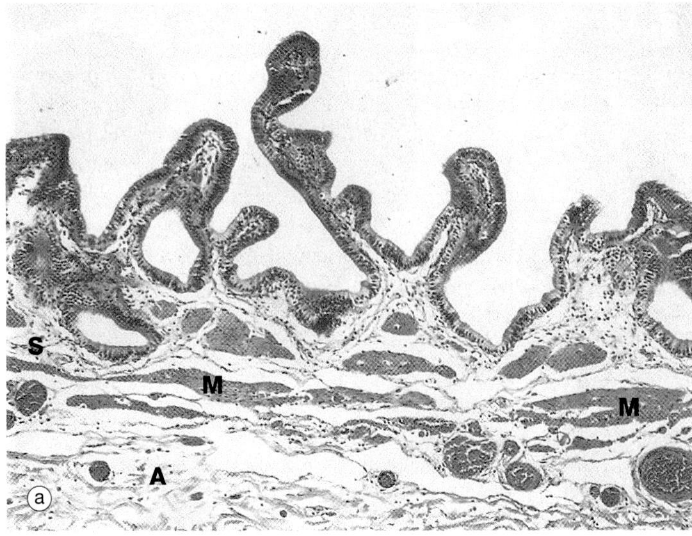

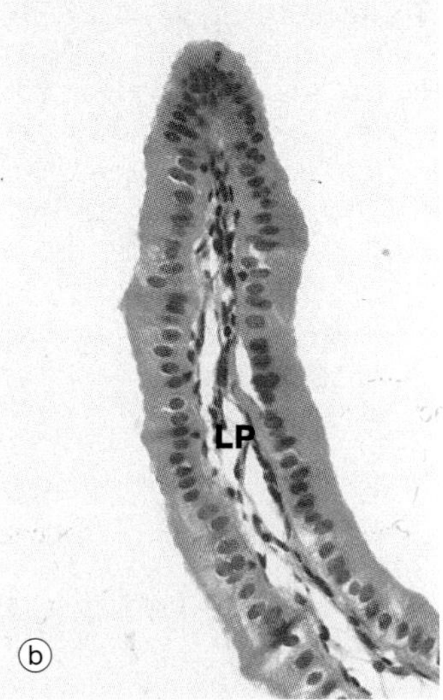

Fig. 15.13 Gall bladder
(a) H & E ×30 (b) H & E ×100 (c) H & E ×10

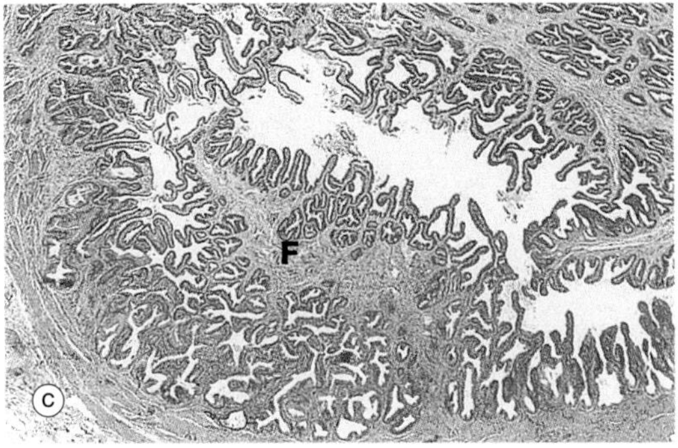

The intrahepatic bile collecting system merges to form ***right*** and ***left hepatic ducts***, which join creating a single large duct, the ***common hepatic duct***. On leaving the liver, this is joined by the ***cystic duct*** which drains the gall bladder. The ***common bile duct*** so formed joins the pancreatic duct to form the short ***ampulla of Vater*** before entering the duodenum. Bile draining down the common hepatic duct is shunted into the gall bladder where it is stored and concentrated. The major bile ducts outside the liver are collectively called the ***extrahepatic biliary tree***.

The gall bladder is a muscular sac lined by a simple columnar epithelium; it has a capacity of about 100 mL in humans. The presence of lipid in the duodenum promotes the secretion of the hormone cholecystokinin-pancreozymin (CCK) by neuroendocrine cells of the duodenal mucosa, stimulating contraction of the gall bladder and forcing bile into the duodenum. Bile is an emulsifying agent facilitating the hydrolysis of dietary lipids by pancreatic lipases.

Micrograph (a) shows the wall of a gall bladder in the non-distended state in which the mucosa is thrown up into many folds. The relatively loose submucosa **S** is rich in elastic fibres, blood vessels and lymphatics, which drain water reabsorbed from bile during the concentration process. The fibres of the muscular layer **M** are arranged in longitudinal, transverse and oblique orientations but do not form distinct layers. Externally, there is a thick collagenous adventitial (serosal) coat **A** conveying the larger blood and lymphatic vessels. In the neck of the gall bladder and in the extrahepatic biliary tree, mucous glands are found in the submucosa; mucus may provide a protective surface film for the biliary tract.

At high magnification in micrograph (b), the simple epithelial lining of the gall bladder is seen to consist of very tall columnar cells with basally located nuclei; numerous short irregular microvilli account for the unevenness of the luminal surface. The lining cells concentrate bile 5–10 fold by an active process, the resulting water passing into lymphatics in the lamina propria **LP**.

Micrograph (c) illustrates the wall of the cystic duct which is formed into a twisted mucosa-covered fold **F** known as the ***spiral valve of Heister***.

The flow of bile and pancreatic juice into the duodenum is controlled by the complex arrangement of smooth muscle known as the ***sphincter of Oddi***. The components of this structure include the ***choledochal sphincter*** at the distal end of the common bile duct, the ***pancreatic sphincter*** at the end of the pancreatic duct and a meshwork of muscle fibres around the ampulla. This arrangement controls the flow of bile and pancreatic juice into the duodenum and at the same time prevents reflux of bile and pancreatic juice into the wrong parts of the duct system. When the choledochal sphincter is closed, bile is directed into the gall bladder where it is concentrated.

Cholelithiasis

Abnormal concentration and precipitation of the constituents of bile may form stones (***calculi***) within the gall bladder or the extrahepatic biliary system. A stone may become impacted in a duct, leading to blockage. Complete blockage of the common bile duct by a stone would lead to failure of bile secretion and clinical ***jaundice***. If the gall bladder is affected by stones then it may become inflamed leading to pain (***chronic cholecystitis***). The term ***cholelithiasis*** is used to refer to formation of stones within the biliary system.

Pancreas

The pancreas is a large gland which, like the liver, develops embryologically as an outgrowth of the primitive foregut. The pancreas has both exocrine and endocrine components; the endocrine pancreas is described in detail in Chapter 17. The exocrine pancreas, which forms the bulk of the gland, secretes an enzyme-rich alkaline fluid into the duodenum via the ***pancreatic duct***. The high pH of pancreatic secretions is due to a high content of bicarbonate ions and serves to neutralise the acidic chyme as it enters the small intestine from the stomach. The pancreatic enzymes degrade proteins, carbohydrates, lipids and nucleic acids by the process of luminal digestion (see Fig. 14.18). Like pepsin in the stomach, the pancreatic proteolytic enzymes trypsin and chymotrypsin are secreted in an inactive form. ***Enterokinase***, an enzyme secreted by the duodenal mucosa, activates protrypsin to form trypsin; trypsin then activates prochymotrypsin to form chymotrypsin. This mechanism prevents autodigestion of the pancreas. The other pancreatic enzymes are secreted in the active form.

Pancreatic secretion occurs continuously, the rate being modulated by hormonal and nervous influences. Secretin, a hormone released by neuroendocrine cells scattered in the duodenum, promotes the secretion of copious watery fluid rich in bicarbonate. Cholecystokinin-pancreozymin (CCK), also derived from duodenal neuroendocrine cells, stimulates the secretion of enzyme-rich pancreatic fluid. Gastrin, secreted by neuroendocrine cells of the gastric pylorus, has a similar action on the pancreas to that of CCK. The pancreas is richly innervated by the autonomic nervous system which also modulates secretory activity.

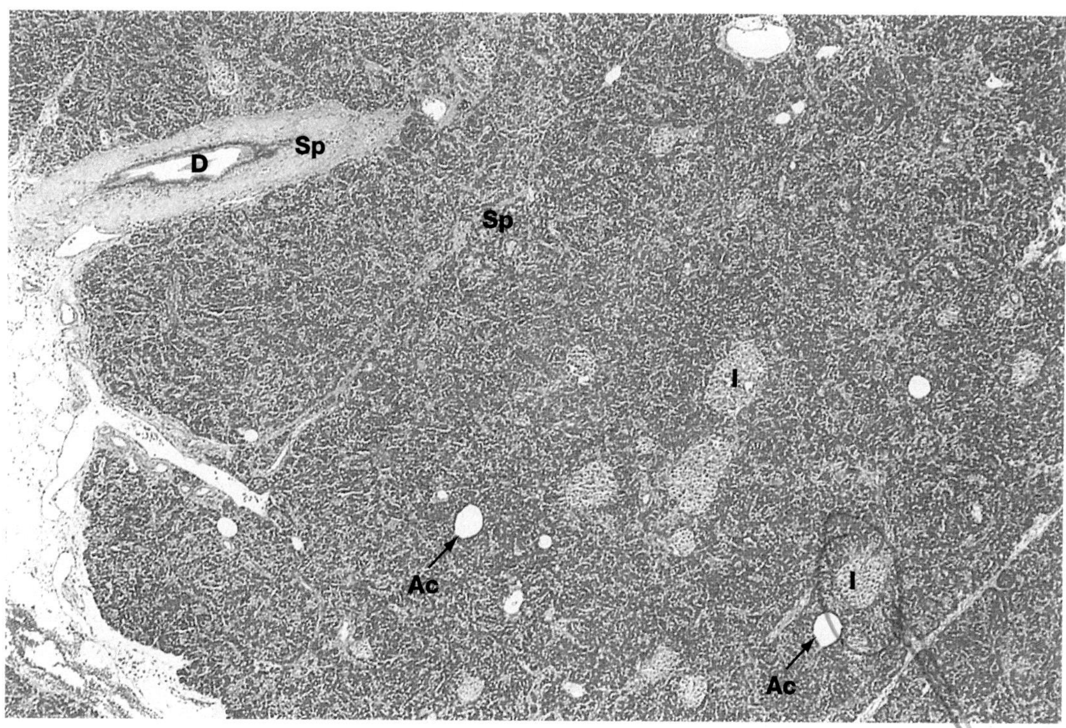

Fig. 15.14 Pancreas
H & E ×45

The pancreas is a lobulated gland covered by a thin collagenous capsule which extends as delicate septa **Sp** between the lobules. The exocrine component of the pancreas consists of closely packed secretory acini which drain into a highly branched duct system. Most of the secretion drains into the main pancreatic duct, which joins the common bile duct to drain into the duodenum via the ampulla of Vater; in most people, a small ***accessory pancreatic duct*** drains into the duodenum more proximally. ***Interlobular ducts*** **D** can be seen in this micrograph; their surrounding supporting tissue reinforces the septal framework.

The endocrine tissue of the pancreas forms ***islets of Langerhans*** **I** of various sizes scattered throughout the exocrine tissue. Occasional adipocytes **Ac** are scattered throughout the parenchyma. These are scanty in young adults but are seen in increasing numbers in older people, reflecting the natural atrophy of the gland with age.

endocrine panc.

A adventitia **Ac** adipocyte **D** interlobular duct **F** mucosal fold **I** islet of Langerhans **LP** lamina propria **M** muscular layer **S** submucosa **Sp** septum

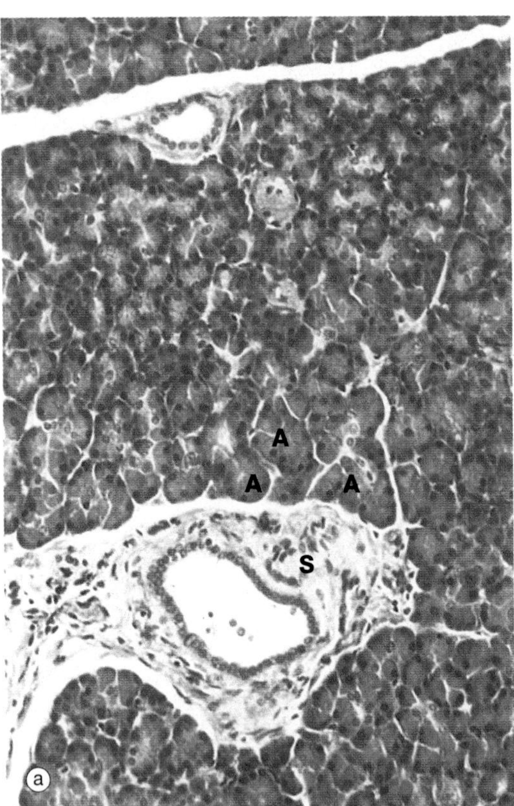

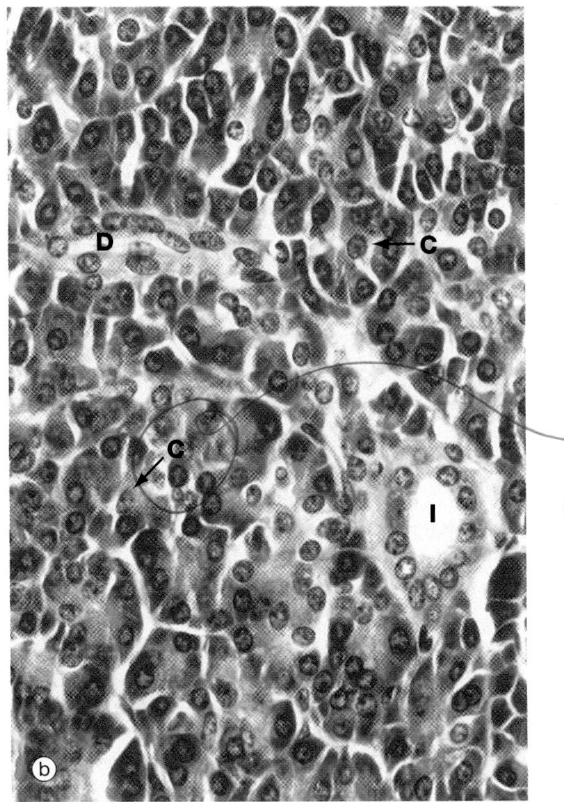

Fig. 15.15 Exocrine pancreas
(a) H & E ×200 (b) H & E ×450 (c) EM ×8500 *(opposite)*

Details of the pancreatic acini and duct system can be seen in these micrographs. Each acinus is made up of an irregular cluster of pyramid-shaped secretory cells, the apices of which surround a minute central lumen which represents the terminal end of the duct system. The smallest of the tributaries are known as ***intercalated ducts***. Adjacent acini are separated by inconspicuous supporting tissue containing numerous capillaries. In histological section, the interacinar spaces tend to appear wider than they do in vivo, due to a fixation artefact. The intercalated ducts drain into small ***intralobular ducts***, which in turn drain into the ***interlobular ducts*** in the septa of the gland. The intercalated ducts are lined by simple low cuboidal epithelium, which becomes stratified cuboidal in the larger ducts. With increasing size, the ducts are invested by a progressively thicker layer of dense collagenous supporting tissue; the wall of the main pancreatic duct contains smooth muscle.

Micrograph (a) shows the general arrangement of the glandular acini **A**. An intralobular duct is seen in upper midfield and a larger interlobular duct in lower midfield, the latter having a much broader sheath of supporting tissue **S**.

At higher magnification in micrograph (b), the cells of each pancreatic acinus have a roughly triangular shape in section, their apices projecting towards a central lumen of a minute duct. The acinar cells are typical protein-secreting cells. The nuclei are basally located and surrounded by basophilic cytoplasm crammed with rough endoplasmic reticulum; the apices of the cells are packed with eosinophilic secretory granules containing proenzymes. The centres of the acini frequently contain one or more nuclei of ***centroacinar cells*** **C** with pale nuclei and sparse pale-stained cytoplasm; these represent the terminal lining cells of intercalated ducts. Cells of similar appearance can be seen between the acini and those of intercalated ducts **D** passing to join the larger intralobular ducts **I**. The cells lining the intercalated ducts secrete water and bicarbonate ions into the pancreatic juice.

The electron micrograph (c) opposite illustrates part of a pancreatic acinus with its central lumen **L**. The pyramid-shaped secretory cells have round basally located nuclei with dispersed chromatin and prominent nucleoli **Nu**, both characteristic features of highly active cells. The basal cytoplasm is packed with lamellar profiles of rough endoplasmic reticulum **rER**, among which elongated mitochondria **M** are scattered. A large Golgi apparatus **G** is located in a supranuclear position and is responsible for packaging enzymes synthesised on the rough endoplasmic reticulum to form zymogen granules. Newly packed secretory or zymogen granules $\mathbf{Z_1}$ are large and much less electron-dense than the smaller mature granules $\mathbf{Z_2}$ which aggregate in the apical cytoplasm. Zymogen granules are released into the acinar lumen by exocytosis; small irregular microvilli associated with this process are seen projecting into the lumen. Note small capillaries **Ca**, a fibroblast **F** and collagen **Coll** in the fine supporting tissue which surrounds the acinus.

A glandular acini **C** centroacinar cells **Ca** capillary **Coll** collagen **D** intercalated ducts
F fibroblast **G** Golgi **I** intralobular ducts **L** lumen **M** mitochondrion **Nu** nucleolus
S support tissues $\mathbf{Z_1, Z_2}$ zymogen granules

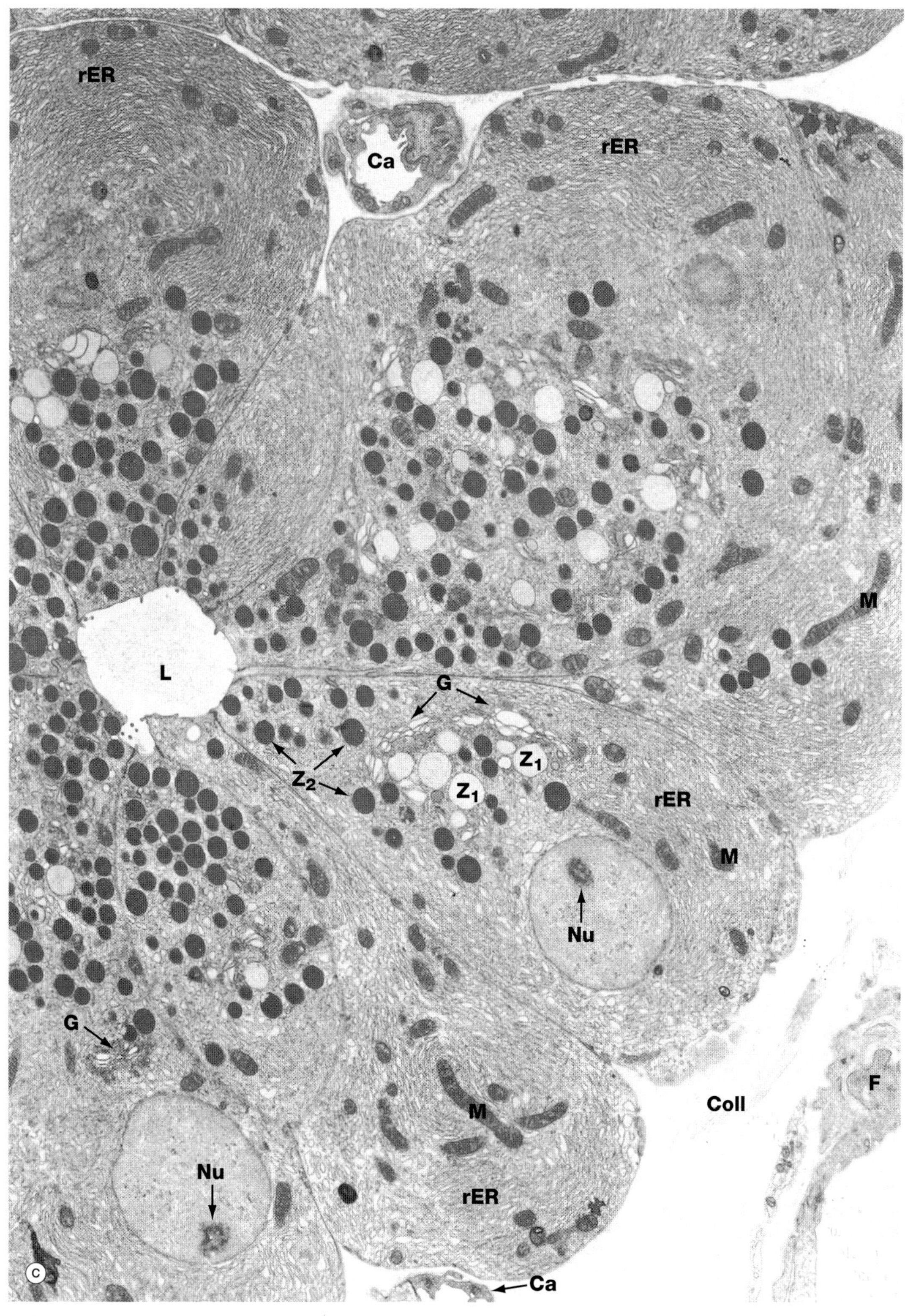

Acute pancreatitis

Damage to the pancreatic acinar cells releases pancreatic enzymes into the local tissues. These powerful enzymes cause death of pancreatic tissue and severe inflammation termed ***acute pancreatitis***. The release of pancreatic lipase causes death of local fat cells (***fat necrosis***). Pancreatic amylase is released and can be detected at high levels in the blood. This is a severe life-threatening condition.

16. *Urinary system*

Introduction

The principal function of the urinary system is the maintenance of water, electrolyte and acid–base homeostasis, which requires that any input into the system is balanced by an equivalent output. The kidney provides the mechanism by which excess water and electrolytes are eliminated from the body while the ureters, bladder and urethra form the storage and outflow tract. A second major function of the urinary system is the excretion of many toxic metabolic waste products, particularly the nitrogenous molecules urea and creatinine, compounds that can conveniently be excreted dissolved in water. The end product of these processes is ***urine***. Since all body fluids are maintained in dynamic equilibrium with one another by the circulatory system, any adjustment in the composition of the blood results in similar changes in the other fluid compartments of the body. Thus regulation of the osmotic concentration of blood plasma by the kidneys (***osmoregulation***) ensures the osmotic regulation of all other body fluids.

The functional and structural unit of the kidney, the ***nephron***, consists of a ***renal corpuscle*** (including the ***glomerulus***) plus a long folded ***renal tubule***. The human kidney contains approximately one million nephrons that perform the functions of osmoregulation and excretion by the following processes:

- Filtration in the glomerulus of most small molecules from blood plasma to form an ultrafiltrate of plasma.
- Selective reabsorption in the tubule of most of the water and some other molecules from the ultrafiltrate, leaving behind excess and waste materials to be excreted.
- Secretion in the tubule of some excretory products directly from blood into the urine.
- Maintenance of the acid–base balance by selective secretion by the tubule of H^+ ions into the urine.

The kidney also has hormonal and metabolic functions:

- **Renin**, synthesised in the kidney, is a component of the ***renin-angiotensin-aldosterone*** mechanism that controls blood pressure.
- **Erythropoietin**, synthesised in the kidney, stimulates the production of erythrocytes in the bone marrow and thus regulates the oxygen-carrying capacity of the blood.
- **Vitamin D**, which regulates calcium balance, is converted to an active form in the kidney.

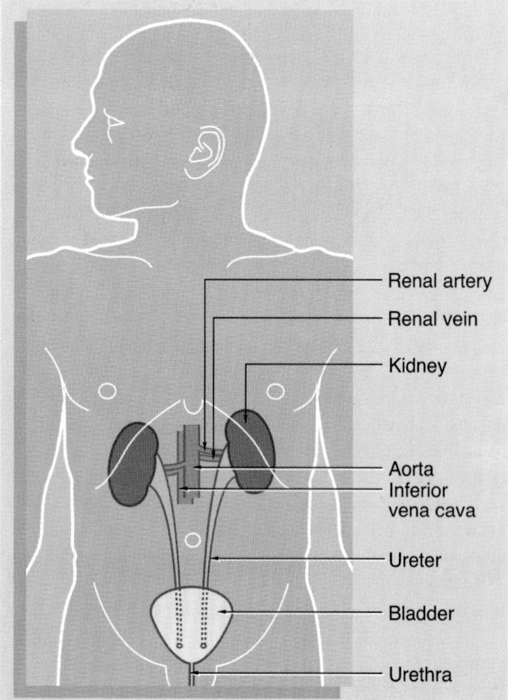

Fig. 16.1 The urinary system

The urinary system comprises two ***kidneys***, two ***ureters***, a ***bladder*** and a ***urethra***. Urine is produced in the kidneys and flows down the ureters to the bladder where it is stored until voided via the urethra. No further modification of the urine takes place after it leaves the kidneys. The kidneys and ureters are found in the retroperitoneum while the urinary bladder is in the anterior part of the pelvis.

Blood is supplied to each kidney by the ***renal arteries***, which arise from the aorta. One or more ***renal veins*** drains each kidney to the inferior vena cava. The total blood volume of the body is circulated through the kidneys about 300 times each day.

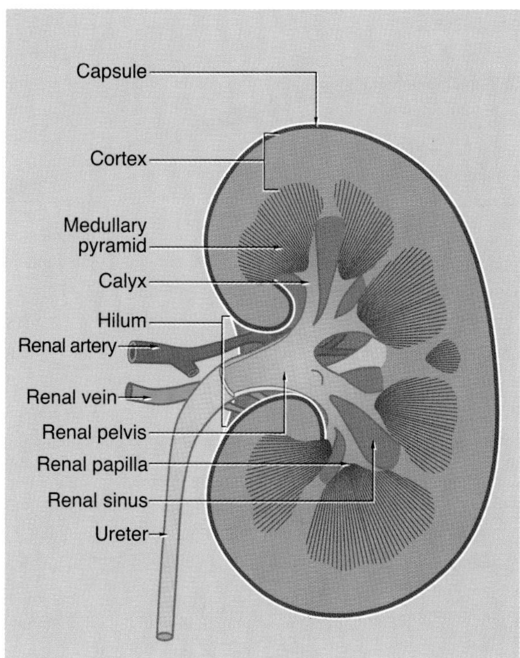

Fig. 16.2 Kidney

The kidney is a bean-shaped organ lying in the upper retroperitoneal area and oriented with the concave surface directed medially. In adults the kidney measures 10–12 cm. The ***hilum*** is the site of entry and exit of the renal blood vessels and the ureter.

The archetypal kidney of lower mammals consists of a single lobe made up of a ***medullary pyramid*** (actually cone-shaped), the base of which is enveloped by the ***cortex*** containing the renal corpuscles and the proximal and distal parts of the tubules. Nephrons arise in the cortex, loop down into the medulla and return to the cortex. From here they drain into ***collecting ducts*** that descend again into the medulla to discharge urine from the apex of the medullary pyramid. The apical part of the pyramid (known as the ***renal papilla***) is enveloped by a funnel-shaped ***renal pelvis***, which represents the dilated proximal part of the ureter.

The human kidney is made up of 10–18 lobes. In the adult the cortical components of the lobes are fused so that the cortex forms a continuous smooth outer zone which extends down between the pyramids. The ***renal medulla*** is made up of multiple medullary pyramids separated by medullary extensions of the cortex. Each renal papilla is surrounded by a branch of the renal pelvis called a ***calyx***; the whole urinary collecting system within the kidney being described as the ***pelvicalyceal system***. The space between the branches of the pelvicalyceal system is filled with fatty supporting tissue and is known as the ***renal sinus***.

The kidney is invested by a tough fibrous capsule, which is surrounded by a thick layer of perinephric fat that is in turn encased in a delicate condensation of connective tissue, known as ***Gerota's fascia***. The fat around the kidney cushions it against trauma.

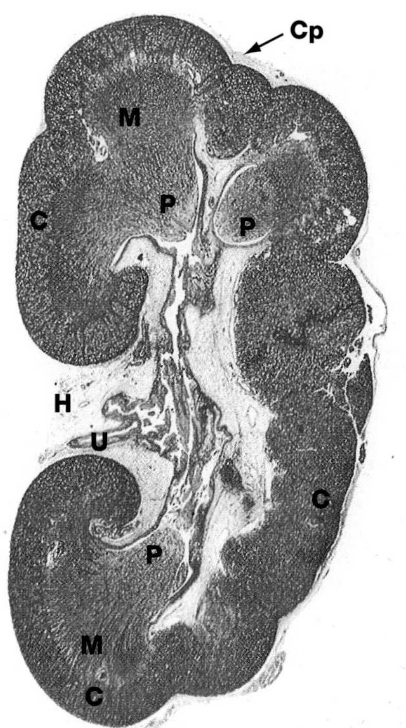

Fig. 16.3 Kidney
H & E ×3

This micrograph of a kidney from a stillborn child illustrates at low power the features of the kidney described in Fig. 16.2. The kidney of a baby has been chosen as it is small enough to section and photograph in its entirety. Furthermore its convex surface is irregular, reflecting the development of the many lobes making up the organ. In histological section, only a single plane through the pelvicalyceal system can be visualised. This plane of section includes the axes of three lobes, the papilla **P** of each one projecting into the central pelvicalyceal space; this drains into the ureter **U** that leaves the kidney via the hilum **H**.

The darker stained cortex **C** can be clearly differentiated from the paler stained medulla **M**. The cortex contains large numbers of tiny spheroidal structures, the developing renal corpuscles (see Fig. 16.4). The medullary pyramids are characterised by the numerous tubules converging towards the tips of the renal papillae. Note the continuity of the cortex throughout the outer zone of the kidney and the cortical extension between the two medullary pyramids at the top of the field. The fibrous capsule **Cp** of the kidney is continuous at the hilum with fatty supporting tissue, which packs the space (known as the ***renal sinus***) between the hilar structures. The renal artery and vein also pass through the hilum but are not seen in this plane of section.

C cortex **Cp** capsule **H** hilum **M** medulla **P** papilla **U** ureter

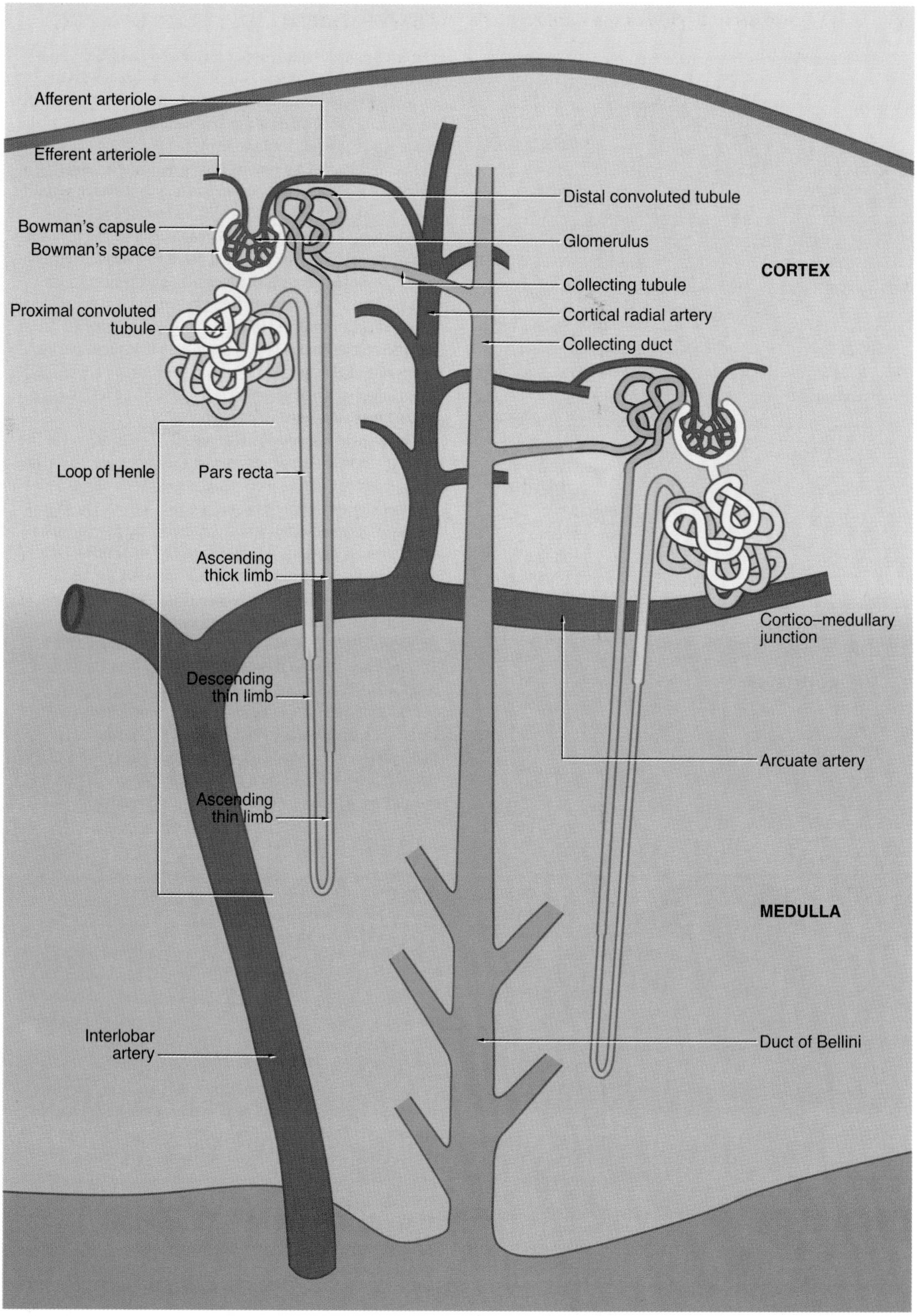

Fig. 16.4 Basic organisation of the nephron, collecting system and renal vasculature

The nephron and collecting system

The nephron, the functional unit of the kidney, consists of two major components, the ***renal corpuscle*** and the ***renal tubule***.

Renal corpuscle. The renal corpuscle is responsible for the filtration of plasma and is a combination of two structures, ***Bowman's capsule*** and the ***glomerulus***.

Bowman's capsule consists of a single layer of flattened cells resting on a basement membrane; it is derived from the distended, blind end of the renal tubule. The glomerulus is a globular network of anastomosing capillaries, which invaginates Bowman's capsule (see Fig. 16.8). Thus the capillary loops of the glomerulus are invested by the ***visceral layer of Bowman's capsule***: a highly specialised layer of epithelial cells called ***podocytes*** (see Fig. 16.13). The visceral layer is reflected around the vascular stalk of the glomerulus to become continuous with the ***parietal layer*** that constitutes Bowman's capsule proper. The space between the two layers is known as ***Bowman's space*** and is continuous with the lumen of the renal tubule; the parietal epithelium of Bowman's capsule is continuous with the epithelium lining the renal tubule.

In the renal corpuscle, water and low molecular weight constituents of plasma are filtered from the glomerular capillaries into Bowman's space to form the

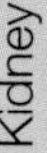

glomerular ultrafiltrate, which then passes into the renal tubule. Thus the filtration barrier between the capillary lumen and Bowman's space consists of the capillary endothelium, the podocyte layer and their common basement membrane known as the ***glomerular basement membrane*** (see Fig. 16.15).

The ***afferent arteriole***, which supplies the glomerulus, and the ***efferent arteriole***, which drains it, enter and leave the corpuscle at the ***vascular pole*** that is usually situated opposite the entrance to the renal tubule, the ***urinary pole*** (see Fig. 16.7).

Renal tubule. The renal tubule extends from Bowman's capsule to its junction with a ***collecting duct***. The renal tubule is up to 55 mm long in humans and is lined by a single layer of epithelial cells. The primary function of the renal tubule is the selective reabsorption of water, inorganic ions and other molecules from the glomerular filtrate. In addition, some inorganic ions are secreted directly from blood into the lumen of the tubule. In humans, glomerular filtrate is produced at a steady rate of approximately 120 mL/min; of this, all but about 1 mL is reabsorbed by the renal tubules giving a normal rate of urine production of around 1 mL/min. The renal tubule has a convoluted shape and has four distinct zones, each of which has a different role in tubular function and a corresponding difference in histological appearance.

1. **The proximal convoluted tubule (PCT)** is the longest, most convoluted section of the tubule and is responsible for the reabsorption of approximately 65% of the ions and water of the glomerular filtrate. PCTs are confined to the renal cortex and make up the greater part of its bulk.
2. **The loop of Henle** includes the distal straight part of the proximal tubule, the ***pars recta***, the ***thin descending*** and ***ascending limbs***, and the ***thick ascending limb***. The difference between these parts is due to differences in the epithelium. The thin segments of the loop of Henle dip down into the medulla where they form a hairpin bend. The length of the loop of Henle varies from short to long depending on the location of the renal corpuscle of the particular nephron. The corpuscles of short-looped nephrons tend to be located in the superficial and midcortical regions, the loops extending very little beyond the corticomedullary junction. Long-looped nephrons are mainly associated with juxtamedullary corpuscles; a small proportion of long loops almost reach the tips of the renal papillae but successively greater numbers turn back at higher levels as necessitated by the tapering shape of the medullary pyramids. The limbs of the loop of Henle are closely associated with parallel wide capillary loops, the ***vasa recta*** (not shown in this diagram), which arise from the efferent arterioles of glomeruli located near the corticomedullary junction. The vasa recta descend into the medulla then loop back on themselves to drain into veins at the junction of the medulla and cortex. The main function of the loops of Henle is to generate a high osmotic pressure in the extracellular fluid of the renal medulla; the mechanism by which this is achieved is known as the ***counter-current multiplier system*** (see Fig. 16.23). In some animals the loop of Henle plays a major role in reabsorption of water from the glomerular filtrate back into the circulation via the vasa recta; however, this function is of lesser importance in the human kidney.
3. **The distal convoluted tubule (DCT)** is a continuation of the thick limb of the loop of Henle after its return to the cortex. Shorter and less convoluted than the PCT, the DCT is responsible for reabsorption of sodium ions, an active process controlled by the adrenocortical hormone ***aldosterone***. Sodium reabsorption is coupled with the secretion of hydrogen or potassium ions into the DCT, the secretion of hydrogen ions resulting in a net loss of acid from the body.
4. **The collecting tubule** is the straight terminal portion of the nephron; several collecting tubules converging to form a ***collecting duct***. The collecting ducts descend through the cortex in parallel bundles called ***medullary rays*** (see Fig. 16.5), progressively merging in the medulla to form the large ***ducts of Bellini*** which open at the tips of the renal papillae to discharge urine into the pelvicalyceal system. The collecting tubules and ducts are not normally permeable to water. However, in the presence of ***antidiuretic hormone (ADH)*** secreted by the posterior pituitary, the collecting tubules and ducts become permeable to water. Thus the high osmotic pressure generated by the counter-current multiplier system into the interstitial tissues of the medulla removes water that is returned to the general circulation via the vasa recta. The loops of Henle and ADH thus provide a mechanism for the production of urine that is hypertonic with respect to plasma.

Renal vasculature

Each kidney is supplied by a single renal artery, which divides in the hilum into two main branches. Each of these gives rise to several ***interlobar arteries***, which ascend between the pyramids to the corticomedullary junction. Here they branch to form the ***arcuate arteries***, which run in an arc-like course parallel to the capsule of the kidney. The arcuate arteries give rise to numerous ***cortical radial (interlobular) arteries*** that radiate towards the capsule, branching to form the afferent arterioles of the glomeruli.

As previously described, the vasa recta form a continuation of the efferent arterioles of juxtamedullary glomeruli and form the microcirculation of the renal medulla. The efferent arterioles of the rest of the cortex divide to form the plexus of capillaries that surround the tubules of the renal cortex. The cortical and medullary capillaries drain via ***cortical radial (interlobular) veins*** to ***arcuate veins*** at the cortico-medullary junction and thence to the ***renal vein***.

The functions of the different parts of the nephron are summarised in Fig. 16.23.

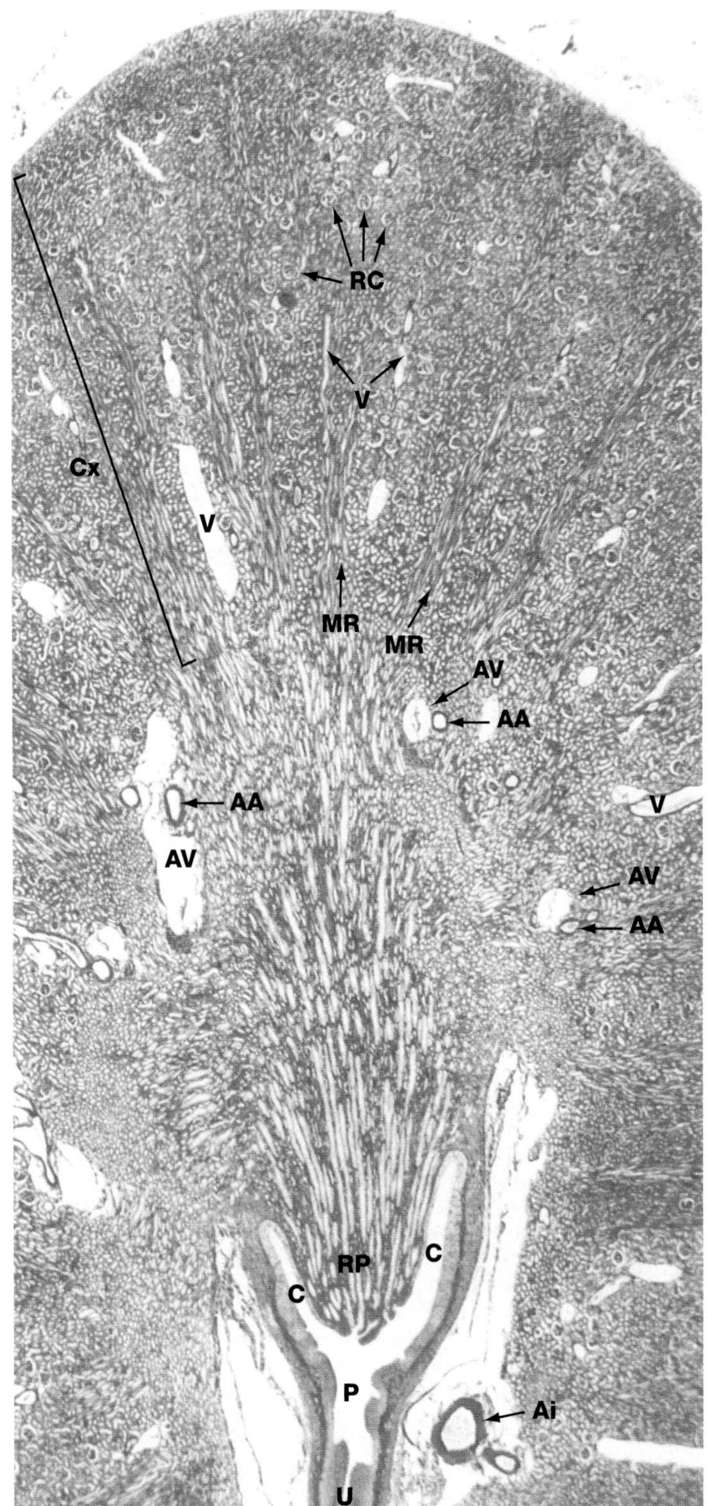

Fig. 16.5 Kidney (monkey)
Jones' methenamine silver
H & E ×12

The basic geography of the kidney can be seen in this unilobar kidney that has been sectioned through the axis of the medullary pyramid. Note the cup-shaped calyx **C** surrounding the renal papilla **RP**. The calyces fuse to form the pelvis **P** that in turn leads to the ureter **U**.

In the cortex **Cx**, numerous renal corpuscles **RC** (200 μm in diameter) are just visible at this magnification. The corpuscles tend to be arranged in parallel rows at right angles to the capsule, separated by interlobular arteries from which they derive their blood supply. Interlobular arteries are too narrow to be identified at this magnification but a number of their accompanying thin-walled interlobular veins **V** are easily seen.

Most of the cortical parenchyma surrounding the renal corpuscles consists of proximal and distal convoluted tubules. From the cortex, ***medullary rays*** **MR** course towards the medulla; they consist of collecting tubules and ducts draining nephrons located high in the cortex. The collecting ducts merge in the medulla to form the larger ducts of Bellini that converge towards the tip of the renal papilla. Although not visible at this magnification, long loops of Henle dip into the medulla between, and parallel with, the collecting ducts. The long, straight vasa recta also dip down into the medulla alongside the loops of Henle; these vessels, too small to be seen at this magnification, absorb water from the loops of Henle and collecting ducts.

The corticomedullary junction is marked by several arcuate arteries **AA** and their associated thin-walled arcuate veins **AV.** Note a large interlobar branch of the renal artery **Ai** in the hilar supporting tissue.

AA arcuate artery **Ai** interlobar artery **AV** arcuate vein **C** calyx **Cx** cortex **G** glomerulus **IA** interlobular artery **MR** medullary ray **P** renal pelvis **RC** renal corpuscles **RP** renal papilla **T** tubule **U** ureter **V** interlobular vein

The renal cortex

The renal cortex is easily identified even at low magnification by the presence of renal corpuscles, which are absent in the renal medulla. However, the bulk of the cortex is occupied by the proximal and distal convoluted tubules. The arcuate arteries and veins help to demarcate the cortex from the medulla.

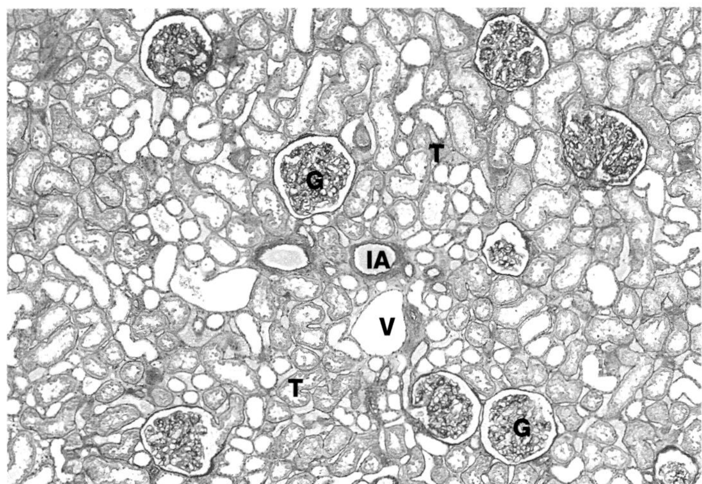

Fig. 16.6 Renal cortex
H & E ×40

At higher magnification, the renal corpuscles are dense rounded structures, the ***glomeruli* G**, surrounded by narrow Bowman's spaces, normally filled with plasma ultrafiltrate. The tubules **T** fill the bulk of the parenchyma between the corpuscles. The cortex consists mainly of proximal convoluted tubules lined by more eosinophilic epithelial cells, with smaller numbers of distal convoluted tubules and collecting tubules. Two interlobular arteries **IA** and veins **V** are also easily identified.

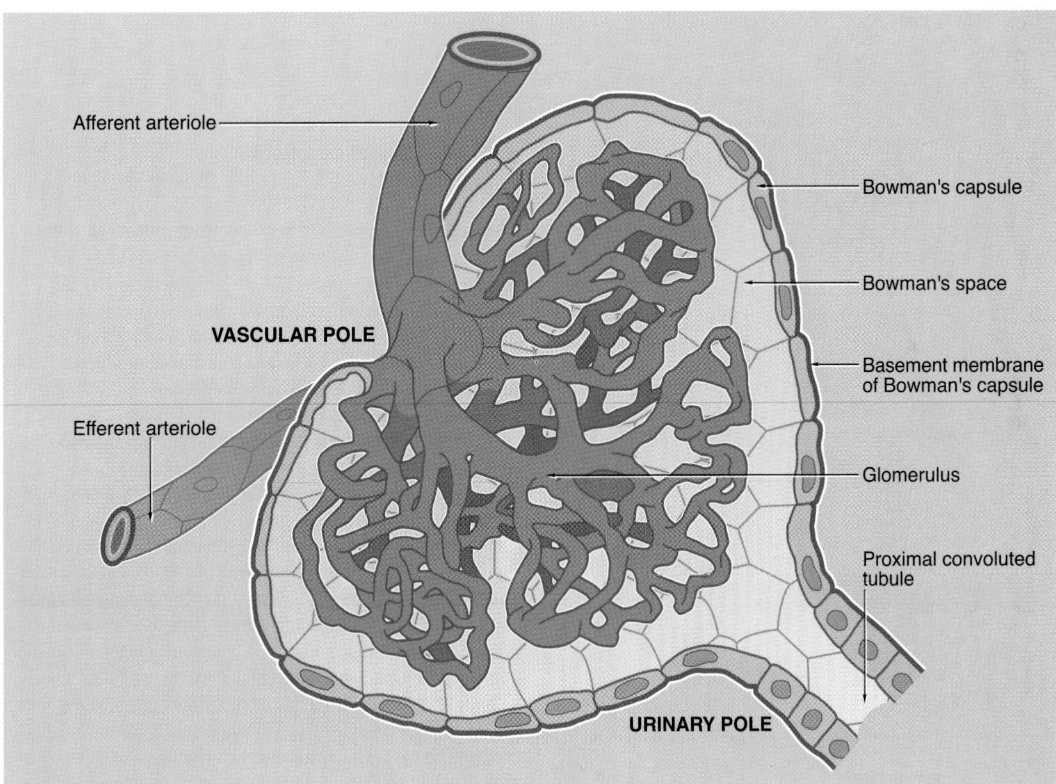

Fig. 16.7 Renal corpuscle

The main structural features of the renal corpuscle are demonstrated in this diagram.

The relatively wide diameter afferent arteriole enters Bowman's capsule at the vascular pole of the renal corpuscle and then branches to form an anastomosing network of glomerular capillaries, each major branch giving rise to a ***lobule***. The glomerulus is thus suspended in Bowman's space from the vascular pole. Although not shown in this diagram, the spaces between the capillary loops in each glomerular lobule are filled by basement membrane-like material called ***mesangium***, which contains ***mesangial cells***.

The efferent vessel draining the glomerulus is unusual in that it has the structure of an arteriole and is thus called the efferent arteriole (rather than the efferent venule). The efferent arteriole is of smaller diameter than the afferent arteriole and a pressure gradient is thus maintained that drives the filtration of plasma into Bowman's space.

The layer of podocytes investing the glomerular capillaries (visceral layer of Bowman's capsule) is not shown in this diagram. At the vascular pole, the podocyte layer is reflected to become continuous with the epithelium of Bowman's capsule proper, which in turn becomes continuous with the first part of the renal tubule, the proximal convoluted tubule.

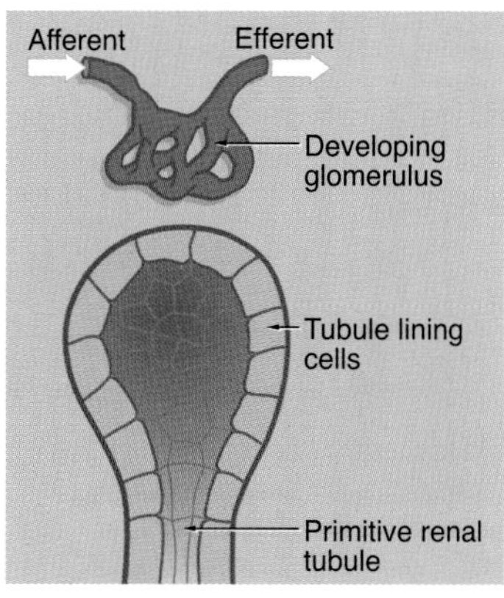

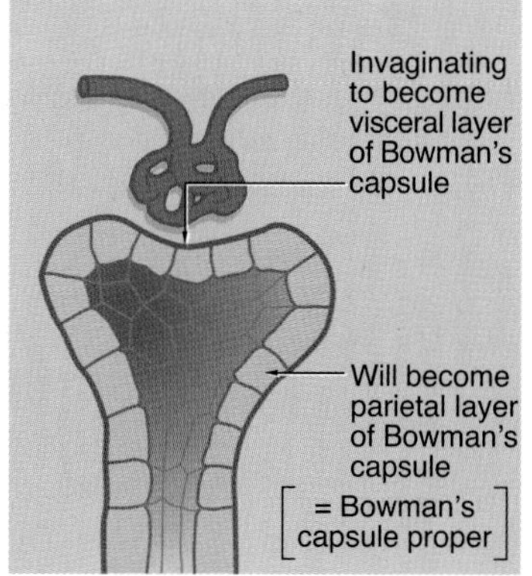

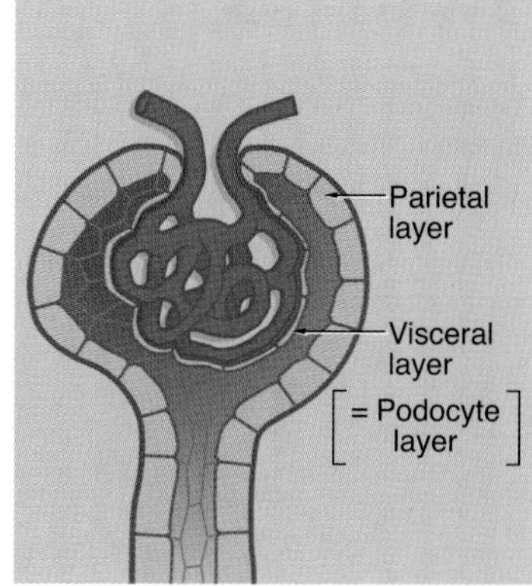

Fig. 16.8 Development of the renal corpuscle

The three dimensional structure of the renal corpuscle can be clarified by studying its development. The renal tubules develop from the embryological ***metanephros*** as blind-ended tubes consisting of a single layer of cuboidal epithelium. The ends of the tubules dilate and become invaginated by a tiny mass of mesoderm tissue that differentiates to form the glomerulus. The layer of invaginated epithelium flattens and differentiates into podocytes that become closely applied to the outer surfaces of glomerular capillaries. Most of the intervening tissue disappears so that the basement membrane of glomerular endothelial cells and podocytes effectively fuse, forming the glomerular basement membrane. A small amount of tissue remains to support the capillary loops and differentiates to form the mesangium. Where the mesangium stretches between the capillary loops, its urinary surface is invested by podocyte cytoplasm with underlying basement membrane.

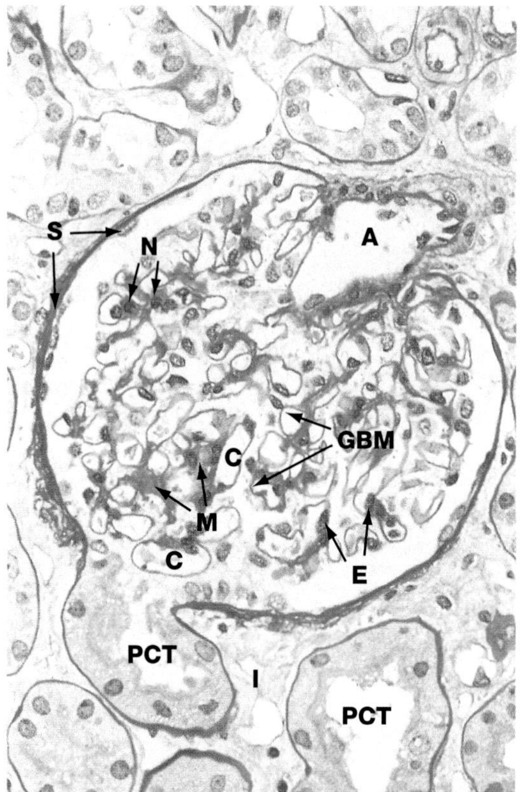

Fig. 16.9 Renal corpuscle
PAS ×300

This renal corpuscle has been sectioned through the vascular pole and shows the afferent arteriole **A** entering the glomerulus. The efferent arteriole is not seen in this plane of section. At the opposite pole (the urinary pole) the start of the proximal convoluted tubule **PCT** can be identified. Other proximal convoluted tubules can be seen cut in various planes of section embedded in the renal interstitium **I**. Glomerular capillaries **C** are cut in transverse, longitudinal and oblique sections. The numerous nuclei in the glomerulus are those of capillary endothelial cells, mesangial cells and podocytes.

The PAS stain picks out the glomerular basement membrane **GBM** and the mesangium **M** that consists of basement membrane-like material. Mesangial cells are found embedded within the mesangium but only their nuclei **N** can be discerned at this magnification. The capillary lumina are lined by endothelial cells **E**.

Note the flattened nuclei of the squamous cells **S** lining Bowman's capsule. This squamous epithelium is continuous with the epithelium of the proximal convoluted tubule and undergoes an abrupt transition to cuboidal form at the urinary pole.

A afferent arteriole **BC** Bowman's capsule **BS** Bowman's space **C** glomerular capillary **E** endothelial cell **GBM** glomerular basement membrane **I** interstitium **M** mesangium **N** mesangial cell nucleus **P** podocyte **PCT** proximal convoluted tubule **S** squamous cell

Glomerulonephritis

This glomerulus is from a patient with ***glomerulonephritis***. Compare this glomerulus with the normal one in Fig. 16.9. Note how the glomerulus seems full of cells and is virtually solid. The glomerular capillary loops are partially obstructed by a mixture of activated endothelial cells and mesangial cells. Less obvious with this staining method is the thickening of the glomerular basement membrane. This patient has the autoimmune disease ***systemic lupus erythematosus*** (***SLE***), and the histological changes in the glomerulus result from the deposition of immune complexes and the response of the intrinsic glomerular cells to these immune complexes. The immune complexes consist of antibodies and antigen, such as double stranded DNA, a normal body component. The clinical symptoms and signs of ***lupus nephritis*** include haematuria, proteinuria including nephrotic syndrome, hypertension and chronic renal failure.

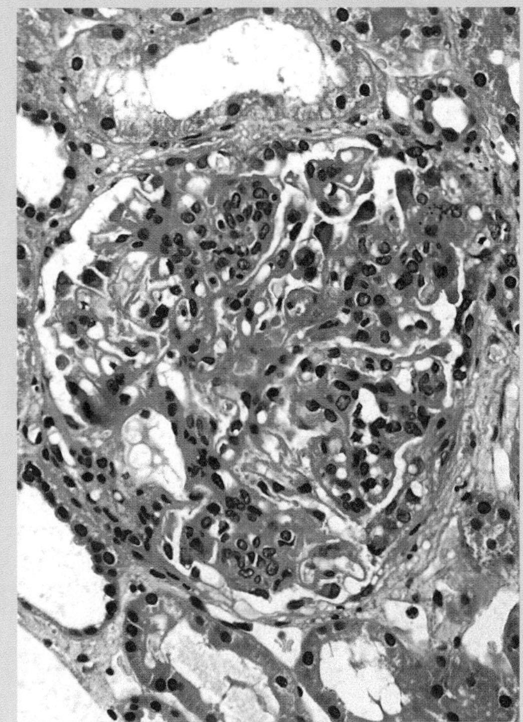

Fig. 16.10 Glomerulonephritis
H & E ×200

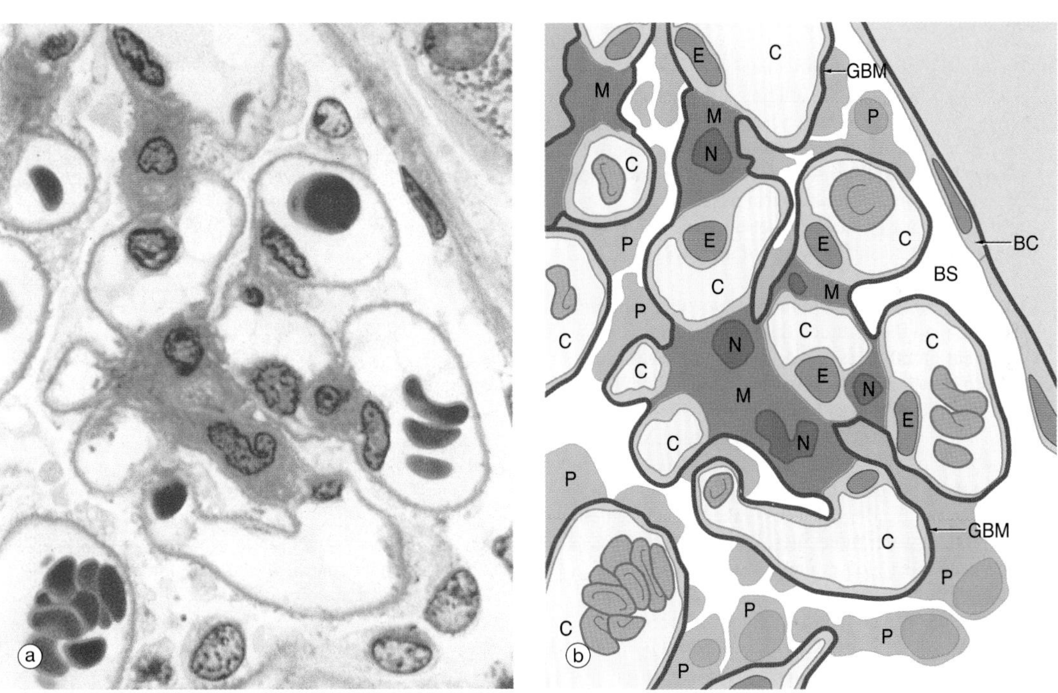

Fig. 16.11 Glomerulus
(a) Thin epoxy resin section, toluidine blue ×1200 (b) Explanatory diagram

Using resin-embedding techniques it is possible to cut thin sections (approximately 0.5–1.0 μm thick) which permit much greater resolution at high magnification.

In this preparation, the glomerular capillaries **C**, some of which contain erythrocytes, are defined by the prominent glomerular basement membranes **GBM**. Occasional capillary endothelial cell nuclei **E** are seen bulging into the capillary lumina. Mesangium **M** consists of material similar to basement membrane and contains mesangial cells, identifiable by their nuclei **N**. Mesangial cells, which are probably modified pericytes, are contractile and are thus able to modify the diameter of the glomerular capillaries in response to vasoactive substances, some of which they themselves produce. Thus mesangial cells have an important role in the control of glomerular function and of blood pressure. They also secrete the mesangial matrix and may have a phagocytic function. The mesangium is separated from the capillary lumen only by a thin layer of fenestrated endothelial cell cytoplasm, the basement membrane of which merges with the mesangial matrix. Thus particulate matter from blood may pass into the mesangium where it can be phagocytosed and degraded by mesangial cells. The podocytes and their basement membrane invest the outer surface of the mesangium.

Podocytes **P** also invest the capillary loops exposed to Bowman's space **BS**. The podocytes have extensive branching pale stained cytoplasm and large round pale stained nuclei. Note the nuclei of two squamous cells of Bowman's capsule **BC**.

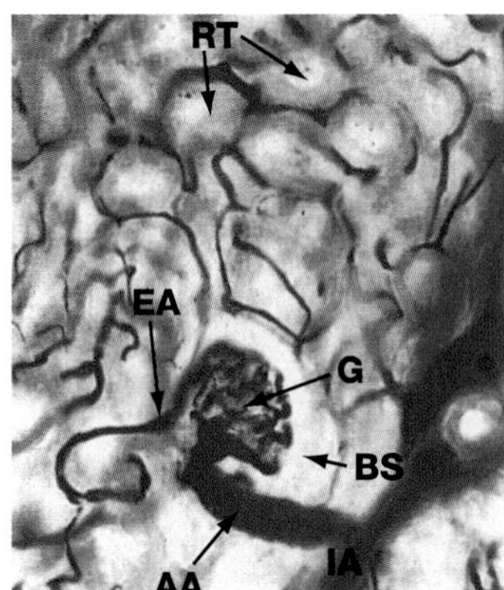

Fig. 16.12 Blood supply of the glomerulus
Carmine-gelatine perfused ×128

This section is from a kidney that has been perfused with a red dye in order to demonstrate the renal blood supply; the nephrons remain unstained.

An interlobular artery **IA** can be seen branching to form the afferent arteriole **AA** of a glomerulus **G**. The efferent arteriole **EA** leaving the glomerulus is of much smaller diameter than the afferent arteriole, an arrangement which maintains pressure within glomerular capillaries necessary for blood plasma to be filtered into Bowman's space **BS**. Blood pressure within the glomerulus is controlled by variation of the diameter of the afferent and efferent arterioles.

In the superficial and midcortex as shown here, efferent arterioles give rise to a network of capillaries which surround the renal tubules **RT**; towards the medulla, efferent arterioles give rise to the vasa recta. Molecules reabsorbed from glomerular filtrate are returned to the general circulation via this capillary network which drains into the renal venous system.

Fig. 16.13 The glomerular filter

During filtration of plasma from glomerular capillaries into the renal tubule, the filtrate passes through three layers: ***capillary endothelium***, ***glomerular basement membrane*** and the ***podocyte layer***. All contribute to the filtration process.

- The capillary endothelium contains numerous large round fenestrations (70–100 nm in diameter) which occupy about 20% of the endothelial surface area. In adults the fenestrations do not exhibit diaphragms as in fenestrated capillaries elsewhere in the body (see Fig. 8.16). Another unusual feature is that the luminal surface of the endothelium is negatively charged due to a surface layer of a glycoprotein called ***podocalyxin***.
- The glomerular basement membrane (approximately 350 nm in adults) is much thicker than other basement membranes and appears to be elaborated by both capillary endothelial cells and podocytes. As with basement membranes elsewhere (see Ch. 4), it consists of a feltwork of type IV collagen, structural glycoproteins (fibronectin and laminin) and proteoglycans rich in heparan sulphate, the interstices of this highly cross-linked structure being occupied by water molecules. By electron microscopy, the glomerular basement membrane consists of three layers, a dense central layer, the ***lamina densa***, with a thinner electron-lucent layer on either side of it, the ***lamina rara interna*** under the endothelium and the ***lamina rara externa*** supporting the podocytes. Both laminae rarae are negatively charged.
- The podocytes have long cytoplasmic extensions called ***primary processes*** that embrace the capillaries, giving rise to short ***secondary foot processes*** (***pedicels***), which interdigitate with those of other primary processes. The secondary foot processes are directly applied to the lamina rara externa and bound to it by fine filaments. The gaps between adjacent secondary foot processes known as ***filtration slits***, are of uniform width (40 nm) and are bridged by ***slit diaphragms***. The slit diaphragm is composed of a single layer of transmembrane protein, ***nephrin***, whose extracellular domains from adjacent foot processes link together rather in the manner of a zip. A layer of negatively charged podocalyxin covers the urinary surface of the podocytes including the slit diaphragms. The intracellular component of nephrin is bound to the actin cytoskeleton of the podocyte, and it has been suggested that the slit diaphragm is in fact a modified tight junction.

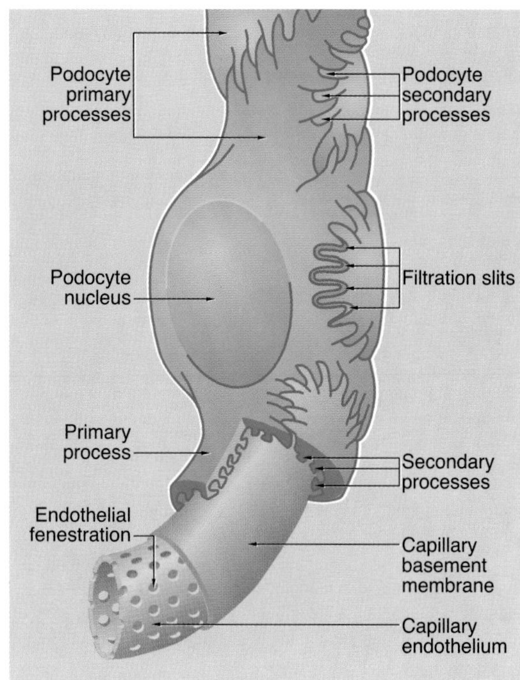

As mentioned at the outset, all layers contribute to the selective filtration barrier. Clinical evidence demonstrates that free haemoglobin (MW 65 000) and smaller molecules pass freely through the glomerular filter, whereas albumin (MW 68 000) and larger molecules are retained. For macromolecules, three factors determine permeability, namely electrical charge, size and configuration. Negatively charged (anionic) molecules are blocked by the negatively charged endothelial cell coat and laminae rarae of the basement membrane, while the meshwork of the lamina densa of the basement membrane discriminates on the basis of molecular size and configuration. The slit diaphragm restricts the passage of any large molecules but its main role is in controlling water flow which is also held back by the colloidal osmotic pressure of retained albumin and other large molecules.

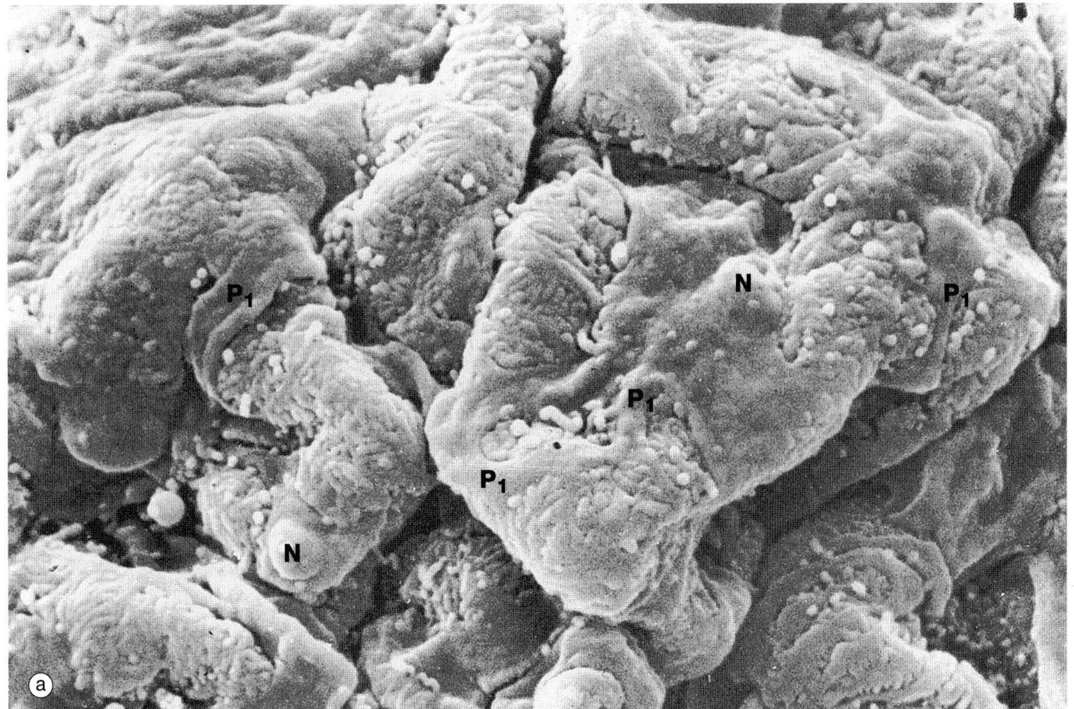

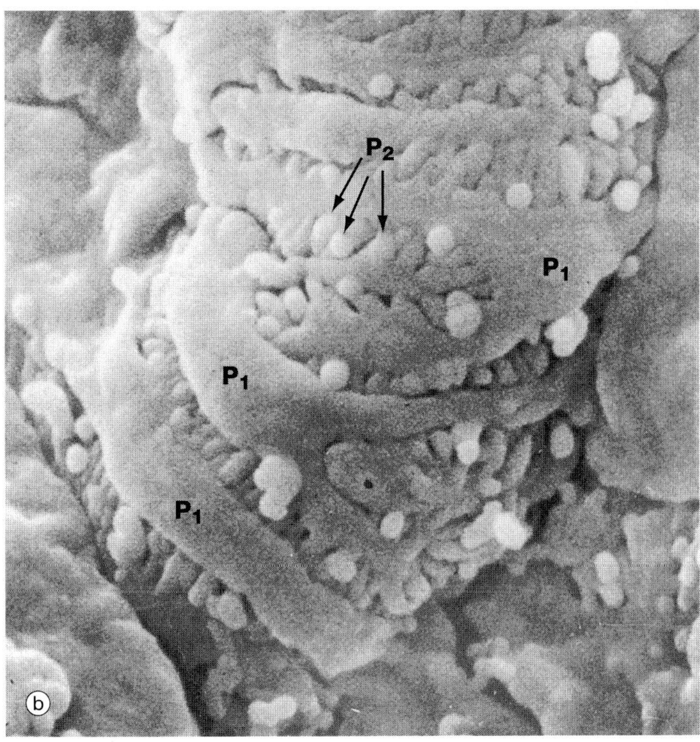

Fig. 16.14 Glomerulus SEM
(a) ×1500 (b) ×6000

Scanning electron microscopy readily demonstrates the three-dimensional relationships of podocytes and their processes that extend like octopus tentacles over the whole surface of the glomerulus.

Micrograph (a) shows part of a glomerular capillary tuft. The capillaries are enveloped by podocytes which have large flattened cell bodies and bulging nuclei **N**. Each podocyte has several long primary processes $\mathbf{P_1}$ that embrace one or more capillaries. Each primary process has numerous secondary ***foot processes*** (***pedicels***), which rest on the lamina rara externa of the glomerular basement membrane.

At higher magnification in micrograph (b), the secondary foot processes $\mathbf{P_2}$ can be seen as extensions of the large primary processes $\mathbf{P_1}$. The secondary foot processes interdigitate with those of other primary processes separated by filtration slits of uniform width.

AA afferent arteriole **BS** Bowman's space **EA** efferent arteriole **G** glomerulus
IA interlobular artery **N** nucleus $\mathbf{P_1}$ primary podocyte process $\mathbf{P_2}$ secondary podocyte process
RT renal tubules

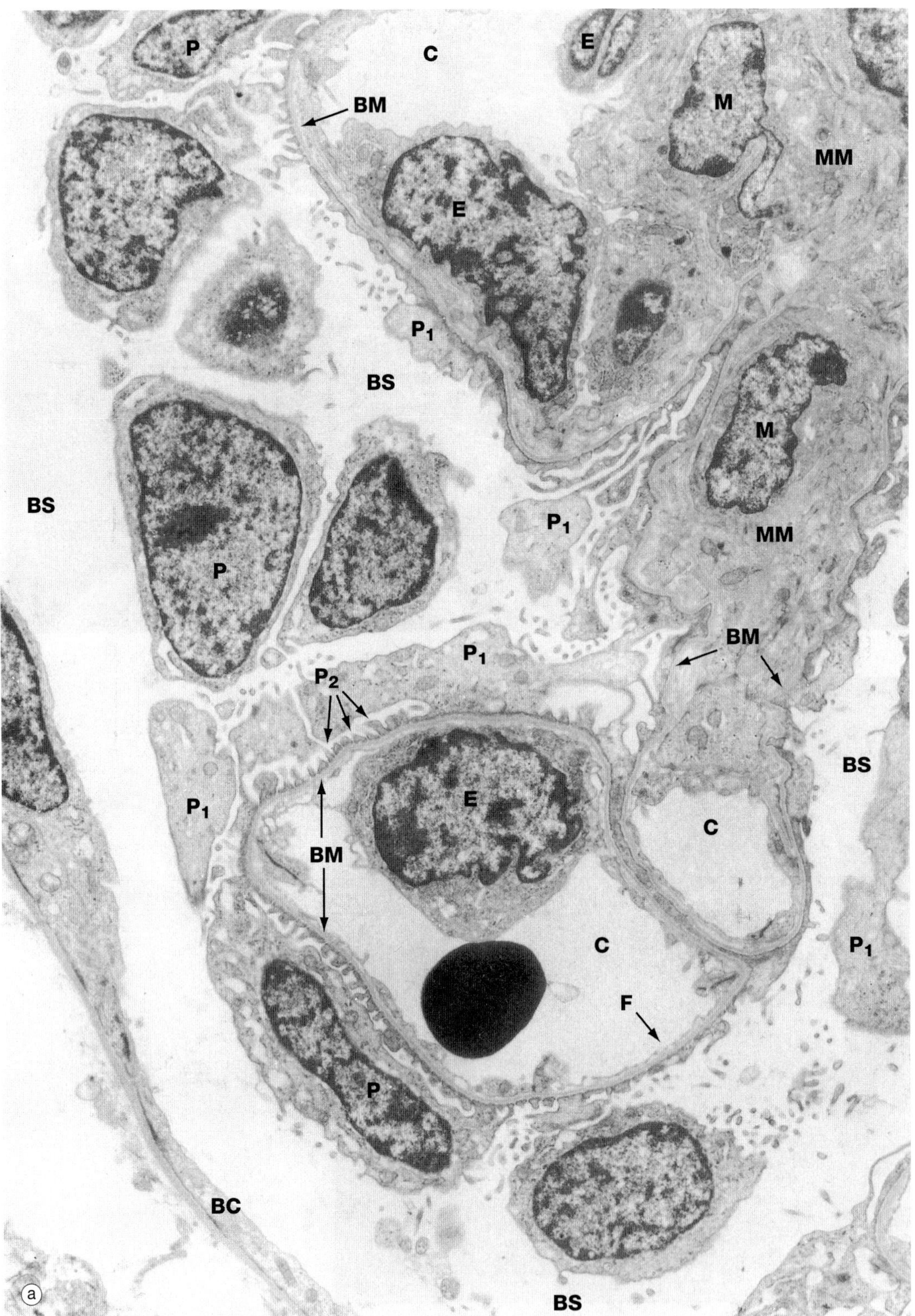
P
C
E
BM
M
MM
E
P1
BS
BS
P
P1
M
MM
BM
P1
P2
BS
P1
E
BM
C
C
P1
F
P
BC
BS
a

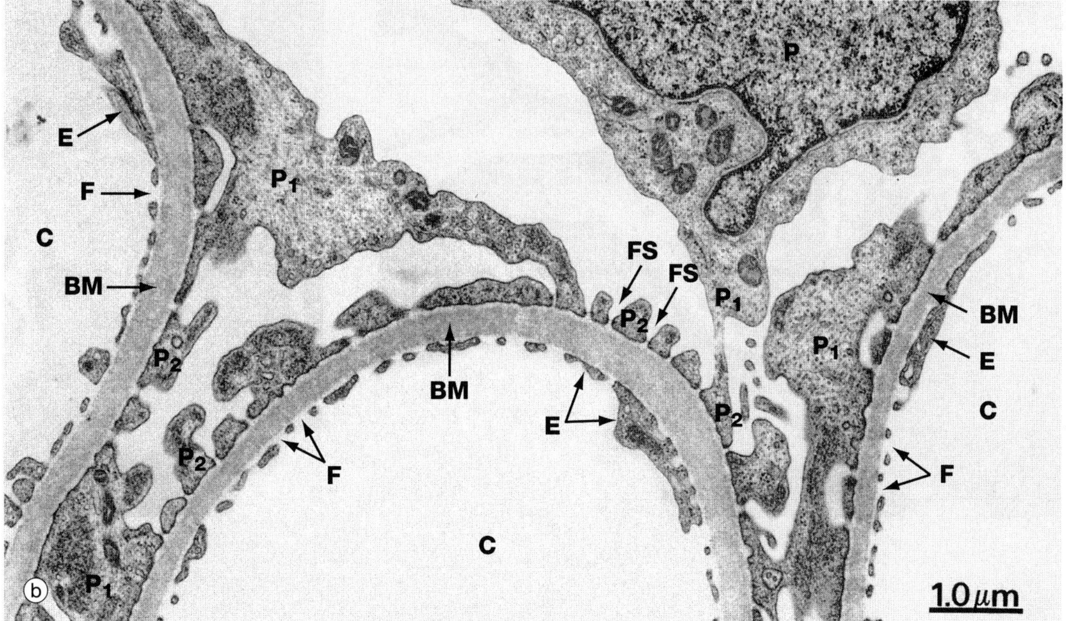

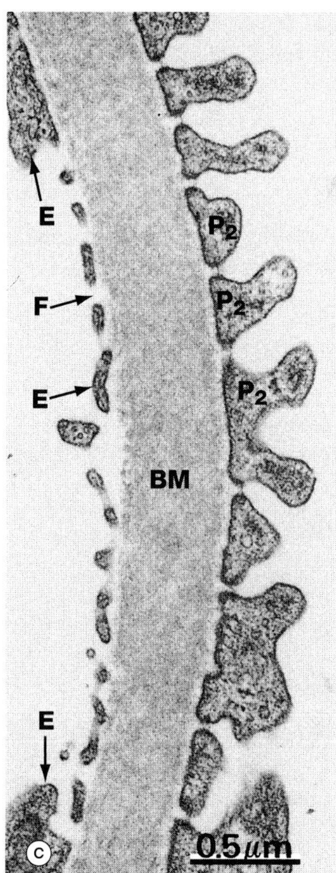

Fig. 16.15 Glomerulus
(a) EM ×4800 *(opposite)* (b) EM ×14 000 (c) EM ×30 000

When examining ultrathin light microscope specimens of glomeruli (e.g. Fig. 16.11) and electron micrographs the podocytes, endothelial cells and mesangium are identified most easily by tracing out the glomerular basement membrane. Micrograph (a) shows several capillary loops **C** lined by a thin layer of fenestrated endothelial cytoplasm. The endothelial cell nuclei **E** can be seen bulging into the capillary lumina. The capillary endothelial fenestrations **F** are better seen at higher magnification in micrographs (b) and (c). The nuclei of several podocytes **P** can be seen, their primary processes P_1 giving rise to numerous secondary foot processes P_2 that rest on the glomerular basement membrane **BM**. At right midfield a branched mesangial stalk comprising mesangial cells **M** and dense mesangial matrix **MM** provides support for the capillary loops. The mesangium is separated from the capillary lumen only by the cytoplasm of the endothelial cells, while the podocytes and their basement membrane continue around the mesangial stalk separating it from Bowman's space. Part of Bowman's capsule **BC** is seen at the periphery, consisting of a squamous epithelial cell and underlying basement membrane. Note the labyrinth of Bowman's space **BS** ramifying throughout the glomerulus.

Micrograph (b) shows three glomerular capillaries **C** lined by attenuated endothelial cytoplasm **E** with wide fenestrations **F**. A podocyte **P** extends several primary foot processes P_1 onto the capillaries, these in turn giving rise to multiple secondary foot processes P_2 separated by filtration slits **FS**. The glomerular basement membrane **BM** separates the podocytes and capillary endothelium. The thickness of the basement membrane appears variable but this is due to the slightly oblique plane of section; the basement membranes are in fact of uniform width.

With further magnification in micrograph (c), the three components of the glomerular filter are seen. The fenestrated capillary endothelium **E** is closely applied to the luminal surface of the glomerular basement membrane **BM**; on the opposite side are podocyte secondary foot processes P_2, separated by filtration slits of uniform width and bridged by the slit diaphragms. The wide central lamina densa of the glomerular basement membrane can be seen bordered on each side by a narrow lamina rara.

BC Bowman's capsule **BM** basement membrane **BS** Bowman's space **C** capillary loop
E endothelial cell **F** fenestrations **FS** filtration slit **M** mesangial cell **MM** mesangial matrix
P podocyte P_1 podocyte primary process P_2 podocyte secondary foot process

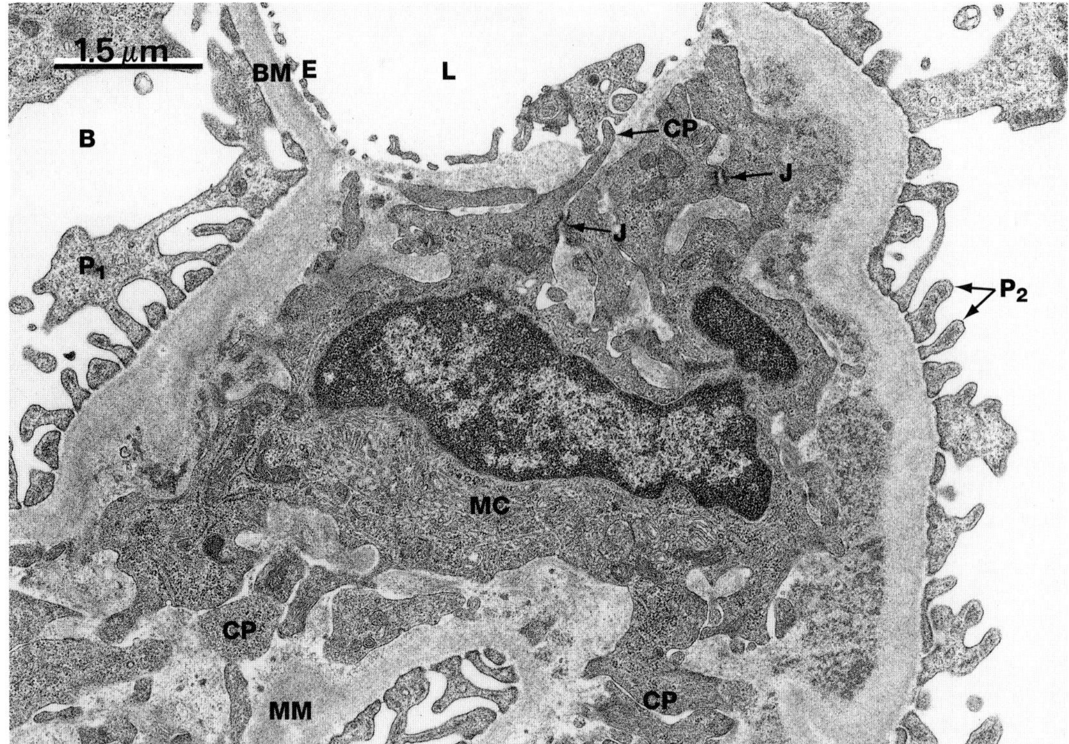

Fig. 16.16 The mesangium (rat)
EM ×14 000

This electron micrograph shows an area of mesangium along with part of a glomerular capillary lumen **L** and part of Bowman's space **B**. The capillary lumen is lined by the delicate fenestrated endothelium **E**. Podocyte primary processes $\mathbf{P_1}$ and secondary foot processes $\mathbf{P_2}$ are easily seen. The mesangium is composed of basement membrane-like material **MM** within which is embedded a mesangial cell **MC**. Mesangial cells have long cytoplasmic processes **CP** that ramify through the mesangium and form cell junctions with the processes of other mesangial cells. Several of these cell junctions **J** can be seen in this field. Thus the mesangial cells form a network supporting the glomerular capillaries. One function of mesangial cells is the secretion of mesangial matrix; they also secrete vasoactive and other factors and phagocytose particles, such as immune complexes, from the blood.

This micrograph demonstrates the close relationship between the mesangial and endothelial cells. These are not separated from each other by a basement membrane and in fact lie within the same basement membrane-bound compartment. Conceptually it might be helpful to consider the mesangium as a modified segment of the glomerular capillary wall. Also in this electron micrograph the morphological difference between the glomerular basement membrane **BM** and the mesangial matrix **MM** is apparent; this reflects the differences in chemical composition between the two.

Diabetic renal disease

Diabetic nephropathy is the most common cause of renal failure in affluent countries. The incidence of type 2 diabetes is increasing, an increase that is felt to be largely due to changing lifestyles with increasing obesity and decreasing exercise although there is little doubt that genetic factors are also important. Usually one of the earliest signs of diabetic nephropathy is proteinuria, which may eventually progress to the nephrotic syndrome and progressive chronic renal failure. The microscopic features in these cases include thickening of the mesangial basement membrane and an increase in mesangial matrix, often called ***diabetic glomerulosclerosis***. Recent research is beginning to tease out the mechanisms underlying these clinical features, including chemical mediators such as transforming growth factor β that induce increased deposition of mesangial matrix in response to high glucose concentrations. However, other factors, including direct podocyte injury and changes in the slit pore membrane, also contribute to the characteristic proteinuria that precedes frank renal failure.

Diabetics also tend to suffer from vascular disease, hypertension and increased infections in the kidney and all of these tend to contribute to the downward spiral towards end stage renal failure.

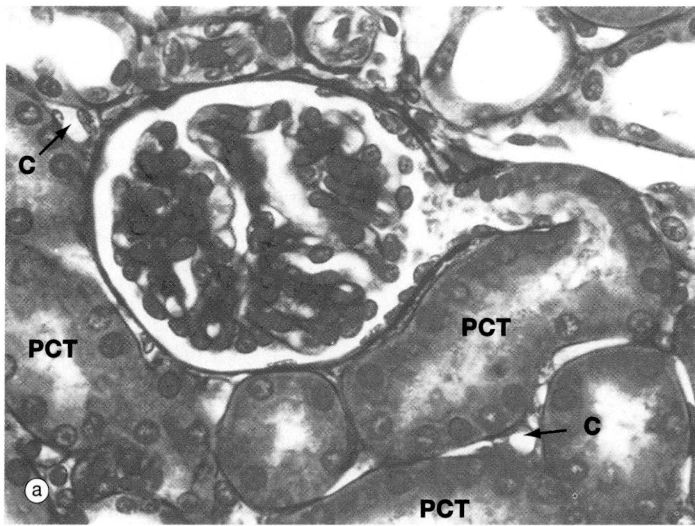

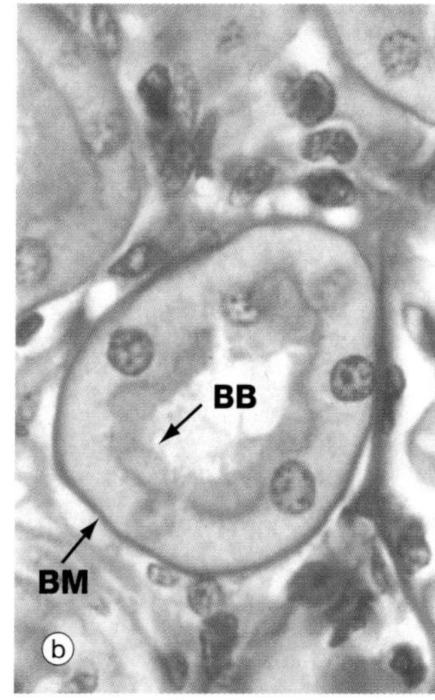

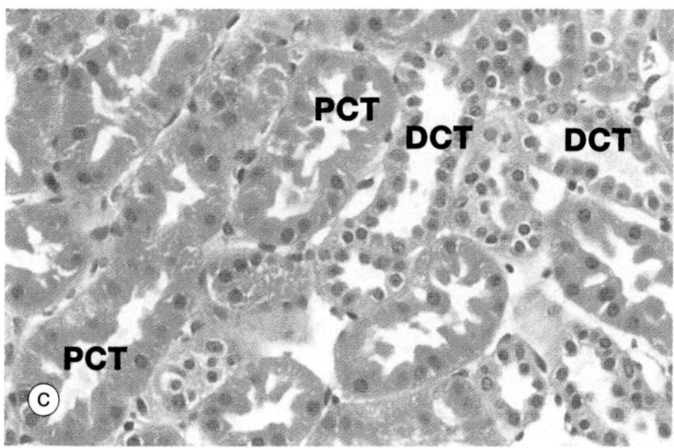

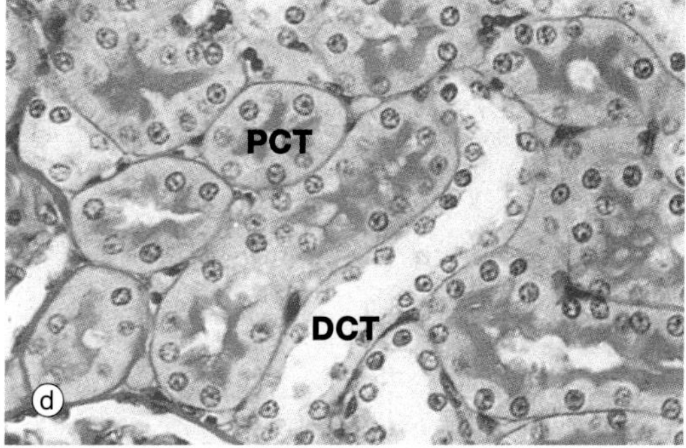

Fig. 16.17 Proximal and distal convoluted tubules
(a) PCT Azan ×480 (b) PCT PAS/haematoxylin ×800 (c) DCT H & E ×200 (d) DCT PAS/haematoxylin ×480

These micrographs compare the appearances of the proximal and distal convoluted tubules. The intervening loop of Henle is discussed in Fig. 16.20. The proximal convoluted tubule (PCT) is a coiled tube measuring approximately 14mm in length and random sections of PCT thus occupy most of the renal cortex. Approximately 65% of the glomerular filtrate is reabsorbed from the PCT, a function reflected in the structure of the epithelial lining.

Micrograph (a) shows a proximal convoluted tubule **PCT** arising from a renal corpuscle; convolutions of the PCT are also seen in longitudinal, oblique and transverse sections. The simple cuboidal epithelium has a prominent blue stained brush border of tall microvilli, increasing the surface area of the plasma membrane some 20-fold. The cytoplasm of PCT epithelial cells stains intensely due to a high content of organelles, principally mitochondria. Basement membranes stain blue by this technique thus highlighting the tubular and glomerular basement membranes and that of Bowman's capsule.

The PAS staining method has been used in micrograph (b) to demonstrate the prominent brush border **BB** projecting into the lumen of the PCT. The brush border is PAS-positive since the surfaces of the microvilli are coated with a prominent glycocalyx (see Fig. 1.2). Like those elsewhere, the basement membrane **BM** supporting the tubular epithelium is strongly PAS-positive. In both micrographs, note that the epithelial cells of the PCT have round nuclei with prominent nucleoli.

A rich network of capillaries **C** arising from the efferent arteriole of the glomerulus (see Fig. 16.12) surrounds the proximal tubules and returns molecules reabsorbed from the glomerular filtrate back into the general circulation.

The distal tubule is a continuation of the thick ascending limb of the loop of Henle after its return to the cortex and forms the third segment of the renal tubule. Distal tubules are thus found within the cortex among the proximal convoluted tubules. The first part of the distal tubule forms the macula densa (see Fig. 16.19) while the remainder makes up the distal convoluted tubule (DCT).

In the DCT sodium ions are reabsorbed from the tubular fluid with one hydrogen or potassium ion being secreted in exchange. This adjustment of acid–base balance is controlled by the hormone ***aldosterone*** secreted by the adrenal cortex.

As seen in micrograph (c), distal convoluted tubules **DCT** may be differentiated from proximal convoluted tubules **PCT** by the absence of a brush border, a larger more clearly defined lumen, more nuclei per cross-section (since DCT cells are smaller than PCT cells) and paler cytoplasm (due to fewer organelles). In addition, sections of DCT are less numerous than sections of PCT since the DCT is much shorter than the PCT. In micrograph (d) the prominent brush border of the PCT is contrasted with the lack of brush border in the DCT.

B Bowman's space **BB** brush border **BM** basement membrane **C** peritubular capillaries
CP mesangial cell cytoplasmic processes **DCT** distal convoluted tubule **E** endothelial cell
J cell junction **L** glomerular capillary lumen **PCT** proximal convoluted tubule **MC** mesangial cell
MM mesangial matrix **P_1** podocyte primary process **P_2** podocyte secondary foot process

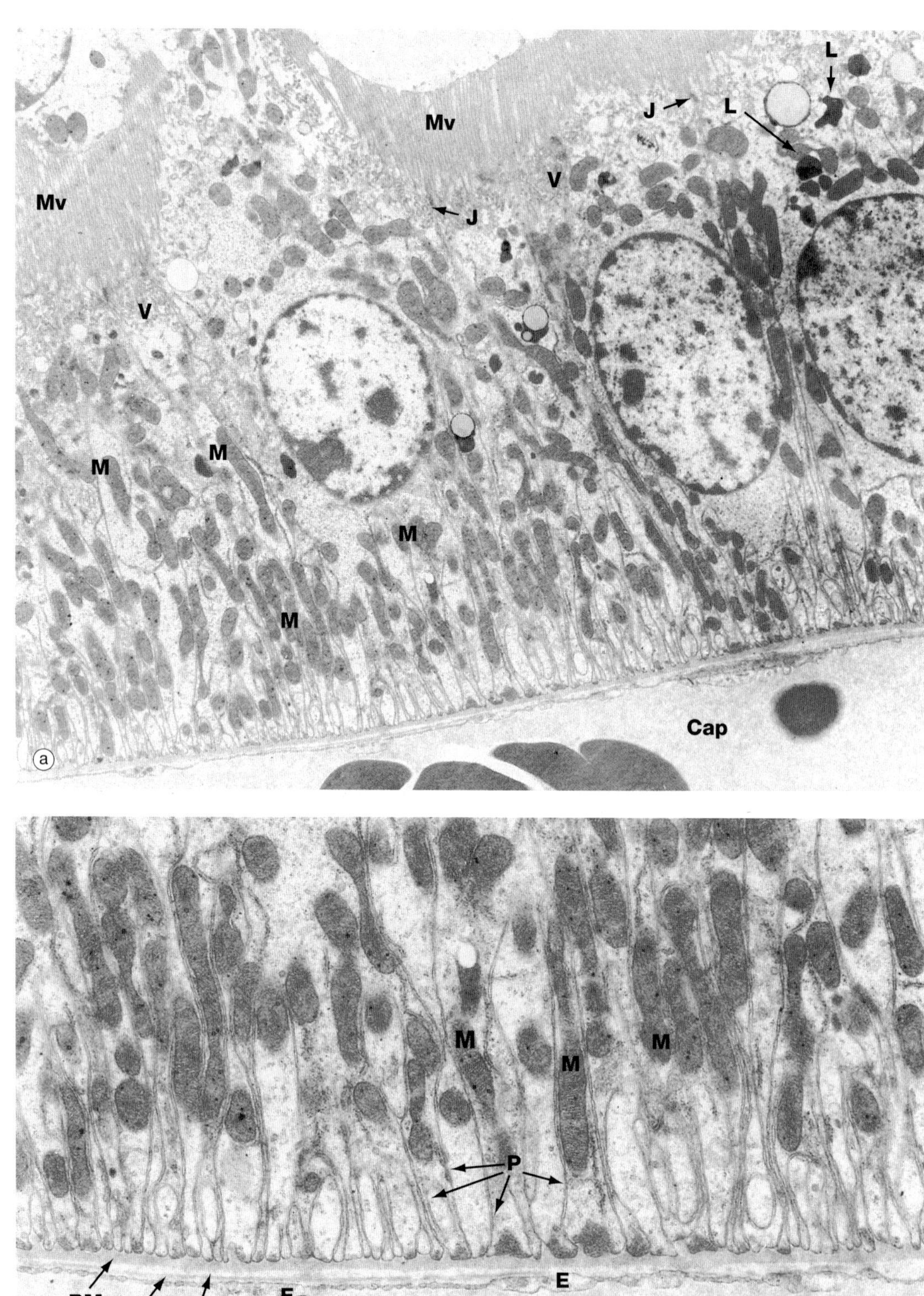

BM basement membrane **BM$_E$** basement membrane of endothelium **Cap** capillary **E** endothelium **J** junctional complex **L** lysosome **M** mitochondrion **Mv** microvilli **P** cell processes **S** supporting tissue **V** pinocytotic vesicle

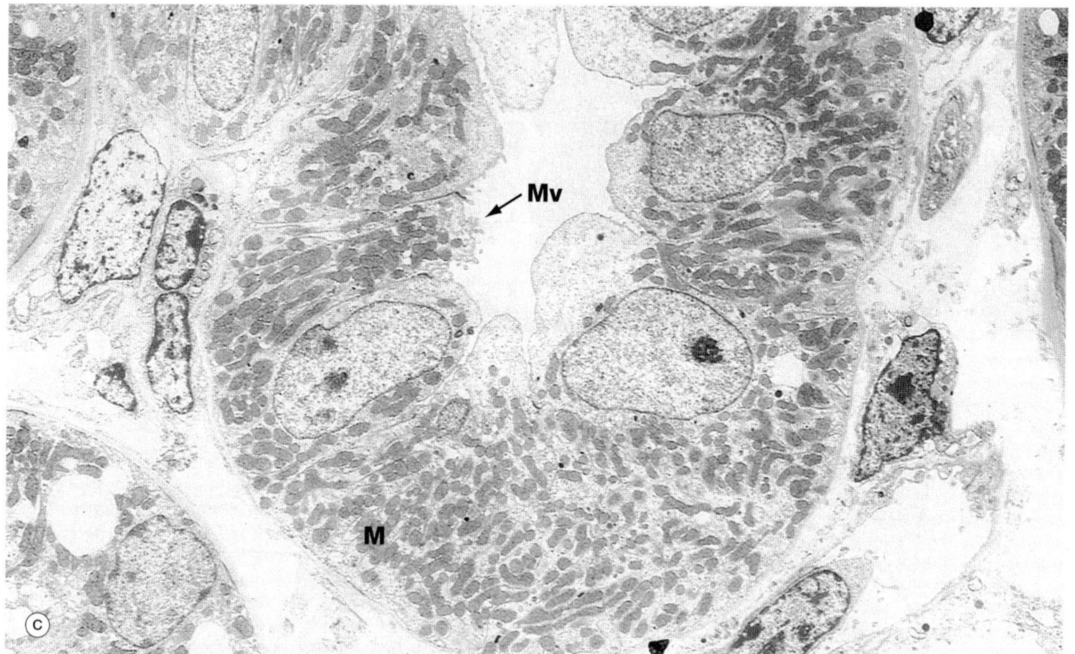

Fig. 16.18 Proximal and distal convoluted tubules
(a) PCT EM ×10 000 *(opposite above)*, (b) PCT EM ×19 000 *(opposite below)* (c) DCT EM ×5000

These electron micrographs compare the ultrastructure of the proximal and distal convoluted tubules. Micrograph (a) of the proximal tubule reveals profuse tall microvilli **Mv** constituting the brush border seen with light microscopy. The cytoplasm immediately beneath the brush border contains many pinocytotic vesicles **V** (that are just visible at this magnification) and lysosomes **L** both of which are involved in reabsorption and degradation of small amounts of protein that have leaked through the glomerular filter. Reabsorbed solutes are transported into surrounding capillaries **Cap** with attenuated endothelium **E** resting on a very thin basement membrane $\mathbf{BM_E}$; note the narrow intervening supporting tissue layer **S** in micrograph (b).

The epithelial cells of the PCT form multiple lateral processes **P** (micrograph (b)) which interdigitate with each other to form a complex ***lateral intercellular space***, with a plasma membrane area equivalent to the luminal plasma membrane. The lateral intercellular space is separated from the lumen of the PCT by a ring of junctional complexes **J** near the luminal surface. The mitochondria **M** in these processes are elongated and arranged at right angles to the basement membrane **BM**. These mitochondria supply ATP for the active transport of Na^+ by the Na^+-K^+ ATPase (sodium pump) located in the basolateral plasma membrane. Thus active transport of Na^+ occurs across the plasma membrane into the lateral intercellular space. This active transport of Na^+ out of the cell is accompanied by facilitated transport into the cells of Na^+, glucose and amino acids by means of transport proteins found in the membrane of the brush border. Almost 100% of the filtered glucose and amino acids is reabsorbed by the PCT.

The distal convoluted tubule (c) has many ultrastructural features in common with the proximal convoluted tubule, in particular the lateral cell interdigitations, and large numbers of mitochondria **M**. The basolateral plasma membrane contains the Na^+-K^+ ATPase which drives active transport of Na^+ ions. The most striking difference is that the DCT lacks a brush border, having only a few irregular microvilli **Mv** at the luminal surface. The DCT cells have less cytoplasm than those of the PCT although the nucleus is of about the same size and consequently occupies much more of the cell. The nuclei of the DCT cells lie close to the luminal surface and tend to bulge into the lumen; the overlying cytoplasm is devoid of mitochondria but contains large numbers of tiny pinocytotic vesicles (not seen at this magnification).

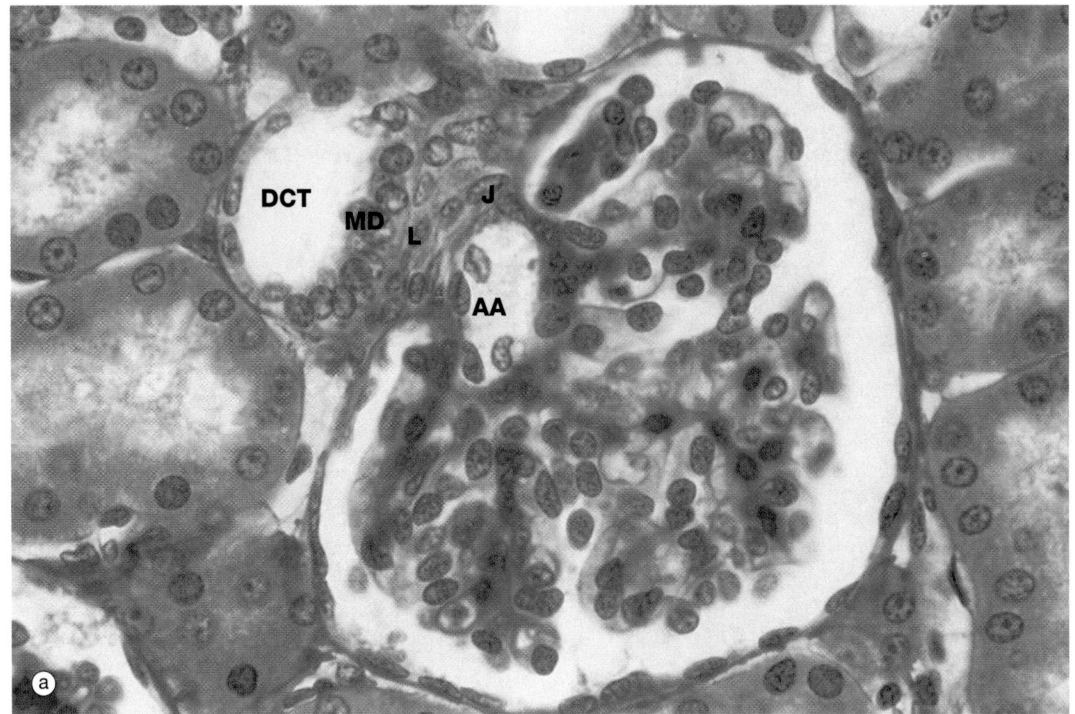

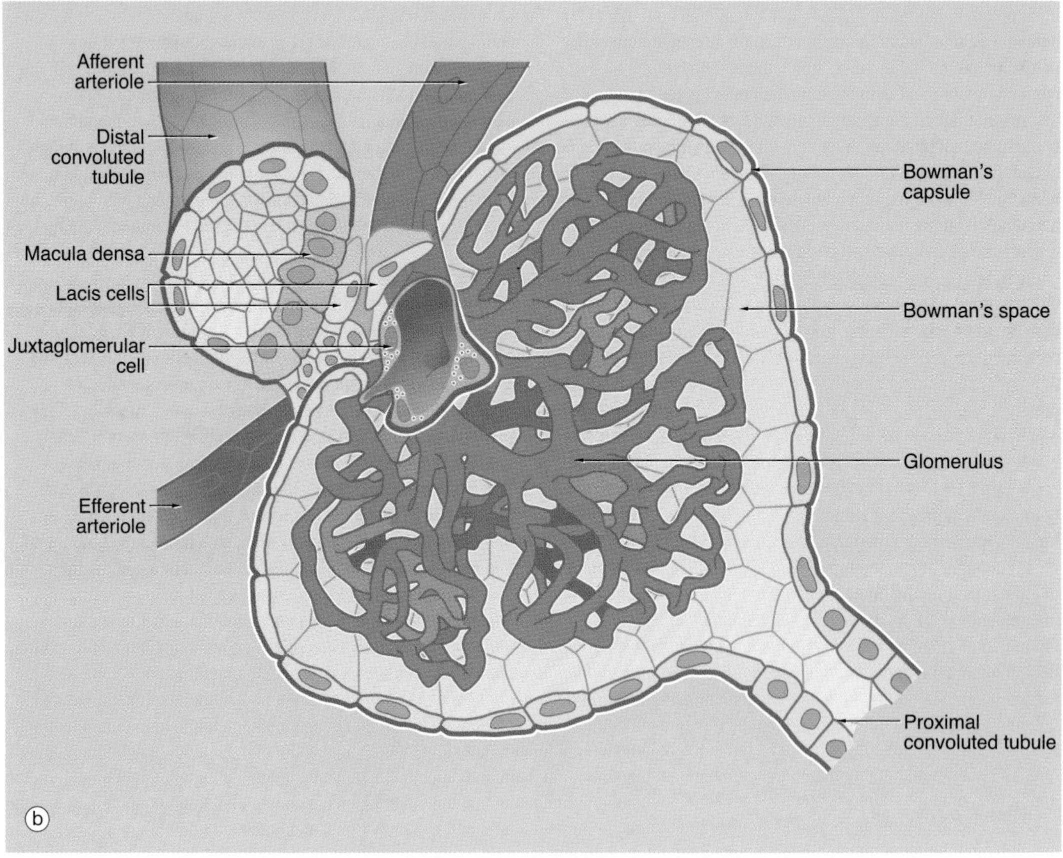

AA afferent arteriole **DCT** distal convoluted tubule **J** juxtaglomerular cells **L** lacis cells **MD** macula densa

Fig. 16.19 Juxtaglomerular apparatus
(a) Azan ×640 *(opposite above)* (b) Explanatory diagram *(opposite below)* (c) Blood pressure control system *(below left)*

The ***juxtaglomerular apparatus*** (***JGA***) is a specialisation of the glomerular afferent arteriole **AA** and the distal convoluted tubule **DCT** of the same nephron and is involved in the regulation of systemic blood pressure via the ***renin-angiotensin-aldosterone mechanism***.

The juxtaglomerular apparatus is made up of three components: the ***macula densa*** of the DCT, renin-secreting ***juxtaglomerular cells*** of the afferent arteriole and ***extraglomerular mesangial cells***.

Macula densa. On returning to the cortex from the renal medulla, the ascending thick limb of the loop of Henle becomes the first part of the distal tubule and comes to lie in the angle between the afferent and efferent arterioles at the vascular pole of the glomerulus. The macula densa **MD** is an area of closely packed, specialised DCT epithelial cells where the DCT abuts the vascular pole of the glomerulus. Compared with other DCT lining cells, the cells of the macula densa are taller and have larger more prominent nuclei situated towards the luminal surface. Mitochondria are scattered throughout the cytoplasm and Na^+ pump activity is absent. The basement membrane between the macula and underlying cells is extremely thin.

The cells of the macula densa are thought to be sensitive to the concentration of sodium ions in the fluid within the DCT; a decrease in systemic blood pressure results in decreased production of glomerular filtrate and hence decreased concentration of sodium ions in the distal tubular fluid.

Juxtaglomerular cells. Juxtaglomerular cells **J** are modified smooth muscle cells of the wall of the afferent arteriole forming a cluster around it just before it enters the glomerulus. Juxtaglomerular cell cytoplasm contains immature and mature membrane-bound granules of the enzyme ***renin***.

Extraglomerular mesangial cells. Also called ***Goormaghtigh cells*** or ***lacis cells*** **L**, these cells form a conical mass, the apex of which is continuous with the mesangium of the glomerulus; laterally it is bounded by the afferent and efferent arterioles and its base abuts the macula densa. The lacis cells are flat and elongated with extensive fine cytoplasmic processes extending from their ends and surrounded by a network ('lacis') of mesangial material. Despite their central location in the JGA, the function of the extraglomerular mesangial cells is not yet clear. The current theory is that these cells participate in the ***tubuloglomerular feedback mechanism*** by which changes in Na^+ concentration at the macula densa give rise to signals that directly control glomerular blood flow. The extraglomerular mesangial cells are thought to be responsible for transmission of a signal arising in the macula densa to the intraglomerular mesangial cells which then contract or relax to make the capillary loops narrower or wider.

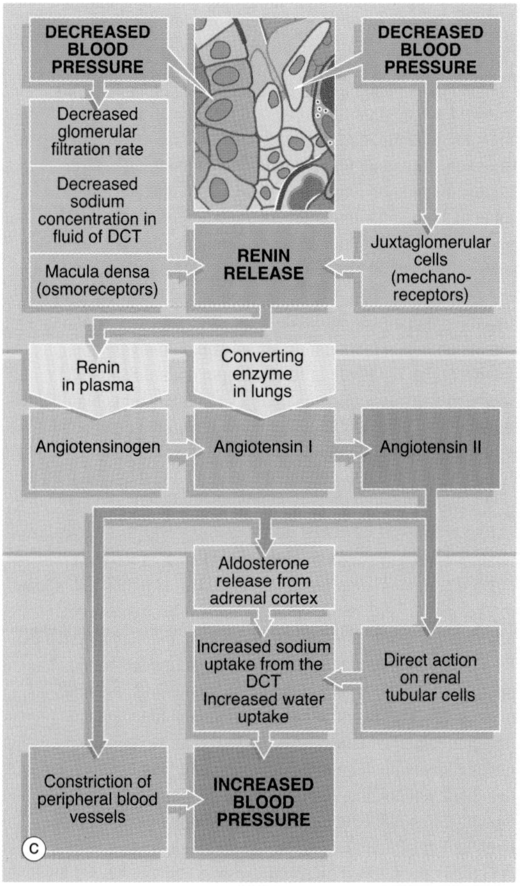

Role of the JGA in the control of blood pressure

The juxtaglomerular apparatus is believed to act as both a baroreceptor and a chemoreceptor; controlling systemic blood pressure by the secretion of renin by the juxtaglomerular cells.

The juxtaglomerular cells are suitably placed to monitor systemic blood pressure, with a fall in blood pressure resulting in renin secretion. Reduction in blood pressure results in reduced glomerular filtration and consequently a lower concentration of sodium ions in the DCT. Acting as chemoreceptors, the cells of the macula densa in some way then promote renin secretion.

Renin diffuses into the bloodstream catalysing the conversion of ***angiotensinogen***, an alpha$_2$-globulin synthesised by the liver, into the decapeptide ***angiotensin I***. In the lungs, ***angiotensin converting enzyme*** (***ACE***) cleaves two amino acids from angiotensin I to form ***angiotensin II*** which is a potent vasoconstrictor.

Angiotensin II raises blood pressure in three ways: constriction of peripheral blood vessels, release of aldosterone from the adrenal cortex and via a direct effect on the renal tubules where it promotes the reabsorption of sodium ions (and therefore water) from the DCT, thus expanding the plasma volume and increasing blood pressure.

As mentioned above, the tubuloglomerular feedback mechanism is also thought to operate at a local level to control glomerular blood flow and therefore indirectly systemic blood pressure.

The renal medulla

The renal medulla consists of closely packed tubules of two types: the loop of Henle and the collecting tubules and ducts as well as the vasa recta. The loop of Henle is a continuation of the proximal convoluted tubule. It dips down into the medulla, where it loops back on itself and returns to the cortex to it's own renal corpuscle, becoming the first part of the distal convoluted tubule.

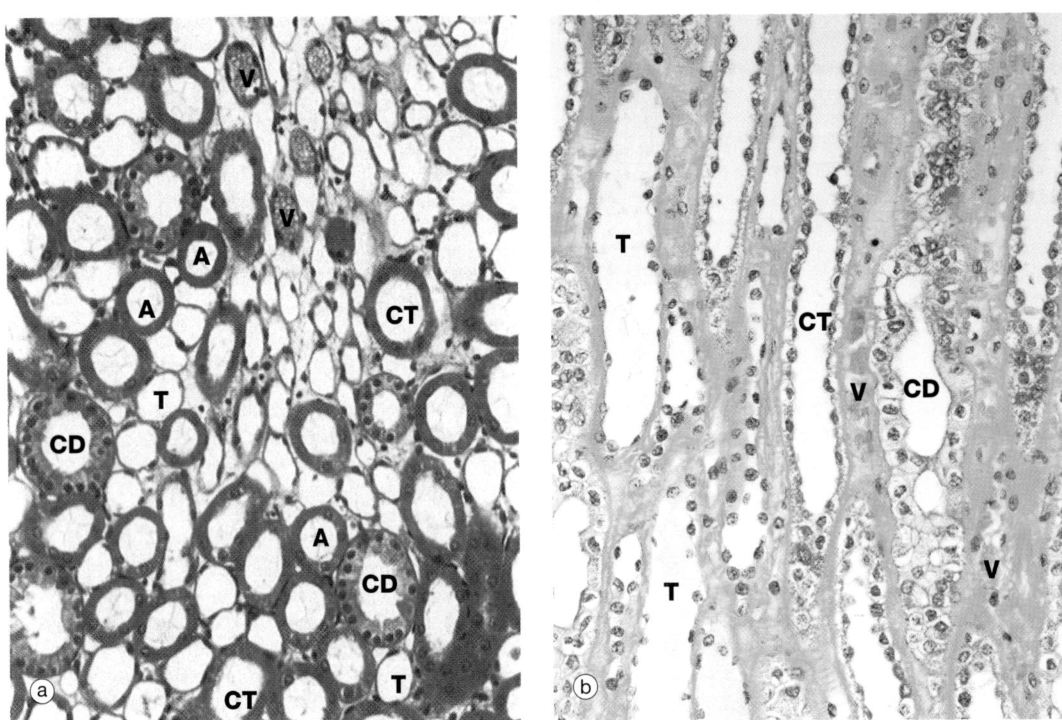

Fig. 16.20 Loop of Henle
(a) H & E, TS ×198 (b) EMSB, LS ×200

The loop of Henle is made up of four parts:

- **The thick descending limb (pars recta of the PCT).**
- **The thin descending limb.**
- **The thin ascending limb.**
- **The thick ascending limb (pars recta of the DCT).**

The thick descending limb is the second, straight part of the proximal tubule that extends down into the outer medulla. There is an abrupt transition to the thin descending limb, which loops down into the medulla for a variable distance. The thin limbs of juxtamedullary nephrons extend down to the inner medulla before turning back on themselves, while those in the outer cortex only extend a short way into the medulla. After the hairpin bend, the tubule becomes the thin ascending limb for a short distance before abruptly changing into the thick ascending limb. Thus the thin descending limb is longer than the thin ascending limb.

The thin limbs **T** have a simple squamous epithelium and may be differentiated from the vasa recta **V** by the absence of erythrocytes and their regular rounded shape in transverse section. Erythrocytes, stained orange by this staining method, are easily seen in the vasa recta in micrograph (b). The thick ascending limbs **A** are lined by low cuboidal epithelium and are also round in cross-section. Neither thick nor thin limbs of the loop of Henle have a brush border. Collecting tubules **CT** have a similar epithelial lining to the ascending limbs but are wider and less regular in shape. The collecting ducts **CD** are easily recognised by their large diameter and pale stained columnar epithelial lining.

The function of the loop of Henle is to produce an increasing osmotic gradient from the cortex to the tip of the renal papilla by the ***counter-current multiplier mechanism*** (see Fig. 16.23). In brief, the parts of the loop of Henle with a thick (cuboidal) epithelium participate in active transport of various ions and molecules out of the lumen and into the interstitium. On the other hand, the thin limbs are lined by a flattened squamous epithelium with little capacity for active transport. The thin descending limb allows free diffusion of H_2O but is fairly impermeable to NaCl, while the thin ascending limb is permeable to NaCl but not to H_2O. The vasa recta take up water from the medullary interstitium and return it to the general circulation.

As the urine flows into the thick ascending limb, active transport of NaCl again occurs and this correlates with the appearances of the epithelium. Here the cuboidal epithelium exhibits basolateral processes that interdigitate with each other forming an extensive basolateral intercellular space in a similar manner to the PCT. This active transport process is fuelled by ATP produced by the many mitochondria found in these processes. The thick ascending limb is also impermeable to water. Tamm–Horsfall protein is a unique glycoprotein produced only by the epithelium of the thick ascending limb. The function of Tamm–Horsfall protein is unknown but various roles such as regulation of blood pressure or prevention of crystallisation have been suggested.

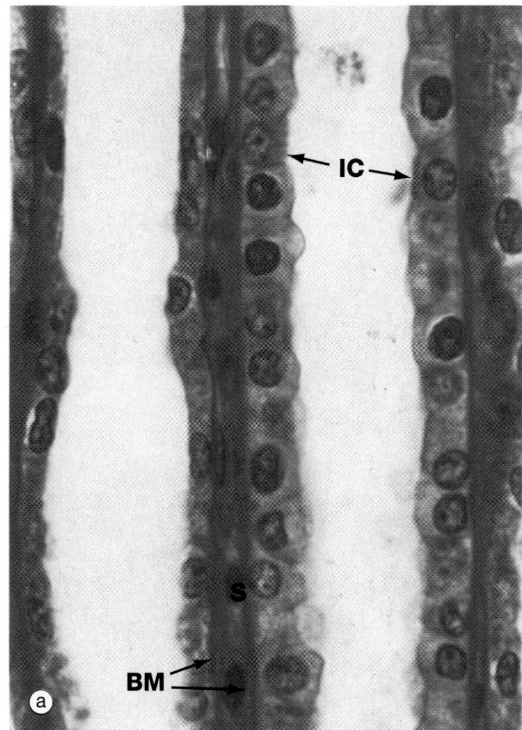

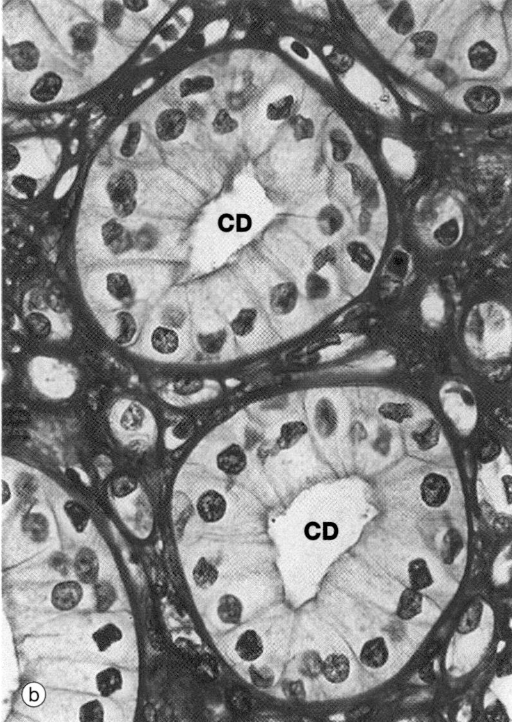

Fig. 16.21 Collecting tubules and ducts
(a) Azan ×750 (b) Azan ×480

The ***collecting tubule***, or ***connecting segment***, joins the distal convoluted tubule to the collecting duct. Several collecting tubules merge to form each collecting duct. The collecting tubules and ducts descend in the medullary rays (see Fig. 16.5) towards the renal medulla where they progressively merge to form the large ducts of Bellini which drain urine from the tip of the renal papilla into the pelvicalyceal system.

The collecting tubules and ducts concentrate urine by passive reabsorption of water into the medullary interstitium following the osmotic gradient created by the counter-current multiplier system of the loops of Henle (see Fig. 16.23). The vasa recta return this water to the general circulation. The amount of water reabsorbed is controlled by ***antidiuretic hormone*** (***ADH***, ***vasopressin***) secreted by the posterior pituitary in response to dehydration. ADH acts by increasing the permeability to water of the collecting tubule and ducts, resulting in retention of water by the body and the production of hypertonic urine. Conversely, ADH secretion is inhibited by water overload and an increased volume of hypotonic urine is thus produced. The collecting tubules and ducts are also the site of H^+ secretion and therefore important in the maintenance of acid–base balance.

The simple low columnar epithelium of the collecting ducts consists of two cell types, ***principal cells*** and ***intercalated cells***. Principal cells have pale cytoplasm with scanty organelles with short microvilli. These cells have prominent infoldings of the basolateral plasma membrane but no lateral interdigitations. Principal cells actively reabsorb Na^+ and secrete K^+ as well as reabsorbing water. Intercalated cells have darker cytoplasm due to the content of multiple mitochondria, polyribosomes and membrane-bound vesicles. These cells secrete H^+ and reabsorb bicarbonate and are thus important in acid–base homeostasis. The number of intercalated cells varies between different parts of the collecting duct and they are virtually absent in the inner medullary segment.

The collecting tubules are lined by a mixture of DCT cells, collecting tubule cells, principal cells and intercalated cells. Overall the epithelium is cuboidal and becomes increasingly tall distally until it merges with the columnar epithelium of the collecting duct.

Micrograph (a) illustrates two collecting tubules in the renal cortex, the tubule on the left being more proximal and the tubule on the right more distal as shown by the flatter cuboidal lining of the former. The majority of the lining cells are relatively poorly stained. The different cell types cannot be differentiated by light microscopy, except for a small number of dark intercalated cells **IC** with surface microvilli. Note the blue stained tubular basement membranes **BM** and narrow intervening supporting tissue **S** mainly occupied by capillaries.

Micrograph (b) is from the renal medulla and illustrates two collecting ducts **CD** surrounded by loops of Henle and vasa recta that cannot be readily distinguished from one another. In the medullary portion of the collecting ducts, principal cells are predominant and no intercalated cells can be seen in this section.

A thick ascending limb of loop of Henle **BM** tubular basement membrane **CD** collecting duct
CT collecting tubule **IC** intercalated cell **S** supporting tissue **T** thin limb of loop of Henle
V vasa recta

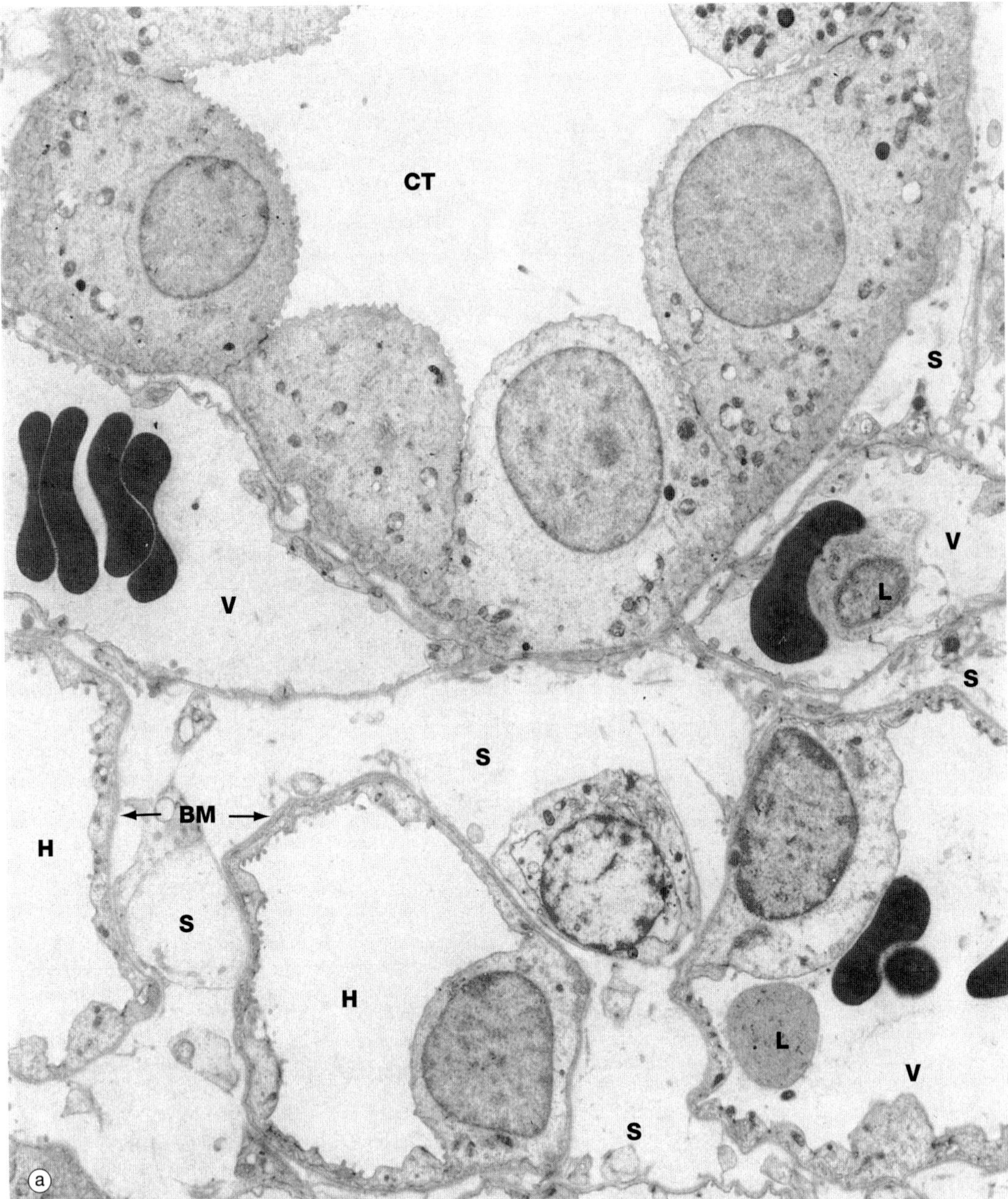

Fig. 16.22 Renal medulla (rat)
(a) EM ×4000 (b) EM ×8000 *(opposite)*

Micrograph (a), a transverse section of the outer medulla, illustrates the ultrastructural features of a collecting tubule **CT**, thin loops of Henle **H** and vasa recta **V**. Lying between the vasa recta and nephrons is the delicate interstitial supporting tissue **S** containing a little collagen along with ***renal interstitial medullary cells (RIMC)***.

The collecting tubule in this section is lined mainly by principal cells whose basal mitochondria associated with infoldings of the plasma membrane can just be identified at this power and are seen clearly in micrograph (b) in the collecting tubule **CT** in the right upper corner. The cells of the thin limbs of loops of Henle are similar to capillary endothelial cells in structure, most of the wall consisting of a thin irregular layer of cytoplasm with a few very short luminal microvilli and the nucleus bulging into the lumen. The epithelium is supported by a thin basement membrane **BM**. The vasa recta can only be readily distinguished from the thin limbs by their content of erythrocytes, occasional leucocytes **L** and precipitated plasma proteins.

The interstitium of the inner medulla in some species, including humans, contains unusual cells called renal interstitial medullary cells. These are illustrated in micrograph (b), a longitudinal section of the medulla, where the cell bodies of two such cells are identifiable by their nuclei **N**. These cells have plentiful lipid droplets **D** within the cytoplasm and long cytoplasmic processes **P** that form a network throughout the loose supporting tissue containing collagen fibrils **C** that fills the intervening space. Interestingly there are also fragments of redundant basal lamina **BL** in the supporting tissue implying that these RIMC may change their position over time. These cells are often arranged at right angles to the collecting tubules **CT** and vasa recta **V**. The function of these cells is not yet clear but they may be involved in the production of prostaglandins and/or hormones that regulate blood pressure.

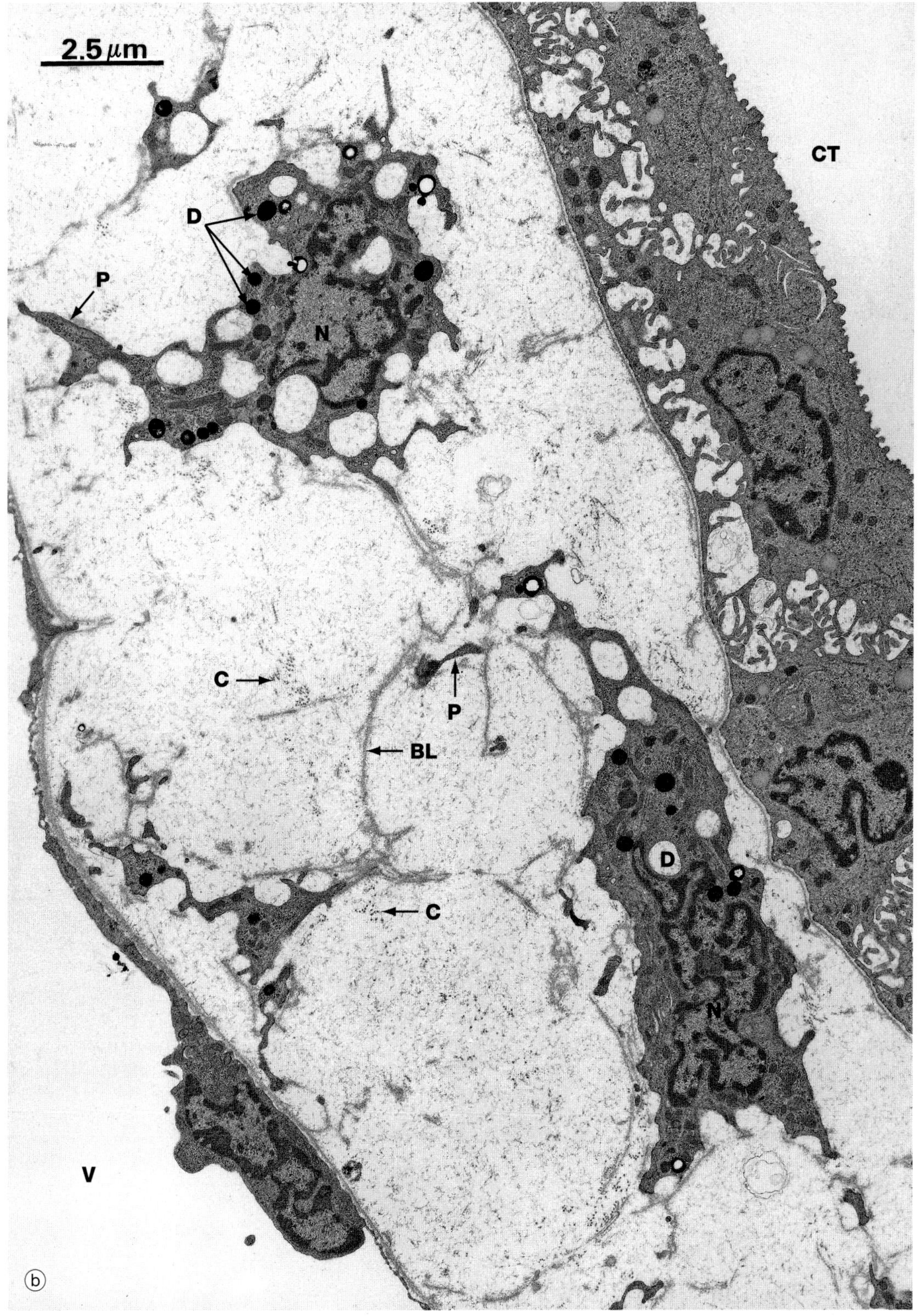

BL basal lamina **BM** basement membrane **C** collagen fibrils **CT** collecting tubule
D lipid droplets **H** loop of Henle **L** leucocyte **N** nucleus of interstitial medullary cell
P cytoplasmic processes of interstitial medullary cell **S** supporting tissue **V** vasa recta

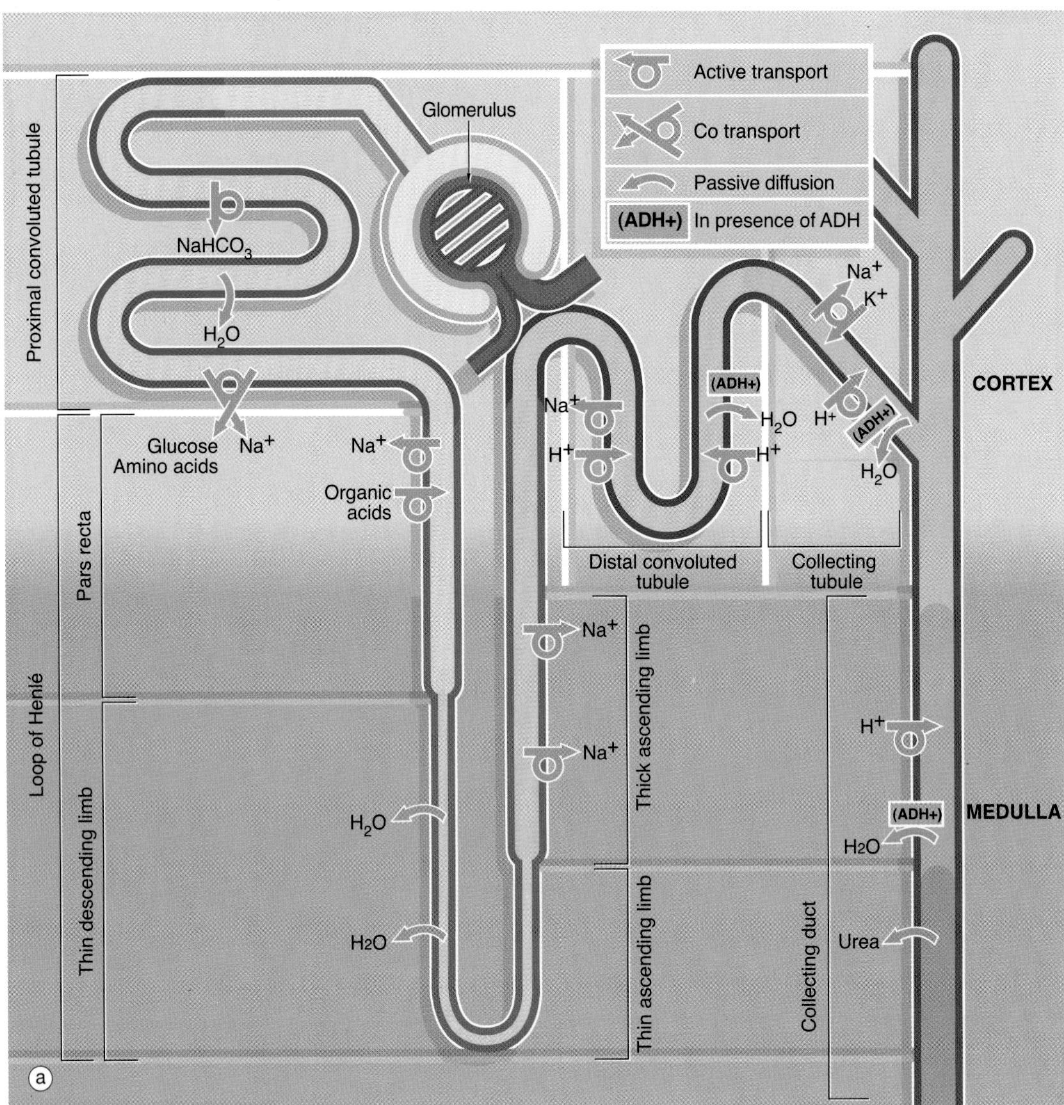

Fig. 16.23 (a) Summary of activities of different parts of the tubule (b) Comparison of epithelial structure in different parts of the renal tubule *(opposite)*

The function of the renal tubule is to transform an ultrafiltrate of plasma into a concentrated solution of waste products such as urea, creatinine, excess H^+ and K^+ and many other substances. At the same time the tubule conserves essential water, Na^+, bicarbonate, amino acids, glucose and low molecular weight proteins. This complex procedure is carried out by a variety of mechanisms in different segments of the tubule including active transport, co-transport, passive diffusion, facilitated diffusion (see Ch. 1) and differential permeability of different parts of the tubule.

The ability of the tubule to produce concentrated urine is dependent on the high osmolarity of the renal medulla, which is created by the unique structure of the loops of Henle and vasa recta dipping down into the medulla. This is known as the ***counter-current multiplier mechanism***. In the presence of ADH, which renders the collecting tubule and duct permeable to water, the high osmolarity of the interstitium of the renal medulla draws water passively out of the tubule and into the medulla where it is carried away by the vasa recta. The counter-current multiplier mechanism is set up by the ability of the thick ascending limb of the loop of Henle to pump large amounts of NaCl into the interstitium against a concentration gradient while remaining impermeable to water. The thin descending limb is permeable to water but not NaCl and water is reabsorbed into the medulla resulting in hyperosmolar urine reaching the hairpin bend of the loop. This water, however, is removed by the vasa recta. The hyperosmolarity of the medulla is also partly due to the high concentrations of urea resulting from passive diffusion of urea from the medullary collecting duct into the interstitium along its concentration gradient.

Diagram (a) outlines the major movements of solutes and water into and out of the different parts of the renal tubule. For further detail of these processes the reader is referred to current physiology texts. The table (b) gives the major morphological features of the epithelium of the different segments of the tubule and correlates them with function.

Fig. 16.23 **(b) Comparison of epithelial structure in different parts of the renal tubule**

Part of tubule	Type of epithelium	Special features	Functional significance
Proximal convoluted tubule (PCT)	Simple cuboidal	Microvilli (brush border)	Facilitated diffusion glucose, amino acids
		Extensive basolateral interdigitations	Na^+ pump
		Plentiful mitochondria	Energy for active transport
Pars recta of proximal tubule	Simple cuboidal	Microvilli (brush border)	Secretion of organic acids
		No basolateral interdigitations	
Thin descending/ ascending limbs	Simple squamous	No basolateral interdigitations or microvilli	No active transport
		Mitochondria scanty	Low energy requirement
Thick ascending limb	Simple cuboidal	Microvilli absent	No facilitated diffusion
		Extensive basolateral interdigitations	Active transport of Na^+
Distal convoluted tubule (DCT)	Simple cuboidal	Extensive basolateral interdigitations	Active transport of Na^+
		Mitochondria plentiful	Energy for active transport
Collecting tubule	Simple cuboidal	Principal cells	Na^+ reabsorption, ADH-dependent H_2O reabsorption K^+ secretion
		Intercalated cells	Acid-base balance, K^+ reabsorption
		Collecting tubule cells	DCT cells Active transport of Na^+
Cortical collecting duct	Simple columnar	Principal cells	Na^+ reabsorption, ADH dependent H_2O reabsorption, K^+ secretion
		Intercalated cells	Acid-base balance, K^+ reabsorption
Medullary collecting duct	Simple columnar	Mainly principal cells	ADH-dependent water reabsorption

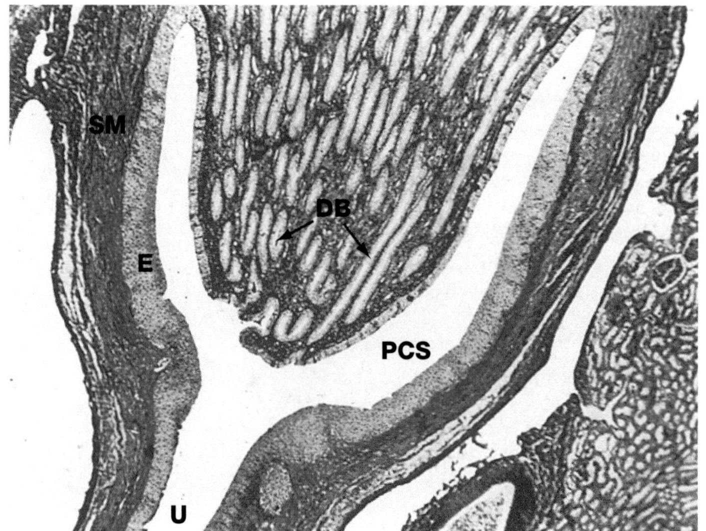

Fig. 16.24 Renal papilla (monkey)
Azan ×30

The renal papilla forms the apex of the medullary pyramid where it projects into the pelvicalyceal space **PCS**. Ducts of Bellini **DB**, the largest of the collecting ducts, converge to drain urine through a number of holes (***cribriform area***) at the tip of the papilla. Between the ducts are the longest loops of Henle and vasa recta, not visible at this magnification. This papilla is a simple papilla, but at the poles of the human kidney the papillae are often fused to form complex papillae.

The pelvicalyceal system represents the proximal end of the ureter **U** and as such is lined by typical urinary (transitional) epithelium **E**. The wall of the pelvis contains smooth muscle **SM**, continuous with that of the ureter.

The lower urinary tract

The lower urinary tract includes the renal pelvis and calyces, the ureters, the urinary bladder and the urethra. The lower urinary tract is specialised for the storage and excretion of urine at a convenient time: no further modification of the urine is possible after it leaves the renal medulla.

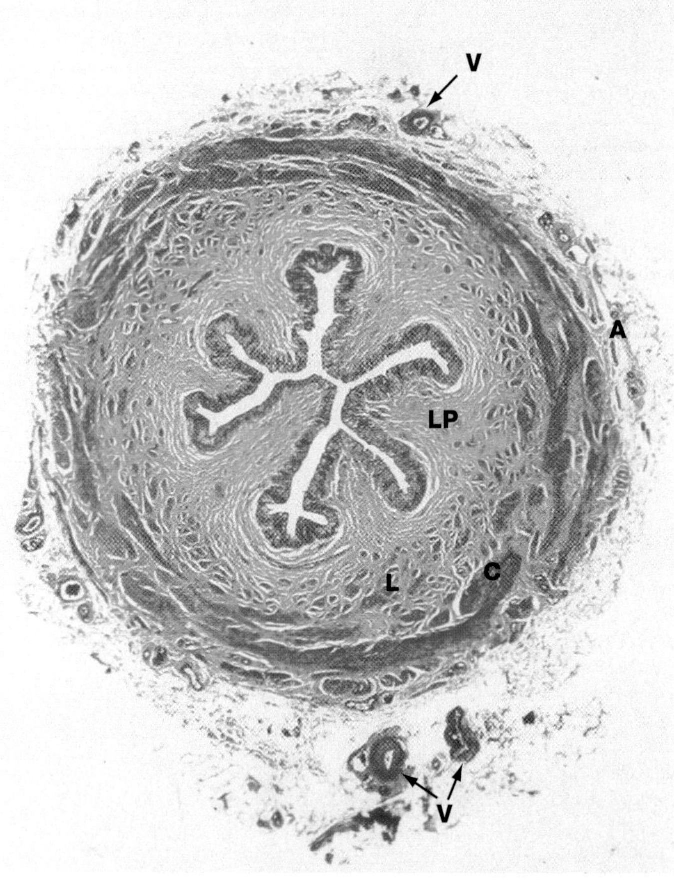

Fig. 16.25 Ureter
Masson's trichrome ×18

The ureters are muscular tubes that carry urine from the kidneys to the bladder. Urine is transported from the pelvicalyceal system as a bolus propelled by peristaltic action of the ureteric wall. The wall of the ureter contains two layers of smooth muscle arranged as an inner elongated spiral but traditionally known as the longitudinal layer **L** and an outer tight spiral traditionally described as the circular layer **C**. Another outer longitudinal layer is present in the lower third of the ureter. However, in reality the three layers are often difficult to distinguish from each other.

The lumen of the ureter is lined by ***transitional epithelium*** (***urothelium***), which is thrown up into folds in the relaxed state allowing the ureter to dilate during the passage of a bolus of urine. Beneath the epithelium is a broad collagenous lamina propria **LP**, the collagen fibres of which are stained greenish-blue in this preparation. Surrounding the muscular wall is a loose collagenous adventitia **A** containing blood vessels **V**, lymphatics and nerves.

A adventitia **C** circular muscle layer of ureter **D** duct of Bellini **E** transitional epithelium
IL inner longitudinal muscle layer of bladder **L** longitudinal muscle layer of ureter **LP** lamina propria
OC outer circular muscle layer of bladder **OL** outer longitudinal muscle layer of bladder
PCS pelvicalyceal space **SM** smooth muscle **U** ureter **Um** umbrella cell **V** blood vessel

Fig. 16.26 Bladder
Masson's trichrome ×12

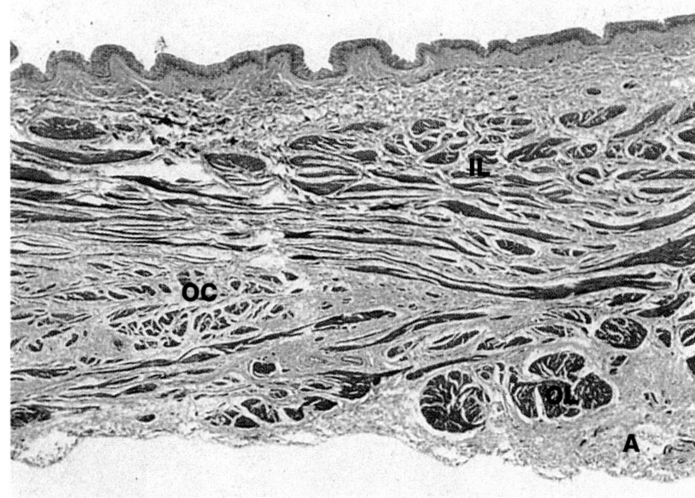

The urinary bladder serves as a urine store in which urine can be held until a convenient time and place for its excretion. The general structure of the bladder wall resembles that of the lower third of the ureters. The wall of the bladder consists of three loosely arranged layers of smooth muscle and elastic fibres that contract during micturition. Note the inner longitudinal **IL**, outer circular **OC** and outermost longitudinal **OL** layers of smooth muscle. As in the ureter, the layers are often difficult to distinguish. The transitional epithelium lining the bladder is thrown into many folds in the relaxed state. A delicate, often incomplete, muscularis mucosa (not identifiable at this magnification) separates the lamina propria from the submucosa in some but not all individuals. The outer adventitial coat **A** contains arteries, veins and lymphatics.

The urethra, the final conducting portion of the urinary tract, is discussed as part of the male reproductive tract in Chapter 18.

Fig. 16.27 Transitional epithelium
H & E ×450

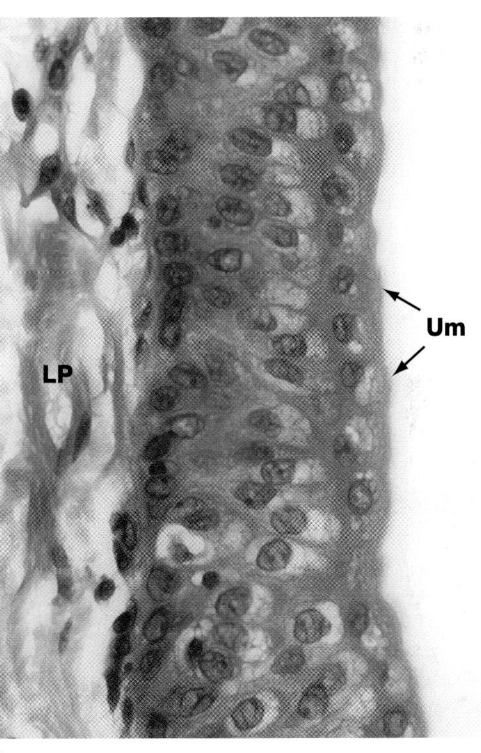

Transitional epithelium, also called urothelium, is found only within the conducting passages of the urinary system for which it is especially adapted. The epithelium is stratified, comprising three to six layers of cells; the number of layers being greatest when the epithelium is least distended at the time of fixation.

The cells of the basal layer are compact and cuboidal in form, while those of the intermediate layers are more columnar with their nuclei orientated at right angles to the basement membrane. The surface cells are called ***umbrella*** or ***dome cells*** **Um** and have unique features that allow them to maintain the impermeability of the epithelium to urine even when at full stretch. This permeability barrier also prevents water from being drawn through the epithelium into hypertonic urine. The umbrella cells are large and ovoid with round nuclei and plentiful eosinophilic cytoplasm; some surface cells are binucleate (not illustrated). The surface outline has a characteristic scalloped appearance and the superficial cytoplasm is fuzzy, indistinct and more intensely stained than the rest of the cytoplasm.

Ultrastructural studies have revealed that much of the surface plasma membrane consists of thickened inflexible ***plaques***, often called ***asymmetrical unit membrane***, interspersed with narrow zones of normal membrane. These normal areas act as 'hinges', allowing sections of the membrane to fold inwards somewhat like a concertina, forming deep clefts and stacks of flattened plasma membrane segments, inappropriately called ***fusiform vesicles***. This structure allows the umbrella cells to expand greatly and quickly when the bladder is distended and the epithelium is at full stretch. Plentiful junctional complexes between the cells maintain the cohesion of adjacent cells. These features of the urothelium allow it to store chemically toxic urine in considerable volumes for quite long periods of time without damage to the tissues.

Urinary epithelium rests on a basement membrane that is often too thin to be resolved by light microscopy. The loose lamina propria **LP** is seen underlying the epithelium.

17. *Endocrine system*

Introduction

The endocrine system is responsible for the synthesis and secretion of chemical messengers known as ***hormones***. Hormones may be disseminated throughout the body by the bloodstream where they may act on specific ***target organs*** or affect a wide range of organs and tissues. Other hormones act locally, often arriving at their site of action by way of a specialised microcirculation. In conjunction with the nervous system, hormones coordinate and integrate the functions of all the physiological systems.

As a general rule, endocrine glands are composed of islands of secretory cells of epithelial origin with intervening supporting tissue, which is rich in blood and lymphatic capillaries. The secretory cells discharge their hormone product into the interstitial spaces from which it is rapidly absorbed into the circulatory system.

Reflecting their active hormone synthesis, cells of the endocrine system have prominent nuclei and abundant mitochondria, endoplasmic reticulum, Golgi bodies and secretory vesicles. The nature of the secretory vesicles varies according to the hormone secreted. There are four main groups of chemicals which can act as hormones:

- Protein and glycoprotein molecules, e.g. insulin, growth hormone, parathormone.
- Small peptide molecules, e.g. vasopressin, products of enteroendocrine cells.
- Amino acid derivatives, e.g. thyroxine, epinephrine and norepinephrine (adrenaline and noradrenaline).
- Steroids derived from cholesterol, e.g. adrenal cortical hormones, ovarian and testicular hormones.

Endocrine cells which produce hormones based on amino acids, peptides and proteins often have characteristic membrane-bound secretory vacuoles with electron-dense central cores (dense core granules).

The endocrine system can be divided into three parts:

- **The major endocrine organs** – in which the sole or major function of the organ is the synthesis, storage and secretion of hormones.
- **Endocrine components within other solid organs** – for example, the endocrine components of the pancreas, ovary, testis and kidney, in the form of clusters of endocrine cells within other tissues.
- **The diffuse endocrine system** – scattered individual hormone cells (or small clumps), usually within an extensive epithelium, e.g. the gastrointestinal and respiratory tract. The major function of these cells is probably ***paracrine***, i.e. acting on adjacent non-endocrine cells rather than entering the bloodstream and producing systemic effects.

Pituitary gland

The ***pituitary gland*** (***hypophysis***) is a small bean-shaped gland, about 1 cm across, at the base of the brain beneath the third ventricle, sitting in a bony cavity in the base of the skull (the ***sella turcica***). The gland is divided into anterior and posterior parts which have different embryological origins, functions and control mechanisms.

The secretion of all pituitary hormones is controlled by the hypothalamus which itself is under the influence of nervous stimuli from higher centres in the brain. Control is mainly by feedback from the levels of circulating hormones produced by pituitary-dependent endocrine tissues.

The pituitary hormones fall into two functional groups:

- Hormones which act directly on non-endocrine tissues: growth hormone (GH), prolactin, antidiuretic hormone (ADH), oxytocin and melanocyte stimulating hormone (MSH).
- Hormones which modulate the secretory activity of other endocrine glands (***trophic hormones***): thyroid stimulating hormone (TSH), adrenocorticotrophic hormone (ACTH) and the gonadotrophic hormones, follicle stimulating hormone (FSH) and luteinising hormone (LH).

Thus the thyroid gland, adrenal cortex and gonads may be described as ***pituitary-dependent endocrine glands***.

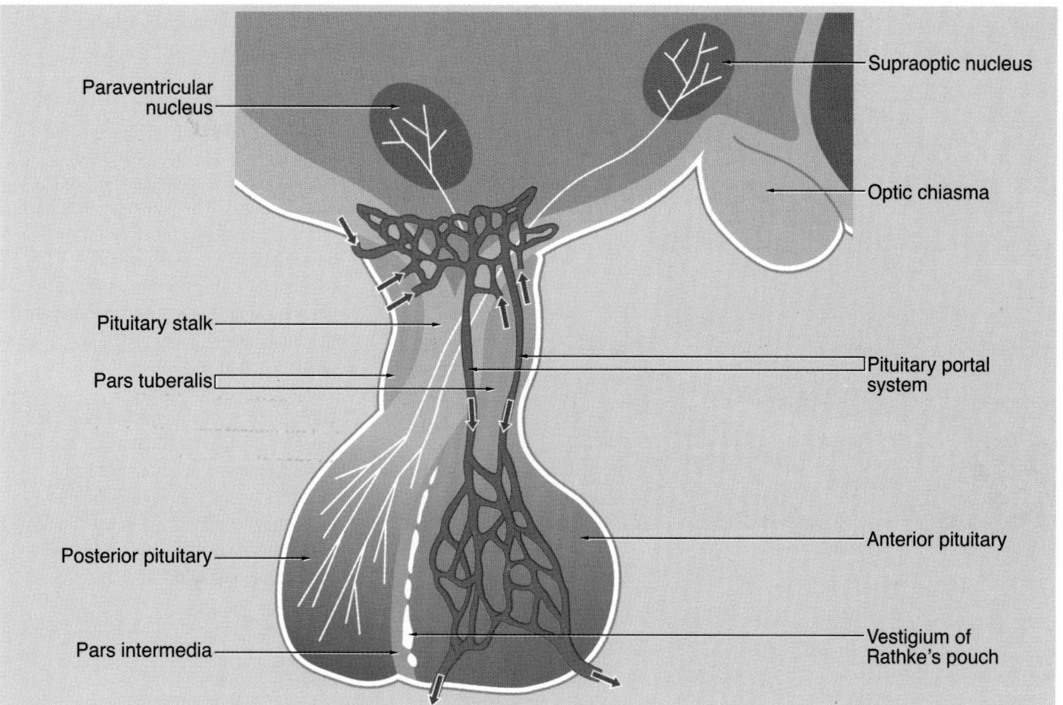

Fig. 17.1 Pituitary gland

The anterior and posterior parts of the pituitary originate from different embryological sources and this is reflected in their structure and function.

- **The posterior pituitary,** also called the ***neurohypophysis*** or ***pars nervosa*** is derived from a downgrowth of nervous tissue from the hypothalamus to which it remains joined by the ***pituitary stalk***.
- **The anterior pituitary** arises as an epithelial upgrowth from the roof of the primitive oral cavity, known as ***Rathke's pouch***. This specialised glandular epithelium is wrapped around the anterior aspect of the posterior pituitary and is often called the ***adenohypophysis***. The adenohypophysis may contain a cleft or group of cyst-like spaces which represent the vestigial lumen of Rathke's pouch. This vestigial cleft divides the major part of the anterior pituitary from a thin zone of tissue lying against the posterior pituitary, known as the ***pars intermedia***. An extension of the adenohypophysis surrounds the neural stalk and is known as the ***pars tuberalis***.

The type and mode of secretion of the posterior pituitary differ greatly from that of the anterior pituitary. The posterior pituitary secretes two hormones. ***antidiuretic hormone*** (***ADH***), also called ***vasopressin***, and the hormone ***oxytocin***, both of which act directly on non-endocrine tissues. ADH is synthesised in the neurone cell bodies of the ***supraoptic nucleus***, and oxytocin is synthesised in those of the ***paraventricular nucleus*** of the hypothalamus. Bound to glycoproteins, the hormones pass down the axons of the hypothalamopituitary tract through the pituitary stalk to the posterior pituitary where they are stored in the distended terminal parts of the axons. Release of posterior pituitary hormones is controlled directly by nervous impulses passing down the axons from the hypothalamus, a process known as ***neurosecretion***.

Hypothalamic control of anterior pituitary secretion is mediated by specific hypothalamic releasing hormones, e.g. ***thyroid stimulating hormone releasing hormone*** (***TSHRH***): exceptions to this rule are prolactin secretion, which is under the inhibitory control of ***dopamine***, and secretion of growth hormone which is controlled by both releasing and inhibitory hormones. These releasing and inhibitory hormones are conducted from the ***median hypothalamic eminence*** to the anterior pituitary by a unique system of ***portal veins*** (the ***pituitary portal system***).

The pars intermedia synthesises and secretes ***melanocyte-stimulating hormone*** (***MSH***); in humans, the pars intermedia is rudimentary and the physiological importance of MSH and the control of its secretion are poorly understood.

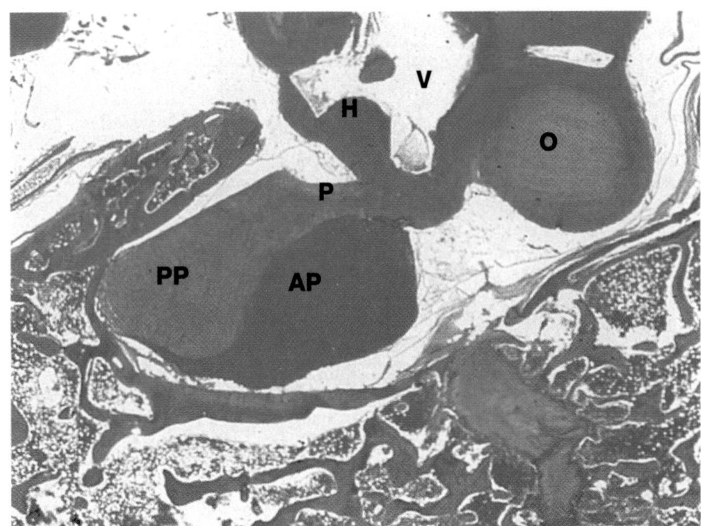

Fig. 17.2 Pituitary gland (monkey)
H & E ×12

This micrograph from a midline section through the brain and cranial floor illustrates the pituitary gland in situ. The pituitary sits in a bony depression in the sphenoid bone, called the ***sella turcica***. The two major components of the gland, the anterior pituitary **AP** and the posterior pituitary **PP**, are easily seen at this magnification. The posterior pituitary is connected to the hypothalamus **H** by the pituitary stalk **P** and, like the hypothalamus, is composed of nervous tissue. Note the close proximity of the third ventricle **V** above the hypothalamus and the optic chiasma **O** anteriorly.

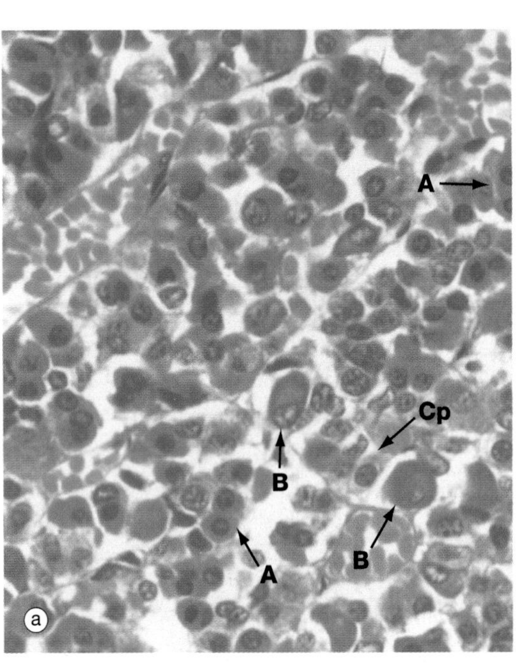

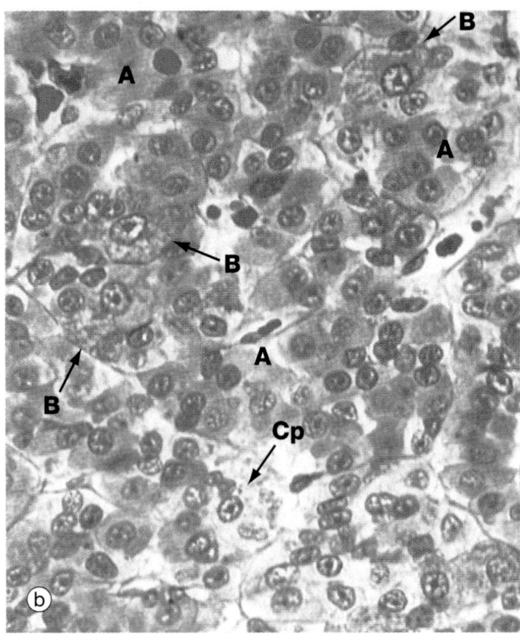

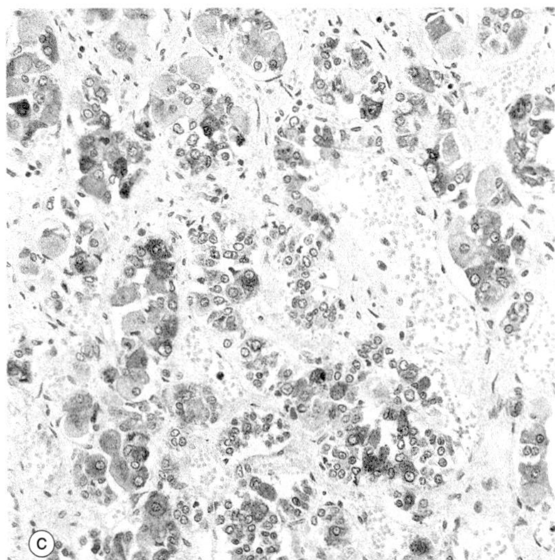

Fig. 17.3 Anterior pituitary
(a) H & E ×480 (b) Azan ×480 (c) Immunoperoxidase for LH ×150 (d) EM ×4270 *(illustration opposite)*

Micrograph (a) is an H&E stained preparation of anterior pituitary and shows two main populations of cells, those with strongly staining cytoplasm (chromophils **A** and **B**) and those with weakly staining cytoplasm (chromophobes **Cp**). Special stains (b) can separate the chromophils further into cells with basophilic cytoplasm (basophils **B)** and acidophils **A**. The most accurate identification of cell types is given by immunocytochemical methods and electron microscopy. These methods show that chromophobes have very few secretory granules but may produce small amounts of any of the hormones.

Micrograph (c) shows a section of anterior pituitary stained by the immunoperoxidase technique for luteinising hormone (LH). The brown stained LH-containing cells can be seen scattered at random among the other cells types.

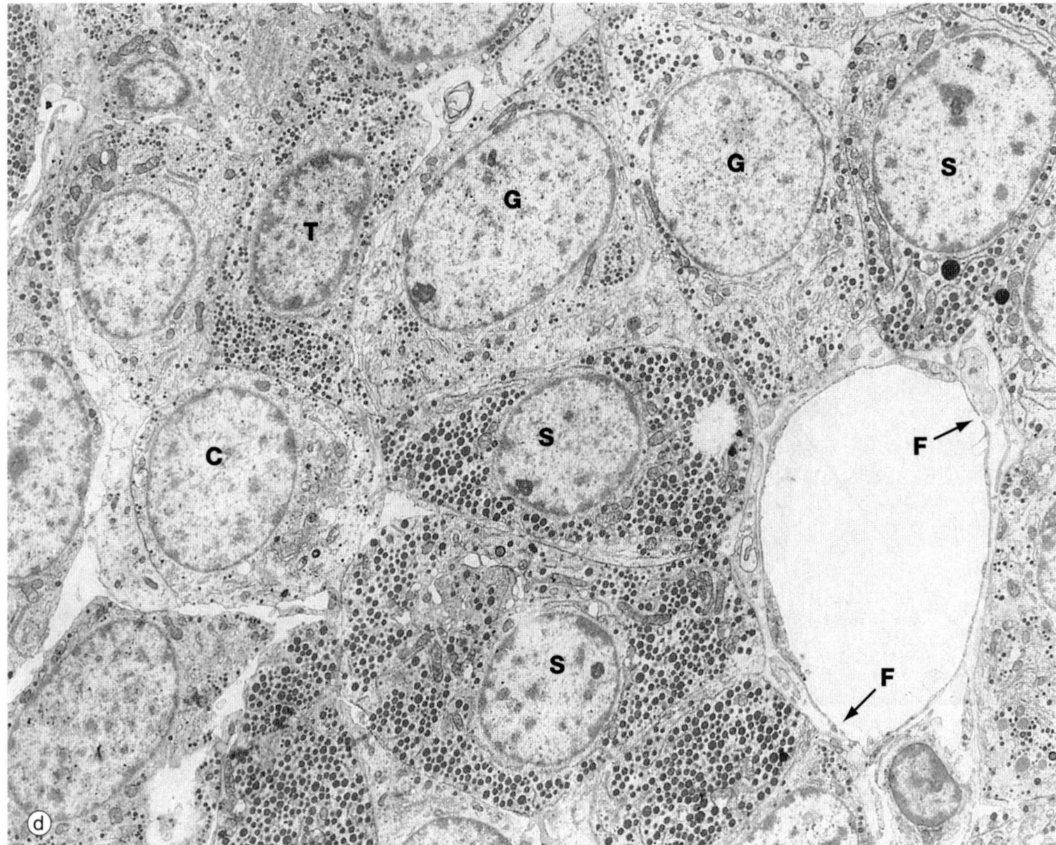

Fig. 17.3 Anterior pituitary (*cont'd*)
(a) H & E ×480 (b) Azan ×480 (c) Immunoperoxidase for LH ×150 *(illustrations opposite)* (d) EM ×4270

The different cell types are now named as follows:

- **Somatotrophs**, the cells responsible for growth hormone secretion, are the most numerous, making up almost half of the bulk of the anterior pituitary.
- **Mammotrophs (lactotrophs)**, the prolactin secreting cells, comprise up to 20% of the anterior pituitary, increasing in number during pregnancy; prolactin controls milk production during lactation.
- **Corticotrophs** secrete ACTH (***corticotrophin***) and constitute about 20% of the anterior pituitary mass. ACTH is a polypeptide which becomes split from a much larger peptide molecule known as ***pro-opiomelanocortin***. ***Lipotropins*** (involved in regulation of lipid metabolism), ***endorphins*** (endogenous opioids) and various species of MSH can be derived from the same molecule; this explains the hyperpigmentation associated with excessive ACTH secretion.
- **Thyrotrophs**, which secrete TSH (***thyrotrophin***), are much less numerous, making up only about 5% of the gland.
- **Gonadotrophs**, the cells responsible for the secretion of FSH and LH, make up the remaining 5% of the anterior pituitary.

In general one cell produces a single hormone, although LH- and FSH-containing secretory granules have been demonstrated within a single cell. The different cell types are not evenly distributed throughout the gland, but rather particular cell types tend to congregate in particular zones of the gland.

The secretory granules of each cell type have a characteristic size, shape and electron density by which the different cell types can be recognised with electron microscopy as in micrograph (d). Somatotrophs **S** are packed with secretory granules of moderate size. Thyrotrophs **T** have smaller granules which tend to be more peripherally located. Gonadotrophs **G** are large cells with secretory granules of variable size. Corticotrophs **C** have sparse secretory granules located at the extreme periphery of the cell.

The clumps and cords of cells have a rich capillary network. The endothelial lining of capillaries in endocrine tissue is characteristically fenestrated (see Fig. 8.16) facilitating the passage of hormones into the sinusoids. Note the fenestrations **F** in the sinusoid seen in micrograph (d).

A acidophils **AP** anterior pituitary **B** basophils **C** corticotroph **Cp** chromophobes
F fenestrations **G** gonadotroph **H** hypothalamus **O** optic chiasma **P** pituitary stalk
PP posterior pituitary **S** somatotroph **T** thyrotroph **V** third ventricle

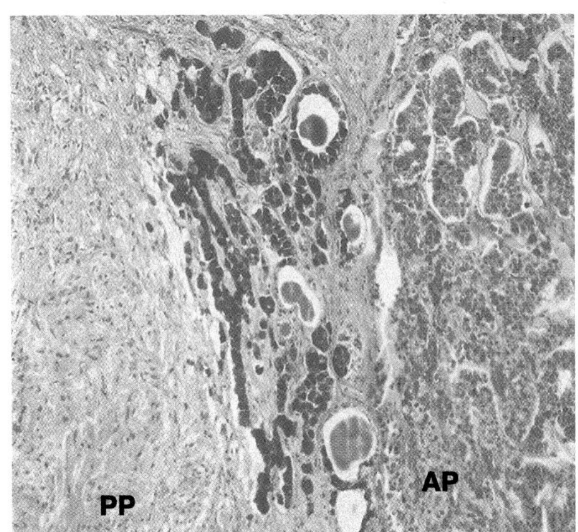

Fig. 17.4 Pituitary: pars intermedia
Isamine blue/eosin ×100

The pars intermedia, like the anterior pituitary, is derived embryologically from Rathke's pouch. The cells are basophilic (stained blue here), lying in irregular clusters between the anterior **AP** and posterior **PP** pituitary. The pars intermedia also contains small cystic spaces filled with eosinophilic material.

Ultrastructurally, the cells of the pars intermedia contain secretory granules similar to those of corticotrophs, and produces pro-opiomelanocortin which splits to produce a number of active hormones (see Fig. 17.3).

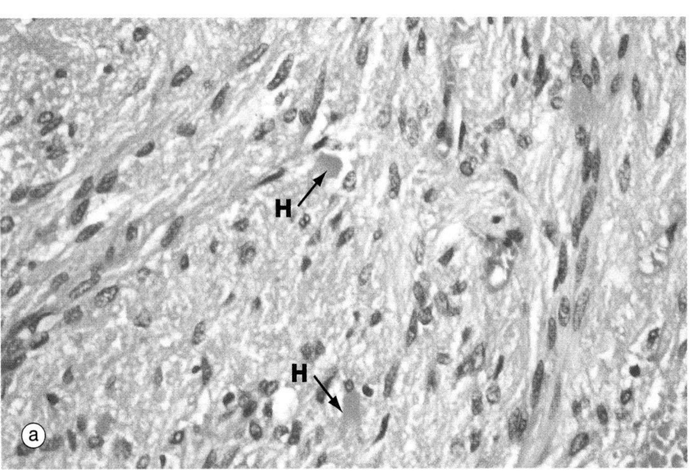

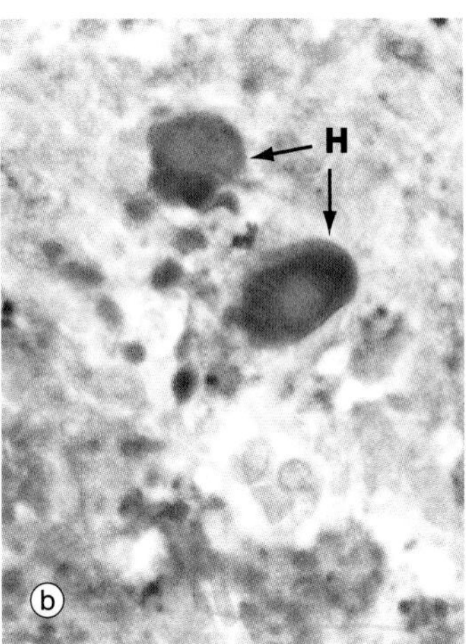

Fig. 17.5 Posterior pituitary
(a) H & E ×200 (b) Immunoperoxidase synaptophysin ×200

The posterior pituitary is largely composed of the ***non-myelinated axons*** of specialised neurones, which have considerable neurosecretory activity. The cell bodies of these neurones are located in the supraoptic and paraventricular nuclei of the hypothalamus, and it is here that the posterior pituitary peptide hormones, oxytocin and arginine vasopressin, are produced. They are passed down the axons in ***neurosecretory granules***, which accumulate in the distended terminations of the axons where they contact capillaries. These distensions are called ***Herring bodies*** **H**. The axons are supported by specialised highly branched glial cells called pituicytes, the cytoplasm of which sometimes contains small amounts of yellowish brown pigment.

Micrograph (a) shows the structure of posterior pituitary; the fibrillar structures are the axons of the hypothalamic neurones with distended terminal Herring bodies **H**, and the nuclei are those of supporting pituicytes.

Micrograph (b) is an immunocytochemical preparation for neurosecretory granules (synaptophysin). Although granules are scattered in the axons, they are particularly concentrated in the round Herring bodies **H**.

Anterior pituitary disorders

The most common disease of the pituitary is ***pituitary adenoma***. These tumours are classified as benign because they do not invade adjacent tissues. However they may have serious or even fatal consequences. They cause their effects by the excessive continuous production of hormone, uncontrolled by any feedback mechanisms. Thus a tumour of corticotrophs secretes excess ACTH, stimulating the adrenals to produce large quantities of corticosteroid, leading to Cushing's disease. Tumours of somatotrophs produce excess growth hormone causing ***gigantism*** in children or ***acromegaly*** in adults. Some pituitary adenomas produce no hormones but grow locally so large that they grow upwards out of the sella turcica to compress and damage the overlying optic chiasma and nerves, leading to vision disturbance and eventual blindness.

The pituitary gland can rarely be destroyed by disease blocking its arterial supply, leading to necrosis of the cells and failure of hormone output (***panhypopituitarism***).

Thyroid gland

The thyroid gland is a butterfly-shaped endocrine gland lying in the neck in front of the upper part of the trachea. The thyroid gland produces hormones of two types:

- Iodine-containing hormones ***tri-iodothyronine*** (***T_3***), and ***thyroxine*** (***tetra-iodothyronine***, ***T_4***); T_4 is converted to T_3 in the general circulation by removal of one iodothyronine unit although a small amount of T_3 is secreted directly. T_3 is much more potent than T_4 and appears to be the metabolically active form of the hormone. Thyroid hormone regulates the basal metabolic rate and has an important influence on growth and maturation particularly of nerve tissue. The secretion of these hormones is regulated by TSH secreted by the anterior pituitary.
- The polypeptide hormone ***calcitonin***; this hormone regulates blood calcium levels in conjunction with parathyroid hormone. Calcitonin lowers blood calcium levels by inhibiting the rate of decalcification of bone by osteoclastic resorption and by stimulating osteoblastic activity. Control of calcitonin secretion is dependent only on blood calcium levels and is independent of pituitary and parathyroid hormone levels.

The thyroid gland is unique among the human endocrine glands in that it stores large amounts of hormone in an inactive form within extracellular compartments in the centre of follicles; in contrast, other endocrine glands store only small quantities of hormones in intracellular sites.

The main bulk of the gland develops from an epithelial downgrowth from the fetal tongue whereas the calcitonin-secreting cells are derived from the ultimobranchial element of the fourth branchial pouch.

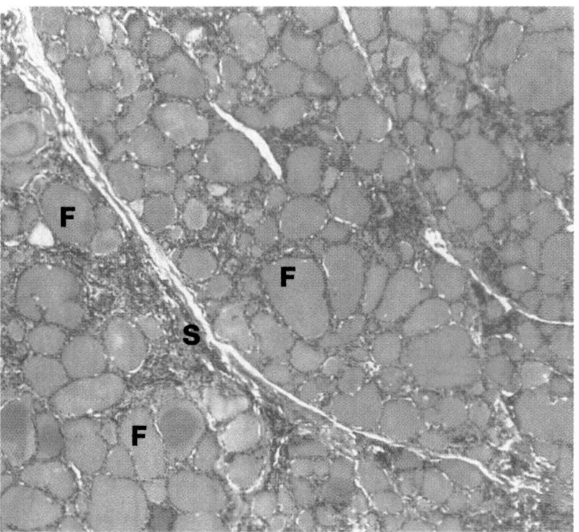

Fig. 17.6 Thyroid gland
H & E ×12

The functional units of the thyroid gland are the ***thyroid follicles***, spheroidal structures composed of a single layer of cuboidal epithelial cells bounded by a basement membrane (see also Fig. 5.28). As seen in this micrograph of a normal active thyroid, the follicles **F** are variable in size and contain a homogeneous colloid material which is stained pink in this preparation.

The thyroid gland is enveloped by a fibrous capsule from which fine collagenous septa **S** extend into the gland, dividing it into lobules. The septa convey a rich blood supply together with lymphatics and nerves.

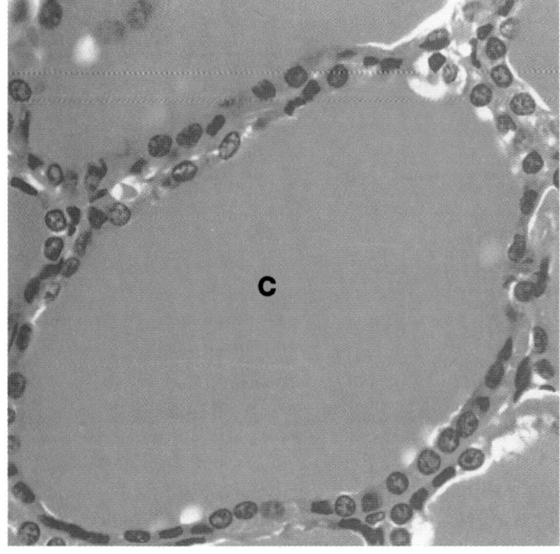

Fig. 17.7 Thyroid follicle – inactive
H & E ×180

Thyroid follicles store ***thyroglobulin***, an iodinated glycoprotein, the storage form of thyroxine (T_4) and tri-iodothyronine (T_3). The follicles are lined by epithelial cells which are initially responsible for the synthesis of the glycoprotein component of thyroglobulin and for the conversion of iodide to iodine, the iodine linking to the glycoprotein in the follicle lumen. When active thyroid hormone is required, the same thyroid epithelial cells remove some of the stored thyroid colloid and detach T_3 and T_4, which then pass through the cell into an adjacent capillary. When inactive, thyroid epithelial cells are simple flat or cuboidal cells, but when actively synthesising or secreting thyroid hormone they are tall and columnar. This micrograph shows inactive epithelial cells lining follicles filled with stored thyroglobulin (colloid **C**).

AP anterior pituitary **C** thyroid colloid **F** thyroid follicle **H** Herring body **PP** posterior pituitary **S** fibrous septum

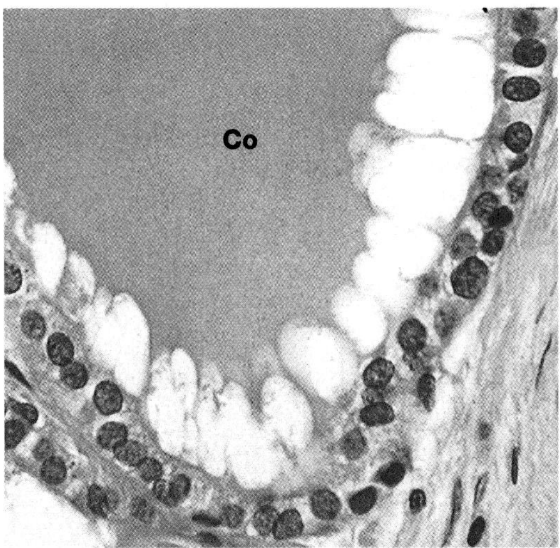

Fig. 17.8 Thyroid follicle – active
H & E ×220

Compare this photomicrograph of an active thyroid follicle with the inactive follicle in Fig. 17.7. The epithelial cells are taller, with more cytoplasm and larger, pale-staining, nuclei, reflecting their increased activity. In this follicle they are extracting stored thyroid colloid **Co** from the lumen and converting it into active thyroid hormones. The scalloped pale edge of the colloid indicates where the colloid has been removed from the follicle lumen.

Thyroid hyperplasia

In the normal thyroid gland in humans, most of the thyroid follicles are full of stored colloid and the epithelium is in the inactive storage phase. Only a few follicles are actively metabolising the stored colloid to release hormone at any time to meet current requirements. This process is under the control of thyroid-stimulating hormone (TSH) secreted by the anterior pituitary.

Sometimes a tumour-like nodule arises in the thyroid gland in which the follicle epithelial cells constantly synthesise and secrete thyroid hormone without a significant inactive storage phase (***nodular hyperplasia***). In another condition (***Graves' disease***) the patient produces an autoantibody (***long-acting thyroid stimulator – LATS***) which mimics TSH and constantly stimulates the thyroid to secrete excess hormone. This affects all the thyroid follicles (***diffuse hyperplasia***), all of which are constantly in an active phase, as shown in Fig. 17.9; the epithelial cells are large and active, and there is marked depletion of stored colloid within the follicles. Both of these patterns of hyperplasia produce the disease called ***thyrotoxicosis***.

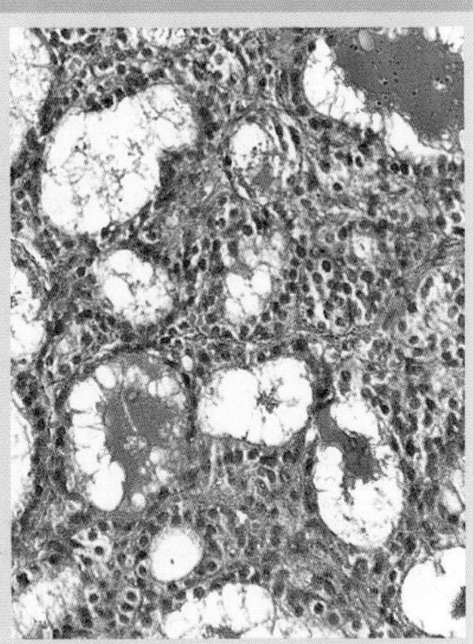

Fig. 17.9 Thyroid hyperplasia
H & E ×90

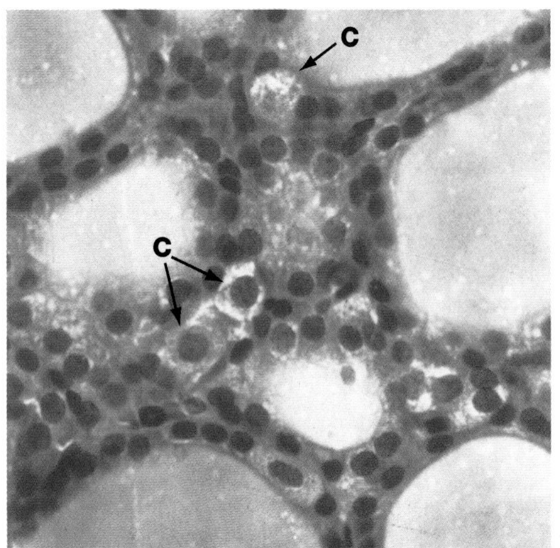

Fig. 17.10 Thyroid C cell
H & E ×150

A second type of endocrine cell with the ultrastructural characteristics of neuroendocrine cells, the ***C cell*** or ***parafollicular cell*** C, is found in the thyroid gland as individual scattered cells in the follicle lining, or as small clumps in the interstices between follicles. They are particularly prominent in dogs where they are identifiable in H & E sections as pale-staining cells with granular cytoplasm but in humans they are much less prominent and can usually only be identified ultrastructurally (see Fig. 17.11), and by immunocytochemical methods. These cells secrete ***calcitonin***, which is a physiological antagonist to parathormone and therefore lowers blood calcium levels by suppressing the osteoclastic resorption of bone.

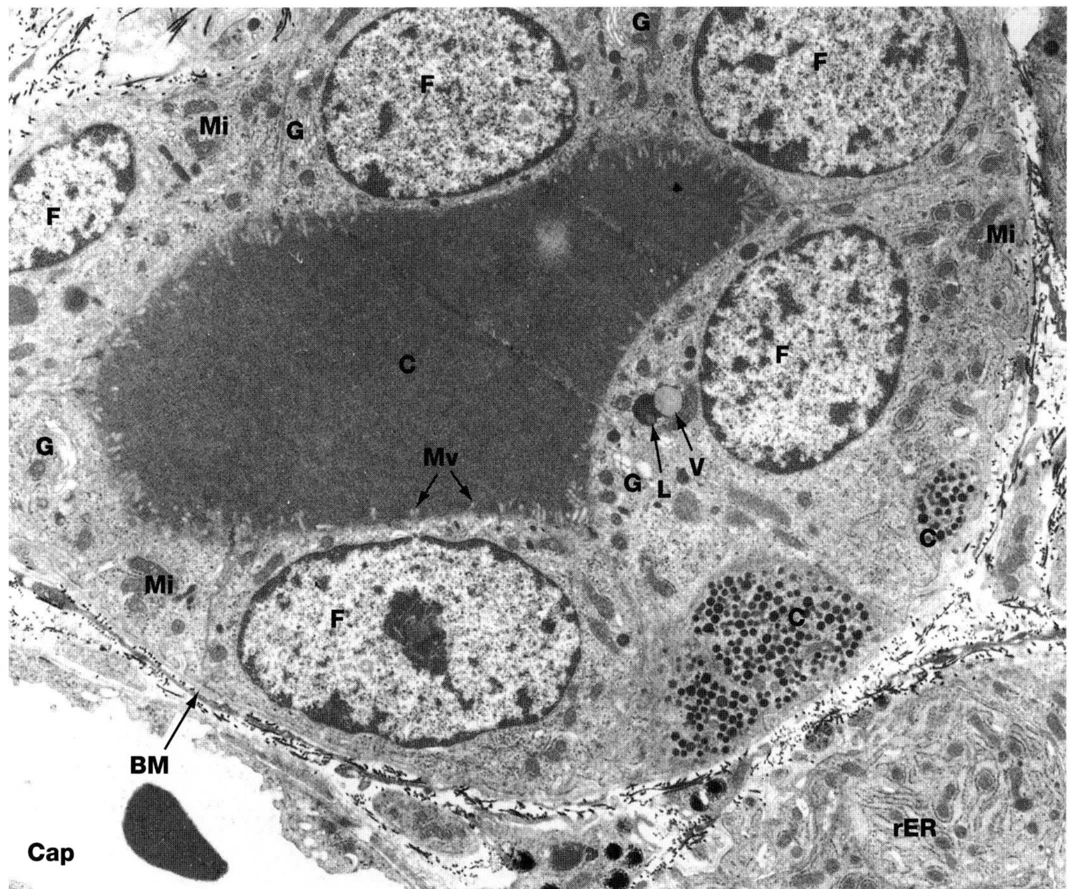

Fig. 17.11 Thyroid follicle (rat)
EM ×6800

This micrograph demonstrates a thyroid follicle composed of cuboidal follicular cells **F** surrounding a lumen containing the homogeneous colloid, thyroglobulin **Co**. A basement membrane **BM** delineates the follicle. Two portions of the cytoplasm of a C cell **C** are seen within the follicular epithelium typically located on the basement membrane and not exposed to the follicular lumen. The cytoplasm contains numerous electron-dense secretory granules of the hormone calcitonin. A fenestrated capillary **Cap** containing an erythrocyte is closely applied to the follicular basement membrane.

Follicular cells concentrate iodide from the blood by means of an iodide pump in the basal plasma membrane. Within the cell, iodide is oxidised to iodine and transported to the follicular plasma membrane where it is released into the follicular lumen. The glycoprotein thyroglobulin is synthesised in the rough endoplasmic reticulum, glycosylated and packaged by the Golgi apparatus, then released into the follicular lumen by exocytosis. Within the follicular lumen (not within the follicular cells), iodine combines with tyrosine residues of the thyroglobulin to form the hormones tri-iodothyronine (T_3) and tetra-iodothyronine (thyroxine, T_4) which remain bound to the glycoprotein in an inactive form.

Secretion of these hormones involves pinocytosis of the thyroglobulin-hormone complex to form cytoplasmic vacuoles; the vacuoles then fuse with lysosomes of the follicular cell cytoplasm and hydrolytic enzymes cleave the hormone from the thyroglobulin. The hormones are released in the basal cytoplasm from which they diffuse into the bloodstream. The synthetic and secretory activity of the thyroid gland is dependent on thyroid stimulating hormone (TSH) secreted by the anterior pituitary.

In this micrograph, rough endoplasmic reticulum **rER** is best demonstrated in the basal aspect of a secretory cell of an adjacent follicle. Mitochondria **Mi** are closely associated with the endoplasmic reticulum and are also scattered throughout the cytoplasm. Golgi complexes **G** are a prominent feature. Small microvilli **Mv** associated with the exocytosis of thyroglobulin and the endocytosis of the thyroglobulin-hormone complex protrude into the follicular lumen. In one cell a vacuole **V** of thyroglobulin-hormone is seen about to fuse with a large lysosome **L**. Electron-dense lysosomes are also seen scattered throughout the cytoplasm.

BM basement membrane **C** C cell **Cap** capillary **Co** colloid **F** follicular cell **G** Golgi **L** lysosome **Mi** mitochondria **Mv** microvilli **rER** rough endoplasmic reticulum **V** vacuole

Parathyroid gland

The parathyroid glands are small oval endocrine glands closely associated with the thyroid gland. In mammals, there are usually two pairs of glands, one pair situated on the posterior surface of the thyroid gland on each side, although occasional individuals possess five or even six parathyroids. The embryological origins of the parathyroid glands are the third and fourth branchial (pharyngeal) pouches. The parathyroid glands regulate serum calcium and phosphate levels via ***parathyroid hormone*** (***parathormone***, ***PTH***).

Parathyroid hormone raises serum calcium levels in three ways:

- Direct action on bone, increasing the rate of osteoclastic resorption and promoting breakdown of the bone matrix.
- Direct action on the kidney, increasing the renal tubular reabsorption of calcium ions and inhibiting the reabsorption of phosphate ions from the glomerular filtrate.
- Promotion of the absorption of calcium from the small intestine; this effect involves vitamin D.

Secretion of parathyroid hormone is stimulated by a decrease in blood calcium levels. In conjunction with calcitonin secreted by the C cells of the thyroid gland, blood calcium levels are maintained within narrow limits. Parathyroid hormone is the most important regulator of blood calcium levels and is essential to life, whereas calcitonin appears to provide a complementary mechanism for fine adjustment and is not essential to life.

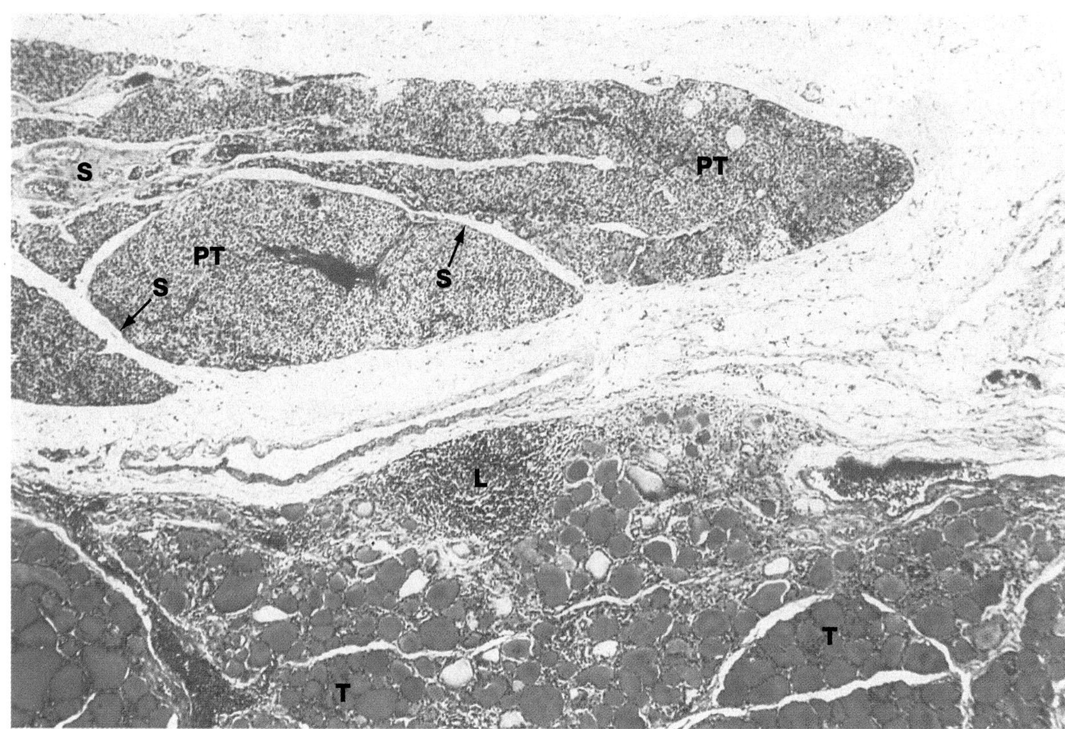

Fig. 17.12 Parathyroid gland
H & E ×45

This micrograph shows a parathyroid gland **PT** characteristically embedded in the capsule of a thyroid gland **T**. Some parathyroids are actually found embedded in the thyroid. The thin fibrous capsule of the parathyroid gland gives rise to delicate septa **S** which divide the parenchyma into nodules of secretory cells; as seen here they are very prone to shrinkage artefact during histological preparation. The septa carry blood vessels, lymphatics and nerves.

Note that in this specimen from a 55-year-old woman, there is some infiltration of the thyroid by lymphocytes **L**: this is a common feature of the ageing thyroid gland, and is often of little clinical significance.

A adipose tissue **C** capillaries **L** lymphocytes **O** oxyphil cells **P** principal or chief cells
PT parathyroid gland **S** fibrous septa **T** thyroid gland

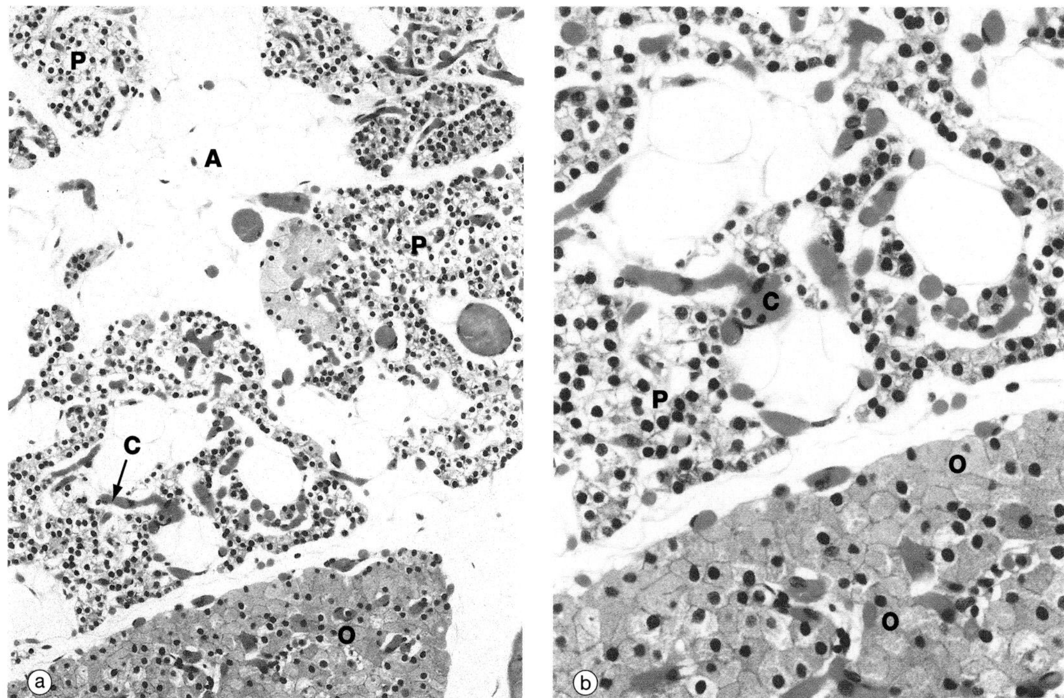

Fig. 17.13 Parathyroid gland
(a) H & E ×150 (b) H & E ×300

Micrograph (a) is a medium power view of normal adult parathyroid showing the glandular elements intermixed with adipose tissue **A**, which begins to accumulate after puberty and makes up 25–40% of the total tissue in normal adults. The glandular cells are of two types: ***chief*** or ***principal cells*** **P** and ***oxyphil cells*** **O**. The glandular cells are arranged as clusters, ribbons or glands.

At higher power, in micrograph (b), the chief cells **P**, are small with round central nuclei and pale eosinophilic or clear cytoplasm. These are the cells which synthesise and secrete PTH. The staining intensity of the cytoplasm depends on whether the cells are actively secreting PTH, in which case the cytoplasm contains plentiful rough endoplasmic reticulum and stains strongly. On the other hand, resting cells have pale cytoplasm and make up about 80% of the total in normal adults.

Oxyphil cells **O**, which tend to occur in nodules, have copious eosinophilic cytoplasm that ultrastructurally is seen to be packed with mitochondria. These cells do not secrete PTH and increase in number with age.

Note the many delicate capillaries **C** between the nests of endocrine cells.

Disorders of the parathyroid gland

The parathyroid glands may either overwork, producing excessive parathormone (***hyperparathyroidism***) or underwork, producing little or no hormone (***hypoparathyroidism***).

The commonest cause of hyperparathyroidism is a benign tumour of one of the parathyroid glands (***parathyroid adenoma***) which constantly produces excessive parathormone, unresponsive to normal feedback mechanisms related to the blood calcium levels. The excess parathormone stimulates excessive osteoclastic erosion of bone (see Fig. 10.6) with the release of bone calcium into the blood to produce ***hypercalcaemia***. The results include bone pain with X-ray abnormalities and an increased risk of kidney stones. This pattern is called ***primary hyperparathyroidism***. ***Secondary hyperparathyroidism*** is a secondary response of all the parathyroid glands to a persistent low serum calcium level in patients with kidney failure who are constantly losing calcium in their urine. The feedback mechanism is triggered and all of the parathyroids become enlarged (***parathyroid hyperplasia***) and secrete excess parathormone in an attempt to bring the serum calcium level back to normal.

Hypoparathyroidism is rare, and is usually due to inadvertent surgical removal of all parathyroid glands during total thyroidectomy.

Adrenal gland

The adrenal (suprarenal) glands are small, flattened endocrine glands which are closely applied to the upper pole of each kidney. In mammals, the adrenal gland contains two functionally different types of endocrine tissue which have distinctly different embryological origins; in some lower animals, these two components exist as separate endocrine glands. The two components of the adrenal gland are the ***adrenal cortex*** and ***adrenal medulla***.

- **Adrenal cortex.** The adrenal cortex has a similar embryological origin to the gonads and, like them, secretes a variety of ***steroid hormones*** all structurally related to their common precursor, ***cholesterol***. The adrenal steroids may be divided into three functional classes, ***mineralocorticoids, glucocorticoids*** and ***sex hormones***. The mineralocorticoids are concerned with electrolyte and fluid homeostasis. The glucocorticoids have a wide range of effects on carbohydrate, protein and lipid metabolism. Small quantities of sex hormones are secreted by the adrenal cortex and supplement gonadal sex hormone secretion.
- **Adrenal medulla.** Embryologically, the adrenal medulla has a similar origin to that of the sympathetic nervous system and may be considered as a highly specialised adjunct of this system. The adrenal medulla secretes the catecholamine hormones, ***adrenaline*** (***epinephrine***) and ***noradrenaline*** (***norepinephrine***).

The control of hormone secretion differs markedly between the cortex and medulla. Glucocorticoid secretion is mainly regulated by the pituitary trophic hormone ACTH, while mineralocorticoid secretion is under the control of the renin-angiotensin system (see Ch. 16). In contrast, the secretion of adrenal medullary catecholamines is directly controlled by the sympathetic nervous system. The function of the adrenal medulla is to reinforce the action of the sympathetic nervous system under conditions of stress, the direct nervous control of adrenal medullary secretion permitting a rapid response.

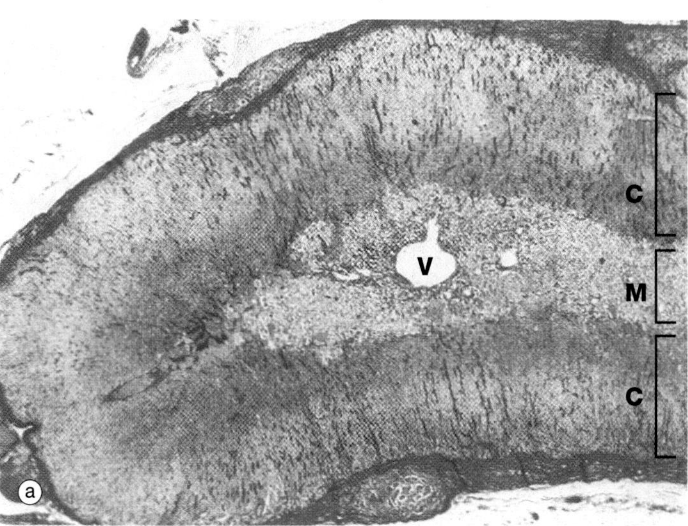

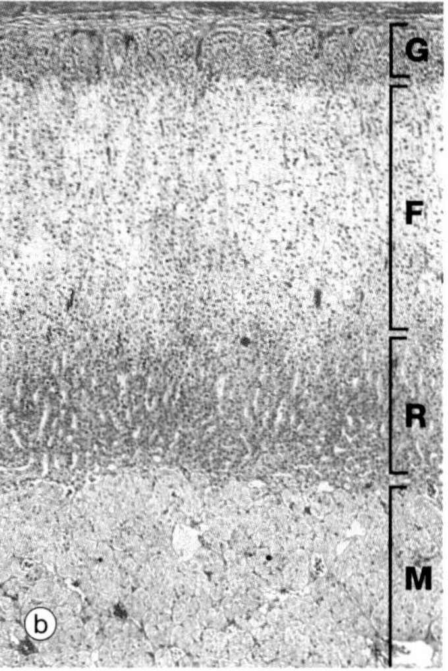

Fig. 17.14 Adrenal gland
(a) Azan ×12 (b) Azan ×20

At low magnification, the adrenal gland is seen to be divided into an outer cortex **C** and a pale stained inner medulla **M**. A dense fibrous tissue capsule, stained blue in this preparation, invests the gland and provides external support for a delicate collagenous framework supporting the secretory cells. A prominent vein **V** is characteristically located in the centre of the medulla.

At higher magnification in micrograph (b), the adrenal cortex can be seen to consist of three histological zones which are named according to the arrangement of the secretory cells: ***zona glomerulosa***, ***zona fasciculata*** and ***zona reticularis***.

The zona glomerulosa **G** lying beneath the capsule contains secretory cells arranged in rounded clusters. The intermediate zona fasciculata **F** consists of parallel cords of secretory cells disposed at right angles to the capsule. The zona reticularis **R**, which lies adjacent to the medulla **M**, consists of small closely packed cells arranged in irregular cords. Often the borders of the zones are less regular and less easily recognised than in this specimen.

C cortex **Cap** capsule **F** zona fasciculata **G** zona glomerulosa **M** medulla **R** zona reticularis **T** trabeculae **V** vein

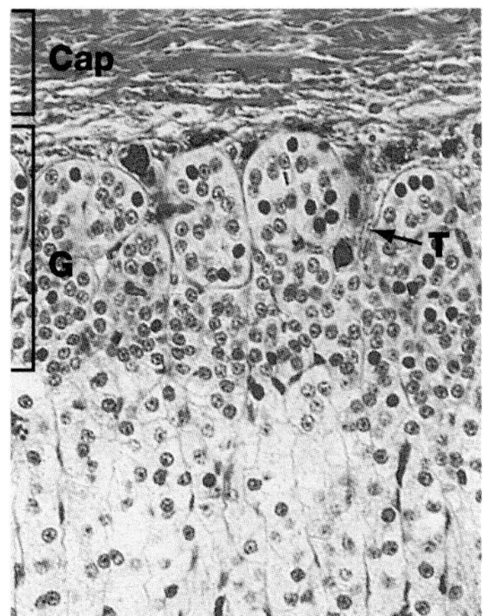

Fig. 17.15 Adrenal cortex: zona glomerulosa
Azan ×128

The zona glomerulosa **G** is composed of cells arranged in irregular ovoid clusters separated by delicate fibrous trabeculae **T** continuous with the fibrocollagenous capsule **Cap**; both the trabeculae and inner capsule contain prominent capillaries. The cells have round nuclei and less cytoplasm than the cells in the adjacent zona fasciculata. The cytoplasm contains plentiful smooth endoplasmic reticulum and numerous mitochondria, but with only scanty lipid droplets.

This zone secretes the mineralocorticoid hormones, principally ***aldosterone***, the secretion of which is controlled by the renin-angiotensin system (see Ch. 16), which in turn is controlled by the macula densa of the distal renal tubule. Aldosterone acts directly on the renal tubules to increase sodium and therefore water retention. This increases extracellular fluid volume, and therefore increases arterial blood pressure. Aldosterone secretion is independent of ACTH control.

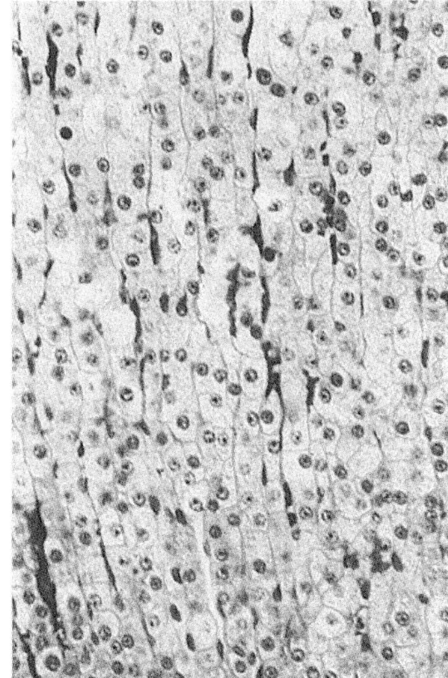

Fig. 17.16 Adrenal cortex: zona fasciculata
Azan ×128

The zona fasciculata is the middle and broadest of the three cortical zones. It consists of narrow columns and cords of cells, often only one cell thick, separated by fine strands of collagen and wide bore capillaries. The cell cytoplasm is abundant and pale staining due to the large number of lipid droplets present; mitochondria and smooth endoplasmic reticulum are also abundant. The zona fasciculata secretes glucocorticoid hormones, mainly cortisol, which have many metabolic effects, one of which is to raise blood glucose levels and increase cellular synthesis of glycogen. They also increase the rate of protein breakdown and the rate of liberation of lipid from tissue stores.

Cortisol secretion is controlled by the hypothalamus via the anterior pituitary trophic hormone ACTH. By this means, many stimuli, such as stress, promote glucocorticoid secretion.

The zona fasciculata is also the site of secretion of small amounts of androgenic sex hormones.

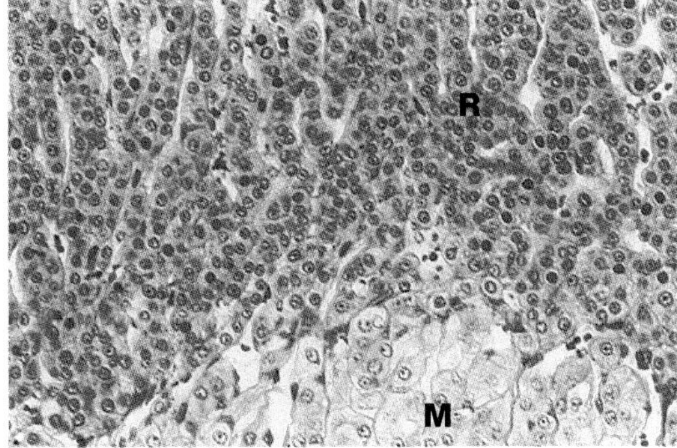

Fig. 17.17 Adrenal cortex: zona reticularis
Azan ×128

The zona reticularis **R** is the thin innermost layer of the adrenal cortex, and lies next to the adrenal medulla **M**. It consists of an irregular network of branching cords and clusters of glandular cells separated by numerous wide diameter capillaries. The zona reticularis cells are much smaller than those of the adjacent zona fasciculata with less cytoplasm. The cytoplasm is darker staining because it contains considerably fewer lipid droplets. Brown lipofuscin pigment (see Fig. 1.15) is sometimes seen in the cells of this layer. The zona reticularis secretes small quantities of androgens and glucocorticoids.

Disorders of the adrenal cortex

Destruction of both adrenals (for example, by autoimmune adrenalitis or, in former years, by tuberculosis) leads to failure of secretion of all adrenal cortical hormones (***hypoadrenalism***), leading to the clinical syndrome called ***Addison's disease*** (weakness, tiredness, skin pigmentation, postural hypotension, hypovolaemia and low blood sodium). More common is ***hyperadrenalism*** where there is excess secretion of one or more of the cortical hormones, mainly glucocorticoids (producing ***Cushing's syndrome***) or mineralocorticoids (producing ***Conn's syndrome***). The excess hormone may be produced by a benign tumour (***adrenal cortical adenoma***) or a malignant tumour (***adrenal cortical carcinoma***), or by ***diffuse hyperplasia*** of the adrenal cortex. In adrenal cortical carcinoma, the excessive output affects all three types of cortical hormone, including androgens, and hirsutism or virilisation are frequently present.

Ectopic ACTH syndrome occurs when some types of tumour elsewhere in the body (e.g. neuroendocrine carcinomas in the lung) secrete excessive amounts of ACTH-like substance which stimulates the zona fasciculata to produce excess glucocorticoids.

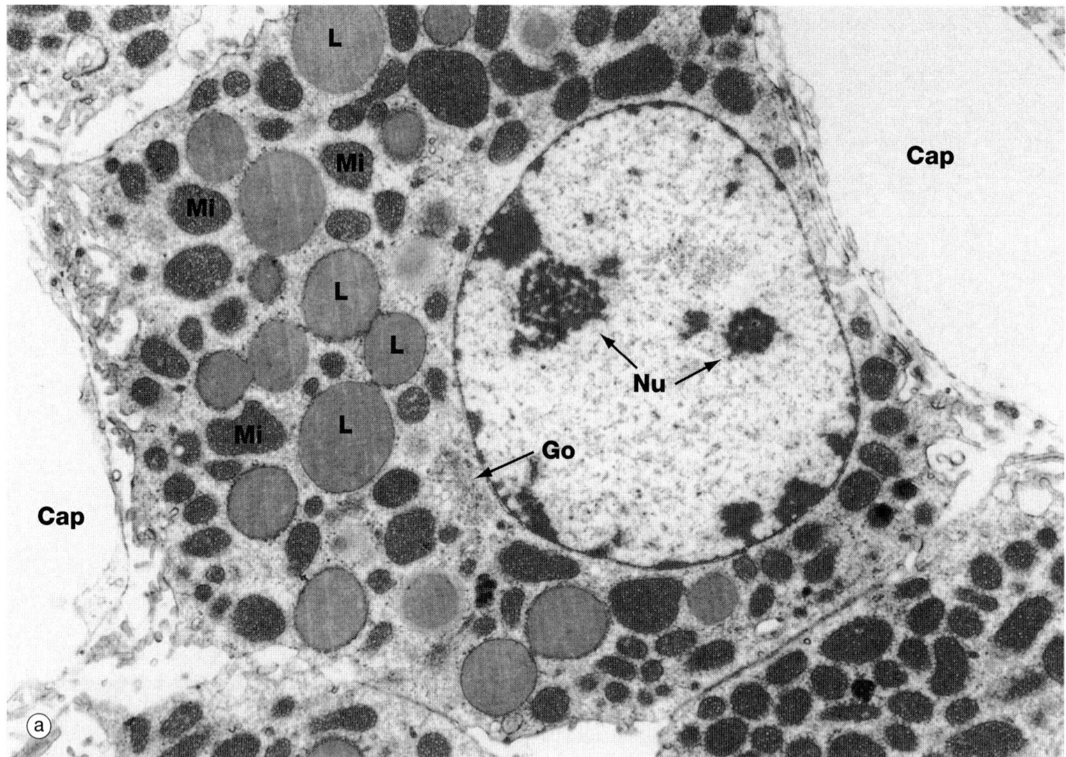

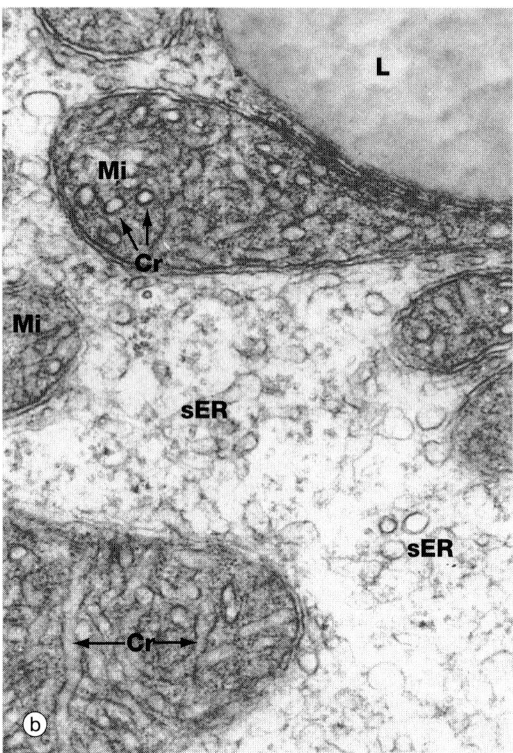

Fig. 17.18 Steroid-secreting cell
(a) EM ×8500 (b) EM ×110 500

These micrographs illustrate the typical ultrastructural features of steroid-secreting cells which are seen not only in the cells of the adrenal cortex but also in the steroid-secreting cells of the ovaries and testes (see Chs 18 and 19). At low magnification in micrograph (a), a secretory cell is seen intimately associated with fenestrated capillaries **Cap**. Note the short microvillous projections of the secretory cell plasma membrane subjacent to the capillary endothelium. The rounded secretory cell nucleus is characterised by one or more prominent nucleoli **Nu**.

The abundant cytoplasm contains many large lipid droplets **L** containing stored cholesterol esters. A small Golgi apparatus **Go** is seen close to the nucleus. Numerous variably shaped mitochondria **Mi** crowd the cytoplasm. As seen in micrograph (b) at high magnification, the mitochondria have unusual, tubular cristae **Cr**. The cytoplasm contains a prolific system of smooth endoplasmic reticulum **sER**.

Synthesis of steroid hormones begins with the liberation of cholesterol esters from lipid droplets. The cholesterol molecule is modified to form a wide range of steroid hormones by enzyme systems found in the smooth endoplasmic reticulum and in the mitochondria.

A adrenaline-secreting cell **C** adrenal cortex **Cap** capillary **Cr** cristae **F** zona fasciculata **G** zona glomerulosa **Go** Golgi **L** lipid droplet **M** medulla **Mi** mitochondria **Na** noradrenaline-secreting cell **Nu** nucleolus **R** zona reticularis **sER** smooth endoplasmic reticulum **V** vein

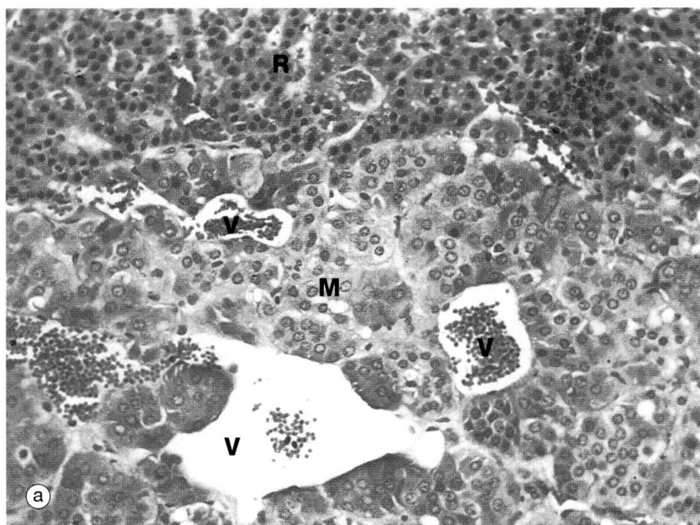

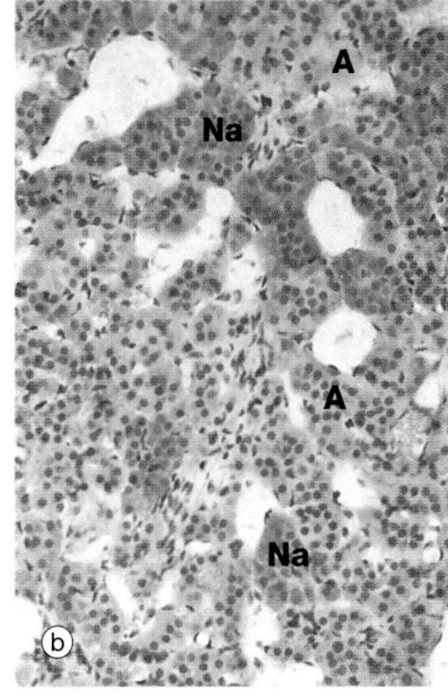

Fig. 17.19 Adrenal medulla
(a) H & E x198 (b) Chrome salt fixation H & E x 200

The adrenal medulla secretes the amines adrenaline (epinephrine) and noradrenaline (norepinephrine) under the control of the sympathetic nervous system. When stained with the standard H & E method the adrenal medulla **M** (micrograph (a)) is composed of clusters of cells with granular, faintly basophilic cytoplasm, with numerous capillaries in their fine supporting stroma. Venous channels **V** draining blood from the sinusoids of the cortex pass through the medulla towards the central medullary vein. This photomicrograph also shows part of the zona reticularis **R** of the cortex.

When fixed in chrome salts (micrograph (b)), the stored catecholamine granules of adrenal medullary cells are oxidised to a brown colour; consequently the name ***chromaffin cells*** was often applied to the secretory cells of the adrenal medulla. Some adrenal medullary cells synthesise noradrenaline; however, the majority synthesise adrenaline by the addition of a further N-methyl group to noradrenaline. Those cells containing noradrenaline **Na** exhibit a much more strongly positive chromaffin reaction than adrenaline-secreting cells **A**. Ultrastructurally the cytoplasm of the medullary cells contains dense core granules similar to those illustrated in Fig. 17.3. The granules in adrenaline secreting cells have a narrow clear halo surrounding the dense core, while those containing noradrenaline have a much wider clear halo around the dense core.

Secretion of catecholamines by the adrenal medulla is controlled by preganglionic neurones of the sympathetic nervous system; thus, the secretory cells of the adrenal medulla are functionally equivalent to the postganglionic neurones of the sympathetic nervous system. Acute physical and psychological stresses initiate release of adrenal medullary hormones. The released catecholamines act on adrenergic receptors throughout the body, particularly in the heart and blood vessels, bronchioles, visceral muscle and skeletal muscle, producing physiological effects very familiar to those who have ever taken a viva voce examination. Adrenaline also has potent metabolic effects such as the promotion of glycogenolysis in liver and skeletal muscle, thus releasing a readily available energy source during stress situations.

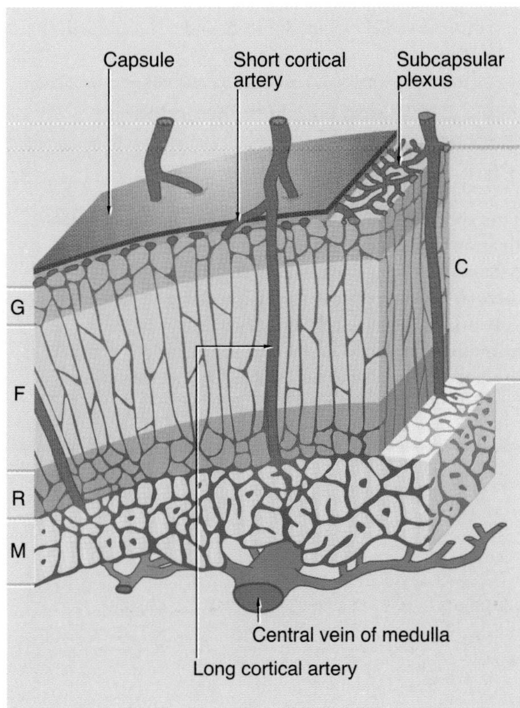

Fig. 17.20 Blood supply of the adrenal

The adrenal gland is supplied by the ***superior***, ***middle*** and ***inferior suprarenal*** arteries, which form a plexus just under the capsule of the gland.

The vascular system of the cortex **C** consists of an anastomosing network of capillary sinusoids supplied by branches of the subcapsular plexus, known as ***short cortical arteries***. The sinusoids descend between the cords of secretory cells in the zona fasciculata **F** into a deep plexus in the zona reticularis **R** before draining into small venules which converge upon the central vein of the medulla **M**. The central medullary veins contain longitudinal bundles of smooth muscle between which the cortical venules enter; contraction of this smooth muscle is thought to dam back cortical blood and thus regulate flow.

The medulla is supplied by ***long cortical arteries*** which descend from the subcapsular plexus through the cortex into the medulla where they ramify into a rich network of dilated capillaries surrounding the medullary secretory cells. The medullary capillaries also drain into the central vein of the medulla. Thus the secretory cells of the medulla are exposed to fresh arterial blood as well as blood rich in adrenocorticosteroids, which are believed to have an important influence on the synthesis of adrenaline by the medulla.

Endocrine pancreas

The pancreas is not only a major exocrine gland (see Ch. 15) but also has important endocrine functions.

The embryonic epithelium of the pancreatic ducts consists of both potential exocrine and endocrine cells. During development, the endocrine cells migrate from the duct system and aggregate around capillaries to form isolated clusters of cells, known as ***islets of Langerhans***, scattered throughout the exocrine glandular tissue. The islets vary in size and are most numerous in the tail of the pancreas. The islets contain a variety of cell types each responsible for secretion of one type of polypeptide hormone.

The main secretory products of the endocrine pancreas are ***insulin*** and ***glucagon***, polypeptide hormones which play an important role in carbohydrate metabolism. Insulin promotes the uptake of glucose by most cells, particularly those of the liver, skeletal muscle and adipose tissue, thus lowering plasma glucose concentration. In general, glucagon has metabolic effects that oppose the actions of insulin. Apart from their role in carbohydrate metabolism, these hormones have a wide variety of other effects on energy metabolism, growth and development.

At least four other types of endocrine cells are present in the islets or else scattered singly or in small groups between the exocrine acini and along the ducts. Their secretory products include ***somatostatin*** (which has a wide variety of effects on gastrointestinal function and may also inhibit insulin and glucagon secretion), ***vasoactive intestinal peptide*** (***VIP***) and ***pancreatic polypeptide*** (***PP***). Another cell type, the enterochromaffin (EC) cell, appears to secrete several different peptides including ***motilin, serotonin*** and ***substance P***.

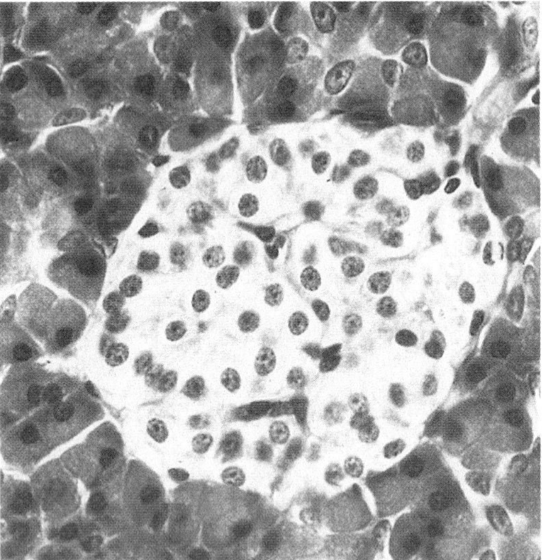

Fig. 17.21 Islet of Langerhans
H & E ×480

The islets of Langerhans are composed of groups of up to 3000 secretory cells supported by a fine collagenous network containing numerous fenestrated capillaries. A delicate capsule surrounds each islet. The endocrine cells are small with a pale stained granular cytoplasm: in contrast, the large cells of the surrounding exocrine pancreatic acini stain strongly.

The endocrine pancreas contains secretory cells of several types: however, in H & E stained preparations, the cell types are indistinguishable from one another and special staining methods are required to differentiate between them. Traditionally, the glucagon-, insulin- and somatostatin-secreting cells have been designated as alpha, beta and delta cells, respectively. However, with the advent of immunoperoxidase methods for identification of secretory products, it is most appropriate to identify cells by their products.

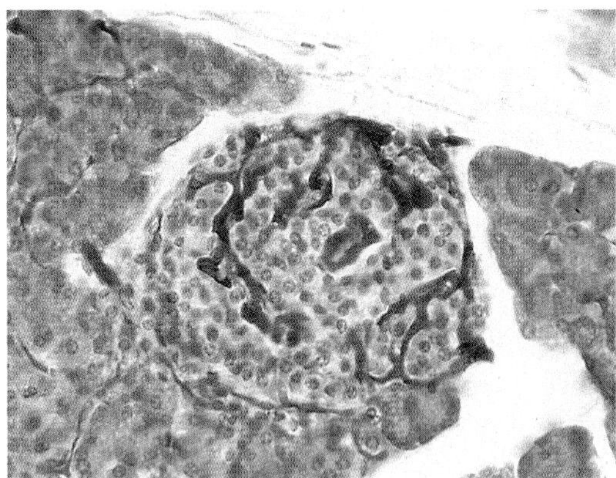

Fig. 17.22 Blood supply of the endocrine pancreas
Carmine perfused/haematoxylin ×128

This specimen was perfused with a red dye before fixation to demonstrate the rich blood supply of the pancreatic islets. Each islet is supplied by as many as three arterioles, which ramify into a highly branched network of fenestrated capillaries, into which the hormones produced in the islet are secreted. The islet is drained by about six venules passing between the exocrine acini to the interlobular veins.

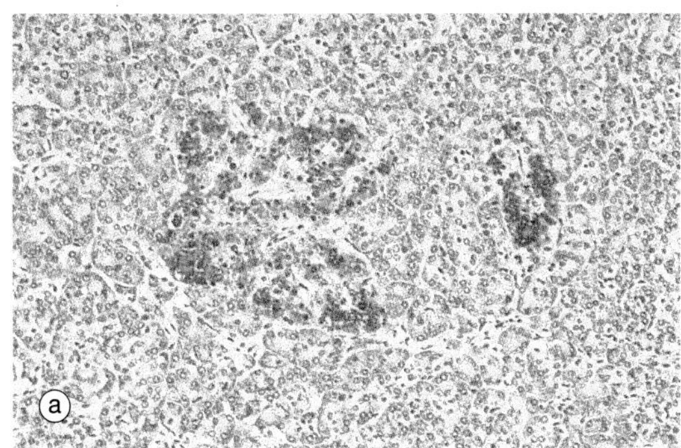

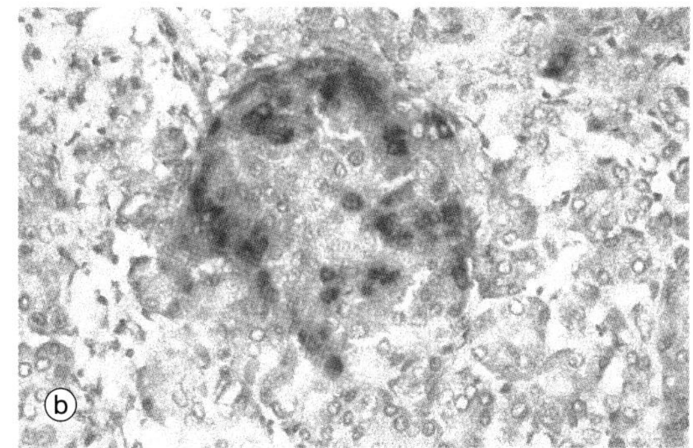

Fig. 17.23 Islet of Langerhans
(a) Immunoperoxidase for insulin ×100 (b) Immunoperoxidase for glucagon ×200

In the past, empirical staining methods were used to demonstrate the different cell types in the islets of Langerhans. These have now been superseded by the immunoperoxidase technique which is able to detect specific intercellular products, in this case insulin and glucagon. The insulin-producing beta cells, which constitute over 60% of the cells in the islet, are stained brown in micrograph (a). Beta cells are distributed throughout the islet while in contrast, glucagon-producing alpha cells (about 25% of the total) are arranged around the periphery (b). Other hormone-producing cells are unstained in these micrographs. The close proximity of these cells facilitates their interaction for control of blood glucose levels and other metabolic functions.

Insulin, a small protein, is synthesised in the rough endoplasmic reticulum as ***preproinsulin*** which is then cleaved to form ***proinsulin***. Proinsulin is cleaved again, this time in the Golgi apparatus, to form insulin, which is then packaged with a small amount of uncleaved proinsulin into membrane-bound secretory granules which remain in the cytoplasm until insulin secretion is triggered.

Disorders of the endocrine pancreas

The islets of Langerhans contain endocrine cells which produce a range of hormones, but the most important disease is that associated with the production and function of insulin.

Diabetes mellitus

Diabetes mellitus is a common and important disease of insulin metabolism, and there are two main types:

- ***Type I diabetes*** usually begins in childhood or adolescence and is the result of loss of endocrine cells in the pancreatic islets, including those which secrete insulin. The islet cell destruction is thought to be due to an abnormal autoimmune response, possibly to a viral infection, and results in insulin deficiency. This has widespread metabolic effects on carbohydrate, protein and fat metabolism, leading to complex metabolic and structural diseases.
- ***Type II diabetes*** begins in late adult life (maturity onset) and is the result of the resistance of target cells to the effect of insulin rather than a failure of insulin production by the pancreatic islets.

Tumours of the islets of Langerhans

Rarely, tumours of the islets of Langerhans may produce disease as a result of excessive secretion of one of the islet hormones, for example an insulin-secreting tumour produces ***hyperinsulinism***, with hypoglycaemic symptoms.

Pineal gland

The pineal gland is a small roughly spherical gland 6–10 mm in diameter, and lies in the midline of the brain, just below the posterior end of the corpus callosum. It represents an evagination of the posterior part of the roof of the third ventricle. It is connected to the brain by a short stalk containing nerve fibres, some of which communicate with the hippocampus. The pineal gland synthesises the hormone ***melatonin*** which acts as an endocrine transducer, inducing rhythmical changes in the endocrine activity of the hypothalamus, pituitary, ovaries and testes in response to changes in light received by the retina. Melatonin production by the pineal is induced by darkness and inhibited by light, probably through sympathetic nerves transmitting messages from the eye through the suprachiasmatic nucleus, central sympathetic pathways and the superior cervical ganglion.

Postulated effects of melatonin in man include an influence on the onset of puberty and body biorhythms. In other animals it plays a role in the timing of seasonal reproductive cycles and, in reptiles and other lower vertebrates is responsible for changing skin colour through its action on melanophores, pigmented cells analogous to melanocytes in mammals. There is still much to learn about the role of melatonin in health and disease in man.

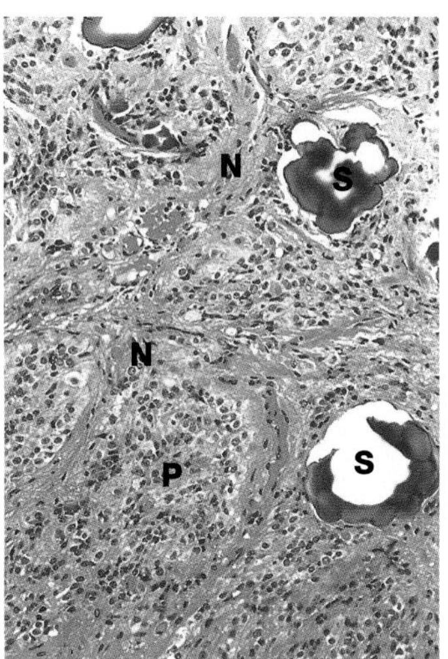

Fig. 17.24 Pineal gland
H & E ×100

The pineal consists of two main cell types: ***pinealocytes*** (***pineal chief cells***) and ***neuroglial cells***. Pinealocytes **P** are highly modified neurones arranged in clusters and cords surrounded by a rich network of fenestrated capillaries. Pinealocytes have round nuclei with prominent nucleoli and granular cytoplasm, and many highly branched processes, some of which terminate near or upon blood vessels. The cytoplasmic granules of pinealocytes contain melatonin and its precursor, serotonin.

The neuroglial cells **N**, which are similar to the astrocytes of the rest of the CNS, are dispersed between the clusters of pinealocytes and in association with capillaries.

A characteristic feature of the ageing pineal is the presence of basophilic extracellular bodies called ***pineal sand*** **S** consisting of concentric layers of calcium and magnesium phosphate in an organic matrix. The calcified pineal can be seen on X-rays of the skull and its position can be a useful guide to pathological conditions causing the midline to be displaced to one side.

Diffuse neuroendocrine system

This is the name given to a scattered system of neuroendocrine cells which secrete hormones and active peptides, some of which act locally to affect the function of adjacent cells (***paracrine***), while others are transmitted in the bloodstream as normal endocrine hormones. Neuroendocrine cells possess characteristic membrane-bound neurosecretory vesicles, usually spherical, with an electron dense central core (dense-core vesicles). Although neuroendocrine-type cells form part of other endocrine organs (e.g. adrenal medulla) and some non-endocrine organs (e.g. islets of Langerhans in the pancreas, juxtaglomerular apparatus in kidney), they are particularly important in the diffuse neuroendocrine system in the gastrointestinal and respiratory tracts.

Gastrointestinal neuroendocrine cells are found scattered in the mucosa of the gastrointestinal tract and in the pancreatic and biliary ducts. These cells secrete more than 20 different peptide and amine hormones including gastrin, secretin, CCK, serotonin, enteroglucagon, somatostatin, substance P, vasoactive intestinal peptide (VIP), bombesin, gastric inhibitory polypeptide (GIP), motilin and pancreatic polypeptide (PP). These hormones constitute a system of interacting mediators, which collectively regulate and coordinate most aspects of gastrointestinal activity in concert with the autonomic nervous system.

While some of these substances are true ***endocrine hormones***, acting at a distance from their site of origin, others are locally acting mediators known as ***paracrine hormones***. A third mechanism of action (***neurocrine***) is by neurotransmitter activity and indeed some of these substances also act as neurotransmitters within the central nervous system (gastrin, VIP, CCK and many others).

The lower respiratory tract contains scattered peptide- and amine-secreting endocrine cells analogous to those in the gastrointestinal tract, which are probably involved in local and autonomically mediated regulation of respiratory tract function particularly in early childhood. The endocrine cells are scattered individually in the epithelium or in clumps (neuroepithelial bodies – see Fig 12.11b) protruding into the airway and have a variety of secretory products including serotonin, calcitonin, bombesin and leu-enkephalin.

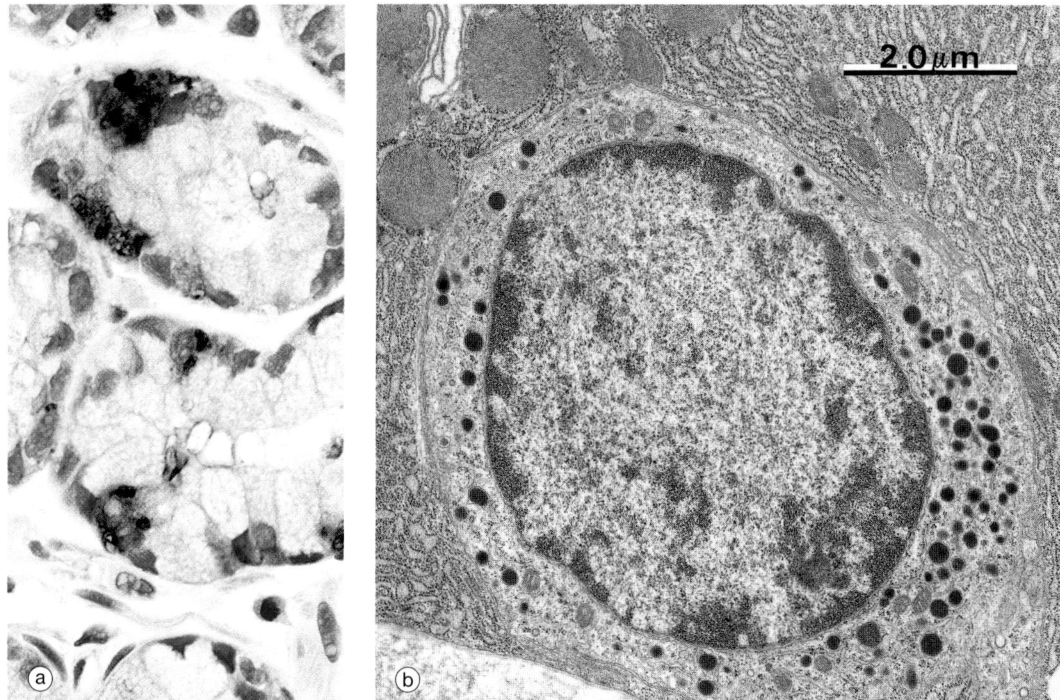

Fig. 17.25 Gastric neuroendocrine cells
(a) Immunoperoxidase ×400 (b) EM ×12 500

Micrograph (a) shows cross-sections of two gastric glands near the base, stained by an immunoperoxidase method for somatostatin. The neuroendocrine cells (brown-black) are pyramidal-shaped with a broad base sitting on the basement membrane of the gland, and a narrower part approaching the lumen of the gland. In so-called 'open-type' mucosal neuroendocrine cells, the narrow end of the cell is in contact with the lumen and its contents.

Micrograph (b) shows a somatostatin-secreting neuroendocrine cell in the gastric mucosa. The cytoplasm contains large numbers of electron-dense neurosecretory vacuoles (dense-core granules); they are mainly spherical, of various sizes, and are particularly concentrated towards the base of the cell.

Tumours of the diffuse neuroendocrine system

The cells of the diffuse neuroendocrine system may occasionally give rise to tumours. The most frequent, and most important, is a highly malignant tumour of neuroendocrine cells of the bronchial tree, called ***small cell (oat cell) carcinoma***. This tumour grows very rapidly and infiltrates and destroys nearby tissues, but also spreads to distant sites such as bones, liver, brain etc. Most of these tumours retain some capacity to synthesise and secrete hormones or hormone-precursor molecules, and rarely excessive secretion of these can cause fatal metabolic disorders. Small cell carcinoma of the lung often secretes an ACTH-like substance which stimulates excessive and uncontrolled secretion of hormones from the adrenal cortex.

The most common tumour of the neuroendocrine cells in the alimentary tract is the ***carcinoid tumour***. These are most common in the small intestine and appendix, and grow slowly. They secrete 5-hydroxytryptamine which usually has no systemic effect because it passes from the tumour in the gut via the hepatic portal vein to the liver where it is broken down into inactive products. Although these tumours are slow-growing, they are potentially malignant and can spread to secondary sites away from the gut. In this case, 5-hydroxytryptamine can enter the systemic blood circulation and produce metabolic effects; this is called ***carcinoid syndrome***.

N neuroglial cells **P** pinealocytes **S** pineal sand

18. *Male reproductive system*

Introduction

The male reproductive system may be divided into four major functional components:

- The ***testes*** or male gonads, paired organs lying in the scrotal sac, are responsible for production of the male gametes, ***spermatozoa***, and secretion of male sex hormones, principally ***testosterone***.
- A system of ducts, consisting of ***ductuli efferentes***, ***epididymis***, ***ductus (vas) deferens*** and ***ejaculatory duct***, collects, stores and conducts spermatozoa from each testis. The ejaculatory ducts converge on the ***urethra*** from which spermatozoa are expelled into the female reproductive tract during copulation.
- Two exocrine glands, the paired ***seminal vesicles***, and the single ***prostate gland***, secrete a nutritive and lubricating fluid medium called ***seminal fluid*** in which spermatozoa are conveyed to the female reproductive tract. ***Semen***, the fluid expelled during ejaculation, consists of seminal fluid and spermatozoa, plus some desquamated duct lining cells.
- The ***penis*** is the organ of copulation. A pair of small accessory glands, the ***bulbourethral glands of Cowper***, secrete a fluid which lubricates the urethra for the passage of semen during ejaculation.

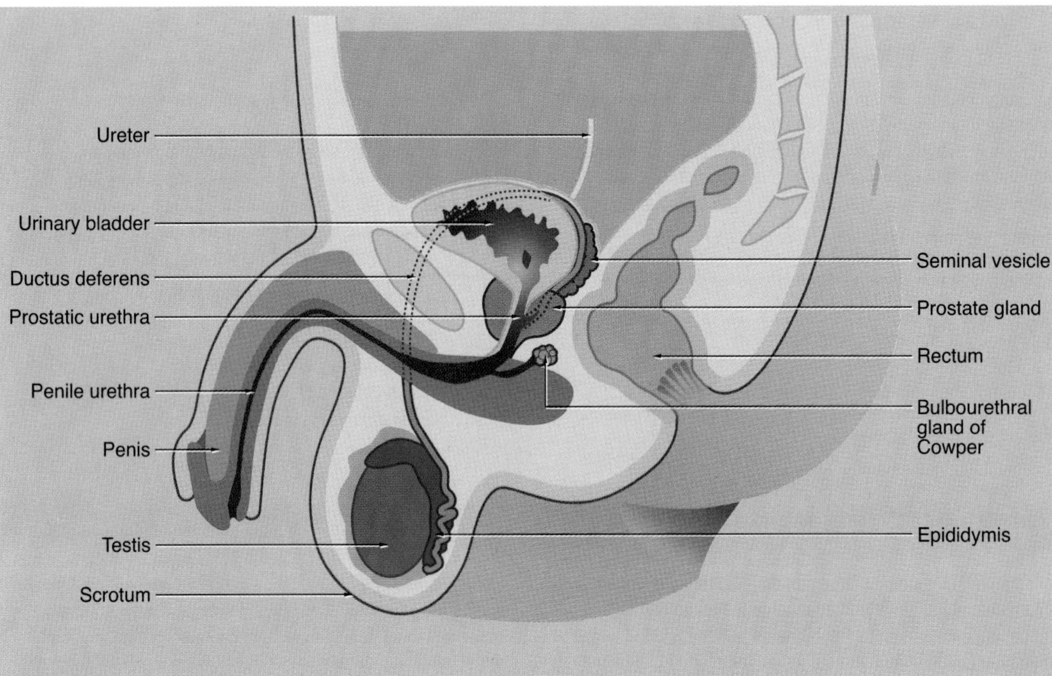

Fig. 18.1 Male reproductive system

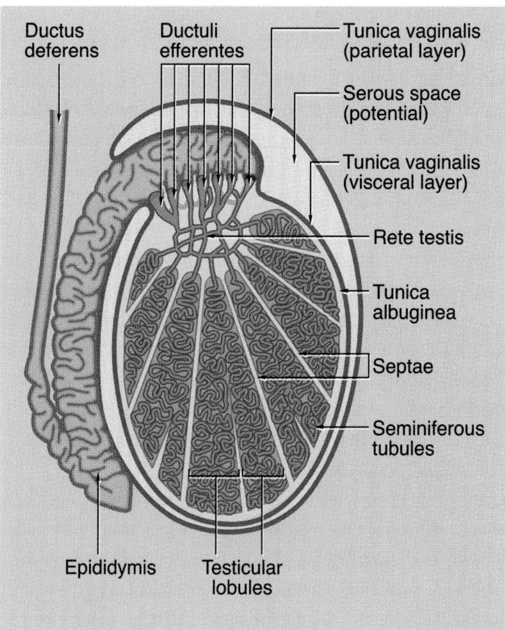

Fig. 18.2 Testis

During embryological development, each testis with the first part of its duct system, blood vessels, lymphatics and nerves, descends from the posterior wall of the peritoneal cavity to the scrotum. During migration, the testis carries with it an investing layer of peritoneum so that in the scrotum the testis is almost completely surrounded by a double layer of mesothelium enclosing a potential space. This double lining is called the ***tunica vaginalis*** and, like the pleura, consists of ***visceral*** and ***parietal layers*** separated by a thin layer of serous fluid. The fluid is secreted by the mesothelial cells and acts as a lubricant, allowing the testis to move freely in the scrotal sac. The visceral layer of the tunica vaginalis rests on the capsule of the testis, the ***tunica albuginea***, which gives rise to numerous incomplete collagenous septa. These divide the testis into about 250 ***testicular lobules***. Within each lobule there are one to four highly convoluted tubes, the ***seminiferous tubules***, in which spermatozoa are produced. The seminiferous tubules converge upon a plexus of channels, the ***rete testis***. From the rete testis, 15 to 20 small ducts, called the ***ductuli efferentes***, conduct spermatozoa to the extremely tortuous first part of the ***ductus deferens***, which is known as the ***epididymis***.

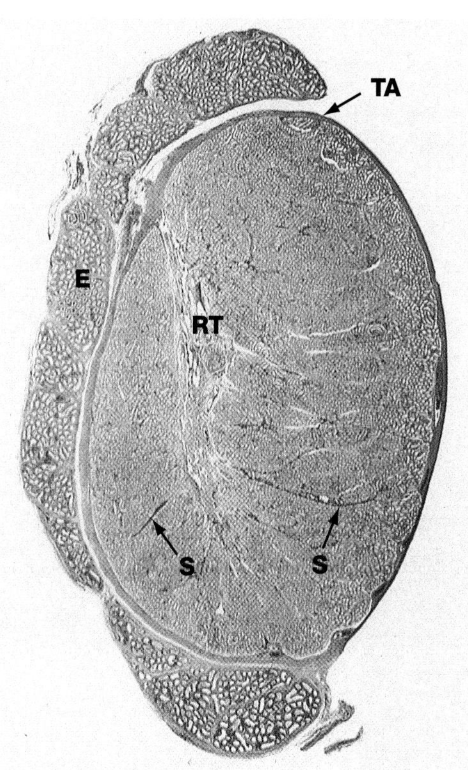

Fig. 18.3 Testis – monkey
H & E ×3

This micrograph illustrates the macroscopic features of a testis; cut in the sagittal plane, it shows the relationship of the epididymis **E** which lies on its posterior aspect. The testis is packed with coiled seminiferous tubules, which can just be seen in various planes of section at this magnification. Groups of up to four seminiferous tubules are segregated into testicular lobules by fine interlobular septa **S**.

The dense fibrous capsule which invests the testis, and which is continuous with many of the interlobular septa, is called the ***tunica albuginea*** **TA** and contains fibroblasts and myofibroblasts, particularly in the posterior aspect, which subject the seminiferous tissue to rhythmic contractions. The deepest layer of the tunica albuginea consists of loose connective tissue containing blood and lymphatic vessels, sometimes called the ***tunica vasculosa***.

Spermatozoa pass from the seminiferous tubules into the rete testis **RT** which is connected to the epididymis via the ductuli efferentes at the upper posterior pole of the testis; the ductuli are not included in the plane of this section. The epididymis is a tightly coiled tube, which forms a compact mass extending down the whole length of the posterior surface of the testis, and is the major site of storage of newly formed spermatozoa. At the lower pole of the testis, the epididymal tube becomes continuous with the relatively straight ductus (vas) deferens, which is not seen in this section.

E epididymis **RT** rete testis **S** interlobular septa **TA** tunica albuginea

Gametogenesis

In all somatic cells, cell division (***mitosis***) results in the formation of two daughter cells, each one genetically identical to the mother cell. Somatic cells contain a full complement of chromosomes (the ***diploid number***) which function as homologous pairs (see Ch. 2). The process of sexual reproduction involves the fusion of specialised male and female cells called ***gametes*** to form a ***zygote***, which has the diploid number of chromosomes. Each gamete contains only half the diploid number of chromosomes, one representative of each pair; this half complement of chromosomes is known as the ***haploid number***.

The production of haploid cells involves a unique form of cell division called ***meiosis***, which occurs only in the germ cells of the gonads during the formation of gametes; meiotic cell division is thus also called ***gametogenesis***. Meiosis involves two cell division cycles of which only the first is preceded by duplication of chromosomes (see Ch. 2). Thus, meiotic cell division of a single diploid germ cell gives rise to four haploid gametes. In the male, each of the four gametes undergoes morphological development into a mature ***spermatozoon***. In contrast, in the female, unequal distribution of the cytoplasm during meiosis results in one gamete gaining almost all the cytoplasm from the mother cell, while the other three acquire almost no cytoplasm; the large gamete matures to form an ***ovum*** and the other three, called ***polar bodies***, degenerate.

The primitive germ cells of the male, the ***spermatogonia***, are present only in small numbers in the male gonads before sexual maturity. After puberty, spermatogonia multiply continuously by mitosis to provide a supply of cells, which then undergo meiosis to form male gametes. In contrast, the germ cells of the female, called ***oogonia***, multiply by mitosis only during early fetal development, thereby producing a fixed complement of cells with the potential to undergo gametogenesis. Gametogenesis in the female is discussed more fully in Chapter 19. The production of male gametes is called ***spermatogenesis*** and the subsequent development of the male gamete into a motile spermatozoon is called ***spermiogenesis***, the whole process taking approximately 70 days; both these processes occur within the testes although final maturation of spermatozoa occurs in the epididymis.

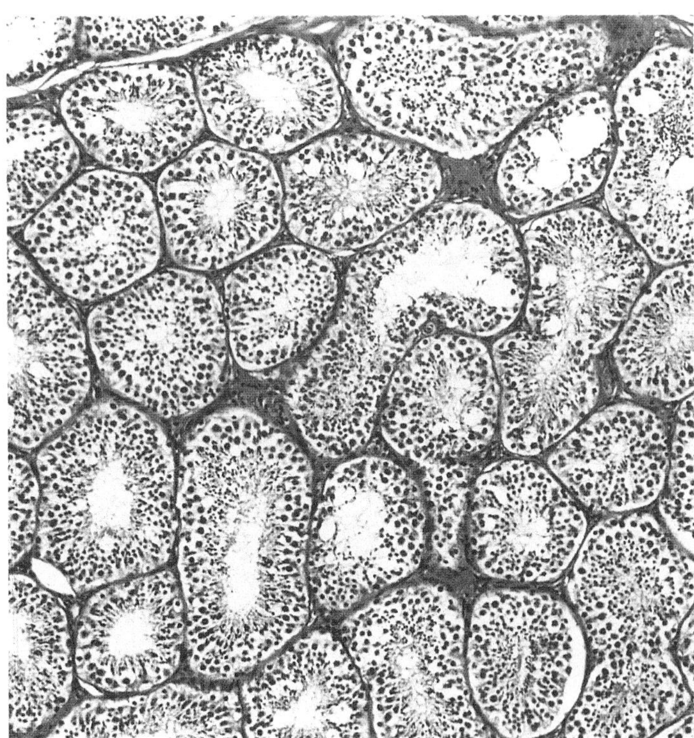

Fig. 18.4 Seminiferous tubules
H & E ×100

This micrograph illustrates seminiferous tubules cut in various planes of section. The seminiferous tubules are highly convoluted and lined by:

- Germ cells in various stages of spermatogenesis and spermiogenesis, which are collectively referred to as the ***spermatogenic series***.
- Non-germ cells called ***Sertoli cells***, which support and nourish the developing spermatozoa.

In the interstitial spaces between the tubules, endocrine cells called ***Leydig cells*** are found either singly or in groups in the supporting tissue.

M myofibroblasts **S_A** spermatogonia type A **S_B** spermatogonia type B **S_1** primary spermatocytes **S_3** spermatids **S_4** spermatozoa **St** Sertoli cells.

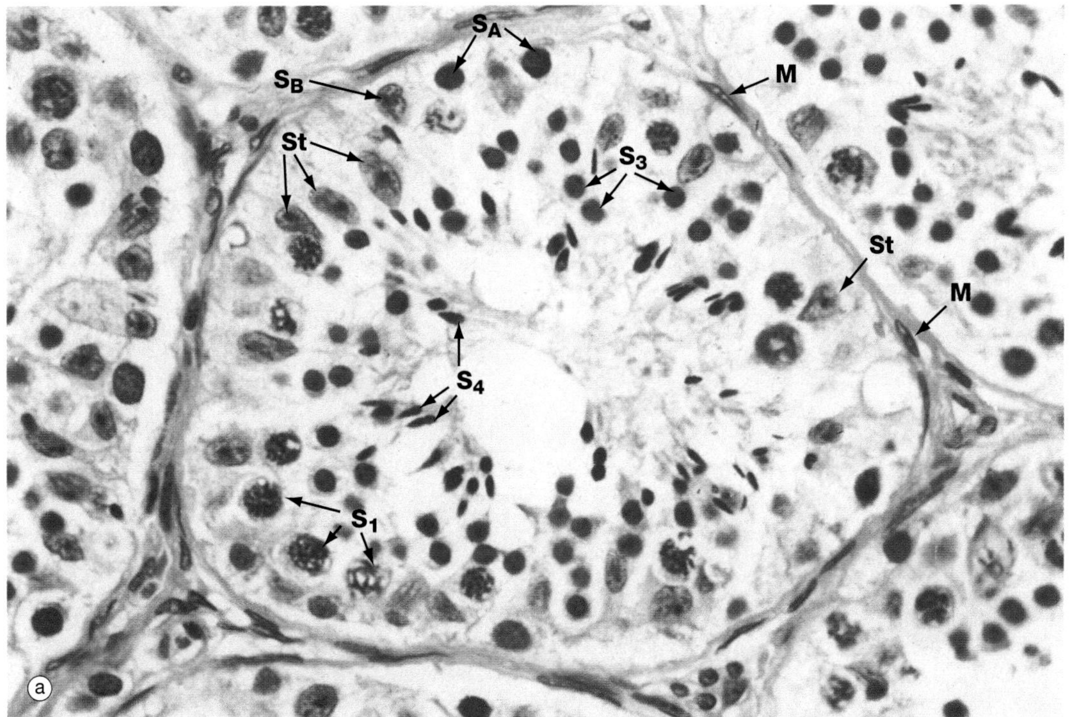

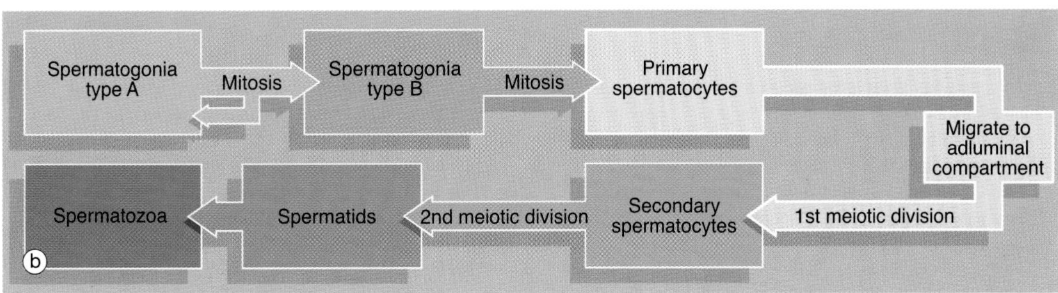

Fig. 18.5 Seminiferous tubule
(a) H & E ×640 (b) Diagram

Micrograph (a) illustrates an adult seminiferous tubule cut in transverse section. The processes of spermatogenesis and spermiogenesis are synchronised, with waves of activity occurring sequentially along the length of each tubule. Thus in a single cross-section of a tubule, not all development phases will be represented (b).

The undifferentiated germ cells, found in the basal compartment of the seminiferous tubule, are called ***type A spermatogonia***. These go through several cycles of mitosis to produce further type A spermatogonia, which maintain the germ cell pool, and ***type B spermatogonia***, which are committed to production of spermatozoa. Spermatogonia type A $\mathbf{S_A}$ are characterised by a large round or oval nucleus with condensed chromatin; peripheral nucleoli and a nuclear vacuole may be prominent. Spermatogonia type B $\mathbf{S_B}$ have dispersed chromatin, central nucleoli, and no nuclear vacuole. Both types of spermatogonia have sparse poorly stained cytoplasm.

Type B spermatogonia undergo further mitotic divisions to produce ***primary spermatocytes***. These migrate to the adluminal compartment of the seminiferous tubule before commencing the first meiotic division. Primary spermatocytes $\mathbf{S_1}$ are readily recognised by their copious cytoplasm and large nuclei containing coarse clumps or thin threads of chromatin; dividing cells may be seen. In humans, the first meiotic division cycle takes approximately 3 weeks to complete, after which time the daughter cells become known as ***secondary spermatocytes***. The smaller secondary spermatocytes rapidly undergo the second meiotic division and are therefore seldom seen.

The gametes thus produced, called ***spermatids*** $\mathbf{S_3}$, then proceed through the long maturation process known as spermiogenesis to become recognisable as spermatozoa. During this process, the nuclei of the spermatids assume the small pointed form of spermatozoa $\mathbf{S_4}$ (see Fig. 18.7). Examination of different sections of the tubules of a normal testis shows about half the spermatogenic cells to be in the late spermatid stage.

During the developmental process, the cells of the spermatogenic series are supported by Sertoli cells **St**, whose nuclei are usually found towards the basement membrane of the seminiferous tubule. The Sertoli cell nucleus is typically triangular or ovoid in shape with a prominent nucleolus and dispersed chromatin.

The basal layer of germinal cells is supported by a basement membrane, which is surrounded by a lamina propria containing several layers of spindle-shaped myofibroblasts **M** and fibroblasts.

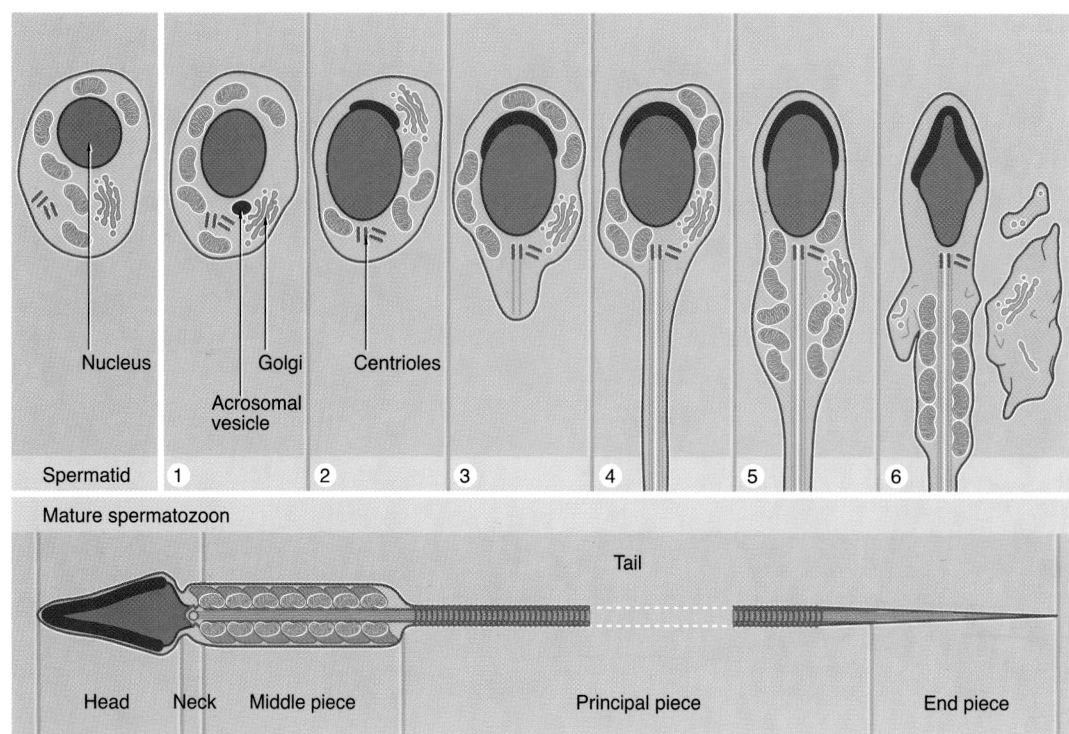

Fig. 18.6 Spermiogenesis

Spermiogenesis is the process by which spermatids, the gametes produced by meiotic division, are transformed into motile mature spermatozoa. This involves the following major stages:

1. The Golgi apparatus elaborates a large vesicle, the ***acrosomal vesicle***, which accumulates carbohydrates and hydrolytic enzymes.
2. The acrosomal vesicle becomes applied to one pole of the progressively elongating nucleus to form a structure known as the ***acrosomal head cap***.
3. Meanwhile, both centrioles migrate to the end of the cell opposite to the acrosomal head cap; the centriole aligned parallel to the long axis of the nucleus elongates to form a flagellum which has a basic structure similar to that of the cilium (see Fig. 5.14).
4. As the flagellum elongates, nine ***coarse fibrils***, which may contain contractile proteins, become arranged longitudinally around the core of the flagellum. Further rib-like fibrils then become disposed circumferentially around the whole flagellum.
5. The cytoplasm migrates to surround the first part of the flagellum. The remainder of the flagellum appears to project from the cell but in fact remains surrounded by plasma membrane. This migration of cytoplasm thus concentrates mitochondria in the flagellar region.
6. As the flagellum elongates, excess cytoplasm is phagocytosed by the enveloping Sertoli cell prior to release of the spermatid into the lumen.

The mitochondria become arranged in a helical manner around the fibrils, which surround the first part of the flagellum.

The structure of fully formed spermatozoa varies in detail from species to species, but conforms to the basic structure seen in this diagram of a human spermatozoon.

Throughout the entire developmental process from spermatogonia to spermatozoa, hundreds of spermatids remain connected to one another by narrow cytoplasmic bridges which only break down upon release of spermatozoa into the lumen of the seminiferous tubule. This explains the synchronous development of spermatozoa at any one part of the tubule.

Sertoli cells are important in the regulation of spermatogenesis and spermiogenesis. Sertoli cells form tight junctions with each other as well as with the developing germ cells. It is well established that high concentrations of androgen hormones secreted by Leydig cells of the testicular interstitium (see Fig. 18.9) are essential for production and maturation of spermatogenic cells. Sertoli cells secrete an androgen-binding protein, which transports testosterone and dihydrotestosterone to the lumen of the seminiferous tubule. These hormones are also necessary for function of the epithelium of the rete testis and epididymis; production of this binding protein is believed to be dependent on the pituitary gonadotrophin, follicle stimulating hormone (FSH).

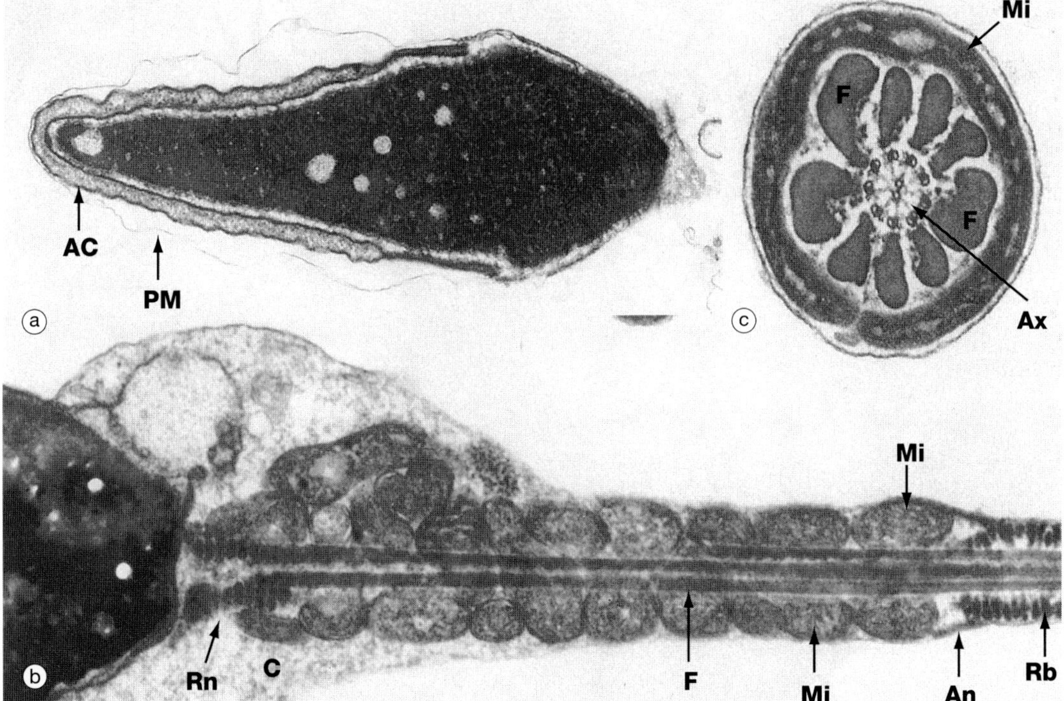

Fig. 18.7 Spermatozoa

(a) Head: EM, LS ×14 000 (b) Neck (middle piece and principal piece): EM, LS ×17 000 (c) Middle piece: EM, TS ×48 000

The ultrastructural features of human spermatozoa are shown in these micrographs. The spermatozoon is an extremely elongated cell (about 65 μm long) consisting of three main components, the ***head***, ***neck*** and ***tail***. The tail is subdivided into three segments, the ***middle piece***, ***principal piece*** and ***end piece*** (see Fig. 18.6).

The head is the most variable structure between different mammalian species. In humans, the head is about 7 μm long and has a flattened pear shape. As seen in micrograph (a), the nucleus, which occupies most of the head, is composed of very condensed chromatin; in humans, this contains a variable number of areas of dispersed chromatin called ***nuclear vacuoles***. Surrounding the anterior two-thirds of the nucleus is the acrosomal cap **AC**, a flattened membrane-bound vesicle containing a range of glycoproteins and a variety of hydrolytic enzymes, principally ***hyaluronidase***; the enzymes disaggregate the cells of the corona radiata and dissolve the zona pellucida during fertilisation (see Ch. 19). Note the plasma membrane **PM**, which has become partially separated during preparation.

The neck is a very short segment connecting the head with the tail. It contains vestiges of the centrioles, one of which gives rise to the axoneme **Ax** of the flagellum which is seen in micrograph (c). The axoneme has the standard 'nine plus two' arrangement of microtubule doublets seen in cilia (see Fig. 5.14). The axoneme of the neck is surrounded by several condensed fibrous rings **Rn** seen in micrograph (b). In human spermatozoa, a significant amount of cytoplasm **C** often remains in the neck region.

The middle piece, the first part of the tail, is about the same length as the head and consists of the flagellar axoneme surrounded by nine ***coarse*** (***outer dense***) ***fibres*** **F** arranged longitudinally. External to this core, elongated mitochondria **Mi** are arranged in a tightly packed helix providing the energy required for flagellar movement. A fibrous thickening beneath the plasma membrane, called the annulus **An**, prevents the mitochondria from slipping into the principal piece. The principal piece, which constitutes most of the tail length, consists of a central core, comprising the axoneme and the nine coarse fibres continuing from the middle piece. Surrounding this core are numerous fibrous ribs **Rb** arranged in a circular manner and seen in micrograph (b). Two of the longitudinal fibrils of the core are fused with the surrounding ribs so as to form ***dorsal*** and ***ventral columns*** extending throughout the length of the principal piece (not illustrated). This arrangement divides the principal piece longitudinally into two functional compartments, one containing three coarse fibrils and the other containing four. Little is known of the mechanism of flagellar motion but this asymmetry may account for the more powerful stroke of the tail in one direction, the so-called 'power stroke'; this can easily be observed in fresh, live preparations of spermatozoa viewed with the light microscope. The end piece, not shown in these micrographs, is merely a short tapering portion of the tail containing the axoneme only.

AC acrosomal cap **An** annulus **Ax** axoneme **C** cytoplasm **F** outer dense fibres
Mi mitochondria **PM** plasma membrane **Rb** fibrous ribs **Rn** fibrous rings

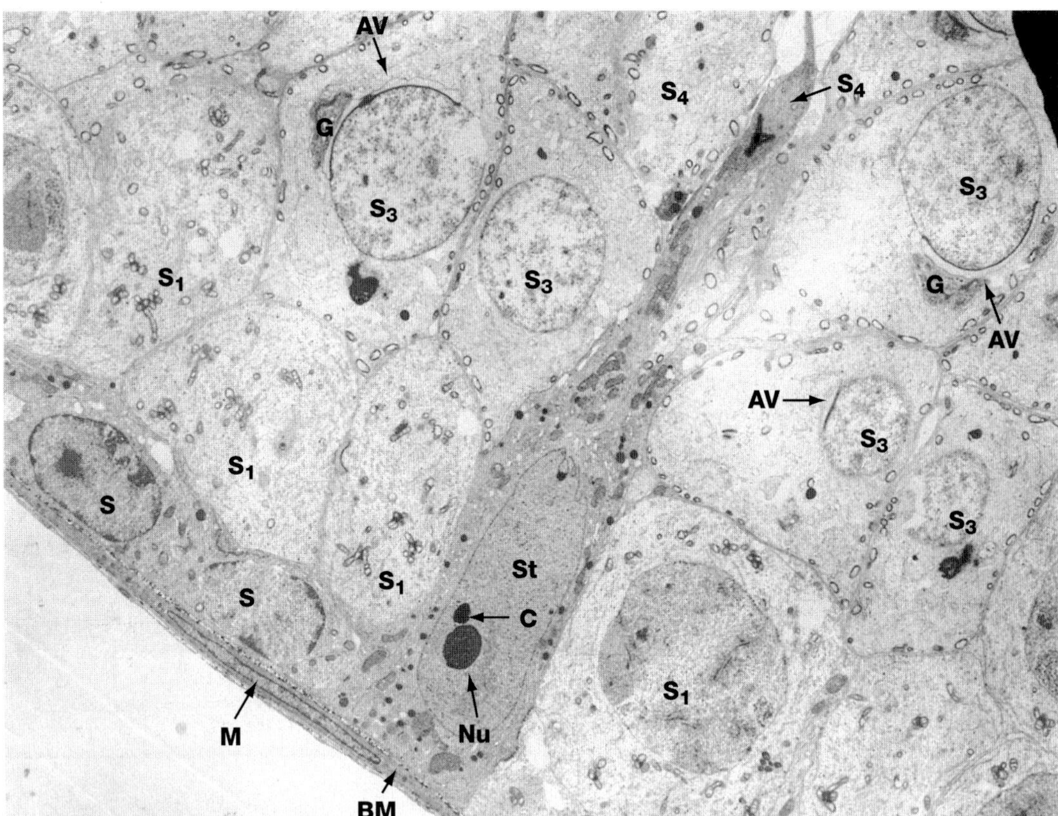

Fig. 18.8 Sertoli cell
EM ×3400

The intimate relationship of a Sertoli cell **St** to cells of the spermatogenic series is demonstrated in this electron micrograph.

The Sertoli cell rests on the basement membrane **BM** of the seminiferous tubule and its cytoplasm extends to the lumen of the tubule. Sertoli cells have an extensive cytoplasm, which ramifies throughout the whole germinal epithelium enclosing all the cells of the spermatogenic series. The cytoplasmic outline of the Sertoli cell is thus highly irregular and constantly changing to permit the progressive movement of developing spermatozoa towards the luminal surface. The oval nucleus of the Sertoli cell is characteristically orientated at right angles to the basement membrane and often exhibits a deep indentation. A prominent nucleolus **Nu** is a constant feature and dense chromatin bodies **C** are often associated with the nucleolus. The cytoplasm contains a moderate number of mitochondria, lipid droplets and a small amount of rough endoplasmic reticulum. Plentiful smooth endoplasmic reticulum is also present as well as lamellar protein arrays known as Charcot–Bottcher crystals (not shown in this cell).

Sertoli cells are bound to one another by junctional complexes containing extensive tight junctions (see Ch. 5). The junctional complex is located towards the basal layer of the spermatogenic epithelium so as to divide the tubule into ***basal*** and ***adluminal compartments***. The latter contains the spermatids which are thus isolated by a ***blood–testis barrier***. The Sertoli cells mediate all metabolic exchange with the systemic compartment. The function of this barrier is to prevent exposure of gametes, which are antigenically different from somatic cells, to the immune system, thus preventing an autoimmune response. Sertoli cells have multiple functions including:

- Secretion of factors which regulate spermatogenesis and spermiogenesis.
- Secretion of factors which regulate the function of Leydig cells and peritubular cells.
- Secretion of ***inhibin*** which regulates hormone production.
- Secretion of tubular fluid.
- Phagocytosis of discarded spermatid cytoplasm.

A variety of cells of the spermatogenic series are seen in this micrograph. Spermatogonia **S** rest upon the basement membrane beneath which is a myofibroblast **M**. Above the germ cell layer, primary spermatocytes $\mathbf{S_1}$ are seen; secondary spermatocytes are short-lived and therefore rarely seen. Spermatids $\mathbf{S_3}$ in different phases of spermiogenesis are seen in upper layers; these cells have developing acrosomal vesicles **AV** elaborated by a large Golgi apparatus **G** (see Fig. 18.6). At the luminal surface, the Sertoli cell partly envelops the head an almost fully formed spermatozoon $\mathbf{S_4}$.

AV acrosomal vesicle **BM** basement membrane **C** chromatin body **G** Golgi apparatus **L** Leydig cell **M** myofibroblast **Nu** nucleolus **S** spermatogonia **SM** smooth muscle **St** Sertoli cell $\mathbf{S_1}$ primary spermatocytes $\mathbf{S_3}$ spermatid $\mathbf{S_4}$ spermatozoon

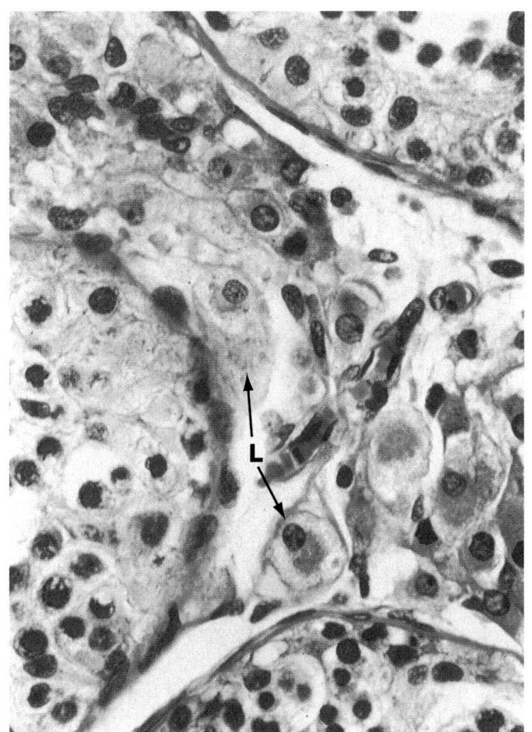

Fig. 18.9 Interstitial (Leydig) cells of the testis
H & E ×480

Leydig cells **L**, the principal cell type found in the interstitial supporting tissue between the seminiferous tubules, synthesise and secrete the male sex hormones and other non-steroid substances. They occur singly or in clumps and are embedded in the rich plexus of blood and lymph capillaries which surrounds the seminiferous tubules. The nucleus is round with dispersed chromatin and one or two nucleoli at the periphery. The extensive eosinophilic cytoplasm contains variable numbers of lipid vacuoles and seen by electron microscopy closely resembles the steroid-secreting cells of the adrenal cortex (see Fig. 17.18). In humans (and wild bush rats), but no other species, Leydig cells also contain elongated cytoplasmic ***crystals of Reinke*** which are large enough to be seen with light microscopy when suitably stained: these crystals are found only in adults but their function is unknown.

Testosterone is the main hormone secreted by Leydig cells. Testosterone is not only responsible for the development of male secondary sexual characteristics at puberty but is also essential for the continued function of the seminiferous epithelium. The secretory activity of Leydig cells is controlled by the pituitary gonadotrophic hormone, luteinising hormone, sometimes called ***interstitial cell stimulating hormone*** (***ICSH***) in the male.

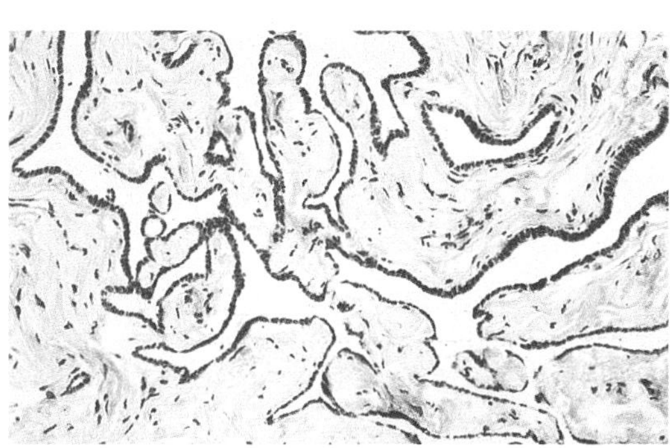

Fig. 18.10 Rete testis
H & E ×128

The seminiferous tubules converge upon the ***mediastinum testis***, which consists of a plexiform arrangement of channels, the ***rete testis***, surrounded by highly vascular collagenous supporting tissue containing myoid cells. The rete testis is lined by a single layer of cuboidal epithelial cells with surface microvilli and a single cilium.

Myoid cell contraction helps to mix the spermatozoa and move them towards the epididymis. The lining epithelium reabsorbs protein and potassium from the seminal fluid. Ciliary activity is presumed to aid the progress of spermatozoa, which do not become motile until after maturation is completed in the epididymis.

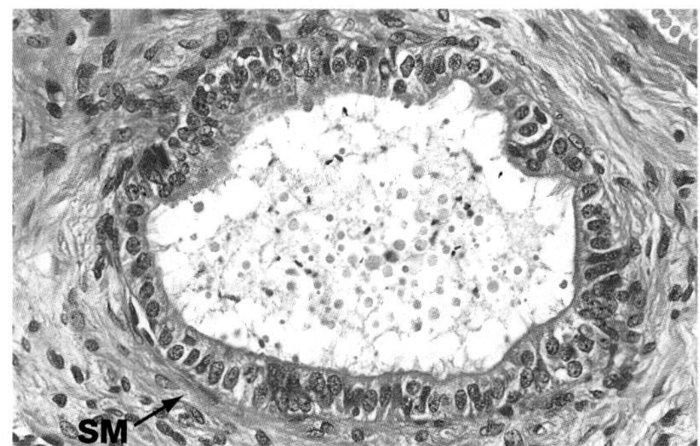

Fig. 18.11 Ductulus efferens
H & E ×200

The rete testis drains into the head of the epididymis via some 15–20 convoluted ducts, the ***ductuli efferentes***. The ductuli are lined by a single layer of epithelial cells, some of which are tall columnar and ciliated and others which are short and non-ciliated: both cell types often contain a brown pigment of unknown composition. Ciliary action in the ductuli propels the still non-motile spermatozoa towards the epididymis. The non-ciliated cells reabsorb some of the fluid produced by the testis. Basal cells, which do not reach the lumen, are also present and probably act as reserve cells. A thin band of circularly arranged smooth muscle **SM** surrounds each ductulus and aids propulsion of the spermatozoa towards the epididymis.

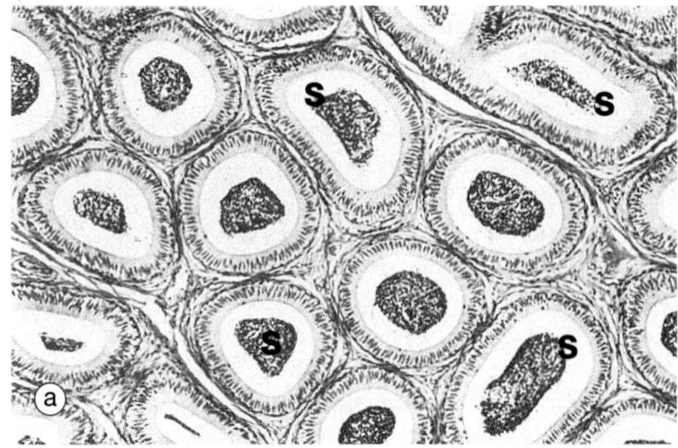

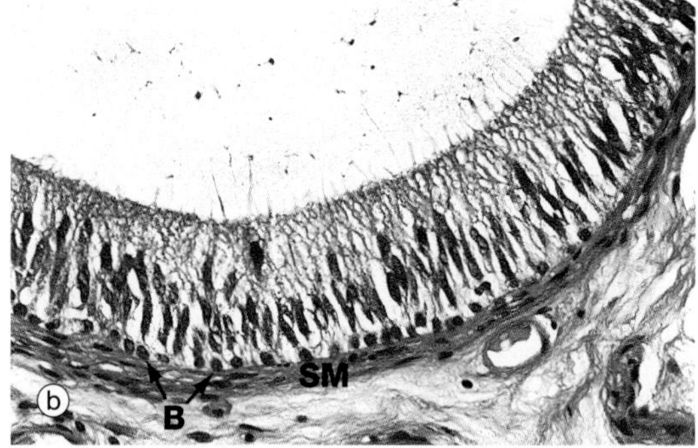

Fig. 18.12 Epididymis
(a) H & E ×50 (b) H & E ×200

The ***epididymis*** is a long extremely convoluted duct extending down the posterior aspect of the testis to the lower pole where it becomes the ductus deferens. The epididymis consists of a ***head*** at the upper pole of the testis, a ***body*** lying along the posterior margin and a ***tail*** at the lower pole of the testis. The major function of the epididymis is the accumulation, storage and maturation of spermatozoa **S**; in the epididymis, the spermatozoa develop motility.

The epididymis is a tube of smooth muscle lined by a pseudostratified epithelium. From the proximal to the distal end of the epididymis, the muscular wall increases from a single circular layer **SM**, as in these micrographs, to three layers organised in the same manner as in the ductus deferens (see Fig. 18.13). Proximally, the smooth muscle exhibits slow rhythmic contractility which gently moves spermatozoa towards the ductus deferens. Distally, the smooth muscle is richly innervated by the sympathetic nervous system which produces intense contractions of the lower part of the epididymis during ejaculation.

The epithelial lining of the epididymis exhibits a gradual transition from a tall pseudostratified columnar form in the head, as seen in micrograph (b), to a shorter pseudostratified form at the tail. The principal cells of the epididymal epithelium bear tufts of very long microvilli, inappropriately called ***stereocilia*** (see Fig. 5.16), which are thought to be involved in absorption of an excess of fluid accompanying the spermatozoa from the testis. The ultrastructure of the cells strongly suggests an additional secretory function, but the nature of epididymal secretory products, if any, remains unknown. Basal cells **B** are prominent at the base of the epithelium.

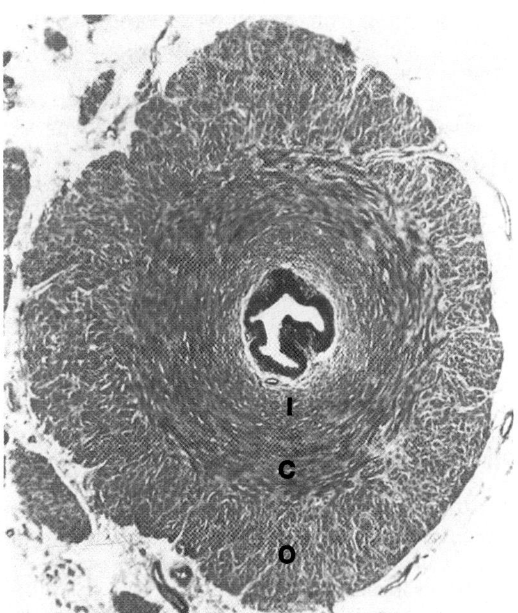

Fig. 18.13 Ductus deferens
H & E ×30

The ***ductus*** (or ***vas***) ***deferens***, which conducts spermatozoa from the epididymis to the urethra, is a thick-walled muscular tube consisting of inner **I** and outer **O** longitudinal layers and a thick intermediate circular layer **C**. Like the distal part of the epididymis, the ductus deferens is innervated by the sympathetic nervous system, producing strong peristaltic contractions to expel its contents into the urethra during ejaculation.

The ductus deferens is lined by a pseudostratified columnar epithelium similar to that of the epididymis (see Fig. 18.12): the epithelial lining and its supporting lamina propria are thrown into longitudinal folds, permitting expansion of the duct during ejaculation. The dilated distal portion of each ductus deferens, known as the ***ampulla***, receives a short duct draining the seminal vesicle, thus forming the short ***ejaculatory duct***; the ejaculatory ducts from each side converge to join the urethra as it passes through the prostate gland.

This specimen was obtained at operation for male sterilisation (***vasectomy***).

B basal cells **C** circular muscle **I** inner longitudinal muscle **L** lipofuscin pigment
M muscular wall **O** outer longitudinal muscle **S** spermatozoa **SM** smooth muscle

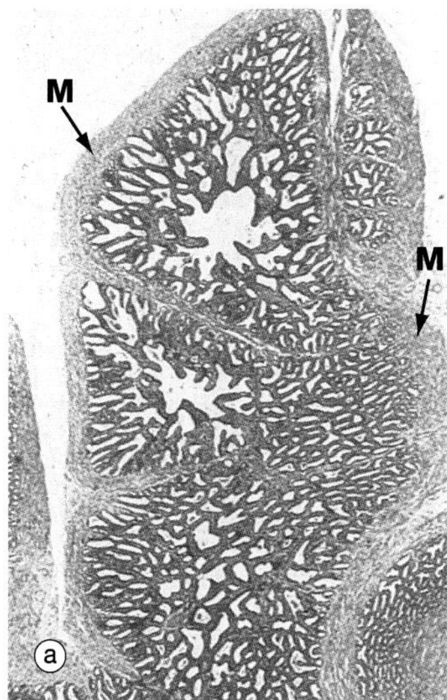

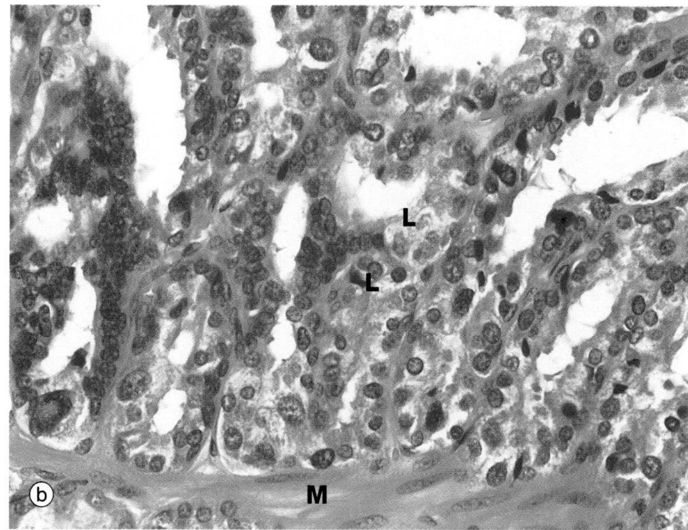

Fig. 18.14 Seminal vesicle
(a) H & E ×10 (b) H & E ×300

Each seminal vesicle is a complex glandular diverticulum of the associated ductus deferens. Between them the seminal vesicles secrete up to 85% of the total volume of seminal fluid, most of the rest being secreted by the prostate gland. The lumen of each seminal vesicle is highly irregular and recessed, giving a honeycombed appearance at low magnification.

The epithelial lining is usually of a pseudostratified tall columnar type and consists of secretory cells with lipid droplets in the cytoplasm giving it a foamy appearance. The seminal vesicles produce a yellowish viscid alkaline fluid containing a wide range of substances, including fructose, fibrinogen, vitamin C and prostaglandins. The epithelial cells often contain brown lipofuscin granules **L** and characteristically have rather variable nuclear shape and size. Both of these features are seen in micrograph (b). Although not thought to store spermatozoa, seminal vesicles are often seen to contain spermatozoa which have probably entered by reflux from the ampulla. The prominent muscular wall **M** is arranged into inner circular and outer longitudinal layers and is supplied by the sympathetic nervous system; during ejaculation, muscle contraction forces secretions from the seminal vesicles into the urethra via the ampullae.

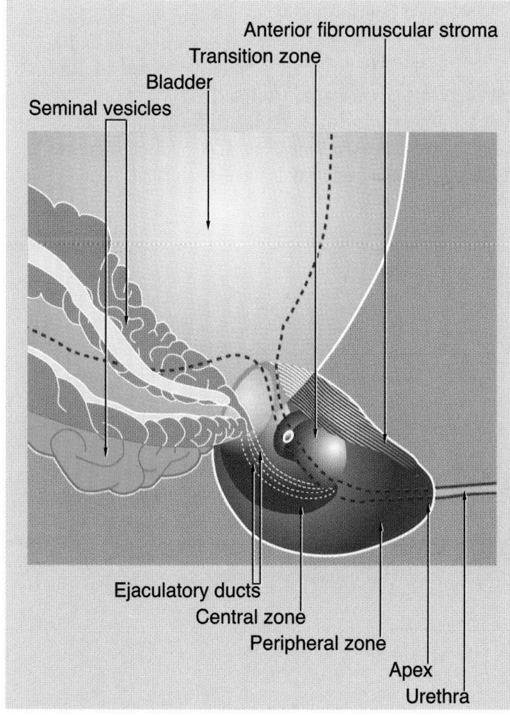

Fig. 18.15 Prostate gland

The prostate gland, which in young adults is about the size of a walnut, surrounds the bladder neck and the first part of the urethra, known as the ***prostatic urethra***. The urethra courses through the prostate to become the ***membranous urethra*** at the apex of the prostate. In the substance of the gland, the urethra merges with the ejaculatory ducts and at this point angles forwards.

The prostate consists of branched tubulo-acinar glands embedded in a fibromuscular stroma. There is a partial capsule enclosing the posterior and lateral aspects of the prostate but the anterior and apical surfaces are bounded by the ***anterior fibromuscular stroma***, a part of the gland consisting, as the name implies, only of collagenous stroma and muscle fibres.

In the past the prostate was described as consisting of a number of ill-defined lobes. However, this terminology has been replaced by the concept of prostate zones and the gland is now described as consisting of four zones of unequal size:

- **The transition zone** surrounds the proximal prostatic urethra and comprises about 5% of the glandular tissue.
- **The central zone** (20%) surrounds the ejaculatory ducts.
- **The peripheral zone** makes up the bulk of the gland (approximately 70%).
- **The anterior fibromuscular stroma** contains no glandular tissue and lies anteriorly.

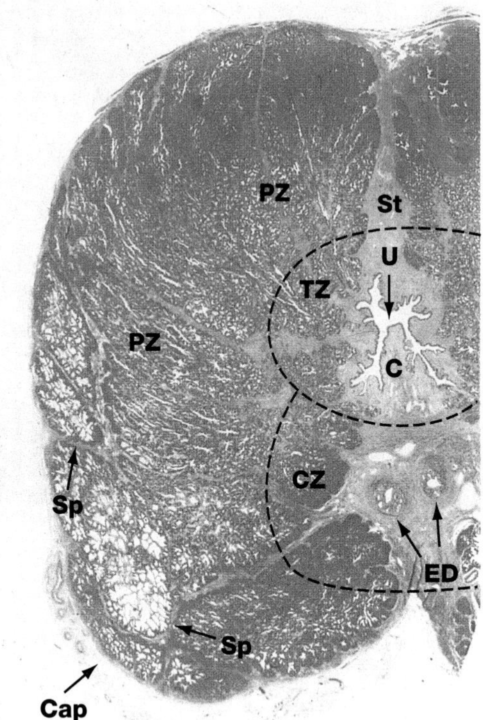

Fig. 18.16 Prostate gland (dog)
H & E ×5

This low power view of the prostate of a dog shows the general architectural features of the gland. The urethra **U** lies centrally surrounded by a fibrous stroma **St**. The ejaculatory ducts **ED** also lie in this central stroma as they course towards their junction with the prostatic urethra. The zones of the prostate are not clearly demarcated from each other anatomically. Partial fibrous septa **Sp** separate the gland into lobules. The transition zone **TZ** surrounds the first part of the prostatic urethra. The central zone **CZ** lies posterior to the transition zone and encircles the ejaculatory ducts. The peripheral zone **PZ** makes up the main bulk of the gland. The ducts of the peripheral zone glands empty into the posterolateral recesses of the urethra on either side of the ***verumontanum*** (***urethral crest***) **C**.

The different zones of the prostate are important because they tend to be the sites of different disease processes. Most cases of carcinoma of the prostate arise in the peripheral zone while the transition zone harbours almost all cases of benign nodular hyperplasia (see below).

At this power the anterior fibromuscular stroma appears continuous with the capsule **Cap** and its content of muscle fibres cannot be discerned.

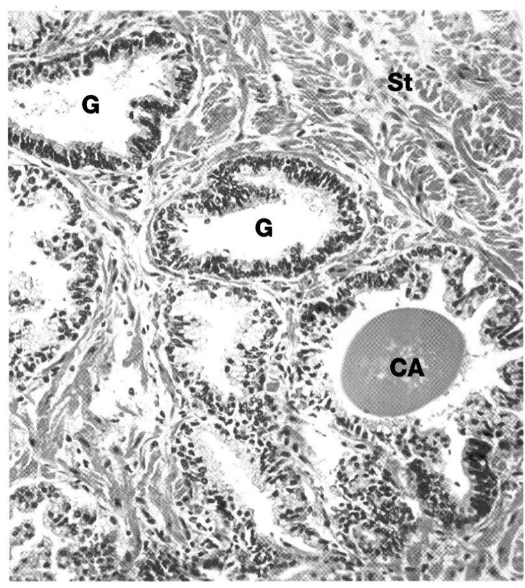

Fig. 18.17 Prostate gland
H & E ×50

The prostate gland is composed of glands and stroma. The supporting stroma **SS** is a mixture of collagenous fibrous tissue and smooth muscle fibres. The glands **G** show a convoluted pattern with the epithelium thrown up into folds, sometimes into almost a papillary pattern.

The secretory product of the prostate, which makes up about half the seminal fluid volume, is a thin liquid rich in citric acid and proteolytic enzymes, including fibrinolysins, which liquefies coagulated semen after it has been deposited in the vagina. Inspissated secretions may accumulate in some glands to form spherical concretions (***corpora amylacea*** **CA**), which increase in number with age and may become calcified.

Common prostatic disease

The most common disease of the prostate is called ***benign prostatic hyperplasia*** and occurs in men over 50. The prostatic glands around the urethra (transition zone – see Fig 18.16) become greatly increased in size and number and the gland lumina become distended by secretions and corpora amylacea. At the same time the stromal smooth muscle fibres become greatly enlarged. This increase in bulk enlarges the prostate gland as a whole, and compresses the urethra, leading to interference with bladder emptying.

C urethral crest **CA** corpora amylacea **Cap** capsule **CC** corpus cavernosum **CS** corpus spongiosum **CZ** central zone **ED** ejaculatory ducts **F** fibrocollagenous tissue **G** gland **PZ** peripheral zone **S** skin **Sp** fibrous septum **SS** supporting stroma **St** fibrous stroma **TZ** transition zone **U** urethra

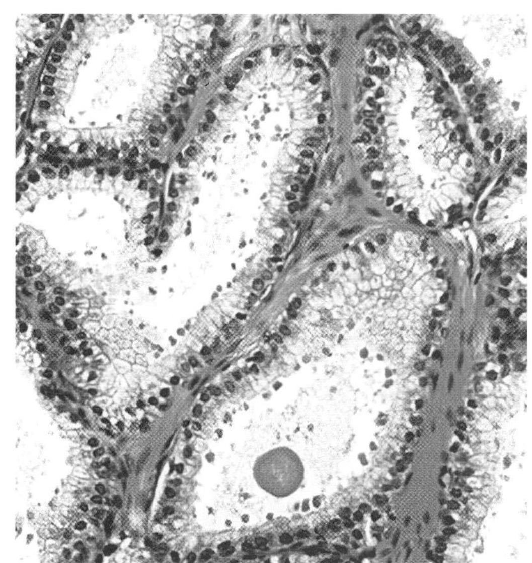

Fig. 18.18 Prostate gland
H & E ×80

This higher magnification picture shows the detail of the epithelium of the prostate glands. The main epithelial type is the tall columnar secretory cell with prominent round basal nuclei and pale-staining cytoplasm. There is also a scanty population of small flat basal cells at the base of the gland, in contact with the basement membrane; these cannot be seen in this micrograph. The glands contain small beads of secretion on the luminal surface, and one corpus amylaceum.

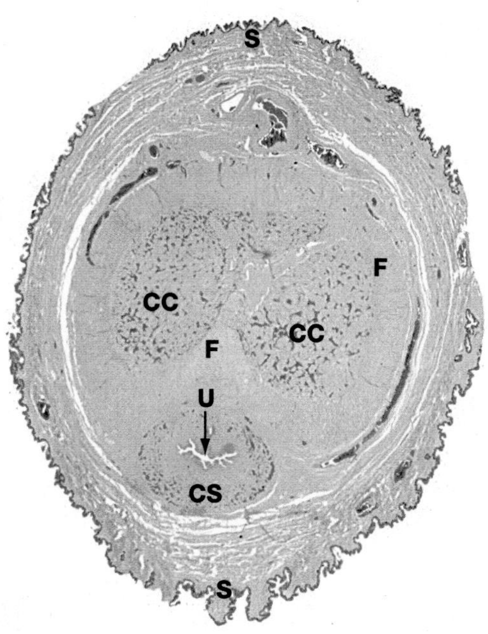

Fig. 18.19 Penis
H & E ×3

This transverse section of the human penis shows the arrangement of the erectile tissues, which exist in the form of three columns. The two dorsal columns are called the ***corpora cavernosa*** **CC** and the single ventral column is the ***corpus spongiosum*** **CS**, through which runs the ***penile urethra*** **U**. At its distal end, the corpus spongiosum expands to form the ***glans penis***. The erectile corpora are enclosed within, and separated by, a fibrocollagenous capsule **F**. The erectile centre of the penis is enclosed in a sheath of skin **S** to which it is connected by a loose subcutis containing prominent blood vessels.

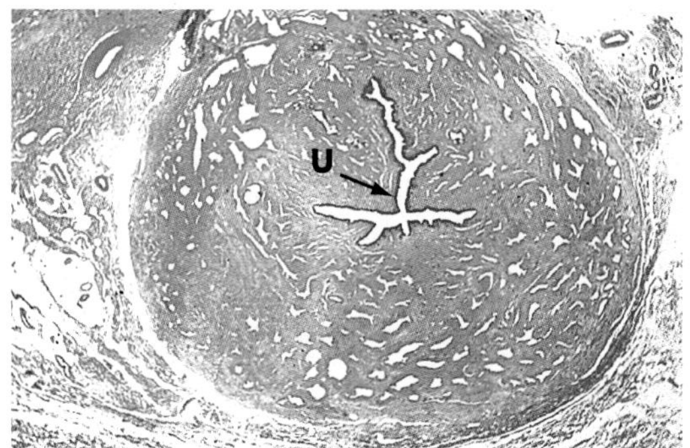

Fig. 18.20 Corpus spongiosum
H & E ×6

The corpus spongiosum is composed of erectile tissue, large irregular interconnected vascular channels with fibrocollagenous stroma between; the stroma contains some smooth muscle fibres. Running through the centre of the corpus spongiosum is the penile urethra **U**. Small paraurethral mucus glands open into the urethra.

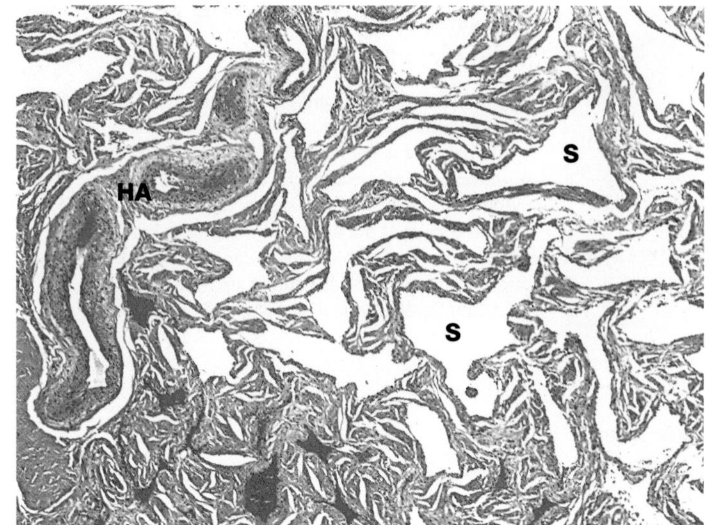

Fig. 18.21 Penile erectile tissue
H & E ×30

The vascular sinuses **S** of the cavernous bodies of the penis are supplied by numerous anastomosing thick-walled arteries and arterioles called ***helicine arteries*** **HA** since they follow a spiral course in the flaccid state. Blood drains from the sinuses via veins which lie immediately beneath the dense fibroelastic tissue investing the cavernous bodies. During erection, dilatation of the helicine arteries, mediated by the parasympathetic nervous system, results in engorgement of the vascular sinuses, which enlarge, compressing and restricting venous outflow. The process is enhanced by relaxation of smooth muscle cells in the trabeculae of the cavernous bodies.

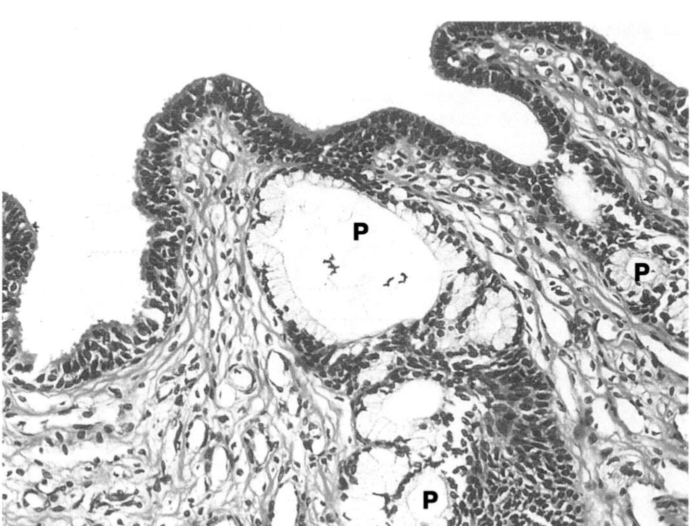

Fig. 18.22 Penile urethra
H & E ×200

Apart from the prostatic urethra, which is lined by transitional epithelium, the male urethra is lined by stratified or pseudostratified columnar epithelium, although small areas of stratified squamous epithelium may also be found in human adult males. The external opening (***urethral meatus***) is lined by stratified squamous epithelium, which becomes continuous with the epithelium of the glans.

The urethra is lubricated by mucoid secretions from the para-urethral glands **P** and the ***bulbo-urethral glands of Cowper*** (see Fig. 18.1), which have a similar, but more discrete, organisation.

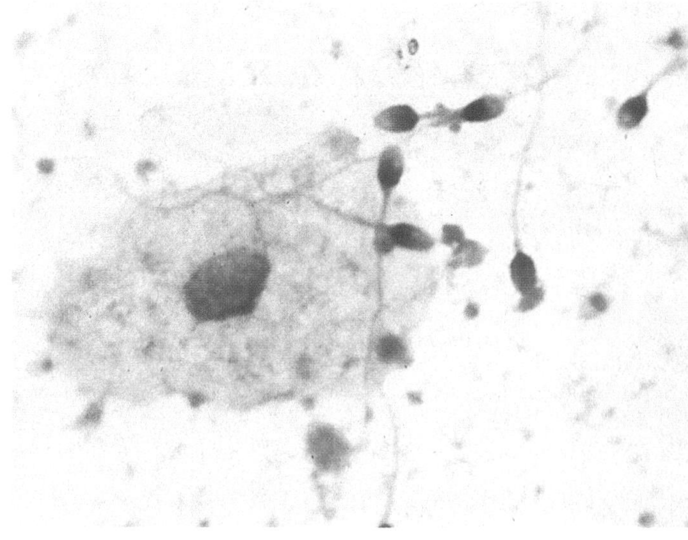

Fig. 18.23 Semen
H & E ×1200

Semen, the product of ejaculation, consists of spermatozoa and seminal fluid which is derived principally from the seminal vesicles and prostate gland. The volume of each human ejaculate is about 3.5 mL containing from 50 to 150 million spermatozoa per mL. In normal fertile human males, up to 25% of the ejaculated spermatozoa are abnormal or degenerate forms. By the time of ejaculation, spermatozoa have matured and acquired the property of motility; nevertheless, they remain incapable of fertilising an ovum until after undergoing a process called ***capacitation*** within the female genital tract.

HA helicine artery **P** paraurethral gland **S** vascular sinus

19. *Female reproductive system*

Introduction

The female reproductive system has six major functions:

- Production of female gametes, the ***ova***, by the process of ***oogenesis***.
- Reception of male gametes, the ***spermatozoa***.
- Provision of a suitable environment for the fertilisation of ova by spermatozoa.
- Provision of an environment for the development of the fetus.
- Expulsion of the developed fetus to the external environment.
- Nutrition of the newborn.

These functions are all integrated by an elegant system of hormonal and nervous mechanisms. The female reproductive system may be divided into three structural units on the basis of function:

- **The ovaries**, which are the site of oogenesis, are paired organs lying on either side of the uterus adjacent to the lateral wall of the pelvis. In sexually mature mammals, ova are released, by the process of ***ovulation***, in a cyclical manner either seasonally or at regular intervals throughout the year. This cycle is suspended during pregnancy. The ovaries are also endocrine organs producing the hormones ***oestrogen*** and ***progesterone***. Both ovulation and ovarian hormone production are controlled by the cyclical release from the anterior pituitary of the gonadotrophic hormones, ***luteinising hormone*** (***LH***) and ***follicle stimulating hormone*** (***FSH***). Oestrogen and progesterone in turn regulate LH and FSH production by feedback mechanisms. Thus ovulation is coordinated with preparation of the uterus to receive the fertilised ovum.
- **The genital tract** extends from near the ovaries to an opening at the external surface and provides an environment for reception of male gametes, fertilisation of ova, development of the fetus and expulsion of the fetus at birth. The genital tract begins with a pair of ***Fallopian tubes***, also called ***oviducts*** or ***uterine tubes***, which conduct ova from the ovaries to the ***uterus*** where fetal development occurs. Fertilisation of ova by spermatozoa occurs within the Fallopian tubes. The uterus is a muscular organ, the mucosal lining of which undergoes cyclical proliferation under the influence of ovarian hormones. This provides a suitable environment for implantation of the fertilised ovum and subsequent development of the ***placenta*** via which the developing fetus is nourished throughout gestation. At birth (***parturition***), strong contractions of the muscular uterine wall expel the fetus through the lower part of the uterus, the ***uterine cervix***, into the birth canal or ***vagina***. The vagina is an expansile muscular tube specialised for the reception of the penis during coitus and for the passage of the fetus to the external environment. At the external opening of the vagina are thick folds of skin, the ***labia***, which along with the ***clitoris*** constitute the ***vulva***.
- **The breasts** are highly modified apocrine sweat glands which, in the female, develop at puberty and regress at menopause. During pregnancy, the secretory components expand greatly in size and number in preparation for milk production (***lactation***).

In the non-pregnant state, the female reproductive system undergoes continuous cyclical changes from puberty to menopause. When ovulation is not followed by the implantation of a fertilised ovum, the thickened mucosal lining, the ***endometrium***, degenerates and a new ovulation cycle commences. In humans, the thickened endometrium is shed in a period of bleeding known as ***menstruation***; the first day of bleeding marks the beginning of a new cycle of endometrial proliferation which is known as the ***menstrual cycle***. In humans, the standard menstrual cycle is of 28 days duration but there is considerable variation among normal individuals. Ovulation usually occurs at the midpoint of the cycle.

In other mammals, the proliferated uterine mucosa is absorbed rather than shed and the female is receptive to the male only during the period of ovulation, which is known as ***oestrus*** (or heat). The remaining part of the cycle is called the ***dioestrus*** and the whole cycle is known as the ***oestrus cycle***.

The general anatomy of the female genital tract is illustrated in Figs 19.1 and 19.2 overleaf.

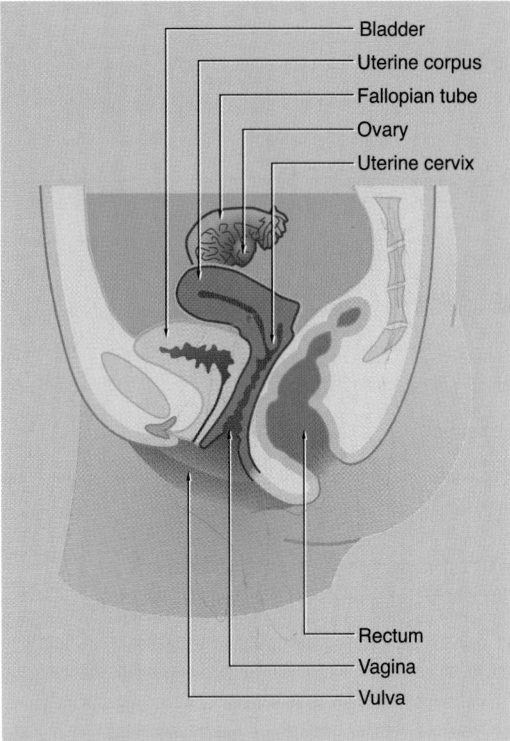

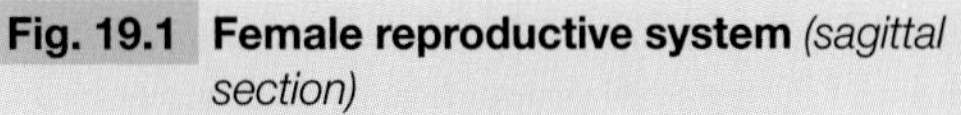

Fig. 19.1 Female reproductive system *(sagittal section)*

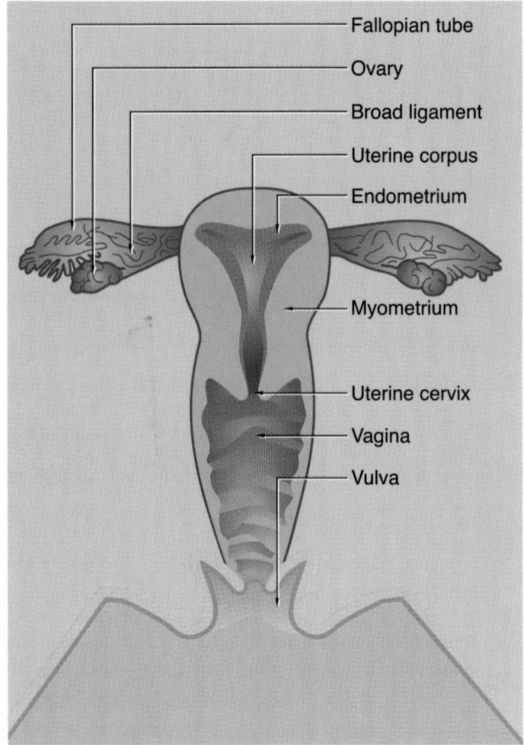

Fig. 19.2 Female reproductive system *(coronal view)*

Fig. 19.3 Ovary *(illustrations opposite)*
(a) Monkey, Azan ×18 (b) Human, H & E ×8

The ovaries of all mammals have a similar basic structure. There are however, considerable variations in accordance with species differences in the ovarian cycle and the stage in the cycle at which the ovary is examined. These micrographs compare the ovarian appearance of the monkey with that of the human.

The ovaries, which are some 3–5 cm long in humans, have a flattened ovoid shape. The body of the ovary consists of spindle-shaped cells, fine collagen fibres and ground substance that together constitute the ***ovarian stroma***. The stromal cells resemble fibroblasts but some contain lipid droplets. Bundles of smooth muscle cells are also scattered throughout the stroma. In the peripheral zone of the stroma, known as the ***cortex***, are numerous ***follicles*** that contain female gametes in various stages of development. In addition, there may also be post-ovulatory follicles of various kinds, namely ***corpora lutea*** (responsible for oestrogen and progesterone production, see Fig. 19.8), degenerate and former corpora lutea (***corpora albicantes***, see Fig. 19.11) and degenerate (atretic) follicles (see Fig. 19.10).

The superficial cortex is more fibrous than the deep cortex and is often called the ***tunica albuginea***. However, unlike the testis, this is not an anatomically distinct capsule. On the surface of the ovary is an epithelial covering, misleadingly called ***germinal epithelium***, which is a continuation of the peritoneum.

In the monkey ovary, numerous follicles **F** are seen in various sizes and states of development. In contrast, developing follicles are difficult to see in the human ovary (b) at this magnification; an active corpus luteum **CL** and several degenerating corpora lutea **D** and corpora albicantes **A** dominate this human ovary.

The central zone of the ovarian stroma, the ***medulla*** **M**, is highly vascular and contains ***hilus cells***, which are morphologically very similar to Leydig cells of the testis. The ovarian artery (a branch of the aorta) and ovarian branches of the uterine artery form anastomoses in the ***mesovarium*** and the ***broad ligament*** **L**. From this arterial plexus approximately 10 coiled arteries, the ***helicine arteries*** **H** enter the hilum of the ovary, best seen in micrograph (a). Smaller branches form a plexus at the corticomedullary junction, giving rise to straight cortical arterioles that radiate into the cortex. Here they branch and anastomose to form vascular arcades giving rise to a rich network of capillaries around the follicles. Venous drainage follows the course of the arterial system, the medullary veins being large and tortuous. Lymphatics arise in the perifollicular stroma, draining to larger vessels, which coil around the medullary veins. Innervation of the ovary is by sympathetic fibres that not only supply blood vessels but also terminate on smooth muscle cells in the stroma around the follicles, possibly playing some part in follicular maturation and ovulation. In micrograph (b), the nearby Fallopian tube **Ft** is included in the plane of section.

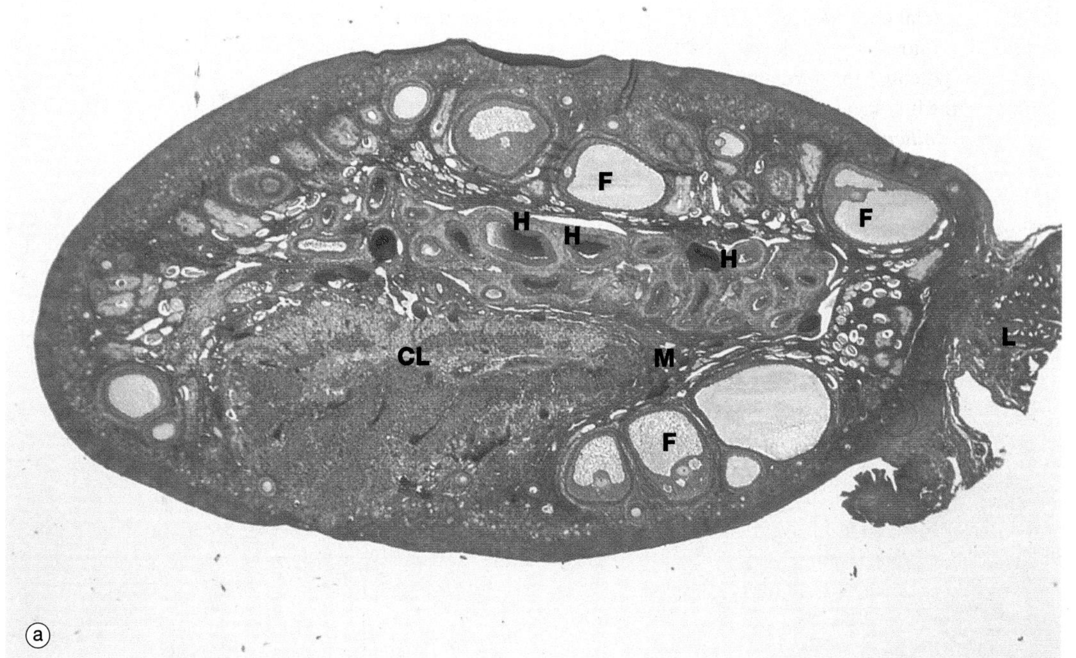

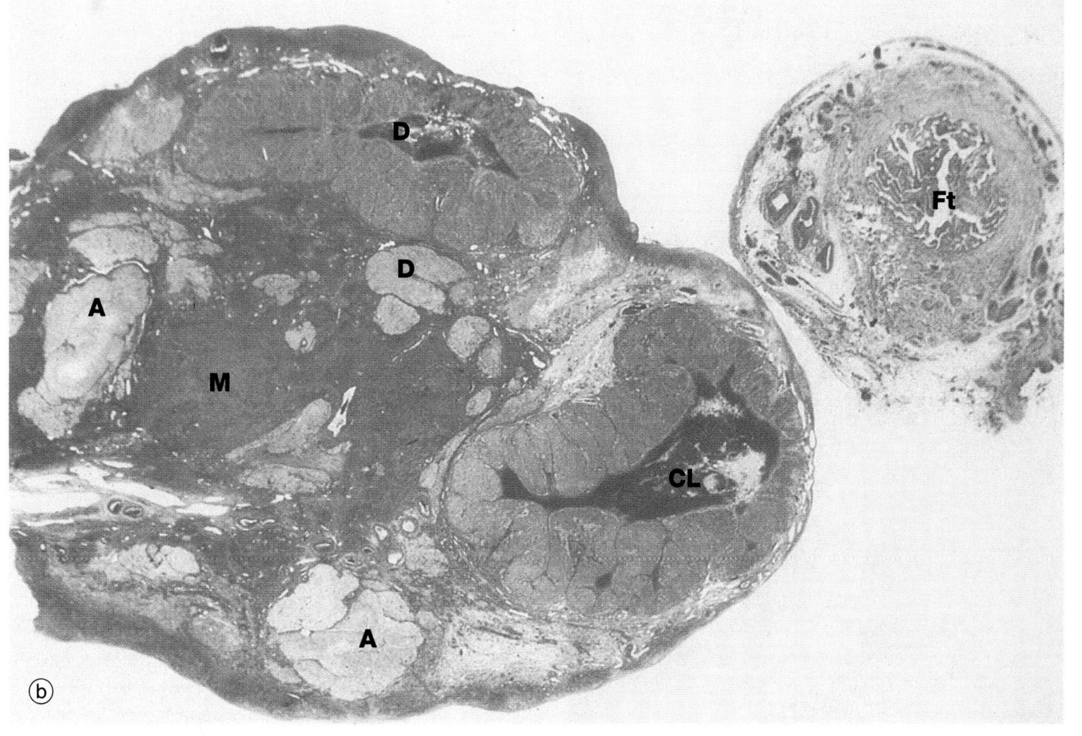

A corpus albicans **CL** corpus luteum **D** degenerating corpus luteum **F** follicle **Ft** Fallopian tube
H helicine artery **L** broad ligament **M** medulla

Follicular development

During early fetal development, primordial germ cells called ***oogonia*** migrate into the ovarian cortex where they multiply by mitosis. By the fourth and fifth months of human fetal development, some oogonia enlarge and assume the potential for development into mature gametes. At this stage they are called ***primary oocytes*** and commence the first stage of meiotic division (see Ch. 2). By the seventh month of fetal development, a single layer of flattened ***follicular cells*** surrounds the primary oocytes to form ***primordial follicles***, of which there are approximately 500 000 in the human ovary at birth. This encapsulation arrests the first meiotic division and no further development of primordial follicles then occurs until after the female reaches sexual maturity. The process of meiotic division is only completed during follicular maturation leading up to ovulation and fertilisation. Thus all the female germ cells are present at birth but the process of meiotic division is only completed some 15–50 years later! In contrast, in males, meiotic division of germ cells commences only after sexual maturity, and formation and maturation of spermatozoa are accomplished within about 70 days (see Ch. 18). Female germ cells may undergo degeneration (***atresia***) at any stage of follicular maturation.

During each ovarian cycle, a cohort of up to 20 primordial follicles is activated to begin the maturation process; nevertheless, usually only one follicle reaches full maturity and undergoes ovulation while the remainder regress before this point. The reason for this apparent wastage is unclear; during maturation, however, the follicles have an endocrine function, which may be far beyond the capacity of a single follicle, and the primary purpose of the other follicles may be to act as an endocrine gland.

Follicular maturation involves changes in the oocyte, the follicular cells and the surrounding stromal tissue. Follicular maturation is stimulated by FSH (follicle stimulating hormone) secreted by the anterior pituitary gland.

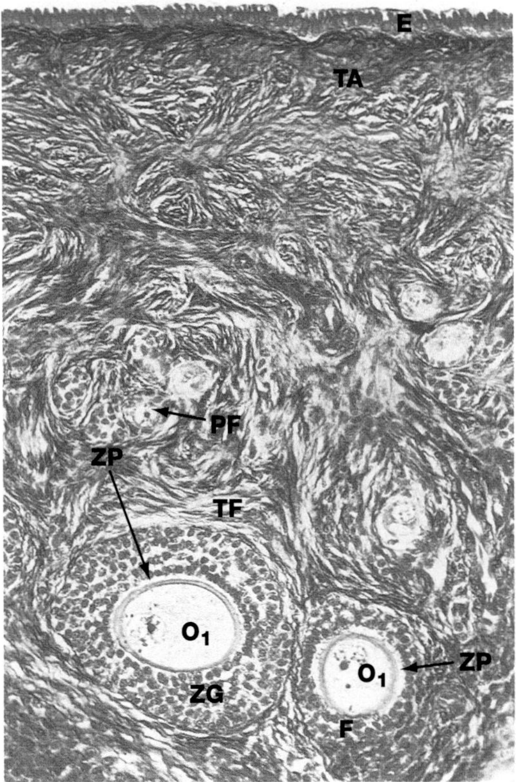

Fig. 19.4 Ovarian cortex (monkey)
Azan ×120

This micrograph, taken from a monkey, shows the typical appearance of follicles in the ovarian cortex and illustrates several stages in early follicular development.

In the mature ovary, undeveloped follicles exist as ***primordial follicles*** **PF** which are composed of a ***primary oocyte*** surrounded by a single layer of flattened follicular cells. The primary oocyte has a large nucleus with dispersed finely granular chromatin, a prominent nucleolus and little cytoplasm.

At the lower right of the field, a primordial follicle has been stimulated, increasing in size to form a ***primary follicle***; its oocyte $\mathbf{O_1}$ has greatly enlarged and the follicular cells **F** have multiplied by mitosis and become cuboidal in shape; they are now known as ***granulosa cells***. A thick homogeneous layer of glycoprotein and acid proteoglycans, the ***zona pellucida*** **ZP**, develops between the oocyte and the follicular cells; both cell types probably contribute to its formation.

With further follicular development as seen in the large follicle at lower left, the surrounding stromal cells begin to form an organised layer around the follicle called the ***theca folliculi*** **TF** separated from the granulosa cells by a basement membrane. Theca cells are derived from the fibroblast-like cells of the ovarian stroma. The primary follicle continues to enlarge and the granulosa cells continue to proliferate, forming a layer several cells thick called the ***zona granulosa*** **ZG**.

Note also in this micrograph, the fibrous tunica albuginea **TA** and the single layer of cuboidal or columnar epithelial cells **E** on the surface of the ovary. This epithelial layer is continuous with the mesothelial lining of the peritoneal cavity and was formerly known as the ***germinal epithelium*** from the mistaken belief that these cells were the origin of the female germ cells.

CO cumulus oophorus **CR** corona radiata **E** epithelial cell **F** follicular cells **FA** follicular antrum
$\mathbf{O_1}$ primary oocyte $\mathbf{O_2}$ secondary oocyte **PF** primordial follicle **TA** tunica albuginea
TE theca externa **TF** theca folliculi **TI** theca interna **ZG** zona granulosa **ZP** zona pellucida

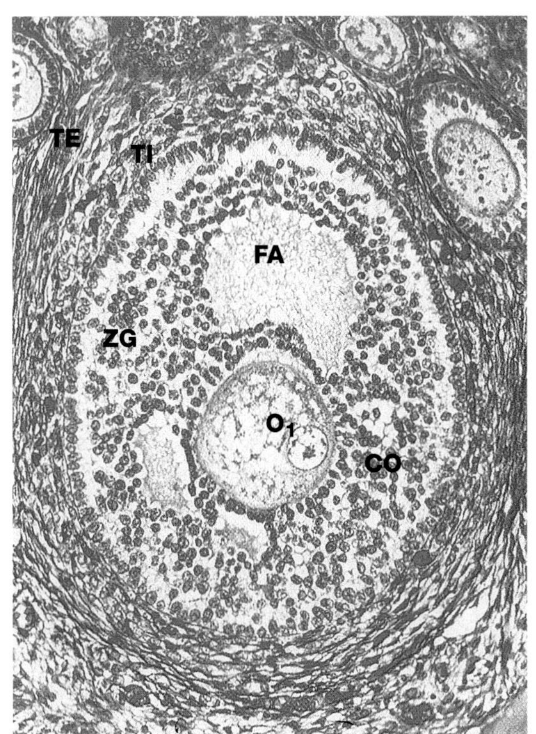

Fig. 19.5 Secondary follicle
Azan ×120

Primary follicles continue to develop to form ***secondary follicles*** and acquire the features seen in this micrograph; by now they are usually situated deeper in the ovarian cortex.

The zona granulosa **ZG** continues to proliferate and within it small fluid-filled spaces appear; these fuse to form the ***follicular antrum*** **FA**, in which follicular fluid accumulates. At this stage, the oocyte $\mathbf{O_1}$ has almost reached its full size and becomes situated eccentrically in a thickened area of the granulosa called the ***cumulus oophorus*** **CO**.

At the periphery of the follicle, the theca folliculi has developed two layers, the ***theca interna*** **TI**, comprising several layers of rounded cells, and the less well-defined ***theca externa*** **TE** consisting of spindle-shaped cells that merge with the surrounding stroma.

The cells of the theca interna have the features of typical steroid-secreting cells (see Fig. 17.18) and produce oestrogen precursors (e.g. androstenedione), oestrogen and, in the preovulatory stage, progesterone. In the ovary these steroid-secreting cells are often described as ***luteinised***. Follicular hormones promote proliferation of the endometrium in readiness for the implantation of a fertilised ovum. The theca externa is composed of flattened stromal cells and has no endocrine function. The granulosa cells also produce hormones from the stage of antral formation onwards; oestrogen is produced from precursors secreted by the theca interna as well as small amounts of intrafollicular FSH and (at ovulation) the FSH inhibitor, ***inhibin F***.

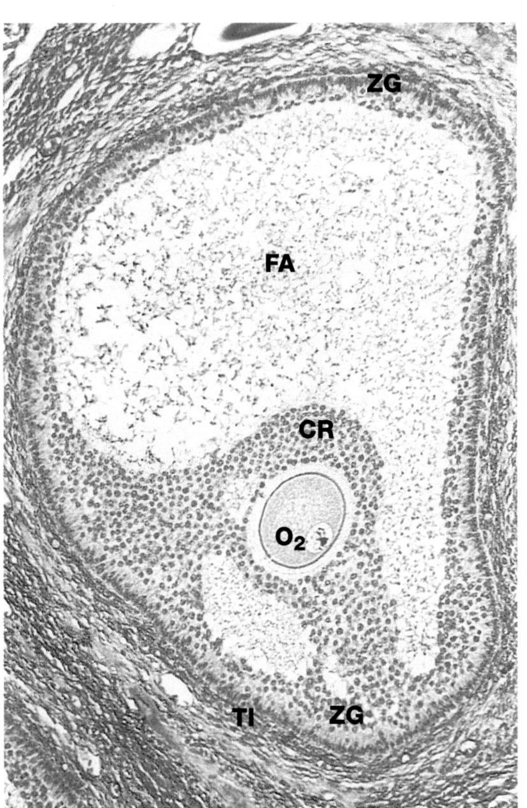

Fig. 19.6 Graafian follicle
Azan ×75

Approaching maturity, further growth of the oocyte ceases and the first meiotic division is completed just before ovulation. At this stage, the oocyte becomes known as the ***secondary oocyte*** and commences the second meiotic division. The first polar body (see Ch. 2), containing very little cytoplasm, remains inconspicuously within the zona pellucida. The follicular antrum **FA** enlarges markedly and the zona granulosa **ZG** now forms a layer of even thickness around the periphery of the follicle. The cumulus oophorus diminishes leaving the oocyte $\mathbf{O_2}$ surrounded by a layer several cells thick, the ***corona radiata*** **CR**, which remains attached to the zona granulosa by thin bridges of cells. Before ovulation, these bridges break down and the oocyte, surrounded by the corona radiata, floats free inside the follicle. Note the surrounding theca interna **TI** consisting of plump luteinised cells. By this stage the follicle has reached between 1.5 and 2.5 cm in diameter and bulges under the ovarian surface. The overlying surface epithelial cells are flattened and atrophic and the thin intervening stroma becomes degenerate and avascular.

At ovulation, the mature follicle ruptures and the ovum, made up of the secondary oocyte, zona pellucida and corona radiata, is expelled into the peritoneal cavity near the entrance to the Fallopian tube. The second meiotic division of the oocyte is not completed until after penetration of the ovum by a spermatozoon.

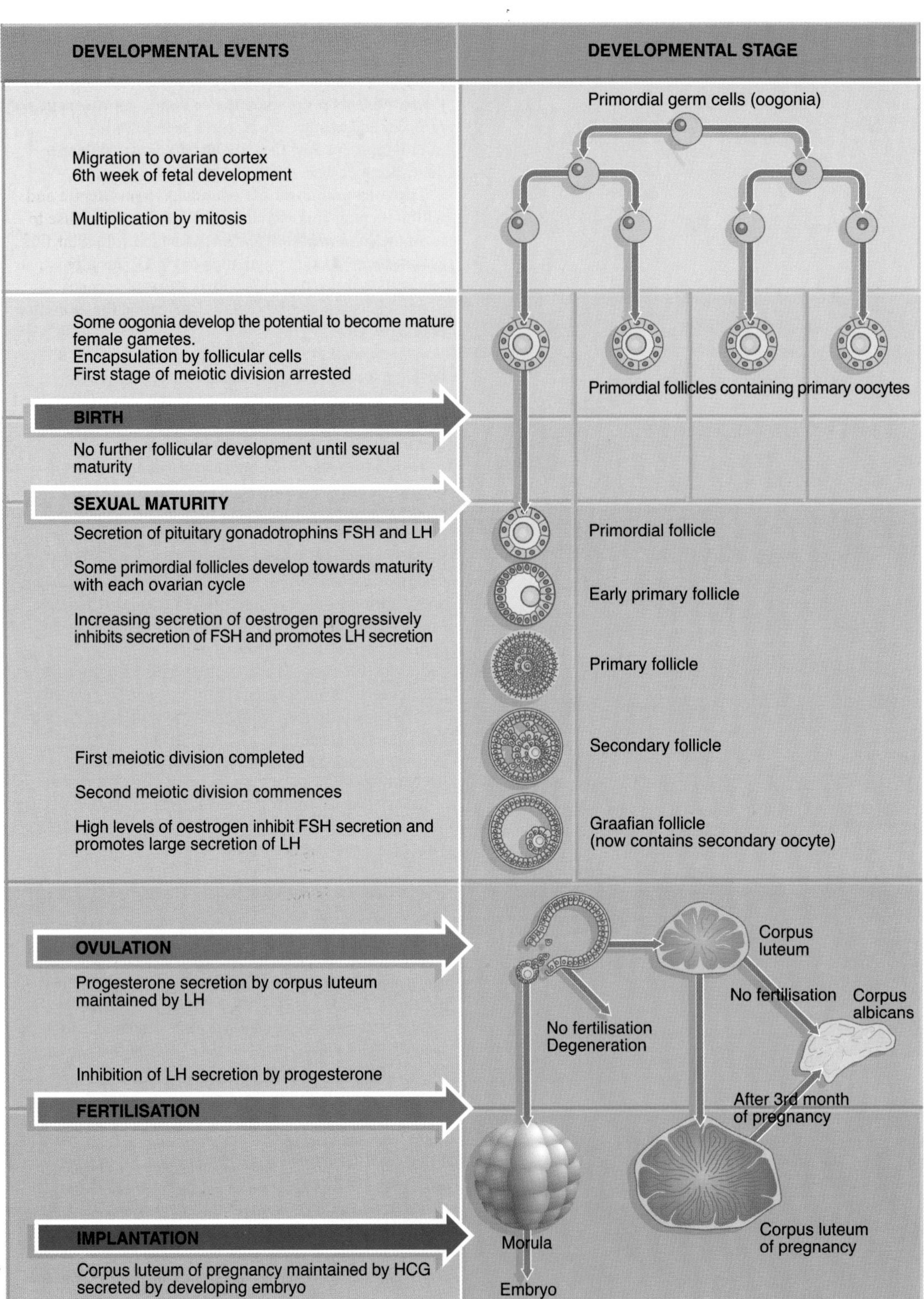

Fig. 19.7 **Follicular development**

B blood clot **G** granulosa lutein cells **S** septum **Sh** vascular sheath of theca cells
T theca lutein cells **TE** theca externa cells **TI** theca interna cells **V** blood vessel

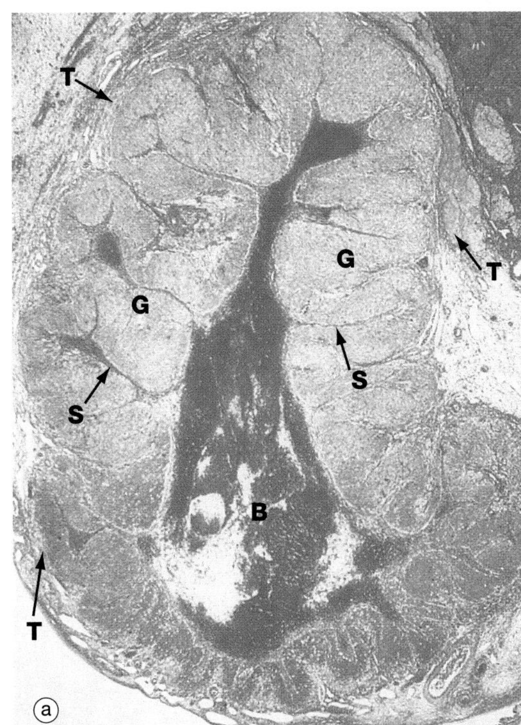

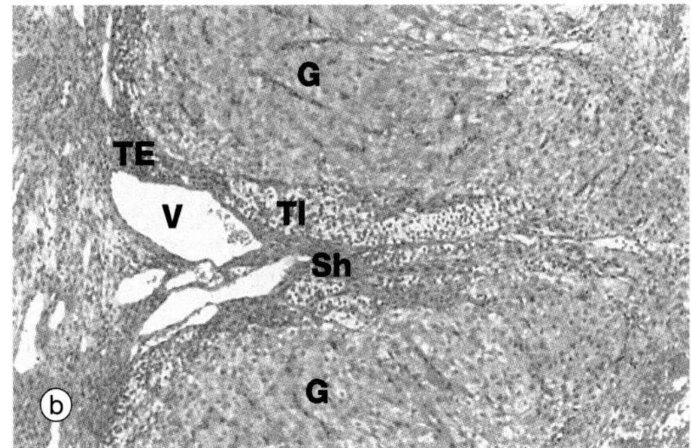

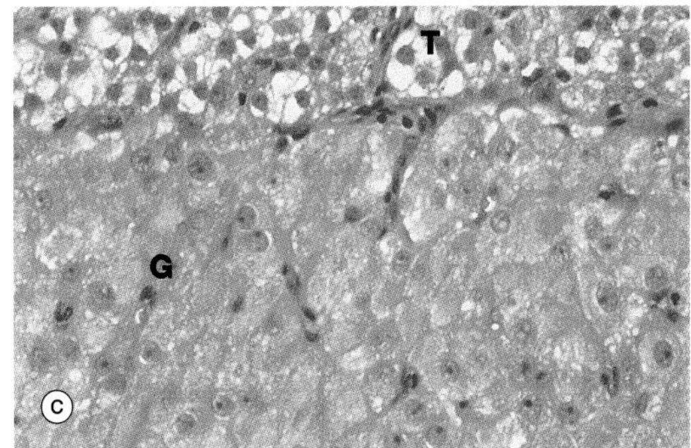

Fig. 19.8 Corpus luteum of menstruation
(a) H & E ×20 (b) H & E ×50 (c) H & E ×200

Following ovulation, the ruptured follicle collapses and fills with a blood clot to form the ***corpus luteum of menstruation***, which has a brief career as an endocrine organ. The corpus luteum of menstruation is about the same size as the antecedent ovulatory follicle, i.e. 1.5–2.5 cm. Under the influence of luteinising hormone (LH) secreted by the anterior pituitary, granulosa cells increase greatly in size and begin secretion of progesterone. The granulosa cells acquire the characteristics of steroid-secreting cells and are now called ***granulosa lutein cells***. Progesterone promotes the changes in the endometrium that make it ready for implantation of the embryo should fertilisation occur (see Figs 19.15–19.19). Thus the cycles of production of oocytes and the preparation of the endometrium (the ***menstrual cycle***) are coordinated by the same set of hormones.

The cells of the theca interna also increase somewhat in size and acquire similar cytoplasmic features to the luteinised granulosa cells. Although interrupted by ovulation, these cells (as well as the granulosa cells) continue to secrete oestrogens, which are necessary to maintain the thickened uterine mucosa. These cells become known as ***theca lutein cells***.

The basement membrane between the zona granulosa and theca interna breaks down and these layers are invaded by capillaries and larger vessels from the theca externa to form a rich vascular network characteristic of endocrine glands.

Progesterone production by the corpus luteum is dependent on LH from the anterior pituitary, but rising progesterone levels inhibit LH production. Without the continuing stimulus of LH, the corpus luteum cannot be maintained and 12–14 days after ovulation it regresses, ultimately forming a functionless ***corpus albicans*** (see Fig. 19.11). Once the corpus luteum regresses, secretion of both oestrogen and progesterone ceases. Without these hormones the endometrial lining of the uterus collapses, resulting in the onset of menstruation.

Micrograph (a) shows a corpus luteum of menstruation. In the centre, the remnant of the post-ovulatory blood clot **B** is seen surrounded by a broad zone of granulosa lutein cells **G** penetrated by septa **S** containing the larger blood vessels. Peripherally, a thin zone of theca lutein cells **T** can be seen. Externally, the corpus luteum is bounded by a zone of condensed stromal tissue representing the theca externa of the antecedent Graafian follicle.

Micrograph (b) shows the margin of a corpus luteum at intermediate magnification. Most of the field is occupied by granulosa lutein cells **G**, large polygonal cells with abundant pale eosinophilic (pink stained) cytoplasm and round nuclei. The cytoplasm contains plentiful smooth endoplasmic reticulum, abundant mitochondria, lipid droplets and some lipofuscin, giving the corpus luteum a yellow colour macroscopically. At the periphery are theca cells which also extend in a finger-like extension forming a sheath **Sh** around blood vessels **V**. The theca externa cells **TE** have darker stained cytoplasm while the luteinised theca interna cells **TI** have pale cytoplasm due to their content of lipid droplets.

At high magnification in micrograph (c), granulosa lutein cells **G** may be compared with theca lutein cells **T**. The eosinophilic cytoplasm of the granulosa lutein cells contains numerous small lipid droplets which give rise to the vacuolated appearance seen in this preparation; their larger spherical nuclei contain one or two prominent nucleoli. Theca lutein cells are smaller, with a more densely staining cytoplasm but with larger lipid vacuoles; their ovoid nucleus has a single large nucleolus. The ultrastructure of the endocrine cells of the corpus luteum is characteristic of all steroid secretory cells (see Fig. 17.18).

As previously described, the granulosa lutein cells secrete progesterone (and a small amount of oestrogen) and the theca lutein cells secrete oestrogen precursors which are converted to oestrogen by the granulosa cells.

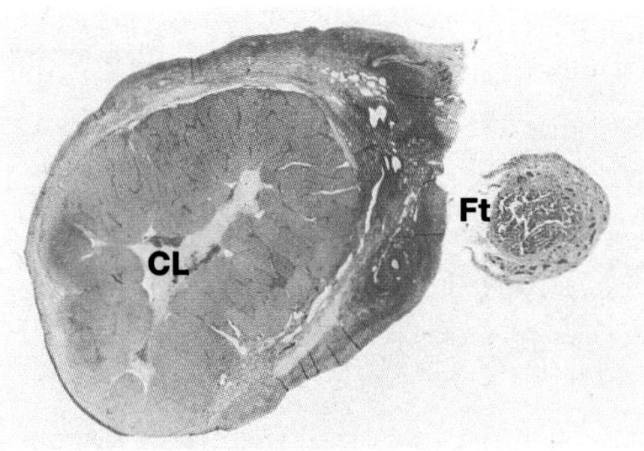

Fig. 19.9 Corpus luteum of pregnancy
H & E ×3

Implantation of a fertilised ovum in the uterine wall interrupts the integrated ovarian and menstrual cycles. After implantation, a hormone called ***human chorionic gonadotrophin*** (***HCG***) is secreted into the maternal circulation by the developing placenta. HCG has an analogous function to LH and maintains the function of the corpus luteum in secreting oestrogen and progesterone until about the 9th week of pregnancy. After this time, the ***corpus luteum of pregnancy*** slowly regresses to form a functionless corpus albicans and the placenta takes over the major role of oestrogen and progesterone secretion until parturition.

This micrograph shows a human ovary during the first trimester of pregnancy. The corpus luteum **CL** is greatly enlarged and by now occupies most of the ovary. The organisation of the corpus luteum of pregnancy is similar to that of menstruation but there are some histological changes that are almost specific for the corpus luteum of pregnancy. In particular the granulosa lutein cells contain hyaline, eosinophilic inclusion bodies that tend to enlarge and then calcify as the pregnancy progresses. Note the adjacent Fallopian tube **Ft**.

Ovarian cysts

Ovarian cysts are common and arise from a wide variety of causes. Most common of all are ***follicular cysts***, due to enlargement of normal follicles, and ***corpus luteum cysts***, which result from a similar expansion of a normal corpus luteum. Other cysts in the ovary arise from more sinister causes including neoplasms. These include epithelial cysts such as the ***serous cystadenoma*** at the benign end of the spectrum, the ***serous cystadenocarcinoma*** at the malignant end and the in-between ***borderline serous tumour***. There is a similar range of ***mucinous tumours***. A fairly common type of ovarian cyst in young women is the ***dermoid cyst*** or ***mature teratoma***, a lesion that is virtually always benign. Another common type of cyst is the ***endometriotic cyst*** or ***endometrioma***, where abnormal deposits of endometrial glands and stroma are found in the ovary and indeed in many other sites in the body. Endometriosis is often associated with infertility as is ***polycystic ovary syndrome***, a condition where multiple follicular cysts are associated with obesity and hirsutism. From this brief and incomplete summary of ovarian cysts, the variety of pathologies and therefore of treatments is clear. Diagnosis often requires biopsy or oophorectomy (removal of the ovary).

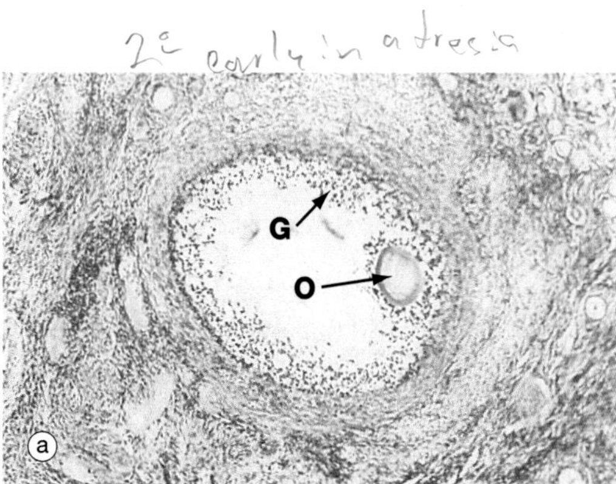

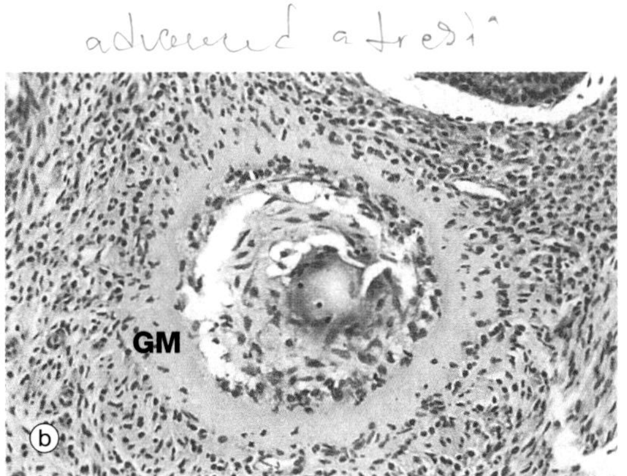

Fig. 19.10 Atretic follicles
(a) H & E ×128 (b) H & E ×128

The process of follicular atresia (degeneration) may occur at any stage in the development of the ovum. By the sixth month of development, the fetal ovary contains several million primordial follicles, yet by the time of birth only about half a million remain. Atresia continues until puberty and thereafter through the reproductive years. In addition, with each ovarian cycle approximately 20 follicles begin to mature, usually all but one becoming atretic at some stage before complete maturity.

The histological appearance of ***atretic follicles*** varies enormously, depending on the stage of development reached and the progress of atresia. The atretic follicle seen in micrograph (a) is a secondary follicle in early atresia; the oocyte **O** has degenerated and the granulosa cells **G** have begun to disaggregate. Advanced atresia, as seen in micrograph (b), is characterised by gross thickening of the basement membrane between the granulosa cells and the theca interna, forming the so-called ***glassy membrane*** **GM**. Atretic follicles are ultimately replaced completely by collagenous tissue known as the ***corpus fibrosum***. Most corpora fibrosa eventually disappear completely. In the postmenopausal woman, primordial follicles are absent and the cortex consists of stroma and corpora albicantes only, with no developing follicles. The postmenopausal ovary is smaller than that in premenopausal women.

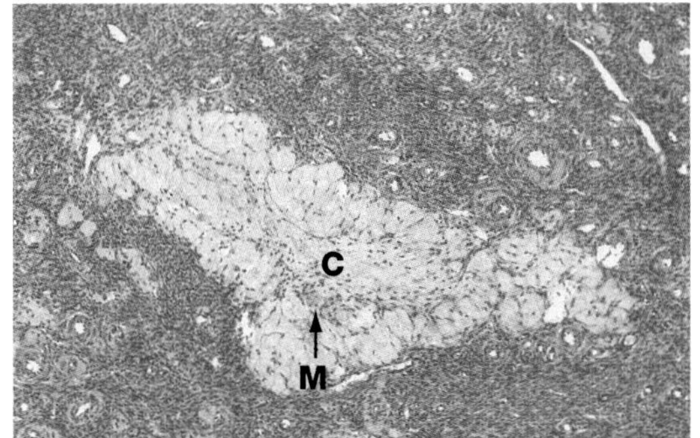

Fig. 19.11 Corpus albicans
H & E ×50

The corpus albicans **C** is the inactive fibrous tissue mass that forms following the involution of a corpus luteum. The secretory cells of the degenerate corpus luteum undergo autolysis and are phagocytosed by macrophages **M**, a few of which, containing cytoplasmic haemosiderin pigment, can be seen here. The vascular supporting tissue regresses to form a relatively acellular collagenous scar containing a few fibroblasts.

In the human ovary, corpora albicantes are a dominant feature, increasing in number with age and often appearing to occupy almost the whole ovarian stroma. However, most regress completely leaving no trace; otherwise the postmenopausal ovary would contain approximately 500 corpora albicantes.

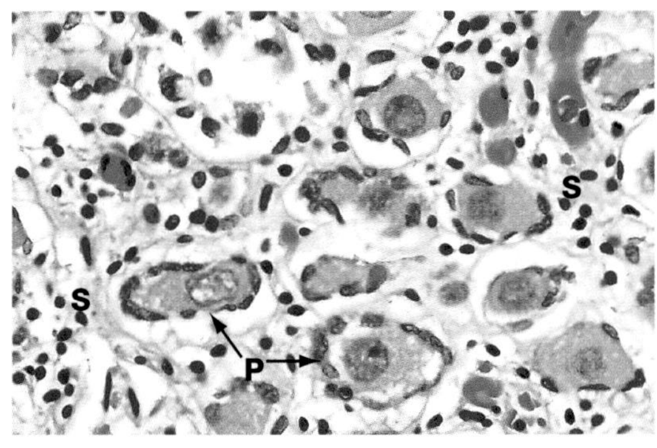

Fig. 19.12 Fetal ovary
H & E ×200

In this micrograph of ovary from a term fetus, the ovarian cortex is seen to be packed with primordial follicles **P**. The surrounding stroma **S** is much more delicate than in an adult woman. These ova are arrested in the first meiotic division and remain so until the onset of puberty signals the waves of maturation of follicles that occur with each cycle in the reproductive years.

The genital tract

The genital tract consists of the Fallopian tubes, uterus and vagina, all of which have the same basic structure: a wall of smooth muscle, an inner mucosal lining and an outer layer of loose supporting tissue. The mucosal and muscular components vary greatly according to their location and functional requirements; the whole tract undergoes cyclical changes under the influence of ovarian hormones released during the ovarian cycle.

The cyclical changes in the genital tract facilitate the entry of ova into the Fallopian tube, the passage of spermatozoa through the uterine cervix and into the Fallopian tube, the passage of the fertilised ovum into the uterus and the implantation and development of the fertilised ovum in the mucosal lining (endometrium) of the uterus. Implantation of a fertilised ovum results in the secretion of hormones that inhibit the ovarian cycle and produce the changes in the genital tract necessary for fetal development and parturition.

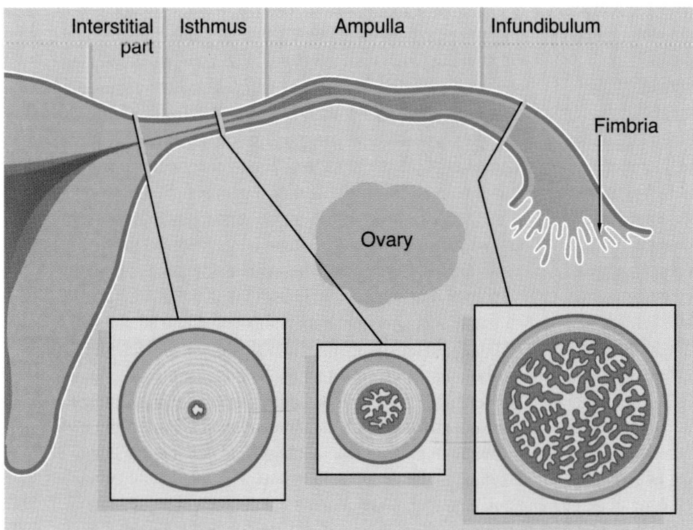

Fig. 19.13 Fallopian tubes

The ***Fallopian tubes*** (also called ***uterine tubes*** or ***oviducts***) carry ova from the surface of the ovaries to the uterine cavity and are also the site of fertilisation by spermatozoa. The Fallopian tube is shaped like an elongated funnel and is divided anatomically into four parts as shown in the diagram.

C corpus albicans **CL** corpus luteum **Ft** Fallopian tube **G** granulosa cells **GM** glassy membrane **M** macrophages **O** oocyte **P** primordial follicle **S** stroma

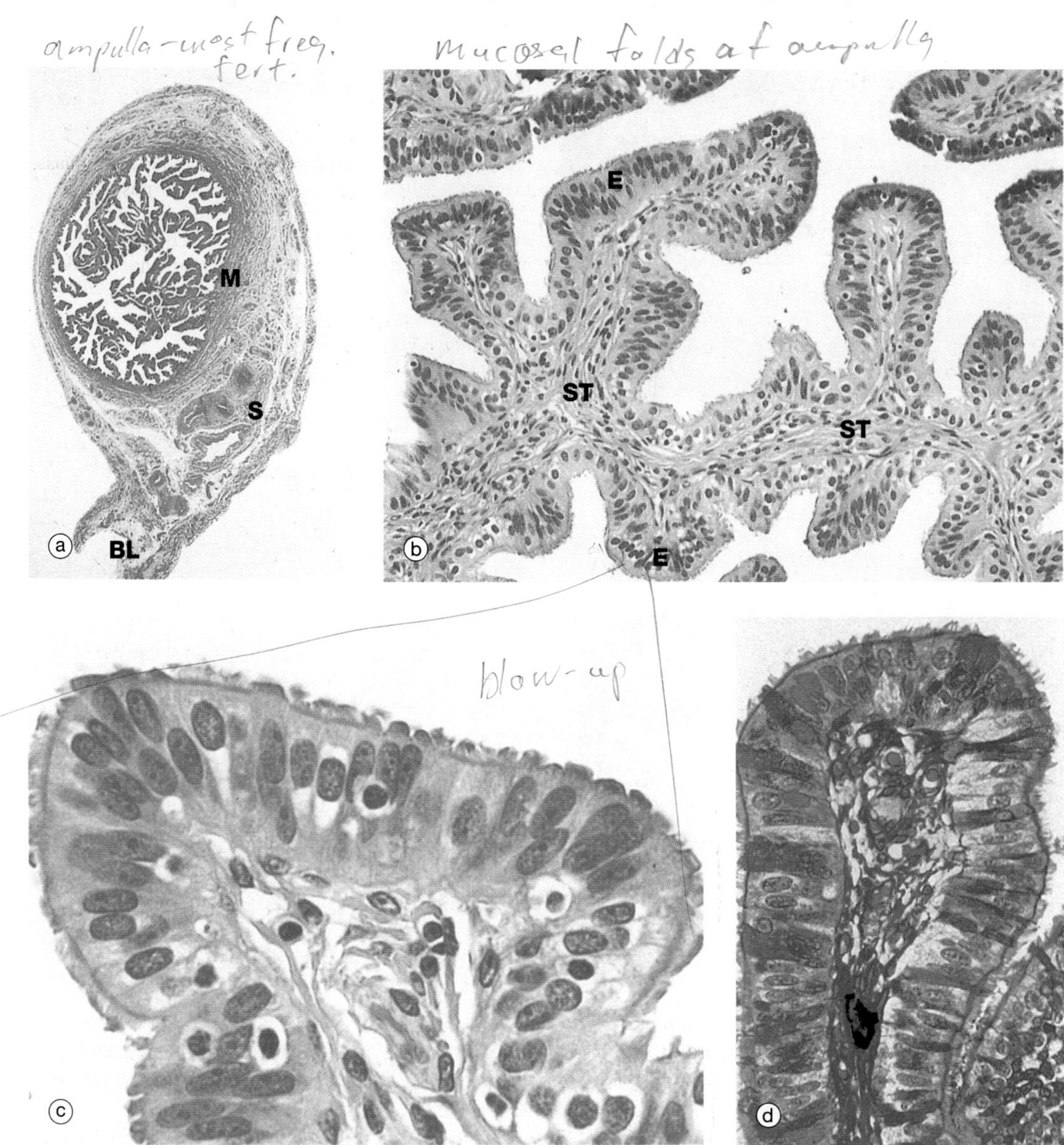

Fig. 19.14 Fallopian tube
(a) H & E ×10 (b) H & E ×150 (c) H & E ×600 (d) Azan ×320

At the time of ovulation, the ***infundibulum*** moves so as to overlie the site of rupture of the Graafian follicle; finger-like projections called ***fimbriae*** extending from the end of the tube envelop the ovulation site and direct the ovum into the tube. Movement of the ovum along the tube is mediated by gentle peristaltic action of the longitudinal and circular smooth muscle layers of the oviduct wall; this is aided by a current of fluid propelled by the action of the ciliated epithelium lining the tube. The mucosal lining of the Fallopian tube is thrown into a labyrinth of branching, longitudinal folds, a feature that is most prominent in the ampulla (a), which is the usual site of fertilisation. Note also in this micrograph, the muscular wall **M** and the vascular supporting tissue of the serosa **S**, which is continuous with the broad ligament **BL**. The serosal layer and broad ligament have a surface lining of mesothelium. The muscular wall has two layers, an inner circular and an outer longitudinal, not discernible at this magnification.

Micrograph (b) focuses on one of the mucosal folds of the ampulla. These have a branching core of vascular supporting tissue **ST** and are invested by a single layer of tall columnar epithelial cells **E**.

Micrograph (c) shows the tip of a mucosal fold at high magnification. The columnar cells of the epithelium are of three types, ***ciliated***, ***non-ciliated secretory*** and ***intercalated cells***. The non-ciliated cells produce a secretion that is propelled towards the uterus by the wave-like beating of the cilia of the ciliated cells, carrying with it the ovum. This secretion probably also has a role in the nutrition and protection of the ovum. The intercalated cells may be a morphologic variant of the secretory cells. The ratio of ciliated to non-ciliated cells and the height of the cells undergo cyclical variations under the influence of ovarian hormones. The ciliated cells are generally shorter than the secretory cells, making the epithelial surface somewhat irregular in outline. Scattered intraepithelial lymphocytes are also present. Micrograph (d) employs a method that stains the secretory cells blue. Note that the collagen of the supporting tissue core of the mucosal fold is also stained blue.

The human menstrual cycle

The uterus is a flattened pear-shaped organ approximately 7 cm long in the non-pregnant state. Its mucosal lining, the ***endometrium***, provides the environment for fetal development; the thick smooth muscle wall, the ***myometrium***, expands greatly during pregnancy and provides protection for the fetus and a mechanism for the expulsion of the fetus at parturition. The endometrium is variable in thickness measuring between 1 mm and 5 mm at different stages of the menstrual cycle. The myometrium makes up the bulk of the uterus measuring up to about 20 mm in a woman of reproductive age (see Fig. 19.2).

In women of child-bearing age, the endometrial lining of the uterine cavity consists of a pseudostratified columnar ciliated epithelium forming numerous simple tubular glands supported by the cellular ***endometrial stroma***. Under the influence of oestrogen and progesterone secreted during the ovarian cycle, the endometrium undergoes regular cyclical changes so as to offer a suitable environment for implantation of a fertilised ovum. These changes are summarized in Fig.19.15 overleaf. For successful implantation, the fertilised ovum requires an easily penetrable, highly vascular tissue and an abundant supply of glycogen for nutrition until vascular connections are established with the maternal vasculature.

The cycle of changes in the endometrium proceeds through three distinct phases, ***menstruation***, ***proliferation*** and ***secretion***; these changes involve both the epithelium and supporting stroma.

- **The menstrual phase:** the first day of menstruation is by convention, taken as the first day of the cycle simply because it is easily identified. This is the phase of endometrial shedding that only occurs if there is failure of fertilisation and/or implantation of the ovum. Progesterone production by the corpus luteum is inhibited by negative feedback on the anterior pituitary thus suppressing LH release and leading to involution of the corpus luteum. In the absence of progesterone, the endometrium cannot be maintained. Reactivation of FSH secretion initiates a new cycle of follicular development and oestrogen secretion; this in turn, initiates a new cycle of proliferation of the endometrium from the endometrial remnants of the previous cycle.

- **The proliferative phase:** the endometrial stroma proliferates becoming thicker and richly vascularised. The simple tubular glands elongate to form numerous long coiled glands that begin secretion coincident with ovulation. The proliferative phase is initiated and sustained until ovulation by the increasing production of oestrogens from developing ovarian follicles.

- **The secretory phase:** release of progesterone from the corpus luteum after ovulation promotes production of a copious thick glycogen-rich secretion by the endometrial glands.

A typical menstrual cycle is 28 days although there is a wide variation among normal women. Menstruation lasts on average 5 days; the proliferative phase continues until about the 14th day when ovulation occurs and the secretory phase begins. The secretory phase culminates at the onset of menstruation on about the 28th day.

The endometrium is divided into three histologically and functionally distinct layers. The deepest or basal layer, the ***stratum basalis***, adjacent to the myometrium, undergoes little change during the menstrual cycle and is not shed during menstruation. The broad intermediate layer is characterised by a stroma with a spongy appearance and is called the ***stratum spongiosum***. The thinner superficial layer, which has a compact stromal appearance, is known as the ***stratum compactum***. The compact and spongy layers exhibit dramatic changes throughout the cycle and both are shed during menstruation; hence they are jointly referred to as the ***stratum functionalis***.

The arrangement of the arterial supply of the endometrium has important influences on the menstrual cycle. Branches of the uterine arteries pass through the myometrium and immediately divide into two different types of arteries, ***straight arteries*** and ***spiral arteries***. Straight arteries are short and pass a small distance into the endometrium, then bifurcate to form a plexus supplying the stratum basalis. Spiral arteries are long, coiled and thick-walled and pass to the surface of the endometrium giving off numerous branches which give rise to a capillary plexus around the glands and in the stratum compactum. Unlike the straight arteries, the spiral arteries are responsive to the hormonal changes of the menstrual cycle. The withdrawal of progesterone secretion at the end of the cycle causes the spiral arteries to constrict and this precipitates an ***ischaemic phase*** that immediately precedes menstruation.

BL broad ligament **E** epithelial cells **M** muscular wall **S** serosa **ST** supporting tissue

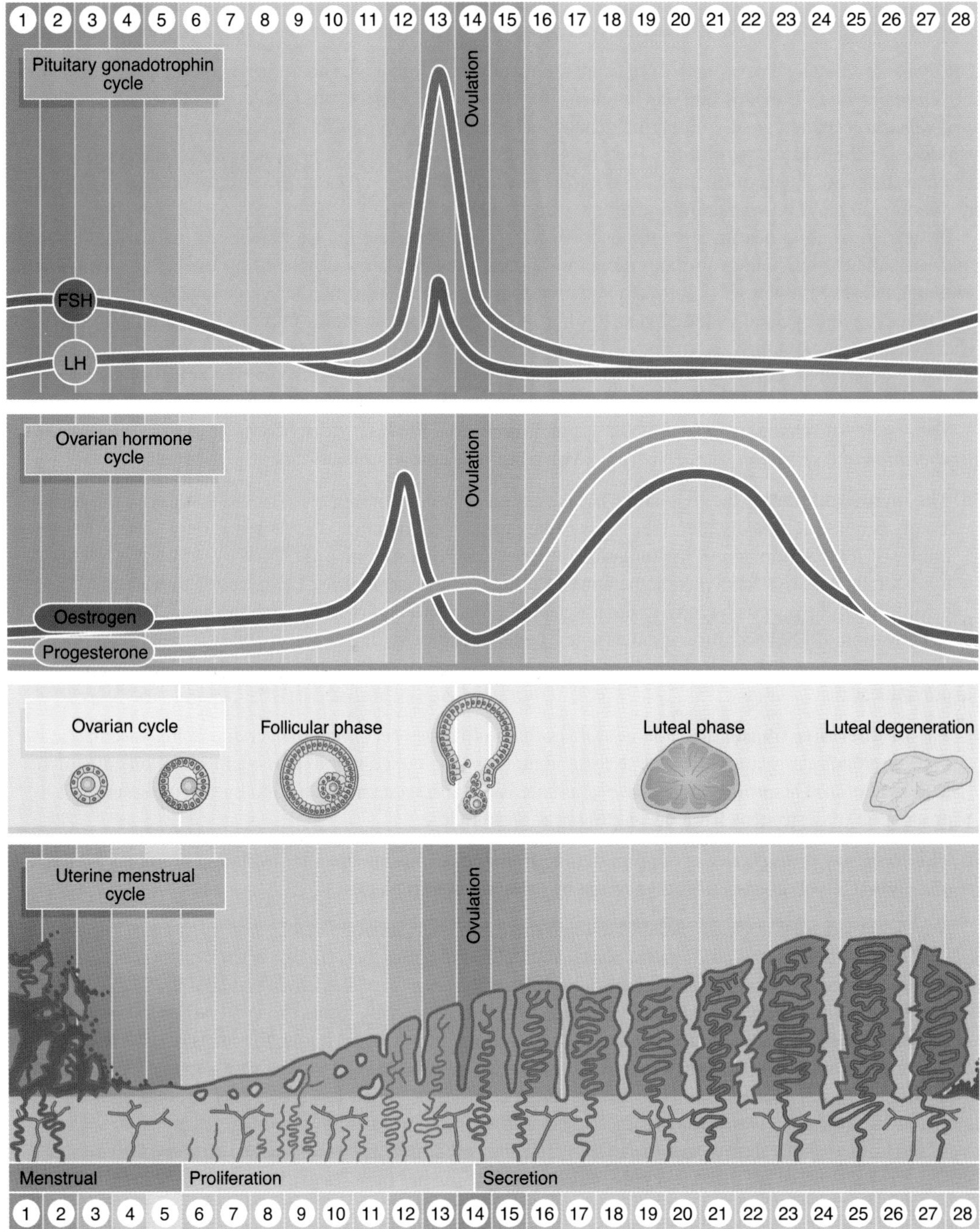

Fig. 19.15 **The hormonal integration of the ovarian and menstrual cycles**

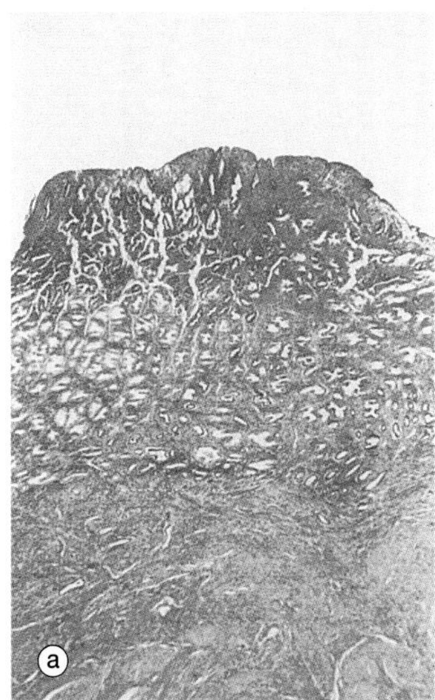

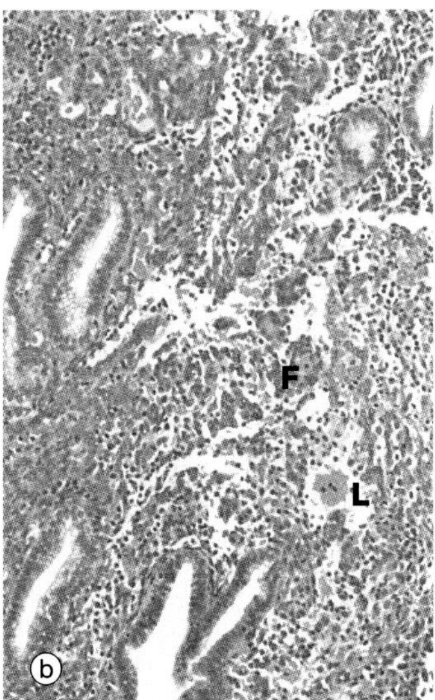

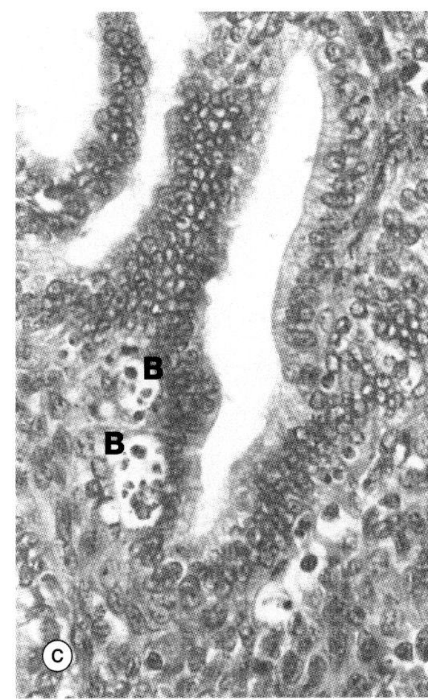

Fig. 19.16 Endometrium: onset of menstruation
(a) H & E ×8 (b) H & E ×100 (c) H & E ×300

In the absence of implantation of a fertilised ovum, degeneration of the corpus luteum results in cessation of oestrogen and progesterone secretion. In turn this initiates spasmodic constriction in the spiral arterioles of the endometrial stratum functionalis **F**. The resulting ischaemia is initially manifest by degeneration of the superficial layers of the endometrium and leakage of blood **L** into the stroma; this is seen in micrographs (a) and (b). Stromal cells disaggregate and the endometrial glands collapse. These features are indicative of early necrosis of glands and stroma. At high magnification in micrograph (c), nuclear debris of endometrial cells (apoptotic bodies) **B** can be seen at the onset of menstruation. These cells have died by apoptosis (see Ch. 2).

Further ischaemia leads to degeneration of the whole stratum functionalis, which is progressively shed as ***menses***. Menses is thus composed of blood, necrotic epithelium and stroma. Normally, menstrual blood does not clot due to the local release of inhibitory (anticoagulant) factors and its expulsion is enhanced by uterine contractions. By day 3–4 of menstruation most of the stratum functionalis has been shed and proliferation of the basal layer of the endometrium has begun again.

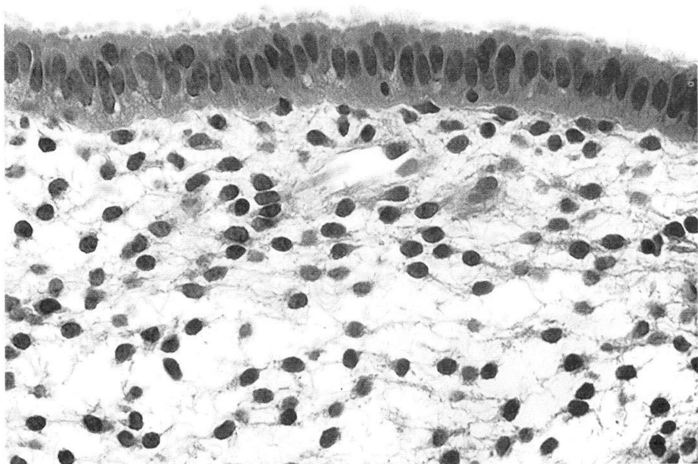

Fig. 19.17 Endometrial surface
H & E ×400

This micrograph illustrates the surface epithelium of the endometrium which is tall columnar in form. Some of the cells bear cilia, the remainder having surface microvilli. Stromal cells have plump spindle-shaped nuclei and scanty cytoplasm. The specimen was obtained during the secretory phase at a time when the stroma is quite oedematous and this can be seen in the clear spaces between the spindle-shaped stromal cells.

B apoptotic bodies **F** stratum functionalis **L** leakage of blood

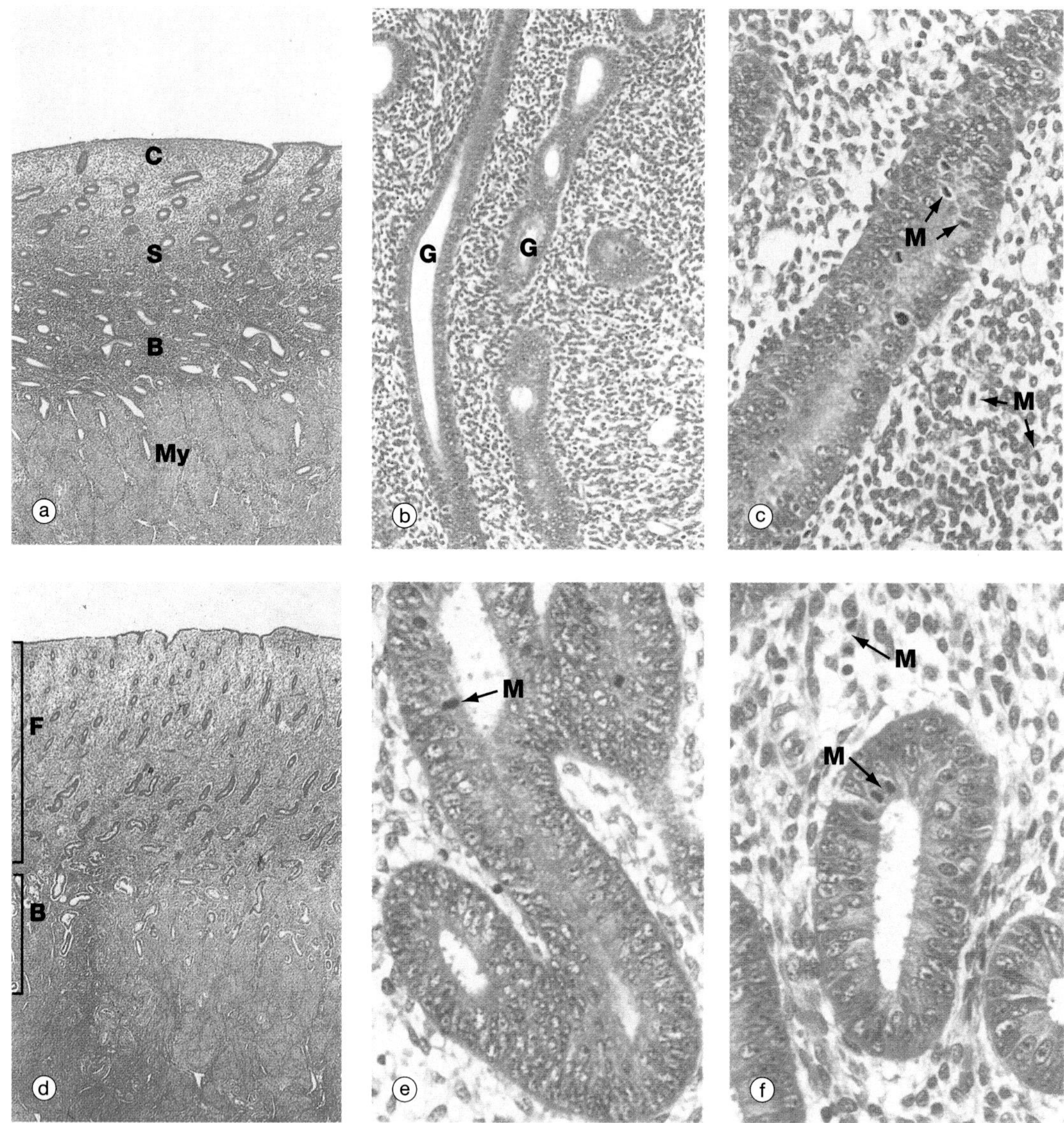

Fig. 19.18 Proliferative endometrium
Early phase: (a) H & E ×20 (b) H & E ×100 (c) H & E ×200; Late phase: (d) H & E ×10 (e) H & E ×100 (f) H & E ×200

Micrograph (a) illustrates early proliferative endometrium at low magnification. At the bottom of the field is the muscular wall, the myometrium **My**. The relatively thin endometrium consists of the stratum basalis **B**, stratum spongiosum **S** and stratum compactum **C**. The glands at this stage are fairly sparse and straight. As the glands, stroma and vessels proliferate, the endometrium gradually becomes thicker. By day 5–6 of the cycle the surface epithelium has regenerated. During the proliferative phase the epithelial cells acquire microvilli and cilia as well as the cytoplasmic organelles required for the secretory phase.

At higher magnification in micrograph (b), the straight tubular form of the endometrial glands **G** can be seen. At very high magnification in micrograph (c), the proliferating glandular epithelium is seen to consist of columnar cells with basally located nuclei exhibiting prominent nucleoli. Mitotic figures **M** can be seen both in the epithelium and in the stroma. Note the highly cellular stroma, almost devoid of collagen fibres.

By the late proliferative stage, shown at low magnification in micrograph (d), the endometrium has doubled in thickness. Note that in contrast to the stratum functionalis **F**, the appearance of the stratum basalis **B** is little changed when compared with the early proliferative phase. With further magnification, micrograph (e) shows that the tubular glands are now becoming coiled and more closely packed. At very high magnification in micrograph (f), mitotic figures **M** are more prevalent in both the glandular epithelium and the supporting stroma. The stroma is also somewhat oedematous at this stage. During the proliferative phase there is a continuum of change that makes the precise dating of the cycle inaccurate in histological specimens. Lymphocytes and occasional lymphoid aggregates are a normal feature of late proliferative phase endometrium but plasma cells are abnormal indicating chronic infection (***endometritis***).

B stratum basalis **C** stratum compactum **F** stratum functionalis **G** endometrial gland
M mitotic figure **My** myometrium **S** stratum spongiosum **Se** secretions **V** vacuoles

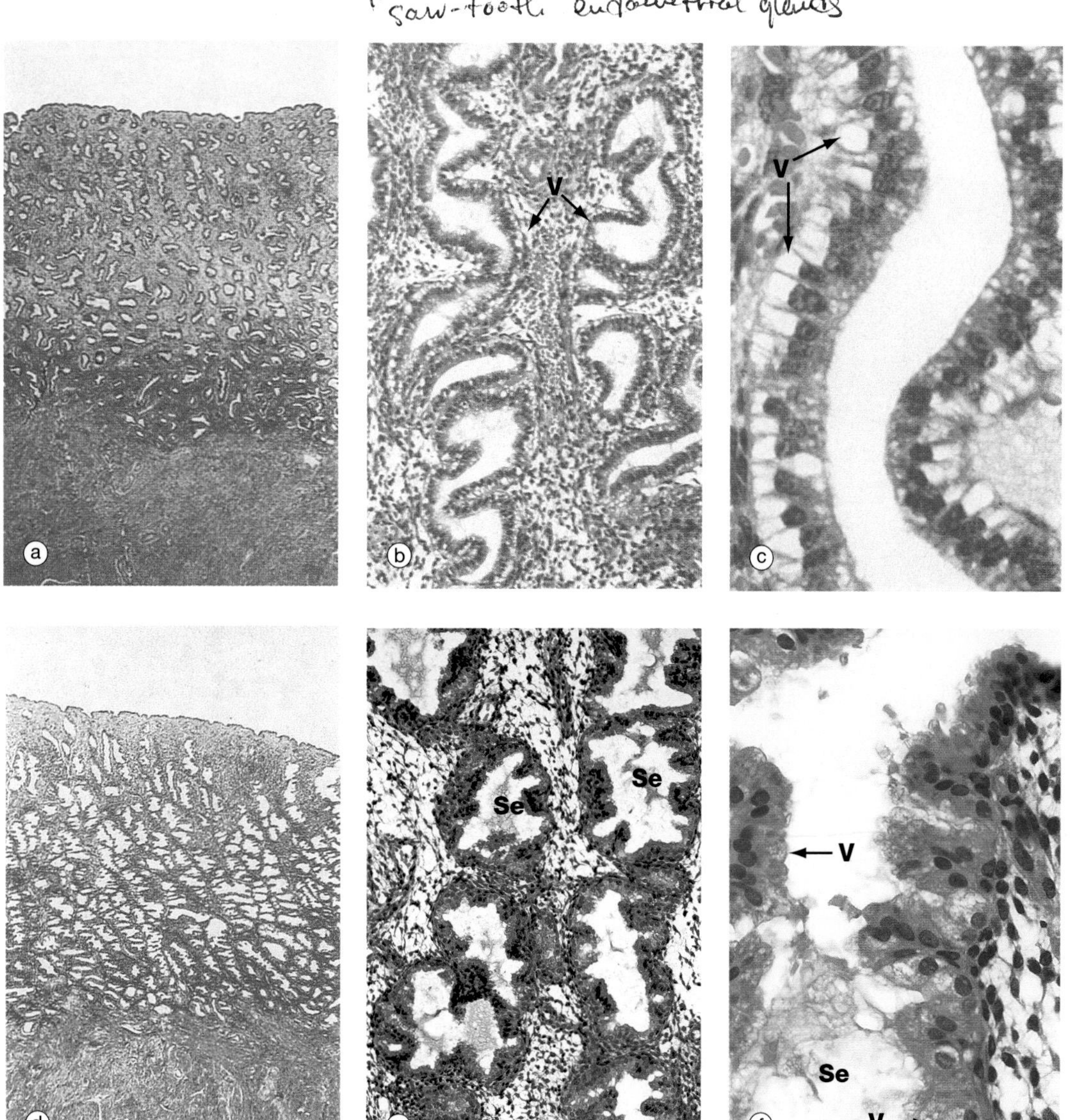

Fig. 19.19 Secretory endometrium
Early phase: (a) H & E ×8 (b) H & E ×50 (c) H & E ×200; Late phase: (d) H & E ×8 (e) H & E ×100 (f) H & E ×400

Ovulation marks the onset of the secretory phase although endometrial cell division continues for several days. At low magnification in micrograph (a), the coiled appearance of the glands is now more pronounced and the endometrium approaches its maximum thickness.

Under the influence of progesterone, the glandular epithelium is stimulated to synthesise glycogen. Initially the glycogen accumulates to form vacuoles **V** in the basal aspect of the cells, thus displacing the nuclei towards the centre of the now tall columnar cells. This ***basal vacuolation*** of the cells appears on day 16 and is the characteristic feature of early secretory endometrium as seen at intermediate and high magnification in micrographs (b) and (c), respectively. Glycogen is an important source of nutrition for the fertilised ovum.

As seen at low and intermediate magnification in micrographs (d) and (e) respectively, the late secretory phase is characterised by a saw-tooth appearance of the glands that contain copious thick glycogen- and glycoprotein-rich secretions **Se**.

At very high magnification in micrograph (f), the cytoplasmic vacuoles **V** can now be seen on the luminal aspect of the cell and the nucleus has returned to its basal position. These vacuoles contain glycogen and glycoproteins that are secreted **Se** into the glandular lumen by apocrine-type secretion. Mitotic figures are absent. The stroma is by now at its most vascular and interstitial fluid begins to accumulate between the stromal cells. ***Endometrial stromal granulocytes***, which are probably large granular lymphocytes, are found in the stroma at this stage. These changes in secretory phase endometrium make more precise dating possible on histological specimens than in the proliferative phase. Such examinations are often carried out in the investigation of infertility.

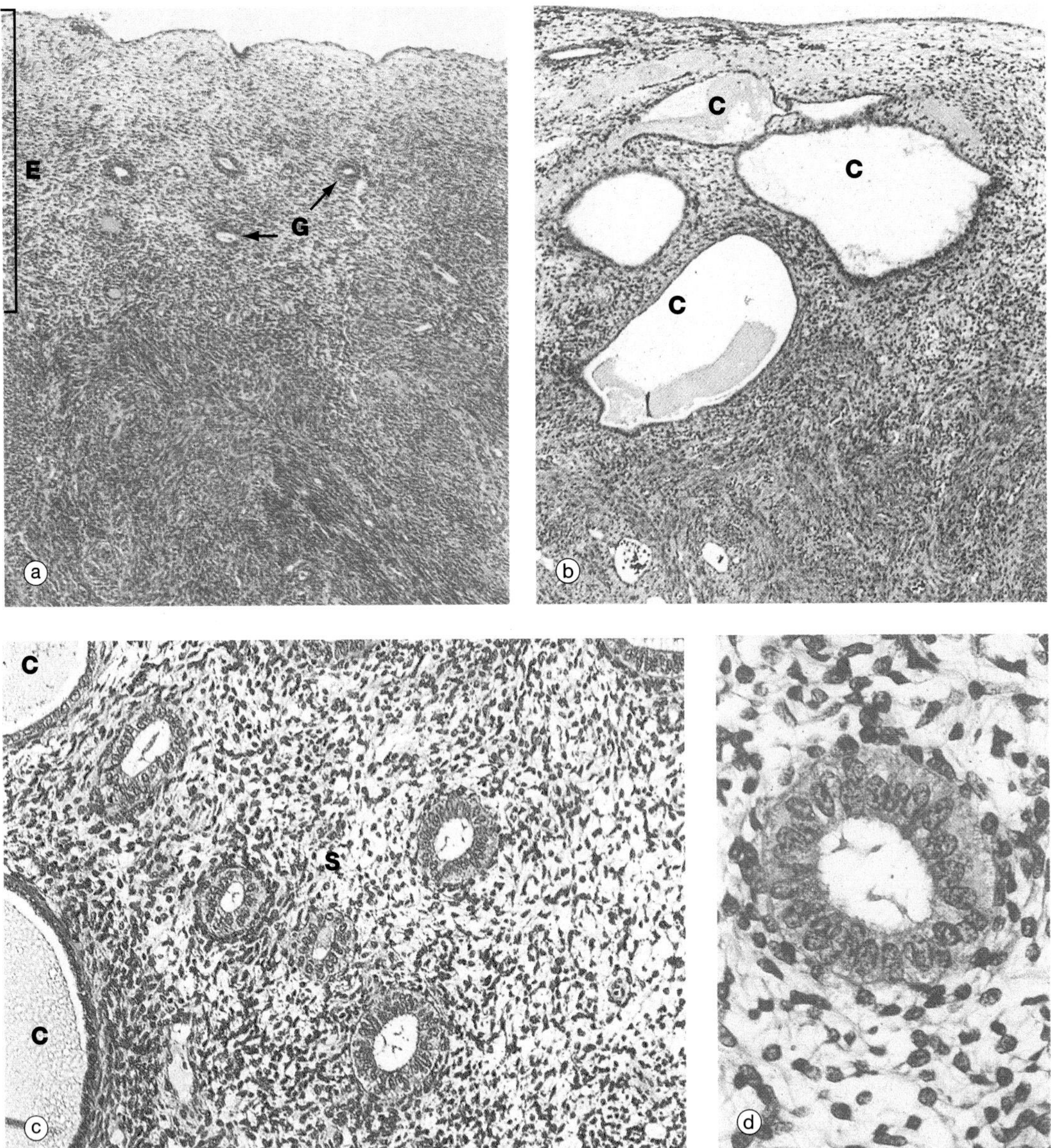

Fig. 19.20 Postmenopausal endometrium
(a) H & E ×60 (b) H & E ×60 (c) H & E ×150 (d) H & E ×400

After the menopause, the cyclical production of oestrogen and progesterone from the ovaries ceases and the whole genital tract undergoes atrophic changes. As seen in micrograph (a), the endometrium **E** is thin, consisting only of the stratum basalis, and the glands **G** are sparse and inactive. As shown in micrograph (b), in some women the glands become dilated to form cystic spaces **C**; the reason for this is unknown but this appearance is so common as to be considered a normal variant.

As shown at higher magnifications in micrographs (c) and (d), the glandular epithelial cells are cuboidal or low columnar with no mitotic figures or secretory activity. The epithelium which lines cystically dilated glands **C**, as shown in micrograph (c), is often flattened. The stroma **S** is much less cellular and contains more collagen fibres than during the reproductive years and no mitotic activity is seen.

The myometrium also becomes atrophic after the menopause and the uterus shrinks to about half its former size.

C cystic gland **E** endometrium **G** gland **L** longitudinal smooth muscle bundle **Ly** leiomyoma **M** myometrium **O** oblique smooth muscle bundle **S** stroma **T** transverse smooth muscle bundle

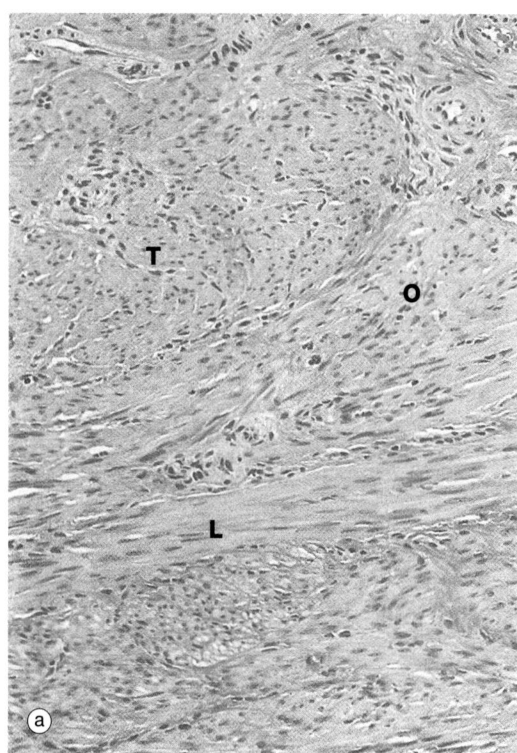

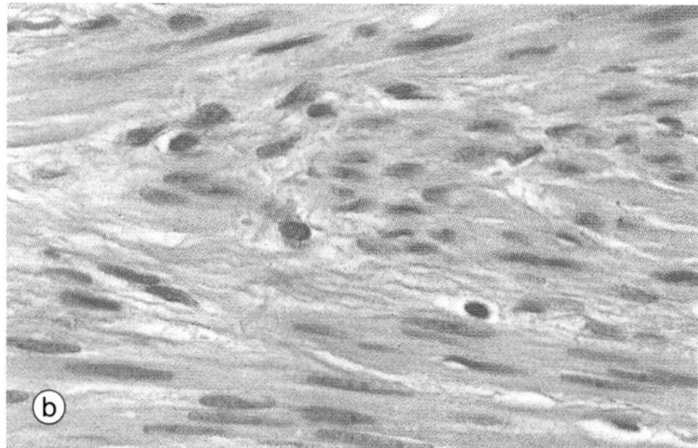

Fig. 19.21 Myometrium
(a) H & E ×150 (b) H & E ×400

The main bulk of the uterus consists of smooth muscle, the ***myometrium***, which is composed of interlacing bundles of long slender fibres arranged in ill-defined layers. This is readily seen in micrograph (a), which contains bundles of fibres in transverse **T**, longitudinal **L**, and oblique sections **O.** Within the muscle is a rich network of arteries and veins supported by collagenous supporting tissue. Micrograph (b) shows detail of the smooth muscle cells at high magnification, highlighting the closeness with which the muscle fibres are packed.

During pregnancy, in response to increased levels of oestrogens, the myometrium increases greatly in size, mainly by increasing cell size (***hypertrophy***), although some increase in cell numbers (***hyperplasia***) due to cell division may also occur.

At parturition, strong contractions of the myometrium are reinforced by the action of the hormone oxytocin secreted by the posterior pituitary. These contractions expel the fetus from the uterus and also constrict the blood supply to the placenta, thus precipitating its detachment from the uterine wall.

Uterine fibroid

The uterine ***leiomyoma***, colloquially known as a ***fibroid***, is a very common benign tumour of women of reproductive age. They tend to increase in size and number with age and cause a range of symptoms including abnormal bleeding, a feeling of pain or dragging in the lower abdomen, urinary frequency if they compress the bladder, and infertility.

As shown in Fig. 19.22, the leiomyoma **Ly** consists of bland smooth muscle fibres that are very like their normal counterparts in appearance. The smooth muscle fibres form whorls and are embedded in a fibrous stroma. The resulting nodule has a very well circumscribed margin and a pseudocapsule of compressed smooth muscle separating it from the normal myometrium **M**. The endometrium **E** is seen at the top of this micrograph. Although this example is a small leiomyoma, they may reach considerable size with 15 cm diameter or larger examples not uncommon. Multiple leiomyomas are very common.

In contrast, ***leiomyosarcomas***, the malignant counterpart of the benign fibroid, are much rarer, occur in older women and are characterised by an infiltrative margin, marked cytologic atypia and mitotic figures.

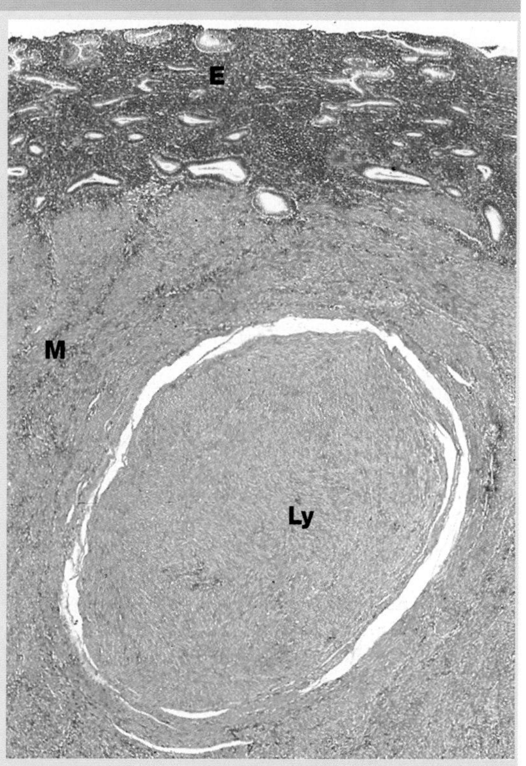

Fig. 19.22 Uterine 'fibroid'
H & E ×40

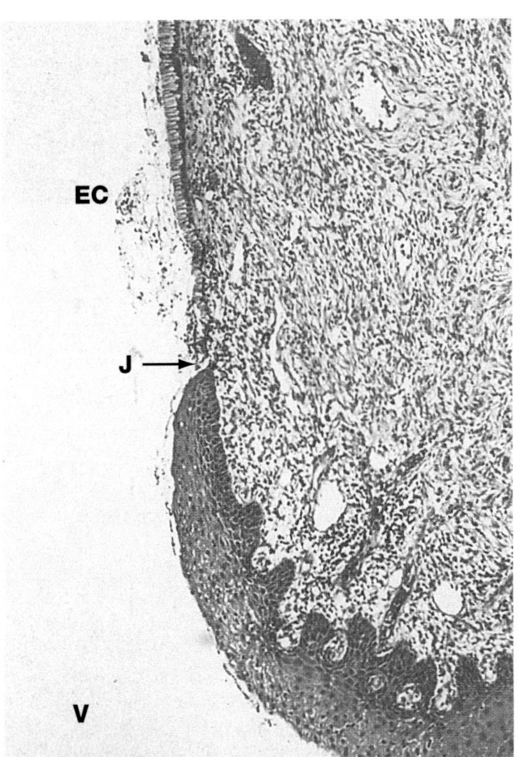

Fig. 19.23 Uterine cervix
H & E ×200

The uterine cervix protrudes into the upper vagina and contains the ***endocervical canal*** linking the uterine cavity with the vagina. The function of the cervix is to admit spermatozoa to the genital tract at the time when fertilisation is possible, i.e. around the time of ovulation, but at other times, including pregnancy, its function is to protect the uterus and upper tract from bacterial invasion. In addition, the cervix must be capable of great dilatation to permit the passage of the fetus during parturition.

As seen in this micrograph, the endocervical canal **EC** is lined by a single layer of tall columnar mucus-secreting epithelial cells. Where the cervix is exposed to the more hostile environment of the vagina **V**, the ***ectocervix***, it is lined by thick stratified squamous epithelium as in the vagina and the vulva. The cells of the ectocervix often have clear cytoplasm due to their high glycogen content (not apparent in this specimen). The junction **J** between the ecto- and endocervical epithelium is quite abrupt and is normally located at the ***external os***, the point at which the endocervical canal opens into the vagina.

The main bulk of the cervix is composed of tough, collagenous tissue containing a little smooth muscle. At the squamocolumnar junction, the cervical stroma is often infiltrated with leucocytes forming part of the defence against ingress of microorganisms.

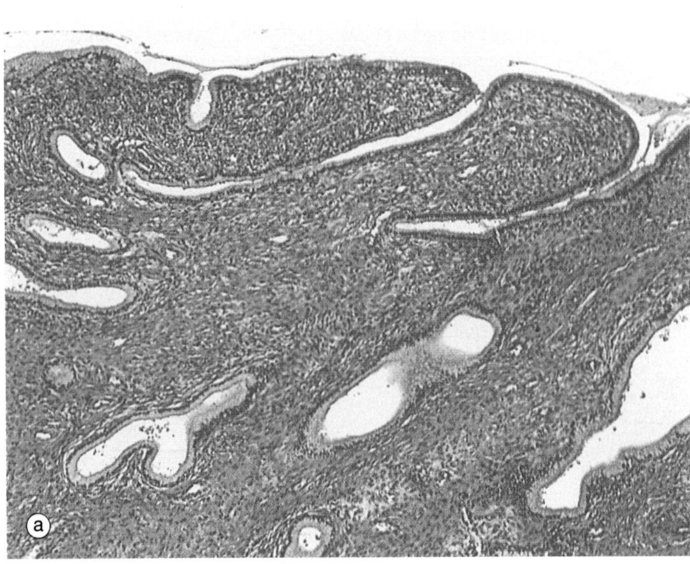

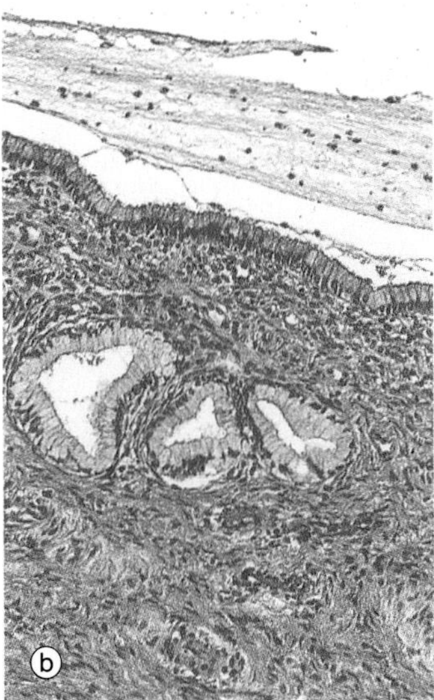

Fig. 19.24 Endocervix
(a) H & E ×60 (b) H & E ×100

As seen in micrograph (a), the mucus-secreting epithelial lining of the endocervical canal is thrown into deep furrows and tunnels giving the appearance in two dimensions of branched tubular glands - hence the rather inaccurate term ***endocervical glands***. The columnar mucus-secreting cells lining the 'glands' are shown at higher magnification in micrograph (b). Note the leucocytic infiltrate in the superficial stroma and the presence of leucocytes in the endocervical mucus on the surface.

During the menstrual cycle, the endocervical epithelium undergoes cyclical changes in secretory activity. In the proliferative phase, rising levels of oestrogen promote secretion of thin watery mucus, which permits the passage of spermatozoa into the uterus around the time of ovulation. Following ovulation, the cervical mucus becomes highly viscid forming a plug that inhibits the entry of microorganisms (and spermatozoa) from the vagina; this is particularly important should pregnancy occur.

A adventitia **E** stratified squamous epithelium **EC** endocervical canal **J** squamocolumnar junction **LP** lamina propria **SM** smooth muscle **V** vagina

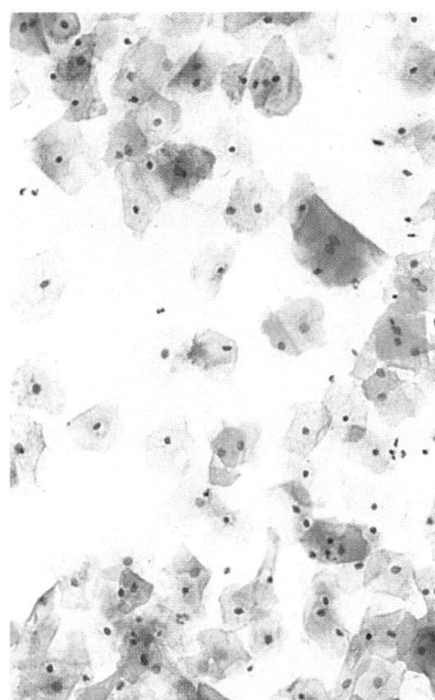

Fig. 19.25 Cervical cytology
Papanicolaou method ×400

The cervical stroma is influenced by the ovarian hormones, particularly oestrogens, which soften the tissues by reducing collagenous cross-linkages and increasing uptake of water by the ground substance. At its most extreme, this provides the means by which the cervix stretches, thins and dilates in late pregnancy and during parturition. To a much lesser extent, similar changes occur during the normal menstrual cycle. One effect of this is that the volume of the cervical stroma varies during each cycle causing eversion of the columnar epithelium near the squamocolumnar junction and exposing it to the vaginal environment. This ***ectropion*** is known colloquially as 'cervical erosions'. This induces the growth of stratified squamous epithelium (***squamous metaplasia***) over the exposed area, considered a normal variant in women of reproductive age. The importance of this ***transformation zone*** is that it may undergo malignant change, causing cancer of the cervix.

This area can be studied by scraping cells from the surface using various types of spatula or brush, smearing them on a glass slide and staining them by the Papanicolaou method (***cervical smear*** or ***Pap test***). This technique is known as ***exfoliative cytology*** and is demonstrated here from a normal healthy cervix. The surface cells of the stratified squamous epithelium have contracted nuclei and are stained pink due to the cytoplasmic keratin; the deeper cells have plump nuclei of normal appearance and the cytoplasm is stained blue/green. An adequate Pap smear should also contain some endocervical cells (demonstrating that the transformation zone has been sampled) as well as cervical mucin and inflammatory cells.

A more recent development of the cervical smear suspends the exfoliated cells in a special medium and layers them evenly onto a glass slide, a technique known as 'ThinPrep'. This gives hugely superior visibility of the cells and improves the ability of the cytologist to see abnormal cells. Various computerised technologies are also becoming available to screen the slides although these are not yet in general use.

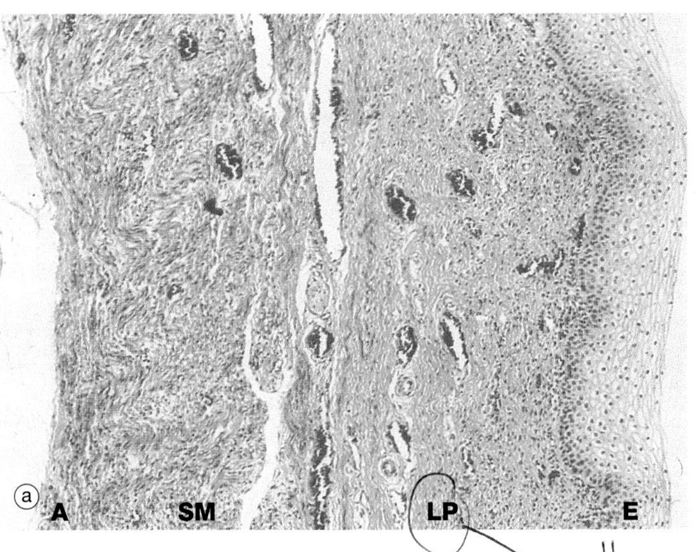

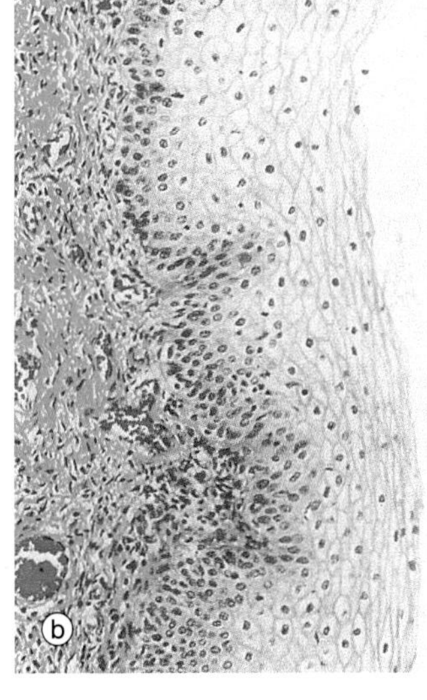

Fig. 19.26 Vagina
(a) Masson's trichrome ×75 (b) Masson's trichrome ×128

The wall of the vagina, micrograph (a), consists of a mucosal layer lined by stratified squamous epithelium **E**, a layer of smooth muscle **SM** and an outer adventitial layer **A**. In the relaxed state, the vaginal wall collapses to obliterate the lumen and the vaginal epithelium is thrown up into folds. The fibrous lamina propria **LP** contains many elastic fibres, has a rich plexus of small veins and is devoid of glands. The vagina is lubricated by cervical mucus, a fluid transudate from the rich vascular network of the lamina propria and mucus secreted by glands of the labia minora. The smooth muscle bundles of the muscular layer are arranged in ill-defined inner circular and outer longitudinal layers. The adventitial layer of the vagina merges with the adventitial layers of the bladder anteriorly and rectum posteriorly.

The combination of a muscular layer and a highly elastic lamina propria and outer adventitia permits the gross distension that occurs during parturition. Conversely, after coitus, involuntary contraction of the smooth muscle layer ensures that a pool of semen remains in the cervical region.

Micrograph (b) illustrates the stratified squamous epithelium that lines the vagina. During the menstrual cycle, this epithelium undergoes cyclical changes in glycogen levels. Throughout the cycle, the superficial cells produce glycogen that is anaerobically metabolized by vaginal commensal bacteria to form lactic acid, which inhibits the growth of pathogenic microorganisms.

The placenta

The placenta is formed from elements of the membranes that surround the developing fetus as well as the uterine endometrium and provides the means for physiological exchange between the fetal and maternal circulations. The structure of the placenta varies greatly from one species to another and the following discussion is thus necessarily confined to the human placenta. At various stages during fetal development, the placenta performs a remarkable range of functions until the fetal organs become functional. These include gaseous exchange, excretion, maintenance of homeostasis, hormone secretion, haemopoiesis and hepatic metabolic functions.

Fig. 19.27 Fertilisation and implantation *(opposite)*

Within about 24–48 hours after ovulation, fertilisation of an ovum by a spermatozoon occurs in the ampulla of the Fallopian tube with the formation of a ***zygote***; the zona pellucida remains intact (see Fig. 19.4). Within 24 hours, the zygote undergoes its first mitotic cell division, the process continuing until there are some 12–16 cells called ***blastomeres***, each with a small portion of the original cytoplasm. The mass, now called a ***morula*** (for its resemblance to a mulberry), remains enclosed by the zona pellucida through which it is nourished by diffusion of oxygen and low molecular weight metabolites from Fallopian tube secretions.

The morula reaches the uterus 2–3 days after fertilisation and begins to absorb uterine fluid forming a central cavity. The ***blastocyst***, as it is now known, consists of a peripheral layer of blastomeres forming the ***trophoblast***, with a mass of cells at one aspect, the ***polar trophoblast***, bulging into the central lumen and known as the ***inner cell mass***. The trophoblast (along with a maternal contribution) eventually gives rise to the placenta while the inner cell mass develops into the embryo. By this time, the blastocyst has grown to about twice the size of the original ovum and the zona pellucida has become quite thin. When the blastocyst has been within the uterine cavity for 2–3 days, the zona pellucida disappears and implantation occurs. The polar trophoblast invades the endometrium so that by the 10th day after conception the blastocyst is completely buried.

The trophoblast gives rise to two layers, an inner ***cytotrophoblast*** layer of mononuclear cells and an outer ***syncytiotrophoblast*** layer formed by fusion of cytotrophoblast cells to form a continuous multinucleate syncytium in which there is no internal cytoplasmic demarcation by plasma membranes. The cytotrophoblast remains as a single layer of cells whereas the syncytiotrophoblast becomes increasingly broad and develops finger-like projections into the endometrium. A third type of trophoblast known as ***intermediate trophoblast*** has histological features intermediate between cytotrophoblast and syncytiotrophoblast and has a major role in invading the endometrium. Within a short time, a sponge-like network of spaces called ***lacunae*** develops within the syncytiotrophoblast, initially filled with tissue fluid and uterine secretions. Soon afterwards, invasion by the intermediate trophoblast causes disintegration of endometrial capillaries with leakage of maternal blood into the lacunae. Progressively the trophoblast envelops maternal capillaries, expanding the lacunar network and establishing an arterial supply and venous drainage system.

By now, the syncytiotrophoblast also secretes a variety of hormones including ***human chorionic gonadotrophin (HCG)***, ***human chorionic somatotrophin*** (previously human placental lactogen, HPL), ***oestrogen*** and ***progesterone*** which are necessary to sustain the endometrial tissues. In the meantime, the blastocyst cavity becomes filled with ***extraembryonic mesoderm*** (mesenchyme) which completely surrounds the early embryo developing from the inner cell mass. The embryo by now comprises plates of ***embryonic endoderm*** and ***ectoderm*** on either side of which lie the ***yolk sac*** and ***amniotic cavities*** enclosed by ***extraembryonic endoderm*** and ***extraembryonic ectoderm***, respectively. Subsequently, a cavity forms within the extraembryonic mesoderm, this ***extraembryonic coelom*** eventually surrounds the developing embryo which remains attached to the trophoblast by a ***connecting stalk*** of extraembryonic mesoderm. The trophoblast, along with the mesodermal layer remaining beneath it, now constitutes the ***chorion***.

Meanwhile the ***trabeculae*** of syncytiotrophoblast and intermediate trophoblast between the lacunae are invaded by columns of cytotrophoblastic cells called ***primary chorionic villi***. These grow out to the periphery and spread out over the interface between the trophoblast and endometrium forming the ***cytotrophoblast shell***. Extraembryonic mesoderm now invades the primary villi which thus develop a mesenchymal core, becoming known as ***secondary chorionic villi***.

By about 2 weeks after implantation (i.e. about 24 days after fertilisation), primitive blood vessels begin to develop in the chorionic mesoderm simultaneously with development of the primitive embryonic circulatory system, the embryo now being too large to rely on mere diffusion for its growth and metabolic requirements. When the mesenchymal cores of the villi become vascularised, they become known as ***tertiary villi*** (not illustrated).

The form of the placenta is essentially established by the end of the fourth month after which the placenta grows in diameter, complementing growth in the size of the uterus.

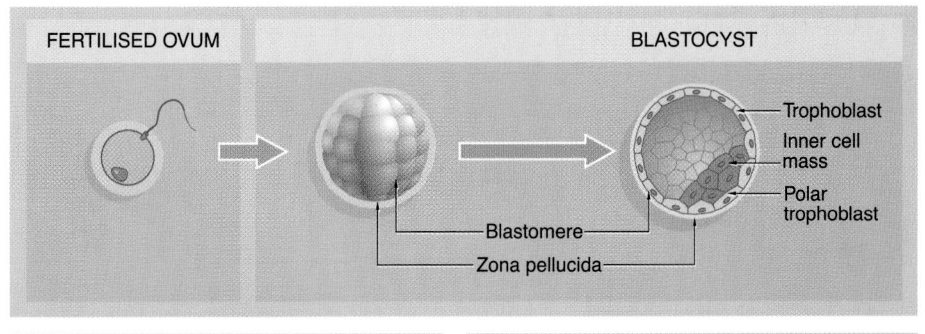

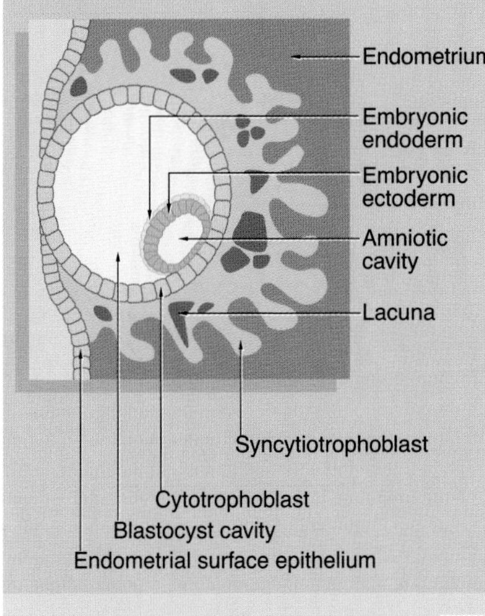

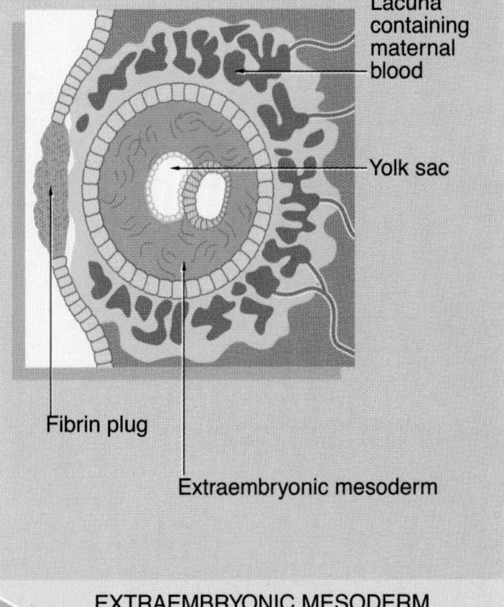

IMPLANTATION OF BLASTOCYST

EXTRAEMBRYONIC MESODERM REPLACES THE BLASTOCYST CAVITY

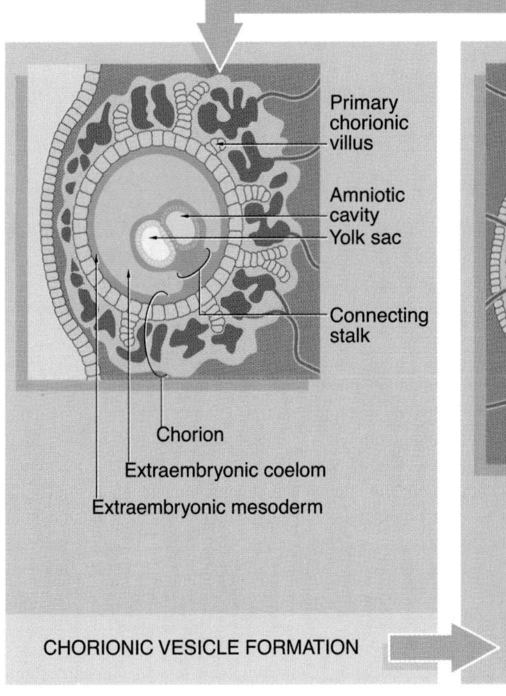

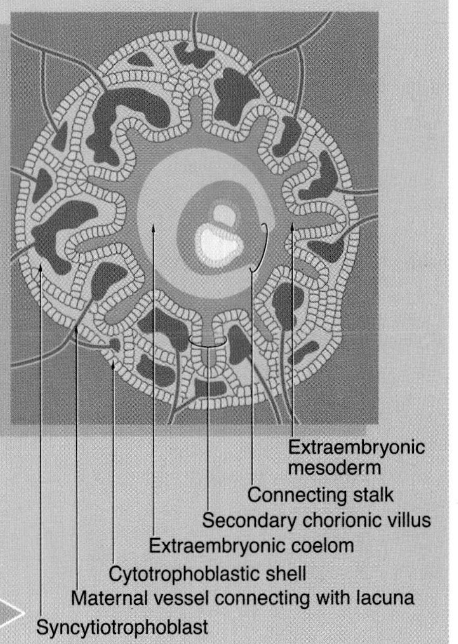

CHORIONIC VESICLE FORMATION

Fig. 19.28 *(caption opposite)*

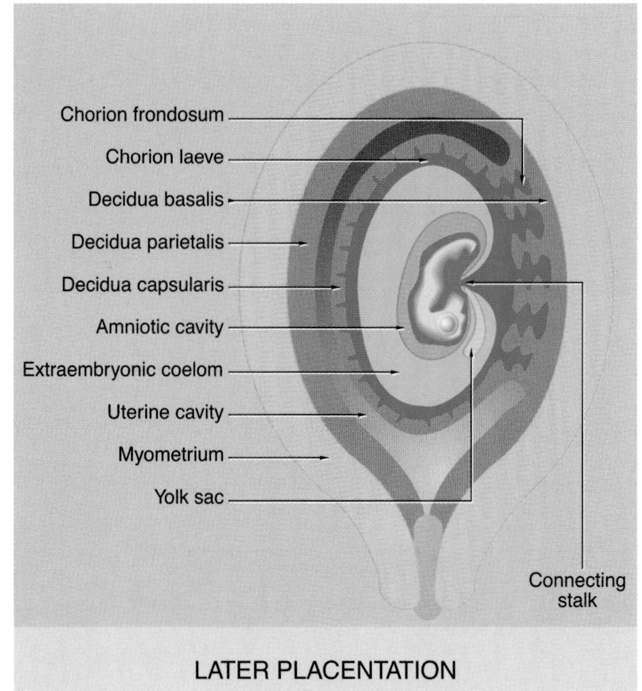

Fig. 19.29 *(caption opposite)*

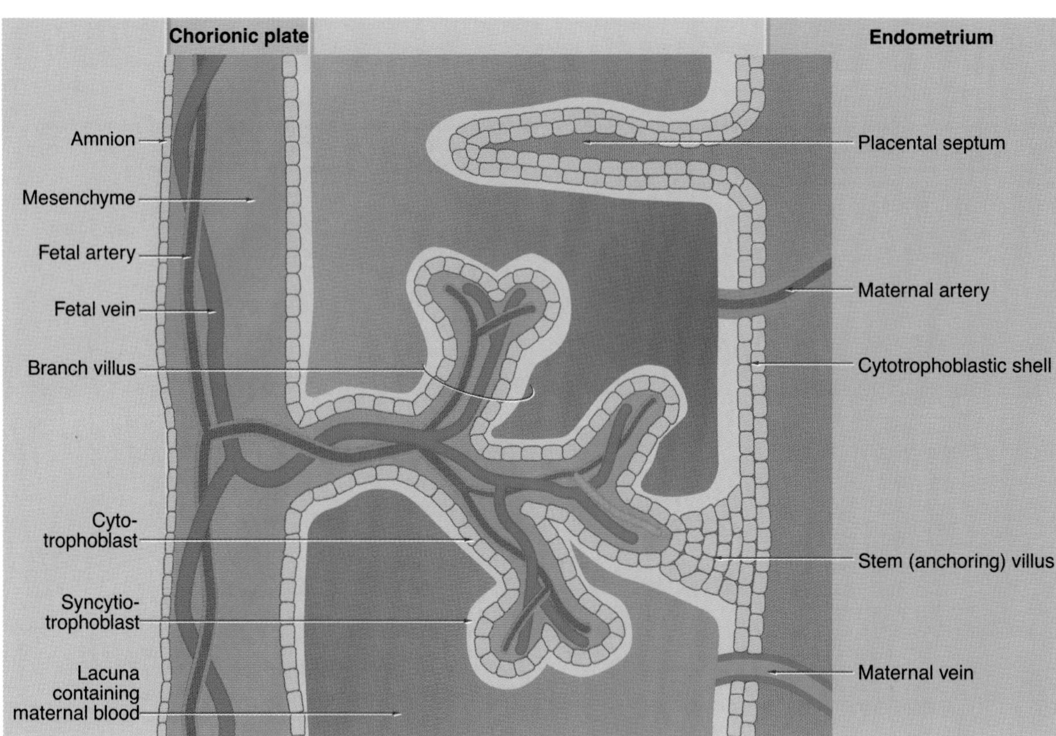

D decidua **G** endometrial gland **I** intermediate trophoblast **S** syncytiotrophoblast cell
V blood vessel

Fig. 19.28 Decidua formation and early placental development *(illustrations opposite, above)*

During the process of implantation, secretion by the syncytiotrophoblast of HCG (which is functionally analogous to luteinising hormone) interrupts the ovarian cycle. This results in growth and proliferation of stromal cells of the endometrial stratum functionalis at the implantation site into large polyhedral ***decidual cells***, a change that has already begun in the late secretory phase. The ***decidua*** beneath the developing embryo is known as the ***decidua basalis*** and with the trophoblast will form the future placenta. The decidua overlying the embryo is known as the ***decidua capsularis*** and the decidual lining of the rest of the uterus is called the ***decidua parietalis***. Ultimately, expansion of the embryo and its enveloping fluid-filled membrane system results in fusion of the capsular and parietal layers of the decidua with complete obliteration of the uterine cavity.

During the first 2 months of embryological development the chorion grows fairly uniformly around the whole periphery of the vesicle. From the third month, the chorion in contact with the decidua basalis develops extensive frond-like villous outgrowths into the decidua becoming known as the ***chorion frondosum***, while the superficial chorion in contact with the decidua capsularis atrophies to become the smooth ***chorion laeve***. Progressively, the chorion frondosum and decidua basalis develop into the flattened placenta and the vessels connecting the chorion to the embryonic circulation become the umbilical cord.

Fig. 19.29 Structure of placental villi *(illustration opposite, below)*

From the time maternal blood appears within the trophoblastic lacunae, the trabeculae between the lacunae become increasingly robust with ***stem villi*** forming anchorage points with the cytotrophoblastic shell. Side branches grow out into the lacunae, progressively forming a complex villous structure. Each villus has a mesenchymal core containing capillaries served by afferent and efferent fetal blood vessels. Between the villous capillaries and the maternal blood is a continuous layer of syncytiotrophoblast supported by a layer of proliferating cytotrophoblast cells. From the fourth month onwards, the cytotrophoblast layer becomes atrophic. As more and more branches are added to the villous tree, the villi become smaller and smaller and the tissue barrier between fetal capillaries and maternal blood is greatly diminished.

As the placenta develops, the decidua basalis regresses so that all that remains are a number of anastomosing septa of maternal supporting tissue projecting into the cytotrophoblastic shell. When the placenta is shed immediately after childbirth, its maternal surface is seen to be divided into about 20 irregular segments called ***cotyledons*** that are demarcated from each other by the positions of the former maternal (placental) septa.

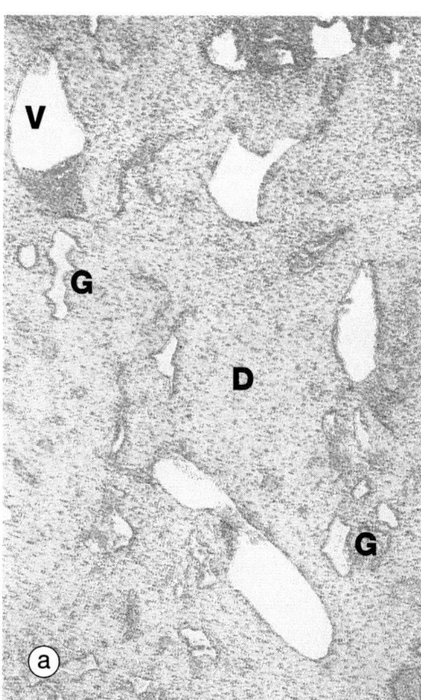

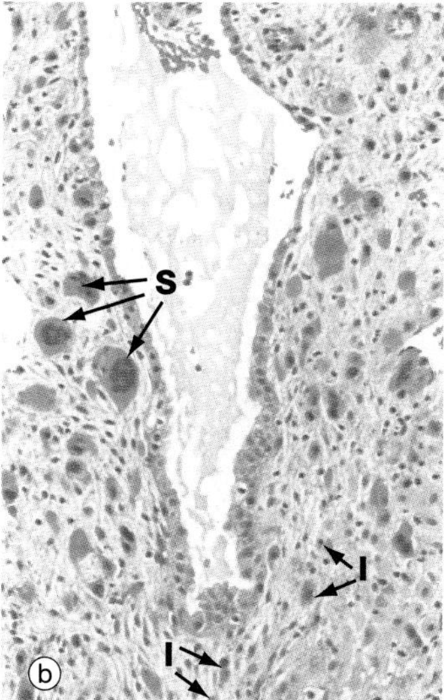

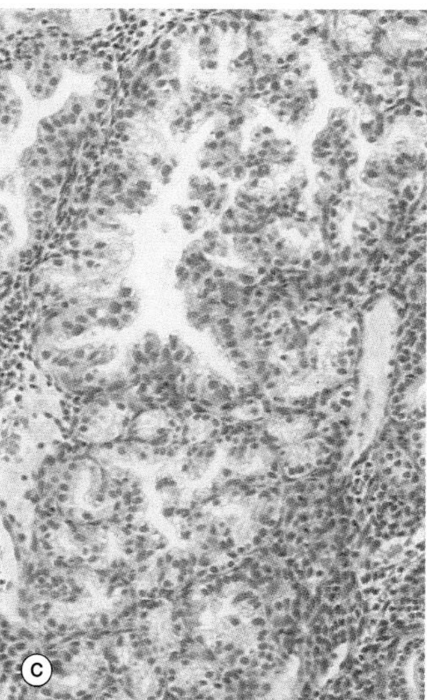

Fig. 19.30 Decidua
(a) H & E ×20 (b) H & E ×100 (c) H & E ×200

Micrograph (a) illustrates decidual change **D** in the endometrial stroma. The decidual cells proliferate and enlarge greatly, their cytoplasm staining pink (eosinophilia) due to the presence of numerous mitochondria and intermediate filaments. Dilated blood vessels **V** and endometrial glands **G** are apparent.

At higher power in micrograph (b), multinucleated syncytiotrophoblast cells **S** can be seen infiltrating the decidua. Intermediate trophoblast cells **I** are actually present in greater numbers than syncytiotrophoblast cells but are less easily identified. In the centre of the field is a dilated gland.

Micrograph (c) shows the deeper part of the endometrium in pregnancy. Here the decidual reaction is inconspicuous but the secretory nature of the glands is greatly exaggerated; it is thus often called ***hypersecretory endometrium***. Note the prominent infolding of the glandular epithelium and the vacuolation of the epithelial cell cytoplasm.

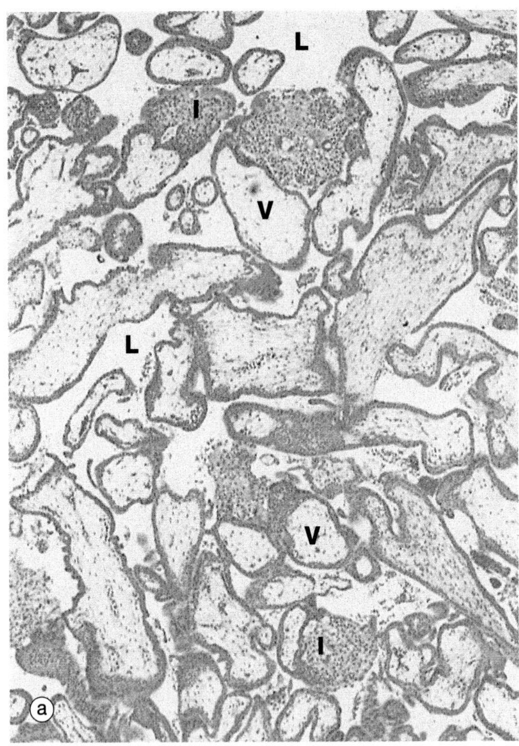

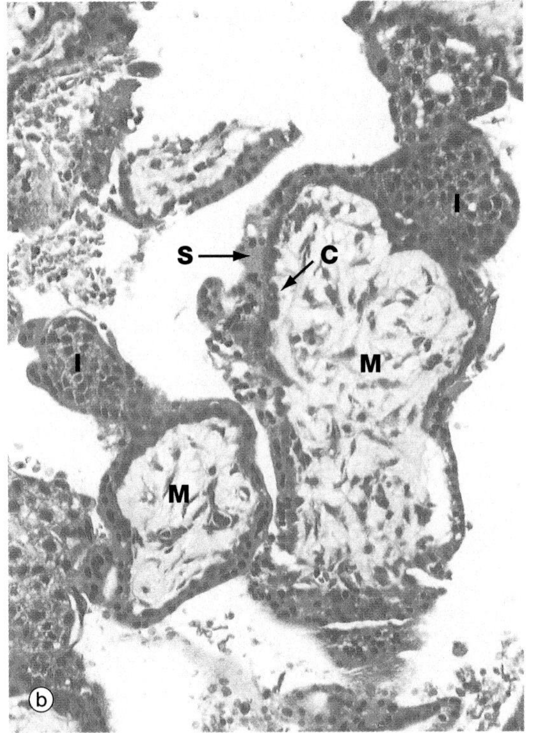

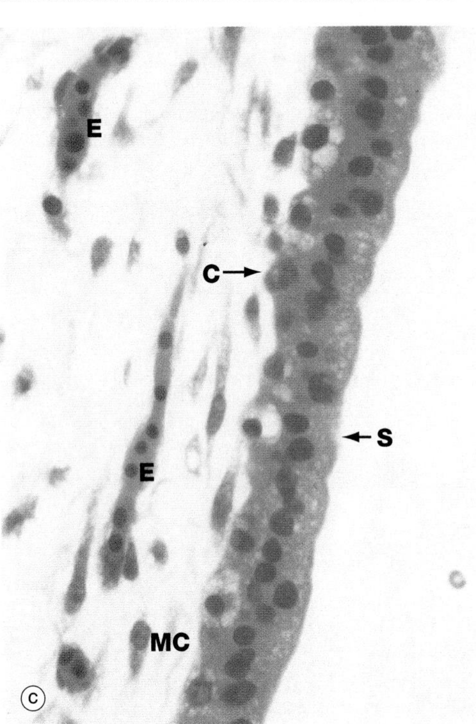

Fig. 19.31 Early placenta
(a) H & E ×50 (b) H & E ×150 (c) H & E ×300

This series of micrographs at increasing magnification shows a placenta at about 6 weeks gestational age. Nucleated fetal erythrocytes **E**, which in humans persist until 9 weeks gestational age, can be seen in the capillary in micrograph (c).

At low magnification in micrograph (a), the main feature is the large numbers of villi **V** projecting into the lacuna system **L** that in vivo would be filled with maternal blood; some villi show evidence of branching. Solid cores of cytotrophoblast and intermediate trophoblast **I** can be seen extending away from the villi to form new branches.

With further magnification in micrograph (b), the villi are seen to have a core of primitive mesenchyme **M**. The villi are invested by trophoblast, comprising an inner layer of cytotrophoblast cells **C** and a broader, outer syncytiotrophoblast layer **S**. In some areas, solid buds of trophoblast can be seen forming new branches. The specimen is a little broken up as it is derived from a curettage specimen following incomplete spontaneous abortion.

Micrograph (c) focuses on the margin of a villus at high magnification, the cellular preservation being again less than ideal due to its origin from a spontaneous miscarriage. The syncytiotrophoblast layer **S** can be distinguished from the single layer of cytotrophoblast cells **C** which are smaller. The mesenchymal cells **MC** are large, with extensive branching cytoplasmic processes, and the intercellular matrix is myxoid due to its high glycosaminoglycans content.

BM basement membrane **C** cytotrophoblast **D** desmosome **E** nucleated erythrocytes
G Golgi apparatus **I** intermediate trophoblast **L** lacuna **M** mesenchyme **MC** mesenchymal cell
Mi mitochondrion **Mv** microvilli **Nu** nucleolus **R** polyribosomes
rER rough endoplasmic reticulum **S** syncytiotrophoblast **sER** smooth endoplastic reticulum **V** villus

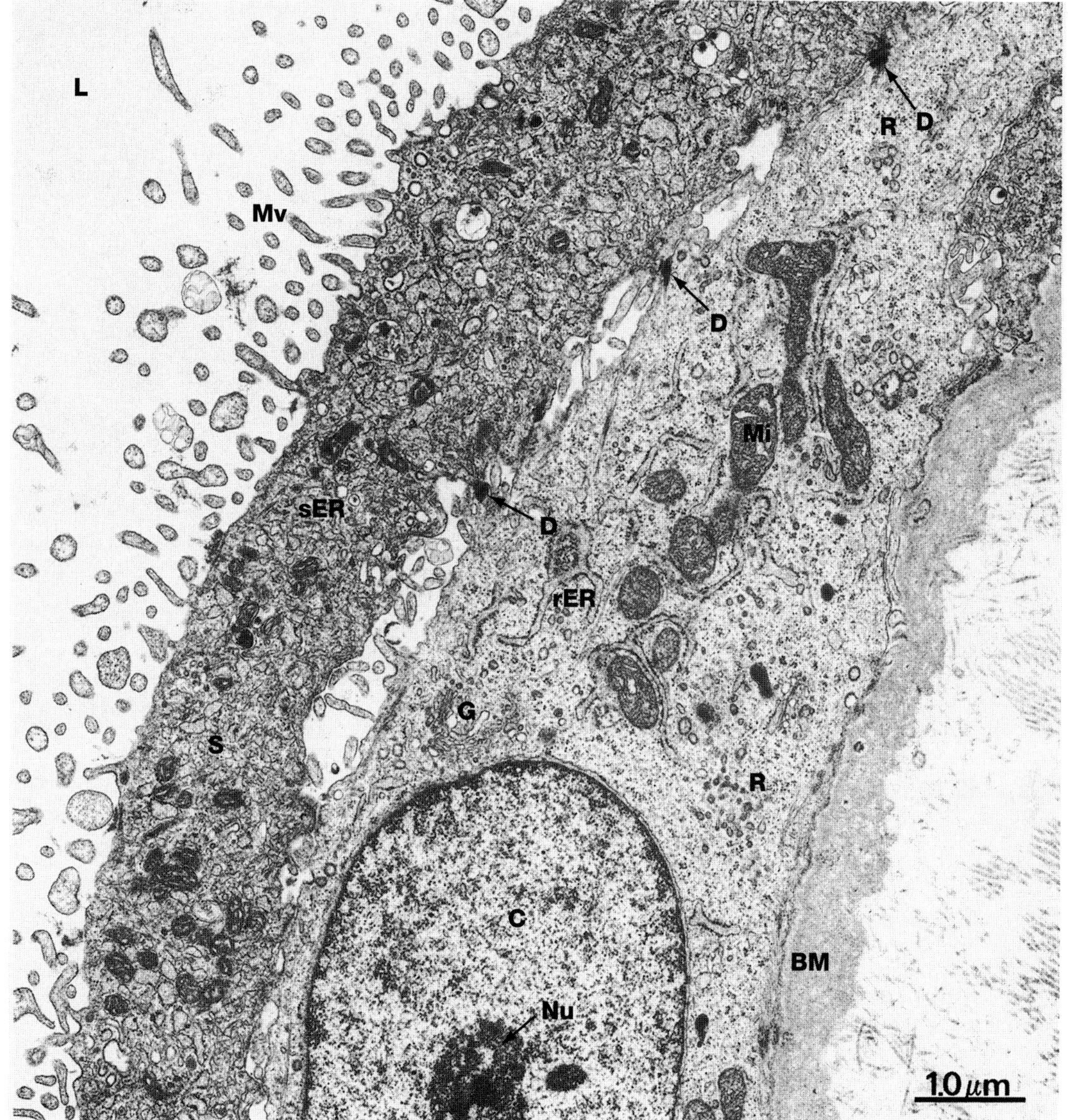

Fig. 19.32 Trophoblast
EM ×16 000

This micrograph shows the general ultrastructural features of the trophoblastic components; these show considerable variation from one region to another and from early to late stages of placental development.

The syncytiotrophoblast **S** typically presents large numbers of irregular microvilli **Mv** to the lacunae **L** greatly enhancing the surface area for physiological exchange. The plasma membranes of the microvilli incorporate a wide variety of enzymes and receptors involved in membrane transfer processes as well as receptors for many hormones and growth factors. Microfilaments extend into the microvilli from a cytoskeletal network concentrated immediately below the free surface. Some areas of the syncytiotrophoblast contain rough endoplasmic reticulum while in others, such as shown here, smooth endoplasmic reticulum **sER** predominates, presumably involved in steroid hormone synthesis.

The cytotrophoblast layer **C** has ultrastructural features of relatively undifferentiated stem cells exhibiting profiles of rough endoplasmic reticulum **rER**, a well-defined Golgi apparatus **G**, relatively few mitochondria **Mi** and numerous polyribosomes **R**. The nucleus is typically large with dispersed chromatin and nucleoli **Nu**. The cytotrophoblast is typically tightly bound to the overlying syncytiotrophoblast by desmosomes **D**, but in some areas, as in this specimen, spaces can be seen between the cell layers; the reason for this is unclear. Separating the cytotrophoblast from the underlying collagenous stroma is a relatively thick basement membrane **BM**.

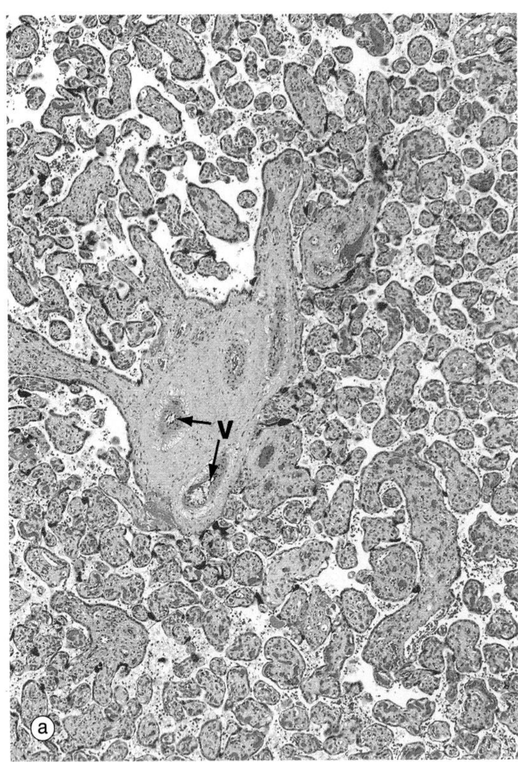

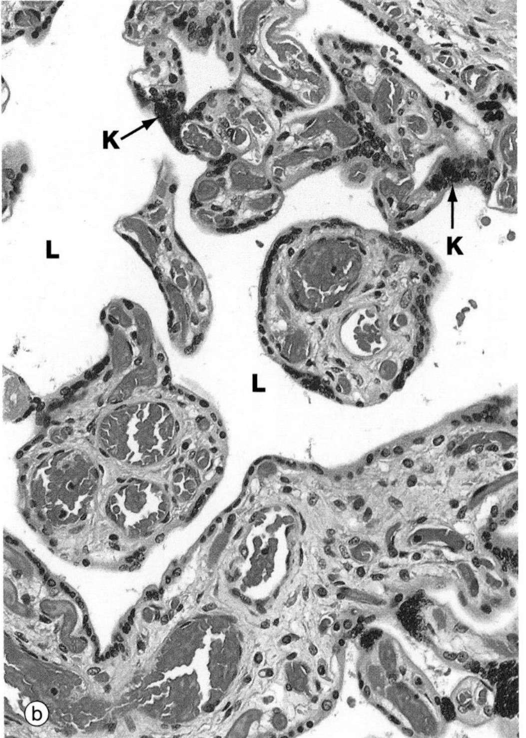

Fig. 19.33 Term placenta
(a) H & E ×40 (b) H & E ×100 (c) H & E ×600

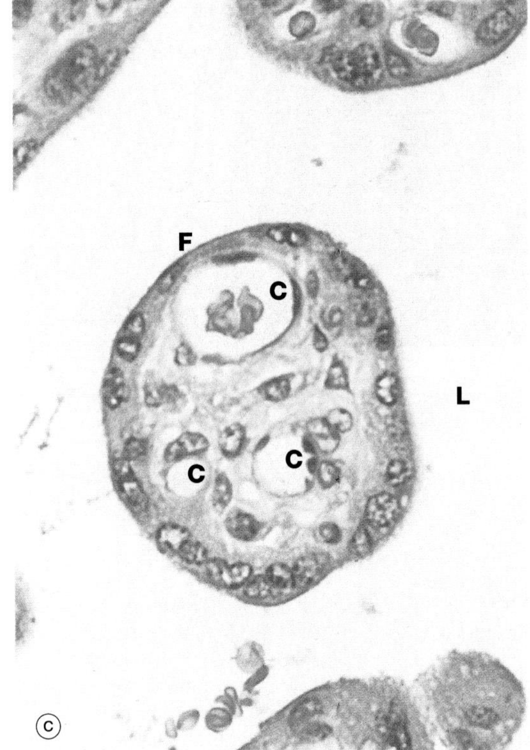

These micrographs illustrate placenta from a full-term fetus.

At low magnification in micrograph (a), huge numbers of villi can be seen cut in various planes of section and varying in diameter from large main stem villi to very small terminal branch villi. Compared with early placenta shown in Fig. 19.31(a), the villous pattern is much more highly developed and the average villous diameter is much smaller, reflecting the extensive branching growth of the villi as the placenta enlarges. Note the large blood vessels **V** in the biggest villi.

Micrograph (b) demonstrates the branching nature of the villi at higher magnification. Compare the marked vascularity of the villous cores with that of the much earlier placenta in Fig. 19.31(b) and the greatly increased villous surface area exposed to the lacunae **L** filled with maternal blood. A feature of the term placenta is the syncytial knot **K**, where syncytiotrophoblast nuclei are aggregated together in clusters leaving zones of thin cytoplasm devoid of nuclei between.

Micrograph (c) focuses on a small branch villus and highlights the proximity of blood in fetal capillaries **C** to maternal blood in the surrounding lacuna **L**. The trophoblast is reduced to a thin layer of syncytiotrophoblast only and the capillaries tend to be located in the periphery of the core. The diffusion barrier between maternal and fetal circulations comprises five layers, namely: trophoblast, trophoblast basement membrane, villous core supporting tissue, capillary endothelial basement membrane and endothelium. In many cases, fetal capillaries are so close to the trophoblast that their basement membranes fuse **F**, reducing the diffusion barrier to only three layers.

A umbilical artery **Am** amniotic membrane **BM** basement membrane **C** capillary
Ch chorionic membrane **D** outer collagenous layer **E** epithelial cells
F fused basement membranes **I** inner collagenous layer of chorionic membrane **In** intermediate zone
K syncytial knot **L** lacunae **M** mesenchymal layer **MC** mesenchymal cells **T** trophoblast
V blood vessel **Ve** umbilical vein **W** Wharton's jelly

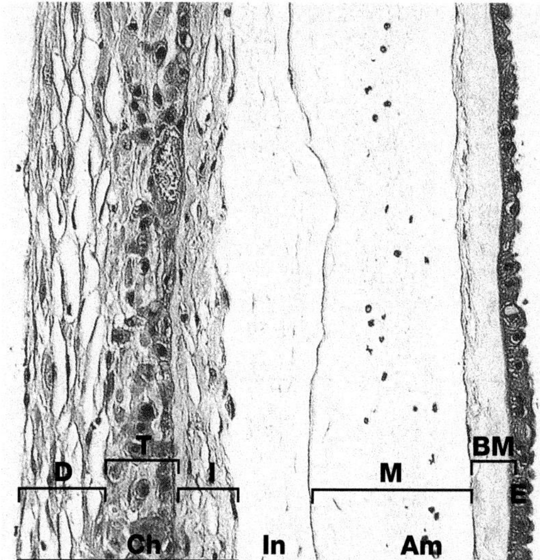

Fig. 19.34 Fetal membranes
H & E ×150

During early development, the embryo is surrounded by the extraembryonic coelom (see Fig. 19.28) but later this becomes obliterated as the amniotic cavity expands to surround the fetus. The outer mesenchymal layer of the amnion then comes to lie in contact with (and often fuses with) the inner mesenchymal layer of the chorion forming the ***chorio-amnion*** or ***fetal membranes***. The two layers are often difficult to separate from one another at birth.

The amniotic membrane **Am** comprises a single layer of epithelial cells **E** derived from extraembryonic ectoderm resting on a thick basement membrane **BM**; beneath this is a delicate avascular mesenchymal layer **M** which is a remnant of the extraembryonic mesoderm. The chorionic membrane **Ch** consists of three layers. A vascular collagenous inner layer **I** is also derived from extraembryonic mesoderm, the ***intermediate zone*** **In** seen here separating it from the amnion represents the remnant of the extraembryonic coelom and varies greatly in thickness. The trophoblast **T** of the chorion laeve is represented by the middle layer of eosinophilic epithelial cells, and the outermost vascular collagenous layer **D** is of maternal origin representing the decidua capsularis (see Fig. 19.28).

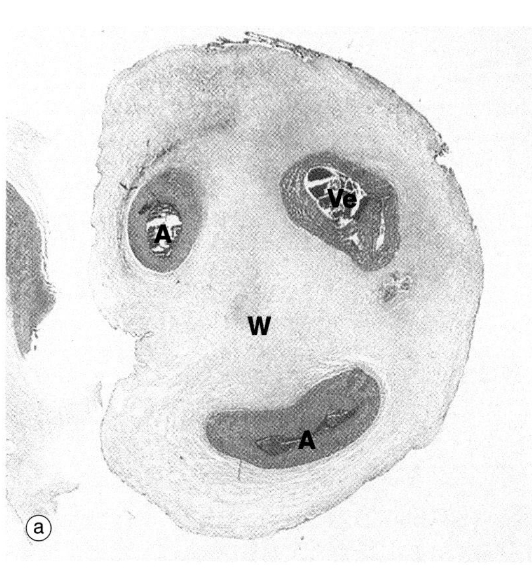

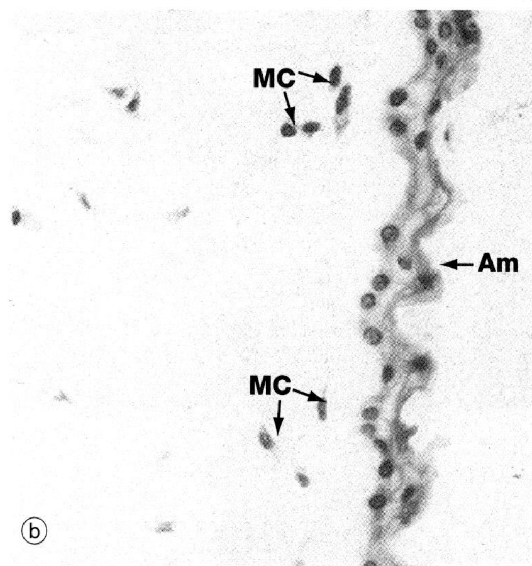

Fig. 19.35 Umbilical cord
(a) H & E ×7.5 (b) H & E ×300

The development of the umbilical cord begins with the formation of the extraembryonic coelom which almost surrounds the early embryo and which remains attached to the chorion by the connecting stalk of mesenchyme (see Fig. 19.28). With further embryonic development, the site of attachment of the connecting stalk becomes located ventrally, just caudal to the point where the ***vitello-intestinal duct*** connects the ***yolk sac*** to the mid-gut. As the embryo grows, the amniotic sac expands greatly, filling the extraembryonic coelom and compressing the vitello-intestinal duct and yolk sac remnant (surrounded by a sleeve of extraembryonic coelom) up against the connecting stalk. These structures ultimately fuse to form the umbilical cord, which now is surrounded by the amnion and amniotic cavity.

By the middle of the fifth month, the remnants of the vitello-intestinal duct, yolk sac and sheath of extraembryonic coelom atrophy and disappear. As seen in micrograph (a), all that remains are two ***umbilical arteries*** **A** and a single ***umbilical vein*** **Ve** embedded in mesenchyme consisting mainly of ground substance and known as ***Wharton's jelly*** **W**. Mesenchymal cells **MC** and surface amnion **Am** are shown at high magnification in micrograph (b). The umbilical arteries convey deoxygenated fetal blood to the placenta while the umbilical vein conveys oxygenated blood back to the fetus.

The breasts (mammary glands) are highly modified apocrine sweat glands (see Fig. 9.11) which develop embryologically along two lines, the ***milk lines***, extending from the axillae to the groins. In humans, only one gland develops on each side of the thorax, although accessory breast tissue may be found anywhere along the milk lines.

The breasts of both sexes follow a similar course of development until puberty, after which the female breasts develop under the influence of pituitary, ovarian and other hormones. Until the menopause, the breasts undergo cyclical changes in activity, which are controlled by the hormones of the ovarian cycle. After menopause, the breasts, like the other female reproductive tissues, undergo progressive atrophy and involution.

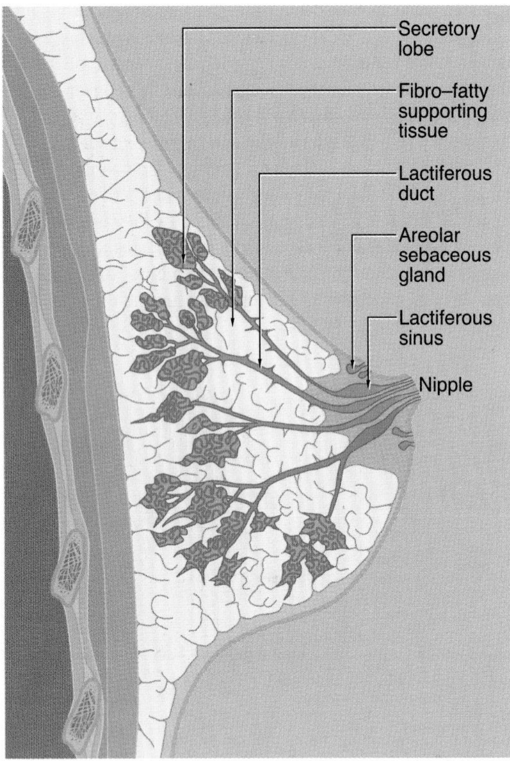

Fig. 19.36 Structure of the breast

This highly schematic diagram illustrates the general organisation of the breast. Each breast consists of 15–25 independent units called ***breast lobes***, each consisting of a compound tubulo-acinar gland (see Fig. 5.26). The size of the lobes is quite variable and the bulk of the breast is made up of a few large lobes that connect to the surface. Immediately before opening onto the surface, the duct forms a dilatation called the ***lactiferous sinus***. Smaller lobes end in blind ending ducts that do not reach the nipple surface. The lobes are embedded in a mass of adipose tissue subdivided by collagenous septa.

The nipple contains bands of smooth muscle orientated in parallel to the lactiferous ducts and circularly near the base; contraction of this muscle causes erection of the nipple.

Within each lobe of the breast, the main duct branches repeatedly to form a number of ***terminal ducts***, each of which leads to a ***lobule*** consisting of multiple ***acini***. Each terminal duct and its associated lobule is called a ***terminal duct-lobular unit***. The lobules are separated by moderately dense collagenous ***interlobular*** tissue, whereas the ***intralobular*** supporting tissue surrounding the ducts within each lobule is less collagenous and more vascular. The skin surrounding the nipple, the ***areola***, is pigmented and contains sebaceous glands that are not associated with hair follicles.

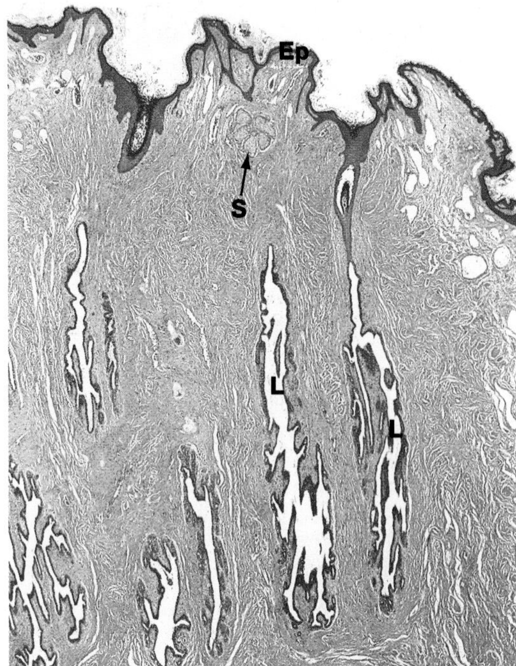

Fig. 19.37 The nipple
H & E ×20

This low magnification micrograph of the nipple demonstrates the structure of the ***lactiferous sinuses*** and shows their connection to the surface of the skin of the nipple. Several lactiferous sinuses **L** are seen coursing through the dermis towards the skin surface. Only the lactiferous sinus on the right can be seen connecting to the surface in this micrograph but this is probably due to a slightly oblique plane of section rather than blind-ending sinuses. The undulating surface of the epidermis **Ep** is seen and a single sebaceous gland **S** is also identifiable. The epithelium of the lactiferous sinuses is similar to that of the ducts in the rest of the breast until close to the surface where the epithelium becomes stratified squamous in type. Carcinoma in situ (see Fig. 19.42) may spread along the lactiferous sinus from the underlying breast lobe and even spread into the surface epidermis, where it is known as ***Paget's disease of the breast***.

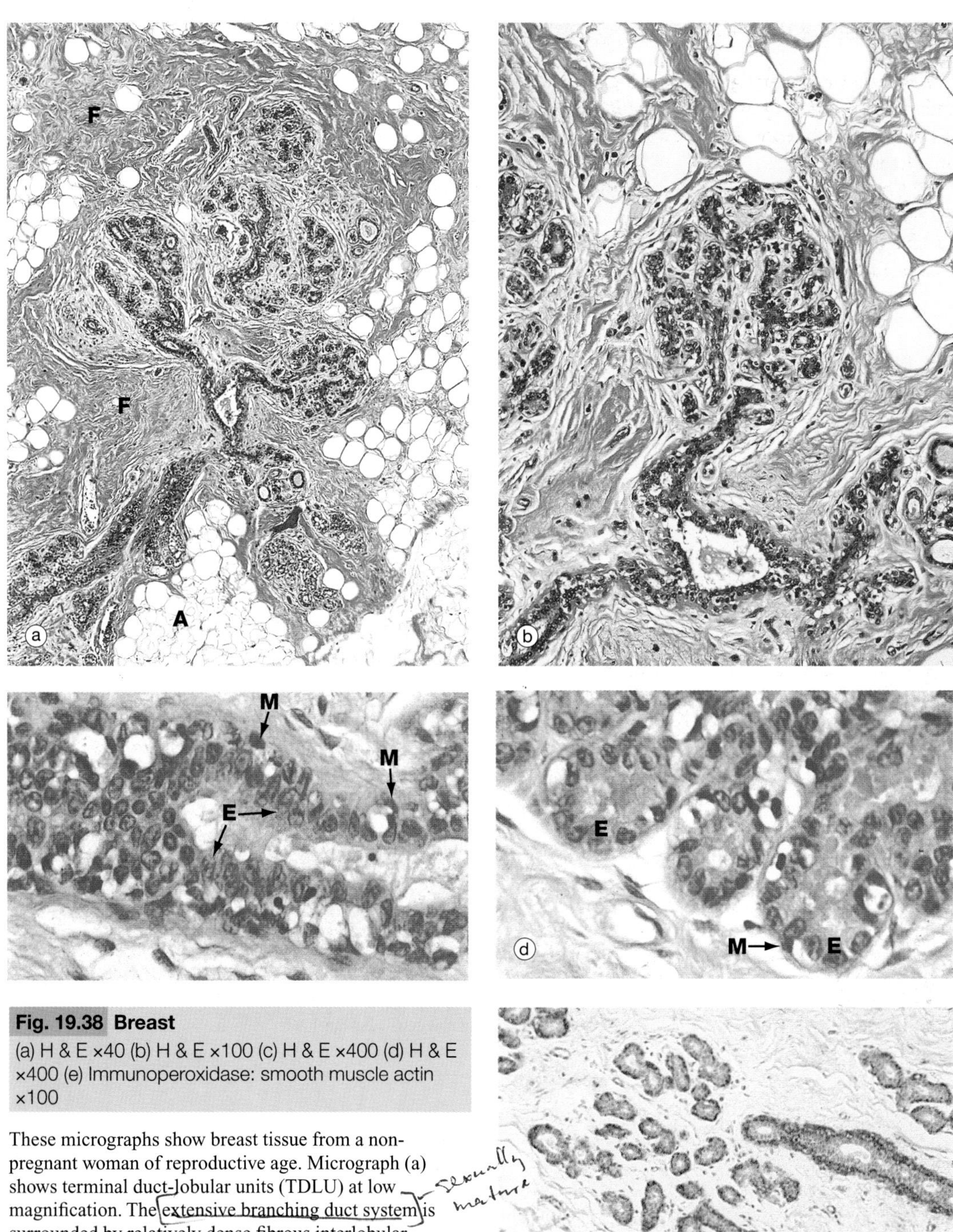

Fig. 19.38 Breast
(a) H & E ×40 (b) H & E ×100 (c) H & E ×400 (d) H & E ×400 (e) Immunoperoxidase: smooth muscle actin ×100

These micrographs show breast tissue from a non-pregnant woman of reproductive age. Micrograph (a) shows terminal duct-lobular units (TDLU) at low magnification. The extensive branching duct system is surrounded by relatively dense fibrous interlobular tissue **F** and adipose tissue **A**. The interlacing (reticular) arrangement of the coarse collagen of the interlobular tissue is seen at higher magnification in micrograph (b), as is the branching duct system of the lobule.

The breast ducts and acini are lined by two layers of cells; a luminal layer of epithelial cells and a basal layer of flattened myoepithelial cells. In the larger ducts, as shown in micrograph (c), the luminal epithelial cells **E** are tall columnar type whereas in the smaller ducts and acini shown in micrograph (d) the epithelial cells are cuboidal. A discontinuous layer of stellate myoepithelial cells **M** with pale cytoplasm surrounds the ductal lining cells. In micrograph (e), which uses the immunoperoxidase technique to stain the myoepithelial cells for actin, the extent and number of the myoepithelial cells (stained brown) are apparent. During the reproductive years, the duct epithelium undergoes mild cyclical changes under the influence of ovarian hormones. Early in the cycle, the duct lumina are not clearly evident but later in the cycle they become more prominent and may contain an eosinophilic secretion.

A adipose tissue **E** epithelial cells **Ep** epidermis **F** fibrous interlobular tissue **L** lactiferous sinus **M** myoepithelial cells **S** sebaceous gland

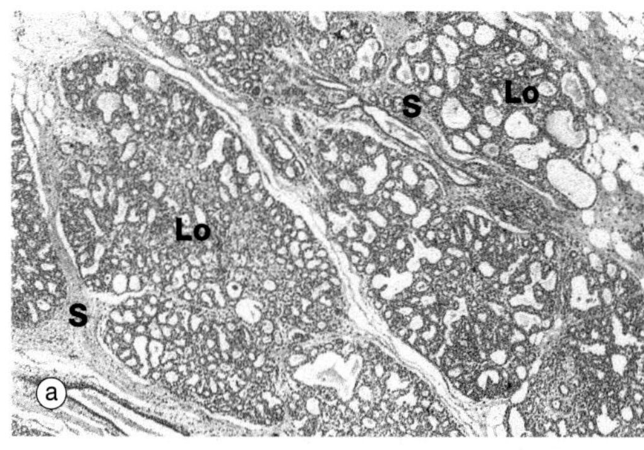

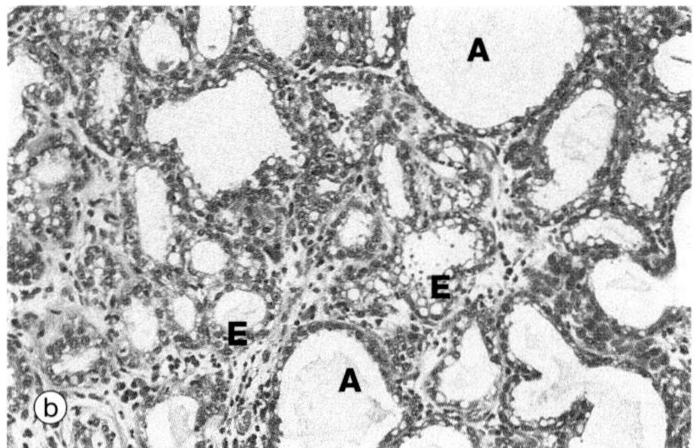

Fig. 19.39 Breast during pregnancy
(a) H & E ×20 (b) H & E ×100

Under the influence of oestrogens and progesterone produced by the corpus luteum and later by the placenta, the terminal duct epithelium proliferates to form greatly increased numbers of secretory acini. Breast proliferation is also dependent on prolactin, human chorionic somatomammotropin (a prolactin-like hormone produced by the placenta), thyroid hormone and corticosteroids.

At low magnification in micrograph (a), the breast lobules **Lo** are seen to have enlarged greatly at the expense of the intralobular tissue and interlobar adipose tissue, although septa **S** of interlobular tissue still remain. At higher magnification in (b) the acini **A** are dilated. The lining epithelial cells **E** vary from cuboidal to low columnar and contain cytoplasmic vacuoles. The intralobular stroma is much less prominent and contains an infiltrate of lymphocytes, eosinophils and plasma cells.

As pregnancy progresses, the acini begin to secrete a protein-rich fluid called ***colostrum***, the accumulation of which dilates the acinar and duct lumina as seen in micrograph (b). Colostrum is the form of breast secretion available during the first few days after birth; it contains a laxative substance and maternal antibodies. Unlike milk, colostrum contains little lipid. Breast secretion is controlled by the hormone prolactin. During pregnancy, prolactin secretion progressively increases but high levels of circulating oestrogens and progesterone suppress its activity.

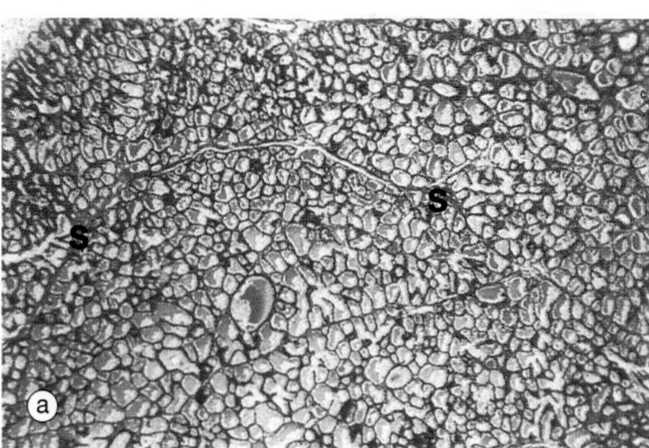

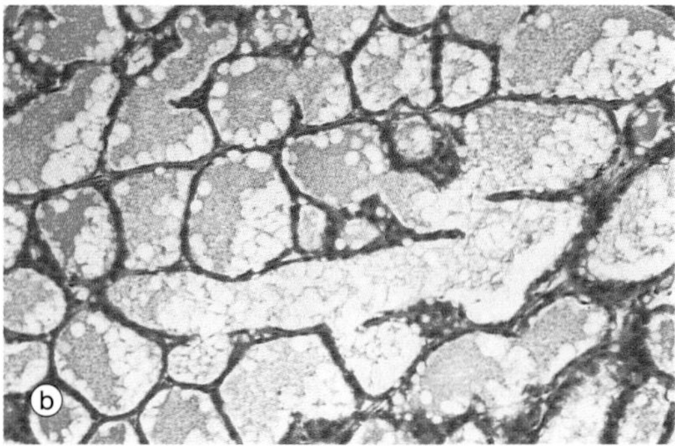

Fig. 19.40 Lactating breast
(a) H & E ×20 (b) H & E ×128

After parturition, the levels of circulating progesterone and oestrogens, which inhibit milk secretion, fall precipitously. Prolactin stimulates milk production in conjunction with several other hormones.

As seen in micrograph (a), the lactating breast is composed almost entirely of acini distended with milk, the interlobular tissue now being reduced to thin septa **S** between the lobules. At higher magnification in (b), the acini are filled with an eosinophilic material containing clear vacuoles caused by lipid droplets dissolved out during tissue preparation. The epithelial cells are flattened and the acini distended by secretions. However, in different areas the epithelium may be thicker and the acinar lumina smaller.

Milk production proceeds for as long as suckling continues and can continue for some years after childbirth. A neurohormonal reflex in which nipple stimulation by suckling causes release of prolactin from the anterior pituitary controls the process. A different neurohormonal reflex, also initiated by suckling, causes the release of the hormone oxytocin from the posterior pituitary. Oxytocin causes contraction of the myoepithelial cells which embrace the secretory acini and ducts, thus propelling milk into the lactiferous sinuses (milk 'let-down'). Withdrawal of the suckling stimulus, and hence the release of pituitary hormones at weaning, results in regression of the lactating breast and resumption of the ovarian cycle.

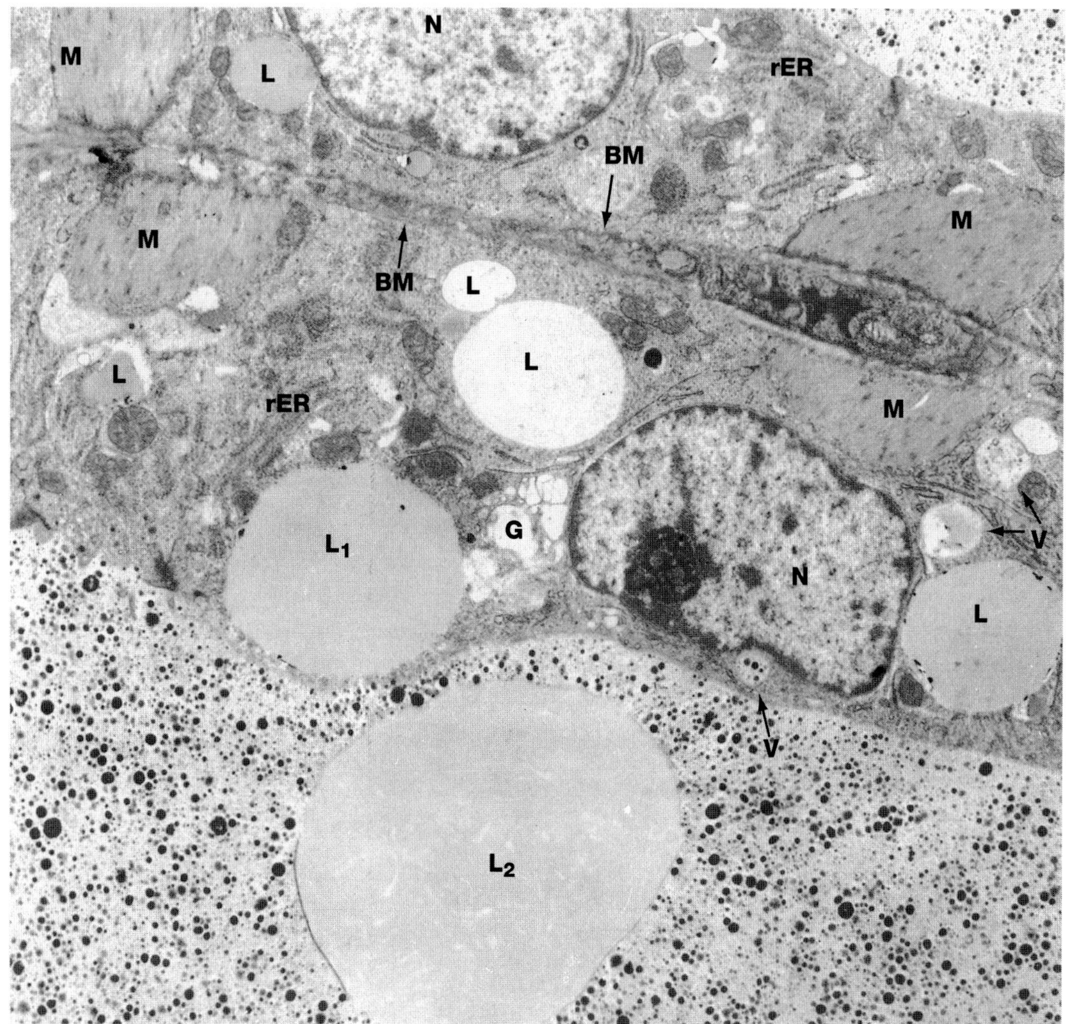

Fig. 19.41 Lactating breast
EM ×9000

This micrograph shows two secretory cells of adjacent acini in a lactating breast. Their nuclei **N** are large with prominent nucleoli. Each acinus is bounded by a basement membrane **BM**, the basement membranes in this example being separated by only a shred of intralobular supporting tissue. Between each basement membrane and the secretory cells are the cytoplasmic processes of myoepithelial cells **M**, contraction of which expels milk from the gland.

The composition of milk varies somewhat during lactation and even during each suckling episode but its main constituents are as follows: water (88%), ions (particularly sodium, potassium, chloride, calcium and phosphate), protein (1.5%, mainly lactalbumin and casein), carbohydrate (7%, mainly lactose), lipids (3.5%, mainly triglycerides), vitamins and antibodies (mainly IgA).

Secretion of different components of the milk occurs by different mechanisms. Water and some ions diffuse freely through the apical cell membrane. Proteins are synthesised on the rough endoplasmic reticulum **rER**, packaged in the Golgi apparatus **G** and secreted in vacuoles **V** by exocytosis; protein in the milk is represented by small electron-dense granules. The Golgi apparatus is extensive and the protein-containing secretory vacuoles also contain a considerable amount of other less electron-dense material including lactose and calcium.

The cytoplasm of the secretory cells contains lipid droplets **L** of various sizes not bounded by membrane; these contain triglycerides, although whether this is derived directly from blood or synthesised in the secretory cells is uncertain. The lipid is discharged by apocrine secretion, which involves the lipid droplet, surrounding cytoplasm and plasma membrane being cast off into the lumen. A large lipid droplet $\mathbf{L_1}$ with thin overlying rim of cytoplasm can be seen in the lower acinus just prior to secretion; an even larger droplet $\mathbf{L_2}$ surrounded by a remnant of cytoplasm and plasma membrane is seen in the lumen close by.

IgA, taken up by receptor-mediated endocytosis at the base of the cell from the bloodstream, is transported across the cell in small membranous vesicles and released by exocytosis into the milk, a process known as transcytosis.

A acinus **BM** basement membrane **E** epithelial cell **G** Golgi apparatus **L** lipid droplet $\mathbf{L_1}$ large lipid droplet $\mathbf{L_2}$ very large lipid droplet **Lo** lobule **M** myoepithelial cell **N** nucleus **rER** rough endoplasmic reticulum **S** septum **V** secretory vacuoles

Breast carcinoma

Carcinoma of the breast is one of the commonest malignant tumours of women, leading to many premature deaths and great morbidity. In many countries, breast cancer screening programs are in operation in the hope that early detection of cancer or even precancerous lesions will cure the disease. Women in the age groups at risk are subjected to mammography, an uncomfortable and undignified procedure that is nevertheless better than dying of breast cancer. Lesions identified at mammography are biopsied and the pathologist determines whether the lesion is indeed a cancer or one of many benign breast lesions that may cause a lump or a mammographic abnormality.

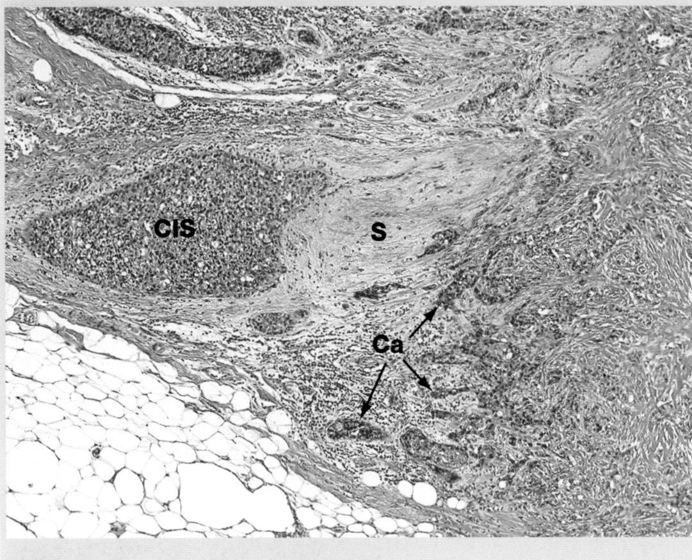

Fig. 19.42 Breast cancer
H & E ×40

This micrograph shows a medium power view of an area of breast carcinoma in a middle-aged woman. The cancer is of the commonest type known as ***ductal carcinoma, NOS*** (not otherwise specified). Note how clusters of malignant epithelial cells **Ca** invade into the normal breast stroma **S**, destroying it. In the left side of the field is a single expanded duct filled and expanded with similar cells: this is an area of ductal carcinoma in situ **CIS**. Breast carcinoma in situ often calcifies allowing the disease to be identified on mammograms. Obviously the earlier the cancer is identified the better the chance of a complete cure.

Fig. 19.43 Summary of the major components of the female reproductive system

Part of the Female genital tract	Illustration	Key features
Ovary	(b)	Primordial and developing follicles embedded in ovarian stroma Surface covering of epithelium (mesothelium) Corpora lutea and corpora albicantes
Fallopian tube	(c)	Muscular wall Folded mucosa Ciliated columnar epithelium
Uterus	(d)	Muscular wall – the myometrium Lining endometrium consisting of glands and stroma – varies with the menstrual cycle
Endocervix	(e)	Bulk consists of a dense fibromuscular stroma Surface has deep clefts lined by simple columnar mucus secreting epithelium
Ectocervix	(f)	Stroma same as for endocervix Stratified squamous non-keratinising surface epithelium
Vagina	(g)	Fibromuscular wall Stratified squamous non-keratinising surface epithelium
Vulva	Not illustrated	Stratified squamous epithelium/modified skin – see Ch. 9
Placenta	(h)	Chorionic villi with core of mesenchyme and double surface layer of trophoblast
Breast (a)	(i)	Stroma consists of adipose tissue with fibrous septa Branching tubulo-acinar glands Glandular epithelium consists of luminal epithelial cells and underlying myoepithelial cells

Ca invasive carcinoma **CIS** carcinoma in situ **S** fibrous breast stroma

Fig. 19.43 Summary of the major components of the female reproductive system
(a) Table (*opposite*) (b–i) (*below*) (b) Azan ×12 (c) H & E ×10 (d) H & E ×10 (e) H & E ×60 (f) H & E ×200
(g) Masson's trichrome ×128 (h) H & E ×150 (i) H & E ×40

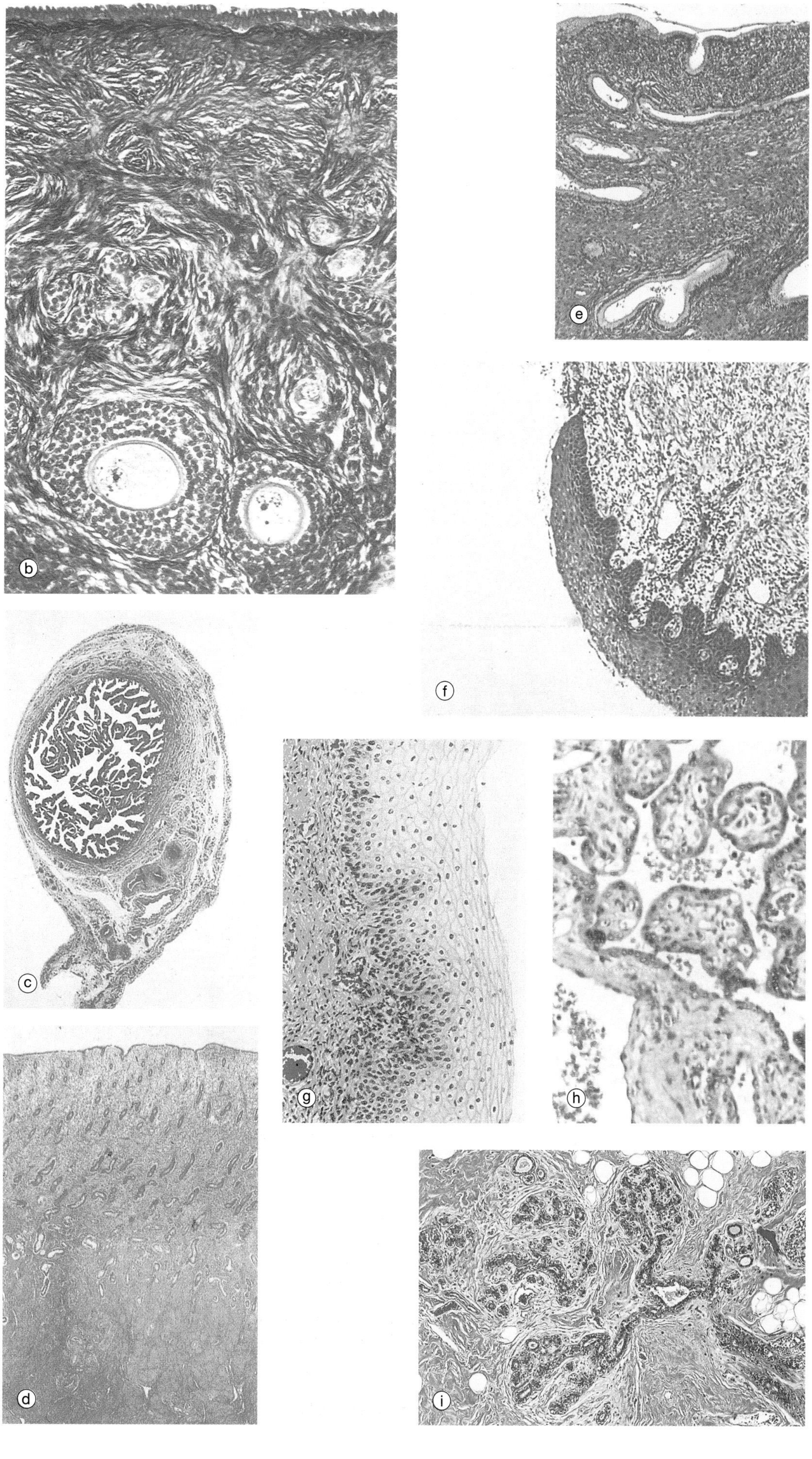

(b)

(c)

(d)

(e)

(f)

(g)

(h)

(i)

20. *Central nervous system*

Introduction

The central nervous system (CNS) consists of the brain and spinal cord, which are composed of ***neurones***, the supporting cells of the CNS (***glial cells***) and blood vessels. The histology of nervous tissue and the meninges which invest the CNS are described in Chapter 7.

Macroscopically, all parts of the CNS are made up of grey matter and white matter, the grey matter containing most of the neurone cell bodies and the white matter the axons; lipid in the myelin sheaths of the axons accounts for the white appearance of the white matter. The distribution of grey matter and white matter differs greatly from one part of the brain to another as does the morphology and arrangement of the neurones.

The histological methods used in the study of the CNS can be divided into four groups:

- Techniques which demonstrate nuclei, cell bodies and their cytoplasmic constituents. Such methods include routine stains such as H & E and more specific methods for demonstrating particular cytoplasmic constituents such as the Nissl method for RNA. These methods show minimal detail of axons and dendrites and the structure of white matter but are useful to highlight the arrangement of neurones, glial cells and blood vessels.
- Myelin methods, e.g. Weigert–Pal or Luxol fast blue, are routinely used in studying the arrangement of grey matter and white matter in the brain stem and spinal cord, as well as abnormalities of myelination. With myelin methods, the white matter stains strongly, the grey matter remaining unstained.
- Immunohistochemical techniques using antibodies against proteins specific to neurones, astrocytes, oligodendroglia or microglia are routinely used to delineate individual cell types, especially in examination of diseases of the nervous system.
- Heavy metal impregnation methods, applied to thick tissue sections, demonstrate overall cell morphology, especially the pattern of branching of axons and dendrites, permitting study of neuronal interconnections. These methods are rarely used today.

Within the CNS, specific terms are used to describe arrangements of cells and their connections:

- The extensive, diffuse arrangement of neurones over the surface of the brain is termed the ***cortex***.
- An arrangement of neuronal cells as a discrete unit is termed a ***nucleus***.
- An arrangement of neuronal cells running along the spinal cord is termed a ***column***.
- A defined bundle of axons running in white matter is termed a ***tract*** or a ***fascicle***.

The CNS develops through growth and complex folding, resulting in distinct convolutions visible on the external surface and in sections. In the cerebral cortex, the crests of folds are termed ***gyri*** while the clefts between folds are termed ***sulci***. In the cerebellum these folds are termed ***folia***.

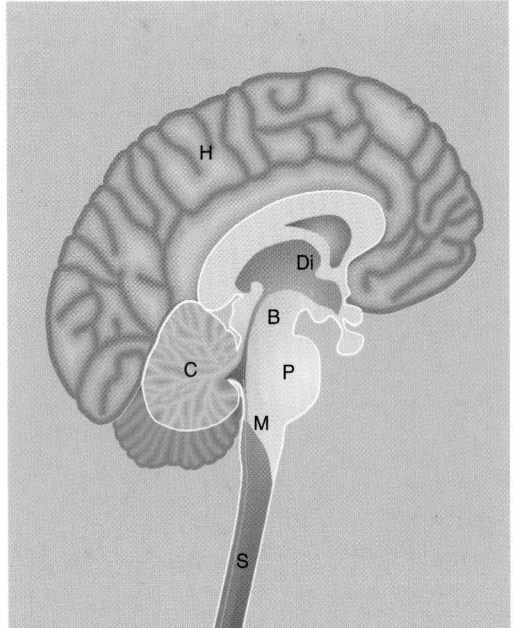

Fig. 20.1 Main anatomic divisions in the central nervous system

This diagram shows the brain and spinal cord viewed in a sagittal section. The main part of the brain consists of the paired ***cerebral hemispheres*** **H**, the outer part of which is the cerebral cortex. Deep within the brain are large grey matter structures which form the ***diencephalon*** **Di**. Included in this region are the ***basal ganglia*** and ***thalamus***. The cerebral hemispheres are connected to structures below by the ***midbrain*** **B**. In this region there are important nuclei including the substantia nigra. The ***pons*** **P** connects to the **medulla M** as well as to the ***cerebellum*** **C**. The ***spinal cord*** **S** extends from the lower end of the medulla.

Fig. 20.2 Spinal cord: cat
Weigert–Pal ×10 (a) Cervical (b) Thoracic (c) Lumbar (d) Sacral

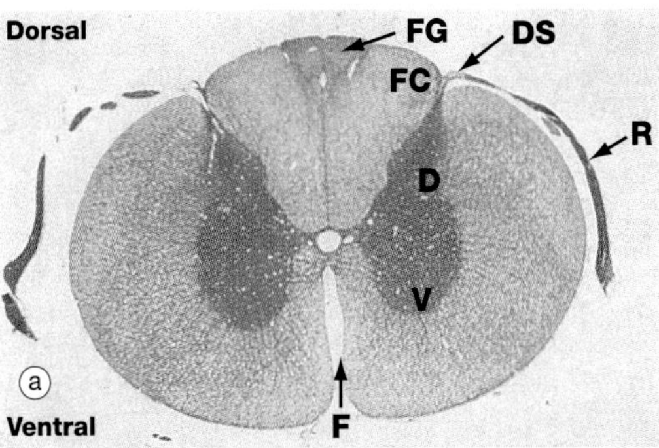

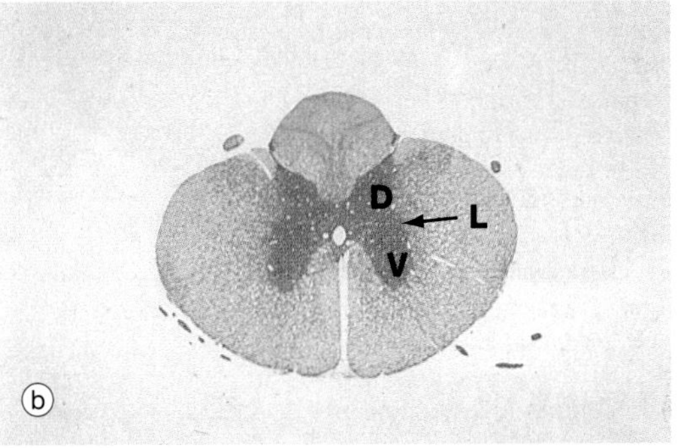

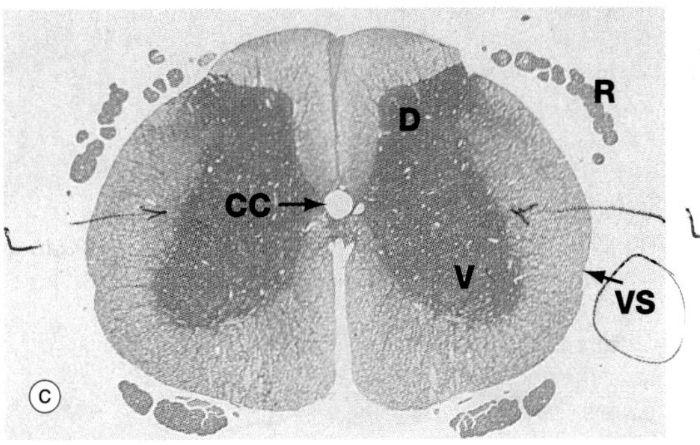

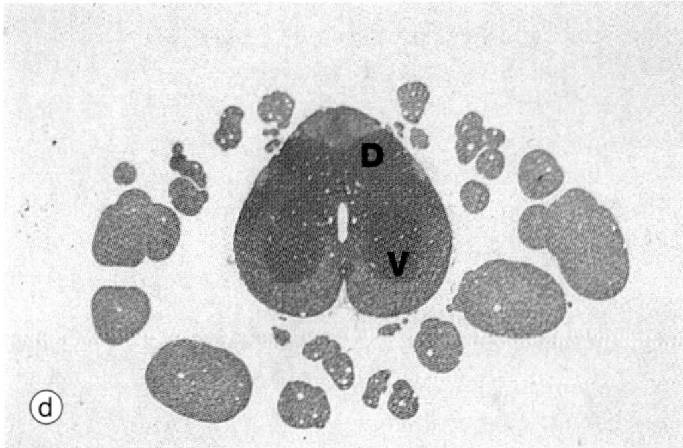

The structure of the spinal cord is basically similar throughout its whole length, with the four main regions demonstrated in this series of micrographs.

In transverse section, the central mass of grey matter has the shape of a butterfly, the ***ventral horns*** **V** being most prominent and containing the cell bodies of the large lower motor neurones. The ***dorsal horns*** **D** are much less prominent and contain the cell bodies of small second order sensory neurones; these relay sensory information to the brain from primary afferent neurones for the modalities of temperature and pain whose cell bodies lie in the dorsal root ganglia. Small ***lateral horns*** **L**, which contain the cell bodies of preganglionic, sympathetic efferent neurones, are found in the thoracic and upper lumbar regions corresponding to the level of the sympathetic outflow from the cord. The volume of grey matter is much more extensive in the cervical and lumbar regions corresponding to the sensory and motor innervation of the limbs and this is reflected in the much greater diameter of the spinal cord in these areas. The ***central canal*** **CC** lies in the ***central commissure*** of grey matter; it is lined by ependymal cells and contains CSF.

The white matter of the spinal cord consists of ascending tracts of sensory fibres and descending motor tracts; passing up the spinal cord towards the brain, more and more fibres enter and leave the cord so that the volume of white matter increases progressively from the sacral to cervical regions.

Externally, the spinal cord has a deep ***ventral median fissure*** **F** but dorsally there is only a shallow dorsal ***midline sulcus***. On each side, a ***dorsolateral sulcus*** **DS** marks the line of entry of the dorsal nerve roots **R**, part of which can be seen in micrographs (a) and (c). The roughly triangular area of white matter between the dorsal horns represents the ascending ***dorsal columns*** which convey fibres for the senses of vibration, proprioception and discriminatory touch to the medulla where they synapse with second order sensory neurones in the ***gracile*** and ***cuneate nuclei***. In the cervical region, each dorsal column is subdivided into two fascicles, the medial ***fasciculus gracilis*** **FG** conveying fibres from the lower limbs, and the lateral ***fasciculus cuneatus*** **FC** conveying fibres from the upper limbs.

Ventrolateral sulci **VS** may be discernible on each side as in micrograph (c), marking the sites of exit of the ventral nerve roots.

The ventrolateral white matter on each side is made up of various ascending and descending tracts, most notably the ***lateral spinothalamic tract*** (pain and temperature), ***ventral spinothalamic tract*** (light touch), ***spinocerebellar tracts*** and ***corticospinal tract*** (motor).

Like the brain, the spinal cord is invested by meninges, the outer surface of the dura mater being loosely connected to the periosteum of the vertebral canal by the denticulate ligaments, and the intervening epidural space being filled with loose adipose tissue and an extensive venous plexus. During development, the vertebral column lengthens to a greater degree than the enclosed spinal cord and the segmental levels of the lower part of the cord therefore lie above the corresponding intervertebral foramina. Consequently, below the cervical region, the nerve roots pursue an increasingly oblique course in the subarachnoid space before passing through the intervertebral foramina; thus they can be seen adjacent to the cord, particularly in the lumbar and sacral regions.

B midbrain **C** cerebellum **CC** central canal **D** dorsal horn **Di** diencephalon
DS dorsolateral sulcus **F** median fissure **FC** fasciculus cuneatus **FG** fasciculus gracilis
H hemisphere **L** lateral horn **M** medulla **P** pons **R** nerve root **S** spinal cord **V** ventral horn
VS ventrolateral sulcus

Fig. 20.3 Medulla oblongata
Weigart–Pal ×4 (a) Upper to mid-level (b) Lower level

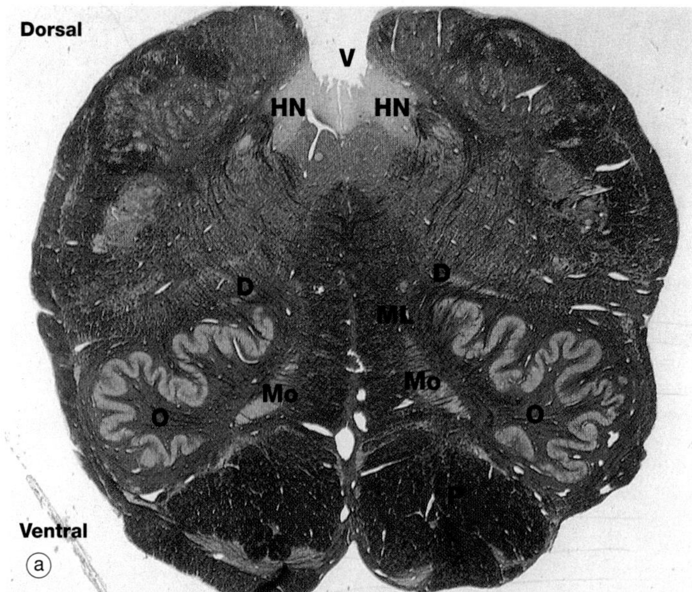

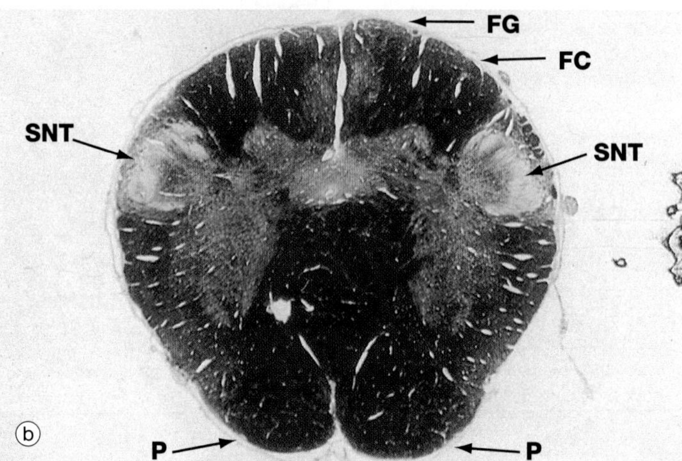

The medulla oblongata, the most distal part of the brain stem, can be roughly divided into upper and lower parts. At the upper medullary level shown in micrograph (a), the fourth ventricle **V** closes to become a narrow central canal which continues down into the spinal cord. Thus the medulla is often divided into an upper, open part and a lower, closed part. The myelin staining method employed in these preparations leaves grey matter relatively unstained.

The most obvious feature of the upper half of the medulla is the ***inferior olivary nucleus*** **O** with its peculiar convoluted appearance in transverse section; adjacent are the smaller ***dorsal*** **D** and ***medial accessory olivary nuclei*** **Mo** which complete the ***inferior olivary complex***. The neurones of the inferior olivary complex relay central and spinal afferent stimuli to the cerebellar cortex.

All of the ascending (sensory) and descending (motor) pathways found in the spinal cord pass through the medulla, although their arrangement in the medulla differs considerably from that in the spinal cord. The most easily recognisable features of these pathways in the medulla are the gracile and cuneate nuclei and fasciculi, and the pyramids.

The dorsal white matter columns of the spinal cord convey ascending proprioceptive, vibration and discriminatory touch fibres from the lower limbs and upper limbs in the ***fasciculus gracilis*** **FG** and ***fasciculus cuneatus*** **FC** respectively. In the similarly situated ***nucleus gracilis*** and ***nucleus cuneatus*** in the dorsum of the medulla, these fibres synapse with cell bodies of second order neurones which then pass upwards to the thalamus via the ***medial lemniscus*** **ML** which lies medial to the olivary complex.

Axons originating in the motor cortex descend through the ***internal capsule***, break up into small bundles in the ***pons***, then converge again in the medulla to form a prominent ventral ***pyramid*** **P** on each side of the medulla; in the pyramids, about 85% of fibres cross to the other side in the ***decussation of the pyramids***.

The medulla also contains the various tracts and nuclei of the eighth to the twelfth cranial nerves as well as the ***spinal nucleus*** and ***tract*** of the ***trigeminal nerve*** which extends from the pons down into the upper cervical cord. The ***spinal nucleus of the trigeminal tract*** **SNT** is easily recognisable dorsolaterally throughout the medulla with its tract of white matter lying superficially. The ***hypoglossal nucleus*** **HN** can also be identified in micrograph (a). In the centre of the lower medulla, grey matter can be seen, still roughly resembling the characteristic butterfly shape seen in sections of the spinal cord; the ventral grey matter horns contain cell bodies of lower motor neurones running in the spinal accessory and first cervical nerves.

D dorsal accessory olivary nucleus **FC** fasciculus cuneatus **FG** fasciculus gracilis
HN hypoglossal nucleus **M** middle cerebellar peduncle **ML** medial lemniscus
Mo medial accessory olivary nucleus **O** inferior olivary nucleus **P** pyramid
SCP superior cerebellar peduncle **SNT** spinal nucleus and tract of trigeminal nerve **V** fourth ventricle

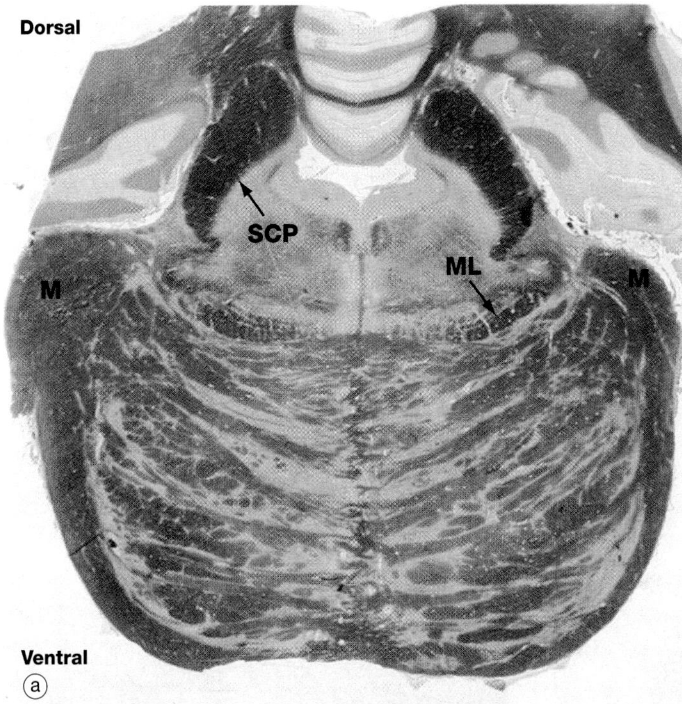

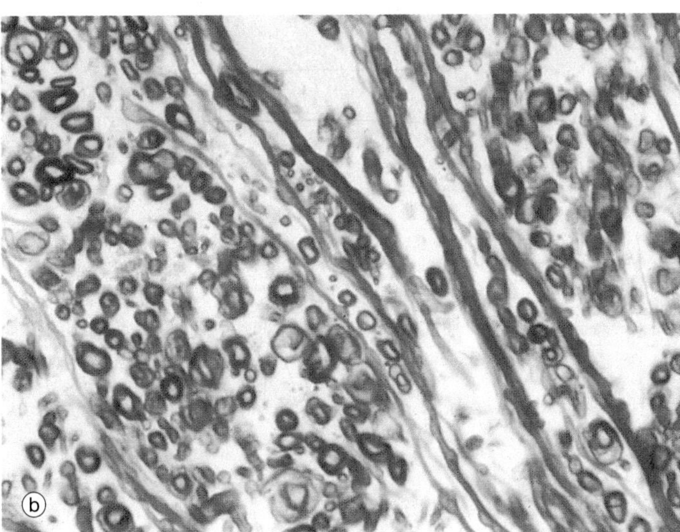

Fig. 20.4 Pons
(a) Mid-level, Weigart-Pal ×3
(b) Basal pons, Weigart-Pal ×480

The pons is the middle portion of the brain stem, lying between midbrain proximally and medulla distally. In transverse section, it comprises two parts, a bulky ventral region (the ***basal pons***) and a smaller dorsal (***tegmental***) region.

The basal pons consists of criss-crossed bundles of longitudinal and transverse fibres between which lie collections of neurone cell bodies known as ***pontine nuclei***. Micrograph (b) shows a small area of this region at high magnification, the myelin investing the axons being stained blue; neurone cell bodies are not stained and are therefore not identifiable. The longitudinal fibres of the basal pons consist of descending fibres of two main types. Firstly, there are axons from the motor cortex passing down to synapse with lower motor neurones of the ventral horns of the spinal cord; on leaving the pons, these axons converge to form the characteristic pyramids (pyramidal tracts) of the medulla. The second group of descending fibres originate in various areas of the cortex and synapse in the pontine nuclei from which fibres then pass in the transverse bundles, crossing the midline to enter the cerebellum via the ***middle peduncles* M**.

The dorsal tegmentum contains the ascending spinothalamic (sensory) tracts and the nuclei of the fifth, sixth and seventh cranial nerves. On each side, the ***medial lemniscus* ML** is readily identifiable; this represents the upward continuation of proprioceptive, vibration and fine touch pathways from the gracile and cuneate nuclei of the medulla. The ***cerebellar peduncles*** are a readily recognisable feature of the pons, the middle peduncle being still present in sections through the mid-pontine level as in micrograph (a); at this level the ***superior peduncles* SCP** are very prominent. The main bulk of the superior cerebellar peduncles is made up of fibres from the central nuclei of the cerebellum passing upwards to the thalamus and then projecting to the motor cortex.

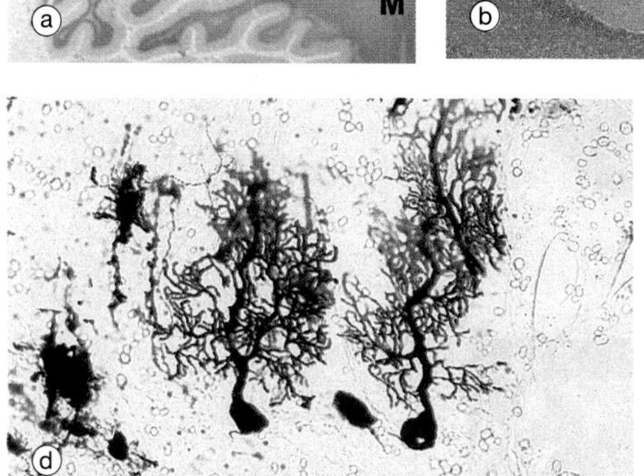

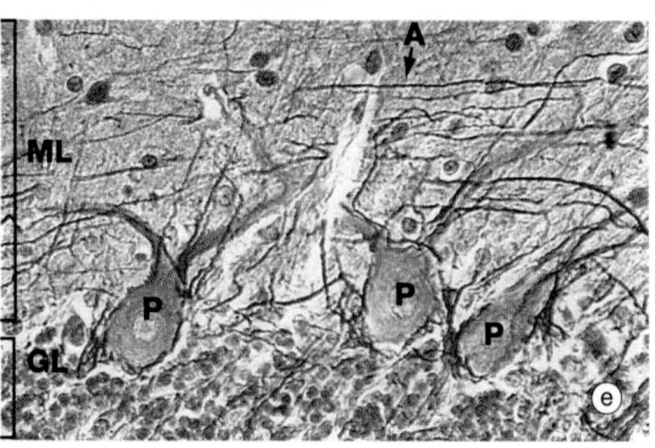

Fig. 20.5 Cerebellum
(a) H & E ×4 (b) H & E ×20 (c) H & E ×320 (d) Golgi-Cox ×320 (e) Bielschowsky/neutral red ×600

The cerebellum, which coordinates muscular activity and maintains posture and equilibrium, consists of a cortex of grey matter with a central core of white matter containing four pairs of nuclei. Afferent and efferent fibres pass to and from the brain stem via inferior, middle and superior cerebellar peduncles linking medulla, pons and midbrain respectively.

As seen in micrograph (a), the cerebellar cortex forms a series of deeply convoluted folds or ***folia*** supported by a branching central medulla **M** of white matter. At higher magnification in micrograph (b), the cortex is seen to consist of three layers. The outer ***molecular layer*** **ML** contains relatively few neurones and large numbers of unmyelinated fibres. The inner ***granular cell layer*** **GL** is extremely cellular. Between the two is a single layer of huge neurones called ***Purkinje cells*** **PL**.

Purkinje cells **P** are seen at higher magnification in micrograph (c); they have very large cell bodies, a relatively fine axon extending down through the granular cell layer **GL**, and an extensively branching dendritic system which arborises into the outer molecular layer **ML**. This extraordinary dendritic system of Purkinje cells is best demonstrated by heavy metal methods as in micrograph (d).

The deep granular cell layer of the cortex contains numerous small neurones, the non-myelinated axons of which pass outwards to the molecular layer where they bifurcate to run parallel to the surface to synapse with the dendrites of Purkinje cells. Micrograph (e) demonstrates the course of granular cell axons in the molecular layer. The axons **A** are stained black with silver and their cell bodies in the granular cell layer **GL** are counter-stained with neutral red. In addition to the Purkinje **P** and granular cells already described, there are three other types of small neurones in the cerebellar cortex, namely ***stellate cells*** and ***basket cells*** scattered in the molecular layer **ML** and ***Golgi cells*** scattered in the superficial part of the granular cell layer. Note black-stained fibrils of basket cells axons surrounding the Purkinje cell bodies **P** in (e).

In simple terms, afferent fibres enter the cerebellum from the brain stem and then pass via the white matter core to make complex connections with granular cells, these in turn connect with Purkinje dendrites via basket cells and other neurones of the cerebellar cortex. The only efferent fibres from the cerebellar cortex are the Purkinje cell axons which pass down through the granular cell layer into the white matter where they synapse in the central nuclei of the cerebellum.

Cerebellar ataxia

Disease that causes damage to Purkinje cells in the cerebellar cortex leads to the development of ***cerebellar ataxia*** in which there is poor co-ordination of voluntary movement. Causes include familial neurodegenerative disease, alcohol abuse, tumours, trauma or hypoxic damage.

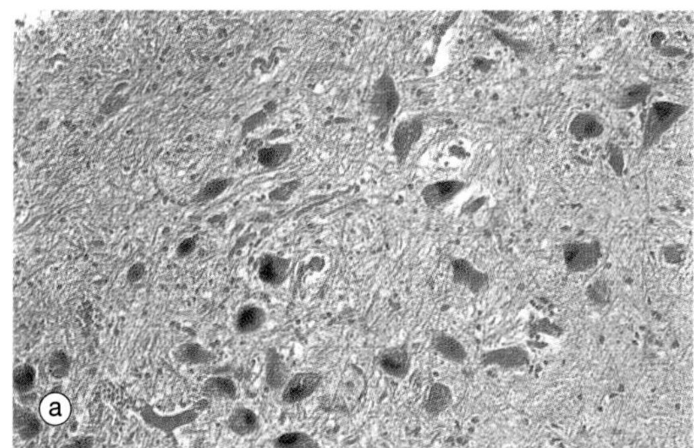

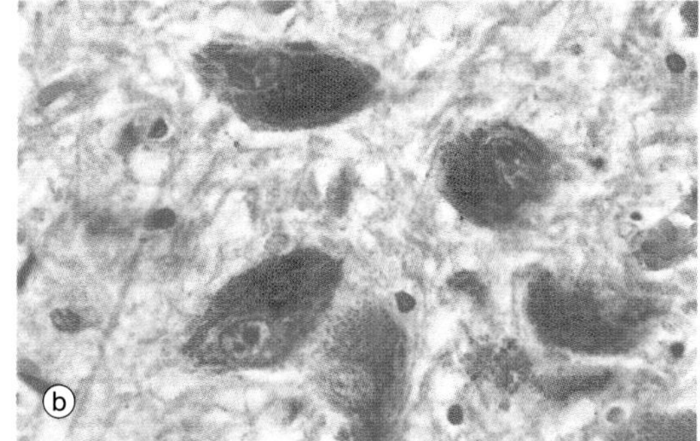

Fig. 20.6 Substantia nigra
(a) H & E ×100 (b) H & E ×400

The substantia nigra is a large mass of grey matter extending throughout the midbrain; on each side it divides the cerebral peduncles into dorsal and ventral parts and in sections of the midbrain, as in micrograph (a), it is easily recognised by neurons containing dark pigment from which its name derives. The substantia nigra has extensive connections with the cortex, spinal cord, corpus striatum and reticular formation and appears to play an important part in the fine control of motor function.

The neurones of the substantia nigra are multipolar in form and in adults the cytoplasm contains numerous granules of neuromelanin pigment as seen in micrograph (b). The pigmented neurones of the substantia nigra contain ***dopamine*** which appears to act as a neurotransmitter causing inhibitory effects particularly on neurones in the corpus striatum.

Neuromelanin is contained in membrane-bound granules. Very little neuromelanin is present at birth, with the amount increasing during childhood and thereafter rising with increasing age. The origin of neuromelanin is still debated, with proposals that it is enzymatically generated or is merely an oxidation byproduct of dopamine synthesis. Functionally it may sequester metals such as iron, as well as toxic organic compounds.

Parkinson's disease

Parkinson's disease is a common neurodegenerative disease usually seen in later life. It is clinically characterised by tremor, muscular rigidity and slowness of movement. Neuropathology shows degeneration and death of neurones in the substantia nigra. This leads to a marked reduction in dopamine levels in the brain that in turn leads to the movement disorder.

Macroscopic examination of the brain of a patient who has died with Parkinson's disease shows abnormal pallor of the substantia nigra correlating with loss of the pigment-containing nigral neurones.

Symptoms can be alleviated by the drug L-dopa, a dopamine precursor which crosses the blood–brain barrier to increase brain dopamine levels.

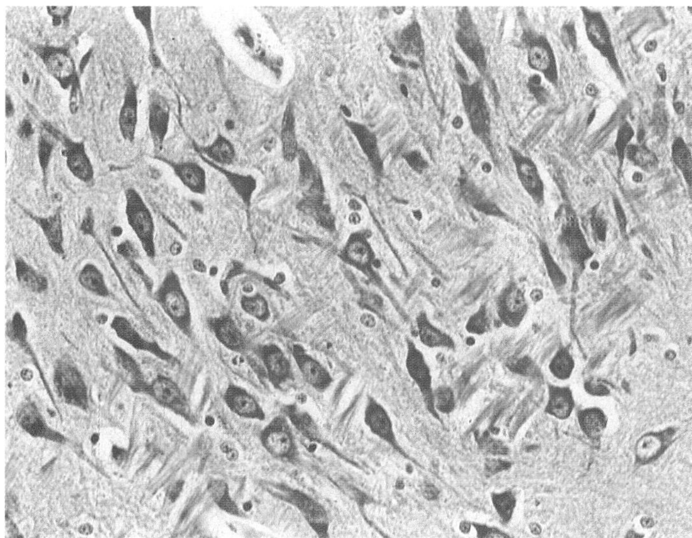

Fig. 20.7 Thalamus H & E ×480

The thalami are large masses of grey matter lying on each side of the third ventricle and comprising the main bulk of the ***diencephalon***, the central core of the cerebrum. Functionally, the thalamus is subdivided into a large number of nuclei including reticular and motor nuclei as well as specific sensory nuclei containing the cell bodies of neurones with axons projecting to the cerebral cortex. The thalamus constitutes an extremely complex relay and integration centre for information from almost all parts of the CNS.

This micrograph shows the histological appearance of a typical thalamic nucleus consisting of a dense aggregation of neurone cell bodies criss-crossed by tracts of afferent and efferent nerve fibres.

A axon **GL** granular layer **M** central branching medulla **ML** molecular layer **P** Purkinje cell
PL Purkinje cell layer

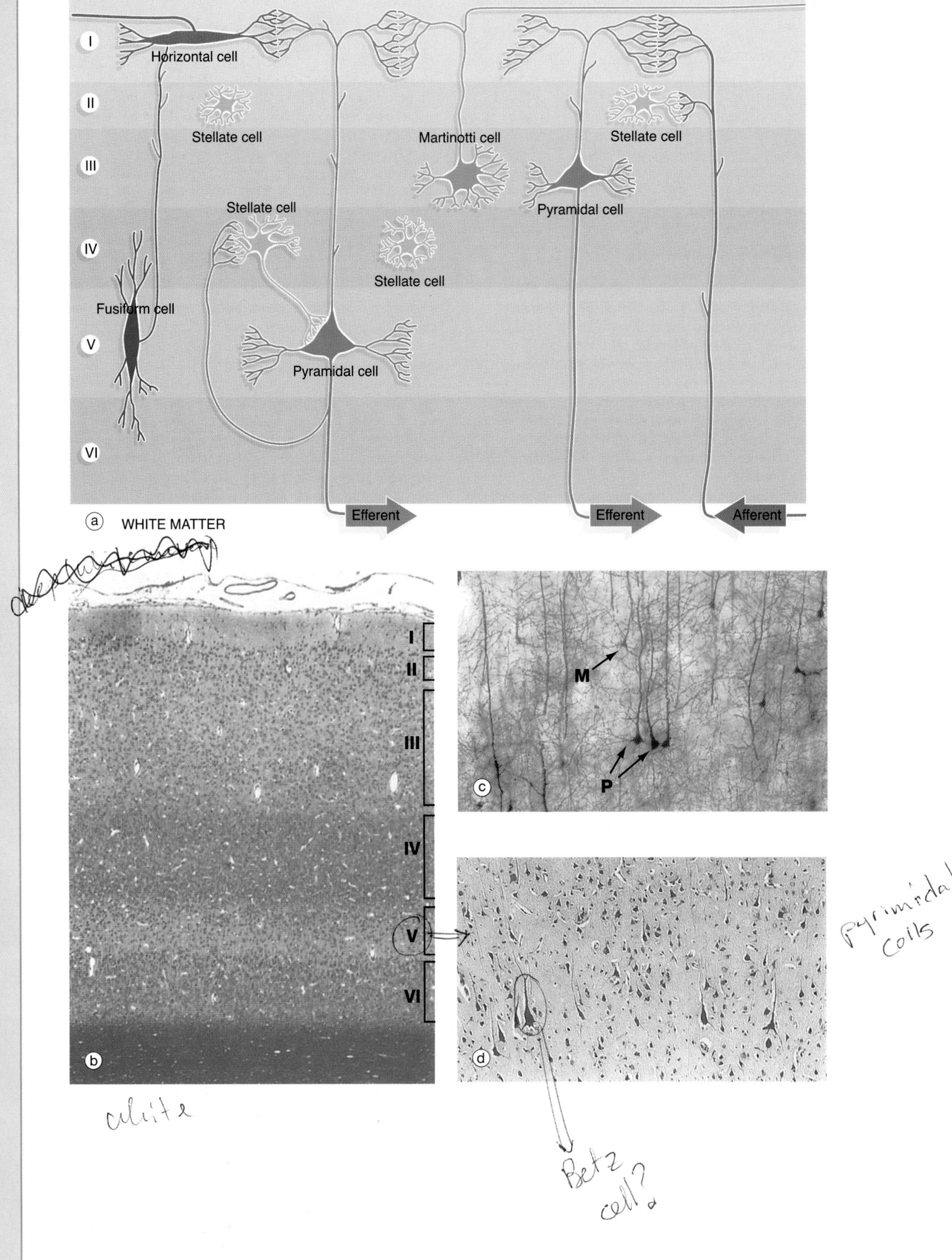

M cell of Martinotti **P** pyramidal cell

Fig. 20.8 Cerebral cortex *(illustrations opposite)*
(a) Neurone cell types (b) Methylene blue ×42 (c) Golgi method ×320 (d) Nissl method ×320

The cerebral hemispheres consist of a convoluted cortex of grey matter overlying the central medullary mass of white matter which conveys fibres between different parts of the cortex and to and from other parts of the CNS.

Histologically, the neurones of the cerebral cortex are divided into five different morphological types which are arranged in several layers. In submammalian species, the major function of the cortex concerns the sense of olfaction (smell) and the neurones are arranged into three layers. In mammals, there has evolved the so-called ***neocortex*** consisting of six layers of neurones. The neocortex includes the ***sensory*** and ***motor areas*** of the cortex as well as the ***association cortex*** and in humans constitutes about 90% of the cerebral cortex. The primitive three-layered pattern persists only in the olfactory cortex and cortical part of the limbic system in the temporal lobe.

Neurone types in the cerebral cortex

The five characteristic types of cortical neurone are shown diagrammatically in (a), the pyramidal and stellate cells being by far the most common type.

- **Pyramidal cells**, as their name implies, have pyramid-shaped cell bodies, the apex being directed towards the cortical surface. A slender axon arises from the base of the cell and passes into the underlying white matter, though in the case of small superficially located cells, the axon may synapse in the deep layers of the cortex. From the apex, a thick branching dendrite passes towards the surface where it has an array of fine dendritic branches. In addition, short dendrites arise from the edges of the base and ramify laterally. The size of the pyramidal cells varies from small to large, the smallest tending to lie more superficially. The huge upper motor neurones of the motor cortex, known as ***Betz cells***, are the largest of the pyramidal cells in the cortex.
- **Stellate (granule) cells** are small neurones with a short vertical axon and several short branching dendrites, giving the cell body the shape of a star; basket and neurogliaform subtypes are also described. With routine histological methods, the cells look like small granules giving rise to their alternative name.
- **Cells of Martinotti** are small polygonal cells with a few short dendrites; the axon extends towards the surface and bifurcates to run horizontally, usually in the most superficial layer.
- **Fusiform cells** are spindle-shaped cells oriented at right angles to the surface of the cerebral cortex. The axon arises from the side of the cell body and passes superficially. Dendrites extend from each end of the cell body branching into deeper and more superficial layers.
- **Horizontal cells of Cajal** are small and spindle-shaped but oriented parallel to the surface. They are the least common cell type and are only found in the most superficial layer where their axons pass laterally to synapse with the dendrites of pyramidal cells.

In addition to neurones, the cortex contains supporting neuroglial cells, i.e. astrocytes, oligodendroglia and microglia.

Layers of the neocortex

As previously stated, the neurones in the neocortex are arranged into six layers, the layers differing in neurone morphology, size and population density. The layers merge with one another rather than being highly demarcated and vary somewhat from one region of the cortex to another depending on cortical thickness and function.

Micrograph (b) illustrates the typical layered appearance of the cerebral cortex, the more detailed characteristics of each layer being as follows:

I. **Plexiform (molecular) layer.** This most superficial layer mainly contains dendrites and axons of cortical neurones making synapses with one another; the sparse nuclei are those of neuroglia and occasional horizontal cells of Cajal.
II. **Outer granular layer.** A dense population of small pyramidal cells and stellate cells make up this thin layer which also contains various axons and dendritic connections from deeper layers.
III. **Pyramidal cell layer.** Pyramidal cells of moderate size predominate in this broad layer, the cells increasing in size deeper in the layer. Martinotti cells are also present.
IV. **Inner granular layer.** This layer consists mainly of densely packed stellate cells.
V. **Ganglionic layer.** Large pyramidal cells and smaller numbers of stellate cells and cells of Martinotti make up this layer, the name of the layer originating from the huge pyramidal (ganglion) Betz cells of the motor cortex.
VI. **Multiform cell layer.** This is so named for the wide variety of differing morphological forms found in this layer. It contains numerous small pyramidal cells and cells of Martinotti, as well as stellate cells, especially superficially, and fusiform cells in the deeper part.

Micrograph (c) shows part of layer V; a thick section is employed, stained with a heavy metal impregnation technique which demonstrates considerable morphological detail. Several pyramidal cells **P** are easily identifiable, the principal dendrite of each (but not the axon) being included in the plane of section. A cell of Martinotti **M** can also be identified by its polygonal shape.

Micrograph (d) also shows layer V but in this case the section is thinner and stained by a routine histological method. In this example there is little morphological detail, nevertheless most of the cells are identifiable as pyramidal cells, increasing in size in the deeper part and including several very large cells.

The synaptic interconnections within the cortex are exceedingly complex, with any one neurone synapsing with several hundred others. However, there are several basic principles of cortical organisation and function:

- Functional units are disposed vertically, corresponding to the general orientation of axons and major dendrites.
- Afferent fibres (their cell bodies lying elsewhere in the CNS) generally synapse high in the cortex with dendrites of efferent neurones, the cell bodies of which lie in deeper layers of the cortex.
- Efferent pathways, typically the axons of pyramidal cells, tend to give off branches which pass back into more superficial layers to communicate with their own dendrites via interneuronal connections involving other cortical cell types.

21. *Special sense organs*

Introduction

The organs of special sense are sophisticated sensory structures in which the specific neural receptors are incorporated in a non-neural structure which enhances and refines the reception of incoming stimuli. The eye and audiovestibular apparatus of the ear are the main special sense organs, but the gustatory (taste) and olfactory (smell) receptors are usually also included in this category.

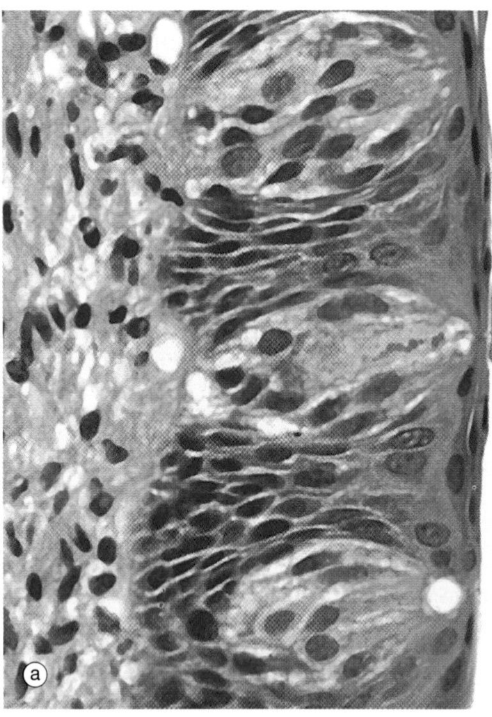

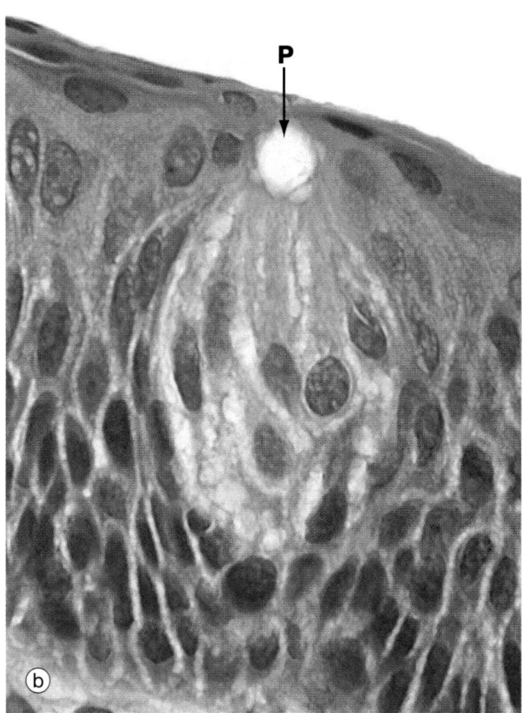

Fig. 21.1 Taste buds
(a) H & E ×200 (b) H & E ×1000

Taste buds, the chemoreceptors for the sense of taste (***gustation***), are in humans mainly located in the epithelium of the circumvallate papillae of the tongue (see Fig. 13.12), although they are also found scattered in other parts of the tongue, palate, pharynx and epiglottis. In the circumvallate papillae, taste buds face into the deep troughs surrounding the papillae as shown in 13.12a. Serous glands, called the ***glands of von Ebner***, secrete a serous fluid into the troughs to act as a solvent for taste provoking substances. The human tongue has approximately 3000 taste buds.

The taste bud is a barrel-shaped organ extending the full thickness of the epithelium and opening at the surface via the taste pore **P**. Each taste bud contains about 50 long spindle-shaped cells which extend from the basement membrane to the taste pore. Classically, two types of cell are described in the taste bud: light ***gustatory cells*** and dark ***supporting*** or ***sustentacular*** cells. A third cell type, the ***basal cell***, is now generally recognised and may constitute the precursor of one or both of the other cell types. Both gustatory and sustentacular cells have long microvilli extending into the taste pore which contains a glycoprotein substance thought to be secreted by the sustentacular cells.

Ultrastructural studies have shown that non-myelinated nerve fibres are associated with both cell types, but there appears to be a more intimate, synapse-like relationship between the nerve fibres and the gustatory cells. Although the gustatory cells are thought to be the taste receptors, the sustentacular cells may also serve some receptor function. Like the oral epithelium, all the cells of the taste bud, which represent highly specialised epithelial cells, are renewed continuously although the gustatory and sustentacular cells are replaced at different rates.

Four taste modalities are recognised: sweet, bitter, acid and salt. Each modality tends to be principally perceived in a specific region of the tongue; however, no structural differences have been demonstrated between taste buds from different areas. The sensations of taste and smell are closely associated and loss of olfactory sense is accompanied by diminished gustatory perception.

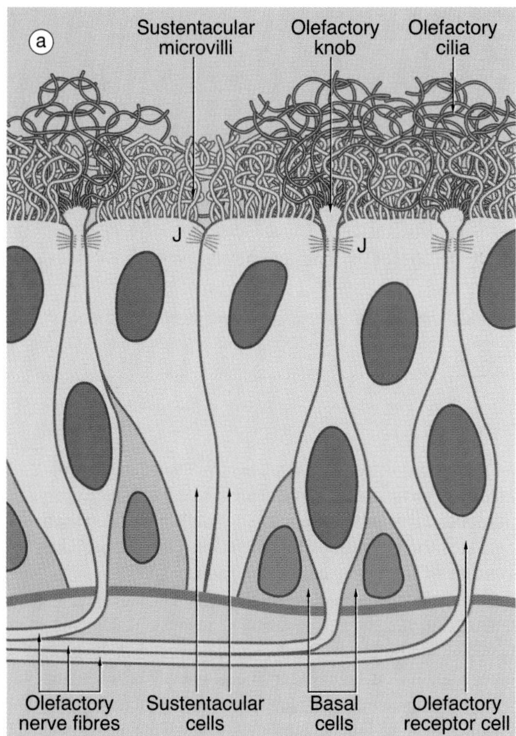

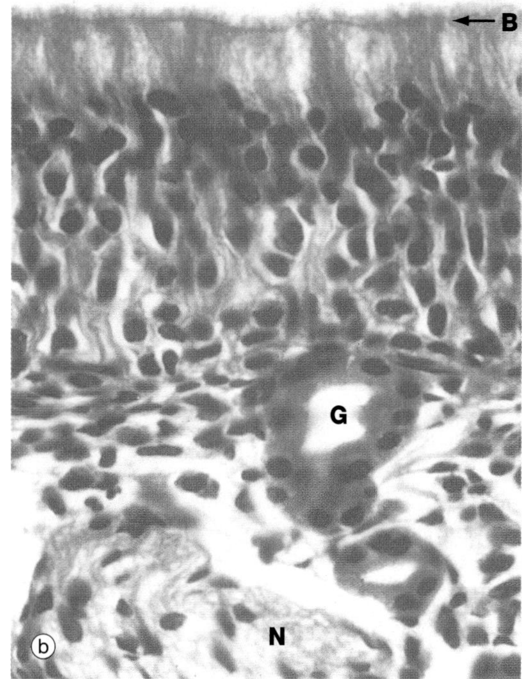

Fig. 21.2 Olfactory receptors
(a) Schematic diagram (b) H & E ×720

The receptors for the sense of smell are located in a modified form of respiratory epithelium called ***olfactory epithelium*** in the nasal cavity; although extensive in some mammals such as the dog, the olfactory epithelium is restricted to a small area in the roof of the nasal cavity in humans. The olfactory epithelium is very tall, pseudostratified columnar in form and contains cells of three types: olfactory receptor cells, supporting epithelial (***sustentacular***) cells and basal epithelial cells.

The ***olfactory receptor cells*** are true bipolar neurones (see Fig. 7.2), the cell bodies of which are located in the middle stratum of the olfactory epithelium. A single dendritic process extends from the cell body to the free surface where it terminates as a small swelling, the ***olfactory knob***, which gives rise to about a dozen extremely long modified cilia. These cilia, or olfactory hairs, contain the usual '9 plus 2' arrangement of microtubules in their proximal portion but become thinner distally where they contain variable numbers of single microtubules in different species. The cilia are non-motile and lie flattened against the epithelial surface in the surface mucous layer. The cilia are the sites of interaction between odiferous substances and the receptor cells. At the basal aspect, each receptor cell gives rise to a single fine non-myelinated axon which penetrates the basement membrane to join the axons of other receptor cells. The bundles of axons pass via about 20 small holes on each side of the ***cribriform plate*** of the ethmoid bone to reach the olfactory bulbs of the forebrain where they synapse with second order sensory neurones.

The supporting or sustentacular cells are elongated with their tapered bases resting on the basement membrane. Many long microvilli extend from their luminal surfaces to form a tangled mat with the cilia of the receptor cells. At the luminal surface, the plasma membranes of the sustentacular and receptor cells are bound together by typical junctional complexes **J**. The functions of the sustentacular cells are poorly understood but they probably provide mechanical and physiological support for the receptor cells. The basal cells are small, conical cells which appear to be stem cells for both olfactory and sustentacular cells.

In histological section, it is difficult to distinguish individual cell types within the olfactory epithelium; however, the nuclei of sustentacular cells occupy the uppermost stratum, those of the receptor cells the middle stratum and those of the basal cells lie close to the basement membrane. Note the terminal bar **B** at the luminal surface representing junctional complexes; note also the fuzzy surface contour representing the tangled meshwork of microvilli and cilia on the surface.

The olfactory epithelium is supported by loose vascular tissue containing bundles of afferent nerve fibres **N** and numerous serous glands called ***Bowman's glands*** **G** which produce the watery surface secretions in which odiferous substances are dissolved.

B terminal bar **G** Bowman's gland **J** junctional complex **N** afferent nerve fibres **P** taste pore

The eye

The eye is the highly specialised organ of photoreception, a process which involves the conversion of light energy into nerve action potentials. The photoreceptors are modified dendrites of two types of nerve cells, ***rod cells*** and ***cone cells***. The rods are integrated into a system which is receptive to light of differing intensity; this is perceived in a form analogous to a black and white photographic image. The cones are of three functional types receptive to the colours blue, green and red and constitute a system by which coloured images are seen. The rod and cone receptors and a system of integrating neurones are located in the inner layer of the eye, the ***retina.*** The remaining structures of the eye serve to support the retina or to focus images of the visual world upon the retina.

In addition, several accessory structures, namely the ***eyelids***, ***lacrimal gland*** and ***conjunctiva***, protect the eye from external damage.

Fig. 21.3 The eye *(illustration opposite)*

The eye is made up of three basic layers: the outer ***corneo-scleral layer***, the intermediate ***uveal layer*** (***uveal tract***) and the inner ***retinal layer***.

Corneo-scleral layer

The corneo-scleral layer forms a tough, fibroelastic capsule which supports the eye. The posterior five-sixths, the ***sclera***, is opaque and provides insertion for the extraocular muscles.

The anterior one-sixth, the ***cornea***, is transparent and has a smaller radius of curvature than the sclera. The cornea is the principal refracting medium of the eye and roughly focuses an image onto the retina; the focusing power of the cornea depends mainly on the radius of curvature of its external surface. The corneo-scleral junction is known as the ***limbus*** and is marked internally and externally by a shallow depression. Running from the junction of the cornea and limbus the surface of the eye is covered by ***conjunctiva*** which is reflected into the eyelids.

Uveal layer

The middle layer, the uvea or uveal tract, is a highly vascular layer which is made up of three components: the ***choroid***, ***ciliary body*** and the ***iris***. The choroid lies between the sclera and retina in the posterior five-sixths of the eye. It provides support for the retina and is heavily pigmented, thus absorbing light which has passed through the retina. Anteriorly, the choroid merges with the ciliary body which is a circumferential thickening of the uvea lying beneath the limbus.

The ciliary body surrounds the coronal equator of the ***lens*** and is attached to it by the ***suspensory ligament*** or ***zonule***. The lens is a biconvex transparent structure, the shape of which can be varied to provide fine focus of the corneal image upon the retina. The ciliary body contains smooth muscle, the tone of which controls the shape of the lens via the suspensory ligament. The lens, suspensory ligament and ciliary body divide the eye into a large compartment containing a thick gel called the ***vitreous body*** and a compartment part in front containing a watery fluid called the ***aqueous humor***.

The iris, the third component of the uvea, forms a diaphragm extending in front of the lens from the ciliary body so as to incompletely divide the anterior compartment into two chambers; these are known by the terms ***anterior*** and ***posterior chamber***. The highly pigmented iris acts as an adjustable diaphragm which regulates the amount of light reaching the retina. The aperture of the iris is called the ***pupil***.

The anterior and posterior chambers contain the aqueous humor, which is secreted into the posterior chamber by the ciliary body and circulated through the pupil to drain into a canal at the angle of the anterior chamber, the ***canal of Schlemm***. The aqueous humor is a source of nutrients for the non-vascular lens and cornea, and acts as an optical medium which is non-refractive with respect to the cornea. The pressure of aqueous humor maintains the shape of the cornea.

The large, posterior compartment of the eye contains a specialised connective tissue largely composed of a transparent gel known as the vitreous body. The vitreous body supports the lens and retina from within as well as providing an optical medium which is non-refractive with respect to the lens. In life, the vitreous body contains a canal which extends from the exit of the optic nerve to the posterior surface of the lens; this ***hyaloid canal*** represents the course of the hyaloid artery which supplies the vitreous body during embryological development. The vitreous body and hyaloid canal are rarely preserved in histological preparations.

Retinal layer

The photosensitive retina forms the inner lining of most of the posterior compartment of the eye and terminates along a scalloped line, the ***ora serrata***, behind the ciliary body. Anterior to the ora serrata, the retinal layer continues as a non-photosensitive epithelial layer which lines the ciliary body and the posterior surface of the iris.

The visual axis of the eye passes through a depression in the retina called the ***fovea*** which is surrounded by a yellow-pigmented zone, the ***macula lutea***. The fovea is the area of greatest visual acuity.

Afferent nerve fibres from the retina converge to form the ***optic nerve*** which leaves the eye through a part of the sclera known as the ***lamina cribrosa***. The retina overlying the lamina cribrosa, the ***optic papilla*** (***optic disc***), is devoid of photoreceptors and thus represents a blind spot.

Inflammatory diseases of the eye

The different compartments of the eye can be the focus of specific inflammatory diseases.

- ***Conjunctivitis*** refers to inflammation of the conjunctival surface of the eye also involving the lining of the eyelids.
- ***Uveitis*** describes inflammation of the uveal tract including the uvea and ciliary body. When uveal inflammation is limited to the iris it is termed ***iritis***.
- Inflammation of the sclera is termed ***scleritis***.
- Certain diseases cause inflammation of the retina termed ***retinitis***.

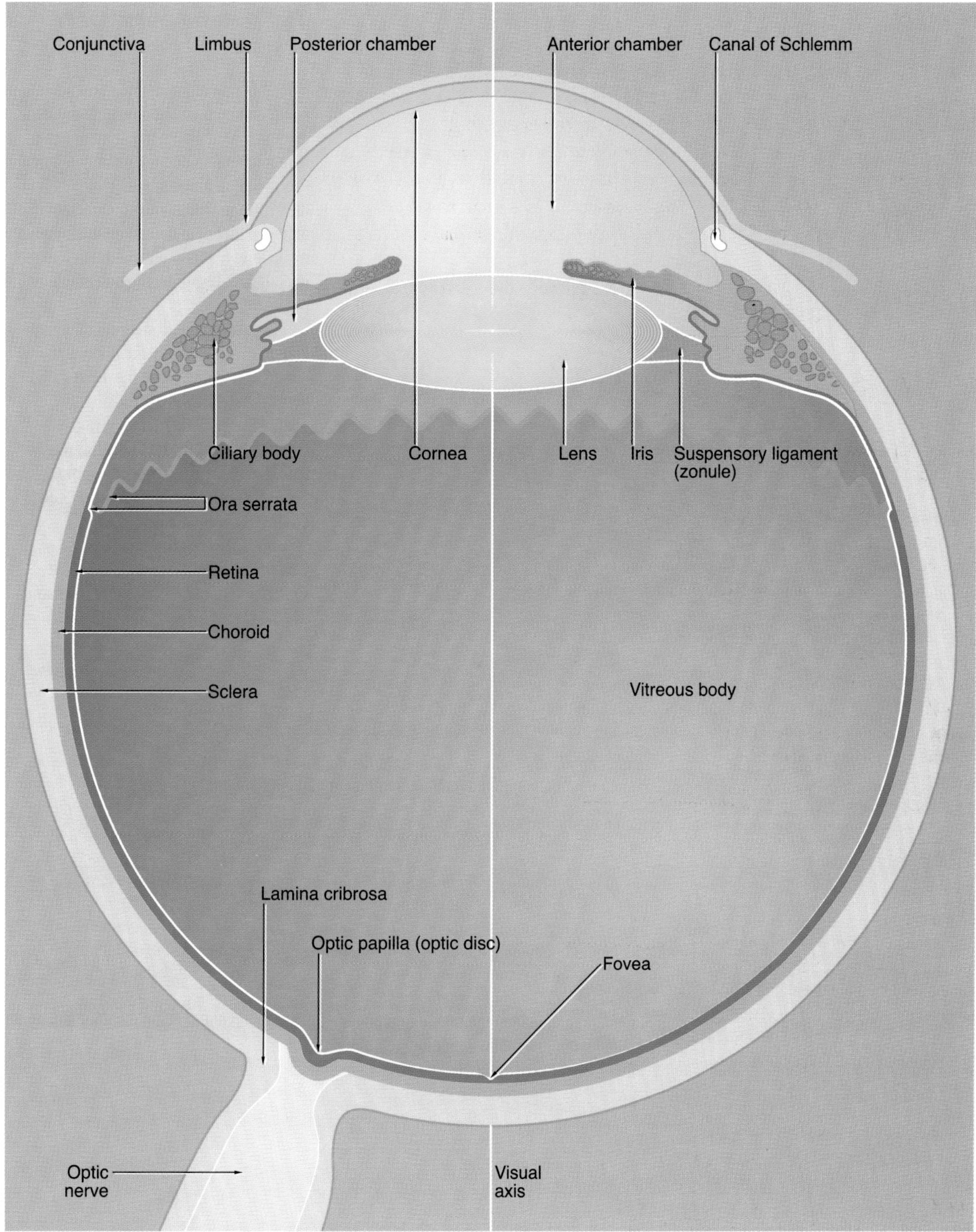

Loss of visual acuity

Loss of visual acuity, leading to blurring of vision, is common and can have several causes.

Certain disorders of the eye cause problems with accommodation such that light is not brought into a correct focus on the retina. For example, ageing is associated with difficulty focusing on objects that are close (***presbyopia***), due to loss of elasticity of the lens.

In other disorders, the normal transparent structures of the eye become opaque and visual acuity is reduced. Diseases of the cornea that cause scarring lead to abnormal opacification and light scattering, reducing visual acuity. Diseases that cause abnormal opacification of the lens (***cataracts***) lead to loss of visual acuity and, when severe, blindness.

The retina may be the seat of several diseases which cause problems with visual acuity. The retina may become detached from the uvea (***retinal detachment***) leading to loss of light perception in the affected part. Any condition that causes loss of the specialised photoreceptors from the retina causes loss of visual acuity. Common conditions affecting the retina include ***macular degeneration*** in which there is loss of specialised retinal cells and ***diabetes mellitus*** in which pathology affecting small blood vessels causes retinal damage and cell death.

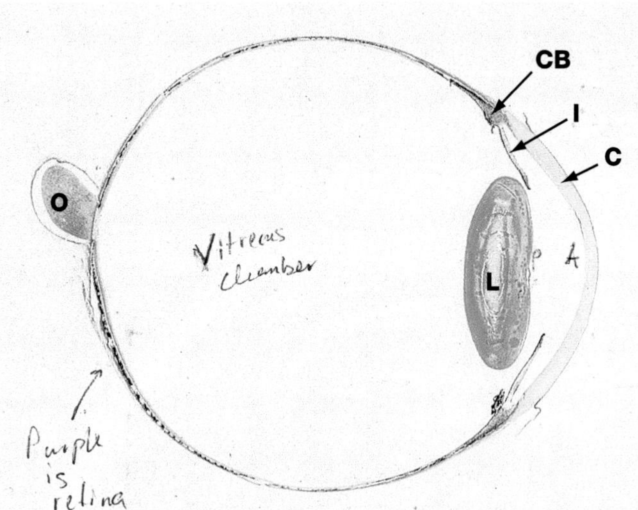

Fig. 21.4 Eye (monkey)
H & E ×5

This horizontal section shows the relative sizes of the components of the eye. At this magnification, the three layers making up the wall of the globe are not readily distinguishable although in the wall of the posterior compartment, the middle layer, the choroid, is recognisable by its high content of pigment.

The other uveal structures, the ciliary body **CB** and iris **I** are readily visible. The lens **L** has been artefactually distorted during preparation and the suspensory ligament by which it is attached to the ciliary body is not preserved. Note the relative thickness of the cornea **C**.

The optic nerve **O** is seen to penetrate the sclera medial to the visual axis; the fovea is not present in this plane of section.

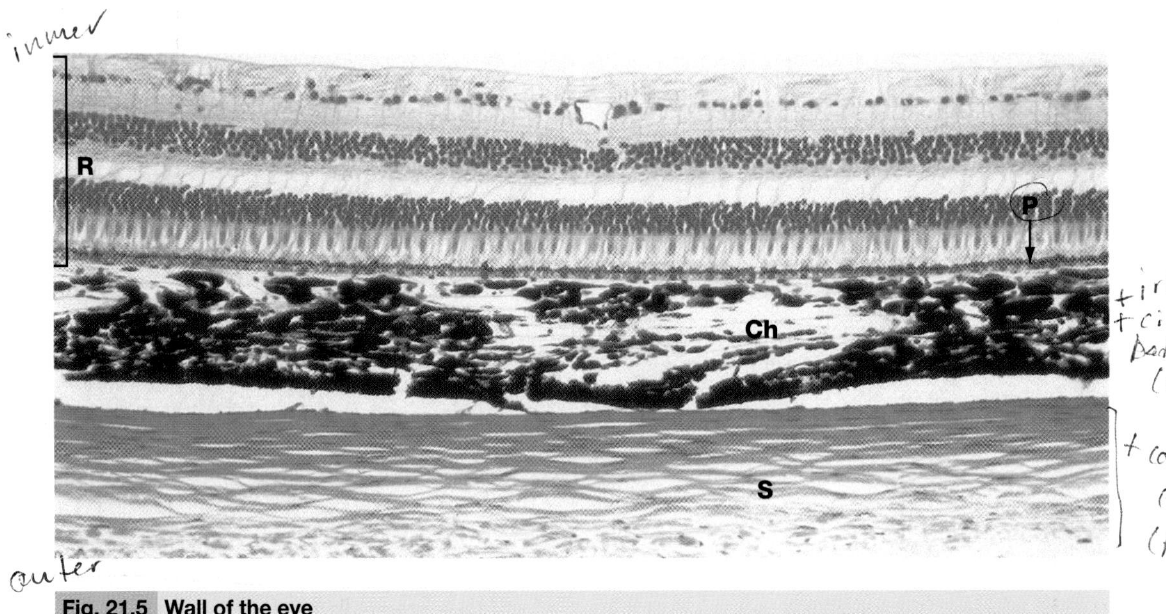

Fig. 21.5 Wall of the eye
H & E ×300

The three layers of the wall of the eye are illustrated in this micrograph.

The inner photosensitive retina is a multilayered structure, the outermost limit of which is defined by a layer of pigmented epithelial cells, the ***pigment epithelium*** **P**.

The choroid **Ch** is a layer of loose vascular supporting tissue lying between the sclera **S** externally and the retina **R** internally. The choroid and retina are separated by a membrane known as ***Bruch's membrane*** which is composed of the basement membranes of the pigmented epithelium of the retina and the endothelium of the choroid capillaries plus intervening layers of collagen and elastin fibres. The blood supply of the uveal layer of the eye is provided by branches of the ophthalmic artery which penetrates through the sclera. Larger vessels predominate in the superficial aspect of the choroid, with a rich capillary plexus in the deeper aspect providing nourishment for the outer layers of the retina by diffusion across Bruch's membrane. The choroid contains numerous large, heavily pigmented melanocytes which confer the dense pigmentation characteristic of the choroid. The pigment absorbs light rays passing through the retina and prevents interference due to light reflection.

The sclera consists of dense fibroelastic tissue, the fibres of which are arranged in bundles parallel to the surface. This layer contains little ground substance and few fibroblasts. The sclera varies in thickness, being thickest posteriorly and thinnest at the coronal equator of the globe.

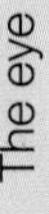

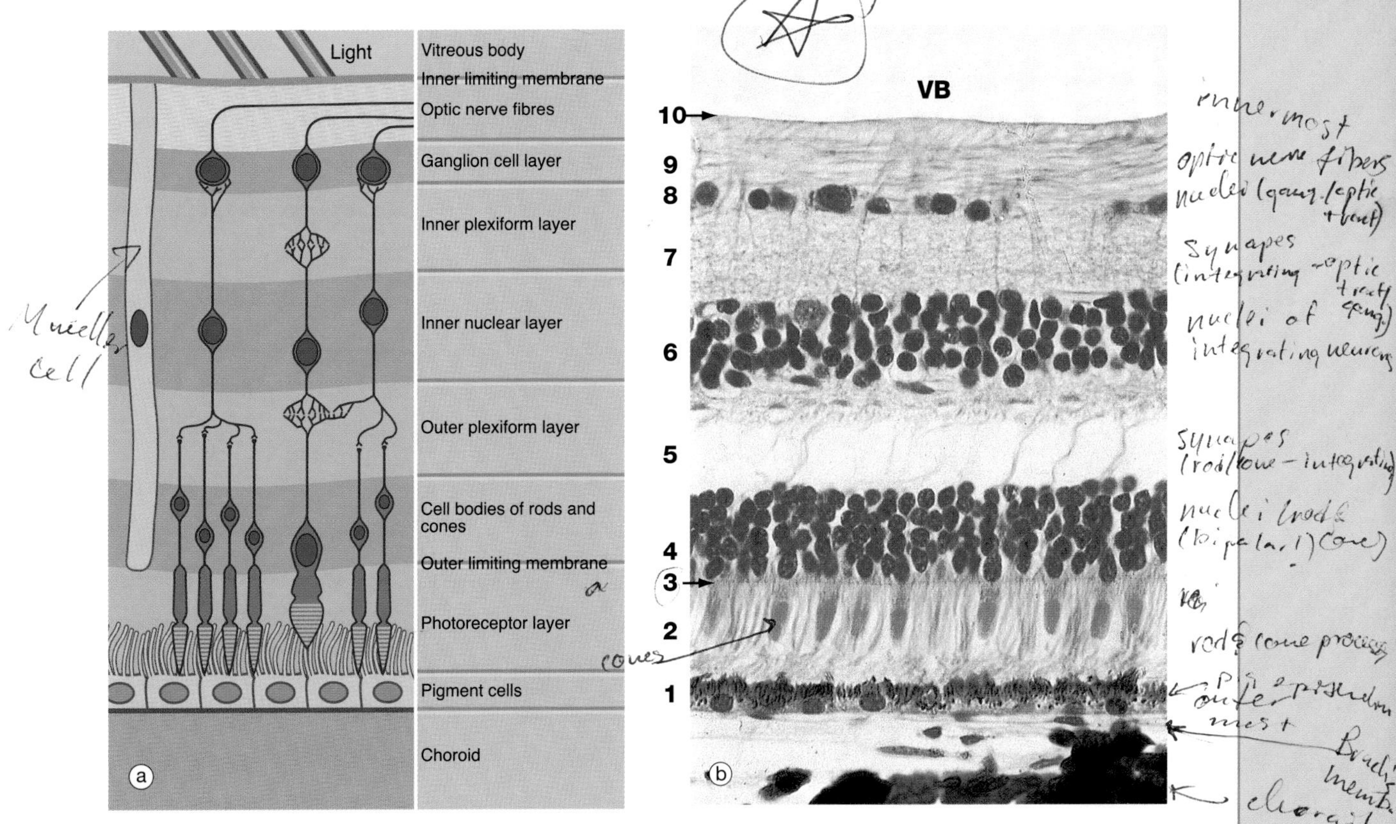

Fig. 21.6 Retina
(a) Schematic diagram (b) H & E ×640

The retina is made up of three cell types: ***neurones***, ***pigmented epithelial cells*** and ***neurone support cells***. The neurones are divided into three functional groups, namely photoreceptor cells (rod cells and cone cells), the cells of afferent fibres passing in the optic nerve, and a group of neurones interposed between the first two types which integrate sensory input from the photoreceptors before transmission to the cerebral cortex. The integrating neurones are further subdivided into three types: ***bipolar cells***, ***horizontal cells*** and ***amacrine cells***.

Histologically, the retina is traditionally divided into 10 distinct histological layers, as shown in the micrograph; the distribution of the different cell types being illustrated in a highly schematic manner in the diagram.

The outermost layer (1) consists of the ***pigmented epithelial cells*** forming a single layer resting on Bruch's membrane which separates them from the choroid. The next layer is the ***photoreceptor layer*** made up of the rod and cone processes (2) with a thin eosinophilic structure known as the ***outer limiting membrane*** (3) separating them from a layer of densely packed nuclei described as the ***outer nuclear layer*** (4). The outer nuclear layer contains the cell bodies of the rod and cone photoreceptors. The almost featureless layer deep to this is known as the ***outer plexiform layer*** (5) and contains synaptic connections between the short axons of the photoreceptor cells and integrating neurones, the cell bodies of which lie in the ***inner nuclear layer*** (6). In the ***inner plexiform layer*** (7), the integrating neurones make synaptic connections with dendrites of neurones whose axons form the optic tract. The cell bodies of the optic tract neurones (***retinal ganglion cells***) comprise the ***ganglion cell layer*** (8). Internal to this is the layer of afferent fibres (9) passing towards the optic disc to form the optic nerve. Finally, the ***inner limiting membrane*** (10) demarcates the innermost aspect of the retina from the vitreous body **VB**. Note in the diagram that only bipolar cells are represented in the integrating cell layer; this layer also contains the cell bodies of the horizontal and amacrine cells as illustrated in Fig. 21.8. Note that light impinging on the retina passes through many layers before reaching the photoreceptor cells.

Towards the left of the diagram there is an extremely elongated support cell extending between inner and outer limiting membranes, which has its nucleus in the same layer as the integrating neurones, the inner nuclear layer. These cells, known as ***Muller cells***, are analogous to the neuroglia of the CNS and have long cytoplasmic processes which embrace and sometimes even encircle the retinal neurones filling all the intervening spaces. Muller cells provide structural support and may also mediate the transfer of essential metabolites such as glucose to the retinal neurones.

The outer limiting membrane is not a true membrane but merely represents the line of intercellular junctions between Muller cells and the photoreceptor cells (shown diagrammatically in Fig. 21.7). In contrast, the inner limiting membrane represents the basement membrane of the Muller cells resting on the vitreous body.

C cornea **CB** ciliary body **Ch** choroid **I** iris **L** lens **O** optic nerve **P** pigment epithelium
R retina **S** sclera **VB** vitreous body

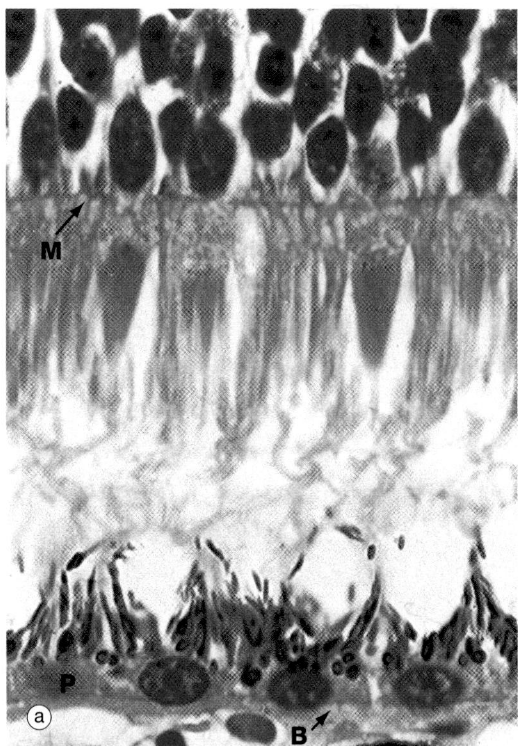

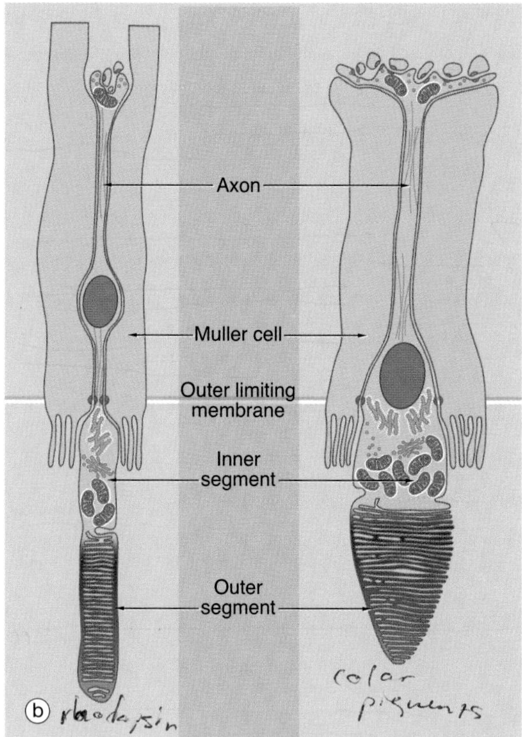

Fig. 21.7 Retinal photoreceptors
(a) H & E ×1200 (b) Schematic diagram

The rod and cone photoreceptor layer of the retina is shown at very high magnification in micrograph (a), the cell bodies of the rod and cone cells lying deep to the outer limiting membrane **M**. Peripherally, the rods and cones mingle with long microvilli extending from the pigmented epithelial cells **P**.

As shown in the diagram (b), the rod photoreceptors are long slender bipolar cells, the single dendrite of each cell extending beyond the outer limiting membrane as the rod proper. The rod proper consists of ***inner*** and ***outer segments*** connected by a thin eccentric strand of cytoplasm containing nine microtubule doublets similar to those of a cilium but without the inner pair of microtubules. The inner segment contains a prominent Golgi apparatus and many mitochondria. The outer segment has a regular cylindrical shape and contains a stack of flattened membranous discs which incorporate the pigment ***rhodopsin*** (visual purple). The membranous discs are continuously shed from the end of each rod and phagocytosed by the pigmented epithelial cells. The discs are continuously replaced from the inner part of the outer segment. In essence, the transduction process involves the interaction of light with rhodopsin molecules which promotes a conformational change in the rhodopsin molecule, thus initiating an action potential. The action potential then passes inwards along the dendrite and axon to the layer of integrating neurones.

Cones are similar in basic structure to the rods but they differ in several details. The outer segment of the cone is a long conical structure about two-thirds the length of a rod and containing a similar number of even more flattened membranous discs. Unlike the situation in the rods, however, the disc membrane is continuous with the plasma membrane so that, on one side, the spaces between the discs are continuous with the extracellular environment. The discs are not shed, although the tips of the cones are invested by processes of pigmented epithelial cells. The cones contain visual pigments similar to rhodopsin, receptive to blue, green and red light, and the mechanism of transduction is probably similar. The bodies of the cone cells are generally continuous with the inner segment of the cone proper without an intervening dendritic process and the nuclei of cone cells thus form a row immediately deep to the outer limiting membrane.

As seen in micrograph (a), the pigmented epithelial cells are cuboidal in shape with the nuclei located basally towards ***Bruch's membrane*** **B**. Apically, the cells are crammed with melanin granules, numerous mitochondria and lipofuscin, a residual product of phagocytosis (see Fig. 1.15a). The pigmented cell microvilli, which are 5–7 μm long, extend between the photoreceptors and, with electron microscopy, are seen to contain membranous lamellae similar to those in the rod outer segments; these appear to disintegrate as they pass deeper into the pigmented cells. In addition to phagocytosis, the pigmented epithelial cells provide structural and metabolic support for the rods and cones and also absorb light, thus preventing back reflection.

Retinal detachment

The specialised photoreceptor cells are normally closely attached to the retinal pigment epithelium so that the pigment epithelium can maintain a vital support function. This junction can be the site of separation of the retinal layers in the condition of ***retinal detachment***. Symptoms include loss of vision corresponding to the detached part of the retina described as 'like a dark curtain' in the visual field. If the retina can be surgically re-attached then vision can be restored.

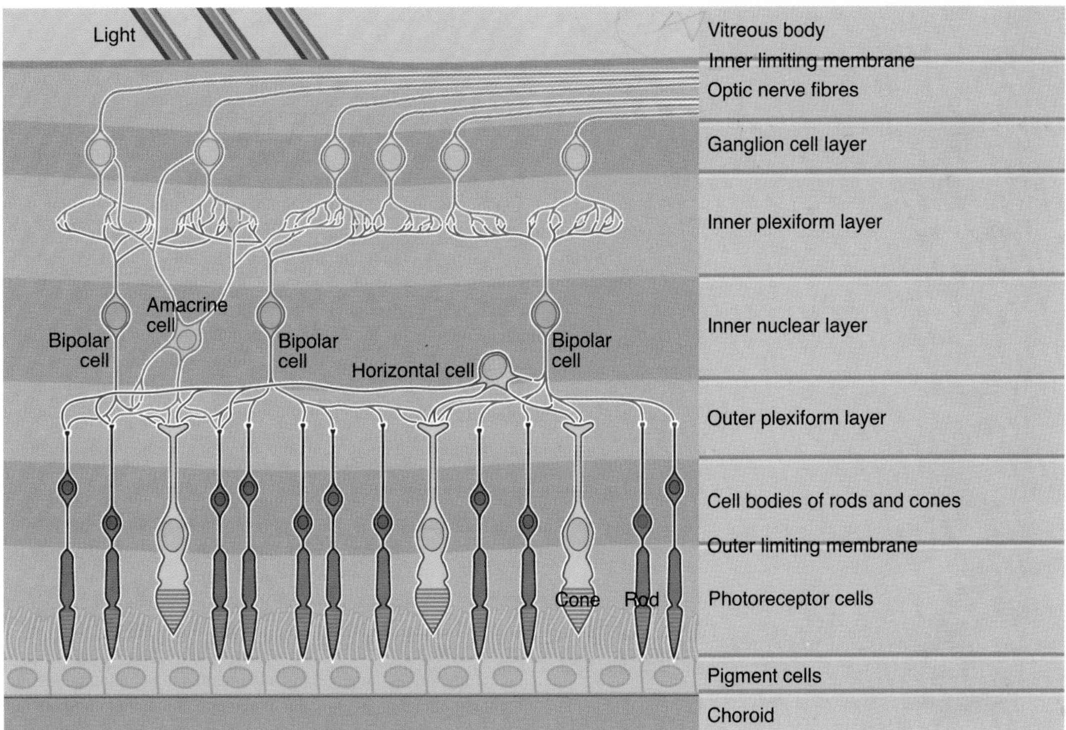

Fig. 21.8 Neuronal interconnections in the retina

This diagram demonstrates the basic pattern of neuronal interconnections between the photoreceptor cells and the afferent neurones of the optic tract. The interneurones consist of three basic cell types, ***bipolar cells***, ***horizontal cells*** and ***amacrine cells***, their cell bodies all being located in the inner nuclear layer (along with those of the supporting Muller cells).

Bipolar cells, the most numerous of the integrating neurones, in general make direct connections between one or more photoreceptors and one or more optic tract neurones as well as with horizontal and amacrine cells. Horizontal cells have several short processes and one long process, the terminal branches of each making lateral connections between adjacent and more distant rods and cones in the outer plexiform layer. Horizontal cells also synapse with the dendrites of bipolar cells. The amacrine cells have numerous dendrites which make connections with bipolar and optic tract neurones in the inner plexiform layer, as well as making occasional feedback connections with photoreceptors in the outer plexiform layer.

As seen in Fig. 21.7(b) opposite, the axons of the rod photoreceptors terminate in spherical processes into which are invaginated their small number of synaptic connections. In contrast, the cone photoreceptors have a flattened pedicle which accommodates hundreds of intercellular contacts.

In all, there are more than 100 million rods and 6 million cones. The cones are particularly dense in the macula and the immediately surrounding area and, in the fovea itself, the photoreceptors are almost exclusively cones. The density of both rods and cones diminishes towards the retinal periphery. The foveal cones have an almost one-to-one relationship with optic tract neurones giving maximal visual discrimination. There are only about 1 million optic tract neurones and the more peripheral the photoreceptors, the greater the number of photoreceptors synapsing with each optic tract neurone. This is consistent with the main function of the more peripheral receptors (predominantly rods), which is for determination of light and dark rather than fine two-point discrimination.

Retinal degenerations

The retina is affected by several diseases classed as retinal degenerations. These lead to loss of specialised photoreceptor cells and progressive loss of visual acuity, often causing total blindness.

Macular degeneration is a condition mainly seen in people over the age of sixty. It is one of the commonest causes of loss of visual acuity in elderly. Abnormal masses of lipid-rich material accumulate in the choroid (***drusen***) leading to failure of support for photoreceptor cells. The macula is the retinal region serving fine detailed colour vision in the centre of the visual field (Fig. 21.9). Loss of receptor cells in this area leads to severe visual impairment but peripheral vision served by rods is preserved.

Retinitis pigmentosa is the name given to a family of inherited degenerative diseases of the retina. There are several genetic forms of disease which all cause death of specialised retinal elements. In the commonest forms there is preferential degeneration of rod cells leading to gradual loss of peripheral vision, sometimes described as 'tunnel vision' as the macula, composed of cones, is affected last.

B Bruch's membrane **M** outer limiting membrane **P** pigment epithelial cells

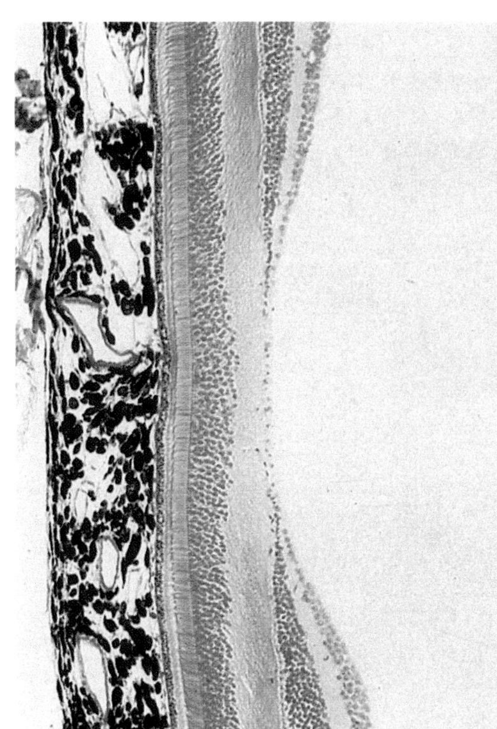

Fig. 21.9 Fovea
Masson's trichrome ×320

The fovea is a conical depression in the retina corresponding to the point where the visual axis of the cornea and lens meets the retina and lying about 4 mm lateral and slightly inferior to the exit of the optic nerve fibres at the optic disc. Consequently, the fovea is the area subject to the least refractory distortion. To complement this, the foveal retina is modified to obtain the maximum photoreceptor sensitivity and is thus the area of the retina with the greatest visual discrimination; however, its function is poor in conditions of low light intensity. Surrounding the fovea is an ovoid yellow area about 1 mm wide called the ***macula lutea***.

As seen in this micrograph, at the fovea the inner layers of the retina are flattened laterally so as to present the least barrier to light reaching the photoreceptors. Retinal blood vessels are absent at the fovea, as can be readily seen with the ophthalmoscope, and the brownish colour of the choroidal melanin shows through the much attenuated retina. At the fovea, the photoreceptors are almost exclusively cones which are elongated and closely packed (approximately 100 000 cones are contained in the fovea). Neuronal interconnections in the bipolar cell layer provide for a one-to-one ratio of these cones to optic nerve fibres which means that each foveal photoreceptor is individually represented at the visual cortex.

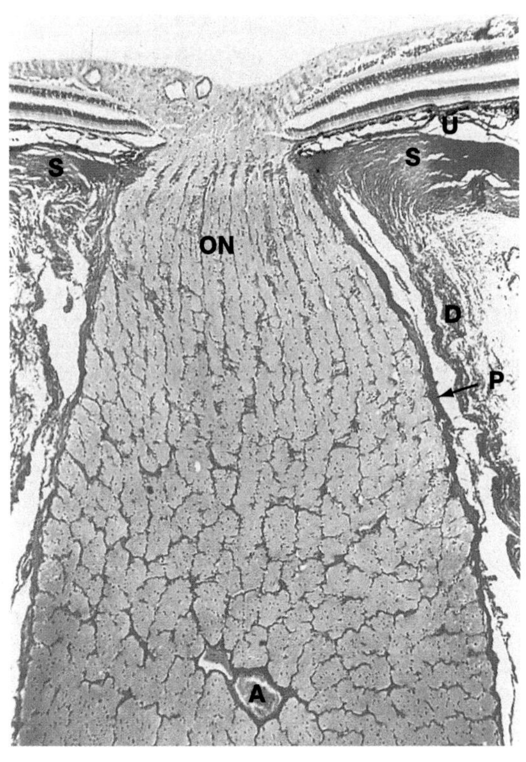

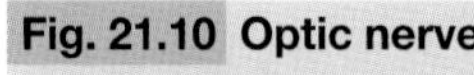

Fig. 21.10 Optic nerve
H & E ×30

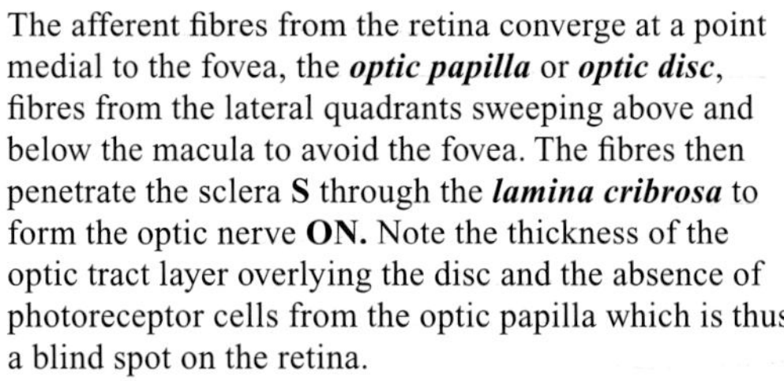

The afferent fibres from the retina converge at a point medial to the fovea, the ***optic papilla*** or ***optic disc***, fibres from the lateral quadrants sweeping above and below the macula to avoid the fovea. The fibres then penetrate the sclera **S** through the ***lamina cribrosa*** to form the optic nerve **ON.** Note the thickness of the optic tract layer overlying the disc and the absence of photoreceptor cells from the optic papilla which is thus a blind spot on the retina.

In their course across the retina, the afferent fibres are not myelinated as this would obstruct light passing to the photoreceptors. Myelination commences at the optic disc which imparts the white colour seen with the ophthalmoscope.

The optic nerve and retina develop embryologically as an outgrowth of the primitive forebrain, and thus the optic nerve is invested by meninges. The ***dura mater*** **D** becomes continuous with its developmental equivalent, the sclera, while the ***pia-arachnoid*** **P** continues into the eye as the uveal tract **U**.

The main blood supply of the retina is provided by the ***central artery of the retina*** **A**, a branch of the ophthalmic artery. This divides at the optic disc into four branches supplying the quadrants of the retina. These vessels course within the optic nerve fibre layer breaking up into a rich capillary network which drains back into a venous system closely following the course of the arterial supply. The vessels are confined to the optic nerve fibre layer, and more superficial layers are dependent on diffusion, the most peripheral retinal layers being supplied likewise from the choroid.

A central artery of the retina **C** ciliary process **CB** ciliary body **CS** canal of Schlemm
D dura mater **E** epithelium **I** iris **ICA** iridocorneal angle **L** lens **M** smooth muscle
ON optic nerve **P** pia-arachnoid **PC** posterior chamber **S** sclera **SL** suspensory ligaments
U uvea

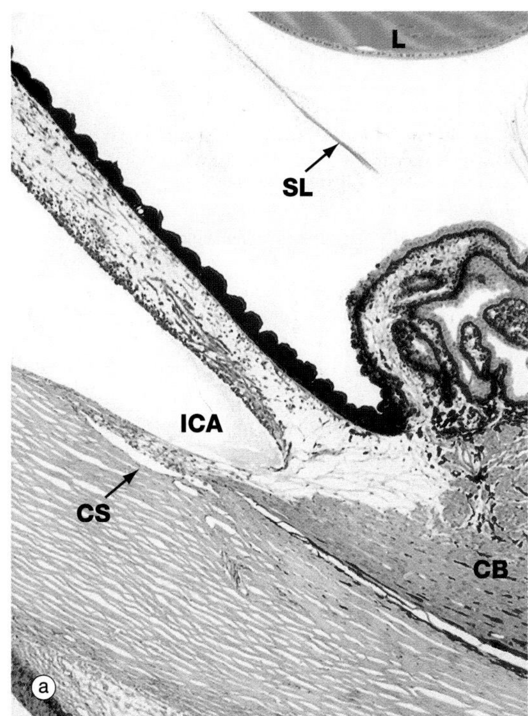

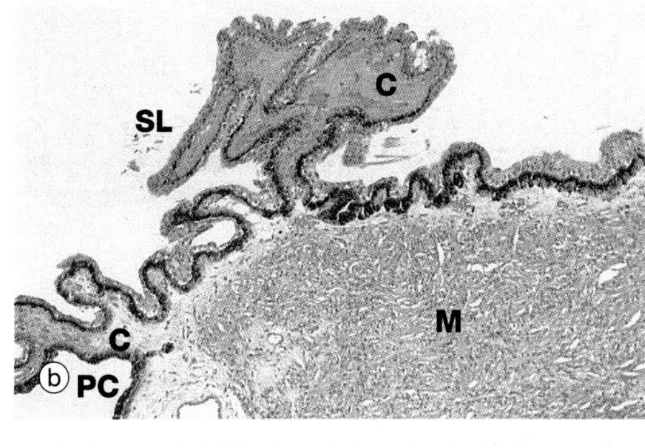

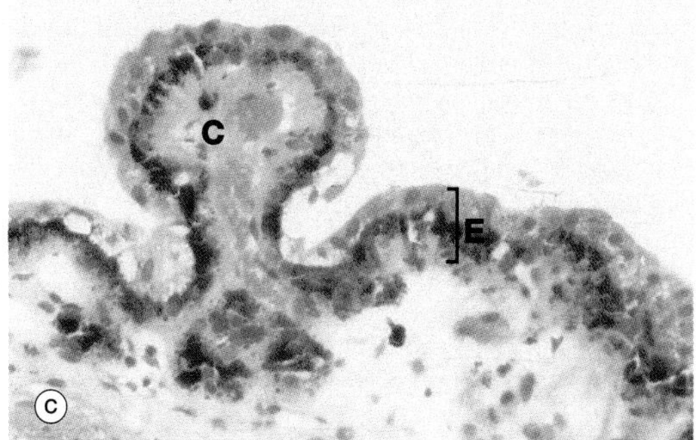

Fig. 21.11 Ciliary body
(a) H & E ×30 (b) H & E ×50 (c) H & E ×200

The ciliary body is a circumferential structure which bulges into the eye between the ora serrata and the limbus (see Fig. 21.3). As seen in micrograph (a), the ciliary body **CB** represents the forward continuation of the choroid layer of the uveal tract of the posterior five-sixths of the wall of the eye and, like it, is highly vascular and contains a considerable amount of dark-staining melanin pigment. Anteriorly, it is continuous with the third component of the uveal tract, the iris **I**, passing in front of the lens **L**.

As seen in micrograph (c), the ciliary body is lined with a double layer of cuboidal epithelium **E**. The deep layer is highly pigmented and represents a forward continuation of the pigmented epithelial layer of the retina, while the surface layer, which is not pigmented, is a non-photosensitive forward extension of the receptor layer of the retina.

The ciliary body is attached to the coronal equator of the lens by the ***suspensory ligaments*** **SL** which consist of extremely fine strands composed of the protein fibrillin. Tension in the suspensory ligament tends to flatten the lens which, in the relaxed state, assumes a more globular shape. The bulk of the ciliary body consists of smooth muscle **M** arranged in such a manner that, when it contracts, tension upon the suspensory ligament is reduced, thus permitting the lens to assume a more convex shape. This mechanism permits fine focusing of images already roughly focused upon the retina by the cornea. The ciliary muscle is innervated by parasympathetic nerve fibres.

From that part of the ciliary body exposed to the angle of the posterior chamber **PC**, there project a number of branching epithelial folds called ***ciliary processes*** **C** with a supporting tissue core rich in fenestrated capillaries. The ciliary processes are responsible for the continuous production of aqueous humor which then circulates into the anterior chamber via the pupil. Aqueous humor is continuously reabsorbed into the ***canal of Schlemm*** **CS** seen at the base of the irido-corneal angle of the anterior chamber **ICA** in micrograph (a).

Aqueous humor is a clear, watery fluid somewhat similar in composition to CSF and hypotonic with respect to plasma. The production of aqueous humor is an active process mediated by the two epithelial layers lining the ciliary processes. Balanced rates of secretion and reabsorption of aqueous humor result in the maintenance of a constant intraocular pressure of about 15 mm of mercury which stabilises the lens and cornea. The flow of aqueous humor also provides for a continuous exchange of metabolites with the cells of the avascular cornea and lens.

Glaucoma

If the drainage of aqueous humor is obstructed then the ciliary body continues to secrete, leading to a sustained increase in the intraocular pressure termed ***glaucoma***. If untreated this causes damage to the neural retina and can cause blindness.

- Some forms of glaucoma are inherited and are associated with abnormal filtration of aqueous at the canal of Schlemm.
- Any disease which causes inflammation or scarring of the iridocorneal angle can leads to glaucoma by blocking the canal of Schlemm.
- Proliferation of blood vessels in the iris root, usually as a response to poor blood supply to the retina, as may happen in patients with diabetes, may block aqueous drainage.

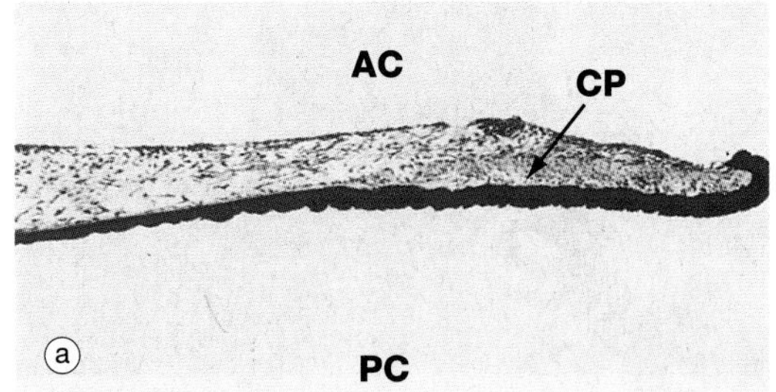

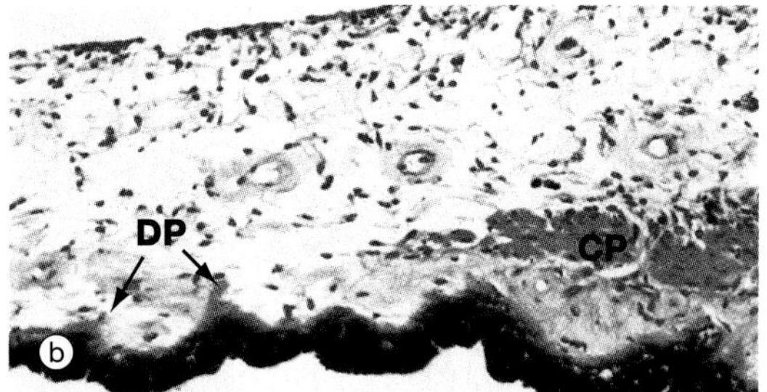

Fig. 21.12 Iris
(a) H & E ×20 (b) H & E ×100

The iris is the most anterior part of the uveal layer of the eye. It arises from the ciliary body and forms a diaphragm in front of the lens, so dividing the anterior compartment of the eye into posterior **PC** and anterior chambers **AC** which communicate via the pupil. The pupillary edge of the iris rests on the anterior surface of the lens in life.

The main mass of the iris consists of loose, highly vascular tissue which is pigmented due to the presence of numerous melanocytes scattered in the stroma. The anterior surface of the iris is irregular and consists of a discontinuous layer of fibroblasts and melanocytes; in the fetus the surface is lined by endothelial cells but these disappear during early childhood. In contrast, the posterior surface is relatively smooth and is lined by epithelium which is derived embryologically as a continuation of the two layers which line the surface of the ciliary body. The surface layer, non-pigmented in the ciliary body, becomes heavily pigmented in the iris such that the individual cells are completely obscured. The deep layer, pigmented in the ciliary body, is transformed in the iris into lightly pigmented myoepithelial cells which constitute the radially orientated ***dilator pupillae muscle*** **DP** of the iris. Even at high magnification (b), these myoepithelial cells are difficult to distinguish.

The constrictor muscle of the pupil (***constrictor pupillae***) **CP** consists of a band of circumferentially oriented smooth muscle fibres situated in the stroma near to the free edge of the iris. Like the smooth muscle of the ciliary body, the constrictor pupillae is innervated by the parasympathetic nervous system, whereas the myoepithelial cells of the dilator pupillae are innervated by the sympathetic nervous system.

The colour of the iris depends on the amount of pigment in the stroma, the amount of pigment in the posterior epithelial layer being relatively constant between individuals. Blue eyes contain little pigment whereas brown eyes have much stromal pigment.

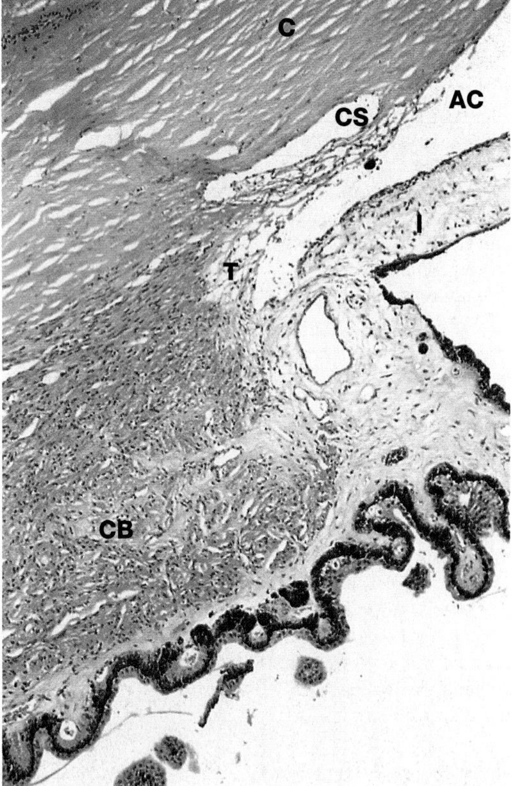

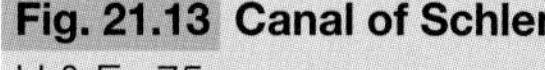
Fig. 21.13 Canal of Schlemm
H & E ×75

The ***canal of Schlemm*** **CS** is a circumferential canal lined by endothelium which is situated in the inner aspect of the corneal margin **C** immediately adjacent to the angle of the anterior chamber **AC**. At the angle of the anterior chamber there is a meshwork of fine collagenous trabeculae **T** lined by endothelium; aqueous humor percolates through the spaces between the trabeculae before reaching the canal of Schlemm. There is no direct communication between the trabecular spaces and the canal of Schlemm, and thus reabsorption of aqueous humor involves passage across two layers of endothelium and intervening supporting tissue. The canal of Schlemm drains via minute channels through the sclera into the episcleral venous system, a pressure gradient being maintained to prevent reflux of blood. Note the close relationship between the root of the iris **I** and the canal of Schlemm. The smooth muscle of the ciliary body **CB** is easily seen in this micrograph.

A lens epithelium **AC** anterior chamber **C** cornea **CA** lens capsule **CB** ciliary body
CP constrictor pupillae **CPR** ciliary process **CS** canal of Schlemm **DP** dilator pupillae
E lens equator **I** iris **J** junction between anterior and posterior lens cells
N nuclei of peripheral lens fibres **PC** posterior chamber **R** retina **T** trabeculae

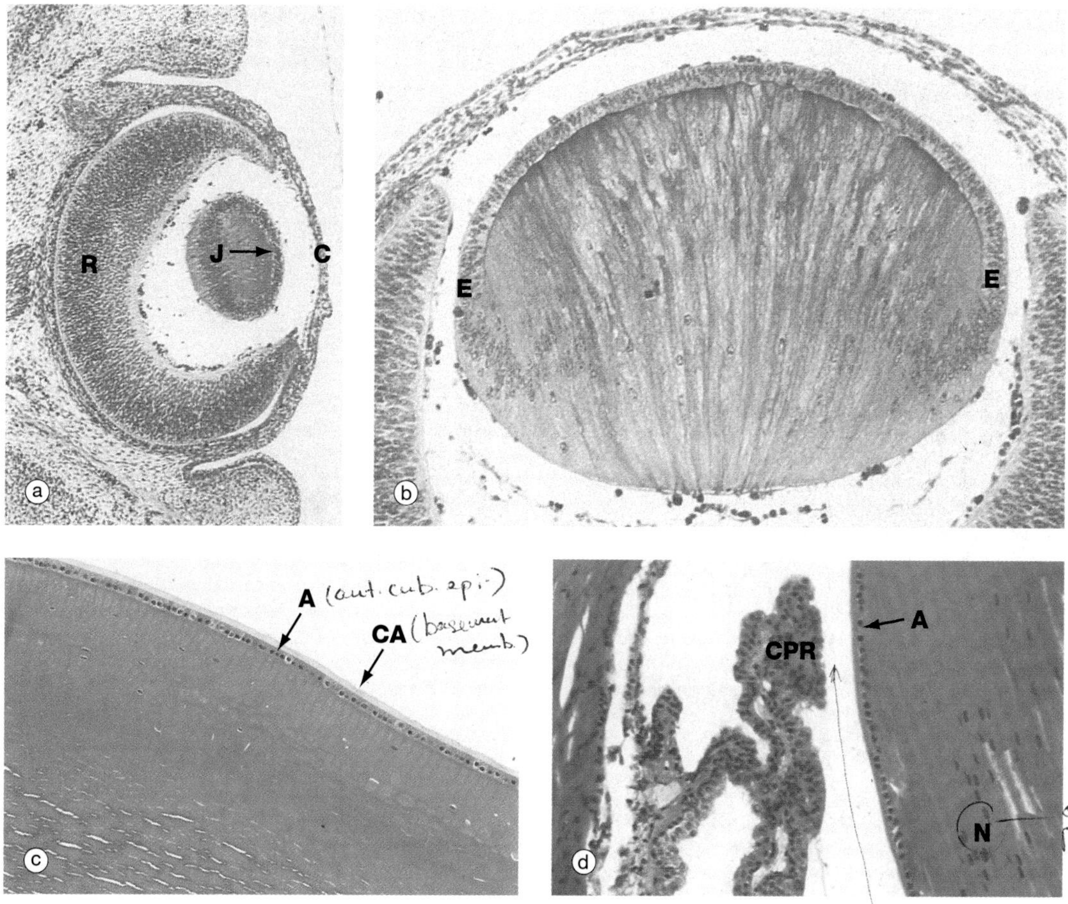

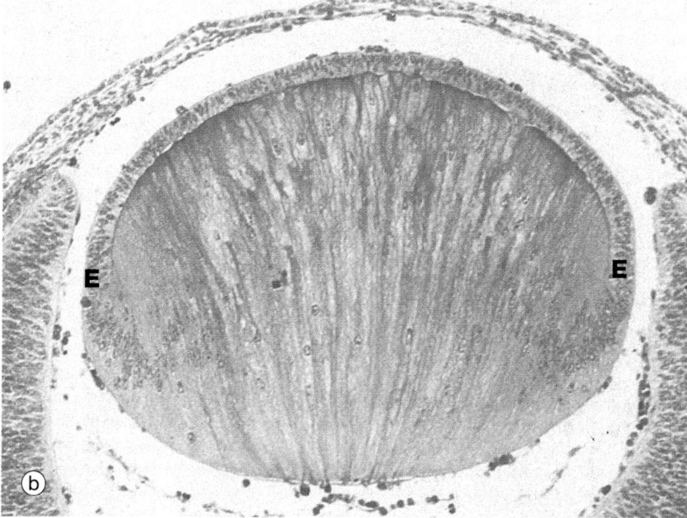

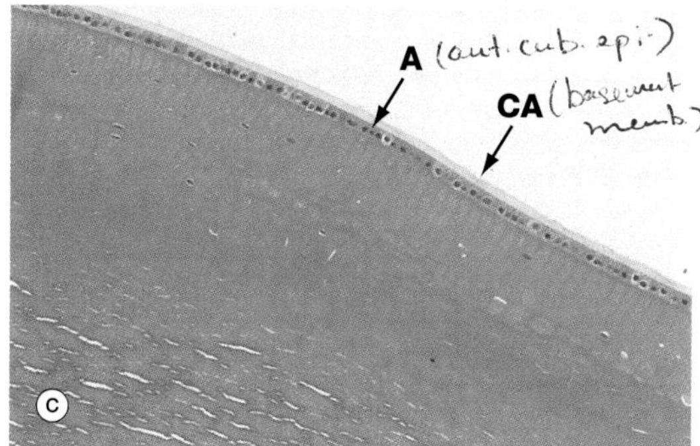

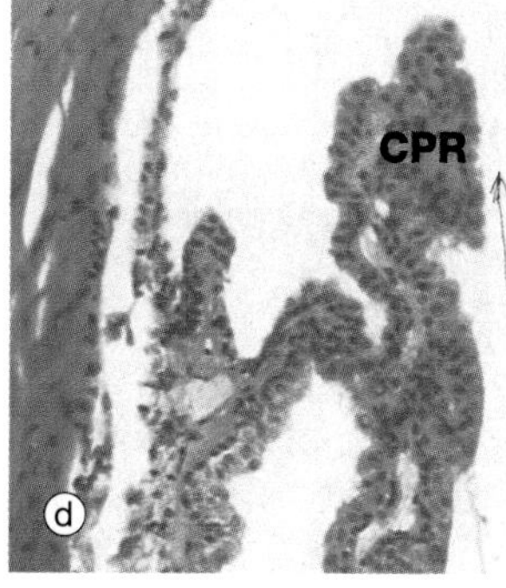

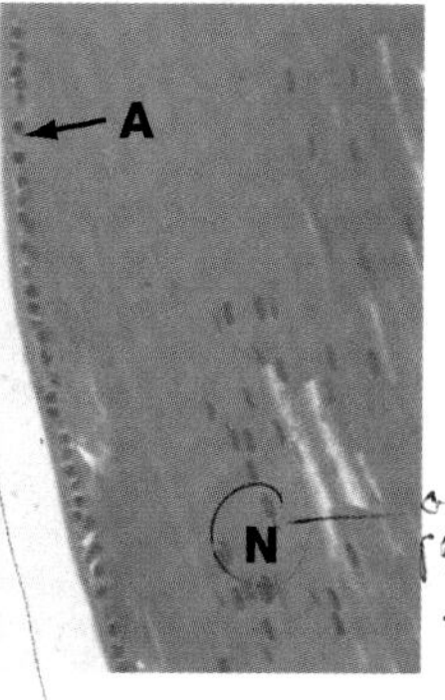

Fig. 21.14 The lens and its development
(a) H & E ×64 (b) H & E ×150 (c) H & E ×100 (d) H & E ×50

The lens is an elastic biconvex structure which, although transparent and apparently amorphous, is almost entirely composed of living cells. The lens cells are highly modified epithelial cells derived embryologically from ectoderm which forms a depression, the lens pit, overlying the embryonic optic vesicle.

With further development, the lens pit becomes deeper, its margins fusing to form the lens vesicle which becomes detached from the surface and sinks deeper to become enveloped by the growing optic vesicle; at this stage the lens vesicle merely consists of a single layer of epithelial cells.

The posterior cells of the lens vesicle now become greatly elongated anteroposteriorly, filling the central cavity of the vesicle. This stage of development is shown in micrograph (a), showing the junction **J** between posterior and anterior cells of the former lens vesicle. Note the developing cornea **C** and retina **R**. The lens cells in the central anteroposterior axis then undergo maturation, as seen in micrograph (b), losing their nuclei to become known as ***lens fibres***. Proliferation of the cells at the lens equator **E** adds further fibres to the central mass, the growth process continuing at a slow rate even into old age.

When fully developed, the lens substance consists of 2000–3000 anucleate fibres, each stretching between anterior and posterior poles of the lens. The fibres have the shape of extremely elongated six-sided prisms, the more peripheral fibres curving to follow the anteroposterior surface contour of the lens. The lens fibres are packed with proteins called ***crystallins*** and the cell membranes of adjacent fibres are fused, leaving little intervening extracellular substance.

The whole lens is enveloped by a thick epithelial basement membrane forming the ***lens capsule*** which is connected via the suspensory ligament to the ciliary body. The anterior lens surface is covered by a single layer of cuboidal cells which retain their nuclei, this layer merging with the residual proliferative cells at the equatorial margin of the lens. This cell layer lies deep to the capsule and is absent posteriorly.

Micrograph (c) shows part of the mature lens including the anterior cuboidal epithelium **A** and lens capsule **CA**. The lens substance is particularly prone to artefactual distortion during histological preparation. Micrograph (d) shows the equatorial region of the lens and nearby ciliary processes **CPR**. Note the anterior epithelial layer **A** and nuclei **N** in the more recently formed peripheral fibres.

Cataracts

The normal lens is translucent and elastic. If there is damage to either the lens fibres or if the normally translucent crystallin proteins aggregate then the lens becomes opaque and light is either diffused or blocked. The lens opacity is called a ***cataract***. Cataracts can occur due to ageing, trauma to the lens, inflammatory diseases within the eye or in response to some metabolic diseases.

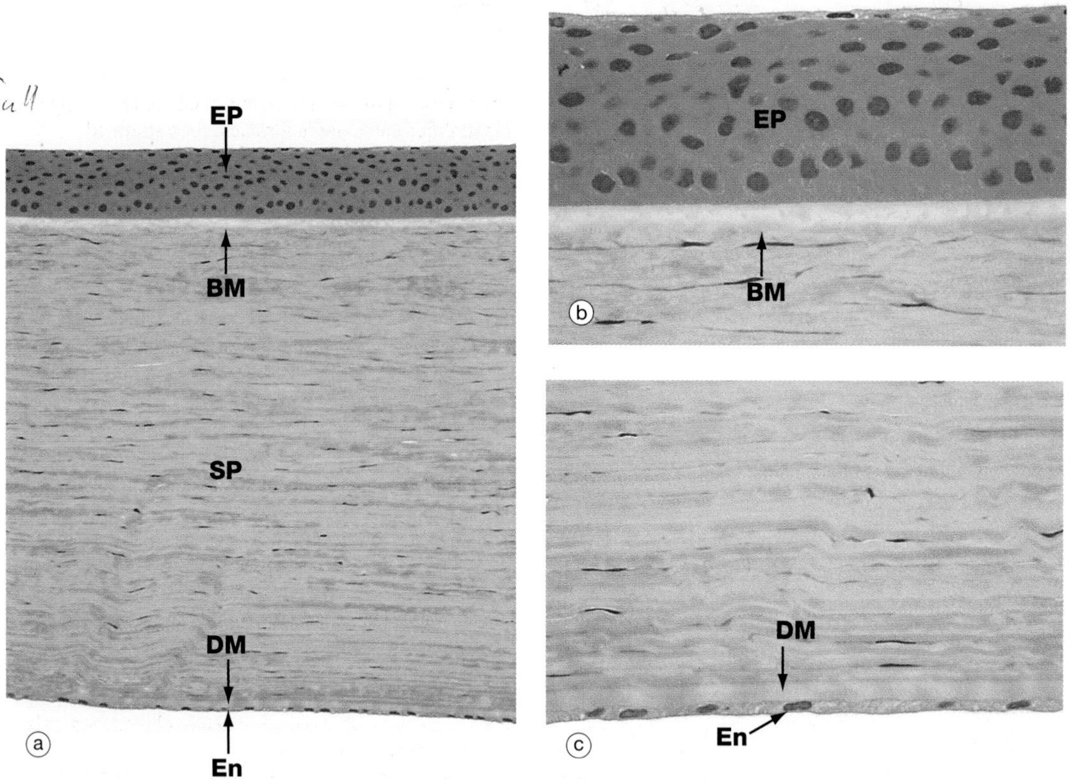

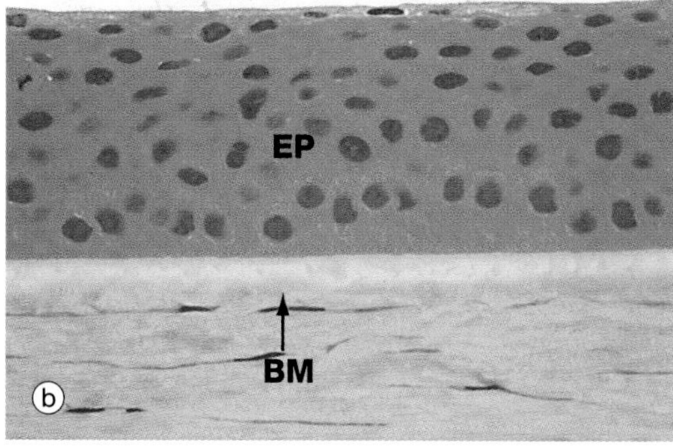

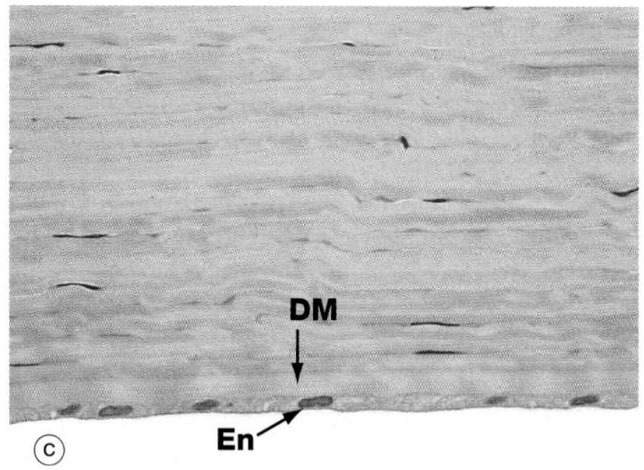

Fig. 21.15 Cornea
(a) H & E ×100 (b) H & E ×200 (c) H & E ×200

The cornea is the thick transparent portion of the corneo-scleral layer enclosing the anterior one-sixth of the eye. The fixed convexity of the external surface provides the principal mechanism for focusing images upon the retina. Micrograph (a) shows the full thickness of the cornea, while micrographs (b) and (c) show the superficial and deep aspects at higher magnification.

The cornea is an avascular structure consisting of five layers. The outer surface is lined by stratified non-keratinised squamous epithelium **EP** about six cells thick. This epithelium rests on a thin basal lamina supported by a thick specialised layer of corneal stroma known as ***Bowman's membrane*** **BM** which is particularly prominent in humans. The bulk of the cornea, the ***substantia propria*** or ***stroma*** **SP**, consists of a highly regular form of dense collagenous tissue forming thin lamellae. Fibroblasts with elongated nuclei and barely visible cytoplasm termed ***keratocytes*** are scattered in the ground substance between the lamellae. The inner surface of the cornea is lined by a layer of flattened endothelial cells **En** which are supported by a very thick basement membrane known as ***Descemet's membrane*** **DM**. The corneal endothelium is highly active in pumping fluid from the substantia propria, preventing excessive hydration which would result in the cornea becoming opaque.

The cornea is sustained by diffusion of metabolites from the aqueous humor and the blood vessels of the limbus; some oxygen is derived directly from the external environment.

There is a rich innervation by free nerve endings, making the cornea very pain sensitive.

Corneal disease

The cornea plays a vital role in refracting light into the eye.

Although the endothelial cell layer looks inconspicuous it is highly active in pumping fluid out of the corneal stroma. If the endothelial cell layer is damaged, or cell numbers are reduced as happens with disease or age, then this fluid pumping function is impaired. Clinically there is blurring of vision as the corneal stroma becomes waterlogged. The corneal epithelium develops areas of separation from Bowman's membrane forming small bullae which are very painful and can lead to ulceration of the surface epithelium.

Diseases which cause inflammation of the cornea, for example viral infection by herpes zoster, can lead to loss of Bowman's membrane and replacement of the normal highly-ordered collagen of the corneal stroma by haphazardly arranged collagenous scar tissue. Corneal scars are not transparent and produce an opacity that interferes with light transmission, so causing poor visual acuity.

If the curvature of the cornea becomes abnormal then there may be loss of visual acuity because light is not focused correctly. An unusual condition called ***keratoconus*** can develop where the cornea develops a conical profile due to remodeling of the corneal collagen.

A damaged cornea may be replaced by a transplant.

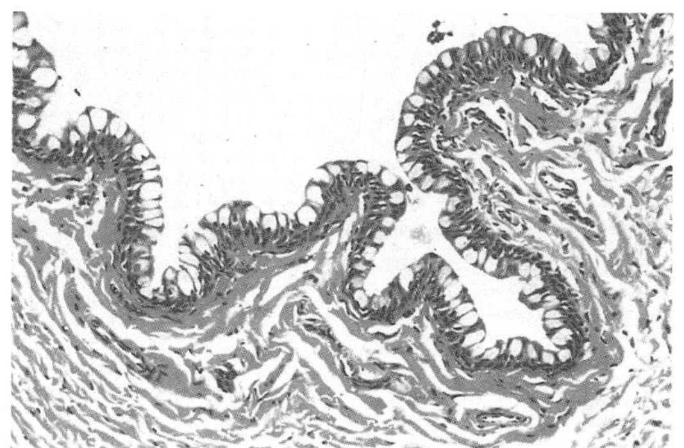

Fig. 21.16 Conjunctiva
H & E ×128

The conjunctiva is the epithelium which covers the exposed part of the sclera and inner surface of the eyelids. It is stratified columnar in form and for a stratified epithelium is unusual in that it contains goblet cells in the surface layers. Melanocytes are found in the basal layer. The conjunctival mucous secretions contribute to the protective layer on the exposed surface of the eye, and allow the eyelids to move freely over the eye.

Beneath the conjunctival epithelium is loose vascular supporting tissue.

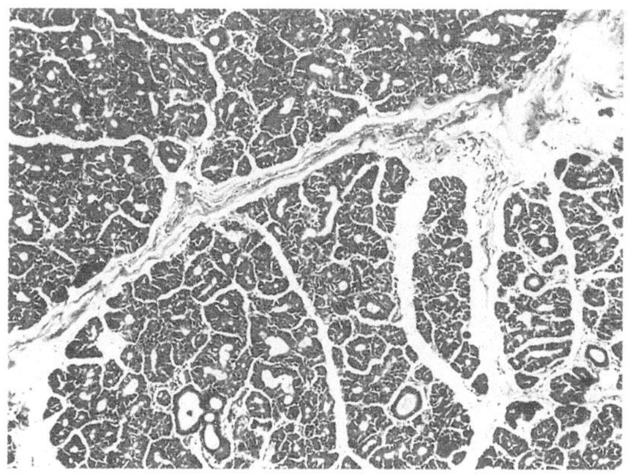

Fig. 21.17 Lacrimal gland
H & E ×150

The lacrimal gland is responsible for the secretion of tears, a watery fluid containing the antibacterial enzyme lysozyme and electrolytes of similar concentration to plasma.

Histologically, the lacrimal glands are similar to the salivary glands in the lobular structure and compound tubulo-acinar form of the secretory units. The secretory cells have the typical appearance of serous (protein-secreting) cells with basally located nuclei and strongly stained granular cytoplasm.

Each gland drains via a dozen or more small ducts into the superior fornix. Tears drain to the inner aspect of the eye and then into the nasal cavity via the nasolacrimal duct.

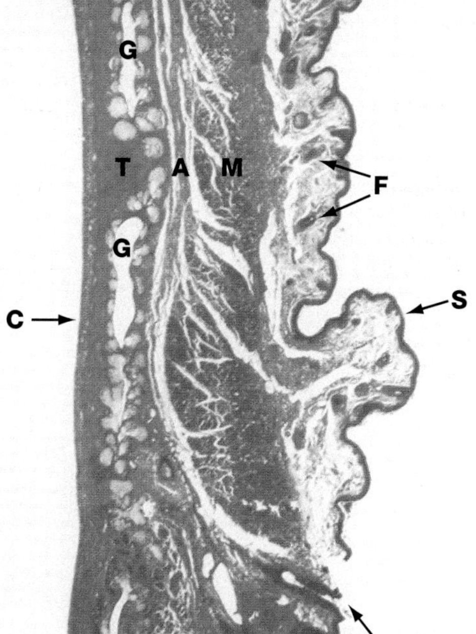

Fig. 21.18 Eyelid
H & E ×16

Each eyelid consists of a dense fibroelastic plate, the ***tarsus*** or ***tarsal plate*** **T**, covered externally by thin, highly folded skin **S** and on the internal aspect by smooth conjunctiva **C**. The skin contains scattered fine hair follicles **F** and the underlying supporting tissue is extremely loose and devoid of fat.

Skeletal muscle **M** of orbicularis oculi (and levator palpebrae in the upper eyelid) lies immediately superficial to the tarsal plate and is separated from it by a layer of supporting tissue **A** which, in the upper lid, represents a forward continuation of the sub-aponeurotic layer of the scalp. The clinical importance of this is that blood or inflammatory exudates collecting above the scalp aponeurosis may track forward into the superficial planes of the eyelid; being extremely lax, this area may become markedly swollen. This supporting tissue layer also contains the sensory nerves of the eyelid.

Within the tarsal plate lie some 12–30 ***tarsal*** (***Meibomian***) ***glands*** **G** oriented vertically and opening at the free margin of the eyelid via minute foramina. These glands are modified sebaceous glands each consisting of a long central duct into which open numerous sebaceous acini. Associated with the eyelashes **E** are sebaceous glands known as the ***glands of Zeis*** and modified apocrine sweat glands known as the ***glands of Moll***. Together, the glands of the eyelid produce an oily layer which is thought to cover the tear layer, thereby preventing evaporation of the tears.

A support tissue **BM** Bowman's membrane **C** conjunctiva **DM** Descemet's membrane
E eyelash **En** corneal endothelium **EP** corneal epithelium **F** hair follicle **G** Meibomian gland
M muscle **S** skin **SP** substantia propria of cornea **T** tarsal plate

The ear

The ear or vestibulo-cochlear apparatus has the dual sensory function of maintenance of equilibrium and hearing (stato-acoustic system).

Structurally the system may be divided into three parts, the ***external ear***, the ***middle ear*** and the ***internal ear***. The specific sensory receptors for both movement and sound are situated in a membranous structure located in the internal ear, while the external and middle ear are concerned with reception, transmission and amplification of incoming sound waves.

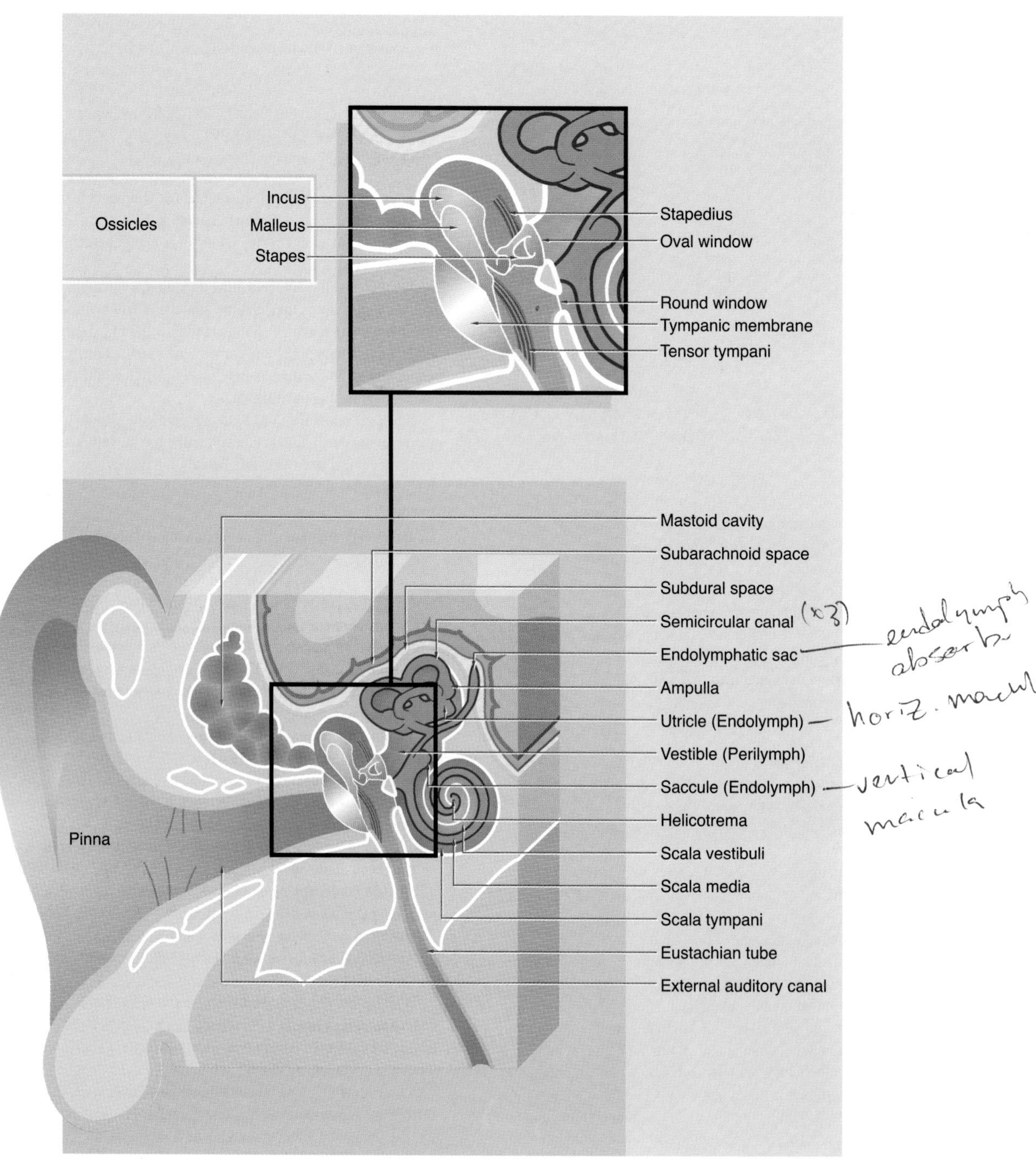

Fig. 21.19 The ear *(illustration opposite)*

The main structural elements of the vestibulo-cochlear apparatus are illustrated in this diagram.

External ear

The external ear is responsible for reception of sound waves which are funnelled onto the ear drum (***tympanic membrane***). It consists of the ***auricle*** (***pinna***), a modified cone-shaped structure composed of elastic cartilage covered by skin, which converges onto the ***external auditory meatus*** (***canal***). Elastic cartilage also forms the wall of the outer third of the canal while the inner two-thirds of the canal lie in the petrous part of the temporal bone. The canal is lined by hairy skin containing sebaceous glands and modified apocrine glands which secrete a waxy material called ***cerumen***.

Middle ear

The middle ear is an air-filled cavity, the ***tympanic cavity***, located in the petrous temporal bone and is separated from the external auditory canal by the tympanic membrane. Sound waves impinging on the tympanic membrane are converted into mechanical vibrations which are then amplified by a system of levers made up of three small bones called ***ossicles*** (the ***malleus***, ***incus*** and ***stapes***) and transmitted to the fluid-filled inner ear cavity. The ossicles articulate with one another via synovial joints and the malleus and incus pivot on tiny ligaments which are attached to the wall of the middle ear cavity. Small slips of muscle, the ***tensor tympani*** and ***stapedius***, pass to the midpoint of the tympanic membrane and stapes bone, respectively, and damp down excessive vibrations which might otherwise damage the delicate auditory apparatus. The middle ear cavity communicates anteriorly with the nasopharynx via the ***auditory*** (***Eustachian***) ***tube*** which permits equalisation of pressure changes with the external environment. Posteriorly, the middle ear cavity communicates with numerous interconnected air spaces which lighten the mass of the mastoid part of the temporal bone. The whole of the middle ear and mastoid cavities are lined by simple squamous or cuboidal epithelium.

Internal ear

The internal ear consists of an interconnected fluid-filled ***membranous labyrinth*** lying within a labyrinth of spaces of complementary shape in the temporal bone (the ***osseous labyrinth***). The membranous labyrinth is bound down to the walls of the osseous labyrinth in various places but in the main is separated from the bony walls by a fluid-filled space. The fluid within the membranous labyrinth is known as ***endolymph*** and the fluid in the surrounding perimembranous space is known as ***perilymph***. The perimembranous space is directly connected with the subarachnoid space and, like the latter, is crossed by delicate fibrous strands and lined by squamous epithelium; the perilymphatic fluid is thus similar in composition to CSF. In contrast, the membranous labyrinth is a closed system with a sac, the ***endolymphatic sac***, lying in the subdural space of the underlying brain. The membranous labyrinth is lined by a simple epithelium except in the endolymphatic sac where the cells are columnar with morphological features suggesting that this is the site of endolymph absorption.

The osseous labyrinth may be divided into three main areas:

- **The vestibule.** The central space of the osseous labyrinth is called the ***vestibule***; it gives rise to three ***semicircular canals*** posteriorly, and to the ***cochlea*** anteriorly. The vestibule contains two components of the membranous labyrinth, namely the ***utricle*** and the ***saccule***, which are connected by a short, Y-shaped duct from which arises the ***endolymphatic duct***. The walls of the utricle and saccule each contain a specialised area of sensory receptor cells known as a ***macula*** (see Fig. 21.27) from which axons pass into the ***vestibular nerve*** as part of sensory inputs to maintain equilibrium. Laterally, the vestibule is separated from the middle ear cavity by a thin bony plate containing two fenestrations or windows. The ***oval window*** is occluded by the base of the stapes bone and its surrounding ***annular ligament*** whereby vibrations are transmitted to the perilymph from the tympanic membrane via the ossicle chain. The ***round window*** is closed by a membrane similar to the tympanic membrane and it is thus sometimes described as the ***secondary tympanic membrane***. This membrane permits vibrations which have passed to sensory receptors for sound to be dissipated.
- **The semicircular canals.** Three semicircular canals arise from the posterior aspect of the vestibule, two being disposed in vertical planes at right angles to one another and the other in a near-horizontal plane. Within each semicircular canal is a semicircular membranous duct filled with endolymph and continuous at both ends with the utricle; near one end of each semicircular membranous duct is a dilated area called the ***ampulla***. In each ampulla, there is a ridge called the ***crista ampullaris*** (see Fig. 21.28) containing sensory receptors with axons converging on the vestibular nerve. Together with the receptors of the maculae of the utricle and saccule, these receptors help maintain balance and equilibrium.
- **The cochlea.** The cochlea occupies a conical, spiral-shaped space in the temporal bone extending from the anterior aspect of the vestibule. The membranous component of the cochlea arises from the saccule and spirals upwards with its blind end attached at the apex of the osseous space. The membranous canal is triangular in cross-section and attached to the bony walls of the cochlea in such a manner as to divide the osseous space into three spiral compartments (see Fig. 21.24). The middle compartment, the ***scala media***, contains endolymph, and the upper and lower compartments contain perilymph. At the base of the cochlea, the upper perilymph compartment is directly continuous with the perilymph of the vestibule and via this space, called the ***scala vestibuli***, vibrations pass through the perilymph towards the apex of the cochlea. At the apex, the scala vestibuli becomes continuous with the lower perilymphatic space of the cochlear spiral via a minute hole called the ***helicotrema***. This lower space terminates at the secondary tympanic membrane covering the round window and 'spent' vibrations are thus dissipated; the lower perilymphatic space is therefore known as the ***scala tympani***. The sensory receptors for sound are located in a spiral shaped structure known as the ***organ of Corti*** shown in detail in Fig. 21.25.

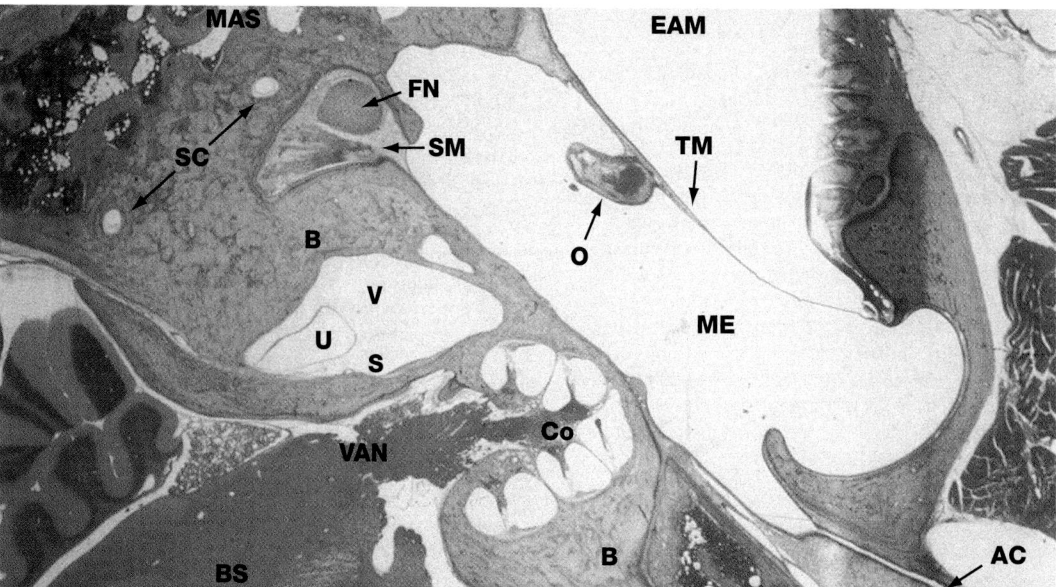

Fig. 21.20 The ear
H & E ×8

This micrograph shows a horizontal section through the vestibulo-cochlear apparatus which lies within the temporal bone **B**. The tympanic membrane **TM** can be seen stretched between the tympanic plate of the temporal bone anteriorly and the lateral part of the petrous temporal bone posteriorly, dividing the external auditory meatus **EAM** from the cavity of the middle ear **ME**. Part of one of the ossicles **O**, the handle of the malleus, can be seen attached to the inner aspect of the tympanic membrane. From the anterior aspect of the middle ear chamber, the auditory canal (Eustachian tube) **AC** passes forwards towards the nasopharynx; in the mastoid part of the temporal bone there are numerous irregular mastoid air spaces **MAS**.

Near the centre of the field is the vestibule of the inner ear **V** containing two delicate membranous structures, the utricle **U** and saccule **S** more anteriorly. Two of the semicircular canals **SC** can be identified deep in the posterior part of the petrous temporal bone. Immediately posterior to the middle ear cavity, the facial nerve **FN** is seen in transverse section as it passes inferiorly; just medial to it lies the stapedius muscle **SM**.

Anterior to the vestibule, the conical spiral of the cochlea **Co** has been cut in longitudinal section through its central bony axis. From the base of the cochlea, the vestibulo-auditory nerve **VAN** passes towards the brain stem **BS**, behind which the cerebellum is easily recognisable.

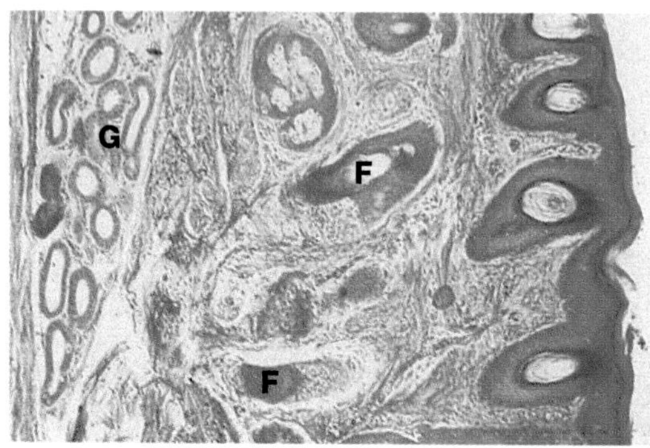

Fig. 21.21 External auditory meatus
H & E ×100

The external auditory meatus is the canal leading from the auricle to the tympanic membrane. The wall of the outer third is formed by elastic cartilage whereas the inner two thirds is formed by the temporal bone. The canal is lined by skin which is devoid of the usual dermal papillae and closely bound down to the underlying cartilage or bone by a dense collagenous dermis. The skin of the outer third (as shown here) has fine hairs and the dermis contains numerous coiled tubular ***ceruminous glands*** **G** which secrete wax (cerumen) and which represent specialised apocrine sweat glands. The ceruminous glands open directly onto the skin surface or into the sebaceous glands associated with hair follicles **F**. The meatal hairs provide protection from foreign bodies while the cerumen protects the skin of the external meatus from moisture and infection.

AC auditory canal **B** temporal bone **BS** brain stem **C** cuticular layer **Ca** cartilage
CB compact bone **Co** cochlea **EAM** external auditory meatus **F** hair follicles
Fi fibrous layer **FN** facial nerve **G** ceruminous gland **M** mucous layer **MAS** mastoid air spaces
ME middle ear **Mu** tensor tympani muscle **O** ossicle **S** saccule **SC** semicircular canals
SM stapedius muscle **TM** tympanic membrane **U** utricle **V** vestibule
VAN vestibuloauditory nerve

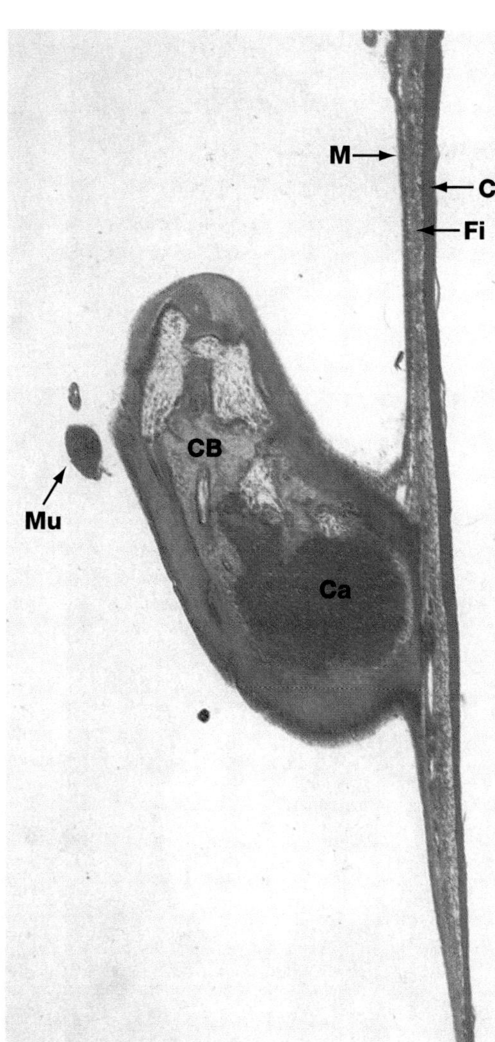

Fig. 21.22 Tympanic membrane and ossicle
H & E ×20

The tympanic membrane (ear drum) is a thin fibrous membrane separating the external auditory canal from the cavity of the middle ear. With the exception of a small triangular area superiorly, the ***pars flaccida***, the membrane is tense (***pars tensa***), being firmly attached to the surrounding bone by a fibrocartilaginous ring. The handle of the malleus is attached to the centre of the membrane, the chain of ossicles pulling the membrane slightly inwards.

The tympanic membrane is made up of three layers: an external ***cuticular layer***, an intermediate ***fibrous layer*** and an inner ***mucous layer***. The cuticular layer **C** consists of thin hairless skin, the epidermis being only about 10 cells thick and the basal layer being flat and devoid of the usual epidermal ridges. The thin dermis contains plump fibroblasts and a fine vascular network.

The intermediate fibrous layer **Fi** consists of an outer layer of fibres radiating from the centre of the membrane towards the circumference and an inner layer of fibres disposed circumferentially at the periphery. These fibres contain a large amount of type II and type III collagen, and a small amount of type I collagen representing a distinct composition especially adapted for the function of the tympanic membrane.

The inner mucous layer **M** represents a continuation of the modified respiratory-type mucous membrane lining the middle ear cavity, but in this situation it is merely a single layer of cuboidal cells devoid of cilia and goblet cells. The underlying lamina propria is thin with a blood supply separate from that of the dermis of the cuticular layer. A similar modified respiratory-type mucosa invests the ossicles, small muscles and nerves exposed to the middle ear cavity.

The ossicles consist of compact bone **CB** formed by endochondral ossification, which accounts for the cartilage **Ca** seen in this specimen from a kitten. Note also the tensor tympani muscle **Mu**.

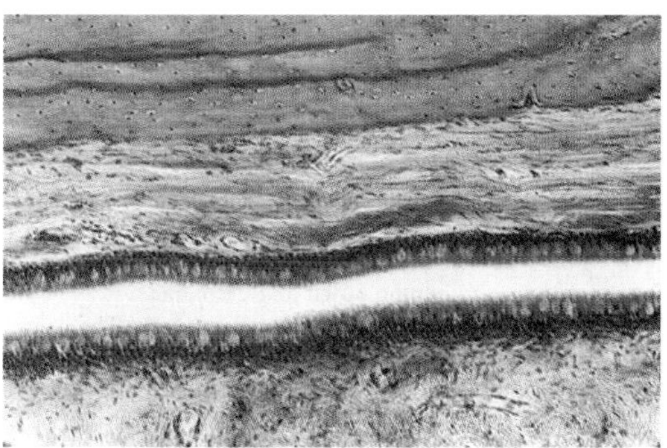

Fig. 21.23 Auditory (Eustachian) canal
H & E ×320

The auditory canal connects the cavity of the middle ear with the nasopharynx and allows for equalisation of air pressure between the middle ear and the external environment. From the middle ear, the tube first passes through bone, but towards the pharynx, the wall is supported on two sides by cartilage and on the remaining two sides by fibrous tissue.

The tube is lined by typical pseudostratified respiratory epithelium with numerous goblet cells particularly towards the pharyngeal end. The ***salpingo-pharyngeus***, ***tensor palati*** and ***levator veli palati*** muscles are connected to the fibrocartilaginous part of the tube causing it to dilate during swallowing.

Conductive deafness

Conductive deafness is caused by disorders that interfere with the conduction of sound through the outer and middle ear, affecting hearing before the sound reaches the cochlea.

- A foreign body, or wax, in the external canal is a common cause of impaired hearing.
- Inflammation affecting the middle ear can result in secretions building up within the middle ear cavity (***otitis media***) which usually resolves with appropriate therapy.
- ***Otosclerosis*** is an inherited disease where the ossicles fuse together, preventing conduction of sound. Surgery can re-establish conduction and restore hearing.

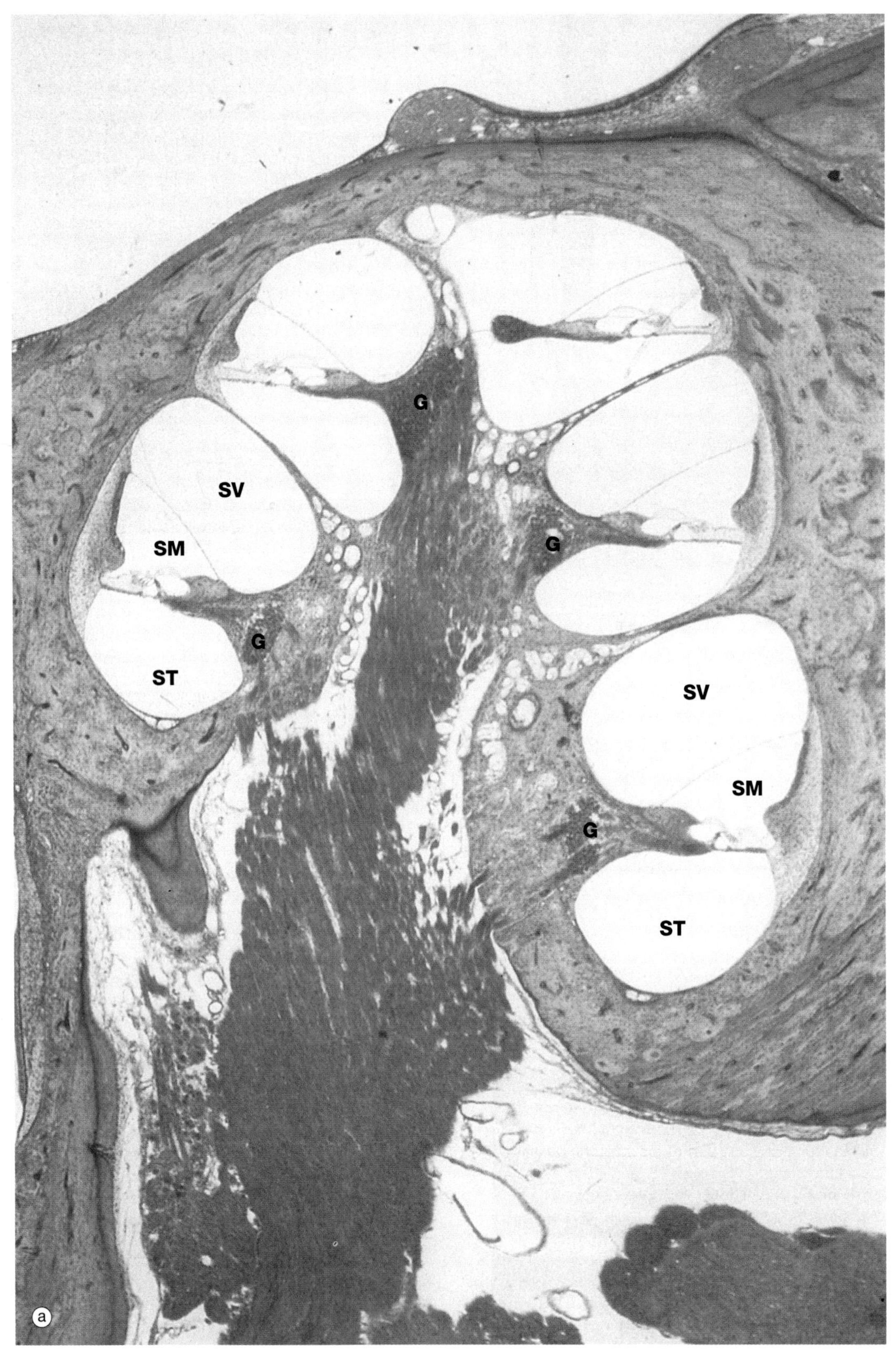

BM basilar membrane **G** spiral ganglion **O** osseous spiral lamina **N** nerve fibres
SL spiral limbus **SLig** spiral ligament **SM** scala media **ST** scala tympani **SV** scala vestibuli
SVasc stria vascularis **VM** vestibular membrane

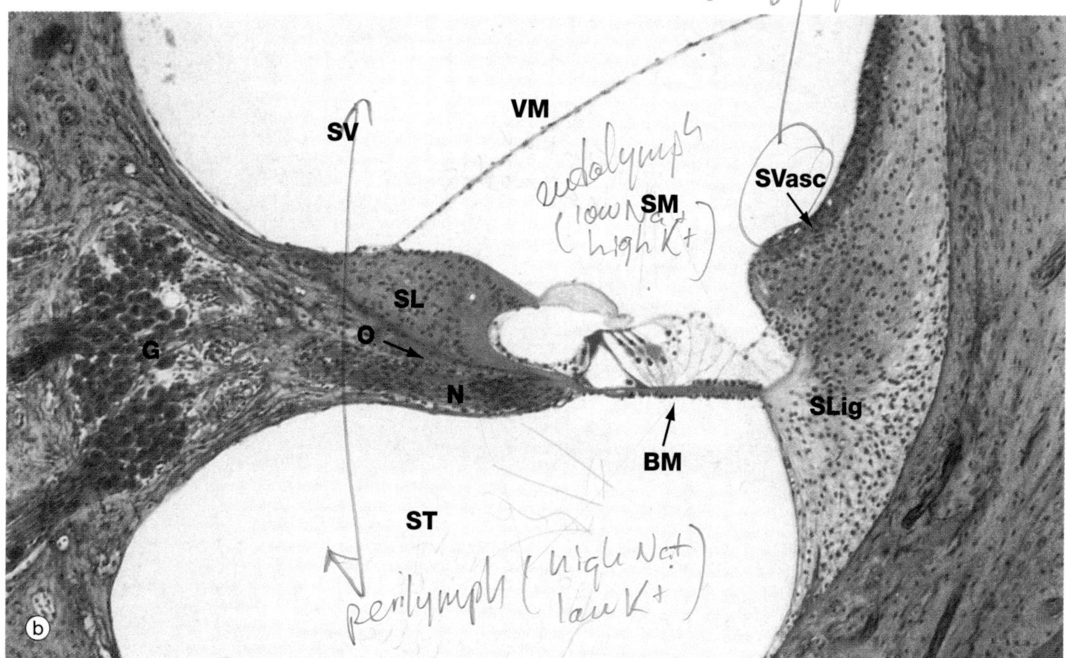

Fig. 21.24 Cochlea
(a) H & E ×20 *(opposite)* (b) H & E ×96

The cochlea is the component of the internal ear which contains the auditory sense organ. The conical spiral-shaped form of the cochlea can be visualised in micrograph (a) which shows a cochlea cut in a plane of section which includes its long bony axis. Note that the cavity in the petrous temporal bone is reminiscent of the space inside a conical snail shell. The cochlea has two-and-a-half full turns and in this section, therefore, five separate cross-sections of the cochlea can be seen, each turn of the spiral being separated from the next by a thin plate of bone. A corkscrew-like bony structure, the ***modiolus***, forms the central axis of the cochlea.

Each turn of the cochlear canal can be seen to be divided into three compartments, shown at higher magnification in micrograph (b). The central compartment, the ***scala media*** **SM**, is roughly triangular in cross-section, with the apex attached to a spicule of bone spiralling outwards from the modiolus and known as the ***osseous spiral lamina*** **O**. Above the free edge of the osseous spiral lamina is a thickened mass of tissue known as the ***spiral limbus*** **SL**. The base of the scala media is thickened and attached to the outer wall of the cochlea. The membrane making up the walls of the scala media represents that part of the membranous labyrinth extending up into the cochlea from the saccule, and the scala media is thus filled with endolymph.

Above the scala media is the ***scala vestibuli*** **SV** originating in the vestibule near the oval window and the base of the stapes; vibrations are conducted towards the apex of the cochlea in the perilymph of the scala vestibuli. Below the scala media is the perilymphatic space which spirals down from the apex to the secondary tympanic membrane, the ***scala tympani*** **ST**.

The membrane separating the scala media and the scala tympani, known as the ***basilar membrane*** **BM**, supports the ***organ of Corti*** which contains the auditory receptor cells; the organ of Corti is described in detail in Fig. 21.25. The cells of the organ of Corti are derived from the simple epithelium lining the membranous labyrinth which embryologically is of ectodermal origin. The basilar membrane is composed of fibrous tissue. Axially, it is attached to the osseous spiral lamina and laterally to the ***spiral ligament*** **SLig** which consists of a marked thickening of the endosteum of the lateral wall of the cochlear canal. The thickened outer wall of the scala media is highly vascular and lined by a stratified epithelium; this area, known as the ***stria vascularis*** **SVasc**, is responsible for maintaining the correct ionic composition of endolymph.

The membrane between the scala media and scala vestibuli, the ***vestibular (Reissner's) membrane*** **VM**, is composed of extremely delicate fibrous tissue lined by simple squamous epithelium on both sides. The scala vestibuli and scala tympani are lined by a simple unspecialised squamous epithelium of mesodermal origin.

In micrograph (b) bundles of afferent nerve fibres **N** can be seen arising from the base of the organ of Corti and converging towards the spiral ganglion **G** in the modiolus at the base of the spiral lamina. These ganglion cells represent the cell bodies of bipolar sensory neurones, and their proximal axons form the auditory component of the eighth cranial nerve (see Fig. 21.26).

Sensory-neural deafness

Sensory-neural deafness is caused by damage to the sensory receptors of the inner ear (the hair cells, organ of Corti) or the auditory nerve leading to the brain.

- Children may be born with sensory-neural deafness due to intrauterine infection or poor oxygen supply near birth. Cochlear implants can restore hearing.
- Exposure to noise can cause loss of hearing due to damage to sensory elements in the organ of Corti.
- Age-related loss of high frequency hearing has been called ***presbycusis***.

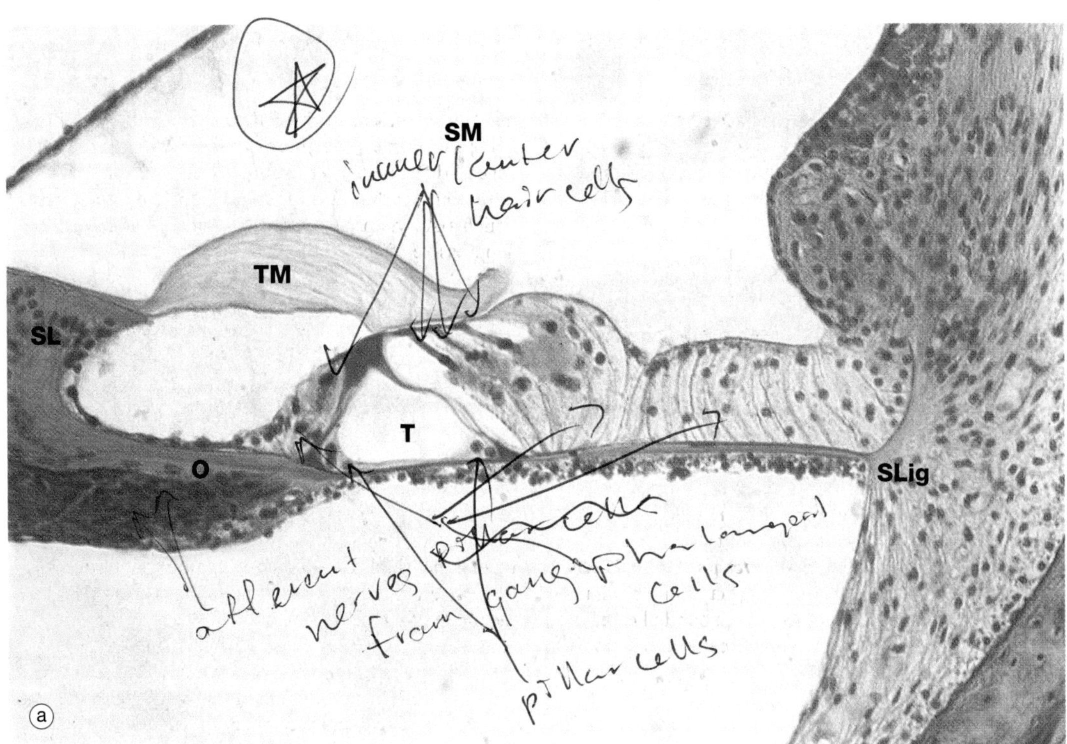

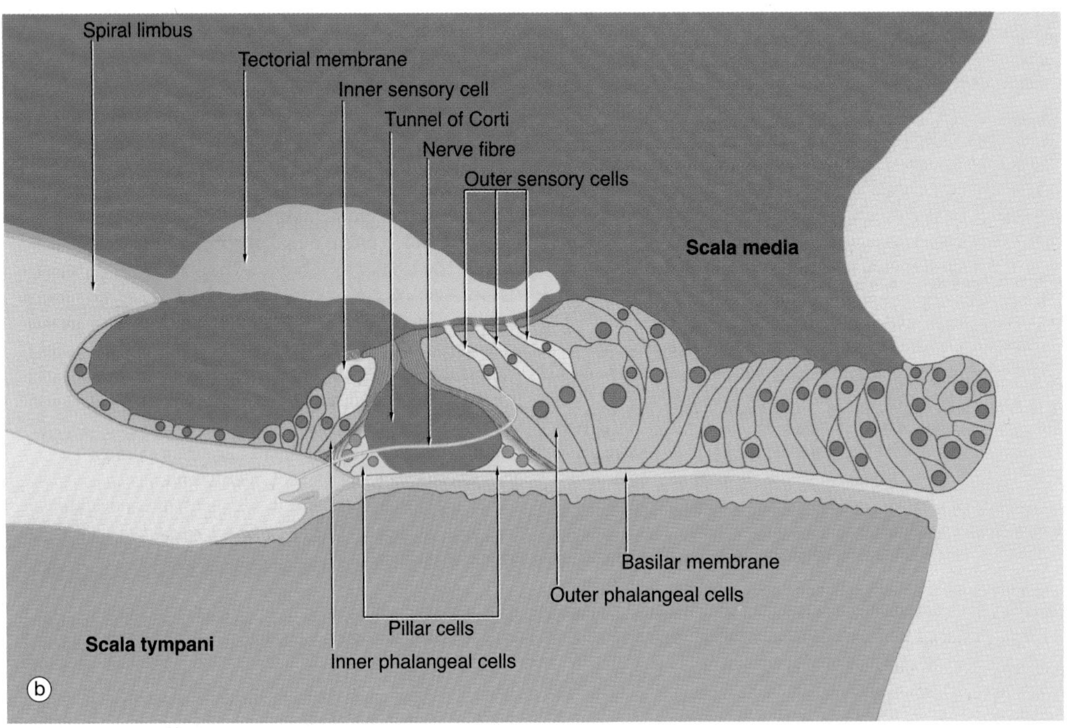

O osseous spiral lamina **SL** spiral limbus **SLig** spiral ligament **SM** scala media
T tunnel of Corti **TM** tectorial membrane

Fig. 21.25 Organ of Corti *(illustrations opposite)*
(a) H & E ×480 (b) Schematic diagram

The organ of Corti is a highly specialised epithelial structure containing receptor cells which convert (transduce) mechanical energy in the form of vibrations into electrochemical energy, resulting in excitation of auditory sensory receptors.

The organ of Corti lies in the scala media **SM** supported on the basilar membrane. The basilar membrane consists of a thin sheet of fibrous tissue stretched between the osseous spiral lamina **O** of the modiolus and the spiral ligament **SLig** laterally; its undersurface, exposed to the scala tympani, is lined by a simple epithelium. The basilar membrane is thinnest at the base of the cochlea and becomes progressively thicker as it spirals towards the apex.

The organ of Corti consists of two basic types of cells, ***sensory (hair) cells*** and ***support cells*** of several different types, including among others the ***inner*** and ***outer pillar cells*** and ***inner*** and ***outer phalangeal cells***. At the centre of the organ is a triangular-shaped canal, the inner tunnel or ***tunnel of Corti*** **T**, bounded on each side by a single row of tall columnar cells called ***pillar cells.*** Each pillar cell contains a dense bundle (pillar) of microtubules and the pillars on either side of the tunnel of Corti converge at the surface and then curve laterally to form a thin, hood-like structure containing small fenestrations. The cell bodies of the pillar cells lie in the acute angles formed by the pillars and the basilar membrane at the floor of the tunnel.

On the inner aspect of the inner row of pillar cells is a single row of flask-shaped cells, the inner phalangeal cells, which support a single row of ***inner sensory*** (***hair***) ***cells***. The phalangeal cells contain microtubules, some of which support the base of the hair cells while others extend to the free surface around the hair cells. Beyond the outer row of pillar cells there are three to five rows of outer phalangeal cells which support the same number of rows of ***outer sensory*** (***hair***) ***cells***. Cytoplasmic extensions of the phalangeal cells extend to the surface between and around the hair cells and their microtubules support the fenestrated hood-like structure formed by the pillar cells. Through the fenestrations project the free ends of the sensory cells. A variety of other specialised epithelial cells provides the remaining support for the organ of Corti.

The sensory cells are known as hair cells because numerous stereocilia, i.e. very long microvilli (see Fig. 5.16), project from their free ends. The stereocilia are embedded in the surface of the ***tectorial membrane***. As previously described, the spiral ganglion of the cochlea contains bipolar cell bodies of first order sensory neurones. From here, axons pass towards the base of the rows of hair cells, those going to the outer hair cells traversing the tunnel of Corti as shown in the diagram (b). The end of each fibre ramifies into a number of dendrites which make synaptic contact with several hair cells; each sensory cell may synapse with dendrites of several different sensory neurones. In addition, inhibitory neurones arising in the brain stem send fibres which also synapse with the sensory cells and exert a suppressive effect.

From the layer of ***border cells*** which cover the ***spiral limbus*** **SL**, there extends a flap-like mass of glycosaminoglycans called the ***tectorial membrane*** **TM** overlying the sensory cells and within which the tips of the stereocilia are embedded.

Function of the organ of Corti

Only an outline of the mechanism of hearing is presented here, molecular details are being discovered at a rapid pace. Sound waves are funnelled into the external auditory meatus and impinge on the tympanic membrane which vibrates at the appropriate frequency. These vibrations are transmitted to the stapes bone via the malleus and incus and, in the process, their amplitude is enhanced about 10-fold. The base of the stapes, which lies in the oval window, conducts the vibrations into the perilymph of the vestibule of the inner ear and pressure waves pass from here into the scala vestibuli of the cochlea. These pressure waves are probably conducted directly to the endolymph of the scala media across the delicate vestibular membrane from which vibrations are induced in the basilar membrane upon which rests the organ of Corti. From here, spent vibrations are transmitted into the perilymph of the scala tympani and dissipated at the secondary tympanic membrane over the round window.

The basilar membrane is thinnest at the base of the cochlea and thickest at the apex. It appears that, at every point on the spiral, the membrane is 'tuned' to vibrate to a particular frequency of sound waves reaching the ear; the overall range of frequencies encompassed is of the order of 11 octaves, with the highest frequencies (pitch) being sensed towards the base of the cochlea and progressively lower frequencies being sensed along the spiral towards the apex. For any given sound frequency, only one specific point of the basilar membrane and organ of Corti is thought to vibrate and thereby activate the appropriate hair cells to initiate afferent sensory impulses which then pass to the auditory cortex of the brain. Deformation of the stereocilia of the hair cells results in either depolarisation or hypopolarisation of the cell membrane, which in turn excites the sensory nerves which synapse with them.

The sensory input from the cochlea is integrated in the brain stem and auditory cortex from which efferent suppressor pathways can modulate receptor activity to enhance auditory acuity.

Inherited deafness syndromes

Approximately 50% of childhood deafness is caused by mutations in specific genes. Many of these genes have been found to code for proteins that affect function of the specialised sensory elements found in the inner ear. Approximately 70% of genetic hearing loss cases are termed nonsyndromic, meaning deafness is the only symptom, and 30% are termed syndromic where deafness is part of a larger set of medical symptoms.

Mutations in genes coding for ***connexin*** proteins, involved in formation of gap junctions account for a large proportion of cases.

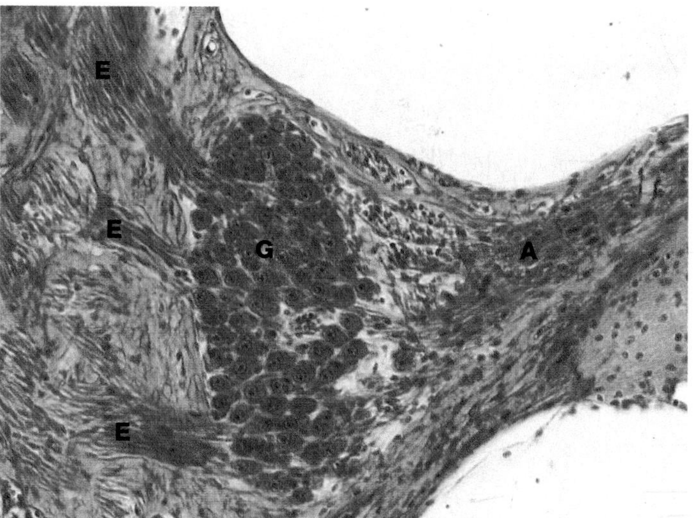

Fig. 21.26 Spiral ganglion
H & E ×320

The spiral ganglion is a spiral-shaped mass of nerve cell bodies lying in a canal at the extremity of the osseous spiral lamina of the modiolus.

As seen in this micrograph, the ganglion cells **G** have the typical appearance of somatic ganglion cells (see Fig. 7.20) and represent the cell bodies of bipolar sensory neurones, relaying information from the receptors of the organ of Corti to the brain.

Note the afferent fibres **A** entering the ganglion from the organ of Corti and numerous bundles of efferent fibres **E** which pass to the centre of the modiolus to form the cochlear nerve, the auditory component of the eighth cranial nerve; the cochlear nerve is readily seen in Fig. 21.24a.

Fig. 21.27 Receptor organs of the saccule and utricle *(illustrations opposite)*
(a) H & E ×480 (b) H & E ×600 (c) Scanning EM ×5000 (d) Schematic diagram

The saccule and utricle are two dilated regions of the membranous labyrinth lying within the vestibule of the inner ear and filled with endolymph. The walls of each are composed of a fibrous membrane which is bound down in places to the periosteum of the vestibule and, in other areas, is attached to the periosteum by fibrous strands, the intervening space being filled with perilymph. Internally, the saccule and utricle are lined by simple cuboidal epithelium but in each there is a small region of highly specialised epithelium called the macula, shown in micrographs (a) and (b), containing receptor cells which contribute part of the sensory input to that part of the brain responsible for maintaining balance and equilibrium. The macula of the utricle is oriented at right angles to that of the saccule.

The maculae are made up of two basic cell types, ***sensory hair cells*** and ***support cells***. The support cells are tall and columnar with basally located nuclei and microvilli at their free surface. The hair cells lie between the support cells, with their larger nuclei placed more centrally. Each hair cell has a single eccentrically located cilium of typical conformation, often called the ***kinocilium*** (see Fig. 5.14), and many stereocilia (long microvilli) projecting from its surface; hence the name hair cells. The 'hairs' are embedded in a thick, gelatinous plaque of glycoprotein probably secreted by the supporting cells; this is lost during histological preparation. At the surface of the glycoprotein layer is a mass of crystals mainly composed of calcium carbonate and known as otoliths. These are shown in micrograph (c).

There are two different forms of hair cells. ***Type I hair cells (goblet cells)*** are bulbous in shape and stain poorly, their nuclei tending to lie at a lower level than those of ***type II hair cells (columnar cells)*** which are more slender in shape. The type I hair cells are invested by a meshwork of dendritic processes of afferent sensory neurones, whereas the type II hair cells have only small dendritic processes at their bases. The hair cells also have synaptic connections with modulatory (inhibitory) neurones from the CNS.

Function of the maculae

The function of the maculae relates mainly to the maintenance of balance by providing sensory information about the static position of the head in space. This is of particular importance when the eyes are closed, or in the dark or under water, and the maculae are consequently more developed in animals other than humans.

When the head is moved from a position of equilibrium, the otolithic membrane tends to move with respect to the receptor cells, causing bending of their stereocilia. When the stereocilia are bent in the direction of the cilium, the receptor cell undergoes excitation and, when the relative movement is in the opposite direction, excitation is inhibited. The orientation of the hair cells in different directions in the maculae causes different hair cells to be stimulated with different positions of the head. The pattern of hair cell stimulation allows the central nervous system to determine the position of the head very accurately with respect to gravity.

The neural pathways of the balance and equilibrium mechanism are complex and the sensory input from the maculae is integrated with that of other proprioceptors, such as muscle spindles to elicit reflex responses directed towards the maintenance of postural equilibrium.

A afferent nerve fibres **E** efferent nerve fibres **G** ganglion cells

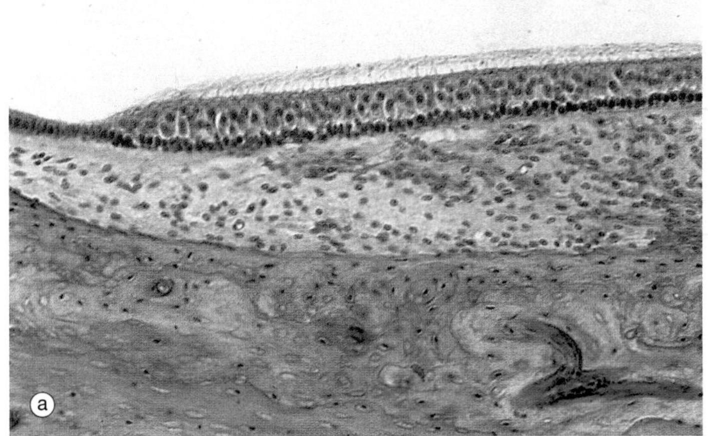

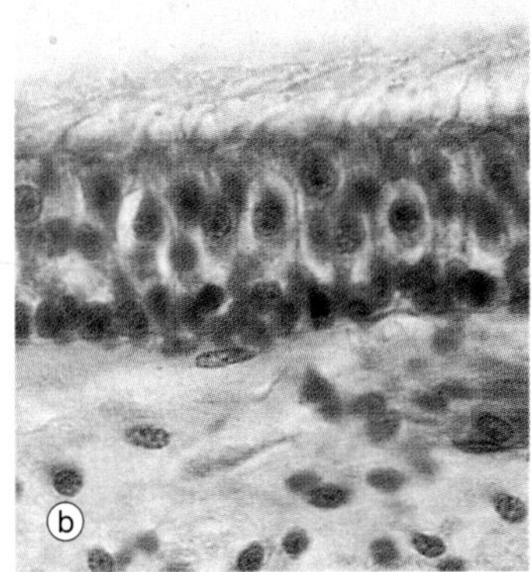

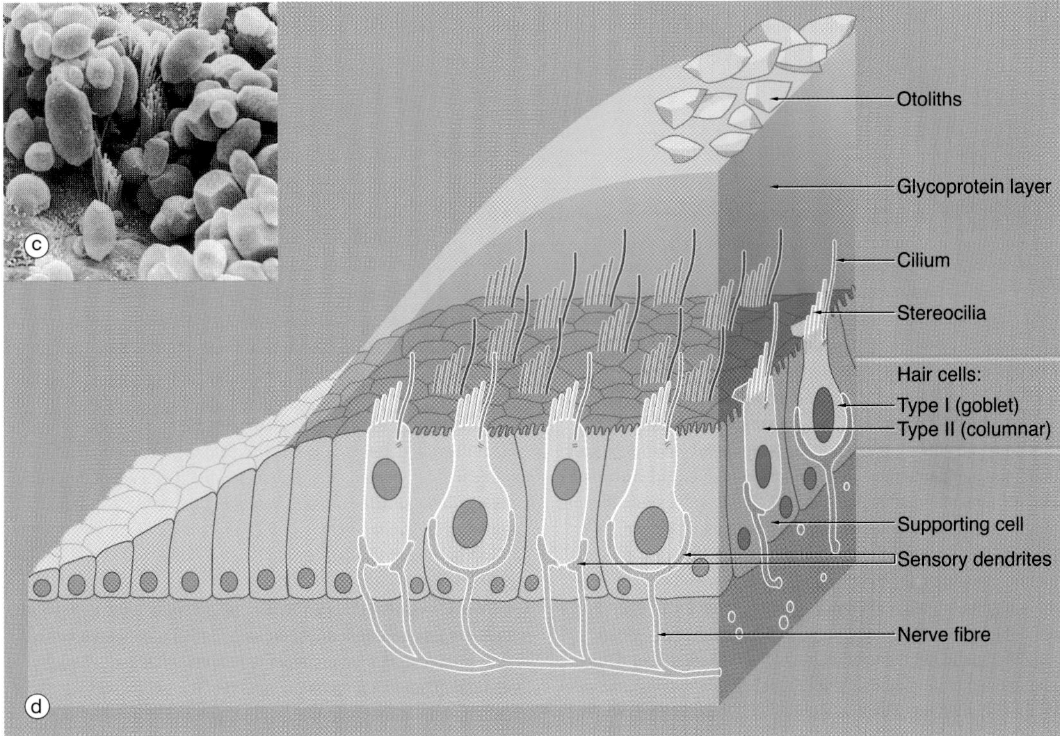

Diseases of the membranous labyrinth system

Ménière's disease is an abnormality of the inner ear. Clinically, affected patients experience dizziness, disturbance of balance (***vertigo***), a high pitched, rushing or roaring sound in the ears (***tinnitus***) and fluctuating hearing loss.

The symptoms of Ménière's disease are associated with an increase in endolymph volume within the membranous labyrinth system. An increase in endolymph volume is believed to cause the membranous labyrinth to swell (endolymphatic hydrops) leading to development of abnormal signalling from receptors. The cause of this increase in endolymph remains uncertain. One possibility is rupture of the membranous labyrinth which allows the endolymph to mix with perilymph.

For patients with mild disease treatment with symptomatic medication can be effective. For patients with debilitating disease surgical ablation of parts of the labyrinthine system are effective, but may involve permanent hearing loss. Infusion of drugs known to be toxic to the sensory-neural apparatus (e.g. gentamicin) in the middle ear is also used for treatment.

Transient dysfunction of the labyrinthine system can be caused by viral infection (***viral labyrinthitis***). Patients develop severe dizziness, vertigo, nausea and vomiting which reaches a peak after about 24 hours and subsequently resolves within a week.

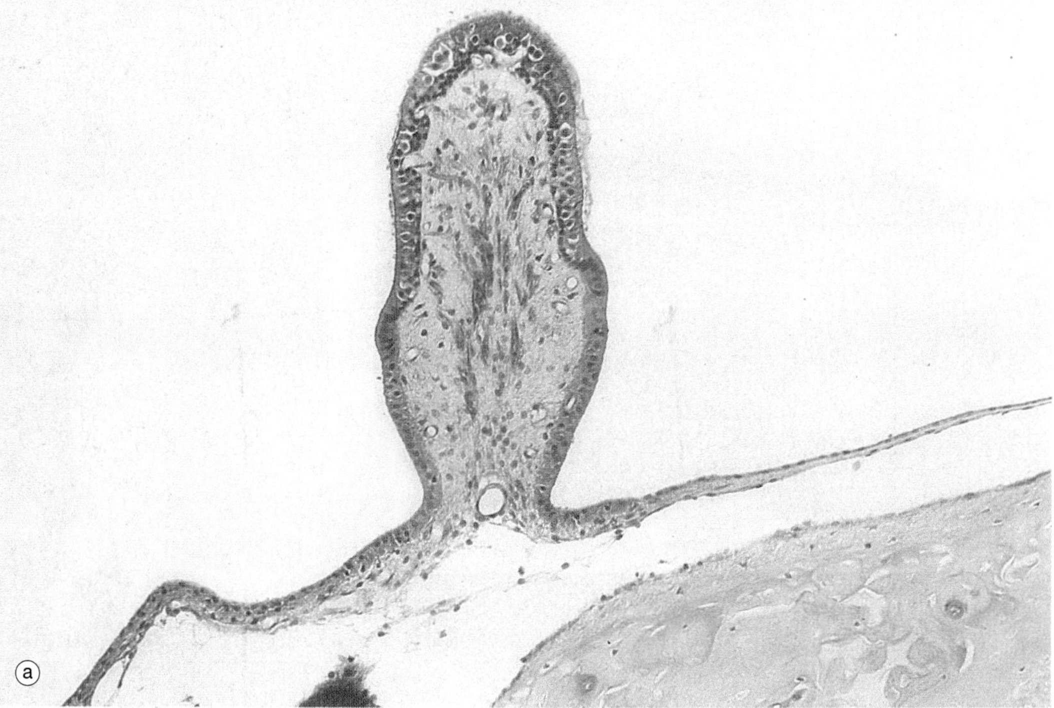

Fig. 21.28 Receptor organs of the semicircular canals
(a) Masson's trichrome ×200 (b) Schematic diagram *(opposite)*

Three semicircular canals arise from the vestibule of the inner ear, each containing a membranous semicircular duct which opens at both ends into the utricle. At one end of each duct is a dilated portion, the ampulla, which contains a receptor organ called the ***crista ampullaris***.

Each crista ampullaris is an elongated epithelial structure situated on a ridge of supporting tissue arising from the membranous wall of the ampulla and oriented at right angles to the direction of flow of the endolymph in the semicircular canal. Structurally, the cristae ampullares bear many similarities to the maculae of the utricle and saccule (see Fig. 21.27). The hair cells are of the same two morphological forms, ***type I*** and ***type II cells***, the former being invested by a basket of sensory dendrites and the latter having small dendritic endings at the base only. The hair cells are supported by a single layer of columnar cells which is continuous with the simple cuboidal epithelium lining the rest of the membranous labyrinth.

Like those of the maculae, the hair cells of the cristae have numerous stereocilia and a single kinocilium, the kinocilium being situated at the margin of the cell nearest to the utricle. The stereocilia and the kinocilia of the hair cells are embedded in a ridge of gelatinous glycoprotein which is tall and cone shaped in cross-section giving rise to the term ***cupula***. In contrast to the macula, the cupula does not contain otolithic crystals. Traces of the cupola can be seen on the surface of the crista ampullaris in micrograph (a), although most of it has been lost during histological preparation of the specimen.

Function of the crista ampullaris

When the head is moved in the plane of a particular semicircular canal, the inertia of the endolymph acts to deflect the cupula in the opposite direction. The stereocilia of the sensory cells are then deflected towards or away from the cilia, resulting in excitation or inhibition, respectively.

In each ear there are three semicircular canals, two at right angles to each other in vertical planes and one in a near-horizontal plane. Each is paired with a semicircular canal in the other ear, the members of each pair being oriented in parallel. The sensory input from the cristae ampullares mainly concerns changes in the direction and rate of movement of the head. Afferent impulses pass via bipolar sensory neurones with cell bodies in the vestibular ganglion which lies at the base of the internal auditory meatus. Afferent fibres pass via the vestibular part of the eighth cranial nerve to the brain stem, cerebellum and cerebral cortex where sensory information from various other sources is integrated for the maintenance of balance, position sense and equilibrium.

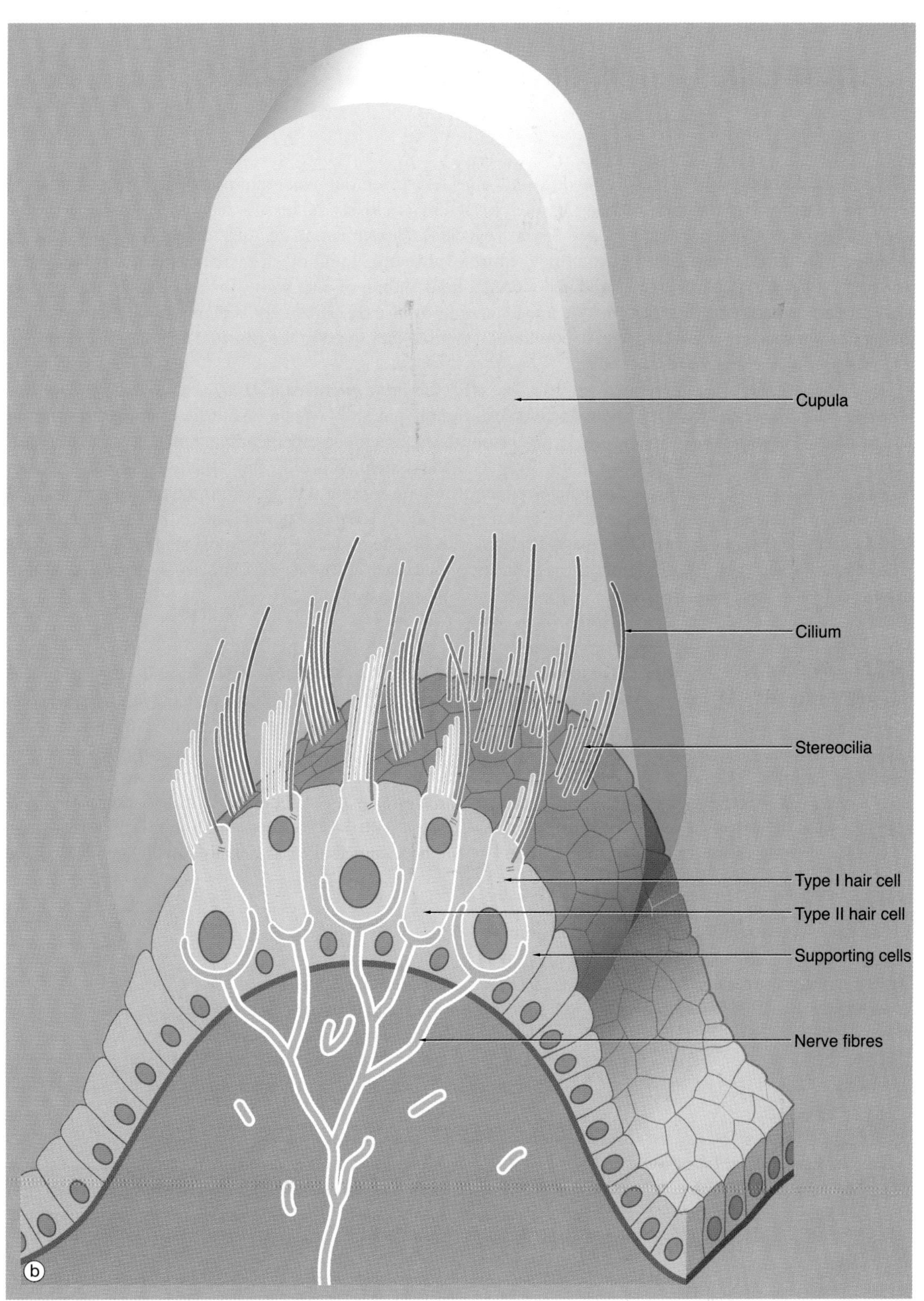
Cupula
Cilium
Stereocilia
Type I hair cell
Type II hair cell
Supporting cells
Nerve fibres
b

Appendix 1: *Introduction to microscopy*

The study of histology, the subject of this text and atlas, is carried out using microscopes of various types in order to visualise the structure of body tissues. Structure is closely related to function and much can be deduced about the function of cells and tissues by careful examination of their component parts. Taken together with information gathered from biochemistry, physiology and other basic sciences, this study can provide a powerful tool to understand the normal functioning of the body. In addition, acquiring this knowledge is a necessary first step for the understanding of disease. Histology is about looking at structure, and in this introductory section we aim to provide some guidelines to assist the absolute beginner in examining and interpreting the images in this book.

This book mainly uses photomicrographs taken with the ***light microscope (LM)*** (colour images) and the ***electron microscope (EM)*** (black and white images). Simply put, the LM and EM differ in ***optical resolution*** and ***available magnification***. In practical terms 'resolution' refers to the capacity of an optical system to reveal detail in a specimen. The resolution available from a conventional LM is only about 0.2 μm. Thus at distances of less than 0.2 μm, objects that are actually separate from one another will appear to merge. In contrast, EM resolution for biological specimens is as little as 1 nm, so that the resolving power is about 200-fold better than LM. In addition, maximum 'available magnification' is limited to about ×1000 in most student LMs, whereas an EM readily achieves 100-fold greater magnification, or about ×100 000. EM images are therefore said to display cell and tissue ***ultrastructure***.

EM images may be two- or three-dimensional

There are two types of electron microscope: ***scanning EM*** and ***transmission EM***. Scanning EM produces three-dimensional (3-D) images, but these are restricted to the surface of the object with the internal structure concealed from view. Transmission EM is so-named because the electron beam must pass through the specimen to form an image. To achieve this, ultrathin sections (50–100 nm) must be cut. Transmission of the electron beam through the tissue results in a 2-D image of the plane of the section. In practice, transmission EM is more informative of biological ultrastructure and these images predominate in this book. We have supplemented these with scanning EM images where it helps with 3-D conceptualisation (cf. Figs 16.14 and 16.15). As a matter of convention the abbreviation EM can be assumed to be a transmission EM, while we have identified scanning EMs as SEM.

Light and electron microscopy are complementary

The strengths of LM and EM differ yet complement one another very effectively. With LM one can observe large areas of a specimen (usually several cm^2). A wide range of staining methods, some empirical, some specific, are available for LM, permitting identification of cell and tissue features; many of these stains are polychromatic, i.e. they produce multiple colours in the specimen which, besides looking pretty, help to identify different components. For certain specimens, sections slightly thicker than usual may be used to demonstrate 3-D features. Thus from LM, students can expect to gain an understanding of overall cell and tissue architecture.

The superior resolution and magnification of EM permit visualisation of many features which simply cannot be seen by LM. Yet in some respects EM is less flexible than LM. For example, the available area in EM specimens is generally less than 1 mm^2 and this may make it difficult to obtain representative fields. Few staining methods are available for EM and these produce only monochromatic (black and white) images. EM is also costly and time-consuming and usually not available to the average student.

Hints for interpreting EMs

Interpretation of EMs can be quite challenging due to the wide range of magnifications available (×500–190 000 in this book). In other words an EM image is not necessarily of very high magnification. In fact, there is an overlap in the magnification ranges of EM and LM. It is a good idea consciously to note the magnification and/or scale bar on each image in the book. The terms ***electron-dense*** and ***electron-lucent*** are used to describe the relative darkness and lightness, respectively, as they appear in transmission EM images. Sections examined by EM are almost featureless unless stained with heavy metals (e.g. uranium and lead salts) that bind to cell and tissue components to varying degrees. Significant binding of metal stain to a particular structure will impede transmission of the electron beam through the specimen at that point; the structure will appear dark grey or black and is said to be electron-dense (really too dense to allow passage of electrons). Other structures with little or no affinity for the stain will appear lighter grey or white and are termed electron-lucent because they permit greater transmission of the electron beam.

A useful starting point in interpreting EMs is to select several commonly found structures that you can confidently identify and memorise their dimensions. These can then be used as 'internal rulers' to gauge the dimensions of numerous other features in the field. For example, plasma membrane and organelle membranes will be visible at medium magnifications as thin electron-dense lines that measure about 10 nm wide. Thus, structures such as intermediate filaments (10 nm in diameter and solid) and microtubules (20–25 nm in diameter but hollow) can be identified. Similarly, individual ribosomes and glycogen particles are 20–30 nm in diameter. Being alert to major size differences between organelle types will instill further confidence. For example, nuclear diameter (5–10 μm in most cells) is up to 10 times greater than the diameter of lysosomes and mitochondria (0.2–1.0 μm) and up to 100 times greater than individual Golgi transport vesicles (50–100 nm). The next step is to actively look for the unique set of features that characterises and distinguishes each organelle and inclusion. For example, only mitochondria and the nucleus possess a double membrane, and in mitochondria the inner of these two membranes is thrown into highly characteristic folds.

High magnification electron micrographs are often required to demonstrate particular features but usually display only a tiny region of the cell. Therefore, do not be surprised if many of the common organelles are not seen in the field. A reliable indicator of high magnification is if an individual membrane appears trilaminar rather than as a single electron-dense line. At low magnification, EM interpretation can actually be more difficult because membranes and the smallest organelles are no longer clearly visible. Get orientated by looking first for the biggest objects, i.e. nuclei and boundaries of the cells themselves, and next for the mid-sized organelles such as mitochondria. Regions of interface between cells and extracellular tissue can give clues about tissue heterogeneity.

Specific localisation methods for LM and EM

The traditional staining techniques of histology, developed in the last two centuries from dyes used in the textile industry, remain valuable and widely used as empirical methods for LM. Subsequently, a range of specific methods was developed, enabling LM visualisation of defined intracellular and extracellular constituents. More recently, technical refinements have allowed conceptually similar specific localisations to be achieved at EM level.

One major group of specific methods, known as ***histochemical techniques***, employs reagents known to react with defined cellular constituents (e.g. lipids, glycogen and DNA) thereby producing selective colouration recognisable by LM. In a subset known as ***enzyme histochemistry*** the activity of enzymes can similarly be demonstrated by staining for their specific substrates or end products; these methods are often applicable for both EM and LM. A further subset, termed ***immunohistochemistry***, has gained rapid acceptance. Immunologically based, this newer method offers high specificity and sensitivity of localisation. In essence, antibodies are raised against specific cellular components (in this context, the antigen) and then conjugated with a visual marker appropriate for LM or EM (e.g. dyes, enzymes, tiny particles of colloidal gold). When the antibody is then applied to the tissue under study, it binds to the antigen. Hence, the site of antibody–antigen binding becomes flagged by the chosen visual marker (e.g. Fig. 1.9; Appendix 2, Notes on staining techniques).

Constraints in LM and EM: aspects of tissue preparation

A problem common both to light and electron microscopy is the need to prevent autolytic degeneration and to preserve cellular ultrastructure. Fixatives such as ***formaldehyde*** and ***glutaraldehyde*** are used for this purpose. ***Fixation*** causes cross-linking of macromolecules, which reduces and often arrests biological activity, at the same time rendering the cells more amenable to staining. Most tissues are too thick to be examined directly in the microscope and must therefore be cut into very thin slices (***sections***). To facilitate the cutting of thin sections, the tissue is usually ***embedded*** in a hard medium such as paraffin wax (LM) or a plastic resin (EM); fixed tissues generally require dehydration with organic solvents before the embedding step. Each stage in the fixation, dehydration, embedding, sectioning and final staining sequence may induce ***artefacts*** (distortions in cell and tissue architecture, e.g. shrinkage). In situations where preservation of biological activity of cell constituents (e.g. enzymes) is the major objective, thin sections for histochemistry can be obtained from minimally fixed or unfixed frozen tissue; such ***frozen sections*** have their own peculiar artefactual distortions. As noted above, unstained sections are quite lacking in contrast when viewed by conventional LM or EM. However, special types of LM (***phase contrast, interference contrast, confocal microscopy***) have been developed to address this limitation and are frequently used, for example, to monitor living tissue cultures.

Appendix 2: *Notes on staining techniques*

Haematoxylin and eosin (H & E)
This is the most commonly used technique in animal histology and routine pathology. The basic dye, haematoxylin, stains acidic structures a purplish blue. Nuclei, ribosomes and rough endoplasmic reticulum have a strong affinity for this dye owing to their high content of DNA and RNA, respectively. In contrast, eosin is an acidic dye which stains basic structures red or pink. Most cytoplasmic proteins are basic and hence cytoplasm usually stains pink or pinkish red. In general, when the H & E staining technique is applied to animal cells, nuclei stain blue and cytoplasm stains pink or red.

Periodic acid–Schiff reaction (PAS)
Staining methods that specifically stain components of cells and tissues are called histochemical staining techniques. Such techniques are invaluable for the understanding of cell and tissue structure and function, and for making a diagnosis on diseased tissues. The PAS reaction stains complex carbohydrates a deep red colour, traditionally described as magenta. The mucin produced by goblet cells of the gastrointestinal and respiratory tracts stains magenta with this technique (and is therefore termed PAS-positive). Basement membranes and the brush borders of kidney tubules and the small and large intestines are also PAS-positive, as is cartilage and to some extent collagen. Glycogen, the intracellular storage form of carbohydrate found in cells such as hepatocytes and muscle cells, is also PAS-positive.

Masson's trichrome
This technique is a so-called connective tissue technique since it is used to demonstrate supporting tissue elements, principally collagen. As its name implies, the staining technique produces three colours: nuclei and other basophilic structures are stained blue; collagen is stained green or blue depending on which variant of the technique is used; and cytoplasm, muscle, erythrocytes and keratin are stained bright red.

Alcian blue
Alcian blue is a mucin stain which may be used in conjunction with other staining methods such as H & E or van Gieson (see below). Certain types of mucin, but not all, are stained blue by the Alcian blue method, as is cartilage. When the technique is combined with van Gieson, the Alcian blue colour becomes green.

van Gieson
This is another connective tissue method in which collagen is stained red, nuclei are blue and erythrocytes and cytoplasm yellow. When used in combination with an elastic stain, elastin is stained blue/black in addition to the results described above. This staining technique is particularly useful for blood vessels and skin.

Reticulin stain
This method demonstrates the reticulin fibres of supporting tissue which are stained blue/black by this technique. Nuclei may be counterstained blue with haematoxylin or red with the dye, neutral red.

Azan
This technique is traditionally classed as a connective tissue method but is excellent for demonstrating fine cytological detail, especially in epithelium. Nuclei are stained bright red; collagen, basement membrane and mucin are stained blue; muscle and red blood cells are stained orange to red.

Giemsa
This technique is a standard method for staining blood cells and other smears of cells, e.g. bone marrow. Nuclei are stained dark blue to violet, background cytoplasm pale blue and erythrocytes pale pink.

Toluidine blue
This stain is one of the few stains which will differentially stain tissues in very thin epoxy resin sections (see Appendix 3), and is particularly used in the high resolution investigation of the structure of the glomerulus in health and disease as well as for high resolution light microscopy of nerves. This dye also stains mast cell granules reddish purple in paraffin sections, a property called 'metachromasia'.

Goldner's trichrome stain
This method is applied to acrylic resin sections (see Appendix 3) of undecalcified bone to distinguish between mineralised bone and unmineralised osteoid, and has a haematoxylin component which also stains the nuclei of osteoblasts, osteocytes, osteoclasts and marrow cells. The von Kossa stain (a silver method) also distinguishes between mineralised bone and osteoid, but shows no cellular detail.

Silver and gold methods

These methods were extremely popular at the end of the nineteenth century and are occasionally used today to demonstrate such fine structures as cell processes, e.g. in neurones, motor end-plates and intercellular junctions. Depending on the method used, the end product is black, brown or golden.

Nissl and methylene blue methods

These techniques use a basic dye to stain the rough endoplasmic reticulum found in neurones; when this is seen as clumps it is called Nissl substance.

Sudan black and osmium

These dyes stain lipid-containing structures such as myelin a brownish-black colour for light microscopy. Osmium is also used as the staining agent that provides contrast in electron microscopy. Grids prepared for electron microscopy are stained with osmium tetroxide in solution. Electron-dense structures are those that have affinity for osmium staining.

Immunohistological techniques

A variety of immunohistological techniques are vital for diagnostic purposes as well as for research. Micrographs employing the immunoperoxidase technique are used in several chapters of this book to highlight specific histological features (see for example Figs 1.9d, 11.7b, and 17.23). For this reason the basic technique is described here in some detail.

Immunohistochemical techniques depend on the exquisite specificity of antibodies for their antigen. Thus any substance (antigen) can be specifically identified provided antibodies for it are available. To demonstrate a particular substance, such as insulin, in sections of tissue, antibodies must be produced. This is done by injecting human insulin into a laboratory animal, which obligingly recognises the human peptide as foreign and produces antibodies to it. A virtually inexhaustible source of antibody can then be created using monoclonal technology. (In actual practice you order a vial of antibody from a recognised supplier.)

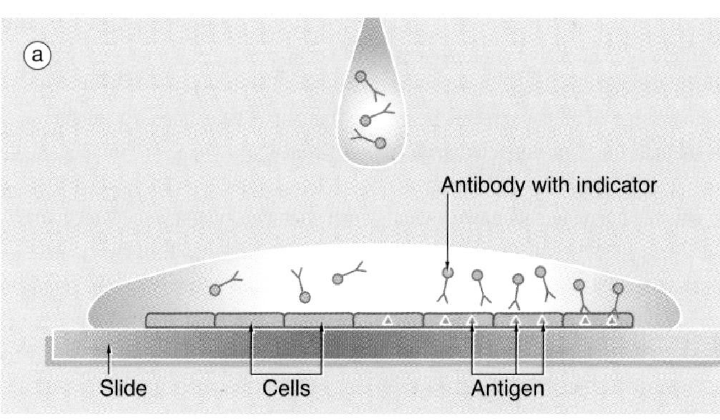

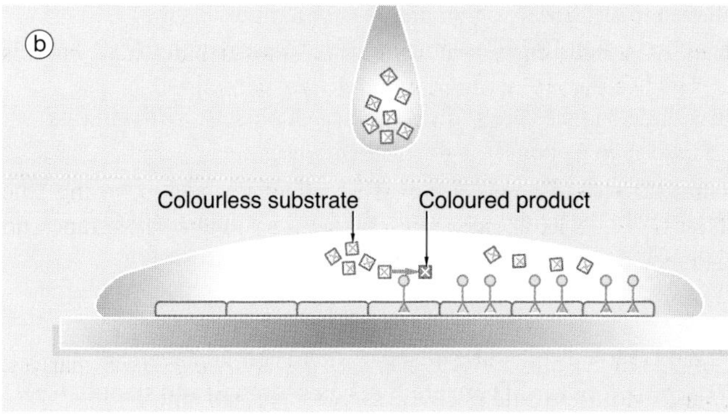

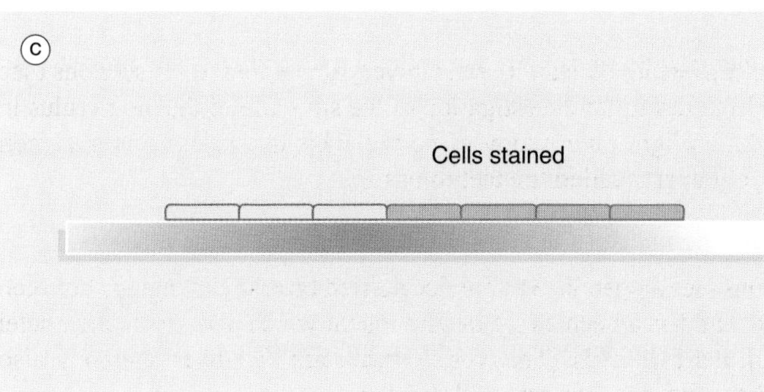

A section of tissue is placed on a glass slide (a) and a solution of antibody is laid over the tissue. The antibody binds to the antigen and excess antibody is washed away so that only cells containing the particular antigen have antibody bound to them. To demonstrate the position of antibody, the antibody is prelinked to an indicator substance. This may be a fluorescent substance such as fluorescein, in which case the technique is known as ***immunofluorescence*** and the position of antibody can be visualised using a fluorescence microscope. It is more useful to bind to the antibody an enzyme that is able to convert a colourless substrate to a coloured product. A solution of the substrate is laid over the tissue section (b) with the bound antibody. After a period of incubation, the coloured product can be seen on the section using an ordinary light microscope (c). An enzyme commonly used for this purpose is horseradish peroxidase and the technique is then called the ***immunoperoxidase*** technique. A further modification of this principle for electron microscopy uses antibodies linked to gold which, as gold is electron-dense, can be detected by electron microscopy (***immunogold labelling***). Many other variants of this technique are available.

Appendix 3: *Glossary of terms*

ATP – adenosine triphosphate is the small molecule used in cells as the primary source of readily available energy.

Basophilic or **haematoxophilic** – structures that stain with the basic dye haematoxylin, one of the components of the standard haematoxylin and eosin (H & E) method (see Appendix 2). Acidic molecules such as DNA and RNA take up this dye, thus acquiring a blue colour.

Complement cascade – a group of enzymes found in inactive form in the blood. Binding of immune complexes or certain bacterial products activates the first enzyme which is then able to activate larger amounts of the second that in turn switches on larger amounts of the third and so on. This cascade can very quickly produce large quantities of effector molecules that fight infection and promote inflammation.

Coronal planes – imaginary vertical planes at right angles to the median/sagittal plane (see below).

Cytokines – proteins or peptides released by cells that convey signals to nearby cells.

Distal – anatomical term meaning further from the centre or the root of a limb, e.g. the ankle is distal to the knee.

DNA – deoxyribonucleic acid is the chemical structure that holds the genetic code, which contains the blueprint for every protein produced by an individual. DNA is found in the nucleus where it forms the chromosomes (see Chapter 2).

Electron-dense – tissue stained for electron microscopy with heavy metals impedes the passage of electrons to a greater or lesser degree depending on the amount of heavy metal bound. Structures that take up large amounts of heavy metal stains are called electron-dense and appear dark grey to black.

Electron-lucent – tissue stained for electron microscopy with heavy metals impedes the passage of electrons to a greater or lesser degree depending on the amount of heavy metal bound. Those structures that bind little heavy metal and allow the passage of the electron beam are said to be electron-lucent and appear white to pale grey.

EM – two-dimensional electron micrograph views of objects, acquired by passing the electron beam through a thin section of the specimen (see Appendix 1). Almost all of the electron micrographs in this book are transmission electron micrographs and are referred to as "EMs". Other authors sometimes use the abbreviation TEM although by convention the abbreviation EM is assumed to be a transmission EM.

SEM – scanning electron micrographs are 3-dimensional views of the surface of objects. SEMs in this book are identified in figure captions as "SEM" (see Appendix 1 for further details).

Eosinophilic or **acidophilic** – these structures stain with the acidic dye eosin, the other component of the standard haematoxylin and eosin (H & E) method. Most cytoplasmic structures are basic and therefore acidophilic to some extent, so that in most tissues the cell cytoplasm stains with eosin and appears pinkish-red.

ER – endoplasmic reticulum is a membrane-bound cytoplasmic compartment where certain chemical reactions take place sequestered from the rest of the cytoplasm. There are two types – rough and smooth (see below).

rER – rough endoplasmic reticulum is studded with ribosomes and is the site of synthesis and processing of proteins for export.

sER – smooth endoplasmic reticulum is a major site of lipid synthesis.

In vivo – occurring in a living body – used in experimental situations to describe events taking place in real life.

In vitro – an experiment taking place outside of a living body, e.g. in a tissue culture dish.

Protein superfamilies – proteins can be grouped into superfamilies by similarities in structure and function. An example is the immunoglobulin superfamily that has a range of functions in antigen recognition and cell–cell interactions.

Proximal – closer to the centre or the root of a limb, e.g. the elbow is proximal to the wrist.

RNA – ribonucleic acid is a chemical structure that exists in three forms – messenger RNA, transfer RNA and ribosomal RNA (see below).

> **mRNA** – messenger RNA is a chemical copy of the sequence of bases in DNA and acts as a template for the synthesis of proteins (see Ch. 1).
>
> **tRNA** – transfer RNA interacts with mRNA during protein synthesis to assemble the amino acids in the correct order to create a particular protein.
>
> **rRNA** – ribosomal RNA is the type of RNA that makes up the physical structure of the ribosome, the site of protein synthesis. Ribosomal RNA controls the docking of tRNA in the correct order as defined by mRNA to produce the correct sequence of amino acids in a particular polypeptide chain.

Sagittal or **median plane** – an imaginary vertical plane through the body, dividing it into right and left halves. Additional paramedian or parasagittal planes are parallel to the sagittal plane.

Section or **tissue section** – a very thin slice of tissue that is prepared in one of a number of ways for staining and microscopic examination:

> **Frozen section** – this type of section is used for urgent diagnosis intra-operatively. The tissue is snap frozen, sections cut and stained and a diagnosis given within a sort space of time (15–30 minutes). The disadvantage of this method is that tissue preservation is not nearly so good as with routine paraffin sections and so diagnosis is more difficult. Frozen sections are also used for immunofluorescence microscopy, certain stains to detect lipids in tissue and for enzyme histochemistry.
>
> **Paraffin sections** – most of the photomicrographs in this book are of paraffin sections. The fixed tissues are dehydrated and infiltrated by hot liquid paraffin wax and cooled until the wax is solid (at room temperature). The wax provides support for the tissue and allows sections as thin as 3 microns to be cut. The wax is dissolved away by an organic solvent and the tissue slice is rehydrated before stains are applied. This procedure requires hours to carry out and most routine tissue sections are processed overnight.
>
> **Resin sections** – in some circumstances, paraffin wax offers inadequate support for tissue sectioning, and resins are used as the embedding medium. Two main types are used. Acrylic resins are harder than paraffin wax and offer greater support when cutting hard tissues such as fingernail and undecalcified bone. A wide range of stains can be applied. Epoxy resins are even harder, and are particularly used in electron microscopy. Using special glass 'knives', very thin sections can be cut and stained with Toluidine blue (see Appendix 2, 'Notes on stains') for very high resolution light microscopy, and even thinner sections (ultrathin sections) stained for transmission electron microscopy.

Index